RACE

and **RACIALIZATION**

RACE
and RACIALIZATION
ESSENTIAL READINGS | **SECOND EDITION**

Edited by **Tania Das Gupta, Carl E. James, Chris Andersen,
Grace-Edward Galabuzi, and Roger C.A. Maaka**

**CANADIAN
SCHOLARS**

Toronto | Vancouver

Race and Racialization: Essential Readings, Second Edition
Edited by Tania Das Gupta, Carl E. James, Chris Andersen, Grace-Edward Galabuzi, and Roger C.A. Maaka

First published in 2018 by
Canadian Scholars, an imprint of CSP Books Inc.
425 Adelaide Street West, Suite 200
Toronto, Ontario
M5V 3C1

www.canadianscholars.ca

Library and Archives Canada Cataloguing in Publication

Race and racialization : essential readings / edited by
Tania Das Gupta, Carl E. James, Chris Andersen, Grace-Edward
Galabuzi, and Roger C.A. Maaka. -- Second edition.

Includes bibliographical references.
Issued in print and electronic formats.
ISBN 978-1-77338-015-5 (softcover).--ISBN 978-1-77338-017-9
(EPUB).--ISBN 978-1-77338-016-2 (PDF)

1. Race. 2. Racism. 3. Race relations. 4. Race awareness.
I. Das Gupta, Tania, 1957- editor

HT1521.R238 2018   305.8   C2017-907183-1
                                          C2017-907184-X

Cover and interior design by Elisabeth Springate
Typesetting by Peggy and Co. Design Inc.

Printed and bound in Canada by Webcom

Contents

PART 3 | RACE, RACISM, AND INSTITUTIONS

PART 4 | PRIVILEGES, MARGINALIZATION, AND RESISTANCE

Preface

In this second edition of *Race and Racialization: Essential Readings*, we build on what we attained in the first anthology, inspired by the feedback that some of our key strategies when putting that edition together have been helpful to readers. What we aspired to do was to draw links between the colonization of Indigenous peoples in various regions— and the colonization of Asians, Africans, the inhabitants of the Americas, Caribbeans, and various "others"—and their linked experiences with "race" and racism under colonial and neo-colonial relationships. In established texts, these experiences in different parts of the globe are examined separately and aimed at different audiences, so that there is no opportunity to draw linkages between our experiences, which may be separated by time and space, but which are connected to the dynamics of capitalist expansion and the search for new lands, resources, markets, and, of course, cheaper labour.

Connected to these imperatives, we wanted to draw a link between, on the one hand, colonization, racism, and race discourse, and their exclusionary and often genocidal effects; and, on the other, the exploitation of labour power of those racialized as "people of colour" in the Americas and the Caribbean, including the slavery of Africans, indentureship of Asians, and today's global deployment of migrant labour. We are also mindful of the basis of colonialism, neocolonialism, neoliberalism, and racism in capitalist expansion and globalization and their intersections with class, gender, sexuality, religion, and other oppressive discourses as they became articulated in concrete ways in people's everyday lives.

This edition of the book was put together in the context of the recent election of billionaire businessman Donald Trump as the president of the United States, following his daily tirades of anti-immigrant, anti-Mexican, and Islamophobic racism; his misogynist and hetero-sexist "jock talk" and ableist mimicry; and his stereotyping of all African Americans as poor and living in crime-ridden neighbourhoods. This was part of his politics of "division" to appeal to the American "citizenry," racialized as white. His win has stunned many and delighted hardline conservatives and racists for whom he is a hero who will "make America great again."

His platform of "Make America Great Again" harkens back to a nostalgic era of "cowboys and Indians," colonial rule, and Cold War–era style dominance of the "free world"; in short, a world where a Western "whiteness" ruled supreme and "the rest" (Hall, 1996) fell in line behind them through violence or consent. It is as if America's greatness was destroyed in the interim period and its "white hegemony" challenged with the election of a Black president, whose legitimacy was questioned by many, including Trump, as a non-American and possibly a Muslim. The discourses of systemic racism and white supremacy in employment were challenged by affirmative action, diversity, and anti-racism. America's so-called greatness had likewise been challenged by Indigenous communities all over the Americas and other settler colonies by their "decolonization" movements, including transnational public actions against oil pipelines and concomitant environmental/human destruction. America's so-called greatness had been challenged by the cries of "Black Lives Matter."

Trump is not unique. He was preceded by Stephen Harper's regime in Canada, who felt it necessary to enact the Zero Tolerance for Barbaric Cultural Practices Act to control immigrants from non-Christian backgrounds, chiefly Muslim immigrants. One of his ministers, Kellie Leitch, who ran for the leadership of the Conservative Party, promised to quiz all new immigrants to determine their adherence to "Canadian values" before their admission. Likewise—despite running on a platform in opposition to Harper of the apparently quintessential Canadian values of tolerance and respect for diversity and difference—current Prime Minister Justin Trudeau has overseen the expansion of pipelines into and across Indigenous territories throughout Canada, and the detainment of immigrants has far outpaced the amount under Harper's regime.

Nor is North America unique in the rise of right-wing racism and xenophobia. The United Kingdom's majority vote to exit the European Union (referred to as Brexit) was largely a show of anti-immigrant sentiment. Similarly, Trump-like rhetoric has been heard in recent elections in the Netherland and France. In fact, these recent iterations of openly anti-immigrant racism have been on the rise in Europe for more than three decades now, most notably personified in France in the figure of Jean-Marie Le Pen, founder of the National Front.

What can history and theoretical debates on race and racialization tell us about such troubling developments? What are the continuing and differing forms of racism (see part 1)? The common variable in all racism is the racializing of individuals and the "othering" of them on the basis of arbitrarily chosen and essentialized "difference(s)" from the dominant group, with a focus on cultural phenotype and the legal categorization of identity as the basis for difference in racialized terms. Further, individuals and groups deemed different are excluded, degraded, cast out, neglected, and sometimes left to perish just because of their physical, religious, and cultural differences. These differences are often hidden in a language of migrancy or, in this latest reiteration of racism, non-belonging to the nation, a language with long and tangled roots in Canada's history. Historically, racism accompanies the global colonialism of Indigenous peoples and produces such systems of exclusion as reserves and reservations; legislated and court mandated legal categories like Canada's Indian Act; residential schools to perpetuate differentiation and genocide wherever it establishes itself; the slavery of African peoples in North and South America; and the indenture of Indians and Chinese peoples in the Caribbean, South America, Africa, Fiji, and other places (see part 2). In addition, it must be remembered that the apartheid system of South Africa—established in the 1960s—was modelled in part on Canada's treatment of status Indians, hence a Canadian export. Settler colonial countries are still characterized by these historical institutions and/or the remaining legacy of such institutions.

Racism is covert, incremental, and systemic (see parts 3B, C, D, and E). It is camouflaged and can be difficult to pinpoint within our education, employment, media, police, and justice systems. In today's diverse societies, with the constant potential for conflict and resistance, the state engages in the politics of commissions, negotiations, co-optations, reconciliations, truth telling, and apologies (see part 3A). One recent example is the celebration of Viola Desmond, who, in 2018, will become the "first Canadian woman" to be on the country's currency—the $10 bill (Annett, 2016). Interestingly, many Canadians, even prominent ones, did not know who Desmond was. Desmond is mistakenly constructed as Canada's Rosa Parks, when Desmond's action against racism and discrimination was some 10 years before Parks's protest. Further, it is intriguing that what brought Desmond to prominence—her action against the discrimination, inequity, and social injustice that Black people face in Canada—is never named by political and civic leaders; rather, they choose to cite her "dignity and bravery," and/or her "courage, strength and determination" as representing important Canadian qualities that "we should all aspire to every day" (Annett, 2016).

The fact that we are differently located and racialized within colonial capitalism, within Canada and globally, sometimes deployed and used against each other, means that there are differences and separations among us. This makes resisting racism and colonialism more complex and challenging. At the same time, new "identities" are produced and solidarities forged that made it possible to fight back. We have organized and are organizing, decolonizing, and resisting everyday (see, in particular, part 4).

THE ORGANIZATION OF THE BOOK

As in the first edition of the book, the editors each worked on their own sections. Part 1 deals with theoretical discussions of "race," presenting the major debates in the literature. Here, Tania Das Gupta took on part 1A (Early Theories of Race), Chris Andersen and Roger C.A. Maaka worked on part 1B (Colonialism and the Construction of Race), and Grace-Edward Galabuzi tackled part 1C (Thinking through Race in the Twenty-First Century).

Part 2 deals with the experiences of colonialism and racism. Roger and Chris decided to completely re-vamp the first part (Indigeneity and Colonialism), while Tania retained the chapters in the second (Colonialism, Slavery, and Indentured Labour).

Part 3 deals with institutional racism. Carl E. James and Tania added the new part 3A (State Multiculturalism—Managing "Difference"). The second part (Racism in the Education System) was handled by Carl; the third (Racism and Employment) by Grace-Edward; the fourth (Racism, the Media, and Popular Culture) by Tania; and the fifth (Racism in the Justice System and Police Force) by Chris.

Finally, Part 4 deals with questions of privilege and marginalization due to "race" as well as resistance. The first part (Race, Privilege, and Identity) was edited by Carl and the second (Resisting Racism) by Tania. Tania also provided overall editorial coordination of the book. The additional annotated readings are intended to provide a means for examining, interrogating, and further discussing the issues raised in various chapters, and to point to future work that could be done.

Despite our effort to be inclusive, gaps undoubtedly exist. There is always room for improvement. Nonetheless, we hope that readers will find this collection provocative and useful in furthering their understanding of "race," racism, racialization, and other intersecting topics.

REFERENCES

Annett, E. 2016. Who's the Woman on Canada's New $10 bill? A Viola Desmond Primer. *Globe and Mail*, December 8. Accessed March 18, 2017. http://www.theglobeandmail.com/news/national/women-on-banknotes-viola-desmond/article33264617.

Hall, Stuart. 1996. The West and the Rest: Discourse and Power. In *Modernity: An Introduction to Modern Societies*, edited by Stuart Hall, David Held, Don Hubert, and Kenneth Thompson, 201–277. Cambridge, MA: Blackwell Publishing.

PART 1

RACE THROUGH TIME

PART 1A

EARLY THEORIES OF RACE

Few words have generated as much debate and controversy as the word *race*. Those of us who think about, study, and write about racism are aware that even today this is an area of tension and division. There are those who employ the word *race* in their work and insist on it, others use it in a critical manner, and some prefer to use other words such as *racialization*. The contemporary debate will be reflected in later chapters. This opening section gives us a sense of the length of this debate, with roots in the seventeenth century and possibly earlier. Admittedly, this debate was taking place among European men, including biologists, geneticists, physicians, philosophers, clergymen, and some of dubious disciplinary origins.

FURTHER READING

Banton, Michael. 1977. *The Idea of Race.* Cambridge, UK: Tavistock Publications.
This book explores the intellectual context within which particular relationships between racial groups emerged. Further, it posits that one cannot separate the sociology of race relations from the history of the idea of "race." In order to understand a certain set of racial relations, one has to understand the knowledge base on which they are based, including how race is understood. Moreover, since the understanding of race has changed over history, one has to have a historical perspective in order to understand both the current knowledge base and the social relationships based on that knowledge. Chapters 3 and 5 in the book are particularly relevant: the former looks at race typology from 1850 onwards, and the latter at social Darwinism.

Graham, Richard, ed. 1990. *The Idea of Race in Latin America.* Austin: University of Texas Press.
This book is a collection of three chapters on Brazil, Argentina, Cuba, and Mexico, focusing on these societies between 1870 and 1940. The authors point out that, following independence from Spain and Portugal, the people in these countries faced the contradiction of having highly mixed societies (ethnically speaking) and yet being dominated by European ideas around racism. The idea that "whitening" the nation through racial mixing would redeem them was dominant, thus demonstrating that racial thinking was hegemonic. This was often reflected in public policies.

Montagu, Ashley. 1965. *The Idea of Race.* **Lincoln: University of Nebraska Press.**
This short book is a collection of three chapters, two of which were lectures that the author gave in 1964. The book differentiates between the "social" and "biological" ideas of race, touching on a variety of writers, including Englishman John Foxe writing in 1570, Aristotle writing in ancient Greece, and Arab scholar Ibn Khaldun writing in 1300. It talks about how the ideology of racism was developed with the combination of both aspects of race, and Montagu systematically argues against it from both biological and social perspectives.

Montagu, Ashley. 1951. *Statement on Race.* **New York: Henry Schuman.**
In the author's own words, this book is "an extended discussion in plain language of the UNESCO statement by experts on race problems." On July 18, 1950, following World War II and the Nazis' extermination of millions of Jews on the basis of alleged racial inferiority, a group of academics issued a statement establishing in writing that race is a myth, as are the notions that race determines mental aptitude, temperament, or social habits. In this book, the author amplifies each section of the statement and discusses the facts and findings on which it is based.

Robb, Peter. 1995. *The Concept of Race in South Asia.* **Delhi: Oxford University Press.**
This collection of essays, largely coming out of a workshop held at the School of Oriental and African Studies in London, explores whether there were homegrown varieties of racial discourses in pre-colonial South Asian texts and to what extent these interacted, co-mingled with, or resisted European race ideology in colonial times. Several chapters deal with how British colonial writings applied racial classifications on Indian subjects. Other chapters explore the extent to which racial perspectives may have influenced oppositional identities as articulated in pan-Islamic and nationalist texts in colonial India.

Chapter 1

Race and Progress[1]

Franz Boas

This chapter is actually an address by Franz Boas as the president of the American Association for the Advancement of Science in 1931. Readers are alerted to the fact that, given the time in which he made this presentation, some of the terminology used by him is highly problematic. While we must critique his use of the term "race" to refer to different groups of people, such as Blacks, whites, Asians, and northern and southern Europeans, his arguments against anti-miscegenation hysteria, sometimes referred to as "race mixing" or even "race degeneration" by eugenic stalwarts, reflect an important debate in the scientific community at that time. Referring to studies of populations from a biological perspective, he argues that wherever there have been populations, there has been mingling among groups and that there is no evidence to suggest that this results in degeneration. He further argues that intense inbreeding sometimes results in health problems and that certain changes in human anatomy can result from environmental, cultural, and social conditions as opposed to human selection. Moreover, there is no biological evidence to connect bodily form and its physical and mental functions. In this connection, he discusses briefly the IQ controversy in the USA. He insists that racial hostility has no biological or natural basis, but rather is socially based.

Permit me to call your attention to the scientific aspects of a problem that has been for a long time agitating our country and which, on account of its social and economic implications, has given rise to strong emotional reactions and has led to varied types of legislation. I refer to the problems due to the intermingling of racial types.

If we wish to reach a reasonable attitude, it is necessary to separate clearly the biological and psychological aspects from the social and economic implications of this problem. Furthermore, the social motivation of what is happening must be looked at not from the narrow point of view of our present conditions but from a wider angle.

The facts with which we are dealing are diverse. The plantation system of the South brought to our shores a large Negro population. Considerable mixture between White masters and slave women occurred during the period of slavery, so that the number of pure Negroes was dwindling continually and the colored population gradually became lighter. A certain amount of intermingling between White and Indian took place, but in the United States and Canada this has never occurred to such a degree that it became an important social phenomenon. In Mexico and many parts of Central and South America it is the most typical case of race contact and race mixture. With the development of immigration the people of eastern and southern Europe were attracted to our country and form now an important part of our population. They differ in type somewhat among themselves, although the racial contrasts are much less than those between Indians or Negroes and Whites. Through Mexican and West Indian immigration another group has come into our country, partly of South European, partly of mixed Negro and mixed Indian descent. To all these must be added the East Asiatic groups, Chinese, Japanese and Filipinos, who play a particularly important role on the Pacific Coast.

The first point in regard to which we need clarification refers to the significance of the term race. In common parlance when we speak of a race we mean a group of people that have certain bodily and perhaps also mental characteristics in common. The Whites, with their light skin, straight or wavy hair and high nose, are a race set off clearly from the Negroes with their dark skin, frizzly hair and flat nose. In regard to these traits the two races are fundamentally distinct. Not quite so definite is the distinction between East Asiatics and European types, because transitional forms do occur among normal White individuals, such as flat faces, straight black hair and eye forms resembling the East Asiatic types; and conversely European-like traits are found among East Asiatics. For Negro and White we may speak of hereditary racial traits so far as these radically distinct features are concerned. For Whites and East Asiatics the difference is not quite so absolute, because a few individuals may be found in each race for whom the racial traits do not hold good, so that in a strict sense we cannot speak of absolutely valid hereditary racial traits.

This condition prevails to a much more marked extent among the different, so-called races of Europe. We are accustomed to speak of a Scandinavian as tall, blond and blue-eyed, of a South Italian as short, swarthy and dark-eyed; of a Bohemian as middle-sized, with brown or gray eyes and wide face and straight hair. We are apt to construct ideal local types which are based on our everyday experience, abstracted from a combination of forms that are most frequently seen in a given locality, and we forget that there are numerous individuals for whom this description does not hold true. It would be a rash undertaking to determine the locality in which a person is born solely from his bodily characteristics. In many cases we may be helped in such a determination by manners of wearing the hair, peculiar mannerisms of motion, and by dress, but these are not to be mistaken for essential hereditary traits. In populations of various parts of Europe many individuals may be found that may as well belong to one part of the continent as to another. There is no truth in the contention so often made that two Englishmen are more alike in bodily form than, let us say, an Englishman and a German. A greater number of forms may be duplicated in the narrower area, but similar forms may be found in all parts of the continent. There is an overlapping of bodily form between the local groups. It is not justifiable to assume that the individuals that do not fit into the ideal local type which we construct from general impressions are foreign elements in the population, that their presence is always due to intermixture with alien types. It is a fundamental characteristic of all local populations that the individuals differ among themselves, and a closer study shows that this is true of animals as well as of men. It is, therefore, not quite proper to speak in these cases of traits that are hereditary in the racial type as a whole, because too many of them occur also in other racial types. Hereditary racial traits should be shared by the whole population so that it is set off against others.

The matter is quite different when individuals are studied as members of their own family lines. Racial heredity implies that there must be a unity of descent, that there must have existed at one time a small number of ancestors of definite bodily form, from whom the present population has descended. It is quite impossible to reconstruct this ancestry through the study of a modern population, but the study of families extending over several generations is often possible. Whenever this study has been undertaken we find that the family lines represented in a single population differ very much among themselves. In isolated communities where the same families have intermarried for generations the differences are less than in larger communities. We may say that every racial group consists of a great many family lines which are distinct in bodily form. Some of these family lines are duplicated in neighboring territories and the more duplication exists the less is it possible to speak of fundamental racial characteristics. These conditions are so manifest in Europe that all we can do is to study the frequency of occurrence of various family lines all over the continent. The differences between the family lines belonging to each larger area are much greater than the differences between the populations as a whole.

Although it is not necessary to consider the great differences in type that occur in a population as due to mixture of different types, it is easy to see that intermingling has played an important part in the history of modern populations. Let us recall to our minds the migrations that occurred in early times in Europe, when the Kelts of Western Europe swept over Italy and eastward to Asia Minor; when the Teutonic tribes migrated from the Black Sea westward into Italy, Spain and even into North Africa; when the Slav expanded northeastward over Russia, and southward into the Balkan Peninsula; when the Moors held a large part of Spain, when Roman and Greek slaves disappeared in the general population, and when Roman colonization affected a large part of the Mediterranean area. It is interesting to note that

Spain's greatness followed the period of greatest race mixture, that its decline set in when the population became stable and immigration stopped. This might give us pause when we speak about the dangers of the intermingling of European types. What is happening in America now is the repetition on a larger scale and in a shorter time of what happened in Europe during the centuries when the people of northern Europe were not yet firmly attached to the soil.

The actual occurrence of intermingling leads us to consider what the biological effect of intermixture of different types may be. Much light has been shed on this question through the intensive study of the phenomena of heredity. It is true we are hampered in the study of heredity in man by the impossibility of experimentation, but much can be learned from observation and through the application of studies of heredity in animals and plants. One fact stands out clearly. When two individuals are mated and there is a very large number of offspring and when furthermore there is no disturbing environmental factor, then the distribution of different forms in the offspring is determined by the genetic characteristics of the parents. What may happen after thousands of generations have passed does not concern us here.

Our previous remarks regarding the characteristics of local types show that matings between individuals essentially different in genetic type must occur in even the most homogeneous population. If it could be shown, as is sometimes claimed, that the progeny of individuals of decidedly distinct proportions of the body would be what has been called disharmonic in character, this would occur with considerable frequency in every population, for we do find individuals, let us say, with large jaws and large teeth and those with small jaws and small teeth. If it is assumed that in the later offspring these conditions might result in a combination of small jaws and large teeth a disharmony would develop. We do not know that this actually occurs. It merely illustrates the line of reasoning. In matings between various European groups these conditions would not be materially changed, although greater differences between parents would be more frequent than in a homogeneous population.

The essential question to be answered is whether we have any evidence that would indicate that matings between individuals of different descent and different type would result in a progeny less vigorous than that of their ancestors. We have not had any opportunity to observe any degeneracy in man as clearly due to this cause. The high nobility of all parts of Europe can be shown to be of very mixed origin. French, German and Italian urban populations are derived from all the distinct European types. It would be difficult to show that any degeneracy that may exist among them is due to an evil effect of intermating. Biological degeneracy is found rather in small districts of intense inbreeding. Here again it is not so much a question of type, but of the presence of pathological conditions in the family strains, for we know of many perfectly healthy and vigorous intensely inbred communities. We find these among the Eskimos and also among many primitive tribes among whom cousin marriages are prescribed by custom.

These remarks do not touch upon the problem of the effect of intermarriages upon bodily form, health and vigor of crosses between races that are biologically more distinct than the types of Europe. It is not quite easy to give absolutely conclusive evidence in regard to this question. Judging merely on the basics of anatomical features and health conditions of mixed populations there does not seem to be any reason to assume unfavorable results, either in the first or in later generations of offspring. The mixed descendants of Europeans and American Indians are taller and more fertile than the pureblood Indians. They are even taller than either parental race. The mixed blood Dutch and Hottentot of South Africa and the Malay mixed bloods of the Island of Kisar are in type intermediate between the two races, and do not exhibit any traits of degeneracy. The populations of the Sudan, mixtures of Mediterranean and Negro types, have always been characterized by great vigor. There is also little doubt that in eastern Russia a considerable infusion of Asiatic blood has occurred. The biological observations on our North American mulattoes do not convince us that there is any deleterious effect of race mixture so far as it is evident in anatomical form and function.

It is also necessary to remember that in varying environment human forms are not absolutely stable, and many of the anatomical traits of the body are subject to a limited amount of change according to climate and conditions of life. We have definite evidence showing changes of bodily size. The stature in European populations has increased materially since the middle of the nineteenth century. War and starvation have left their effects upon the children growing up in the second decade of our century. Proportions of the body change with occupation. The forms of the hand of the laborer and that of the musician reflect their occupations. The changes in head form that have been observed are analogous to those observed in animals under varying conditions of life, among lions born in captivity or among rats fed with different types of diet. The extent to which geographical and social environment may change bodily form is not known, but the influences of outer conditions have to be taken into consideration when comparing different human types.

Selective processes are also at work in changing the character of a population. Differential birth-rate, mortality and migration may bring about changes in the hereditary composition of a group. The range of such changes is limited by the range of variation within the original population. The importance of selection upon the character of a population is easily overestimated. It is true enough that certain defects are transmitted by heredity, but it cannot be proved that a whole population degenerates physically by the numerical increase of degenerates. These always include the physically unfit, and others, the victims of circumstances. The economic depression of our days shows clearly how easily perfectly competent individuals may be brought into conditions of abject poverty and under stresses that only the most vigorous minds can withstand successfully. Equally unjustified is the opinion that war, the struggle between national groups, is a selective process which is necessary to keep mankind on the onward march. Sir Arthur Keith, only a week ago, in his rectoral address at the University of Aberdeen is reported to have said that "Nature keeps her human orchard healthy by pruning and war is her pruning hook." I do not see how such a statement can be justified in any way. War eliminates the physically strong, war increases all the devastating scourges of mankind such as tuberculosis and genital diseases, war weakens the growing generation. History shows that energetic action of masses may be released not only by war but also by other forces. We may not share the fervor or believe in the stimulating ideals; the important point is to observe that they may arouse the same kind of energy that is released in war. Such a stimulus was the abandonment to religion in the middle ages, such is the abandonment of modern Russian youths to their ideal.

So far we have discussed the effects of heredity, environment and selection upon bodily form. We are not so much concerned with the form of the body as with its functions, for in the life of a nation the activities of the individual count rather than his appearance. There is no doubt in my mind that there is a very definite association between the biological make-up of the individual and the physiological and psychological functioning of his body. The claim that only social and other environmental conditions determine the reactions of the individual disregards the most elementary observations, like differences in heart beat, basal metabolism or gland development; and mental differences in their relation to extreme anatomical disturbances of the nervous system. There are organic reasons why individuals differ in their mental behavior.

But to acknowledge this fact does not mean that all differences of behavior can be adequately explained on a purely anatomical basis. When the human body has reached maturity, its form remains fairly stable until the changes due to increasing age set in. Under normal conditions the form and the chemical constitution of the adult body remain almost stable for a number of years. Not so with bodily functions. The conditions of life vary considerably. Our heart beat is different in sleep and in waking. It depends upon the work we are doing, the altitude in which we live, and upon many other factors. It may, therefore, well be that the same individual under different conditions will show quite different reactions. It is the same with other bodily functions. The action of our digestive tract depends upon the quality and quantity of the food we consume. In short, the physiological reactions of the body are markedly adjusted to conditions of life. Owing to this many individuals of different organic structure when exposed to the same environmental conditions will assume a certain degree of similarity of reaction.

On the whole it is much easier to find decided differences between races in bodily form than in function. It cannot be claimed that the body in all races functions in an identical way, but that kind of overlapping which we observed in form is even more pronounced in function. It is quite impossible to say that, because some physical function, let us say the heart beat, has a certain measure, the individual must be White or Negro—for the same rates are found in both races. A certain basal metabolism does not show that a person is a Japanese or a White, although the averages of all the individuals in the races compared may exhibit differences. Furthermore, the particular function is so markedly modified by the demands made upon the organism that these will make the reactions of the racial groups living under the same conditions markedly alike. Every organ is capable of adjustment to a fairly wide range of conditions, and thus the conditions will determine to a great extent the kind of reaction.

What is true of physiological function is equally true of mental function. There exists an enormous amount of literature dealing with mental characteristics of races. The blond North-Europeans, South Italians, Jews, Negroes, Indians, Chinese have been described as though their mental characteristics were biologically determined. It is true, each population has a certain character that is expressed in its behavior, so that there is a geographical distribution of types of behavior. At the same time we have a geographical distribution of anatomical types, and as a result we find that a selected population can be described as having a certain anatomical type and a certain kind of behavior. This, however, does not justify us in claiming that the anatomical type determines behavior. A great error is committed when we allow ourselves to draw this inference. First of all it would be necessary to prove that the correlation between bodily form and behavior is absolute, that it is valid not only for the selected spot, but for the whole population of the given type, and, conversely, that the same behavior does not occur when the types of bodily build differ. Secondly, it would have to be shown that there is an inner relation between the two phenomena.

I might illustrate this by an example taken from an entirely different field. A particular country has a specific climate and particular geological formation. In the same country is found a certain flora. Nevertheless, the character of soil and climate does not explain the composition of the flora, except in so far as it depends upon these two factors. Its composition depends upon the whole historical evolution of plant forms all over the world. The single fact of an agreement of distribution does not prove a genetic relation between the two sets of observations. Negroes in Africa have long limbs and a certain kind of mental behavior. It does not follow that the long limbs are in any way the cause of their mental behavior. The very point to be proved is assumed as proved in this kind of argumentation.

A scientific solution of this problem requires a different line of approach. Mental activities are functions of the organism. We have seen that physiological functions of the same organism may vary greatly under varying conditions. Is the case of mental reactions different? While the study of cretins and of men of genius shows that biological differences exist which limit the type of individual behavior, this has little bearing upon the masses constituting a population in which great varieties of bodily structure prevail. We have seen that the same physiological functions occur in different races with varying frequency, but that no essential qualitative differences can be established. The question must be asked whether the same conditions prevail in mental life.

If it were possible to subject two populations of different type to the same outer conditions the answer would not be difficult. The obstacle in our way lies in the impossibility of establishing sameness of conditions. Investigators differ fundamentally in their opinion in regard to the question of what constitutes sameness of conditions, and our attention must be directed, therefore, to this question.

If we could show how people of exactly the same biological composition react in different types of environment, much might be gained. It seems to me that the data of history create a strong presumption in favor of material changes of mental behavior among peoples of the same genetic composition. The free and easy English of Elizabethan times contrast forcibly with the prudish Mid-Victorian; the Norse Viking and the modern Norwegian do not impress us as the same; the stern Roman republican and his dissolute descendant of imperial times present striking contrasts.

But we need more tangible evidence. At least in so far as intelligent reaction to simple problems of everyday life is concerned, we may bring forward a considerable amount of experimental evidence that deals with this problem. We do not need to assume that our modern intelligence tests give us a clue to absolutely biologically determined intelligence—whatever that may mean—they certainly do tell us how individuals react to simple, more or less unfamiliar, situations. At a first glance it would seem that very important racial differences are found. I refer to the many comparative tests of the intelligence of individuals of various European types and of Europeans and Negroes. North Europeans tested in our country were found as a whole decidedly superior to South Europeans, Europeans as a whole to Negroes. The question arises, what does this mean? If there is a real difference determined by race, we should find the same kind of difference between these racial types wherever they live. Professor Garth has recently collected the available evidence and reaches the conclusion that it is not possible to prove a difference due to genetic factors, that rather all the available observations may be easily explained as due to differences in social environment. It seems to me the most convincing proof of the correctness of this view has been given by Dr. Klineberg, who examined the various outstanding European types in urban and rural communities in Europe. He found that there is everywhere a marked contrast between rural and urban populations, the city giving considerably better results than the country and that furthermore the various groups do not follow by any means the same order in city and country; that the order rather depends upon social conditions, such as the excellence of the school systems and conflicts between home and school. Still more convincing are his observations on Negroes. He examined a considerable number of Negroes in southern cities who had moved to the city from rural districts. He found that the longer they lived in the city the better the results of the tests came to be, so that Negroes who had lived in the city for six years were far superior to those who had just moved to the city. He found the same result when studying Negroes who had moved from the south to New York, an improvement with the time of residence in New York. This result agrees with Brigham's findings for Italians who had lived for varying periods in the United States. It has often been claimed, as was done in the beginning by Brigham, that such changes are due to a process of selection, that more poorly endowed individuals have migrated to the country in late years and represent the group that has just come to the city. It would be difficult to maintain this in view of the regularity with which this phenomenon reappears in every test. Still, Dr. Klineberg has also given definite evidence that selection does not account for these differences. He compared the records of the migrating groups with those who remained behind. The records collected in Nashville and Birmingham showed that there is no appreciable difference between the two groups. The migrants were even a little below those who stayed at home. He also found that the migrants who came to New York were slightly inferior to those who remained in the South.

I have given these data in some detail, because they show definitely that cultural environment is a most important factor in determining the results of the so-called intelligence tests. In fact, a careful examination of the tests shows clearly that in none of them has our cultural experience been eliminated. City life and country life, the South and the North present different types of cultural background to which we learn to adapt ourselves, and our reactions are determined by these adaptations, which are often so obscure that they can be detected only by a most intimate knowledge of the conditions of life. We have indications of such adaptations in other cases. It would seem that among the Plains Indians the experience of girls with bead work gives to them a superiority in handling tests based on form. It is highly desirable that the tests should be examined with greatest care in regard to the indirect influence of experience upon the results. I suspect strongly that such influences can always be discovered and that it will be found impossible to construct any test in which this element is so completely eliminated that we could consider the results as an expression of purely biologically determined factors.

It is much more difficult to obtain convincing results in regard to emotional reactions in different races. No satisfactory experimental method has been devised that would answer the crucial question, in how far cultural background and in how far the biological basis of personality is responsible for observed differences. There is no doubt that individuals do differ in this respect on account of their biological constitution. It is very questionable whether the same may be said of races, for in all races we find a wide range of different types of personality. All that we can say with certainty is that the cultural factor is of greatest importance and might well account for all the observed differences, although this does not preclude the possibility of biologically determined differences. The variety of response of groups of the same race but culturally different is so great that it seems likely that any existing biological differences are of minor importance. I can give only a few instances. The North American Indians are reputed as stoic, as ready to endure pain and torture without a murmur. This is true in all those cases in which culture demands repression of emotion. The same Indians, when ill, give in to hopeless depression. Among closely related Indian tribes certain ones are given to ecstatic orgies, while others enjoy a life running in smooth conventional channels. The buffalo hunter was an entirely different personality from the poor Indian who has to rely on government help, or who lives on the proceeds of land rented by his White neighbors. Social workers are familiar with the subtle influence of personal relations that will differentiate the character of members of the same family. Ethnological evidence is all in favor of the assumption that hereditary racial traits are unimportant as compared to cultural conditions. As a matter of fact, ethnological studies do not concern themselves with race as a factor in cultural form. From Waitz on, through Spencer, Tylor, Bastian, to our times, ethnologists have not given serious attention to race, because they find cultural forms distributed regardless of race.

I believe the present state of our knowledge justifies us in saying that, while individuals differ, biological differences between races are small. There is no reason to believe that one race is by nature so much more intelligent, endowed with great will power, or emotionally more stable than another, that the difference would materially influence its culture. Nor is there any good reason to believe that the differences between races are so great that the descendants of mixed marriages would be inferior to their parents. Biologically there is no good reason to object to fairly close inbreeding in healthy groups, nor to intermingling of the principal races.

I have considered so far only the biological side of the problem. In actual life we have to reckon with social settings which have a very real existence, no matter how erroneous the opinions on which they are founded. Among us race antagonism is a fact, and we should try to understand its psychological significance. For this purpose we have to consider the behavior not only of man, but also of animals. Many animals live in societies. It may be a shoal of fish which any individuals of the same species may join, or a swarm of mosquitoes. No social tie is apparent in these groups, but there are others which we may call close societies that do not permit any outsider to join their group. Packs of dogs and well-organized herds of higher mammals, ants and bees are examples of this kind. In all these groups there is a considerable degree of social solidarity which is expressed particularly by antagonism against any outside group. The troops of monkeys that live in a given territory will not allow another troop to come and join them. The members of a closed animal society are mutually tolerant or even helpful. They repel all outside intruders.

Conditions in primitive society are quite similar. Strict social obligations exist between the members of a tribe, but all outsiders are enemies. Primitive ethics demand self-sacrifice in the group to which the individual belongs, deadly enmity against every outsider. A closed society does not exist without antagonisms against others. Although the degree of antagonism against outsiders has decreased, closed societies continue to exist in our own civilization. The nobility formed a closed society until very recent times. Patricians and plebeians in Rome, Greeks and barbarians, the gangs of our streets, Mohammedan and infidel, and our modern nations are in this sense closed societies that cannot exist without antagonisms. The principles that hold societies together vary enormously, but common to all of them are social obligations within the group, antagonisms against other parallel groups.

Race consciousness and race antipathy differ in one respect from the social groups here enumerated. While in all other human societies there is no external characteristic that helps to assign an individual to his group, here his very appearance singles him out. If the belief should prevail, as it once did, that all red-haired individuals have an undesirable character, they would at once be segregated and no red-haired individual could escape from his class no matter what his personal characteristics might be. The Negro, the East Asiatic or Malay who may at once be recognized by his bodily build is automatically placed in his class and not one of them can escape being excluded from a foreign closed group. The same happens when a group is characterized by dress imposed by circumstances, by choice, or because a dominant group prescribe for them a distinguishing symbol—like the garb of the medieval Jews or the stripes of the convict—so that each individual no matter what his own character may be, is at once assigned to his group and treated accordingly. If racial antipathy were based on innate human traits this would be expressed in interracial sexual aversion. The free intermingling of slave owners with their female slaves and the resulting striking decrease in the number of full-blood Negroes, the progressive development of a half-blood Indian population and the readiness of intermarriage with Indians when economic advantages may be gained by such means, show clearly that there is no biological foundation for race feeling. There is no doubt that the strangeness of an alien racial type does play an important role, for the ideal of beauty of the White who grows up in a purely White society is different from that of a Negro. This again is analogous to the feeling of aloofness among groups that are characterized by different dress, different mannerisms of expression of emotion, or by the ideal of bodily strength as against that of refinement of form. The student of race relations must answer the question whether in societies in which different racial types form a socially homogeneous group, a marked race consciousness develops. This question cannot be answered categorically, although interracial conditions in Brazil and the disregard of racial affiliation in the relation between Mohammedans and infidels show that race consciousness may be quite insignificant.

When social divisions follow racial lines, as they do among ourselves, the degree of difference between racial forms is an important element in establishing racial groupings and in creating racial conflicts.

The actual relation is not different from that developing in other cases in which social cleavage develops. In times of intense religious feeling denominational conflicts, in times of war national conflicts take the same course. The individual is merged in his group and not rated according to his personal value.

However, nature is such that constantly new groups are formed in which each individual subordinates himself to the group. He expresses his feeling of solidarity by an idealization of his group and by an emotional desire for its perpetuation. When the groups are denominational, there is strong antagonism against marriages outside of the group. The group must be kept pure, although denomination and descent are in no way related. If the social groups are racial groups we encounter in the same way the desire for racial endogamy in order to maintain racial purity.

On this subject I take issue with Sir Arthur Keith, who in the address already referred to is reported to have said that "race antipathy and race prejudice nature has implanted in you for her own end—the improvement of mankind through racial differentiation." I challenge him to prove that race antipathy is "implanted by nature" and not the effect of social causes which are active in every closed social group, no matter whether it is racially heterogeneous or homogeneous. The complete lack of sexual antipathy, the weakening of race consciousness in communities in which children grow up as an almost homogeneous group; the occurrence of equally strong antipathies between denominational groups, or between social strata—as witnessed by the Roman patricians and plebeians, the Spartan Lacedaemonians and Helots, the Egyptian castes and some of the Indian castes—all these show that antipathies are social phenomena. If you will, you may call them "implanted by nature," but only in so far as man is a being living in closed social groups, leaving it entirely indetermined what these social groups may be.

No matter how weak the case for racial purity may be, we understand its social appeal in our society. While the biological reasons that are adduced may not be relevant, a stratification of society in social groups that are racial in character will always lead to racial discrimination. As in all other sharp social groupings the individual is not judged as an individual but as a member of his class. We may be reasonably certain that whenever members of different races form a single social group with strong bonds, racial prejudice and racial antagonisms will come to lose their importance. They may even disappear entirely. As long as we insist on a stratification in racial layers, we shall pay the penalty in the form of interracial struggle. Will it be better for us to continue as we have been doing, or shall we try to recognize the conditions that lead to the fundamental antagonisms that trouble us?

NOTE

1.   Address of the president of the American Association for the Advancement of Science, Pasadena, June 15. *Science*, N.S., vol. 74. (1931) pp. 1–8.

Chapter 2

The Concept of Race[1]

Ashley Montagu

This chapter by Ashley Montagu, an address on genetics from 1962, makes a case for abandoning the use of the term "race" and suggests using other terms to refer to different groups of people, terms such as "ethnic groups" or "genogroups." Readers can explore whether these words suggested by him are acceptable or not in light of some current writings that assert that even seemingly neutral concepts such as "ethnicity" are subject to social construction and power relations. Nevertheless, Montagu's main argument in favour of throwing out problematic terms used to build "the master's house" and searching for new ones is worth considering. Further, he critiques the "scientific" approach of making conclusions about human species on the basis of what other animal species do or don't do, because, as he argues, one cannot equate all animal groupings with human groupings, as the latter, unlike the former, are subject to "culture, that is to say, the man-made [sic] part of the environment" in addition to nature. His opposition to the use of "race" in studying populations is based on the fact that the word has a very problematic set of associations and assumptions underlying it, such as those based in race typology; he insists that it is impossible to use the word in any other way.

In this paper I desire to examine the concepts of race as they are used with reference to man. I shall first deal with the use of this term by biologists and anthropologists, and then with its use by the man-on-the-street, the so-called layman—so-called, no doubt, from the lines in Sir Philip Sidney's sonnet:

> I never drank of Aganippe well
> Nor ever did in shade of Tempe sit,
> And Muses scorn with vulgar brains to dwell;
> Poor layman I, for sacred rites unfit.

I shall endeavor to show that all those who continue to use the term "race" with reference to man, whether they be laymen or scientists, are "for sacred rites unfit." Once more, I shall, as irritatingly as the sound of a clanging door heard in the distance in a wind that will not be shut out, raise the question as to whether, with reference to man, it would not be better if the term "race" were altogether abandoned.

At the outset it should, perhaps, be made clear that I believe, with most biologists, that evolutionary factors, similar to those that have been operative in producing raciation in other animal species, have also been operative in the human species—but with a significant added difference, namely, the consequences which have resulted from man's entry into that unique zone of adaptation in which he excels beyond all other creatures, namely culture, that is to say, the man-made part of the environment.

On the evidence it would seem clear that man's cultural activities have introduced elements into the processes of human raciation which have so substantially modified the end-products that one can no longer equate the processes of raciation in lower animals with those which have occurred in the evolution of man. The factors of mutation, natural selection, drift, isolation, have all been operative in the evolution of man. But so have such factors as ever-increasing degrees of mobility, hybridization, and social selection, and it is the effects of these and similar factors which, at least so it has always seemed to me, makes the employment of the term "race" inapplicable to most human populations as we find them today.

Of course there exist differences, but we want a term by which to describe the existence of these differences. We do not want a prejudiced term which injects meanings which are not there into the differences. We want a term which as nearly mirrors the conditions as a term can, not one which falsifies and obfuscates the issue.

Terminology is extremely important, and I think it will be generally agreed that it is rather more desirable to allow the conditions or facts to determine the meaning of the terms by which we shall refer to them, than to have pre-existing terms determine the manner in which they shall be perceived and ordered, for pre-existing terms constitute pre-existing meanings, and such meanings have a way of conditioning the manner in which what we look at shall be perceived. Each time the term "race" is used with reference to man, this is what, I think, is done.

The term "race" has a long and tortured history. We cannot enter upon that here. The present-day usage of the term in biological circles is pretty much the sense in which it was used in similar circles in the 19th century, namely, as a subdivision of a species the members of which resemble each other and differ from other members of the species in certain traits. In our own time valiant attempts have been made to pour new wine into the old bottles. The shape of the bottle, however, remains the same. The man-on-the-street uses the term in much the same way as it was used by his 19th century compeer. Here physical type, heredity, blood, culture, nation, personality, intelligence, and achievement are all stirred together to make the omelet which is the popular conception of "race." This is a particularly virulent term, the epidemiology of which is far better understood by the social scientist than by the biologist—who should, therefore, exercise a little more caution than he usually does when he delivers himself on the subject.

The difficulty with taking over old terms in working with problems to which they are thought to apply is that when this is done we may also take over some of the old limitations of the term, and this may affect our approach to the solution of those problems. For what the investigator calls "the problem of human races" is immediately circumscribed and delimited the moment he uses the word "races." For "race" implies something very definite to him, something which in itself constitutes a solution, and the point I would like to make is that far from the problem meaning something like a solution to him, it should, on the contrary, constitute itself in his mind as something more closely resembling what it is, namely, a problem requiring investigation.

Instead of saying to himself, as the true believer in "race" does, "Here is a population, let me see how it fits my criteria of 'race,'" I think it would be much more fruitful of results if he said to himself, instead, "Here is a population, let me go ahead and find out what it is like. What its internal likenesses and differences are, and how it resembles and how it differs from other populations. And then let me operationally describe what I have found," that is, in terms of the data themselves, and not with reference to the conditions demanded by any pre-existing term.

The chief objection to the term "race" with reference to man is that it takes for granted as solved problems which are far from being so and tends to close the mind to problems to which it should always remain open. If, with ritual fidelity, one goes on repeating long enough that "the Nordics" are a race, or that "the Armenoids" are, or that "the Jews" are, or that races may be determined by their blood group gene frequencies, we have already determined what a "race" is, and it is not going to make the slightest difference whether one uses the old or the new wine, for we are back at the same old stand pouring it into the old bottles covered with the same patina of moss-like green.

It is the avoidance of this difficulty that T.H. Huxley had in mind when in 1865, he wrote, "I speak of 'persistent modifications' or 'stocks' rather than of 'varieties,' or 'races,' or 'species,' because each of these last well-known terms implies, on the part of its employer, a preconceived opinion touching one of those problems, the solution of which is the ultimate object of the science; and in regard to which, therefore, ethnologists are especially bound to keep their minds open and their judgments freely balanced" (1865, 209–10).

It is something to reflect upon that, a century later, this point of view has still to be urged.

In the year 1900, the French anthropologist Joseph Deniker published his great book, simultaneously in French and in English, *The Races of Man*. But though the title has the word in it, he objected to the term "race" on much the same grounds as Huxley. The whole of his introduction is devoted to showing the difficulties involved in applying to man the terms of zoological nomenclature. He writes, "We have presented to us Arabs, Swiss, Australians, Bushmen, English, Siouan Indians, Negroes, etc., without knowing if each of these groups is on an equal footing from the point of view of classification."

"Do these real and palpable groupings represent unions of individuals which, in spite of some slight dissimilarities, are capable of forming what zoologists call 'species,' 'subspecies,' 'varieties,' in the case of wild animals, or 'races' in the case of domestic animals? One need not be a professional anthropologist to reply negatively to this question. They are *ethnic groups* formed by virtue of community of language, religion, social institutions, etc., which have the power of uniting human beings of one or several species, races, or varieties, and are by no means zoological species; they may include human beings of one or of many species, races, or varieties." "They are," he goes on to say, "theoretic types" (1900, 2–3).

When, in 1936, Julian Huxley and A.C. Haddon published their valuable book on "race," *We Europeans*, they took pains to underscore the fact that "the existence of ... human sub-species is purely hypothetical. Nowhere does a human group now exist which corresponds closely to a systematic sub-species in animals, since various original sub-species have crossed repeatedly and constantly. For the existing populations, the non-committal term *ethnic group* should be used.... All that exists today is a number of arbitrary ethnic groups, intergrading into each other" (1936, 106). And finally, "The essential reality of the existing situation ... is not the hypothetical sub-species or races, but the *mixed ethnic groups*, which can never be genetically purified into their original components, or purged of the variability which they owe to past crossing. Most anthropological writings of the past, and many of the present fail to take account of this fundamental fact" (1936, 108). "If *race* is a scientific term," these authors point out, "it must have a genetic meaning" (1936, 114).

Haddon, as an anthropologist, was familiar with Deniker's book, and it is possible that the noncommittal term "ethnic group" was remembered by him as one more appropriately meeting the requirements of the situation and thus came to be adopted by both authors in their book. It was from this source, that is from Huxley and Haddon, that I, in turn, adopted the term "ethnic group" in 1936 and have consistently continued to use it since that time. The claim is that the noncommittal general term "ethnic group" meets the realities of the situation head on, whereas the term "race" does not. Furthermore, it is claimed that "ethnic group" is a term of heuristic value. It raises questions, and doubts, leading to clarification and discovery. The term "race," since it takes for granted what requires to be demonstrated within its own limits, closes the mind on all that.

It is of interest to find that quite a number of biologists have, in recent years, independently raised objections to the continuing use of the term "race," even, in some cases, when it is applied to populations of lower animals. Thus, for example, W.T. Calman writes, "Terms such as 'geographical race,' 'form,' 'phase,' and so forth, may be useful in particular instances but are better not used until some measure of agreement is reached as to their precise meaning" (1949, 14). Hans Kalmus writes, "A very important term which was originally used in systematics is 'race.' Nowadays, however, its use is avoided as far as possible in genetics" (1948, 45). In a later work Kalmus writes, "It is customary to discuss the local varieties of humanity in terms of 'race.' However, it is unnecessary to use this greatly debased word, since it is easy to describe populations without it" (1958, 30). G.S. Carter writes that the terms "'race,' 'variety,' and 'form' are used so loosely and in so many senses that it is advisable to avoid using them as infraspecific categories" (1951, 163). Ernst Hanhart objects to the use of the term "race" with reference to man since he holds that there are no "true races" among men (1953, 545). Abercrombie, Hickman, and Johnson, in their *A Dictionary of Biology* (1951), while defining species and subspecies consistently, decline even a mention of the word "race" anywhere in their book. L.S. Penrose in an otherwise highly favorable review of Dunn and Dobzhansky's excellent *Heredity, Race and Society*, writes that he is unable "to see the necessity for the rather apologetic retention of the obsolete term 'race,' when what is meant is simply a given population differentiated by some social, geographical or genetical character, or … merely by a gene frequency peculiarity. The use of the almost mystical concept of race makes the presentation of the facts about the geographical and linguistic groups … unnecessarily complicated" (1952, 252).

To see what Penrose means, and at the same time to make our criticism of their conception of "race," let us turn to Dunn and Dobzhansky's definition of race. They write, in the aforementioned work, "Races can be defined as populations which differ in the frequencies of some gene or genes" (1952, 118). This definition at once leads to the question: Why use the word "race" here when what is being done is precisely what should be done, namely, to describe populations in terms of their gene frequency differences? What, in point of fact, has the antiquated, mystical conception of "race" to do with this? The answer is: Nothing. Indeed, the very notion of "race" is antithetical to the study of population genetics, for the former traditionally deals with fixed clear-cut differences, and the latter with fluid or fluctuating differences. It seems to me an unrealistic procedure to maintain that this late in the day we can re-adapt the term "race" to mean something utterly different from what it has always most obfuscatingly and ambiguously meant.

We may congratulate ourselves, and in fact often do, that the chemists of the late 18th and early 19th centuries had the good sense to throw out the term "phlogiston" when they discovered that it corresponded to nothing in reality, instead of attempting to adapt it to fit the facts which it was not designed to describe, and of which, indeed, it impeded the discovery for several centuries. The psychologists of the second decade of this century had the good sense to do likewise with the term "instinct" when they discovered how, like a bunion upon the foot, it impeded the pilgrim's progress toward a sounder understanding of human drives (Bernard 1924).

It is simply not possible to redefine words with so longstanding a history of misuse as "race," and for this, among other cogent reasons, it is ill-advised. As Simpson has said, "There … is a sort of Gresham's Law for words; redefine them as we will, their worst or most extreme meaning is almost certain to remain current and to tend to drive out the meaning we prefer" (1953, 268).

For this reason alone it would appear to me unwise to afford scientific sanction to a term which is so embarrassed by false meanings as is the term "race." There is the added objection that it is wholly redundant, and confusingly so, to distinguish as a "race" a population which happens to differ from other populations in the frequency of one or more genes. Why call such populations "races" when the operational definition of what they are is sharply and clearly stated in the words used to convey what we mean, namely, populations which differ from one another in particular frequencies of certain specified genes? Surely, to continue the use of the word "race" under such circumstances is to exemplify what A.E. Housman so aptly described as "calling in ambiguity of language to promote confusion of thought" (1933, 31).

When populations differ from each other in the frequency of the sickle-cell gene or any other gene or genes, all that is necessary is to state the facts with reference to those populations. That is what those populations are in terms of gene frequencies. And those are the operative criteria which we can use as tools or concepts in giving an account of the realities of the situation—the actual operations.

I have thus far said nothing about the anthropological conception of "race" because this is to some extent yielding to genetic pressure, and because the future of what used to be called the study of "race" lies, in my view, largely in the direction of population genetics. The older anthropological conception of "race" still occasionally lingers on, suggesting that it is perhaps beyond the reach both of scientific judgment and mortal malice. Insofar as the genetic approach to the subject is concerned, many anthropologists are, as it were, self-made men and only too obviously represent cases of unskilled labor. However, my feeling is that they should be praised for trying rather than blamed for failing. The new anthropology is on the right track.

Recently Garn and Coon (1955) have attempted to adapt the terms "geographic race," "local race," and "microgeographical race," for use in the human species. They define, for example, "A geographical race" as, "in its simplest terms, a collection of (race) populations having features in common, such as a high gene frequency for blood group B, and extending over a geographically definable area" (1955, 997).

In this definition I think we can see, in high relief as it were, what is wrong with the continuing use of the term "race." The term "geographical race" immediately delimits the group of populations embraced by it from others, as if the so-called "geographical race" were a biological entity "racially" distinct from others. Such a group of populations is not "racially" distinct, but differs from others in the frequencies of certain of its genes. It was suggested by the UNESCO group of geneticists and physical anthropologists that such a group of populations be called a "major group" (Montagu 1951, 173–82). This suggestion was made precisely in order to avoid such difficulties as are inherent in the term "geographical race." Since Garn and Coon themselves admit that "geographical races are to a large extent collections of convenience, useful more for pedagogic purposes than as units for empirical investigation" (1955, 1000), it seems to me difficult to understand why they should have preferred this term to the one more closely fitting the situation, namely, "major groups." It is a real question whether spurious precision, even for pedagogical purposes, or as an "as if" fiction, is to be preferred to a frank acknowledgment, in the terms we use, of the difficulties involved. Garn and Coon are quite alive to the problem, but it may be questioned whether it contributes to the student's clearer understanding of that problem to use terms which not only do not fit the conditions, but which serve to contribute to making the student's mind a dependable instrument of imprecision, especially in view of the fact that a more appropriate term is available.

The principle of "squatter's rights" apparently applies to words as well as to property. When men make a heavy investment in words they are inclined to treat them as property, and even to become enslaved by them, the prisoners of their own vocabularies. High walls may not a prison make, but technical terms sometimes do. This, I would suggest, is another good reason for self-examination with regard to the use of the term "race."

Commenting on Garn's views on race, Dr. J.P. Garlick has remarked, "The use of 'race' as a taxonomic unit for man seems out of date, if not irrational. A hierarchy of geographical, local and micro-races is proposed, with acknowledgements to Rensch and Dobzhansky. But the criteria for their definition are nowhere made clear, and in any case such a scheme could not do justice to the many independent fluctuations and frequency gradients shown by human polymorphic characters. Surely physical anthropology has outgrown such abstractions as 'Large Local Race.... Alpine: the rounder-bodied, rounder-headed, predominantly darker peoples of the French mountains, across Switzerland, Austria, and to the shores of the Black Sea'" (1961, 169–70).

Garn and Coon do not define "local races" but say of them that they "can be identified, not so much by average differences, but by their nearly complete isolation" (1955, 997). In that case, as Dahlberg (1942) long ago suggested, why not call such populations "isolates"?

"Microgeographical races" also fail to receive definition, but are described as differing "only qualitatively from local races." In that case, why not use some term which suggests the difference?

In short, it is our opinion that taxonomies and terms should be designed to fit the facts, and not the facts forced into the procrustean rack of pre-determined categories. If we are to have references, whether terminological or taxonomical, to existing or extinct populations of man, let the conditions as we find them determine the character of our terms or taxonomies, and not the other way round.

Since what we are actually dealing with in human breeding populations are differences in the frequencies of certain genes, why not use a term which states just this, such as *genogroup*, and the various appropriate variants of this?[2] If necessary, we could then speak of "geographic genogroups," "local genogroups," and "microgenogroups." A genogroup being defined as a breeding population which differs from other breeding populations of the species in the frequency of one or more genes. The term "genogroup" gets as near to a statement of the facts as a term can. The term "race" goes far beyond the facts and only serves to obscure them. A *geographic genogroup* would then be defined as a group of breeding populations characterized by a marked similarity of the frequencies of one or more genes.

A *local genogroup* would be one of the member populations of a geographic genogroup, and a *microgenogroup* a partially isolated population with one or more gene frequency differences serving to distinguish it from adjacent or nonadjacent local genogroups.

It is to be noted that nothing is said of a common heredity for similarity in gene frequencies in a geographic genogroup. The common heredity is usually implied, but I do not think it should be taken for granted, except within the local genogroups and the microgenogroups. One or more of the genogroups in a geographic genogroup may have acquired their frequencies for a given gene quite independently of the other local populations comprising the geographic genogroup. This is a possibility which is, perhaps, too often overlooked when comparisons are being made on the basis of gene frequencies between populations, whether geographic or not.

But this must suffice for my criticism of the usage of the term "race" by biologists and anthropologists. I wish now to discuss, briefly, the disadvantages of the use of this term in popular usage, and the advantages of the general term "ethnic group."

The layman's conception of "race" is so confused and emotionally muddled that any attempt to modify it would seem to be met by the greatest obstacle of all, the term "race" itself. It is a trigger word. Utter it, and a whole series of emotionally conditioned responses follow. If we are to succeed in clarifying the minds of those who think in terms of "race" we must cease using the word, because by continuing to use it we sanction whatever meaning anyone chooses to bestow upon it, and because in the layman's mind the term refers to conditions which do not apply. There is no such thing as the kind of "race" in which the layman believes, namely, that there exists an indissoluble association between mental and physical characters which make individual members of certain "races" either inferior or superior to the members of certain other "races." The layman requires to have his thinking challenged on this subject. The term "ethnic group" serves as such a challenge to thought and as a stimulus to rethink the foundations of one's beliefs. The term "race" takes for granted what should be a matter for inquiry. And this is precisely the point that is raised when one uses the noncommittal "ethnic group." It encourages the passage from ignorant or confused certainty to thoughtful uncertainty. For the layman, as for others, the term "race" closes the door on understanding. The phrase "ethnic group" opens it, or at the very least, leaves it ajar.

In opposition to these views a number of objections have been expressed. Here are some of them. One does not change anything by changing names. It is an artful dodge. Why not meet the problem head-on? If the term has been badly defined in the past, why not redefine it? Re-education should be attempted by establishing the true meaning of "race," not by its existence. It suggests a certain blindness to the facts to deny that "races" exist in man. One cannot combat racism by enclosing the word in quotes. It is not the word that requires changing but people's ideas about it. It is a common failing to argue from the abuse of an idea to its total exclusion. It is quite as possible to feel "ethnic group prejudice" as it is to feel "race prejudice." One is not going to solve the race problem this way.

Such objections indicate that there has been a failure of communication, that the main point has been missed. The term "ethnic group" is not offered as a substitute for "race." On the contrary, the term "ethnic group" implies a fundamental difference in viewpoint from that which is implied in the term "race." It is not a question of changing names or of substitution, or an artful dodge, or the abandonment of a good term which has been abused. It is first and foremost an attempt to clarify the fact that the old term is unsound when applied to man, and should therefore not be used with reference to him. At the same time "ethnic group," being an intentionally vague and general term, is designed to make it clear that there is a problem to be solved, rather than to maintain the fiction that the problem has been solved. As a general term it leaves all question of definition open, referring specifically to human breeding populations, the members of which are believed to exhibit certain physical or genetic likenesses. For all general purposes, an "ethnic group" may be defined as one of a number of breeding populations, which populations together comprise the species *Homo sapiens*, and which individually maintain their differences, physical or genetic and cultural, by means of isolating mechanisms such as geographic and social barriers.

The re-education of the layman should be taken seriously. For this reason I would suggest that those who advocate the redefinition of the term "race," rather than its replacement by a general term which more properly asks questions before it attempts definitions, would do well to acquaint themselves with the nature of the laymen as well as with the meaning of the phenomena to which they would apply a term which cannot possibly be redefined. If one desires to remove a prevailing erroneous conception and introduce a more correct one, one is more likely to be successful by introducing the new conception with a distinctively new term rather than by attempting redefinition of a term embarrassed by longstanding unsound usage. Professor Henry Sigerist has well said that "it is never sound to continue the use of terminology with which the minds of millions of people have been poisoned even when the old terms are given new meanings" (1951, 101).

There is, apparently, a failure on the part of some students to understand that one of the greatest obstacles to the process of re-education would be the retention of the old term "race," a term which enshrines the errors it is designed to remove. The deep implicit meanings this term possesses for the majority of its users are such that they require immediate challenge whenever and by whomsoever the term "race" is used.

Whenever the term "race" is used, most people believe that something like an eternal verity has been uttered when, in fact, nothing more than evidence has been given that there are many echoes, but few voices. "Race" is a word so familiar that in using it the uncritical thinker is likely to take his own private meaning for it completely for granted, never thinking at any time to question so basic an instrument of the language as the word "race." On the other hand, when one uses the term "ethnic group," the question is immediately raised, "What does it mean? What does the user have in mind?" And this at once affords an opportunity to discuss the facts and explore the meaning and the falsities enshrined in the word "race," and to explain the problems involved and the facts of the genetic situation as we know them.

The term "ethnic group" is concerned with questions; the term "race" is concerned with answers, unsound answers, where for the most part there are only problems that require to be solved before any sound answers can be given.

It may be difficult for those who believe in what I.A. Richards has called "The Divine Right of Words" to accept the suggestion that a word such as "race," which has exercised so evil a tyranny over the minds of men, should be permanently dethroned from the vocabulary, but that constitutes all the more reason for trying, remembering that the meaning of a word is the action it produces.

NOTES

1. Presented at the University Seminar on Genetics and the Evolution of Man, Columbia University, December 6, 1959.
2. The term "genogroup" was suggested to me by Sir Julian Huxley during a conversation on September 29, 1959.

REFERENCES

Abercrombie, M., C.J. Hickman, and M.L. Johnson. 1951. *A dictionary of biology*. Harmondsworth: Penguin Books.

Bernard, L.L. 1924. *Instinct*. New York: Henry Holt and Co.

Calman, W.T. 1949. *The classification of animals*. New York: John Wiley and Sons.

Carter, G.S. 1951. *Animal evolution*. New York: Macmillan Co.

Dahlberg, G. 1942. *Race, reason and rubbish*. New York: Columbia University Press.

Deniker, J. 1900. *The races of man*. London: The Walter Scott Publishing Co. Ltd.

Dunn, L.C., and Th. Dobzhansky. 1952. *Heredity, race and society*. Rev. ed. New York: The New American Library of World Literature.

Garlick, J.P. 1961. Review of *Human races and Readings on race*, by S.M. Garn. *Annals of Human Genetics* 25:169–70.

Garn, S.M., and C.S. Coon. 1955. On the number of races of mankind. *American Anthropologist* 57:996–1001.

Hanhart, E. 1953. Infectious diseases. In *Clinical genetics*, ed. Arnold Sorsby. St. Louis: Mosby.

Housman, A.E. 1933. *The name and nature of poetry*. New York: Cambridge University Press.

Huxley, J.S., and A.C. Haddon. 1936. *We Europeans: a survey of "racial" problems*. New York: Harper and Bros.

Huxley, T.H. 1865. On the methods and results of ethnology. *Fortnightly Review*. Reprinted in *Man's place in nature and other anthropological essays*. London: Macmillan Co., 1894.

Kalmus, H. 1948. *Genetics*. Harmondsworth: Pelican Books.

———. 1958. *Heredity and variation*. London: Routledge and K. Paul.

Montagu, M.F. Ashley. 1951. *Statement on race*. Rev. ed. New York: Henry Schuman.

Penrose, L.S. 1952. Review of *Heredity, race and society*, by Dunn and Dobzhansky. *Annals of Human Eugenics* 17:252.

Sigerist, H. 1951. *A history of medicine*. Vol. 1. New York: Oxford University Press.

Simpson, G.G. 1953. *The major features of evolution*. New York: Columbia University Press.

Chapter 3

The Classification of Races in Europe and North America: 1700–1850

Michael Banton

The final piece in this section, a 1987 article by Michael Banton, provides a genealogy of the term "race" in Europe. He argues that early writings based in biblical thinking reveal a deep-seated assumption of monogenesis (single origin) and the importance of environmental effects on phenotypical differences, as well as a lack of interest in the classification of "races." Referring to many writers, he demonstrates that although slavery and colonialism were well entrenched by the seventeenth century, and although racial feelings and structures were the norm, these did not develop into an intellectual ("scientific") tradition of "race typology" until the early to mid-nineteenth century. While earlier the word "race" had been associated with lineage, it later became associated with "variety," "type," or "class" and thus with the theory of polygenesis (separate origins). The latter evolved in some writings to an association with phenotypical, cultural, and even national differences. Banton suggests that although there was no agreement on the meaning of "race" among biologists and anthropologists, and although race typologists were opposed to imperialism on grounds that "inferior races" could not adapt to Western European ways, the word "race" gained popularity due to political and scientific developments in the mid- to late nineteenth century.

The classification of *homo sapiens* into varieties was a feature of eighteenth-century natural history, and must be seen in that context. That classifactory enterprise appears, at least to start with, to have been independent of the increased use of the word "race" or its equivalent in several West European languages. [...]

The dominant view at that time was that everything in the world was the work of the Creator. It was expressed in John Milton's *Paradise Lost* (1677) as he described the creation of each of the most familiar animals. As the naturalist John Ray declared in 1688, "the number of true species in nature is fixed and limited and, as we may reasonably believe, constant and unchangeable from the first creation to the present day." Differences between living things were to be traced backed to the intentions of the Creator and explanations took the form of genealogies. Any discussion of differences between humans had to assume that they were all descended from a single original pair (the doctrine of monogenesis).

LINEAGE AND VARIETY IN PARALLEL

The naturalists who devised the first classifications were primarily interested in plants, but believed, reasonably enough, that the principles underlying the classification of plants must apply to all living things, for all were the works of the same Creator. The modern pioneer in the study of natural history was an English clergyman, John Ray (1627–1705), author of *The Wisdom of God Manifested in the Works of the Creation*. John P. Greene, in his very useful study of the rise of evolutionary biology, *The Death of Adam* (1957, p. 15), testifies that in Ray's mind there was no scientific problem in the natural order; it was God's work. Yet in his praise of the Creator there was a lurking anxiety that indicated the direction from which his static view of the universe was to be challenged. Even a believer had difficulty discerning God's design. There were the species created by God, but there were also "accidents" of variation in the size and colour of specimens, in the number of leaves, and so on. Just as Ray would not accept that a black cow and a white cow, or two similar fruits with a different taste, were necessarily separate species, so he would make no such distinction between a Negro and a European. [...]

Immanuel Kant (1724–1804), the great philosopher, concluded from his study of human variation that the only character invariably transmitted from one generation to another was that of skin colour. [...] Both he and Buffon amplified some of the stereotypes of their age but rejected the polygenist claim that the different varieties of *homo* derived from separate creations.

The most careful eighteenth-century classification of humans was that by the German anatomist J.F. Blumenbach (1752–1840), the author (in Latin) of *On the Natural Variety of Mankind*. [...] In 1770 he divided *homo* into four divisions, but in the second (1781) edition of his book, he introduced the five-fold classification that was to become famous. These five varieties he called Caucasian, American, Mongolian, Malay and Ethiopian, the second and fourth being seen as intermediates between the other varieties. Blumenbach collected evidence of Negro accomplishments to bolster his belief in the unity of the human species. The variations within that species were, he thought, differences of degree arising from the general biological process of degeneration (by which he seems to have meant not deterioration but the modification that arises as one generation succeeds another). Changes of climate and the domestication of a species could accelerate this process. [...]

As Greene (1957, pp. 221–2) remarks, most of the eighteenth-century writers on race were more concerned to explain the origins of races than to classify them. Samuel Stanhope Smith, indeed, dismissed attempts at classification as "a useless labour" since it was so difficult to draw the necessary distinctions. [...] Only when the general processes responsible for variation were understood would it be possible to explain particular kinds of variation, like the differences between Caucasians and Ethiopians. To this problem there were three main kinds of response. The popular answer was to regard variation as the result of divine intervention, blackness being a curse or punishment upon the descendants of Ham. The second answer was that environmental influences, in some as yet unexplained manner, gave rise to variations which were then inherited. The third kind of answer was that the variations had been there all along, having been part of the Creator's intention. [...]

To discover the relations between the internal and external history of racial thought in this period, it is necessary to examine the work of particular authors in relation to the movements of their time. In producing theoretical explanations of physical and cultural variation, the authors may have been influenced by the assumptions about about human variation which they shared with other members of their societies who were not engaged in scientific enquiries. [...] The theories of the scientists may in turn have contributed to the assumptions of the age. There would appear to have been an interaction between racial theories on the one hand and racial consciousness on the other. The problematical nature of that interaction has often been overlooked, sometimes through a superficial reading of a passage in Eric Williams' *Capitalism and Slavery*. Williams wrote:

> Slavery in the Caribbean has been too narrowly identified with the Negro. A racial twist has therefore been given to what is basically an economic phenomenon. Slavery was not born of racism; rather, racism was the consequence of slavery. Unfree labor in the New World was brown, white, black and yellow; Catholic, Protestant and Pagan (1944, p. 7).

The thrust of this argument lies in the first sentence. There was no reason for Williams to deny that there were white prejudices against blacks before New World slavery. There is now no reason for anyone else to deny that such prejudices were increased by slavery. To take the matter further, however, it is essential to separate the various strands that constitute the complex now known as racism.

As is so often the case, the historical record offers less evidence than might be desired, but there is little that cannot be harmonized with the thesis that men and women have used differences of physique and culture to draw boundaries and exclude competitors whenever it has suited them to do so. In the early conflicts with the Spaniards Sir Francis Drake was ready to enter alliances with the Negro refugees from Spanish settlements who were called Cimarrons. There was little evidence of white prejudice then. But when the whites in seventeenth-century Virginia perceived the native Americans as a threat, or wanted their land, then the prejudice appeared. Edmund S. Morgan (1975, pp. 327, 331, 386) concluded that, to start with, English servants seem not to have resented the substitution of African servants for more of their own kind, but from the late 1660s the Virginia assembly deliberately set out to raise the status of lower-class whites by fostering contempt for blacks and native Americans. "Racism thus absorbed in Virginia the fear and contempt that men in England, whether Whig or Tory, monarchist or republican, felt for the inarticulate lower classes. Racism made it possible for white Virginians to develop a devotion to the equality that English republicans had declared to be the soul of liberty...." This was the era in which the institution of permanent black slavery was becoming established in the United States. The readiness of the English to use differences of physique and culture to this end may also have been influenced by the assumptions which they brought with them to the New World.

By the standards of the twentieth century, scarcely any Englishmen of the eighteenth century were racially conscious. A few who had returned to England after living in the West Indies might be so described, but their influence was limited. At that time the word race was rarely used either to describe peoples or in accounts of differences between them. Anthony J. Barker (1978) has studied the literature of this period more thoroughly than any other author. He reports that there was a theory of African inferiority at this time, but that it is not to be found in the works of the intellectuals. [...] When, after about 1787, the debate about the abolition of the slave trade started, it was conducted within a framework of existing knowledge. For the abolitionists the central issues were the doubtful morality and necessity of the trade. Only a handful of pro-slavery writers asserted that blacks were inferior; most pointedly rejected such views except in so far as they contended that only Negroes could work in extreme heat. [...]

One of the major eighteenth-century changes in the external conditions likely to influence racial thought was the Declaration of Independence of the United States in 1776. A majority of the whites chose to break away from the country with which they had previously identified themselves. They had to create a new sense of national identity. They decided that what should distinguish their nation would be political institutions designed to create a more perfect union, to establish a higher standard of justice and to insure domestic tranquility. Forgetting the Afro-Americans, some of them looked to the seventeenth-century radical belief that Anglo-Saxon institutions were the source of political liberty. This belief had been used to counter the claim of kings to rule by divine right and it was paralleled by a similar belief in France that freedom had been brought to the country from the Germany described by Tacitus. In France, in England, and in the United States, the first political use of a concept of race was in the context of struggles between whites, and it used race in the sense of lineage rather than type (Horsman, 1982; Poliakov, 1974).

New World slave owners had been aware from an early period that blacks did not suffer much from yellow fever and malaria, though these diseases devastated European populations (on the slave ships about 20 per cent of the crew died on each voyage). There were other diseases from which blacks suffered more severely, like cholera, tuberculosis, whooping cough, tetanus and some with a dietary origin (Kiple and King, 1981). These differences, together with the obvious tensions and conflicts of interest inherent in so unequal a relationship as that of slavery, might be expected to have encouraged theories of racial inequality. Therefore the judgement of a leading historian, George M. Fredrickson (1971, p. 43), is of particular interest. He has found that prior to the 1830s, although black subordination was widespread in the United States, and whites commonly assumed that Negroes were inferior "open assertions of *permanent* inferiority were exceedingly rare."

LINEAGE AND VARIETY CONFUSED

The academic study of racial relations has been dominated by scholars from the English-speaking world, and particularly by social scientists who have either grown up in the United States or have unconsciously taken over assumptions originating there. Scientific reasoning requires precise definitions, yet much research in this field has been based on the conceptions of race which are current among ordinary members of the North American public, relatively untouched by the studies which have exposed the cultural bias. Because of the economic power of the United States and the highly developed nature of its mass communications media, that country's folk definitions of race have been transmitted to other regions as if they represented universal categories within social science instead of reflecting the very special way in which relations between reds, whites and blacks developed in United States history. To start with, other languages lacked any words corresponding to the meaning of race in American English; they have had to find or devise translations, but the correspondence is not always very close. It is important, therefore, to examine the manner in which the word has acquired its present meanings.

Changes in the West European languages were closely linked. Colette Guillaumin (1972, p. 19), who has studied French usage, found that at the beginning of the nineteenth century there was an important change. She wrote "the term 'race' itself acquired the sense of human group as it lost its narrower sense of lineage." While race continued to mean lineage for many people (and indeed continues to the present day to retain that sense), it acquired the *additional* significance of designating a class or type of animal or human.

The change can be seen in Cuvier's great work *The Animal Kingdom* first published in Paris in 1817. Near the beginning is a section entitled "Variétés de l'espèce humaine" which starts:

Quoique l'espèce humaine paraisse unique, puisque tous les individus peuvent se mêler indistinctement, et produire des individus féconds, on y remarque de certaines conformations héréditaires qui constituent ce qu'on nomme des *races*.

This usage, which made race and variety synonymous, seems to have worried Cuvier's first English translator, for in the 1827 London translation the last sentence appears as "... which constitute what are called *varieties*." In several of the passages where Cuvier wrote race, this translator put variety. Yet in the next English translation (published in New York in 1831) the sentence runs "... which constitute what are termed races" and "race" is used thereafter.

It is easy to understand how race and variety came to appear synonymous. To start with, in English and French writing, race was used to designate a lineage or a line of descent. Then, in natural history, people began to classify plants and animals, and named the least general classes genera, species and varieties. Similar specimens were classed together. They were similar because they were of common descent. So membership in a historically constituted unit (race) and membership in a classification made at a moment in time with little information about antecedents (genus, species or variety) seemed two ways of saying the same thing. That they were not may be clarified by a simple example. According to the Old Testament, Moses was a Levite who married a Midionite woman, Zipporah, who bore him two sons, Gershon and Eliezer. Later he married an Ethiopian woman (his brother and sister "spoke against him" for doing so). Imagine that this wife also bore him a son. That son would be just as much of the race of Levi as Gershon and Eliezer. But if some contemporary anthropologist had set out to classify the individuals, Moses, Gershon and Eliezer would have been accounted Semites and Moses' third son a hybrid; he would not have been assigned to the same "race" as Gershon, Eliezer and Moses, using race in the sense of variety. [...]

In 1784 Johann Gottfried von Herder in *Ideen zur Philosophic der Geschichte der Menschheit* had protested about those who

> have thought fit to employ the term races for four or five divisions, according to regions
> or origin or complexion. I see no reason for employing this term. Race refers to a
> difference of origin, which in this case either does not exist or which comprises in each
> of these regions or complexions the most diverse "races" (Herder, 1969, p. 284).

Kant criticized Herder for his "inadequate and unsympathetic treatment of race." Some (e.g. Dover, 1952) have argued that Herder's conception of the nation implied a distinctive variety of humanity with permanent and inherited characters of its own, and that this was more dangerous than the classifications he opposed. Whatever view be taken of this, the observations of Kant and Herder should have suggested to their contemporaries that an equation of "race" with "variety" was not to be taken for granted. After Cuvier's book had been translated, the English physician James Cowles Prichard noticed what was happening, and in 1836 he protested, "races are properly successions of individuals propagated from any given stock." He objected to the tendency to use the word "as if it implied a distinction in the physical character of a whole series of individuals" (quoted at greater length in Banton, 1977, p. 30). Prichard was respected as an authority on matters of race but his warning passed unheeded.

Thus it came about that race in English and French confused descent with phenotypical classification, though in both these languages the word continued to be used to denote commonality of descent and so was sometimes equated with nation as well. In Italian, the use of *razza* seems very similar, having on occasion the sense either of lineage or variety. German usage is not very different, with the addition that the same word covers what in English would be "breed"—as in *Hunderasse* (French also fails to differentiate breed from race). In Russian, the equivalent word is a nineteenth-century addition to the vocabulary, having the sense of variety and with less of the ambiguities of the West European languages. In the many languages which derive from Sanskrit, however, the possibilities for misunderstanding European usage seem greater. In Sanskrit the two words closest to "race" are *jātá* and *vansá*, the former translated as "race, kind, sort, class, species," the latter as "pedigree or genealogy";

both are close to the sense of race as lineage and lack the taxonomic connotations of variety or sub-species. In Arabic, the word *unsur* seems close to race as lineage and would be used in a translation of a reference to "the ethnic minority problem," but there is in addition the word *jins*, corresponding to the Greek *genos* and translating race as variety. In Japanese, *jinshu* was probably introduced in the nineteenth century to translate race as variety, so that the language has three words: *shu* for species, *henshu* for variety and *jinshu* for a human race constituted by people sharing common physical characteristics; in the written form all these words share the character for seed. In Chinese, race can be translated by *renzhong* which, when written, combines two characters, one for "human" and the other for "species" or "type." Another possible translation is *zhongzu*, which combines the second character of renzhong with one representing class, or group with common characteristics, or, on its own, race or nationality. It would therefore seem possible that the confusion Cuvier failed to discourage has been spread to other languages.

The specialists consulted about the problem of finding equivalents for the different senses of race in English refer to the associations that words have because of the other connections in which they are used in the lives of the peoples who speak these languages.[1] Translation often causes difficulty, but it would appear that the possibilities of misunderstanding with respect to ideas of race and racial relations are greater than usual. Readers from outside West Europe and North America might bear this in mind when considering the loose way in which the word was used in some languages during the nineteenth and early twentieth centuries.

THE DOCTRINE OF RACIAL TYPES

[...] Faced with the evidence of human diversity, eighteenth-century scholars such as Buffon and Blumenbach, and their succesors like Samuel Stanhope Smith and Prichard, had inclined to the theory that all humans had a common origin (monogenesis), but hidden agencies associated with either their environments or their habits had caused them to diversify; some varieties had made greater progress because of their opportunities and social institutions; relations between varieties were seen in moral terms. By contrast, Cuvier had maintained that the differences had been the result of a great catastrophe, since which these had remained without change; ability to progress, and the character of inter-racial relations were determined by the inherent capacities of races.

The man who, in the United States, did most to develop the thesis that the different varieties of *homo* represented permanent types was the Philadelphian physician Samuel George Morton, but it is difficult to tell how far he was directly influenced by Cuvier. In 1830 Morton chose to deliver a lecture on the skulls of the five varieties identified by Blumenbach. Being unable to obtain sufficient skulls for his purpose, he started his own collection. To start with Morton was very cautious in the conclusions he drew, but he became bolder as his views gained support, and he lived in an environment in which many white Americans were ready to welcome a theory that both stated blacks to be inferior and advanced an explanation for it. Morton became the leader of a school which denied that blacks and whites were varieties of the species *homo*. They argued that *homo sapiens* was the genus and that it was divided into several species. Blacks and whites were separate species. [...] The question was whether these differences had a physical origin, implying permanent inferiority, or whether they had an environmental origin, in which case the backward peoples could be expected to catch up. [...]

The perspective which sees the efforts of Morton and his successors as the working out of one from a limited number of possible solutions to a problem within the field of natural history (though not only within that field), is strengthened by the evidence which shows very similar arguments to have been developed, almost independently and virtually simultaneously, in several other countries. Chronologically the first of the books to set out the typological view systematically was *The Natural History of the Human Species* (1848) by Charles Hamilton Smith, a retired English army officer who counted himself a disciple and friend of Cuvier's. Next came the Scottish anatomist, Robert Knox, another pupil of Cuvier's, who published a set of lectures, *The Races of Men*, in London in 1850. Then, in 1853–55, the four volumes of Count Arthur de Gobineau's *Essai sur l'inégalité des races humaines* was published in Paris; the first volume is the only one to have been translated into English and it is this which has attracted all the attention. Gobineau was apparently unacquainted with the work of the other typologists, though he had noticed Morton's table of the cranial capacity of skulls of different races when it was reprinted in a German book, and gave it a prominent place in his own argument. Next there appeared in Philadelphia in 1854 a very substantial work edited by J.C. Nott and G.R. Gliddon entitled *Types of Mankind*. Nott and Gliddon were much more aware of the work of like-minded contemporary scholars and they pulled the available arguments together.

It has been customary to refer to the writing of Smith, Knox, Gobineau, Nott and Gliddon as "scientific racism," yet their key concept was not race but type. One source of dispute about the definition of racism can therefore be avoided by referring to their school as that of racial typology. It should be noted that while these five authors agreed on some major propositions, there were differences between them, particularly with respect to the questions of hybridity and acclimatization. [...]

The line of argument developed by Morton, Knox and Nott is the true polygenesis, denying the religious belief that all humans were descended from Adam and Eve. Yet the differences among the typologists were small by comparison with the principles on which they agreed. They shared a belief that variations in the constitution and behaviour of individuals were the expression of differences between underlying types of a relatively permanent kind. In classifying these variations, they treated physical and cultural differences as equally characteristic of types. How people behaved was as relevant to classification as their size and shape. Obviously, descriptions and classifications of ways of behaving were far more subjective and liable to distortion than those based upon physical measurements, but the typologists were usually quite unconcerned about this. [...] The typologists also agreed in seeing human groupings, including nations, as the expression of biological types and in interpreting racial antagonism in the same way. Some have seen their arguments as little more than the rationalization of personal prejudice, but this is a very superficial view. There were other writers in the middle years of the century, especially in the United States, who compiled volumes about the superiority of whites over blacks. The typological theory was more persuasive than such works because it was less particular. It claimed to account for the characters of all the races of the world by reference to principles which also explained the distribution of particular kinds of plants and animal life. It was a theory with considerable intellectual pretension, and, in a pre-Darwinian world, of some plausibility.

The typologists were passionately concerned with the affairs of their generation. For most it was important to resist the representatives of organized religion who claimed to determine the proper scope of scientific research. The European typologists were impressed by the revolutions of 1848. Knox saw them as the struggle of races and thought they demonstrated the truth of what he had been preaching. De Gobineau presented his *Essay* as a commentary upon the causes underlying the events of that year. Though there were upheavals overseas which would be seen in racial terms (like the American Civil War), the focus was upon problems nearer home (such as the conflict in Ireland). The whole thrust of typological reasoning was that the colonization of overseas territories was doomed to failure; Knox, for example, scorned "that den of all abuses, the office of the Colonial Secretary." The 1850s and 1860s were not a time when the British wished to expand their overseas possessions; indeed Gladstone's cabinet of 1868 is sometimes taken to mark the high point of *anti*-imperial sentiment. Not until later in the century is it worthwhile hunting for links between racial consciousness and imperialism.

In the United States, white Southerners were divided along class lines, but both classes defended slavery on Biblical grounds, leading Stanton (1960, p. 194) to conclude that "the South turned its back on the only respectable defence of slavery it could have taken up." This requires some qualification. For decades there had been a Southern Bourbon tradition which defended slavery as an institution independently of any question of racial difference. Non-slave holding whites disliked it. Some aspired to become slave holders themselves and many were anxious to protect and increase their privileges at the expense of black workers. With the extension of the suffrage in the 1830s to white males by the weakening of property-owning qualifications, the white workers' influence grew and the planter class had to adjust to their beliefs, demands and phobias (Fredrickson, 1971, pp. 69–70). In a changed political atmosphere what had earlier seemed an irreligious mode of reasoning got a more sympathetic welcome.

A FURTHER CONFUSION

By the late 1850s, therefore, discussion of racial issues displayed what to a later generation might appear a contradiction. On the one hand the word "race" had come into greatly increased use in English, French and other West European languages to refer to social units which would nowadays be designated peoples or perhaps nations. On the other hand, firstly, there was no agreement amongst natural historians or anthropologists about the definition of race, and, in particular, whether it was to be equated with species or variety. Secondly, those who had done most to draw attention to racial explanations within anthropology, the typologists who took the position of Knox and Nott, had argued that racial types were suited to their historical environments and could not acclimatize to new ones. Their doctrine contended that imperialism was folly. Thirdly, those within the typological school who most deviated from the "no acclimatization" principle, and were most inclined to argue for white superiority, were C.H. Smith and Gobineau. Smith was the least well-known of these authors and de Gobineau's four volumes made little initial impact. As Poliakov (1974, p. 206) writes, de Gobineau's views on race were resolutely ignored by all his French contemporaries except Ernest Renan and Taine, and they did not start to attract attention until they were taken up in Germany in the 1880s (but cf. Barzun 1965, pp. 61–77).

Why, then, was the idea of race so popular, and why did it become even more influential? Two considerations seem important. Firstly, the idea of race became associated with that of nation and it proved useful to nineteenth-century nationalist movements, perhaps because of the very confusion as to its meaning in natural history. Secondly, throughout the nineteenth century evolutionary thought was gathering strength, receiving a major boost from Darwin in 1859, though strongly associated in many people's minds with the works of Herbert Spencer. Throughout this period there were major problems concerning the means by which evolution might operate. Some of these could not be solved before the rediscovery in 1900 of the principles earlier formulated by Mendel, but important as that was, it was by no means the end of the story. The early Mendelians thought that the new experimental evidence had dealt a death blow to selection theory since a particulate theory of inheritance implied to them a discontinuity in evolution (Mayr, 1982, p. 547). Thus the confusion in the biological understanding of human variation in the latter part of the nineteenth century cannot be understood apart from the history of science. Biologists were confused because they were ignorant of principles which later generations regard as the true explanations, and such confusion is unavoidable.

NOTE

1.   Colleagues at the University of Bristol have been most helpful in assisting me with this question. I would like to thank Rohit Barot, David Chambers, Michael Costello, D.H. Higgins, Richard Peace, Rodney Sampson and Frank Shaw. Professor J. Derek Latham wrote to me about usage in Arabic and Mrs Hiroko Minamikata about Japanese. I fear that I have been unable to integrate all that they kindly told me.

REFERENCES

Banton, M. 1977. *The Idea of Race*. London: Tavistock.

Barker, A.J. 1978. *The African Link: British Attitudes to the Negro in the Era of the Atlantic Slave Trade, 1550–1807*. London: Frank Cass.

Barzun, J. 1937. *Race: A Study in Modern Superstition*. New York: Harcourt Brace Revised ed. New York: Harper, 1965.

Bendyshe, T. 1865. The History of Anthropology. *Memoirs read before the Anthropological Society of London*, Vol. 1, pp. 335–458.

Blumenbach, J.F. 1865. *The Anthropological Treatises of Johann Friedrich Blumenbach*.... London: Anthropological Society of London.

Buffon, G.L. 1971. *De l'homme*. Présentation et notes de Michèle Duchet. Paris: Maspero.

Dover, C. 1952. The Racial Philosophy of Johann Herder. *British Journal of Sociology*, Vol. 3, pp. 124–33.

Fredrickson, G.M. 1971. *The Black Image in the White Mind: The Debate on Afro-American Character and Destiny, 1817–1914*. New York: Harper and Row.

Fryer, P. 1984. *Staying Power: The History of Black People in Britain*. London: Pluto.

Gobineau, Comte de. 1853–55. *Essai sur l'inégalité des races humaines*. Paris: Firmin-Didot.

Greene, J.P. 1957. *The Death of Adam: Evolution and its Impact on Western Thought*. New York: Mentor Books.

Guillaumin, C. 1972. *L'idéologie raciste: genèse et langage actuelle*. Paris: Mouton.

Herder, J.G. von. 1969. *On Social and Political Culture* (selections). Cambridge: Cambridge University Press.

Horsman, R. 1982. *Race and Manifest Destiny: The Origins of American Racial Anglo-Saxonism*. Cambridge, Mass.: Harvard University Press.

Kiple, K.F., and King, V.H. 1981. *Another Dimension to the Black Diaspora: Diet, Disease, and Racism*. Cambridge: Cambridge University Press.

Knox, R., 1850. *The Races of Men: A Fragment*. 2nd ed. 1862, subtitled *A Philosophical Enquiry into the Influence of Race over the Destinites of Nations*. London: Renshaw.

Mayr, E. 1982. *The Growth of Biological Thought: Diversity, Evolution, Inheritance*. Cambridge, Mass.: Harvard University Press.

Morgan, E.S. 1975. *American Slavery, American Freedom: The Ordeal of Colonial Virginia*. New York: Norton.

Morton, S.G. 1839. *Crania Americana; or, a Comparative View of the Skulls of Various Aboriginal Nations of North and South America, to which is prefixed an Essay on the Varieties of the Human Species*. Philadelphia and London.

Morton, S.G. 1844. *Crania Aegyptica; or, Observations on Egyptian Ethnography, Derived from Anatomy, History, and the Monuments*. Philadelphia and London.

Nott, J.C., and Gliddon, S.G. 1854. *Types of Mankind; or, Ethnological Researches*. Philadelphia: Lippincott.

Poliakov, L. 1974. *The Aryan Myth: A History of Racist and Nationalist Ideas in Europe*. London: Chatto, Heinemann.

Smith, C.H. 1848. *The Natural History of the Human Species*. Edinburgh: Lizars.

Smith, S.S. 1810. *An Essay on the Causes of the Variety of Complexion in the Human Species*. 2nd ed., reprinted Cambridge, Mass.: Harvard University Press, 1965.

Stanton, W. 1960. *The Leopard's Spots: Scientific Attitudes towards Race in America, 1815–59*. Chicago: University of Chicago Press.

Williams, E.E., 1944. *Capitalism and Slavery*. Chapel Hill: University of North Carolina Press.

PART 1B

COLONIALISM AND THE CONSTRUCTION OF RACE

Although contemporary scholars from a wide range of disciplines have reached a general (if unstable) consensus that no solid scientific evidence exists explaining the validity of race, science has historically played a crucial role in upholding and explaining the validity not only of the classification of different races, but also the notion that the white or Caucasian race was superior to all others. Science and philosophy contemporaneously defended the existing racial hierarchies of both Europe and North America. The four readings in this section examine some of the reasons why, as well as the different ways in which Western nation-states attempted to colonize non-Western, largely non-Christian societies.

FURTHER READING

Barakan, Elazar. 1996. *The Retreat of Scientific Racism: Changing Concepts of Race in Britain and the United States between the World Wars*. Cambridge, UK: Cambridge University Press.

This book examines the handling of the concept of race in both anthropology and biology, comparing American and British approaches. It traces the move away from focusing on physical traits to focusing on social conditions as determinants of behaviour. The author argues that changing social conditions throughout the twentieth century have been more influential in the decline of scientific racism than any scientific considerations.

Memmi, Albert. 1965. *The Colonizer and the Colonized*. Boston: Beacon Press.

First published in 1957, this is one of the classics in the field, one that made public the detrimental affect of colonization on the colonizer as well as the colonized. Although in most parts of the world the older exigent forms of colonization have long since disappeared, there are still many regions where colonization is rationalized by both overt and covert forms of racism.

Watson, Peter. 2005. *Ideas: A History from Fire to Freud.* **London: Weidenfeld & Nicolson.**
Section 21, "The 'Indian' Mind: Ideas in the New World"
Section 33, "The Uses and Abuses of Nationalism and Imperialism"
These two readings from a recent survey of the history of ideas examine the origins of many of the ideas surveyed by Gustav Jahoda and Edward Said in this section. Watson offers a non-ideological perspective focusing on their historical context and treating them as noteworthy and influential in the history of ideas.

Chapter 4

Towards Scientific Racism

Gustav Jahoda

In this 1999 chapter, Gustav Jahoda traces the ways in which respected German and French thinkers of the late seventeenth and early eighteenth centuries grappled intellectually with the issue of whether the different races could reasonably be said to belong to different species, and if so, where the "Black race" fell between Caucasians and apes. This debate gave rise to nascent theories about how to differentiate between races, including examining the shape of the skull and making determinations about the beauty, ugliness, or adaptability of different races (i.e., those who could tolerate pain or wide swings in temperature, or heal more quickly, or eat a wider range of less refined food were considered "backward," while those who suffered in physical situations were more likely to be seen as part of advanced or superior civilizations). In particular, Jahoda explains the ways in which the craniology developed by a French scientist (i.e., taking measurements of skulls and their facial angles) not only became the scientific standard for differentiating between the races, but also was positioned as support for the racial theories about the similarities between the Black race and apes.

The debate in Germany reflected the changing climate of opinion, progressively tilting against the Enlightenment view of savagery as a stage in the evolution of humanity. The debate was wide-ranging, including Herder and Kant, but I shall concentrate on a small group of key figures in close contact, the most outstanding of whom was Blumenbach, whose views were diametrically opposed to those of Meiners, his colleague at the University of Gottingen. Meiners was a polygenist who wrote in defence of slavery, Blumenbach a monogenist who stressed the unity of the human species. Their personal styles were equally contrasting: Meiners a speculative philosopher with a heavy ideological commitment, Blumenbach a sober scientist concerned with empirical evidence.

There was also Soemmering, who had been a close friend of Blumenbach while they were undergraduates. Another friend of Soemmering's was Johann Georg Forster (1754–94), who while still in his teens had accompanied his father on Cook's second voyage. Blumenbach, it will be recalled, had been critical of Soemmering's book; but Soemmering's other friend, Forster, was much more ambiguous in his response, seemingly not wishing to offend. He declared that, not being an anatomist himself, he was not qualified to judge, but he suggested to Soemmering that he should mention the decisive argument for the humanity of the Negroes, namely their capacity for speech. Forster's views are set out most clearly in his critique of two essays by Kant on the subject of race. Accusing Kant of applying philosophical categories without reference to empirical reality, he warmly recommended Soemmering's book. Forster's adherence to the Great Chain is indicated by his reference to "the fruitful thought, that everything in creation is linked by small steps [Nuancen]" (Forster [1786] 1969, Vol. 2, p. 85). In a lengthy and rather convoluted passage he discussed the relationship between whites, blacks and apes in the series of animals on earth. It boils down to the statement that, though among the various human types blacks most closely resemble the apes, there remains a critical gap: "Thus an ape-like human is no ape" (p. 86). Forster was unable to make up his mind as regards monogeny or polygeny, but while uncertain about some issues he clearly abhorred slavery, making an emotional appeal against the animalization entailed by its practice.

As will already have become apparent, the major figure who stressed the full humanity of blacks was Johann Friedrich Blumenbach (1752–1840), professor of medicine and natural history, who is generally regarded as the founder of physical anthropology. He had become inspired by his teacher Buttner, who possessed a fine collection of naturalia and frequently displayed at his lectures travel books with illustrations of exotic peoples. Blumenbach later assembled a famous collection of skulls, and throughout his life remained an avid reader of travel reports; but unlike many others, notably his colleague Meiners, Blumenbach was a critical reader. He went so far as to arrange the reports about particular peoples in chronological order, and compared them. He found quite striking contradictions and inconsistencies, noting also that if a work was regarded as a *locus classicus*, the tendency was merely to copy it (cf. Plischke 1937). Blumenbach had scant regard for the doctrine of the Great Chain, certainly treating it as inapplicable within the human species. Moreover, he was rather sceptical about a number of then current beliefs, such as the supposed "fact" that savage women give birth as easily as animals.

Blumenbach's major work was his *De generis humani varietate nativa* ([1795] 1865), which pioneered an empirical approach to the classification of races by the shape of the skull. He refuted some of Linnaeus' more extravagant notions, showing, for instance, that albinos are not a separate species but people who suffer from an infirmity that affects both skin and eyes. He also went to great trouble to investigate and disprove some of the stories used by Linnaeus to support his contentions.[1] Blumenbach did not devise any system of measurement but proposed a method of comparison whereby skulls, with the lower jaws removed, are placed on a surface and viewed from above, the so-called *norma verticalis*. In practice he made little use of his method and did not base his classification on it. The reason why it is important is that it led in the 19th century to the elaboration of the "cephalic index" (i.e. the ratio of the breadth of the skull to its length expressed as a percentage) by Anders Retzius (1796–1860), which subsequently became one of the main tools of craniology.

Of chief concern here are Blumenbach's views about racial differences, based on the study of both his extensive collection of skulls and of the contemporary travel literature. In his view, skull shapes suggest a division into five major races, namely Caucasian, Mongolian, Ethiopian, American and Malaysian. He enthused about the beauty and symmetry of a young female Georgian skull, which probably accounts for his view that the Caucasian is the highest type and also the original race from which others were subsequently derived by a process he called "degeneration." For him this term had no negative connotations, and he meant by it a diversification resulting from the influence of climatic and other factors that came to be transmitted by heredity. At the same time Blumenbach rejected any sharp dividing lines between such races, emphasizing the unity of humankind as a species:

> No variety of mankind exists, whether of colour, countenance, or stature, etc., so singular
> as not to be connected with others of the same kind by such an imperceptible transition,
> that it is very clear that all are related and only differ from each other in degree. ([1795]
> 1865, pp. 98–9)

It must be admitted that in his earlier writings Blumenbach had painted a rather unflattering portrait of the physical characteristics of "Ethiopians," as he had initially termed Africans; he described them variously as having a "knotty forehead," "puffy lips" and being often "bandy-legged." Later he radically shifted his position, possibly as a result of a personal encounter.[2] Certainly in his later years he made a point of getting to know Africans, reading the literature about them, and collecting and measuring African skulls. As a result, he criticized others who depicted blacks as inferior or even as a separate species, stressing that Africans have the same mental abilities and potential as the rest of humanity. He referred to "the good disposition and faculties of our black brethren" and devoted several pages to citing examples of black ability, concluding as follows:

> there is no so-called savage nation known under the sun which has so much distinguished
> itself by such examples of perfectibility and original capacity for scientific culture, and

thereby attached itself so closely to the most civilized nations of the earth, *as the Negro.* (Blumenbach [1795] 1865, p. 312; emphasis in original)

Blumenbach was later extensively cited by writers such as the anatomist Tiedermann (1837), who were concerned to show that blacks are full members of the human family rather than intermediate between humans and apes. Blumenbach was strongly opposed to the teachings of Meiners, a defender of slavery, whom Soemmering had called "the beloved philosopher of our fatherland" (1784, p. xiii). The views propagated by Meiners were distasteful to Blumenbach, though as a colleague in Gottingen he attacked him only obliquely.

Christoph Meiners (1747–1816) described himself as "a teacher of wordly wisdom [Weltweisheit]," in other words a philosopher. He was a man of immense erudition who exerted considerable influence in his time. Like Vico, the ambitious Meiners wanted to found a "new science" dealing with the nature of man, his past and his future. Unlike Vico's, his teachings were fundamentally based on ideas of racial and sexual inequality and did not endure, though they were temporarily resurrected by Nazi race theorists. The wide range of his writings, and their reception, have been surveyed by Rupp-Eisenreich (1983), and I shall merely present some selected aspects relevant to my theme.

Nowadays Meiners usually rates only a cursory mention in histories of anthropology, focused on his idiosyncratic criteria for the classification of races. In his *Sketch of the history of mankind* (Meiners 1785) he proposed that "One of the most important characteristics of tribes and peoples is beauty or ugliness" (p. 43), claiming that only people of Caucasian stock (but excepting Slavs) deserve the epithet of beauty. While in this early work it was only one, albeit an important criterion for the classification of peoples, it later became for him *the* major one. In a subsequent lengthy article Meiners (1788) sought to document in detail the characteristics of the "ugly peoples." Those of mongoloid descent, he alleged, resemble "the feeble-minded or lunatics of our continent inasmuch as they have much thicker skulls and much larger heads" (p. 280). In American savages the hair grows almost down to their eyebrows; in China women are preferred whose eyes are as piggish [schweinsartig] as possible; the faces of Negroes have an apish appearance; and so on.

In other writings Meiners (1787) put forward a theory concerning what may be roughly translated as the "adaptability" of different peoples, with a strong accent on the animality of the "ugly races." Meiners started with the observation that humans have settled in the most diverse climatic conditions and utilize a wide range of foodstuffs, unlike animals confined to a narrow ecological range and limited to certain kinds of nourishment. Yet paradoxically humans are more sensitive to pain and adverse weather, suffer more illnesses and recover more slowly from injuries, and cannot cope with raw or indigestible foods.

While this is true of humans in general, there are substantial variations in adaptability among the different races of man:

> The more intelligent and noble people are by nature, the more adaptable, sensitive, delicate and soft is their body; on the other hand, the less they possess the capacity and disposition towards virtue, the more they lack adaptability; and not only that, but the less

sensitive are their bodies, the more can they tolerate extreme pain or the rapid alteration of heat and cold; the less they are exposed to illnesses, the more rapidly their recovery from wounds that would be fatal for more sensitive peoples, and the more they can partake of the worst and most indigestible foods … without noticeable ill effects. (Meiners 1787, pp. 211–2)

Belief in such hardiness of the backward races formed at that time part of the conventional wisdom, pushed by Meiners to greater extremes. For him the noblest race were the Celts, and he points out that they were able to conquer various parts of the world. Yet they are more sensitive to heat and cold, fall more easily prey to sickness, and their delicacy is shown by the fact that they are fussy about what they eat.

The Slavs are clearly an inferior race, less sensitive and more resistant to disease. This is illustrated by a series of anecdotes: for instance, Russians are content with rough food and can eat poisonous fungi without coming to any harm; other Slavs bake sick people in an oven and then make them roll in the snow—saunas were not fashionable in Meiners' Germany. Below the Slavs are the peoples of the Middle East and Asia, all limited in intelligence and of an evil disposition, which goes together with lack of adaptability and insensitivity.

Meiners went on to discuss the Negroes and Americans who "approach animals most closely." With regard to the Negroes, he referred to the anatomical studies of Soemmering, expressing his conviction that it is not only their colour but their whole bodily structure that governs their capacities, dispositions and emperament. Thus in the Negroes the parts of the head concerned with the mastication of food, i.e. jaw muscles and bones, and teeth, are much bigger and stronger than those of Europeans. Their heads are larger, but the brain is smaller and the nerves coarser. They can eat practically anything, such as raw and stinking rotten meat. Their females give birth as easily as wild beasts. They are seldom ill, even in the West Indies where they are maltreated, and can endure any amount of pain "as if they had no human, barely animal, feeling." Meiners tells the story of a Negro, condemned to death by slow-burning fire; when his back was already half cooked, he asked for a pipe and smoked it placidly. Lest this evoke some admiration in the reader, Meiners added: "If one wanted to attribute this quiet endurance of [suffering] not to the lack of feeling of the thick-skinned and coarse-nerved Negro, but to his steadfastness, then one would have to rate [the lowest kinds of animals] more highly than the greatest heroes of antiquity and modern times" (1787, p. 230).

If the Negroes are bad, according to Meiners, the Americans are even worse. [...] Other confabulations abound: American skulls are so thick that, as the Spanish conquerors found, the best blades shatter on them. Their skin is thicker than that of an ox. They can walk naked in the hottest sun as well as the coldest winter. The Americas harbour the most gluttonous monsters—they can feed on all kinds of foul offal, drink the most polluted water and consume without ill effect vast quantities of alcohol that would kill the strongest beast. They live to a ripe old age, without diminution of their strength: one can see 100-year-old men jumping on to their horses as easily as the fittest youngsters. They seldom suffer illness, and make miraculous recoveries from the severest wounds. There is a lengthy account of the self-inflicted wounds of their endurance tests and their unbelievable cruelty to their enemies, described in lovingly grisly detail over several pages.

At the same time, the Americans are not only the most unfeeling of peoples, they are also the least adaptable: they cannot get used to other climates, food or modes of life. When the Jesuits brought Indians to their mission, they began to die in large numbers. They were, Meiners argued, quite unable to adapt to their changed circumstances, lapsing into a deadly melancholy. Examples of this kind abound, without any suggestion that European diseases might have been the cause. Here again Meiners seemed anxious lest the reader be led to draw the wrong conclusion, namely that the Americans are so happy in their way of life that depriving them of it kills them:

> one can only conclude from this that the unfeeling Americans are … so lacking in adaptability that they are almost as little able as wild beasts to get used to another climate, and even more so to other kinds of food and modes of life. (Meiners 1787, p. 246)

Meiners greatly expanded on these and other themes in a large work entitled *Researches on the variations in human nature* (1815). It contains more alleged anatomical details of various races, and their supposed sexual peculiarities are examined in prurient detail. For instance, men in north-east Asia are said to have very small genitals and their women, by contrast, very large ones; owing to this misfit, the women disdain their own men, preferring Russians and Cossacks. In addition, American (Indian) women and Negresses are said to have always shown a decided preference for Europeans; this was a stereotypical theme in the (male-authored) literature on blacks. Meiners failed to explain why black women should be so keen on white men, given the fact that he dwelt in some detail on the extraordinarily large and "animal-like" penis of Negro males. Generally he maintained that unduly weak (as among American Indians) and unduly strong sexual drives (as among Africans, Chinese, Japanese and peoples of the South Sea Islands) were equally bad—only Europeans have it just right.

I should make it clear once again that the above is certainly not a balanced account of Meiners' approach. His writings contain many sensible and perceptive passages; for instance, some of his comments on the abilities and shortcomings of various peoples foreshadow topics of study by 20th-century cross-cultural psychologists.[3] Nonetheless, the notion of the permanent inferiority and animal-likeness of the "ugly races" runs as a constant thread through most of his writings. His reading was wide but quite uncritical; furthermore, he was apt to select from the mass of material which he perused those aspects that fitted in with his thesis.

I have dealt with Meiners at some length, since his ideas were the subject of lively, often critical discussions. He was read by the young Hegel, and probably contributed to Hegel's demonic image of Africa, which he described as a place where one can find the most terrible manifestations of human nature (Hegel [1832] 1992, Vol. 12, pp. 120–9).

REACTION IN FRANCE: VIREY AND THE HUMAN-LIKENESS OF APES

The writings of Meiners, with their strident ideological message, were widely understood as applying the lessons of history to the contemporary situation. In a French translation of one of his works the preface refers to the decadence of Rome with its "multitudes of slaves and foreigners … in such a corrupting atmosphere they degraded by their admixture the entire mass of the people" (cited in Rupp-Eisenreich 1983, p. 135). A similar line was taken by the Nazi historian von Eickstedt who wrote in praise of Meiners, coupling his name with that of Virey and others like him. There is in fact evidence that Virey was familiar with the writings of Meiners (Rupp-Eisenreich 1985). However, apart from the denigration of savages, their approaches to the issue did not have much in common. Unlike Meiners, Virey was a believer in the Great Chain and argued most vigorously in the style of Long and White. Moreover, in order to render his often bizarre arguments of the close relation between blacks and apes more plausible, he took over some old notions about the supposedly remarkable accomplishments of apes.

Jules Virey (1775–1847) was a naturalist and professor of pharmacy, a follower of Rousseau and a fervent admirer of Buffon.[4] Nonetheless he was, unlike Buffon, a polygenist who believed that humans consist of separate species. His *Histoire naturelle du genre humain* was essentially a work of popularization that achieved a wide circulation. In the first edition, published in 1801, he, rather like Meiners, dichotomized humans into fair and dark; in later ones he used Camper's "facial angle" to categorize races, a notion to which I shall return. In the earlier editions there are passages indicating that his imagination ran along much the same lines as Long's, as, for instance, in the passage [...] about the sexual congress in darkest Africa between Negresses and satyrs. That passage was left out in later editions, which abandoned the poetry of dark passions and assumed a somewhat more detached tone. Nonetheless, Virey voiced some quaint ideas, such as his belief that colours influence the character of everything in organic nature. Thus he said that white animals are mostly innocent and guileless, while black ones are violent and nasty; this, he suggested, applied even to flowers: white ones are harmless, and dark ones are often poisonous. This comes oddly from someone who practised pharmacy!

According to Virey, Negroes are deficient in "morality," a term used by him in a very broad sense to include thought and knowledge, political and religious ideas. While lacking in moral relationships with each other, they have relatively more physical ones:

> negresses abandon themselves to love with transports unknown anywhere else: they have large sexual organs, and those of the negroes are proportionately voluminous; for generally, as the organs of generation acquire great activity among humans, so the intellectual faculties suffer a loss of energy. (Virey 1824, Vol. II. pp. 45–6)

This "energy theory," as I will show in due course, gained further prominence later in the 19th century. Elsewhere Virey contended that Negro intelligence is less active because of "the narrowness of the cerebral organs." For the same reason the heads of their infants are smaller, which accounts for the ease with which savage women give birth.

Virey constantly harped on the "animality" of blacks:

Moreover, the negro brutally abandons himself to the most villainous excesses; his soul is, so to say, more steeped in the material, more encrusted in animality, more driven by purely physical appetites....

    If man consists mainly of his spiritual faculties, it is incontestable that the negro is less human in this respect; he is closer to the life of brutes, because we see him obeying his stomach, his sexual parts, in sum his senses, rather than reason. (Virey 1834, Vol. 2, p. 117)

The most extreme degradation, according to Virey, is to be found among the Hottentots, whose physique he characterized as being similar to that of the great apes. Their rudimentary speech, almost like the clucking of guinea-fowl, is close to the muffled cluckings of orang-utans. They, together with Papuans, display "extreme resemblances" to apes. Actually the Negroes themselves, averred Virey, recognize their parentage with the apes, whom they regard as savage and lazy Negroes.

The counterpoint to this tirade is a chapter on orang-utans, spelling out in detail their human-like behaviour as supposedly noted by observers. They easily learn things like eating at table using cutlery and a tooth-pick, making their beds, and even playing the flute. They can be taught to dress themselves, tie their shoe-laces, and the females have a well-developed sense of modesty. As regards modesty, if this were true, then by Virey's own logic female apes would be closer to white women than black ones! At any rate, for him all this proved the family resemblance between the higher apes and what for him was the lowest form of humanity. Virey conceded at one point that he did not pretend blacks and apes were of the same species, but on the very same page also commented:

when one notes how much the orang-outan shows the signs of intelligence, how much his morals [moeurs], his actions, his habits are analogous to those of negroes, how much he is susceptible to education, it seems to me that one cannot disagree that the least perfect of blacks is very close to the first of the apes. (Virey 1834, Vol. 2, p. 118)

Virey's strategy was to humanize the anthropoid apes and dehumanize the blacks (see figure 4.1). As might have been expected, Virey's views, like those of Long,[5] were well received and extensively borrowed across the Atlantic, since they provided ammunition for defenders of slavery. For example, Gwenebault (1837), who acknowledged his debt to Virey, referred to the "extreme lasciviousnes of negro women … their simple and animal mode of living" (p. 94). He conveyed the impression that practically everything they do is animal-like, including even their manner of resting: "Europeans sit on chairs, Asiatics cross-legged on earth or carpets, but the Negro either in Africa or New Guinea … remains squatting on his haunches, like the monkey" (p. 106). Apart from his success in America, Virey was also for a time widely read in France, and his work went through several editions. But many of his views were so patently absurd that it was difficult to take him seriously, and his writings later fell into well-deserved oblivion.

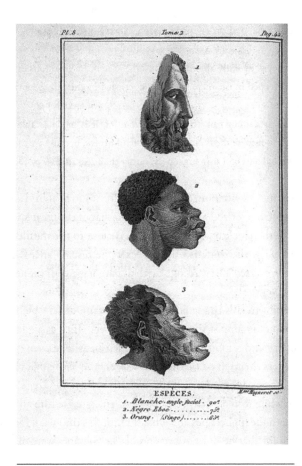

Figure 4.1: A classical Greek profile juxtaposed with those of a "Negro" and an ape. Note the incipient "muzzle" of the "Negro," approximating to that of the ape (i.e. progressively lower "facial angle"). *Source*: Virey (1824)

CAMPER'S "FACIAL ANGLE"

The mode of classification that came to be adopted by Virey, and subsequently many others, had been devised by Camper. Previous classifications of human types had been based on criteria that were largely arbitrary, and there had been no clear way of deciding between them. The work of Camper from the 1760s onwards seemed to offer the promise of an objective criterion which involved measurement, the hallmark of science. Camper is often still only remembered as the man who first introduced quantification[6] thereby paving the way for the craniological measures (see figure 4.2) that became ever more elaborate as the 19th century progressed (e.g. Baker 1974; Curtin 1965).

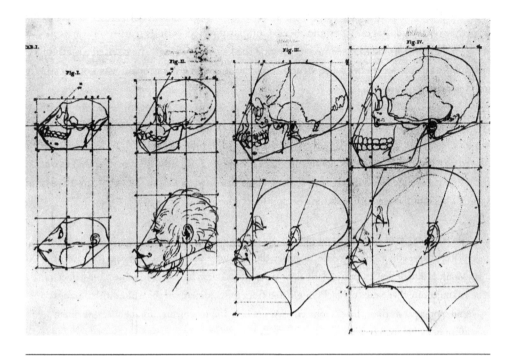

Figure 4.2: Camper's illustration of "facial angles" *Source*: Camper (1794).

While the "facial angle" as such has often been mentioned and explained, and will therefore be only summarily described in a footnote,[7] an important aspect of the story is less well known, namely the fact that the method introduced by Camper came to be interpreted in a manner he had never intended, and that was quite contrary to his own views (Visser 1990). In effect, it was hijacked by those who believed in, and wished to prove, the existence of a racial hierarchy from the noble European to the lowest savage.

Petrus Camper (1722–89), a versatile Dutchman, was not only an outstanding comparative anatomist but also an artist and sculptor of great skill. A staunch monogenist, he emphasized in his lectures the unity of mankind, and the relative superficiality of differences he attributed to environmental causes. This did not mean a lack of interest in the varieties of forms encountered in nature. On the contrary, in his posthumously published *Works* (1794) he recounted his fascination, from an early age, with differences between animals and human races. He also studied theories of art from the Greeks onwards, noting that most European artists painted Negroes with the faces of Europeans.

Camper looked for some principle according to which the appearances of various human groups could be captured, which would also serve as a guide for their correct artistic representation. At the same time he was concerned with the concept of beauty, whose most perfect expression he saw in classical Greek sculpture. Convinced that the artists of antiquity must have worked to some abstract rules which enabled them to achieve the perfect harmony of their creations, he wanted to rediscover them. Concentrating on heads, he collected skulls of people of different ages, sexes and races. Comparing their various features, he arrived at a structural characteristic that seemed to provide the key. Accordingly, he devised a method for the quantitative assessment of the structure of the skull, whose rationale was both aesthetic and scientific.[8]

Camper identified "facial angle" as a major source of error in the representation of different races, an idea he presented to the Academy of Drawing in 1770. He also noted that facial angles displayed a regular decline from Greek and Roman busts (90–95°) to European (80°), Negro (70°), and orang-utan (58°) heads. Thus the angle could be said to correspond to a scale from ape via savage to civilized, and Camper was of course well aware of that. In discussing some of his comparative illustrations he commented:

> The assemblage of cranium, and profiles of two apes, a negro and a Calmuck, in the first place, may perhaps excite some surprise: the striking resemblance between the race of Monkies and of Blacks, particularly upon a superficial view, has induced some philosophers to conjecture that a race of blacks originated from the commerce of the whites with ourangs and pongos; or that these monsters, by gradual improvements, finally became man. (Camper 1794, p. 32)

In writing this, Camper was merely mentioning speculations that were widespread in his time, and went on to refute them forcefully. He denied that the range of facial angles corresponds to a scale of superiority–inferiority, and never linked it to the Great Chain. Camper specifically stated that the resemblance between Negro and ape as regards a projecting jaw is merely superficial, and that there is an unbridgeable gulf between them, while there is no significant difference between whites and blacks. He also stated that everybody was descended from a single pair, it being immaterial whether that pair was black or fair. Subsequent changes, he suggested, were brought about by environmental factors such as climate, nutrition, manners, customs and education. Camper's work, originally published in 1792, received much acclaim and was soon translated into French, German and English. The only critical voice was that of Blumenbach who had two reservations: first, he objected to the facial angle being treated as the only criterion for racial classification, which Camper in fact had never claimed; second, he questioned the validity of the method because of the arbitrariness of the baseline, a critique that was justified.

The subsequent fate of Camper's ideas was an unfortunate one, since in spite of his explicit disclaimers, the regular gradient from Greek perfection to apes was later taken by many of his successors to reflect a fundamental biological feature. Visser (1990) suggests a number of reasons why this occurred. Well before publication, Camper's work had become known through informal channels, and he himself described it personally to Blumenbach and Soemmering among others. One important source of distortion was a summary of his 1770 address prepared by the then director of the Academy of Drawing. In this summary facial angles were directly linked to the doctrine of the Great Chain, and as the summary was widely circulated, also in translation, its misrepresentation gained broad currency. Moreover, it appealed to those who believed in the affinity between blacks and apes. This was true for Soemmering, White and Virey, who used this distorted version to bolster their own views. Opponents of the ape-connection theory, such as James Cowles Prichard (1786–1848), mistakenly criticized Camper on the same basis. But it was the adoption and elaboration of that version by the great Cuvier that had the most fateful consequences. The importance of Camper's "facial angle" is evident from the fact that it was applied by craniologists for most of the 19th century, and Broca (1874) devised a so-called "goniometer" for its more accurate measurement. It was not until a Congress of the German Anthropological Society in 1882 that a revised eye–ear plane came to be substituted for Camper's "facial angle" (Hoyme 1953).

Hence, paradoxically, a measure devised by a convinced monogenist for the purpose of analysing aesthetic principles became a prime tool in the hands of 19th-century race theorists for demonstrating the proximity between blacks and apes. The manner in which this occurred will be the topic of the next chapter. [...]

NOTES

1. He was able to establish that the famous "Wild Peter" had been the mute mental defective child of a widower, turned out of his home by a new stepmother. Or again, he rebuked with gentle wit some of Linnaeus' categorizations:

    > The custom of making women thin by a particular diet is very ancient, and has prevailed amongst the most refined nations, so politeness and respect forbid us to class it, with Linnaeus, amongst deformities. (Blumenbach [1795] 1865, p. 128)

2. During a visit to Switzerland,

    > he saw from behind a female form which struck him by its harmonious and beautiful shape. He spoke to the girl, who turned her face on Blumenbach, and he saw to his stupefaction the features of an African lady.... Blumenbach was enchanted ... [and his] delight reached its height when he realised that the girl was not only beautiful, but also witty and sensible. (Debrunner 1979, pp. 142–3)

    Blumenbach seems to have had quite a flirtation with her, and the experience clearly made a great impression on him.

3. Such topics include what Meiners described as their lack of visual judgement, which his examples indicate relate to what would now be called visual space perception (1815, Vol. 3, p. 222). On the other hand, he mentioned their good visual memory (pp. 224–5), and certain manual skills. Yet overall he asserted their complete unfitness for arts and sciences (p. 223).

4. For a detailed account of Virey's life and teachings cf. Benichou and Blanckaert (1988).

5. It is not clear whether Virey had actually read Long; although he referred to some publications in English, I have not come across any direct reference to Long. Nonetheless, in view of the prevalence of scholarly exchanges at that period it is virtually certain that Virey was familiar with Long's work.

6.   At about the same time Daubenton (1764) proposed a measure of the angle of the head
      in both animals and men, relating to the position of the hole at the base of the skull
      ("Le grand trou occipital") through which the nerves pass into the brain. According to
      Barzun (1938), "Daubenton was measuring in degrees the position of the head on top of the
      spinal column and correlating the measure of that angle with the amount of will-power in
      the several races" (p. 52). This was not in the *Mémoire* I consulted, nor was I able to trace
      any other one where it appeared.

7.   The method which Camper devised may be briefly outlined as follows. He placed a skull in
      a position where the orifices of the ears and the lowest part of the nasal aperture were level,
      and this he somewhat arbitrarily designated as the horizontal. He then drew a line between
      the forehead and the foremost part of the front teeth, ignoring any intersection with the
      nasal bones. The angle between those two lines came to be known as the "facial angle." A
      high angle is one where the forehead is more or less on a vertical line with the chin, while a
      low value indicates a forward projection of the jaw in relation to the cranium, a characteristic
      that came to be known as "prognathism" (cf. Baker 1974; Cowling 1989; Curtin 1965).

8.   For more detail cf. Blanckaert (1987) or Gould (1991).

REFERENCES

Baker, J.R. 1974. *Race.* London: Oxford University Press.

Barzun, J. 1938. *Race: A study in modern superstition.* London: Methuen.

Benichou, C., and C. Blanckaert. 1988. *Julien-Joseph Virey.* Paris: Vrin.

Blanckaert, C. 1987. Les "vissitudes de l'angle facial" et les débuts de la craniométrie. *Revue de
    Synthèse* 4e série, No. 3–4, p. 417.

Blumenbach, Johann Friedrich. [1795] 1865. *The anthropological treatises of Johann Friedrich
    Blumenbach*, trans. and ed. Thomas Bendyshe. London: The Anthropological Society.

Camper, Petrus. 1794. *The works of the later Professor Camper*, trans. T. Cogan. London: Dilly.

Cowling, M. 1989. *The artist as anthropologist.* Cambridge: Cambridge University Press.

Curtin, P.D. 1965. *The image of Africa.* London: Macmillan

Daubenton, M. 1764. Mémoire sur les différences de la situation de grand trou occipital dans
    l'homme et dans les animaux. *Mémoires de l'Académie des Sciences* 1 (September).

Debrunner, H.W. 1979. *Presence and prestige: Africans in Europe.* Basel: Basler Afrika Bibliographien.

Forster, Georg. [1786] 1969. Noch etwas über die Menschenrassen. In *Wekre* (4 vols.). Frankfurt:
    Insel.

Gould, S.J. 1991. Petrus Camper's angle. In *Bully for Brontosaurus.* London: Hutchinson Radius.

Gwenebault, J.H. 1837. *The natural history of the Negro Race.* Dowling: South Carolina.

Hegel, Georg Wilhelm Friedrich. [1832] 1992. *Vorlesungen über die Philosophie der Gerschichte.* In
    Werke, Vol 12. Frankfurt-arn-Main: Suhrkamp.

Hoyme, L.E. 1953. Physical anthropology and its instruments: an historical study. *Southwestern
    Journal of Anthropology* 9: 408–30

Long, Edward [under pseudonym "A Planter"]. 1772. *Candid Reflection upon a judgement … on what is commonly called the Negroe-Cause.* London.

———. 1774. *History of Jamaica.* 3 vols. London.

Meiners, Christoph. 1785. *Grundriss der Geschichte der Menschheit.* Lerngo: Meyer.

———. 1787. Ueber die grosse Verschiedenheit der Biegsamkeit und Unbiegsamkeit, der Härte und Weichheit der verschiedenen Stamme, und racen der Menschen. *Göttingisches Magazin* 1: 210–46.

———. 1788. Einige Betrachtungen über die Schönheit der menschlichen Bildung un über den Hang aller hässlichen Völker, sich noch rnehr zu verhässlichen. *Göttingisches Magazine* 2: 270–92.

———. 1815. Unter Suchungen über die Verschied enheiten der Mrnschennaturen. 3 vols. Tübingen: Cotta.

Plischke, H. 1937. *Johann Friedrich Blumenbach's Einfluss auf die Entdeskungreisenden seiner Zeit.* Hörtingen: Vandenhoeck & Ruprecht.

Rupp-Eisenreich, B. (1983). Des choses occultes en histoire des sciences humanines: Le destin de la "science nouvelle" de Christoph Meiners. *L'Ethnographie* LXXIX: 131–83.

———. 1985. Christoph Meiners et Joseph-Marie de Gérando: Un chapitre du comparatisme anthropologique. In D. Droixhe and P.-P. Jossiaux (eds.), *L'homme des Lumières et la découverle de l'autre.* Brussels: Université Libre de Bruxelles.

Soemmering, Samuel Thomas. 1784. *Ueber die körpliche Verschiedenheit de Negers vom Europaer.* Frankfurt.

Tiedermann, F. 1837. *Das Hurn des Negers mit dem des Europäers und Orang-Outans nerglichen.* Heidelberg: Winter.

Virey, Jules J. 1801. *Histoire naturelle du genre humain.* 2 vols. Paris.

———. 1824. *Histoire naturelle du genre humain.* 3 vols. Brussels: Wahlen.

———. 1834. *Histoire naturelle du genre humain.* 3 vols. Brussels: Hauman.

Visser, R. 1990. Die Rezeption der Anthropologie Petrus Campers. In G. Mann and F. Dumont (eds), *Die Natur des Menschen.* Stuttgart: Fischer.

White, Charles. 1799. *An account of the Regular Gradation in Man.* London: Dilly.

Chapter 5

The Dark Matter: Race and Racism in the Twenty-First Century

Howard Winant

In this piece, critical race theory doyen Howard Winant speaks on the power of race and racial discourse as co-constitutive of modernity and modern society. Fixing the concept of race to its role as ballast for the growth of modern capitalism, Winant briefly explores the ways in which previous forms of differentiating (e.g., othering) were distinctively shaped by the growth of modernity, capitalism, and Enlightenment dynamics and power.

INTRODUCTION

Race and racism may be termed the 'dark matter' of the modern epoch. 'Dark matter,' as you know, makes up much of the universe. Invisible, it possesses mass and gravitational attraction (what gravity is, however, is still up for debate; that's another story).

This rhetorical device begins with a crude analogy, but it suggests a lot of detailed comparisons. Race was invented along with the modern era; this was a historic swing that itself took several centuries to accomplish. It involved the lift-off of capitalism, a big bang of sorts: primitive accumulation, worldwide European seaborne empire, the Westphalian state system, conquest and settlement, the African slave trade, and the advent of enlightenment culture. The invisibility of the dark matter then—the darker peoples of that time—was not complete: in fact they were not invisible at all as 'matter,' as something that mattered. They were invisible as people. 'The turning of Africa into a warren for the commercial hunting of blackskins,' as Marx (1967: 351) puts it.

I won't go much into the comparisons here. Empire, slavery, augmented state power, and the dialectic of enlightenment as well, can all be seen as racial dynamics, in which absolutism's grasping and violent claws tore at the 'others,' seeking to dominate their bodies and their lands. What absolutist rule did not destroy it attempted to use for its own purposes.

Systems of rule and exploitation have advanced a great deal since the bad old days of maximum depredation that characterized the 'way of death' (Miller, 1988) in Africa or the 'entombment of mines of the aboriginal populations' (Marx again). That rapacity launched the modern world. Today, race and racism retain their predatory characteristics, their disregard for most of mankind. They continue *from above* as an ongoing war against the weak, the 'dark matter' of the world, who are still more 'matter' than people. An institutionalized forgetting of the provenance and meaning of race ('colorblindness') dismisses and disguises this war, this coercion and violence.

Race and racism also work *from below*, as matters of resistance (racism continues as something to be resisted), and as frameworks for alternative identities and collectivities. Though there has been endless suffering, the subaltern social strata, the 'dark matter,' has proved itself in resistance (in many ways, not all) to rule by the racial regime. The (partial) autonomy of people of color, combined with their sheer numbers and their continuing indispensability to the regime—as labor, citizens/denizens/migrants, as 'multitude,' and even as 'bare life'—suggests that they can never be effectively ruled again as they were in the past. Still a significant degree of absolutism endures, much of it organized along racial lines. 'Deathscapes' anybody? 'Bare life'? (Mbembe, 2003; Agamben, 1998). As Judith Butler (2007) notes: 'We have become accustomed over recent years to the argument that modern constitutions retain a sovereign function and that a tacit totalitarianism functions as a limiting principle within constitutional democracies.'

To provide a credible theoretical account of race and racism is always a challenge. To do so in the 21st century, a period that is putatively 'post-civil rights,' post-apartheid, and 'colorblind,' is to run political and intellectual risks. My comments here are necessarily provisional, work-in-progress. In these few pages I cannot hope to offer anything definitive or comprehensive. Where race is concerned, we are in a notably contradictory age: the 'post-civil rights' period, the age of Obama, is also the age of neoliberalism, itself a political-economic phenomenon whose racial dimensions go largely unrecognized. Here I confine myself to situating the present in the *longue durée* of racial history that is, I believe, largely contiguous with the modern world-system's history.

The essay proceeds through a series of brief and interconnected topical vignettes: In the next section, 'We Come from the Abyss,' I discuss the world-historical origins of race and racism in the absolutist regimes of the past. In 'The Abyss Is Still Here,' I point to the substantial continuities of the racial present with those regimes. That theme continues in '"Deathscapes" and Development,' where I also introduce the notion, drawn from Myrdal, of 'circular and cumulative development.' In 'The Race Concept over the *Longue Durée*' I explore the vicissitudes of the race-concept itself. Next, in 'Accumulation by Dispossession' and 'The World-Historical Shitpile of Race,' I apply David Harvey's account of neoliberalism to the racial present. In 'Yet That's Not the Whole Story' and 'A Crisis of Race and Racism?' I address the contrariety and instability of race and racism in the present. [...]

WE COME FROM THE ABYSS

We can begin with an understanding that racism is a living relic of absolutism. Consider Ruth Wilson Gilmore's valuable definition; she characterizes racism as '… the state-sanctioned or extra-legal production and exploitation of group-differentiated vulnerability to premature death' (Gilmore, 2007: 28).

Using 'premature death' as a biostatistical variable, we can venture some crude figures: *Indigenous deaths* in the Americas in the first century of European rule totaled c. 42 million/80% of the total (lowest credible estimate). Deaths directly attributable to the Atlantic slave trade look like this: 8–10 million in Africa (some through war and raiding, most through forced marches and in coastal internment); 10–12 million in the 'middle passage'; and 5 million in Jamaican 'seasoning' camps alone. The estimated Brazilian slave death rate before age 35 is c. 80% for 200+ years! At a world scale the abyss is almost impossible to contemplate. If we continue the point into the 20th century, we can see that 'merely' the post–Second World War wars of national liberation took the lives—and this is a very crude estimate—of c. 80 million souls.[1]

THE ABYSS IS STILL HERE

We come from the abyss—and the abyss has a sort of a racially-stratified character. But the abyss is also *still here*. Here I will mention just a few dimensions of the ongoing modern world (racial) system, which as I argue is not all that modern: the absolutist residue recurs once again.

Greed kills: A neglected lesson of the so-called War on Terror is that the world's North, if only for its own security (but for a lot of other reasons as well), has not terminated its ceaseless exploitation of the global South. It cannot; this is its lifeblood. The consumerism of 'McWorld' is built on a planetary sweatshop. The world's poor are largely peasants and superexploited workers, the dark-skinned sharecroppers and field hands of a global corporate plantation.

Climate change is a global racism issue: The world's South is far more vulnerable to global warming. The hottest and poorest countries on the planet are being hit first and hardest by rising temperatures. Environmental racism is now about much more than dumping of toxic substances: it's about drought, famine, forced migration, corporate agriculture and mining … These are supremely familiar historical events.

Colonialism is not over: The European colonial powers could not sustain their empires after the Second World War, a fact they sometimes had to be taught the hard way, through armed revolutions. But they had learned by the 1960s that indirect rule works better than explicit empire anyway. Setting up spheres of influence throughout the now 'independent' global South allowed for a level of pillage and depredation unimaginable during the bad old days of overt colonialism. After the Second World War, the US became the chief neocolonialist power (Nkrumah, 1966).

'DEATHSCAPES' AND DEVELOPMENT

'Deathscape' is the term used by Achille Mbembe to describe the 'postcolony.' We could also apply it to Gaza, to North Philadelphia (where I worked for many years), or to the Western Region Detention Facility at San Diego. The latter is one of an extensive archipelago of immigrant prisons where constitutional rights (and human rights) are below minimal. Circa 50,000 people are presently detained in the US on strictly immigration violations. The overall US prison population is now in the 2.7 million range.

How should we understand the range of policing, carceral practices, and racial profiling involved in—or required for—the maintenance of the post–civil rights/post-imperial system? Some have argued that war is the appropriate framework and indeed I have used that term above. I would prefer to invoke a few other concepts, however.

One of these is 'development.' From Gunnar Myrdal's work I draw the idea of 'cumulative and circular development.' This appears in *An American Dilemma* in early form, but later operates as a master concept in Myrdal's arguments against global inequality and what was then termed 'underdevelopment' on a world scale.

Bringing in the 'cumulative and circular' idea allows us to account both for the reiteration of practices of racial oppression and of anti-racist resistance. That's the 'circular' part. We can furnish endless examples of reiterative racial practices: in immigration/xenophobia, racial 'science,' recursive stereotypes about the racialized 'other's' laziness, criminality, and so on. Imperialism too has reiterative dimensions, as does the struggle against it. For example the post–Second World War national liberation movements recapitulated many organizational and ideological features of the 19th-century revolutions against European colonialism in the Americas (Haiti, Gran Colombia, Mexico, and elsewhere). They were broadly parallel 'racial projects.'[2] The anti-racist/abolitionist dimension of these 19th-century struggles reappeared in the 20th-century linkage between national liberation in the periphery and black liberation in the metropoles.

With the 'cumulative' idea I want to highlight the convergence of various racial projects that had earlier been distinct substantively or geographically. 'Profiling' is an instance of substantive convergence I want to stress. It was originally an aggressive racist style of policing; it now exceeds the criminological context in which it was first developed and extends to the racist gaze more generally. Race serves as a multi-use political technology for organizing and explaining any form of social conflict, both in social science and in everyday life/commonsense. John Solomos and Les Back point out that racism is 'a scavenger ideology, which gains its power from its ability to pick out and utilize ideas and values from other sets of ideas and beliefs in specific socio-historical contexts' (Solomos and Back, 1996: 18–19; see also Fredrickson, 2003: 8). This interpellative adaptability—to scavenge for *ressentiment*, xenophobia, religious dogma, or a host of other proclivities or projections—is a highly developed, indeed central, component of racism. In other words, the ready availability of race as an 'explanation' for deviance from some attributed norm becomes more intelligible when we recognize both the ease with which racial distinctions are made—their 'ocularity'—and when we simultaneously admit the breadth and depth of racial awareness in much of the modern world.

Geographically too there has always been a convergence of 'styles' of racial oppression. Cooper and Stoler (1997) point out how cultures of coercion that were developed in imperial peripheries were imported back to the UK, France, and other European imperial metropoles. Nikhil Singh (2012) notes that today US efforts to police the globe parallel US efforts to police the ghettos and barrios. 'National security' doctrines give way to 'human security' doctrines as networking, contracting, and training (by the US, Israel, Brazil, and others) cooperate and learn from each other (Amar, 2013). State terror remains available (the 'iron fist') but softer forms of power (the 'velvet glove') are preferable in 'reformed' racist polities.

In the same way, insurgent groups converge on strategies that target similar oppressive regimes, whether or not they exhibit similar racist features. The 'Bloody Sunday' marchers in 1973 in Northern Ireland sang 'We Shall Overcome.' Consider the parallels between the Arab Spring and Occupy: both collective actions were more 'class-' and 'youth-' oriented than explicitly anti-racist, but they taught and learned from each other; they both drew on recent anti-colonial and anti-racist traditions.

THE RACE CONCEPT OVER THE *LONGUE DURÉE*

From the social to the biological and back again … reiteration once again. When the colonial encounter happened and the African slave trade began, the race concept didn't yet exist. Some precursors can be identified. These are chiefly the distinctions between 'civilized' and 'barbarous' peoples, which go back at least to the Greeks (Hannaford, 1996), and the quasi- biological stigmatization of Jews and Muslims by the Inquisition under the doctrine of *limpieza de sangre*: possession or lack of pure—that is, Christian—blood. In a more general way, however, categorization of peoples was not primarily corporeally-based, not attached to the body, not 'biopolitical' (Foucault via Stoler, 1995), in the premodern world. It was more like what we would today call cultural or ethnic: religious, linguistic, territorial.

The 'otherness' of peripheral subjects varied by empire, of course. To the pioneering Portuguese and Spanish, Africans were not so strange, since the Iberian peninsula had been ruled by Africans—Maghrebines mostly, but there were sub-Saharan (black) Africans around too—for more than half a millennium. The *reconquista* was still a recent event when the European seaborne empires were first launched—notably by Portugal and then Spain, more than a century before the British and the French (Thornton, 1998).

Still, the indigenous peoples of the Western Hemisphere were as unknown a population to the Portuguese and Spanish as they were to the British, French, and Dutch. Hence the famous debate between Bartolomé de las Casas and Juan Ginés de Sepúlveda in 1550 Valladolid, and a century later António Vieira's profound defense of the indigenous peoples, and to some extent of the enslaved Africans of Brazil (on las Casas and Vieira see Todorov, 1985; Cohen, 1998, Blackburn, 1997).

The Brits, French, and Dutch were late-comers, but not as benighted about Africa and Africans as, say, Winthrop Jordan would have us believe. In large measure they learned from the Portuguese: not only about who the natives and blacks were but about how to traffic them and how to exploit them.

The race concept arose out of the social and political need to dominate enslaved and conquered people, and conversely out of the social and political imperative for resistance against those practices. Because the occupying powers had to be able to distinguish native from settler, enslaved from 'free,' they gravitated toward 'optical' or phenomic criteria to organize their regimes. For the same reason the occupied and enslaved peoples of African descent and of the Americas—those who survived the onslaughts of the European empires—had also to employ these optical frameworks of social classification. So race developed as a highly practical political technology of oppression and resistance. Of course this was in practice a complex process, not so bilaterally a matter of 'us and them'; there were enslaved Europeans, African and indigenous slave-traders, ethnic differences among Africans, and so on. But the general point holds: between free and slave, between native and settler, between oppressor and oppressed, a 'colorline' arose, not all at once, but over the early years of empire and Atlantic slavery. Social, not biological, construction.

In turn and over a longer time period, biological concepts of race developed out of the sociopolitical distinction of race. These were the products of enlightenment: they reified and essentialized what had previously been sociopolitical categories. In a broad sense, the biologizing of race may be understood as rationalization, both in the commonsense meaning of that term and in the Weberian sense of modernization and legitimation. Consider the underlying logics of 'enlightened' racial discourse—the *mission civilisatrice*, the white man's burden, or manifest destiny—from this standpoint: 'It's just common sense: these practices may seem unjust, but when you look deeper you will discover that they are uplifting and domesticating. Such obviously primitive and backward people cannot be afforded full human status; they are more 'natural,' more driven by desire than reason, less inclined to work, less cultivated …,' and so on. These attributions remain common today, especially on the right, and also in 'commonsense.' From the Weberian standpoint the stages of legitimation proceed from lower to higher, both ontogenetically and phylogenetically. The 'lower orders' are *naturally* lower. Slavery and empire were more modern, more developed, more rational systems of authority than were the 'primitive' societies which empire supplanted or subordinated. Evolutionary doctrine, both before and after Darwin (notably in the view of Francis Galton, Darwin's cousin and the founder of eugenics), further naturalized the previously sociopolitical phenomenon of race: not only 'social Darwinism' but the mere presence of a worked-out and admirable theory of the evolution of species tended to hierarchize the human race along the lines of biologically attributable differences. Thus what had begun as a social distinction of political convenience was transformed into a natural condition: something eternal, perhaps tragic, but ineluctable.

Not until the turn of the 20th century did there emerge any serious effort to reinterpret race as social and political. By that time the biologization of race was taken for granted, immured in both science and commonsense. Racial identity and difference had long been linked to the putatively rational and hierarchical order of the planet, where empire and racial 'caste' were established social conventions. Indeed race and class had now tacitly merged in the national doctrines of the 'advanced' countries, and on the world stage as well. Race in particular was seen as absolute and permanent, as evidenced by the rise of eugenics.

In this historical and theoretical context the critique of racial biology must be recognized as a very impressive intellectual achievement. Its provenance, as Du Bois (2007 [1935]) certainly makes clear, lies in abolitionism, first in the Haitian revolution but most spectacularly in the US Civil War and its aftermath, in which black people not only overthrew the system of slavery but called into question (as the Haitians had also done; cf. James, 1989 [1938]) the viability of the imperial order itself. The achievements of black people in and after the War (Hahn, 2005) led directly to the first scientific refutations of biologistic racism, carried out by such people as George Washington Williams, Kelly Miller, Anna Julia Cooper, William Monroe Trotter, and Du Bois himself. It was black social scientists, then, who first launched the drive to reinterpret—or re-reinterpret—race as a social construct. These people were largely ignored; they were vindicated only after the fall of eugenics during and after the Second World War and the dawn of the civil rights era. But their arguments were presented again—independently reinvented or in some sense derived from the earlier black scholars' work—by the Chicago sociologists in the 1920s (Park, Frazier, Johnson, Cox). The return of the sociopolitical concept of race is an inconvenient truth.

ACCUMULATION BY DISPOSSESSION

David Harvey's (2003) concept reworks Marx's idea of 'primitive accumulation' and brings the coercive basis of race rule forward into our age of neoliberalism. Here again is the continuity of absolutism. Primitive accumulation, extra-economic coercion—boy, Marx was right about that! Maybe he didn't go far enough: 'the turning of Africa into a warren for the commercial hunting of black skins' was pretty good, but Marx, along with Weber and Durkheim, still tended to valorize capitalist depredation as a necessary way-station in the historical march forward of civilization: towards collective self-rule (in Marx's case),[3] toward more deeply legitimate authority (in Weber's case), and toward a more 'organic' and inclusive solidarity (in Durkheim's case).

Maybe Marx didn't fully comprehend slavery as the first transnational business, or the most central one anyway. Maybe he didn't fully grasp radical pragmatist notions of politics in the way that DuBois did in *Black Reconstruction*, or C.L.R. James did with his concept of 'self-activity' (James et al. 2005 [1958]), or in earlier form in *The Black Jacobins* ... Those works are centered on some notions of race-based (and of course class-based) self-emancipation, what Robin Kelley might call 'freedom dreams.' They converge with Deweyan notions of 'situated creativity' and 'self-reflective action,' if those terms can be properly racialized and fully politicized as well.

Wherever we locate Marx on the path to those concepts, we must recognize that he still did a pretty good job at recognizing that the accumulation of capital is *always* violent, *always* coercive, and that the racial dimension is at least involved. After all, 'labor cannot emancipate itself in the white skin when in the black skin it is branded' (Marx, 1967: 329).

THE WORLD-HISTORICAL SHITPILE OF RACE

Structural racism—an odious stinkpile of shit left over from the past and still being augmented in the present—has been accumulated by 'slavery unwilling to die,'[4] by empire, and indeed by the entire racialized modern world system. The immense *waste* (Feagin et al., 2001, drawing on Bataille) of human life and labor by these historically entrenched social structures and practices still confronts us today, in the aftermath of the post–Second World War racial 'break.' Our anti-racist accomplishments have reduced the size of the pile; we have lessened the stink. But a massive amount of waste still remains. So much racial waste is left over from the practice of racial domination in the early days of empire and conquest to the present combination of police state and liberalism! Indeed it often seems that this enormous and odious waste pinions the social system under an immovable burden. How often have despair and hopelessness overcome those who bore this sorrow? How often have slave and native, peon and *maquiladora*, servant and ghetto-dweller, felt just plain 'sick and tired' (Nappy Roots, 2003), encumbered by this deadening inertia composed of a racial injustice that could seemingly never be budged? How often, too, have whites felt weighed down by the waste, the guilt and self-destruction built into racism and the 'psychological wage'?

Yet racial politics is always unstable and contradictory. Racial despotism can never be fully stabilized or consolidated. Thus at key historical moments, perhaps rare but also inevitable, the sheer weight of racial oppression—*qua* social structure—becomes insupportable. The built-up rage and inequity, the irrationality and inutility, and the explosive force of dreams denied are mobilized politically in ways that would have seemed almost unimaginable earlier.

Racism remains formidable, entrenched as a structuring feature of both US and global society and politics. Indeed it often seems impossible to overcome.

YET THAT'S NOT THE WHOLE STORY

We are so used to losing! We can't see that the racial system is in crisis both in the US and globally. Large-scale demographic and political shifts have overtaken the modern world (racial) system, undermining and rearticulating it. During and after the Second World War a tremendous racial 'break' occurred, a seismic shift that swept much of the world (Winant, 2001). The US was but one national 'case' of this rupture, which was experienced very profoundly: racial transformations occurred that were unparalleled since at least the changes brought about by the US Civil War. Omi and I (1994)—and many, many others—have proposed that the terrain of racial politics was tremendously broadened and deepened after the War. The increased importance of race in larger political life not only grounded the modern civil rights movement but shaped a whole range of 'new social movements' that we take for granted today as central axes of political conflict. In earlier stages of US history it had not been so evident that 'the personal is political'—at least not since the end of Reconstruction. From the explicit racial despotism of the Jim Crow era to the 'racial democracy' (of course still very partial and truncated) of the present period … : that is a big leap, people.

In the modern world there were always black movements, always movements for racial justice and racial freedom. The experience of injustice, concrete grievances, lived oppression, and resistance, both large and small, always exists. It can be articulated or not, politicized or not. These movements, these demands, were largely excluded from mainstream politics before the rise of the civil rights movement after the War. Indeed, after the Second World War, in a huge 'break' that was racially framed in crucial ways, this 'politicization of the social' swept over the world. It ignited (or reignited) major democratic upsurges. This included the explicitly anti-racist movements: the modern civil rights movement, the anti-apartheid movement, and the anti-colonial movement (India, Algeria, Vietnam, etc.). It also included parallel, and more-or-less allied, movements like 'second-wave' feminism, LGBTQ (*née* gay liberation) movements, and others.

In short, the world-historical upheaval of the Second World War and its aftermath were racial upheavals in significant ways: the periphery against the center, the colored 'others' against 'The Lords of Human Kind' (Kiernan, 1995). These movements produced:

- Demographic, economic, political, and cultural shifts across the planet
- The destruction of the old European empires
- The coming and going of the Cold War
- The rise of the 'new social movements,' led by the black movement in the US

And this is only the start of what could be a much bigger list.

A CRISIS OF RACE AND RACISM?

'[C]risis,' Gramsci famously wrote, 'consists precisely in the fact that the old is dying and the new cannot be born: in this interregnum, morbid phenomena of the most varied kind come to pass' (1971: 276). Using the Gramscian formula, I suggest that there is such a crisis of race and racism. On the one hand, the old verities of established racism and white supremacy have been officially discredited, not only in the US but fairly comprehensively around the world. On the other hand, racially-informed action and social organization, racial identity and race consciousness, continue unchecked in nearly every aspect of social life! On the one hand, the state (many states around the world) now claims to be colorblind, non-racialist, racially democratic; while on the other hand, in almost every case, those same states *need* race to rule. Consider in the US alone: race and electoral politics, race and social control, race and legal order … Why don't our heads *explode* under the pressures of such cognitive dissonance? Why doesn't manifest racial contradiction provoke as much uncertainty and confusion in public life and political activity as it does in everyday experience? Are we just supposed to pretend that none of this is happening? Can anyone really sustain the view that they are operating in a nonracial, 'colorblind' society?

The 'colorblind' claim is that one should not 'notice' race. For if one 'sees' race, one wouldn't be 'blind' to it, after all.[5] But what happens to race-consciousness under the pressure (now rather intense in the US, anyway) to be 'colorblind'? Quite clearly, racial awareness does not dry up like a raisin in the sun. Not only does it continue as a matter of course in everyday life, but in intellectual, artistic, and scientific (both social and natural) life race continues to command attention.[6]

'Colorblind' ideologies of race today serve to impede the recognition of racial difference or racial inequality based on claims that race is an archaic concept, that racial inclusion is already an accomplished fact, and so on. Just so, persistent race-consciousness highlights racial differences and particularities. 'Noticing' race can be linked to despotic or democratic motives, framed either in defense of coercion, privilege, and undeserved advantage, or invoked to support inclusion, human rights, and social justice (Carbado and Harris, 2008; see also Brown et al., 2003). [...]

NOTES

This essay was first presented as the keynote address at 'The Problem of the Twenty-First Century: Race and Racism in and beyond the United States' conference, held at the University of Illinois, Urbana-Champaign in October 2012. Thanks to Professors Moon-Kie Jung, Zsusza Gille, David Roediger, Elizabeth Esch, David Wilson, and numerous other conference participants. © Howard Winant 2012

1. Please accept my disclaimers for not providing sources on these numbers. They are based on extensive digging into the genocide literature. To list writings on this theme would explode the bibliography and give an air of authority that is not really justified. Also, I am not attempting to account for the vast range of genocidal consequences, or indeed other consequences, of the Atlantic slavery complex: for example, demographic or ecological effects, as discussed by Zuberi (1995), Miller (1988), or Vansina (1990). My effort here is to signal the scope of the coercion, violence, and destruction that were visited upon African-descent peoples in the death march toward the modern world.

2. This is a term from Omi's and my work on racial formation (Omi and Winant, 1994).

3. See Anderson's (2010) historical sociological account of the vicissitudes of *Marx at the Margins*.

4. 'Some badges of slavery remain today. While the institution has been outlawed, it has remained in the minds and hearts of many white men. Cases which have come to this Court depict a spectacle of slavery unwilling to die' (Douglas, 1968: 445; see also Feagin, 2000: 25).

5. Colorblindness is an abhorrent term, a neologism twice over. First and most obviously it is rooted in an ophthalmic condition that has no relevance to race, unless we understand race as being 'about' skin color, a deep reductionism in the term's meaning. Second, the term appears in the dissent of Justice John Marshall Harlan in the 1896 *Plessy* case, where the Justice's insistence that 'Our Constitution is Colorbind' coexists blissfully with a range of support claims for eternal white superiority and supremacy (see Gotanda, 1995).

6.   For example the status of the racialized body is a major subject across many of these
      fields. The resurgence of a new racial biologism (mainly via genomics) is a pressing
      question in the biological and social sciences. Racial demographics are shifting in many
      countries, not just in the US, but also globally across both the North-South and West-East
      axes, posing new political and cultural questions.

REFERENCES

Agamben G (1998) *Homo Sacer: Sovereign Power and Bare Life*, trans Heller-Roazen D. Stanford, CA:
      Stanford University Press.

Amar P (2013) *The Security Archipelago: Human-Security States, Sexuality Politics, and the End of
      Neoliberalism*. Durham, NC: Duke University Press.

Anderson KB (2010) *Marx at the Margins*. Chicago, IL: University of Chicago Press.

Blackburn R (1997) *The Making of New World Slavery: From the Baroque to the Modern, 1492–1800*.
      New York, NY: Verso.

Brown MK, Carnoy M, Currie E et al. (2003) *Whitewashing Race: The Myth of a Colorblind Society*.
      Berkeley, CA: University of California Press.

Butler J (2007) 'I merely belong to them.' *London Review of Books* 29(9): 26–28.

Carbado DW and Harris CI (2008) Taking initiative on initiatives: Examining Proposition 209 and
      beyond: The new racial preferences. *California Law Review* 96: 1139–1214.

Cohen T (1998) *The Fire of Tongues: Antonio Vieira and the Missionary Church in Brazil and Portugal*.
      Stanford, CA: Stanford University Press.

Cooper F and Stoler AL (1997) Between metropole and colony: Rethinking a research agenda.
      In: Cooper F and Stoler AL (eds) *Tensions of Empire: Colonial Cultures in a Bourgeois World*.
      Berkeley, CA: University of California Press.

Douglas WO (1968) Concurring in *Jones v. Alfred H. Mayer Co.*, 392 US 409.

Du Bois WEB (2007 [1935]) *Black Reconstruction in America: An Essay toward a History of the Part
      which Black Folk Played in the Attempt to Reconstruct Democracy in America, 1860–1880*. New
      York, NY: Oxford University Press.

Feagin JR (2000) *Racist America: Roots, Current Realities, and Future Reparations*. New York,
      NY: Routledge.

Feagin JR, Vera H, and Batur P (2001) *White Racism: The Basics*. New York, NY: Routledge.

Fredrickson GM (2003) *Racism: A Short History*. Princeton, NJ: Princeton University Press.

Gilmore RW (2007) *Golden Gulag: Prisons, Surplus, Crisis, and Opposition in Globalizing California*.
      Berkeley, CA: University of California Press.

Gotanda N (1995) A critique of 'our constitution is color-blind.' In: Crenshaw K et al. (eds) *Critical
      Race Theory: The Key Writings that Formed the Movement*. New York, NY: New Press.

Gramsci A (1971) *Selections from the Prison Notebooks*, eds Hoare Q and Nowell-Smith G. New York,
      NY: International Publishers.

Hahn S (2005) *A Nation under Our Feet: Black Political Struggles in the Rural South from Slavery to
      the Great Migration*. Cambridge, MA: Harvard University Press.

Hannaford I (1996) *Race: The History of an Idea in the West*. Baltimore, MD: Johns Hopkins University Press.

Harvey D (2003) The new imperialism: Accumulation by dispossession. *Socialist Register* 40: 63–87.

James CLR (1989 [1938]) *The Black Jacobins: Toussaint L'Ouverture and the San Domingo Revolution*. New York, NY: Vintage.

James CLR, Lee G and Castoriadis C (2005 [1958]) *Facing Reality*. Chicago, IL: Charles H. Kerr.

Kiernan VG (1995) *The Lords of Human Kind: European Attitudes to Other Cultures in the Imperial Age, 4th edn*. Serif Publishing (Open Library).

Marx K (1967) *Capital, Vol. 1*. New York, NY: International Publishers.

Mbembe A (2003) Necropolitics. *Public Culture* 15(1): 11–40.

Miller JC (1988) *Way of Death: Merchant Capitalism and the Angolan Slave Trade, 1730–1830*. Madison, WI: University of Wisconsin Press.

Myrdal, Gunnar (1962) *An American Dilemma*. New York, NY: McGraw-Hill.

Nappy Roots (2003) Sick and tired. *Wooden Leather*. Atlantic Records.

Nkrumah K (1966) *Neo-Colonialism: The Last Stage of Imperialism*. New York, NY: International Publishers.

Omi M and Winant H (1994) *Racial Formation in the United States: From the 1960s to the 1990s, 2nd edn*. New York: Routledge.

Singh N (2012) Racial formation in an age of permanent war. In: HoSang DM, LaBennett O, and Pulido L (eds) *Racial Formation in the Twenty-First Century*. Berkeley, CA: University of California Press.

Solomos J and Back L (1996) *Racism and Society*. New York, NY: St. Martin's Press.

Stoler AL (1995) *Race and the Education of Desire: Foucault's History of Sexuality and the Colonial Order of Things*. Durham, NC: Duke University Press.

Thornton J (1998) *Africa and Africans in the Making of the Atlantic World, 1400–1680, 2nd edn*. New York, NY: Cambridge University Press.

Todorov T (1985) *The Conquest of America: The Question of the Other*, trans. Howard R. New York, NY: Harper and Row.

Vansina J (1990) *Paths in the Rainforests: Toward a History of Political Tradition in Equatorial Africa*. Madison, WI: University of Wisconsin Press.

Winant H (2001) *The World Is a Ghetto: Race and Democracy Since World War II*. New York, NY: Basic Books.

Zuberi T [Antonio McDaniel] (1995) *Swing Low, Sweet Chariot: The Mortality Cost of Colonizing Liberia in the Nineteenth Century*. Chicago, IL: University of Chicago Press.

Chapter 6

Latent and Manifest Orientalism

Edward W. Said

Spawning a distinctive field of literature after him, Edward Said argued that, far from representing a true or accurate depiction of a particular region, "the Orient" instead constituted a systematic regime of representation within which Westerners thought about, came to "know," and ultimately attempted to colonize the diversity of Indigenous nations in specific geographic spaces. Importantly, Said argues that Westerners' sense of the geographical regions they came to perceive as "the Orient" did not reflect any reality, but instead represented the prejudices and stereotypes that Westerners held about "Orientals." In this chapter from his 1978 book *Orientalism*, Said argues that over time certain sets of observations about the Orient solidified into natural or taken-for-granted truths (usually depicting the Orient as backward or deficient and Western society as dominant and superior). Said refers to this bedrock of truth that shaped the opinions of the vast majority of Orientalists (i.e., those who studied the Orient) as "latent Orientalism." Thus, despite the apparently diverse sets of views and knowledges produced with respect to the Orient (what Said refers to as "manifest Orientalism"), all writers relied in one way or another on a construction of the Orient as fundamentally different from—and inferior to—"the West."

In Chapter One, I tried to indicate the scope of thought and action covered by the word *Orientalism*, using as privileged types the British and French experiences of and with the Near Orient, Islam, and the Arabs. In those experiences I discerned an intimate, perhaps even the most intimate, and rich relationship between Occident and Orient. Those experiences were part of a much wider European or Western relationship with the Orient, but what seems to have influenced Orientalism most was a fairly constant sense of confrontation felt by Westerners dealing with the East. The boundary notion of East and West, the varying degrees of projected inferiority and strength, the range of work done, the kinds of characteristic features ascribed to the Orient: all these testify to a willed imaginative and geographic division made between East and West, and lived through during many centuries. In Chapter Two my focus narrowed a good deal. I was interested in the earliest phases of what I call modern Orientalism, which began during the latter part of the eighteenth century and the early years of the nineteenth. Since I did not intend my study to become a narrative chronicle of the development of Oriental studies in the modern West, I proposed instead an account of the rise, development, and institutions of Orientalism as they were formed against a background of intellectual, cultural, and political history until about 1870 or 1880. Although my interest in Orientalism there included a decently ample variety of scholars and imaginative writers, I cannot claim by any means to have presented more than a portrait of the typical structures (and their ideological tendencies) constituting the field, its associations with other fields, and the work of some of its most influential scholars. My principal operating assumptions were—and continue to be—that fields of learning, as much as the works of even the most eccentric artist, are constrained and acted upon by society, by cultural traditions, by worldly circumstance, and by stabilizing influences like schools, libraries, and governments; moreover, that both learned and imaginative writing are never free, but are limited in their imagery, assumptions, and intentions; and finally, that the advances made by a "science" like Orientalism in its academic form are less objectively true than we often like to think. In short, my study hitherto has tried to describe the *economy* that makes Orientalism a coherent subject matter, even while allowing that as an idea, concept, or image the word *Orient* has a considerable and interesting cultural resonance in the West.

I realize that such assumptions are not without their controversial side. Most of us assume in a general way that learning and scholarship move forward; they get better, we feel, as time passes and as more information is accumulated, methods are refined, and later generations of scholars improve upon earlier ones. In addition, we entertain a mythology of creation, in which it is believed that artistic genius, an original talent, or a powerful intellect can leap beyond the confines of its own time and place in order to put before the world a new work. It would be pointless to deny that such ideas as these carry some truth. Nevertheless the possibilities for work present in the culture to a great and original mind are never unlimited, just as it is also true that a great talent has a very healthy respect for what others have done before it and for what the field already contains. The work of predecessors, the institutional life of a scholarly field, the collective nature of any learned enterprise: these, to say nothing of economic and social circumstances, tend to diminish the effects of the individual scholar's production.

A field like Orientalism has a cumulative and corporate identity, one that is particularly strong given its associations with traditional learning (the classics, the Bible, philology), public institutions (governments, trading companies, geographical societies, universities), and generically determined writing (travel books, books of exploration, fantasy, exotic description). The result for Orientalism has been a sort of consensus: certain things, certain types of statement, certain types of work have seemed for the Orientalist correct. He has built his work and research upon them, and they in turn have pressed hard upon new writers and scholars. Orientalism can thus be regarded as a manner of regularized (or Orientalized) writing, vision, and study, dominated by imperatives, perspectives, and ideological biases ostensibly suited to the Orient. The Orient is taught, researched, administered, and pronounced upon in certain discrete ways.

The Orient that appears in Orientalism, then, is a system of representations framed by a whole set of forces that brought the Orient into Western learning, Western consciousness, and later, Western empire. If this definition of Orientalism seems more political than not, that is simply because I think Orientalism was itself a product of certain political forces and activities. Orientalism is a school of interpretation whose material happens to be the Orient, its civilizations, peoples, and localities. Its objective discoveries—the work of innumerable devoted scholars who edited texts and translated them, codified grammars, wrote dictionaries, reconstructed dead epochs, produced positivistically verifiable learning—are and always have been conditioned by the fact that its truths, like any truths delivered by language, are embodied in language, and what is the truth of language, Nietzsche once said, but

> a mobile army of metaphors, metonyms, and anthropomorphisms—in short, a sum of human relations, which have been enhanced, transposed, and embellished poetically and rhetorically, and which after long use seem firm, canonical, and obligatory to a people: truths are illusions about which one has forgotten that this is what they are.[1]

Perhaps such a view as Nietzsche's will strike us as too nihilistic, but at least it will draw attention to the fact that so far as it existed in the West's awareness, the Orient was a word which later accrued to it a wide field of meanings, associations, and connotations, and that these did not necessarily refer to the real Orient but to the field surrounding the word.

Thus Orientalism is not only a positive doctrine about the Orient that exists at any one time in the West; it is also an influential academic tradition (when one refers to an academic specialist who is called an Orientalist), as well as an area of concern defined by travelers, commercial enterprises, governments, military expeditions, readers of novels and accounts of exotic adventure, natural historians, and pilgrims to whom the Orient is a specific kind of knowledge about specific places, peoples, and civilizations. For the Orient idioms became frequent, and these idioms took firm hold in European discourse. Beneath the idioms there was a layer of doctrine about the Orient; this doctrine was fashioned out of the experiences of many Europeans, all of them converging upon such essential aspects of the Orient as the Oriental character, Oriental despotism, Oriental sensuality, and the like. For any European during the nineteenth century—and I think one can say this almost without qualification—Orientalism was such a system of truths, truths in Nietzsche's sense of the word. It is therefore correct that every European, in what he could say about the Orient, was consequently a racist, an imperialist, and almost totally ethnocentric. Some of the immediate sting will be taken out of these labels if we recall additionally that human societies, at least the more advanced cultures, have rarely offered the individual anything but imperialism, racism, and ethnocentrism for dealing with "other" cultures. So Orientalism aided and was aided by general cultural pressures that tended to make more rigid the sense of difference between the European and Asiatic parts of the world. My contention is that Orientalism is fundamentally a political doctrine willed over the Orient because the Orient was weaker than the West, which elided the Orient's difference with its weakness.

This proposition was introduced early in Chapter One, and nearly everything in the pages that followed was intended in part as a corroboration of it. The very presence of a "field" such as Orientalism, with no corresponding equivalent in the Orient itself, suggests the relative strength of Orient and Occident. A vast number of pages on the Orient exist, and they of course signify a degree and quantity of interaction with the Orient that are quite formidable; but the crucial index of Western strength is that there is no possibility of comparing the movement of Westerners eastwards (since the end of the eighteenth century) with the movement of Easterners westwards. Leaving aside the fact that Western armies, consular corps, merchants, and scientific and archaeological expeditions were always going East, the number of travelers from the Islamic East to Europe between 1800 and 1900 is minuscule when compared with the number in the other direction.[2] Moreover, the Eastern travelers in the West were there to learn from and to gape at an advanced culture; the purposes of the Western travelers in the Orient were, as we have seen, of quite a different order. In addition, it has been estimated that around 60,000 books dealing with the Near Orient were written between 1800 and 1950; there is no remotely comparable figure for Oriental books about the West. As a cultural apparatus Orientalism is all aggression, activity, judgment, will-to-truth, and knowledge. The Orient existed for the West, or so it seemed to countless Orientalists, whose attitude to what they worked on was either paternalistic or candidly condescending—unless, of course, they were antiquarians, in which case the "classical" Orient was a credit to *them* and not to the lamentable modern Orient. And then, beefing up the Western scholars' work, there were numerous agencies and institutions with no parallels in Oriental society.

Such an imbalance between East and West is obviously a function of changing historical patterns. During its political and military heyday from the eighth century to the sixteenth, Islam dominated both East and West. Then the center of power shifted westwards, and now in the late twentieth century it seems to be directing itself back towards the East again. My account of nineteenth-century Orientalism in Chapter Two stopped at a particularly charged period in the latter part of the century, when the often dilatory, abstract, and projective aspects of Orientalism were about to take on a new sense of worldly mission in the service of formal colonialism. It is this project and this moment that I want now to describe, especially since it will furnish us with some important background for the twentieth-century crises of Orientalism and the resurgence of political and cultural strength in the East.

On several occasions I have alluded to the connections between Orientalism as a body of ideas, beliefs, clichés, or learning about the East, and other schools of thought at large in the culture. Now one of the important developments in nineteenth-century Orientalism was the distillation of essential ideas about the Orient—its sensuality, its tendency to despotism, its aberrant mentality, its habits of inaccuracy, its backwardness—into a separate and unchallenged coherence; thus for a writer to use the word *Oriental* was a reference for the reader sufficient to identify a specific body of information about the Orient. This information seemed to be morally neutral and objectively valid; it seemed to have an epistemological status equal to that of historical chronology or geographical location. In its most basic form, then, Oriental material could not really be violated by anyone's discoveries, nor did it seem ever to be revaluated completely. Instead, the work of various nineteenth-century scholars and of imaginative writers made this essential body of knowledge more clear, more detailed, more substantial—and more distinct from "Occidentalism." Yet Orientalist ideas could enter into alliance with general philosophical theories (such as those about the history of mankind and civilization) and diffuse world-hypotheses, as philosophers sometimes call them; and in many ways the professional contributors to Oriental knowledge were anxious to couch their formulations and ideas, their scholarly work, their considered contemporary observations, in language and terminology whose cultural validity derived from other sciences and systems of thought.

The distinction I am making is really between an almost unconscious (and certainly an untouchable) positivity, which I shall call *latent* Orientalism, and the various stated views about Oriental society, languages, literatures, history, sociology, and so forth, which I shall call *manifest* Orientalism. Whatever change occurs in knowledge of the Orient is found almost exclusively in manifest Orientalism; the unanimity, stability, and durability of latent Orientalism are more or less constant. In the nineteenth-century writers I analyzed in Chapter Two, the differences in their ideas about the Orient can be characterized as exclusively manifest differences, differences in form and personal style, rarely in basic content. Every one of them kept intact the separateness of the Orient, its eccentricity, its backwardness, its silent indifference, its feminine penetrability, its supine malleability; this is why every writer on the Orient, from Renan to Marx (ideologically speaking), or from the most rigorous scholars (Lane and Sacy) to the most powerful imaginations (Flaubert and Nerval), saw the Orient as a locale requiring Western attention, reconstruction, even redemption. The Orient existed as a place isolated from the mainstream of European progress in the sciences, arts, and commerce. Thus whatever good or bad values were imputed to the Orient appeared to be functions of some highly specialized Western interest in the Orient. This was the situation from about the 1870s on through the early part of the twentieth century—but let me give some examples that illustrate what I mean.

Theses of Oriental backwardness, degeneracy, and inequality with the West most easily associated themselves early in the nineteenth century with ideas about the biological bases of racial inequality. Thus the racial classifications found in Cuvier's *Le Règne animal*, Gobineau's *Essai sur l'inégalité des races humaines*, and Robert Knox's *The Races of Man* found a willing partner in latent Orientalism. To these ideas was added second-order Darwinism, which seemed to accentuate the "scientific" validity of the division of races into advanced and backward, or

European-Aryan and Oriental-African. Thus the whole question of imperialism, as it was debated in the late nineteenth century by pro-imperialists and anti-imperialists alike, carried forward the binary typology of advanced and backward (or subject) races, cultures, and societies. John Westlake's *Chapters on the Principles of International Law* (1894) argues, for example, that regions of the earth designated as "uncivilized" (a word carrying the freight of Orientalist assumptions, among others) ought to be annexed or occupied by advanced powers. Similarly, the ideas of such writers as Carl Peters, Leopold de Saussure, and Charles Temple draw on the advanced/backward binarism[3] so centrally advocated in late-nineteenth-century Orientalism.

Along with all other peoples variously designated as backward, degenerate, uncivilized, and retarded, the Orientals were viewed in a framework constructed out of biological determinism and moral-political admonishment. The Oriental was linked thus to elements in Western society (delinquents, the insane, women, the poor) having in common an identity best described as lamentably alien. Orientals were rarely seen or looked at; they were seen through, analyzed not as citizens, or even people, but as problems to be solved or confined or—as the colonial powers openly coveted their territory—taken over. The point is that the very designation of something as Oriental involved an already pronounced evaluative judgment, and in the case of the peoples inhabiting the decayed Ottoman Empire, an implicit program of action. Since the Oriental was a member of a subject race, he had to be subjected: it was that simple. The *locus classicus* for such judgment and action is to be found in Gustave Le Bon's *Les Lois psychologiques de l'évolution des peuples* (1894).

But there were other uses for latent Orientalism. If that group of ideas allowed one to separate Orientals from advanced, civilizing powers, and if the "classical" Orient served to justify both the Orientalist and his disregard of modern Orientals, latent Orientalism also encouraged a peculiarly (not to say invidiously) male conception of the world. I have already referred to this in passing during my discussion of Renan. The Oriental male was considered in isolation from the total community in which he lived and which many Orientalists, following Lane, have viewed with something resembling contempt and fear. Orientalism itself, furthermore, was an exclusively male province; like so many professional guilds during the modern period, it viewed itself and its subject matter with sexist blinders. This is especially evident in the writing of travelers and novelists: women are usually the creatures of a male power-fantasy. They express unlimited sensuality, they are more or less stupid, and above all they are willing. Flaubert's Kuchuk Hanem is the prototype of such caricatures, which were common enough in pornographic novels (e.g., Pierre Louys's *Aphrodite*) whose novelty draws on the Orient for their interest. Moreover the male conception of the world, in its effect upon the practicing Orientalist, tends to be static, frozen, fixed eternally. The very possibility of development, transformation, human movement—in the deepest sense of the word—is denied the Orient and the Oriental. As a known and ultimately an immobilized or unproductive quality, they come to be identified with a bad sort of eternality: hence, when the Orient is being approved, such phrases as "the wisdom of the East."

Transferred from an implicit social evaluation to a grandly cultural one, this static male Orientalism took on a variety of forms in the late nineteenth century, especially when Islam was being discussed. General cultural historians as respected as Leopold von Ranke and

Jacob Burckhardt assailed Islam as if they were dealing not so much with an anthropomorphic abstraction as with a religio-political culture about which deep generalizations were possible and warranted: in his *Weltgeschichte* (1881–1888) Ranke spoke of Islam as defeated by the Germanic-Romanic peoples, and in his "Historische Fragmente" (unpublished notes, 1893) Burckhardt spoke of Islam as wretched, bare, and trivial.[4] Such intellectual operations were carried out with considerably more flair and enthusiasm by Oswald Spengler, whose ideas about a Magian personality (typified by the Muslim Oriental) infuse *Der Untergang des Abendlandes* (1918–1922) and the "morphology" of cultures it advocates.

What these widely diffused notions of the Orient depended on was the almost total absence in contemporary Western culture of the Orient as a genuinely felt and experienced force. For a number of evident reasons the Orient was always in the position both of outsider and of incorporated weak partner for the West. To the extent that Western scholars were aware of contemporary Orientals or Oriental movements of thought and culture, these were perceived either as silent shadows to be animated by the Orientalist, brought into reality by him, or as a kind of cultural and intellectual proletariat useful for the Orientalist's grander interpretative activity, necessary for his performance as superior judge, learned man, powerful cultural will. I mean to say that in discussions of the Orient, the Orient is all absence, whereas one feels the Orientalist and what he says as presence; yet we must not forget that the Orientalist's presence is enabled by the Orient's effective absence. This fact of substitution and displacement, as we must call it, clearly places on the Orientalist himself a certain pressure to reduce the Orient in his work, even after he has devoted a good deal of time to elucidating and exposing it. How else can one explain major scholarly production of the type we associate with Julius Wellhausen and Theodor Nöldeke and, overriding it, those bare, sweeping statements that almost totally denigrate their chosen subject matter? Thus Nöldeke could declare in 1887 that the sum total of his work as an Orientalist was to confirm his "low opinion" of the Eastern peoples.[5] And like Carl Becker, Nöldeke was a philhellenist, who showed his love of Greece curiously by displaying a positive dislike of the Orient, which after all was what he studied as a scholar.

A very valuable and intelligent study of Orientalism—Jacques Waardenburg's *L'Islam dans le miroir de l'Occident*—examines five important experts as makers of an image of Islam. Waardenburg's mirror-image metaphor for late-nineteenth- and early-twentieth-century Orientalism is apt. In the work of each of his eminent Orientalists there is a highly tendentious—in four cases out of the five, even hostile—vision of Islam, as if each man saw Islam as a reflection of his own chosen weakness. Each scholar was profoundly learned, and the style of his contribution was unique. The five Orientalists among them exemplify what was best and strongest in the tradition during the period roughly from the 1880s to the interwar years. Yet Ignaz Goldziher's appreciation of Islam's tolerance towards other religions was undercut by his dislike of Mohammed's anthropomorphisms and Islam's too-exterior theology and jurisprudence; Duncan Black Macdonald's interest in Islamic piety and orthodoxy was vitiated by his perception of what he considered Islam's heretical Christianity; Carl Becker's understanding of Islamic civilization made him see it as a sadly undeveloped one; C. Snouck Hurgronje's highly refined studies of Islamic mysticism (which he considered the essential part of Islam) led him to a harsh judgment of its crippling limitations; and Louis Massignon's extraordinary identification with Muslim theology, mystical passion, and poetic art kept him curiously unforgiving to Islam for what he regarded as its unregenerate revolt against the idea of incarnation. The manifest differences in their methods emerge as less important than their Orientalist consensus on Islam: latent inferiority.[6]

Waardenburg's study has the additional virtue of showing how these five scholars shared a common intellectual and methodological tradition whose unity was truly international. Ever since the first Orientalist congress in 1873, scholars in the field have known each other's work and felt each other's presence very directly. What Waardenburg does not stress enough is that most of the late-nineteenth-century Orientalists were bound to each other politically as well. Snouck Hurgronje went directly from his studies of Islam to being an adviser to the Dutch government on handling its Muslim Indonesian colonies; Macdonald and Massignon were widely sought after as experts on Islamic matters by colonial administrators from North Africa to Pakistan; and, as Waardenburg says (all too briefly) at one point, all five scholars shaped a coherent vision of Islam that had a wide influence on government circles throughout the Western world.[7] What we must add to Waardenburg's observation is that these scholars were completing, bringing to an ultimate concrete refinement, the tendency since the sixteenth and seventeenth centuries to treat the Orient not only as a vague literary problem but—according to Masson-Oursel—as "un ferme propos d'assimiler adéquatement la valeur des langues pour pénétrer les moeurs et les pensées, pour forcer même des secrets de l'histoire."[8]

I spoke earlier of incorporation and assimilation of the Orient, as these activities were practiced by writers as different from each other as Dante and d'Herbelot. Clearly there is a difference between those efforts and what, by the end of the nineteenth century, had become a truly formidable European cultural, political, and material enterprise. The nineteenth-century colonial "scramble for Africa" was by no means limited to Africa, of course. Neither was the penetration of the Orient entirely a sudden, dramatic afterthought following years of scholarly study of Asia. What we must reckon with is a long and slow process of appropriation by which Europe, or the European awareness of the Orient, transformed itself from being textual and con-templative into being administrative, economic, and even military. The fundamental change was a spatial and geographical one, or rather it was a change in the quality of geographical and spatial apprehension so far as the Orient was concerned. The centuries-old designation of geograph-ical space to the east of Europe as "Oriental" was partly political, partly doctrinal, and partly imaginative; it implied no necessary connection between actual experience of the Orient and knowledge of what is Oriental, and certainly Dante and d'Herbelot made no claims about their Oriental ideas except that they were corroborated by a long *learned* (and not existential) trad-ition. But when Lane, Renan, Burton, and the many hundreds of nineteenth-century European travelers and scholars discuss the Orient, we can immediately note a far more intimate and even proprietary attitude towards the Orient and things Oriental. In the classical and often temporally remote form in which it was reconstructed by the Orientalist, in the precisely actual form in which the modern Orient was lived in, studied, or imagined, the *geographical space* of the Orient was penetrated, worked over, taken hold of. The cumulative effect of decades of so sovereign a

Western handling turned the Orient from alien into colonial space. What was important in the latter nineteenth century was not *whether* the West had penetrated and possessed the Orient, but rather *how the* British and French felt that they had done it.

The British writer on the Orient, and even more so the British colonial administrator, was dealing with territory about which there could be no doubt that English power was truly in the ascendant, even if the natives were on the face of it attracted to France and French modes of thought. So far as the actual space of the Orient was concerned, however, England was really there, France was not, except as a flighty temptress of the Oriental yokels. There is no better indication of this qualitative difference in spatial attitudes than to look at what Lord Cromer had to say on the subject, one that was especially dear to his heart:

> The reasons why French civilisation presents a special degree of attraction to Asiatics and Levantines are plain. It is, as a matter of fact, more attractive than the civilisations of England and Germany, and, moreover, it is more easy of imitation. Compare the undemonstrative, shy Englishman, with his social exclusiveness and insular habits, with the vivacious and cosmopolitan Frenchman, who does not know what the word shyness means, and who in ten minutes is apparently on terms of intimate friendship with any casual acquaintance he may chance to make. The semi-educated Oriental does not recognise that the former has, at all events, the merit of sincerity, whilst the latter is often merely acting a part. He looks coldly on the Englishman, and rushes into the arms of the Frenchman.

The sexual innuendoes develop more or less naturally thereafter. The Frenchman is all smiles, wit, grace, and fashion; the Englishman is plodding, industrious, Baconian, precise. Cramer's case is of course based on British solidity as opposed to a French seductiveness without any real presence in Egyptian reality.

> Can it be any matter for surprise [Cromer continues] that the Egyptian, with his light intellectual ballast, fails to see that some fallacy often lies at the bottom of the Frenchman's reasoning, or that he prefers the rather superficial brilliancy of the Frenchman to the plodding, unattractive industry of the Englishman or the German? Look, again, at the theoretical perfection of French administrative systems, at their elaborate detail, and at the provision which is apparently made to meet every possible contingency which may arise. Compare these features with the Englishman's practical systems, which lay down rules as to a few main points, and leave a mass of detail to individual discretion. The half-educated Egyptian naturally prefers the Frenchman's system, for it is to all outward appearance more perfect and more easy of application. He fails, moreover, to see that the Englishman desires to elaborate a system which will suit the facts with which he has to deal, whereas the main objection to applying French administrative procedures to Egypt is that the facts have but too often to conform to the ready-made system.

Since there is a real British presence in Egypt, and since that presence—according to Cromer—is there not so much to train the Egyptian's mind as to "form his character," it follows therefore that the ephemeral attractions of the French are those of a pretty damsel with "somewhat artificial charms," whereas those of the British belong to "a sober, elderly matron of perhaps somewhat greater moral worth, but of less pleasing outward appearance."[9]

Underlying Cromer's contrast between the solid British nanny and the French coquette is the sheer privilege of British emplacement in the Orient. "The facts with which he [the Englishman] has to deal" are altogether more complex and interesting, by virtue of their possession by England, than anything the mercurial French could point to. Two years after the publication of his *Modern Egypt* (1908), Cromer expatiated philosophically in *Ancient and Modern Imperialism.* Compared with Roman imperialism, with its frankly assimilationist, exploitative, and repressive policies, British imperialism seemed to Cromer to be preferable, if somewhat more wishy-washy. On certain points, however, the British were clear enough, even if "after a rather dim, slipshod, but characteristically Anglo-Saxon fashion," their Empire seemed undecided between "one of two bases—an extensive military occupation or the principle of nationality [for subject races]." But this indecision was academic finally, for in practice Cromer and Britain itself had opted against "the principle of nationality." And then there were other things to be noted. One point was that the Empire was not going to be given up. Another was that intermarriage between natives and English men and women was undesirable. Third—and most important, I think—Cromer conceived of British imperial presence in the Eastern colonies as having had a lasting, not to say cataclysmic, effect on the minds and societies of the East. His metaphor for expressing this effect is almost theological, so powerful in Cromer's mind was the idea of Western penetration of Oriental expanses. "The country," he says, "over which the breath of the West, heavily charged with scientific thought, has once passed, and has, in passing, left an enduring mark, can never be the same as it was before."[10]

In such respects as these, nonetheless, Cromer's was far from an original intelligence. What he saw and how he expressed it were common currency among his colleagues both in the imperial Establishment and in the intellectual community. This consensus is notably true in the case of Cromer's viceregal colleagues, Curzon, Swettenham, and Lugard. Lord Curzon in particular always spoke the imperial lingua franca, and more obtrusively even than Cromer he delineated the relationship between Britain and the Orient in terms of possession, in terms of a large geographical space wholly owned by an efficient colonial master. For him, he said on one occasion, the Empire was not an "object of ambition" but "first and foremost, a great historical and political and sociological fact." In 1909 he reminded delegates to the Imperial Press Conference meeting at Oxford that "we train here and we send out to you your governors and administrators and judges, your teachers and preachers and lawyers." And this almost pedagogical view of empire had, for Curzon, a specific setting in Asia, which as he once put it, made "one pause and think."

I sometimes like to picture to myself this great Imperial fabric as a huge structure like some Tennysonian "Palace of Art," of which the foundations are in this country, where they have been laid and must be maintained by British hands, but of which the Colonies are the pillars, and high above all floats the vastness of an Asiatic dome.[11]

With such a Tennysonian Palace of Art in mind, Curzon and Cromer were enthusiastic members together of a departmental committee formed in 1909 to press for the creation of a school of Oriental studies. Aside from remarking wistfully that had he known the vernacular he would have been helped during his "famine tours" in India, Curzon argued for Oriental studies as part of the British responsibility to the Orient. On September 27, 1909, he told the House of Lords that

our familiarity, not merely with the languages of the people of the East but with their customs, their feelings, their traditions, their history and religion, our capacity to understand what may be called the genius of the East, is the sole basis upon which we are likely to be able to maintain in the future the position we have won, and no step that can be taken to strengthen that position can be considered undeserving of the attention of His Majesty's Government or of a debate in the House of Lords.

At a Mansion House conference on the subject five years later, Curzon finally dotted the i's. Oriental studies were no intellectual luxury; they were, he said,

a great Imperial obligation. In my view the creation of a school [of Oriental studies—later to become the London University School of Oriental and African Studies] like this in London is part of the necessary furniture of Empire. Those of us who, in one way or another, have spent a number of years in the East, who regard that as the happiest portion of our lives, and who think that the work that we did there, be it great or small, was the highest responsibility that can be placed upon the shoulders of Englishmen, feel that there is a gap in our national equipment which ought emphatically to be filled, and that those in the City of London who, by financial support or by any other form of active and practical assistance, take their part in filling that gap, will be rendering a patriotic duty to the Empire and promoting the cause and goodwill among mankind.[12]

To a very great extent Curzon's ideas about Oriental studies derive logically from a good century of British utilitarian administration of and philosophy about the Eastern colonies. The influence of Bentham and the Mills on British rule in the Orient (and India particularly) was considerable, and was effective in doing away with too much regulation and innovation; instead, as Eric Stokes has convincingly shown, utilitarianism combined with the legacies of liberalism and evangelicalism as philosophies of British rule in the East stressed the rational importance of a strong executive armed with various legal and penal codes, a system of doctrines on such matters as frontiers and land rents, and everywhere an irreducible supervisory imperial authority.[13] The cornerstone of the whole system was a constantly refined knowledge of the Orient, so that as traditional societies hastened forward and became modern commercial societies, there would be no loss of paternal British control, and no loss of revenue either. However, when Curzon referred somewhat inelegantly to Oriental studies as "the necessary furniture of Empire," he was putting into a static image the transactions by which Englishmen and natives conducted their business and kept their places. From the days of Sir William Jones the Orient had been both what Britain ruled and what Britain knew about it: the coincidence between geography, knowledge, and power, with Britain always in the master's place, was complete. To have said, as Curzon once did, that "the East is a University in which the scholar never takes his degree" was another way of saying that the East required one's presence there more or less forever.[14]

But then there were the other European powers, France and Russia among them, that made the British presence always a (perhaps marginally) threatened one. Curzon was certainly aware that all the major Western powers felt towards the world as Britain did. The transformation of geography from "dull and pedantic"—Curzon's phrase for what had now dropped out of geography as an academic subject—into "the most cosmopolitan of all sciences" argued *exactly* that new Western and widespread predilection. Not for nothing did Curzon in 1912 tell the Geographical Society, of which he was president, that

> an absolute revolution has occurred, not merely in the manner and methods of teaching geography, but in the estimation in which it is held by public opinion. Nowadays we regard geographical knowledge as an essential part of knowledge in general. By the aid of geography, and in no other way, do we understand the action of great natural forces, the distribution of population, the growth of commerce, the expansion of frontiers, the development of States, the splendid achievements of human energy in its various manifestations.
>
> We recognize geography as the handmaid of history.... Geography, too, is a sister science to economics and politics; and to any of us who have attempted to study geography it is known that the moment you diverge from the geographical field you find yourself crossing the frontiers of geology, zoology, ethnology, chemistry, physics, and almost all the kindred sciences. Therefore we are justified in saying that geography is one of the first and foremost of the sciences: that it is part of the equipment that is necessary for a proper conception of citizenship, and is an indispensable adjunct to the production of a public man.[15]

Geography was essentially the material underpinning for knowledge about the Orient. All the latent and unchanging characteristics of the Orient stood upon, were rooted in, its geography. Thus on the one hand the geographical Orient nourished its inhabitants, guaranteed their characteristics, and defined their specificity; on the other hand, the geographical Orient solicited the West's attention, even as—by one of those paradoxes revealed so frequently by organized knowledge—East was East and West was West. The cosmopolitanism of geography was, in Curzon's mind, its universal importance to the whole of the West, whose relationship to the rest of the world was one of frank covetousness. Yet geographical appetite could also take on the moral neutrality of an epistemological impulse to find out, to settle upon, to uncover—as when in *Heart of Darkness* Marlow confesses to having a passion for maps.

I would look for hours at South America, or Africa, or Australia, and lose myself in all the glories of exploration. At that time there were many blank spaces on the earth, and when I saw one that looked particularly inviting on a map (but they all look that) I would put my finger on it and say, When I grow up I will go there.[16]

Seventy years or so before Marlow said this, it did not trouble Lamartine that what on a map was a blank space was inhabited by natives; nor, theoretically, had there been any reservation in the mind of Emer de Vattel, the Swiss-Prussian authority on international law, when in 1758 he invited European states to take possession of territory inhabited only by mere wandering tribes.[17] The important thing was to dignify simple conquest with an idea, to turn the appetite for more geographical space into a theory about the special relationship between geography on the one hand and civilized or uncivilized peoples on the other. But to these rationalizations there was also a distinctively French contribution.

By the end of the nineteenth century, political and intellectual circumstances coincided sufficiently in France to make geography, and geographical speculation (in both senses of that word), an attractive national pastime. The general climate of opinion in Europe was propitious; certainly the successes of British imperialism spoke loudly enough for themselves. However, Britain always seemed to France and to French thinkers on the subject to block even a relatively successful French imperial role in the Orient. Before the Franco-Prussian War there was a good deal of wishful political thinking about the Orient, and it was not confined to poets and novelists. Here, for instance, is Saint-Marc Girardin writing in the *Revue des Deux Mondes* on March 15, 1862:

La France a beaucoup à faire en Orient, parce que l'Orient attend beaucoup d'elle. Il lui demande même plus qu'elle ne peut faire; il lui remettrait volontiers le soin entier de son avenir, ce qui serait pour la France et pour l'Orient un grand danger: pour la France, parce que, disposée a prendre en mains la cause des populations souffrantes, elle se charge le plus souvent de plus d'obligations qu'elle n'en peut remplir; pour l'Orient, parce que tout peuple qui attend sa destinée de l'étranger n'a jamais qu'une condition précaire et qu'il n'y a de salut pour les nations que celui qu'elles se font elles-mêmes.[18]

Of such views as this Disraeli would doubtless have said, as he often did, that France had only "sentimental interests" in Syria (which is the "Orient" of which Girardin was writing). The fiction of "populations souffrantes" had of course been used by Napoleon when he appealed to the Egyptians on their behalf against the Turks and for Islam. During the thirties, forties, fifties, and sixties the suffering populations of the Orient were limited to the Christian minorities in Syria. And there was no record of "l'Orient" appealing to France for its salvation. It would have been altogether more truthful to say that Britain stood in France's way in the Orient, for even if France genuinely felt a sense of obligation to the Orient (and there were some Frenchmen who did), there was very little France could do to get between Britain and the huge land mass it commanded from India to the Mediterranean.

Among the most remarkable consequences of the War of 1870 in France were a tremendous efflorescence of geographical societies and a powerfully renewed demand for territorial acquisition. At the end of 1871 the Société de géographic de Paris declared itself no longer confined to "scientific speculation." It urged the citizenry not to "forget that our former preponderance was contested from the day we ceased to compete ... in the conquests of civilization over barbarism." Guillaume Depping, a leader of what has come to be called the geographical movement, asserted in 1881 that during the 1870 war "it was the schoolmaster who triumphed," meaning that the real triumphs were those of Prussian scientific geography over French strategic sloppiness. The government's *Journal officiel* sponsored issue after issue centered on the virtues (and profits) of geographical exploration and colonial adventure; a citizen could learn in one issue from de Lesseps of "the opportunities in Africa" and from Gamier of "the exploration of the Blue River." Scientific geography soon gave way to "commercial geography," as the connection between national pride in scientific and civilizational achievement and the fairly rudimentary profit motive was urged, to be channeled into support for colonial acquisition. In the words of one enthusiast, "The geographical societies are formed to break the fatal charm that holds us enchained to our shores." In aid of this liberating quest all sorts of schemes were spun out, including the enlisting of Jules Verne—whose "unbelievable success," as it was called, ostensibly displayed the scientific mind at a very high peak of ratiocination—to head "a round-the-world campaign of scientific exploration," and a plan for creating a vast new sea just south of the North African coast, as well as a project for "binding" Algeria to Senegal by railroad—"a ribbon of steel," as the projectors called it.[19]

Much of the expansionist fervor in France during the last third of the nineteenth century was generated out of an explicit wish to compensate for the Prussian victory in 1870–1871 and, no less important, the desire to match British imperial achievements. So powerful was the latter desire, and out of so long a tradition of Anglo-French rivalry in the Orient did it derive, that France seemed literally haunted by Britain, anxious in all things connected with the Orient to catch up with and emulate the British. When in the late 1870s, the Société académique indo-chinoise reformulated its goals, it found it important to "bring Indochina into the domain of Orientalism." Why? In order to turn Cochin China into a "French India." The absence of substantial colonial holdings was blamed by military men for that combination of military and commercial weakness in the war with Prussia, to say nothing of long-standing and pronounced colonial inferiority compared with Britain. The "power of expansion of the Western races," argued a leading geographer, La Roncière Le Noury, "its superior causes, its elements, its influences on human destinies, will be a beautiful study for future historians." Yet only if the white races indulged their taste for voyaging—a mark of their intellectual supremacy—could colonial expansion occur.[20]

From such theses as this came the commonly held view of the Orient as a geographical space to be cultivated, harvested, and guarded. The images of agricultural care for and those of frank sexual attention to the Orient proliferated accordingly. Here is a typical effusion by Gabriel Charmes, writing in 1880:

On that day when we shall be no longer in the Orient, and when other great European powers will be there, all will be at an end for our commerce in the Mediterranean, for our future in Asia, for the traffic of our southern ports. *One of the mast fruitful sources of our national wealth will be dried up.* (Emphasis added)

Another thinker, Leroy-Beaulieu, elaborated this philosophy still further:

A society colonizes, when itself having reached a high degree of maturity and of strength, it procreates, it protects, it places in good conditions of development, and it brings to virility a new society to which it has given birth. Colonization is one of the most complex and delicate phenomena of social physiology.

This equation of self-reproduction with colonization led Leroy-Beaulieu to the somewhat sinister idea that whatever is lively in a modern society is "magnified by this pouring out of its exuberant activity on the outside." Therefore, he said,

Colonization is the expansive force of a people; it is its power of reproduction; *it is its enlargement and its multiplication through space*; it is the subjection of the universe or a vast part of it to that people's language, customs, ideas, and laws.[21]

The point here is that the space of weaker or underdeveloped regions like the Orient was viewed as something inviting French interest, penetration, insemination—in short, colonization. Geographical conceptions, literally and figuratively, did away with the discrete entities held in by borders and frontiers. No less than entrepreneurial visionaries like de Lesseps, whose plan was to liberate the Orient and the Occident from their geographical bonds, French scholars, administrators, geographers, and commercial agents poured out their exuberant activity onto the fairly supine, feminine Orient. There were the geographical societies, whose number and membership outdid those of all Europe by a factor of two; there were such powerful organizations as the Comité de l'Asie française and the Comité d'Orient; there were the learned societies, chief among them the Société asiatique, with its organization and membership firmly embedded in the universities, the institutes, and the government. Each in its own way made French interests in the Orient more real, more substantial. Almost an entire century of what now seemed passive study of the Orient had had to end, as France faced up to its transnational responsibilities during the last two decades of the nineteenth century.

In the only part of the Orient where British and French interests literally overlapped, the territory of the now hopelessly ill Ottoman Empire, the two antagonists managed their conflict with an almost perfect and characteristic consistency. Britain was *in* Egypt and Mesopotamia; through a series of quasi-fictional treaties with local (and powerless) chiefs it controlled the Red Sea, the Persian Gulf, and the Suez Canal, as well as most of the intervening land mass between the Mediterranean and India. France, on the other hand, seemed fated to hover over the Orient, descending once in a while to carry out schemes that repeated de Lesseps's success with the canal; for the most part these schemes were railroad projects, such as the one planned across more or less British territory, the Syrian-Mesopotamian line. In addition France saw itself as the protector of Christian minorities—Maronites, Chaldeans, Nestorians. Yet together, Britain and France were agreed in principle on the necessity, when the time came, for the partition of Asiatic Turkey. Both before and during World War I secret diplomacy was bent on carving up the Near Orient first into spheres of influence, then into mandated (or occupied) territories. In France, much of the expansionist sentiment formed during the heyday of the geographical movement focused itself on plans to partition Asiatic Turkey, so much so that in Paris in 1914 "a spectacular press campaign was launched" to this end.[22] In England numerous committees were empowered to study and recommend policy on the best ways of dividing up the Orient. Out of such commissions as the Bunsen Committee would come the joint Anglo-French teams of which the most famous was the one headed by Mark Sykes and Georges Picot. Equitable division of geographical space was the rule of these plans, which were deliberate attempts also at calming Anglo-French rivalry. For, as Sykes put it in a memorandum,

> it was clear ... that an Arab rising was sooner or later to take place, and that the French and ourselves ought to be on better terms if the rising was not to be a curse instead of a blessing....[23]

The animosities remained. And to them was added the irritant provided by the Wilsonian program for national self-determination, which, as Sykes himself was to note, seemed to invalidate the whole skeleton of colonial and partitionary schemes arrived at jointly between the Powers. It would be out of place here to discuss the entire labyrinthine and deeply controversial history of the Near Orient in the early twentieth century, as its fate was being decided between the Powers, the native dynasties, the various nationalist parties and movements, the Zionists. What matters more immediately is the peculiar epistemological framework through which the Orient was seen, and out of which the Powers acted. For despite their differences, the British and the French saw the Orient as a geographical—and cultural, political, demographical, sociological, and historical—entity over whose destiny they believed themselves to have traditional entitlement. The Orient to them was no sudden discovery, no mere historical accident, but an area to the east of Europe whose principal worth was uniformly defined in terms of Europe, more particularly in terms specifically claiming for Europe—European science, scholarship, understanding, and administration—the credit for having made the Orient what it was now. And this had been the achievement—inadvertent or not is beside the point—of modern Orientalism.

There were two principal methods by which Orientalism delivered the Orient to the West in the early twentieth century. One was by means of the disseminative capacities of modern learning, its diffusive apparatus in the learned professions, the universities, the professional societies, the explorational and geographical organizations, the publishing industry. All these, as we have seen, built upon the prestigious authority of the pioneering scholars, travelers, and poets, whose cumulative vision had shaped a quintessential Orient; the doctrinal—or doxological—manifestation of such an Orient is what I have been calling here latent Orientalism. So far as anyone wishing to make a statement of any consequence about the Orient was concerned, latent Orientalism supplied him with an enunciative capacity that could be used, or rather mobilized, and turned into sensible discourse for the concrete occasion at hand. Thus when Balfour spoke about the Oriental to the House of Commons in 1910, he must surely have had in mind those enunciative capacities in the current and acceptably rational language of his time, by which something called an "Oriental" could be named and talked about without danger of too much obscurity. But like all enunciative capacities and the discourses they enable, latent Orientalism was profoundly conservative—dedicated, that is, to its self-preservation. Transmitted from one generation to another, it was a part of the culture, as much a language about a part of reality as geometry or physics. Orientalism staked its existence, not upon its openness, its receptivity to the Orient, but rather on its internal, repetitious consistency about its constitutive will-to-power over the Orient. In such a way Orientalism was able to survive revolutions, world wars, and the literal dismemberment of empires.

The second method by which Orientalism delivered the Orient to the West was the result of an important convergence. For decades the Orientalists had spoken about the Orient, they had translated texts, they had explained civilizations, religions, dynasties, cultures, mentalities—as academic objects, screened off from Europe by virtue of their inimitable foreignness. The Orientalist was an expert, like Renan or Lane, whose job in society was to interpret the Orient for his compatriots. The relation between Orientalist and Orient was essentially hermeneutical: standing before a distant, barely intelligible civilization or cultural monument, the Orientalist scholar reduced the obscurity by translating, sympathetically portraying, inwardly grasping the hard-to-reach object. Yet the Orientalist remained outside the Orient, which, however much it was made to appear intelligible, remained beyond the Occident. This cultural, temporal, and geographical distance was expressed in metaphors of depth, secrecy, and sexual promise: phrases like "the veils of an Eastern bride" or "the inscrutable Orient" passed into the common language.

Yet the distance between Orient and Occident was, almost paradoxically, in the process of being reduced throughout the nineteenth century. As the commercial, political, and other existential encounters between East and West increased (in ways we have been discussing all along), a tension developed between the dogmas of latent Orientalism, with its support in studies of the "classical" Orient, and the descriptions of a present, modern, manifest Orient articulated by travelers, pilgrims, statesmen, and the like. At some moment impossible to determine precisely, the tension caused a convergence of the two types of Orientalism. Probably—and this is only a speculation—the convergence occurred when Orientalists, beginning with Sacy, undertook to advise governments on what the modern Orient was all about. Here the role of the specially trained and equipped expert took on an added dimension: the Orientalist could be regarded as the special agent of Western power as it attempted policy vis-à-vis the Orient. Every learned (and not so learned) European traveler in the Orient felt himself to be a representative Westerner who had gotten beneath the films of obscurity. This is obviously true of Burton, Lane, Doughty, Flaubert, and the other major figures I have been discussing.

The discoveries of Westerners about the manifest and modern Orient acquired a pressing urgency as Western territorial acquisition in the Orient increased. Thus what the scholarly Orientalist defined as the "essential" Orient was sometimes contradicted, but in many cases was confirmed, when the Orient became an actual administrative obligation. Certainly Cromer's theories about the Oriental—theories acquired from the traditional Orientalist archive—were vindicated plentifully as he ruled millions of Orientals in actual fact. This was no less true of the French experience in Syria, North Africa, and elsewhere in the French colonies, such as they were. But at no time did the convergence between latent Orientalist doctrine and manifest Orientalist experience occur more dramatically than when, as a result of World War I, Asiatic Turkey was being surveyed by Britain and France for its dismemberment. There, laid out on an operating table for surgery, was the Sick Man of Europe, revealed in all his weakness, characteristics, and topographical outline.

The Orientalist, with his special knowledge, played an inestimably important part in this surgery. Already there had been intimations of his crucial role as a kind of secret agent *inside* the Orient when the British scholar Edward Henry Palmer was sent to the Sinai in 1882 to gauge anti-British sentiment and its possible enlistment on behalf of the Arabi revolt. Palmer was killed in the process, but he was only the most unsuccessful of the many who performed similar services for the Empire, now a serious and exacting business entrusted in part to the regional "expert." Not for nothing was another Orientalist, D.G. Hogarth, author of the famous account of the exploration of Arabia aptly titled *The Penetration of Arabia* (1904),[24] made the head of the Arab Bureau in Cairo during World War I. And neither was it by accident that men and women like Gertrude Bell, T.E. Lawrence, and St. John Philby, Oriental experts all, posted to the Orient as agents of empire, friends of the Orient, formulators of policy alternatives because of their intimate and expert knowledge of the Orient and of Orientals. They formed a "band"—as Lawrence called it once—bound together by contradictory notions and personal similarities: great individuality, sympathy and intuitive identification with the Orient, a jealously preserved sense of personal mission in the Orient, cultivated eccentricity, a final disapproval of the Orient. For them all the Orient was their direct, peculiar experience of it. In them Orientalism and an effective praxis for handling the Orient received their final European form, before the Empire disappeared and passed its legacy to other candidates for the role of dominant power.

Such individualists as these were not academics. We shall soon see that they were the beneficiaries of the academic study of the Orient, without in any sense belonging to the official and professional company of Orientalist scholars. Their role, however, was not to scant academic Orientalism, nor to subvert it, but rather to make it effective. In their genealogy were people like Lane and Burton, as much for their encyclopedic autodidacticism as for the accurate, the quasi-scholarly knowledge of the Orient they had obviously deployed when dealing with or writing about Orientals. For the curricular study of the Orient they substituted a sort of elaboration of latent Orientalism, which was easily available to them in the imperial culture of their epoch. Their scholarly frame of reference, such as it was, was fashioned by people like William Muir, Anthony Bevan, D.S. Margoliouth, Charles Lyall, E.G. Browne, R.A. Nicholson, Guy Le Strange, E.D. Ross, and Thomas Arnold, who also followed directly in the line of descent from Lane. Their imaginative perspectives were provided principally by their illustrious contemporary Rudyard Kipling, who had sung so memorably of holding "dominion over palm and pine."

The difference between Britain and France in such matters was perfectly consistent with the history of each nation in the Orient: the British were there; the French lamented the loss of India and the intervening territories. By the end of the century, Syria had become the main focus of French activity, but even there it was a matter of common consensus that the French could not match the British either in quality of personnel or in degree of political influence. The Anglo-French competition over the Ottoman spoils was felt even on the field of battle in the Hejaz, in Syria, in Mesopotamia—but in all these places, as astute men like Edmond Bremond noted, the French Orientalists and local experts were outclassed in brilliance and tactical maneuvering by their British counterparts.[25] Except for an occasional genius like Louis Massignon, there were no French Lawrences or Sykeses or Bells. But there were determined imperialists like Étienne Flandin and Franklin-Bouillon. Lecturing to the Paris Alliance française in 1913, the Comte de Cressaty, a vociferous imperialist, proclaimed Syria as France's own Orient, the site of French political, moral, and economic interests—interests, he added, that had to be defended during this "âge des envahissants impérialistes"; and yet Cressaty noted that even with French commercial and industrial firms in the Orient, with by far the largest number of native students enrolled in French schools, France was invariably being pushed around in the Orient, threatened not only by Britain but by Austria, Germany, and Russia. If France was to continue to prevent "le retour de l'Islam," it had better take hold of the Orient: this was an argument proposed by Cressaty and seconded by Senator Paul Doumer.[26] These views were repeated on numerous occasions, and indeed France did well by itself in North Africa and in Syria after World War I, but the special, concrete management of emerging Oriental populations and theoretically independent territories with which the British always credited themselves was something the French felt had eluded them. Ultimately, perhaps, the difference one always feels between modern British and modern French Orientalism is a stylistic one; the import of the generalizations about Orient and Orientals, the sense of distinction preserved between Orient and Occident, the desirability of Occidental dominance over the Orient—all these are the same in both traditions. For of the many elements making up what we customarily call "expertise," style, which is the result of specific worldly circumstances being molded by tradition, institutions, will, and intelligence into formal articulation, is one of the most manifest. It is to this determinant, to this perceptible and modernized refinement in early-twentieth-century Orientalism in Britain and France, that we must now turn.

NOTES

1. Friedrich Nietzsche, "On Truth and Lie in an Extra-Moral Sense," in *The Portable Nietzsche*, ed. and trans. Walter Kaufmann (New York: Viking Press, 1954), pp. 46–7.

2. The number of Arab travelers to the West is estimated and considered by Ibrahim Abu-Lughod in *Arab Rediscovery of Europe: A Study in Cultural Encounters* (Princeton, NJ: Princeton University Press, 1963), pp. 75–6 and passim.

3. See Philip D. Curtin, ed., *Imperialism: The Documentary History of Western Civilization* (New York: Walker & Co., 1972), pp. 73–105.

4. See Johann W. Fück, "Islam as an Historical Problem in European Historiography since 1800," in *Historians of the Middle East*, ed. Bernard Lewis and P.M. Holt (London: Oxford University Press, 1962), p. 307.

5. Ibid., p. 309.

6. See Jacques Waardenburg, *L'Islam dans le miroir de l'Occident* (The Hague: Mouton & Co., 1963).

7. Ibid., p. 311.

8. R. Masson-Oursel, "La Connaissance scientifique de l'Asie en France depuis 1900 et les variétés de l'Orientalisme," *Revue Philosophique* 143, nos. 7–9 (July–September 1953): 345.

9. Evelyn Baring, Lord Cromer, *Modern Egypt* (New York: Macmillan. Co., 1908), 2: 237–8.

10. Evelyn Baring, Lord Cromer, *Ancient and Modern Imperialism* (London: John Murray, 1910), pp. 118, 120.

11. George Nathaniel Curzon, *Subjects of the Day: Being a Selection of Speeches and Writings* (London: George Allen & Unwin, 1915), pp. 4–5, 10, 28.

12. Ibid., pp. 184, 191–2. For the history of the school, see C.H. Phillips, *The School of Oriental and African Studies, University of London, 1917–1967: An Introduction* (London: Design for Print, 1967).

13. Eric Stokes, *The English Utilitarians and India* (Oxford: Clarendon Press, 1959).

14. Cited in Michael Edwardes, *High Noon of Empire: India under Curzon* (London: Eyre & Spottiswoode, 1965), pp. 38–9.

15. Curzon, *Subjects of the Day*, pp. 155–6.

16. Joseph Conrad, *Heart of Darkness*, in *Youth and Two other Stories* (Garden City, NY: Doubleday, Page, 1925), p. 52.

17. For an illustrative extract from de Vattel's work, see Curtin, ed., *Imperialism*, pp. 42–45.

18. Cited by M. de Caix, *La Syrie*, in Gabriel Hanotaux, *Histoire des colonies françaises*, 6 vols. (Paris: Société de l'histoire nationale, 1929–33), 3: 481.

19. These details are to be found in Vernon McKay, "Colonialism in the French Geographical Movement," *Geographical Review* 33, no. 2 (April 1943): 214–32.

20. Agnes Murphy, *The Ideology of French Imperialism, 1817–1881* (Washington: Catholic University of America Press, 1948), pp. 46, 54, 36, 45.

21. Ibid., pp. 189, 110, 136.

22. Jukka Nevakivi, *Britain, France, and the Arab Middle East, 1914–1920* (London: Athlone Press, 1969), p. 13.
23. Ibid., p. 24.
24. D.G. Hogarth, *The Penetration of Arabia: A Record of the Development of Western Knowledge Concerning the Arabian Peninsula* (New York: Frederick A. Stokes, 1904). There is a good recent book on the same subject: Robin Bidwell, *Travellers in Arabia* (London: Paul Hamlyn, 1976).
25. Edmond Bremond, *Le Hedjaz dans la guerre mondiale* (Paris: Payor, 1931), pp. 242 ff.
26. Le Comte de Cressaty, *Les Intérêts de la France en Syrie* (Paris: Floury, 1913).

Chapter 7

The West and the Rest:
Discourse and Power

Stuart Hall

Building on the theoretical insights of Said's Orientalism from the previous chapter, Stuart Hall (1996) examines perhaps one of the most hallowed social constructs in the Western world, the very idea of "the West": its character, its boundaries, and its coherence as a subject of study and as a valid differentiating principle of societies. Specifically, Hall examines how a discourse of "the West" established itself in a seemingly natural differentiation against "the other" (for example, Said's "the Orient"). Hall underlines the importance of discourse as a crucial medium between the production of knowledge and the subsequent representation of reality. In other words, the very act of talking about and creating knowledge about something shapes the ways we understand and act upon it. For example, notions of beauty may differ drastically from region to region, differences that result from how they are embedded in different discourses. According to Hall, powerful discourses (like that of "the West") successfully reproduce themselves by borrowing from and folding within themselves earlier discourses.

Like Said, Hall makes the point that "the West" as a regime of knowledge relied heavily on archival documents, myth and folklore, travellers' tales, fictional writings, and government reports; each of these forms of knowledge played a role in how "the West" became constructed in government, intellectual circles, and the popular imagination. Also like Said, Hall emphasizes that with sufficient time and effort, certain ways of understanding and talking about the world can become so natural or taken for granted that they come to be seen as "true" and, in doing so, make it difficult for alternative understandings of the world to take root (in our society for example, think about the difficulties for discourses that position beauty as "inner" to do battle with externalized, physical images of beauty).

DISCOURSE AND POWER

This article will examine the formation of the languages or "discourses" in which Europe began to describe and represent the *difference* between itself and the "others" it encountered in the course of its expansion. We are now beginning to sketch the formation of the "discourse" of "the West and the Rest." However, we need first to understand what we mean by the term "discourse."

What Is a "Discourse"?

In commonsense language, a discourse is simply "a coherent or rational body of speech or writing; a speech, or a sermon." But here the term is being used in a more specialized way. By "discourse," we mean a particular way of *representing* "the West," "the Rest," and the relations between them. A discourse is a group of statements which provide a language for talking about—i.e. a way of representing—a particular kind of knowledge about a topic. When statements about a topic are made within a particular discourse, the discourse makes it possible to construct the topic in a certain way. It also limits the other ways in which the topic can be constructed.

A discourse does not consist of one statement, but of several statements working together to form what the French social theorist Michel Foucault (1926–84) calls a "discursive formation." The statements fit together because any one statement implies a relation to all the others: "They refer to the same object, share the same style and support 'a strategy ... a common institutional ... or political drift or pattern'" (Cousins and Hussain, 1984, pp. 84–5).

One important point about this notion of discourse is that it is not based on the conventional distinction between thought and action, language and practice. Discourse is about the production of knowledge through language. But it is itself produced by a practice: "discursive practice"—the practice of producing meaning. Since all social practices entail *meaning*, all practices have a discursive aspect. So discourse enters into and influences all social practices. Foucault would argue that the discourse of the West about the Rest was deeply implicated in practice—i.e. in how the West behaved towards the Rest.

To get a fuller sense of Foucault's theory of discourse, we must bear the following points in mind.

1. A discourse can be produced by many individuals in different institutional settings (like families, prisons, hospitals, and asylums). Its integrity or "coherence" does not depend on whether or not it issues from one place or from a single speaker or "subject." Nevertheless, every discourse constructs positions from which alone it makes sense. Anyone deploying a discourse must position themselves *as if* they were the subject of the discourse. For example, we may not ourselves believe in the natural superiority of the West. But if we use the discourse of "the West and the Rest," we will necessarily find ourselves speaking from a position that holds that the West is a superior civilization. As Foucault puts it, "To describe a ... statement does not consist in analyzing the relations between the author and what he

[*sic*] says … ; but in determining what position can and must be occupied by any individual if he is to be the subject of it [the statement]" (Foucault, 1972, pp. 95–6).

2. Discourses are not closed systems. A discourse draws on elements in other discourses, binding them into its own network of meanings. Thus, as we saw in the preceding section, the discourse of "Europe" drew on the earlier discourse of "Christendom," altering or translating its meaning. Traces of past discourses remain embedded in more recent discourses of "the West."

3. The statements within a discursive formation need not all be the same. But the relationships and differences between them must be regular and systematic, not random. Foucault calls this a "system of dispersion": "Whenever one can describe, between a number of statements, such a system of dispersion, whenever … one can define a regularity … [then] we will say … that we are dealing with a *discursive formation*" (Foucault, 1972, p. 38).

These points will become clearer when we apply them to particular examples, as we do later in this article.

Discourse and Ideology

A discourse is similar to what sociologists call an "ideology": a set of statements or beliefs which produce knowledge that serves the interests of a particular group or class. Why, then, use "discourse" rather than "ideology"?

One reason which Foucault gives is that ideology is based on a distinction between *true* statements about the world (science) and *false* statements (ideology), and the belief that the facts about the world help us to decide between true and false statements. But Foucault argues that statements about the social, political, or moral world are rarely ever simply true or false; and "the facts" do not enable us to decide definitively about their truth or falsehood, partly because "facts" can be construed in different ways. The very language we use to describe the so-called facts interferes in this process of finally deciding what is true and what is false.

For example, Palestinians fighting to regain land on the West Bank from Israel may be described either as "freedom fighters" or as "terrorists." It is a fact that they are fighting; but what does the fighting *mean*. The facts alone cannot decide. And the very language we use—"freedom fighters/terrorists"—is part of the difficulty. Moreover, certain descriptions, even if they appear false to us, can be *made* "true" because people act on them believing that they are true, and so their actions have real consequences. Whether the Palestinians are terrorists or not, if we think they are, and act on that "knowledge," they in effect become terrorists because we treat them as such. The language (discourse) has real effects in practice: the description becomes "true."

Foucault's use of "discourse," then, is an attempt to sidestep what seems an unresolvable dilemma—deciding which social discourses are true or scientific, and which false or ideological. Most social scientists now accept that our values enter into all our descriptions of the social world, and therefore most of our statements, however factual, have an ideological dimension. What Foucault would say is that knowledge of the Palestinian problem is produced by competing discourses—those of "freedom-fighter" and "terrorist"—and that each is linked to a contestation over power. It is the outcome of *this* struggle which will decide the "truth" of the situation.

You can see, then, that although the concept of "discourse" sidesteps the problem of truth/falsehood in ideology, it does *not* evade the issue of power. Indeed, it gives considerable weight to questions of power since it is power, rather than the facts about reality, which makes things "true": "We should admit that power produces knowledge.... That power and knowledge directly imply one another; that there is no power relation without the correlative constitution of a field of knowledge, nor any knowledge that does not presuppose and constitute ... power relations" (Foucault, 1980, p. 27).

Can a Discourse Be "Innocent"?

Could the discourse which developed in the West for talking about the Rest operate outside power? Could it be, in that sense, purely scientific—i.e. ideologically innocent? Or was it influenced by particular class interests?

Foucault is very reluctant to *reduce* discourse to statements that simply mirror the interests of a particular class. The same discourse can be used by groups with different, even contradictory, class interests. But this does *not* mean that discourse is ideologically neutral or "innocent." Take, for example, the encounter between the West and the New World. There are several reasons why this encounter could not be innocent, and therefore why the discourse which emerged in the Old World about the Rest could not be innocent either.

First, Europe brought its own cultural categories, languages, images, and ideas to the New World in order to describe and represent it. It tried to fit the New World into existing conceptual frameworks, classifying it according to its own norms, and absorbing it into western traditions of representation. This is hardly surprising: we often draw on what we already know about the world in order to explain and describe something novel. It was never a simple matter of the West just looking, seeing, and describing the New World/the Rest without preconceptions.

Secondly, Europe had certain definite purposes, aims, objectives, motives, interests, and strategies in setting out to discover what lay across the "Green Sea of Darkness." These motives and interests were mixed. The Spanish, for example, wanted to

1. get their hands on gold and silver;
2. claim the land for Their Catholic Majesties; and
3. convert the heathen to Christianity.

These interests often contradicted one another. But we must not suppose that what Europeans said about the New World was simply a cynical mask for their own self-interest. When King Manuel of Portugal wrote to Ferdinand and Isabella of Spain that "the principal motive of this enterprise [da Gama's voyage to India] has been ... the service of God our Lord, and our own advantage" (quoted in Hale, 1966, p. 38)—thereby neatly and conveniently bringing God and Mammon together into the same sentence—he probably saw no obvious contradiction between them. These fervently religious Catholic rulers fully believed what they were saying. To them, serving God and pursuing "our advantage" were not necessarily at odds. They lived and fully believed their own ideology.

So, while it would be wrong to attempt to reduce their statements to naked self-interest, it is clear that their discourse was molded and influenced by the play of motives and interests across their language. Of course, motives and interests are almost never wholly conscious or rational. The desires which drove the Europeans were powerful; but their power was not always subject to rational calculation. Marco Polo's "treasures of the East" were tangible enough. But the seductive power which they exerted over generations of Europeans transformed them more and more into a myth. Similarly, the gold that Columbus kept asking the natives for very soon acquired a mystical, quasi-religious significance.

Finally, the discourse of "the West and the Rest" could not be innocent because it did not represent an encounter between equals. The Europeans had outsailed, outshot, and outwitted peoples who had no wish to be "explored," no need to be "discovered," and no desire to be "exploited." The Europeans stood, vis-à-vis the Others, in positions of dominant power. This influenced what they saw and how they saw it, as well as what they did not see.

Foucault sums up these arguments as follows. Not only is discourse always implicated in *power*, discourse is one of the "systems" through which power circulates. The knowledge which a discourse produces constitutes a kind of power, exercised over those who are "known." When that knowledge is exercised in practice, those who are "known" in a particular way will be subject (i.e. subjected) to it. This is always a power-relation. (See Foucault, 1980, p. 201.) Those who produce the discourse also have the power to *make it true*—i.e. to enforce its validity, its scientific status.

This leaves Foucault in a highly relativistic position with respect to questions of truth because his notion of discourse undermines the distinction between true and false statements—between science and ideology—to which many sociologists have subscribed. These epistemological issues (about the status of knowledge, truth, and relativism) are too complex to take further here. However, the important idea to grasp now is the deep and intimate relationship which Foucault establishes between discourse, knowledge, and power. According to Foucault, when power operates so as to enforce the "truth" of any set of statements, then such a discursive formation produces a "regime of truth."

Let us summarize the main points of this argument. Discourses are ways of talking, thinking, or representing a particular subject or topic. They produce meaningful knowledge about that subject. This knowledge influences social practices, and so has real consequences and effects. Discourses are not reducible to class-interests, but always operate in relation to power—they are part of the way power circulates and is contested. The question of whether a discourse is true or false is less important than whether it is effective in practice. When it is effective—organizing and regulating relations of power (say, between the West and the Rest)—it is called a "regime of truth."

REPRESENTING "THE OTHER"

So far, the discussion of discourse has been rather abstract and conceptual. The concept may be easier to understand in relation to an example. One of the best examples of what Foucault means by a "regime of truth" is provided by Edward Said's study of Orientalism. In this section, I want to look briefly at this example and then see how far we can use the theory of discourse and the example of Orientalism to analyze the discourse of "the West and the Rest."

Orientalism

In his book *Orientalism*, Edward Said analyzes the various discourses and institutions which constructed and produced, as an object of knowledge, that entity called "the Orient." Said calls this discourse "Orientalism." Note that, though we tend to include the Far East (including China) in our use of the word "Orient," Said refers mainly to the Middle East—the territory occupied principally by Islamic peoples.

Also, his main focus is French writing about the Middle East. Here is Said's own summary of the project of his book:

> My contention is that, without examining Orientalism as a discourse, one cannot possibly understand the enormously systematic discipline by which European culture was able to manage—and even produce—the Orient politically, sociologically, militarily, ideologically, scientifically and imaginatively during the post-Enlightenment period. Moreover, so authoritative a position did Orientalism have that I believe no one writing, thinking, or acting on the Orient could do so without taking account of the limitations on thought and action imposed by Orientalism. In brief, because of Orientalism, the Orient was not (and is not) a free subject of thought and action. This is not to say that Orientalism unilaterally determines what can be said about the Orient, but that it is the whole network of interests inevitably brought to bear on (and therefore always involved in) any occasion when that peculiar entity "the Orient" is in question.... This book also tries to show that European culture gained in strength and identity by setting itself off against the Orient as a sort of surrogate and even underground self. (Said, 1985, p. 3)

We will now analyze the discourse of "the West and the Rest," as it emerged between the end of the 15th and 18th centuries, using Foucault's ideas about "discourse" and Said's example of "Orientalism." How was this discourse formed? What were its main themes—its "strategies" of representation?

The "Archive"

Said argues that "In a sense Orientalism was a library or archive of information commonly … held. What bound the archive together was a family of ideas and a unifying set of values proven in various ways to be effective. These ideas explained the behaviour of Orientals; they supplied Orientals with a mentality, a genealogy, an atmosphere; most important, they allowed Europeans to deal with and even to see Orientals as a phenomenon possessing regular characteristics" (Said, 1985, pp. 41–2). What sources of common knowledge, what "archive" of other discourses, did the discourse of "the West and the Rest" draw on? We can identify four main sources:

1. **Classical knowledge:** This was a major source of information and images about "other worlds." Plato (c. 427–347 B.C.) described a string of legendary islands, among them Atlantis which many early explorers set out to find. Aristotle (384–322 B.C.) and Eratosthenes (c. 276–194 B.C.) both made remarkably accurate estimates of the circumference of the globe which were consulted by Columbus. Ptolemy's *Geographia* (2nd century A.D.) provided a model for map-makers more than a thousand years after it had been produced. Sixteenth-century explorers believed that in the outer world lay, not only Paradise, but that "Golden Age," place of perfect happiness and "springtime of the human race," of which the classical poets, including Horace (65–8 B.C.) and Ovid (43 B.C.–A.D. 17), had written.

    The 18th century was still debating whether what they had discovered in the South Pacific was Paradise. In 1768 the French Pacific explorer Bougainville renamed Tahiti "The New Cythera" after the island where, according to classical myth, Venus first appeared from the sea. At the opposite extreme, the descriptions by Herodotus (484–425 B.C.) and Pliny (A.D. 23–79) of the barbarous peoples who bordered Greece left many grotesque images of "other" races which served as self-fulfilling prophecies for later explorers who found what legend said they would find. Paradoxically, much of this classical knowledge was lost in the Dark Ages and only later became available to the West via Islamic scholars, themselves part of that "other" world.

2. **Religious and biblical sources:** These were another source of knowledge. The Middle Ages reinterpreted geography in terms of the Bible. Jerusalem was the center of the earth because it was the Holy City. Asia was the home of the Three Wise Kings; Africa, that of King Solomon. Columbus believed the Orinoco (in Venezuela) to be a sacred river flowing out of the Garden of Eden.

3. **Mythology:** It was difficult to tell where religious and classical discourses ended and those of myth and legend began. Mythology transformed the outer world into an enchanted garden, alive with misshapen peoples and monstrous oddities. In the 16th century, Sir Walter Raleigh still believed he would find, in the Amazon rainforests, the king "El Dorado" ("The Gilded One") whose people were alleged to roll him in gold which they would then wash off in a sacred lake.

4. **Travellers' tales:** Perhaps the most fertile source of information was travellers' tales—a discourse where description faded imperceptibly into legend. The following 15th century German text summarizes more than a thousand years of travellers' tales, which themselves often drew on religious and classical authority:

In the land of Indian [sic] there are men with dogs' heads who talk by barking [and] … feed by catching birds…. Others again have only one eye in the forehead…. In Libya many are born without heads and have a mouth and eyes. Many are of both sexes…. Close to Paradise on the River Ganges live men who eat nothing. For … they absorb liquid nourishment through a straw [and] … live on the juice of flowers…. Many have such large underlips that they can cover their whole faces with them…. In the land of Ethiopia many people walk bent down like cattle, and many live four hundred years. Many have horns, long noses and goats' feet…. In Ethiopia towards the west many have four eyes … [and] in Eripia there live beautiful people with the necks and bills of cranes…. (quoted in Newby, 1975, p. 17)

A particularly rich repository was Sir John Mandeville's *Travels*—in fact, a compendium of fanciful stories by different hands. Marco Polo's *Travels* was generally more sober and factual, but nevertheless achieved mythological status. His text (embellished by Rusticello, a romance writer) was the most widely read of the travellers' accounts and was instrumental in creating the myth of "Cathay" ("China," or the East generally), a dream that inspired Columbus and many others.

The point of recounting this astonishing mixture of fact and fantasy which constituted late medieval "knowledge" of other worlds is not to poke fun at the ignorance of the Middle Ages. The point is (a) to bring home how these very different discourses, with variable statuses as "evidence," provided the cultural framework through which the peoples, places, and things of the New World were seen, described, and represented; and (b) to underline the conflation of fact and fantasy that constituted "knowledge." This can be seen especially in the use of analogy to describe first encounters with strange animals. Penguins and seals were described as being like geese and wolves respectively; the tapir as a bull with a trunk like an elephant, the opossum as half-fox, half-monkey.

A "Regime of Truth"

Gradually, observation and description vastly improved in accuracy. The medieval habit of thinking in terms of analogies gave way to a more sober type of description of the fauna and flora, ways of life, customs, physical characteristics, and social organization of native peoples. We can here begin to see the outlines of an early ethnography or anthropology.

But the shift into a more descriptive, factual discourse, with its claims to truth and scientific objectivity, provided no guarantees. A telling example of this is the case of the "Patagonians." Many myths and legends told of a race of giant people. And in the 1520s, Magellan's crew brought back stories of having encountered, in South America, such a race of giants whom they dubbed *patagones* (literally, "big feet"). The area of the supposed encounter became known as "Patagonia," and the notion became fixed in the popular imagination, even though two Englishmen who visited Patagonia in 1741 described its people as being of average size.

When Commodore John Byron landed in Patagonia in 1764, he encountered a formidable group of natives, broad-shouldered, stocky, and inches taller than the average European.

They proved quite docile and friendly. However, the newspaper reports of his encounter wildly exaggerated the story, and Patagonians took on an even greater stature and more ferocious aspect. One engraving showed a sailor reaching only as high as the waist of a Patagonian giant, and The Royal Society elevated the topic to serious scientific status. "The engravings took the explorers' raw material and shaped them into images familiar to Europeans" (Withey, 1987, pp. 1175–6). Legend had taken a late revenge on science. [...]

This is where the notion of "discourse" came in. A discourse is a way of talking about or representing something. It produces knowledge that shapes perceptions and practice. It is part of the way in which power operates. Therefore, it has consequences for both those who employ it and those who are "subjected" to it. The West produced many different ways of talking about itself and "the Others." But what we have called the discourse of "the West and the Rest" became one of the most powerful and formative of these discourses. It became the dominant way in which, for many decades, the West represented itself and its relation to "the Other." In this article, we have traced how this discourse was formed and how it worked. We analyzed it as a "system of representation"—a "regime of truth." It was as formative for the West and "modern societies" as were the secular state; capitalist economies; the modern class, race, and gender systems; and modern, individualist, secular culture—the four main "processes" of our formation story.

Finally, we suggest that, in transformed and reworked forms, this discourse continues to inflect the language of the West, its image of itself and "others," its sense of "us" and "them," its practices and relations of power towards the Rest. It is especially important for the languages of racial inferiority and ethnic superiority which still operate so powerfully across the globe today. So, far from being a "formation" of the past, and of only historical interest, the discourse of "the West and the Rest" is alive and well in the modern world. And one of the surprising places where its effects can still be seen is in the language, theoretical models, and hidden assumptions of modern sociology itself.

REFERENCES

Cousins, M., and Hussain, A. 1984. *Michel Foucault.* London: Macmillan.

Foucault, M. 1972. *The Archeology of Knowledge.* London: Tavistock.

Foucault, M. 1980. *Power/Knowledge.* Brighton: England, Harvester.

Hale, J.R., et al. 1966. *Age of Exploration.* The Netherlands: Time-Life International.

Mandeville, Sir J. 1964. *The Travels.* New York: Dover.

Newby, E. 1975. *The Mitchell Beazley World Atlas of Exploration.* London: Mitchell Beazley.

Said, E.W. 1985. *Orientalism: Western Concepts of the Orient.* Harmondsworth: England, Penguin.

Withey, L. 1987. *Voyages of Discovery: Captain Cook and the Exploration of the Pacific.* London: Hutchinson.

PART 1C

THINKING THROUGH RACE
IN THE TWENTY-FIRST CENTURY

This section introduces a number of theoretical debates about race and racialization. This collection of articles explores the treatment of race and racialization by thinkers from a variety of perspectives, drawing on sociological, spatial, political, and other orientations, and representing varied academic disciplines, traditions, and discourses from Asia, Africa, Canada, Europe, and the United States, among others. The chapters also address how racialization is taking on a religious character and the complexities that arise when religion is used to structure the racialization of societies from Islamic, Hindu, and Jewish perspectives.

To a lesser degree, the chapters also take up the tension between race and class. However, it is mostly hinted at in the explorations of contemporary forms of racialization, especially in metropolitan labour markets increasingly dependent on migrant labour from racialized populations of the global South. Yet this migration flow raises questions about the evolving nature of racism as a tool of exclusion and marginalization in the epicentres of globalized economies in the global North.

FURTHER READING

Gilroy, Paul. 1987. *"There Ain't No Black in the Union Jack": The Cultural Politics of Race and Nation*. London: Hutchinson.

Gilroy demonstrates the enormous complexity of racial politics in England today. Exploring the relationships among race, class, and nation as they have evolved over the past 20 years, he highlights racist attitudes that transcend the left-right political divide. He challenges current sociological approaches to racism as well as the ethnocentric bias of British cultural studies.

Goldberg, David Theo. 1990. *Anatomy of Racism*. Minneapolis: University of Minnesota Press.

This collection of essays discusses the persistent and multifarious nature of racism. By exposing historical as well as contemporary forms of racist practices, discourses, and expressions, the author shows that racism, though constantly undergoing transformations, remains a significant constant. The implications for social identity are highlighted and collective resistance and opposition to racism are voiced.

Miles, Robert. 1989. *Racism.* **New York: Routledge.**

In *Racism*, Miles powerfully depicts the evolution and expansion of the dynamic concept of racism. From debates on "racism as ideology" to debates on "institutional racism" and the "new racism," Miles illuminates the central place of the concept in historical and contemporary capitalist societies. He argues that racism is best seen as an ideology, and that while it does not describe a biological or material fact, the concept should continue to be used in sociological analysis.

UNESCO. 1980. *Sociological Theories: Race and Colonialism.* **Paris: UNESCO.**

In this volume, various authors address the concept of race within the context of traditional and contemporary sociological theories. Drawing on the theories of Weber, Marx, and Durkeim, as well as pluralist, rational choice, and dependency theories, the authors in this volume show how race is integral to the ways in which societies have been structured in particular historical periods.

Winant, Howard. 1994. *Racial Conditions: Politics, Theory, Comparisons.* **Minneapolis: University of Minnesota Press.**

This book addresses the gaps in our understanding of contemporary racial dynamics, and develops a powerful theoretical approach to the vast subject of race. The author argues that race cannot be understood as a "social problem" or as a "survivor" of earlier, more benighted ages. The key to Winant's analysis is racial formation theory, an approach he refines and advances as he considers a wide range of contemporary controversies in racial theory and politics. Among these are the relationship between race and class, as well as the racial dimensions of gender, diaspora, colonialism, and fascism.

Chapter 8

Does "Race" Matter? Transatlantic Perspectives on Racism after "Race Relations"

Robert Miles and Rudy Torres

Miles and Torres (1996) pose the essential question regarding the validity and value of race as a concept and an explanatory category. Drawing on long-standing polemics with other academics, they rhetorically ask the question: Do races exist? And if not, what use is an analytical framework that assumes their existence? Their chapter challenges what they see as the essentialism of race within the dominant "race relations" paradigm, widely used as a policy and academic framework utilizing race as an analytical category (Banton, 1967). Pointing to the double meaning contained in Cornel West's title *Race Matters* (1994), they interrogate the notion of race as useful, arguing that the tendency among social scientists to reify race for the purposes of understanding how processes of racialization persist and have material meaning directly leads to the reproduction of the very phenomenon many claim to oppose—validating racialization. They suggest that a simple solution would be to take seriously the high profile refutation of the ideology of race and abandon the use of race as a social scientific analytical tool.

*The discourse promoting resistance to racism must not prompt identification with
and in terms of categories fundamental to the discourse of oppression. Resistance
must break not only with practices of oppression, although its first task is to do that.
Resistance must oppose also the language of oppression, including the categories
in terms of which the oppressor (or racist) represents the forms in which resistance is
expressed. (Goldberg 1990:313–14)*

In April 1993, one year after the Los Angeles civil unrest, a major US publisher released a book with the creatively ambiguous title *Race Matters* by the distinguished scholar Cornel West. The back cover of the slightly revised edition published the following year categorized it as a contribution to both African American studies and current affairs. The latter was confirmed by the publisher's strategy of marketing the book as a "trade" rather than as an "academic" title: this was a book for the "American public" to read. And the American public was assured that they were reading a quality product when they were told that its author had "built a reputation as one of the most eloquent voices in America's racial debate."

Some two years later, the *Los Angeles Times* published an article by its science writer under the headline "Scientists Say Race Has No Biological Basis." The opening paragraph ran as follows:

Researchers adept at analyzing the genetic threads of human diversity said Sunday that the concept of race—the source of abiding cultural and political divisions in American society—simply has no basis in fundamental human biology. Scientists should abandon it.

And on the same day (20 February 1995), the *Chronicle of Higher Education* reproduced the substance of these claims in an article under the title "A Growing Number of Scientists Reject the Concept of Race." Both publications were reporting on the proceedings of the American Association for the Advancement of Science in Atlanta.

If "the concept of race … simply has no basis in fundamental human biology," how are we to evaluate Professor West's assertion that "Race Matters"? If "race" matters, then "races" must exist! But if there are no "races," then "race" cannot matter. These two contributions to public political debate seem to reveal a contradiction. Yet within the specific arena of academic debate there is a well-rehearsed attempt to dissolve the contradiction, which runs as follows. It is acknowledged that, earlier this century, the biological and genetic sciences established conclusively in the light of empirical evidence that the attempt to establish the existence of different types or "races" of human beings by scientific procedures had failed. The idea that the human species consisted of a number of distinct "races," each exhibiting a set of discrete physical and cultural characteristics is therefore false, mistaken. The interventions reported as having been made in Atlanta in February 1995 only repeat what some scientists have been arguing since the 1930s. Yet the fact that scientists have to continue to assert these claims demonstrates that the contrary is still widely believed and articulated in public discussion.

Because this scientific knowledge has not yet been comprehensively understood by "the general public" (which not only persists in believing in the existence of "races" as biologically discrete entities but also acts in ways consistent with such a belief), it is argued that social scientists must employ a *concept* of "race" to describe and analyze these beliefs, and the discrimination and exclusion that are premised on this kind of classification. In other words, while social scientists know that there are no "races," they also know that things believed to exist (in this case "races") have a real existence for those who believe in them and that actions consistent with the belief have real social consequences. In sum, because people believe that "races" exist (i.e. because they utilize the *idea* of "race" to comprehend their social world), social scientists need a *concept* of "race."

Or do they? This chapter will explore the reasons why this question needs to be asked. It will also answer it by suggesting that social scientists do not need to, and indeed should not, transform the *idea* of "race" into an analytical category and use "race" as a *concept*. Pre-eminent amongst the reasons for such an assertion is that the arenas of academic and political discourse cannot be clinically separated. Hence Professor West, in seeking to use his status as a leading Afro-American scholar to make a political intervention in current affairs by arguing that "Race Matters," is likely to legitimate and reinforce the widespread public belief that "races" exist irrespective of his views on this issue. For if this belief in the existence of "races" was not widespread, there would be no news value in publishing an article in a leading daily US newspaper that claims that "Race Has No Biological Basis."

CRITICIZING "RACE" AS AN ANALYTICAL CATEGORY

We begin this exploration by crossing the Atlantic in order to consider the issue as it has been discussed in Britain since the early 1950s. As we shall see, the development of the British discussion has in fact been influenced substantially by the preconceptions and language employed in the US: the use of "race" as an analytical category in the social sciences is a transatlantic phenomenon.

It is now difficult to conceive, but forty years ago no one would have suggested that "Race Matters" *in* Britain. The idea of "race" was employed in public and political discussion, but largely only in order to discuss "the colonies": the "race problem" was spatially located beyond British shores in the British Empire and especially in certain colonies, notably South Africa. It is relevant to add that this too had not always been so. During the nineteenth and early twentieth centuries, it was widely believed that the population of Britain was composed of a number of different "races" (e.g., the Irish were identified as being "of the Celtic race") and, moreover, migration to Britain from central and eastern Europe in the late nineteenth century was interpreted using the language of "race" to signify the Jewish refugees fleeing persecution (e.g., Barkan 1992:15–165). But, as the situation in the port city of Liverpool after the First World War suggested (e.g., Barkan 1992:57–165), the language of "race" used to refer to the interior of Britain was to become tied exclusively to differences in skin colour in the second half of the twentieth century. What, then, was the "race" problem that existed beyond the shores of Britain?

Briefly expressed, the problem was that, or so it was thought, the colonies were spatial sites where members of different "races" (Caucasian, White, African, Hindoo, Mongoloid, Celts: the language to name these supposed "races" varied enormously) met and where their "natures" (to civilize, to fight, to be lazy, to progress, to drink, to engage in sexual perversions, etc.) interacted, often with tragic consequences. This language of "race" was usually anchored in the signification of certain forms of somatic difference (skin colour, facial characteristics, body shape and size, eye colour, skull shape) which were interpreted as the physical marks which accompanied, and which in some unexplained way determined, the "nature" of those so marked. In this way, the social relations of British colonialism were explained as being rooted simultaneously in the biology of the human body and in the cultural attributes determined by nature.

But the "race" problem was not to remain isolated from British shores, to be contained there by a combination of civilization and violence. All Her Majesty's subjects had the right of residence in the Motherland, and increasing numbers of them chose to exercise that right as the 1950s progressed. Members of "coloured races," from the Caribbean and the Indian subcontinent in particular, migrated to Britain largely to fill vacancies in the labour market but against the will of successive governments (Labour and Conservative) who feared that they carried in their cheap suitcases not only their few clothes and personal possessions but also the "race problem" (e.g., Joshi and Carter 1984, Solomos 1989, Layton-Henry 1992). By the late 1950s, it was widely argued that, as a result of "coloured immigration," Britain had imported a "race" problem: prior to this migration, so it was believed, Britain's population was "racially homogeneous," a claim that neatly dispensed with not only earlier racialized classifications of both migrants and the population of the British Isles but also the history of interior racisms.

The political and public response to immigration from the Caribbean and the Indian subcontinent is now a well-known story (e.g., Solomos 1989, Layton-Henry 1992), although there are a number of important by-ways still to be explored. What is of more interest here is the academic response. A small number of social scientists (particularly sociologists and anthropologists) wrote about these migrations and their social consequences using the language of everyday life: *Dark Strangers* and *The Colour Problem* were the titles of two books that achieved a certain prominence during the 1950s, and their authors subsequently pursued distinguished academic careers. Considered from the point of view of the 1990s, these titles now seem a little unfortunate, and perhaps even a part of the problem insofar as they employ language that seems to echo and legitimate racist discourses of the time.

But can the same be said for two other books that became classic texts within the social sciences: Michael Banton's *Race Relations* (1967) and John Rex's *Race Relations in Sociological Theory* (1970)? Both were published in the following decade and were widely interpreted as offering different theoretical and political interpretations of the consequences of the migration to, and settlement in, Britain of British subjects and citizens from the Caribbean and the Indian subcontinent. And indeed they did offer very different analyses. Notably, Rex sought to reinterpret the scope of the concept of racism to ensure that it could encompass the then contemporary political discourses about immigration. Such discourse avoided any direct references to an alleged hierarchy of "races" while at the same time referring to or implying the existence of different "races." Banton interpreted this shift in discourse as evidence of a decline in racism, a conclusion that was to lead him to eventually reject the concept of racism entirely (1987).

But what is more remarkable is that, despite their very different philosophical and theoretical backgrounds and conclusions, they shared something else in common. Both Banton and Rex mirrored the language of everyday life, incorporated it into academic discourse and thereby legitimated it. They agreed that Britain (which they both analyzed comparatively with reference to the US and South Africa) had a race relations problem, and Rex in particular wished to conceptualize this problem theoretically in the discipline of sociology. In so doing, both premised their arguments on the understanding that scientific knowledge proves that "races" do not exist in the sense widely understood in everyday common sense discourse: if "race" was a problem, it was a social and not a biological problem, one rooted in part at least in the continued popular belief in the existence of "races." Indeed, John Rex had been one of the members of the team of experts recruited by UNESCO to officially discredit the continuing exploitation of nineteenth-century scientific knowledge about "race" by certain political groups and to educate the public by making widely known the more recent conclusions of biological and genetic scientists (Montagu 1972).

The concept of "race relations" seemed to have impeccable credentials, unlike the language of "dark strangers," for example. This is in part because the notion was borrowed from the early sociology of the "Chicago School" in the US which, amongst other things, was interested in the consequences of two contemporaneous migrations: the early twentieth-century migration from the southern to the northern states of "Negroes" fleeing poverty (and much more besides) in search of wage labour and the continuing large-scale migration from Europe to the US. As a result of the former migration, "Negro" and "white races" entered, or so it was conceptualized, into conflicting social relations in the burgeoning industrial urban areas of the northern states and sociologists had named a new field of study. "Coloured migration" to British cities after 1945 provided an opportunity for sociologists to import this field of study into Britain: Britain too now had a "race relations" problem.

Moreover, for Rex at least, "race relations situations" were characterized by the presence of a racist ideology. Hence, the struggle against colonialism could now be pursued within the Mother Country "herself: by intervening in the new, domestic race relations problem on the side of the colonized victims of racism, one could position oneself against the British state now busily seeking a solution to that problem through the introduction of immigration controls intended specifically to prevent 'coloured' British subjects from entering the country." Such was the rush to be on the side of the angels that few, if any, wondered about what the angels looked like and whether there was any validity in the very concept of angel.

There was a further import from the US that had a substantial impact on the everyday and academic discourses of race relations in the late 1960s and early 1970s in Britain: the struggle for civil rights and against racism on the part of "the blacks" in the US (the notion of "Negro" had now run its course and, like "coloured" before it, it had been ejected into the waste-bin of politically unacceptable language). This movement had the effect of mobilizing not only many blacks in Britain but also many whites politically inclined towards one of several competing versions of socialist transformation. And if radical blacks were busy "seizing the time" in the names of anti-racism and "black autonomy," there was little political or academic space within which radically-inclined white social scientists could wonder about the legitimacy and the consequences of seizing the language of "race" to do battle against racism. For it was specifically in the name of "race" that black people were resisting their long history of colonial oppression: indeed, in some versions of this vision of liberation, contemporary blacks were the direct descendants and inheritors of the African "race" which had been deceived and disinherited by the "white devils" many centuries ago. In this "race war," the white race was soon to face the day of judgement.

Possession of a common language and associated historical traditions can blind as well as illuminate. It is especially significant that both the Left and the Right in Britain looked across the Atlantic when seeking to analyze and to offer forecasts about the outcome of the race relations problem that both agreed existed within Britain. The infamous speeches on immigration made by the MP Enoch Powell in the late 1960s and 1970s contained a great deal of vivid imagery, refracting the current events in US cities and framing them as prophecies of what was inevitably going to happen in due course in British cities if the "alien wedge" was not quickly "repatriated." At the same time, the Left drew political inspiration from the black struggle against racism and sought to incorporate aspects of its rhetoric, style, and politics. Hence, while there was disagreement about the identity of the heroes and the villains of race relations in the US, there was fundamental agreement that race relations there provided a framework with which to assess the course of race relations in Britain. Even legislation intended to regulate race relations and to make racialized discrimination illegal refracted the "American experience."

As a result, the academic response to the race relations problem in Britain was largely isolated both from the situations elsewhere in Europe—and particularly in northwest Europe which was experiencing a quantitatively much more substantial migration than that taking place in Britain—and from academic and political writing about those situations. Two features of those situations are pertinent to the argument here.

First, the nation states of northwest Europe had recently experienced either fascist rule or fascist occupation, and therefore had suffered the direct consequences of the so-called "final solution to the Jewish question" which sought to eliminate the "Jewish race." Hence, the collective historical memory of most of the major cities of northwest Europe was shaped by the genocide effected against the Jews and legitimated in the name of "race," even if that historical memory was now the focus of denial or repression. Second, this experience left the collective memory especially susceptible to the activities of UNESCO and others seeking to discredit the idea of "race" as a valid and meaningful descriptor. Hence, the temporal and spatial proximity of the Holocaust rendered its legitimating racism (a racism in which the idea of "race" was explicit and central) an immediate reality: in this context, few people were willing to make themselves vulnerable to the charge of racism, with the result that suppressing the idea of "race," at least in the official and formal arenas of public life, became a political imperative.

The political and academic culture of mainland northwest Europe has therefore been open to two developments which distinguish it from that existing in the British Isles. First, in any debate about the scope and validity of the concept of racism, the Jewish experience of racism is much more likely to be discussed, and even to be prioritized over any other. Second, the idea of "race" itself became highly politically sensitive. Its very use as a descriptor is more likely to be interpreted in itself as evidence of racist beliefs and, as a result, the idea is rarely employed in everyday political and academic discussion, at least not in connection with domestic social relations. However, in Britain, given the combination of the colonial migration and the multiple ideological exchange with the US, there were far fewer constraints on the everyday use of the idea of "race" and on a redefinition of the concept of racism. As a result, the latter came to refer exclusively to an ideology held by "white" people about "black" people which was rooted in colonial exploitation and in capitalist expansion beyond Europe.

Having recognized the relative distinctiveness of the political and academic space in northwest Europe and then having occupied that space, one can view those social relations defined in Britain and the US as race relations from another point of view. For there is no public or academic reference to the existence of race relations in contemporary France or Germany. It then becomes possible to pose questions that seem not to be posed from within these intimately interlinked social and historical contexts. What kinds of social relations are signified as race relations? Why is the idea of "race" employed in everyday life to refer only to certain groups of people and to certain social situations? And why do social scientists unquestioningly import everyday meanings into their reasoning and theoretical frameworks in defining "race" and "race relations" as a particular field of study? As a result, what does it mean for an academic to claim, for example, that "race" is a factor in determining the structure of social inequality or that "race" and gender are interlinked forms of oppression? What is intended and what might be the consequences of asserting as an academic that "race matters"?

These are the kinds of question that one of the present authors has been posing for nearly fifteen years (e.g., Miles 1982, 1984, 1989), influenced in part by the important writing of the French theorist Guillaumin (1972, 1995). The answers to these questions lead to the conclusion that one should follow the example of biological and genetic scientists and refuse to attribute analytical status to the *idea* of "race" within the social sciences, and thereby refuse to use it as a descriptive and explanatory *concept*. The reasoning can be summarized as follows (cf. Miles 1982:22–43; 1993:47–9).

First, the idea of "race" is used to effect a reification within sociological analysis insofar as the outcome of an often complex social process is explained as the consequence of some thing named "race" rather than of the social process itself. Consider both the recent publication of *The Bell Curve* (1994) by Richard J. Hernstein and Charles Murray and the authors' common assertion that "race" determines academic performance and life chances. The assertion can be supported with statistical evidence that demonstrates that, in comparison with "black people," "white people" are more likely to achieve top grades in school and to enter the leading universities in the US. The determining processes are extremely complex, including amongst other things parental class position, active and passive racialized stereotyping, and exclusion in the classroom and beyond. The effects of these processes are all mediated through a previously racialized categorization into a "white/black" dichotomy which is employed in everyday social relations. Hence, it is not "race" that determines academic performance; rather, academic performance is determined by an interplay of social processes, one of which is premised on the articulation of racism to effect and legitimate exclusion. Indeed, given the nineteenth-century meanings of "race," this form of reification invites the possibility of explaining academic performance as the outcome of some quality within the body of those racialized as "black."

Second, when academics who choose to write about race relations seek to speak to a wider audience (an activity which we believe to be fully justified) or when their writings are utilized by non-academics, this unwittingly legitimates and reinforces everyday beliefs that the human species is constituted by a number of different "races," each of which is characterized by a particular combination of real or imagined physical features or marks and cultural practices. When Professor West seeks to persuade the American public that "Race Matters," there is no doubt that he himself does not believe in the existence of biologically defined "races," but he cannot control the meanings attributed to his claim on the part of those who identify differences in skin colour, for example, as marks designating the existence of blacks and whites as discrete "races." Unintentionally, his writing may then come to serve as a legitimation not only of a belief in the existence of "race" as a biological phenomenon but also of racism itself. He could avoid this outcome by breaking with the race relations paradigm.

Third, as a result of reification and the interplay between academic and common sense discourses, the use of "race" as an analytical concept incorporates a notion which has been central to the evolution of racism into the discourse of antiracism, thereby sustaining one of the conditions of the reproduction of racism within the discourse and practice of antiracism.

For these reasons, the idea of "race" should not be employed as an analytical category within the social sciences, and it follows from this that the object of study should not be described as race relations. Hence, we reject the race relations problematic as the locus for the analysis of racism. But we do not reject the concept of racism. Rather, we critique the race relations problematic in order to retain a concept of racism which is constructed in such a way as to recognize the existence of a plurality of historically specific racisms, not all of which employ explicitly the idea of "race." In contrast, the race relations paradigm refers exclusively to either black/white social relations or social relations between "people of colour" and "white people," with the result that there is only one racism, the racism of whites which has as its object and victim people of colour (e.g., Essed 1991). Moreover, as is increasingly recognized in the academic literature of the past decade, many recent and contemporary discourses which eschew use of the idea of "race" nevertheless advance notions that were previously a referent of such an idea. We can only comprehend contemporary discourses that dispense with the explicit use of the idea of "race" and those discourses which naturalize and inferiorize white populations if we rescue the concept of racism from the simultaneous inflation and narrowing of its meaning by the intersection of the academic and political debates that have taken place in Britain and the US since the end of the Second World War.

REFLECTIONS ON THE RACIALIZATION OF THE US BY THE AMERICAN ACADEMY

When one views the contemporary academic debate about racism in the US both from this analytical position and from Europe, one is struck by the following things. First, when compared with the mid- and late 1960s, it is now an extremely contested debate, and one in which many voices are heard arguing different positions. On the one hand, writers such as Wellman (1993) continue to assert that racism remains the primary determinant of social inequality in the US, while on the other writers such as Wilson claim that the influence of racism has declined substantially, to the point where it cannot be considered to be a significant influence on current structures of inequality (1987). Between these two positions, one finds writers such as West who assert that the continuing impact of racism has to be assessed in terms of its relationship with the effects of class, sexism, and homophobia (e.g., 1994:44). Moreover, it is a debate in which the voices of "Afrocentrists" (e.g., Karenga 1993) and "black feminists" (e.g., hooks 1990) have become extremely influential over the past two decades, while at the same time a "black" conservative intellectual tradition has emerged and attracted increasing attention (e.g., Sowell 1994).

Second, it remains a debate in which it is either largely taken for granted or explicitly argued that the concept of racism refers to an ideology and (in some cases) a set of practices, of which black people are the exclusive victim: racism refers to what "white" people think about and do to "black" people. While the concept of institutional racism goes further by eschewing any reference to human intentionality, it retains the white/black dichotomy in order to identify beneficiary and victim. Thus the scope of the concept of racism is very narrowly defined: the centrality of the white/black dichotomy denies by definition the possibility that any group other than white people can articulate, practise or benefit from racism and suggests that only black people can be the object or victim of racism.

Some of West's writing illustrates this difficulty. He clearly distinguishes himself from those he describes as black nationalists when he argues that their obsession with white racism obstructs the development of the political alliances that are essential to effecting social changes, changes that will alleviate the suffering of black people in the US, and that white racism alone cannot explain the socio-economic position of the majority of black Americans (1994:82, 98–99). Moreover, he goes so far as to suggest that certain black nationalist accounts "simply mirror the white supremacist ideals we are opposing" (1994:99). Yet he seems reluctant to identify any form of racism other than white racism. In his carefully considered discussion of what he describes as "Black-Jewish relations," he employs a distinction between black anti-Semitism and Jewish anti-black racism (1994:104; see also Lerner and West 1995:135–56) which suggests that these are qualitatively different phenomena: Jews articulate racism while blacks express anti-Semitism. This interpretation is reinforced by his assertion that black anti-Semitism is a form of "xenophobia from below" which has a different institutional power when compared with "those racisms that afflict their victims from above" (1994:109–110) even though he claims that both merit moral condemnation.

A similar distinction is implicit in the recent writing of Blauner (1992) who, partly in response to the arguments of one of the present authors, has revised his position significantly since the 1960s. Blauner returns to the common distinction between "race" and ethnicity, arguing that the "peculiarly modern division of the world into a discrete number of hierarchically ranked races is a historic product of Western colonialism" (1992:61). This, he argues, is a very different process from that associated with ethnicity. Hence, Blauner refrains from analyzing the ideologies employed to justify the exclusion of Italians and Jews in the US in the 1920s as racism: these populations are described as "white ethnics" who were "viewed racially" (1992:64). Concerning the period of fascism in Germany, Blauner refers to genocide "where racial imagery was obviously intensified" (1992:64), but presumably the imagery could never be intensified to the point of warranting description as racism because the Jews were not "black." Yet, as we shall see shortly in the case of West's writing, Blauner comes very close to breaking with the race relations problematic when he argues that

> Much of the popular discourse about race in America today goes awry because ethnic
> realities get lost under the racial umbrella. The positive meanings and potential of ethnicity
> are overlooked, even overrun, by the more inflammatory meanings of race. (1992:61)

Third, it is a debate which is firmly grounded in the specific realities of the history and contemporary social structure of the US, or rather a particular interpretation of those particular realities. It is perhaps not surprising therefore that scholars of racism in the US have shown so little interest in undertaking comparative research, although there are important exceptions. Some comparative work has been undertaken which compares the US with South Africa (e.g., van den Berghe 1978; Fredrickson 1981), and a comparison between the US and England achieved prominence some twenty years ago (Katznelson 1976; for a recent analysis, see Small 1994). More recently, the "neo-conservative" Sowell (1994) has chosen a comparative international arena to demonstrate what he sees as the explanatory power of his thesis, although it is arguable whether this constitutes a contribution to the sociology of racism. But the vast bulk of work on racism by scholars in the US focuses on the US itself. This may be explained as the outcome of a benign ethnocentrism, but one wonders whether it is not also a function of the limited applicability of a theory of racism that is so closely tied to the race relations paradigm and a black/white dichotomy that it has limited potential to be used to analyze social formations where there is no "black" presence.

Yet there is evidence of an increasingly conscious unease with this race relations paradigm and the black/white dichotomy. For example, as we have already noted, West argues in a recent book that "race matters":

> Race is the most explosive issue in American life precisely because it forces us to confront the
> tragic facts of poverty and paranoia, despair and distrust. In short, a candid examination of
> *race* matters takes us to the core of the crisis of American democracy. (1994:155–56)

But he also argues that it is necessary to formulate new frameworks and languages in order not only to comprehend the current crisis in the US but also to identify solutions to it (1994:11). Indeed, he asserts that it is imperative to move beyond the narrow framework of "dominant liberal and conservative views of race in America," views which are formulated with a "worn-out vocabulary" (1994:4). But it seems that West does not accept that the idea of "race" itself is an example of this exhausted language, for he employs it throughout with apparently little hesitation, despite the fact that he believes that the manner in which "we set up the terms for discussing racial issues shapes our perception and response to these issues" (1994:6). Later in the book, he seems to be on the verge of following through the logic of this argument to its ultimate conclusion when he argues that the Clarence Thomas/Anita Hill hearings demonstrate that "the very framework of racial reasoning" needs to be called into question in order to reinterpret the black freedom struggle not as an issue of "skin pigmentation and racial phenotype" but, instead, as an issue of ethics and politics (1994:38). And yet West cannot follow through the logic of this argument to the point of acknowledging that there cannot be a place for the use of "race" as an analytical concept in the social sciences.

But there is a transatlantic trade in theories of racism and this is now a two-way trade. Some scholars in the US are not only aware of debates and arguments generated in Europe (including those contributions which question some of the key assumptions that characterize the debate in the US), but some have also acknowledged and responded to one of the present authors, who has criticized both the use of "race" as an analytical concept and the way in which the concept of racism has been inflated (e.g., Miles 1982, 1989, 1993). Recent contributions by Wellman (1993), Blauner (1992), Omi and Winant (1993, 1994), and Goldberg (1993) all refer to and comment on these arguments, with varying degrees of enthusiasm. Interestingly, they all seem to ignore the writing of Lieberman and his associates (e.g., Lieberman 1968; Reynolds 1992) in the US, who argue for a position which overlaps in important respects the one outlined here.

Goldberg offers perhaps the most complex and thoughtful response in the course of a wide-ranging and, in part, philosophically inspired analysis of contemporary racisms and of the conceptual language required to analyze them. His important analysis requires a more extended evaluation than is possible in the limited space available here, so we have chosen to focus instead on the work of Omi and Winant. This is in part because their writing has already had considerable influence in both the US and Britain, partly because of the way in which some of their key concepts have parallels in the equally influential work of Gilroy (1987). And this influence is deserved. There is much to admire and to learn from their theoretical and conceptual innovations. We prefer to employ a concept of *racialized* formation (rather than racial formation), but we agree that racialized categories are socially created, transformed, and destroyed through historical time (1994:55). We can recognize that it is essential to differentiate between "race" (although we do not use "race" as a *concept* but rather we capture its use in everyday life by referring to the *idea* of "race") and the concept of racism, a distinction that allows us to make a further distinction between racialization and racism (although Omi and Winant refer to this as a distinction between racial awareness and racial essentialism; compare

Omi and Winant 1994:71 with Miles 1989: 73–84). And we also agree that it is essential to retain the concept of racism to identify a multiplicity of historically specific racisms, with the consequence that there is "nothing inherently white about racism" (Omi and Winant 1994:72; see also 1994:73, and compare with Miles 1989:57–60; 1993). Wellman (1993:3) is simply mistaken when he claims that Miles argues that racism is not a useful concept.

It is important to highlight these areas of agreement prior to considering Omi and Winant's defence of the use of the idea of "race" as an analytical concept in the social sciences in order to indicate both the innovations that they have effected within the discussion in the US about racism and their failure to pursue the logic of these innovations to their ultimate conclusion. Partly as a result of their emphasis upon the way in which the idea of "race" has been socially constructed and reconstructed, there is now a debate within the literature in the US about the theoretical and analytical status of the idea of "race." Other scholars in the US have made important contributions to the development of this debate, notably Lieberman (1968), Fields (1990), and Roediger (1994). Fields' work is especially significant because it reaches a conclusion that is close to that reached by one of the present authors (see Miles 1982; 1993:27–52). Omi and Winant have criticized Fields' conclusions in the course of defending their continued use of "race" as analytical concept and it is therefore important to reflect upon the arguments and evidence that they have employed.

Omi and Winant offer two criticisms of the position that the idea of "race" should be analyzed exclusively as a social or ideological construct (1993:5). First, they suggest that it fails to recognize the social impact of the longevity of the concept of "race." Second, they claim that, as a result of this longevity, "race is an almost indissoluble part of our identities," a fact that is not recognized by those who argue that "race" is an ideological construct. They are mistaken on both counts. The writing of Miles highlights the historical evolution of the meanings attributed to the idea of "race" and, for example in his discussions of colonialism and of the articulation between racism and nationalism, stresses the way in which the idea of belonging to the "white race" was central to the construction of the identity of the British bourgeoisie and working class (1982, 1993). Indeed, these claims can be refuted simply by citing a quotation from Fields (1990:118) that Omi and Winant themselves reproduce (1993:5). Fields writes:

> Nothing handed down from the past could keep race alive if we did not constantly reinvent and re-ritualise it to fit our own terrain. If race lives on today, it can do so only because we continue to create and re-create it in our social life, continue to verify it, and thus continue to need a social vocabulary that will allow us to make sense, not of what our ancestors did then, but of what we choose to do now.

Thus Fields certainly does not deny that in the contemporary world people use the idea of "race" to classify themselves and others into social collectivities and act in ways consistent with such a belief, actions which collectively produce structured exclusion. And, hence, Omi and Winant's critique is shown to be vacuous. Fields' key objective is to critique the way in which historians invoke the idea of "race" to construct explanations for events and processes in the past, and her critique applies equally to the work of sociologists such as Omi and Winant who have reinvented and re-ritualized the idea of "race" to fit their own terrain within the academy (which is after all only one more arena of social life). Let us examine how Omi and Winant reinvent and thereby reify the idea of "race" in the course of their sociological analysis. Consider the following claim: "One of the first things we notice about people when we meet them (along with their sex) is their race" (1994:59). Elsewhere, they argue that "To be raceless is akin to being genderless. Indeed, when one cannot identify another's race, a microsociological 'crisis of interpretation' results ..." (1993:5). How are we to interpret this assertion? While they also claim that "race is ... a socially constructed way of differentiating human beings" (1994:65), the former assertion is at the very least open to interpretation as suggesting that "race" is an objective quality inherent in a person's being, that every human being is a member of a "race," and that such membership is inscribed in a person's visible appearance. It is in the interstices of such ambiguity that the idea of "race" as a biological fact does not just "live on" but is actively recreated by social scientists in the course of their academic practice.

This argument commonly stimulates incomprehension on the part of scholars in the US, who echo arguments employed in some critiques of this position in Britain. Thus, it is often said, "How can you deny analytical status to the idea of race and ultimately the existence of race when blacks and whites are so obviously different and when all the evidence demonstrates that their life chances differ too?" In responding to this question, it is necessary first to problematize what it takes for granted, specifically that the "black/white" division is *obvious*. The quality of *obviousness* is not inherent in a phenomenon, but is the outcome of a social process in the course of which meaning is attributed to the phenomenon in a particular historical and social context. The meaning is learnt by those who are its subject and object. They therefore learn to habitually recognize it, and perhaps to pass on this signification and knowledge to others, with the result that the quality of obviousness attributed to the phenomenon is reproduced through historical time and social space.

Skin colour is one such phenomenon. Its visibility is not inherent in its existence but is a product of signification: human beings identify skin colour to *mark* or symbolize other phenomena in a historical context in which other significations occur. When human practices include and exclude people in the light of the signification of skin colour, collective identities are produced and social inequalities are structured. It is for this reason that historical studies of the meanings attributed to skin colour in different historical contexts and through time are of considerable importance. And it is in relation to such studies that one can enquire into the continuities and discontinuities with contemporary processes of signification which sustain the obviousness of skin colour as a social *mark*. Historically and contemporarily, differences in skin colour have been and are signified as a mark which suggests the existence of different "races." *But people do not see "race": rather, they observe certain combinations of real and sometimes imagined somatic and cultural characteristics which they attribute meaning to with the idea of "race."* A difference of skin colour is not essential to the process of marking: other somatic features can be and are signified in order to racialize. Indeed, in some historical circumstances, the absence of somatic difference has been central to the powerful impact of racism: the racialized "enemy within" can be identified as a threatening presence even more effectively if the group is not "obviously different" because "they" can be imagined to be everywhere.

Omi and Winant reify this social process and reach the conclusion that all human beings belong to a "race" because they seek to construct their analytical *concepts* to reproduce directly the common sense ideologies of the everyday world. Because the idea of "race" continues to be widely used in everyday life in the US (and Britain) to classify human beings and to interpret their behaviour, Omi and Winant believe that social scientists must employ a *concept* of race. This assumption is the source of our disagreement with them. We argue that one of the contemporary challenges in the analysis of racisms is to develop a conceptual vocabulary that explicitly acknowledges that people use the *idea* of "race" in the everyday world while simultaneously refusing to use the idea of "race" as an analytical *concept* when social scientists analyze the discourses and practices of the everyday world. It is not the *concept* of "race" that "continues to play a fundamental role in structuring and representing the social world" (Omi and Winant 1994:55) but rather the *idea* of "race," and the task of social scientists is to develop a theoretical framework for the analysis of this process of structuring and representing which breaks completely with the reified language of biological essentialism. Hence, we object fundamentally to Omi and Winant's project of developing a critical theory of the *concept* of "race" (1993:6–9) because we also recognize the importance of historical context and contingency in the framing of racialized categories and the social construction of racialized experiences (cf. Omi and Winant 1993:6): we believe that historical context requires us to criticize all concepts of "race," and this can be done by means of a concept of racialization. Omi and Winant's defence of the concept of "race" is a classic example of the way in which the academy in the US continues to racialize the world.

Furthermore, the concept of racialization employed by Omi and Winant is not fully developed, nor do they use it in a sustained analytical manner, because it is grounded in "race relations" sociology, a sociology that reifies the notion of "race" and thereby implies the existence of "racial groups" as monolithic categories of existence. Additionally, they fail to take into account the impact of the social relations of production within the racialization process. We, on the other hand, advance the position that the process of racialization takes place and has its effects in the context of class and production relations and that the idea of "race" may indeed not even be explicitly articulated in the racialization process (see Miles 1989, 1993).

CONCLUSION

West begins the first essay in his book *Race Matters* with a reference to the Los Angeles riots of April 1992. He denies that they were either a "race riot or a class rebellion." Rather, he continues,

> ... this monumental upheaval was a multi-racial, trans-class, and largely male display of social rage.... Of those arrested, only 36 percent were black, more than a third had full-time jobs, and most claimed to shun political affiliation. What we witnessed in Los Angeles was the consequence of a lethal linkage of economic decline, cultural decay, and political lethargy in American life. Race was the visible catalyst, not the underlying cause. (1994:3–4)

And he concludes by claiming that the meaning of the riots is obscured because we are trapped by the narrow framework imposed by the dominant views of "race" in the US.

The *Los Angeles Times* Opinion Editor, Jack Miles, rendered a different version of the narrow framework of the black/white dichotomy. In an essay in the October 1992 issue of the *Atlantic Monthly* entitled "Blacks vs Browns," Miles suggested that Latinos were taking jobs that the nation, by dint of the historic crimes committed against them, owed to African Americans. He blamed Latinos for the poverty in African American communities—a gross misattribution of responsibility—while reinforcing "race" as a relevant category of social and analytical value. His confusion was revealing: the "two societies, one black, one white—separate and unequal" dichotomy made famous by the 1968 report of the National Advisory Commission on Civil Disorders cannot provide an analytical framework to deconstruct the post-Fordist racialized social relations of the 1990s.

The meaning of West's argument is constructed by what is not said as much as by what is. There is a silence about the definition of "race riot": presumably, the events of April 1992 would have been a race riot if the principal actors had been "blacks" and "whites." Hence, West refers only to "race" as the visible catalyst: Rodney King was "obviously black" and the policemen who arrested him were "obviously white." But the riots themselves did not fit the race relations paradigm because the rioters and those who became the victims of the riot were not exclusively blacks and whites. Indeed, as the media were framing the events of April 1992 in black/white terms in the great melodrama of race relations, the first image across the airwaves was of men atop a car waving the Mexican flag! Thus, "Hispanic" may signify presumptively as "white" in the ethno-"racial" dynamics that rest on a system of neat racialized categories, but this has little to do with the popular understanding and experience of Latinos. The outcome of such practices has led to superficial analysis of the full impact of the riots within the context of a changing political economy. The analytical task is therefore to explain the complex nature of the structural changes associated with the emergence of the post-Fordist socio-economic landscape and the reconfigured city's racialized social relations.

Perhaps half of the businesses looted or burned were owned by Korean Americans and another third or so were owned by Mexican Americans/Latinos and Cuban Americans. Those engaged in the looting and burning certainly included African Americans, but poor, recent, and often undocumented immigrants and refugees from Mexico and Central America were equally prominent. Of those arrested, 51% were Latinos and 36% were African Americans. And, of those who died in the civil unrest, about half were African Americans and about a third were Latinos. All this is only surprising if one begins with the assumption that the events were or could have been "race riots." But such an assumption is problematic for two reasons.

First, academics, media reporters, and politicians "conspired" to use the vocabulary of "race" to make sense of the Los Angeles riots because it is a central component of everyday, commonsense discourse in the US. And when it became overwhelmingly apparent that it was not a black/white riot, the language of "race" was nevertheless unthinkingly retained by switching to the use of the notion of "multiracial" in order to encompass the diversity of historical and cultural origins of the participants and victims. Therefore while the race relations paradigm was dealt a serious blow by the reality of riots, the vocabulary of "race" was retained. But—and here we find the source of West's unease—the idea of "race" is so firmly embedded in common sense that it cannot easily encompass a reference to Koreans or Hispanics or Latinos, for these are neither black nor white. It is thus not surprising that pundits and scholars such as West stumble over "racial" ambiguity. The clash of racialized language with a changing political economy presents challenges for scholars and activists alike.

Second, if one had begun with an analysis grounded simultaneously in history and political economy rather than with the supremely ideological notion of race relations, one would have quickly concluded that the actors in any riot in central Los Angeles would probably be *ethnically* diverse. Large-scale inward migration from Mexico and Central America and from southeast Asia into California has coincided with a restructuring of the Californian economy, the loss of major manufacturing jobs, and large-scale internal migration within the urban sprawl of "greater" Los Angeles, with the consequence that the spatial, ethnic, and class structure that underlay the Watts riots of 1965 had been transformed into a much more complex set of relationships. The most general conditions were structural in nature, and thus the decline and shift in the manufacturing base in Los Angeles was not unique but represented a shift in the mode of capital accumulation worldwide (from Fordist to Flexible). In order to analyze those relationships, there is no need to employ a concept of "race": indeed, its retention is a significant hindrance. But it is also necessary to draw upon the insights consequent upon the creation of the concept of *racisms*. The complex relationships of exploitation and resistance, grounded in differences of class, gender, and ethnicity, give rise to a multiplicity of ideological constructions of the racialized Other. For, while the idea of "race" does not matter outside the process of racialization, to which academics are active contributors, the racisms employed in Los Angeles and elsewhere to naturalize, inferiorize, exclude, and sustain privilege certainly *do* matter.

REFERENCES

Banton, M. (1967). *Race Relations*. London: Tavistock.

———. (1987). *Racial Theories*. Cambridge: Cambridge University Press.

Barkan, E. (1992). *The Retreat of Scientific Racism: Changing Concepts of Race in Britain and the United States Between the Wars*. Cambridge: Cambridge University Press.

van den Berghe, P.L. (1978). *Race and Racism: A Comparative Perspective*. New York: John Wiley.

Blauner, B. (1992). "Talking Past Each Other: Black and White Languages of Race," *The American Prospect* 10: 55–64.

Essed, P. (1991). *Understanding Everyday Racism: An Interdisciplinary Theory*. Newbury Park, Cal.: Sage.

Fields, B.J. (1990). "Slavery, Race and Ideology in the United States of America," *New Left Review* 181: 95–118.

Fredrickson, G.M. (1981). *White Supremacy*. New York: Oxford University Press.

Gilroy, P. (1987). *"There Ain't No Black in the Union Jack": The Cultural Politics of Race and Nation*. London: Hutchinson.

Goldberg, D.T. (1990). "The Social Formation of Racist Discourse." In D.T. Goldberg (ed.), *Anatomy of Racism.* Minneapolis: University of Minnesota Press.

———. (1993). *Racist Culture: Philosophy and the Politics of Meaning.* Oxford: Blackwell.

Guillaumin, C. (1972). *L'Idéologie Raciste.* Paris: Mouton.

———. (1995). *Racism, Sexism, Power and Ideology.* London: Routledge.

hooks, b. (1990). *Yearning: Race, Gender and Cultural Politics.* Boston: South End Press.

Joshi, S., and Carter, B. (1984). "The Role of Labour in the Creation of a Racist Britain." *Race and Class* 25(3): 53–70.

Karenga, M. (1993). *Introduction to Black Studies.* Los Angeles: University of Sankore Press.

Katznelson, I. (1976). *Black Men, White Cities.* Chicago: University of Chicago Press.

Layton-Henry, Z. (1992). *The Politics of Immigration.* Oxford: Blackwell.

Lerner, M., and West, C. (1995). *Jews and Blacks: Let the Healing Begin.* New York: G.P. Putnam's Sons.

Lieberman, L. (1968). "The Debate Over Race: A Study in the Sociology of Knowledge." *Phylon* 39: 127–41.

Miles, R. (1982). *Racism and Migrant Labour: A Critical Text.* London: Routledge and Kegan Paul.

———. (1984). "Marxism versus the 'Sociology of Race Relations.'" *Ethnic and Racial Studies* 7(2): 217–37.

———. (1989). *Racism.* London: Routledge.

———. (1993). *Racism After "Race Relations."* London: Routledge.

Montagu, A. (1972). *Statement on Race.* London: Oxford University Press.

Omi, M., and Winant, H. (1993). "On the Theoretical Status of the Concept of Race." In C. McCarthy and W. Crichlow (eds.), *Race, Identity and Representation.* New York: Routledge.

———. (1994). *Racial Formation in the United States: From the 1960s to the 1990s,* 2nd. ed. New York: Routledge.

Rex, J. (1970). *Race Relations in Sociological Theory.* London: Weidenfeld and Nicolson.

Reynolds, L.T. (1992). "A Retrospective on 'Race': The Career of a Concept." *Sociological Focus.* 25(1): 1–14.

Roediger, D. (1994). *Towards the Abolition of Whiteness: Essays on Race, Politics and Working Class History.* London: Verso.

Small, S. (1994). *Racialized Barriers: The Black Experience in the United States and England in the 1980s.* London: Routledge.

Solomos, J. (1989). *Race and Racism in Contemporary Britain.* London: Macmillan.

Sowell, T. (1994). *Race and Culture: A World View.* New York: Basic Books.

Wellman, D. (1993). *Portraits of White Racism,* 2nd. ed. Cambridge: Cambridge University Press.

West, C. (1994). *Race Matters.* New York: Vintage Books.

Wilson, W.J. (1987). *The Truly Disadvantaged.* Chicago: University of Chicago Press.

Chapter 9

When Place Becomes Race

Sherene H. Razack

Sharene Razack's 2002 chapter best illustrates the materiality of "race" as it goes beyond the symbolic representation that Miles and Torres suggest, seeking to materialize race in its colonial context and pointing to the spatiality of racialization in a critical project aimed at "unmapping" the processes of white supremacists and their deployment of political, economic, and social power in structuring racialized hierarchies, especially in whiter settler colonies such as Canada, the US, Australia, and New Zealand.

Razack seeks to investigate "how place becomes race" and how race becomes imbued with such social and historical meaning that it helps create empires. She is concerned with how processes that are racially implicated, such as conquest, colonization, and cultural genocide, acquire a benign character through the mythologies of white settlement as a process of civilization. The deeply racist validation of violent settler processes of displacement and dispossession assume the mythology of the land as uninhabited, an empty space willing and inviting, perhaps even beckoning—just as a woman in skimpy clothing is said to invite rape. The subsequent acts of development do not erase the stench of the original plunder, although it is masked by the claims of nation-building that become racialized as exclusively European, negating the labour and exploitation of the people of colour who toiled as cheap labour on the railways (as they covered the confiscated land), on the farms, in the mines, and in the factories, or negating the Aboriginals dispossessed of their commercial trade and starved through economic exclusion.

In 1983, commenting on section 97 (b) of the *Indian Act*, which made it an offence for a person to be intoxicated on an Indian reserve, a judge of the Manitoba Court of Appeal commented that its logic was both spatial and racial: "Place becomes race," he concluded succinctly of the now repealed section,[1] This book explores *how* place becomes race through the law. The authors examine drinking establishments, parks, slums, classrooms, urban spaces of prostitution, provincial parliaments, the location of mosques, and national borders, exploring how such spaces are organized to sustain unequal social relations and how these relations shape spaces. To highlight our specific interest in how the constitution of spaces reproduces racial hierarchies, we examine the spatial and legal practices required in the making and maintaining of a white settler society.

A white settler society is one established by Europeans on non-European soil. Its origins lie in the dispossession and near extermination of Indigenous populations by the conquering Europeans. As it evolves, a white settler society continues to be structured by a racial hierarchy. In the national mythologies of such societies, it is believed that white people came first and that it is they who principally developed the land; Aboriginal peoples are presumed to be mostly dead or assimilated. European settlers thus *become* the original inhabitants and the group most entitled to the fruits of citizenship. A quintessential feature of white settler mythologies is, therefore, the disavowal of conquest, genocide, slavery, and the exploitation of the labour of peoples of colour. In North America, it is still the case that European conquest and colonization are often denied, largely through the fantasy that North America was peacefully settled and not colonized.

For example, delivering the prestigious Massey lectures for the year 2000, the well-known Canadian scholar Michael Ignatieff takes to task Aboriginal leader Ovide Mercredi and Aboriginal scholar and judge Mary Ellen Turpel for using the term "settler-colonials" when referring to the Europeans who colonized Canada: "To speak this way, as if settlement were merely a form of imperial domination, is to withhold recognition of the right of the majority to settle and use the land we both share." In this view, violent colonization simply did not happen:

> Throughout centuries of collaboration between newcomers and aboriginal nations, Native peoples have always accepted, with varying degrees of willingness, the fact that being first possessors of the land is not the only source of legitimacy for its use. Those who came later have acquired legitimacy by their labours; by putting the soil under cultivation; by uncovering its natural resources; by building great cities and linking them together with railways, highways, and now fibre-optic networks and the Internet. To point out the legitimacy of non-aboriginal settlement in Canada is not to make a declaration about anyone's superiority or inferiority, but simply to assert that each has a fair claim to the land and that it must be shared.[2]

Mythologies or national stories are about a nation's origins and history. They enable citizens to think of themselves as part of a community, defining who belongs and who does not belong to the nation. The story of the land as shared and as developed by enterprising settlers is manifestly a racial story. Through claims to reciprocity and equality, the story produces European settlers as the bearers of civilization while simultaneously trapping Aboriginal people in the pre-modern, that is, before civilization has occurred. Anne McClintock has described this characterization of Indigenous populations as one which condemns them to anachronistic space and time.[3] If Aboriginal peoples are consigned forever to an earlier space and time, people of colour are scripted as late arrivals, coming to the shores of North America long after much of the development has occurred. In this way, slavery, indentureship, and labour exploitation—for example, the Chinese who built the railway or the Sikhs who worked in the lumber industry in nineteenth-century Canada—are all handily forgotten in an official national story of European enterprise.

The national mythologies of white settler societies are deeply spatialized stories. Although the spatial story that is told varies from one time to another, at each stage the story installs Europeans as entitled to the land, a claim that is codified in law. In the first phase of conquest, we see the relationship between law, race, and space in the well-known legal doctrine of *terra nullius*, or empty, uninhabited lands. As Dara Culhane has shown in the case of British colonialism, already inhabited nations "were simply legally *deemed to be uninhabited* if the people were not Christian, not agricultural, not commercial, not 'sufficiently evolved' or simply in the way." In land claim cases launched by Aboriginal nations in Canada, Culhane points out, when Aboriginal people "say today that they have had to go to court to prove they exist, they are speaking not just poetically, but also *literally*."[4]

When more European settlers arrive and the settler colony becomes a nation, a second installment of the national story begins to be told. In Canada, this is the story of the "empty land" developed by hardy and enterprising European settlers. In our national anthem, Canadians sing about Canada as the "True North Strong and Free," an arctic land unsullied by conquest. This land, as both Carl Berger and Robert Shields have shown, is imagined as populated by white men of grit, a robust Northern race pitting themselves against the harshness of the climate. "These images," Carl Berger points out, "denote not merely geographical location or climactic condition but the combination of both, moulding racial character."[5]

The imagined rugged independence and self-reliance of the European settlers are qualities that are considered to give birth to a greater commitment to liberty and democracy. If Northern peoples are identified with strength and liberty, then Southern peoples are viewed as the opposite: degenerate, effeminate, and associated with tyranny.[6] Racialized populations seldom appear on the settler landscape as other than this racial shadow; when they do, as David Goldberg writes, they are "rendered transparent ... merely part of the natural environment, to be cleared from the landscape—urban and rural—like debris."[7] In the Canada of the national mythology, there are vast expanses of open, snow-covered land, forests, lakes, and the occasional voyageur (trapper) or his modern-day counterpart in a canoe. So compelling is this spatial vision of pristine wilderness that a contemporary advertising campaign for Stanfield's underwear is able to proclaim: a Canadian is someone who knows how to make love in a canoe.

In the 1990s there is a third, equally spatialized development of the national story. The land, once empty and later populated by hardy settlers, is now besieged and crowded by Third World refugees and migrants who are drawn to Canada by the legendary niceness of European Canadians, their well-known commitment to democracy,[8] and the bounty of their land. The "crowds" at the border threaten the calm, ordered spaces of the original inhabitants. A specific geographical imagination is clearly traceable in the story of origins told in anti-immigration rhetoric, operating as metaphor but also enabling material practices such as the increased policing of the border and of bodies of colour.

The September 11, 2001, terrorist attacks on the World Trade Center in New York City and on the Pentagon in Washington (attacks in which over three thousand people lost their lives) have deeply intensified the policing of bodies of colour. Like the United States, Canada has proposed an *Anti-Terrorism Act*[9] that will give sweeping powers to police to identify, prosecute, convict, and punish suspected terrorists. With terrorist activity broadly defined, a person can be arrested without a warrant and detained for more than twenty-four hours solely on the basis that the police have suspicions of terrorist activity. Already many men of Arab descent or who are Arab looking have been detained indefinitely, often in solitary confinement. The incarceration of Japanese Canadians in camps during the Second World War [...] readily comes to mind.

With its purpose to give the state a chance to sort out who is a terrorist and who is not, the *Anti-Terrorism Act* draws inspiration from a number of existing and proposed changes to Canada's *Immigration Act* that established a two-tier structure of citizenship. For example, the Act penalizes Convention refugees without documents (in contravention of the United Nations 1951 Convention and the 1967 Protocol Relating to the Status of Refugees) and requires them to wait three years before enjoying the benefits of full citizenship. Politicians justify the penalty on the grounds that the original inhabitants have a legitimate right to defend themselves from the massive influx of foreign bodies who possess few of the values of honesty, decency, and democracy of their "hosts." Refugees, it is argued, must be given time to learn respect for Canadian culture, and original citizens must be given time to know who they can trust.[10]

To contest white people's primary claim to the land and to the nation requires making visible Aboriginal nations whose lands were stolen and whose communities remain imperilled. It entails including in the national story those bodies of colour whose labour also developed this land but who are not its first occupants. It is to reveal, in other words, the racialized structure of citizenship that characterizes contemporary Canada. The contributors to this book propose to undertake this by unmapping the primary claim. "To unmap," Richard Phillips notes, is not only to denaturalize geography by asking how spaces come to be but also "to undermine world views that rest upon it."[11] Just as mapping colonized lands enabled Europeans to imagine and legally claim that they had discovered and therefore owned the lands of the "New World," unmapping is intended to undermine the idea of white settler innocence (the notion that European settlers merely settled and developed the land) and to uncover the ideologies and practices of conquest and domination.

In unmapping, there is an important relationship between identity and space. What is being imagined or projected on to specific spaces and bodies, and what is being enacted there? Who do white citizens know themselves to be and how much does an identity of dominance rely upon keeping racial Others firmly *in place*? How are people kept in their place? And, finally, how does place become race? We ask these questions here in the fervent belief that white settler societies can transcend their bloody beginnings and contemporary inequalities by remembering and confronting the racial hierarchies that structure our lives.

In tracking dominance spatially, this book joins in the virtual explosion of books in the 1990s that pay attention to the material and symbolic constitution of actual spaces. It is perhaps true, as some have speculated, that the popularity of spatial theory has something to do (ironically) with the colonial mastery that maps and concrete spaces provide.[12] We feel in control and anchored in something real when we can think and talk about a specific street, town, or region.[13] Spatial theory lends itself to so much "specificity," I tell my graduate class on Race, Space, and Citizenship, seizing the opportunity to encourage theory grounded in an empirical base. But the attraction to the concrete is also bound up with the hope that we can pin down something about racialization processes that are directly experienced as spatial. When police drop Aboriginal people outside the city limits leaving them to freeze to death, or stop young Black men on the streets or in malls, when the eyes of shop clerks follow bodies of colour, presuming them to be illicit, when workplaces remain relentlessly white in the better paid jobs and fully "coloured" at the lower levels, when affluent areas of the city are all white and poorer areas are mostly of colour, we experience the spatiality of the racial order in which we live.

The geographical turn in critical theory may falsely reassure us that we have mapped how white supremacy works, yet it promises a stronger connection between everyday life and scholarship, and a closer connection to radical politics. The contributors hope that our engagement with spatial theory will yield insight into the multiple ways in which whites secure their dominance in settler societies. For the most part, we focus on the geographical spaces of Canada, inviting others who consider both Canadian and other geographies to examine the role of Canadian law in producing and sustaining a racial social order.

It must be said at the outset that our focus on racial formations is automatically a focus on class and gender hierarchies as well. Racial hierarchies come into existence through patriarchy and capitalism, each system of domination mutually constituting the other. The lure of a spatial approach is precisely the possibility of charting the simultaneous operation of multiple systems of domination. As Edward Soja explains in *Postmodern Geographies*, "the spatiality of social life is stubbornly simultaneous, but what we write down is successive because language is successive."[14] To consider, for example, the multiple systems that constitute spaces of prostitution, we must talk about the economic status of women in prostitution, the way in which areas of prostitution are marked as degenerate space that confirms the existence of white, respectable space, the sexual violence that brings so many young girls to prostitution, and so on. Yet, beginning with any one practice privileges a particular system and leaves the impression that it is that system that is pre-eminent. A spatial analysis can help us to see the operation of all the systems as they mutually constitute each other.

POINTS OF ENTRY: SPACE AS AN OBJECT OF STUDY

What an interdisciplinary collection on space such as this one gains from geography must be clarified from the start. The academic world is still largely discipline bound: geographers sometimes think they own the concepts associated with space, legal scholars guard the gates to the study of the law, and sociologists lay claim to social identities and social inequality as their own objects of study. The gate keeping is not merely a turf war, that is, a contest over who has the right to teach and write about whom and where. Rather, each discipline has approached its "proper" objects of study with specific questions in mind. Further, each has its own critical traditions. Borrowing from a variety of disciplines increases the risk that something of the depth of these scholarly projects will be lost. Geographers have not failed to express their concern that those of us eager to assume the language of geography sometimes end up taking as our "unexamined grounding a seemingly unproblematic, common sense notion of space as a container, a field, a simple emptiness in which all things are 'situated' or 'located.'"[15]

The risk, duly noted here, is that non-geographers are not well qualified to engage in spatial theory. While we acknowledge from the start a partial and incomplete access to each discipline, we deliberately reject the boundaries created by them. If there is anything we have learned about racial projects it is that they come into being and are sustained through a wide number of practices, both material and symbolic. The study of the creation of racial hierarchies demands nothing less than the tools of history, sociology, geography, education, and law, among other domains of knowledge. In an effort to delineate the interdisciplinary approach that is the basis of this book, I provide below an outline of the core ideas that have engaged the contributors, providing the reader with a kind of schematic guide to the starting points we each had in mind and offering an indication of the limits contained here.

SPACE AS A SOCIAL PRODUCT

To question how spaces come to be, and to trace what they produce as well as what produces them, is to unsettle familiar everyday notions. Space seems to us to be empty. Either we fill it with things (houses, monuments, bridges) or nature fills it with trees, a cold climate, and so on. Space, in this view, is innocent. A building is just a building, a forest just a forest. Urban space seems to evolve naturally. We think, for example, that Chinatowns simply emerged when Chinese people migrated in sufficient numbers to North America and decided to live together. Slums and wealthy suburbs seem to evolve naturally. In the same way that spaces appear to develop organically, so too the inhabitants of spaces seem to belong to them. If the slum or the housing project has a disproportionate number of Black or Aboriginal people, it is thought to be simply because such people lack the education and training to obtain the jobs, and thus the income, that would enable them to live in a wealthy suburb. Perhaps, we often reason, poor districts are simply occupied by recently arrived immigrants who will, in time, move up to more affluent spaces.

If we reject the view that spaces simply evolve, are filled up with things, and exist either prior to or separate from the subjects who imagine and use them, then we can travel along two theoretical routes. First, we can consider the materiality of space, for example, the fact that a large number of workers must be housed somewhere. The buildings in which they live, perhaps the rooming houses built by their wealthy bosses, become a particular kind of space which we might say was shaped by capitalism and the class system. Here space is the result of unequal economic relations. A second approach is to consider the symbolic meaning of spaces. The rooming houses of the workers mean something specific in our context. Perhaps they represent poverty to us and enable us to understand ourselves as located in a social system where status derives from one's position in the means of production.

By itself, each of these approaches to understanding space is limited, as Henri Lefebvre argues. A theory of space, he maintains, has to cut through the dominant notion of space as innocent and as more real "than the 'subject,' his thought and his desires [sic]," but it also had to avoid reducing space to the status of a "message" (what it can tell us about social relations) and the inhabiting of it to the status of a "reading" (deciphering the codes of social space and how we perform it).[16] To treat space this way is to remain on a purely descriptive level that does not show the dialectical relationship between spaces and bodies. It does not show how the symbolic and the material work through each other to constitute a space.

Lefebvre's project, as Eugene McCann observed, "was to write a history of space by relating certain representations of space to certain modes of production through time."[17] Lefebvre saw, for instance, that capitalism relied upon and produced what he called "abstract space," which, McCann notes, is commodified and bureaucratized space arranged in the interests of capital and produced as a concerted attempt to define the appropriate meaning of public space and what citizens can do in it. Lefebvre proposes the concept of social space, as indistinguishable from mental and physical space, and as containing the social relations of production and reproduction. In his widely cited formulation, Lefebvre identified three elements (perceived, conceived, and lived space) in the production of social space.

First, perceived space emerges out of spatial practices, the everyday routines and experiences that install specific social spaces. For example, the daily life of a tenant in a government-sponsored housing project includes the rhythm of daily life (the buses one must take to work, the spaces through which one must walk), how people know themselves in it, as well as how they are known in it, and what the space accomplishes in relation to other spaces. Through these everyday routines, the space comes to perform something in the social order, permitting certain actions and prohibiting others. Spatial practices organize social life in specific ways. In the case of the housing project, it organizes, among other things, who will be able to walk in green spaces and who will not.

Second, conceived space entails representations of space, that is, how space is conceived by planners, architects, and so on. Here we might consider how the housing project was initially conceptualized, perhaps as a cleaning up of slums and a collecting of the poor into units that are centralized in the city but nonetheless peripheral to it.[18] Third, lived space is space "directly lived through its associated images and symbols, and hence the space of 'inhabitants' and 'users,' but also of some artists and perhaps of those, such as a few writers and philosophers who describe and aspire to do more than describe."[19] For the tenant, the housing project may be experienced as racialized space in which communities of colour both experience their marginal condition and resist it. Perhaps people gather on street corners to socialize, defying the containment offered by the buildings and imagining them instead as symbols of community. In lived space (representational space), the users of the space interpret perceived space (spatial practices), and conceived space (representations of space).

In her study of the homeless body, Samira Kawash offers a compelling example of how we might consider space as a social product by attending to the social hierarchies that sustain and are sustained by the idea of abstract public space. Drawing on Rosalyn Deutsche's analysis of how exclusions from public space are officially justified by representing the space as a unity that must be protected from conflict (in effect, Lefebvre's abstract space), Kawash discusses Deutsche's example of the padlocking after dark of a public park in New York. The padlocked park produces as illegitimate the homeless who might use the park to sleep, while neighbourhood groups in favour of the padlocking are produced as legitimate users and natural owners of public space.[20]

The homeless body is constituted as "the corporeal mark of the constitutive outside of the realm of the public."[21] That is, it is through this body that we know who is a citizen and who is not. Through its presence as a material body that occupies space, but as one that is consistently denied space through a series of violent evictions, the homeless body confirms what and who must be contained in order to secure society. The war on the homeless, evident in so many cities in the last few years (including the passage of restrictions on sleeping in public space, on begging, "bum-proof" bus shelters, and restrictions on "squeegee kids" in public space), must be seen as "the production of an abject body against which the public body of the citizen can stand."[22]

It is important to note how symbolic and material processes work together to produce these respectable and abjected bodies. When public toilets are systematically closed, the homeless have no choice but to perform bodily functions in public, a produced mark of degeneracy that only confirms who is respectable. The violent evictions that produce the homeless body are therefore a "constitutive violence"; they make possible subjects who are legitimate and those who are not.[23] Kawash's exploration of the production of the illegitimate homeless body makes it clear that the production of space is also the production of excluded and included bodies, an aspect of the production of space illustrated in the work of Michel Foucault.

THE BODY IN SPACE

It is from Michel Foucault that many of us learned to think about the production of subjects in space. In his work, we encounter the body marked as degenerate and its opposite, the bourgeois body marked as respectable. Foucault believed that space was fundamental in any exercise of power.[24] Foucault begins his analysis with the establishment in the seventeenth century of "enormous houses of confinement,"[25] of the Hôpital Général for housing the poor and the unemployed, the asylums for the insane, and extends it to prisons and schools to consider what was meant by the physical segregation of marginal populations, an exclusionary practice characteristic of the liberal state. He proposed that the bourgeois citizen of the state, the figure who replaced the earlier orders, distanced himself from the aristocracy and the lower orders of this earlier hierarchy by developing an identity premised on close control over the manner of living. The new citizen subject was a figure who, through self-control and self-discipline, achieved mastery over his own body. The self-regulating bourgeois subject had to be spatially separated from the degeneracy, abnormalcy, and excess that would weaken both him and the bourgeois state. Bodies that crossed "the frontier of bourgeois order"[26] were segregated, not for the purpose of punishment, but for moral regulation. The poor and the unemployed, housed in the Hôpital Général were to be trained not to be idle; asylums set themselves the task of producing moral subjects cleansed of everything that opposed the essential virtues of the society; prisons revolved around a political technology of the body, morally reforming inmates.

What sets the period of the establishment of states and citizen subjects in the eighteenth century apart from previous periods in Europe is the treatment of the body as object and target of power on a scale that did not exist before. While in every society there were constraints, prohibitions, and obligations on the body, what was new, according to Foucault, was the practice of exercising upon the body such micro processes as disciplining bodies to produce "subjected and practised bodies, 'docile' bodies." In the school, the barracks, the hospital, or the workshop, "the smallest fragment of life" becomes subject to minute calculation, "a codification that partitions as closely as possible time, space, movement." Timetables, specific, repeated movements, continual examinations, penalties for latenesses, absences, inattention: all these capture and fix individuals, placing them in a field of surveillance. Discipline "makes individuals" but the making requires a "mechanism that coerces by means of observation." Architecture had to render visible people's movement and conduct and thus to convey that one was always seen and known: "This infinitely scrupulous concern with surveillance is expressed in the architecture by innumerable petty mechanisms." By means of such surveillance, two kinds of bodies are produced: the normal and the abnormal body, the former belonging to a homogenous social body, the latter exiled and spatially separated.[27]

Kathleen Kirby elaborates on the individual body's relationship to space in the social/spatial configurations described above. Focusing on the respectable body, she argues, as Foucault did, that Enlightenment individualism is "inextricably tied to a specific concept of space and the technologies invented for dealing with that space."[28] Kirby explains how the bourgeois citizen, the Enlightenment individual, and the figure Kirby calls "the Cartesian subject" are reducible to the same graphic schema: "The 'individual' expresses a coherent, consistent, rational space paired with a stable, organized environment."[29] Cartography (the science of mapping), Kirby observes, both expresses this new subjectivity and enables it to exist. The subject who maps his space and thereby knows and controls it, is also the imperial man claiming the territories of others for his own; the inventor of *terra nullius*. The Cartesian or the mapping subject achieves his sense of self through keeping at bay and in place any who would threaten his sense of mastery. Maps sought to measure, standardize, and bind space, keeping the environment on the outside. Mapping the "New World" enabled Samuel de Champlain, for instance, to feel himself master of the lands he would eventually claim for the king of France. Only occasionally revealing himself to be overwhelmed by a landscape he does not know, Champlain, at such moments, considers the land itself (and its inhabitants) as inherently chaotic and unstable.[30] His sense of self is directly derived from controlling rigid boundaries and specific practices of knowledge production to create racial space, that is, space inhabited by the racial Other.

Kirby's account of the Cartesian subject in space, a subject privileged enough to choose to be in unfamiliar landscapes, may be usefully contrasted with Radhika Mohanram's account of its opposite, the Black body. Mohanram describes the two bodies in terms of their racial and spatial attributes: "First, whiteness has the ability to move; second, the ability to move results in the unmarking of the body. In contrast, blackness is signified through a marking and is always static and immobilizing."[31] To explain how the two bodies are imagined in a racial social order, Mohanram uses a text of the anthropologist Lévi-Strauss in which he explains human intellectual activity and compares two ways of knowing—that of the engineer and the bricoleur (handyman).[32] Although Lévi-Strauss does not suggest that one way of knowing is a more primitive form of thought than the other, Mohanram shows how, in Lévi-Strauss's narrative, the engineer is white and male, a figure who is able to connect the laws of physics and chemistry in anthropological discourse, while the bricoleur is the native, the indigenous scientist who uses intuition, imagination, and signs to know the world. The engineer has science to guide him; the bricoleur has intuition. Significantly, while the bricoleur can only classify perceived differences, the engineer's scientific system enables him to classify things not yet seen.

Thinking of Mary Louise Pratt's description of the European naturalists and cartographers who roamed Europe's colonies classifying plants and making maps with their scientific knowledge, and thus creating a European discourse about a non-European world,[33] Mohanram reflects on how the bricoleur, a pre-capitalist and pre-modern figure, is tied to place while the engineer, located within capitalism and modernity, has the freedom to roam. Noting the same two figures in Alfred Cosby's book *Ecological Imperialism*, where Europeans are described as shaping the environment of the Americas to their advantage, Mohanram comments that the European settler becomes the disembodied Universal Subject, "a subject who is able to take anyone's place." The Indigene, on the other hand, remains "immobile against the repeated onslaught of the settler."[34] For the settler, it is through movement from European to non-European space that he comes to know himself, a journey that materially and symbolically secures his dominance.

GENDER, TRANSGRESSION, AND JOURNEYS THROUGH SPACE

We know the black body by its immobility and the white body by its mobility. However, bodies are gendered and when we speak of subjects coming to know themselves in and through space, we are speaking of identity-making processes that are profoundly shaped by patriarchy. It is not only that men and women come to know themselves as dominant or subordinate in different ways. It is also that dominant masculinities and femininities exist symbiotically. In *Mapping Men and Empire*, Richard Phillips examines Victorian adventure stories showing, in the case of Robert Ballantyne's novels, how the journeys of male heroes through nineteenth-century Canada enable their coming to manhood through encounters with the rugged Canadian wilderness and its "wild Indians." Heroic boys learn the "rough life" and return home to women and civilization confirmed in their mastery and ready to assume the responsibilities of patriarchs. Careful to note that readers have agency when they enter into such fantasies, what Phillips nonetheless underlines is the process through which individuals gain a sense of self in and through space, by moving from civilized to liminal and back again to civilized space.

Liminal space is the border between civilized and primitive space, the space inhabited by savages whom civilized men vanquish on every turn. The subject who comes to know himself through such journeys first imagines his own space as civilized, in contrast to the space of the racial Other; second, he engages in transgression, which is a movement from respectable to degenerate space, a risky venture from which he returns unscathed; and third, he learns that he is in control of the journey through individual practices of domination. In the boys' adventure stories, white masculinity is confirmed when the boy hero punches out an Indian who is cruel to dogs.[35] Here the young white boy comes to know himself as white and in control, and as possessing superior values, a knowledge gained through the bodies and spaces of the racial Other. He also learns his place through white girls and women who stand as the marker of home and civility.

As Radhika Mohanram observes, it is as "feminine women" that white women are co-opted into imperial ventures as keepers of the imperial hearth.[36] Thus for white girls, Phillips points out, confined to domestic and enclosed material space, journeys into liminal space and contact with the Other in adventure stories required a gender transgression. Paradoxically, refusing their gender-specific imperial role in the home and undertaking such an imperial journey enabled girls to understand themselves as part of the colonial project and as potential settlers.

The journeys through the metaphorical space of the adventure stories have their material expression. Young white boys and girls learned something of who they were through such stories and the stories promoted popular support for imperialism. Phillips is rightfully emphatic, however, in noting that the novels of colonial culture did not "cause" colonialism.[37] The novels suggest the relationship between space, identity, and racial domination, a relationship I describe as a racial journey into personhood. Today, the identity-making processes of such journeys are evident in women's participation in development work in the Third World, where, as development workers, women of the First World can know themselves as autonomous, competent, and good through their interactions with Third World peoples and their efforts to "help" them.[38] Their development activities fix the natives, confining them to their environment and mode of thought and making them available to be assisted into modernity.[39] We might also see a racial journey into personhood taking place when Northern peacekeepers leave their own "civilized" spaces determined to save Southern nations from their own chaos.[40]

The identity-making processes at work in journeys from respectable to degenerate space are multiple and gendered. The processes described above do not show what the spaces might mean to the subordinate person in the encounter, for example. How might the Indian in Ballantyne's Canadian adventure stories experience the encounter differently from the young white boys? To return to Kathleen Kirby's example of Samuel de Champlain, when Champlain is lost, the land is experienced as chaotic, wild, and untamed, something it would not have seemed to the Aboriginal nations whom Champlain encountered. As well, we cannot presume that subordinate peoples were merely dominated. There is a spatiality to their resistance, which we do not take up to any great extent in this book.

SPACE AND INTERLOCKING SYSTEMS OF OPPRESSION

To interrogate bodies travelling in spaces is to engage in a complex historical mapping of spaces and bodies *in relation*, inevitably a tracking of multiple systems of domination and the ways in which they come into existence in and through each other. Spatial theorists have not generally used an interlocking approach. For example, in many anthologies devoted to gender and space,[41] woman remains an undifferentiated category with an occasional article on women of colour as a variation on the original model. That race, gender, and class hierarchies structure (rather than simply complicate) each other is not considered. For example, in their work on the segregation of large numbers of women into poorly paid jobs in Worcester, Massachusetts, Susan Hanson and Geraldine Pratt focus on the social and economic geographies of women's lives as compared with men's lives. They note that occupational segregation begins at home, that suburbs make it difficult to combine work and home, and that neighbourly networks facilitate participation in the workforce.[42] These patterns largely apply to white women, something the authors do not interrogate. More significantly, the patterns are themselves embedded in an economy in which, for example, Black women clean the houses of white suburban women. Had Hanson and Pratt considered how their locality was historically produced as a white space, exploring for instance how it comes to be that 70 per cent of the largely white working-class population has lived there for forty years, they might have seen how the gendered conditions they explore are profoundly shaped by a racial economy.

Similar erasures are evident in work on geography and disability. For example, in her review of the edited collection *Mind and Body Spaces: Geographies of Illness, Impairment and Disability*, Sheila Gill identifies what is elided when the category of analysis is an uncomplicated notion of disability. Articles in this collection discuss, among other topics, the ableism of nineteenth-century architecture theory, the spatial dimensions of the "mental deficiency" asylum, and the moral topography of intemperance yet pay no attention to the context of imperial expansion and colonialism. The result is that "mental deficiency" in nineteenth-century Canada is understood as largely unconnected to the eugenics movement and to the making of a white Canada. That a disproportionate number of new immigrants were confined to the asylums and a vigorous discourse about preserving the health of the white race was in place do not interrupt the text's central raceless narrative about "feeblemindedness."[43]

Race also strangely disappears in some geographical work on cities in spite of the fact that difference is a sustained feature of urban spaces and geographers have long paid attention to how the city is experienced differently.[44] Jane Jacobs explains how this erasure of race is most likely to happen. Many of the spatial features of cities, including gentrification, mega-developments, large malls, and heritage buildings are understood primarily as hallmarks of postmodernity. That is, it is clear that globalization has resulted in the growth of international cities in which financial activities are concentrated. Cities are characterized increasingly by a polarization of labour—young professionals in the information and financial sectors on one end and large pools of migrant labour in the service sector on the other. Inequalities are understood here as class inequalities, sometimes complicated by race (for example, the argument that people of colour are overrepresented in the lower levels of the labour market).

Such monocausal explanations, Jacobs argues, ignore the way that "postmodernity manufactures difference in service of its own consuming passions." Older racial orders are reshaped and revitalized in the new globalized conditions. To keep imperialism in sight, Jacobs recommends a closer attention to how spaces are mapped together. "Imperialism," she reminds us, "in whatever form, is a global process—it occurs across regions and nations—but even in its most marauding forms it necessarily takes hold in and through the local."[45] Her reminder is an important one, not only because it instructs us to explore how spaces are linked but also because it insists that we abandon monocausal explanations in favour of those that pay attention to interlocking systems of oppression.

Two steps mark our interlocking approach. First, we examine how the systems mutually constitute each other, an analysis aided by Jacobs's advice to map how spaces are linked. Second, we pursue how all the systems of domination operate at the local level, a task facilitated by attending to material and symbolic constitution of specific spaces. Our goal is to identify legal and social practices that reproduce racial hierarchies. For us, a spatial approach is one way, among others, to uncover processes of racialization. The concept we have all worked with is simply expressed by Radhika Mohanram: racial difference is also spatial difference.[46] Making the same point, David Goldberg writes: "Racisms become institutionally normalized in and through spatial configuration, just as social space is made to seem natural, a given, by being conceived and defined in racial terms."[47]

To denaturalize or unmap spaces, then, we begin by exploring space as a social product, uncovering how bodies are produced in spaces and how spaces produce bodies. This, in turn, entails an interrogation of how subjects come to know themselves in and through space and within multiple systems of domination. We draw on spatial theorists, including, but not limited to, Lefebvre, Foucault, and on a wide range of postcolonial scholars (Mohanram, Phillips, Kirby, and others). Additionally, each chapter draws on scholars who consider colonial space, city space, suburban space, institutional space, and so on. What ties the collection together, however, is the central idea of national space, in this instance, the space of a white settler society. Our concern is to tell the national story as a racial and spatial story, that is, as a series of efforts to segregate, contain, and thereby limit, the rights and opportunities of Aboriginal people and people of colour. [...]

These nine chapters, which cover two coasts of Canada, its Prairies, and the borders between Canada and the United States and the United States and Mexico, show us in intricate detail how the law is used to protect the interests of white people. Each author challenges the racelessness of law and the amnesia that allows white subjects to be produced as innocent, entitled, rational, and legitimate. We are encouraged to ask on what basis our emancipatory projects lie and are reminded not to forget history. The chain of events that begins with eviction and moves through "burials, denials, and complicities through time" must be resurrected. We must find ways to move beyond law's insistence on abstract individuals without histories. The tracing of the constitution of spaces through law and the mapping of the hierarchical social relations they create and sustain is one way of beginning. *Race, Space, and the Law* proposes some initial methodologies for this work of denaturalization, the work of asking how spacial divisions by race come into existence and are sustained.

NOTES

1. *R. v. Hayden*, Manitoba Court of Appeal, Monnin C,J,M., Hall and Philp JJ.A. Judgment delivered by Hall J.A. *Western Weekly Reports* [1983] 6 W.W.R. at 659.

2. Michael Ignatieff, *The Rights Revolution* (Toronto: House of Anansi Press, 2000), pp. 123–4.

3. Anne McClintock, *Imperial Leather: Race, Gender and Sexuality in the Colonial Contest* (New York: Routledge, 1995), p. 130.

4. Dara Culhane, *The Pleasure of the Crown: Anthropology, Law and First Nations* (Burnaby, BC: Talonbooks, 1998), p. 48.

5. Carl Berger, "The True North Strong and Free," in Peter Russell, ed., *Nationalism in Canada* (Toronto: McGraw-Hill, 1966), p. 5; Robert Shields, *Places on the Margins: Alternative Geographies of Modernity* (New York: Routledge, 1991), p. 162.

6. Berger, "The True North Strong and Free," p. 5.

7. David Goldberg, *Racist Culture: Philosophy and the Politics of Meaning* (Oxford: Blackwell Publishers, 1993), p. 186.

8. Ignatieff, *The Rights Revolution*, p. 10.

9. "Government of Canada Introduces Anti-Terrorism Act," Department of Justice Canada, <http://canada.justice.gc.ca/ en/news/nr/200i/doc_27785.html>, November 13, 2001.

10. Sherene H. Razack, "'Simple Logic': Race, the Identity Documents Rule and the Story of a Nation Besieged and Betrayed," *Journal of Law and Social Policy* 15 (2000), pp. 181–209.

11. Richard Phillips, *Mapping Men and Empire: A Geography of Adventure* (New York: Routledge, 1997), p. 143.

12. Steve Pile and Michael Keith, eds., *Geographies of Resistance* (New York: Routledge, 1997), p. 6.

13. See, for example, N. Smith and C. Katz, "Grounding Metaphor: Towards a Spatialized Politics," in Michael Keith and Steve Pile, eds., *Place and the Politics of Identity* (New York: Routledge, 1993), pp. 67–83, discussed in David Morley, *Home Territories: Media, Mobility and Identity* (New York: Routledge, 2000), pp. 7–8.

14. Edward W. Soja, *Postmodern Geographies: The Reassertion of Space in Critical Social Theory* (London: Verso Press, 1989), p. 247.

15. Julie Kathy Gibson-Graham, "Postmodern Becomings: From the Space of Form to the Space of Potentiality," in Georges Benko and Ulf Strohrnayer, eds., *Space and Social Theory* (Oxford: Blackwell Publishers, 1997), p. 307, discussing N. Smith and C. Katz, "Grounding Metaphor: Towards a Spatialized Politics," in Keith and Pile, eds., *Place and the Politics of Identity*, pp. 67–83.

16. Henri Lefebvre, *The Production of Space*, trans. Donald Nicholson-Smith (Oxford: Blackwell Publishers, 1991), p. 7.

17. Eugene J. McCann, "Race, Protest, and Public Space: Contextualizing Lefebvre in the US City," *Antipode* 31,2 (1999), p. 169.

18. Goldberg, *Racist Culture*, p. 198.

19. Lefebvre, *The Production of Space*, p. 39.

20. Samira Kawash, "The Homeless Body," *Public Culture* 10,2 (1998), p. 323.

21. Ibid., p. 329.

22. Ibid., p. 325.

23. Ibid., pp. 332, 337.

24. Michel Foucault, "Space, Power, Knowledge," interview with Paul Rabinow, trans. Christian Hubert, in Paul Rabinow, ed., *The Foucault Reader* (New York: Pantheon, 1984) p. 252.

25. Foucault, "Madness and Civilization," in Rabinow, ed., *The Foucault Reader*, p. 124.

26. Ibid., p. 131.

27. Ibid., pp. 181–2, 184, 189, 191.

28. Kathleen Kirby, "Re:Mapping Subjectivity: Cartographic Vision and the Limits of Politics," in Nancy Duncan, ed., *Body Space: Destabilizing Geographies of Gender and Sexuality* (New York: Routledge, 1996), p. 44.

29. Ibid.

30. Ibid., p. 48.

31. Radhika Mohanram, *Black Body: Women, Colonialism, and Space* (Minneapolis: University of Minnesota Press, 1999), p. 4.

32. A bricoleur undertakes odd jobs and is a jack of all trades. Since the term as used in Lévi-Strauss has no English equivalent, it is usually not translated. Lévi-Strauss uses bricolage to describe a characteristic feature of mythical thought. David Macey, *The Penguin Dictionary of Critical Theory* (London: Penguin, 2000), p. 52.

33. Mary Louise Pratt, *Imperial Eyes: Travel Writing and Transculturation* (New York: Routledge, 1992).

34. Mohanram, *Black Body*, pp. 11, 14, 15; Alfred W. Crosby, *Ecological Imperialism: The Biological Expansion of Europe, 900–1900* (Cambridge: Cambridge University Press, 1986).

35. Phillips, *Mapping Men and Empire*, p. 60.

36. Mohanram, *Black Body*, p. 167.

37. Phillips, *Mapping Men and Empire*, p. 68.

38. Barbara Heron, "Desire for Development: The Education of White Women as Development Workers" (Ph.D. diss., University of Toronto, 1999).

39. Arjun Appadurai, "Putting Hierarchy in Its Place," *Cultural Anthropology* 3,1 (1988), pp. 36–49. See also Mohanram, *Black Body*, p. 11, for a discussion of Appadurai.

40. Sherene H. Razack, "From the 'Clean Snows of Petawawa': The Violence of Canadian Peacekeepers in Somalia," *Cultural Anthropology* 15,1 (2000), pp. 127–63.

41. See, for example, Erica Carter, James Donald, and Judith Squires, eds., *Space and Place: Theories of Identity and Location* (London: Lawrence and Wishart, 1993); Gillian Rose, *Feminism and Geography: The Limits of Geographical Knowledge* (Minneapolis: University of Minnesota Press, 1993); Doreen B. Massey, *Space, Place and Gender* (Minneapolis: University of Minnesota Press, 1994); Women and Geography Study Group, *Feminist Geographies: Explorations in Diversity and Difference* (Harlow: Longman, 1997); Rosa Ainley, ed., *New Frontiers of Space, Bodies and Gender* (New York: Routledge, 1998); Elizabeth Kenworthy Teather, *Embodied Geographies: Space, Bodies and Rites of Passage* (New York: Routledge, 1999).

42. Susan Hanson and Geraldine Pratt, *Gender, Work, and Space* (New York: Routledge, 1995).

43. Sheila Gill, "Review of *Mind and Body\Spaces: Geographies of Illness, Impairment and Disability*, edited by Ruth Butler and Hester Parr," *Revue Canadienne Droit et Société/ Canadian Journal of Law and Society* 15,2 (2000), pp. 228–34.

44. Ruth Fincher and Jane M. Jacobs, "Introduction," in Ruth Fincher and Jane M. Jacobs, eds., *Cities of Difference* (London: The Guilford Press, 1998), p. 2.

45. Jane M. Jacobs, *Edge of Empire: Postcolonialism and the City* (New York: Routledge, 1996), pp. 33–4.

46. Mohanram, *Black Body*, p. 3.

47. Goldberg, *Racist Culture*, p. 185.

SELECTED BIBLIOGRAPHY

Berger, Carl. "The True North Strong and Free." In Peter Russell, ed. *Nationalism in Canada.* Toronto: McGraw-Hill, 1966.

Carter, Erica, James Donald, and Judith Squires, eds. *Space and Place: Theories of Identity and Location.* London: Lawrence and Wishart, 1993.

Culhane, Dara. *The Pleasure of the Crown: Anthropology, Law and First Nations.* Burnaby, BC: Talonbooks, 1998.

Fincher, Ruth, and Jane M. Jacobs, eds. *Cities of Difference.* London: The Guilford Press, 1998.

Goldberg, David. *Racist Culture: Philosophy and the Politics of Meaning.* Oxford: Blackwell Publishers, 1993.

Heron, Barbara. "Desire for Development: The Education of White Women as Development Workers." PhD Dissertation, The Ontario Institute for Studies in Education of University of Toronto, 1999.

Jacobs, Jane M. *Edge of Empire: Postcolonialism and the City.* New York: Routledge, 1996.

Kawash, Samira. "The Homeless Body." *Public Culture* 10,2 (1998).

Kirby, Kathleen. "Re-Mapping Subjectivity: Cartographic Vision and the Limits of Politics." In Nancy Duncan, ed. *Body Space: Destabilizing Geographies of Gender and Sexuality*. New York: Routledge, 1996.

Lefebvre, Henri. *The Production of Space*. Trans. Donald Nicholson-Smith. Oxford: Blackwell Publishers, 1991.

McCann, Eugene J. "Race, Protest, and Public Space: Contextualizing Lefebvre in the US City." *Antipode* 31,2 (1999), pp. 163–84.

McClintock, Anne. *Imperial Leather: Race, Gender and Sexuality in the Colonial Contest*. New York: Routledge, 1995.

Mohanram, Radhika. *Black Body: Women, Colonialism, and Space*. Minneapolis: University of Minnesota Press, 1999.

Phillips, Richard. *Mapping Men and Empire: A Geography of Adventure*. New York: Routledge, 1997.

Pile, Steve, and Michael Keith, eds. *Geographies of Resistance*. New York: Routledge, 1997.

Pratt, Mary Louise. *Imperial Eyes: Travel Writing and Transculturation*. London: Routledge, 1992.

Rabinow, Paul, ed. *The Foucault Reader*. New York: Pantheon, 1984.

Razack, Sherene. "From the 'Clean Snows of Petawawa': The Violence of Canadian Peacekeepers in Somalia." *Cultural Anthropology* 15,1 (2000), pp. 127–63.

———. "'Simple Logic': Race, the Identity Documents Rule and the Story of a Nation Besieged and Betrayed." *Journal of Law and Social Policy* 15 (2000), pp. 181–209.

Rose, Gillian. *Feminism and Geography: The Limits of Geographical Knowledge*. Minneapolis: University of Minnesota Press, 1993.

Soja, Edward W. *Postmodern Geographies: The Reassertion of Space in Critical Social Theory*. London: Verso Press, 1989.

Chapter 10

Is There a "Neo-Racism"?

Etienne Balibar

Balibar's focus is on the evolving deployment of race in response to "new threats" to Eurocentric ethnicity in France and the rest of Europe—especially the nationalist political formations. It provides a new and contemporary dimension of the debate on the concept of race. Balibar's 1991 article assumes the transition to a "new" basis for the processes of racialization, one that goes beyond the biological and genetic rationalizations. What Balibar suggests is that a form of racism has emerged in the post–Cold War period to coincide with the multicultural nature of Europe's metropolitan centres. The reality of the South-North internationalization of population movements informs Balibar's formulation and the transnational character of the form of racism emerging with it. He points particularly to the use of immigration as a "substitute" for race in the development of a consciousness that supports or sustains social closure in French society, enabling what he calls "racism without races." Cultural difference, previously the very basis for anti-racism action, then becomes naturalized and formalized as a basis for what Taguieff has referred to as "differentialist racism"—a form of racism based on the validity of difference that otherwise underpins contemporary popular notions of diversity, multiculturalism, and anti-racism.

To what extent is it correct so speak of a neo-racism? The question is forced upon us by current events in forms which differ to some degree from one country to another, but which suggest the existence of a transnational phenomenon. The question may, however, be understood in two senses. On the one hand, are we seeing a new historical upsurge of racist movements and policies which might be explained by a crisis conjuncture or by other causes? On the other hand, in its themes and its social significance, is what we are seeing only a *new* racism, irreducible to earlier "models," or is it a mere tactical adaptation? I shall concern myself here primarily with this second aspect of the question.[1]

First of all, we have to make the following observation. The neo-racism hypothesis, at least so far as France is concerned, has been formulated essentially on the basis of an internal critique of theories, of discourses tending to legitimate policies of exclusion in terms of anthropology or the philosophy of history. Little has been done on finding the connection between the newness of the doctrines and the novelty of the political situations and social transformations which have given them a purchase. I shall argue in a moment that the theoretical dimension of racism today, as in the past, is historically essential, but that it is neither autonomous nor primary. Racism—a true "total social phenomenon"—inscribes itself in practices (forms of violence, contempt, intolerance, humiliation and exploitation), in discourses and representations which are so many intellectual elaborations of the phantasm of prophylaxis or segregation (the need to purify the social body, to preserve "one's own" or "our" identity from all forms of mixing, interbreeding or invasion) and which are articulated around stigmata of otherness (name, skin colour, religious practices). It therefore organizes affects (the psychological study of these has concentrated upon describing their obsessive character and also their "irrational" ambivalence) by conferring upon them a stereotyped form, as regards both their "objects" and their "subjects." It is this combination of practices, discourses and representations in a network of affective stereotypes which enables us to give an account of the formation of a racist community (or a community of racists, among whom there exist bonds of "imitation" over a distance) and also of the way in which, as a mirror image, individuals and collectivities that are prey to racism (its "objects") find themselves constrained to see themselves as a community.

But however absolute that constraint may be, it obviously can never be cancelled out as constraint *for its victims*: it can neither be interiorized without conflict (see the works of Memmi) nor can it remove the contradiction which sees an identity as community ascribed to collectivities which are simultaneously denied the right to define themselves (see the writings of Frantz Fanon), nor, most importantly, can it reduce the permanent excess of actual violence and acts over discourses, theories and rationalizations. From the point of view of its victims, there is, then, an essential dissymmetry within the racist complex, which confers upon its acts and "actings out" undeniable primacy over its doctrines, naturally including within the category of actions not only physical violence and discrimination, but words themselves, the violence of words in so far as they are acts of contempt and aggression. Which leads us, in a first phase, to regard shifts in doctrine and language as relatively incidental matters: should we attach so much importance to justifications which continue to retain the same structure (that of a denial of rights) while moving from the language of religion into that of science, or from the language of biology into the discourses of culture or history, when in practice these justifications simply lead to the same old acts?

This is a fair point, even a vitally important one, but it does not solve all the problems. For the destruction of the racist complex presupposes not only the revolt of its victims, but the transformation of the racists themselves and, consequently, *the internal decomposition of the community created by racism*. In this respect, the situation is entirely analogous, as has often been said over the last twenty years or so, with that of sexism, the overcoming of which presupposes both the revolt of women and the break-up of the community of "males." Now, racist theories are indispensable in the formation of the racist community. There is in fact no racism without theory (or theories). It would be quite futile to inquire whether racist theories have emanated chiefly from the elites or the masses, from the dominant or the dominated classes. It is, however, quite clear that they are "rationalized" by intellectuals. And it is of the utmost importance that we enquire into the function fulfilled by the theory-building of academic racism (the prototype of which is the evolutionist anthropology of "biological" races developed at the end of the nineteenth century) in the crystallization of the community which forms around the signifier, "race."

This function does not, it seems to me, reside solely in the general organizing capacity of intellectual rationalizations (what Gramsci called their "organicity" and Auguste Comte their "spiritual power") nor in the fact that the theories of academic racism elaborate an image of community, of original identity in which individuals of all social classes may recognize themselves. It resides, rather, in the fact that the theories of academic racism mimic scientific discursivity by basing themselves upon visible "evidence" (whence the essential importance of the stigmata of race and in particular of bodily stigmata), or, more exactly, they mimic the way in which scientific discursivity articulates "visible facts" to "hidden causes" and thus connect up with a spontaneous process of theorization inherent in the racism of the masses.[2] I shall therefore venture the idea that the racist complex inextricably combines a crucial function of *misrecognition* (without which the violence would not be tolerable to the very people engaging in it) and a "will to know," a violent *desire for* immediate *knowledge* of social relations. These are functions which are mutually sustaining since, both for individuals and for social groups, their own collective violence is a distressing enigma and they require an urgent explanation for it. This indeed is what makes the intellectual posture of the ideologues of racism so singular, however sophisticated their theories may seem. Unlike for example theologians, who must maintain a distance (though not an absolute break, unless they lapse into "gnosticism") between esoteric speculation and a doctrine designed for popular consumption, historically effective racist ideologues have always developed "democratic" doctrines which are immeditately intelligible to the masses and apparently suited from the outset to their supposed low level of intelligence, even when elaborating elitist themes. In other words, they have produced doctrines capable of providing immediate interpretative keys not only to what individuals are *experiencing* but to what they *are* in the social world (in this respect, they have affinities with astrology, characterology and so on), even when these keys take the form of the revelation of a "secret" of the human condition (that is, when they include a *secrecy effect* essential to their imaginary efficacity: this is a point which has been well illustrated by Leon Poliakov).[3]

This is also, we must note, what makes it difficult to *criticize* the content and, most importantly, the influence of academic racism. In the very construction of its theories, there lies the presupposition that the "knowledge" sought and desired by the masses is an elementary knowledge which simply justifies them in their spontaneous feelings or brings them back to the truth of their instincts. Bebel, as is well known, called anti-Semitism the "socialism of fools" and Nietzsche regarded it more or less as the politics of the feeble-minded (though this in no way prevented him from taking over a large part of racial mythology himself). Can we ourselves, when we characterize racist doctrines as strictly demagogic theoretical elaborations, whose efficacy derives from the advance response they provide for the masses' desire for knowledge, escape this same ambiguous position? The category of the "masses" (or the "popular") is not itself neutral, but communicates directly with the logic of a naturalization and racization of the social. To begin to dispel this ambiguity, it is no doubt insufficient merely to examine the way the racist "myth" gains its hold upon the masses; we also have to ask why other sociological theories, developed within the framework of a division between "intellectual" and "manual" activities (in the broad sense), are unable to fuse so easily with this desire to know. Racist myths (the "Aryan myth," the myth of heredity) are myths not only by virtue of their pseudo-scientific content, but in so far as they are forms of imaginary transcendence of the gulf separating intellectuality from the masses, forms indissociable from that implicit fatalism which imprisons the masses in an allegedly natural infantilism.

We can now turn our attention to "neo-racism." What seems to pose a problem here is not the *fact* of racism, as I have already pointed out—practice being a fairly sure criterion (if we do not allow ourselves to be deceived by the denials of racism which we meet among large sections of the political class in particular, which only thereby betrays the complacency and blindness of that group)—but determining to what extent the relative novelty of the language is expressing a *new* and lasting articulation of social practices and collective representations, academic doctrines and political movements. In short, to use Gramscian language, we have to determine whether something like a hegemony is developing here.

The functioning of the category of *immigration* as a substitute for the notion of race and a solvent of "class consciousness" provides us with a first clue. Quite clearly, we are not simply dealing with a camouflaging operation, made necessary by the disrepute into which the term "race" and its derivatives has fallen, nor solely with a consequence of the transformations of French society. Collectivities of immigrant workers have for many years suffered discrimination and xenophobic violence in which racist stereotyping has played an essential role. The interwar period, another crisis era, saw the unleashing of campaigns in France against "foreigners," Jewish or otherwise, campaigns which extended beyond the activities of the fascist movements and which found their logical culmination in the Vichy regime's contribution to the Hitlerian enterprise. Why did we not at that period see the "sociological" signifier definitively replace the "biological" one as the key representation of hatred, and fear of the other? Apart from the force of strictly French traditions of anthropological myth, this was probably due, on the one hand, to the institutional and ideological break which then existed between the perception of immigration (essentially European) and colonial experience (on the one side, France "was being invaded," on the other it "was dominant") and, on the other hand, because of the absence of a new model of articulation between states, peoples and cultures on a world scale.[4] The two reasons are indeed linked. The new racism is a racism of the era of "decolonization," of the reversal of population movements between the old colonies and the old metropolises, and the division of humanity within a single political space. Ideologically, current racism, which in France centres upon the immigration complex, fits into a framework of "racism without races" which is already widely developed in other countries, particularly the Anglo-Saxon ones. It is a racism whose dominant theme is not biological heredity but the insurmountability of cultural differences, a racism which, at first sight, does not postulate the superiority of certain groups or peoples in relation to others but "only" the harmfulness of abolishing frontiers, the incompatibility of life-styles and traditions; in short, it is what P.A. Taguieff has rightly called a *differentialist racism*.[5]

To emphasize the importance of the question, we must first of all bring out the political consequences of this change. The first is a destabilization of the defences of traditional anti-racism in so far as its argumentation finds itself attacked from the rear, if not indeed turned against itself (what Taguieff excellently terms the *"turn-about effect"* of differentialist racism). It is granted from the outset that races do not constitute isolable biological units and that in reality there are no "human races." It may also be admitted that the behaviour of individuals and their "aptitudes" cannot be explained in terms of their blood or even their genes, but are the result of their belonging to historical "cultures." Now anthropological culturalism, which is entirely orientated towards the recognition of the diversity and equality of cultures—with only the polyphonic ensemble constituting human civilization—and also their transhistorical *permanence*, had provided the humanist and cosmopolitan anti-racism of the post-war period with most of its arguments. Its value had been confirmed by the contribution it made to the struggle against the hegemony of certain standardizing imperialisms and against the elimination of minority or dominated civilizations—"ethnocide." Differentialist racism takes this argumentation at its word. One of the great figures in anthropology, Claude Lévi-Strauss, who not so long ago distinguished himself by demonstrating that all civilizations are equally complex and necessary for the progression of human thought, now in "Race and Culture" finds himself enrolled, whether he likes it or not, in the service of the idea that the "mixing of cultures" and the suppression of "cultural distances" would correspond to the intellectual death of humanity and would perhaps even endanger the control mechanisms that ensure its biological survival.[6] And this "demonstration" is immediately related to the "spontaneous" tendency of human groups (in practice national groups, though the anthropological significance of the political category of nation is obviously rather dubious) to preserve their traditions, and thus their identity. What we see here is that biological or genetic naturalism is not the only means of naturalizing human behaviour and social affinities. At the cost of abandoning the hierarchical model (though the abandonment is more apparent than real, as we shall see), *culture can also function like a nature*, and it can in particular function as a way of locking individuals and groups a priori into a genealogy, into a determination that is immutable and intangible in origin.

But this first turn-about effect gives rise to a second, which turns matters about even more and is, for that, all the more effective: if insurmountable cultural difference is our true "natural milieu," the atmosphere indispensable to us if we are to breathe the air of history, then the abolition of that difference will necessarily give rise to defensive reactions, "interethnic" conflicts and a general rise in aggressiveness. Such reactions, we are told, are "natural," but they are also dangerous. By an astonishing volte-face, we here see the differentialist doctrines themselves proposing to *explain racism* (and to ward it off).

In fact, what we see is a general displacement of the problematic. We now move from the theory of races or the struggle between the races in human history, whether based on biological or psychological principles, to a theory of "race relations" within society, *which naturalizes not racial belonging but racist conduct*. From the logical point of view, differentialist racism is a meta-racism, or what we might call a "second-position" racism, which presents itself as having drawn the lessons from the conflict between racism and anti-racism, as a politically operational theory of the causes of social aggression. If you want to avoid racism, you have to avoid that "abstract" anti-racism which fails to grasp the psychological and sociological laws of human population movements; you have to respect the "tolerance thresholds," maintain "cultural distances" or, in other words, in accordance with the postulate that individuals are the exclusive heirs and bearers of a single culture, segregate collectivities (the best barrier in this regard still being national frontiers). And here we leave the realm of speculation to enter directly upon political terrain and the interpretation of everyday experience. Naturally, "abstract" is not an epistemological category, but a value judgement which is the more eagerly applied when the practices to which it corresponds are the more concrete or effective: programmes of urban renewal, anti-discrimination struggles, including even positive discrimination in schooling and jobs (what the American New Right calls "reverse discrimination"; in France too we are more and more often hearing "reasonable" figures who have no connection with any extremist movements explaining that "it is anti-racism which creates racism" by its agitation and its manner of "provoking" the mass of the citizenry's national sentiments).[7]

It is not by chance that the theories of differentialist racism (which from now on will tend to present itself as the *true anti-racism* and therefore the true humanism) here connect easily with "crowd psychology," which is enjoying something of a revival, as a general explanation of irrational movements, aggression and collective violence, and, particularly, of xenophobia. We can see here the double game mentioned above operating fully: the masses are presented with an explanation of their own "spontaneity" and at the same time they are implicitly disparaged as a "primitive" crowd. The neo-racist ideologues are not mystical heredity theorists, but "realist" technicians of social psychology....

In presenting the turn-about effects of neo-racism in this way, I am doubtless simplifying its genesis and the complexity of its internal variations, but I want to bring out what is strategically at stake in its development. Ideally one would wish to elaborate further on certain aspects and add certain correctives, but these can only be sketched out rudimentarily in what follows.

The idea of a "racism without race" is not as revolutionary as one might imagine. Without going into the fluctuations in the meaning of the word "race," whose historiosophical usage in fact predates any re-inscription of "genealogy" into "genetics," we must take on board a number of major historical facts, however troublesome these may be (for a certain anti-racist vulgate, and also for the turn-abouts forced upon it by neo-racism).

A racism which does not have the pseudo-biological concept of race as its main driving force has always existed, and it has existed at exactly this level of secondary theoretical elaborations. Its prototype is anti-Semitism. Modern anti-Semitism—the form which begins to crystallize in the Europe of the Enlightenment, if not indeed from the period in which the Spain of the *Reconquista* and the Inquisition gave a statist, nationalistic inflexion to theological anti-Judaism—is *already* a "culturalist" racism. Admittedly, bodily stigmata play a great role in its phantasmatics, but they do so more as signs of a deep psychology, as signs of a spiritual inheritance rather than a biological heredity.[8] These signs are, so to speak, the more revealing for being the less visible and the Jew is more "truly" a Jew the more indiscernible he is. His essence is that of a cultural tradition, a ferment of moral disintegration. Anti-Semitism is supremely "differentialist" and in many respects the whole of current differentialist racism may be considered, from the formal point of view, *as a generalized anti-Semitism.* This consideration is particularly important for the interpretation of contemporary Arabophobia, especially in France, since it carries with it an image of Islam as a "conception of the world" which is incompatible with Europeanness and an enterprise of universal ideological domination, and therefore a systematic confusion of "Arabness" and "Islamicism."

This leads us to direct our attention towards a historical fact that is even more difficult to admit and yet crucial, taking into consideration the French national form of racist traditions. There is, no doubt, a specifically French branch of the doctrines of Aryanism, anthropometry and biological geneticism, but the true "French ideology" is not to be found in these: it lies rather in the idea that the culture of the "land of the Rights of Man" has been entrusted with a universal mission to educate the human race. There corresponds to this mission a practice of assimilating dominated populations and a consequent need to differentiate and rank individuals or groups in terms of their greater or lesser aptitude for—or resistance to—assimilation. It was this simultaneously subtle and crushing form of exclusion/inclusion which was deployed in the process of colonization and the strictly French (or "democratic") variant of the "White man's burden." I return in later chapters to the paradoxes of universalism and particularism in the functioning of racist ideologies or in the racist aspects of the functioning of ideologies.[9]

Conversely, it is not difficult to see that, in neo-racist doctrines, the suppression of the theme of hierarchy is more apparent than real. In fact, the idea of hierarchy, which these theorists may actually go so far as loudly to denounce as absurd, is reconstituted, on the one hand, in the practical application of the doctrine (it does not therefore need to be stated explicitly), and, on the other, in the very type of criteria applied in thinking the difference between cultures (and one can again see the logical resources of the "second position" of meta-racism in action).

Prophylactic action against racial mixing in fact occurs in places where the established culture is that of the state, the dominant classes and, at least officially, the "national" masses, whose style of life and thinking is legitimated by the system of institutions; it therefore functions as an undirectional block on expression and social advancement. No theoretical discourse on the dignity of all cultures will really compensate for the fact that, for a "Black" in Britain or a "*Beur*" in France, the assimilation demanded of them before they can become "integrated" into the society in which they already live (and which will always be suspected of being superficial, imperfect or simulated) is presented as progress, as an emancipation, a conceding of rights. And behind this situation lie barely reworked variants of the idea that the historical cultures of humanity can be divided into two main groups, the one assumed to be universalistic and progressive, the other supposed irremediably particularistic and primitive. It is not by chance that we encounter a paradox here: a "logically coherent" differential racism would be uniformly conservative, arguing for the fixity of *all* cultures. It is in fact conservative, since, on the pretext of protecting European culture and the European way of life from "Third Worldization," it utopianly closes off any path towards real development. But it immediately reintroduces the old distinction between "closed" and "open," "static" and "enterprising," "cold" and "hot," "gregarious" and "individualistic" societies—a distinction which, in its turn, brings into play all the ambiguity of the notion of culture (this is particularly the case in French!).

The difference between cultures, considered as separate entities or separate symbolic structures (that is, "culture" in the sense of *Kultur*), refers on to cultural inequality within the "European" space itself or, more precisely, to "culture" (in the sense of *Bildung*, with its distinction between the academic and the popular, technical knowledge and folklore and so on) as a structure of inequalities tendentially reproduced in an industrialized, formally educated society that is increasingly internationalized and open to the world. The "different" cultures are those which constitute obstacles, or which are established as obstacles (by schools or the norms of international communication) to the acquisition of culture. And, conversely, the "cultural handicaps" of the dominated classes are presented as practical equivalents of alien status, or as ways of life particularly exposed to the destructive effects of mixing (that is, to the effects of the material conditions in which this "mixing" occurs).[10] This latent presence of the hierarchic theme today finds its chief expression in the priority accorded to the individualistic model (just as, in the previous period, openly inegalitarian racism, in order to postulate an essential fixity of racial types, had to presuppose a differentialist anthropology, whether based on genetics or on *Völkerpsychologie*): the cultures supposed implicitly superior are those which appreciate and promote "individual" enterprise, social and political individualism, as against those which inhibit these things. These are said to be the cultures whose "spirit of community" is constituted by individualism.

In this way, we see how the *return of the biological theme* is permitted and with it the elaboration of new variants of the biological "myth" within the framework of a cultural racism. There are, as we know, different national situations where these matters are concerned. The ethological and sociobiological theoretical models (which are themselves in part competitors) are more influential in the Anglo-Saxon countries, where they continue the traditions of Social Darwinism and eugenics while directly coinciding at points with the political objectives of an aggressive neo-liberalism.[11] Even these tendentially biologistic ideologies, however, depend fundamentally upon the "differentialist revolution." What they aim to explain is not the constitution of races, but the vital importance of cultural closures and traditions for the accumulation of individual aptitudes, and, most importantly, the "natural" bases of xenophobia and social aggression. Aggression is a fictive essence which is invoked by all forms of neo-racism, and which makes it possible in this instance to displace biologism one degree: there are of course no "races," there are only populations and cultures, but there are biological (and biophysical) causes and effects of culture, and biological reactions to cultural difference (which could he said to constitute something like the indelible trace of the "animality" of man, still bound as ever to his extended "family" and his "territory"). Conversely, where pure culturalism seems dominant (as in France), we are seeing a progressive drift towards the elaboration of discourses on biology and on culture as the external regulation of "living organisms," their reproduction, performance and health. Michel Foucault, among others, foresaw this.[12]

It may well be that the current variants of neo-racism are merely a transitional ideological formation, which is destined to develop towards discourses and social technologies in which the aspect of the historical recounting of genealogical myths (the play of substitutions between race, people, culture and nation) will give way, to a greater or lesser degree, to the aspect of psychological assessment of intellectual aptitudes and dispositions to "normal" social life (or, conversely, to criminality and deviance), and to "optimal" reproduction (as much from the affective as the sanitary or eugenic point of view), aptitudes and dispositions which a battery of cognitive, sociopsychological and statistical sciences would then undertake to measure, select and monitor, striking a balance between hereditary and environmental factors.... In other words, that ideological formation would develop towards a "post-racism." I am all the more inclined to believe this since the internationalization of social relations and of population movements within the framework of a system of nation-states will increasingly lead to a rethinking of the notion of frontier and to a redistributing of its modes of application; this will accord it a function of social prophylaxis and tie it in to more individualized statutes, while technological transformations will assign educational inequalities and intellectual hierarchies an increasingly important role in the class struggle within the perspective of a generalized techno-political selection of individuals. In the era of nation-enterprises, the true "mass era" is perhaps upon us.

NOTES

1.   It was only after writing this article that Pierre-André Taguieff s book, *La Force du préjugé. Essai sur le racisme et ses doubles* (La Découverte, Paris, 1988), became known to me. In that book he considerably develops, completes and nuances the analyses to which I have referred above, and I hope, in the near future, to be able to devote to it the discussion it deserves.

2.   Colette Guillaumin has provided an excellent explanation of this point, which is, in my opinion, fundamental: "The activity of categorization is *also* a *knowledge activity*.... Hence no doubt the ambiguity of the struggle against stereotypes and the surprises it holds in store for us. Categorization is pregnant with knowledge as it is with oppression." (*L'Idéologie raciste. Genèse et langage actuel*, Mouton, Paris/The Hague, 1972, pp. 183 *et seq.*)

3.   L. Poliakov, *The Aryan Myth: A History of Racist and Nationalist Ideas in Europe*, transl. E. Howard, Sussex University Press, Brighton, 1974; *La Causalité diabolique: essais sur l'origine des persécutions*, Calmann-Lévy, Paris, 1980.

4.   Compare the way in which, in the United States, the "Black problem" remained separate from the "ethnic problem" posed by the successive waves of European immigration and their reception, until, in the 1950s and 60s, a new "paradigm of ethnicity" led to the latter being projected on to the former (cf. Michael Omi and Howard Winant, *Racial Formation in the United States*, Routledge & Kegan Paul, London, 1986).

5.   See in particular his "Les Présuppositions définitionnelles d'un indéfinissable: le racisme," *Mots*, no. 8, 1984; "L'Identité nationale saisie par les logiques de racisation. Aspects, figures et problèmes du racisme différentialiste," *Mots*, no. 12, 1986; "L'Identité française au miroir du racisme différentialiste," *Espaces* 89, *L'identité française*, Editions Tierce, Paris, 1985. The idea is already present in the studies by Colette Guillaumin. See also Véronique de Rudder, "L'Obstacle culturel: la différence et la distance," *L'Homme et la société*, January 1986. Compare, for the Anglo-Saxon world, Martin Barker, *The New Racism: Conservatives and the Ideology of the Tribe*, Junction Books, London, 1981.

6.   This was a lecture written in 1971 for UNESCO, reprinted in *The View from Afar*, transl. J. Neugroschel and P. Hoss, Basic Books, New York, 1985; Cf. the critique by M. O'Callaghan and C. Guillaumin, "Race et race ... la mode 'naturelle' en sciences humaines," *L'Homme et la société*, nos. 31–2, 1974. From a quite different point of view, Lévi-Strauss is today attacked as a proponent of "anti-humanism" and "relativism" (cf. T. Todorov, "Lévi-Strauss entre universalisme et relativisme," *Le Débat*, no. 42, 1986; A. Finkielkraut, *La Défaite de la pensée*, Gallimard, Paris, 1987). Not only is the discussion on this point not closed; it has hardly begun. For my own part, I would argue not that the doctrine of Lévi-Strauss "is racist," but that the racist theories of the nineteenth and twentieth centuries have been constructed within the conceptual field of humanism; it is therefore impossible to distinguish between them on the basis suggested above (see my "Racism and Nationalism," chapter 3 in *Race, Nation, Class: Ambiguous Identities* [London and New York: Verso, 1991]).

7.   In Anglo-Saxon countries, these themes are widely treated by "human ethology" and "sociobiology." In France, they are given a directly culturalist basis. An anthology of these ideas, running from the theorists of the New Right to more sober academics, is to be found in A. Béjin and J. Freund, eds., *Racismes, antiracismes*, Méridiens-Klincksieck, Paris, 1986. It is useful to know that this work was simultaneously vulgarized in a mass-circulation popular publication, *J'ai tout compris*, no. 3, 1987 ("Dossier choc: *Immigrés: demain la haine*" edited by Guillame Faye).

8. Ruth Benedict, among others, pointed this out in respect of H.S. Chamberlain: "Chamberlain, however, did not distinguish Semites by physical traits or by genealogy; Jews, as he knew, cannot be accurately separated from the rest of the population in modern Europe by tabulated anthropomorphic measurements. But they were enemies because they had special ways of thinking and acting. 'One can very soon become a Jew ...' etc." (*Race and Racism*, Routledge & Kegan Paul, London, 1983 edn., pp. 132 *et seq.*). In her view, it was at once a sign of Chamberlain's "frankness" and his "self-contradiction." This self-contradiction became the rule, but in fact it is not a self-contradiction at all. In anti-Semitism, the theme of the inferiority of the Jew is, as we know, much less important than that of his irreducible otherness. Chamberlain even indulges at times in referring to the "superiority" of the Jews, in matters of intellect, commerce or sense of community, making them all the more "dangerous." And the Nazi enterprise frequently admits that it is an enterprise of *reduction* of the Jews to "subhuman status" rather than a consequence of any *de facto* subhumanity: this is indeed why its object cannot remain mere slavery, but must become extermination.

9. See *Race, Nation, Class*, chapter 3, "Racism and Nationalism."

10. It is obviously this subsumption of the "sociological" difference between cultures beneath the institutional hierarchy of Culture, the decisive agency of social classification and its naturalization, that accounts for the keenness of the "radical strife" and resentment that surrounds the presence of immigrants in schools, which is much greater than that generated by the mere fact of living in close proximity. Cf. S. Boulot and D. Boyson-Fradet, "L'Echec scolaire des enfants de travailleurs immigrés," *Les Temps modernes*, special number: "L'Immigration maghrébine en France," 1984.

11. Cf. Barker, *The New Racism*.

12. Michel Foucault, *The History of Sexuality*, vol. 1, *An Introduction*, transl. Robert Jurley, Peregrine, London, 1978.

Chapter 11

The Relationship between Racism and Anti-Semitism

Michael Banton

It is not always possible to distinguish forms of religious discrimination from other types of discrimination. That is especially the case when dealing with a people subject to varied forms of oppression and exclusion that transcend religion. Banton (1992) explores whether there is value to characterizing religious discrimination against Jews—anti-Semitism—as racist. Banton argues against the "exceptionality" of anti-Semitism on the grounds that all forms of discrimination have common features and so the focus should be less on characteristics and more on the identification of the cause. In that vein, he is inclined to focus on the economic and social causes of discrimination as opposed to the psychological (hatred). But this characterization misses the emotional scars that arise from the memory of the atrocities suffered by the victims of anti-Semitism in repeated pogroms in history and eventually in the Jewish Holocaust. And, while Banton may not agree, maintaining the category of anti-Semitism as a particular form of racism could be important in organizing protection against repeating the crimes of the past, a strong case for both remembering and sustaining the specificity of the anti-Semitic crimes of the last century.

In 1975 the United Nations General Assembly voted by seventy-five to thirty-five to adopt Resolution 3379 which "determines that Zionism is a form of racism and racial discrimination." It has sometimes been suggested that antisemitic feelings lay behind this Resolution. But only a moment's reflection is needed to appreciate that whether or not Zionism is racism, and whether or not criticism of Israeli policies is antisemitic, depends upon the meanings given to the key terms. Both concepts—racism and antisemitism—have been of great rhetorical value in mobilizing opinion against grievous evils, and both can be used in interpreting the history of these evils. Neither, however, is useful for social analysis or for the designing of counter-measures.

THE UNITED NATIONS

At the end of 1959 there were attacks on Jewish burial grounds and synagogues in West Germany, followed by similar attacks in some other European countries. The concern which they generated led to a proposal in 1961 that the General Assembly should prepare a convention that would impose on those states choosing to accede to it a legal obligation to prevent manifestations of racial and national hatred. Some states argued that it should also cover religious discrimination. But the eventual decision favoured two separate declarations and conventions: one on racial discrimination and one on religious discrimination. Opposition to combining the two came from some of the Arab delegations, and reflected the Arab-Israeli conflict; however, it might have been difficult in any event to cover them both in the same document. Many delegations, particularly those from Eastern Europe, did not consider questions of religion to be as important as those of race.

The International Convention on the Elimination of All Forms of Racial Discrimination was adopted in 1965. In 1970, monitoring the implementation of its provisions by State Parties began. Israel ratified the Convention in 1979. The Declaration on the Elimination of All Forms of Intolerance and of Discrimination Based on Religion or Belief was adopted in 1981. A draft convention which would give, for the ratifying states, legal effect to the principles in the Declaration was prepared in 1967 but its progress has been slow.

When Resolution 3379—declaring Zionism a form of racism—was proposed, one particular charge was that the Israeli Law of Return discriminated on racial grounds and was in breach of Article 1 (1) of the International Convention which states that racial discrimination:

> shall mean any distinction, exclusion, restriction or preference based on race, colour, descent, or national or ethnic origin which has the purpose or effect of nullifying or impairing the recognition, enjoyment or exercise, on an equal footing, of human rights and fundamental freedoms in the political, economic, social, cultural or any other field of public life.

The charge against the Israeli law seems justified. If in no other way, the Law of Return discriminates on the basis of descent. Article 11 of the Convention offers a procedure whereby a State Party—if it considers that another State Party is not giving effect to the provisions of the Convention—may raise the issue of possible non-compliance. Even if Israel had been a State Party to the Convention in 1975, this procedure could not have been used, since Article 1 (2) states: "This Convention shall not apply to distinctions, exclusions, restrictions or preferences made by a State Party to this Convention between citizens and non-citizens." This exception protects Israel against any charge that the Law of Return breaches the Convention. (It also protects the government of the United Kingdom against charges that its immigration legislation is discriminatory.)

In 1969, the General Assembly designated 1971 as "International Year to Combat Racism and Racial Discrimination" which later developed into the "Decade for Action to Combat Racism and Racial Discrimination" (starting in 1973)—followed later by a "Second Decide." The Programme of Action was the responsibility of the entire General Assembly, not just the State Parties to the International Convention. It therefore offered scope for a resolution against Israel even though that country was not then a party to the Convention.

The vote in favour of the 1975 Resolution was a diplomatic defeat for Israel, and it has provided a basis for many criticisms of that state's policies. The extent to which those criticisms are justified is not at issue here. But the entire episode has been a striking illustration of just how important rhetoric can be in international politics. Any proposition about the nature and form of an "ism" has a flexible character that can be exploited in debate but cannot provide the necessary precision for legal proceedings. Such propositions can also be used persuasively in social analyses which assume that a social pattern can be understood only by placing it in a wider historical context. Thus in *Caste, Class and Race* (New York, 1948), Oliver C. Cox distinguished between antisemitism and racism—he used the phrase "race-prejudice," but in a manner corresponding to the post-1968 meaning of "racism" (p. 393). Antisemitism, he said, is a form of social intolerance directed towards the conversion, expulsion or eradication of a specific minority; racism, on the other hand, serves to rationalize and justify exploitation. The Jew is hated for being different; black people are expected to remain different—and subordinate.

From this point of view, racism is a historical phenomenon associated with the expansion of the capitalist world; it has a definite beginning and therefore can have a definite end. Some Jews might interpret antisemitism as having a definite historical meaning, albeit a very different one: namely, proof that the Jews are indeed the chosen people. One early Zionist thinker, Leon Pinsker, describing the status of Jews in Gentile societies, presented antisemitism in just that way when he argued: "He must be blind indeed who will assert that the Jews are not *the chosen people*, the people chosen for universal hatred." Since many people find it difficult to accept that human history has no meaning other than that which is read into it, propositions which promise to explain history can have enormous appeal.

THE GROUNDS OF DISCRIMINATION

The concept of intent is central to criminal law in most countries. Thus, it is not intrinsically wrong to walk out of a shop with goods that have not been paid for, but it is an offence to knowingly deprive someone of his or her property. Discrimination has not been criminalized in every country; in some it has been made a civil wrong. But whatever form the prohibition takes, it usually rests on a concept close to that of intent—namely, that there have been unlawful grounds for a particular action. It is not wrong to dismiss workers who happen to be black or Jewish, but it is wrong to dismiss them *because* they are black or Jewish, i.e. on the grounds of ethnic origin.

The International Bill of Human Rights declares that such rights must be available "without distinction of any kind, such as race, colour, sex, language, religion, political or other opinion, national or social origin, property, birth or other status." Not every country prohibits all these forms of discrimination. The United Kingdom, for example, prohibits discrimination on grounds of race, colour, sex and national origin in Great Britain; whereas in Northern Ireland it prohibits discrimination on grounds of sex, religion and political belief only, maintaining that there is no need to prohibit racial discrimination there. The prohibitions cover both direct and indirect discrimination—that is, both actions stemming from an unlawful purpose and those having an unlawful effect.

There are some ambiguities in the present international law against discrimination, as well as possible inconsistencies between direct and indirect discrimination. For example, it seems clear that, within the territory controlled by the State of Israel, there is discrimination against Arabs: they are treated less favourably because they are Arabs. But is this on racial, religious or political grounds? It could be very difficult for a court to decide. This difficulty should not, however, be used as a basis for complaint about the law on human rights. It should rather be seen as an indication of how hard it is to draft laws against discrimination. Given the nature of the problem, it might be a source of satisfaction that so much progress has already been made. The International Convention on the Elimination of All Forms of Racial Discrimination was drafted with an eye to the gross violations of human rights occurring at that time, the 1960s, in South Africa and in the Deep South of the United States, where the lines of discrimination were drawn very clearly. It will take time to adapt it to the different circumstances of the Middle East, to East Asia, to the Hindu caste system and to the discrimination suffered by the indigenous peoples of South America.

When the Universal Declaration of Human Rights came to the UN General Assembly for adoption, four Muslim states abstained from voting because of Article 18 which declares that the right to freedom of thought includes a person's right "to change his religion or belief." The Muslims averred that their co-religionists did not have a right to abandon their faith. This objection influenced the drafting of the International Declaration on the Elimination of All Forms of Intolerance and of Discrimination Based on Religion or Belief, and led to the complaint that the Declaration failed to protect a right acknowledged earlier. Communist delegates also argued that the use of the word "religion" did not explicitly extend the principle of tolerance to atheists, so the first reference to "religion" was expanded to read "religion or whatever belief of his choice." From the believers' standpoint, there is a fundamental difference between a divine order they are not free to dispute or qualify, and a human right which lies on the same plane as other human rights, all of which have to be simultaneously accommodated. The difficulties experienced by several western legislatures in coming to terms with differing beliefs about abortion are another example of the same conflict.

In the court-room or the lecture hall it may be possible to distinguish religious discrimination from discrimination on the grounds of race or political opinion; but in everyday life such distinctions may not be so obvious. The intensity of caste-based discrimination in some parts of India is illustrated by a recent report of an incident in which a young man and a young woman of different castes fell in love; this so scandalized some of the villagers that they forced the fathers of these two young people to kill them in a public assembly. Whether this was religious discrimination or some other kind seems almost irrelevant compared to the enormity of the conduct. The political philosophy of Hitler's Nazis elaborated a particular idea of race as part of its interpretation of the human past and its future; displaying many features of religion itself, Nazism was set against traditional Christian beliefs. Many terrorists (Armenian, Basque, Irish, Palestinian, Sikh, Tamil, etc.) dedicate their lives to upholding a faith in their nation's historic rights—sometimes in spite of knowing that most of their compatriots do not share their convictions. In recent times, some white South Africans and some Israeli settlers have gunned down people whose very presence they thought incompatible with their group's historic destiny; according to some definitions, such behaviour would also count as a form of terrorism. These examples may be contentious. They are adduced simply to call into question any assumption that religion can easily be distinguished from other grounds of discrimination.

Religious belief is often said to impose upon believers obligations of a non-negotiable character. Yet for some people beliefs about race and political opinion are just as inflexible; while others who consider themselves religious accept that the tenets of their faith have to be reinterpreted in the light of changing circumstances. Since these circumstances include a very pressing need to live in peace with others of different faiths, some are ready to engage in dialogues and develop mutual understanding.

Such considerations indicate that, since Jews can be discriminated against on a number of grounds other than those of race, there is no merit in regarding antisemitism as a form of racism. Indeed, it could be said that the notion of antisemitism became obsolete with the foundation of the State of Israel since it is often difficult to distinguish hostility towards Jews from hostility towards Israeli policies.

THE SOURCES OF DISADVANTAGE

Discrimination is not the only cause of inequality between groups. Its importance can be measured by a consideration of racial disadvantage—that is, any form of handicap associated with assignment to a racial group. The evidence of such handicaps are well displayed in the labour market, in the under-representation of women and members of ethnic minorities in preferred occupations. This situation might arise simply because such persons have not applied for these positions—casual observation would suggest that in Britain the number of Jews who want to become engineers is proportionately' much lower than the number who want to become doctors or lawyers.

A category of persons may also be under-represented when for some reason their labour is less highly valued. There are four principal reasons why the services of members of a minority race may be less valuable: nature, experience, motivation and investment. First, people in some groups may be of different physical stature or health and, on average, less suited to heavy work, for example. Second, immigrant workers may have less experience than native workers in the use of equipment; they may be less skilled and have less knowledge about how to perform tasks. Third, motivations vary. Refugees, for example, may be less career-orientated than economic migrants and native workers because their aspirations are set upon return to their home country. Minority workers may believe (perhaps with justification) that they have little chance of obtaining certain jobs and never apply for them—an example of supply being affected by perceptions of demand. Fourth, groups differ in their attitudes towards children. In some, parents like to have many children (a reflection of circumstances in their country of origin); in others, parents prefer to have fewer children and to invest more of their time, emotional energy and money on their upbringing so that they enter the labour market with more valuable skills.

Discrimination occurs when an employer has less demand for the services of some category of workers even though, objectively, their labour is equally valuable. The three main reasons for this are taste, risk and profit.

It is customary to speak of consumers exercising taste when they buy one sort of product rather than another, whether the product be a foodstuff, a brand of petrol or an item of clothing. But if people selling houses want to sell to purchasers from the same group as themselves, that too is an expression of taste. If it is a white person who wants to sell to another white, and a black person offers a higher price than any white person is willing to pay, there must come a point at which the vendor agrees to a sale. If whites would pay, say, £100,000 and the black person has to bid up to £110,000 in order to buy, the difference of £10,000 represents the price which the vendor puts upon his or her taste; for the purchaser it represents a "colour tax." The concept of taste can be applied in other situations. Workers of one racial group may resist the recruitment of workers of another because of their taste for associating only with their own kind, and so on.

Risk arises when information is lacking about the consequences that will result from an action. Buyers and sellers do not know how a market will react to future considerations. They are short of information about probable futures; it takes time and money to get the facts which would help them make the predictions on which their policies will have to depend. They will be averse from taking risky decisions when the consequences of mistakes will be costly. Engaging minority workers may seem just such a risk, and if the employer never engages any he will never find out whether his initial assumption was correct. Since some discrimination results from estimates about differential frequencies of risk associated with different groups, and since the same argument applies to the recruitment of women workers, what has been called the statistical theory of racism and sexism has been developed.

If employers want to make the maximum profit, they cannot afford to bother about the economically irrelevant characteristics of their customers or employees. But many employers are not that set on profit, and most markets fall very far short of perfect competitiveness. The simplest example is that of a monopoly—one seller, many buyers—in which the seller is able to exploit a position of power in order either to charge a higher price or to be less efficient. Another example is a monopsony—one buyer, many sellers—such as the South African mining industry in which employers, seeking black labour, established a common recruiting agency to enlist workers at standard rates, paying them less than they would have done had they been bidding against one another. Having created a monopsony, they benefited from the greater bargaining power it gave them. South Africa has offered an example of a triangular relationship between the (white) employer, the higher-paid (white) section of the labour force and the lower-paid (black) section which was, until recently, forbidden to form trade unions. Because the higher-paid section had greater bargaining power it could get a greater share of the wages bill and therefore profit from its position of strength. State regulation of the labour market permitted the two white sections to profit from the black section's weaker position. How that profit was (and is) divided is an empirical issue to be investigated case by case, but the example does illustrate the way in which the search for profit can lead to discrimination and thereby to disadvantage.

This sort of analysis can be extended to other markets, like housing and, to some extent, the health services and education; but it must always be remembered that markets are embedded in political processes. It is governments that decide what can be bought and sold, and according to what rules. There is a plausible argument that ideologues who want to maintain racial, religious or political boundaries fear markets because they can dissolve such boundaries. For example, if people are permitted to put a price on their tastes when selling houses, they may breach an established pattern of segregation. Therefore segregationists will try either to restrict their freedom of action or threaten them with dire consequences for ignoring the prejudices of others. A series of studies of local communities in the Deep South of the United States in the 1930s showed how whites were brought up to regard any move towards social equality between blacks and whites as positively immoral; for them, certain kinds of contact with blacks were considered harmful. Any white person who stepped out of line could be subjected to tremendous pressure—and any black person could be killed. It was possible for a poor white to rent a house from a black landlord but the relationship had to be strictly commercial and open to public scrutiny. Differences of wealth could not threaten the colour line. A market analysis needs to be extended to explain the constraints upon transactions, and how it is that some markets adjust to racial boundaries.

An account of the relationship between racism and antisemitism should cover questions of disadvantage, including the relationship between racial discrimination and discrimination against Jews. The above discussion sketches the outlines of the argument that all forms of group disadvantage (including those based on sex or gender) have common features and can be explained by the use of a body of general concepts. Discrimination is a normal feature of social life, since it can be observed in some form wherever groups exist. When there are opportunities for gain, patterns of discrimination can be elaborated to an extent that is contrary to the economic interests even of those who believe that they benefit from them. The cultural representation of group differences may conceal this. All societies will include individuals with psychopathological tendencies; these may find a release in group hostilities, and may be more influential where discrimination is institutionalized. Because of differing circumstances, instances of group hostility necessarily have some unique features, but minority members are sometimes inclined to exaggerate the uniqueness of their group's suffering. The social scientist seeks the general causes of discrimination and hatred within the more powerful groups by studying psychology and economic relationships. The starting point of analysis is the identification of cause, not the characteristics of victims. Generalizations about antisemitism are misleading if they imply that hostility towards Jews is of a special kind.

THE PRESENT AND THE PAST

Addressing the German Parliament in May 1985, Richard von Weiszacker, President of the Federal Republic, said:

> Whoever closes his eyes to the past becomes blind to the present.... Precisely because we seek reconciliation, we must remember that reconciliation without remembering is impossible. Every Jew, wherever he may be, has internalized the experience of the millions of murders, not only because people cannot forget such horror, but also because the memory belongs to the Jewish faith.

The force of that statement is not lessened by the observation that the memory of suffering is important to other groups as well. It recalls a conversation with a black scholar in the United States. Referring to recent calculations that the number of Africans caught up in the Atlantic slave trade were fewer than previously thought, he said: "The Jews say that six million died in the camps; we say that twelve million came in the ships." To him, it was important that the suffering be remembered not just by the descendants of the victims but also by the descendants of those who had been responsible. The accusation of racism has carried a heavy emotional charge because so many white people feel as guilty about how whites have treated blacks during the past four hundred years as about present economic disparities. It might be worthwhile sometime to study the nature of this sentiment more closely and to compare it with Gentile guilt about antisemitism.

Racism and antisemitism are ideas used today to define patterns in the abuse of human rights in the past, and to stimulate action designed to reduce the likelihood of their being repeated in the future. Before 1968, "racism" designated a doctrine but thereafter its significance was broadened to incorporate attitudes and practices. This extension brought many positive benefits. At the United Nations it contributed powerfully to a massive mobilization against *apartheid*, the policies of the South African government, and for decolonization of Angola, Mozambique, Namibia and Zimbabwe. It led to a much greater than expected number of accessions to the International Convention on the Elimination of All Forms of Racial Discrimination—more than might have been achieved had states appreciated the comprehensiveness of the Convention's definition of racial discrimination.

Within particular states, the idea of racism has entered the public consciousness. A 1991 opinion poll in Britain found that 97 per cent of the white respondents were willing to answer the question "Do you think Britain as a society is very racist, fairly racist, fairly non-racist or completely non-racist?" Sixty-seven per cent considered Britain to be racist to some extent, which is evidence of a major change over the last twenty-five years.

The idea of racism has provided the foundation for an attack on some of the conditions which generate discrimination. For example, it has been used to encourage school teachers to develop less ethnocentric approaches in the classroom. The underlying moral concern can be appreciated better by comparing recent attitudes towards racism with those towards crime—also a normal feature of human societies. People accept that there will always be crime and that policies must simply aim to keep it in check, balancing restraints against freedoms. The same might be said of discrimination but racism is understood as something pathological which could and should be eliminated. It is not excused in the way that crime is excused.

One difficulty in conceiving of racism as an impersonal force is the link between the noun "racism" and the adjective "racist," now in such common use. The concept has become an epithet. The accusation of racism is disabling. The accuser claims a moral superiority; the accused has not so much to defend an action as to demonstrate a purity of intention, which is necessarily difficult since all persons—accusers as well as accused—are impelled by a medley of motivations and associations. The black scholar referred to earlier insisted that no black person should ever criticize another black person in public. When it was objected that criticism could then come only from whites, and that there would therefore be a suspicion that it was racially motivated, he replied that this could not be helped. Solidarity was essential to the black cause. Partly because of this outlook some blacks in responsible positions have abused their powers. Whites have been afraid to criticize them for fear of being called "racist"; blacks have been silent because of the demand for solidarity.

Parallels with the accusation of antisemitism are weak however. Gentiles have not felt equally guilty about the past mistreatment of Jews. Responsibility for the Holocaust has been pinned on Germans, on Nazis and on those who collaborated with the Nazis. The silence of the world while the "Final Solution" was being attempted has been excused by professions of ignorance of what was going on at the time, and the pressures of war-time priorities.

A CONCLUSION

Nothing is gained by defining antisemitism as a form of racism. They are both political ideas used in interpreting experience and in organizing protection against the repetition of past evils. They have stimulated attempts to understand the factors in human society which give rise to—and magnify—group hostilities, but neither racism nor antisemitism belongs in the battery of analytical concepts of social science which are useful in identifying the causes of hostility or in planning measures to reduce disadvantage. Both of them are emotion-laden, especially for the victims of group hostility. Both tend to be eurocentric, reflecting particular events in the history of Europe and of European expansion into Africa and the Americas, so that people in other regions of the world sometimes conclude that such issues are not their concern. Both racism and antisemitism relate to hateful experiences; their contemplation easily leads to pessimism.

The last half-century's international struggle to define and protect human rights offers an escape from this conceptual cul-de-sac. The relative success of the human rights movement offers hope for a better future. It seeks to cultivate values that can be acknowledged in all regions of the world, and it can be guided by research into the factors which threaten human rights. Three-quarters of the world's states, as parties to the International Convention on the Elimination of All Forms of Racial Discrimination, have accepted an obligation to provide legal remedies for racial discrimination. In several countries recently, antisemitic writings have been condemned by courts which, while recognizing the right to freedom of expression, have held that the exercise of that right must not infringe the human rights of Jewish citizens. In the twenty-first century, concern with racism and antisemitism will increasingly be brought within the new framework constructed by the movement for human rights.

POSTSCRIPT

An illustration of some of the difficulties attaching to references to antisemitism in international bodies was provided at the 41st session of the United Nations Committee for the Elimination of Racial Discrimination in 1992. The Report of the Committee to the General Assembly concerning the 10th periodic report of Austria states at paragraph 185: "Some members expressed concern over the results of a Gallup Poll conducted in Austria in 1991 in which up to 20 per cent of those interviewed did not recognize the equal rights of Jews in economic life." The response of the state representative appears in paragraph 192: "As for anti-Semitism, the only danger came from organized antisemitic organizations or movements and not from individuals who were free to hold whatever opinions they wished regarding Jews." The Committee's "concluding observations" on the Austrian report read "The Committee was disturbed to learn that in Austria, as in other parts of Europe, there were signs of an increase in racism, xenophobia and anti-Semitism, and readiness to ignore the rights of members of ethnic groups, including Jews."

The concluding observations were adopted only after an animated discussion which involved 14 of the 18 members of the Committee and which took longer than might be expected. I served as Country Rapporteur for the consideration of the Austrian report and in this capacity proposed a set of concluding observations which included: "The Committee was disturbed to learn that, according to a Gallup Poll conducted in 1991, significant numbers of Austrians did not recognize the equal rights of Jews in economic life." This was challenged by one of my colleagues as representing my views only. He said that he was not disturbed by the results of a mere opinion poll; until recently the Chancellor of Austria had been Jewish. Moreover an opinion poll on antisemitism covered not only Jews, but also Arabs—as the Gallup Poll would know. Some members did not wish to single out Austria; others thought there were good reasons to do so. Some nationals of Asian and African countries say that antisemitism (i.e. hostility towards Jews just because they are Jews) is a purely European phenomenon, so that it is acceptable to refer to antisemitism only if it is clear that it refers to Europe alone. Some felt that the result of the discussion was to weaken an observation that should have been stronger. In due course a public record of the Committee's 951st meeting will be available through the UN information centre.

Chapter 12

Global Apartheid? Race and Religion in the New World Order

Ali A. Mazrui

Mazrui (1993) situates the emergence of religion as a prominent basis for distinguishing state and social action in the context of international events in the post–Cold War period. The re-emergence of long-suppressed parochial bases of social mobilization gives religion new social currency. But it also identifies it as a target of Western antipathy in the post-communist period and a possible basis for a new clash of civilization. It is this concern, the politicization of Islam by its adherents as well as its adversaries, on which Mazrui focuses. With the increasing political salience of Islamophobia in the time of the "long war against terror," we also see the re-assertion of white supremacy and the mission of civilization imbued in the calls for a new imperial posture for those whose resolve is to pacify Islamic populations as the only way of ensuring the national security of Western or non-Islamic populations. The ideological conjuncture between racialization of religion and the clash of civilization seems more apparent today than when Mazrui wrote, in the aftermath of the first Gulf War; in the context of the "long war" it seems more real and potentially enduring.

Now that secular ideological divisions between the East and West have declined in relevance, are we witnessing the re-emergence of primordial allegiances? Are we witnessing new forms of *retribalization* on the global arena—from Natal in South Africa to Bosnia and Herzegovina, from Los Angeles to Slovakia? In Europe, two levels of retribalization are discernible. In Eastern Europe, *microretribalization* is particularly strong. Microretribalization is concerned with microethnicity, involving such conflicts as Serbians versus Croats, Russians versus Ukrainians, and Czechs versus Slovaks.

On the other hand, Western Europe shows strides in regional integration despite hiccups as the 1992 referendum in Denmark against the Maastricht Treaty. Regional integration can be *macroretribalization* if it is race-conscious. Macroretribalization can be the solidarity of white people, an arrogant pan-Europeanism greater in ambition than anything seen since the Holy Roman Empire.

Is the white world closing ranks in Eastern Europe and the West? Will we see a more united, and potentially more prosperous, white world presiding over the fate of a fragmented and persistently indigent black world in the twenty-first century? Put in another way, now that apartheid in South Africa is disintegrating, is there a global apartheid in the process of formation? With the end of the Cold War, is the white world closing ranks at the global level—in spite of current divisions within individual countries such as Yugoslavia? Is the danger particularly acute between black and white people?

In addition to the black-white divide in the world, Muslim countries, in particular, may have reason to worry in the era after the Cold War. Will Islam replace communism as the West's perceived adversary? Did the West exploit the Gulf War of 1991 to put Islam and its holiest places under the umbrella of Pax Americana? It is to these issues that we turn.

BETWEEN IDEOLOGY AND RACE

There was a time when the white people of the Soviet Union colonized fellow white people of Eastern Europe while at the same time Soviet weapons and money aided black liberation. In other words, Moscow was an imperial power in Europe and a liberating force in Africa. At the global level, alliances for or against imperialism did not coincide with racial differences. Indeed, the liberation of black people from white minority governments in Africa would probably have been delayed by at least a generation without the support of white socialist governments during the days of the Cold War.

The end of the Cold War ended inter-white rivalries in the Third World. On the positive side, this meant an earlier end to African civil wars. The war in Eritrea would not have lasted thirty years had there been no external material support and encouragement. The war in Angola would not have lasted a decade and a half if the Cold War had ended sooner. Similar things can be said of the war in Mozambique, which was a child of external racist manipulation.

On the negative side, former members of the Warsaw Pact lost all interest in supporting Third World causes. Leninist anti-imperialism seems to be as dead as other aspects of Leninism. V.I. Lenin added to Marxism some elements that are responsible for the present crisis of socialism worldwide. These factors included a vanguard party; democratic centralism; statism; and Marxism as an ideology of development, which in the end failed to deliver economic goods.

But Lenin also rescued Marxism from ethnocentrism and racism. Karl Marx's historical materialism once applauded British imperialism in India as a force that was destroying older precapitalist Hindu forms, propelling the country towards capitalism as a higher phase. Friedrich Engels also applauded French colonization of Algeria as two steps forward in the social evolutionary process. In other words, Engels and Marx were so Eurocentric that their paradigm legitimated European imperialism.

It was Lenin, however, who put European Imperialism on trial with his book, *Imperialism: The Highest Stage of Capitalism.*[1] From then on, Marxism-Leninism became one of the major anti-imperialist forces of twentieth-century history. Now that even Marxists in Eastern Europe are de-Leninized, socialist anti-imperialism has declined. White socialists are far less likely to support black liberation today than they were two or three decades ago. De-Leninization strengthened the bonds between white socialists and white imperialists. For now, the process of de-Leninization is quite comprehensive. What were once Africa's comrades in arms against colonialism are now collaborators with apartheid in South Africa.

The demise of Leninism in Eastern Europe resulted in the decline of antiracism and anti-imperialism as well. Some Eastern European countries in 1990 moved almost obscenely toward full resumption of relations with the apartheid regime in South Africa before the racist structure had begun to be dismantled. Some newly democratized Eastern European countries started to violate international sanctions against Pretoria even before they held their first multiparty elections. The Soviet Union in 1990 used a subsidiary of a South African company, DeBeers, to market diamonds for Moscow—something that would have been unthinkable before *glasnost* and *perestroika.* Liberalization among the former Warsaw Pact members meant their greater readiness to do business with the world's leading racist regime, Pretoria.

BETWEEN IDEOLOGY AND RELIGION

Meanwhile, another tilt was taking place—not a shift from ideology to race, but a transition from anticommunism to anti-Islamism. Western fears of Islam are centuries older than Western fears of communism. But in recent times, Western anti-Islamic tendencies were ameliorated by the indisputable superiority in technological and military power held by the West. Western nervousness about Islam was also ameliorated by the West's need for Muslim allies in its confrontation with the Soviet Union and the Warsaw Pact.

Three things occurred in the last quarter century to affect this shift. First, some elements in the Muslim world learned that those who are militarily weak have one strategy of last resort against the mighty—terrorism. They became convinced that terrorism was no worse than any other kind of warfare; if anything, it killed far fewer civilians than conventional, let alone nuclear, warfare.

As the fear of communism receded in the 1980s, however, the West felt freer to be tough about terrorism from the Muslim world. Libya was bombed. Syria was put into diplomatic cold storage. US ships went to the Persian Gulf in the midst of the Iran-Iraq War to intimidate Iran and protect Kuwaiti ships. In the process, the United States shot down an Iranian civilian airliner and killed all—over three hundred passengers—on board.

Second, if terrorism becomes the weapon of the militarily weak, nuclear weapons are for the technologically sophisticated. While some elements of the Muslim world were experimenting with terrorism and guerrilla warfare, others explored the nuclear option and other weapons of mass destruction. Ancient Western worries about Islam were rekindled. Egypt must be bribed to sign the Nuclear Nonproliferation Treaty whether or not Israel complied. Pakistan must be stopped from acquiring a nuclear capability. And Iraq must be given enough rope to hang itself over Kuwait so that all Iraqi weapons of mass destruction could then be destroyed.

The third reason for Western anxiety about Islam was the importance of Muslim oil for Western industry. Although Western technological power was still preeminent and undisputed, its dependence on Middle Eastern oil made it vulnerable to political changes in the Muslim world—changes of the magnitude of the revolution in Iran or of Iraq's annexation of Kuwait.

It seems almost certain that Muslims became the frontline military victims of the new world order while Blacks became the frontline economic victims of this emerging global apartheid. Muslims, especially in the Middle East, felt the firing power of US guns and US-subsidized Israeli planes. Blacks felt the deprivations of economic exploitation and neglect.

The military victimization of Muslims took either the direct form of Western bombing, as in the war against Iraq, or the surrogate Western aggression of heavily subsidizing Israel without adequately criticizing its repressive and military policies. There have also been Western double standards of crying "foul" when Muslim killed Muslim (as when Arab Iraqis repressed Kurds), but remaining apathetic when the Indian array committed atrocities in Kashmir.

Was the Gulf War against Iraq part of global apartheid? Aspects of the war were certainly ominous including Soviet submissiveness to the United States, Western hegemony in the United Nations, the attempted recolonization of Iraq after the war, and Western insensitivity to the killing of over two hundred thousand Iraqis. It was not a war; it was a massacre. Admittedly, it was triggered by Iraq's unforgivable aggression against Kuwait. But Bush, in turn, was more keen on saving time than saving lives. He refused to give sanctions enough time, even if it meant killing hundreds of thousands of Iraqis.

The coalition against Iraq was multiracial. Its leadership was decidedly and unmistakably white. Bush regarded the war against Iraq as the first major war of the new world order. Perhaps one day we will also lament the Gulf War as the first major war of the era of global apartheid. Just when we thought apartheid in South Africa was over, apartheid on a global scale reared its ugly head.

The apparent demise of Soviet and East European anti-imperialism hurt the Muslim world in other ways. When a US ship shot down an Iranian civilian airliner over international airspace, the new Soviet Union under Gorbachev did not attempt to rally the world against this act of manslaughter committed by Americans. Would the Iranian airliner have been shot down if there was a chance that European passengers were on board? Would Soviets have been silent if Soviet citizens were aboard? Moscow said it was deliberately not going to follow the accusatory precedent set by the United States in 1983 when Washington led the world in vigorously denouncing the Soviet Union's shooting down of a Korean civilian airliner. When the Soviets shot down South Korea's Flight 007, the Cold War was still on. Many of the passengers killed were Westerners, including a US Congressman. The United States served as the conscience of the world. But when a US battleship shot down the Iranian airliner, the Cold War was ending, there was no reason to believe that any Westerners or Soviet citizens were on board, and the USSR refused to serve as the conscience of the world and to denounce this fatal "accident."

If there is global apartheid in formation, how will it affect the European Soviet Union in relation to the Asian Soviet Union? One out of five citizens of the former USSR was a Muslim, and the Muslim pace of natural reproduction was much faster than that of non-Muslims. One future scenario could be an alliance between the Russian Federation and the Muslim republics. Indeed, the possibility of a Muslim president of the USSR was already in the cards, although with much reduced power. Gorbachev even considered appointing a Muslim vice president.

No less likely a scenario is one in which the European parts of what used to be the Soviet Union would align more closely to the newly integrated Western Europe, while the Muslim parts of the former USSR developed relationships with the rest of the Muslim world and Third World. Pakistan is now seeking new markets in places such as Uzbekistan and may open a consulate there. Turkey is seeking a new role in that part of the Muslim world. Such a trend would once again reinforce global apartheid. There is even a risk that the former Muslim republics would become Russian Bantustans, "backyards" with even less power than they had before.

But not all aspects of the newly emerging global apartheid may be detrimental to Muslim interests globally. After all, the new world order is predicated on the foundation of Pax Americana. An imperial system values stability and peace (hence the "pax"), but on its own imperial terms. Objectively, the main obstacle to peace in the Middle East since the 1970s is Israel. Will Pax Americana not only force Israel and the Arabs to the negotiating table, but compel them to consider exchanging land for peace as well? Indeed, will the Gulf War against Iraq turn out to be the undoing of Israel as we have so far known it?

Before he went to war against Iraq, George Bush vowed that there was no linkage between the Gulf crisis and the wider Arab-Israeli conflict. Almost as soon as the war was over, Secretary of State James Baker started a series of diplomatic trips in order to start a peace process in the Arab-Israeli conflict. There was de facto linkage. The Gulf War that Bush and his allies launched was not really a war; it was a massacre. On the other hand, Desert Storm temporarily made Bush so strong in domestic politics that he was able to stand up to the pro-Israeli lobby and defy the Israeli prime minister. George Bush may turn out to be the toughest president on Israel since Eisenhower. Are there signs that the Gulf War may turn out to be the beginning of the political undoing of the old, defiant Israel after all?

Israel's political decline in Washington, although modest, may be due to two very different factors: the end of the Cold War and the new US-Arab realignments following the Gulf

War. The end of the Cold War, as indicated, reduced the strategic value of Israel to the United States. It also increased Syria's desire to be friends with the United States. Israel may become a less intimate friend to the United States; Syria has already become less objectionable as an adversary to the United States. The Gulf War provided a test for US-Syrian realignment. Damascus and Washington moved closer as a result of the Gulf War.

Most commentators focused on the political and economic losses the Palestinians sustained as a result of the Gulf War. Few noted that this was balanced, at least to some degree, by the political losses sustained by Israel as a result of a new US-Arab realignment and by the popularity of George Bush in the aftermath of the war. The popularity was great enough to withstand the criticism of the pro-Israeli lobby, at least for one year.

On the other hand, the end of the Cold War also reduced the strategic value of Pakistan to the Western world. Pressures on Pakistan to conform to Western prescriptions have already increased and its nuclear credentials have become even more of an issue in its relations with the United States. As far as the West is concerned, Islam must on no account be nuclearized. This means (1) stopping Pakistan from developing nuclear capability, (2) destroying Iraq's capacity in weapons of mass destruction, (3) neutralizing Egypt by getting it to sign the Nuclear Non-Proliferation Treaty, (4) coopting Syria into pro-Western respectability, and (5) preventing Qaddafy from buying nuclear credentials.

On the other hand, the United States' conventional capability—although originally targeted at the Second World of Socialist countries—in reality tended to be used against the Third World. There were disproportionate numbers of Muslim victims. Under the Reagan and Bush administrations the United States (1) bombed Beirut from the sea, (2) invaded Grenada, (3) bombed Tripoli and Bengazi in Libya, (4) hijacked an Egyptian plane in international airspace, (5) shot down an Iranian civilian aircraft in the Gulf and killed all on board, (6) invaded Panama and kidnapped General Manuel Noriega, and (7) bombed Iraqi cities as part of an anti-Saddam coalition. More than two-thirds of the casualties of US military activity since the Vietnam War were Muslims, amounting to at least a quarter of a million, and possibly half a million, Muslim deaths.

BETWEEN IDEOLOGY AND ECONOMICS

If the first military victims of global apartheid were disproportionately Muslims, the first economic victims of global apartheid may be Blacks. The good news is that Europe, in spite of Yugoslavia and the fragmentation of the Soviet Union, is carrying forward the torch of continental unification and regional integration. The bad news is that countries such as France, often "champions of African interests" in world affairs, are beginning to turn their eyes away from Africa toward Europe.

In the struggle against old style narrow nationalism and the nation-state, Western Europe led the way. The Treaties of Rome created the European Economic Community (EEC) in March 1957 and set the stage for wider regional integration. In 1992, an enlarged European Community achieved even deeper integration as more walls between members disappeared (or came down). The former German Democratic Republic was reunited with the Federal Republic of Germany as part of this wider Europe. And the newly liberated Eastern European countries are seeking new links with the European Community, further eroding narrow nationalism and enlarging regional integration. Yugoslavia and the Soviet Union, torn by ethnic separatism, still manifest in the European areas an eagerness to be accepted into the wider European fraternity. The decline of socialist ideology throughout Eastern Europe is accompanied by a resurgence of primordial culture. Marxism has either died or been de-Leninized, but a pan-European identity is reasserting itself on a scale greater than the Holy Roman Empire.

Marxism-Leninism, while it lasted, was transracial. It made European Marxists seek allies and converts among people of color. But European identity is, by definition, Eurocentric. It increases the chances of pan-Europeanism. The bad news is that pan-Europeanism can carry the danger of cultural chauvinism and even racism.

Anti-Semitism has been on the rise in Eastern Europe as an aspect of this cultural chauvinism. And racism and xenophobia in the reunified Germany have reached new levels. Racism in France took its highest toll among North Africans. And all over Europe, there is a new sense of insecurity among immigrants who are of a darker hue than the local populations; some of the immigrants farther north may even be Portuguese mistaken for Turks or North Africans. Where does xenophobia end and racism begin? An old dilemma once again rears its head.

Then there is the racial situation in the United States with all its contradictions. On the one hand, the country produced the first black governor of a state (Virginia) and the first black mayor of New York City. On the other hand, in 1991 the state of Louisiana produced a startling level of electoral support for David Duke, a former member of the Ku Klux Klan and former advocate of Nazi policies. Duke got a majority of the white votes that were cast, but lost the election because of the other votes. In April 1992, a mainly white jury in California found that beating and kicking of a black suspect (Rodney King) while he was down was not excessive use of force. The verdict sparked some of the worst riots in US history in Los Angeles in which nearly sixty people were killed.

George Bush exploited white racial fears in the presidential electoral campaign of 1988. A television commercial of the Bush campaign exploited to the utmost the image of a black convict, Willie Horton, who had been prematurely "furloughed" in Massachusetts and who killed again. The television commercial was probably a significant factor behind George Bush's victory in the 1988 presidential election.

Meanwhile, the Supreme Court of the United States moves farther and farther to the right, endangering some of the interracial constitutional gains of yesteryear. The new right wing Supreme Court legalized atrocities, ranging from violence by prison wardens to kidnapping by US agents in countries such as Mexico. The economic conditions of the black underclass in the United States are as bad as ever. Poverty, drug abuse, crime, broken homes, unemployment, infant mortality, and now the disproportionate affliction by AIDS are a stubborn part of the black condition in the United States.

The holocausts of the Western hemisphere continue to inflict pain and humiliation on native Americans and descendants of enslaved Africans. Approximately 40 percent of the prisoners on death row in the United States are African Americans. The jails, mortuaries, and police cells still bear anguished testimony to the disproportionate and continuing suffering of US holocausts. In the United States today, there are possibly more male descendants of enslaved Africans in prison than in college.

Equally ominous on a continental scale is the economic condition of Africa. The continent still produces what it does not consume, and consumes what it does not produce. Agriculturally, many African countries have evolved dessert and beverage economies, producing cocoa, coffee, tea, and other incidentals for Northern dining tables. In contrast, Africa imports the fundamentals of its existence from basic equipment to staple foods. In addition, Africa is liable to environmental hazards that lead to drought and famine in certain areas. The Horn of Africa and the Sahel were particularly prone to these ecological deprivations.

The external factors that retarded Africa's economic development included price fluctuations and uncertainties about primary commodities, issues over which Africa had very little say. The debt crisis in Africa is also a major shackle on the pace of development. Although the debts of African countries are modest compared with countries such as Brazil and Mexico, it is important to remember that African economies are not only smaller, but also more fragile than those of the major Latin American states. The West demonstrated more flexibility in recent times about Africa's debt crisis, and some Western countries extended debt forgiveness. Speedy action toward resolving the debt problem would be a contribution in the fight against the forces of global apartheid.

Just as African societies are becoming more democratic, African states exert less influence on the global scene than ever. African people are increasing their influence on their governments just when African countries are losing leverage on the world system. As the African electorate is empowered, the African countries are enfeebled.

Africa's international marginalization does include among its causes the absence of the Soviet bloc as a countervailing force in the global equation. A world with only one superpower is a world with less leverage for the smaller countries in the global system. Africa's marginalization is also a result of the re-emergence of Eastern European countries as rivals for Western attention and Western largesse.

Africa is also being marginalized in a world of such mega-economies as an increasingly unified North America, an increasingly unified European Community, an expanding Japanese economy, and some of the achievements of the member states of the Association of South East Asian Nations (ASEAN). In the economic domain, global apartheid is a starker and sharper reality between white nations and black nations than between white nations and some of the countries of Asia.

In the United Nations and its agencies, Africa is also marginalized, partly because Third World causes have lost the almost automatic support of former members of the Warsaw Pact. On the contrary, former members of the Socialist bloc are now more likely to follow the US lead than to join forces with the Third World. Moreover, the African percentage of the total membership of the UN system is declining. In 1991, five new members were admitted to the UN, none of them African (the two Koreas and three Baltic states). The disintegration of

Yugoslavia and the Soviet Union has resulted in at least ten more members. The numerical marginalization of Africa within the world body is likely to continue.

In the financial world, the power of the World Bank and the International Monetary Fund (IMF) not only remains intact, but is bound to increase in the era of global apartheid. It was once said of a British monarch that the power of the king has increased, is increasing and ought to diminish. This philosophy is especially applicable to the power of the World Bank in Africa. Unfortunately, all indications continue to point in the direction of greater escalation of Africa's dependence upon such international financial institutions.

On the other hand, the World Bank sometimes acts as an ambassador on behalf of Africa, coaxing Japan, for example, to allocate more money for African aid. The World Bank may help to persuade Western countries to bear African needs in mind even as the West remains mesmerized by the continuing drama in the former Soviet Union and Eastern Europe. At its best, the World Bank can be a force against the drift towards global apartheid. But at its worst, the World Bank is an extension of the power of the white races over the darker peoples of the globe.

It is virtually certain that German money is already being diverted from Tanzania and Bangladesh toward the newly integrated East Germany, to compensate the Soviet Union for its cooperation with German reunification. Before long, larger amounts of Western money will be going to Poland, Hungary, the Czech and Slovak republics, and the newly independent republics of Lithuania, Latvia, and Estonia.

Western investment in former Warsaw Pact countries may also be at the expense of investment in Africa. Western trade may also be redirected to some extent. Now that white Westerners and Easterners no longer have an ideological reason for mutual hostility, are their shared culture and race acquiring more primary salience? Are we witnessing the emergence of a new Northern solidarity as the hatchets of the Cold War are at last buried? Are Blacks the first economic victims of this global apartheid?

CONCLUSION

Are we witnessing new forms of retribalization and race consciousness just as the more local-ized apartheid of South Africa is coming to an end? I argued that if there is a new world order, its first economic victims will be black people of Africa, the Americas, Europe, and elsewhere. I also argued that the new world order's first military victims are Muslims; about half a million have been killed by the West or Western-subsidized initiatives since the Vietnam War. Palestinians, Libyans, Iraqis, and Lebanese are among the casualties. Since World War II, far more Muslims have been killed by the West than have citizens of the former Warsaw Pact, from the Suez War of 1956 to the Gulf War of 1991.

One advantage of the old East-West divide was that it was transracial and interracial. White socialist countries supported black liberation fighters militarily against white minority governments in Africa. But now the former Socialist countries are among the least supportive of Third World causes. In the UN, the former communist adversaries are often more cooper-ative with Washington than are some Western allies. In reality, Paris is more independent of

Washington than is Moscow since the Gorbachev revolution.

With regard to this new world order, are there racial and racist differences between the Western response to Iraqi aggression against Kuwait in 1990 and to Serbia's aggression against Bosnia and Herzegovina in 1992? Both Bosnia and Kuwait had prior international recognition as sovereign states. Both had prior historical links with the countries that committed aggression against them, Serbia and Iraq respectively. Bosnia and Serbia had once been part of Yugoslavia; Kuwait and Iraq had once been part of the same province of the Ottoman Empire. Iraq in 1990 had territorial appetites masquerading as a dispute over oil wells between Iraq and Kuwait; Serbia had territorial appetites masquerading as protection of ethnic Serbs in Bosnia.

The West, under the leadership of the Bush administration, said to Iraqi aggression: "This will not stand!" To end Iraqi aggression in Kuwait, the West and its allies bombed Baghdad and Basra. To end Serbian aggression in Bosnia, was the West in 1992 prepared to bomb Belgrade? If not, why not? Did the reasons include racism? Was it all right to bomb Arab populations thousands of miles away, but insupportable to bomb fellow Europeans next door?

The new idea of creating a European army answerable to the European Community, as well as to NATO, also seemed to draw a sharp distinction between "military intervention" outside Europe and "peacekeeping" within Europe.

According to Joseph Fitchett, writing for the *International Herald Tribune*:

> Braving Bush administration objections, France and Germany are proceeding … to establish a substantial joint military force that could assume functions previously reserved for NATO.
>
> Conceived as the core for a future European army, the proposed Euro-corps is supposed to ready the equivalent of two divisions by 1995 for military intervention outside Europe and for peacekeeping and other, as yet undefined, operations within Europe.[2]

Is there a clear reluctance to shed European blood among some nations, such as France and Britain, which have very recently shed Arab and Muslim blood?

Regarding the war in Bosnia, Anthony Lewis of the *New York Times* said in 1992:

> The Americans and Europeans have plenty of warplanes, based near enough … to take command of the air…. We could have said to Mr. Milosevic, and still could: Stop your aggression at once, or our military aircraft will control your skies. Not just over Dubrovnik or Sarajevo, but over Belgrade…. The failure of nerve and imagination in the face of Serbian aggression is Europe's as well as America's. But Mr. Bush raised expectations so high in the Gulf War that disappointment naturally focused on him. What happened to the man who three days after Iraq grabbed Kuwait said, "This will not stand"?[3]

Was it a "failure of nerve" on the part of the United States or Europe? Or was it a triumph of macroracial empathy? It was easier to remember British planes bombing Baghdad in 1991 than to imagine British planes bombing Belgrade in 1992. And US planes bombing Sarajevo or Dubrovnik in the 1990s in order to save them seems distasteful. It was easier to bomb parts of Kuwait in 1991 and would be easier to rebomb Tripoli and Baghdad in 1992 and 1993.

Long before the end of the Cold War, I had occasion to worry publicly about a "global caste system" in the making. I argued in a book published in 1977 that the international stratification did not have the flexibility and social mobility of a class structure, but had some of the rigidities of caste:

> If the international system was, in the first half of the twentieth century a class system, it is now moving in the direction of rigidity. We may be witnessing the consolidation of a global caste structure.... Just as there are hereditary factors in domestic castes, so there are hereditary elements in international castes. Pre-eminent among those factors is the issue of *race*.... If people of European extraction are the Brahmins of the international caste system, the Black people belong disproportionately to the caste of the untouchables. Between the highest international caste [Whites] and the lowest [Blacks] are other ranks and estates such as Asians.[4]

What prevented this global caste system from becoming global apartheid at that time was, ironically, the Cold War, which divided the white world ideologically. Rivalry between the two white power blocs averted the risk of racial solidarity among the more prosperous whites. The white world was armed to the teeth against each other. This was unlike apartheid in South Africa. At the global level, we had Brahmins at dagger points.[5]

But there is now a closing of ranks among the white peoples of the world. The ethnic hiccups of Yugoslavia and the Soviet Union notwithstanding, and after allowing for Denmark's caution and Britain's relative insularity, the mood in Europe is still toward greater continental union. Pan-Europeanism is reaching levels greater than anything experienced since the Holy Roman Empire. The question that arises is whether this new pan-European force, combined with the economic trend towards a mega–North America, will produce a human race more than ever divided between prosperous white races and poverty-stricken Blacks. Is a global macroretribalization in the making?

The era of global apartheid coincided with the era of a unipolar world—a global system with only one superpower. The declining fear of communism may reactivate an older Western fear of Islam. The location of petroleum disproportionately in Muslim lands, combined with the tensions of the Arab-Israeli conflict, cost the Muslim world upward of half a million lives as a result of military actions by the United States and its allies during the Reagan and Bush administrations. The main victims were Libyans, Iranians, Lebanese, Palestinians, and, most recently, Iraqis.

Race and religion remain potent forces in global affairs. Historically, race has been the fundamental divisive factor between Westerners and people of African descent almost everywhere. Religion has been the fundamental divisive factor between Westerners and people of Muslim culture almost everywhere. Was the collapse of the Berlin Wall in 1989 the beginning of the racial reunification of the white world? Did the Gulf War of 1991 put the holiest places of Islam under the imperial umbrella of Pax Americana? Is the twentieth century getting ready to hand over to the twenty-first century a new legacy of global apartheid? The trends are ominous, but let us hope that they are not irreversible.

NOTES

1. V.I. Lenin, *Imperialism: The Highest Stage of Capitalism* (New York: International Publishers, 1939).

2. Joseph Fitchett, "Paris and Bonn to Form the Nucleus of a 'Euro-corps,'" *International Herald Tribune* (14 May 1992).

3. Anthony Lewis, "What was that About a New World Order?" *International Herald Tribune* (18 May 1992).

4. Ali A. Mazrui, *Africa's International Relations: The Diplomacy of Dependency and Change* (Boulder, CO: Westview Press, 1977): 7–8.

5. Gernot Kohler used the concept of "global apartheid" in a working paper published for the World Order Models Project (Gernot Kohler, *Global Apartheid*, New York: World Order Models Project, Institute for World Order, Working Paper No. 7, 1978). His definition of apartheid did not require a fundamental solidarity within the privileged race. My definition does.

Chapter 13

The Lore of the Homeland: Hindu Nationalism and Indigenist "Neoracism"

Chetan Bhatt

In Bhatt's (2000) chapter, Hindu nationalism can be seen as representing a form of indigenist neo-racism. Bhatt is looking at how national lore is resurrected and constructed in ways that theoretically undermine the project of "diversity" and "multiculturalism" by asserting notions of cultural absolutism among South Asian communities. In this instance, race becomes deployed not only as a political force, but also as a reactionary ideology that informs right-wing political projects by traditional victims of racism—racialized populations themselves.

Bhatt's contribution focuses on the Hindutva nationalist movement in India (and in the Indian diaspora) and its deployment of the race concept based on heredity as a cultural phenomenon, as opposed to a biological one. He concludes then that the uses and abuses of the race concept in Hindutva are very close to those in Western "race thinking," certainly much closer than is usually assumed or imagined. On this basis, we can also see how the Hindutva modes would travel transnationally, from India to Europe, presenting a convergence of the instrumentality of neo-racism from above and below that could provide it validity for the exclusions it imports.

INTRODUCTION

Conventional Western paradigms of race and ethnic relations sociology, as well as the political practices of anti-racism, have undergone significant internal evaluation over the last decade. This has been partly the result of the political conflicts over varieties of authoritarian anti-racism and identity politics since the mid-1980s. Sociological paradigms around race and class have also been interrogated and developed in a number of feminist interventions over the same period (Solomos and Back 1996). Many of the recent debates on globalisation and European integration have shifted emphasis away from some of the more parochial aspects of ethnic and race relations sociology of the last two decades. However, perhaps the most significant challenge to the theorisation of "race" or racism, the ethnographic assessment of minority communities or the policy framework of multicultural pluralism has been the rise since the mid-1980s of ethnic and cultural absolutist movements in South Asian communities in the UK. The impact of the Rushdie affair is well known, and established the vulnerable nature of the secularism that was inherent in the projects of "Asian" or "black" politics. The affair also exposed an absence in political sociology of a serious and sustained consideration of the specificity of the politics of the South Asian experience in the UK, especially in a way that did not reduce the latter to an ethnography of cultural habits or to "black anti-racism." If there has been a rapid, though uneven move away from the secular politics of black liberation and anti-racism towards issues of primarily religious and ethnic difference, it is still the case that "race" has retained an importance for some black political formations. For example, a concept of "race," and a claim about the value of "racial" attributes is as important for some varieties of Afrocentricity as it is for the right-wing, neo-nazi and racist political formations that are animating contemporary European politics.

This essay explores the importance of "race thinking" in the new Hindu authoritarian religious movements that are dominating both Indian politics and the Hindu diaspora. These movements are variously labelled "Hindu nationalism," the sangh parivar,[1] the Hindutva movement or "Hindu cultural nationalism." Their particular formations of "race" may be very different from western scientific or cultural "racial" paradigms. Because of the relative unfamiliarity within mainstream western sociology of South Asian politics and history, and in particular the substantive historical, political and cultural configurations of Hinduisms, the essay is broadly introductory. Much can be learned from the experience of religious and ethnic conflict in India during and since the colonial period. Many of the political languages of multiculturalism, secularism, diversity and discrimination that are important in the west have a longer pedigree in South Asian politics and administration and indeed have been fundamental to (and fundamentally contested in various ways) in Indian politics. The depth of the debates in India about these matters can inform discussions of these issues in progressive British multicultural sociology and political theory. It also needs remembering that multiculturalist discourse itself arose in the period of colonial administrative theory and practice, especially in the New World, South Asia and central Africa. Many of its older languages survive in surprisingly similar forms in contemporary western race and ethnic relations theory.

The Hindutva movement condenses numerous themes about ethnogenesis, religious author-itarianism, cultural absolutism, the nature of secular postcolonial citizenship, majority-minority relations, and "racial" and ethnic hatred that often appear separately in other examples of contemporary religious and ethnic conflict. In this sense, Hindutva ideology can represent a universal example of the numerous directions that absolutist and totalitarian ideologies can travel in the late modern period. Similarly, in describing Hindutva ideology using conventional theoretical paradigms, none of the analytical concepts of "race," racism, religion, ethnicity or culture on their own suffice, but all are deeply relevant in a combination that perhaps requires a new description, as perhaps do many other contemporary "absolutist ideologies of indigenism."

Hindutva ideology presents a highly overdetermined ontology of *ethnos* and *xenos*. There is, for example, a powerful hereditarian "race concept" in Hindutva but this has little to do with western scientific racism proper. It is instead related to, and often indistinguishable from a sep-arate hereditarian discourse of culture, religion and ethnicity. If the opposition between biology and culture has often been used to analytically situate western racisms, it is important to consider how "culture" already contains powerful epistemic resources that can provide for a sentimentalist racism that is never obliged to take actual biology or science seriously but can still contain a hereditary or genetic core, the latter frequently articulated through primordial origin myths, and the tropes of breeding, cultivation, blood and lineage. This kind of "racism"[2] is virtually definitive of Hindutva discourse (Jaffrelot 1995, Bhatt 1997). There is a different equally relevant Hindutva "civilisational-nationalist" discourse that need not necessarily be hereditarian, but can convincingly be called "racist," and in many ways presents a paradigmatic case of "monocultural neoracism." There is yet another purely "metaphysical ethnology" that arises in Hindutva ide-ology (Bhatt 1999). In this sense, the Hindutva movement has created a distinctive ontology of selves and others that is not easily captured by many of the theoretical discourses typically used to analyse racism. We shall however see later that the relations between Hindutva and western "race thinking" are historically closer and deeper than is usually imagined.

An assessment is presented below that some South Asian ideological formations have come close in form and content to versions of classical fascism and Nazism. This may seem a stark judgment, especially when applied to some of the political formations arising from minority communities who may already face structural discrimination or "racial" inequality in the west. The ethical challenge is indeed to keep equally abreast of both issues in all their dense historical and social complexity and without reducing each to the other. In doing so, it is necessary to move away from a distinct "metaphysics of innocence" (an explicit disavowal of the capacity for ethical judgement that travels beyond the rhetorical labour that is required to uphold the unity of one's ownmost identity or being), that accompanies much discussion of the victims of racism and discrimination and engage in a deeper and more reflexive consideration of the global and national processes of South Asian community formation and representation that by and large overwhelm the binary syntax of racism and anti-racism. Indeed, it is precisely the normative location of those communities within the nexus of British racial discourse (or sociological racialisation) that has prevented more comprehensive assessments of some of the far right-wing movements and networks that claim to represent those communities.

It finally needs emphasising that the discussion below is about Hindu nationalism, and not about vernacular, cultural, historical or ascetic forms of Hinduism, or their attendant beliefs and practices in South Asian communities. However, some general points about the relation between Hindutva and Hinduism are necessary. The Hindutva movement has attempted to blur the distinctions between its novel ideology and historical Hinduisms in general, and has mobilised various strategies of obfuscation and indigenist claims about incommensurability to achieve this. In doing so, the Hindutva movement reproduces a grand epistemology about Hinduism that fundamentally subverts the methods of history and historical sociology. In this view, Hinduism or its essence is in some fundamental way unchanging and primordial (Hindutva is indeed based on this "essence"). The extraordinarily complex histories of sects, caste development and change, and the social, political and cultural processes that eventually led in the modern period to the idea of Hinduism are grossly simplified and reified—in essence, they are stagnated. The similarity with western thinking (for example, Marxism) about South Asian social formations during the colonial period is obvious. In this Hindutva conception, ideas such as brahminism, sanatana dharma ("the eternal religion") and so forth are detached from the historical processes in which they developed and mobilised as self-evident signifiers of a contemporary identity. In this sense, "Hinduism" becomes an abstraction, an empty but normative signification of something that exists above and beyond the histories of societies and cultures. The temporal schemes of Hindu mythology are applied to contemporary histories (indeed, a realism is claimed for mythic temporalities). The Hindutva movement also supplies other grand linear historiographies, one of which, like James Mill, simply divides Indian history into ancient (Vedic-Aryan), medieval (Muslim-Mughal) and modern (colonial British) hermetic periods (Thapar 1996a). Much of the structure and power of Hindutva discourse is derived by intentionally blending (and confusing) mythic, archaeological, medieval, colonial and contemporary time, space and event.

A second aspect of Hindutva methodology has included reliance on some traditional Hindu conceptual schemes and tropes, especially, but not exclusively, selective components of brahminism. Within many forms of traditional Hinduism, its many texts, symbols, myths and iconography are subject to compounded and variant meanings. In the cultural ecology of traditional Hinduism, conceptions of mythic, historical and contemporary times and spaces can cohabit the same intellectual universe without contradiction. That these layered religious and secular concepts may be seen, from an external gaze, to accumulate epistemological or ontological anomalies is viewed as irrelevant to their purposes. This is a distinctive characteristic of many Hinduisms: through processes of accretion, conflict, epistemic breaks, interpolation, fabulations, refabulations and retellings, Hinduism invests its symbols (in the broadest sense) with a vast number of meanings that remain together in a shifting hermeneutic and semiotic alliance. This is a self-conscious process (rather than a consequence of linguistic theory) which is sometimes referred to as periphrasis, but in an important sense it is its opposite: a symbol is invested with a large number of mundane and metaphysical aspects that are known, in various hybrid, syncretistic ways by Hindus who may otherwise belong to differing sects.[3]

Hindutva exploits these characteristics around time, space, event, symbol and myth by appropriating the symbols of Hinduism and rearticulating their various layered cultural and religious meanings into a politically ordered, "syndicated" and homogeneous Hinduism (Thapar 1991). This has also been identified as a key characteristic of the history of brahminism, which mobilised similar strategies to incorporate within itself, hegemonise, politically exploit or reach a complex syncretic negotiation with other movements, such as Buddhism, Jainism and the numerous bhakti (devotional) sects. Consequently, the Hindutva movement has been interpreted by some writers as a legacy of the same historical tendency within dominant forms of brahminism (Lele 1995). It certainly is the case that the Hindutva movement has been brahmin-led and dominated, and reliant on north-Indian brahminic metaphysics or ideals (such as the glorification of Vedic and Upanishadic religion and sanatana dharma) rather than other metaphysical narratives produced by other castes and sects, including dalit movements.

THE HINDUTVA FAMILY

Hindu nationalism has a long and complex ideological history that owes much to the formation of, and indigenous Indian negotiation with, European Romantic and British colonial knowledges about Indian social formations, their cultural and epistemic products, their histories and their antiquity. In their paradoxical way, the antecedents of Hindu nationalism are located precisely in that period from the mid-eighteenth to the late-nineteenth-century Europe, and in that divergence between Enlightenment secular rationality and Romantic affective primordialism whose product was itself an unsettled "secular nationalism," the latter phrase perhaps capturing a key instability within modernity.

However, the birth of contemporary Hindu nationalism is usually traced to, and just after, the inter-war period, from 1916–25, during which two organisations, the Hindu Mahasabha (The Great Assembly of Hindus) and its "semi-rival," the Rashtriya Swayamsevak Sangh (RSS, the National Volunteer-Servers Organisation) were formed. Hindu nationalism's key, but by no means only ideologue was Vinayak Damodar Savarkar, an anti-colonial revolutionary hero and founder of the Mahasabha, who in 1923 presented the novel idea of Hindutva, the essence or "beingness" of a Hindu. Hindutva was a hereditarian conception, born from the time the intrepid Aryans entered India and whose "blood commingled" with that of the original inhabitants of India.[4] For Savarkar, a Hindu could be defined as someone who considers India as their fatherland, motherland and holy-land and "who inherits the blood of that race whose first discernible source could be traced back" to the Vedic Aryans (Savarkar [1923] 1989: 115).

Savarkar's formulation of Hindutva considerably influenced Keshav Baliram Hedgewar, the founder of the paramilitary Rashtriya Swayamsevak Sangh (RSS, formed in 1924) as well as Madhav Golwalkar, the RSS's second leader. Golwalkar extended strands of Hindutva to develop an extraordinarily modern, Nazi-like racial idea of Hinduness, most clearly elaborated in his *We—or our nationhood defined* (1939).[5] The RSS is the core ultra-nationalist organisation of the Hindutva movement and has about 2.5 million members in India. It has emphasised since its beginning a novel organisational method that owes practically nothing to Hindu traditions. This is the shaka, a regimented and regulated system of boy-scout discipline involving physical games and exercise, nationalist ideological inculcation and martial arts. The RSS recruits its members from among young and very young boys, reflecting a conscious "catch them young" policy. It has a distinctive uniform based on the British colonial police uniform—khaki shorts, white shirt, black cap—which evokes variously both considerable amusement and fear. Its supreme emblem, "the true preceptor," is the saffron flag. This is saluted as a symbol of the Hindu nation with a bodily gesture that cannot but invoke for an onlooker the period of the 1930s and 1940s in Germany. The RSS has developed several mantras that extol the glory of a united Hindu society or nation. It celebrates six main festivals (*utsavs*) a year, several of which are traditional Hindu festivals, but the traditional pedagogies of these festivals are heavily slanted towards the secular-nationalist concerns of the sangh: political unity and social cohesion among Hindus, a celebration of Hindu strength and nationhood, and worship of the nation and motherland. It would be extremely difficult to conceptualise the cultural, symbolic and ideological content of RSS philosophy as anything other than anti-traditional, especially its explicit secular deification of nation and nationalism. Its organisational structure is hierarchical, centralised and based on the principle of *ek chalak anuvartita* (devotion to the One Supreme Leader). An obsession with organisation and discipline sums up the RSS's quotidian philosophy. However, its wider aim is to literally take individual after individual "and mould them for an organised national life."

> The ultimate vision of our work, which has been the living inspiration for all our organisational efforts, is a perfectly organised state of our society wherein each individual has been moulded into a wider ideal of Hindu manhood and made into the living limb of the corporate personality of society. (Golwalkar 1966: 61)

Deendayal Upadhyaya, an RSS member and one of the founders of the Jana Sangh political party, precursor to the contemporary Bharatiya Janata Party (BJP) developed many of Savarkar's and Golwalkar's ideas into a simplistic corporatist social and political philosophy, Integral Humanism, which became increasingly important from the mid-1960s. This defined an ideal social order as an organic unity (based on *ekatmata*, "the unifying principle" or "oneness") in which *karna* ("desire," especially bodily desire) and *artha* ("wealth," but including political and economic instrumental need), are to be subsumed under the greater principle of *dharma* ("natural law," order and duty) for the ideal of *moksha* ("salvation" or liberation) (Upadhyaya 1991). Integral Humanism now forms the main ideological plank of the contemporary BJP and is based on a view of the ideal social formation as one regulated by Hindu *dharma* (religion, ethical code) which is seen as transcendent and prior to the exigencies of the state and civil society. As in Golwalkar's mystical cultural nationalism, Upadhyaya's philosophy stresses the *a priori* nature of the cultural-dharmic field which exists above and beyond the social and political histories of nations and societies and is indeed the condition for them. Integral Humanism also emphasises an organicist view of the social formation and state–civil society relations, the latter, and indeed all social relations, to be conceived of as non-conflictual and non-contradictory if *dharmic* principles are followed.

The RSS created several other organisations of which the Vishwa Hindu Parishad (VHP, World Hindu Council), formed in the 1960s and representing a federation of Hindu religious leaders, and the BJP created in 1980 out of the RSS remnants of the Jana Sangh, are the most important. From the 1960s onwards, and especially from the early 1980s, one can speak of the formation of a mass far-right-wing Hindu social movement which perhaps reached its peak in the successful campaign to destroy the medieval Mughal mosque, the Babri masjid, in 1992. In 1998, the BJP formed India's government under a broad, shaky coalition and entered the world's political stage by ordering the explosion of five nuclear devices, including allegedly a thermonuclear device, at the Pokharan test site in northern India.[6]

Aside from its political successes, the Hindutva movement has developed formidable, in several respects unique, cultural and ideological strategic practices in Indian civil society that have not been matched by recent secular movements. The emphasis on slow patient work in civil society should be noted, and indeed the RSS often calls itself the largest voluntary organisation in the world. Its self-conscious and deep cultural strategy attempts to intervene in the detail of the ecology, vernacular practices and beliefs of everyday Hinduisms, to reconstitute these into a new habitus, a way of practising and thinking about Hinduism and its relation to the life-world that reappears as innate, natural and instinctive, despite its historical newness and fabrication. The Vedas, Puranas and epics become palimpsests, simplified icons of the new Hinduism. An attempt is made to rearticulate many vernacular Hinduisms, and their epics, myths or devotionalism into a political (that is, a secular) idiom in a way that seeks to fundamentally alter the cultural meanings and symbolic import of religious forms and artefacts. These "neotraditional" methods aim to make their intended subjects not more religious but more political.

The complex and compounded histories of Hinduisms, Buddhism, Sikhism, Jainism and South Asian Islam over several millennia, as well as the complexities of the economic, social, political and cultural formations in the Indian sub-continent are shielded from followers in favour of a monologic view of history and of the social formation as an elementary, easily intelligible totality made up of just Hindus and just minorities, and the conflicts between the latter. The parameters of state or civil society are reduced to ones solely of religious belonging. Culture is a simple inventory of the cultural artefacts that tell stories of a golden age or a glorious and endless war. The familiar temporal scheme of many ethnic absolutist movements is also evident. "Historicity," and "a revenge against history" are customary tropes. History is typically imagined as commencing from an ancient primordial and sublime origin, a temporally illegible utopia that falters because of Hindu failure in faith, or external aggression or both. This is followed by a period of medieval (Muslim) or modern (British) degradation and oppression and a long unflinching war that drives time forward. The present dystopian moment is one of Hindu renewal and identity formation. Futurity is closed with the establishment of a perfected and powerful Hindu utopia.

War metaphors are central to the political language of the Hindutva movement. The movement has identified the domestic "enemies" that have placed "Hindu society under siege"—communism ("Soviet Imperialism"), western influences ("Christian" or "Western Imperialism" or "Macaulayism") and Muslims ("Islamic Imperialism"). India's Muslim population is already articulated as a minority that has been *appeased* for too long by previous governments. India's traditional military adversaries, the belligerent and aggressive Pakistan, as well as China, are joined by Bangladesh, the latter seen in Hindutva political language as a source of Islamic "demographic aggression" against, and "infiltration" of, India (because of Bangladeshi migration into India). The extremely volatile situation in Kashmir is already conceivable as a war by proxy.

The "anti-imperialist" rhetoric of Hindu nationalism, as in many varieties of Islamism, is less to do with the history of British economic imperialism and political domination. Apart from its banning after the murder of Gandhi, and its paramilitary activities in the Punjab during Partition, the RSS was conspicuously absent from the Indian liberation movement that it now seeks to own. Its anti-imperialism is however related to a xenophobic religious-cultural indigenism that is to be cultivated against what are seen as foreign influences. It is also axiomatic that Hindu nationalism reduces all social identities and social, economic and political processes to bare religious signifiers—Hindu and Muslim/Christian, the former conceived of as tolerant, peaceful and inclusive of all Hindu sects, which are seen to include Buddhism, Jainism and Sikhism, and the latter as monolithic, intolerant and violent. This disembedding of complex major or quotidian social, cultural and political processes and identities into pure religious signifiers of self and other is a familiar authoritarian strategy in which the democratic ideals of people, citizenship and individual autonomy are reconstituted into antagonistic, permanently separate religious collectives (Panikkar 1997). It also raises a deeper question about why modern democracies tend to problematise minorities. Hindu nationalism also undertakes the familiar metaphoric substitution of the nation by the idea of the national, or social or human body; conversely, minorities, especially Muslims, are seen as a polluting presence within that body. Consequently, Hindu nationalism is dangerously obsessed with Muslim demography, reproduction and fertility (see, for example, Lal 1990). Within the Hindutva repertoire of blood and belonging, Muslims are for the most part Hindus "whose original Hindu blood has been unaffected by alien adulteration" but who have betrayed their original faith or were coerced into Islam, and now constitute the traitorous fifth column in the Hindu nation. This ambiguity about blood, allegiance and betrayal is suggestively primordial. It is also extremely similar to Serbian (and Croat) nationalist discourses about Bosnian, Croat or Albanian Muslims who have transgressed their "original" Slavic or Croat "blood heritage."

"Global" Hindutva

A significant feature of Hindu nationalism has been its international network and form of organisation. The RSS and the VHP have established an organisational presence in over 150 countries, virtually everywhere that Hindus have settled because of indentured labour, migrant labour, economic migration, as refugees or through the more recent professional economic migration of NRIs (non-resident Indians) to the US and Canada. (In RSS hagiography, the first overseas *sangh shaka* was formed aboard a ship of South Asian migrants and labourers heading from Bombay to Kenya in 1946, and the first non-Indian *shaka* formed in Kenya the following year.) In the west, the RSS, the VHP and the supporters of the BJP are extremely (USA) or relatively (UK and Europe) well organised. However, the sociological features of Hindutva in Britain and the US are dissimilar, and related to the different processes of migration and settlement, as well as the different socio-economic characteristics of South Asian communities in the respective countries. US Hindutva is primarily organised through the VHP (the latter being perhaps the main RSS platform) and the Overseas Friends of the BJP (OFBJP). Its key feature is "silicon Hindutva," the relatively large influence of Hindu nationalism and RSS-VHP ideology on professional, educated and relatively wealthy American NRIs and their families, especially physicists and computer scientists. Indeed, the key US Hindutva activists are natural scientists. Youth and children are involved in RSS activities through the distinctively American summer camp tradition or through various Hindu Students Councils at various US campuses. The US Hindutva phenomenon reflects a characteristic global process of ultra-nationalism by a relatively young community of professionals and students that has chosen to leave India, and yet supports financially the Hindutva movement "at home" and attempts to dominate the representation of Hindus or India in the US media and within political fora. In both areas it has been very successful.

In the UK, the Hindutva movement, first organisationally established in 1973 (though it is claimed that the first *sangh shaka* was formed in the mid-1960s), has been subject to a longer more complex and varied process of South Asian community formation and settlement and the rise of communal-religious conflict in recent years. Both the RSS and the VHP are well established in the UK. Perhaps their most important events were the Virat Hindu Sammelan organised in Milton Keynes in 1989 and attended by some 50,000 Hindus, as well as their Hindu Sangam in Bradford in 1984. The RSS's current UK structure reflects the centralist structure of its Indian parent. This includes the idiosyncratic titles and tiers that RSS members and officers have: executives (*sanghchalak*), organisers (*karyawahas*), guides/intellectuals (*bauddhiks*), teachers (*mukya shikshaks*), probationary officers (*vistaraks*) and full-time officers (*pracharaks*). The RSS women's affiliate in the UK, the Rashtriya Sevika Samiti, has a parallel national structure. The RSS has branches across the UK, and several regional offices. It is organised by region (*vibhag*), city (*nagar*) and local branch (*shaka*) level. There are over 20 regular *shakas* as well as *sevika samitis* in London (mainly in west London, Brent, Newham and Essex). Organisationally, the RSS is strongest in the South East and Midlands, though with a strong presence in Bradford, Oldham, Manchester and Bolton. Attendance at its regular *shakas* is fairly low, ranging from 15 at a local *shaka* or *samiti* to 150 at a city level event involving both men and women. However, at public events, the RSS can muster a much larger attendance of local Hindus, invited Asian guests and other local dignitaries, the latter typically local councillors and officers. In some areas, the RSS has managed to cultivate extremely strong and regular associations with the local authority, the city council, education authorities or political parties. The National Hindu Students Federation (NHSF), which, like many of its US counterparts, uses a key RSS corporate slogan ("A vision in action") is still fairly small in comparison with other student bodies. It is dominated by RSS-Hindutva philosophy and several officers of its central executive are RSS members or younger RSS officers, including RSS *vistaraks*. It receives its instructions from the RSS and its main officers indeed meet at RSS head offices. Its political orientation can be gauged from the title of one of its leaflets—*The smokescreen of 'Asian Unity'*—establishing a Hindu youth agenda (NHSF 1996). During the campaigns in the mid-1990s by the National Union of Students against the activities of the fringe Islamic fundamentalist Hizb ut Tahrir, the NHSF joined Jewish and gay student groups in demanding its banning. A key claim in their national campaign against the "religious persecution" of Hindu university students was the forced conversion to Islam of young Hindu women by the Hizb—a curious transplantation of an Indian VHP agenda onto UK campuses.

The political concerns of the RSS family in the UK and US have revolved around several main themes: the authoritarian policing of the popular representation of Hinduism; the organisational, cultural, historical and national representation of Hindu communities in official public and policy fora; the desecularisation of the languages of minority South Asian political negotiation; the assertion of one particular kind of militant Hindu identity with self-evident needs that have to be articulated, typically antagonistically in diverse political processes; and the mobilisation of community support for BJP-RSS-VHP ventures in India. The RSS has faced little sustained political opposition in the UK except for activities of the small South Asian secular left, some strands within the women's movement and, indirectly, by progressive and syncretic South Asian youth cultures whose transgressions, "blasphemies" and "sin" they increasingly seek to discipline, even though such Semitic concepts are typically alien to Hinduisms. Hindu nationalist sensitivities about the representation of Hindu icons, texts, symbols and especially deities are particularly acute and it would not be surprising if the authoritarian surveillance of the representation of images, idols and text came to dominate much of their activism in the UK, just as it has with many Islamist groups. Indeed the equivalence and convergence in political activism and language between ostensibly adversarial fundamentalisms, Christian, Jewish, Islamic or Hindu, is a key sociological feature.

Cultural Incommensurability and the Field of Intellectual Production

One dominant aspect of the political projects of many fundamentalist movements is the claim that their conceptual and epistemic schemes are unique and not capable of translation and comprehension from a "foreign" or "western" gaze. These absolutist claims about cultural incommensurability are remarkably similar to those made within many recent western postmodern or postcolonial theoretical writings. Religious fundamentalism has indeed provided the empirical example for the most obscurantist varieties of cultural and epistemic relativism in some contemporary multicultural theory. However, it needs emphasising that apart from its many epistemological problems, claims about cultural incommensurability can never be self-evident but are an intrinsic part of the political strategy employed by fundamentalist movements to disavow the legitimacy of oppositional political critiques. The claim is made that reason and rationality, arbitrarily identified as "western," cannot legitimately provide a foundation for the critique of Hindu nationalism since the latter, in the form of its metaphysical spirituality, exists prior to the emergence of reason itself (Bhatt 1997).

Cultural incommensurability and its sibling strategy, the self-conscious cultivation of epistemic vagueness in core political concepts, is a key tactic of the Hindutva movement. However, despite the consistent and vigorous claims of the Hindutva movement that concepts such as "*dharma*" and "*rashtra*" are untranslatable into western concepts of "religion" and "nation-state" or "nationalism," many of the aims of Hindutva movement are based on very familiar modern-authoritarian political conceptions. The Hindutva movement is primarily a majoritarian movement that demands, to differing degrees, an exclusive Hindu *rashtra* or Hindu nation-state which provides the precepts for the obligations of citizenship for all those, including all minorities, who live within the national territory. A Hindu *rashtra* is frequently, though not always, conceived to be genuinely secular and reflecting simply the "Hindu ethos," "Hindu civilisation" or Hindu *dharma* that has moulded and shaped the lives of Hindus, Buddhists, Jains and Sikhs over a period seen to be commencing from some ineffable, primordial moment. In this register, Hindu *dharma* is presented as secular and non-discriminatory. Consequently, it is frequently claimed that Hinduism and the Hindu nation-state are the basis for a genuine secularism. The Indian Supreme Court in its wisdom indeed made the appalling judgement in the mid-1990s that Hindutva was, like Hinduism, intrinsically secular (M. Rama Jois 1996).

Dharma is a key trope in Hindu nationalist political language. Its meaning is held to be both ineffable and totalising and this is central to the manner of its use by the Hindutva movement. It is also monotonously claimed that *dharma* is unique and untranslatable from a foreign gaze. In many varieties of Hinduism, *dharma* has compounded meanings that include religion, religious law (as in jurisprudence), a religious code of conduct, way of life, an ethics, or more broadly the natural order of things, "natural law," the righteous path, following the ordinances of sacred revelation or tradition, "the way things are" or "the way things ought to be." There are many sect and subcaste *dharmashastras*[7] ("law books") that can govern or inform the lives of Hindus to widely varying degrees. In the practical lives of Hindus, *dharma* is more mundane. In many (north Indian) Hindu sects or subcastes, *dharma* can define rules for, for example, caste mixing and marriage, birth and death rites, gender relations, food and the compulsion to respect one's parents. It is a fundamentally religious, typically ritualistic conception. However, in Hindu nationalism it is disingenuously claimed to be secular since *dharma* is held to be the basis for Hinduism's unique traditional tolerance and reverence for all paths towards the Ineffable. The typical religious source used by many secularists and Hindu nationalists alike, is Rig Veda 1:164:46, "It is of one existence that the sages speak in many ways."[8] However, arguably, "tolerance" was an attribute ascribed to Hinduism, and against Islam, in the modern colonial period, and was dependent on the reformative strands of modern Hinduism that eventually culminated in Gandhianism. Similarly, the ahistoricised conception of *dharma* promoted in Hindu nationalism is a distinctly brahminic one, the ideal of *sanatana dharma*, the eternal ethical order of things. These ideas of Hindu *dharma* are claimed to be unique, and Hinduism is held to be a unique code for human and natural existence that cannot be compared with other religious traditions. Hinduism in this view is a complete universal order for life,[9] whereas Christianity and Islam are simply religious ideologies.

Hinduism, in this sense, is articulated in the Hindutva movement as not a religion at all but an eternally valid ethical code, a distinct orientation to the temporal and spiritual world, the natural social and political order, the fulfilment of civilisation and a world-view for humankind. It cannot, therefore, be compared with or comprehended by external western or Islamic paradigms. If Hinduism (Hindu *dharma*) can be conceptualised not as a religion but as an incommensurable civilisational ethos, a further claim can be made that Hinduism is itself a tolerant genuinely secular way of being and not a religion as such. Descriptions such as fundamentalism, fascism, authoritarianism can be dismissed as western concepts that are inapplicable to Hinduism (see for example Goel [1983] 1994a, Frawley 1995a). Consequently, state and civil society can be *dharmic* and secular, even as all citizens can be compelled to live by Hindu *dharma* and love and adulation for the Hindu nation.

This kind of holistic revolutionary conservatism is not, however, simply the package of prejudice and exclusivist identity politics that emerges in its political languages. The Hindutva movement has cultivated its own "field of intellectual production: (Bourdieu 1991). Whatever the critical rational evaluation of its intellectual content, Hindu nationalism is a deeply intellectual enterprise and it would be a fundamental error to reduce its intellectual and cultural strategy to "chauvinism" or propaganda, or to reduce its political trajectory to only that of seeking elected power or political representation. In Hindu nationalism one can speak of the creation of a major revisionist project around nation, state, civil society, culture, religion, ethnicity, metaphysics and human origins. Its form is manifest in the now incalculably large body of literature produced or fundamentally influenced by far-right-wing Hindu nationalist ideologues. This has attempted to breach the boundaries and methods of research and verification within several intellectual disciplines, including social and cultural history, ancient and medieval history, archaeology, philosophy and metaphysics, anthropology, sociology, political science, religious studies, natural science and mathematics, education and pedagogy, astronomy, linguistics, comparative philology and human geography. In the process the Hindutva movement has managed to carve out a characteristic intellectual field. This has a typically antagonistic conceptual border (anti-secular, anti-Muslim, anti-marxist, anti-western) that is necessary for its reproduction. Its intellectual content is reproduced by a relatively large and international orbit of writers and critics. Its political languages and academic-nationalist thematics are discrete, distinguishable, and broadly unified. Its intellectual disagreements occur within its own field and mutually reinforce the field itself, but much of the core and productive nationalist content and its "thematic and lexical ramifications" are shared.

THE LONG NINETEENTH CENTURY

The intellectual antecedents of both the Hindutva movement and of many modern Hinduisms are complex and related to several ideological currents, prominent from the mid-1850s that were concerned to represent, and in many ways recreate Hinduism in relation to modern political and social systems during a period of colonial domination. There are several aspects of this complex and diverse period of the mid-nineteenth-century "Hindu Renaissance" that are worth noting briefly because they have important contemporary resonances. This period can also be viewed as reconstructive of certain strands of especially, but not exclusively, elite, brahminic or higher-caste Hindu thinking. In the face of the challenge and ethical claims of colonial Christianity, several mostly elite organisations undertook the project of demonstrating the ethical content or superiority of an intellectual Hinduism that was concerned to shed what was perceived as its polytheism and idolatry and its backward practices regarding the status of women and the injustice of the caste system. Both the liberal Brahmo Samaj (1828) and the "fundamentalist" Arya Samaj (1875) can be seen as representative of some of these strands.

As important was the necessity of negotiating with key political concepts that made a modernist Hinduism thinkable: nation, the people, citizenship, self-determination, representation, equality, autonomy, state and civil society. Put differently, how could elite Hinduism reconstruct itself within the framework of modern procedural, bureaucratic, scientific and technical rationality? How could Hinduism simultaneously negotiate both secular rationality and affective nationalism in a period of colonial and imperial domination? Perhaps the third important strand was an intense negotiation with, and recovery of, important philosophical aspects of Vedic and Upanishadic Hinduism, which elite Hinduism could use to develop an epistemic and ethical resource both for modernity and against western colonial modernity. A related and powerful syncretic current from within the nineteenth century "Hindu Renaissance" that continued to resonate deeply in numerous, otherwise antagonistic conceptions of modern Hinduism in this century was the belief not only in the universality of Hinduism but of its relevance outside India. Hinduism was not necessarily superior to other religious or ideological systems, though that claim was (and is) enunciated often enough, but rather that its metaphysical resources and epistemic and ethical systems, especially those of tolerance, peace, pluralism, and organicist reverence for all of creation provided a foundational example for all other ideological and political systems. Hinduism's revelation was the *a priori* for all other religious systems. Hinduism in some fundamental way could not be compared to any other religion, just as India was a country unlike any other. In this register, deeply resonant in the contemporary Hindutva movement, Hinduism was the seat of all religion and revelation, just as India was the cradle of all civilisation.

The Aryas: Philology and Ethnology

Another important though often ambiguous strand emerged during the nineteenth century that was concerned with the recovery of the Hindu present by cultivating its primordial past. This was quite fundamentally reliant on the discoveries from the mid-eighteenth century of both British philology and Germany Indology. The contemporary Hindutva movement also closely follows the epistemic trajectory of early Indology, expressed through that early German love affair with India during the late eighteenth century, in the period during and after the French revolution. Charles Wilkins's translation of Sanskrit and Sir William Jones's discovery in the 1780s of the philological similarities between Greek, Latin and archaic Sanskrit, and his discussions of the antiquity and perfection of the Sanskrit language and its grammar, provided rich material for those who sought a new, non-Biblical, and importantly a non-Semitic, non-Hebraic origin for "the obscurer portions" of European, especially German history and civilisation (Poliakov 1974). In Germany and to a lesser degree France, from the eighteenth century onwards, this became a major justification for the fascination with India.

Frederick Schlegel's *On the language and wisdom of the Indians* (Schlegel 1849), published in 1808, contained several key points that were to become so effective later: India received the primordial revelation (and, he added, the primordial errors); world civilisation emerged either from Indian migration out of India or from Indian influence; Greek, Latin, Hebraic and Arabic language and mythology are already both superseded and captured in Sanskrit and in the Vedic religion; Indian spiritual and mystical reverence for a "northern place" was the basis for Indian outward migration, which led ultimately to the formation of the Teutonic races in northern Europe.[10]

For Schlegel the Teutons were descendants of the primordial Indians (for his brother August Wilhelm, Germany was the "orient of Europe"). Similar themes were to differing degrees embraced by other writers. India was seen as the site of the first revelation (Herder) or civilisation (Kant, among numerous Enlightenment thinkers, including the encylopaedists). Hinduism's key concepts, such as "metempsychosis" provided other writers with a "pessimistic immortalism" which was contrasted with life-denying ethics of Judaeo-Christianity (Schopenhauer). However, much of this "arche-philology" became immensely complicated towards the late eighteenth century. Max Muller, the British-German Indologist, had in the mid-1800s argued comprehensively for the popularisation of "the technical term, Aryan" to refer to the group of languages which Frederick Schlegel had earlier called "Indo-Germanic" and Franz Bopp had called "Indo-European" (various other names were popular in Britain, including "Japhetic," "Sanskritic" or "Mediterranean"). "Aryan," which was borrowed from the archaic Sanskrit *arya*[11] and the Zend Avestan *airya*, "had the advantage of being short, and being of foreign origin lending itself more easily to any technical definition" (Muller 1881: 205). Muller also explicitly and often inadvertently created a convergence between the *arya* language and the *arya* people, itself reflective of a problematic disciplinary equivalence between comparative philology and ethnology that was to have such horrifying consequences in this century. Some of this was based on translations of the Rig Veda which, it was claimed, showed the Aryans as both a warrior race and one that was distinctly organised on racial-colour and "nobility"[12] hierarchies (caste). The *aryas*, it was claimed, had a definitive xenology whose victims were the ("dark-skinned, stub-nosed") *dasyus*, *mlecchas* ("foreigners" or "barbarians") and other non-*arya* speaking groups (Thapar 1996a).

The third, and perhaps consequential focus was on the origins of the Aryans. Schlegel's original lineage was increasingly modified (a project that continues to today) and the primordial Aryan homeland moved westwards and northwards out of India proper and settled variously in Persia, the Caucasus, the Russian steppe, "Atlantis," Lithuania or the Balkans generally, the Mediterranean or Greece, Germany, Scandinavia, Eire and even the North Pole.[13]

Max Muller, exasperated by many of these debates, retracted his earlier discussions of the Aryans as a racial rather than a linguistic group, and was eventually to conclude that the primordial Aryan linguistic homeland was "somewhere in Asia" (Muller 1888: 127). However, Aryanist thinking had already travelled widely and by the mid 1800s in the hands of Joseph Arthur de Gobineau, became a fully-fledged theory of white Aryan-noble racial supremacy. In the case of Houston Stewart Chamberlain, Wagner and the Bayreuth Circle, it became a vicious anti-semitism (Mosse 1966), a refraction of an earlier metaphysics in which the Judeo-Christian and the Hindu-Buddhist were antagonistically polarised (Schopenhauer 1890).

Aryanism and Hindutva

The importance of Aryanism for the contemporary Hindutva movement has been highlighted by the Indian historian Romila Thapar (1996b). A distinctive variety of Aryanist thinking, often metonymically linked to a separate hereditarian discourse, aspects of which were already embedded in many varieties of Hinduism, became an important current from the late nineteenth century in colonial India itself. Hindu discussions about Aryan origins are probably best represented in the speeches and writings of the nationalist activist and spiritualist Aurobindo Ghose during the early part of this century. Aurobindo, a spiritual source of emulation for both the Hindutva movement and for some remarkably reactionary strands of a burgeoning "New Age evolutionism" (Danino and Nahar 1996), stated that Aryans were autochthonous to India and the theory of an Aryan migration into or invasion of India was a British colonialist myth that sought to deny India's unique, superlative nature.

However, Hindutva appropriations of Aryanism only really became important after the 1930s. For the founders of the contemporary Hindutva movement, western Aryanism presented an obvious epistemic problem. The evidences of English and German comparative linguistics and Indology suggested Aryans entered from outside physical India, and hence the idea of an immemorial originary cultural hearth in which the physical land, culture and people intermingled to give rise to Hindu civilisation is already disturbed at its origin by a founding presence which is alien to the land. In the 1920s Savarkar indeed initially argued for a hybrid origin for Vedic civilisation: it was the mixture of the blood of the Aryans and the people they encountered that gave rise to Vedic-Hindu civilisation, though evidently only the Aryan blood was of any consequence. Savarkar articulated the birth of Vedic civilisation through a Lamarckian conception whereby the physical land and environment impressed upon, and was conversely affected by the Aryan people so as to instil a unique *hereditary* quality to land, culture and people. Savarkar provided an archetypal genealogy of cultural hearth and reverence for the land, imagined as the first and best land of the Aryans. The essence of Aryan culture was *hindutva*, the "beingness" of a Hindu that defines a common nation (*rashtra*), race (*jati*) and civilisation (*sankskriti* culture). Hindutva is transmitted patrilinearly by blood and apprehended by a *feeling*, a structure of emotion that makes a Hindu realise his or her true connection with the sublime civilisation of the Vedic Aryans (Savarkar [1923] 1989). Savarkar's powerful "race concept" combines land, heredity, affect, an ancestral blood community, and an originary Vedism. But, at least in its earlier form, it still depended on an external invasive event.

In later Hindutva writers, just as in Aurobindo's writings, this hybrid, syncretic Aryan origin for Hinduism is simply rejected and, in a fundamentally instructive move, Schlegel's (and indeed the Enlightenment's) original thesis is resurrected. For Golwalkar, the RSS's second and perhaps most important "Supreme Guide and Philosopher," the idea of an Aryan invasion of India was a product of colonialism, aimed to denigrate Hindus. Against this view, Golwalkar stated that Hindus had existed in India from time immemorial: "Undoubtedly … we Hindus have been in undisputed and undisturbed possession of this land for over 8 or even 10 thousand years before the land was invaded by any foreign race." (Golwalkar [1939] 1944)

FROM LANGUAGE TO ARCHAEOLOGY

[…] It is exactly around these issues the Hindutva movement and its western New Age[14] apologists have forcefully intervened over the last few years in an imposing revisionist project that has regenerated an epistemic obsession with primordial Aryanism in many Hindutva or Hinducentric circles (Gupta 1996; Singh 1995; Sethna 1989, 1992; Talageri 1993a, 1993b; Rajaram 1995; Rajaram and Frawley 1997; Shendge 1996; Danino and Nahar 1996; Kak 1989 and 1992; Feuerstein, Kak and Frawley 1995). The rewriting of history, both medieval[15] and ancient, has become a dominant theme in the literary outpourings of the Hindutva movement, as well as of other Hinducentric efforts. The project appropriated by the Hindutva movement may well be dependent on a recent intellectual reassessment of India's and Pakistan's antiquity in which more recent archaeological and geographical discoveries might suggest that the Indus Valley civilisations were both more extensive and older than may have been assumed. However, the pace of actual archaeological scholarship, the possibilities of rethinking Indian antiquity against western colonial distortions, and the speculations and fancies of Hindu nationalists have become mixed up in these recent interventions. The Hindutva movement has instead attempted to set the agenda for debate and create "commonsense" world-views about India's and Pakistan's antiquity that shortcut the methods of traditional scholarship, and which would have relied, in different circumstances, on a necessary mobilisation of the whole critical intellectual process itself.

It is in the interests of the Hindutva movement to claim, despite the archaeological and linguistic evidence to the contrary, that the Indus Valley civilisation was Aryan in language, culture, ethnicity and "nobility," Vedic in religion, and Sanskritic in civilisation. Several other consequences immediately follow, for such claims imply that Aryans were autochthonous and not usurpers, that a fundamentally Aryan civilisation was the first world civilisation, that all other civilisations were its direct or indirect products, that the differentiations between Indo-Aryan and other Indian languages are colonial racist fabrications, and that, instead, all Indian languages and cultural products are essentially derived from one ethnic, indigenous, non-invasive Aryan culture and civilisation. This, of course, also provides a far greater lineage for Hinduism, and confirms not only its primordial antiquity, but its superlative and original genesis in that first civilisational hearth, "the best land of the Aryans." The congruence of this Aryan "prehistory" with that developed in early German orientalism, and its exact mirroring in the western racial Aryanism that animated the pre-Nazi and Nazi periods, is less important than the general Aryan primordialism that all these tendencies share.

Much of this unsettled Hindutva Aryanist thinking, which can itself be cloaked in volkish "anti-racist" and "anti-imperialist" rhetoric, illustrates how *varieties of Aryanism* are important to contemporary politics, and that Aryanism continues to be a resource for origin myths that are not completed by the kind of specifically western white Aryanism that dominated Europe, and especially Germany, earlier this century. In late modernity, authoritarian movements have arisen again that seek to ideologically combine an organic and holistic natural social order, a purified nationality, a primeval mysticism, and a belief in a superlative civilisation that was created by an ancestral community of blood.

NOTES

I would like to thank John Solomos, Jane Hindley and Parita Mukta for comments on an earlier draft.

1. Or just "sangh," whose meaning sits suggestively between "organisation" and "society."

2. The term "racism" is used in describing aspects of Hindutva discourse throughout the essay despite its very different meanings in many contemporary western debates about "race" and racism. This is acknowledged to he a deeply problematic area and its taxonomic difficulties are symptomatic of a wider epistemic shift that is necessary in thinking through a range of absolutist ideologies of primordial indigenism.

3. "Sect" is a misleading term in relation to branches of Hinduism, or varieties of Hindu belief and practice, but is used for convenience.

4. Savarkar's genesis of Hindutva is worth contrasting with, for example, Gobineau's or Houston Stewart Chamberlain's or Alfred Rosenberg's view of the racial degradation of the Aryans once their blood mixed with that of the original Indians.

5. It is likely that Golwalkar's *We ...* was a paraphrasing of Savarkar's brother, Babarao's earlier work.

6. The appeal to religious sensibilities during the nuclear tests should be noted. The tests, like those undertaken in the 1970s, were conducted on Buddha purnima. The Vishwa Hindu Parishad has declared the test site holy and is planning to build there a temple to the Mother Goddess (*shaktipeeth*, a "seat of strength") that symbolises India's resurgence as a nuclear power. "We are no longer eunuchs," declared the Shiv Sena. Some parivar activists wanted to distribute sand from the site throughout India as a religious symbol and offering, though this idea was abandoned because of possible harmful radiation. If the literal worship and deification of nuclear bombs whose only purpose is mass human destruction seems obscene, it also illustrates how far the contemporary representatives of Hinduism have travelled from Hinduism itself. The inevitable claim that nuclear weapons

are traditional to Hinduism was also made: the fire god Agni in the Vedas was proof, it was said, that the ancient Hindus possessed nuclear bombs, *India Abroad* 22.S.98.

7.   The *Manu Dharmashastra* is often held to be the archaic basis for many other (north Indian Hindu) *dharmic* regulations that may use, or oppose, its precepts. But the point is that *dharma* is an abstract term for an extremely widely varying series of caste or subcaste, sect and regional regulations.

8.   The full verse (Griffith translation, 1896) is: "They call him Indra, Mithra, Varuna, Agni, and he is heavenly nobly-winged Garutman. To what is One [Reality], sages give many a title [name]: they call it Agni, Yama, Matarisvan.'

9.   This exact claim is, of course, also made in Islamist and other fundamentalist movements.

10. This critical idea of the mountainous cold north derived from an interpretation of the Rig Veda and the reverence with which the Aryans held mountains, possibly the Himalayas, has influenced numerous writers, up to the present period. Kant held this cradle to be Tibet, and later writers assumed the Caucasus. A north pole origin for the Aryans gained currency from various interpretations of the Rig Veda and was pronounced again this century by Tilak, a founder and leader of the Indian National Congress.

11. The word *arya* occurs over 30 times in the ancient Sanskrit Rig Veda, and may have been used in this and in the ancient Persian Zend Avesta as a description of self by the putative groups who composed the original versions of these texts. It is also used much more freely in later Indian Buddhist texts to describe a quality, usually considered to be "noble."

12. What it translated as "nobility" or "noble" in western thinking requires a much fuller discussion than can be provided here, especially because the western use of the concept of nobility has been so fundamentally important in the histories of "race thinking." Similarly, the ease with which aristocratic ideals, nobility, culture and hierarchy are translated into their archaic Hindu counterparts (and vice versa) require much further elaboration. "Nobility" is also of considerable importance for Hindutva apologists for the caste system and for arya xenology.

13. Childe (1926) is an earlier overview, useful for illustrating both an abhorrence of racism and a warrior or dynamic quality to the Aryan. For the current state of debate on Aryan origins and homeland, see Mallory (1989). Renfrew (1987) is perhaps the main scholarly western advocate for an Indian Aryan homeland. The recent, numerous Indian and Hindutva contributions are discussed below, and tend to argue for an Aryan primordial homeland in the east, especially in northern- or central-eastern India.

14. The relation between some syncretic western spiritual movements and varieties of deep conservatism, including racism and racial Aryanism, are considerable. The transmutation of some strands of the New Thought movement and some strands of Theosophy in the earlier parts of this century into a specifically Aryan religion, Ariosophy, which formed the epistemic content for Nazism's natural religion has been brilliantly described by Goodrick-Clarke (1985). It is important to note the marriage between the far-right Hindutva ideology and western New Ageism in the works of writer like David Frawley (1994, 1995a, 1995b),

who is both a key apologist for the Hindutva movement and author of various New Age books on Vedic astrology, oracles and yoga. Similarly, Subhash Kak, a collaborator on a work that is both distinctively New Ageist and rehearses the Hindutva obsession with a arya-Vedic primordialism (Feuerstein, Kak and Frawley 1995), is also a Hindu nationalist writer who has a substantial publications record on Aryans in *Mankind Quarterly*, perhaps the most important academic racist eugenicist journal in the west.

15. The revision of medieval Indian history is at least as important to the Hindutva project, and in many respects far more important for its immediate political purposes than the obsession with ancient India, but cannot be discussed here for reasons of space. However, it should be noted that historical revisionism around the medieval, especially Mughal period constitutes a monumental project for the Hindutva movement. The project is single-minded in its desire to demonstrate that the medieval period was one of Muslim religious conquest and oppression of non-aggressive and tolerant Hindus. Virtually everything disagreeable within Hinduism is traced to this period and viewed as either as a consequence of Islamic rule or as an intrinsic attribute of Islam that has polluted Hinduism. This includes caste and caste discrimination, tribe formation, purdah, harems, bonded labour systems, corruption, poverty, women's oppression, educational backwardness, obscurantism, alongside the more typical discussions of religious oppression of Hindus, genocide, minorityism and so forth (Lal 1992, 1994, 1995; Rai 1993, 1994). Everything considered agreeable with Hinduism, especially wars that can be reinterpreted from the gaze of the present as simply "heroic Hindu resistance against Muslim invaders," is celebrated within this historical revisionism. See Goel [1983] 1994a.

REFERENCES

Bhatt, C. 1997. *Liberation and Purity.* London: UCL Press.

Bhatt, C. 1999. "Ethnic absolutism and the authoritarian spirit." *Theory, Culture and Society* 16(2).

Bourdieu, P. 1991. *The Political Ontology of Martin Heidegger.* Cambridge: Polity.

Childe, V.G. 1926. *The Aryans.* London: Kegan Paul.

Danino, M., and Nahar, S. 1996. *The Invasion That Never Was.* Mysore: Mira Aditi.

Dhavalikar, M.K. 1995. *Cultural Imperialism: Indus Civilisation in Western India.* New Delhi: Books and Books.

Feuerstein, G., Kak, S., and Frawley, D. 1995. *In Search of the Cradle of Civilisation.* Wheaton, Ill.: Quest.

Frawley, D. 1994. *The Myth of the Aryan Invasion of India.* New Delhi: Voice of India.

Frawley, D. 1995a. *Hinduism: the Eternal Tradition.* New Delhi: Voice of India.

Frawley, D. 1995b. *Arise Arjuna: Hinduism and the Modern World.* New Delhi: Voice of India.

Gautier, F. 1994. *The Wonder That Is India.* New Delhi: Voice of India.

Goel, S.R. [1983] 1994a. *Defence of Hindu Society.* New Delhi: Voice of India.

Goel, S.R. 1994b. *Heroic Hindu Resistance to Muslim Invaders.* New Delhi: Voice of India.

Golwalkar, M.S. [1939] 1944. *We, Or Our Nationhood Defined*, second edn. Nagpur: Bharat Publications.

Golwalkar, M.S. 1966. *Bunch of Thoughts*. Bangalore: Vikrama Prakashan.

Goodrick-Clarke, N. 1985. *The Occult Roots of Nazism*. New York: New York University Press.

Gupta, S.P. 1996. *The Indus-Saraswati Civilisation: Origins, Problems, Issues*. Delhi: Pratibha Prakashan.

Jaffrelot, C. 1995. "The idea of the Hindu race." In P. Robb, ed., *The Concept of Race in South Asia*. Delhi: Oxford University Press.

Jois, M.R. 1996. *Supreme Court Judgment on Hindutva: An Important Landmark*. New Delhi: Suruchi Prakashan.

Kak, S.C. 1989. "Indus writing," *Mankind Quarterly* 30: 113–118.

Kak, S.C. 1992. "The Indus tradition and the Indo-Aryans," *Mankind Quarterly* 32: 195–213.

Lal, K.S. 1990. *Indian Muslims—Who Are They?* New Delhi: Voice of India.

Lal, K.S. 1992. *The Legacy of Muslim Rule in India*. New Delhi: Aditya Prakashan.

Lal, K.S. 1994. *Muslim Slave System in Medieval India*. New Delhi: Aditya Prakashan.

Lal, K.S. 1995. *Growth of Scheduled Tribes and Castes in Medieval India*. New Delhi: Voice of India.

Lele, J. 1995. *Hindutva: The Emergence of the Right*. Madras: Earthworm Books.

Mallory, J.P. 1989. *In Search of the Indo-Europeans: Language, Archaeology, Myth*. London: Thames & Hudson.

Mosse, G.L. 1966. *The Crisis of German Ideology*. London: Weidenfeld & Nicholson.

Muller, F.M. 1881. *Selected Essays on Language, Mythology and Religion*, vol. I. London: Longmans, Green & Co.

Muller, F.M. 1888. *Biographies of Words and The Home of the Aryas*. London: Longmans, Green & Co.

Panikkar, K.N. 1997. *Communal Threat Secular Challenge*. Madras: Earthworm Books.

Poliakov, L. 1974. *The Aryan Myth: A History of Racist and Nationalist Ideas in Europe*. London: Chatto Heinemann.

Rai, B. 1993. *Demographic Aggression Against India*. Chandigarh: B.S. Publishers.

Rai, B. 1994. *Is India Going Islamic?* Chandigarh: B.S. Publishers.

Rajaram, N.S. 1995. *The Politics of History: Aryan Invasion Theory and the Subversion of Scholarship*. New Delhi: Voice of India.

Rajaram, N.S., and Frawley, D. 1997. *Vedic Aryans and the Origins of Civilisation*. New Delhi: Voice of India.

Renfrew, C. 1987. *Archaeology and Language*. Cambridge: University Press.

Savarkar, V.D. [1923] 1989. *Hindutva—Who is a Hindu?* sixth edn. Bombay: Veer Savarkar Prakashan.

Schlegel, F. 1849. *Aesthetic and Miscellaneous Works*. London: Henry G. Bohn.

Schopenhauer, A. 1890. *Studies in Pessimism*. London: George Allen & Unwin.

Sethna, K.D. 1989. *Ancient India in a New Light*. New Delhi: Aditya.

Sethna, K.D. 1992. *The Problem of Aryan Origins From an Indian Point of View*, second edn. New Delhi: Aditya Prakashan.

Shendge, M.J. 1996. *The Aryas: Facts without Fancy or Fiction*. New Delhi: Abhinav.

Singh, B. 1995. *The Vedic Harappans*. New Delhi: Aditya Prakashan.

Solomos, J., and Back, L. 1996. *Racism and Society*. London: Macmillan.

Talageri, S.G. 1993a. *Aryan Invasion Theory and Indian Nationalism*. New Delhi: Voice of India.

Talageri, S.G. 1993b. *The Aryan Invasion Theory: A Reappraisal*. New Delhi: Aditya Prakashan.

Thapar, R. 1991. "A historical perspective on the story of Rama." In S. Gopal, ed., *The Anatomy of a Confrontation*. New Delhi: Penguin.

Thapar, R. 1996a. *Ancient Indian Social History: Some Interpretations*. London: Sangarn.

Thapar, R. 1996b. "The theory of Aryan race and India: history and polities." *Social Scientist* 24, 1–3, Jan-Mar.

Upadhyaya, D. 1991. *Ideology and Perception, Part. II: Integral Humanism*. New Delhi: Suruchi Prakashan.

Wheeler, M. 1963. *Early India and Pakistan to Ashoka*. London: Thames & Hudson.

PART 2

COLONIALISM AND RACISM

PART 2A

INDIGENEITY AND COLONIALISM

Globally, Indigenous peoples continue to assert and articulate their sovereignties in the face of "all the forces" (Erasmus, 1977, 3–4) that have attempted to diminish, denigrate, or dismiss them. As it turns out, however, the relationship between indigeneity and colonialism is a good deal more complex than our tendency to speak about it in the singular would indicate. In many cases, Indigenous peoplehood has been severely impacted (though, importantly, not erased) by centuries of colonial projects based on a desire for territory and natural resources, and an innate sense of natural superiority over Indigenous relationships to land and systems of governing.

In this section, though we remain cognizant of the material inequalities wrought by colonialism, we wish to emphasize instead the ways that Indigenous peoples and our social and political orders have called into question several of the fundamental underlying assumptions that such deficit-based arguments have tended to be anchored in. In particular, we highlight the work of a growing cadre of award-winning Indigenous scholars, whose work has profoundly critiqued the discourses of legitimacy that sit at the base of colonial social relations. This work has also sophisticatedly traced the narrowness of colonial assumptions and the ways that this narrowness has strangulated more complex accountings of indigeneity.

Together, these readings offer powerful testimony to the ways that Indigenous scholars have not merely resisted the simplistic, plastic accounts of indigeneity that have served as currency in more colonial, conventional accounts of their cultures and peoplehood. In addition to their diagnostic sophistication, these readings have offered alternative ways forward, profoundly *different* ways to conceive not only of indigeneity, but also of the relationship between Indigenous peoples and colonialisms more broadly.

REFERENCE

Erasmus, George. 1977. "We the Dene." In *Dene Nation: The Colony Within*, edited by Mel Watkins, 3–4. Toronto: University of Toronto Press.

FURTHER READING

Blaut, J.M. 1993. *The Colonizer's Model of the World: Geographic Diffusionism and Eurocentric History.* **New York: The Guilford Press.**
The author challenges the proposition that Western civilization is superior to other civilizations and argues that the "West"—a hallmark of more than three centuries of intellectual thought—is an ideology of colonialism. In particular, Blaut explains that the rise of European nation-states as international superpowers is a direct result of the exploitative effects of colonialism itself.

Francis, Daniel. 1992. *The Imaginary Indian: The Image of the Indian in Canadian Culture.* **Vancouver: Arsenal Pulp Press.**
Using a wide array of popular cultural icons, including paintings, travel writings, and fictional accounts, Daniel Francis explores the ways in which the image of the "Indian" was constructed and entrenched in the consciousness of nineteenth-century Anglo-Canadians. In particular, he explores the ways in which the dominant ideology of the "vanishing Indian" impacted the explosion of motifs (many of which were state-sponsored) around "indigeneity" as a respectable art form.

Wolf, Eric. 1997. *Europe and the People without History.* **Berkeley: University of California Press.**
Using history and anthropology, along with other social sciences, the author offers a Marxian analysis of the imperial expansion of Western Europe and explains how Indigenous peoples were incorporated, to their detriment, into capitalist societies. Disciplinarily, Wolf tethers anthropological insights to a global political economy framework in the interests of understanding the complex and myriad ways in which Indigenous societies and economies came to be interconnected with larger global/colonial forces.

Chapter 14

Everyday Decolonization: Living a Decolonizing Queer Politics

Sarah Hunt and Cindy Holmes

In this excerpt from Sarah Hunt and Cindy Holmes's 2015 article in the *Journal of Lesbian Studies*, the authors take an "everyday" approach to discussing colonialism, exploring the notion of decolonization at the level of interpersonal relationships, in contrast to the more typical focus on public spaces, like those of community coalitions (2015, 156). More specifically, Hunt and Holmes emphasize the importance of a decolonial queer praxis, which seeks to dismantle the heteronormativity of settler colonialism, a crucial point that is all too often rendered invisible by other and otherwise sophisticated deconstructions.

[...]

The material reality of colonial dispossession is often overlooked in conversations in non-Indigenous queer and trans communities about creating a sense of home and safety in these lands. Thus, we choose to foreground these tensions in our conversation about decolonial queer geographies of allyship. We first discuss friendships and intimate relationships as spaces in which allyship can be fostered (de Leeuw, Cameron, & Greenwood, 2012) within the everyday engagements of a decolonial queer praxis, and then share some specific examples of allyship in our families.

Friendships can provide opportunities for enacting allyship and a decolonial queer praxis, while raising questions about reciprocity and accountability across axes of difference. Our friendship developed initially within the context of our scholarly work, but it was deepened through conversations that made clear our mutual interests in issues of violence, power, and colonialism. We also shared involvement in queer and social justice circles in Coast Salish territories, and developed several collaborations, which allowed both our personal connection, and academic collaborations, to deepen. Thus, our friendship developed through undertaking collaborative action to foster cross-cultural conversation about colonialism, violence, gender, and space, rather than just acknowledging these shared interests on an intellectual level. Through these connections, Sarah and her partner also developed a friendship with Cindy's child—an intergenerational friendship of solidarity that honors and celebrates her child's nonconforming gender expression and identity. This desire to *do* something or to be changed through shared experience and knowledge is emphasized by Jeanette Armstrong's (1995) statement: "there's no point in sharing this with you, if it's only going to excite you for a day and then you go your way. You're wasting my time and your time. If you're willing to do something I'm willing to talk with you" (p. 299).

Relatedly, Sarah de Leeuw, Emilie Cameron, and Margo Greenwood (2012) emphasize the importance of relationships in Indigenous systems of knowledge and practice, framing their cross-cultural friendship as one space in which critical interrogation can contribute to decolonizing their geographic praxis as researchers. Friendships such as these require developing trust and communication across differences, challenging one another, and creating solidarity with one another. However, friendships can also be spaces in which the tensions of confronting colonialism and White privilege can necessarily arise as "a medium through which dominant sociocultural ideas are at once contested *and* reproduced" (emphasis in original) (Bunnell et al., 2012, p. 492). Bunnell et al. (2012) make the point that "friendships require ... active, ongoing and necessarily reciprocal work" (p. 493), but allyship within friendships does not always require reciprocity on the part of the individual who is socially marginalized. Instead, we suggest that allyship requires *accountability* on the part of members of the dominant group and is not predicated on reciprocity by those who are marginalized.

Intimate relationships with partners or lovers raise a different set of questions about enacting decolonial practices across axes of race, gender, class, sexuality, and so on. As cisgender queer women, we have been in intimate relationships with genderqueer and trans partners in which we have enacted allyship by providing intimate support and care for partners encountering transphobia and heteronormativity in daily life. This requires undertaking self-education and self-reflection, particularly as our intimate relationships are spaces of reciprocal support in a different way than our friendships.

However, for Indigenous people, intimate partnerships are also spaces in which questions of colonialism and White privilege can arise. For Sarah, decolonizing queer relationships requires that her partner undertake some form of self-reflection on their role as an ally to her work in Indigenous communities and the personal toll this work can take. Important work has been done on the role of SOFFAs (Significant Others, Friends, Family and Allies of Trans People) in relation to cisgender allyship with trans people (Cook-Daniels, n.d.), and some recent work has begun to address the roles and responsibilities of White settler queer and trans people to Indigenous queer, trans, and Two-Spirit people as an urgent issue of concern for queer and trans communities (Riggs, 2010; Morgensen, 2011). However, there remains a disturbing lack of commitment by White settlers to challenging racism and colonialism in queer and trans communities (including within friendships and intimate relationships) and practicing a politics of accountability to Indigenous people and people of color. A decolonial queer praxis requires that we continue to ask why these questions are marginal to discussions of allyship in queer relationships. Additionally, in the context of their relationships, White settler queer and trans people can challenge one another to think about how issues such as home ownership and parenting can become spaces to think through a decolonial queer politic.

Within her own family, Sarah has experienced being Indigenous and being queer with the support and understanding of her White, heterosexual single mom. She did not grow up thinking her Indigeneity was separate from her family, but was indeed integrally connected to her relationship with her mom, who played an important role in educating her about histories of colonialism and resistance. Sarah's mom was involved in political activism and community organizing long before she met Sarah's dad. She spent a number of years supporting the work of Indigenous women who were trying to change the *Indian Act* so their Indian status no longer hinged on whom they married. It was in relationship with her mom that Sarah developed her identity as Indigenous, mixed-race, and as an activist, as she taught Sarah about colonialism, social justice, and definitions of community that were not rooted in identity politics but in everyday actions. Importantly, at a young age, Sarah had opportunities to think about reconciling her Indigenous identity and heritage with her European settler heritage. Sarah also visited her dad at his home in Victoria where she witnessed him practicing their culture as a master carver. His decolonial teachings were different than those practiced by her mom, as he continued to create Indigenous culture through his artwork, participating in potlatches and speaking about their history and current politics.

When she was 14, Sarah and her mom moved to a mobile home on the traditional territories of the Songhees people, now called the Songhees Indian reserve. As a mixed-heritage Indigenous person living with her White mom, Sarah occupied a hybrid space in this community. Here, Sarah saw, and continues to see, her mother's solidarity politics unfold in how she enacts her relationships. She is involved in the ongoing hustle and bustle of life in this community, baking brownies for loonie-toonie fundraisers,[1] bringing food to families in mourning when a loved one is lost, attending cultural events, and visiting regularly with her neighbors. During fishing season, neighbors stop in front of her home to drop off salmon for her. Kids come by with care packages when she is sick. As an Indigenous person, Sarah has come to value these everyday actions as a true measure of her mom's respectful approach to living as a non-Indigenous person within a mostly native community. It is in these intimate acts of reciprocity that her relationships of allyship are formed. Importantly, these relationships unfold in the context of her ongoing self-education about colonialism, Indigenous culture, history, and resistance that inform her acts of allyship with her daughter.

Sarah's mom has also been an important queer ally, both to Sarah and to her partner. She has attended many gay pride parades and other queer community events, actively participating in these spaces even without Sarah's presence. However, the allyship is not just one way, as Sarah also demonstrates allyship with her single mother, who raised Sarah while struggling to make ends meet. These dynamics of solidarity across their interconnected identities and positionalities are central to putting a decolonizing politic into practice in their relationship. Sarah has invited her mom to collaborate on an article about her mother's work at a residential school during her twenties. Challenging assumptions about what allyship looks like, this collaboration involves Sarah, as an Indigenous academic, using her educational skills and privilege to facilitate her mother reflecting on her time at a residential school as a non-Indigenous woman. Sarah sees this as enacting her decolonial politics as an Indigenous person, exposing rarely heard perspectives on the colonial spaces of residential schools while confronting the assumptions about power relations between Indigenous and non-Indigenous people. However, the collaboration also requires that they navigate around complex questions of power, colonialism, voice, and identity in recalling what is a painful and difficult time both for Sarah's mom personally and for Indigenous peoples. These emotional conversations can be sites of change, growth, and strengthened understanding.

In reflecting on allyship and decolonization, Cindy is aware that the very act of telling "White settler stories of allyship" is always fraught with tensions, given that White settler narratives of good intentions and benevolence have been a historical foundation of White settler identity formation (Srivastava, 2005; Regan, 2010). How can White queers talk about allyship without positioning themselves as better than other White queers, or without perpetuating narratives that maintain White supremacy by propping up White settlers as benevolent saviors of the "oppressed other"? While sharing stories of the everyday practices of White settlers resisting White supremacy may be a necessary part of decolonization, it is not a neutral or uncomplicated process.

For Cindy, practices of allyship in her family are not only within relationships across differences (in the case of being a cisgender ally to her gender nonconforming child and partner, or her White, heterosexual parents' allyship to her and other LGBTQ people) but also practices of allyship that involve resisting White settler colonialism and racism, for example as a White parent raising a White child, and in relationships with other White extended family members. Since welcoming their child into the world, Cindy and her partner have consciously tried to parent from what might be called "a critical social justice framework" that makes connections between multiple systems of domination. Early on, they talked about their vision for their family and how they wanted to live their anti-racist feminist and queer politics as parents. At the core of their parenting philosophy is a commitment to promoting critical literacy for social justice within their family, including conversations that raise questions to help their child develop critical thinking skills about the world around her with a focus on issues of equity and justice. An analysis about White supremacy and the history of colonialism in Canada is central to these conversations, which take place around the kitchen table, on their way home from school, or while reading stories together. Together, Cindy's family discusses age-appropriate questions that disrupt the dominant White settler mythology about Canada and what this means for them as White settlers today—rejecting what Paulette Regan (2010) calls the "self-congratulatory version of Canadian history" (p. 70) and "the benevolent peacemaker myth" that form the basis of settler identity (p. 11). It necessarily involves having ongoing conversations that challenge the pervasive colonial narratives about "thanksgiving," "Canada Day," and "explorers," bringing a critical and decolonial lens to examining news media, books, toys, music, films, and more. It also involves having conversations with children that help illuminate the connections between colonialism and the enforcement of a hetero/cisnormative gender binary, such as through discussion of the way Euro-colonial gender hierarchies were imposed on all Indigenous children at residential schools, as well as the histories of Two-Spirit people.

Practicing decolonial allyship within a White settler queer family also means deepening an understanding of the way colonial narratives may be embedded within "social justice," "intersectional," or "critical literacy" discourses and practices despite their claim to do the opposite. For example, it has been important to Cindy that the story her child hears (and tells) about Indigenous people in Canada is not only a story of oppression but also of resistance and resilience. She has sought out children's books written by Indigenous authors that center Indigenous knowledge, community, and resistance such as *Secret of the Dance* (Spalding & Scow, 2006), a story told from the point of view of a Kwakwaka'wakw boy whose family defied the British Columbia government by holding a forbidden potlatch. And yet, she remains concerned that the stories of land theft, poverty, the ongoing traumatic effects of residential schools, and the colonial policies and laws that deny Indigenous sovereignty are more central in her child's understanding of Indigenous people than stories of resilience and strength. Similarly, she is troubled by the way these conversations may re-center Whiteness by focusing on the "oppression of the other" without sustained examination of how Whiteness is *produced* or how colonialism shapes their sense of self as White settlers. Cindy and her partner recognize the importance of not only making Whiteness visible to themselves as White queer people, but regularly discussing how they are implicated.

In conversations with her child about their family heritage, Cindy tries to hold the tension of honoring their ancestors while clearly naming their family's role in colonization as some of the early European colonizers. For example, three years ago her eight-year-old child initiated this conversation:

> *K:* I love you Mommy.
>
> *C:* I love you too.
>
> *K:* Do you love everyone in our family?
>
> *C:* Of course! I love you, Mum, Rosebud, Nana, all of our aunts, uncles, cousins, nephews, and our friends who are family to us, like Aunt Caroline.
>
> *K:* And our ancestors?
>
> *C:* Oh yes! I love our ancestors too.
>
> *K:* Well not all of them … we don't love our England ancestors who came over here and did the whole stealing the land from the Aboriginal people.
>
> *C:* Oh … those ancestors. Umm, right. Well, that's a really good question. Do we love people who do things that are wrong? Could we hate what they did, but love the people?
>
> *K:* Well, I'm not sure. I care about the Aboriginal people and what happened to them.

C: I do too. That's a really interesting and important question you are asking.

K: Yeah.

C: It's not easy to figure that out, is it?

K: No, it isn't.

Recently, this conversation about their family's role in settler colonialism surfaced while working on a school project to create a family tree. As Cindy and her child talked about their English, Irish, and Scottish ancestors who came to Turtle Island in the early-to-mid 1800s, her child struggled again with the painful reality of their intimate connection to this violent history. They said: "I don't like to think of them as my family. What they did was horrible. Why did they do that?" For Cindy and her partner, it is important to make space for these and other uncomfortable conversations as a necessary part of resisting racial amnesia (Razack, 2002) and the familiar White settler narratives of innocence and denial of conquest and genocide, and thus moving toward White settler practices of accountability to Indigenous people and people of color in Canada.[2] Throughout this process, Cindy also tries to acknowledge to her child that she does not always have "the answer," makes mistakes, and is going through an ongoing unsettling, unlearning process alongside them. As Paulette Regan (2010) reminds us: "Settler stories as counter narratives that create decolonizing space are both interior and relational. As such, they require us to risk revealing ourselves as vulnerable 'not knowers' who are willing to examine our dual positions as colonizer-perpetrators and colonizer-allies" (p. 28).

Another necessary yet uncomfortable family conversation is the way they benefit from past and present White settler colonialism, which has allowed them to buy property on stolen Coast Salish land. Although referring to oneself as a "visitor" on unceded and traditional Coast Salish territories does acknowledge that the land belongs to Indigenous peoples, it also can mask the reality that Cindy's family benefits materially from owning land and this ability to buy land is directly related to other forms of prior land theft of her White settler ancestors (and her partner's) that date back to the early 1800s in the territories of the Six Nations of the Grand River and the Saugeen Ojibway Nation. Engaging in critical dialogue about these issues within their family and community (including asking how we can address accountability at a *material level*) is an important part of everyday decolonization.

But critical self-reflexive conversations among White family members around the kitchen table are insufficient on their own. Once again, this highlights the importance of embracing a "both/and" approach to allyship that honors the intimate and often invisible practices of decolonization in home and family spaces, but connects them with other acts of solidarity with Indigenous people taking place across much wider sociospatial contexts as well. Participating in public rallies, marches, and direct actions supporting Indigenous sovereignty, attending Indigenous art exhibits, visiting Indigenous cultural centers, signing petitions, writing letters, making monetary donations, and volunteering to support Indigenous initiatives are only a few of the other forms of solidarity that must accompany acts of decolonial allyship in the White queer settler family home. In this way, we can also see how these geographies of allyship are relational.

CONCLUDING THOUGHTS ON THE INTIMATE GEOGRAPHIES OF ALLYSHIP

In this essay, we have attempted to provoke thought and conversation that challenges common understandings of allyship. We have not provided a clear path or model for allyship, queering, nor decolonization. Rather, we hope to have exposed some of the tensions, dynamics, and unresolved questions at the heart of decolonial processes in our everyday queer lives. Within the spaces of our homes, families, and communities, we have opportunities to develop long-term processes of challenging our assumptions about how we perform queerness, whiteness, Indigeneity, cisgender privilege, and a whole range of other identities. We would like to conclude by highlighting that an active engagement across geographies of allyship requires that we remain open and flexible to shift the strategies and terms of our work with one another. This is especially true within our intimate family relationships and friendships with whom we move across various socio-political spaces and contexts.

Drawing on the work of Jessica Danforth (2011), we ask how these intimate geographies create meaningful opportunities to enact "consensual allyship," which requires ongoing dialogue and relationship-building. Danforth writes "solidarity and allyship are great in theory but when imposed they replicate the same oppression we're resisting" (n.p.). This speaks to the previously discussed importance of troubling White settler narratives founded on good intentions, which have allowed settlers to overlook the potentially harmful outcomes of their well-intentioned actions. These "good intentions" can also be enacted within and across our closest relationships, as we try to "protect" our loved ones from the violence of racist, transphobic, or homophobic systems and interactions. In our daily movement within the intimate geographies of our relationships, we are challenged to avoid speaking *for* our loved ones and our relatives without their consent while also creating spaces in which we can be called upon as allies when desired. As an Indigenous person, Sarah is also continually challenged to find ways to clarify how her friends and family members can enact decolonial allyship in ways that feel positive. Cindy, on the other hand, is challenged to unmask and unlearn White settler colonial ways of thinking and being in the world, and to listen and learn from Indigenous people. In our own friendship, we encourage one another to have conversations about appropriate forms of allyship with our family members and friends, so that we are prepared to act when needed. As the examples within our own families demonstrate, consensual allyship in our homes and intimate relationships can provide meaningful and important ways to put our decolonial queer politics into action.

Thus, we want to end by raising questions about our own families and relationships that we encourage others to raise in their everyday lives. A decolonial queer praxis requires that we engage in the complexities of re-orienting ourselves away from White supremacist logics and systems and toward more respectful and accountable ways of being in relation to one another and the lands we live on, while not appropriating Indigenous knowledge. How do White settlers become informed by Indigenous worldviews and systems of knowledge while taking responsibility for White privilege and shifting power relations? These need to be seen as queer family issues—questions we are compelled to discuss with one another.

[...]

NOTES

1. Widely held among First Nations communities in BC, these fundraisers are an alternative to auctions. The format involves purchasing tickets worth one or two dollars and using them to enter a drawing for auction items, allowing people with very little money to have the possibility of winning. The terms "Loonie" and "Toonie" are nicknames commonly used to refer to Canada's one and two dollar coins, respectively.

2. While writing, we considered a reviewer's suggestion to complicate the narrative of "bad ancestors" by discussing histories of imperialism and economic hardship that led many of our European settler ancestors to come to Turtle Island—histories both Cindy and Sarah discuss within their families. However, we argue it is important to examine the effects of centering *this* story in a conversation about White settler allyship and accountability to Indigenous people in Canada. When we interrupt the story of Indigenous genocide to complicate it with stories about the "original" hardship or oppression of the White settlers in Europe, we have to ask how this may work in the service of White supremacy and upholding the White settler mythology of innocence (Razack, 2002) regardless of whether this was the intention or not.

BIBLIOGRAPHY

Armstrong, J. (1995). Jeanette Armstrong. In D. Jensen (Ed.), *Conversations about nature, culture, and eros* (pp. 282–299). San Francisco, CA: Sierra Club Books.

Bunnell, T., Yea, S., Peake, L., Skelton, T., and Smith, M. (2012). Geographies of friendship. *Progress in Human Geography 36*(4), 490–507.

Cook-Daniels, L. (n.d.). *Social change and justice for all: The role of SOFFAs in the trans community.* Retrieved from http://forge-forward.org/wp-content/docs/CLAGS-SOFFA-social-justice.pdf

Danforth, J. (2011). Twitter feed. October 10, 2011.

de Leeuw, S., Cameron, E., and Greenwood, M. (2012). Participatory and community-based research, Indigenous geographies and the spaces of friendship: A critical engagement. *The Canadian Geographer 56*(2), 180–194.

Morgensen, S.L. (2011). *Spaces between us: Queer settler colonialism and indigenous decolonization.* Minneapolis, MN: University of Minnesota Press.

Razack, S. (2002). *Race, space and the law: Unmapping a white settler society.* Toronto, Canada: Between the Lines Press.

Regan, P. (2010). *Unsettling the settler within: Indian Residential Schools, truth telling, and reconciliation in Canada.* Vancouver, Canada: University of British Columbia Press.

Riggs, D.W. (2010). On accountability: Towards a white middle-class queer "post identity politics identity politics." *Ethnicities 10*(3), 344–357.

Spalding, A., and Scow, A. (2006). *Secret of the dance.* Victoria, BC: Orca Book Publishers.

Srivastava, S. (2005). You're calling me a racist? The moral and emotional regulation of anti-racism and feminism. *Signs: Journal of Women and Culture in Society 31*(1), 29–62.

Chapter 15

Native American DNA: Tribal Belonging and the False Promise of Genetic Science

Kim TallBear

The second reading in this section, from Dakota scholar Kim TallBear's award-winning *Native American DNA* (2013), explores how the rise of genetic science as a powerful scientific discourse has impacted how we conceive of "Native American community and belonging." Despite its own pretentions, TallBear convincingly demonstrates the inability of genetic science to offer objective criteria to provide answers about who is and is not Native American, in ways that other forms of association or belonging do not. She also powerfully demonstrates the extent to which such "truth-making" and "truth-telling" discourses have been invested in not just by scientists but by Native American tribes as well (particularly those dealing with financial windfalls, like from casinos). She also persuasively lays out the tricky ground that Indigenous scholars and policy actors must tread as they attempt to both harness and refuse these powerful discourses, institutions, and practices.

[...]

Scientists and the public alike are on the hunt for "Native American DNA."[1] Hi-tech genomics labs at universities around the world search for answers to questions about human origins and ancient global migrations. In the glossy world of made-for-television science, celebrity geneticist Spencer Wells travels in jet planes and Land Rovers to far-flung deserts and ice fields. Clad in North Face® gear, he goes in search of indigenous DNA that will provide a clearer window into our collective human past.

Others—housewives, retirees, professionals in their spare time—search for faded faces and long-ago names, proof that their grandmothers' stories are true, that there are Indians obscured in the dense foliage of the family tree. Some are meticulous researchers, genealogists who want to fill in the blanks in their ancestral histories. They combine DNA testing with online networking to find their "DNA cousins." Some have romantic visions of documenting that "spiritual connection" they've always felt to Native Americans. A few imagine casino payouts or free housing, education, and health care if they can get enrolled in a Native American tribe. Applicants to Ivy League and other top-ranked schools have had their genomes surveyed for Native American DNA and other non-European ancestries with the hope of gaining racial favor in competitive admissions processes. Former citizens of Native American tribes ejected for reasons having to do with the financial stakes of membership have sought proof of Native American DNA to help them get back onto tribal rolls.[2] One mother—herself an adoptee from a Native American biological mother—sought a DNA test in order to forestall legal termination of her parental rights. If she could represent herself and her child as genetically Native American, she hoped to invoke the Indian Child Welfare Act, which inhibits the adoption of children away from Native American parents and communities.[3]

WHAT IS NATIVE AMERICAN DNA?

To understand Native American DNA, it is not enough to discuss simply what genetic scientists say they are looking for in their samples—though I will do that shortly. It is also important to look back at how Native American bodies have been treated historically, for knowledge-producing cultures and practices that shaped earlier research continue to influence the way science is done today. Biophysical scientists have for several centuries crafted and refined particular questions, terminologies, and methods in their studies of Native American and other marginalized bodies. Native American bodies, both dead and living, have been sources of bone, and more recently of blood, spit, and hair, used to constitute knowledge of human biological and cultural history. In the nineteenth and early twentieth centuries, the American School of Anthropology rose to worldwide prominence through the physical inspection of Native American bones and skulls plucked from battlefields or from recent gravesites by grave robbers–cum–contract workers for scientists. It was certainly distasteful work to scavenge decomposing bodies and boil them down so bones could be sent more easily to laboratories clean and ready for examination.

But two justifications emerged for the work, justifications that will ring familiar in my analysis of genetic scientists' treatment of Native Americans' DNA. First, this sort of research was and is for the good of knowledge, and knowledge, it was and is supposed, is for the good of all, despite complaints by Native Americans then and now about research purposes and methods. Second, the Indians were seen as doomed to vanish before the steam engine of westward expansion. Today, "indigenous peoples" are doomed to vanish through genetic admixture. The idea was then and is now that they should be studied before their kind is no more. It is not the means but the ends that science keeps its sights on.

Given that background, what, in technical terms, is Native American DNA? In the early 1960s, new biochemical techniques began to be applied to traditional anthropological questions, including the study of ancient human migrations and the biological and cultural relationships between populations. The new subfield of molecular anthropology was born, sometimes also called anthropological genetics.[4] Sets of markers or nucleotides in both mitochondrial DNA (mtDNA) and in chromosomal DNA were observed to appear at different frequencies among different populations. The highest frequencies of so-called Native American markers are observed by scientists in "unadmixed" native populations in North and South America. These markers are the genetic inheritance of "founder populations," allegedly the first humans to walk in these lands that we now call the Americas.

On the order of millennia, anthropological geneticists want to understand which human groups, or "populations," are related to which others, and who descended from whom. Where geographically did the ancestors of different human groups migrate from? What were their patterns of geographic migration, and when did such migrations occur? In the genomes of the living and the dead, scientists look for molecular sequences—the "genetic signatures" of ancient peoples whom they perceive as original continental populations: for example, Indo-Europeans, Africans, Asians, and Native Americans. Native American DNA, as a (threatened and vanishing) scientific object of study, can help answer what are, for these scientists, pressing human questions.

Unlike scientists or consumers of genetic-ancestry tests, I stretch the definition of Native American DNA beyond its usual reference to "New World" genetic ancestry traceable either through female mtDNA and male Y-chromosome lines or through more complex tests that combine multiple markers across the genome to trace ancestry. I include the "DNA profile" as I examine the material and social work that Native American DNA does in the world. Commonly used in criminal cases, this test has been referred to as a "DNA fingerprint." Within an individual's genome, multiple sets of genetic markers are examined. They act like a genetic fingerprint to identify an individual at a very high probability. As a parentage test, the same form of analysis shows genetic relatedness between parent and child. When used by U.S. tribes and Canadian First Nations as part of conferring citizenship (also called "enrollment"), the DNA fingerprint becomes essentially a marker of Native Americanness. More than genetic-ancestry tests that target "Native American" as a race or panethnic category, the DNA profile is helping to reconfigure the concept of tribe.

Technically, the DNA profile promises only to identify an individual or close biological kin relationship. But one must have a basic grasp of several types of complex knowledges simultaneously—molecular knowledges and their social histories, and practices of tribal citizenship—or the DNA profile is likely to be taken as a powerful marker of Native American identity. Those who understand its technical limitations—say, DNA-testing-company scientists and marketers—do not have a deep historical or practical understanding of the intricacies of tribal enrollment. Nor do they tend to understand the broader political frame circumscribing their work, how their disciplines have historically fed from marginalized bodies. Tribal folks know these politics and histories well—we live day in and day out with enrollment rules, and we all know about the Native American Graves Protection and Repatriation Act (NAGPRA)—but we do not know the molecular intricacies of the test. Where knowledge is lacking, gene talk—the idea that essential truths about identity inhere in sequences of DNA—misleads us. DNA tests used by tribes are simply statements of *genetic* parentage that tribal governments have made regulatory decisions to privilege instead of or along with other forms of parent-child relationship documentation, such as birth or adoption certificates. Tribes increasingly combine DNA tests with longer-standing citizenship rules that focus largely on tracing one's genealogy to ancestors named on "base rolls" constructed in previous centuries. Until now, tribal enrollment rules have been articulated largely through the symbolic language of "blood." Like many other Americans, we are transitioning in Indian Country away from blood talk to speaking in terms of what "is coded in our DNA" or our "genetic memory." But we do it in a very particular social and historical context, one that entangles genetic information in a web of known family relations, reservation histories, and tribal and federal-government regulations.

A Culmination of History and Narrative

Clearly, mtDNA lineages A, B, C, and D, and X- or Y-chromosome lineages M, Q3, and M3 are not simply objective molecular objects. These molecular sequences, or "markers"—their patterns, mutations, deletions, and transcriptions that indicate genetic relationships and histories—have not been simply uncovered in human genomes; they have been conceived in ways shaped by key historical events and influential narratives. Native American DNA as it is usually defined refers to molecules that track deep genetic and geographic ancestries (sometimes they code for genetic traits, often not) amplified from blood or saliva—less often from bone and hair—via chemicals and laboratory devices. The concept of Native American DNA is also conditioned by complex software that calculates frequency distributions of markers among different populations of the world from whom biological samples have been taken.[5]

But Native American DNA could not have emerged as an object of scientific research and genealogical desire until individuals and groups emerged as "Native American" in the course of colonial history. Without "settlers," we could not have "Indians" or "Native Americans"—a pan-racial group defined strictly in opposition to the settlers who encountered them. Instead, we would have many thousands of smaller groups or peoples defined within and according to their own languages, as Diné, Anishinaabeg, or Oceti Sakowin, for example. It is the arrival of the settler in 1492 and many subsequent settlements that frame the search for Native American DNA before it is "too late," before the genetic signatures of the "founding populations" in the Americas are lost forever in a sea of genetic admixture.

Of course, mixing is predicated on the notion of purity. The historical constitution of continental spaces and concomitant grouping of humans into "races" is the macro frame of reference for the human-genome-diversity researcher. Scientists who trace human migrations do not tell a story from the standpoint of those peoples who were encountered; they tell a story from the standpoint of those who did the encountering—those who named and ordered many thousands of peoples into undifferentiated masses of "Native Americans," "Africans," "Asians," and "Indo-Europeans." Standing where they do—almost never identifying as indigenous people themselves—scientists who study Native American migrations turn and look back over their shoulders with desire to know the "origins" of those who were first encountered when European settlers landed on the shores of these American continents.

In human genome diversity research, faith in the origins gets operationalized as "molecular origins." This refers to ancestral populations that are inferred for an individual based on a specific set of genetic markers, a specific set of algorithms for assessing genetic similarity, and a specific set of reference populations.[6] But each of those constitutive elements operates within a loop of circular reasoning. Particular, and particularly pure, biogeographic origins must be assumed in order to constitute the data that supposedly reveals those same origins. Native American DNA as an object could not exist without, and yet functions as a scientific data point to support the idea of, once pure, original populations. Notions of ancestral populations, the ordering and calculating of genetic markers and their associations, and the representation of living groups of individuals as reference populations all require the assumption that there was a moment, a human body, a marker, a population back there in space and time that was a biogeographical pinpoint of originality. This faith in originality would seem to be at odds with the doctrine of evolution, of change over time, of becoming.

The populations and population-specified markers that are identified and studied mirror the cultural, racial, ethnic, national, and tribal understandings of the humans who study them. Native American, sub-Saharan African, European, and East Asian DNAs are constituted as scientific objects by laboratory methods and devices, and also by discourses or particular ideas and vocabularies of race, ethnicity, nation, family, and tribe. For and by whom are such categories defined? How have continental-level race categories come to matter? And why do they matter more than the "peoples" that condition indigenous narratives, knowledges, and claims?

The answer to this last question is not because favored scientific categories are more objectively true. Privileging the concept of genetic population enables the sampling of some bodies and not others. An Anishinaabeg with too many non-Anishinaabeg ancestors won't count as part of an Anishinaabeg "population." To make things even more complicated, a scientist may draw blood from enrolled members of the Turtle Mountain Band of Chippewa Indians at a reservation in North Dakota and call her sample a "Turtle Mountain Chippewa" sample. At the same time, she may have obtained "Sioux" samples from multiple other scientists and physicians who took them at multiple sites (on multiple reservations or in urban Indian Health Service hospitals) over many years. In the first instance, we have a "population" circumscribed by a federally recognized tribal boundary. In the second, we have a "population" circumscribed by a broader ethnic designation that spans multiple tribes. There is often little categorical consistency between different study samples. That is because samples are delineated and named differently depending on where they are obtained and on how that government or institution organizes its citizenry or service population. There are histories of politics that *inhere in* the samples. Added to that are the politics *imposed onto* the samples by researchers who enforce subsequent requirements for the data, namely, that usable samples come only from subjects who possess a certain number of grandparents from within said population.

But such problems have done little to undermine the authority of scientists on questions of Native American origins and identity that precede study of our genome diversity. In the "real world" of power and resource imbalances, in which some peoples' ideas and knowledge are made to matter more than others, genetic markers and populations named and ordered by scientists play key roles in the history that has come to matter for the nation and increasingly the world. If such narratives are rescripting what is historically salient, they risk rescripting what is socially and politically salient with real material consequences. Native American DNA is material-semiotic.[7] It is supported by and threads back into the social-historical fabric to (re) constitute the categories and narratives by which we order life. Indigenous political authorities and identities, as well as land and resource claims, are at stake.

[...]

NOTES

1. I will refrain from consistently putting scare quotes around "Native American DNA" or referring to it as "so-called Native American DNA," which could be tedious for the reader. But rest assured that I mean the constituted and not simply found nature of that object in every instance.

2. Deborah A. Bolnick et al., "The Science and Business of Genetic Ancestry Testing," *Science*, October 19, 2007, 399–400; Amy Harmon, "DNA Gatherers Hit Snag: Tribes Don't Trust Them," *New York Times*, December 10, 2006; Paul Harris, "The Genes That Build America," *London Observer*, July 15, 2007, 22–27; Brendan Koerner, "Blood Feud," *Wired* 13, no. 9 (September 2005); John Simons, "Out of Africa," *Fortune*, February 19, 2007, 39–43. Takeaway Media Productions, *Motherland: A Genetic Journey*, (London: Takeaway Media Productions, 2003), Film; Henry Louis Gates Jr., "The Promise of Freedom," *African American Lives*, episode 2, directed by Leslie Asako Gladsjo, aired February 1, 2006, PBS; and Howard Wolinsky, "Genetic Genealogy Goes Global," *EMBO Reports* 7, no. 11 (2006): 1072–1074.

3. Kim TallBear, field notes and personal conversation with legal expert working in this area.

4. Jonathan Marks, "What Is Molecular Anthropology? What Can It Be?" *Evolutionary Anthropology* 11, no. 4 (2002): 131–135.

5. Deborah A. Bolnick, "Individual Ancestry Inference and the Reification of Race as a Biological Phenomenon," in *Revisiting Race in a Genomic Age*, ed. Barabara Koenig, Sandra Soo-Jin Lee, and Sarah Richardson (New Brunswick, N.J.: Rutgers University Press, 2008), 70–88; and Kenneth M. Weiss and Jeffrey C. Long, "Non-Darwinian Estimation: My Ancestors, My Genes' Ancestors," *Geneome Research* 19, no. 5 (2009): 703–710.

6.   Sandra Soo-Jin Lee et al., "The Illusive Gold Standard in Genetic Ancestry Testing," *Science*, July 3, 2009, 38–39.

7.   Donna Haraway, "Morphing the Order: Flexible Strategies, Feminist Science Studies, and Primate Revisions," in *Primate Encounters*, ed. Shirley Strum and Linda Fedigan (Chicago: University of Chicago Press, 2000), 398–420.

Chapter 16

Mohawk Interruptus: Political Life across the Borders of Settler States

Audra Simpson

Mohawk scholar Audra Simpson's award-winning *Mohawk Interruptus* (2014) takes up the notion of refusal, and in doing so, disrupts the otherwise hegemonic power of nation-states' claims to Indigenous territory and, ultimately, their own legitimacy. She does so by emphasizing a politics of refusal through an analysis of her own community's (the Mohawks of Kahnawà:ke, located near Montreal) efforts to retain their political and cultural sovereignty in the face of a Canadian state that defaults to the assumption that it no longer exists. Simpson sets out a nuanced argument for what it means to refuse such assumptions, and the manner in which anthropology in particular is implicated in such deeply colonial discourses.

[...]

To speak of Indigeneity is to speak of colonialism and anthropology, as these are means through which Indigenous people have been known and sometimes are still known (Pagden 1982).[1] In different moments, anthropology has imagined itself to be a voice, and in some disciplinary iterations, *the* voice of the colonized (Said 1989; Paine 1990). This modern interlocutionary role had a serious material and ideational context: it accorded with the imperatives of Empire and in this, specific technologies of rule that sought to obtain space and resources, to define and know the difference that it constructed in those spaces, and to then govern those within (Asad 1979; Said [1978] 1994, 1989). Knowing and representing people within those places required more than military might; it required the methods and modalities of knowing—in particular, categorization, ethnological comparison, linguistic translation, and ethnography.

These techniques of knowing were predicated upon a profound need, as the distributions in power and possibility that made Empire also made for the heuristic and documentary requirements of an ecclesiastical, metropolitan, and administrative readership. This readership derived its interest in "new worlds" or "discovered" or "settling spaces" explicitly for interests of conversion, a "harvest of souls" in the language of French Jesuits to New France in the sixteenth century (Mealing 1963; Blackburn 2000). The Jesuits' letters to France gave accounts of their mission, on the progress of learning Indigenous languages, on mapping, and on their need for provisions, but, most important, they provided accounts of Indigenous "culture" and "belief," on geography, on the mechanics of conversion that were of such a protoethnological discourse that they have been used to reconstruct (with archaeology) authoritative accounts of, for example, Huron and Iroquois history (Trigger 1988, 1991). Linda Colley's unique history of Empire moves through genders and locations to demonstrate that Empire indeed required these stories of captivity and regaled them, but also that Empire was very much an uneven process and was work. Here she argues that during the Seven Years' War, "the British learnt first hand the sheer physical extent and complexity of the lands they and their settlers had so casually accumulated. It was now that they were made to realize how varied the people of North America were, and the degree to which their own white settlers were more than simply mirrors of themselves. And it was now that they came to understand far more vividly than before that, for all their dwindling numbers, Native Americans could still be highly dangerous as well as potentially useful, and necessarily had to be taken seriously" (2002, 172).

Thus English and French readers enjoyed "the captivity narrative" of ensnared settlers within an emergent New England and New France (along with Algeria and Australia) that regaled readers with stories of Indigenous brutality, sexuality, paganism, and at times kindness, while also learning about the politics, governance, and gender configurations of these places and peoples in the seventeenth and eighteenth centuries.[2] These protoethnographies and ethnologies had not only an administrative, missionizing, and governmental use; they also serve as an important (albeit explicitly positioned) archive for regional, cultural, and broader senses of history, anthropology, and literature in the present.[3] These sometimes very popular accounts made their way to governments as stories of the difference that "culture'" stood in for in these "new" places.[4]

These accounts were required for governance, but also so that those in the metropole might know themselves in a way that fit with the global processes under way. Like "race" in other contexts, "'culture" was (and still is in some quarters) the conceptual and necessarily essentialized space standing in for complicated bodily and exchange-based relationships that enabled and marked colonial situations in Empire: warfare, commerce, sex, trade, missionization. Culture described the difference that was found in these places and marked the ontological endgame of each exchange: a difference that had been contained into neat, ethnically defined territorial spaces that now needed to be made sense of, ordered, ranked, governed, and possessed.[5] This is a form of politics that is more than representational, as this was a governmental and disciplinary possession of bodies *and* territories, and included existent forms of philosophy, history, and social life that Empire sought to speak of and for.

In this chapter I will argue that if we take this historical form of ethnological representation into account, we might then be able to come up with techniques of representation that move away from "difference" and its containment, from the ethnological formalism and fetishism. … I am interested in the way that cultural analysis may look when difference is *not* the unit of analysis; when culture is disaggregated into a variety of narratives rather than one comprehensive, official story; when proximity to the territory that one is engaging in is as immediate as the self. What, then, does this do to ethnographic form? I will argue that when we do this type of anthropological accounting, "voice" goes hand in hand with sovereignty at the level of enunciation, at the level of method, and at the level of textualization. Within Indigenous contexts, when the people we speak of speak for themselves, their sovereignty interrupts anthropological portraits of timelessness, procedure, and function that dominate representations of their past and, sometimes, their present.

When I first started this research as a graduate student, I found portraits of Indigenous peoples, in particular Haudenosaunee peoples, to be strange in light of the deeply resistant, self-governing, and relentlessly critical people I was working with. When I started to do my work on a topic that simply matters to the Mohawks of Kahnawà:ke—the question of who we are, and who we shall be for the future—I found the anthropological histories on the Iroquois and methods used for cultural analysis to be exceedingly narrow, ritualistic, and procedural, so much so that they could only see certain peoples and practices, that they privileged particular communities and peoples in ways that stressed harmony and timelessness even where there was utter opposition to and struggle against the state. These "patterns" were evident in the canon just delineated in the previous chapter [of the original book]. Again, this is more than a representational problem or a superficially representational problem. The people that I worked with care deeply about ceremony and tradition, but hinged those concerns to the language and practices of nationhood, citizenship, rights, justice, proper ways of being in the world, the best way to be in relation to one another, political recognition, and invigorating the Mohawk language. They did not talk about the usual anthropological fare that dominated the prodigious amount of research done on "the Iroquois" and, sometimes, on them. They clearly had and have critiques of state power, hegemony, history, and even one another that made them appear anomalous, if not aberrant, to the literature written about them. Recall J.N.B. Hewitt's quote that Kahnawa'kehró:non had "forgotten," "confused," and "perverted" what they knew of tradition.

This was, and is, an assessment of knowledge and a simultaneous statement of judgment and value—and one that is ignorant or dismissive of the scene of dispossession and the complicated history of this place and, as such, is unfair. And so it was that I sought to figure out why this was and reveal it. I asked questions about the questions that mattered to the community and I had to write in certain ways, as these matters belonged to Kahnawà:ke and yet were being used to vilify the community and to vilify sovereignty in the mainstream press. Their discussions had import for much larger questions concerning *just* forms of dominion, sovereignty, or citizenship. I want to reflect upon the dissonance between the representations that were produced and what people say about themselves (imperfectly glossed here as "voice"), and I want to do this now in order to ask what knowledge and representation might look like in disciplinary form and analysis when we account for histories such as the one sketched out above. To further that goal, I consider what analysis will look like, or sound like, when the goals and aspirations of those we talk to inform the methods and the shape of our theorizing and analysis.

What we saw from the Morgan and Parker history in the previous chapter [of the original book] is the not-so-subtle relationship between territorial dispossession and science—the way in which Iroquois dispossession provided the occasion for the initial dialogue between Ely Parker and Lewis Henry Morgan. More than merely an occasion to chat, the process of elimination that marks the settler-colonial project shapes these dialogues, as it was the inevitability of the decline, of the death of Indigeneity that shaped the form that Morgan's inquiry would take. The sturdy, the salient, the apparent, the lively sense of an imminent *cultural* death that made for certain things that mattered in the ethnological and ethnographic eye—the rituals, the songs that accompanied these rituals, the precise translation of wampum, the affixing and then dating of wampum—all of these forms of authentication in fact adjudicated a sense of deep skepticism that accompanied the difference that presented itself to Morgan's successors (such as the Tuscarora J.N.B. Hewitt), when things did not appear as they should have. Part of this fetishized, deeply controlled canonical approach to "culture as the pure," "culture as tradition," "culture as what is prior to settlement" disavows or pushes away its context of articulation: the political project of dispossession and containment, as it actually works to contain, to fetishize and entrap and distill Indigenous discourses into memorizable, repeatable rituals for preservation against a social and political death that was foretold but did not happen.

PARTICULAR WAYS OF KNOWING

Thus, context is key for getting at what you can't get at until you account for all this. More specifically, unlike anthropologies of the past, accounting for Empire and colonialism and doing so in the context of "settler societies" (code for proximal-to, or once "Indigenous") is now a sturdy subfield within anthropology and informs most if not all contemporary analysis within those geopolitical spaces. This is owing to political currents, critiques, and philosophical trends outside of and within anthropology that have embedded the discipline within the history of colonialism, have highlighted ethics and form, and pluralized the places and peoples that are now considered viable for ethnographic analysis. Although more critically inflected than in the past, anthropological analyses of Indigeneity may still occupy the "salvage" and "documentary" slot and rely on enduring categories that emerged in moments of colonial contact, and that still reign supreme in some quarters. In those moments, people left their own spaces of self-definition and "became." But this category did not explicitly *state* or theorize the shared experience of having their lands alienated from them or that they would be understood in particular ways. This shared condition might be an innocent tale of differential access to power, of differing translations of events, were there a level field of interpretation within which to assert those different translations, as well as an agreed-upon vocabulary for comparison. No situation is "innocent" of a violence of form, if not content, in narrating a history or a present for ourselves. But like the law and its political formations that took things from Indigenous peoples, academic disciplinary forms had to be contended with too. Anthropology and the "law" (both, necessarily, reified here) mark two such spaces of knowledge and contention that have serious implications for Indigenous peoples in the present (Baker 1998, 2010).

As an example, Aileen Moreton-Robinson cites Captain Cook's 1770 account of the people he first encountered in what is now Australia. It was "stated that the Indigenous people of Australia had no form of land tenure because they were uncivilized, which meant the land belonged to no-one and was available for possession under the doctrine of *terra nullius*" (2004, 75–88). This legal doctrine of "empty land" held sway in Australia until the High Court overturned it in 1992 with the Mabo decision, and it offers stark testimony to the distinct power of one account over another in defining not only difference but establishing *presence,* by establishing the terms of even being seen: a historical perceptibility that empowered possibilities of self- and territorial possession in the present (Russell 2005). We see in this example how historical perceptibility was used, and is still used, to *claim,* to define capacities for self-rule, to apportion social and political possibilities, to, in effect, empower and disempower Indigenous peoples in the present. Such categorical forms of recognition and misrecognition are indebted to deep philosophical histories of seeing and knowing; tied to legal fiat, they may enable disproportionately empowered political forms (such as "Empire" or particular nation-states, such as the United States, Canada, and Australia) to come into being in a very short time. Without that category of knowing and its concomitant force, land could not be wrested from those who belong to it and to whom it rightfully belongs.

Thus concepts have teeth, and teeth that bite through time. By legally acknowledging the presence of Indigenous peoples in Australia, Mabo enabled Indigenous peoples there to finally claim legal title to their ancestral territories. Yet they could only do so after 215 years of settler occupation that coincided with 215 years of their continued presence on their own lands.[6] These historical and legal effacements of Indigeneity are predicated upon accounts such as Cook's, accounts that became histories that dialectically informed theories, which then emboldened the laws of nationstates. The traffic between theory and event moved colonies into nationstates. This trafficking disabled future claims of Indigenous occupation and ownership of territory because, in part, their own voices were imperceptible, or unknowable, or unimportant, or were sieved through analytics or narrative forms that interpreted their aspirations in ways that were not their own and/or were unrecognizable (Andersen and Hokowhitu 2007).

[...]

NOTES

1. The emphasis here on the knowledge of Indigenous peoples is not to forgo the importance of that knowledge in Indigenous self-making or forms of either intersubjective recognition of institutional and political arrangements that speak to these formulations. "Indigenous" is a category of peoplehood that emerges formally in international politics in 1919 with a reference to Indigeneity in the League of Nations *Covenant of the League of Nations*, whereby the Greek government, after expropriating large landed estates, will give part of the land to "indigenous peasant proprietors, but the larger part is being used for the settlement of refugees" (n.d., 418). There is also recognition (or identification) of Indigenous peoples as a subject of concern for the International Labor Organization in 1957's C107 Indigenous and Tribal Populations Convention, which was concerned with those who were "tribal or semi-tribal," defined as groups/persons who "although they are in the process of losing their tribal characteristics, are not yet integrated into the national community." This definition gets revised through time (Niezen 2003). Key to both this definition of them and their construction (self or otherwise) is the consciousness of the global experience of colonization, dispossession, and containment, which stretches this category to include those who are subjected to similar forms of power, force, and definition. A question then emerges as to whether Indigeneity would exist prior to settlement and anthropology and whether it is made only in these interstices. I would say that (a) politically it must know itself as having been in place prior to both, and (b) it is made in its present form through these matrices. As with blackness or queerness, it is made in its present form against whiteness or straightness but has its own varying, deeply differentiated, and sovereign histories away from both. I am indebted to Dawn Wells for research on the literature on Indigeneity that helped in the formulation of this definitional account.

2. See also John Smith 1624; Issac Jogues 1655; Thomas Rowlandson 1682—all in Gordon Sayre 2000.

3. Colin Calloway 1992; John Demos 1994; Evan Haefeli and Kevin Sweeney 2003; Bruce Trigger 1985, 1991; Michelle Burnham 1997.

4. Bernard Cohn 1987; Nicholas Thomas 1994; Patrick Wolfe 1999; Mary Louise Pratt 1992.

5. Peter Pels and Oscar Salemink (1999, 19) trace the anthropological "culture" concept back to the eighteenth century, to Johann Gottfried Herder's notion of a nation that is necessarily differentiated from others, and possessing a history that was generated internally and shaped by language. Note that Patchen Markell 2003 has an entire chapter on the influence of Herder's version of culture on the Canadian political theorist, Charles Taylor.

6. This is not to say that all Indigenous peoples in Australia (or what is now the United States or Canada) remained in situ from first contact. Their histories of mobility (whether forced or voluntary) provide fodder for the question of land rights today, as the definition of "ancestral territory" often presumes fixity of place. For nuanced accounts of this territorial presumption as legal impasses, see Elizabeth Povinelli 2002; Paul Nadasy 2005; Antonia Mills 1994. I am grateful to Nadia Abu El-Haj for pushing me on this.

BIBLIOGRAPHY

Andersen, Chris and Brendan Hokowhitu. 2007. "Whiteness: Naivety, Void and Control." *Junctures: The Journal for Thematic Dialogue* 8.

Asad, Talal. 1979. "Anthropology as the Analysis of Ideology." *Man* 14:607–627.

Baker, Lee D. 1998. *From Savage to Negro: Anthropology and the Construction of Race.* Berkeley: University of California Press.

Baker, Lee D. 2010. *Anthropology and the Radical Politics of Culture.* Durham, NC: Duke University Press.

Blackburn, Carole. 2000. *"Harvest of Souls": The Jesuit Missions and Colonialism in North America, 1632–1650.* Montreal: McGill-Queens University Press.

Burnham, Michelle. 1997. *Captivity and Sentiment: Cultural Exchange in American Literature, 1621–1861.* Hanover: University Press of New England.

Calloway, Colin G. 1992. *North Country Captives: Selected Narratives of Indian Captivity from Vermont and New Hampshire.* Hanover: University Press of New England.

Cohn, Bernard. 1987. *An Anthropologist among the Historians and Other Essays.* Delhi: Oxford University Press.

Colley, Linda. 2002. *Captives: The Story of Brtiain's Pursuit of Empire and How Its Soldiers and Civilians Were Held Captive by the Dream of Global Supremacy, 1600–1850.* New York: Pantheon.

Demos, John. 1994. *The Unredeemed Captive: A Family Story from Early America.* New York: Alfred A. Knopf Press.

Haefeli, Evan, and Kevin Sweeney. 1997. "Revisiting The Redeemed Captive: New Perspectives on the 1704 Attack on Deerfield." In *After King Phillips War: Presence and persistence in Indian, New England,* 229–271. Edited by Colin G. Calloway. Hanover: University Press of New England.

Hewitt, J.N.B. 1892. "Legend of the Founding of the Iroquois League." *American Anthropologist* 5(2):131–148.

Hewitt, J.N.B. 1929. "The Culture of The Indians of Eastern Canada." In *Explorations and Field-work of the Smithsonian Institution in 1928,* 179–182. Washington, DC: Smithsonian Institution Press.

League of Nations. n. d. *The Covenant of the League of Nations.* http://avalon.law.yale.edu/20th_century/leagcov.asp.

Markell, Patchen. 2003. *Bound by Recognition.* Princeton, NJ: Princeton University Press.

Mealing, 1963. S.R., ed. 1963. *The Jesuit Relations and Allied Documents: A Selection.* Ottawa: Carleton University Press.

Mills, Antonia. 1994. *Eagle Down Is Our Law: Witsuwit'en Law, Feasts and Land Claims.* Vancouver: UBC Press.

Moreton-Robinson, Aileen. 2004. "Whiteness, Epistemology and Indigenous Representation." In *Whitening Race: Essays in Social and Cultural Criticism,* 105–136. Edited by Aileen Moreton-Robinson. Canberra: Aboriginal Studies Press.

Morgan, Lewis-Henry. [1851] 1996. *League of the Iroquois.* Introduction by William N. Fenton. Secaucus, NJ: Carol Publishing Book.

Morgan, Lewis-Henry. [1877] 1985. *Ancient Society.* Introduction by Elisabeth Tooker. Tuscon: University of Arizona Press.

Nadasdy, Paul. 2005. *Hunters and Bureaucrats: Power, Knowledge and Aboriginal-State Relations in the Southern Yukon.* Vancouver: University of British Columbia Press.

Niezen, Ronald. 2003. *The Origins of Indigenism: Human Rights and the Politics of Identity.* Berkeley: University of California Press.

Padgen, Anthony. 1982. *The Fall of Natural Man: The American Indian and the Origins of Comparative Ethnology.* Cambridge: Cambridge University Press.

Paine, 1990. "Our Authorial Authority." *Culture* 9:35–47.

Pels, Peter, and Oscar Salemink. 1999. "Introduction: Locating the Colonial Subjects of Anthropology." In *Colonial Subjects: Essays on the Practical History of Anthropology,* 1–52. Edited by Peter Pels and Oscar Salemink. Ann Arbor: University of Michigan Press.

Povinelli, Elizabeth A. 2002. *The Cunning of Recogntion: Indigenous Alterities and Australian Multiculturalism.* Duham, NC: Duke University Press.

Pratt, Mary Louise. 1992. *Imperial Eyes: Travel Writing and Transculturation.* London: Routledge.

Russell, Peter H. 2005. *Recognizing Aboriginal Title: The Mabo Case and Indigenous Resistance to English-Settler Colonialism.* Toronto: University of Toronto Press.

Said, Edward. 1989. "Representing the Colonized: Anthropology's Interlocutors." *Critical Inquiry* 15(2):205–225.

Said, Edward. [1978] 1994. *Orientalism.* New York: Vintage Books.

Sayre, Gordon. 2000. *American Captivity Narratives.* New York: Houghton Mifflin.

Thomas, Nicholas. 1994. *Colonialism's Culture: Anthropology, Travel, and Government.* Princeton, NJ: Princeton University Press.

Trigger, Bruce G. 1985a. *Natives and Newcomers: Canada's "Heroic Age" Reconsidered.* Montreal: McGill Queen's University Press.

Trigger, Bruce G. 1985b. "The Past as Power: Anthropology and the North American Indian." In *Who Owns the Past?,* 11–40. Edited by Isabel McBryde. Melbourne: Oxford University Press.

Trigger, Bruce G. 1988. *The Children of Aataentsic: The Huron People to 1660.* Montreal: McGill-Queen's Press.

Trigger, Bruce G. 1991. "Early Native and North American Responses to European Contact: Romantic versus Rationalistic Interpretations." *Journal of American History* 77(4):1195–1215.

Wolfe, Patrick. 1999. *Settler Colonialism and the Transformation of Anthropology: The Politics and Poetics of an Ethnographic Event.* London: Cassel.

Chapter 17

White Possession and Indigenous Sovereignty Matters

Aileen Moreton-Robinson

In the final reading in this section, an excerpt from the introduction to her award-winning *The White Possessive* (2015), Indigenous scholar Aileen Moreton-Robinson explores the complex relationship between race and Indigeneity and does so through an analysis of the power of whiteness and what she terms "white possessiveness" in mediating that relationship in the cauldron of colonialism. Following on her nuanced analyses of these social relations and in sympathetic critique of Simpson's emphasis on refusal, Moreton-Robinson lays out the stakes (and the dangers) of using "cultural difference" for establishing markers of Indigeneity. This intervention is a crucially important one to the extent that Canadian (and even American) scholars have failed to systematically trace the co-constitutive relationships between race and Indigeneity, and the manner in which this has aided and abetted colonial projects.

The problem with white people is they think and behave like they own everything.
—Dennis Benjamin Moreton (personal communication, April 10, 2005)

It seems apt to begin with a quote from my recently departed Gami (uncle) because he was a humble, kind, and wise man. Gami's words succinctly encapsulate what I am striving to reveal. … While writing this introduction, race as a socially constructed phenomenon is busy doing its work within Australia, measuring Aboriginality by the shade of skin color. It is as though race travels back and forth in time to show us its indeterminacy, seductively enticing us to commit ourselves to its truths. We know not its origins, as a form of exclusion, though there is some consensus that the manifestation of race, conceptualized as having biological form, emerged in the seventeenth century, occurring simultaneously with the rise of liberal democracy. Indigenous peoples did not produce this history, but the conditions under which we live shape our experiences of how well race and state operate in tandem to condition each other.[1] It takes a great deal of work to maintain Canada, the United States, Hawai'i, New Zealand, and Australia as white possessions. The regulatory mechanisms of these nation-states are extremely busy reaffirming and reproducing this possessiveness through a process of perpetual Indigenous dispossession, ranging from the refusal of Indigenous sovereignty to overregulated piecemeal concessions. However … it is not the only way the possessive logics of patriarchal white sovereignty are operationalized, deployed, and affirmed. I use the concept "possessive logics" to denote a mode of rationalization, rather than a set of positions that produce a more or less inevitable answer, that is underpinned by an excessive desire to invest in reproducing and reaffirming the nation-state's ownership, control, and domination. As such, white possessive logics are operationalized within discourses to circulate sets of meanings about ownership of the nation, as part of commonsense knowledge, decision making, and socially produced conventions.

Subjects embody white possessive logics. A leading Australian conservative journalist, Andrew Bolt, was found guilty in 2011 of breaching the Racial Discrimination Act 1975 on two counts, accusing "fair-skinned" Aboriginal people of only claiming their Aboriginal identity in order to gain access to social and economic benefits. The presiding judge, Justice Bromberg, found that Bolt's articles were not written in good faith, contained factual errors, and were offensive.[2] Across the Pacific, in the United States, the case of Baby Veronica continues to play out in the media after the Supreme Court ruled that her Cherokee father's parental rights, under the Indian Child Welfare Act (ICWA), should not be privileged over those of the white adoptive parents.[3] We could ask what it is that links these two seemingly unrelated cases across an expanse of ocean. Perhaps the answer lies in what is common to both. As racial signifiers the "Aborigine" and the "Cherokee" are presupposed as being "known," and they can be used by the courts to assess the identity and parental attributes of those whose bodies are deemed to be marked by this racial knowledge. The courts operationalize a patriarchal white possessive logic through the way in which they rationalize the nonexistence of race while simultaneously deploying it through their racial signifiers "Aboriginal" and "Cherokee."

Race indelibly marks the law's possessiveness. At the turn of the twentieth century, the founding white fathers of Australia's federation feared that nonwhite races would want to invade the country. They were concerned with white racial usurpation and dispossession and took action to ensure that Australia would be a nation controlled by and for whites. Their possessive logics were embedded in the law through the passage of the Immigration Restriction Act 1901, which the new federal government implemented in the form of the White Australia Policy. Australia was not the only nation-state to use immigration legislation as a means to regulate and keep out nonwhite populations. The United States produced the Naturalization Act of 1790, which was designed explicitly for whites only, while Canada's and New Zealand's nineteenth-century Immigration Acts strongly preferred the migration of British citizens to their shores. The development of these different pieces of immigration legislation, though at different times in history, illustrates that there are inextricable connections between white possessive logics, race, and the founding of nation-states. As will become evident … it is one of the ways that the logics of white possession and the disavowal of Indigenous sovereignty are materially and discursively linked.

Race matters in the lives of all peoples; for some people it confers unearned privileges, and for others it is the mark of inferiority. Daily newspapers, radio, television, and social media usually portray Indigenous peoples as a deficit model of humanity. We are overrepresented as always lacking, dysfunctional, alcoholic, violent, needy, and lazy, whether we are living in Illinois, Auckland, Honolulu, Toronto, or Brisbane. For Indigenous people, white possession is not unmarked, unnamed, or invisible; it is hypervisible. In our quotidian encounters, whether it is on the streets of Otago or Sydney, in the tourist shops in Vancouver or Waipahu, or sitting in a restaurant in New York, we experience ontologically the effects of white possession. These cities signify with every building and every street that this land is now possessed by others; signs of white possession are embedded everywhere in the landscape. The omnipresence of Indigenous sovereignties exists here too, but it is disavowed through the materiality of these significations, which are perceived as evidence of ownership by those who have taken possession. This is territory that has been marked by and through violence and race. Racism is thus inextricably tied to the theft and appropriation of Indigenous lands in the first world. In fact, its existence in the United States, Canada, Australia, Hawai'i, and New Zealand was dependent on this happening. The dehumanizing impulses of colonization are successfully acted upon because racisms in these countries are predicated on the logic of possession. Yet, from our respective standpoints, Indigenous studies scholarship has rarely interrogated the mutual constitution of the possessiveness of patriarchal white sovereignty and racialization. Perhaps to a large degree this is an outcome of the development of Indigenous studies shaped by the rights discourse that emerged in the late 1960s and early 1970s.

INDIGENOUS STUDIES AS CULTURAL DIFFERENCE

Debates by Indigenous scholars over what constitutes the field of Indigenous studies began in the early 1970s and were primarily informed by the global Indigenous political movement for self-determination and sovereignty. Crow Creek Sioux scholar and elder Elizabeth Cook-Lynn argues that in the United States a concerted address about what should constitute Native American studies was made by Indian scholars at Princeton University in March 1970.[4]

Discussions were centered on the defense of Indigenous lands and nationhood, as well as Indigenous knowledges and rights. After this initial gathering, further symposiums were held and the disciplinary principles of Native American studies were developed. Native American studies would focus on the endogenous study of Indigenous cultures and history with Indigenous belief systems constituting its bases so that it differentiated itself from the traditional disciplines that pursued exogenous studies of Native American communities. Two key concepts would be epistemic drivers in developing the discipline: Indigenousness and Sovereignty. Indigenousness would encompass culture, place, and philosophy and Sovereignty would include history and law.

Across the Pacific Ocean, and writing a year earlier, Māori scholar Mason Durie gave an overview of the development of Māori studies in New Zealand universities. He noted that the field was uncomfortably constituted by "being an area of study in its own right, an academic discipline, and a potential component of every other area of study."[5] While acknowledging that Māori studies has been "enriched by the several disciplines of law, science, linguistics, anthropology, philosophy, history, education and sociology," Durie argued that Māori philosophies, worldviews, language, and methods formed the basis of Māori studies within the academy.[6] It is a Māori-centered approach to producing knowledge that is neither exclusively traditional nor Western in orientation. He noted that "a greater emphasis on whanau (family models) group learning, and peer support as well as the observation of some customary practices … tend to distinguish Māori studies" as it is taught by Māori scholars. This Indigenous focus on an endogenous approach to history, language, politics, culture, literature, and traditions is also reflected in the development of Native studies in Canada, Kanaka Maoli studies in Hawai'i, and, to a lesser degree, Aboriginal and Torres Strait Islander studies in Australia.

The Indigenous endogenous approach to Indigenous studies discursively centers the Indigenous world as the object of study. The corpus of knowledge that Indigenous scholars have produced over the past four decades has been primarily concerned with expressing and theorizing the specificities of our cultural differences in multiple forms in order to stake our claim in the production of knowledge about us. This early scholarship is extremely important, but it has developed alongside, not through, a rigorous engagement with the traditional disciplines that have shaped Indigenous scholarship. In making this point, I am not condemning Indigenous scholarship to a state of existential oblivion, nor am I denying that ethnographic refusal exists in the production of this knowledge.[7] What I am arguing is that an unintended consequence of the Indigenous endogenous approach to knowledge production is the reification of cultural difference. We compel "culture" to function discursively as a category of analysis in the process of differentiation, while the exogenous disciplinary knowledges that have been produced about us operationalize "race" as the marker of our difference, even when defining Indigenous "cultures."

[…]

NOTES

1.   I acknowledge that there are thousands of Indigenous peoples around the world. I use the terms Indigenous and Aboriginal interchangeably within the Australian context. Otherwise, my use of the term Indigenous in this book is restricted to Native Americans, Kanaka Maoli, Maōri, First Nations, Métis, Aborigines, and Torres Strait Islanders.

2.   Federal Court of Australia. *Eatock v. Bolt* [2011] FCA 1103 (September 28, 2011), http://www.austlii.edu.au/cgibin/sinodisp/au/cases/cth/FCA/2011/1103.html?stem=0&synonyms=0&query=Bolt.

3.   Supreme Court of the United States. *Adoptive Couple v. Baby Girl*, 570 U.S. (2013), http://www.supremecourt.gov/opinions/12pdf/12-399_q86b.pdf.

4.   Elizabeth Cook-Lynn, "Who Stole Native American Studies?" *Wicazo Sa Review* 12, no. 1 (Spring 1997): 9–28.

5.   Mason Durie, "The Development of Maōri Studies in New Zealand Universities," *He Pukenga Korero, Nghuru* 1, no. 2 (1996): 22–25.

6.   Ibid., 24.

7.   Audra Simpson, "On Ethnographic Refusal: Indigeneity, 'Voice,' and Colonial Citizenship," *Junctures*, no. 9 (December 2007): 67–80.

PART 2B

COLONIALISM, SLAVERY, AND INDENTURED LABOUR

The chapters in this section provide a glimpse of the effects of colonialism and its associated labour forms in different social formations, particularly such labour forms as slavery and indentureship. Readers will see that the effects of these labour forms have been economic, social, cultural, political, psychological, and spiritual. Taken together, these effects have fundamentally shaped societies, the subjectivities of oppressed people, and their relationships with members of dominant groups.

FURTHER READING

Bhaba, Homi. 2002. "Of Mimicry and Man: The Ambivalence of Colonial Discourse." In *Race Critical Theories: Text and Context*, edited by Philomena Essed and David Theo Goldberg, 113–122. Malden, MA: Blackwell Publishers.
In the tradition of Fanon, Bhaba combines psychological perspectives with post-colonial concerns in the formation of subjectivities and inter-subjectivities. It illustrates that colonialism had an effect not only at the economic and political level, but also at the level of psycho-social existence. The colonial project of assimilating the "native" was never complete so long as the difference between the colonizer and the colonized was maintained in order to preserve colonial power. The partial imitation of British men that colonialism produced—what Bhaba calls the "mimic man"—turned out to be a "menace" because his ambivalence preserved a space for subversion. What happened to "mimic woman" has been theorized by other writers.

Fanon, Frantz. 1963. *The Wretched of the Earth.* New York: Grove Press
This is an English translation of Fanon's work on colonization and decolonization in Africa, with a preface by Jean-Paul Sartre. In this work, Fanon discusses in detail the political, economic, cultural, and mental health effects of colonialism, colonial war, and violence on the colonized. Chapters deal with the inherent polarization between the colonizer and the colonized ("settlers" and "natives"), as well as the stark violence perpetrated against the latter by the former through the state apparatus and its individual representatives. Fanon argues that power relations in the colony are different from those in the "mother" country in that ruling is done through force alone, not through consent. Colonization produces two worlds in the colonies, one in which the "settler" lives and the other in which

the "native" lives; the two are presented as diametrical opposites (by the colonial regime), with the former embodying everything that is good and virtuous and the latter embodying that which is evil and inferior. Fanon then explores the effects of such social and political arrangements on the subjectivities of the colonized through a class analysis. In particular, he engages in a fascinating exploration of the position of bourgeois African intellectuals and their separation from the rank and file. He discusses the economic, political, and cultural limitations of the post-colonial situation when this national intellectual class takes over the government. In contrast, he argues for the revolutionary potential of the peasantry in such countries.

Fanon, Frantz. 1967. *Black Skin, White Masks*. **New York: Grove Press.**
This is an English translation of Fanon's seminal text in which he explores the psychological effects of colonialism and racism on the Black man, predominantly from his own subject position. Fanon contends that colonization and racism produce a desire in the Black man to be white. In chapters 2 and 3, he discusses the impact of these dynamics on intimate relations between Blacks and whites, the former chapter dealing with the relationship of the woman of colour and the white man. The book also includes critiques of other contemporary writers, as well as considerations of the Black man's struggles to discover his identity in a white-dominated world. Fanon takes the provocative position of arguing that what is represented as blackness is a white construct. This work provides a rare and early revelation of the intersections of colonialism, racism, psychology, and intimacy, one that has spawned many other contemporary writings in related areas.

Mehta, Brinda. 2004. *Diasporic (Dis)Locations: Indo-Caribbean Women Writers Negotiate the Kala Pani*. **Kingston, Jamaica: University of West Indies Press.**
This book focuses on the experiences and literary expressions of Indian Hindu women who braved the treacherous Kala Pani (Atlantic Ocean) to lead new lives marked by indentureship in the Caribbean. For many this was a flight from Hindu patriarchal family relations to lives of relative social, economic, and sexual "freedom," particularly in the context of the demographic imbalance in which women were a minority among indentured labourers. This book examines the expression of diasporic Indian womanhood in recent critical and creative writings by Indo-Caribbean women.

Tharu, Susie. 1999. "Tracing Savitri's Pedigree: Victorian Racism and the Image of Women in Indo-Anglian Literature." In *Recasting Women: Essays in Indian Colonial History*, edited by Kumkum Sangari and Sudesh Vaid, 254–268. New Brunswick, NJ: Rutgers University Press.

In the post-colonial tradition of Fanon and Bhaba, Tharu throws light on the subjectivities of colonized women, in particular upper-class and upper-caste Hindu women from Bengal, the seat of British colonial power in India. In this critical essay, the author deconstructs a number of Indo-Anglian nationalist writings by women in the context of British colonial domination. She argues that, in an effort to dispute racist and Orientalist constructions of Indian women and men—for instance, the stereotype of them as weak and immoral—Indo-Anglian writers constructed heroines who embodied Victorian virtues of chastity, purity, and freedom in a way that was typically associated with European women. Indeed, the combination of indigenous purity, sacrifice, and spiritual strength were portrayed as vital for the defeat of colonialism. However, the author argues that in this process of constructing the feminine figure of the martyr, patriarchy was not completely dismantled; there was an assertion of racial equality (and thus a confirmation of the idea of race); and there was an obfuscation of the exploitation of ordinary men and women, lest a negative light be thrown on Indians.

Chapter 18

Of Our Spiritual Strivings

W.E.B. Du Bois

W.E.B. Du Bois, writing at the turn of the twentieth century, discussed "double consciousness" in the context of the post-Reconstruction United States. He asked, "How does it feel to be a problem?" Just as Frantz Fanon spoke about being objectified, Du Bois spoke about "a world which yields [the black man] no true self-consciousness." He argued that the formal freedom from slavery had not brought "real" freedom, in that most African Americans still lived in the shadows of slavery, in utter poverty, with broken homes, having to deal with war, racism, and capitalism. Du Bois argued, "To be a poor man is hard, but to be a poor race in a land of dollars is the very bottom of hardships." He ends with the positive assertion that African Americans have a great deal to offer the country, riches and resources that have come out of struggle and sorrow.

O water, voice of my heart, crying in the sand,
All night long crying with a mournful cry,
As I lie and listen, and cannot understand
The voice of my heart in my side or the voice of the sea,
O water, crying for rest, is it I, is it I?
All night long the water is crying to me.

Unresting water, there shall never be rest
Till the last moon droop and the last tide fail,
And the fire of the end begin to burn in the west;
And the heart shall be weary and wonder and cry like the sea,
All life long crying without avail,
As the water all night long is crying to me.
                    —Arthur Symons

Between me and the other world there is ever an unasked question: unasked by some through feelings of delicacy; by others through the difficulty of rightly framing it. All, nevertheless, flutter round it. They approach me in a half-hesitant sort of way, eye me curiously or compassionately, and then, instead of saying directly, How does it feel to be a problem? they say, I know an excellent colored man in my town; or, I fought at Mechanicsville;[2] or, Do not these Southern outrages make your blood boil? At these I smile, or am interested, or reduce the boiling to a simmer, as the occasion may require. To the real question, How does it feel to be a problem? I answer seldom a word.

And yet, being a problem is a strange experience,—peculiar even for one who has never been anything else, save perhaps in babyhood and in Europe. It is in the early days of rollicking boyhood that the revelation first bursts upon one, all in a day, as it were. I remember well when the shadow swept across me. I was a little thing, away up in the hills of New England, where the dark Housatonic[3] winds between Hoosac and Taghkanic to the sea. In a wee wooden schoolhouse, something put it into the boys' and girls' heads to buy gorgeous visiting-cards—ten cents a package—and exchange. The exchange was merry, till one girl, a tall newcomer, refused my card,—refused it peremptorily, with a glance. Then it dawned upon me with a certain suddenness that I was different from the others; or like, mayhap, in heart and life and longing, but shut out from their world by a vast veil. I had thereafter no desire to tear down that veil, to creep through; I held all beyond it in common contempt, and lived above it in a region of blue sky and great wandering shadows. That sky was bluest when I could beat my mates at examination-time, or beat them at a foot-race, or even beat their stringy heads. Alas, with the years all this fine contempt began to fade; for the worlds I longed for, and all their dazzling opportunities, were theirs, not mine. But they should not keep these prizes, I said; some, all, I would wrest from them. Just how I would do it I could never decide: by reading law, by healing the sick, by telling the wonderful tales that swam in my head,—some way. With other black boys the strife was not so fiercely sunny: their youth shrunk into tasteless sycophancy, or into silent hatred of the pale world about them and mocking distrust of every-thing white; or wasted itself in a bitter cry, Why did God make me an outcast and a stranger in mine own house? The shades of the prison-house closed round about us all: walls strait and stubborn to the whitest, but relentlessly narrow, tall, and unscalable to sons of night who must plod darkly on in resignation, or beat unavailing palms against the stone, or steadily, half hopelessly, watch the streak of blue above.[4]

After the Egyptian and Indian, the Greek and Roman, the Teuton and Mongolian, the Negro is a sort of seventh son,[5] born with a veil,[6] and gifted with second-sight in this American world,—a world which yields him no true self-consciousness, but only lets him see himself through the revelation of the other world. It is a peculiar sensation, this double-consciousness,[7] this sense of always looking at one's self through the eyes of others, of measuring one's soul by the tape of a world that looks on in amused contempt and pity. One ever feels his two-ness,—an American, a Negro; two souls, two thoughts, two unreconciled strivings; two warring ideals in one dark body, whose dogged strength alone keeps it from being torn asunder.

The history of the American Negro is the history of this strife,—this longing to attain self-conscious manhood, to merge his double self into a better and truer self. In this merging he wishes neither of the older selves to be lost. He would not Africanize America, for America has too much to teach the world and Africa. He would not bleach his Negro soul in a flood of white Americanism, for he knows that Negro blood has a message for the world. He simply wishes to make it possible for a man to be both a Negro and an American, without being cursed and spit upon by his fellows, without having the doors of Opportunity closed roughly in his face.[8]

This, then, is the end of his striving: to be a co-worker in the kingdom of culture, to escape both death and isolation, to husband and use his best powers and his latent genius. These powers of body and mind have in the past been strangely wasted, dispersed, or forgotten. The shadow of a mighty Negro past flits through the tale of Ethiopia the Shadowy and of Egypt the Sphinx. Throughout history, the powers of single black men flash here and there like falling stars, and die sometimes before the world has rightly gauged their brightness. Here in America, in the few days since Emancipation, the black man's turning hither and thither in hesitant and doubtful striving has often made his very strength to lose effectiveness, to seem like absence of power, like weakness. And yet it is not weakness,—it is the contradiction of double aims. The double-aimed struggle of the black artisan—on the one hand to escape white contempt for a nation of mere hewers of wood and drawers of water, and on the other hand to plough and nail and dig for a poverty-stricken horde—could only result in making him a poor craftsman, for he had but half a heart in either cause. By the poverty and ignorance of his people, the Negro minister or doctor was tempted toward quackery and demagogy; and by the criticism of the other world, toward ideals that made him ashamed of his lowly tasks. The would-be black *savant* was confronted by the paradox that the knowledge his people needed was a twice-told tale to his white neighbors, while the knowledge which would teach the white world was Greek to his own flesh and blood. The innate love of harmony and beauty that set the ruder souls of his people a-dancing and a-singing raised but confusion and doubt in the soul of the black artist; for the beauty revealed to him was the soul-beauty of a race which his larger audience despised, and he could not articulate the message of another people. This waste of double aims, this seeking to satisfy two unreconciled ideals, has wrought sad havoc with the courage and faith and deeds of ten thousand thousand people,—has sent them often wooing false gods and invoking false means of salvation, and at times has even seemed about to make them ashamed of themselves.

Away back in the days of bondage they thought to see in one divine event the end of all doubt and disappointment; few men ever worshipped Freedom with half such unquestioning faith as did the American Negro for two centuries. To him, so far as he thought and dreamed, slavery was indeed the sum of all villainies, the cause of all sorrow, the root of all prejudice; Emancipation was the key to a promised land of sweeter beauty than ever stretched before the eyes of wearied Israelites.[9] In song and exhortation swelled one refrain—Liberty; in his tears and curses the God he implored had Freedom in his right hand. At last it came,—suddenly, fearfully, like a dream. With one wild carnival of blood and passion came the message in his own plaintive cadences:—

> "Shout, O children!
> Shout, you're free!
> For God has bought your liberty!"[10]

Years have passed away since then,—ten, twenty, forty; forty years of national life, forty years of renewal and development, and yet the swarthy spectre sits in its accustomed seat at the Nation's feast. In vain do we cry to this our vastest social problem:—

> "Take any shape but that, and my firm nerves
> Shall never tremble!"[11]

The Nation has not yet found peace from its sins; the freedman has not yet found in freedom his promised land. Whatever of good may have come in these years of change, the shadow of a deep disappointment rests upon the Negro people,—a disappointment all the more bitter because the unattained ideal was unbounded save by the simple ignorance of a lowly people.

The first decade was merely a prolongation of the vain search for freedom, the boon that seemed ever barely to elude their grasp,—like a tantalizing will-o'-the-wisp, maddening and misleading the headless host. The holocaust of war, the terrors of the Ku-Klux Klan,[12] the lies of carpetbaggers,[13] the disorganization of industry, and the contradictory advice of friends and foes, left the bewildered serf with no new watchword beyond the old cry for freedom. As the time flew, however, he began to grasp a new idea. The ideal of liberty demanded for its attainment powerful means, and these the Fifteenth Amendment gave him.[14] The ballot, which before he had looked upon as a visible sign of freedom, he now regarded as the chief means of gaining and perfecting the liberty with which war had partially endowed him. And why not? Had not votes made war and emancipated millions? Had not votes enfranchised the freedmen? Was anything impossible to a power that had done all this? A million black men started with renewed zeal to vote themselves into the kingdom. So the decade flew away, the revolution of 1876 came,[15] and left the half-free serf weary, wondering, but still inspired. Slowly but steadily, in the following years, a new vision began gradually to replace the dream of political power,—a powerful movement, the rise of another ideal to guide the unguided, another pillar of fire by night after a clouded day. It was the ideal of "book-learning"; the curiosity, born of compulsory ignorance, to know and test the power of the cabalistic letters of the white man, the longing to know. Here at last seemed to have been discovered the mountain path to Canaan; longer than the highway of Emancipation and law, steep and rugged, but straight, leading to heights high enough to overlook life.

Up the new path the advance guard toiled, slowly, heavily, doggedly; only those who have watched and guided the faltering feet, the misty minds, the dull understandings, of the dark pupils of these schools know how faithfully, how piteously, this people strove to learn. It was weary work. The cold statistician wrote down the inches of progress here and there, noted also where here and there a foot had slipped or some one had fallen. To the tired climbers, the horizon was ever dark, the mists were often cold, the Canaan was always dim and far away. If, however, the vistas disclosed as yet no goal, no resting-place, little but flattery and criticism, the journey at least gave leisure for reflection and self-examination; it changed the child of Emancipation to the youth with dawning self-consciousness, self-realization, self-respect. In those sombre forests of his striving his own soul rose before him, and he saw himself,—darkly as through a veil;[16] and yet he saw in himself some faint revelation of his power, of his mission. He began to have a dim feeling that, to attain his place in the world, he must be himself, and not another. For the first time he sought to analyze the burden he bore upon his back, that dead-weight of social degradation partially masked behind a half-named Negro problem. He felt his poverty; without a cent, without a home, without land, tools, or savings, he had entered into competition with rich, landed, skilled neighbors. To be a poor man is hard, but to be a poor race in a land of dollars is the very bottom of hardships. He felt the weight of his ignorance,—not simply of letters, but of life, of business, of the humanities; the accumulated sloth and shirking and awkwardness of decades and centuries shackled his hands and feet. Nor was his burden all poverty and ignorance. The red stain of bastardy, which two centuries of systematic legal defilement of Negro women had stamped upon his race, meant not only the loss of ancient African chastity, but also the hereditary weight of a mass of corruption from white adulterers, threatening almost the obliteration of the Negro home.

A people thus handicapped ought not to be asked to race with the world, but rather allowed to give all its time and thought to its own social problems. But alas! while sociologists gleefully count his bastards and his prostitutes, the very soul of the toiling, sweating black man is darkened by the shadow of a vast despair. Men call the shadow prejudice, and learnedly explain it as the natural defence of culture against barbarism, learning against ignorance, purity against crime, the "higher" against the "lower" races.[17] To which the Negro cries Amen! and swears that to so much of this strange prejudice as is founded on just homage to civilization, culture, righteousness, and progress, he humbly bows and meekly does obeisance. But before that nameless prejudice that leaps beyond all this he stands helpless, dismayed, and well-nigh speechless; before that personal disrespect and mockery, the ridicule and systematic humiliation, the distortion of fact and wanton license of fancy, the cynical ignoring of the better and the boisterous welcoming of the worse, the all-pervading desire to inculcate disdain for everything black, from Toussaint[18] to the devil,—before this there rises a sickening despair that would disarm and discourage any nation save that black host to whom "discouragement" is an unwritten word.

But the facing of so vast a prejudice could not but bring the inevitable self-questioning, self-disparagement, and lowering of ideals which ever accompany repression and breed in an atmosphere of contempt and hate. Whisperings and portents came borne upon the four winds: Lo! we are diseased and dying, cried the dark hosts; we cannot write, our voting is vain; what need of education, since we must always cook and serve? And the Nation echoed and enforced this self-criticism, saying: Be content to be servants, and nothing more; what need of higher culture for half-men? Away with the black man's ballot, by force or fraud,—and behold the suicide of a race! Nevertheless, out of the evil came something of good,—the more careful adjustment of education to real life, the clearer perception of the Negroes' social responsibilities, and the sobering realization of the meaning of progress.

So dawned the time of *Sturm und Drang*:[19] storm and stress to-day rocks our little boat on the mad waters of the world-sea; there is within and without the sound of conflict, the burning of body and rending of soul; inspiration strives with doubt, and faith with vain questionings. The bright ideals of the past,—physical freedom, political power, the training of brains and the training of hands,—all these in turn have waxed and waned, until even the last grows dim and overcast. Are they all wrong,—all false? No, not that, but each alone was over-simple and incomplete,—the dreams of a credulous race-childhood, or the fond imaginings of the other world which does not know and does not want to know our power. To be really true, all these ideals must be melted and welded into one. The training of the schools we need to-day more than ever,—the training of deft hands, quick eyes and ears, and above all the broader, deeper, higher culture of gifted minds and pure hearts. The power of the ballot we need in sheer self-defence,[20]—else what shall save us from a second slavery? Freedom, too, the long-sought, we still seek,—the freedom of life and limb, the freedom to work and think, the freedom to love and aspire. Work, culture, liberty,—all these we need, not singly but together, not successively but together, each growing and aiding each, and all striving toward that vaster ideal that swims before the Negro people, the ideal of human brotherhood, gained through the unifying ideal of Race; the ideal of fostering and developing the traits and talents of the Negro, not in opposition to or contempt for other races, but rather in large conformity to the greater ideals of the American Republic, in order that some day on American soil two world-races may give each to each those characteristics both so sadly lack. We the darker ones come even now not altogether empty-handed: there are to-day no truer exponents of the pure human spirit of the Declaration of Independence than the American Negroes; there is no true

American music but the wild sweet melodies of the Negro slave; the American fairy tales and folk-lore are Indian and African; and, all in all, we black men seem the sole oasis of simple faith and reverence in a dusty desert of dollars and smartness. Will America be poorer if she replace her brutal dyspeptic blundering with light-hearted but determined Negro humility?[21] or her coarse and cruel wit with loving jovial good-humor? or her vulgar music with the soul of the Sorrow Songs?

Merely a concrete test of the underlying principles of the great republic is the Negro Problem, and the spiritual striving of the freedmen's sons is the travail of souls whose burden is almost beyond the measure of their strength, but who bear it in the name of an historic race, in the name of this the land of their fathers' fathers, and in the name of human opportunity.

And now what I have briefly sketched in large outline let me on coming pages tell again in many ways, with loving emphasis and deeper detail, that men may listen to the striving in the souls of black folk.

NOTES

1. The verse is Arthur Symons, "The Crying of Waters." The music is a Negro spiritual, "Nobody Knows the Trouble I've Seen." In every chapter but the last, Du Bois uses this structure of epigraphs: a passage of verse (usually from an American or European poet, but in one case from the Bible and in another from the *Rubaiyat of Omar Khayyam*), followed by a bar of music from the songs of American slaves. On the significance of this structure, especially the choice and origins of the spirituals, see Eric J. Sundquist, *To Wake the Nations: Race in the Making of American Literature* (Cambridge, Mass.: Harvard University Press), 490–539.
2. Mechanicsville was a Civil War battle fought on June 26, 1862, just east of Richmond, Virginia.
3. Housatonic is the river that flows through Great Barrington, Massachusetts.
4. In a composition he wrote as an undergraduate at Harvard, Du Bois may have expressed resentment that had been prompted by this childhood experience. Entitled "The American Girl," the essay describes the girl as an "eye-sore" whose face is "more shrewd than intelligent, arrogant than dignified, silly than pleasant, and pretty than beautiful." See Herbert Aptheker, ed., *Against Racism: Unpublished Essays, Papers, Addresses, 1887–1961, W.E.B. Du Bois* (Amherst: University of Massachusetts Press, 1985), 20. "The shades of the prison-house closed round us all" explicitly echoes William Wordworth's ode "Intimations Of Immortality From Recollections Of Early Childhood," lines 67–68. See chapter 12, note 10.
5. The figure of the seventh son carries multiple meanings. Apparently revising Hegel's philosophy of history, Du Bois adds the Negro to Hegel's story of six world-historical peoples (see pp. 12–13). In African American folklore, the seventh son is said to be distinguished in some way, to be able to see ghosts, and to make a good doctor. See

Newbell Niles Puckett, *Folk Beliefs of the Southern Negro* (New York: Dover, 1969); Elsie Clews Parsons, *Folk-Lore of the Sea Islands, South Carolina* (Cambridge, Mass.: American Folklore Society, 1923); and Melville Herskovitz, *The Myth of the Negro Past* (1941; reprint, Boston: Beacon Press, 1958).

6. In African American folklore, a child born with a caul, a veil-like membrane that sometimes covers the head at birth, is said to be lucky, to be able to tell fortunes, and to be a "double-sighted" seer of ghosts. In some West African folk traditions, a child born with a caul is thought to possess a special personality endowed with spiritual potency. For biblical allusions to the veil, see Exodus 34.33–35; 2 Corinthians 13.13–18; Matthew 27.51; Hebrews 6.19, 10.20; and Isaiah 25.7. Also see the sources in note 5 of this chapter.

7. For an introduction to the literature on double consciousness, see Dickson D. Bruce Jr., "W.E.B. Du Bois and the Idea of Double Consciousness," *American Literature* 64 (June 1992): 299–309. Also see page 26, note 21.

8. Du Bois in this passage echoes the most prominent philosophers and poets writing in the European romantic tradition (such as William Blake, Samuel Taylor Coleridge, Friedrich Schiller, and Georg Wilhelm Friedrich Hegel) by promoting the creation of a unified self that synthesizes and preserves diverse elements. Though the American Negro was captured in Africa and forced into slavery in America, he knows no nostalgia for an African "self" that was untainted by the experience of America. Rather, his is a quest for a better, truer, and more encompassing self, the search for a mode of integrity that merges his African and newly acquired American identities yet retains them as distinct. On the romantic philosophers and poets, see M.H. Abrams, *Natural Supernaturalism* (New York: Norton, 1971).

9. Du Bois envisions blacks in America as the Old Testament Jews (Israelites) who have yet to escape the land of their captivity (Egypt) and enter the promised land (Canaan). On the late-nineteenth-century tradition of African American religious and political thought that gives rise to this imagery, see David W. Wills, "Exodus Piety: African-American Religion in an Age of Immigration," in *Minority Faiths and the American Protestant Mainstream*, ed. David O'Brien and Jonathan Sarns (Urbana: University of Illinois Press, 1998).

10. From the Negro spiritual "Shout, O Children!"

11. Shakespeare, *Macbeth*, 3.4.102–3.

12. The Ku Klux Klan is the white fraternal terrorist organization created in 1866 by Confederate veterans in Pulaski, Tennessee. Its members altered the Greek word for circle, *kuklos*, and invented their name. During Reconstruction in the South, the Klan engaged in widespread violence against blacks and their white Republican supporters.

13. Carpetbaggers were northern politicians and businessmen who moved to the South after the Civil War, allegedly to exploit the devastation of the South and the political vacuum left by the defeat of the Confederacy.

14. The Fifteenth Amendment to the US Constitution passed Congress in February 1869 and was ratified by the states in March 1870. It provided that voting rights "shall not be denied ... on account of race, color, or previous condition of servitude." The Fifteenth Amendment

was a moderate measure; it did not specifically outlaw qualifications tests for the right to vote. But it did represent the federal government's key role as guarantor of rights during Reconstruction.

15. In the disputed presidential election of 1876, Republican Rutherford B. Hayes defeated Democrat Samuel J. Tilden. In three southern states, Louisiana, Florida, and South Carolina, the voting returns were disputed, with fraud and intimidation charged by both sides. The election was settled by a congressional committee that declared Hayes the winner in the three contested states as well as by a political compromise (known as the Compromise of 1877) between the two parties. The "revolution" refers to southern Democratic threats to secede from the Union or march on Washington, D.C., early in the crisis. This "revolution" also represented the abandonment of the freedpeople in the South by the Republican Party.

16. See 1 Corinthians 13.12: "For now we see through a glass, darkly; but then face to face: now I know in part; but then shall I know even as also I am known."

17. Du Bois alludes to the belief, prevalent in the nineteenth century, that there exist several races of human beings that can be ranked hierarchically. For example, Count Arthur de Gobineau, in his *Essay on the Inequality of Human Races* (1853–1855), held that the white race possessed qualities (such as love of freedom, honor, and spirituality) that made it superior to the yellow and black races.

18. Toussaint L'Ouverture (1746–1803) was the leader of the Haitian revolution of 1791. A former slave, he became a brilliant general, led the forces that overthrew French rule in Sainte Domingue, and established himself as ruler of the new government by 1796. Toussaint was eventually captured by the French and died in France in 1803.

19. Literally in English, "storm and stress," the term *Sturm und Drang* was used for a literary movement in Germany during the last quarter of the eighteenth century. In general, the writings of the Sturm und Drang movement were intensely personal, emphasizing emotional experience and spiritual struggle. The work that perhaps best captures the spirit of the movement is Johann Wolfgang von Goethe's novel *Die Leiden des Jungen Werthers* (*The Sorrows of Young Werther*), published in 1774.

20. Appealing to the necessity of self-defense to justify an extension of the franchise was common in the nineteenth century and echoed utilitarian arguments for democracy made by philosophers Jeremy Bentham and James Mill. On Bentham's and Mill's views, see C.B. Macpherson, *The Life and Times of Liberal Democracy* (Oxford: Oxford University Press, 1977), 23–43.

21. Du Bois echoes the commencement speech he delivered at Harvard in June 1890, "Jefferson Davis as a Representative of Civilization." The speech describes the contrast between the brutal civilization of Jefferson Davis, president of the Confederacy, and the personal submissiveness of the Negro. See Aptheker, *Against Racism*, 14–16. Also see page 125 in chapter 8 of *Souls*.

SELECTED BIBLIOGRAPHY

Aptheker, Herbert, ed. *Against Racism: Unpublished Essays, Papers, Addresses. 1887–1961, W.E.B. Du Bois*. Amherst: University of Massachusetts Press, 1985.

Sundquist, Eric J. "Swing Low: *The Souls of Black Folk*." In *To Wake the Nations: Race in the Making of American Literature*. Cambridge: Harvard University Press, 1993.

Chapter 19

Capitalism and Slavery

Eric Williams

Moving away from the psychological and spiritual, Eric Williams (1970) brings home the point that colonialism, specifically the plantation economy in the Caribbean, was at its root an exploitative economic system based on slave labour. The sugar trade was accompanied by the West African slave trade, which was the jurisdiction of various Portuguese, English, French, Dutch, and Swedish companies. Williams writes that the slave trade became "an international free-for-all." Free trade was a matter of great debate in the seventeenth century, as it is today, but in the earlier period it dealt with "slaves as commodities" as well as with consumer products. It was hardly a concern for slave traders that three out of every ten Africans died on the voyage through the Middle Passage. Neither was it a concern for plantation owners that one in three Africans died within the first three years after landing. Africans were in fact "objectified," a theme that Frantz Fanon took to a psychological level. The so-called triangular trade, involving European traders and shopkeepers, West African traders and enslaved people, and Caribbean plantation owners, filled the coffers of European monarchies, traders, and entrepreneurs.

"There is nothing which contributes more to the development of the colonies and the cultivation of their soil than the laborious toil of the Negroes." So reads a decree of King Louis XIV of France, on August 26, 1670. It was the consensus of seventeenth-century European opinion. Negroes became the "life" of the Caribbean, as George Downing said of Barbados in 1645. The "very being" of the plantations depended on the supply of Negroes stated the Company of Royal Adventurers of England trading to Africa to King Charles II in 1663. Without Negroes, said the Spanish Council of the Indies in 1685, the food needed for the support of the whole kingdom would cease to be produced and America would face absolute ruin. Europe has seldom been as unanimous on any issue as it has been on the value of Negro slave labour.

In 1645, before the introduction of the sugar economy, Barbados had 5,680 Negro slaves, or more than three able-bodied white men to every slave. In 1667, after the introduction of the sugar industry, the island, by one account, contained 82,023 slaves, or nearly ten slaves to every white man fit to bear arms. By 1698 a more accurate estimate of the population gave the figures as 2,330 white males and 42,000 slaves, or a ratio of more than eighteen slaves to every white male.

In Jamaica the ratio of slaves to whites was one to three in 1658, nearly six to one in 1698. There were 1,400 slaves in the former year, 40,000 in the latter. The ratio of slaves and mulattoes to whites increased from more than two to one in Martinique in 1664 to more than three to one in 1701. The coloured population amounted to 2,434 in 1664 and 23,362 in 1701. In Guadeloupe, by 1697, the coloured population outnumbered the whites by more than three to two. In Grenada in 1700 the Negro slaves and mulattoes were more than double the number of whites. In the Leeward Islands and in St. Thomas the whites steadily lost ground.

By 1688 it was estimated that Jamaica required annually 10,000 slaves, the Leeward Islands 6,000, and Barbados 4,000. A contract of October, 1675, with one Jean Oudiette, called for the supply of 800 slaves a year for four years to the French West Indies. Four years later, in 1679, the Senegal Company undertook to supply 2,000 slaves a year for eight years to the French Islands. Between 1680 and 1688 the Royal African Company supplied 46,396 slaves to the British West Indies, an annual average of 5,155.

The Negro slave trade became one of the most important business enterprises of the seventeenth century. In accordance with sixteenth-century precedents its organisation was entrusted to a company which was given the sole right by a particular nation to trade in slaves on the coast of West Africa, erect and maintain the forts necessary for the protection of the trade, and transport and sell the slaves in the West Indies. Individuals, free traders or "interlopers," as they were called, were excluded. Thus the British incorporated the Company of Royal Adventurers trading to Africa, in 1663, and later replaced this company by the Royal African Company, in 1672, the royal patronage and participation reflecting the importance of the trade and continuing the fashion set by the Spanish monarchy of increasing its revenues thereby. The monopoly of the French slave trade was at first assigned to the French West India Company in 1664, and then transferred, in 1673, to the Senegal Company. The monopoly of the Dutch slave trade was given to the Dutch West India Company, incorporated in 1621. Sweden organised a Guinea Company in 1647. The Danish West India Company, chartered in 1671, with the royal family among its shareholders, was allowed in 1674 to extend its activities to Guinea. Brandenburg established a Brandenburg African Company, and established its first trading post on the coast of West Africa in 1682. The Negro slave trade, begun about 1450 as a Portuguese monopoly, had, by the end of the seventeenth century, become an international free-for-all.

The organisation of the slave trade gave rise to one of the most heated and far-reaching economic polemics of the period. Typical of the argument in favour of the monopoly was a paper in 1680 regarding the Royal African Company of England. The argument, summarised, was as follows: firstly, experience demonstrated that the slave trade could not be carried on without forts on the West African Coast costing £20,000 a year, too heavy a charge for private traders, and it was not practicable to apportion it among them; secondly, the trade was exposed to attack by other nations, and it was the losses from such attacks prior to 1663 which had resulted in the formation of the chartered company; thirdly, the maintenance of forts and warships could not be undertaken by the Company unless it had an exclusive control; fourthly, private traders enslaved all and sundry, even Negroes of high rank, and this led to reprisals on the coast; finally, England's great rival, Holland, was only waiting for the dissolution of the English company to engross the entire trade.

The monopolistic company had to face two opponents: the planter in the colonies and the merchant at home, both of whom combined to advocate free trade. The planters complained of the insufficient quantity, the poor quality, and the high prices of the slaves supplied by the Company; the latter countered by pointing out that the planters were heavily in debt to it, estimated in 1671 at £70,000, and, four years later, at £60,000 for Jamaica alone. The British merchants claimed that free trade would mean the purchase of a larger number of Negroes, which would mean the production of a larger quantity of British goods for the purchase and upkeep of the slaves.

The controversy ended in a victory for free trade. On July 5, 1698, Parliament passed an act abrogating the monopoly of the Royal African Company, and throwing open the trade to all British subjects on payment of a duty of ten per cent *ad valorem* on all goods exported to Africa for the purchase of slaves.

The acrimonious controversy retained no trace of the pseudo-humanitarianism of the Spaniards in the sixteenth century, that Negro slavery was essential to the preservation of the Indians. In its place was a solid economic fact, that Negro slavery was essential to the preservation of the sugar plantations. The considerations were purely economic. The slaves were denominated "black ivory." The best slave was, in Spanish parlance, a "piece of the Indies," a slave 30 to 35 years old, about five feet eleven inches in height, without any physical defect. Adults who were not so tall and children were measured, and the total reduced to "pieces of the Indies." A contract in 1676 between the Spaniards and the Portuguese called for the supply of 10,000 "tons" of slaves; to avoid fraud and argument, it was stipulated that three Negroes should be considered the equivalent of one ton. In 1651 the English Guinea Company instructed its agent to load one of its ships with as many Negroes as it could carry, and, in default, to fill up the ship with cattle.

The mortality in the Middle Passage was regarded merely as an unfortunate trading loss, except for the fact that Negroes were more costly than cattle. Losses in fact ran quite high, but such concern as was evinced had to deal merely with profits. In 1659, a Dutch slaver, the *St. Jan*, lost 110 slaves out of a cargo of 219—for every two slaves purchased, one died in transit to the West Indies. In 1678, the *Arthur*, one of the ships of the Royal African Company, suffered a mortality of 88 out of 417 slaves—that is, more than 20 per cent. The *Martha*, another ship, landed 385 in Barbados out of 447 taken on the coast—the mortality amounted to 62, or a little less than 15 per cent. The *Coaster* lost 37 out of 150, a mortality of approximately 25 per cent. The *Hannibal*, in 1694, with a cargo of 700 slaves, buried 320 on the voyage, a mortality of 43 per cent; the Royal African Company lost £10 and the owner of the vessel 10 guineas on each slave, the total loss amounting to £6,560. The losses sustained by these five vessels amounted to 617 out of a total cargo of 1,933, that is, 32 per cent. Three out of every ten slaves perished in the Middle Passage. Hence the note of exasperation in the account of his voyage by the captain of the *Hannibal*:

> No gold-finders can endure so much noisome slavery as they do who carry Negroes; for those have some respite and satisfaction, but we endure twice the misery; and yet by their mortality our voyages are ruin'd, and we pine and fret our selves to death to think we should undergo so much misery, and take so much pains to so little purpose.

The lamentations of an individual slave trader or sugar planter were drowned out by the seventeenth-century chorus of approbation. Negro slavery and the Negro slave trade fitted beautifully into the economic theory of the age. This theory, known as mercantilism, stated that the wealth of a nation depended upon its possession of bullion, the precious metals. If, however, bullion was not available through possession of the mines, the new doctrine went further than its Spanish predecessor in emphasising that a country could increase its stock by a favourable balance of trade, exporting more than it imported. One of the best and clearest statements of the theory was made by Edward Misselden, in his *Circle of Commerce*, in 1623:

> For as a pair of scales is an invention to show us the weight of things, whereby we may discern the heavy from the light ... so is also the balance of trade an excellent and politique invention to show us the difference of weight in the commerce of one kingdom with another: that is, whether the native commodities exported, and all the foreign commodities imported do balance or over-balance one another in the scale of commerce.... If the native commodities exported do weigh down and exceed in value the foreign commodities imported, it is a rule that never fails that then the kingdom grows rich and prospers in estate and stock: because the overplus thereof must needs come in treasure.... But if the foreign commodities imported do exceed in value the native commodities exported, it is a manifest sign that the trade decayeth, and the stock of the kingdom wasteth apace; because the overplus must needs go out in treasure.

National policy of the leading European nations concentrated on achieving a favourable balance of trade. Colonial possessions were highly prized as a means to this end; they increased the exports of the metropolitan country, prevented the drain of treasure by the purchase of necessary tropical produce, and provided freights for the ships of the metropolis and employment for its sailors.

The combination of the Negro slave trade, Negro slavery and Caribbean sugar production is known as the triangular trade. A ship left the metropolitan country with a cargo of metropolitan goods, which it exchanged on the coast of West Africa for slaves. This constituted the first side of the triangle. The second consisted of the Middle Passage, the voyage from West Africa to the West Indies with the slaves. The triangle was completed by the voyage from the West Indies to the metropolitan country with sugar and other Caribbean products received in exchange for the slaves. As the slave ships were not always adequate for the transportation of the West Indian produce, the triangular trade was supplemented by a direct trade between the metropolitan country and the West Indian islands.

The triangular trade provided a market in West Africa and the West Indies for metropolitan products, thereby increasing metropolitan exports and contributing to full employment at home. The purchase of the slaves on the coast of West Africa and their maintenance in the West Indies gave an enormous stimulus to metropolitan industry and agriculture. For example, the British woollen industry was heavily dependent on the triangular trade. A parliamentary committee of 1695 emphasised that the slave trade was an encouragement to Britain's woollen industry. In addition, wool was required in the West Indies for blankets and clothing for the slaves on the plantations.

Iron, guns and brass also figured prominently in the triangular trade and the ancillary West Indian trade. Iron bars were the trading medium on a large part of the West African coast, and by 1682 Britain was exporting about 10,000 bars of iron a year to Africa. Sugar stoves, iron rollers, nails found a ready market on the West Indian plantations. Brass pans and kettles were customarily included in the slave trader's cargo. [...]

Barbados was the most important single colony in the British Empire, worth almost as much, in its total trade, as the two tobacco colonies of Virginia and Maryland combined, and nearly three times as valuable as Jamaica. The tiny sugar island was more valuable to Britain than Carolina, New England, New York and Pennsylvania together. "Go ahead, England, Barbados is behind you," is today a stock joke in the British West Indies of the Barbadian's view of his own importance. Two and a half centuries ago, it was no joke. It was sound politics, based on sound economics. Jamaica's external trade was larger than New England's as far as Britain was concerned; Nevis was more important in the commercial firmament than New York; Antigua surpassed Carolina; Montserrat rated higher than Pennsylvania. Total British trade with Africa was larger than total trade with Pennsylvania, New York and Carolina. In 1697 the triangular trade accounted for nearly ten per cent of total British imports and over four per cent of total British exports. Barbados alone accounted for nearly four per cent of Britain's external trade.

Mercantilists were jubilant. The West Indian colonies were ideal colonies, providing a market, directly as well as indirectly, through the slave trade, for British manufactures and foodstuffs, whilst they supplied sugar and other tropical commodities that would otherwise have had to be imported from foreigners or dispensed with entirely. The West Indies thus contributed to Britain's balance of trade in two ways, by buying Britain's exports and by rendering the expenditure of bullion on foreign tropical imports unnecessary. On the other hand, the mainland colonies, Virginia and Maryland, and, to a lesser extent, Carolina excepted, where the conditions of labour and production duplicated those of the West Indies, were nuisances; they produced the same agricultural commodities as England, gave early evidence of competing with the metropolitan countries in manufactured goods as well, and were rivals in fishing and shipbuilding.

The British economists enthused. Sir Josiah Child in his *New Discourse of Trade* in 1668, wrote:

> The people that evacuate from us to Barbados, and the other West India Plantations ... do commonly work one Englishman to ten or eight Blacks; and if we keep the trade of our said plantations entirely to England, England would have no less inhabitants, but rather an increase of people by such evacuation, because that one Englishman, with the Blacks that work with him, accounting what they eat, use and wear, would make employment for four men in England ... whereas peradventure of ten men that issue from us to New England and Ireland, what we send to or receive from them, doth not employ one man in England.

In 1690, Sir Dalby Thomas stated that every white man in the West Indies was one hundred and thirty times more valuable to Britain than those who stayed at home:

> Each white man, woman, and child, residing in the sugar plantations, occasions the consumption of more of our native commodities, and manufactures, than ten at home do—beef, pork, salt, fish, butter, cheese, corn, flour, beer, cyder, bridles, coaches, beds, chairs, stools, pictures, clocks, watches; pewter, brass, copper, iron vessels and instruments; sail-cloth and cordage; of which, in their building, shipping, mills, boiling, and distilling-houses, field-labour and domestic uses, they consume infinite quantities.

Charles Davenant, perhaps the ablest of the seventeenth-century economists, estimated at the end of the century that Britain's total profit from trade amounted to two million pounds. Of this figure the plantation trade accounted for £600,000, and the re-export of plantation produce for £120,000. Trade with Africa, Europe and the Levant brought in another £600,000. The triangular trade thus represented a minimum of 36 per cent of Britain's commercial profits. Davenant added that every individual in the West Indies, white or Negro, was as profitable as seven in England.

What the West Indies had done for Seville in Spain in the sixteenth century, they did for Bristol in England and Bordeaux in France in the seventeenth. Each town became the metropolis of its country's trade with the Caribbean, though neither Bristol nor Bordeaux enjoyed the monopoly that had been granted to Seville. In 1661 only one ship, and that ship a Dutch one, came to Bordeaux from the West Indies. Ten years later twelve ships sailed from that port to the West Indies, and six returned from there. In 1683 the number of sailings to the sugar islands had risen to twenty-six. La Rochelle for a time eclipsed Bordeaux. In 1685 forty-nine ships sailed from that port to the West Indies. Nantes also was intimately connected with West Indian trade; in 1684 twenty-four ships belonging to the port were engaged in West Indian trade.

As a result of the triangular trade Bristol became a city of shopkeepers. It was said in 1685 that there was scarcely a shopkeeper in the city who had not a venture on board some ship bound for Virginia or the West Indies. The port took the lead in the struggle for the abrogation of the Royal African Company's monopoly, and in the first nine years of free trade shipped slaves to the West Indies at the rate of 17,883 a year. In 1700 Bristol had forty-six ships in the West Indian trade.

The basis of this astounding commercial efflorescence was the Negro slaves, "the strength and sinews of this western world." In 1662 the Company of Royal Adventurers trading to Africa pointed to the "profit and honour" that had accrued to British subjects from the slave trade, which King Charles II himself described as that "beneficial trade … so much importing our service, and the enriching of this Our Kingdom." According to Colbert in France, no commerce in the world produced as many advantages as the slave trade. Benjamin Raule exhorted the Elector of Prussia, on October 26, 1685, not to be left behind in the race: "Everyone knows that the slave trade is the source of the wealth which the Spaniards wring out of the West Indies, and that whoever knows how to furnish them slaves, will share their wealth. Who can say by how many millions of hard cash the Dutch West India Company has enriched itself in this slave trade!" At the end of the seventeenth century all Europe, and not England only, was impressed with the words of Sir Dalby Thomas: "The pleasure, glory and grandeur of England has been advanced more by sugar than by any other commodity, wool not excepted."

The Negro slave trade in the eighteenth century constituted one of the greatest migrations in recorded history. Its volume is indicated in the following table, prepared from various statistics that are available.

Average annual importations do not provide a complete picture. In 1774 the importation into Jamaica was 18,448. In fourteen of the years 1702–1775, the annual importation exceeded 10,000. Imports into Saint-Domingue averaged 12,559 in the years 1764–1768; in 1768 they were 15,279. In 1718 Barbados imported 7,126 slaves. During the nine months in which Cuba was under British occupation in 1762, 10,700 slaves were introduced. The British introduced 41,000 slaves in three years into Guadeloupe whilst they were in occupation of the island during the Seven Years' War.

These large importations represented one of the greatest advantages which the slave trade had over other trades. The frightful mortality of the slaves on the plantations made annual increments essential. Consider the case of Saint-Domingue. In 1763 the slave population amounted to 206,539. Imports from 1764 to 1774 numbered 102,474. The slave

TABLE 19.1

YEARS	COLONY	IMPORTATION	AVERAGE IMPOR-TATION PER YEAR
1700–1786	Jamaica	610,000	7,000
1708–1735 & 1747–1766	Barbados	148,821	3,100
1680–1776	Saint-Domingue	800,000	8,247
1720–1729	Antigua	12,278	1,362
1721–1730	St. Kitts	10,358	1,035
1721–1729	Montserrat	3,210	357
1721–1726	Nevis	1,267	253
1767–1773	Dominica	19,194	2,742
1763–1789	Cuba	30,857	1,143
1700–1754	Danish Islands	11,750	214

population in 1776 was 290,000. Thus, despite an importation of over one hundred thousand, without taking into account the annual births, the increase of the slave population in thirteen years was less than 85,000. Taking only importations into consideration, the slave population in 1776 was 19,000 less than the figure of 1763 with the importations added, and the imports for one year are not available.

A much clearer illustration of the mortality is available for Barbados. In 1764 there were 70,706 slaves in the island. Importations to 1783, with no figures available for the years 1779 and 1780, totalled 41,840. The total population, allowing for neither deaths nor births, should, therefore, have been 112,546 in 1783. Actually, it was 62,258. Thus, despite an annual importation for the eighteen years for which statistics are available of 2,324, the population in 1783 was 8,448 less than it was in 1764, or an annual decline of 469. [...]

Thus, after eight years of importations, averaging 4,424 a year, the population of Barbados was only 3,411 larger. 35,397 slaves had been imported; 31,897 had disappeared. In 1770 and 1771 the mortality was so high that the importation in those years, heavy though it was, was not adequate to supply the deficit. Half the population had had to be renewed in eight years.

In 1703 Jamaica had 45,000 Negroes; in 1778, 205,261, an average annual increase from all causes of 2,109. Between 1703 and 1775, 469,893 slaves had been imported, an average annual importation of 6,807. For every additional slave in its population, Jamaica had had to import three. The total population in 1778, excluding births and based only on imports, should have been 541,893, and that figure excludes imports for 1776, 1777 and 1778. Allowing 11,000 a year for those three years, the total population in 1778 should have been 547,893. The actual population in that year was less than forty per cent of the potential total.

Economic development has never been purchased at so high a price. According to one of the leading planters of Saint-Domingue, one in every three imported Negroes died in the first three years. To the mortality on the plantations must be added the mortality on the slave ships. On the slave ships belonging to the port of Nantes in France, that mortality varied from 5 per cent in 1746 and 1774 to as high as 34 per cent in 1732. For all the slave cargoes transported by them between 1715 and 1775, the mortality amounted to 16 per cent. Of one hundred Negroes who left the coast of Africa, therefore, only 84 reached the West Indies; one-third of these died in three years. For every 56 Negroes, therefore, on the plantations at the end of three years, 44 had perished.

The slave trade thus represented a wear and tear, a depreciation which no other trade equalled. The loss of an individual planter or trader was insignificant compared with the basic fact that every cargo of slaves, including the quick and the dead, represented so much industrial development and employment, so much employment of ships and sailors, in the metropolitan country. No other commercial undertaking required so large a capital as the slave trade. In addition to the ship, there was its equipment, armament, cargo, its unusually large supply of water and foodstuffs, its abnormally large crew. In 1765 it was estimated that in France the cost of fitting out and arming a vessel for 300 slaves was 242,500 livres. The cargo of a vessel from Nantes in 1757 was valued at 141,500 livres; it purchased 500 slaves. The cargo of the *Prince de Conty*, of 300 tons, was valued at 221,224 livres, with which 800 slaves were purchased.

Large profits were realised from the slave trade. The *King Solomon*, belonging to the Royal African Company, carried a cargo worth £4,252 in 1720. It took on 296 Negroes who were sold in St. Kitts for £9,228. The profit was thus 117 per cent. From 1698 to 1707 the Royal African Company exported from England to Africa goods to the value of £293,740. The Company sold 5,982 Negroes in Barbados for £156,425, an average of £26 per head. It sold 2,178 slaves in Antigua for £80,522, an average of £37 per head. The total number of Negroes imported into the British islands by the Company in these years was 17,760. The sale of 8,160 Negroes in Barbados and Antigua, less than half the total imports into all the islands, thus realised 80 per cent of the total exports from England. Allowing an average price of £26 per head for the remaining 9,600 Negroes, the total amount realised from the sale of the Company's Negroes was £488,107. The profit on the Company's exports was thus 66 per cent. For every three pounds' worth of merchandise exported from England, the Company obtained two additional pounds by way of profit.

The Negroes taken on by the *Prince de Conty* on the coast of Africa averaged 275 livres each; the survivors of the Middle Passage fetched 1,300 livres each in Saint-Domingue. In 1700 a cargo of 238 slaves was purchased by the Danish West Indies at prices ranging from 90 to 100 rixdollars. In 1753 the wholesale price on the coast of Africa was 100 rixdollars; the retail price in the Danish West Indies was 150 to 300 rixdollars. In 1724 the Danish West India Company made a profit of 28 per cent on its slave imports; in 1725, 30 per cent; 70 per cent on the survivors of a cargo of 1733 despite a mortality in transit of 45 per cent; 50 per cent on a cargo of 1754. It need occasion no surprise, therefore, that one of the eighteenth-century slave dealers admitted that, of all the places he had lived in, England, Ireland, America, Portugal, the West Indies, the Cape Verde Islands, the Azores, and Africa, it was in Africa that he could most quickly make his fortune.

The slave trade was central to the triangular trade. It was, in the words of one British mercantilist, "the spring and parent whence the others flow"; "the first principle and foundation of all the rest," echoed another, "the mainspring of the machine which sets every wheel in motion." The slave trade kept the wheels of metropolitan industry turning; it stimulated navigation and shipbuilding and employed seamen; it raised fishing villages into flourishing cities; it gave sustenance to new industries based on the processing of colonial raw materials; it yielded large profits which were ploughed back into metropolitan industry; and, finally, it gave rise to an unprecedented commerce in the West Indies and made the Caribbean territories among the most valuable colonies the world has ever known.

Examples must suffice. In 1729 the British West Indies absorbed one-quarter of Britain's iron exports, and Africa, where the price of a Negro was commonly reckoned at one Birmingham gun, was one of the most important markets for the British armaments industry. In 1753 there were 120 sugar refineries in England—eighty in London, twenty in Bristol. In 1780 the British West Indies supplied two-thirds of the six and a half million pounds of raw cotton imported by Britain. Up to 1770 one-third of Manchester's textile exports went to Africa, one-half to the West Indian and American colonies. In 1709 the British West Indies employed one-tenth of all British shipping engaged in foreign trade. Between 1710 and 1714, 122,000 tons of British shipping sailed to the West Indies, 112,000 tons to the mainland colonies. Between 1709 and 1787, British shipping engaged in foreign trade quadrupled; ships clearing for Africa multiplied twelve times and the tonnage eleven times.

The triangular trade marked the ascendancy of two additional European ports in the eighteenth century, Liverpool in England and Nantes in France, and further contributed to the development of Bristol and Bordeaux, begun in the seventeenth century. [...]

Liverpool's exports to Africa in 1770 read like a census of British manufactures: beans, brass, beer, textiles, copper, candles, chairs, cider, cordage, earthenware, gunpowder, glass, haberdashery, iron, lead, looking glasses, pewter, pipes, paper, stockings, silver, sugar, salt, kettles.

In 1774 there were eight sugar refineries in Liverpool. Two distilleries were established in the town for the express purpose of supplying slave ships. There were many chain and anchor foundries, and manufacturers of and dealers in iron, copper, brass and lead in the town. In 1774 there were fifteen roperies. Half of Liverpool's sailors were engaged in the slave trade, which, by 1783, was estimated to bring the town a clear annual profit of £300,000. The slave trade transformed Liverpool from a fishing village into a great centre of international commerce. The population rose from 5,000 in 1700 to 34,000 in 1773. It was a common saying in the town that its principal streets had been marked out by the chains, and the walls of its houses cemented by the blood, of the African slaves. The red brick Customs House, blazoned with Negro heads, bore mute but eloquent testimony to the origins of Liverpool's rise by 1783 to the position of one of the most famous—or infamous, depending on the point of view—towns in the world of commerce. [...]

Magnum est saccharum et prevalebit! Great is sugar, and it will prevail! Mercantilists were jubilant. The colonies, wrote Horace Walpole, were "the source of all our riches, and preserve the balance of trade in our favour, for I don't know where we have it but by the means of our colonies." An annual profit of 7s per head was sufficient to enrich a country, said William Wood; each white man in the colonies brought a profit of over seven pounds, twenty times as much. The Negro slaves, said Postlethwayt, were "the fundamental prop and support" of the colonies, "valuable people," and the British Empire was "a magnificent superstructure of American commerce and naval power on an African foundation." Rule Britannia! Britannia rules the waves. For Britons never shall be slaves.

But the sons of France arose to glory. France joined in the homage to the triangular trade. "What commerce," asked the Chamber of Commerce of Nantes, "can be compared to that which obtains men in exchange for commodities?" Profound question! The abandonment of the slave trade, continued the Chamber, would be inevitably followed by the ruin of colonial commerce; "whence follows the fact that we have no branch of trade so precious to the State and so worthy of protection as the Guinea trade." The triangular trade was incomparable, the slave trade precious, and the West Indies perfect colonies. "The more colonies differ from the metropolis," said Nantes, "the more perfect they are.... Such are the Caribbean colonies: they have none of our objects of trade; they have others which we lack and cannot produce."

But there were discordant notes in the mercantilist harmony. The first was opposition to the slave trade. In 1774, in Jamaica, the very centre of Negro slavery, a debating society voted that the slave trade was not consistent with sound policy, or with the laws of nature and of morality. In 1776 Thomas Jefferson wrote into the Declaration of Independence three paragraphs attacking the King of England for his "piratical warfare" on the coast of Africa against people who never offended him, and for his veto of colonial legislation attempting to prohibit or restrain the slave trade. The paragraphs were only deleted on the representations of the states of South Carolina, Georgia and New England. Two petitions were presented to Parliament, in 1774 and 1776, for abolition of the slave trade. A third, more important, was presented in 1783 by the Quakers. The Prime Minister, Lord North, complimented them on their humanity, but regretted that abolition was an impossibility, as the slave trade had become necessary to every nation in Europe. European public opinion accepted the position stated by Postlethwayt: "We shall take things as they are, and reason from them in their present state, and not from that wherein we could hope them to be.... We cannot think of giving up the slave-trade, notwithstanding my good wishes that it could be done."

The second discordant note was more disturbing. Between 1772 and 1778, Liverpool slave traders were estimated to have lost £700,000 in the slave trade. By 1788 twelve of the thirty leading houses which had dominated the trade from 1773 had gone bankrupt. Slave trading, like sugar production, had its casualties. A slave trader in 1754, as his supreme defence of the slave trade, had adumbrated that "from this trade proceed benefits, far outweighing all, either real or pretended mischiefs and inconveniencies." If and when the slave trade ceased to be profitable, it would not be so easy to defend it.

The third discordant note came also from the British colonies. The British Government's ambition was to become the slave carriers and sugar suppliers of the whole world. Britain had fought for and obtained the *asiento*. The supply of slaves to foreign nations became an integral part of the British slave trade. Of 497,736 slaves imported in Jamaica between 1702 and 1775, 137,114 had been re-exported, one out of every four. In 1731, imports were 10,079; re-exports, 5,708. From 1775 to 1783, Antigua imported 5,673 slaves and re-exported 1,972, one out of every three. Jamaica resorted to its seventeenth-century policy, an export tax on all Negroes re-exported. In 1774, the Board of Trade, on the representation of the slave traders of London, Liverpool and Bristol, disallowed the law as unjustifiable, improper and prejudicial to British commerce, pointed out that legislative autonomy in the colonies did not extend to the imposition of duties upon British ships and goods or to the prejudice and obstruction of British commerce, and reprimanded the Governor of the island for dereliction of duty in not stopping efforts to "check and discourage a traffic … beneficial to the nation."

SELECTED BIBLIOGRAPHY

Davenant, Charles. *Discourse on the Trade and Publick Revenues of England*. London, 1698. (There are other useful writings of Davenant, all of which can be found in C. Whitworth (ed.), *The Political and Commercial Works of Charles Davenant*, London, 1781).

Postlethwayt, M. *The National and Private Advantages of the African Trade considered*. London, 1746.

———. *The Universal Dictionary of Trade and Commerce*. London, 1751.

———. *Great Britain's Commercial Interest explain'd and improv'd*. London, 1759.

———. *The African Trade, the Great Pillar and Support of the British Plantation Trade in North America*. London, 1765.

Thomas, Sir Dalby. *An Historical Account of the Rise and Growth of the West India Colonies, and of the Great Advantages they are to England, in respect to Trade*. London, 1690.

Wood, W. *A Survey of Trade*. London, 1718.

———. *The Importance of the Sugar Colonies to Great Britain*. London, 1731.

———. *Some Considerations humbly offer'd upon the Bill now depending in the House of Lords, relating to the Trade between the Northern Colonies and the Sugar-Islands*. London, 1732.

Chapter 20

Prelude to Settlement: Indians as Indentured Labourers

Verene Shepherd

Next to slave labour, indentured labour represented for plantation owners the next best source of workers. Verene Shepherd's 1994 chapter speaks to the experience of thousands of Indians who were brought over to work as plantation labourers in Jamaica from the middle of the nineteenth century to about 1917. (Even larger numbers of Indian labourers were brought to Trinidad and Guyana.) In addition to the economic, political, and psychological implications of colonialism explored in earlier chapters, this chapter reflects on the social and cultural implications of being colonized and racialized. Shepherd writes of Indian men and women of diverse linguistic, religious, caste, and class origins being "herded" together and being introduced to, yet segregated from, African Jamaicans. "A new kind of 'Indian' identity began to emerge," an Indian-Jamaican identity. Demographic realities affected gender relations and family and household formations in ways that were distinctive from other Caribbean and South American countries. The legacy of these realities remains even today.

According to A.E. Smith, "… the system of indentured servitude was the most convenient system next to slavery by which labour became a commodity to be bought and sold."[1] Its applicability to colonial requirements had been suggested as early as 1582 by Sir George Peckham[2] and, indeed, had its precedent in the ancient institution of apprenticeship. In the case of Jamaica, indentureship pre-dated the abolition of African slavery, having been applied to white servants in the seventeenth century. It was extended to immigrants imported between 1835 and 1916. It was, however, most extensively applied to the Indians.

The system of Indian indentureship not only provided the basis for the development of a settled Indian community in Jamaica, but also had far-reaching implications for the later history of Indian settlers. In the passage from Indian village to the immigration depot, the long sea voyage and then residence on a Jamaican plantation, the indentured labourer went through a series of profound shifts in his or her social environment. These inevitably facilitated cultural change.

In the first place, as Benedict noted with reference to Mauritius, Indian labourers were herded together with little regard to regional origin, caste, religion or linguistic group.[3] This led to intra-culturation between different Indian groups which might not have had contact prior to their arrival in the Caribbean, so that a new kind of "Indian" identity began to emerge. Second, contact with managers and other workers on the estate, no matter how limited, started the process of inter-culturation to both Euro- and Afro-creole norms, though this became more pronounced later. Third, though the estate managers maintained a degree of residential and occupational separation between Indians and Afro-Jamaicans, inevitably the juxtaposition of the two groups led to some social contact and, at the very least, the formation of perceptions about the ethnic other. These perceptions, which frequently took a racially stereotyped form, themselves played a part in the formation of an Indo-Jamaican ethnic identity. This came about both in terms of how Indians felt they were perceived by others and sometimes in an enlarged sense of difference from their Afro-Jamaican neighbours. Fourth, the very patterns of work on the plantation were socially and psychologically transforming. The person who set out from village India was part of a caste society whose way of life had changed little over the past centuries. On the plantation began the complex process of change from peasant to proletarian.

In reviewing the experience of indentureship and its implications for the settlement period, this chapter examines the origins of the indentured workers who came to Jamaica, their demographic composition and the salient features of how the indentureship system affected their lives as workers on the estates.

I. ORIGINS OF INDIAN INDENTURED SERVANTS

[…] The process of recruitment was similar for all colonies and, as it has been amply described elsewhere,[4] only a brief account is given here. Recruitment was carried out by men licensed by the Protector of Emigrants, but employed by Sub-Agents who manned the up-country depots at which emigrants were assembled prior to their journey to Madras or Calcutta for embarkation. Licensed recruiters often appointed assistants—*Kutty Maistries* in Madras, *Arkatias* in North India—who travelled around the villages to obtain recruits. Recruiters were paid by commission. Though perhaps the only practicable method of payment, this was accompanied by many abuses which at times led to the cancellation of licences. Unlicensed recruiters, however, often operated undetected.[5] [...]

In general, the pattern of recruitment for other Caribbean colonies was not vastly different, except that by the time that places such as the Windwards began to import Indians, competition with the Assam tea gardens had caused recruitment to shift away from the "Hill Coolies." Jamaica, Trinidad, Guyana and Suriname tapped the same areas, though the source of emigrants was not always the same for each colony for each year. In most cases, the demand for Trinidad and Guyana was filled first, leaving recruiters for Jamaica and Suriname to fill their quota as best they could. This was a reflection of the fact that Jamaica was less popular as a destination for Indians. Repatriation was inefficient and wages were lower than in other colonies.

This brief survey of the areas of recruitment reveals that the Indians who came to Jamaica did not represent a homogeneous group. They came from different linguistic and cultural zones. On the estates, therefore, Tamil and Hindi speakers, Hindus and Muslims would meet with creole Jamaicans and learn the lingua franca of the estate—an early area of cultural adaptation.

II. DEMOGRAPHIC COMPOSITION OF THE INDENTURED INDIANS

[...] Muslims (referred to at times in the Emigration Passes as "Musalmans") formed only a minority of the immigrants introduced to Jamaica and the rest of the Caribbean. Of the 607 imported on the *Indus* in 1907, only 93 were Muslims.[6] Planters were not keen on their importation and only in a few cases did they form the majority on any shipment.[7] Reporting on the arrival of the *Rhine* from Calcutta in 1899 the Protector remarked that there was an unusually large number of "Musalmans" amongst the shipment. This fact he lamented on the grounds that "... these invariably cause trouble among the rest on the properties to which they are allotted."[8] [...]

The most significant demographic characteristic of Indian immigrants to Jamaica and the rest of the diaspora was the disproportionate number of males. This was despite an ordinance stipulating a ration of 40 females to every 100 males and the higher commission paid for the recruitment of females.[9] There were a few years (1892 and 1893 were exceptions) when the obligatory number of women was obtained for emigration. Several reasons have been advanced to explain the failure. First, planters seemed to have preferred to import married women accompanying their husbands. The majority of women opting for emigration, however, were single women (some being widows and women kidnapped in the pilgrim centres) whose dispatch to the colonies was discouraged unless they formed part of an emigrating family. The planters saw women as desirable immigrants only in the light of their ability to satisfy the domestic and sexual needs of male workers and would support single women only if they formed permanent attachments to male labourers on arrival. The feeling was that "a woman who is not occupied otherwise than in cooking her husband's food is more likely to get into mischief." This was an euphemism for "sexual mischief," the planters being of the view that single women were generally prostitutes and "women of doubtful character."[10] However, despite planter preference, the majority of women imported to the region were single—often disguised as married women, emigrating with professing "husbands" and "children."[11] This latter fact means that any figure relating to the number of married women dispatched to the colonies in any one year must be treated with caution. There must be doubts, for example, over the unusually high proportion of married women on the 1893 shipment to Suriname—67%, compared to 45% to Guyana and 27% to Jamaica.[12] [...] This low percentage for Jamaica was replicated in other years. On the *Indus* of 1905 for example, only 29% of the 217 women were married and accompanied by spouses.[13] A similar trend was observed on the *Indus* in 1906 where out of 442 emigrants, 114 were women. Out of the 114, 38 were married and 76 single.[14] Whether married or single, women were underrepresented on each shipment down to 1916—a trend set from the earliest importation of 1845 when out of 261 immigrants only 28, or 11%, comprised women.[15] Indeed, it would be safe to say that women comprised less than one-third of each shipload of immigrants imported to Jamaica from the 1880s.

A second reason for the low importation of women was that up to 1910, no family with more than two children was allowed to emigrate. The view was that large numbers of children increased the risk of epidemics at the depot and on board the ships and the planters were unwilling to incur maintenance expenses for large numbers of children. Thus, up to 1913, no commissions were paid for the recruitment of children under 12. However, in an effort to increase the proportion of women in the colonies, recruiters were given financial incentives for the recruitment of girls after 1913. This, though, had little effect. Up to 1916, when Jamaica obtained the last shipment of Indian immigrants, no significant improvement was noted in the proportion of women dispatched to the island. Combined with the much smaller numbers of Indians in Jamaica, this sexual disparity no doubt played a role in the greater prevalence of Indians marrying outside their group than occurred in Trinidad or Guyana.

III. THE INDENTURESHIP EXPERIENCE

(a) Allocation to Estates, Work and Wages

Between 1845 and 1916, an estimated 37,000 Indian immigrants entered the island and served their period of indentureship on properties located primarily in the parishes of St. Andrew, St. Mary, Portland, Clarendon, Westmoreland, St. Catherine and St. Thomas-in-the-East (simply St. Thomas after 1867). After their arrival in the island (first at Port Royal and then on to various disembarkation depots) immigrants were dispatched in carts, schooners or by rail to the properties on which they were to serve out their indentures. These were the ones who after examination by the Medical Board on arrival were found to be "fit for service" and who were then issued with certificates of indenture. Despite the length and rigours of the journey from India—particularly before the use of steam ships in 1906—those rejected as "unfit" were remarkably few.[16]

In the early years of immigration, Indians seem to have been allocated to estates in batches of about 20, but between 1891 and 1916 some estates received as few as four and others as many as 63 from single shipments. [...] The geographical distribution of immigrants indicated by the parish breakdown was replicated on other shipments. In comparison to Trinidad and Guyana where much larger numbers of Indians were densely concentrated, in Jamaica a much smaller number was widely dispersed, though there were concentrations in areas of high sugar and banana production. Thus, in Jamaica, the land area into which Indians were absorbed— particularly after their employment on banana estates—was larger than in Trinidad and Guyana where estates were concentrated in comparatively smaller ecological zones.[17] The patterns in Martinique and Guadeloupe were much like that of Jamaica.[18] Commenting on the implications of this pattern of settlement for the maintenance of a strong ethnic/cultural identity, Erlich noted that "... whatever strengths existed in the small number that came were shattered by the small numbers in which they were parcelled out."[19] Even when there was the possibility of movement off the estates into villages and the increase of the Indian population by natural means or the addition to their numbers through further importations, there were other factors militating against any significant growth in the Indian population in the island. These included repatriation, the lack of continuous importations and socio-economic factors frustrating the evolution of "Indian villages."

On the estates, Jamaican proprietors employed a variety of measures in an effort to render Indian immigrants a more controllable labour force than Afro-Jamaican labourers. The main strategy was, of course, to secure Indian labourers under indentured contracts. The rationale for such contracts was that when labour was not sufficiently cheap and servile, the free play of market forces had to be interrupted and an element of extra-economic compulsion introduced. Planters constantly agitated for longer contracts, though at first the British Government only allowed one-year contracts. By 1850 the Government had relented sufficiently to allow three-year contracts; this was because Indians from the 1845–47 batches had generally refused to re-indenture after the first year. The provision had been that after serving out the first contract year they were at liberty to enter into contracts for periods not exceeding one year with any planter for whom they wished to work. By 1848, for example, it was clear that a lack of super-vision and the Indians' understandable disinclination to renew their contracts posed problems for the proprietors. A parish-by-parish survey conducted by the press in that year revealed that a large number had become vagrants and mendicants and that poverty was widespread among them.[20] These factors combined with reactions to the Sugar Duties Act of 1846 led to the suspension of immigration in 1848. In the 1850s, however, there were renewed calls for the resumption of Indian immigration—but under more stringent control and longer contracts. Importations restarted in 1860 and by 1862, five-year contracts were general throughout the region. This was confirmed by section 30 of Jamaica Law 23 of 1879 which clarified and amplified earlier laws and with minor adjustments regulated Indian immigration to Jamaica. Sections 41 and 43 of the Law provided that at the expiration of this five-year period immi-grants could enter into fresh contracts of one-year duration in each case. They could choose their employers the second time round. Nevertheless, while such second contracts were in force, "Second Term Coolies," as re-indentureds were called, were subject to the provisions of the immigration laws just as if they were under indenture.

Up to 1921, indentured and "time-expired" Indians worked side by side on the estates; and until re-indentureship was abolished by Law 20 of 1891, a small percentage of "time-expired" immigrants regularly renewed their contracts. In supporting the abolition of re-indenture, the Protector indicated that few Indians in Jamaica made use of this provision because it was not a necessary condition for securing employment—at least not in times of buoyancy in the main economic sectors. [...] In times of economic depression, however, "time-expireds" were the first to suffer. At such times the availability of surplus Afro-Jamaican labourers and the obligation to hire indentured servants deprived the ex-indentured labourer of work.

Before the beginning of the period of contract, each labourer was issued with agricultural implements, cooking utensils and a suit of clothing. Trousers were made out of oznaburgh and shirts out of striped Holland or flannelette. Women's clothes were made from brown calico and striped Holland. This represented a further break in tradition and the demise of the dhoti and sari for many. New immigrants were supplied with rations, for the first few months but thereafter, provided food out of their wages.[21]

On sugar estates, indentured labourers worked in gangs supervised by either an Indian or Afro-Jamaican headman or "driver." Indian "drivers" were selected solely on the basis of their ability to implement plantation routine—not according to caste or religion. Thus low castes could be placed over high caste, Muslims over Hindus, and so on—factors which forced inter-ethnic interaction. Indian labourers naturally preferred Indian headmen or sirdars, who, according to Chimman Lai and James McNeil "... are more cheerfully obeyed if the latter are sure that the former's control is exercised with the full knowledge and approval of the employer."[22]

The classification of gangs followed closely that of slavery, with strength and physical condition, age and gender being important criteria for the worker's allocation. Thus the weeding gang was invariably composed of the less physically able, and some women. At times there was also an invalid gang comprising children and convalescents. In Jamaica the criterion of "race" was also applied. Planter preference for Afro-Jamaican labourers for heavier tasks, combined with the stereotype of the physically weak Indian, caused certain gangs to consist heavily of blacks; correspondingly, certain tasks referred to as "womens' work" tended to be assigned specifically to Indians—male or female.[23] However, the list of tasks performed by Indian labourers [...] including digging stumps, preparing the land, planting and reaping indicates that ethnic factors in allocating work were not absolute. For instance, contrary to popular belief, Indian labourers were employed in sugar factory work.[24]

Work on banana plantations and livestock pens was less regimented, but even on these units the gang system often prevailed. On banana plantations, a similar stereotype regarding the physical capacity of the Indian directed "delicate work" such as pruning bananas, to Indian labour gangs. Other tasks on banana estates ranged from hoeing grass, billing, forking and trenching to heading and carting. Greater dependence on Indian labourers in Trinidad and Guyana meant that such stereotypes could not be allowed to have any significant impact on the allocation of work.

The Indian's life—whether employed on pen, sugar estate or banana plantation—was arranged according to the schedule devised by the plantation. Neither routine nor tasks bore any relationship to caste or religion.[25] About the only restriction which respected caste and religious sensibilities was the direction that Hindus should not be given jobs which involved the handling of meat. Governor Manning claimed that none were so employed in Jamaica,[26] but as Indians worked on livestock farms it is unclear whether this denial was accurate.[27]

During their first three months in the colony, immigrants were required to do nine hours of day labour for six days a week. In Jamaica labourers were paid at the rates of l/6d a day for men of 16 years and upwards and 9d per day for women and children between the ages of 12 and 16. Wages in Trinidad and Guyana were only slightly higher. In Trinidad, a minimum wage of 1/1d a day was stipulated in the indenture contract.[28] [...]

The rates for tasks on banana estates also varied but generally some were more remunerative than others. Cutting, heading, wrapping and carting fruits were the highest paying tasks while among the lowest paid were hoeing and fencing. As cocoa cultivation was generally interspersed with banana cultivation, the Indians also were engaged in pruning and picking cocoa. The wages for these activities were low. [...] Such low wages affected the Indians' ability to leave the estates for village settlement.

Wage rates were not always promptly paid; neither did the employers always pay the correct wage rates or provide jobs to enable the immigrants to earn sufficient wages. This was despite the responsibility of the Protector of Immigrants to ensure that the correct rates were paid. [...]

(b) Accommodation on the Estate

Indentured immigrants were housed in barracks on the estates on which they worked. As in Guyana and Trinidad, the fact that Indians were housed separately from Afro-Jamaicans was a most important factor for the encouragement of Indian cultural retention.[29] Barracks in Jamaica were similar to those in other colonies and were essentially long ranges of buildings divided into rooms of 120 square feet with a covered verandah five feet in width. Detached huts were also found in Jamaica. The mean height of rooms was from nine feet upwards. Floors were boarded and raised from 18 to 24 inches above ground level. In some cases rammed earth raised well above the ground was used. Regulations were laid down to ensure proper ventilation and latrine facilities for the occupants of these buildings,[30] but despite the constant warnings of Medical Officers who visited each estate monthly, these regulations were not always carried out. Indeed, sanitation around the barracks was so poor that immigrants were constantly plagued with ankylostomiasis.[31]

(c) Medical Care

A multiplicity of laws were established to govern immigrants' health experiences under the system of indenture. At first, estates maintained their own hospitals. After 1869, the system of treating patients in estate hospitals in Jamaica was abandoned. Thus Jamaican estates were less self-enclosed than those in Guyana which were more self-sufficient. The abandonment of estate hospitals was not welcomed by all. It was thought, for example, that the treatment of minor ailments in the hospitals increased the number of days labourers were absent from work and facilitated malingering.[32] The Acting Protector, F.N. Isaacs, suggested in 1914 that to offset this tendency, the Medical Department should furnish each estate with dressings and medicines with simple directions for their use. This could be administered for minor ailments by a "responsible" person.[33] [...]

The main illnesses for which immigrants were admitted to hospital were anaemia, ulcers, malaria and phititis. These diseases weakened victims considerably and caused them to be readmitted frequently to hospital. Abas Ali of Agualta Vale Estate in St. Mary, for example, was admitted to hospital for malaria 20 times between 1906 and 1909. The high incidence of illness revealed in the statistics speaks of human misery, but the loss of labour through sickness was also a serious problem for the employers. As usual, though, it was the employers who were able to mitigate the situation to their own advantage. Large numbers of immigrants had their period of indenture extended to take account of periods of sickness; very few were freed on account of ill-health.

(d) Control and Resistance

In addition to contracts, estate residency and gang labour, Jamaican proprietors made extensive use of penal clauses and restrictive labour laws to render Indians a "controllable" work force. These regulations represented an elaborate system of coercion which included laws curtailing freedom of movement outside the estates. In order to lodge a complaint against an employer, for example, the immigrant first had to obtain permission from that same employer to leave the estate and go to the Protector of Immigrants' office. The rationale for this attempt to confine Indians within the physical boundaries of the estate was that like slaves before them, Indians were prone to marronage and had to be restrained from such "vagabond" instincts. A number of punitive devices were also imposed upon indentured workers for what were deemed "offences against the labour law." Such offences included "unlawful" absence from work, downright refusal to labour, "wilful indolence," feigned illness and general malingering. Punishment for such offences ranged from the extra-legal methods of floggings to heavy fines and imprisonment. Furthermore, time spent in prison was simply added to the length of immigrants' indentures. Contrary to the once prevalent myth of the "docile coolie," there is much evidence that Indians in Jamaica as in other receiving colonies, employed a variety of strategies both to resist and to register their disaffection with repressive aspects of the system,

This has added another dimension to resistance studies in the region. While still dominated by a focus on slave resistance, the historiography reflects the increasing attention being paid to protest among indentured labourers. [...] It is not an easy task to determine whether all forms of non-cooperation on the part of indentured immigrants constituted resistance.[34] [...]

The myth of the docile Indian, in Jamaica, was shattered by the frequency of malingering, "wilful indolence," unlawful absence from work and downright refusal to work. According to

Law 23 of 1879 (Section 95 (15)), these offences were regarded as serious breaches of contract and conviction made the labourer liable up to a £3 fine. The fact that such offences formed a large percentage of the cases brought before the Resident Magistrate and the Protector of Immigrants in each year attests to the fact that the threat of fines did not deter the Indians. In 1914–15 alone, a total of 256 cases of wilful indolence were brought before the Resident Magistrates and the Protector. Many employers described the Indians as incorrigible idlers who would never reform even though they were continually punished. However, this did not deter employers and the courts from making extensive use of the labour laws and their penalties. As the Protector of Immigrants, Charles Doorly, admitted, punishment was very often only applied, "...by way of setting an example to others on the property who perhaps are not too zealously inclined."[35]

Refusal to work and "unlawful" absence also accounted for a number of the cases before the Protector and the Magistrates. In 1914–15, 123 cases of downright refusal to work were recorded and 70 cases of "unlawful" absence. Careful records of "unlawful" absence were kept. [...] When compared to the total number of indentured workers, however, these percentages become less significant. In fact, between 1911 and 1916, only 1.55 days on average were lost per year on account of absence from work. [...]

More violent signs of discontent were organised strikes, riots and protest marches to the Protector of Immigrants or to the police station.

Strikes, riots and protest marches occurred throughout the indentureship period, though they were more marked in the twentieth century. These were usually spontaneous and localised and never reached the proportion of planned island-wide revolts. The usual reasons for strikes, riots and protest marches were non-payment of wages or the failure of employers to pay wages on time, disputes over task work, dissatisfaction with the headmen, disputes over rations and ill-treatment. In some cases, violence accompanied strikes. In all cases, the aim of action was to gain better working conditions for all indentured servants and force employers to conform to the terms of contracts. [...]

The Indian leaders of these riots, strikes or protest marches were usually seasoned immigrants. Walter Rodney has reported the planter view that fresh arrivals were more malleable, which was why the planters favoured the continual influx of new Indian immigrants.[36]

Political resistance was resorted to when other methods had failed. In theory, immigrants had access to the courts for legal redress for grievances, and they did sometimes take their employers to court for breaches of the "beneficent" clauses of the immigration ordinances. In theory, too, the magistrates were obliged to move against planters who breached their legal obligations. However, the reality was that immigrants regularly went before the courts as victims of a legal system which brought the force of the law directly on the side of the planters. Indeed, in Jamaica, only in very isolated cases were employers convicted and fined, as for example, in 1913, when the overseer of an estate in Portland was prosecuted for assaulting an Indian worker.[37] [...]

However, neither personal intransigence nor collective resistance brought about the abolition of indentureship or any greater freedom for the indentured population. Despite the frequency of desertion, no free extra-estate communities developed which could "have formed the basis of residential separation. Freedom came through the expiration of contracts and the ten-year compulsory period of residence, through release from indenture on account of disability or by commutation of the unexpired portion of indentures. Between 1907 and 1915 it was recorded that the annual average release from indenture because of physical disability was 4%. Some of those released from indenture settled in the island adding to the resident population. Abolition of the system of indentureship, however, had to await developments in India.

(e) Abolition of Indentureship

Whilst the conditions of indentured labourers in Jamaica and other colonies was the subject of much official investigation from the 1870s to 1913, such recommendations as were made after these investigations only brought about certain minor changes and did not seriously affect the essential nature of the system. Indeed, even some of the attempts to bring about minor improvement were frustrated. [...]

Ultimately, it took the concerted efforts of Mahatma Gandhi, C.F. Andrews and Gokhale to bring about the demise of the system of indentured labour migration in 1917. As the details of that effort have been well documented elsewhere, and as they are necessarily external to Jamaica, they will not be recounted here.[38] However, what is less well known is that economic factors in Jamaica had already led to the cessation of immigration in 1916, although Guyana and Trinidad continued their importations.

Consequently, the news from India of the proposed abolition of indentured immigration was not received in Jamaica with any great alarm and engendered no great public comment in the press.[39] [...]

Indentureship was, then, an inescapable experience in the lives of Indian immigrants in the Caribbean. It operated similarly in all colonies and therefore was not a crucial variable in the observed differences in the cultural adaptation of Indians in Jamaica and in other receiving colonies such as Trinidad and Guyana. The plantation experience began the process of indigenization. However, though it provided the first contact with Afro-Jamaicans, its arrangements for residential separation helped to foster some Indian cultural retention in the non-working hours. At the same time, however, the nature of the estates as "total institutions," organised to deliver regimented labour, had a severe impact on Indian culture, particularly on language, dress and family life. And though the impact of the estate was not ineradicable, as the experience of Indians in Trinidad and Guyana shows, there was no similar pattern of movement off the estates in Jamaica. In Trinidad and Guyana it was this which led to the development of communities organised around Indian cultural patterns, albeit modified. It will be seen that such communities, which greatly facilitated cultural retention, did not develop in Jamaica.

NOTES

1.   A.E. Smith, *Colonists in Bondage: White Servitude and Convict Labor in America, 1607–1706* (Chapel Hill: University of North Carolina Press, 1947), p. 4.

2.   Ibid.

3.   B. Benedict, *Indians in a Plural Society: A Report on Mauritius* (London: HMSO, 1961), p. 26.

4.   See for example, H. Tinker, *A New System of Slavery: The Export of Indian Labour Overseas, 1830–1920* (Oxford: Oxford University Press, 1974), and P. Saha, *Emigration of Indian Labour, 1834–1900*, New Delhi: People's Publishing House, 1970.

5.   See CO 571/3 "Notes on Colonial Emigration."

6.   CGF 1B/9/141 Papers of the SS *Indus*, 1907.

7.   CGF 1B/SM43, Nominal Roll, SS *Mutlah*, 1913.

8.   *Governor's Report on the Blue Book, 1898–99* (Kingston: Gov't. Printing Office, 1899).

9.   In 1914, for example, 60 rupees were paid for male recruits and 100 rupees for each female. See CO 571/3. Emigration Agent Gibbes to the Under-Secretary of the State in the Colonial Office.

10. See V.A. Shepherd, "Indian Women in Jamaica, 1845–1945," in F. Birbalsingh (ed.), *Indenture and Exile: The Indo-Caribbean Experience* (Toronto: Tsar Press, 1989), pp. 100–107, and CO 571/3, Gibbes to the Under-Secretary.

11. Shepherd, p. 100.

12. IORE 4 vii A(l)1893.

13. CGF IB/9/34 and 38, Papers of the *Indus*, 1905.

14. CGF 1B/9/35B, Papers of the *Indus*, 1906.

15. CGF IB/9/3, Papers of the *Blundell*. 1845. See also V.A. Shepherd, "Aspects of the condition of Indian Female Plantation Workers in Jamaica During the Indentureship and Post-Indentureship Periods," unpublished paper submitted for R. Reddock (ed.), *Reader on Plantation Women* (forthcoming).

16. Small sailing ships and barques were used up to 1906. These ranged from 500 to 1,000 tons. One of the smallest ships to Jamaica was the *Wentworth* which was 521 tons. The *Mullah*, one of the largest, was 2,153 tons. Sailing ships took up to six months to arrive in the colonies with a resultant high mortality rate. Seventy-five of the 308 passengers despatched on the *Rajasthan* in 1860 died. The *Humber* of 1872 recorded a 13% death rate. By 1910, however, better medical supervision and steam ships had cut the journey and the mortality rate. The latter ranged between 1 and 4% by 1916.

17. A.S. Erlich, "History, Ecology and Demography in the British Caribbean: An Analysis of East Indian Ethnicity," *Southwestern Journal of Anthropology* 27, no. 2 (1971), pp. 173–176.

18. E. Moutoussamy, "Indianness in the French West Indies," in Birbalsingh (ed.), *Indenture and Exile*, p. 28.

19. Erlich, p. 176.

20. CO 142/7, *Morning Journal*, 3 Aug. 1847 and 15 May 1847. See also Parliamentary Paper No. 399, Vol. XLV, 1847–48.

21. CGF IB/9/17, "Laws operating in 1903 for the treatment of Coolies," Immigration Office, 6 March 1903.

22. Gt. Britain Parliament, 1915. *Report of Chimman Lai and James McNeil on East Indian Immigration* (London: HMSO, 1915), p. 213.

23. Sanderson Commission, Evidence of Sir Arthur Blake, Governor, 6 May 1909, Sec. 2637.

24. J. Weller, *East Indian Indenture in Trinidad* (Rio Piedras, Puerto Rico: Institute of Caribbean Studies, 1967), p. 3.

25. B. Brereton, "The Experience of Indentureship, 1845–1917," in J. La Guerre (ed.), *Calcutta to Caroni: The East Indians of Trinidad* (Port of Spain: Longman Caribbean, 1974), p. 29.

26. Sec. 50, Law 23,1879.

27. Ibid.

28. CSO IB/5/11/5, Jamaica Legislative Council Debates, Session of 24 Oct. 1912.

29. W. Rodney, *A History of the Guyanese Working People, 1881–1905* (London: Heinemann Educational Books Ltd., 1981), p. 17.

30. Ibid., p. 201.

31. This disease was caused by the hookworm which developed in the intestines of the person afflicted and was indicated by an anaemic condition. It was spread by the ova in the faeces of the afflicted person. Fully 75% of the working classes of India suffered from this debilitating and often fatal disease.

32. *Report of Chimman Lai and James McNeil*, p. 202. Also CGF 1B/9/28, Isaacs to the Managers of Estates, 17 April 1914.

33. Protector of Immigrants, Isaacs, to the Manager of Estates, 1914.

34. G.M. Frederickson and C. Lasch, "Resistance to Slavery," *Civil War History* 13 (1967), pp. 315–329.

35. Protector of Immigrants' Report, Jamaica, 1910–11.

36. Rodney, *A History of the Guyanese Working People*, p. 155.

37. PIR 1913–1914.

38. Correspondence No. 20, Protector of Immigrants Papers, Jamaica Archives, Protector to the Colonial Secretary, n.d., 1902.

39. Tinker, *A New System of Slavery*, p. 194.

BIBLIOGRAPHY

Primary Sources

I. MANUSCRIPTS

PUBLIC RECORD OFFICE, LONDON
Selected volumes from the following classes:
CO 571: Immigration Correspondence

JAMAICA ARCHIVES
CSO 1B/S/11/1 to 22, Legislative Council Debates
CSO 1B/5/75 to 77, Original Correspondence and Copies of Original Correspondence from the Colonial Secretary's Office
CGF 1B/9, 1845–1950, Immigration Department Papers of the Protector of Immigrants.

II. PRINTED

INDIA OFFICE LIBRARY AND RECORDS
PP Vol. XLV, (353), 1847–48

REPORTS AND PAPERS
Gt. Britain. Parliament, 1915. *Report by James McNeil and Chimman Lal on East Indian Emigration.* London: HMSO, 1915.

GOVERNMENT OF INDIA
IOR Collection V/24/1208-14, 1875–1916, Annual Reports on Emigration from the Port of Calcutta.

GOVERNMENT OF JAMAICA
Jamaica Annual Reports (which included Reports of the Immigration Department), 1879–1938.

NEWSPAPERS
Morning Journal

Secondary Sources

BOOKS

Benedict, B. *Indians in a Plural Society: A Report on Mauritius*. London: HMSO, 1961.

Birbalsingh, F. (ed). *Indenture and Exile: The Indo-Caribbean Experience*. Toronto: Tsar Press, 1989.

Brereton, B. *A History of Modern Trinidad, 1783–1962*. Kingston, Port of Spain, London: Heinemann Educational Books Ltd., 1981.

Rodney, W. *A History of the Guyanese Working People, 1881–1905*. Kingston, Port of Spain, London: Heinemann Educational Books Ltd., 1981.

Saha, P. *Emigration of Indian Labour, 1834–1900*. New Delhi: Peoples Publishing House, 1970.

Smith, A.E. *Colonists in Bondage: White Servitude and Convict Labour in America, 1607–1776*. USA: University of North Carolina Press, 1947.

Tinker, H. *A New System of Slavery: The Export of Indian Labour Overseas, 1830–1920*. London: Oxford University Press, 1974.

Weller, J.A. *The East Indian Indenture in Trinidad*, Caribbean Monograph Series, No. 4. Puerto Rico: Institute of Caribbean Studies, University of Puerto Rico, 1968.

ARTICLES

Erlich, A.S. "History, Ecology, and Demography in the British Caribbean: An Analysis of East Indian Ethnicity." *Southwestern Journal of Anthropology* 27, 2 (1971).

Frederickson, G.M., and Lasch, C. "Resistance to Slavery." *Civil War History* 13 (1967).

Shepherd, V.A. "Aspects of the Condition of Indian Female Plantation Workers in Jamaica During the Indentureship and Post-Indentureship Period." In R. Reddock (ed.), *Reader in Plantation Women*, forthcoming.

PART 3

RACE, RACISM, AND INSTITUTIONS

PART 3A

STATE MULTICULTURALISM— MANAGING "DIFFERENCE"

Today, societies face many challenges brought about, in part, by world migration, residential patterns, religious and cultural differences, and a heightened sense of social justice. For many Western societies, the resulting economic, political, social, and cultural conditions create environments that demand ongoing education and action that take into account how individuals' situations are related to and mediated by the structures of society. To address these demands, multiculturalism (interculturalism in Quebec) policies and programs have been introduced—often in response to challenges and agitation by racialized members of society as they seek recognition of their presence, with corresponding full participation and equality of opportunities. But multiculturalism as a neo-liberal discourse represents an understanding that all ethnic and racial groups are able to fully participate in their societies irrespective of cultural differences, thus masking inequity and stratification based on ethnicity, language, religion, race (or colour), citizenship (or immigrant status), class, and related differences that exist among members of the population. The discourse holds, first, that society is democratic and meritocratic and the laws, policies, and regulations that exist sufficiently provide members the freedom and opportunity to achieve their aspirations regardless of race, ethnicity, gender, social class, etc. In such a context, special measures that might help to address an individual's failure to participate fully in the society and/or attain their aspirations are considered unnecessary, for it is individual efforts that count and not structural or systemic factors. Second, the discourse holds that multicultural policies, legislation, and programs are useful to complement society's democratic principles and thereby facilitate the integration and/or accommodation of immigrants and minorities.

The chapters in this section present how multiculturalism is articulated and operationalized in Canada and elsewhere. Canada remains a country where multiculturalism is seen as a mark of success in the way it accommodates and responds to its diverse population. There, the notion of cultural difference tends to be applied to those ethnic or racial groups whose values, customs, and practices are seen as different from the societal norms because of their race (or colour), ethnicity, language, and/or "accent"; for other groups, their differences are based on the fact that they are immigrants or "foreign."

FURTHER READINGS

Bannerji, Himani. 2000. *The Dark Side of the Nation: Essays on Multiculturalism, Nationalism and Gender.* **Toronto: Canadian Scholars' Press.**
A collection of critical essays on multiculturalism, nationalism, and gender, generally as well as more specifically in the context of Canada. From an anti-racist feminist Marxist position, Bannerji argues that both "culture" and "multiculturalism" are double-edged swords. As ideological instruments of the colonial capitalist state, the latter becomes "official or elite" in form (as opposed to "popular" multiculturalism), used to obfuscate class, gender, or racial relations, thereby occluding solidarities and alliances across cultures and ethnicities—an effective strategy to "manage" resistance to structural inequalities through consensus. Popular multiculturalism, on the other hand, refers to a vision of culture that is socially formed and fluid in character, which can become emancipatory, as in the case of revolutionary poetry, for instance. The essays in the book are all geared to critiquing official multicultural projects, including more recent formulations such as "diversity."

Chazan, May, Lisa Helps, Anna Stanley, and Sonali Thakkar. 2011. *Home and Native Land: Unsettling Multiculturalism in Canada.* **Toronto: Between the Lines.**
This anthology, from the 2007 conference "From Multicultural Rhetoric to Anti-Racist Action" held at the University of Toronto, presents a variety of vantage points on multiculturalism policy, but all from a critical perspective. It brings together a conversation involving Aboriginal, immigration, labour, and critical race scholars. They reflect on the entrenchment of multiculturalism in all aspects of Canadian life. Several of the authors, including Glen Coulthard, Brian Egan, and Emilie Cameron, argue that the politics of recognition—so central in the discourse of multiculturalism—has seeped into the politics of reconciliation with the Aboriginal community. They further state that this discourse has not helped, indeed it has hindered, land claims and decolonizing efforts. Critical race scholar Nandita Sharma argues that multiculturalism has homogenized all immigrants into one category, thus obfuscating differences of class and coloniality. In the end, this anthology asserts that multiculturalism is not a "failed" project from the perspective of the state, because it allows it to manage immigrants, migrants, Aboriginal peoples, and poverty all at the same time.

Hage, Ghassan. 2000. *White Nation: Fantasies of White Supremacy in a Multicultural Society.* **New York: Routledge.**

In critically analyzing the multicultural discourse of Australia, Ghassan Hage describes how "tolerant white multiculturalists" of that country maintain their power. He argues that these multiculturalists position Aboriginal people and immigrants as people who can be pacified with benefits provided by the state. But as Hage shows, both Aboriginals and immigrants actively challenge white control, demanding recognition of their presence and their issues, which they expect will lead to their full participation in the society.

Walcott, Rinaldo. 2011. "Into the Ranks of Man: Vicious Modernism and the Politics of Reconciliation." In *Cultivating Canada: Reconciliation through the Lens of Cultural Diversity,* **edited by Ashok Mathur, Jonathan Dewar, and Mike DeGagne, 343–349. Ottawa: Aboriginal Healing Foundation.**

This essay in a thought-provoking anthology reflects on the ambiguity the author feels towards reconciliations and apologies initiated by a settler colonial state, most recently vis-à-vis the Aboriginal peoples in Canada. He argues that these gestures are to invite colonized and violated communities such as Indigenous peoples and Blacks into a Euro-Western conception of humanity that is based on designating "others" as sub-human or infra-human. As such, it does not end colonial violence, nor does it recognize different conceptions of humanity. However, he states that it could be the beginning of a deeper collective exploration of what "being human" entails, not just from a Euro-Western point of view, but from multiple perspectives, leading to "new modes of being human."

Chapter 21

Language, Race, and the Impossibility of Multiculturalism

Eve Haque

This question of maintaining national unity is the recurrent conundrum that drives the re-working and reiteration of formulations for belonging, with the contemporary formula of "multiculturalism in a bilingual framework" as the most durable of all. In this chapter, Eve Haque (2012) explores how, in Canada, language—as bilingualism—came to be the site for articulating exclusions that can no longer be stated in terms of race and ethnicity. To get at this question, Haque explores how the liberal paradox of racist differentiation lies at the heart of universal identity (Goldberg, 1993) and its counterpart in the mobilization of language in contemporary multicultural nation-building. She argues that "this is accomplished by embedding a racial hierarchy by way of a contradiction in the use of culture through the proxy of language, thus foreclosing its openness even as racial differentiation is disavowed and the possibility of language as a universal community is declared. In the case of Canada, this is concretely achieved through, among other means, the policy of 'multiculturalism within a bilingual framework,' which emerged directly out of the work of the Royal Commission on Bilingualism and Biculturalism."

On 30 October 1995, the night of the sovereignty referendum in Quebec, Premier Jacques Parizeau became infamous for his comment that 'money and ethnic votes' had defeated the sovereigntist cause. The vote was an incredibly close victory for the 'No' side (a margin of 53,000 votes), which may have fuelled the frustration that drove Parizeau to make his remarks. His speech, in particular the comment regarding the role of ethnic voters, triggered major national media coverage, analysis, and discussion. Within the next twenty-four hours Parizeau had tendered his resignation, and over the next few months he virtually disappeared from public and political life.

What is interesting about this incident is not so much Parizeau's speech, which sustained a surfeit of media analysis, commentary, and public discussion on all sides of the debate, but rather his own explanation of his controversial remarks, made years later in an hour-long documentary about his life. This documentary, entitled *Public Enemy Number One* (2003), directed and narrated by journalist Francine Pelletier, traces Parizeau's early life and the build-up to his successful political career. The climax comes near the end of this documentary, when Parizeau explains what he meant by his 'money and ethnic votes' comment:

> It's true that we were beaten … but by what? By money and ethnic votes. I know that I'm supposed to be a fascist … I'm supposed to be a racist but I never put anyone in jail. I never prevented anyone from saying what they wanted to … and it's true that I can't be compared to that great democrat Pierre Elliot Trudeau who put 500 people in jail … It's not 'hating'? I've tried to describe reality as I saw it … It's true we know now that that love-in cost more than twice what the Yes campaign and No campaign were authorized to spend for the full campaign … so I said it … money … yes indeed … The ethnic vote—the words might not have been very well chosen—but the fact is that that is what happened … the non-francophone vote … and I'm not talking here … I'm talking language … I'm not talking … ethnic origin or whatever … that's why my words were not necessarily well chosen but … it was a language issue—the non-francophones more than usually as was the case voted No and some polls were zero—I had never seen that … (Cartier and Henriquez, 2003)

Although Parizeau holds firm to his position and backs it with analysis, he also tries to unpack exactly what he meant by 'the ethnic vote.' In this portion of the documentary, Parizeau, who had been quite articulate until then, starts to struggle. He begins by admitting that his words 'might not have been very well chosen.' In his attempt to delineate exactly who was covered by the term 'ethnic,' he notes that what he had in mind was not 'ethnic origin or whatever' but rather language: 'it was a language issue.' Significantly, he is not specifying the Quebec anglophone minority either, for then he could simply name it as such; instead, he is trying to find a way to identify the 'No' voters among the 'non-francophone' and, by extension, non-anglophone groups. If this is not a group of voters/non-voters that can be acceptably delineated through 'ethnic origin'—for, after all, this is what ignited the country-wide storm of reaction against Parizeau's speech—then Parizeau's own effort to find the acceptable words and offer the appropriate explanation ('that's why my words were not necessarily well chosen') reveals that language was a good substitute: 'I'm talking language.'

Parizeau's explanation provides an entry point into the central questions of this chapter. More than a semantic slip, Parizeau's shift onto the terrain of language to clarify and support his comments was illustrative of the convenient alibi for racial ordering that can be provided by a multicultural nation established on the foundation of a putatively open linguistic duality—articulated in national policy as 'multiculturalism within a bilingual framework.' Yet I am not interested in vilifying Parizeau, nor the political position from which he speaks; rather, I wish to use his comments as a basis from which to explore questions about language, race, and nation-building. The animating question of my analysis is this: how, in Canada, did language come to be the site for articulating exclusions which can no longer be stated in terms of race and ethnicity? To get at this question requires investigating how the liberal paradox of racist differentiation that lies at the heart of universal identity (Goldberg, 1993) finds its counterpart in the mobilization of language in contemporary multicultural nation-building. I argue that this is accomplished by embedding a racial hierarchy by way of a contradiction in the use of culture through the proxy of language, thus foreclosing its openness even as racial differentiation is disavowed and the possibility of language as a universal community is declared. In the case of Canada, this is concretely achieved through, among other means, the policy of 'multiculturalism within a bilingual framework', which emerged directly out of the work of the Royal Commission on Bilingualism and Biculturalism.

THE ROYAL COMMISSION

The Royal Commission on Bilingualism and Biculturalism (1963–70), commonly known as the B and B Commission, was established by the Liberal government of Lester B. Pearson as a response to growing nationalist sentiment among French Canadians in Quebec, and the mandate of the commission, as laid out in its terms of reference, was primarily to:

> inquire into and report upon the existing state of bilingualism and biculturalism in Canada and to recommend what steps should be taken to develop the Canadian Confederation on the basis of an equal partnership between the two founding races, taking into account the contribution made by the other ethnic groups to the cultural enrichment of Canada and the measures that should be taken to safeguard that contribution. (Royal Commission on Bilingualism and Biculturalism, *Book I,* 1967, Appendix I)

The terms of reference go on to specify that this would include determining the extent of bilingualism in the federal bureaucracy, the role of the public and private sectors in promoting English-French harmony, and the opportunities open to both English and French Canadians for becoming bilingual. Central to the commission's view of Canada, especially in its early phase, was the notion that the country rested on an equal partnership between the English and French 'founding races'[1] and that the reality of this partnership needed to be fully recognized in national institutions and society at large. In time, as this vision was challenged by non-English and non-French Canadians during the commission, it evolved into what became known as 'multiculturalism within a bilingual framework'.

The B and B Commission was struck at a particular historical juncture when a confluence of many factors meant that Canada had to rearticulate its formulation for nation-building and belonging. This commission of inquiry operated as an apparatus to systematize the principles underlying policy—which, in turn, was expressed in language that observed the rules of objective knowledge or facts. The commission began with Preliminary Hearings after which a *Preliminary Report* was issued (1965) and then the main commission of inquiry began with cross country Public Hearings followed by a few years of a research phase, and completed with the eventual publication of a multi-volume final report. During the research and analysis phase of the inquiry leading up to publication of the volumes of the final report, the heterogeneity of submissions from the 'public' during the public hearings was constructed through the commission's interpretative and organizational practices into the textual reality of the final report. Some key moves during the course of the inquiry included the construction of a singular crisis between the 'two founding races' to support the embedded hierarchy within the terms of reference, despite myriad petitions from 'other ethnic groups'[2] during the preliminary hearings.

With the publication of the *Preliminary Report*, the public hearings began and other ethnic groups pushed for a shift from *bi-* to *multi-* cultural belonging. Subsequently, as the commission's research program expanded, expertise was rallied to confer legitimacy on the commission's findings, and a rationale began to emerge for excluding Indigenous groups from the inquiry's scope. Also, the basis of the inquiry was starting to shift from race and ethnicity to the terrain of language and culture; specifically, the shift from overt racial distinctions between founding and other ethnic groups onto the terrain of language and culture meant that racial exclusions could be disavowed even as they were smuggled back in through the contradictory operation of language and culture. This strategy emerged just as obvious, biologically based racial exclusions became increasingly politically and socially disreputable; therefore, particular cultural forms—especially language—became essential ascriptions for the constitution and exclusion of various groups along racialized lines. Consequently, language was identified as a fundamental element of culture by the commission and mobilized as an essential component of culture for the founding races, even as it was deemed to be a private and peripheral element of culture for other ethnic groups. With the appearance of *Book I* (1967) of the final report, these new perspectives became clear: Indigenous groups were decisively removed from the purview of the inquiry, and a contradictory mechanism whereby culture and language would operate to reinscribe the now-disavowed racial and ethnic hierarchy of the original terms of reference was put into place. As well, *Book I* made it obvious that delineating the precise workings of an equal partnership between the two founding groups would require the Other—that is, the Indigenous and ethnic others. All of this was further underlined in *Book IV* (1969) where integration emerged as the means through which other ethnic groups, later in the inquiry referred to as cultural groups, would be peripherally located in relation to the two founding groups. A series of recommendations that embodied this unequal relationship was entrenched by Prime Minister Trudeau's limited acceptance, in the House of Commons (1971), of *Book IV* of the final report as the declaration of a new Multiculturalism Policy (1971), but all within a bilingual framework. Thus, by fixing narrow definitions of 'multicultural' and 'integration' in federal legislation, through the Official Languages Act (1969) and the Multiculturalism Policy (1971), claims for substantive and collective forms of recognition from the state for other ethnic groups could be limited. In this way, with the concurrent changes to immigration legislation—the move from race and regional preferences to a points system for immigration—that were also taking place in the 1960s, language and culture were mobilized through the national formulation of multiculturalism within a bilingual framework in order to incorporate people into the contemporary, racialized hierarchy of belonging and citizenship rights.

NATION BUILDING AFTER THE B AND B COMMISSION

In sum, the Royal Commission's goal was to develop a new, unisonant formulation for nation-building; one that could preserve white-settler dominance at the same time as it disavowed its racialized exclusions. For the commission, the answer lay in the model of a bilingual and bicultural nation and in the entrenchment of asymmetrical collective-language rights through a contradictory operation of language and culture, and this disparity was justified by the purported openness of language to the integration of other ethnic groups into the official-language collectives. The workings of this contradictory mechanism were detailed for the first time in the paradigmatic blue pages of *Book I*, which laid out definitions of key terms—among them, language, culture, bilingualism, and ethnicity. Blodgett states that *Book I* can be read as the 'discursive origin for the discussion of ethnicity in Canada' (Blodgett, 1990, 15), and as John Porter notes, determining the limits of the commission's principal terms was a challenging endeavour:

> Book I, The Official Languages, is preceded by a General Introduction printed on blue paper, which discusses the key words of the terms of reference of the Commission. These blue pages contain, in the English language at least, some of the most elegant sophistry about culture, language, society, and other concepts of importance to sociologists and anthropologists … The blue pages are important because they generate a mythology of culture which goes far beyond any scientific understanding or use of the word. This condition detracts greatly from the convincing case the Commission makes for bilingualism, because their arguments become obscured by ideological, contradictory, and often nonsensical statements about culture, cultural identity, cultural heritage, cultural equality and so forth. (Porter, 1969, 112)

Porter also makes the important point that these blue pages were able, for the first time at the national level, to generate a new mythology about culture in Canada, setting out a story of belonging that could be couched in linguistic and cultural terms while the effects were organized along racial and ethnic lines. It was through the Royal Commission, therefore, that a new mythology of national belonging appeared—one that could ostensibly claim to envision a pluralist and open nation, multicultural within a bilingual framework.

This national mythology has proven to be durable, becoming naturalized in the under-standing of everyday life in a putatively pluralist and open society. In addition, the changes to immigration policy that were taking place concurrently with the emergence of this national mythology provided the basis for contemporary manifestations of the racial ordering of 'immi-grant' others. In the present, Will Kymlicka's (1995) liberal theory of multicultural citizenship and the Charter of Rights and Freedoms can both be seen as examples of the commission's legacy, and yet they both leave unanswered the question of how to think through alternative ways of nation-building and national belonging.

Etienne Balibar discusses the relationship between language, race, and nation in order to unravel the purported openness of linguistic community in the monolingual hegemony of France. As a classic example of modern nation-building, Balibar asserts, the nation-state of France instituted a community that is always a 'fictive ethnicity' against a background of uni-versalistic representation (Balibar, 1991, 96). However, as Balibar says, this invites questions. If national identity is based on a 'fictive ethnicity, "How can ethnicity be produced?" and in particular, "how can it be produced in such a way that it does not appear as fiction, but as the most natural of origins?"' (ibid.). For Balibar, the answer lies in the complementarity between language and race, which roots national character in the people. As he explains, 'they consti-tute two ways of rooting historical populations in a fact of "nature" (the diversity of languages and the diversity of races appearing predestined), but also two ways of giving a meaning to their continued existence, of transcending its contingency' (ibid., 97). He continues that it is crucial that the national language should 'appear to be the very element of the life of a people,' and that all linguistic practices should feed into a single 'love of the language' which is the 'mother tongue,' since this mother tongue is 'the ideal of a common origin projected back beyond learning processes and specialist forms of usage and which, by that very fact, becomes the metaphor for the love fellow nationals feel for one another' (ibid.).

The complement to this is that the language community is not enough to produce ethnic-ity, because, by definition, linguistic construction of identity is *open* (Balibar, 1991, 98). That is, although a mother tongue cannot be chosen, it is still possible to 'learn' languages and to 'turn oneself into a different kind of bearer of discourse' (ibid.). With respect to a linguistic community, Balibar concludes that 'ideally, it "assimilates" anyone, but holds no one' (ibid., 99). Thus, for language to be tied down to what he calls 'the frontiers of a particular people,' it needs an extra degree of particularity or principle of closure and exclusion, which is that of being part of a common race (ibid.). This is what Balibar refers to as a second-degree fiction, which, although a fiction, derives a material effectiveness from the everyday practices and relations structuring the lives of individuals. The language community creates equality only by 'naturalizing' the social inequality of linguistic practices, but the race community dissolves social inequalities in an ambivalent 'similarity' by ethnicizing the social difference into a division between the 'genuinely' and 'falsely' national (ibid., 100).

Balibar provides a cogent analysis of how race forecloses the openness of linguis-tic community in the construction of the modern nation-state. However, in Canada, the nation-building project cannot draw upon a uniform history of origins to organize the demarcation of 'genuine' and 'false' nationals, or 'us' and 'them.' Race necessarily operates differently, in this case through the contradiction of language and culture, in order to foreclose the purportedly open linguistic communities of the nation. Michelle Anne Lee (2003) discusses the tension that multiculturalism, or the politics of diversity, introduces into the inherent dialectic of 'us' and 'them' and embeds in modernist notions of nationalism. She states: 'Nationalism consistently requires some clear demarcation of "us" in distinction from "them." Multiculturalism, on the other hand, purports a discourse that requires "them" continually to become part of "us," *as defined by the dominant culture* tolerating and choosing to accept, or not, other cultures' (Lee, 2003, 111, emphasis in original).

Engineering how 'them' would become a part of 'us' within the dominant framework of bilingualism and biculturalism was a central preoccupation of the B and B Commission, and the project ultimately was realized in the Official Languages Act of 1969 and the Multiculturalism Policy of 1971. Lee does not see multiculturalism as opposed to standard models of nationalism as much as she sees it as an extension of them:

> For newer, more pluralistic societies that do not find their basis for legitimacy in historical continuity, however, challenges also abound. A multicultural society must deal with the realities that recent growth generated by large-scale, economic-driven migration presents. They must also respond to what is now perceived by many members of the imagined community as an *essentially* pluralistic history. (Lee, 2003, 111, emphasis in original)

In the present, this relatively recent construction of multicultural nationalism, now more than forty years, is a naturalized '*essentially* pluralistic history' of Canada. It can incorporate the continuous and contemporary advent of economically driven migration into a similar historical continuity without disrupting the embedded contradiction which maintains the racialized hierarchy of belonging. As Lee explains, in multicultural notions of nation-building, 'direct calls to respect and acknowledge ethnic diversity in a single nation still position a particular group as possessing the power to make such a choice' (ibid., 112). Yet the powerful appeal of this model lies in the fact that, regardless, 'the invention of multicultural tradition is one that diverse members can all and equally commit themselves to' (ibid.). So, today, multicultural nationalism has a powerful, discursive force as an inclusive and equitable model of nation-building.

In Canada, the full formulation is *multiculturalism within a bilingual framework*, but these elements have to a large extent been sheared apart in current political discourse. At least at the federal level, bilingualism has come to almost exclusively signify questions about Quebec nationalism and anxieties about separation. And multiculturalism has become, at least in English-dominant Canada, a discourse about the inclusion and exclusion of racialized Others while it also ingrains the '*essentially* pluralist history' required to maintain the national mythology of a pluralistic society. Even though the limitations on inclusion organized through the contradictory operation of language and culture still continue to function in the present despite their discursive separation, it is vital that the two elements remain discursively interconnected if the white-settler foundations of the nation are to be evident. As Mary Kirtz (1996) states, 'The "bilingual framework" continues to determine the boundaries of the debate over national identity, boundaries beyond which multiculturalism cannot travel and within which ethnic identity must effect its limited transformations' (20). It is bilingualism, as the realization of collective language rights for some, that functions in tandem with multiculturalism as a limiting agent by foreclosing the purported openness of the nation's official linguistic communities.

The ability of language to construct a putatively open community should not be underestimated. As Uli Linke (2003) states in her analysis of linguistic purism and nation-building in Germany: 'This formative power of linguistic systems, which provides centralized regimes with the capacity to absorb and assimilate a diversity of subjects, seems to exhibit a democratic propensity. But such a making of nationals is inherently coercive: through the medium of language, and its strategic deployment in citizenship and immigration politics' (156). Although substantively different from German nationalism, Canadian multicultural nationalism is also based on the purported 'democratic propensity' of language, and the inherent coercion of language as it is deployed through citizenship and immigration in Germany finds its counterpart in Canada as well. Specifically, the emergence of multiculturalism within a bilingual framework in the late 1960s and early 1970s was more than just a new discourse of national mythology; it was also a formulation for national unity that subsequently established a particular system for the racial ordering of 'immigrant' Others. That is, during the course of the B and B Commission, while white-settler national belonging was being rearticulated on the terrain of language and culture, parallel changes were taking place in Canadian immigration policy—which was also moving away from explicitly stated racial preferences. These changes to immigration policy, which began in 1962, meant that by the late 1960s and early 1970s radical changes were occurring in the number and source of immigrants coming to Canada. The result was that, by the time Trudeau responded to the recommendations of *Book IV* in 1971, concerns about the balance between the founding dualities had to be considered, since the increasing number of immigrants was seen as one of the main demographic threats to national unity. In addition, as overt racial preferences for articulating national unity and immigration policy were being jettisoned, the racial composition of the immigrant population began to shift dramatically. Specifically, as source countries for immigration expanded beyond Europe and encompassed more of the global South, more visibly racialized groups were immigrating to Canada, thereby linking these critical changes in immigration policy to the system of racial ordering installed through the policy of multiculturalism in a bilingual framework.

THE LEGISLATIVE ENTRENCHMENT OF 'MULTICULTURALISM WITHIN A BILINGUAL FRAMEWORK'

In the present, the normalization of this racial ordering is clear in Kymlicka's (1995) theory of multicultural citizenship. It is instructive to examine this liberal theory of pluralism not only because Kymlicka's framework has become a dominant and ubiquitous model for multicultural citizenship and nation-building, but also because it reveals the durability of the racial ordering that the formulation of multiculturalism within a bilingual framework originally established.

Kymlicka makes a distinction between what he terms 'national minorities'—in Canada, these are the English, French, and a homogenized Indigenous grouping—who are 'distinct and potentially self-governing societies incorporated into a larger state'; and 'ethnic minorities,' who are 'immigrants who have left their national community to enter another society' (Kymlicka, 1995, 79). The key distinction is that national minorities, at the time of their incorporation, constituted an 'ongoing societal culture and may have or had rights regarding language and land use' (ibid.), whereas ethnic minorities came 'voluntarily,' are not 'nations,' and do not occupy homelands but are scattered throughout the nation-space. These distinctions are based on rationales that closely recall the commission's own reasons for eventually conferring collective language rights on founding groups only, and Kymlicka, like the commission, disavows that these are racial distinctions; instead, he sees them as cultural: 'In talking about national minorities, therefore, I am not talking about racial or descent groups, but about cultural groups' (ibid., 23). For immigrants, their distinctiveness is 'manifested primarily in their family lives and in voluntary associations, and is not inconsistent with institutional integration' since 'they still participate within the dominant institutions of the dominant culture(s) and speak the dominant language(s)' (ibid., 14). In fact, 'immigrants (except the elderly) … in Canada, must learn either of the two official languages' (ibid., 14–15). As Kymlicka states, '[T]he commitment to ensuring a common language has been a constant feature of the history of immigration policy' (ibid.). Again, this logic closely recapitulates the narrow reasoning of the integration model that emerged to locate other ethnic groups in relation to the founding dualities in the B and B Commission's *Book IV.*

Kymlicka does admit that there are 'hard cases' which do not fit into either category, with examples being African-Americans, Hutterites, and refugees, among others. However, based on his main group divisions, he has no problem articulating a well-planned hierarchy of 'group-differentiated citizenship' rights. He also gives language as an example of this group-differentiated right, stating that 'the real issue in evaluating language rights is why they are group specific—that is, why francophones should be able to demand court proceedings or education in their mother tongue at public expense when Greek- or Swahili-speakers cannot' (Kymlicka, 1995, 46). For Kymlicka, it is clear that language rights are a major component of the national rights of French Canadians; and furthermore, since immigrant groups are not national minorities, they should not have similar language rights (ibid.). Overall, this hierarchy of rights is presented as a tidy and neat formula. For example, in response to the common charge that at one time even the dominant 'national minorities' were immigrants to the New World, Kymlicka differentiates between English and French colonists and present-day migrants. As he notes, 'there was a fundamentally different set of expectations accompanying colonization and immigration—the former resulted from a deliberate policy aimed at the systematic recreation of an entire society in a new land; the latter resulted from individual and familial choices to leave their society and join another existing society' (ibid., 95). Therefore, the discriminatory project of collective language rights only for some—the national minorities—is premised on a differentiation in migration history, an idea similar to the claims of prior history which were advanced during the commission. Also, the notion of immigration as a choice, which emerged during the commission's public hearings, is a central rationale throughout Kymlicka's theory.

Kymlicka uses the theme of 'choice' as a prime justificatory principle in his gross differentiation of rights between 'national minorities' and 'immigrants': 'After all, most immigrants (as distinct from refugees) choose to leave their own culture' and 'they have uprooted themselves, and they know when they come that their success, and that of their children, depends on integrating into the institutions of English-speaking society' (Kymlicka, 1995, 96). This concept of 'choice' also allows Kymlicka to make statements about the right of immigrants to live and work in their own culture: 'Immigration is one way of waiving one's right' and 'in deciding to uproot themselves, immigrants voluntarily relinquish some of the rights that go along with their original national membership' (ibid.). He is therefore careful to explain that, with respect to the policies designed to accommodate immigrant cultural difference, 'all of these measures take the form of adapting the institutions and practices of the mainstream society so as to accommodate ethnic differences, not of setting up a separate societal culture based on the immigrants' mother tongue' (ibid., 97). In Kymlicka's theory, the foundations of the white-settler *bi*-nation—in his words the 'societal culture'—are a given, and the racial ordering they entrench remains unexamined.

There have been many cogent critiques of Kymlicka's theory that address the depth of historical amnesia upon which his idea of liberal toleration and inclusion is founded. For example, scholars have questioned his idea that immigrants 'choose' to migrate, stating that this ignores the conditions for economic and political survival that imperialism and circuits of global capital have created for many in the global South; as well, they have pointed to the fact that in Kymlicka's model of nation-building, immigrants are forever frozen into the category of 'immigrant' (Padolsky, 2000; Razack, 1998). Other scholars take issue with the form of liberalism he uses, the definition of culture he adopts, and the distinctions he makes between different groups of minorities, in addition to the political and philosophical underpinnings of his work (Parekh, 1997; Young, 1997; Choudhry, 2002). But Kymlicka's theory of multicultural citizenship remains the intellectual basis of the current formulation of multiculturalism within a bilingual framework. It preserves the rationales for the hierarchy of rights that emerged through the B and B Commission, even as it acknowledges group-based claims for Indigenous peoples—albeit only in a limited way that regards these peoples as a homogenized and unspecified grouping without a distinctive history.

The influence of Kymlicka's theory of multicultural nationalism is widespread, and, while it is extensively debated, it is nonetheless used across disciplines to address questions of language, society, and nation-building (see May, 2001). Since language is a key marker of levels of rights and citizenship in his theory, there is also an increasing engagement with Kymlicka's ideas in the area of language rights (see Patten, 2001). Kymlicka acknowledges that "group-differentiated citizenship rights' are a central element of his theory. In so doing, he makes explicit the contradiction that is lodged at the core of multiculturalism within a bilingual framework; that is, the extension of group rights only to national minorities while ethnic minorities have the standard guarantees of 'freedoms' and choices, or individual rights. Kymlicka's justification is built on historical claims and demographic rationales similar to those used by the B and B Commission, making the link between the two explicit. Based on Kymlicka's rationales, group-differentiated citizenship rights are posited as a rational solution to the dilemma of constructing the unisonant multicultural nation, yet this also elides the disparity in citizenship between the two groupings.

Chantal Mouffe (2001) argues that the liberal logic is a 'logic of the assertion of rights,' and she draws on Arendt's notion of the 'right to have rights' to maintain that it is only 'through being a democratic citizen' that it is possible to have the full exercise of human rights (107). However, the entrenchment of group-differentiated citizenship rights, predicated on a particular reading of national history, makes the assumption of equal citizenship for all members of the polity impossible. Yet this is precisely the formulation that Kymlicka proposes. In the present, his theory of multicultural citizenship, with its mistaken assumption that all members of the polity are equal as citizens, remains enshrined in the Canadian Charter of Rights and Freedoms.

Before the Royal Commission on Bilingualism and Biculturalism, the only provision for language rights in the constitution of Canada lay in section 133, which allowed the use of English and French both in Parliament and the federal court system and required that laws were written in both English and French. In the wake of the Royal Commission, the expanded set of English and French language rights in the Official Languages Act became part of the Charter of Rights and Freedoms—and was then embedded in the Canadian constitution with its repatriation in 1982 and the subsequent passing of the Constitution Act. Thus, with the Charter as part of the constitution, the collective language rights of the founding groups were entrenched as fundamental rights in Canada; language rights were established in sections 16 to 23 of the Charter, guaranteeing English and French official-language status and ensuring both as the languages of Parliament, federal-level public services, and the courts, as well as ensuring official-language minority educational rights across Canada. In addition, section 27 of the Charter was included as the 'multicultural clause' to ensure that the Charter was interpreted in a manner consistent with the preservation and enhancement of the multicultural heritage of Canadians.

In an article that analyses Pierre Trudeau's campaign speeches and various government documents from the late 1960s, Robert Charles Vipond traces the logic of Trudeau's entrenchment of language rights in the Charter as a way of ensuring that citizenship would be seen as a fundamental individual right and as the foundation of a deep sense of belonging (Vipond, 1996, 186). According to this reasoning, it was possible to support the constitutional protection of individual rights and the constitutional protection of language rights, for the two were cut from the same cloth; bilingualism was one of the 'fundamental liberties which make us feel proud of being Canadian' (ibid., 183). Language rights could be explained and defended under both rubrics of citizenship—that is, as rights and as belonging—since, as Vipond states,

'Trudeau spoke of minority language rights both as fundamental individual rights and as the foundation for creating a deep sense of belonging, and he moved seamlessly between them as if, by finding an element common to both ideas of citizenship, he could somehow fuse them' (ibid., 186). Vipond draws on Tuohy's notion of 'institutional ambivalence' (in Vipond, 1996, 186) to argue that putting language rights first was Trudeau's way of reconciling the tension between these two notions of citizenship as rights and as belonging. And putting them in the Charter in such a way that he could harness other rights—but not language rights—to the override provision of section 33, the 'notwithstanding clause,'[3] was Trudeau's way of institutionalizing this ambivalence (ibid., 186-7).

Terrence Meyerhoff examines the legacy of this 'institutional ambivalence' by considering language rights in the Charter against multicultural rights, as outlined in the Charter's section 27. In his analysis, the collective rights of linguistic dualism, entrenched through the language rights of the Charter, result in a disparity between ethnic minorities and official-language minorities with respect to the rights and status each enjoy (Meyerhoff, 1993-4, 918). Meyerhoff reveals that section 27 has almost never been interpreted to contain any collective rights at all and that 'case law suggests that section 27 is not treated as a substantive provision'; rather, it is at best 'merely an interpretive provision with little impact on other rights' (ibid., 953). In fact, language rights constrain the definition of multiculturalism in the Charter, signalling the genealogical connection of these Charter provisions to the B and B Commission, and in particular to Trudeau's inauguration of a limited and specified definition of multiculturalism through the Multiculturalism Policy of 1971.

Meyerhoff also states that 'the Charter structure reflects the influence linguistic dualism … has had on shaping multiculturalism and language rights. The upshot of linguistic dualism, as legislation, policy and the Charter exhibit, is a disparity between the rights and status—as to language and culture—afforded official language minorities compared to ethnic minorities' (Meyerhoff, 1993-4, 961). The implications of this relationship of rights are clear; there is an inconsistency in the stated, egalitarian definition of multiculturalism, amounting to an entrenchment of cultural inequality, and these inconsistencies suggest linguistic assimilation and racial ordering, both of which are antithetical to the cultural equality and pluralism that multicultural policy purports to promote (ibid., 967-9).

Meyerhoff begins with the legal inconsistencies that the Charter has promulgated in the present before returning to the contradiction between language and culture that the B and B Commission had set into place for the organization of a hierarchy of belonging—or, in Kymlicka's terms, 'group-differentiated citizenship' rights. In short, the commission's original formulation of multiculturalism within a bilingual framework still speaks to the powerful national mythology it has created, with legal decisions consistently upholding it. As Meyerhoff and Vipond conclude, language rights as envisioned and entrenched by Trudeau, first in the Official Languages Act and then in the Multiculturalism Policy, and eventually as 'institutional ambivalence' in the Charter, did not provide the platform for national unity he had hoped for. Meyerhoff has termed Canada's model of language rights and multiculturalism, premised upon linguistic dualism and a narrow definition of multiculturalism, as 'a weak reed for nation building' and national unity (Meyerhoff, 1993–4, 973). This question of main-taining national unity is the recurrent conundrum that drives the reworking and reiteration of formulations for belonging, with multiculturalism in a bilingual framework as the most durable of all.

MOVING TOWARDS UNCONDITIONAL BELONGING

We are thus left with the problem of how to promote national unity in a multicultural milieu without establishing a hierarchical relation of rights, without short-circuiting full citizenship rights through a contradiction between language and culture, and without putting into place a racially based social order. This problem has resonance for all states that have to contend with the challenge of addressing minority rights without reverting to an explicitly racial and ethnic form of nationalism.

These are complex issues for which there are no simple formulas or easy models, if exclusions are to be avoided. Perhaps trying to think through the conundrum of national unity and minority rights in a putatively multicultural state requires a questioning of some of the fundamental bases of organizing national inclusion. The preliminary consideration, then, probably has to be about the boundaries that construct any notion of inclusion, whether these are national boundaries or cultural ones (Clifford, 1988). Perhaps Jacques Derrida's radical rethinking of *hospitality* is an entry point into this issue.

Derrida (2000) differentiates between a conditional hospitality and an unconditional hospitality, stating that conditional hospitality is the welcoming of the Other within the limits of the law whereby the host remains the master of the home and retains his authority. Meyda Yegenoglu (2003) draws a parallel between this model of hospitality and multiculturalism, stating: 'The place from which multiculturalist tolerance welcomes the particularity of the other, fortified by codifications such as affirmative action and other legal measures, is what precisely enables the disavowed and inverted self-referentiality of racist hospitality which by emptying the host's position from any positive content asserts its superiority and sovereignty' (10). This is what Yegenoglu calls the inherent paradox of multiculturalism's conditional and lawful welcoming of the Other as guest, best exemplified by immigration laws. The multicultural figure is the 'limit figure' 'which brings into crisis the clear distinction between what is inside and what is outside,' the figure that marks 'cultural and national boundaries' (ibid., 11).

Unconditional hospitality, on the other hand, is the ethics, not law, of hospitality, where hospitality is infinite and cannot be limited—that is, regulated—by a nation's political or juridical practices (Derrida, 2000). Therefore, unconditional hospitality is a reversal, an 'interruption of a full possession of a place called home,' and, as Yegenoglu states, 'the question of hospitality cannot be reduced to a multiculturalist tolerance, for there is no longer a question of limiting, restricting, or regulating tolerance of the other' (Yegenoglu, 2003, 20). Between these two limits of hospitality, the conditional and the unconditional, is an *aporia* where the impossibility of hospitality lies. Yet this is a productive impossibility, since the principle of unconditionality is the driving force behind the possibility of a revision of the law of hospitality (ibid., 25): 'As Derrida notes, the law is perfectible and there is progress to be performed on the law that will improve the conditions of hospitality. The condition of laws on immigration has to be improved without claiming that unconditional law should become an official policy. The very desire for unconditional hospitality is what regulated the improvement of the laws of hospitality' (ibid., 22).

The driving force behind the impossibility of unconditional hospitality strains the boundaries of nation and culture, or immigration laws and multicultural tolerance, even though these boundaries can likely never be jettisoned. Unconditional hospitality, as the demand for the immediate transformation of present conditions of hospitality—and as a way to encourage the transformation of the regulations that produce the boundaries of nation and culture—may provide another approach to the conundrum of national unity and multicultural nation-building. Derrida's idea of hospitality, although perhaps not having immediate policy implications, might nevertheless lead to general guiding principles about how we can begin to rethink nation and community. In particular, when questions of 'who we are' reach a crisis point, even symbolic and bureaucratic exercises such as inquiries and commissions may provide a space for counter-discourses and a reimagining of who we are or might become. In the present, the ongoing anxieties and crises about the place of the Other in the nation emerge out of a contradictory set of rights and hierarchical relations, put into place through our current federal formulation of multiculturalism within a bilingual framework, which delineates groupings, their rights, and their mode of national belonging. These crises indicate that our current formulation gives rise to principles for nation-building which cannot accommodate who we are and have become since the B and B Commission was inaugurated.

If we are to seriously reconsider our 'social imaginary' (Castoriadis, 1987) in ways that respond substantively to these crises of national belonging without reproducing a racially based social order, then perhaps the productive impossibility of unconditional hospitality might serve to dislodge the bilingual framework of the anemic state multiculturalism that currently underpins the normalized, white-settler narrative of two founding nations—a narrative that dates back only about forty years to the B and B Commission. Furthermore, this driving force of unconditional hospitality might be harnessed to provide guiding principles for the inquiry into and revision of laws of hospitality governing immigration, citizenship, and refugees, among other areas. Perhaps we can use this principled desire for unconditional hospitality in our next, and overdue, exercise of reimagining nation, community, and belonging.

NOTES

1. 'Founding races' is the phrase used by the Royal Commission in their terms of reference to refer to the English and French communities of Canada. The use of 'races' to refer to the French and English groups in Canada can be traced back in Canadian history, most notably to Lord Durham's report of 1839.

2. 'Other ethnic groups' is how all non-French, non-British and non-Indigenous groups were referred to at the start of the Royal Commission.

3. The notwithstanding clause is often called an 'override clause'; it allows Parliament or the legislature of a province to declare in an Act of Parliament or of the legislature that the Act or a provision will operate notwithstanding a provision included in section 2 or sections 7 to 15 of the Charter for up to a period of five years.

REFERENCES

Balibar, Etienne. 1991. 'The Nation Form: History and Ideology.' In Balibar and I. Wallerstein, eds., *Race, Nation, Class: Ambiguous Identities*. London: Verso. 86–106.

Blodgett, E.D. 1990. 'Ethnic Writing in Canadian Literature as Paratext.' *Signature*, 3: 13–27.

Canada. 1971. 8 October. 'Federal Government's Response to Book IV of the Report of the Royal Commission on Bilingualism and Biculturalism: Document Tabled in the House of Commons.' Sessional Paper 283-4/101B, Appendix: 8583-4.

Cartier, C., and P. Henriquez (producers), and F. Pelletier (director/narrator). 2003. *Jacques Parizeau, Public Enemy Number One* [motion picture]. Canada: Macumba International.

Castoriadis. C. 1987. *The Imaginary Institution of Society*. Cambridge, Mass.: MIT Press.

Choudhry, S. 2002. 'National Minorities and Ethnic Immigrants: Liberalism's Political Sociology.' *Journal of Political Philosophy*, 10(1): 54–78.

Clifford, James. 1988. *The Predicament of Culture: Twentieth Century Ethnography, Literature, and Art*. Cambridge, Mass.: Harvard University Press.

Derrida, J. 2000. *Of Hospitality: Anne Dufourmantelle Invites Jacques Derrida to Respond*. R. Bowlby, trans. Stanford, Calif.: Stanford University Press.

Goldberg, D.T. 1993. *Racist Culture*. Oxford, U.K.: Blackwell.

Kirtz, M.K. 1996. 'Old World Traditions, New World Inventions: Bilingualism, Multiculturalism, and the Transformation of Ethnicity.' *Canadian Ethnic Studies*, 28(1): 8–21.

Kymlicka, W. 1995. *Multicultural Citizenship*. Oxford, U.K.: Clarendon Press.

Lee, M.A. 2003. 'Multiculturalism as Nationalism: A Discussion of Nationalism in Pluralistic Nations.' *Canadian Review of Studies in Nationalism*, 30: 103–23.

Linke, U. 2003. 'There is a Land Where Everything Is Pure: Linguistic Nationalism and Identity Politics in Germany.' In D.S. Moore, J. Kosek, and A. Pandian, eds., *Race, Nature and the Politics of Difference*. Durham, N.C.: Duke University Press. 149-74.

Meyerhoff, T. 1993, 1994. 'Multiculturalism and Language Rights in Canada: Problems and Prospects for Equality and Unity.' *American University Journal of International Law and Policy*, 9: 913–1013.

May, S. 2001. *Language and Minority Rights*. London: Longman.

Mouffe, C. 2001. 'Every Form of Art Has a Political Dimension.' Interview by R. Deutsche, B.W. Joseph, and T. Keenan. *Grey Room*, 2 (winter): 98–125.

Padolsky, E. 2000. 'Multiculturalism at the Millennium.' *Journal of Canadian Studies*, 35(1): 138–60.

Patten, A. 2001. 'Political Theory and Language Policy.' *Political Theory*, 29(5): 691–715.

Parekh, B. 1997. 'Dilemmas of Multicultural Theory of Citizenship.' *Constellations*, 4(1): 54–62.

Porter, J. 1969. 'Bilingualism and the Myths of Culture.' *Review of Canadian Sociology and Anthropology*, 6(2): 111–19.

Razack, S. 1998. *Looking White People in the Eye.* Toronto: University of Toronto Press.

Royal Commission on Bilingualism and Biculturalism. 1965. 1 February. *A Preliminary Report of the Royal Commission on Bilingualism and Biculturalism.* Ottawa: Queen's Printer.

———. 1967. 8 October. *Book I: The Official Languages.* Ottawa: Queen's Printer.

———. 1969. 23 October. *Book IV: The Cultural Contribution of the Other Ethnic Groups.* Ottawa: Queen's Printer.

Vipond, R.C. 1996. 'Citizenship and the Charter of Rights: The Two Sides of Pierre Trudeau.' *International Journal of Canadian Studies*, 14 (fall): 179–92.

Yegenoglu, M. 2003. 'Liberal Multiculturalism and the Ethics of Hospitality in the Age of Globalization.' *Postmodern Culture*, http://www.iath.virginia.edu/pmc/text-only/issue.103/13.2yegenoglu.txt (accessed 13 January 2005).

Young, I.M. 1997. 'A Multicultural Continuum: A Critique of Will Kymlicka's Ethnic-nation Dichotomy.' *Constellations*, 4(1): 49–53.

Chapter 22

Immigrants, Multiculturalism, and the Welfare State

Carl E. James

Using the framework of colour-blindness, James discusses the question: What does multiculturalism make possible for immigrants and ethnoracial minoritized group members in a society? In doing so, he argues that because culture is mainly conceptualized as possessed by people whose values, attitudes, and behaviours are static and observable in people who are "visibly different" and "foreign"—based on colour—they will be forever marked and their full participation in a society structured by inequity will always be a struggle. In this original chapter, James reviews incidents in European societies, paying particular attention to Sweden, arguing that there is a need for states to re-conceptualize how they deal with or respond to their racialized population. He suggests that if racialized members of societies are to fully participate in and enjoy the same freedom, access, and opportunities as their white counterparts, then their "difference" with regard to race must be acknowledged and their experiences based on racism must be addressed.

In many societies, the existence of a multicultural policy or multicultural programs is perceived as sufficient to address the resulting diversity, but growing tensions, conflicts, and hostilities indicate that multiculturalism, as understood and practiced, is insufficient and ineffective in addressing the concerns and needs of all members of the society, particularly racialized members. In this chapter, I discuss the extent to which notions of multiculturalism, which form the basis of policies, programs, and practices pertaining to the integration and participation of immigrants and minoritized people, have helped to produce the acceptance—and not just tolerance—of cultural differences among members of the society. A relevant question here might be: What does multiculturalism make possible for immigrants and ethnoracial minoritized group members in a society where their culture—specifically their values, attitudes, and behaviours—is understood mainly as related to their "foreignness" and not structured by their treatment in the society where they live, work, play, and learn? I argue that because the cultures of immigrants and minoritized members of the society are conceptualized as static, archaic, and observable (because their practices are different from the norm), and because those cultures are carried in the bodies of people perceived to be physically different because of "appearance" pertaining to race or religion, then as long as their "difference" continues to exist they will always be considered "foreign"; the problems they encounter in society will be regarded as product of their own making—a suggestion that they have been unable to let go of their foreignness. I suggest that attributing the experiences and circumstances of minorities to "their culture" masks the racism, xenophobia, Islamophobia, and other such mechanisms of differentiation that permeate society. These mechanisms are maintained by society's claim of colour-blindness, rooted in multiculturalism.

COLOUR-BLIND PERSPECTIVE

We are living in an era when nations claim to take a multicultural, egalitarian, and democratic approach to dealing with the ethnic, religious, and racial diversity of their populations. This claim is rooted in the political ideology of individual rights and social welfare. Such common everyday assumptions enable these states, and for the most part its White citizens, to believe that the state's normative liberal values and goals make opportunities equally accessible to everyone. But this colour-blind approach leaves unacknowledged the significant role that race plays not only in shaping identities, but also in determining the social location that individuals and group members come to occupy in the society, as well as their access to power and resources. As Ferber (2007) points out, a colour-blind perspective is also based on the assumption that racism "is a thing of the past and the playing field has been leveled; therefore, if anyone is not successful, it is a result of his or her own poor choices." Cultural differences and not racism is used to explain the inequality that exists between racial groups (p. 14).

The belief in the liberalism and egalitarianism of the state that frames colour-blind ideology contributes to the notion that every citizen, irrespective of gender, race, sexuality, and class, can succeed within the existing social, political, and economic structure of the society as long as they work hard enough and persevere with their goals (Caouette & Taylor, 2007,

p. 84). Meritocracy provides individuals a rationale for explaining why some people thrive and others do not. Or, as Amanda Lewis points out in her article about studying whites and whiteness in the era of colour-blindness, the "racial ideologies in particular provide ways of understanding the world that make sense of racial gaps in earnings, wealth, and health such that whites do not see any connection between their gain and others' loss." (2004, p. 633). In this way, Whites are led to believe that it is the responsibility of the disadvantaged person to overcome barriers since equal opportunity has been provided to all (Caouette & Taylor, 2007, p. 85). What Briskin terms the "bootstrap message" (quoted in Schick & St. Denis, 2003) ignores systemic barriers while also denying the ubiquitous nature, or everyday assumptions and practices, of Whites that secures their privileged status. In this regard, cultural rationale or cultural differences are used to justify the variations in racial positions and circumstances, suggesting that the situations in which people find themselves are not a consequence of race but culture—in this way, the cultural traits of minoritized group members are pathologized, seen as deficient, and put forward as the "real reason" for a person's lack of success.

The colour-blind perspective operates to dehistoricize and decontextualize the experiences of racialized members of society. For instance, Schick and St. Denis (2003) observed that White pre-service teachers in Canada "are often unaware of, or choose to forget, how disadvantage has been constructed historically" (p. 1). In this regard, Canada's ongoing and inherently racial and colonial settlement is often regarded as a thing of the past bearing little consequence on contemporary social relations. In the same manner, Montgomery's (2005) examination of grade 10 high school history textbooks during the 1960s to 2000 concluded that "racism is imagined to be the exception and fighting against racism the norm" (p. 438). Such implications foster an ongoing perception of Canada as fair and just. In this context, racial incidents are treated as isolated individual problems and perpetrated largely by individuals with negative attitudes and ignorant of the cultural differences of racialized individuals (Montgomery, 2005). In other words, racists are seen as members of "fringe" groups (such as Nazis or KKK members) and operate outside of society's norms, as opposed to reflecting society's ideals.

Based on the liberal notion that we are all part of the human race, it is common to hear individuals say: "I don't see race. I see people as people." Such a statement is meant to reflect the goodness and innocence of the speakers (Schick & St. Denis, 2003, p. 7). But what people fail to recognize in this assertion is the White position from which they speak and how much the meaning of their claim is informed and measured by the boundaries of Whiteness. Disavowing one's complicity in systems of oppression, as Lewis (2004) argues, "makes us blind to the effects of color," and how colour continues to serve as an inherent element in maintaining dominant power relations (p. 636).

The consequences of colour-blindness are well documented. For instance, in their US study of how colour-blindness affects people in their workplaces, Plaut, Thomas, and Goren (2009) found that in cases where racial and ethnic differences were ignored, racialized people felt more pressure to fit in "almost seamlessly into the White norms" of their workplace, making them "less engaged in their work." In the Swedish context, colour-blindness contributes to a situation in which, as Masoud (1997) notes, "cultural discrimination"—"a new kind of discrimination"—contributes to gross inequities that have significant impacts, specifically on immigrants and racial minority refugees in various parts of society (p. 177).

Addressing colour-blindness, and by extension the larger operating political ideology that keeps it in place, requires acknowledgment of Whiteness and its hegemonic role in preserving and reinforcing cultural beliefs, racial bias, and the exclusion of minoritized members of society (Henry & Tator, 2009). Examining the hegemonic structure of Whiteness is necessary if we are to change the taken-for-granted practices that often go unnoticed by Whites, which maintain the privilege of colour-blindness that White people enjoy at the expense of racialized members of society. Indeed, as Masoud (1997) argues with reference to Sweden, the state has a responsibility to implement laws that are inclusive of the realities of immigrants and refugees, and in so doing discard the mono-cultural paradigm upon which it has operated.

In what follows, I use this framework of colour-blindness to review incidents in European societies that have focused attention on the plight of immigrant and racialized members of these societies. I then go on to discuss some issues in Sweden that suggest a need for a re-conceptualization of how the state should be responding to the diversity of its population. I conclude by suggesting that if immigrants and minoritized members of Swedish society are to be indeed integrated, then their "difference" with regard to race must be acknowledged and their experiences based on racism and discrimination must be addressed.

DISQUIET IN THE DIVERSE POPULATIONS OF EUROPE: CHALLENGES AND RESPONSES[1]

It is fair to say that the positive attitudes towards the amicable and harmonious co-existence of ethnic, racial, and religious groups in western countries have become considerably more negative since the bombing of the World Trade Center in New York on September 11, 2001 (9/11). In fact, the benefits that were once thought might be accrued from having immigrant and minoritized group members "maintain" and "celebrate" their cultures in western societies have been called into question. Much of this has to do with bombings that have occurred in Britain and Spain, riots in France and England, and unconditional attacks on religious and racial minorities in many European cities. These events have informed the tone of the discourse of multiculturalism not only in the countries in which these incidents occurred, but in other countries including Canada.

In March 2004, a series of organized train bombings were carried out during rush hour in Madrid three days before Spain's general elections, killing 191 people and wounding 1,800. The UK's *Guardian* called the attacks "the worst Islamist attack in European history" and went on to say that "the bombings were carried out by a group of young men, mostly from North Africa, who were, according to prosecutors, inspired by a tract on an al-Qaida-affiliated web-site that called for attacks on Spain … to exploit the coming general elections … [and ensure] the victory of the Socialist party and the withdrawal of Spanish forces [from Iraq]" (Hamilos, 2007). The attacks in Madrid were followed by nationwide protests and demonstrations.[2] But the official investigation that followed indicated that while the accused had links to Morocco, they were residents of Spain; there was no direct connection to al-Qaida, only that the attack was "inspired" by them.

More than a year later (July 7, 2005, also referred to as the 7/7 bombings), the public transport system in London, England, was attacked in a series of suicide bombs during the morning rush hour. The bombings were a response to Britain's involvement in the Iraq war and other conflicts. Fifty-two commuters were killed and 700 injured; the four suicide bombers were also killed. The attack was the largest on London's transit system in history. In his opening remarks in the report by the Greater London Authority (2006), Chairman Richard Barnes stated that: "What happened in London on 7 July 2005 could happen in any country, in any city, at any time. Ordinary people going about their everyday lives, were suddenly swept up in a maelstrom of extraordinary events over which they had no control." That the accused bombers were born in Britain and prided themselves on being British Muslims was of concern to many Britons. Tariq Modood captured the mood of members of the society in the following comment:

> The fact that most of the individuals involved were born and/or brought up in Britain, a country that had afforded them or their parents refuge from persecution, poverty and freedom of worship, led many to conclude that multiculturalism had failed—or, worse still, was to blame for the bombings. The multinational commentary in the British media included William Pfaff who stated that 'these British bombers are a consequence of a misguided and catastrophic pursuit of multiculturalism' (Pfaff 2005), Gilles Kepel observing that the bombers 'were the children of Britain's own multicultural society' and that the bombings have 'smashed' the implicit social consensus that produced multiculturalism 'to smithereens' (Kepel 2005), and Martin Wolf concluding that multiculturalism's departure from the core political values that must underpin Britain's community 'is dangerous because it destroys political community … (and) demeaning because it devalues citizenship. In this sense, at least, multiculturalism must be discarded as nonsense.' (2007, p. 12)

In Paris, France, the riots of October 2005 were another incident that brought into focus the tension and conflicts that are inherent in diverse societies, and what happens when disadvantaged members seek fair and equitable treatment and opportunities. The riots in the housing projects in the suburbs of Paris were triggered by the deaths of two youth and the injury of one (of Turkish, Malian, and Tunisian backgrounds) who were electrocuted while trying to avoid "identity checks" conducted by police. According to the *New York Times* (2005), the group of teenagers "all fled in different directions to avoid the lengthy questioning that youths in the housing projects say they often face from the police. They say they are required to present identity papers and can be held as long as four hours at the police station, and sometimes their parents must come before the police will release them." Commenting on the riots, the social conditions of racialized people, and "France's indecisive and problematic response to the larger question of how to maintain a stable and diverse society," Gereluk and Race (2007, p. 115) write that "issues of racial discrimination towards immigrants and particularly towards Muslims," as well as "allegations of police brutality and harassment," underpin the issues that brought about the riots in France. So too is the reality that obtaining employment is difficult for individuals with "Arab-sounding" names and immigrants whose applications are "systematically discarded." According to Gereluk and Race, "whether this is a perceived or real problem is irrelevant: the perceptions of Muslims are that French citizens are hostile to them" (2007, p. 115). The authors continued: "France's stance on pluralism has always been forthright in its protection of the civic republican tradition. The legislative ban on conspicuous religious symbols in schools highlights their starkly different approach to multicultural values and tensions as compared with other countries, such as Britain and Canada" (p. 116).

Similarly, in Birmingham, England, in October 2005, riots between African-Caribbean and Asian (Pakistani) youth yet again highlighted the "social problems and divisions" between these communities (Gereluk & Race 2007, p. 114), but more importantly, the enduring and simmering tensions that exist among the disenfranchised, specifically racialized, members of the society that periodically erupt. Racism-related incidents evident in many European countries speak to the particular situation of marginalized members of these societies, immigrants and citizens alike. As *Global News Digest* reported, "from Russia to Germany to Denmark, and from France to Britain, people of color are facing increasing trends in racism that make life far more difficult and hazardous than for the average citizen in any of these countries" (Akwani, 2006, p. 15; see also Bunar, 2007; and Bideke & Bideke, 2007 on protests in Malmö, Sweden). In some cases, people of colour are seen as foreigners and attacked or beaten on the streets (as in Russia and Germany), resulting in deaths and long-term injuries.

While the situation for racialized citizens and immigrants in these countries are difficult, it is often further compounded by their religious identities, specifically Muslims (as noted above).[3] The incidents in Amsterdam are a case in point. The killing of Theo van Gogh[4] in November 2004 precipitated retaliatory violent acts and arson attacks on mosques and Islamic schools, and counter-attacks against Christian churches. These actions are evidence of the complicated and problematic role of religious diversity post-9/11, particularly with regard to Muslims in Christian societies.[5] In this case, the murder of van Gogh by an Amsterdan-born young Muslim of Dutch-Moroccan parents—and the related protection of Ayaan Hirsi Ali, his collaborator on the film, due to death threats, which perciptated anger among Muslims—point to the tensions that adherence to religious dogma sometimes produce. Further contributing to the tensions in Dutch society was the fact that Hirsi Ali, a Somali-born Muslim,[6] spoke out against the religious and cultural freedoms (such as it was) afforded by society. She argued that multicultural practices in the Netherlands and Canada, which unquestioningly allow immigrant cultures to be protected, contribute to the negation of the rights of Muslim women in ways that Sharia Law affords (Hirsi Ali, 2005).

In their recently published book, *Islamophobia: Making Muslims the Enemy*, Peter Gottshalk and Gabriel Greenberg (2008) write that the publication in the Danish newspaper *Jyllands-Posten* of images depicting the Prophet Muhammad in September 2005 is a notable example of how Islamophobia operates in Western societies to bring about and maintain intolerance toward Muslims. At issue were 12 editorial cartoons negatively depicting the Prophet Muhammad, commissioned by the cultural editor of the newspaper. Offended by the publication, a Dutch Muslim approached the newspaper and the Danish government seeking redress, but none was granted. When a similar attempt by ambassadors of Muslim-majority nations to meet with the Danish government was turned down, scholars at Al-Azhar University in Cairo and the secretary general of the Arab League in Lebanon condemned the images and action of the newspaper, all of which contributed to a global protest when Muslims around the world learned of the cartoons through the Islamic conference held in Mecca (Gottshalk & Greenberg, 2008, p. 1). Commenting on the protest, Gottshalk and Greenberg write,

> Once more the familiar pattern unfolded, as some Muslims reacted violently to apparently an insignificant event that seemed the latest battlefront in the West's holding action to preserve inalienable rights against ever threatening Islamic intolerance. Although the Muslims involved never represented more than a fraction of a fraction of the world's more than one billion Muslims, their vociferous fury only confirmed a western image of Muslim intolerance and Islamic otherness. (2008, p. 1)[7]

While European societies struggled with the various demands of their ethnically and racially diverse populations,[8] North Americans similarly struggled to keep a lid on the potential problems with minority and immigrant disenchantment and dissatisfaction over racial profiling, high unemployment, disadvantages in education, and other such issues, many of which are related to racism. In the United States, the longstanding problems of racism and Islamophobia (particularly since 9/11) continued to produce familiar outcries by African Americans, Latino/as, and other racialized group members. And in Canada, with its official policy of multicultural policy since 1971, the events in Europe, particularly the Paris riots, not only had Canadians asking whether such violence could "happen here" (Valpy, 2005), but also signaled, as the *Globe and Mail* (Jiménez, 2007) declared, "a warning that Canada, long considered a model of integration, won't be forever immune from the kind of social disruption that has plagued Europe, where marginalized immigrant communities have erupted in discontent, with riots in the Paris suburbs in the fall of 2005" (p. A1; see also Gereluk & Race, 2007).

In the section that follows, I reflect on the Swedish context, noting how it grapples with changes in society that are brought about, in part, by the influx of immigrants, many of them non-Europeans and racially and religiously different from the people (particularly Finns) who traditionally immigrated to Sweden. In fact, Bunar (2007) writes that "during the past 30 years, Sweden has increasingly become a multiethnic society. Of 9 million inhabitants, more than 1.1 million were born in another country, and additionally, 8,000,000 Swedish born persons have one or both parents born abroad" (p. 166). How Sweden—a country known for its "general welfare model, social liberalism, and generous refugee policy" (Bunar, 2007, p. 166)—responds to its increasing ethnic, racial, religious, and cultural diversity is explored below.

SWEDEN'S STRUGGLES WITH ITS GROWING CULTURAL AND RELIGIOUS DIVERSITY

In a major report that explored minority communities' experiences with racism and discrimination in Sweden, Bideke and Bideke (2007) found that discrimination is experienced everyday by immigrant and minoritized members of society irrespective of how long they have resided in the country. This is contrary to the generally held belief about the generosity of the state in its provision of integration services. This finding indicates that irrespective of immigrant and minoritized individuals' familiarity with Swedish society, its services, and its institutions, systemic factors operate to disenfranchise them. The report also observed that there is a rise in discrimination in the areas of housing, education, employment, health care, and the media. Of note was the steady increase since 1997 in the number of reported hate crimes affecting racial, ethnic, and religious minorities (see also Bunar, 2007, p. 172). According to the Swedish National Council for Crime Prevention, some 2,575 hate crimes related to xenophobia, anti-Semitism, and Islamophobia were reported during 2006 (Bideke & Bideke, 2007, p. 14); these included things such as "cross burning in the victim's garden to arson in refugee camps" (Bunar 2007, p. 168). Significant here is that, contrary to popular opinion, it is not the "ideologically conscious White power group" members who are committing the crimes, but individuals with no "connections to White power groups" (Bunar 2007, p. 172). This is an indication that racial, ethnic, and religious minorities are more likely to be victimized or discriminated against by the average Swedish citizen, pointing to the fact that racism and discrimination are indeed a societal problem and not merely perpetrated by a select few extremists.

Furthermore, victims of racism and discrimination are not necessarily recent immigrants to Sweden. They are the Saamis, Sweden's indigenous people who have been in the region for centuries, and the Romas, who have long resided in the region. In this regard, we can appreciate the fact that Sweden has always been a multiracial society and the circumstances today of these groups are sufficient indication of the historical and structural reality of racism and discrimination in the country. Mathisen (2000) writes that lasting discourses pertaining to the Othering of the Saami were created, reproduced, and maintained through ethnographies, which contributed to a perception of them as "too primitive to civilize," and at the same time attempting to preserve their exoticism and "exotic" culture. The effect of the hegemonic relationship between the Swedes and the Saami people contributes to the stigmatization, and the desolate conditions, in which they live today (Mathisen, 2000).

Adopted Korean children have been living in Sweden since the 1960s.[9] Hubinette (2006) argues that the adoption of Asian children "underscores the Orientalist imagery at work, where, in many western countries, Asian children are widely perceived as being docile, submissive, clever, hardworking, quiet and undemanding—besides being cute, childlike and petite" (Hubinette, 2006, p. 6). He continues to say that, for western people, "these children were objects of rescue fantasies and relief projects for European homeland populations" (Hubinette, 2006, p. 5). It is possible, then, that these perceptions continue to operate in the consciousness of Swedes and as they come to terms with the fact that these Korean-born children are indeed Swedes. And just as Korean Swedes struggle to be seen as Swedes and negotiate the related stereotypes, so too do mixed-race children. In her article "Working Harder to Be the Same: Everyday Racism among Young Men and Women in Sweden," Hallgren (2007) relates that mixed-race children with one Swedish parent "occupy an uncertain identity." Some of this came from their experiences with racialization. For instance, Hallgren's respondents reported that whenever they misbehaved or were seen as lacking in manners, their behaviours were attributed to their non-Swedish or racialized parent. Maria is a case in point: she recalled that her Swedish-born grandmother used to tell her and her siblings that their "naughty" behaviours had to do with their African origin (Hallgren, 2007, p. 329). It is not surprising that these children's experiences with stereotyping would negatively affect their participation in society, as well as their educational performance and outcome (Caballero, Haynes, & Tilkky, 2007).

Research has shown that immigrant and racialized students do poorly in the Swedish school system, resulting in high rates of drop-out. Their low level of performance has been attributed to experiences with racism and stereotyping from teachers; a lack of teachers that reflect these students' racial and cultural backgrounds; and receiving little to no recognition of their differences. As well, being in learning environments where they are not exposed to or effectively socialized in the Swedish language and culture have resulted in poor academic performance and underachievement (Axelsson, 2002; Bideke & Bideke, 2007; Caballero, Haynes & Tilkky 2007; Gomes 2003; Haglund 2005; Hallgren 2005; James, 2001). On the issue of discrimination, statistics from the Ombudsman against Ethnic Discrimination reveal that in 2007 some 61 cases of ethnic discrimination in education were received, "of which 46 complaints concerned discrimination in schools and 15 complaints concerned discrimination in universities and higher education." The report goes on to state that the Ombudsman "did not file a lawsuit in any of these 61 cases" (Bideke & Bideke, 2007, p. 11). It has been established that the students most likely to experience discrimination and related educational problems, like high rates of drop-out, tend to come from communities like Botkyrka where, as Gomes (2003) shows using 1998 information, over one-third of children leave school after the compulsory nine years of schooling, and another third drop out before the end of the three-year secondary school cycle (p. 35).

In spite of Sweden's adoption of the multiculturalism policy in 1974 and the reform of home language teaching in 1977 (Sjörgen, 1997; Runblom, 1998; Masoud, 1997), the education system continues to be one in which immigrant students are "Othered" and racialized, and the superiority of Swedishness and the Swedish language predominate (Haglund, 2005, p. 71). The use of a mono-cultural, rather than a multicultural, approach to teaching is one of the greatest contributing factors to the disenfranchisement of immigrant students in the education system—a system in which immigrant children are also bullied by Swedish students because, among other things, they either cannot speak Swedish well or have foreign sounding names (Hallgren, 2005).

In such a context, students' underperformance and disengagement from schooling is more likely a product of the educational system's—and by extension society's—failure to integrate and fully support minoritized students, not any "deficiency" that is so often attributed to them (Haglund, 2005; Caballero, Haynes, & Tilkky 2007).

As in the area of education, there is extensive documentation of the discrimination immigrants experience in the labour market sector (Bideke & Bideke, 2007; Masoud, 1997; Gomes, 2003). The reasons are similar: foreign sounding names and stereotypes about the abilities and skills of immigrants and minoritized people. According to Bideke and Bideke (2007), several studies published by the Institute for Labour Market Evaluation show the impact of stereotyping on the employment situation of immigrants. One study (by Agerstrom and colleagues, 2007, in Bideke & Bideke, 2007) explored the impact of stereotyping on the work performance of immigrants, and revealed that employers and students associated Arab Muslim men with lower working capacity than men with Swedish origin; in terms of accessing employee mobility from assembly line work to higher positions within a company, immigrants are often overlooked because they are seen as incapable of grasping the necessary concepts to succeed (Mahon, 1994). As Runblom (1998) observed in his work, people with darker skin colour and with names that sounded strange to Swedes found it hard to secure jobs despite good qualifications and job experience. Other studies corroborated this observation that people with non-Nordic names have a difficult time even getting interviews (Gomes, 2003). In fact, Carlsson and Rooth (2007) found that job applicants with Middle Eastern–sounding names were half as likely as their Swedish-sounding name counterparts to receive callbacks for jobs, even though they had equivalent resumes. The callbacks for Middle Eastern applicants were less from a male recruiter and a small firm employer.

In 1997/1998, national policies were passed making the ethnic and racial diversification of workplaces mandatory, especially in government and government agencies; however, citizenship has operated as a barrier for many immigrants, thus preventing them from attaining jobs in these areas (Dingu-Kyrkland, 2007). Therefore, given the situation in which immigrant and minorities find themselves, it is understandable that they would experience high unemployment, poverty, and lower income than their Swedish counterparts. Indeed, as Gomes (2003) writes: "Possibly the most painful form of discrimination has occurred when [immigrants] did not get jobs for which they were qualified. They pinpoint the reason as 'they have the wrong colour'" (p. 69).

The cumulative effect of these experiences likely contributes to conflicts within families and communities, even violence (Gereluk & Race, 2007). This result is even more concerning when we consider that many immigrants and minorities mostly live in homogeneous immigrant/minoritized communities characterized by high population density, ethnic and language diversity, high unemployment, and poverty; they often live in semi-detached houses or "large apartment blocks, characteristic of the early seventies," the majority of which are owned and managed by a housing company belonging to town councils (Gomes, 2003, p. 52). There tends to be visible boundaries to these communities: In Botkyrka, for instance (a community and school I visited in the spring of 2009), Sjörgen (1997) writes that the buildings were initially set up in the early to mid-1970s to accommodate roughly 35,000 occupants made up of Swedish families with two adults working in what used to be a "prosperous semi-industrial, semi-agricultural community" (p. 44). The residences were later converted to accommodate the influx of immigrants and refugees that arrived in Sweden in the 1970s. It is estimated that today some 100 different nationalities or birthplaces, and even more languages, are represented in North Botkyrka, and the children born in the area often start school without having heard much Swedish, due to the minimal or lack of exposure to Swedish language and culture (Sjörgen 1997, p. 45). In the school I visited, the principal and teachers were concerned with meeting the needs of the students, many of whom were Muslim, and some had left the school to attend an exclusive Muslim school. While sending their children to the Muslim school is an attempt to give their children a better chance of succeeding in Sweden, the fact still remains that the families continue to reside in stigmatized communities considered to be crime-ridden and full of deviant people (Gomes, 2003).

TOWARDS A PROGRAM OF *REAL* GENEROSITY AND SOCIAL WELFARE

If immigrants and minoritized members of Western societies are indeed to enjoy cultural freedom, social welfare, and equal opportunity like all other citizens of these societies, then there must be a recognition of their differences and the role that race plays in the construction and responses to their differences. That race operates in racialized members' experiences in education, employment, housing, and in the services they receive from the welfare state, point to the fact that the colour-blind approach and the pervasiveness of white hegemony need to be acknowledged and addressed. Simply declaring a nation to be a multicultural state and pouring money into small anti-racism initiatives, as the government of Sweden did (Bunar 2007), is insufficient. Indeed, as Bunar goes on to point out, such initiatives tend to be "too few, too weak" with little to no "political influence" to have the necessary impact "on racist sentiments and hate crimes in the country" (Bunar 2007, p. 169). In other words, the initiatives have been too small-scale, obscure, resource-starved, and always victim and never perpetrator-focused to have the necessary and intended impacts on the problems at hand. What is needed, as Sisneros, Stakeman, Joyner, and Schmitz suggest, is multiculturalism from a critical perspective, one that allows moving

> beyond the goal of learning about and appreciating diversity to engage in an exploration of the multiple and complex power relations of difference and the mechanisms of oppression that operate in society. The examination of multiculturalism and oppression from a critical perspective involves an analysis of the systems that maintain and perpetuate inequality, with the presumption of a commitment to egalitarianism through action. (2008, p. 3)

In this way, if racist and xenophobic incidents or hate crimes, which contribute to obstacles such as poor language skills, limited educational attainment, unemployment, and poor living conditions, are to be avoided, then immigrant and minoritized members of society must be given opportunities through school, employment, recreational, and neighbourhood life to have a real exchanges with Swedes, and be supported in their aspirations.

NOTES

1. A version of this section appears in James (2010).
2. See http://www.guardian.co.uk/world/2007/oct/31/spain.
3. Recall that in September 2005, a series of 12 cartoons were published in one of Denmark's largest daily newspapers, *Jyllands-Posten*. The cartoons, regarded as racist and Islamophobic because of their caricature depictions of the Prophet Mohammed, created protests (at times violent) in many North American and European communities.
4. Theodoor van Gogh was a Dutch filmmaker, director, and producer who, working from a script written by Ayaan Hirsi Ali, created a 10-minute movie that tells the stories of four abused Muslim women. The title of the movie, *Submission*, is said to be a translation of the word "Islam" into English.
5. It should be noted that in Turkey, a predominantly Muslim country, wearing the hijab is not permitted because of its desire to remain a secular society. However, in societies like France, Muslims have waged numerous community and legal battles for their right to wear the hijab.
6. Ayaan Hirsi Ali was also elected as a member of the Dutch House of Representatives in 2003, and resigned her parlimentary seat following the political crisis over the allegation that she gave false information to secure asylum in the Netherlands.
7. It is of note that, as Gottshalk and Greenberg report, "three years before this controversy the same editor for *Jyllands-Posten* turned down cartoons satirizing the resurrection of Jesus," claiming that it would "'provoke an outcry' among Christians" (p. 2); he reasoned that his different reaction to the cartoons has to do with the fact that he did not commission the one of Jesus.
8. Writing of the situation in Britain, Tariq Modood (2007) notes: "In 2004, a swathe of civil society fora and institutions of the centre-left or the liberal-left held seminars or produced special publications with titles like 'Is Multiculturalism Dead?', 'Is Multiculturalism Over?', 'Beyond Multiculturalism' etc. This critical, sometimes savage, discourse reached a new peak with the London Bombings of 7 July 2005 ('7/7') and the abortive bombings of '21/7'" (p. 12).
9. Hubinette (2003) notes that the adoptions of Korean children peaked in the mid-1980s when a whole industry was set up to support adoptions in South Korea during modernization, and slowed down in the 90s following international and domestic criticism.

REFERENCES

Akwani, Obi. 2006. Racism Against Blacks is a Growing Trends in Europe. *Global News Digest*, June 10. http://imdiversity.com/villages/global/racism-against-blacks-is-a-growing-trend-in-europe.

Axelsson, M. 2002. "Educating Language Minority Students." In *Reflections on Diversity and Change in Modern Sweden*, edited by N.B. Gomes, A. Bigestans, L. Mugnusson, and I. Ramberg, 278–292. Botkyrka, Sweden: The Multicultural Centre.

Bideke, M., and Bideke, M. 2007. *Racism in Sweden*. European Network Against Racism (ENAR) Shadow Report. Stockhom: ENAR.

Bunar, N. (2007). "Hate Crimes against Immigrants in Sweden and Community Responses." *American Behavioral Scientist* 51: 166–181.

Caballero, C., Haynes, J., and Tilkky, L. 2007. "Researching Mixed Race in Education: Perceptions, Policies and Practices." *Race, Ethnicity and Education* 10(3): 345–362.

Caouette, J., and Taylor, D.M. 2007. "'Don't Blame Me For What My Ancestors Did': Understanding the Impact of Collective White Guilt." In *The Great White North? Exploring Whiteness, Privilege, and Identity in Education*, edited by P. Carr and D. Lund, 77–94. Rotterdam: Sense Publishers.

Carlsson, M., and Rooth, D.-O. 2007. "Evidence of Ethnic Discrimination in the Swedish Labor Market." *Labour Economics* 14: 716–729.

Dingu-Kyrklund, E. 2007. "Citizenship, Migration, and Social Integration in Sweden: A Model for Europe." In *CERIS Working Paper Series, No. 52*, edited by M.J. Doucet. Toronto: Centre for Excellence in Research in Immigrant Settlement (CERIS).

Ferber, A.L. 2007. "The Construction of Black Masculinity: White Supremacy Now and Then." *Journal of Sport & Social Issues* 31(1): 11–24.

Gereluk, D., and Race, R. 2007. "Multicultural Tensions in England, France and Canada: Contrasting Approaches and Consequences." *International Studies in Sociology of Education* 17 (1/2): 113–129.

Gomes, N. 2003. "Who Do We Want To Be and Who Does Society Allow Us To Be?" In *As True As Our Lives: A Study Based on Interviews with Minority Young Women in Sweden, Ireland, Portugal and Italy*, edited by N. Gomes, 31–70. Turin, Italy: WFM.

Gottshalk, P., and Greenberg, G. 2008. *Islamophobia: Making Muslims the Enemy*. Lanham, MD: Rowman & Littlefield Publishers, Inc.

Greater London Authority. 2006. *Report of the 7 July Review Committee*. London: London Assembly, City Hall. http://docplayer.net/31103613-Report-of-the-7-july-review-committee-report.html.

Haglund, C. 2005. "Voices of the Margin and the Center: Languages, identifications, and New Allegiances in Multilingual Sweden." In *Quality and diversity in Higher Education: Experiences from Intercultural Teacher Education*, edited by A. Sjogren and I. Ramburg, 65–83. Tumba, Sweden: Multicultural Centre.

Hallgren, C. 2005. "Working Harder To Be the Same: Everyday Racism among Young Men and Women in Sweden." *Race, Ethnicity and Education* 8(3): 319–342.

Hamilos, Paul. 2007. "The Worst Islamist Attack in European History." *The Guardian*, October 31. http://www.guardian.co.uk/world/2007/oct/31/spain.

Henry, F. and Tator, C. 2009. *The Colour of Democracy: Racism in Canadian Society*. Toronto: Nelson Thomson.

Hirsi Ali, A. (2005). "Unfree under Islam: Shariah Endangers Women's Rights, from Iraq to Canada." *The Wall Street Journal*, August, 16.

Hubinette, T. 2006. "Between European Colonial Trafficking, American Empire Building and Nordic Social Engineering: Rethinking International Adoption from a Postcolonial and Feminist Perspective." *The Faroe Islands, Act 3*.

Hubinette, T. 2003. "The Adopted Koreans of Sweden and the Korean Adoption Issue." *The Review of Korean Studies* 6(1): 251–266.

James, C.E. 2010. *Seeing Ourselves: Exploring Race, Ethnicity and Culture.* Toronto: Thompson Education Publishing.

James, C.E. 2001. "Making Teaching Relevant: Toward an Understanding of Students' Experiences in a Culturally 'Different' Sweden." *Pedagogy, Culture and Society* 9(3): 407–426.

Jiménez, Marina. 2007. "How Canadian Are You?" *The Globe and Mail,* January 12. Retrieved May 10, 2017. http://www.theglobeandmail.com/news/national/how-canadian-are-you/article18138461.

Lewis, A. 2004. "'What Group?' Studying Whites and Whiteness in the era of 'color-blindness.'" *Sociological Theory* 22(4): 623–646.

Mahon, R. 1994. "Wage Earners and/or Co-Workers?: Contested Identities." In *Swedish Social Democracy: A Model in Transition*, edited by W. Clement and R. Mahon, 347–372. Toronto: Canadian Scholars Inc.

Masoud, K. 1997. *Distorted Integration: Clientization of Immigrants in Sweden.* Uppsala, Sweden: Uppsala University.

Mathisen, S.R. 2000. "Travels and narratives: Itinerant constructions of a homogenous Saami heritage." In *Folklore, Heritage Politics and Ethnic Diversity*, edited by P.J. Anttonen, A. Siikala, S.R. Mathisen, and L. Magnusson, 179–205. Sweden: Multicultural Centre.

Modood, T. 2007. *Multiculturalism: A Civic Idea.* Cambridge: Polity Press.

Montgomery, K. 2005. "Imagining the Antiracist State: Representations of Racism in Canadian History Textbooks." *Discourse: Studies in the Cultural Politics of Education* 26(4): 427–442.

New York Times. 2005. "Youths Empathize with 3 Teens Who Fled Police." *New York Times*, November 7. Retrieved May 10, 2017. http://www.denverpost.com/2005/11/07/youths-empathize-with-3-teens-who-fled-police.

Plaut, V.C., Thomas, K.M., and Goren M.J. 2009. "Is Multiculturalism or Colour Blindness Better for Minorities?" *Journal of Psychological Science* 20(3): 444–446.

Runblom, H. (1998). *Current Sweden: Sweden as a Multicultural Society.* The Swedish Institute No. 418, Stockholm.

Schick, C., and St. Denis, V. (2003). "What Makes Anti-Racist Pedagogy in Teacher Education Difficult? Three Popular Ideological Assumptions." *Alberta Journal of Education Research* 49(1): 55–69.

Sisneros, J., Stakeman, C., Joyner, M.C., and Schmitz, C.L. (2008). *Critical Multicultural Social Work.* Chicago: Lyceum Books Inc.

Sjörgen, A. (1997). *Language and Environment: A cultural approach to education for minority and immigrant students.* Botkyrka, Sweden: Multiculturalism Centre.

Valpy, Michael. (2005). "Could It Happen Here? As Riots Rage across France, Troubling Parallels Emerge among Children of Canada's Visible-Minority Immigrants." *The Globe and Mail,* November 12, A1. Retrieved May 10, 2017. http://www.yorku.ca/goldring/clippings/Could_it_happen_here.pdf.

Chapter 23

South Asian Canadian Histories of Exclusion

Alia Somani

Alia Somani's paper (2015) explores the experiences of South Asians in Canada, and focuses on two historical events that have become sites of critical inquiry and have prompted discussions about belonging and inclusivity. The first event is the *Komagata Maru* incident, or the deliberate turning away of Punjabi migrants who arrived in Canada in 1914 as British subjects looking to settle in a British dominion. The second is the 1985 bombing of Air India Flight 182, an event which was not publicly understood as a "Canadian tragedy" until recently, even though almost 300 Canadians lost their lives in the explosion. Somani, who reads a selection of history textbooks as discursive accounts of the Canadian nation, considers how the *Komagata Maru* and Air India cases have been remembered or, significantly, forgotten in Canada, and thus how memories of the past have shaped the nation. She suggests that although there has been a hegemonic erasure of histories of racial exclusion—a national forgetting—this forgetting has been challenged from below by writers and artists who have deliberately and unapologetically made attempts to remember past traumas. Somani focuses on a short story by Bharati Mukherjee titled "The Management of Grief" and a museum exhibit by Ajmer Rode and Jarnail Singh called "The Komagata Maru Stories" in order to show that writers and artists have not only recovered the past, but in the process, also remapped the present.

INTRODUCTION

When Canada's Minister of Defense Harjit Sajjan spoke in the House of Commons on February 1, 2016, Conservative MP Jason Kenney attacked him in a manner that many suggested had connotations of racism: "English-to-English translation," he shouted ("Kenney Tweets Defense"). Although Kenney denied the accusations of racism and insisted that what he was heckling was the "coherence" of Sajjan's response rather than his ability to speak English, his attack against the Minister of Defense raised an important question: would the same kind of attack against a decorated war veteran have been made had the Minister of Defense been a member of the dominant white Canadian community rather than a brown-skinned Canadian sporting a turban? Indeed, those who accused Kenney of racism seemed to be reading his response as I do: as discursively positioning Sajjan as the inferior and subordinate other—as the outsider—in a Canadian nation imagined as white and English speaking. I begin with this incident in part because it might be understood as a reminder of the complex relationship that South Asian Canadians today have in relation to the nation. One the one hand, those who trace their origins to South Asia occupy numerous positions of power in Canada; Sajjan himself, for example, is one of four South Asians appointed to Prime Minister Justin Trudeau's newly formed cabinet. On the other hand, members of the South Asian diaspora are often framed as outsiders in the dominant national imaginary, as having a particular kind of "brownness" that marks them as not quite Canadian.

It is perhaps because South Asians occupy a precarious position in Canada, teetering on the border between belonging and alienation, acceptance and rejection, that they are haunted by two historical events that symbolize racial exclusion. The first event is the 1914 *Komagata Maru* incident, in which 376 British subjects of Indian origin sailed to Vancouver aboard a Japanese steamship with the aim of settling in Canada, a British dominion. For two months, however, the passengers were detained in Burrard Inlet by government officials determined to "keep Canada white," and 355 of them were finally barred from entry and forced to return to India. The second event is the 1985 bombing of Air India Flight 182, which claimed the lives of 329 people, 280 of whom were Canadian citizens, most of South Asian origin. It has been well documented that the bombing was "the result of a conspiracy conceived, planned, and executed in Canada" and that "[m]ost of its victims were Canadian" (Rae 2); in its aftermath, however, Canada failed to accept responsibility for what had happened. In *The Sorrow and the Terror: The Haunting Legacy of the Air India Tragedy*, a journalistic account, Clark Blaise and Bharati Mukherjee argue that the investigation began with the racist assumption that the bombing was "a foreign, exotic event, a tragedy planned by 'not quite' Canadians in a 'not quite' Canada, with victims who were themselves 'not quite' ours" (xi). Both the *Komagata Maru* incident and the Air India bombing, despite their differences, have been understood in the South Asian Canadian imaginary in remarkably similar ways—as examples of South Asian Canadian exclusion and as events that raise questions about the Canadian state's promise of inclusion of racialized others.

In recent years, a rather striking proliferation of texts on the *Komagata Maru* and Air India cases has emerged. Even more interesting is that these texts have come out in various forms, including novels, short stories, museum exhibits, inquiries, websites, illustrated books, apologies, and so on. There have been, for instance, novels such as Anita Rau Badami's *Can You Hear the Nightbird Call?* (2006), illustrated books such as Ali Kazimi's *Undesirables: White Canada and the* Komagata Maru (2011), and websites such as Simon Fraser University's digital archive of documents on the *Komagata Maru* case (2012). In this paper, I argue that, though these fragments might appear to be insignificant when read in isolation from one another, collectively they can be understood as a sign that the once obscured stories of South Asian Canadians and their exclusions are increasingly emerging in the public sphere and national consciousness. In other words, I argue that we might read this "new" body of texts as evidence that, despite the nation's reluctance to admit having committed wrongs, the once hidden stories of the *Komagata Maru* incident and the Air India bombing are beginning to appear in the public consciousness, to seep into the national imaginary, and to occupy a more visible space in the text of the Canadian nation.

In *Imagined Communities: Reflections on the Origins and Spread of Nationalism*, Benedict Anderson suggests that the modern nation can shift and change, depending on how it is imagined. For Anderson, the nation exists in the minds of those who see themselves as belonging to a shared temporal, geographical, and affective space, even though they might never meet one another face to face. As he writes, the modern nation is "imagined" "because the members of even the smallest nation will never know most of their fellow-members, meet them, or even hear from them, yet in the minds of each lives the image of their communion" (6). For Anderson, the birth of print-capitalism made it possible "for rapidly growing numbers of people to think about themselves, and to relate themselves to others, in profoundly new ways" (36). Specifically, he notes that the novel and newspaper, insofar as they tied together events occurring simultaneously but in different geographical locations, replicated the structure of the nation itself and thus invited readers into precisely the kind of imaginative realm necessary to "'think' the nation" and bring it into being (22).

Drawing on Anderson's work, I want to consider the possibility that, if nations are indeed "imagined spaces," if they achieve unity from the shared imaginings of their members, then they can change when our collective imaginings change: that is, when we "'think' the nation" differently. Beneath Canada's traditions of tolerance, peace, and good governance and its image of multicultural goodness are the hidden, if not deliberately forgotten, histories of racial oppression and violence: the decimation of Aboriginal peoples, the imposition of a Chinese head tax, the internment of Japanese Canadians, the turning away of the *Komagata Maru*, the destruction of Africville, and the failure to acknowledge the Air India bombing as Canadian. To marginalize such histories or erase them from the narrative of the nation is not only symbolically to write out the presence of minority communities for which these histories are of particular importance but also to recast Canada as a white nation. In contrast, to recuperate and retrieve these forgotten events from the depths of Canada's historical archives is to force the nation to recognize and remember minority communities and their histories and thus to grant them inclusion in the nation. That is, a conscious and deliberate remembering of the nation's forgotten past can serve strategically to alter the composition and text of the Canadian nation, to remember it, and in so doing ultimately to transform it into a more heterogeneous space.

My argument is influenced by the work of Homi K. Bhabha, who suggests that the nation is always tied up with narrative. Whereas the nation tends to project a phantasmatic account of national progress, a linear march forward across space and time, Bhabha suggests that (subaltern) counternarratives "disturb those ideological maneuvers through which 'imagined communities' are given essential identities" by rewriting the nation as fractured rather than cohesive, heterogeneous rather than homogeneous (300). He draws on but also critiques Anderson's argument that the nation is characterized by a certain temporality, namely that of simultaneity and synchronicity, and he reads this temporality as mere illusion, as subterfuge, concealing and containing the nation's inner divisions and fractures. For Anderson, each person reading the newspaper at the same time *is* the nation; but for Bhabha, "the space of the modern nation is never simply horizontal" (293); it is both synchronic and diachronic, and thus its linearity is always at risk of being ruptured by multiple counternarratives. In his formulation, therefore, the struggle for narrative power is essentially a struggle to write the history of the nation.

My point, then, is that the modern nation is not a timeless geopolitical entity that emerges organically but a symbolic space that comes into being through narrative, through a process of remembering and forgetting past events. As Daniel Coleman suggests, in order to produce and sustain its public persona, "to sit comfortably with [its] claims of multicultural civility," Canada has had to engage in a conscious (and violent) discourse of forgetting (8). It has had to *forget* the violence perpetrated against racialized minorities, the genocidal atrocities committed against Indigenous peoples, and a "whole range of injustices in between them" (8). Against "official" forgetting, minority groups attempt to map their histories onto the nation's public record, a space in which those histories might be memorialized and etched into the dominant national consciousness. In this paper, I examine two texts that do precisely that: Bharati Mukherjee's short story "The Management of Grief" and Ajmer Rode and Jarnail Singh's museum exhibit the "*Komagata Maru* Stories."

CANONICAL HISTORY TEXTBOOKS

Before exploring these creative fictions in detail, however, I want to track the national imaginary by turning to a reading of Canadian history textbooks from the 1940s to the present day. I believe that if we are to understand how the nation comes into being through narration, a study of textbooks, many of which are taught in schools, is necessary. As Louis Althusser reminds us, schools are part of the ideological state apparatus: "the school ... teaches 'know-how,' but in forms which ensure subjection to the ruling ideology or the mastery of its 'practice'" (133). My logic is derived in part from the work of the late postcolonial scholar Edward Said. In *Orientalism*, Said argues that the Orient does not simply exist but is also discursively created through texts. Similarly, I would argue that the Canadian nation is not just there but is also produced through a range of discursive formations. Canonical history textbooks, because we tend to think of them as authoritative discursive formations and object-ive accounts of the nation, are particularly valuable as objects of study. Thus, I want to turn to a reading of Canadian history textbooks in order to see what is remembered and what is forgotten, and to consider how the narrative of the nation might have shifted over time.

In Canada, two of the most well-known texts—Arthur Lower's *Colony to Nation: A History of Canada* published in 1947 and Donald Creighton's *The Story of Canada*, first published in 1959 and then as a second edition in 1971—narrativize the nation in ways that we might predict: by omitting histories such as the *Komagata Maru* incident and by representing Canada as a story of white triumphalism in which explorers and settler-invader subjects, all of whom are white and all of whom are male, emerge as heroic and celebratory figures. Lower registers some of the histories of racial discrimination (e.g., the Chinese head tax) but only to justify and sanction them, and Creighton, writing some twelve years later, tends to overlook them entirely.[1] Subtle differences aside, both Lower and Creighton represent the nation as a struggle between the French and the English, and in so doing they imagine the nation as coming into being because of the valiant efforts of its imperial founders, its white forces.

In Canadian history textbooks emerging from the 1990s on, we can see a shift in the way that the nation is imagined: thus, texts such as Alvin Finkel et al.'s two-volume *History of the Canadian Peoples* (1993) and J.M. Bumsted's *A History of the Canadian Peoples* (1998) reinsert histories of ordinary people and minority groups, even though they maintain the same kind of narrative trajectory as earlier texts, tracing Canada's movement "from colony to nation." What is different in these accounts is the tone in which history is recorded: it is less authoritative than earlier accounts of the nation and more conscious of the multiplicity of historical perspectives. Take, for instance, *History of the Canadian Peoples: 1867 to the Present* (Finkel, Conrad, and Strong-Boag). In the introduction, the authors acknowledge that "most academic histories written before 1970 either ignored, or treated unsympathetically, women, people of colour, and issues relating to private life" (xiii). Texts from the 1990s are framed as being more inclusive, as histories written from below. Rather than naturalizing racist ideologies and thus implicitly condoning them, as some of the earlier texts had done, these texts also draw attention to and critique racial violence. Bumsted, for example, begins by documenting what he calls the "invasion" rather than the "arrival" of European settler subjects and the eradication of Native populations. He also critiques Canada's treatment of the Chinese when he explains that the Canadian railway "was built on the backs of Chinese coolies" (215). Yet there are limits to this new inclusive perspective. Because these Canadian history textbooks retain the shape of earlier ones in terms of their basic chronology, minority histories continue to be framed as marginal in relation to the ostensibly more important narrative of the struggle between the French and the English. In these texts, therefore, there is still no mention of the *Komagata Maru* incident, and no reference to the Air India bombing, even though the texts claim to trace Canada's history from the colonial period to the 1990s.

More recent history textbooks such as Margaret Conrad and Alvin Finkel's *Canada: A National History* and Roger Riendeau's *A Brief History of Canada* are not dramatically different from those written a decade earlier, except in one instance: they include the *Komagata Maru* incident as part of the history of Canada, though they do so in ways that are sometimes problematic. In Riendeau's account of the *Komagata Maru* incident, the name of the ship is never mentioned; it is simply referred to as an "alien" ship (229), and the event is not registered in the index of the book. Similarly, though Conrad and Finkel discuss the *Komagata Maru* incident in their account, they seem to overlook its complexity and the full extent of its violent underpinnings. Rather than noting that the passengers aboard the ship were threatened at gunpoint and forced to leave Canadian shores, for example, Conrad and Finkel frame the turning away as a much more civil act, and as a matter of legality, describing the passengers as being "[d]etained on board for two months in Vancouver harbour while their case was heard before the courts" and then being "ordered to leave" (291). These historical retellings show us that there are contradictory pressures at work: on the one hand, a desire to ascertain and record historical "truth"; on the other hand, a reluctance to admit that the country had racist national policies.

Thus, whereas the early texts engage in a straightforward disavowal of diasporic traumas, the most recent texts reveal not only a desire to write histories that recognize racial minorities and their exclusions as part of the Canadian story but also a certain reluctance to displace hegemonic accounts of the nation. The fact that these textbooks still fail to mention the Air India bombing—now understood to be the worst case of aviation terrorism in the history of Canada—might be read as proof of their reluctance to countenance histories of racial exclusion. After all, to recognize the Air India bombing and Canada's failings in its aftermath would be to undermine a narrative of progress that these texts seem to maintain and to raise dangerous questions about the ongoing history of racial exclusion and the treatment of minority communities in Canada. Yet we cannot ignore the fact that, when read chronologically, these textbooks reveal that there has been a subtle shift in the national imaginary, a gradual albeit reluctant move from forgetting to remembering. Cautiously, I want to attribute this shift to the efforts of writers, artists, and activists who have done the hard work of inserting forgotten histories into the national imaginary and sought to remember the nation differently.

CREATIVE FICTIONS

Among the creative fictions that revisit diasporic histories of exclusion and trauma are Mukherjee's short story "The Management of Grief" and Rode and Singh's museum exhibit the "*Komagata Maru* Stories." On one level, these texts engage in a straightforward process of memorializing events such as the *Komagata Maru* incident and Air India bombing and placing them on the map of the nation. "The Management of Grief" recuperates the experiences of the families of the victims in the aftermath of the Air India bombing and draws attention to their interactions with the Canadian state. Rode and Singh's exhibit puts together a (visual and written) account of the *Komagata Maru* incident, one that focuses particular attention on the passengers aboard the ship. But these texts, in addition to recovering South Asian Canadian histories, also comment on and complicate the politics of remembering and forgetting.

Published in 1988 as part of a collection of short stories titled *The Middleman and Other Stories*, "The Management of Grief" tells the story of a fictional woman named Shaila Bhave, whose two sons and husband have died in the bombing. In the opening scene, members of the South Asian community have gathered in her home in Toronto to mourn their loss. Her friend, Kusum, whose husband and younger daughter have died in the explosion, questions her faith in god, while her older daughter, Pam, projects onto her mother her own feelings of regret for having survived the tragedy because of her refusal to join her family on their trip to India. She says, "You think I don't know what Mummy's thinking. *Why her?* that's what. That's sick! Mummy wishes my little sister were alive and I were dead" (182). Shaila has perhaps the most unexpected response to the trauma: she cannot weep. In spite of all the commotion that surrounds her (there are two radios going, the television is on, members of the South Asian Canadian community have filled her house, the phone is ringing, and reporters have arrived at the door), Shaila is trapped by an unbearable sense of calmness, a feeling, she explains, that is "[n]ot peace, just a deadening quiet" (180).

In her insistence on capturing the complexity of the tragedy, Mukherjee not only imaginatively reconstructs the scene of diasporic grief in the wake of the bombing but also draws attention to two important details. First, she shows us that members of the South Asian Canadian community are divided in the aftermath of the explosion. The young boys, we are told, are muttering "Sikh Bomb, Sikh Bomb," in response to which the adult men "bow their heads in agreement" (180).[2] As I will show, Mukherjee addresses and dissolves this divisiveness by the end of the story. Second, she shows us that members of the dominant white Canadian community are absent from the scene of diasporic grief. Drawing attention to this absence, one of the men in Shaila's home complains that the preacher on the television carries on as if nothing has happened, in response to which Shaila thinks that it is because "we're not that important" (180).

Throughout the story, Mukherjee suggests that, for many of the families of the victims, the experience of loss is exacerbated by the state's uncaring response and its refusal to treat the bombing as a Canadian event. In the story, the multicultural state is embodied in the figure of Judith Templeton, a social worker appointed by the provincial government to "reach out" to the bereaved, or the "relatives," as they are called. "Multiculturalism?" asks Shaila when Templeton arrives at her house. "[P]artially," Templeton responds, but she insists that she does much more (182). The seemingly sarcastic tone with which Shaila poses the question suggests that we should be suspicious of the role that the multicultural state plays in helping the families of the victims with their grief. Templeton is the face of official multiculturalism: she is polite, neat, and well turned out, and her mandate is almost entirely bureaucratic. As she explains to Shaila, "We want to help but our hands are tied in so many ways. We have to distribute money to some people, and there are legal documents—these things can be done" (183). Here Mukherjee wants us to see that the state does not really care about the families of the victims. Instead, it wants to "manage" minorities and their emotions and to make certain that the past is forgotten. Thus, whereas critics such as Deborah Bowen have read the title of Mukherjee's story as a reference to the ways in which the victims are "managing their grief" (54), I suggest that we should read it as a sardonic reference to the disciplinary technologies used by the state to placate the families, to ensure that their feelings are kept under control, that they are dispersed and deflected rather than encouraged—put simply, that they forget the past.

Mukherjee shows us that one way in which the Canadian multicultural state tries to "manage" the emotions of the bereaved is by understanding them through the lens of textbook psychology. Templeton, for example, explains to Shaila that she has created charts to track the progress of the families and a list of those who have accepted the trauma and moved on. "Acceptance means you speak of your family in the past tense and you make active plans for moving ahead with your life," she says (192). Her research, she tells Shaila, has been drawn from textbooks on managing grief that outline four stages that the bereaved must pass through: rejection, depression, acceptance, and reconstruction. Although Shaila responds to Templeton politely, telling her that she "has done impressive work" (192), she is suspicious of the state's insistence on forgetting the past. Rather than letting go, Shaila welcomes the visions of her family, who visit her at night: "How do I tell Judith Templeton that my family surrounds me, and that like creatures in epics, they've changed shapes? ... I cannot tell her my days, even my nights, are thrilling" (192). Templeton's formulaic and impersonal method of dealing with grief reminds us that the state has not been affected by what happened, that it only wants to effect closure on the past.

Mukherjee's critique of the multicultural state echoes the argument made by Sherene Razack at the 2006 inquiry into the bombing: behind the nation's civil façade is an assumption that certain lives matter more or, as Judith Butler would say, that some lives are more grievable than others. This assumption, Razack says, is tied to the way in which the nation has been narrativized—as a "white settler society" in which racialized minorities are "consigned to the role of guests and late arrivals in the national imagination" (5). Mukherjee, by resuscitating the eclipsed histories of diasporic communities and enshrining them in the collective consciousness, narrativizes the nation differently, as a space in which diasporic histories are incorporated into the nation. But she also complicates the politics of remembering and forgetting by encouraging a certain kind of remembering of the past.

The point becomes clear in the story when Shaila accompanies Templeton to the house of an elderly Sikh couple whose sons have died in the bombing. Shaila is initially reluctant to visit them and explains to Templeton that "[t]hey are Sikh. They will not open up to a Hindu woman" (193). However, she discovers a profound sense of connection to them when she visits their home. She understands their reluctance to sign legal documents not as an indication of their stubborn inflexibility, as the state does, but as a sign of their strength, a sign that they have not yet given up hope, that they have not forgotten. As a parent who lost her sons, Shaila feels connected to the Sikh couple. She is angry with the state, which seems to be saying to the bereaved "sign the papers, finish things off," and she wants to explain to Templeton that the elderly couple's actions are justifiable, that she understands them. The connectedness between Shaila and the Sikh couple marks a turning point in the story: against state forgetting, diasporic remembering is framed as being useful in the formation of the new nation but only, as Mukherjee reminds us, when that remembering unites the diasporic community around shared memories of loss.

Like Mukherjee, Rode and Singh recognize the importance of resurrecting and preserving diasporic histories. The "*Komagata Maru* Stories," which features paintings by Singh and a narrative account by Rode, was exhibited in Surrey at the Newton Cultural Centre and then in Abbotsford during the summer of 2011. The exhibit does not capture the history of the event in its entirety; rather, like most of the narratives on South Asian Canadian histories of trauma, it constitutes a fragment of the past. As a museum exhibit, the "*Komagata Maru* Stories" can be read as a particularly powerful shaper of public consciousness. In this case, the "*Komagata Maru* Stories" not only memorializes the forgotten history of members of the South Asian Canadian community but also brings visitors back to the site of the original trauma: that is, to British Columbia, where the ship was turned away.

The exhibit features on one wall a chronological account of the *Komagata Maru* incident from the departure of the ship from Hong Kong, to the struggles of the passengers who remained locked in Vancouver's harbour for two months, fighting for their rights as British subjects to settle in Canada, and finally to the forced return of the passengers to India. Thus, viewers are encouraged to explore and retrace what the narrative accompaniment tells us are the "key incidents of the *Komagata Maru*'s stay off the Vancouver coast." On another wall is a large portrait of Gurdit Singh, the Sikh businessman who led the journey of the *Komagata Maru*. Juxtaposed against an ethereal sky-blue background, he is represented as formidable and even godlike. The size of the portrait, together with its placement at the centre of the exhibit, serves to highlight the importance of Singh as a historical figure. Against the forgetting of the journey of the *Komagata Maru* in history textbooks, the exhibit asks us to remember Singh and to trace the struggles of the passengers in 1914.

The "*Komagata Maru* Stories" memorializes the incident not only as a Sikh history but also as part of a larger Indian history and a Canadian history. Rode and Singh, in their insistence on showing us that the passengers aboard the *Komagata Maru* were barred from Canada because they were Indian, remember the tragedy as a shared struggle, one that cuts across communal (or religious) divisions. For instance, in one image, which depicts the passengers aboard the ship as they arrive in Vancouver, we can see that among the Sikh men, identifiable by their beards and turbans, are a Muslim man in a fez hat and a clean-shaven Hindu man sporting a Gandhi cap. The image of the passengers aboard the ship reflects the cosmopolitan Indian nation and constructs the *Komagata Maru* incident as a secular struggle around which Hindus, Muslims, and Sikhs are united against oppression and racial injustice.

The exhibit not only partakes of the process of memorializing diasporic histories but also suggests, perhaps even more explicitly than Mukherjee's short story, that remembering the past is necessary. Thus, the first image in the exhibit, which depicts members of the South Asian Canadian community discussing the fate of the passengers with their lawyer, J. Edward Bird, is accompanied by text suggesting that to forget the past runs the risk of repeating it. The narrative reads as follows: "These paintings and narratives tell us that unless we realize the injustice done to the *Komagata Maru* passengers, unless we acknowledge our past mistakes, unless we purge racism and casteism from our conscience and social conduct, the phantom of the *Komagata Maru* will continue to haunt us." Two things are worth noting here. First, the exhibit seems to insist on the importance of remembering the past in the present and of incorporating it into the national consciousness. Second, the reference to the injustice of caste draws attention to another important dimension of the event. As Rode himself informed me in an interview in December 2012, many of the passengers aboard the ship were high caste and wealthy, and some of them practised untouchability and caste prejudice in Punjab:

> It's probably a bit of a touchy thing which never surfaces in our dialogues on *Komagata Maru*. What I meant was that these people on the *Komagata Maru* and from here, they were fighting against injustice and Canadian racism, and at the same time most of the people were doing the same thing: that is, committing the same crimes back in India against lower castes. So the *Komagata Maru* incident is very complicated.

The images in the exhibit, many of which depict the passengers wearing suits, vests, and ties, seem to support Rode's statement: the men might have enjoyed a certain amount of (caste and class) privilege in relation to some of their fellow countrymen. The exhibit therefore offers a complex understanding of the *Komagata Maru* incident, one that refuses to be reduced to a binary struggle between "white Canadians" and "brown Hindus," "perpetrators" and "victims"; it also seems to suggest that the passengers aboard the ship can be neither cast as "abject victims" nor uncritically celebrated as "revolutionary heroes." Yet the exhibit clearly shows that the barring of the passengers was an act of racial injustice and that they suffered tremendous hardship at Canada's border.

Throughout the exhibit, Rode and Singh challenge the nation's image of multicultural benevolence and point to its dark (and deliberately forgotten) history of racial violence. Thus, they depict Canadian officials of the period and reconstruct the racist proclamations that were part of public discourse in 1914. In one narrative account, we are told that the historical figure of H.H. Stevens, a Conservative Member of Parliament, was "rabidly against any Indians landing on Canadian shores" and that, in one of his speeches made at Dominion Hall in Vancouver, he proclaimed that he intended "to stand up absolutely on all occasions on this one great principle—of a *white country and a white British Columbia*" (emphasis added). According to historian Peter Ward, Stevens was a "leading anti-Oriental spokesman" who publicly "voiced the central concern of west coast nativists, the belief that unassimilable Asian immigrants threatened the province's cultural homogeneity" (91). By invoking the figure of Stevens and representing him as a proponent of white Canada, just as Ward does, the "*Komagata Maru* Stories" draws attention to and documents the history of racism and violence against South Asians in Canada in the early twentieth century; it also forces viewers to acknowledge a past that the nation has forgotten. The exhibit suggests that, just as it is necessary to remember the passengers aboard the ship for any acts of injustice that they might have perpetrated, so too it is crucial to recall the violence perpetrated by the Canadian state. Perhaps more importantly, it is through the process of recalling such details, such complexities, that Rode and Singh seem to insist that the injustice *was* real, that the tragedy *did* take place, and that we *should* remember it.

CONCLUSION

Both Rode and Singh's exhibit and Mukherjee's short story are part of the "new" and growing body of diasporic texts that seek to memorialize South Asian Canadian histories of exclusion, a body of texts that I mentioned at the outset of this paper and that I would like to return to here. When responses to the *Komagata Maru* and Air India cases first appeared, they took forms that we might expect: historical accounts, journalistic reports, literary fictions, and documentary films; later, though, texts appeared in forms such as apologies, inquiries, museum exhibits, websites, and so on. Mukherjee's short story is part of the early wave of texts on diasporic traumas, whereas Rode and Singh's exhibit can be understood as part of a more recent wave of artistic work. Together, therefore, these texts draw attention to just how widespread and diverse the remembering has become.

Two "texts" perhaps worth noting in the story of the changing nation are the official apologies. In 2010, Prime Minister Stephen Harper issued an apology to the families of the victims of Air India. In 2016, Prime Minister Justin Trudeau issued an official apology in the House of Commons for the *Komagata Maru* incident. Although an apology had already been made for the *Komagata Maru* incident in 2008 by Prime Minister Stephen Harper, it was rejected by many activists who said that it should have been made in Parliament rather than in a park. Official apologies, as I have argued elsewhere, constitute a form of state forgetting: in apologizing, the state seems to say "let's get over the past and move on." But these apologies, because they are forced to revisit the past, can in fact shore up historical memory, even though that might not have been the intention (Somani 4–5). By demanding an apology for the *Komagata Maru* incident in the House of Commons, South Asians activists seemed to be saying: "We want Canada's past wrongs to go on the official record; we want a nation that remembers."

Today, the archive of texts on South Asian Canadian histories of exclusion is growing at such a rate that the nation's attempts to forget are regularly thwarted, and the hegemonic narrative of the nation is swiftly undermined. Thus, I read this archive, this new body of texts, as a sign of hope, but also as a reminder that events like the *Komagata Maru* incident and the Air India bombing continue to be relevant and that the fight for a more just and inclusive nation—for a "new" nation—is not yet over.

NOTES

1. Lower, for example, mentions and justifies the Chinese Exclusion Act: "Even before its completion the Canadian Pacific Railway had begun to arrange for steamer service across the Pacific. Most of the British Columbian sections of the road had been built by Chinese labour and that experience had decided British Columbians that the Asiatic was not going to be allowed to crowd into their province and swamp its white population. Against the Chinese, Canada built up such defenses as the 'head-tax'" (446). Since Lower acknowledges histories of oppression and seems to approve of them as markers of

Canadian independence, his text can be read as engaging in a different kind of forgetting, one that contributes to the ongoing subjugation of racialized minorities.

2.   The bombing of Flight 182 was allegedly committed by Sikh extremists in Canada responding to Prime Minister Indira Gandhi's 1984 raid of the Golden Temple, her assassination by her two Sikh bodyguards, and the state-sponsored attack against Sikhs that followed.

WORKS CITED

Althusser, Louis. "Ideology and Ideological State Apparatuses (Notes towards an Investigation)." *Lenin and Philosophy and Other Essays by Louis Althusser*. Trans. Ben Brewster. New York: Monthly Review Press, 1971. 85–126. Print.

Anderson, Benedict. *Imagined Communities: Reflections on the Origin and Spread of Nationalism*. London: Verso, 1983. Print.

Badami, Anita Rau. *Can You Hear the Nightbird Call?* Toronto: Knopf Canada, 2006. Print.

Bhabha, Homi K. "DissemiNation: Time, Narrative, and the Margins of the Modern Nation." *Nation and Narration*. Ed. Homi K. Bhabha. London: Routledge, 1990. 291–320. Print.

Blaise, Clark, and Bharati Mukherjee. *The Sorrow and the Terror: The Haunting Legacy of the Air India Tragedy*. 2nd ed. Markham: Penguin, 1988. Print.

Bowen, Deborah. "Spaces of Translation: Bharati Mukherjee's 'The Management of Grief.'" *ARIEL: A Review of International English Literature* 28.3 (1997): 47–60. Print.

Bumsted, J.M. *A History of the Canadian Peoples*. Toronto: Oxford UP, 1998. Print.

Butler, Judith. *Precarious Life: The Powers of Mourning and Violence*. London: Verso, 2004. Print.

Coleman, Daniel. *White Civility: The Literary Project of English Canada*. Toronto: University of Toronto Press, 2006. Print.

Conrad, Margaret, and Alvin Finkel. *Canada: A National History*. Toronto: Longman, 2003. Print.

Creighton, Donald. *The Story of Canada*. Toronto: Macmillan of Canada, 1959. Print.

———. *The Story of Canada*. 2nd ed. Toronto: Macmillan of Canada, 1971. Print.

Finkel, Alvin, Margaret Conrad, and Cornelius Jaenen. *History of the Canadian Peoples: Beginnings to 1867*. Vol. 1. Toronto: Copp Clark Pitman, 1993. Print.

Finkel, Alvin, Margaret Conrad, and Veronica Strong-Boag. *History of the Canadian Peoples: 1867 to the Present*. Vol. 2. Toronto: Copp Clark Pitman, 1993. Print.

Kazimi, Ali. *Undesirables: White Canada and the* Komagata Maru. Vancouver: Douglas and McIntyre, 2011. Print.

"Kenney Tweets Defense of 'English to English' Heckle of Sajjan." *CBC News* 2 Feb. 2016. Web.

"*Komagata Maru*: Continuing the Journey." Simon Fraser University, 2012. Web.

"*Komagata Maru* Stories." By Ajmer Rode and Jarnail Singh. Surrey, BC: Newton Cultural Centre, 2011. Exhibit.

Lower, Arthur. *Colony to Nation: A History of Canada*. Toronto: Longmans, Green and Company, 1947. Print.

Mukherjee, Bharati. "The Management of Grief." *The Middleman and Other Stories*. New York: Grove Press, 1988. 179–97. Print.

Rae, Bob. "Lessons to Be Learned." Ottawa: Her Majesty the Queen in Right of Canada, 2005. Web.

Razack, Sherene. "The Impact of Systemic Racism on Canada's Pre-Bombing Threat Assessment and Post-Bombing Response to the Air India Bombings." Report submitted to the Inquiry into the Bombing of Air India. 12 Dec. 2007. Report.

Riendeau, Roger. *A Brief History of Canada*. 2nd ed. New York: Facts on File, 2007. Print.

Rode, Ajmer, and Jarnail Singh. Interview with the authors. 12 Dec. 2012.

Said, Edward. *Orientalism*. New York: Vintage, 1978. Print.

Somani, Alia. "The Apology and Its Aftermath: National Atonement or the Management of Minorities?" *Postcolonial Text* 6.1 (2011): 1–18. Web.

Ward, Peter. *White Canada Forever: Popular Attitudes and Public Policy towards Orientals in British Columbia*. 3rd ed. Montreal: McGill-Queen's University Press, 1978. Print.

Chapter 24

Building the Future: A Time for Reconciliation

Gerard Bouchard and Charles Taylor

Between 2006 and 2007, many Quebecers, predominantly white, perceived a "cultural crisis" given a number of requests by members of various groups for religious and cultural accommodations in public settings, such as schools, recreation centres, hospitals, and municipal councils. To these Quebecers, the requests seemed to compromise their "core" values, such as secularism. Further, the requests seemed to be compromising gender equality, identified as another core social value. The media played a role in heightening social tension. To respond to this situation, the then Quebec premier established a Commission on Accommodation Practices Related to Cultural Differences. This chapter first includes a few examples of the kinds of accommodation requests made, followed by the summary of the final report of the Commission. The Quebec state appealed to its citizens to negotiate and compromise in each case at the institutional level rather than relying on courts, which tend to be formal and adversarial. Quebec's approach to handling "difference" through "interculturalism" was reconfirmed, which tries to reconcile cultural diversity of the population with its integration policy through "open secularism" and a common language—French.

A TIME OF TURMOIL (FROM MARCH 2006 TO JUNE 2007)

1. The kirpan and the "Multani affair"
    *   On March 2, 2006, the Supreme Court reversed the decision of the Court of Appeal and ruled that the Superior Court judgment authorizing Gurbaj Singh Multani to wear his kirpan in school allowed for the reconciliation of the boy's religious freedom and the safety of other students. This decision was widely debated in the Québec media.

2. The controversy over the frosted windows in a YMCA
    *   In March 2006, the management of the YMCA du Parc in Montréal decided to replace in one of its exercise rooms the regular glass in four windows equipped with blinds with frosted glass. The decision stemmed in part from a request from the Yetev Lev Orthodox Jewish congregation, which assumed the cost of purchasing and installing the windows.
    *   Between October 1 and November 15, 2006, members of the YMCA circulated a petition demanding that management remove the frosted glass.
    *   On November 7, 2006, a Montréal daily published on the front page the first article on this affair.
    *   On March 19, 2007, the management of the YMCA du Parc announced at a press conference that it would replace the frosted glass with regular glass equipped with blinds.

3. The wearing of a turban in the Port of Montréal
    *   On March 9, 2006, a Montréal daily reported that, in order to accommodate Sikh truck drivers, the Maritime Employers Association was prepared to revise its rules concerning the wearing of a hard hat in the Port of Montréal.

4. Separate swimming sessions
    *   On May 10, 2006, a Montréal daily revealed that several days earlier the administration of the École secondaire Antoine-Brossard, on the South Shore of Montréal, had allowed three Muslim students to take the final exam in their swimming class under special conditions. Female staff supervised the exam and tables were used to cover the windows of the swimming pool to ensure that no man might see the girls in their bathing suits.
    *   On December 13, 2006, a Montréal daily reported that men who were attending their children's exams in a swimming class at the YWCA in downtown Montréal were asked to leave the pool area to avoid indisposing Muslim women who were taking a swimming class in the pool at the same time.

5. Requests for health care provided by female physicians
    • In July 2006, the Centre hospitalier de l'Université de Montréal (CHUM) decided to have pregnant women who visited its establishments sign a declaration stipulating that the centre could not guarantee that they would be treated by a female physician.
    • This topic appeared sporadically in the media between September and November 2006.

6. Prayers at municipal council meetings
    • On September 22, 2006, the Québec Human Rights Tribunal ordered Ville de Laval to halt the practice of reciting a prayer at public meetings of the municipal council. The Mouvement laïque québécois had filed the initial complaint with the Commission des droits de la personne et des droits de la jeunesse on behalf of an individual in 2001. It should be noted that other similar requests have been submitted since then.

7. The "directive" issued by the Service de police de la Ville de Montréal
    • On October 30, 2006, *L'heure juste*, the internal monthly newsletter of the Service de police de la Ville de Montréal, published a cultural factsheet that proposed to its female police officers to ask their male colleagues to intervene when dealing with men from the Hasidic Jewish community. [...]

8. The halal menu in a childcare centre
    • On November 7, 2006, a Montréal television network announced that the Commission des droits de la personne et des droits de la jeunesse was examining a complaint filed against the CPE Gros Bec by a Muslim father who demanded that his two sons not eat any dish containing non-halal meat.
    • On March 20, 2007, the Commission released an opinion asking the childcare centre "to apply the accommodation measure proposed by the complainer and to avoid serving non-halal meat to his children." It also enjoined the childcare centre to pay the complainer $4,000 "in the form of moral damages for the breach of his rights."
    • The board of directors of the childcare centre decided not to carry out these measures and the Commission instituted legal action against the childcare centre before the Human Rights Tribunal.

9. The kosher refrigerator at the Hôpital Sainte-Justine
    • On November 14, 2006, a Montréal television network revealed that the Hôpital Sainte-Justine had allowed Hasidic Jews to install a refrigerator in which to store kosher food while waiting for medical attention. The authorization was granted when the snack bar was renovated in June 2002.

10. Prenatal classes at the CLSC de Parc-Extension
    - On November 16, 2006, a Montréal daily noted that a local community service centre (CLSC) in a multi-ethnic neighbourhood in Montréal was apparently prohibiting men from taking part in prenatal classes because of the religious beliefs of certain women clients.

[...]

12. The controversy surrounding Christmas decorations
    - On December 14, 2006, the session of the National Assembly of Québec ended with a polemic concerning the wishes expressed by the party leaders. Jean Charest and André Boisclair extended their wishes for "happy holidays" without uttering the word "Christmas." Mario Dumont said in the National Assembly: "You will allow me a reasonable accommodation to wish Quebecers a proper 'Merry Christmas.'" [...]

13. Home health care services on the Shabbat
    - On December 15, 2006, a Montréal daily reported that the CSLC Thérèse-de-Blainville granted various forms of reasonable accommodation to patients from the Boisbriand Hasidic Jewish community. Nurses were apparently offering home health care services to patients who usually went to the clinic but were unable to do so during the Shabbat. They also apparently had to comply with a specific dress code when intervening in the community.

[...]

16. The survey on Quebecers' racism
    - On January 15, 2007, a Léger Marketing survey conducted on behalf of three Montréal media revealed that 59% of Quebecers say that they are racist.

17. Mario Dumont's open letter on accommodation
    - On January 16, 2007, Mario Dumont released an open letter in which he denounced political leaders' submission and collapse and the "old reflex of the minority" that encourages Quebecers to "give in" and "collectively fade into the background" when the time comes to assert their values.

18. The crucifix in the National Assembly
    - On January 19, 2007, a Montréal daily reported André Boisclair's remarks to the effect that the crucifix does not seem to belong in the National Assembly.

19. An exemption from music class
    - On January 23, 2007, a Montréal television network reported that Muslim students from the Commission scolaire Marguerite-Bourgeoys were exempted from compulsory music classes since, according to one interpretation of it, the Koran prohibits the practising of certain musical instruments.

20. Parking in Outremont
    - In January 2007, the Outremont borough council decided to prolong the lifting of the prohibition on parking in certain streets during Jewish religious holidays in order to accommodate members of the Hasidic community.
    - On June 26, 2007, a Montréal daily revealed that representatives of two Catholic parishes in Outremont had sent to the mayor of the borough a letter requesting the lifting of the prohibition on parking near two churches during Sunday services and other religious holidays.

21. Hérouxville's "life standards"
    - On January 26, 2007, a Montréal daily published the first article on Hérouxville's "life standards."

[…]

26. The prohibition on wearing the hidjab during a soccer tournament
    - On February 25, 2007, during an indoor soccer tournament in Laval, an 11-year-old female player on an Ottawa-area team refused to remove her hidjab to participate in the competition. The media reported the incident the same day.

[…]

28. Police searches
    - On March 9, 2007, a Montréal daily revealed a dispute between the Fraternité des policiers et des policières and the management of the Service de police de la Ville de Montréal concerning policies to be adopted in respect of ethnic minorities, in particular searches of veiled women.

29. Muslim prayers in a sugarhouse
    - On March 11, 2007, 40-odd Muslims engaged in prayer in the dance hall of a sugarhouse in the Montérégie region, following the noon meal.
    - On March 19, 2007, a Montréal daily published an article entitled "Cabanes à sucre accommodantes. Soupe aux pois sans porc et prière dans la salle de danse" ("Accommodating sugarhouses. Pork-free pea soup and prayers in the dance hall") based on testimony from a customer who was shocked by this practice. The main Montréal, Québec and Toronto media broadcast the news.

30. The dismissal of a trainee female prison guard

   - On March 13, 2007, a Montréal television network revealed that Québec's correctional services had refused to allow a Muslim woman wearing a headscarf (deemed to be unsafe) to pursue her training to become a prison guard.

31. The Chief Electoral Officer of Québec and voting with the face completely covered

   - On March 22, 2007, a Montréal daily carried the following front-page headline: "Le DGE le confirme : Voter masqué, c'est legal" ("The Chief Electoral Officer of Québec has confirmed it: It's legal to vote with your face covered"). The article revealed that, in conjunction with training for polling station staff, a representative of the Chief Electoral Officer of Québec pointed out that the identification procedure stipulated in the *Election Act* allowed women whose faces were completely covered to vote on March 26, 2007.

32. A hotel reservation during Passover

   - On March 24, 2007, a daily reported that a Gatineau hotel had rented its 129 rooms to a group of 350 Orthodox Jews during Passover (April 2 to 10). Under the agreement negotiated, the group would have exclusive use of the hotel's fitness centre and pool for three days. The agreement aroused dissatisfaction among certain regular members of the Santé Spa club, who were unable to use the hotel's facilities on those three days.

I: MANDATE AND INVESTIGATION

A. Mandate

On February 8, 2007, Québec Premier Jean Charest announced the establishment of the Consultation Commission on Accommodation Practices Related to Cultural Differences in response to public discontent concerning reasonable accommodation. The Order in Council establishing the Commission stipulated that it had a mandate to: *a*) take stock of accommodation practices in Québec; *b*) analyse the attendant issues bearing in mind the experience of other societies; *c*) conduct an extensive consultation on this topic; and *d*) formulate recommendations to the government to ensure that accommodation practices conform to Québec's values as a pluralistic, democratic, egalitarian society.

We could have broached the Commission's mandate in two ways, i.e., in a broad sense or in a narrow sense. The narrower sense would consist in confining the Commission's investigation to the strictly legal dimension of reasonable accommodation. The second approach would be to perceive the debate on reasonable accommodation as the symptom of a more basic problem concerning the sociocultural integration model established in Québec since the 1970s. This perspective called for a review of interculturalism, immigration, secularism and the theme of Québec identity. We decided to follow the second course in order to grasp the problem at its source and from all angles, with particular emphasis on its economic and social dimensions. The school-to-work transition and professional recognition, access to decent living conditions and the fight against discrimination are indeed essential conditions for ensuring the cultural integration of all citizens into Québec society.

B. Our Investigation

The Commission had at its disposal a budget of $5 million, which enabled it to carry out a number of activities. We commissioned 13 research projects carried out by specialists from Québec universities. A number of research instruments were developed, including a typology designed to classify the arguments in the briefs submitted and the e-mails that we analysed. We organized 31 focus groups with individuals from different milieus in Montréal and the regions. We held 59 meetings with experts and representatives of sociocultural organizations. We also set up an advisory committee comprising 15 specialists from various disciplines.

As for the public consultations, we commissioned four province-wide forums, organized by the Institut du Nouveau Monde, in which over 800 people participated. The Commission held sessions in 15 regions, in addition to Montréal, for a total of 31 days of hearings. The public responded very generously to our appeal by submitting more than 900 briefs. We read all of these texts and discussed them with their authors during 328 hearings, during which we heard testimony from 241 individuals. In the centres where hearings were held, we organized 22 evening citizens' forums open without restriction to the public and broadcast live or pre-recorded by a number of television networks, which attracted a total of 3,423 participants. Each forum, which lasted for nearly three hours, afforded, on average, 40 participants from all social backgrounds to take the floor and express their opinions. Between August 2007 and January 2008, the Commission also operated a Website that afforded the public opportunities to engage in exchanges (over 400,000 visits).

Between January and March 2008, we drafted our report with a view to *a*) producing our analyses and recommendations in keeping with the path that Québec has followed; *b*) emphasizing the search for balance and compromise; *c*) highlighting citizen action and heightening awareness among individual and community interveners of their responsibility; *d*) taking into account Quebecers' basic choices in recent decades; *e*) allowing for the expression of differences in public space; and *f*) putting the theme of integration in equality and reciprocity at the forefront of our reflections.

II: SOURCES OF THE ACCOMMODATION CRISIS

A. A Crisis of Perception

After a year of research and consultation, we have come to the conclusion that the foundations of collective life in Québec are not in a critical situation. Our investigation did not reveal to us a striking or sudden increase in the adjustments or accommodation that public institutions allow, nor did we observe that the normal operation of our institutions would have been disrupted by such requests, which is eloquently confirmed by the very small number of accommodation cases that ends up before the courts.

We also observed a certain discrepancy between practices in the field, especially in the education and health sectors, and the feeling of discontent that has arisen among Quebecers. An analysis of debate on the question of accommodation in Québec reveals that 55% of the cases noted over the past 22 years, i.e., 40 cases out of 73, were brought to the public's attention during the period March 2006 to June 2007 alone. The investigation of the cases that received the most widespread media attention during this period of turmoil reveals that, in 15 of 21 cases, there were striking distortions between general public perceptions and the actual facts as we were able to reconstitute them. In other words, the negative perception of reasonable accommodation that spread in the public often centred on an erroneous or partial perception of practices in the field. Our report describes several cases that confirm this conclusion.

B. Anxiety over Identity

Sudden media enthusiasm and rumours contributed to the crisis of perception, although they alone cannot explain the current of dissatisfaction that spread among a large portion of the population. The so-called wave of accommodation clearly touched a number of emotional chords among French-Canadian Quebecers in such a way that requests for religious adjustments have spawned fears about the most valuable heritage of the Quiet Revolution, in particular gender equality and secularism. The result has been an identity counter-reaction movement that has expressed itself through the rejection of harmonization practices. Among some Quebecers, this counter-reaction targets immigrants, who have become, to some extent, scapegoats. What has just happened in Québec gives the impression of a face-off between two minority groups, each of which is asking the other to accommodate it. The members of the ethnocultural majority are afraid of being swamped by fragile minorities that are worried about their future. The conjunction of these two anxieties is obviously not likely to foster integration in a spirit of equality and reciprocity.

We can conclude that Quebecers of French-Canadian ancestry are still not at ease with their twofold status as a majority in Québec and a minority in Canada and North America. However, we should also point out that a number of Western nations are experiencing malaises that resemble those expressed during debate on accommodation. A comparison of the situation in Québec with that in several European countries reveals that a number of fears that may be warranted elsewhere are not necessarily justified here.

III: SOCIAL NORMS

One of the key sources of anxiety mentioned during our consultations concerns the putative absence of guidelines to handle accommodation or adjustment requests. However, over the years, Québec society has adopted an array of norms and guidelines that form the basis of a "common public culture." In our report, we allude to these reference points that must guide the process of evaluating requests, with particular emphasis on the social norms that would benefit from clarification, more specifically as regards integration, intercultural relations and open secularism.

A. Reasonable Accommodation and Concerted Adjustment

The field of harmonization practices is complex and there is more than one way to define and delineate it. Among the criteria, we have decided to give priority to the framework for handling requests, which leads us to distinguish between the legal route and the citizen route. Under the legal route, requests must conform to formal codified procedures that the parties bring against each other and that ultimately decree a winner and a loser. Indeed, the courts impose decisions most of the time. The legal route is that of reasonable accommodation. Requests follow a much different route under the second path, which is less formal and relies on negotiation and the search for a compromise. Its objective is to find a solution that satisfies both parties and it corresponds to concerted adjustment.

Generally speaking, we strongly favour recourse to the citizen route and concerted adjustment, for several reasons: *a*) it is good for citizens to learn to manage their differences and disagreements; *b*) this path avoids congesting the courts; and *c*) the values underlying the citizen route (exchanges, negotiation, reciprocity, and so on) are the same ones that underpin the Québec integration model. In quantitative terms, we have noted, moreover, that most requests follow the citizen route and only a small number rely on the courts.

Moreover, our investigation revealed that, in the case of both the citizen route and the legal route, the fear of a domino effect is unfounded. Indeed, several criteria allow us to evaluate accommodation or adjustment requests. Such requests may be rejected if they lead to what jurists call undue hardship, i.e., an unreasonable cost, a disruption of the organization's or the establishment's operations, the infringement of other people's rights or the undermining of security or public order. A number of public institutions have already sought inspiration in the legal guideline of undue hardship to define evaluation methods that take into account their distinctive features. We also observed that many milieus have acquired solid expertise in the realm of intercultural relations and harmonization practices.

B. Interculturalism

Often mentioned in academic papers, interculturalism as an integration policy has never been fully, officially defined by the Québec government, although its underlying principles were formulated long ago. This shortcoming should be overcome, all the more so as the Canadian multiculturalism model does not appear to be well adapted to conditions in Québec.

Generally speaking, it is in the interests of any community to maintain a minimum of cohesion. It is subject to that condition that a community can adopt common orientations, ensure participation by citizens in public debate, create the feeling of solidarity required for an egalitarian society to function smoothly, mobilize the population in the event of a crisis, and take advantage of the enrichment that stems from ethnocultural diversity. For a small nation such as Québec, constantly concerned about its future as a cultural minority, integration also represents a condition for its development, or perhaps for its survival.

That is why the integrative dimension is a key component of Québec interculturalism. According to the descriptions provided in scientific documentation, interculturalism seeks to reconcile ethnocultural diversity with the continuity of the French-speaking core and the preservation of the social link. It thus affords security to Quebecers of French-Canadian origin and to ethnocultural minorities and protects the rights of all in keeping with the liberal tradition. By instituting French as the common public language, it establishes a framework in society for communication and exchanges. It has the virtue of being flexible and receptive to negotiation, adaptation and innovation.

C. Open Secularism

Liberal democracies, including Québec, all adhere to the principle of secularism, which can nonetheless be embodied in different systems. Any secular system achieves some form of balance between the following four principles: 1) the moral equality of persons; 2) freedom of conscience and religion; 3) the separation of Church and State; and 4) State neutrality in respect of religious and deep-seated secular convictions.

Certain systems impose fairly strict limits on freedom of religious expression. For example, France recently adopted restrictive legislation governing the wearing of religious signs in public schools. There are three reasons why we believe that this type of restrictive secularism is not appropriate for Québec: *a*) it does not truly link institutional structures to the outcomes of secularism; *b*) the attribution to the school of an emancipatory mission directed against religion is not compatible with the principle of State neutrality in respect of religion and non-religion; *c*) the integration process in a diversified society is achieved through exchanges between citizens, who thus learn to get to know each other (that is the philosophy of Québec interculturalism), and not by relegating identities to the background.

Open secularism, which we are advocating, seeks to develop the essential outcomes of secularism (first and second principles) by defining institutional structures (third and fourth principles) in light of this objective. This is the path that Québec has followed historically, as witnessed by the Proulx report, which also promotes open secularism.

IV: HARMONIZATION PRACTICES: ELEMENTS OF A POLICY

In light of the social norms that we delineate in our report, we are proposing a number of general key directions aimed at guiding the interveners and individual Quebecers concerned by harmonization practices. However, it is important to note that adjustment requests must be evaluated on a case-by-case basis and that there may be exceptions to general rules.

1. Pursuant to the norms and guidelines that we are formulating, adjustment requests that infringe gender equality would have little chance of being granted, since such equality

is a core value in our society. In the health care sector as in all public services, this value disqualifies, in principle, all requests that have the effect of granting a woman inferior status to that of a man.

2. Coeducation is an important value in Québec society but it is not as fundamental as gender equality. As a general guideline, coeducation should, however, prevail everywhere possible, for example when students are divided into classes, in swimming classes, and so on.

3. As for prayer rooms in public establishments, our position reflects the opinion that the Commission des droits de la personne et des droits de la jeunesse adopted on February 3, 2006. The opinion states that educational establishments are not obliged to set up permanent prayer rooms. However, it is entirely in keeping with the spirit of adjustments to authorize for the purpose of prayer the use of rooms that are temporarily unoccupied. Certain exceptions are made in the case of penitentiaries, hospitals or airports since the individuals who must remain there are not free to visit a church if they so desire.

4. Still in keeping with the notion of the separation of Church and State, we believe that the crucifix must be removed from the wall of the National Assembly, which, indeed, is the very place that symbolizes the constitutional state (a reasonable alternative would be to display it in a room devoted to the history of Parliament). For the same reason, the saying of prayers at municipal council meetings should be abandoned in the many municipalities where this ritual is still practised. On the other hand, the installation of an erub does not infringe the neutrality of the State and thus may be authorized provided that it does not inconvenience other people.

5. The same reasoning leads to respect for dietary prohibitions and to allow in class the wearing of an Islamic headscarf, a kippah or a turban. The same is true of the wearing of the headscarf in sports competitions if it does not jeopardize the individual's safety. It should be noted that all of these authorizations promote integration into our society.

6. Applicants who are intransigent, reject negotiation and go against the rule of reciprocity will seriously compromise their approach, e.g., this would be true of a student who refused any compromise concerning dress to participate in a swimming class.

7. Requests must seek to protect or restore a right. Thus, we believe that non-Christian religious holidays are legitimate since they rectify an inequality. Conversely, requests must not infringe other people's rights. This criterion forbids the exclusion of certain scientific works in a classroom library or opposition by a parent to a blood transfusion necessary for his child's survival.

8. In keeping with the aim of the education system, students must not be exempted from compulsory courses. However, a student may be authorized to abandon a music course for another equivalent course in the case of an optional activity.

V: AN EVOLVING QUEBEC

Regardless of the choices that our society makes to meld cultural differences and contemplate a common future, such choices will be largely doomed to failure if several conditions are not present.

1. Our society must combat underemployment, poverty, inequality, intolerable living conditions and various forms of discrimination.

2. French-speaking Québec must not succumb to fear, the temptation to withdraw and reject, nor don the mantle of a victim. It must reject the scenario of inevitable disappearance, which has no future.

3. Another mistake would be to conceive the future of pluriethnicity as so many juxtaposed separate groups perceived as individual islets, which would mean replicating in Québec what is the most severely criticized in multiculturalism.

4. French-Canadian Quebecers have unpleasant memories of the period when the clergy wielded excessive power over institutions and individuals. It would be unfair that this situation leads them to direct at all religions the painful feeling inherited from their Catholic past.

5. Quebecers of French-Canadian origin must also be more aware of the repercussions on minority groups of their anxieties. Minority groups have undoubtedly been alerted recently by the image of an ethnocultural majority that is apparently unsure of itself and subject to outbursts of temper.

However, several factors seem to bode well for the edification of a promising future. The upcoming generations are displaying considerable openness in their way of perceiving and experiencing intercultural relations. A number of recent surveys have not revealed a clear rift between Montréal and the regions from the standpoint of perceptions of accommodation. Reliable studies reveal that, contrary to certain perceptions, the Montréal area is not ghettoized. We believe that the process of edifying a common identity is firmly under way in numerous areas that must be emphasized, i.e., the use of French, the sharing of common values, the promotion of a Québec collective memory, intercommunity initiatives, civic participation, artistic and literary creation and the adoption of collective symbols. In keeping with the rule of law and the imperatives of pluralism, the identity that we are edifying must be able to develop as a citizen culture, and all Quebecers must be able to invest in it, recognize themselves in it and develop in it.

PART 3B

RACISM IN THE EDUCATION SYSTEM

In an inequitable society, education is often thought to be "the great equalizer." But is this the case? Is education equally accessible to *all* members of the society, including racialized students? Given the meritocratic ethos that is thought to inform the Western education system, it is incumbent on educators, government, and policy makers to create an education system that takes into account the diversity of today's student population, and thereby shape schooling and education practices that are relevant and responsive to students in relation to their racial, ethnic, gender, class, language, religious, sexual, generational, and geographic (i.e., region/nation/urban/rural) differences that are structured by inequities.

In this section, the authors discuss the impact of colonialism and racism on the education of racialized students, specifically Indigenous, Black, and mixed-race students in Canada and Britain. They demonstrate that the existing hegemonic and socially constructed meanings of race operate in ways that disenfranchise, essentialize, homogenize, and misrepresent the realities of Indigenous people of Canada and mixed-race Black students in Britain. In doing so, the authors argue that for these and other racialized students, schooling and education fail to meet, or be responsive to, their needs, interests, concerns, and aspirations. Therefore, what is needed is an approach to education that recognizes the cultural and social capital that students bring to their learning, helps them to exercise agency, and recognizes the ways in which colonialism, racism, and xenophobia have operated to discipline, assimilate, erase, and/or make invisible their presence in their societies. The complex, shifting, multi-layered and community-informed (ethnoracial and/or geographic) cultural identification of students' differences must be taken into account, for those differences are relevant to the schooling and educational processes of students and their parents. Such differences represent the diversity of the student population and must be reflected in textbooks, course content, curricula materials, pedagogical approaches, and other learning resources used with students, thereby enabling a teaching/learning environment that will be responsive to students, relevant to their learning, and suitable for the productive lives they wish to have in the society.

FURTHER READING

Campbell, Carl. 1992. *Colony and Nation: A Short History of Education in Trinidad and Tobago, 1834–1986*. **Kingston, Jamaica: Ian Randle Publishers.**

This book reports in brief (134 pages) on the development of an education system in the twin island states of Trinidad and Tobago in the Caribbean. Starting from the time of slavery and ending with the 1980s, Campbell tells the story of the role that colonialism has played in schooling and education in these former British colonies. While there are similarities with the development of education in many of the former British Caribbean colonies, the settlement of Trinidad and the post-slavery population—comprising Africans, Indian indentured labourers, and smaller numbers of Chinese and Europeans—make for important differences in post-colonial Trinidad and Tobago.

Coté-Meek, Sheila. 2014. *Colonized Classrooms: Racism, Trauma and Resistance in Post-Secondary Education*. **Winnipeg: Fernwood Publishing.**

Building on her more than twenty years' experiences as a student of Anishnaabe descent and a university teacher of Indigenous students, Sheila Coté-Meek tells of the emotional labour involved in learning and teaching about the historical and contemporary violence of colonialism. Employing in-depth interviews with Indigenous students, professors, and Elders—all of whom are involved in post-secondary education—the text explores the experiences of Indigenous students and instructors in classrooms where colonialism operates to instill sadness, shame, and anger among students and instructors alike. Coté-Meek writes that teaching and learning about colonization is a daunting, emotion-laden task; hence, standard normative pedagogical approaches do not apply. And she suggests that while the classroom is necessarily a space of violence and trauma, it can also be a space of healing and resistance.

Dei, George Sefa, and Arlo Kempf. 2013. *New Perspectives on African-Centred Education in Canada*. **Toronto: Canadian Scholars' Press.**

In this book, Dei and Kempf provide an overview of African-centred schooling in the Canadian context. Starting with an in-depth look at the creation of an Africentric public school within the Toronto District School Board, it tells the story of the movement behind that school's creation and lays bare a rich history of activism, organization, and resistance on the part of numerous African Canadian communities and their allies. The book presents a critical overview of the issues facing racialized students and offers a unique vision of African-centred education as a strategy for student engagement and social transformation. The authors offer a comprehensive analysis of the media controversy surrounding African-centred schools, as well as candid reflections on the personal challenges of fighting a largely unpopular battle.

Gilmour, R.J., Davina Bhandar, Jeet Heer, and Michael C.K. Ma, eds. 2012. *Too Asian?: Racism, Privilege, and Post-Secondary Education.* **Toronto: Between the Lines.**
Too Asian takes its title from a 2010 *Maclean's* magazine article written by Nicholas Kohler and Stephanie Findlay in their "Guide to Canadian Universities" issue. The article was widely condemned and criticized for its xenophobia and anti-Asian racism. *Too Asian* is an edited collection that lays out how these sentiments in Canadian society are not new but consistent with the long history and trajectory of these "structures of feelings" in Canada. The contributors explore the racial myths about Asians; the illusion of meritocracy; how diversity, employment equity, and affirmative action are taken up in Canadian and American universities; and how colonial and imperialist legacies are engaged in educational spaces. The text interrogates the problematic "model minority" discourse that is often used to describe Asian Canadians and Americans.

Jarvie, Grant, ed. 1991. *Sport, Racism, and Ethnicity.* **London: Falmer.**
In this edited book, Jarvie and his contributors explore the role of race in the identity formation, race consciousness, participation, and achievement of racial minorities in relation to sports and recreational activities. They examine male and female athletes' experiences with racism in Britain, Canada, South Africa, and the United States, as well as how sports influence the academic performance and outcome of minority, particularly Black and Asian, students.

Karumanchery, Leeno, ed. 2005. *Engaging Equity: New Perspectives on Anti-racist Education.* **Calgary: Detselig Enterprises Ltd.**
This anthology consists of 10 chapters, the last of which is written by the author. In this chapter he addresses the need for developing a process of education that is equitable for minority students. Each contributor addresses the effects of systemic/institutional racism on the schooling and education of students and teachers in Canada, the United States, and Britain.

Lee, Stacey J. 2001. "More than 'Model Minorities' or 'Delinquents': A Look at Hmong American High School Students." *Harvard Educational Review* **71(3): 505–28.**
In this article, Lee challenges the popular stereotype of Asians as high-achieving "model minorities." With data from her ethnographic study of 1.5- and second-generation Hmong American students, Lee discusses the variations that exist between these two genera-tions of students in terms of how their relationships with the dominant society, family and economic circumstances, perceptions of their opportunities, and educational experiences affect their attitudes towards school. Based on her findings, Lee suggests possible ways in which schools "can better serve these students."

Lynn, Marvin. 2004. "Inserting the 'Race' into Critical Pedagogy: An Analysis of 'Race-Based Epistemologies.'" *Educational Philosophy and Theory* **36(2): 153–65.**
In this article the author addresses the question of whether critical pedagogy as an approach in education adequately incorporates issues of race and racism. He reveals what both critical pedagogy and Afrocentricity (with its focus on race) have in common—among other things, both can be referred to as "epistemologies of transformation and liberation" operating from the vantage point of oppressed people and people of colour.

McCarthy, Cameron, Warren Crichlow, Greg Dimitriadis, and Nadine Dolby, eds. 2005. *Race, Identity, and Representation in Education.* **2nd ed. New York: Routledge.**
This very popular edited collection features authors who work in many different educational settings, mainly in the Unites States but also in Canada and Australia. This second edition also gives consideration to the discourse of race in the post-9/11 context. Authors take up issues such as multiculturalism, identity, whiteness, and imperialism, showing the complex-ity, fluidity, and contradictions of race in relation to the educational experiences of students.

Chapter 25

Working to Reconcile: Truth, Action, and Indigenous Education in Canada

Celia Haig-Brown

In this chapter, Haig-Brown reviews some of the history and current circumstances of schooling for and with Indigenous peoples in Canada. She argues that the acquisition of this knowledge is a starting place in the long journey toward reconciliation and more positive relationships between Indigenous and non-Indigenous peoples. If we begin with a question—Whose traditional land are you on at this moment?—truth becomes a guiding principle. Over the years, Indigenous-inspired initiatives and interventions into government policies and practices reveal persistent efforts to redress the negative effects of schooling. A dominant recurring theme is the need for Indigenous control of education, starting with the National Indian Brotherhood's response to Canada's 1969 White Paper and concluding with the 2015 Truth and Reconciliation Commission's yet-to-be-realized Calls to Action. Truth-telling, working to reconcile, and moving to a deeper understanding of our relationships to one another and to this land: these are the goals of Indigenous education in Canada.

The intensity and duration of the campaign to capture Indian minds and hearts reflects the importance accorded to this aspect of nation-building. Control of education goes to the heart of the movement for self-government, a battle Canada fought with Great Britain in the nineteenth century, as Amerindians are waging it with Canada today.
    —Dickason 1992, 338

For over a century, the central goals of Canada's Aboriginal policy were to elimin-ate Aboriginal governments; ignore Aboriginal rights; terminate the Treaties; and, through a process of assimilation, cause Aboriginal peoples to cease to exist as distinct legal, social, cultural, religious, and racial entities in Canada. The estab-lishment and operation of residential schools were a central element of this policy, which can best be described as "cultural genocide."
    —Truth and Reconciliation Commission 2015, 1

INTRODUCTORY WORDS

I want to begin with an acknowledgement of the original occupants of the Land on which I am currently residing and working as an uninvited guest. This complex territory has been and con-tinues to be the home of many Indigenous peoples including members of the Haudenosaunee Confederacy, the Anishnabek Nation, the Wendat, and the Métis Nation. I also want to acknowledge the Mississaugas of the New Credit First Nation. As a non-Indigenous person liv-ing with this Land, I have been taught this protocol of acknowledgment by many First Nations friends, colleagues, and students. I capitalize Land concurring with Sandra Styres who writes, "Land *is* spiritual, emotional and relational; Land *is* experiential; Land *is* conscious—Land *is* a fundamental living being.... Connections to Land are deeply intimate, relational, fluid and spiritually dynamic." (2017, 47, 51; italics in the original).

A starting place for engaging with the topic of this chapter is to ask yourself three ques-tions: (1) Whose traditional Lands are you on at this moment? (2) What do you know of the people who have lived and continue to live here? (3) Whose interests are served when you can or cannot answer these questions? One way to think about the historical and contempor-ary circumstances of the relationships between and amongst Land, Indigenous peoples, and non-Indigenous peoples within Canada is this: Consider the actual material Land on which you, or the building you are occupying, is standing. If it were possible to use laser vision of a particular, perhaps still to be developed, kind, you would be able to look deep into the ground beneath you and see the patterns of footprints that have walked in this place since time began. Some say since time immemorial. At some point in your careful examination, the first human footprints appear. This is the first Indigenous person walking on this particular piece of Land, soon followed by others. Creation stories, histories, and scientific theories give many explanations of how and when people came to be walking here. And as Thomas King tells us, "The truth about stories is that's all we are." (2003, 32). Over the next thousands of years, many more footprints of Indigenous peoples and other beings leave imprints. Then comes the moment when the first non-Indigenous footprints appear. And the mix begins until this very day when you walked into the space where your footprints mingle with and layer on all those historical and contemporary ones, each and every one coming into relationship with Land, Indigenous peoples, and each other. This holds true whether you are Indigenous, non-Indigenous, recent arrival, or long-term occupant.

Now the question becomes how can we move to have all those tenuous human associations in good relation with one another and, most importantly, with the Land? A possible response lies with cautious and thoughtful education. Even as we know that education alone rarely stops racism, knowledge is powerful and has powerful effects. What would it mean for all of us to know the stories and histories of the Land, human existence and movement, and those footprints, and find ways to recognize and respect their histories, our varied roles and responsibilities in those stories, and the resulting contemporary circumstances, whether levels of privilege or levels of injustice? Would reconciliation become a possibility as people begin the work needed to address injustices and come to understand more deeply the privileges accrued from Indigenous peoples through Land theft and legal sleight-of-hand?

A comment on terminology used in this chapter is necessary. In the quotations above, one reads the terms *Amerindian* and *Aboriginal*; in the text following there are the names of specific nations as well as the term *Indigenous*. As the chapter unfolds, the terms *Indian* and *Native American* will appear. What is most important to recognize is that terminology is highly political and can be used strategically. It can erase or inform identities, histories, and differences. To begin with, there are the general terms: Indian, Amerindian, Aboriginal, and Indigenous. The first is, of course, a homogenizing misnomer applied to the various nations of people living in the Americas when they first discovered Europeans landing on their shores. It is also the name of existing federal policy, the Indian Act, which continues to apply to individuals who are government-recognized first peoples of Canada. *Amerindian* is used by some historians to distinguish Indigenous peoples of the Americas from the people of India (e.g., Sioui 1992; Dickason 1992). *Aboriginal* became favoured over the terms *Indian* and *Native* for a period of time and still, in the Constitution of Canada, refers to Indian, Inuit, and Métis peoples. The term Indigenous is used globally to designate a direct and historical relationship with a Land, some say from time immemorial. There is no final verdict on terms for groups of people or even the individuals within a specific group. Context and circumstances matter, and language and group designations shift over time. Most important is to respect the names that people have for themselves and never assume that one name fits all circumstances or that a name that works today will necessarily be appropriate tomorrow.

This chapter builds on a premise: colonization has affected and continues to affect all of us in nearly every facet of our lives. As Ania Loomba tells us, "by the 1930s, colonies and ex-colonies covered 84.6 per cent of the land surface of the globe." (2005, 3). Schooling is a place where understandings of the particular history of colonization of what has come to be called Canada can and should be taken up. Through revealing the truths of the impacts of colonization, some form of reconciliation between and among Indigenous and non-Indigenous peoples living within

these Lands may become possible. Canadians across the country are recognizing the importance of such a goal as they become more aware of what has been well hidden, and strategically
forgotten, in school and university curricula for decades. Indigenous peoples are insisting that
their continuous presence in their traditional Lands, within the cities and throughout the country of Canada, can no longer be denied or dismissed. Many Indigenous people, along with their
supporters, are also insisting that the truth of this country's Land theft, treaty violation, and
blatantly racist laws be a part of the formal education of all Canadians. The accrued benefits
to some, which have led to hardship and poverty for so many Indigenous peoples living on
remnants of their traditional Lands, must be recognized and redressed. Only then is there any
possibility of reconciling our relationships with one another and with this Land.

Examining the impact of colonialism on education, particularly the age of residential
schooling[1]; moving to consider efforts at integration of "Indian" students into public schools;
pondering the effects of Indigenous peoples' interventions in educational policies and practices; and coming full circle to the Truth and Reconciliation Commission's official Calls
to Action: these may be seen as the four dimensions of Indigenous schooling in Canada.
Imagining moments on a dynamic circle allows the reader to see each of these aspects as
interrelated and yet simultaneously distinct within the constant flow of time.

This chapter examines the introduction of schooling for and about Indigenous peoples as
well as its continuing shifts. It explores aspects of the changes imposed on traditional land-
based education through the efforts of colonizers, their governments, and churches to control
Indigenous peoples, their movements, and access to their Land. A series of Indigenous-inspired
initiatives and interventions into government policies and practices reveal their persistent
efforts to redress the negative effects of schooling. The chapter concludes with a focus on
current calls to action for Indigenous control of both schooling and education and respectful
representation of Indigenous histories and contemporary circumstances for all students in
Canada as one aspect of moving toward reconciliation.

COLONIZING EDUCATION

The deliberately ambiguous subheading of this part of the chapter refers to both the colonizing
of existing traditional education and the imposition of colonial forms of education, i.e., schooling, on Indigenous peoples. A consideration of education in Canada starts with the Land
and Indigenous peoples. As the late historian Olive Dickason tells us, the Nation of Canada
was layered upon more than 50 existing nations (1992, 11). In each of those nations, families
educated their children as an integral part of the lifelong processes of becoming adults and
eventually elders. Education was not separate from the everyday activities of the community.
In the words of Jean-Paul Restoule:

> The community and the environment were the classroom. Just about anyone in the community
> was a potential teacher and also a potential learner. It was happening in the extended family,
> in kinship relations. It was happening from other knowledgeable people in the community.

> And it was very highly context-dependent learning. The teacher often knew who it was they were teaching quite intimately. And they knew what they were prepared for and importantly what they were not prepared for. People learn when they are ready to learn. (Restoule n.d.)

Shortly after the colonizers arrived on the scene, some Indigenous people expressed an interest in European-based learning. In numerous contexts, requests were made for schooling for their children that would add to existing community-based knowledge. What is often overlooked are the underlying expectations that Indigenous people had for schooling. Olive Dickason brings to light the persisting hope. She writes:

> When Amerindians had asked for schools during treaty negotiations, they had envisioned them as a means of preparing their children for the new way of life that lay ahead. They had in mind a partnership with whites as they worked out their own adaptations, and saw educational facilities as a right guaranteed by the treaty, by which the government had promised 'to preserve Indian life, values, and Indian government authority.' The whites, however, saw another purpose for schools: their use as instruments for assimilation. (1992, 333)

Similar sentiments can be found when Indigenous peoples met with governments from one side of the country to the other, throughout the decades—regardless of the purported topic of the meeting (see, for example, Haig-Brown 1995, 50–76).

Starting in 1620, boarding schools for Indigenous youth were established in New France, in an area now within the province of Quebec. Récollet and then Jesuit missionaries saw the schools as one way to settle the people and make them more available for conversion to Christianity (Miller 1996, 39–40). For the most part these early experiments were abandoned as they failed one after the other. However, by the mid-nineteenth century, those lessons forgotten, new energy for settling, evangelizing, and contributing to the developing economy brought churches and government together to begin the serious business of establishing residential schools across the country. Not only would they allow the opportunity to train Indigenous youth into a labour force for the industrial and agrarian development of the new country, they would also serve to interfere with Indigenous peoples' freedom of movement, to remove children from their opportunities for traditional forms of education and to facilitate increasing settlement on and exploitation of Lands often taken illegally or under extreme duress from their Indigenous families. Peter Schmalz recounts the situation of the Credit River Anishinaabek in 1847. Having established themselves as successful farmers in southern Ontario, the purported goal of government policy, when the settlers wanted more Land, the Anishinaabe farmers were forced to leave their farms, abandoning the work they had done to create them, and move north.

> One scholar observed that 'only when the government's intention not to give them secure title to their reserve was made clear did [Chief Joseph] Sawyer and his council consider leaving the Credit River. The squatters were taking over their land for nothing. (Schmalz 1991, 145)

Figure 25.1: This circle is placed on turtle's back in recognition of Turtle Island, a name used by some Indigenous people for North America. In the Anishinaabe Creation story told to me separately by Alan Corbiere and Kaaren Dannenmann, Turtle's back is the place where Land begins. Thomas King writes, "There is a story that I know. It's about the earth and how it floats in space on the back of a turtle" (2003, 1). *Source:* Graphic created by Ryan Koelwyn.

RESIDENTIAL SCHOOLS

As the government of Canada has now acknowledged, residential schools were a fundamental tool of colonization and an explicit effort to eradicate Indigeneity and Indigenous peoples from Canada's "body politic." The Province of Canada in 1847 published a report based on the ideas of Egerton Ryerson. It formed the basis for future directions in policy for Indian education and, with Confederation, strongly influenced the development of schooling for Indigenous people (Prentice and Houston 1975, 218). Clearly expressed is white people's perception of the superiority of the European culture, the need "… to raise them [the Indians] to the level of the whites," and the ever-increasing pressure to take control of Land out of Indian hands. The general recommendations of the report were that Indians remain under the control of the Crown rather than provincial authority, that efforts to Christianize the Indians and settle them in communities be continued, and finally that schools, preferably manual labour ones, be established under the guidance of missionaries (Prentice and Houston 1975, 220). Cultural and racial oppression was becoming written policy. Within the discussion of the recommendations is the following comment:

> Their education must consist not merely of the training of the mind, but of a weaning from the habits and feelings of their ancestors, and the acquirements of the language, arts and customs of civilized life. (Prentice and Houston 1975, 220)

What clearer statement of an effort to destroy a culture could exist? Indeed, as the United Nations Convention on the Prevention and Punishment of the Crime of Genocide states in Article II, genocide means "any of the following acts committed with intent to destroy, in whole or in part, ethnical, racial or religious group, as such … (e) Forcibly transferring children of the group to another group" (United Nations 1948, n.p.). This necessity of removing parental influence, another tool of cultural destruction, is further developed by Rev. Peter Jones, a Indigenous convert to Christianity, in Ryerson's report:

> It is a notorious fact, that the parents in general exercise little or no control over their children, allowing them to do as they please. Being thus left to follow their own wills, they too frequently wander about the woods with their bows and arrows, or accompany their parents in their hunting excursions. (Prentice and Houston 1975, 221)

As noted earlier in the chapter and expanded upon below, the activities described were one of the main forms of traditional education for Indigenous people: children learned by observing and following their parents and by gradually moving into doing the tasks expected of adults.

As the federal government focused more strongly on what came to be called "the Indian problem"—that is, their persistent drive to control Indigenous peoples and particularly their Lands—they increasingly saw schools playing a major role in achieving those goals. Following the establishment of the Indian Act of 1876, a consolidation of existing legislation, the federal government formally took over education of Indians, working in concert with the churches in what was seen to be a cost-saving mechanism (Dickason 1992, 333). Almost immediately, N.F. Davin was commissioned to report on industrial schools established for Indigenous people (Native Americans) in the United States. Out of his report came the recommendations that led to the subsequent establishment of many residential schools across Canada. In the introduction to the report, Davin made reference to President Grant's policy on the Indian question:

> The industrial school is the principal feature of the policy known as "aggressive civilization." (Davin 1879, 1)

Other comments show that some of Davin's attitudes were reinforced by politicians involved with schools for Native Americans in the US. One point, which frequently arose in discussions of education for Indigenous peoples, was that working with adults or children in day schools was ineffective.

> The experience of the United States is the same as our own as far as the adult Indian is concerned. Little can be done with him…. The child, again, who goes to a day school learns little, and what he learns is soon forgotten, while his tastes are fashioned at home, and his inherited aversion to toil is in no way combatted. (Davin 1879, 2)

Positively endorsing the notion of residential schools for Indians in Canada, Davin's final comment is "… if anything is to be done with the Indian, we must catch him very young" (1879, 12).

In 1887, L. VanKoughnet, then Deputy Superintendent General of Indian Affairs, again stressed the need for schools for Indigenous children. Incidentally, he also subtly acknowledged indebtedness and injustices perpetrated as "white brothers" have "taken over" possessions and opportunities for success. He wrote to the Right Honourable John A. Macdonald:

> That the country owes to the poor Indian to give him all that will afford him an equal chance of success in life with his white brother, by whom he has been supplanted (to use no stronger expression) in his possessions, goes without saying, and the gift for which we pray on his behalf, with a view to the discharge of this just debt, is the education of his children in such a way as will put beyond question their success in after life. (VanKoughnet 1887, 1)

While this report recommended the establishment of day schools, residential schools were favoured by the federal government. By 1920 amendments to the Indian Act included compulsory school attendance of Indian children and industrial or boarding schools for Indians (Miller and Lerchs 1978, 115). Following these amendments were other minor ones relating to education. It is interesting to note that in the 1920 House of Commons discussion of changes to the Indian Act, Deputy Superintendent General Duncan Campbell Scott stated clearly the idea that Indian cultures as such were to be eliminated.

… Our object is to continue until there is not a single Indian in Canada that has not been absorbed into the body politic and there is no Indian question, and no Indian department, that is the whole object of this Bill. (Miller and Lerchs 1978, 114)

A CASE STUDY: KAMLOOPS INDIAN RESIDENTIAL SCHOOL

A more detailed examination of the establishment of one residential school in British Columbia, the Kamloops Indian Residential School (KIRS), in 1893, typifies what went on across the country. The resonances with the first schools established by religious orders in Quebec in the early seventeenth century, as mentioned earlier in the chapter, are striking. The involvement of the government and the refusal to abandon them, even when so many were clearly suffering, are the primary distinctions. George Manuel, the Secwepemc leader and author, writes, "all areas of our lives which were not occupied by the Indian agent were governed by the priest" (Manuel and Posluns 1974, 63). While the government espoused assimilation of the Indian through Christianization and civilization, it turned the implementation of the task over to the religious orders in schools—priests, nuns, and brothers. The Secwepemc, the Indigenous people on whose traditional territory the Kamloops school was established, saw childhood and education as an inseparable part of the ongoing process of life and living.

> The methods used to teach skills for everyday living and to instill values and principles were participation and example. Within communities, skills were taught by every member, with Elders playing a very important role. Education for the child began at the time he or she was born. The child was prepared for his role in life whether it be hunter, fisherman, wife, or mother. This meant that each child grew up knowing his place in the system…. Integral to the traditional education system was the participation of the family and community as educators. (Jack 1985, 9)

In the early part of the twentieth century, James Teit, an ethnographer who learned Secwepemctsin, the language of the Kamloops people, wrote extensively of the Secwepemc people's lifestyle. Children had few required responsibilities or duties until they reached puberty. They were, however, expected to play a role in the everyday functioning of the family and community. Teit points out that children of the Nlaka'pamux, a closely related tribe to the south, had some restrictions. They had to rise early, wash frequently in cold water, and limit their play after sunset. Secwepemc children also participated in a complex ceremony twice a year called "whipping the children" in which they were encouraged to overcome fear and ultimately demonstrate courage (Teit 1900, 308–309). Puberty brought an intense focus on training. Girls, assisted by a grandmother, mother, or aunt, spent a year in isolation practising all the work that women must do. Boys, isolated for shorter periods of time, followed a similar pattern when their voices changed or they dreamed of women, arrows, and canoes, but their training could last several years (Teit 1909, 587–590). In addition to this specialized training, in the evenings, in particular seasons, the elders spent much time telling stories to all, which included embedded ethical concepts and values important to the people.

In stark contrast, in the residential schools, children were removed from their families and communities, placed in large groups—although isolated from older and opposite sex siblings—and tied into tightly controlled daily routines. The adults with whom they had contact had very definite ideas about discipline and the children's need for changes in language, beliefs, and lifestyle. European dedication to notions of their own superiority as well as their religious commitments blinded the priests and nuns to the ways of the people with whom they were engaging. The Oblates of Mary Immaculate (OMI), a religious order founded in 1812 in France, ran the Kamloops school for most of its existence. Their first involvement with North America came in response to a request from the bishop of Montreal; from there, a small group of Oblates moved west, arriving in Oregon in 1847. Here, the ethnocentric philosophies that were to guide much of the Oblate missionary work in British Columbia were put into action. In his "Instructions on Foreign Missions" the founder of the order, de Mazenod, wrote:

> Every means should therefore be taken to bring the nomad tribes to abandon their wandering life and to build houses, cultivate fields and practise the elementary crafts of civilized life. (Whitehead 1981, 118)

Second only to insisting that the Indigenous people abandon their own spiritual beliefs and take up Christianity was the push for them to abandon their migratory ways of living. It had proved very difficult to minister to people who were seasonally on the move.

Fort Kamloops, a North West Company trading post founded in 1812 and, since time immemorial, an important site of winter homes for the Secwepemc, was a logical site for the establishment of a mission. Father Demers was the first Oblate missionary to visit the Kamloops area in 1842. In 1878, Father Grandidier was appointed rector and bursar of the permanent St. Louis Mission near Kamloops. Father Lejacq served as supervisor from 1880 to 1882, succeeded by Father Lejeune in 1883. Although the Oblates had been operating a school for the children in a different location, in 1893 they took control of the permanent residential school. Father A.M. Carion served as director of the school, with some brief time away, until 1916. Although the priests frequently travelled to preach to the Indigenous bands of the area, they controlled the direction of the school. Father Carion, in a report from Kamloops Indian Residential School, states:

> We keep constantly before the mind of the pupils the object which the government has in view … which is to civilize the Indians and to make them good, useful and law-abiding members of society. A continuous supervision is exercised over them, and no infraction of the rules of morality and good manners is left without due correction. (Cronin 1960, 215)

In British Columbia, as throughout the rest of Canada, the missionaries and governments worked hand in hand to deal with the "Indian problem." Government saw the religious order's role in controlling Indigenous peoples as most beneficial. Rather than sending soldiers and guns, the governments had the missionaries, who insisted that the people practice religion, limit their movements, take up an agrarian lifestyle, and abandon the very substance of their cultures. Although their impact on the people was very different from the whiskey trade and profit-seeking exploitation of some Europeans, it was more subtle at first, and therefore could be considered a more dangerous exploitation in that the Oblates created a growing need for themselves in Indigenous people's lives. Because the missionaries had more extensive knowledge of Jesus Christ than Indigenous people, once converted, they had to rely on the priests as the source for their religious experiences. Only priests could say Mass and offer the sacraments, essential to the practising Catholic. Missing Mass on Sunday was a deadly sin.

Residential schools were seen as a prime opportunity to take the efforts to enforce change even further. Here the students could be isolated from the cultural influences of their parents and a daily, systematic inculcation of Christian theory and practice became possible. Students were expected to attend from August to June and visits from home were strictly limited. Over many years, the use of English was mandatory and many students were punished severely for speaking their mother tongue, even when newly arrived at the schools. These efforts to prohibit Indigenous languages attacked the very base of culture. The permanent residential school near Kamloops was built on land purchased by the government at the edge of what is now the Kamloops Indian Reserve No. 1. It was across the river from the town and several miles from the Secwepemc village itself, making it more difficult for family to visit and students to run away. In 1890, three two-storey wooden buildings were completed at the present site (now owned by the Tk'emlups te Secwepemc). The buildings included separate dormitories for boys and girls, a living area for teachers, classrooms, and a play area.

After a faltering start under the guidance of lay teacher Michael Hagan, the school was taken over by the Oblates in 1893. The Sisters of St. Ann worked with the girls. Sister Mary Joachim, who started at the school in 1890, left and returned in 1894 when the Oblates took over and remained until her death in 1907 (*Kamloops Souvenir Edition* 1977, 8). In 1923, the new brick building was completed to replace the one destroyed by fire: it remains standing today. Throughout most of its operation as a school until its closure in 1966, the KIRS was run by the Oblates and the Sisters of St. Ann. In the usual male-female and class-based hierarchy within the Church, the Oblate priests controlled policy and served as administrators while the Sisters were expected to work obediently as teachers, child care workers, and supervisors along with the Oblate brothers—the labourers of the order.

Most students who attended the school fell within the governmental jurisdiction called the Kamloops Agency. This area included the southern Shuswap Bands of Bonaparte, ChuChua, Skeetchestn, Kamloops, Adams Lake, Chase, Neskonlith, and several bands of Thompson Indians of the Nicola Valley. In relation to the changing names mentioned above, it is interesting to note that these groups are now using names much closer to their original ones, before the colonizers' Anglicization and/or erasure of the names Indigenous peoples had for themselves. For example, the Shuswap are the Secwepemc; Bonaparte is

Stuctwewsemc; ChuChua is Simpcw; Kamloops is Tk'emlúps; and the Thompson Indians are the Nlaka'pamux. Nlaka'pamux people from the Nicola Valley could choose to send children to St. Joseph's School in Lytton if they were Protestant and to St. Louis Mission in Kamloops if they were Catholic. In addition, some children from the Tsilhqot'in and coastal bands attended the school. Following British Columbia's McKenna-McBride Royal Commission hearings (1912–1916), day schools were built in several First Nations communities located some distance from Kamloops. Rising birth rates after the devastation of smallpox and other introduced European diseases, and enforced attendance after 1920, provided students not only for day schools but also an increasing number for the residential school.

Despite what some may want to claim as good intentions, the Oblates' real goal to convert the Indigenous people was simultaneously an inhuman effort to destroy their cultures and languages. Robin Fisher summarizes missionary efforts, at that time, as follows:

> Because the missionaries did not separate Western Christianity and Western civilization, they approached Indian culture as a whole and demanded a total transformation of the Indian proselyte. Their aim was the complete destruction of the traditional integrated Indian way of life. The missionaries demanded even more far-reaching transformation than the settlers and they pushed it more aggressively than any other group of whites. (1977, 144–145)

Throughout Canada, similar schools had been and were being established. Children were often forcibly taken from their parents, sometimes for months and even years at a stretch. For the most part, the students attending the schools were being prepared to perform menial, gender-specific jobs or lead a life of dependency on governments. Much more sinisterly, the schools were the sites of sexual and physical abuse, rampant communicable diseases, and frequent deaths. Children ran away, sometimes in the dead of winter. Letters home from the students telling of dire circumstances were censored and sometimes not sent at all. As will be noted later in the chapter, these aspects are now well-documented and the focus of ongoing reparations. Edward Ahenakew, a member of the Cree Nation, a residential school graduate, and an ordained minister uses a fictional elder's account to give his critique of the schools. Beyond the diseases and trauma spread through the schools, his critique addresses the dependency that the schools fostered in the students who did survive their horrors.

> As for those who do live, who survive and who graduate from the school at the age of eighteen, during every day of their training they have acted under orders. Nothing they did was without supervision. They did not sweep a floor, wash dishes, clean stables, without first being told to do so, and always there would be a member of the staff to show them each step. They never needed to use their own minds and wills. They came to think it would be wrong if they went their own way. Now discipline and expediency in life are good, but will and initiative are better. (1973, 133)

RESISTANCE, TRUTH, AND RECONCILIATION

How is it that the schools finally came to an end? And what took so long? From 1884 to 1951 the potlatch, an economic system that included dances and feasting, had been outlawed (Tennant 1990, 52, 122): this legal control had further been extended to any gathering of Indians. The restrictions, in place for so many years, seriously affected the people's ability to gather to collectively address land claims or treaty issues, or protest the residential school system. Although Indigenous peoples had been railing against the situations arising in the schools whenever there was an authorized gathering, not until 1946 was there any official commitment to even listen to the concerns, disappointments, and, amazingly, the persisting aspirations for sound education from Indigenous peoples. A tantalizing hint of real possibility for change in official attitude and in the expressed intent of Department of Indian Affairs policy, although ultimately disappointing, was contained in the words of J. Allison Glen, Minister of Mines and Resources. He declared: "The Indian ... should retain and develop many of his Indigenous Characteristics, and ... ultimately assume the full rights and responsibilities of democratic citizenship" (Miller and Lerchs 1978, 130). In 1946, discussions began for a complete revamping of the Indian Act.

For the first time, and only after initial strong resistance by committee members, Indigenous input was actually permitted into the hearings for the revisions. Andrew Paull, President of the North American Indian Brotherhood, appeared before the Special Joint Committee. He was highly critical of the committee's lack of Indian representation. He condemned the existing Act as "an imposition, the carrying out of the most bureaucratic and autocratic system that was ever imposed upon any people in this world of ours" (Special Joint Committee 1947, 247). He spoke strongly for Indian self-government, in some ways in indirect support of Glen's words, as he commented that what was needed was

> ... to lift up the morale of the Indians in Canada. That is your first duty. There is no use in passing legislation about this or that if you do not lift up the morale of the people. The only way you can lift up the morale of any people is to let the members look after themselves and look after their people. (427)

His words fell upon deliberately deaf ears.

In 1947, anthropologist Diamond Jenness told the Committee what it had been wanting to hear. His disconcertingly titled "Plan for Liquidating Canada's Indian Problems within 25 Years" (Special Joint Committee 1947, 310–311) recommended the abolition of Indian reserves and the establishment of an integrated educational system as the basis for assimilation. The never-ceasing attempt by the now dominant majority society to make the Indian disappear continued unabashed through this revision of the Indian Act. "The new Indian Act did not differ in many respects from previous legislation" (Miller and Lerchs 1978, 149). It did, however, serve as the beginning of the end for many residential schools because it allowed for Indian attendance in the public school system.

One of the major divergences between traditional Indigenous ways of knowing and conceptions of knowledge and dominant European forms exists between oral tradition and written evidence. When Chief Justice of the Supreme Court of Canada Antonio Lamer, in his written judgement, accepted and commented on oral tradition as well as oral histories as sound legal evidence, a transformation in relations between the courts and representations of traditional Indigenous knowledge occurred (Supreme Court 1997, n.p.). With all of its shortcomings as a product of our existing legal system, this step pushed back against years of refusing such forms of evidence (see Pinder 1990). In the interim, strategic Indigenous scholars, politicians, educators, families, and community members had become more than proficient at writing policy documents and briefs as contributions to the persistent demands for changes to schools and schooling.

One of the first formal interventions came from the Indigenous leaders of the National Indian Brotherhood in 1970 as they responded directly and firmly to Minister of Indian Affairs and Northern Development Jean Chrétien's White Paper of 1969, which once again proposed to do away with Indians, this time through removal of existing "discriminatory" legislation and services that affected Indian people. While the proposed legislation may have seemed on first glance as a move towards equality, it sadly, or perhaps deviously, appeared to lack any depth of understanding of equity and history. Even as it tried to argue that it was placing Indians as defined by the Indian Act more squarely into mainstream Canada, it also excused at least some existing, unrecognized debts, unsettled land claims, treaty violations, and commitments on the part of non-Indian citizens and governments. Indigenous response contained in the policy *Indian Control of Indian Education* (National Indian Brotherhood, 1972) remains a classic and relevant document as it argues for changes in schooling and posits local control and parental responsibility as the guiding principles for education. While acknowledging that the move to integrate Indian students into provincially funded public schools, begun in the 1950s, should have been a positive one, the authors point out that:

> In the past it has been the Indian student who was asked to integrate: to give up his [sic] identity, to adopt new values and a new way of life…. Integrated educational programs must respect the reality of racial and cultural differences by providing a curriculum which blends the best from the Indian and non-Indian traditions…. The success of integration hinges on these factors: parents, teachers, pupils (both Indian and white) and curriculum. (National Indian Brotherhood 1972, 25)

This incisive 38-page document, one might say unfortunately, stands the test of time. Serving as something of a summary of those official inquiries that follow, it addresses the need for dramatic changes to Indigenous programming at all levels, including support for Indigenous languages; teacher and counsellor training; improvement of facilities and educational services for Indigenous students; and, as noted above, the need for culturally-responsive integration of Indigenous students into the public schools. In an oft-quoted introduction the authors say:

> Unless a child learns about the forces which shape him [sic]: the history of his people, their values and customs, their language, he will never really know himself or his potential as a human being. Indian culture and values have a unique place in the history of mankind. The Indian child who learns about his heritage will be proud of it. The lessons he learns in school, his whole school experience, should reinforce and contribute to the image he has of himself as an Indian. (National Indian Brotherhood 1972, 9)

These wise words resonate for all children and all cultures but have special significance for the first peoples of the Land now called Canada. Their histories as the starting point for all citizens' relationships with one another are material for all children, Indigenous and non-Indigenous, to learn. From there, Indigenous knowledge teaches all of us that knowing our origins, including the levels of privilege that allow some of us to be here as uninvited guests on Indigenous Lands, is fundamental to being in good relationships with one another and with the Land.

With far too little accomplished as a result of the policy paper's impact on education, the next significant opportunity for change came in 1991 with the appointment of Royal Commission on Aboriginal Peoples (RCAP). Unlike *Indian Control of Indian Education*, the results of this one yielded "5 volumes and approximately 4000 pages of text" (Institute on Governance 1997, 4). Tellingly, the section focused on education is entitled "Aboriginal Control of Aboriginal Education: Still Waiting" (Canada 1996, n.p.). Resonating clearly with the earlier document, the summary report calls for new education programs that emphasize Indigenous perspectives at all levels from child to elder; teacher education that addresses Indigenous content and attracts prospective teachers from Indigenous communities; and jurisdiction by Indigenous governments. Persistence in the face of disappointing results becomes a recurring theme. In March of 2016, Paul Chartrand, one of the original commissioners for RCAP, was interviewed by CBC regarding his thoughts on the implementation of the recommendations. The title of the article says it all: "20 Years Since Royal Commission on Aboriginal Peoples, Still Waiting for Change" (Troian 2016, n.p.).

The next country-wide initiative on the part of Indigenous peoples and their organizations focused on the lasting impacts of residential schools, a topic raised forcefully in the RCAP reports. Following long struggles on the part of former students to have governments, churches, and the people of Canada recognize the damage the schools had done, on May 8, 2006, the Indian Residential Schools Settlement Agreement was finalized. Arising out of class action litigation, the Agreement provided $125 million for a (five year) Aboriginal Healing Foundation, $60 million for Truth and Reconciliation Funding, and $20 million for Commemoration Funding. To individual former students, $10,000 for the first year of attendance and $3,000 for each additional year was granted, along with "a process" to allow those who suffered sexual, serious physical, or psychologically damaging effects to get additional payments of between $5,000 and $275,000. While some found the settlements a satisfactory recognition, many others commented that money could never make up for what had happened. Still others found themselves once more victimized by unethical lawyers, some of whom have been penalized for their crimes (Marshall 2013, n.p.).

Two years later, in 2008, then Prime Minister Stephen Harper, head of Canada's federal government, reminiscent of US President Grant's words so long ago, apologized for Canada's role in "aggressive assimilation" led by the residential schools. While it was an important gesture, Shauna MacKinnon of the Canadian Centre for Policy Alternatives had this to say four years later:

> The Harper apology did not wipe away the damage done by residential schools and colonization generally.... What is needed is a commitment to a new policy direction.... This must include investment in the long term healing of Aboriginal and non-Aboriginal people through decolonization and cultural reclamation, together with increased and longer term investment in literacy, education and training, housing and job creation. (Mackinnon 2012, n.p.)

THE TRUTH AND RECONCILIATION COMMISSION

The year of the apology, 2008, was also the year that the Truth and Reconciliation Commission of Canada (TRC) was created out of the Residential Schools Settlement Agreement. The three-person commission headed by Honourable Justice Murray Sinclair began the work of finally listening to and actually hearing the stories of those who had attended and worked in the schools and, then, leading Canada and Aboriginal and non-Aboriginal (their words) peoples toward reconciliation. Over the 6 years of its operations, the TRC held 7 national events in large urban centres and 238 days of local hearings in 77 smaller communities across the country. More than 6,750 statements came from the survivors as they were called. There were 96 interviews with former staff and their children. In 2015, its work completed, the commission filed its 535-page final report.

The Truth and Reconciliation Commission is a tremendously significant move in the history of Canada's relationship with the 50 plus nations on which it is overlaid. Much more remains to be done. Although a few school staff came forward, the bulk of the truth telling came from former students. While partial truths may be all that is ever achievable, the silence of those who continue to benefit directly or indirectly from the removal of Indigenous peoples from their Lands is striking. The continuing possession of those Lands by non-Indigenous peoples and organizations highlights the reasons for the numerous active land claims across the country based on both violations of formal treaties and in recognition of the endless hectares of unceded territories. There are still those, primarily non-Aboriginal people, who say that it is time to get over it. But the TRC has now given Canada an indelible testament to the need for redress beyond acknowledgement. And as Wab Kinew writes, "If reconciliation is to be possible, both sides need to move, and Indigenous people have already come a very long way." (2015, 90)

Perhaps moves toward reconciliation might start with looking at the meaning of the word. The Oxford Dictionary indicates that *to reconcile* is to restore friendly relations between, or alternatively, to make someone accept something disagreeable or unwelcome. Apparently drawing on the first definition, the report of the TRC notes, "To some people, reconciliation is the re-establishment of a conciliatory state. However, this is a state that many Aboriginal people assert never has existed between Aboriginal and non-Aboriginal people" (2015, 6). The Commission itself "defines reconciliation as an ongoing process of establishing and maintaining respectful relationships" (2015, 11). Perhaps more significant is the way that Indigenous knowledge keepers consider the word.

> While Elders and Knowledge Keepers across the land have told us that there is no specific word for "reconciliation" in their own languages, there are many words, stories, and songs, as well as sacred objects such as wampum belts, peace pipes, eagle down, cedar boughs, drums, and regalia, that are used to establish relationships, repair conflicts, restore harmony, and make peace. (TRC 2015, 12)

The Truth and Reconciliation Commission and its reports arose from the Indian Residential Schools Settlement, but it has brought Canada face-to-face with something much more significant, with relevance for schools. Glen Coulthard states, in relation to the government's apology, that there must be recognition of the colonial past and the colonial present. There must be action taken to address the much broader system of land dispossession, systematic efforts at "political domination, and cultural genocide of which the residential school formed only a part" (2014, 125). Coulthard goes on to say,

> … Genuine reconciliation is impossible without recognizing Indigenous peoples' right to freedom and self-determination, instituting restoration by *returning enough of our lands* so that we can regain economic self-sufficiency and honouring our treaty relationships. (2014, 127)

In Canada, the survivors of residential schools are with us still and many have told their stories prior to, during, and following the Truth and Reconciliation Commission hearings. The children and grandchildren of those former students have felt the direct effects of efforts at what the TRC has named *cultural genocide*.

Throughout this chapter it has been blatantly clear that Indigenous education within the country now called Canada has been consistently focused on resistance to colonialism; Indigenous refusal of colonizers' efforts to erase cultures, including language, land rights, and responsibilities; and the ceaseless desire for sound education for all. As Eber Hampton (1995) posited in his well-known article "Towards a Redefinition of Indian Education," relentlessness is one of the standards: in this case, the relentless quest of Indigenous people for western (or white man's) education without compromising Indigenous languages, cultures, and communities, accompanied at this moment in time with calls to return to the treaties, return to the teachings (e.g., values, theory), and return to being in good relation with one another. It is no longer possible to ignore the relentless and persistent historical and contemporary strength of Indigenous peoples in their rightful claims to land and their wish to acquire "white man's education" and its benefits without abandoning their own languages, cultures, and teachings. The words of Canada's Truth and Reconciliation Commission on the legacy of residential schools, Indigenous relationships, and the larger implications of their impact bring us full circle:

> …. "reconciliation" is about establishing and maintaining a mutually respectful relationship between Aboriginal and non-Aboriginal peoples in this country. For that to happen, there has to be awareness of the past, acknowledgement of the harm that has been inflicted, atonement for the causes, and action to change behaviour. We are not there yet. (TRC 2015, 6)

Truth-telling, working to reconcile, and a deep understanding of our relationships to one another and to this Land: these are the goals of Indigenous education in Canada. These are admirable and achievable goals for all.

NOTE

1. Much of my understanding of Indian residential schools began in the 1980s with former students who spoke to me in the course of my masters thesis research. This chapter draws on that work (Haig-Brown, 1988).

REFERENCES

Ahenakew, Edward. 1973. *Voices of the Plains Cree*. Edited and introduced by Ruth M. Buck. Toronto: McClelland and Stewart Limited.

Canada. 1996. Royal Commission on Aboriginal Peoples. *People to People, Nation to Nation: Highlights from the Report of the Royal Commission on Aboriginal Peoples*. Accessed May 22, 2017. http://www.aadnc-aandc.gc.ca/eng/1100100014597/1100100014637#chp5.

Coulthard, Glen. 2014. *Red Skin, White Masks: Rejecting the Colonial Politics of Recognition*. Minneapolis: University of Minnesota Press.

Cronin, Kay. 1960. *Cross in the Wilderness*. Vancouver: Mitchell Press.

Davin, Nicholas F. 1879. *Report on Industrial Schools for Indians and Halfbreeds*. Ottawa, March 14. PABC RG 10 Vol. 6001 File 1-1-1, Pt. 1.

Dickason, Olive Patricia. 1992. *Canada's First Nations: A History of the Founding Peoples from Earliest Times*. Toronto: Oxford University Press.

Fisher, Robin. 1977. *Contact and Conflict*. Vancouver: University of British Columbia Press.

Haig-Brown, Celia. 1988. *Resistance and Renewal: Surviving the Indian Residential School*. Vancouver: Tillacum Library.

———. 1995. *Taking Control: Power and Contradiction in First Nations Adult Education*. Vancouver: University of British Columbia Press.

Hampton, Eber. 1995. Towards a Redefinition of Indian Education. In Marie Battiste and Jean

Barman, *First Nations Education in Canada: The Circle Unfolds*, 5–46. Vancouver: UBC Press.

Institute on Governance. 1997. *Summary of the Final Report of the Royal Commission on Aboriginal Peoples*. Ottawa: Institute on Governance. Accessed May 22, 2017. http://iog.ca/wp-content/uploads/2012/12/1997_April_rcapsum.pdf.

Jack, Rita. 1985. "Legacy of the Indian Residential School." *Secwepeme Cultural Arts Magazine* 1(1): 9.

Kamloops Souvenir Edition. 1977. Kamloops Indian Residential School, May 21. Secwepemc Cultural Education Society.

Kinew, Wab. 2015. *The Reason You Walk: A Memoir*. Toronto: Viking Canada.

King, Thomas. 2003. *The Truth About Stories*. Toronto: Anasi Press.

Loomba, Ania. 2005. *Colonialism/Postcolonialism*. 2nd Ed. New York: Routledge.

MacKinnon, Shauna. 2012. *Fast Facts: The Harper 'Apology': Residential Schools and Bill C-10*. Winnipeg: Canadian Centre for Policy Alternatives Manitoba Office. Accessed May 23, 2017. https://www.policyalternatives.ca/publications/commentary/fast-facts-harper-apology-residential-schools-and-bill-c-10.

Manuel, George, and Michael Posluns. 1974. *The Fourth World: An Indian Reality*. Toronto: Collier-MacMillan.

Marshall, Tabitha. 2013. *Indian Residential Schools Settlement Agreement*. Accessed May 23, 2017. http://www.thecanadianencyclopedia.ca/en/article/indian-residential-schools-settlement-agreement/.

Miller, J.R. 1996. *Shingwauk's Vision: A History of Native Residential Schools*. Toronto: University of Toronto Press.

Miller, Kahn-Tineta, and George Lerchs. 1978. *The Historical Development of the Indian Act*. Ottawa(?): Treaties and Historical Research Branch, PRE Group, Indian and Northern Affairs.

National Indian Brotherhood. 1972. *Indian Control of Indian Education*. Ottawa: National Indian Brotherhood,

Pinder, Leslie Hall. 1990. *The Carriers of No: After the Land Claims Trial*. Vancouver: Lazara Press.

Prentice, Alison L., and Susan E. Houston. 1975. *Family, School and Society In Nineteenth-Century Canada*. Toronto: Oxford University Press.

Restoule, Jean-Paul. n.d. A Short History of Indigenous Education in Canada. Pre-contact learning VIDEO 1. Accessed May 17, 2017. https://www.oise.utoronto.ca/abed101/a-short-history-of-indigenous-education-in-canada/.

Schmalz, Peter S. 1991. *The Ojibway of Southern Ontario*. Toronto: University of Toronto Press.

Sioui, Georges E. 1992. *For An Amerindian Autohistory: An Essay on the Foundations of a Social Ethic*. Ottawa: Carleton University Press.

Special Joint Committee of the Senate and the House of Commons Appointed to Examine and Consider the Indian Act. 1947. *Minutes of Proceedings and Evidence No. 1*. Ottawa: King's Printer.

Styres, Sandra. 2017. *Pathways for Remembering and Recognizing Indigenous Thought in Education: Philosophies of Iethi'nihsténha Ohwentsia'kékha (Land)*. Toronto: University of Toronto Press.

Supreme Court Judgements. 1997. *Delgamuukw v. British Columbia*. 3 SCR 1010 Accessed May 22, 2017. https://scc-csc.lexum.com/scc-csc/scc-csc/en/item/1569/index.do.

Teit, James. 1909 [1975]. *The Shuswap*. New York: AMS Press.

———. 1900 [1975]. *The Thompson Indians of British Columbia*. New York: AMS Press.

Tennant, Paul. 1990. *Aboriginal Peoples and Politics: The Indian Land Question in British Columbia, 1849–1989*. Vancouver: University of British Columbia.

Troian, Martha. 2016. "20 Years Since Royal Commission on Aboriginal Peoples, Still Waiting for Change." *CBC News*, March 3. Accessed May 23, 2017. http://www.cbc.ca/news/indigenous/20-year-anniversary-of-rcap-report-1.3469759.

Truth and Reconciliation Commission of Canada. 2015. *Honouring the Truth, Reconciling for the Future: Summary Report of the Final Report of the Truth and Reconciliation Commission of Canada*. Ottawa: Queen's Printer.

United Nations. 1948. No. 1021. *Convention on the Prevention and Punishment of the Crime of Genocide*. Adopted by the General Assembly of the United Nations on 9 December 1948. Accessed May 22, 2017. http://www.ohchr.org/EN/ProfessionalInterest/Pages/CrimeOfGenocide.aspx.

VanKoughnet, L. 1887. *Letter to John A. MacDonald*. Ottawa, August 26. PABC RG 10 Vol. 6001 File 1-1-1, Pt. 1.

Whitehead, Margaret. 1981. *The Cariboo Mission: A History of the Oblates*. Victoria: Sono Nis Press.

Chapter 26

Intersectionality, Critical Race Theory, and the Primacy of Racism: Race, Class, Gender, and Dis/ability in Education

David Gillborn

This chapter explores the utility of intersectionality as an aspect of critical race theory (CRT) in education. Drawing on research with Black middle-class parents in England, the chapter explores the intersecting roles of race, class, and gender in the construction and deployment of dis/ability in education. Gillborn (2015) concludes that intersectionality is a vital aspect of understanding race inequity but that racism retains a primacy for critical race scholars in three ways: empirical primacy (as a central axis of oppression in the everyday reality of schools), personal/autobiographical primacy (as a vital component in how critical race scholars view themselves and their experience of the world), and political primacy (as a point of group coherence and activism).

My title today will displease many people. For some, it will be too provocative; any attempt to place race and racism on the agenda, let alone at the *center* of debate, is deeply unpopular. In the academy we are often told that we are being too crude and simplistic, that things are more complicated than that, that we're being essentialist and missing the *real* problem— of social class (cf. Maisuria, 2012). In politics and the media, race-conscious scholarship is frequently twisted 180 degrees and represented as *racist* in its own right. By focusing on racist inequity, and challenging a colorblind narrative that sees only millions of individuals engaged in meritocratic competition, critical race theory (CRT) is itself accused of racism. This argument was most dramatically played out in the disgusting posthumous attacks on Professor Derrick Bell, in March 2012, when recordings of him and (the then student) Barak

Obama were paraded in the U.S. media in a shallow attempt to smear the President. Initially broadcast by the right-wing web-based "news" site Breitbart.com (Adams, 2012), the story was rapidly relayed by *Fox News* (Martel, 2012) and picked up internationally, for example, by Britain's most influential national newspaper, *The Daily Mail* (Keneally & Gye, 2012). The blogosphere echoed to entries such as "RECORDS SHOW RACIST BIGOT DERRICK BELL TWICE VISITED WHITE HOUSE IN 2010" (http://tundratabloids.com/2012/03/records-show-racist-bigot-derrick-bell-twice-visited-white-house-in-2010), while *Fox News* featured Bill O'Reilly describing Bell as "anti-White" and Sarah Palin calling him a "radical college racist professor."[1] Similar attacks have been rehearsed by academic detractors keen to portray CRT as peddling a view of White people—*all* White people—as universally and irredeemably racist. The following is from a university professor and prominent educational commentator in the United Kingdom:

> For all its supposed academic credentials, critical race theory boils down to one simple claim: "If you are white you are racist!" ... Critical race theorists will dismiss my claim as absurd, but that is because they avoid saying what they really think. The fact that their basic, shared assumption is never stated—that is, if you are white you are racist—allows their views to be promoted ... (Hayes, 2013)

For scholars capable of more nuanced understanding, this article's title may still cause unease; isn't it contradictory to link the idea of "intersectionality" and the "*primacy*" of racism in the same sentence? In the first part of this article, therefore, I address the notion of intersectionality and its relationship to CRT. I then use qualitative research with Black middle-class parents in England as the empirical site to explore the intersection of numerous bases of inequity (including race, class, gender, and dis/ability).[2] Finally, I set out the arguments for understanding the primacy of racism, *not* as a factor that is the only or inevitably the most important aspect of every inequity in education, but in terms of racism's primacy as an empirical, personal, and political aspect of critical race scholarship.

CRT AND INTERSECTIONALITY

There is no single unchanging statement of the core tenets and perspectives that make up CRT but most authoritative commentaries identify a similar set of characteristic assumptions and approaches (cf. Crenshaw, Gotanda, Peller, & Thomas, 1995; Delgado & Stefancic, 2001; Gillborn & Ladson-Billings, 2010; Tate, 1997; Taylor, 2009); key among these perspectives is an understanding that "race" is socially constructed and that "racial difference" is invented, perpetuated, and reinforced by society. In this approach, racism is understood to be complex, subtle, and flexible; it manifests differently in different contexts, and minoritized groups are subject to a range of different (and changing) stereotypes. Critical race theorists argue that the majority of racism remains hidden beneath a veneer of normality and it is only the more crude and obvious forms of racism that are seen as problematic by most people:

Because racism is an ingrained feature of our landscape, it looks ordinary and natural to persons in the culture. Formal equal opportunity—rules and laws that insist on treating blacks and Whites (for example) alike—can thus remedy only the more extreme and shocking forms of injustice, the ones that do stand out. It can do little about the business-as-usual forms of racism that people of color confront every day. (Delgado & Stefancic, 2000, p. xvi)

CRT challenges ahistoricism by stressing the need to understand racism within its social, economic, and historical context (Matsuda, Lawrence, Delgado, & Crenshaw, 1993). Scholars working within CRT place particular emphasis on the experiential knowledge of people of color and challenge common assumptions about "meritocracy" and "neutrality" as camouflage for the interests of dominant groups (Tate, 1997, p. 235). Similarly, CRT adopts a view of "Whiteness" as a socially constructed and malleable identity:

"Whiteness" is a racial discourse, whereas the category "white people" represents a socially constructed identity, usually based on skin colour. (Leonardo, 2009, p. 169)

White-*ness*, in this sense, refers to a set of assumptions, beliefs, and practices that place the interests and perspectives of White people at the center of what is considered normal and everyday. Critical scholarship on Whiteness is not an assault on White people themselves; it is an assault on the socially constructed and constantly reinforced power of White identifications, norms, and interests (Ladson-Billings & Tate, 1995). It is possible for White people to take a genuine, active role in deconstructing Whiteness but such "race traitors" (Ignatiev, 1997) are relatively uncommon. A particularly striking element of CRT (and one seized upon by conservative critics during the Breitbart attacks in 2012) is its understanding of *White supremacy*. In contrast to commonsense understandings of the term (which denote the most extreme and obvious kinds of fascistic race hatred) in CRT White supremacy refers to the operation of much more subtle and extensive forces that saturate the everyday mundane actions and policies that shape the world in the interests of White people (see Ansley, 1997).

For all of its emphasis on the central role of racism in shaping contemporary society, many CRT scholars are keen to explore how raced inequities are shaped by processes that also reflect, and are influenced by, other dimensions of identity and social structure: This is where the notion of intersectionality is crucial.

"Intersectionality" is a widely used (and sometimes misused) concept in contemporary social science. The term addresses the question of how multiple forms of inequality and identity inter-relate in different contexts and over time, for example, the inter-connectedness of race, class, gender, disability, and so on. The term originated in the work of U.S. critical race theorist Kimberlé Crenshaw (1995) but has been deployed widely across the social sciences to the point where it is sometimes viewed as a "buzzword," whose frequent iteration often belies an absence of clarity and specificity (Davis, 2008). In an attempt to bring some clarity back to the discussion of intersectionality, it is instructive to look at how Crenshaw has applied it to real-world problems. In addition to being a professor of law at University of California, Los Angeles (UCLA), Crenshaw is co-founder and executive director of the African American Policy Forum (AAPF; http://aapf.org/) and the AAPF's (n.d.) approach to intersectionality is especially useful:

> Intersectionality is a concept that enables us to recognize the fact that perceived group membership can make people vulnerable to various forms of bias, yet because we are simultaneously members of many groups, our complex identities can shape the specific way we each experience that bias.
>
> For example, men and women can often experience racism differently, just as women of different races can experience sexism differently, and so on.
>
> As a result, an intersectional approach goes beyond conventional analysis in order to focus our attention on injuries that we otherwise might not recognize … to 1) analyze social problems more fully; 2) shape more effective interventions; and 3) promote more inclusive coalitional advocacy. (p. 3)

So, intersectionality—as envisaged by Crenshaw and other critical race activists—has two key elements: First, an *empirical* basis; an intersectional approach is needed to better understand the nature of social inequities and the processes that create and sustain them (i.e., to "analyze social problems more fully"). Second, and this connects to CRT's earliest roots as a movement of engaged legal scholars, intersectionality has a core *activist* component, in that an intersectional approach aims to generate coalitions between different groups with the aim of resisting and changing the status quo.

The AAPF's concise and direct statement on intersectionality is valuable in cutting through the layers of debate and obfuscation that often surround the concept. In particular, the AAPF highlight the importance of intersectionality as a tool (of analysis and resistance) rather than as an academic tactic or fashion. Similarly, Richard Delgado (like Crenshaw, one of the founders of CRT) has highlighted the need to remain clear-sighted about our goals rather than become engaged in never-ending academic games of claim and counter-claim. As Delgado (2011) notes, intersectionality can be taken to such extreme positions that the constant sub-division of experience (into more and more identity categories) can eventually shatter any sense of coherence:

> … intersectionality can easily paralyze progressive work and thought because of the realization that whatever unit you choose to work with, someone may come along and point out that you forgot something. (p. 1264)

As Delgado points out, identity categories are infinitely divisible, and so the uncritical use of intersectionality could lead to the paralysis of critical work amid a mosaic of never-ending difference. In contrast, I want to return to a more critical understanding of intersectionality— as a tool of critical race analysis and intervention. To understand how racism works, we need to appreciate how race intersects with other axes of oppression at different times and in different contexts, but we must try to find a balance between remaining sensitive to intersectional issues without being overwhelmed by them. In an attempt to explore this further, in the following section I draw upon empirical data gathered as part of a 2-year qualitative investigation into the educational strategies of the Black middle classes.[3] The analysis explores the day-to-day life of Black parents and children as they negotiate the social construction of dis/ability within education and, in particular, the processes of labeling in relation to so-called "special educational needs" (SEN).

RESEARCHING EDUCATION AND BLACK MIDDLE CLASSES

The empirical data in this chapter are drawn from a 2-year project funded by the Economic and Social Research Council (ESRC) and conducted with my colleagues Stephen J. Ball, Nicola Rollock, and Carol Vincent.[4] The project began with an explicit focus on how *race* and *class* intersect in the lives of Black middle-class parents. This focus arose from a desire to speak to the silences and assumptions that have frequently shaped education research, policy, and practice in the United Kingdom where middle-class families are generally assumed to be White, and minoritized families—especially those who identify their family heritage in Black Africa and/or the Caribbean—are assumed to be uniformly working class (see Rollock, Gillborn, Vincent, & Ball, 2015). By interviewing Black parents employed in higher professional and managerial roles, we hoped to gain a more nuanced and critical understanding of race-class intersections.[5]

The project sample was limited to parents who identify as being of Black Caribbean ethnic heritage. This group was chosen because the Black Caribbean community is one of the longest established racially minoritized groups in the United Kingdom, with a prominent history of campaigning for social justice, and yet they continue to face marked educational inequalities in terms of achievement and expulsion from school (Gillborn, 2008; John, 2006; Sivanandan, 1990; Warmington, 2014). At the time of the interviews (2009–2010), all the parents had children between the ages of 8 and 18; a range that spans key decision-making points in the English education system. As is common in research with parents, most interviewees were mothers but the project team also wanted to redress common deficit assumptions about Black men (McKenley, 2005; Reynolds, 2010) and so we ensured that a fifth of the sample were fathers. All the parents are in professional/managerial jobs within the top two categories of the National Statistics Socio-Economic Classification (NS-SEC) and most live in Greater London (although we also included parents from elsewhere across England). Parents volunteered to take part, responding to adverts that we placed in professional publications and on the web. Once our initial round of 62 interviews had been completed, utilizing a technique that has proven successful in the past, we then re-interviewed 15 parents chosen to facilitate greater exploration of the key emerging themes and questions. In total, therefore, 77 interviews provide the original data for the project.

Our interviews explored parents' experiences of the education system (including their memories of their own childhood and their current encounters as parents), their aspirations for their children and how their experiences are shaped by race/racism and social class. The project team comprised three White researchers and one Black researcher; respondents were asked to indicate in advance whether they preferred a Black interviewer, a White interviewer, or had no preference, and those preferences were met accordingly. Following the interviews, around half (55%) felt that interviewer ethnicity had made a difference and almost all of these felt that rapport with a Black researcher had been an advantage. The team is split evenly between men and women, and two of us have a declared dis/ability.

"SPECIAL EDUCATION" AND THE INTERSECTION OF RACE, CLASS, GENDER, AND DISABILITY

The terms "race" and "disability" have a lot in common: Both are usually assumed to be relatively obvious and fixed, but are actually socially constructed categories that are constantly contested and redefined. Historically both have operated to define, segregate, and oppress. Received wisdom views both "race" and "disability" as individual matters, relating to identity and a person's sense of self, but a critical perspective views them as socially constructed categories that actively re/make oppression and inequality (Annamma, Connor, & Ferri, 2013; Beratan, 2008; Leonardo & Broderick, 2011). In the United States, for example, Christine Sleeter (1987) has argued that the category "learning disabilities" emerged as a strategic move to protect the children of White middle-class families from possible downward mobility through low school achievement. Whereas *some* labels might be advantageous, for example by securing additional dedicated resources, it is clear that certain other dis/ability labels are far from positive. In both the United States and the United Kingdom, there is a long history of Black youth being over-represented in segregated low-status educational provision, usually disguised beneath blanket terms like "special" or "assisted" education (Tomlinson, 2014). Some of the earliest critical research on race inequities in the English educational system focused on the intersection of race and dis/ability (Coard, 1971; Tomlinson, 1981) and, despite the decades that have passed since those pioneering studies, the issue emerged as a key element in the interviews with contemporary Black middle-class parents: 15 of our interviewees (around a quarter) mentioned dis/ability or related issues during their interviews and some important and disturbing patterns became clear. In the following sections, I review our key findings in relation to three simple questions: First, what processes lead to a "special needs" assessment being made? Second, what happens after the assessment? Finally, whose interests are being served by the schools' reactions to, and treatment of, Black middle-class parents and children in relation to the question of dis/ability? My concern, therefore, is to understand the experiences of Black middle-class parents and their children as they encounter labels being used against them or alternatively how they attempt to use labels to access additional resources; I am interested in how racism intersects with other aspects of oppression (especially class and gender) in the processes that *make, assert,* and *contest* the meaning of dis/ability in schools.[6]

Assessing "Special" Needs

The British government's advice for parents of children with disabilities (Department for Children, Schools and Families [DCSF], 2009) describes a series of stages that should lead to a child's needs being assessed and met:

- The parents and/or school identify that the child is having problems.
- An assessment is arranged through the school or the local authority.
- The nature of the child's needs is identified and adjustments are recommended.
- The school then acts on these recommendations and the student is better able to fulfill their potential.

In our data, there is only a single case that comes close to this model, where the school expressed concern to the parent, and they worked together harmoniously throughout the process. In every other case, it was the parent—not the school—who identified a problem and sought an assessment. This involves parents drawing on both their *economic* capital (to finance expensive specialist assessments) and their *cultural* and *social* capital (often using friendship and professional networks to help negotiate the system). In each of these cases, the school seemed content to assume that the students' poor performance was all that could be expected. Here, Rachel[7] describes how her son was criticized for not paying attention:

> I took [my son] to get him educationally assessed and they said that he had dyslexia … I took him up to Great Ormond Street [Hospital] to get his hearing tested and they said he can't hear half of what's going on. So when the teachers are always saying "he's distracted and not paying attention," he can't hear … they were just very happily saying [he] doesn't pay attention, [he] doesn't do this, [he] doesn't do that, but, you know, *he can't hear* … (Rachel, Senior Solicitor, Private Sector)

According to official guidance where there is a sharp discrepancy between a student's performance on different sorts of task, this can be seen as indicating a possible learning difficulty (Developmental Adult Neuro-Diversity Association [DANDA], 2011). In our research, where Black children's performance was at stake, schools seemed happy to assume that the lowest level of performance was the "true" indicator of their potential.

> A discrepancy was emerging, in that she would get a B for a piece of work that she had spent time doing [at home] and then she would get a D or an E even [for timed work in class]. So I then contacted the school and said, "Look there's a problem here." And they just said, "Well, she needs to work harder." So they were actually not at all helpful and I ended up having a row with the Head of Sixth Form because she accused me of being *"a fussy parent."* And what she said was that my daughter was working to her level, which was the timed essay level, she was working to a D. (Paulette, Psychologist)

Following an independent assessment (that revealed dyslexia) and a move to a private institution (that made the recommended adjustments) Paulette saw a dramatic improvement in her daughter's attainment. In her A (Advanced) level examinations at age 18, Paulette's daughter went from gaining two passes at Grade E and one ungraded (fail) result, to three passes, all at Grade B.

In our interviews, there were two cases where the school made the first move to initiate a formal assessment for special educational needs in a way that shocked and angered the students' parents. In both cases, the school's action served to divert attention from racism in the school and refocus attention on a supposed individual deficit in the Black child. For example, when Felicia told her son's school about him being racially bullied the reaction was initially encouraging:

> the Head of Year was quite shocked and quite encouraging in terms of our conversation; calling and saying, you know, "Really sorry. We've let you down; we've let [your son] down; we didn't know this was happening" ... But nothing happened ... My son's class teacher had said to my son that I'm asking *too much* but not to tell me ... I got this telephone call out of the blue one Sunday afternoon, from his class teacher, suggesting that he have some *test*—I can't remember exactly how this conversation went because it was such a shock; it was five o'clock on Sunday afternoon—that there might be some reason for his under-performing: not the racism at the school that I told them about, but there might be some reason, that he might have some *learning difficulties*. (Felicia, Senior Solicitor)

Similarly, Simon described how his son was expelled for reacting violently to racist harassment. In a situation that directly echoes previous research on the over-representation of Black students in expulsions (Blair, 2001; Communities Empowerment Network, 2005; Wright, Weekes, & McGlaughlin, 2000), the school refused to take account of the provocation and violence that the young man had experienced at the hands of racist peers and, instead, chose to view his actions in isolation and Simon's son was labeled as having "behavior and anger management" problems:

> ... someone called him a "black monkey" and he responded by beating him up ... I just don't think the school really understood the impact, or how isolated pupils can feel when they stand out physically, and that's just something that I don't think they get. (Simon, Teacher)

On two occasions in our data, therefore, Black middle-class parents complained that schools had wrongly taken the initiative in seeking a SEN assessment as a means of shifting the focus away from racism in their institution and onto a supposed individual deficit within the Black child. In both instances, the child was male. In contrast, schools proved reluctant to support an assessment in every case where Black middle-class parents themselves felt that their child might have an unrecognized learning difficulty.

Schools' Reactions to SEN Assessments

Having used their class capitals to access formal SEN assessments, despite the inaction of their children's schools, Black middle-class parents in our research then faced the task of making the schools aware of the assessments and seeking their cooperation in making any reasonable adjustments that had been suggested. In a minority of cases the school simply refused to act on the assessment but in most cases the school made encouraging noises but their actions were at best patchy, at worst non-existent. For example, when Nigel's son was diagnosed with autism, the recommended adjustments included the use of a laptop in class. Nigel was prepared to buy the machine himself but the school refused to allow its use: "We had a long conversation with the head [principal], who we were very friendly with, and they said that it would set a precedent" (Nigel, Human Resources Manager). Although disappointing, the school's reaction to Nigel's request was at least clear; Linda's experiences were more typical. She found that, although adjustments were agreed with a senior teacher (the "Year Head" in charge of the relevant age cohort) and the specialist SEN coordinator, not all teachers knew about them or accepted them. In several cases, the school's lack of action started to look like deliberate obstruction (despite their kind words). Similarly, Lorraine feels that she lost 2 years of education struggling to get her daughter's school to deliver on their promises:

> I have a daughter who now has been diagnosed with autism, I actually do want to get much more involved in the school and how they deal with her. But I think for the school it's easier if they don't get involved with me. So, for instance, going in and having meetings; her Head of Year says, "Oh, you know, I understand now, we'll do this, we'll do that" and then that just doesn't happen ... there were *constant* visits to try to get them to take some kind of action to help ... You know, at first I thought it was me not being forceful enough, but as I said, I was accompanied by a clinical psychologist who tried to get them to help as well and they failed. (Lorraine, Researcher, Voluntary Sector)

Our data suggest, therefore, that Black parents—even *middle-class* ones who are able to mobilize considerable class capitals (both social and economic)—have an incredibly difficult time getting their children's needs recognized and acted upon. In contrast, schools appear much more ready to act on more negative dis/ability labels. As Beth Harry and Janette Klingner (2006) note, in relation to the United States, Black (African American) students face much higher levels of labeling (what they term "*risk rates*") in SEN categories "that depend on clinical judgment rather than on verifiable biological data" (p. 2). These patterns have a long history and they continue today: The most recent comprehensive study of SEN demographics in the United Kingdom (Lindsay, Pather, & Strand, 2006) revealed that rates of Black over-representation are especially pronounced in the category defined as "Behavioral, Emotional, & Social Difficulties," where Black students are more than twice as likely to be labeled as their White peers.[8] This category of student are often removed from mainstream provision and placed in segregated units. One of our interviewee parents visits such units as part of her work. She reported her distress at witnessing what she described as the "brutalization" of Black boys in segregated provision within a state-funded secondary (high school). Here, we can see the intersection of gender (the all-male grouping) alongside race, class, and dis/ability:

> I don't know for what reason [but] they were in a kind of different [part of the school] …
> they weren't in the main school building … The class was predominantly Black, not many
> students but they were really unruly, and I was really shocked at how unruly they were …
> the SenCo [special needs coordinator] said to me, she said, "Well, that's what you get."
> (Paulette, Psychologist)

In a direct parallel to the racialized impact of tracking in the United States (Oakes, 1990; Oakes, Joseph, & Muir, 2004; Watamabe, 2012), in the United Kingdom as students move through high school, they are increasingly likely to be taught in hierarchically grouped classes (known as "sets") which are known to place disproportionate numbers of Black students in the lowest ranked groups (Araujo, 2007; Ball, 1981; Commission for Racial Equality [CRE], 1992; Gillborn, 2008; Gillies & Robinson, 2012; Hallam, 2002; Hallam & Toutounji, 1996; Tikly, Haynes, Caballero, Hill, & Gillborn, 2006). Paulette was in no doubt that the cumulative impact of these processes had a dramatically negative impact on the Black boys she observed:

> … the boys are in sets from the time they come in and those boys are in the bottom sets.
> And the bottom set has been written off as boys who are just not going to get anywhere.
> And literally they kind of turn into animals, they really had, because of the way that they
> had been treated and because of the expectations … And I just felt that there was something
> that that school—you know it sounds crazy—but something that that school did, actually
> *did*, to particular Black boys … And I just think, I just thought that what it is, is that maybe
> the school just brutalizes those children, *unintentionally*. Am I making sense? (Paulette,
> Psychologist)

Paulette went on to describe the fate of a Black student whom she had known for some time. Despite prior attainment in primary school that was "good" to "average," the high school interpreted the SEN label as automatically signaling a generic and untreatable deficit:

> because he had dyslexia they had put him in bottom sets for everything, even though he was
> an able student. So from year seven [aged 11], what do you do? He just became completely
> de-motivated, completely disaffected. He had completely given up. And that was such a
> shock to me, it was such a shock. (Paulette, Psychologist)

This boy's fate is particularly significant. Many young people achieve highly despite dyslexia; indeed, it is exactly the kind of learning disability that—as I noted earlier—Sleeter (1987) views as an explicit part of attempts to protect the educational privilege of *White* middle-class America. Under the right circumstances (with sensible adjustments to pedagogy and through the use of simple assistive technologies), the student might have had a very different experience. But in this school, the combination of SEN and race seemed to automatically condemn the student to the very lowest teaching groups where his confidence and performance collapsed.

The Intersections of Race, Class, Gender, and Dis/ability: Whose Interests Are Being Met?

All children with special educational needs should have their needs met. (DCSF, 2009, p. 5)

The British Education Department's official guide for parents is unequivocal about whose interests should be at the heart of the system, but this is *not* happening and *racism* is deeply implicated. Drawing on data gathered as part of the largest-ever qualitative study of the experiences and perspectives of Black middle-class parents in England (Rollock et al., 2015), I have shown that when it comes to understanding *when* and *how* certain dis/ability categories are mobilized, in the case of Black British students from middle-class homes, it is not the needs of the Black child that are being served but the interests of an institutionally racist education system. Let me recap on the evidence to this point. On the matter of assessment, Black middle-class parents generally had to make their own arrangements for formal assessment in the face of school indifference or opposition. The most striking exceptions to this pattern were two cases where, following racist incidents of aggression against Black boys, the schools suggested an assessment and shifted the focus onto the individual student who suffered the abuse and away from institutional failings.

Numerous qualitative studies have revealed chronically low teacher expectations for Black students to be the norm in many British schools (cf. Gillborn & Mirza, 2000; Gillborn, Rollock, Vincent, & Ball, 2012); consequently, when faced with a sharp discrepancy in performance on different tasks, rather than view this as a potential indicator of a learning dis/ability, our interviewees reported that teachers were generally content simply to accept the lower level of attainment as indicative of the student's "true" potential. When Black parents attempted to rebuff these assumptions by producing privately financed assessments, the school's most common reaction was to sound welcoming and interested, but to behave in ways that are at best patchy and, at worst, obstructive and insulting. Unfortunately, this obstructive attitude does not reflect a *general* reluctance to mobilize dis/ability labels, rather it seems to apply to particular labels (specific or moderate "learning difficulties") that might positively benefit the Black child by seeing them access additional resources. In contrast, labels that apply "behavioral" judgments within a SEN framework continue to be applied with disproportionate frequency against Black students and this was reflected in the interview data, often leading to segregation from the social and academic mainstream, and ultimately decimating the students' academic performance.

Despite the reassuring and inclusive tone of government rhetoric, and in contrast to the often encouraging initial verbal response from schools, in reality the Black middle-class parents' experiences suggest that the needs of the Black child go largely unmet within a system that uses dis/ability labels as a further field of activity where racist inequities are created, sustained, and legitimized. The field of "special" education has long been recognized as a complex and fraught area where race and class influences can significantly shape students' experiences (cf. Artiles & Trent, 1994; Artiles, Trent, & Palmer, 2004; Oliver, 1996; Tomlinson, 2014). The data reported here suggest that *class advantage fails to protect in the face of entrenched racism*. Despite their considerably enhanced social and economic capitals, for Black middle-class parents, the field of dis/ability and SEN appears to be a context where they are excluded from the potential benefits (of legitimate adjustments and dedicated resources) but remain subject to the disadvantages of low expectations, segregation, and exclusion.

Gender has not featured in this article to the same extent as the other principal axes of differentiation (race, class, and dis/ability), but it has been a constant presence in the background. In particular, Black middle-class parents expressed particular concern for male children who could fall foul of heightened surveillance in schools and the attentions of police and gang members on the street (cf. Gillborn et al., 2012). In the present account, gender is also an important part of the context whereby it was male students who made up the segregated and "brutalized" bottom set in isolated provision away from the mainstream school building (reported by Paulette) and it was boys who were referred for assessment following their racist victimization by White peers.

CONCLUSION: THE PRIMACY OF RACISM

> The challenge underpinning any serious analysis of *race as a social relationship* is how to understand its false dimensions while refusing to relegate race and racialisation to the epiphenomenal dog-kennel. For critical race theorists, race is not reducible to false consciousness; nor is it mere "product" or "effect." (Warmington, 2011, p. 263, emphasis in original)

Dis/ability (like race and gender) masquerades as natural, fixed, and obvious: I recall teaching a masters' class, where most students were schoolteachers, when someone argued that although certain forms of identity and inequity can be complex, "disability is *obvious*." I was tempted to challenge this assertion by asking whether the student realized that I was dis/abled? He would probably have been shocked to learn that, having spent more than four decades of my life hiding the painfully slow rate at which I can read and process written information, I had recently been formally assessed as having a "specific learning disability." Despite the assumptions that are schooled into us, social identities and inequities are socially constructed and enforced. As the "social model" of disability has made clear, even the most pronounced so-called "impairments" only become disabling when confronted by socially constructed problems and assumptions, for example, "not being able to walk or hear being made problematic by socially created factors such as the built environment … and the use of spoken language rather than sign language" (Beratan, 2012, p. 45). Consequently, critical social researchers, whatever dimension(s) of identity and inequity they wish to grapple with, are faced with making sense of the constant mutability and complexity of our social worlds. As I hope I have made clear to this point, an *intersectional* understanding of the social can be a distinct advantage when trying to understand how particular inequities are re/made in places like schools. Drawing on a study of the educational strategies of Black middle-class parents in England, I have argued that even a brief exploration of their experiences of dis/ability requires some appreciation of the intersecting dimensions of race, class, and gender. This is not the same as the kind of intersectional trap that Richard Delgado (2011) warns can ultimately paralyze activist work. It is in relation to that danger that I wish to conclude by addressing the primacy of racism for critical race scholars.

From the very beginning of CRT as a recognizable movement, and through to the present day, detractors have sought to misrepresent the approach (Crenshaw, 2002; Delgado, 1993; Gillborn, 2010; Warmington, 2011). To try to avoid any further misunderstanding, therefore, before explaining what I mean by the "primacy of racism," it may be useful if I begin by explicitly stating what I do *not* mean. I do not assume that racism is the *only* issue that matters (this should be obvious from my statements about intersectionality and the experiences of the Black middle-class above), neither do I believe that racism is *always* the most important issue in understanding every instance of social exclusion and oppression that touches the lives of minoritized people. Similarly, I am not suggesting that there is some kind of hierarchy of oppression, whereby members of any single group (however defined) are assumed to always be the most excluded or to always have a perfect understanding of the processes at work.

So, what *do* I mean by the primacy of racism? My argument is that there are at least three ways in which racism unapologetically remains a primary concern for critical race theorists.[9] First, there is *the empirical primacy of racism*; that is, when we study how racist inequity is created and sustained, racist assumptions and practices are often *the* crucial issue when making sense of how oppression operates. Racist inequity is influenced by numerous factors (including gender, class, dis/ability), but we must not shy away from naming the central role that racism continues to play. The case of SEN and race in England is instructive; here the most personal and supposedly individual issues (dis/ability and impairment) are revealed as not merely *socially* constructed, but as *racially* patterned and oppressive.

Second, there is the issue of the *personal or autobiographical primacy of race*, that is, the dimension of the social world, of our lived reality, that we as scholars foreground in making sense of our experiences and shaping our interventions and agency. Many scholars who view themselves as working from a critical and/or activist perspective can identify an issue that touches them most deeply, often viscerally (see Allan & Slee, 2008; Orelus, 2011). Some begin with social class inequity, others with gender, sexuality, or dis/ability: Critical race theorists tend to start with race/racism. This does not blind us to other forms of exclusion and we surely have as much right as any other critic to begin with the issue that—for us—touches us most deeply and which generates our most important experiences and ambitions for change. In the words of Zeus Leonardo (2005), critical race scholars "privilege the concept of race as the point of departure for critique, not the end of it" (p. xi). This may sound unremarkable but, as John Preston and Kalwant Bhopal (2012) have noted, race-conscious scholarship is frequently challenged to defend itself in ways that other radical perspectives are not:

> When speaking about "race" in education, many of us have been faced with the question "What about class/gender/sexuality/disability/faith?" whereas rarely are speakers on these topics ever asked, "What about 'race?'" A focus on "race" in analysis is indicative, for some academics, as a sign of pathology or suspicion. (p. 214)

A third way in which racism remains a prime concern for critical race scholars relates to the activist component so central to the founding of the movement, that is, the *political primacy of racism*. As Kimberlé Crenshaw et al. (1995) argued in one of the foundational CRT texts, for many critical race scholars, *resisting* racial oppression is a defining characteristic of the approach:

> Although Critical Race scholarship differs in object, argument, accent, and emphasis, it is nevertheless unified by two common interests. The first is to understand how a regime of white supremacy and its subordination of people of color have been created and maintained … The second is a desire not merely to understand the vexed bond between law and racial power but to change it. (p. xiii)

If we are to change the racial (and racist) status quo, we must refuse the growing main-stream assertion that racism is irrelevant or even non-existent. A shared analysis of the racism that patterns everyday life can provide a powerful point of coherence for activism and political strategy. We live at a time when racist inequities continue to scar the economy, education, health, and criminal justice systems (Equality & Human Rights Commission [EHRC], 2010) but when merely *naming* racism as an issue is sufficient to generate accusations of "playing the race card"—the supposed "special pleading" that Derrick Bell's "rules of racial standing" analyze so brilliantly (Bell, 1992, p. 111)—or, worse still, we are judged to be acting in ways that are racist against White people. At this time, it is more important than ever that we take our cue from Derrick Bell and have the courage to say the unsay-able and follow through in our actions. We can *use* intersectionality, but we must not be silenced by it. Bell's legacy demands nothing less.

AUTHOR'S NOTE

This article is based on my opening keynote address to the conference "Race, Citizenship, Activism, and the Meaning of Social Justice for the 21st Century: The Legacy of Professor Derrick Bell," the 6th annual conference of the Critical Race Studies in Education Association (CRSEA), held at Teacher's College, Columbia University, New York City, New York, June 2012. The analysis draws on and extends ideas that also appear in Rollock, Gillborn, Vincent, and Ball (2015). The interview project (ESRC RES-062-23-1880) was conceived, executed, and analyzed by Stephen J. Ball, Nicola Rollock, Carol Vincent, and myself.

DECLARATION OF CONFLICTING INTERESTS

The author(s) declared no potential conflicts of interest with respect to the research, authorship, and/or publication of this article.

FUNDING

The research reported in this paper was funded by the Economic & Social Research Council (grant # ESRC RES-062-23-1880)

NOTES

1. These are verbatim transcripts from excerpts included in a feature where Professor Bell's widow answers the claims. Video available at http://talkingpointsmemo.com/muckraker/derrick-bell-s-widow-speaks-about-outrage-against-her-late-husband.

2. I follow Annamma, Connor, and Ferri (2013) in using "dis/ability" to highlight the way in which the traditional form (disability) "overwhelmingly signals a specific inability to perform culturally defined expected tasks (such as learning or walking) that come to define the individual as primarily and generally 'unable' to navigate society. We believe the '/' in disability disrupts misleading understandings of disability, as it simultaneously conveys the mixture of ability and disability" (p. 24).

3. School students categorized as "Black" (including those officially listed as "Black Caribbean," "Black African," and "Black Other" but excluding those of dual ethnic heritage) account for 4.4% of those in the final stage of compulsory schooling in state-maintained schools in England as a whole but for 32.3% of children in inner London, 21.3% of London as a whole, and 11.3% of Birmingham, England's "second city" (Department for Education [DfE], 2012, Table 3).

4. "The Educational Strategies of the Black Middle Classes" was funded by the Economic and Social Research Council (ESRC RES-062-23-1880): Professor Carol Vincent was the principal investigator.

5. We restricted our sample to people whose occupations place them in the top two categories of the eight which make up the National Statistics Socio-Economic Classification (NS-SEC); an occupationally based classification that has been used for all official statistics and surveys in the United Kingdom since 2001 (Office for National Statistics, 2010).

6. I am *not* asking questions of over- and under-representation, as if there were some objective *real* notion of dis/ability into which Black middle-class students should gain rightful admittance or avoid wrongful categorization (see Annamma et al., 2013).

7. All interviewee names are pseudonyms.

8. The most recent major study of these issues found that, relative to White British students, Black Caribbean students are 2.28 times more likely, and "Mixed White & Caribbean" 2.03 times more likely to be categorized as "Behavioral, Emotional, & Social Difficulties" (BESD; Lindsay, Pather, & Strand, 2006, Table 5a).

9. I do not presume to speak for all critical race scholars nor do I seek to mandate a single "CRT" (critical race theory) position: My purpose here is help arrest the slide into endless meaningless subdivisions of intersectionality and diversity ad infinitum and restate the courageous and bold determination that characterized the beginnings of the movement.

REFERENCES

Adams, J.C. (2012). *Obama's beloved law professor: Derrick Bell*. Retrieved from http://www.breitbart.com/Big-Government/2012/03/08/obamas-beloved-law-professor-derrick-bell

African American Policy Forum. (n.d.). *A primer on intersectionality*. New York, NY: Columbia Law School.

Allan, J., & Slee, R. (Eds.). (2008). *Doing inclusive educational research*. Rotterdam, The Netherlands: Sense Publishers.

Annamma, S.A., Connor, D., & Ferri, B. (2013). Dis/ability critical race studies (DisCrit): Theorizing at the intersections of race and dis/ability. *Race Ethnicity and Education*, *16*, 1–31.

Ansley, F.L. (1997). White supremacy (and what we should do about it). In R. Delgado & J. Stefancic (Eds.), *Critical white studies: Looking behind the mirror* (pp. 592–595). Philadelphia, PA: Temple University Press.

Araujo, M. (2007). "Modernising the comprehensive principle": Selection, setting and the institutionalisation of educational failure. *British Journal of Sociology of Education*, *28*, 241–257.

Artiles, A., & Trent, S.C. (1994). Overrepresentation of minority students in special education: A continuing debate. *Journal of Special Education*, *27*, 410–437.

Artiles, A., Trent, S.C., & Palmer, J.D. (2004). Culturally diverse students in special education: Legacies and prospects. In J.A. Banks & C.A. McGee Banks (Eds.), *Handbook of research on multicultural education* (pp. 716–735). San Francisco, CA: Jossey-Bass.

Ball, S.J. (1981). *Beachside comprehensive: A case-study of secondary schooling*. Cambridge, UK: Cambridge University Press.

Bell, D. (1992). *Faces at the bottom of the well: The permanence of racism*. New York, NY: Basic Books.

Beratan, G.D. (2008). The song remains the same: Transposition and the disproportionate representation of minority students in special education. *Race Ethnicity and Education*, *11*, 337–354.

Beratan, G.D. (2012). *Institutional ableism & the politics of inclusive education: An ethnographic study of an inclusive high school* (Unpublished doctoral thesis). Institute of Education, University of London, England.

Blair, M. (2001). *Why pick on me? School exclusions and black youth*. Stoke-on-Trent, UK: Trentham.

Coard, B. (1971). *How the West Indian child is made educationally subnormal in the British School System*. London, UK: New Beacon Books. (Reprinted in *Tell it like it is: How our schools fail Black children*, pp. 27–59, by B. Richardson, Ed., 2005, London, UK: Bookmarks.)

Commission for Racial Equality. (1992). *Set to fail? Setting and banding in secondary schools*. London, England: Author.

Communities Empowerment Network. (2005). Zero tolerance and school exclusions [Special issue]. *CEN Newsletter, 5*(6), 1–4.

Crenshaw, K.W. (1995). Mapping the margins: Intersectionality, identity politics, and violence against women of color. In K. Crenshaw, N. Gotanda, G. Peller, & K. Thomas (Eds.), *Critical race theory: The key writings that formed the movement* (pp. 357–383). New York, NY: New Press.

Crenshaw, K.W. (2002). The first decade: Critical reflections, or "a foot in the closing door." *UCLA Law Review, 49*, 1343–1372.

Crenshaw, K.W., Gotanda, N., Peller, G., & Thomas, K. (1995). Introduction. In K. Crenshaw, N. Gotanda, G. Peller, & K. Thomas (Eds.), *Critical race theory: The key writings that formed the movement* (pp. xiii–xxxii). New York, NY: New Press.

Davis, K. (2008). Intersectionality as buzzword: A sociology of science perspective on what makes a feminist theory successful. *Feminist Theory, 9*, 67–85.

Delgado, R. (1993). On telling stories in school: A reply to Faber and Sherry. (Reprinted in *Foundations of critical race theory in education*, pp. 340–348, by E. Taylor, D. Gillborn, & G. Ladson-Billings, Eds., 2009, New York, NY: Routledge)

Delgado, R. (2011). Rodrigo's reconsideration: Intersectionality and the future of critical race theory. *Iowa Law Review, 96*, 1247–1288.

Delgado, R., & Stefancic, J. (2000). Introduction. In R. Delgado & J. Stafancic (Eds.), *Critical race Theory: The cutting edge* (2nd ed., pp. 1–14). Philadelphia, PA: Temple University Press.

Delgado, R., & Stefancic, J. (2001). *Critical race theory: An introduction*. New York: New York University Press.

Department for Children, Schools and Families. (2009). *Special educational needs (SEN)—A guide for parents and carers*. Nottingham, UK: Author.

Department for Education. (2012). *GCSE and equivalent attainment by pupil characteristics in England, 2010/11, statistical first release SFR 03/2012*. London, UK: Author.

Developmental Adult Neuro-Diversity Association. (2011). *What is neuro-diversity?* Retrieved from http://www.danda.org.uk/ pages/neuro-diversity.php

Equality & Human Rights Commission. (2010). *How fair is Britain? Equality, human rights and good relations in 2010. The first triennial review*. London, UK: Author.

Gillborn, D. (2008). *Racism and education: Coincidence or conspiracy?* New York, NY: Routledge.

Gillborn, D. (2010). Full of sound and fury, signifying nothing? A reply to Dave Hill's "Race and class and in Britain: A critique of the statistical basis for critical race theory in Britain." *Journal for Critical Education Policy Studies, 8*, 78–107. Retrieved from http://www.jceps. com/?pageID=article&articleID=177

Gillborn, D., & Ladson-Billings, G. (2010). Critical race theory. In P. Peterson, E. Baker, & B. McGaw (Eds.), *International encyclopedia of education* (Vol. 6, pp. 341–347). Oxford, UK: Elsevier.

Gillborn, D., & Mirza, H.S. (2000). *Educational inequality: Mapping race, class and gender—A synthesis of research evidence* (Report #HMI 232). London, UK: Office for Standards in Education.

Gillborn, D., Rollock, N., Vincent, C., & Ball, S.J. (2012). "You got a pass, so what more do you want?": Race, class and gender intersections in the educational experiences of the Black middle class. *Race Ethnicity and Education, 15,* 121–139.

Gillies, V., & Robinson, Y. (2012). "Including" while excluding: Race, class and behaviour support units. *Race Ethnicity & Education, 15,* 157–174.

Hallam, S. (2002). *Ability grouping in schools: A literature review.* London, UK: Institute of Education University of London.

Hallam, S., & Toutounji, I. (1996). *What do we know about the grouping of pupils by ability? A research review.* London, UK: Institute of Education University of London.

Harry, B., & Klingner, J.K. (2006). *Why are so many minority students in Special Education? Understanding race and disability in schools.* New York, NY: Teachers College Press.

Hayes, D. (2013). *Teaching students to think racially.* Retrieved from http://www.spiked-online.com/site/article/13459/

Ignatiev, N. (1997). How to be a race traitor: Six ways to fight being white. In R. Delgado & J. Stefancic (Eds.), *Critical white studies: Looking behind the mirror* (p. 613). Philadelphia, PA: Temple University Press.

John, G. (2006). *Taking a stand: Gus John speaks on education, race, social action & civil unrest 1980–2005.* Manchester, UK: The Gus John Partnership.

Keneally, M., & Gye, H. (2012). "We hid this during the election": Obama ally confesses he covered up "race" video Andrew Breitbart threatened to release before his death. *Mail Online.* Retrieved from http://www.dailymail.co.uk/news/article-2111679/Andrew-Breitbart-Obama-race-video-Charles-Ogletree-hid-Derrick-Bell-support-speech-2008-election.html

Ladson-Billings, G., & Tate, W.F. (1995). Toward a critical race theory of education. *Teachers College Record, 97,* 47–68.

Leonardo, Z. (2005). Foreword. In Z. Leonardo (Ed.), *Critical pedagogy and race* (pp. xi–xv). Oxford, UK: Blackwell.

Leonardo, Z. (2009). *Race, whiteness, and education.* New York, NY: Routledge.

Leonardo, Z., & Broderick, A. (2011). Smartness as property: A critical exploration of intersections between whiteness and disability studies. *Teachers College Record, 113,* 2206–2232.

Lindsay, G., Pather, S., & Strand, S. (2006). *Special educational needs and ethnicity: Issues of over- and under-representation* (Research Report RR757). London, UK: Department for Education and Skills.

Maisuria, A. (2012). A critical appraisal of critical race theory (CRT): Limitations and opportunities. In K. Bhopal & J. Preston (Eds.), *Intersectionality and "race" in education* (pp. 76–96). London, UK: Routledge.

Martel, F. (2012). *Hannity debuts Breitbart Obama college video reveals "controversial" hug with embattled professor.* Retrieved from http://www.mediaite.com/tv/hannity-debuts-breitbart-obama-college-video-media-hid-video-of-obama-hugging-professor/

Matsuda, M.J., Lawrence, C.R., Delgado, R., & Crenshaw, K.W. (Eds.). (1993). *Words that wound: Critical race theory, assaultive speech, and the first amendment.* Boulder, CO: Westview Press.

McKenley, J. (2005). *Seven black men: An ecological study of education and parenting*. Bristol, UK: Aduma Books.

Oakes, J. (1990). *Multiplying inequalities: The effects of race, social class, and tracking on students' opportunities to learn mathematics and science*. Santa Monica, CA: RAND.

Oakes, J., Joseph, R., & Muir, K. (2004). Access and achievement in mathematics and science: Inequalities that endure and change. In J.A. Banks & C.A.M. Banks (Eds.), *Handbook of research on multicultural education* (2nd ed., pp. 69–90). San Francisco, CA: Jossey-Bass.

Office for National Statistics. (2010). *Standard occupational classification 2010* (Vol. 3, The National Statistics Socio-Economic Classification: [Rebased On SOC2010] user manual). Retrieved from http://www.ons.gov.uk/ons/guide-method/classifications/current-standard-classifications/soc2010/soc2010-volume-3-ns-sec–rebased-on-soc2010–user-manual/index.html

Oliver, M. (1996). *Understanding disability: From theory to practice*. London, UK: Macmillan.

Orelus, P. W. (Ed.). (2011). *Rethinking race, class, language, and gender: A dialogue with Noam Chomsky and other leading scholars*. Boulder, CO: Rowman & Littlefield.

Preston, J., & Bhopal, K. (2012). Conclusion: Intersectional theories and "race": From toolkit to "mash-up." In K. Bhopal & J. Preston (Eds.), *Intersectionality and "race" in education* (pp. 213–220). London, UK: Routledge.

Reynolds, T. (2010). Lone mothers not to blame. *Runnymede Bulletin*, Issue 361, p. 11.

Rollock, N., Gillborn, D., Vincent, C., & Ball, S.J. (2015). *The colour of class: The educational strategies of the Black middle classes*. London, UK: Routledge.

Sivanandan, A. (1990). *Communities of resistance: Writings on black struggles for socialism*. London, UK: Verso.

Sleeter, C. (1987). Why is there learning disabilities? A critical analysis of the birth of the field in its social context. In T.S. Popkewitz (Ed.), *The formation of school subjects: The struggle for creating an American institution* (pp. 210–237). New York, NY: Falmer Press.

Tate, W.F. (1997). Critical race theory and education: History, theory, and implications. In M.W. Apple (Ed.), *Review of research in education* (Vol. 22, pp. 195–247). Washington, DC: American Educational Research Association.

Taylor, E. (2009). The foundations of critical race theory in education: An introduction. In E. Taylor, D. Gillborn, & G. Ladson-Billings (Eds.), *Foundations of critical race theory in education* (pp. 1–13). New York, NY: Routledge.

Tikly, L., Haynes, J., Caballero, C., Hill, J., & Gillborn, D. (2006). *Evaluation of aiming high: African Caribbean Achievement Project* (Research Report RR801). London, UK: Department for Education and Skills.

Tomlinson, S. (1981). *Educational subnormality: A study in decision-making*. London, UK: Routledge & Kegan Paul.

Tomlinson, S. (2014). *The politics of race, class and special education: The selected works of Sally Tomlinson*. London, UK: Routledge.

Warmington, P. (2011). Some of my best friends are Marxists: CRT, sociocultural theory and the "figured worlds" of race. In K. Hylton, A. Pilkington, P. Warmington, & S. Housee (Eds.), *Atlantic crossings: International dialogues on critical race theory* (pp. 263–283). Birmingham, UK: Sociology, Anthropology, Politics (C-SAP), The Higher Education Academy Network, University of Birmingham.

Warmington, P. (2014). *Black British intellectuals and education: Multiculturalism's hidden history.* London, UK: Routledge.

Watamabe, M. (2012). Tracking in US schools. In J.A. Banks (Ed.), *Encyclopedia of diversity in education* (Vol. 4, pp. 2182–2184). Los Angeles, CA: SAGE.

Wright, C., Weekes, D., & McGlaughlin, A. (2000). *"Race," class and gender in exclusion from school.* London, UK: Routledge.

Chapter 27

"A Raw, Emotional Thing": School Choice, Commodification, and the Racialized Branding of Afrocentricity in Toronto, Canada

Kalervo N. Gulson and P. Taylor Webb

In this chapter, Gulson and Taylor (2013) contend that neo-liberal education policy, which supports the creation of schooling choices in public education systems, is reshaping, conflating, and branding ethnicity. They make these points with reference to school choice in Toronto, Canada, and the establishment of an Africentric school in that city. The authors argue that one of the registers within which education and ethnicity in Toronto operates relates to the conflation of commodification, ethnicity, and geography, and that this conflation indicates one of the limits of school choice as a possible way to redress Black student disadvantage. They suggest education policy, which enables the establishment of ethno-centric schools, enters the realm of other debates about race, equity, and difference that include the practices of marketing and branding.

Demands for change are often framed in the language of school choice and mar-
kets, but they can also be seen as a demand for recognition in a plural democracy
and a critique of the cultural assumptions that underpin current versions of the
common school ... (Gaskell, 2001: 32)

Mark this term: empowerment. In the post-colony it connotes privileged access to
markets, money, and material enrichment. In the case of ethnic groups, it is frankly
associated with finding something essentially their own and theirs alone, something
of their essence, to sell. In other words, a brand. (Comaroff & Comaroff, 2009: 15,
original emphasis)

In September 2009, just over 100 students entered the classrooms of the Africentric Alternative School (AAS) for the first time. The AAS opened as an elementary school within the existing Sheppard Public School in Brookwell Park in the north-west of Toronto, Canada. This school was one of four elementary schools that opened in September 2009 as part of a Toronto school choice policy framework—the 'alternative schools' programme—that allows for the *establishment* of new schools by parents and other interested parties.

[…] Toronto, like many other cities, has a local education quasi-market, with a combination of state control and market mechanisms (Taylor, 2009). Quasi-markets engender a focus on the role of the individual as a responsible consumer, and the processes and outcomes of choice (Olssen et al., 2004). While a quasi-market valorises the 'consumer-parent', there is less emphasis on the idea of the 'producer-parent' who can play a role in establishing schools. This is a particular formation of choice policy that permits the creation of separate, publicly funded educational spaces (Wells et al., 1999). In the case of Toronto, the Toronto District School Board (TDSB) supports the development of alternative schools, which not only presumes parents can choose to send their children to existing schools, but provides the capacity to establish schools. There are now more than 40 elementary and secondary alternative schools in Toronto (Toronto District School Board, 2012).

And yet, in the case of the latest alternative schools established in 2009, *only* the AAS—a small school in a city-wide Toronto District School Board system with 600 schools and close to 300,000 students—near the intersection of Keele Street and Sheppard Avenue West, an intersection in an area of the city not often included in any tourist guides for Toronto, isolated by the surrounding gargantuan urban freeways and adjacent to the mid-town airport, only this small school managed to evoke equal parts support and outrage when it was proposed. The other three 'alternative' schools were proposed and approved with nary a whimper of controversy.

In this paper, we use the example of the differential treatment of the AAS to contend that neo-liberal education policies which supports choice, like the alternative school programme, are reshaping, conflating and branding ethnicity in racialised quasi-school markets. In so doing, school choice policies provide new conditions for, and have reshaped the possibilities of, equity. We suggest this is similar to Fraser's (2009) proposition that forms of politics such as second-wave feminism are far more complicated, and possibly contradictory, under neo-liberal conditions; that is "[a]spirations that had a clear emancipatory thrust in the context of state-organised capitalism assumed a far more ambiguous meaning in the neo-liberal era" (Fraser, 2009: 108). While we might quibble over whether state-organised capitalism is an equally apt description of neo-liberal reforms, the notion of ambiguous meaning, and what Fraser calls "dangerous liaisons" with neo-liberalism, are salient ideas in relation to school choice.

White, middle-class parents and students are often identified as the main beneficiaries and strategic users of school choice policies (Ball, 2003). However, the possibility of parent and community driven establishment of schools is shifting the parameters of opportunity, access and equity; they "help redefine educational opportunities as the creation of separate spaces" (Wells et al., 1999: 175). Education policy supporting school choice of existing schools now permits parents and other stakeholders to *establish new public schools*. Rather than merely advocating choice as the opportunity to attend different types of schools, policy *conflates both the provision and choosing of education*. What is being enabled, therefore, are new forms of what might be termed government-funded "ethno-centric" (Wells et al., 1999) schools that are developing in the Asia-Pacific, North America and Europe through a variety of different school choice mechanisms. These schools—charter schools in the United States, publicly funded 'private' schools in Australia, 'free schools' in the United Kingdom, for example—are often affiliated with ethnic or cultural groups. This includes religious denominations that are 'minority' and/or racialised populations in nation-states, such as Afro-Caribbean in Canada, Muslim in Australia, and Latino/a in the United States. We use the example of the AAS as one such type of school, the first established in Toronto since the 1980s, to look at the links between ethnicity, race and education policy. We locate this problem within an understanding of ethnicity taken as both "increasingly the stuff of existential passion, of the self-conscious fashioning of meaningful, morally anchored selfhood" and as "*also* becoming more corporate, more commodified, more implicated than ever before in the economics of everyday life" (Comaroff & Comaroff, 2009: 1, original emphasis).

[...] Second, we outline the policy environment pertaining to school choice in Toronto and the establishment of alternative schools. This includes discussing broader shifts towards ethno-centric schools, and how school choice provides a form of self-fashioning and empowerment for different groups. We then link ideas of empowerment with notions of racialised commodification and ethnicity in Toronto. In this section, we argue that one of the registers within which education and ethnicity in Toronto operates relates to the conflation of racialised commodification and geography, and that this conflation indicates one of the limits of school choice as an equity project.

We conclude by suggesting school choice policy operates on the premise that the provision of schooling choices is a neutral market. Thus, a 'neutral market' effectively depoliticises education through the commodification of ethnic identities while providing the opportunity for the creation of separate ethno-centric schools. While choice opens up agency as an option in social justice projects, it also complicates other forms of collective action as part of anti-racist projects. [...] We aim to show that, counter to the notion of neutral markets, education policy that enables the establishment of ethno-centric schools such as the AAS enters into, and constitutes, the realm of other debates about equity, race and difference, including the practices of marketing and branding.

METHODOLOGY

[...] Our goal in this paper is to use the example of the AAS in Toronto to illustrate the ways that education policy frames the discourses of recognition and equality are tangled with discourses of ethnic commodification and neo-liberal policies of school choice.

Data Generation

The data were generated from over 1000 school, district and community documents (e.g., provincial and school board policy texts, meeting minutes, newspaper editorials) and other media (such as video footage from school board meetings, documentary films) from the 1992–2012 period, and we explored how these texts signified and conceptualised the links between policy and identity. In 2012, we supplemented this archival work with eight semi-structured interviews with stakeholders including community representatives and School Board Trustees. The latter are elected officials of the school board with a mix of those who voted for and against the school proposal. For reasons of anonymity, in this paper we do not indicate how trustees voted and we name all as 'trustees,' even if they are ex-members. [...]

EDUCATION POLICY, SCHOOL CHOICE AND "ALTERNATIVE SCHOOLS" IN TORONTO

> *The school was a raw emotional thing. There was … a hurly burly man, we were all in there punching and kicking and fighting and yelling, there was no structure, no process, no framework, no nothing. (Black Canadian, Trustee A, TDSB)*

The provision of 'alternative' schools in Toronto emerged as part of a broader movement in the 1960s and 1970s around 'free schools', co-operative parent teacher elementary schools, and community, conservative elementary schools (M. Levin, 1979). In the 1980s and 1990s, alternative schools—many of which had culture or language bases and were underpinned by different groups' desires to have control over, and make more culturally relevant, their children's schooling—were part of contests about schooling in Ontario, and challenges to "an Anglocentric, Protestant and bourgeois regime" (Dehli, 1996b: 78). As one TDSB trustee notes:

> [T]he old Toronto board, established what it called alternative schools which essentially were sort of grassroots, a bunch of parents want a school of a certain kind of methodology or a focus and … [the board would] say 'OK' and then they would turn their

neighbourhood school into that, that was the basis for a lot of the so-called alternative schools. (Trustee B, TDSB)

A parallel to this counter-political form of alternative schools were those established by white, middle-class parents who were intervening in school debates and articulating participation as consumers: "These are the groups who have adopted a cultural script of consumer democracy in education" (Dehli, 1996b: 83). [...]

In 2007, the TDSB attempted to formalise its definition of an 'alternative school' as:

> Sites that are unique in pedagogy, forms of governance and staff involvement, and have strong parental and/or student involvement; environments vary and provide an educational experience suited to individual learning styles/preferences and/or needs (Quan, 2007: Appendix A-1).

The new iteration of 'alternative schools' reinforces school choice as both parents choosing to send their children to existing schools, and *actually establishing a school*. Individuals or groups are able to propose a school and, if they meet the requirement of the board, the trustees vote on the proposal. Schools that were created by parents or other educational stakeholders, post-2007, and have been listed on the TDSB website as alternative schools, included the AAS and the following: the Da Vinci Alternative School, a school based on Waldorf and Steiner education; the Grove Community School, with a social justice and environmental focus; and the Equinox Alternative School that has a holistic learning and teaching approach (Toronto District School Board, 2012). [...]

While the latter three schools were not challenged publicly,[1] or at the very least there was little reported contestation, the AAS was created through numerous public meetings, and entered the maelstrom of the complicated politics of race and equity in the Toronto school district (McGaskell, 2005). Two Black Canadian female 'community activists', Donna Harrow and Angela Wilson, for example, drove the AAS. These two activists were variously lauded or vilified throughout the process of establishing the school (Weiss, 2010). In an interview for a documentary on the AAS called "Our School" (Weiss, 2010), Donna Harrow noted:

> And yeah, there are other alternative schools but those same people who were against all of this [the AAS] had no idea how many alternative schools, what kind of alternative schools, but because this one came up, and there was the big hullabulloo about the Black focused school, of course, 'they're going to say, well no I don't agree with this.' (Weiss, 2010: Film time 14.03–14.36)

This recounting of uninformed yet vehement opposition to the idea of a Black-focused school indicates how choice policy and its ostensive neutrality enters the realm of differentiation and racialisation of provision; that some forms of choice are seen as discomforting, unsettling and dangerous and others as normal or natural (Gulson & Webb, 2012). In

Toronto, this differentiation depends on how the AAS is positioned in relation to the historical disadvantage of Black students. In the Toronto school district in 2006, 12% or 31,800 students identified as Black (Yau et al., 2011). Over 40% of Black students are underachieving in relation to the district standards (Toronto District School Board, 2009). In the 1990s, the extent of Black student disadvantage and racism in Toronto was well known, with the 1992 "Royal Commission on Learning" making extensive recommendations about Black-focused education (Ontario Government/African Canadian Community Working Group, 1992). Between 1992 and 2007 there were myriad moves to include a Black-focused curriculum in Toronto schooling, as well as proposals to develop separate Afrocentric schools. These schools were posited as counters to a Eurocentric focus in the curriculum, sites for Black role models, and as ways of engaging Black students who were not completing school (Dei, 1995, 1996). Despite this extensive focus on Black education, progress on systemic equity initiatives was complicated by the amalgamation of the school boards (McCaskell, 2005).

The AAS as a 'choice' initiative therefore took place against this backdrop of 20–30 years of attempts to rectify Black student disadvantage, and repudiations of those attempts. In June 2007 a feasibility report was prepared for an Africentric Alternative School, after being requested by Black Canadian community members. In November and December 2007 community meetings were held under the aegis of the TDSB, about the school in conjunction with meetings on the education of Black students more generally in Toronto. The trustees approved the school, 11 votes to 9, in a fiery and controversial school board meeting in 2008, televised live. As one trustee noted:

> This was one of the biggest debates in TDSB history, perhaps of ... school history in the country. (Trustee E, TDSB)

Representing different parts of the city, the trustees were celebrated or pilloried for voting for or opposing the school.[2] Some trustees were physically assaulted and received death threats in response to how they voted (both 'for' and 'against'). For, within a normalised policy environment that has long supported the establishment of parent- and stakeholder-led schooling initiatives under the alternative school programme, the AAS, as distinct from the environment school, or the holistic learning school, became the touchstone for all sorts of debates about the future of Toronto—Black student achievement, the management of diversity in Toronto, equity and equality. Therefore, even before it was established the AAS stalked the landscape of Torontonian education like a policy apparition (Webb & Gulson, 2012); even the threat of its existence evoked uncertainty, doubt and fear as part of the policy process. The primary opposition, for example, to the establishment of the AAS was framed in the media as a particular form of re-segregation within the TDSB public school system. The spectre of segregation was raised repeatedly in local media regarding the general ideas of Black-focused schools in Ontario (James, 2011), and specifically in relation to the AAS. For some opponents, the spectre of segregation that was to be manifest in the AAS was both an historical and a-historical reference; historical when the opposition made links to segregated schooling in North America, a-historical when the opposition ignored low student achievement and historical exclusion within public schooling—that is, racism within public schools (James, 2011). The school was caught in a maelstrom of concern over race, ethnicity and equity not only in Toronto, but Canada more broadly. As a Black Canadian trustee noted:

> … there were weeks and weeks of public consultations and people coming into the boardroom. And you know, those kinds of public consultations really attract the lunatic fringe, right? Like people who couldn't string a coherent sentence together, but were having this deeply emotional response because again they couldn't come to grips with whatever it is they were feeling, you know, and get up and kind of rant and rave, and sometimes not even talk about issues related to Black focus school. It's really because a locus for people's discomfort. You name it, public education, the Black community, with poverty, with geography, with the city, like it became this thing. (Black Canadian, Trustee A, TDSB)

In the rest of the paper we discuss this differentiated treatment within the realm of choice policy, in two ways. The first emphasise the empowerment in the market—closely related to new forms of recognition and agency, the capacity and permission to act, and self-fashioning around ethnicity in education afforded by ethno-cultural schools like the AAS. The second looks at how the school is, we contend, enmeshed with and constitutive of the racialised cultural politics of the city. This latter section is intended to complicate the notion of empowerment in relation to ethnicity and commodification.

AFROCENTRICITY INC.?: ETHNICITY, CHOICE AND EMPOWERMENT

Education policy is, of course somewhat axiomatically, about change: "it offers an imagined future state of affairs, but in articulating desired change always offers an account somewhat more simplified than the actual realities of practice" (Rizvi & Lingard, 2010: 5). School choice policy in the form of alternative schools offered the possibility for parents to take control of parts of Black education in Toronto. This is related to a politics of recognition that has, for the past 20 years or so, been played out through and enabled by marketised educational policy in various iterations in different countries and cities—such as open enrolment, changing school establishment regulations, vouchers and charters (Wells et al., 1999). That is, the individualised form of neo-liberal participation as based on parental freedom to choose has also been part of "a demand for recognition in a plural democracy and a critique of the cultural assumptions that underpin current versions of the common school" (Gaskell, 2001: 32–33).

School choice policies can enable the development and establishment of ethno-centric schools and curricula based on ideas of identity and recognition (Rofes & Stulberg, 2004). This includes opportunities to develop ethnic-specific curricula for Native Hawaiians (Buchanan & Fox, 2004), Native Americans (Belgarde, 2004), African Americans (Shujaa, 1988, 1992;

Yancey, 2004), Black Canadians (Dei, 2005) and Aboriginal Canadians (Archibald et al., 2011). Afrocentric schools in particular have a lineage tracing back to community-based or 'free school movements', and the notion of 'independent Black institutions' in the United States (Shujaa, 1992), with contemporary iterations continuing across many states of the United States including Ohio, Missouri, Washington and California, and Afrocentric curricula initiatives in Nova Scotia, Canada (Dei, 1995; Ginwright, 2000). In the case of the Canadian AAS, the school website states: "A unique feature of the AAS will be the integration of the diverse perspectives, experiences and histories of people of African descent into the provincial mandated curriculum" (Africentric Alternative School, 2011).

School choice policies and the emergence of ethno-centric schools within this policy frame can thus enunciate ideas of choice, freedom and equality. The politics surrounding this, however, are complex and at times contradictory. We might see the opportunities afforded by the establishment of ethno-centric schools as part of providing members of an enterprising cultural group with opportunities to speak for themselves and to take responsibility for themselves against persistent and historical educational inequalities. And we might read the AAS as enmeshed in a similar kind of politics—that is in the absence over 20 years of any substantive addressing of Black disadvantage at a systemic level, and with the reduction of equity focus in the new school board, the market becomes the modality for equality. As Donna Harrow identified, a school like the AAS can be borne out of endemic procrastination and obfuscation, of systemic rejection or belittling of the issue of Black student disadvantage, except during moments of crisis. In talking about why the AAS took so long to be established, remembering that Black-focused schools had been recommended as legitimate and important initiatives in Toronto since the 1990s, Donna Harrow suggests:

> I think it took long because we're all very comfortable, and we've become very complacent in how we treat students in our schools, and more specifically, how we treat students of colour within our schools. It has been suggested time and time and time again, and we will have a shooting in a school, we will have a death in a school, and somebody else will recommend ... [a Black focused school], and everybody says, 'yeeah, great idea! We really should deal with this because students, Black students self esteem is down a hole and we need to do something about it'. And we talk and we nod and we smile, and then we forget about it. (Weiss, 2010: Film time 11.00–11.56)

We might see, furthermore, that the market requires certain types of compromises. Lipman (2011) posits the idea of TINA—*There Is No Alternative*—to discuss how Black and Latina/o parents and community members in the United States have become involved in the setting up of charter schools, including highly corporatised models. If we apply this more broadly to choice options like alternative schools in Toronto, what is enabled by neo-liberal education policy is complex, for "people are recruited into neo-liberal forms of governmentality, even if they also, simultaneously, seek to resist some of its effects" (Bondi, 2005: 499). In a sociological sense, TINA may be a politics of belonging, a kind of politics that seeks practices of inclusion and empowerment. However, because TINA is marketised and racialised it is a politics that certainly produces a "politics of self-separation" (Dei, 2005) that pivots on determining who has the authority to place themselves and their children within particular schools to practice discrete forms of care, and how ethno-centric schools are constituted in an education market (Gulson & Webb, 2012). This has led some scholars to argue that education and economic policies that promote the choice and creation of schools with an ethno-centric identity are a new force in educational politics that is simultaneously "progressive" and "conservative" (Pedroni, 2007). This complicated nature is represented by accusations that ethno-centric schools are merely tokenistic. As one TDSB trustee argues:

> I also think one of the things that can be problematic about some of these [ethnic and cultural focused] schools is you say 'well we'll set up a school for …[these groups]' and that might be beneficial for couple hundred kids, but that doesn't mean that anybody else in the system is getting an opportunity to have that kind of programming…. But what about the 249,905 [other students in the TDSB], I mean those kids are still, if we're not making an effort to teach them that knowledge as well then I don't think we're doing the right thing. (Trustee B, TDSB)

In this sense, the trustee makes a claim that indicates how school choice policies—and alternative schools that educate small numbers of students—are poor mechanisms to address historic inequalities. This presumes, as we noted above, that there has not been advocacy for collective change in Black student educational provision in Toronto over the past 30 years. The AAS will not, obviously, address the educational needs of all Black students in Toronto; nonetheless, what this school does achieve, within a choice framework, is an intervention into the discourses of educational inequality. As we have noted previously: "In the end, school choice policy is also a politics of *no longer waiting*" (Webb et al., 2012). Spider Jones, a Black Canadian radio host, suggests a similar thing when he proposes that opposition to the AAS tended to be skewed.

> First of all you get a perspective from basically, with all due respect white guys, that have never grown up in the projects or understand the problems. I think many of them mean well, but there's a difference between meaning well and understanding that we live in desperate times. And in desperate times, you take desperate measures, nothing else is working. (Weiss, 2010: Film time 16.16–16.44)

And as a Black Canadian trustee suggested:

> It was all about how do you meet the needs of the students and their families? And it wasn't that an Africentric school was the answer. It was that there wasn't one answer. (Black Canadian, Trustee A, TDSB)

The AAS transmutes across and through different discourses of difference, pain, poverty and privilege; discourses that delineate the possibilities of culture, identity and recognition in arguments for equity. For instance, Ginwright (2000) wonders, in relation to the possibilities of social justice through Afrocentric schooling, "what are the limits and possibilities for using racial and cultural identity as a solution to reforming urban schools?" (p. 88). For our purposes, we also wonder what limits and possibilities are afforded by racial and cultural identities in urban school reform initiatives within quasi-school markets. Ethnicity, racialisation and culture do not stand apart from the market, but form and are produced as integral features of urban school reform predicated on neo-liberal choice factors. As a Black Canadian TDSB trustee contends:

> I think there's no doubt that because we live in a society that's geared toward individualism this is where choice becomes kind of a double-edged sword, right, because on the one hand choice is about empowerment and being able to make decisions for your family, for your-self, and for whatever, your children, and on the other hand it becomes about entitlement.
>
> … I think as a culture [in Toronto], we're not set up to have these conversations about how systemic oppression or barriers work, your fallback is to frame it on that individual level which is about choice. (Black Canadian, Trustee A, TDSB)

School choice policy is both the opportunity and responsibility to be entrepreneurial—as care of the self in neo-liberal policy frames (Brown, 2003; Dean, 1999; Foucault, 2005). We might also see this within what Comaroff and Comaroff (2009) identify as "empowerment."

> Mark this term: *empowerment*. In the post-colony it connotes privileged access to markets, money, and material enrichment. In the case of ethnic groups, it is frankly associated with finding something essentially their own and theirs alone, something of their essence, to sell. In other words, a brand. (Comaroff & Comaroff, 2009: 15)

To be clear, we are not suggesting that having something to sell—that is, a Black-focused school—is the impetus for the Black activists and supporters who established the school, nor what underpinned trustee support at the board level. Nonetheless, it is a precondition for a new TDSB alternative school to differentiate itself from other schools—and these schools are seen as part of claiming a 'market share' of students. We are, therefore, interested in how a black-focused school becomes both subject to, and can take advantage of, the education market. An ethno-centric school is therefore dangerous in Foucault's sense: "My point is not that everything is bad, but that everything is dangerous, which is not exactly the same as bad. If everything is dangerous, then we always have something to do" (Foucault, 1983: 231–232). Cultural and ethnic identity—strategically and opportunistically essentialised—is mobilised and enabled within neo-liberal education policy regimes that are racialised (Gulson, 2011; Goldberg, 2009). Nevertheless, as we discuss and conceptualise in the next section, empowerment is a fraught and fragile concept for policy and the unintended consequences of policy are played out in multicultural cities like Toronto.

RECOGNITION IN THE CITY: RACIALISED GEOGRAPHIES OF ETHNICITY, IDENTITY AND EDUCATION

We posit there are at least two ways to understand the relationships between the discourses of recognition and identity and the discourse of school choice. First, Toronto's geography and its history provide registers that recognise and identify different racial and ethnic identities. Second, school choice policy mechanisms that emphasise empowerment and neo-liberal ideas of equality provide different registers that enunciate ethnic recognition and identity. We discuss these ideas next.

The ASS raises a series of key questions concerning identity and ethno-centric schools or, in this particular case, what is 'Black' in Black-focused education, and does it differ from Afrocentricity? In other words, what are the aims of ethno-centric schools in relation to particular forms of identity, curriculum and pedagogy (Dumas, 2009)? Further, how does defining Afrocentricity point to its possible role as a powerful assertion in marketised forms? These issues had relevance in the framing of the ASS—that is, what it would mean to have a Black-focused or Afrocentric school in Toronto. The trustees were not shy about addressing this question, nor its contested and complex nature:

> I mean with the Africentric curriculum for those couple of hundred kids that are there, they are learning lots about African cultures because I would emphasise that there is more than one culture in Africa, and two, not to think so is to essentialise the African experience you would be amazed how many people say things like 'oh go learn African culture'. (Trustee B, TDSB)

> But again, another philosophical debate about who counts and who doesn't and one of the real, the really legitimate arguments about what is involved in a Black focus school, right, ... [it's about] who gets to define Blackness. (Black Canadian, TDSB Trustee A)

> When we used the word 'Africentric' we have to be very careful with myself being an African-Canadian. I think we need to look at those words very carefully and sort of decide how we're gonna use it and where we're going to go ... we had a lot of discussions around the word, the term, what it really meant and were we alienating other groups from coming into the school simply because of that. (Black Canadian, TDSB Trustee D)

The constituting of Afrocentricity is, of course, not only the purview of those who proposed the AAS—it also enters the market of schooling where potential clients and opponents are given opportunities to provide input into its existence and development. It similarly allows the TDSB to demonstrate it is doing 'something' about Black schooling:

I think it's probably more true now because now [the AAS is] a selling point and … how diverse their Toronto school board is and you could send your child here and here and here and…. (Black Canadian, Trustee A, TDSB)

For our purposes, the problems of recognition pivot on the extent to which recognition and the concomitant ideas of ethnic identity are used in developing choice schools. That is, as Fraser notes, we are concerned with how markets tame politics (Fraser, 2009). Likewise, Shujaa (1992), in study of parental choice of independent Afrocentric schools, pointedly states:

… I am concerned about the uses to which Afrocentricity has been put. Too often is has come to be regarded as a quantity rather than a quality, and, in some instances, even as a commodity that can be bought and sold. (Shujaa, 1992: 158)

We want to take this point and look at how this idea of commodity and ethnicity has some salience to understanding how the AAS was posited differentially from other alternative schools in Toronto. Cities and education systems, through policy, have long constituted and classified what is possible and prevented; especially governing the ways that difference is produced and reconfigured through and due to race (Gulson, 2011; also see Lipman, 2011). Cities have also been sites in which ethnicity has operated as different forms of capital. We suggest that one way to understand how ethnicity functions as capital in Toronto is to understand that, prior to World War II, Toronto was primarily a WASP (White, Anglo-Saxon, Protestant) city. After the war, the city's migrant make-up changed, to the point that it is now the most ethnically and culturally diverse city in Canada (Buzzelli, 2001), as noted by some trustees.

… for all intents and purposes Toronto's a black city. (Black Canadian, Trustee A, TDSB)

… we live in a more identity conscious city than anyone else…. (Jewish Canadian, Trustee D, TDSB)

The spatial politics of the AAS were rooted within this geographical history in which the resistance to the school is constituted and constitutive of race and ethnic relations established within the city of Toronto. For instance, Trustee F noted how resistance to the AAS was also rooted in concessions about the school's location in the city.

Local councillors basically pushed back, I was surrounded by councillors that voted against it and if you're gonna vote against it the political will on the ground is not gonna see it happen. So they want it up in the northwest corner of the city where we have the highest concentrations of communities of African extraction. They wanted it up there. (Trustee F, TDSB)

When asked to explain how the city of Toronto was racially stratified, the trustee noted that:

> ethnic communities tend to congregate [in Toronto] around religious institutions, churches, mosques, synagogues, community centres, shops so you do have people of national extractions living in a community. (Trustee F, TDSB)

The spatial politics of Toronto were not created by the AAS; rather, the AAS was located on a highly contentious grid of racialisations already mapped onto the city in particular ways. For instance, the politics of segregation regarding the AAS were intertwined with the spatial politics of the city. Trustee F noted that his support of the AAS was partially due to calling out the inherent racialised segregation of Toronto already. He stated that in a meeting he said to other trustees:

> "If you wanna talk about segregation you go look at your Claude Watson [TDSB school, primarily black population] over there, your North Toronto Secondary [TDSB school, primarily white population]." It was like whoa, so they backed off of [their critique of the AAS]. (Trustee F, TDSB)

The establishment of the AAS was in part due to how it fitted on Toronto's grid of race, ethnicity and class. More importantly, for our purposes, the racialised commodification of ethnicity occurred—in part—through the movements through the city. In other words, alternative choice schools in TDSB are 'open boundaries' that destabilise the historical practices of catchment and provide consumers of race-based education with a market in which to participate. Through these movements, a market for choice schools was developed and the commodification of race followed through the selection and consumption of the AAS. Trustee F noted:

> I also messaged on school boundaries and the reality was ... if you wanna talk about so-called segregation you go look at these school boundaries, don't lecture my Afrocentric parents, let's start removing these school boundaries and make sure there's more integration. (Trustee F, TDSB)

Here, the term 'integration' is used in relation to a city already marketised in relation to difference. Toronto is a city that has identified its neighbourhoods through explicit conflation of place with the ethnicity of the 'original' migrants: Little Italy, Greektown, Koreatown and India Bazaar. As multiple generations of migrants have left these parts of the city, like other multicultural cities around the world such as Sydney and London, these names have remained as part of emerging 'cultural to quarters' that are connected both to an historical remnant of migrant collectivism and to commodification (Keith, 2005; Pugliese, 2007).

Ethnicity and identity in contemporary Toronto therefore operates within an already presumed sense of collective commercialisation. It is in the gentrified inner areas of the city, and now the most affluent part of the city (Hulchanski, 2010) and the site of the old Toronto board, and where most alternative schools are located that ethnicity and commodification are most clearly in tandem. Hackworth and Rekers (2005) suggest that as inner city areas like Little Italy or India Bazaar have changed demographically their function as commodity has intensified—in combinations of "commodified culture and traditional landscapes" (p. 216)—as part of the consumptive practices of the new (white) middle classes of inner-city gentrification. Different neighbourhoods are identified as business improvement areas, and then reference ethnicity in the title such as Greektown; local ethnic identity is 'managed' by these improvement associations to varying degrees. Difference becomes tied to a commodity—e.g., restaurants—that communicate these differences in essentialised forms to the 'outside' world. In this way, the governance of the city is tied not just to incorporating the multiculture, but to the *creation* of racialisations and ethnicity. As Osborne and Rose (1999) suggest, from the 19th century onwards, "the government of the city becomes *inseparable from the continuous activity of generating truths about the city*" (p. 739, original emphasis).

In Toronto, the policy frames that link business improvement with ethnicity also provide an indication as to the possibilities and limits of empowerment in relation to cultural identity. Some forms of ethnic difference are more palatable when constituted as an area that is to be consumed. When consumption is tied to education—such as the AAS in an education market—notions such as Black and Africentric move onto more fraught terrain than a neighbourhood with 'authentic' cuisine or 'A Thousand Villages' ethnic free-trade wares. The AAS was a form of ethnicity that was intelligible in the racialised geography of the city—the school invoked the threat of race, rather than benign difference and diversity (see Gulson, 2011; Goldberg, 2009). If a city like Toronto has one set of discourses that considers ethnicity as a marketable and essentialised form, then this reduces the nuances and complexities of how other discourses of ethnicity in the education market may be mobilised by Black Canadian parents and students towards equitable purposes. As such, the AAS, while able to be established through policy, is cast loose by the ostensive neutrality of choice policy and enters the registers of commodification and ethnicity that are racialised and (re)articulated in Toronto.

CONCLUSION

> I was really driven to say there is a hierarchy of racism in our city and Black people are at the bottom of it and First Nations people are at the bottom of it. But they're just less obvious, you know. And again those were the race conversations that nobody wants to have. (Black Canadian female, Trustee A, TDSB)

As Rizvi and Lingard (2011) note, "a commitment to market values in education does not entirely involve a rejection of a concern for social equity, but it does suggest that the meaning of equity is re-articulated" (p. 9). This is choice as part of neo-liberal governmentality and new forms of affinity and community within marketised forms (Miller & Rose, 2008), which reshapes policy "not by entirely eliminating equity concerns but rather by embedding them within choice and accountability frameworks" (Forsey et al., 2008: 15). Education policy seems to now demand the entrepreneurial self and the self as, paradoxically, the collective production of educational equity. As we have noted: "In a re-articulation of equality, education policy now develops markets of care for entrepreneurial, innovative, and particular selves" (Webb et al., 2012, p. 6).

Neo-liberal policy also depends on the racialised and marketised reconfiguring of space—about which parts of the city are deemed acceptable for the consumption of ethnicity. For the creation of separate spaces such as the AAS is, of course, not uncoupled from the histories and geographies of schooling systems and cities. When an Africentric school is proposed in Toronto, it is enabled within a choice framework but enters the domain not just of education but of how ideas of ethnicity may be constituted and marketed/branded within the city. That is, the AAS is *not* treated in the same way as other proposed alternative schools—rather there is extensive racialised contestation over who has the right to define the parameters of the market, that is, which alternative schools are acceptable—and also a debate over who controls culture. This is both an opportunity and problem, for the commodification of culture then runs the risk of being reduced to property (Gilroy, 2006).

The cultural politics of policy are thus incredibly complex in relation to ethno-centric schools like the AAS, for these politics repudiate the notion, endemic in school choice research, that agency in education markets is the purview of the white, middle class and a concomitant lack of agency for people of colour (for critiques, see Lipman, 2011; Pedroni, 2007). What we are seeing in a policy sense is that policy normalisation of the creation of separate spaces of educational opportunity, in which school choice policies are in the form of establishing separate spaces, is now the complicated and contradictory new forms of cultural recognition, survival and agency (Webb et al., 2012; Lipman, 2011). And we might ask whether, simultaneously, neo-liberal education policy is limiting our capacity to imagine new forms of cultural transformation in schools and the city.

ACKNOWLEDGEMENTS

This research was supported by a *Canadian Social Sciences and Humanities Research Council* Standard Research Grant. We would like to thank the two anonymous reviewers for their useful comments, and Carl James for his feedback on an earlier version of this paper.

NOTES

1. The Grove School has been the subject of tabloid journalism (see http://www.torontosun.com/2012/05/07/what-are- they-teaching-our-kids).
2. The spatial politics of the TDSB, and the identification of place with trustees, is noteworthy yet beyond the remit of this paper.

REFERENCES

Africentric Alternative School. (2011). Africentric Alternative School. http://www.tdsb.on.ca/SchoolWeb/_site/viewitem.asp?siteid=10423&pageid=19951&menuid=23019 (Accessed 30.05.2011).

Archibald, J.A., Rayner, A. and Big Head, R. (2011). Community responses to creating a school or model with an Aboriginal focus. http://www.vsb.bc.ca/sites/default/files/11April18_sp_op_commIII_item1.pdf (Accessed 23.10.2011).

Ball, S.J. (2003). *Class strategies and the education market: The middle classes and social advantage.* London: Routledge.

Belgarde, M.J. (2004). Native American charter schools: Culture, language, and self-determination. In *The emancipatory promise of charter schools: Towards a progressive politics of school choice,* E. Rofes, & L. Stulberg (eds.), 107–124. Albany: State University of New York Press.

Bondi, L. (2005). Working the Spaces of Neoliberal Subjectivity: Psychotherapeutic Technologies, Professionalisation and Counselling. *Antipode,* 37(3), 497–514.

Brown, W. (2003). Neo-liberalism and the End of Liberal Democracy. *Theory and Event,* 7. http://muse.jhu.edu/journals/theory_and_event/v007/7.1brown.html.

Buchanan, N. and Fox, R. (2004). Back to the future: Ethno-centric charter schools in Hawai'i. In *The emancipatory promise of charter schools: Towards a progressive politics of school choice,* E. Rofes and L. Stulberg (eds.), 77–106. Albany: State University of New York Press.

Buzzelli, M. (2001). From Little Britain to Little Italy: An Urban Ethnic Landscape Study in Toronto. *Journal of Historical Geography,* 27(4), 573–587.

Comaroff, J.L. and Comaroff, J. (2009). *Ethnicity, Inc.* Chicago: The University of Chicago Press.

Dean, M. (1999). *Governmentality: Power and rule in modern society.* Thousand Oaks, CA: SAGE Publications.

Dehli, K. (1996b). Travelling Tales: Education Reform and Parental 'Choice' in Postmodern Times. *Journal of Education Policy,* 11(1), 75–88.

Dei, G.J.S. (1995). Examining the Case for 'African-Centred' Schools in Ontario. *McGill Journal of Education,* 30(2), 179–198.

Dei, G.J.S. (1996). The Role of Afrocentricity in the Inclusive Curriculum in Canadian Schools. *Canadian Journal of Education,* 21(2), 170–186.

Dei, G.J.S. (2005). The case for black schools. *The Toronto Star.* http://www.diversitywatch.ryerson.ca/media/cache/blackschoolsdei_star_feb4.htm (Accessed 23.11.2011).

Dumas, M.J. (2009). What is this 'Black' in Black education?: Imagining a cultural politics without guarantees. In *Handbook of cultural politics of education,* Z. Leonardo (ed.), 403–422. Rotterdam: Sense Publishers.

Forsey, M., Davies, S. and Walford, G. (2008). The globalisation of school choice? An introduction to key issues and concerns. In *The globalisation of school choice,* M. Forsey, S. Davies and G. Walford (eds.), 9–26. Oxford: Symposium.

Foucault, M. (1983). On the genealogy of ethics: An overview of a work in progress. In *Michel Foucault: Beyond structuralism and hermeneutics*, 2nd ed., H. Dreyfus & P. Rabinow (eds.), 229–252. Chicago: The University of Chicago Press.

Foucault, M. (2005). *The hermeneutics of the subject: Lectures at the College de France, 1981–1982*. New York: Picador.

Fraser, N. (2009). Feminism, Capitalism and the Cunning of History. *New Left Review,* 56, 97–117.

Gaskell, J. (2001). The Public in Public Schools: A School Board Debate. *Canadian Journal of Education,* 26(1), 19–36.

Gilroy, P. (2006). Multiculture in Times of War: An Inaugural Lecture Given at the London School of Economics. *Critical Quarterly,* 48(4), 27–45.

Ginwright, S.A. (2000). Identity for Sale: The Limits of Racial Reform in Urban Schools. *The Urban Review,* 32(1), 87–104.

Goldberg, D.T. (2009). *The threat of race: Reflections on racial neoliberalism*. Oxford: Wiley-Blackwell.

Gulson, K.N. (2011). *Education policy, space and the city: Markets and the (in)visibility of race*. New York: Routledge.

Gulson, K.N. and Webb, P.T. (2012). Education Policy Racialisations: Afrocentric Schools, Islamic Schools and the New Enunciations of Equity. *Journal of Education Policy,* 27(6), 697–709.

Hackworth, J. and Rekers, J. (2005). Ethnic Packaging and Gentrification: The Case of Four Neighbourhoods in Toronto. *Urban Affairs Review,* 41(2), 211–236.

Hulchanski, J.D. (2010). *The three cities within Toronto: Income polarization among Toronto's neighbourhoods, 1970–2005*. Toronto: Cities Centre—University of Toronto.

James, C.E. (2011). Multicultural education in a color-blind society. In *Intercultural and Multicultural Education: Enhancing Global Connectedness*, C.A. Grant & A. Portera (eds.), pp. 191–210. New York: Routledge.

Keith, M. (2005). *After the cosmopolitan? Multicultural cities and the future of racism*. London: Routledge.

Levin, M. (1979). Review of 'Understanding the Alternative Schools Movement: The Re-Transformation of the School' by Daniel L. Luke. *Curriculum Inquiry,* 9(4), 337–349.

Lipman, P. (2011). *The new political economy of urban education: Neoliberalism, race and the right to the city*. New York: Routledge.

McGaskell, T. (2005). *Race to equity: Disrupting educational inequality*. Toronto: Between the Lines.

Miller, P. and Rose, N. (2008). *Governing the present: Administering economic, social and personal life*. Cambridge: Polity Press.

Olssen, M., Codd, J. and O'Neill, A. (2004). *Education policy: Globalization, citizenship and democracy*. London: Sage Publications.

Ontario Government/African Canadian Community Working Group (1992). *Towards a new beginning: The report and action plan of the four-level government/African Canadian community working group*. Toronto.

Osborne, T. and Rose, N. (1999). Governing Cities: Notes on the Spatialisation of Virtue. *Environment and Planning D: Society and Space,* 17, 737–760.

Pedroni, T.C. (2007). *Market movements: African American involvement in school voucher reform.* New York: Routledge.

Pugliese, J. (2007). Whiteness, diasporic architecture and the cultural politics of space. In *Constellations of the transnational: Modernity, culture, critique,* S. Dasgupta (ed.), 23–49. Amsterdam and New York: Rodopi.

Quan, D. (2007). *Briefing note: Alternative schools: Update on implementation of directional statements and operational procedure.* Toronto: Toronto District School Board.

Rizvi, F. and Lingard, B. (2010). *Globalizing educational policy.* London: Routledge.

Rizvi, F. and Lingard, B. (2011). Social Equity and the Assemblage of Values in Australian Higher Education. *Cambridge Journal of Education,* 41(1), 5–22.

Rofes, E. and Stulberg, L. (eds.) (2004). *The emancipatory promise of charter schools: Towards a progressive politics of school choice.* Albany: State University of New York Press.

Shujaa, N.J. (1988). Parental Choice of an Afrocentric Independent School: Developing an Explanatory Theory. *Sankofa,* 2, 22–25.

Shujaa, M.J. (1992). Afrocentric Transformation and Parental Choice in African American Independent Schools. *The Journal of Negro Education,* 61(2), 148–159.

Taylor, C. (2009). Choice, Competition, and Segregation in a United Kingdom Education Market. *American Journal of Education,* 115, 549–568.

Toronto District School Board. (2009). Improving success for Black students: Questions and answers. http://www.tdsb.on.ca/_site/viewItem.asp?siteid=9998&menuid=10863&pageid=9585 (Accessed 13.05.2012).

Toronto District School Board. (2012). Alternative schools. http://www.tdsb.on.ca/_site/View-Item.asp?siteid=122&menuid=490&pageid=379 (Accessed 10.08.2012).

Webb, P.T. and Gulson, K.N. (2012). Policy Prolepsis in Education: Encounters, Becomings and Phantasms. *Discourse: Studies in the Cultural Politics of Education,* 33(1), 87–99.

Webb, P.T., Gulson, K.N. and Pitton, V. (2012). The neo-liberal education policies of epimeleia heautou: Caring for the self in school markets. *Discourse: Studies in the Cultural Politics of Education.* DOI: 10.1080/01596306.2012.739465.

Weiss, A.A. (Writer). (2010). *Our school.* Canada: Aaron A. Weiss Communications.

Wells, A.S., Lopez, A., Scott, J. and Holme, J.J. (1999). Charter Schools as Postmodern Paradox: Rethinking Social Stratification in An Age of Deregulated School Choice. *Harvard Educational Review,* 69(2), 172–205.

Yancey, P. (2004). Independent black schools and the charter movement. In *The emancipatory promise of charter schools: Towards a progressive politics of school choice,* E. Rofes, & L. Stulberg (eds.), 125–158. Albany: State University of New York Press.

Yau, M., O'Reilly, J., Rosolen, L. and Archer, B. (2011). *Census portraits: Understanding our students' ethno-racial backgrounds.* Toronto: Toronto District School Board Research & Information Services.

Chapter 28

Black Mixed-Race British Males and the Role of School Teachers: New Theory and Evidence

Remi Joseph-Salisbury

While increasing attention has been paid to the educational barriers facing young Black men, much of this tends to be predicated on a homogenized understanding of Blackness. The failure to recognize the heterogeneity of blackness means that scant consideration has been given to the particular racialized experiences of Black mixed-race men. By focusing specifically on young Black mixed-race men's perspectives of schooling and teachers, this chapter by Remi Joseph-Salisbury (2016) seeks to redress this problem. The chapter highlights barriers to education, how Black mixed-race men resist, and potential interventions for change.

Whilst there remains a crisis of Black marginality both inside and outside of the British academe, the Black mixed-race[1] male is yet further overlooked in scholarly work. To advance our understanding of Black Britain, we must consider the growing Black mixed-race population. Whilst education has been a key site for Black activism (Andrews, 2014; Warmington, 2014), the Black mixed-race male, despite notably low attainment and high exclusion rates, remains a salient omission from the activist and scholarly work focusing on ethnic minority educational experiences (Tikly et al., 2004; Williams, 2011). In highlighting both commonalities and differences between Blackness and Black-mixedness, this chapter does not seek to do the politically damaging work of fragmenting Britain's Black population, but rather, to move towards a reconceptualisation of Blackness that adequately reflects the experiences of a growing segment of its population. As Stuart Hall (1996, 443) teaches us:

There is no sense in which a new phase in black cultural politics could replace the earlier one. Nevertheless it is true that as the struggle moves forward and assumes new forms, it does to some degree *displace*, reorganize and reposition the different cultural strategies in relation to one another.

Drawing on new data from twenty semi-structured interviews, carried out with Black mixed-race males aged between 18 and 27, this chapter seeks to respond to the scarcity of literature focusing on Black mixed-race educational experiences.

According to school census data the Black mixed-race male population have lower levels of attainment than the average white students and Black mixed-raced females average at GCSE level[2] (DfE, 2014a). Black mixed-race males are also overrepresented in school exclusions (DfE, 2014b). These rates greatly exceed the average and are comparable to the rates of Black males (of two Black parents). Such disproportionality in exclusion rates has presented long-standing tensions between Black communities and the education system (Coard, 1971; Gillborn and Gipps, 1996). The marketisation and neoliberalisation of education has seen the re-emergence of this problem with schools increasingly likely to remove pupils who may impact negatively upon league table scores (Osler and Hill, 1999). Whilst there has been some low level recognition from policy initiatives (DfES, 2003; Richardson, 2005), significant and sustained interventions are yet to be made. In offering a contribution to this sparsely theorised area it is hoped that this chapter can add to growing pressure for intervention.

This chapter focuses on the role of teachers in the education and racialisation of the Black mixed-race male. The first half of the chapter will highlight problems in the teaching force; low teacher expectations, self-fulfilling prophecies and teachers' handling of racist incidents. The second half of the chapter will consider potential interventions. Here the chapter will consider to what extent a racial diversification of the workforce can be effective in raising attainment and improving experiences. Throughout, the chapter will seek to demonstrate how the Black mixed-race male must be considered as part of a more nuanced conception of Blackness.

EDUCATIONAL BARRIERS

Low Teacher Expectations and Stereotypes

Low teacher expectations have long been cited as a barrier facing Black communities in education. More recently this has been recognised to be a barrier for the Black mixed-race male (Tikly et al., 2004; Williams, 2011). Low expectations have been noted to limit the achievements of pupils in a number of ways. Bernard Coard (1971) demonstrated how Black pupils (at a time when Black mixed-race pupils would often have been considered Black (Tizard and Phoenix, 2002)) were disproportionately and unfairly filtered in to schools for the *educationally subnormal*. Teacher stereotypes have also led to disproportionately high rates of exclusion. Low teacher expectations have seen low achieving ethnic minority groups entered for lower-tier

GCSE examinations, which restricts the grade that can be achieved. On this point, Gillborn (2014, 34) states that teacher expectations

> tend to be systematically lower than warranted by their performance in class. These stereotypes exert a powerful influence on students' opportunities to succeed, making it less likely that they will gain access to high status courses and resulting in their being disproportionately placed in the lowest teaching groups, where teachers cover less of the curriculum, thus giving students a reduced chance of achieving the highest grades.

The introduction of the English baccalaureate has perpetuated the disadvantages of tiered exam entrances and 'immediately widened inequalities of achievement' (Ibid., 33). As a mark of academic achievement, the baccalaureate requires higher pass grades in core subjects as opposed to the previous five GCSEs that were a marker of success. This new assessment becomes intertwined with racialised barriers when we realise that the baccalaureate is unattainable for the majority of students; only 21.6% of students are entered in to all the subject examinations required to attain the qualification (Gillborn, 2014).

Low teacher expectations are often built upon stereotypical views and 'teachers' perceptions are often limited and misinformed' (Williams, 2011, xiii). Whilst findings supported Tikly et al.'s (2004, 50) claim that 'times have gone where … it [racism] would be a blatant comment', there were instances in which teachers displayed 'a little underlying racism'. This was recognised by Josh, a participant in my research:

> It's hard sometimes but I think teachers often speak to mixed kids differently, or suspect we might have issues. Not as if a teacher is going to run up to me and call me a nigger but they do treat you different, they make assumptions. It's just hard to challenge with it being more subtle.

In the excerpt from Josh above, we see that although he believes his mixedness results in his differential treatment, he also makes reference to an insult predicated upon his Blackness. This racialisation is dependent upon phenotype and physical clue; some participants recognised being racialised predominantly as Black whilst others felt their appearance meant that they were predominantly racialised as mixed. However, the vast majority felt that they were racialised simultaneously and interchangeably as Black and as mixed-race. This is consistent with findings from Aspinall and Song (2013) who found that, much like the Black male, the Black mixed-race male has limited identity options. For the Black mixed-race male, these were generally confined to mixedness and Blackness.

Research participant James noted the commonalities with Blackness but also the unique aspects of being racialised as mixed-race:

> Mixed-race people and black people are in the same boat, they're both discriminated, both stereotyped but a mixed-race person could be even more stereotyped.

Stereotypes facing Black males predicate on notions of rebellious, anti-school attitudes and hyper-masculinity (Sewell, 1997). Such stereotypes have also proven pervasive in the Black mixed-race context (Tikly et al., 2004). These stereotypes facing Black mixed-race males, as James testifies, coalesce with the somewhat less recognised, yet longstanding, stereotypical views of Black/white mixedness. Born out of fears over the degenerative embodiment of miscegenation, these pathologies, though heavily jettisoned from academic thought, can be traced, in 'sociological' work, to Everett Stonequist's (1961) marginal-man thesis in which he posited that the Black mixed-race individual suffers from maladjustment and identity confusion due to their positioning between Black and white worlds. Williams (2011, 30) study finds evidence of such views amongst teachers: 'They are bound to struggle with their identity. They can't see where they fit in.'

Trevor Phillips, then head of the Equality and Human Rights Commission, shows how such notions have permeated contemporary British society. In 2007 he described mixed-race people as being susceptible to 'identity stripping' due to their precarious position between two communities (Aspinall and Song, 2013). Given his recent misleading and racist assault on Black Britain,[3] both on the screen in a Channel 4 documentary *Things We Won't Say About Race That are True* and accompanying article in the right wing *Daily Mail*, it should come as no surprise that he pathologises mixedness in such a way (Phillips, 2015). We also see the recurrent notion of troubled home lives, attributable to the incompatibility of the two distinct cultures of their parents, often leaving single parent families. This stereotype, a residual effect of anti-miscegenation rhetoric, is evident in the 1930 pseudo-academic *Fletcher Report* in which Fletcher (1930, 26) contends of the Black mixed-race children of Liverpool, 'there is little harmony between the parents … and there appears to be little future for the children'. Williams (2011, 32) again shows how such views are held by teachers today, with one participant in her study saying, 'I think where things are unsettled at home—like they can be—it has a negative impact on the child.' Despite their prevalence, such views have been debunked by academic work (Caballero and Edwards, 2010; Twine, 2010).

Participants were also keen to note that whilst race was a salient factor, such stereotypes were often bound up with social class. The combination of being Black mixed-race, working-class and male resulted in further disadvantage:

> I think a lot for me was being working-class or being off the estate, I mean there was stuff about race as well but being working class was significant. (Kyle)

The importance of class has been highlighted in work on Black students; further research needs to look more closely at the intersection of social class for Black mixed-race students.

As stereotypes of mixedness exist alongside, and often coalesce with, stereotypes of Blackness, educators' understanding of Black mixedness must reflect this. Where viewing the Black mixed-race population as mixed, as some scholars and activists have sought to do, may preclude salient experiences of Blackness, viewing these pupils as a specific section of the Black population can create interventions in which mixedness can be acknowledged without an inadvertent disregarding of Blackness. Such an intervention would negate potential divisiveness between Black and Black mixed-race students, and in Black politics.

Self-Fulfilling Prophecies

Participants felt they were often the victim of low teacher expectations. Such low expectations have the potential to create a self-fulfilling prophecy. Merton (1968, 477) defines this state that has pervaded understandings of the Black male in education:

> The self-fulfilling prophecy is, in the beginning, a false definition of the situation evoking a new behaviour which makes the original false conception come 'true'. This specious validity of the self-fulfilling prophecy perpetuates a reign of error. For the prophet will cite the actual course of events as proof that he was right from the very beginning.

Commentators like Sewell (1997) have recognised the damaging role of low teacher expectations on Black male achievement. Heidi Mirza (BBC, 2008) asserts this point:

> We see structures that categorise black boys as failing and having bad behaviour—and then it's borne out.... We need to talk about expectations and self-fulfilling prophecies. We need to reverse some of these entrenched stereotypes.

Importantly here, Mirza notes the systemic nature of low teacher expectations. Such processes are not the result of individual teacher attitudes but, more worryingly, are a consequence of an institutionally racist, white supremacist system. The current study found evidence of such processes predicating, for the Black mixed-race male, on Blackness *and* mixedness. Participant Reece refers to the negative perception of his Blackness:

> I know while I was at school they just see us as the Black lads. Black lads that aren't interested in school and just want to cuss, but the school wasn't interested in us either so I'm not sure where that starts. They didn't care about me because they already marked me as disinterested and not the school-type, so I didn't care about them.

Rather than challenging and exploring disinterest in an attempt to raise attainment, the school was perceived to reciprocate, perpetuate and perhaps even create disinterest. Prudence Carter (2003, 148), in her work on working class African American students, argues that culturally illiterate teachers' misreading performances of Blackness oftentimes resulted in a misguided stereotype. The imposition of this stereotype was perceivable to the students. As one of her participants puts it, 'I had friends that ... were very smart. They were very, very smart, and the teachers think that they are not smart.' Taylor, a research participant in my study, shows how negative perceptions of mixedness led to his adoption of what might be considered an anti-school attitude:

> They acted like I was troubled, like it would be harder for me to learn and didn't treat me
> with the same respect as other kids. They spend too much time listening to stereotypes and
> believing them, and not enough time getting to know the kid and finding out about them.
> As it happens I wasn't particularly confused and my parents were cool but I'm not pissing
> about with teachers who've already got me marked. There are other routes than education.

In this extract from Taylor, we see how he feels the imposition of a confused state
was misguided and unjust. We also see how the imposition led to his rejection of school
and his move towards *other routes*. Through these two excerpts we see how stereotypes of
Blackness and mixedness both have the potential to lead to self-fulfilling prophecies for
this population.

Williams (2011, xiv) suggests that low teacher expectations often leave Black mixed-race
pupils 'far too prepared to live down to the stereotype'. However scholars must be wary of pathol-
ogising the Black mixed-race male and must maintain an awareness of the systemic racialised
failures of the education system that manifest as barriers to achievement. Aaron spoke in my
research about resisting low teacher expectations, using such views as motivation to achieve:

> They don't expect mixed-race pupils to do well. So that's why I made sure I did, made sure
> I'd make it to university. I like proving people wrong. I enjoyed challenging the stereotypes,
> so then maybe teachers will rethink! Having said that though, I don't think that should take
> the emphasis away from the schools and the teachers. It still should be the schools that make
> changes to accommodate the students. Not the other way round. Kids are just kids, and for
> some the stereotypes might go the other way.

Whilst this is a positive attitude, and a success story (assuming educational attainment
is the primary goal), we must be wary of heralding such exceptional cases as evidence of an
absence of racialised barriers. Such examples must not be used as a stick with which to beat
those Black mixed-race males who are unable, for a range of reasons, to overcome barriers. The
onus must remain firmly on the education system. A teacher in Williams's (2011, 31) research
suggests that school changes can challenge barriers presented by low teacher expectations:

> It's important for schools to help them see their backgrounds as a positive thing. It supports
> all our work with families and helping pupils achieve their full potential. If they see we
> value them and where they've come from they will be happier in school and they'll be more
> prepared to learn.

Given the shared history and experiential commonalities, such learning for Black mixed-
race students can take place alongside that of Black peers. What is important however, is
that the complexity of Blackness and Black mixedness is unpacked in a mutually-supportive,
non-ascriptive, environment. One participant, Trent, spoke of being included in a project
targeting Black Caribbean males that failed to unpack the complexity of his identity:

that whole project was engineered to do with race. Now, I wouldn't say it was racism because usually people associate racism with a negative undertone, a negative outcome. This wasn't that it was a positive thing but it made me think of that, erm, I loved the project and I loved the teacher, I got along with her really well the only thing I didn't like about it was, it was engineered for Black Caribbean boys.

Here, Trent acknowledges the positivity of the intervention, he 'loved the project'. What concerned him however, was the ascription of a racial identity. He continues:

I just didn't like the fact that I was classified, I was very much aware of the fact that I was classified as being a Black Caribbean boy, I always thought well, no I'm not. I'm a little bit different to them in the sense that I'm mixed-race.

It must be seen as a pedagogical error for a teacher to ascribe an identity to a student. This is of fundamental importance to any intervention made. Indeed, Black mixed-race students may identify in a number of different ways, including white, and should be facilitated to do so (Root, 1996). Emancipatory teaching should seek to work *with* students to create an environment in which identity discussions can be held (Freire, 2005).

Trent goes on to explain how, since his peer group were black and he felt that he was often seen as Black, that he would be comfortable in such a group. Trent does not argue for a specifically mixed group, but for an expansion or reconceptualisation of Blackness. Speaking hypothetically about a prospective child in such a group he felt questions must be posed:

My child is mixed-race, what would you intend to do to represent them within this project? because that's important, they're not just Caribbean … is there anything we can do with the name?

Historical figures such as Malcolm X, Mary Seacole and W.E.B. Du Bois, and more contemporarily, Barack Obama could all be used to facilitate discussions around Blackness and Black mixedness. Such discussions may have enabled Trent to feel a greater sense of validation within the project.

Handling of Racist Incidents

Teachers' handling of racist incidents was a major site of participant criticism. Despite Tikly et al. (2004, 44) highlighting the 'need to protect all mixed heritage pupils from racist bullying', several participants felt 'let-down' and unsupported by teachers when racist incidents occurred. Where racist incidents did occur they were too often dealt with in a manner that failed to reflect their seriousness. Discussing an incident in which he felt let down, Josh held that rather than a 'talking to', the pupil who had called him a racist name should have received, 'at least a suspension, second time would be exclusion. No doubt about that in my mind'.

Other participants shared Josh's views that the handlings of racist incidents were insufficient. Owing to a perception of a soft approach to racism two participants resorted to violence. Talking of an incident where he was called 'nigger' Harry elucidated:

> Well, punishment probably wouldn't be enough; I wouldn't feel like justice had been done if the teachers dealt with it, what's an afternoon detention?… I ended up smashin' him up at the bus stop but then I got suspended for that.

We may observe here how the failures of teachers to deal with incidents in a manner proportionate to the seriousness attributed by the victim can lead to a downward spiral for the Black mixed-race male. Harry felt that he needed to take the matter into his own hands. In doing so Harry may have inadvertently fulfilled the stereotypes attributed to him as a Black mixed-race male; confused, angry, confrontational and anti-school. We see here the complex way in which self-fulfilling prophecies may play out. A robust initial response from the school may have negated the violence and the perpetuation of the stereotype. Reflecting on the incident, Harry said, 'I thought that was wrong because he didn't get suspended I thought we both should of.' Although Harry's example is a particularly pertinent one, several participants recalled similarly negative experiences and a subsequent lack of faith in the school and teachers. Whilst participants primarily directed their criticisms at individual teachers, it became clear that a more robust school level policy for dealing with racist incidents would prove effective. It is unclear to what extent individual teachers, educated in a fundamentally racist education system, would have the expertise to deal with such incidents (Bourdieu, 1974, Tomlinson, 2008). Invisibility from policy proved to be to the detriment of the Black mixed-race male in these instances. We may see how such invisibility operates through what Delgado and Stefancic (2001) describe as *structural determinism*. As teachers are socialised in a racist structure that seeks to preserve conditions of inequity, they are unable to 'envision and name a new or different concept that could lead to greater racial justice' (Anderson, 2015, 4). Whilst racist abuse was generally invisible, an awareness of the unique experiences of the Black mixed-race population, who received racial prejudice from both white and Black peers, was further invisible. Tikly et al. (2004, 84), in their study of Black mixed-race pupils, found that the high-achieving schools in their sample had 'effective systems in place for recording of racist incidents and bullying and for responding to these'.

Lloyd, a participant educated in an inner city, racially mixed school suggested another solution,

> I think one advantage of having more ethnic minority staff is that they'd understand racism and perhaps be more empathetic. I'd feel better approaching a minority teacher to discuss racism.

The idea of a diversification of the workforce was a recurrent theme throughout the research. As responses showed, however, this was more complex than merely introducing a few teachers of a darker hue.

Interventions: A Diverse Workforce?

Children learn more from what you are than what you teach. (W.E.B. Du Bois, in Griffin, 2012, 60)

The recruitment of teaching staff from diverse backgrounds has long been cited as an intervention to challenge the underachievement of certain groups (Gordon, 2002; Ross, 2001). Research conducted in 2012 found that 93.3% of the school workforce were white (DfE, 2013), compared to 85.5% of England's total population (ONS, 2011). A multitude of barriers to the retention of teachers who are not white have been noted (McNamara et al., 2009; Mirza and Meetoo, 2012). A disproportionate number of staff of colour occupy non-teaching and unqualified positions (BBC, 2002) and there is recognition of a 'glass ceiling' preventing these reaching more senior roles (Menter et al., 2003; Osler, 1997). Participants problematised the underrepresentation of Black, Black mixed-race and all teachers of colour.

Black Role Models

If they see black teachers, they will aspire to be teachers themselves. (Asthana, 2007)

The complex relationship between Blackness and mixedness is evident when we consider the function of role models. When asked about role models Jamie said this:

> Yeah I think Black teachers do good for mixed-race kids in school. I mean we have one Black parent and one white. We got the white role models so just need some Black as well.

Tyrone, identifying with Blackness, expressed similar views:

> More Black teachers need to be in schools because of the Black people in the schools, they need someone to look up to and relate to, they might be looking up seeing all these rucks and thinking 'where are the black teachers?', subconsciously giving the message that we're not good enough, we're not successful.

In both these instances participants feel that the introduction of more Black role models would prove advantageous. We see the vast commonality between Black and Black mixed-race males. The response from Tyrone suggests that white teachers are unable to provide 'someone to look up to' for him. In referring to a 'we', Tyrone positions himself outside of the white hegemonic education system and as part of a Black mixed group. Indeed, the privilege and security of whiteness is not an option Tyrone feels is available; he finds his identity in Blackness and mixedness. This becomes problematic when we see the British education system (and Western society at large) transmit a message that Blackness is inferior. Here we see, once more, how stereotypes and self-fulfilling prophecies come to fruition. The failure of the education system to provide role models for pupils leads to the internalisation of the idea that 'we're not good enough, we're not successful'. In many cases, the internalisation of the idea means it is borne out.

Whilst the above excerpts highlight the commonalities with Blackness, other participants did recognise the specific needs of the Black mixed-race male. Whilst for Jamie (above) the provision of role models was merely additive (a white role model plus a Black role model is sufficient) for others mixed-race was something more than this and needed to be reflected in any diversification:

> I guess ideally you'd have the broadest range of teachers that is at least as diverse as the population; mixed-race should be included in that. (Daz)
>
> We need mixed-race role models in schools, the population is growing and we need people to look up to. (Jack)

Not only do these comments show the need to move beyond simplistic understandings of Blackness and mixedness but also the vast heterogeneity in Black mixed-race experiences. Like Daz, participants felt that the school workforce should reflect society and provide representation for all pupils. Maylor (2006, 2) suggests, '[h]aving a teaching force that better represents society is critical because of the character, ubiquity, pervasiveness, duration and importance of teaching as a social activity.' The specific importance of a diverse teaching force for those of mixed-race was further highlighted by Tikly et al. (2004, 9) who found the schools in which mixed-race students were 'high achieving' were those that 'reflected diversity … amongst the staff'. The report recommended that schools look to recruit more black and mixed-race teachers as part of a wider diversification, suggesting that this 'can help to affirm mixed heritage identities and challenge the negative stereotypes'.

More than Just Race

It is a mistake to assume that because someone is from a particular ethnic group … that they will respond in a generalistic way. (Morrison, 2008)

Research suggests that it is not enough for the teacher to be someone of the same colour, but it needs to be someone that does not believe the stereotypes. (Phoenix, 2014)

Whilst maintaining that workforce diversification was ideal, participants also felt that it should be about more than race and that teaching ability should be the primary criterion. Jamal made this point, 'the teacher's ability doesn't matter to skin colour'. Positive relationships with white teachers and negative relationships with Black teachers further undercut simplistic assumptions that the introduction of ethnic minority teachers would offer an instantaneous solution. Tyrone, talking of positive experiences with a white teacher, challenges such assumptions:

> I had a teacher that came to the school at the time I was starting to fail and I ended up in her class, she was such an inspiration, she was genuinely interested in me and she even found out about my performances in other classes … she also helped out a couple of other mixed-race kids, I really think she targeted us like that and I'll never forget that.

A number of scholars have sought to (at least partially) shift the focus away from the calls to recruit more Black teachers, and have emphasised the importance of 'culturally responsive teaching' (Gay, 2000) or, as Ladson-Billings (1995) puts it, 'culturally relevant pedagogy'. Such an intervention affirms that teachers, regardless of racial background, must 'develop the knowledge, skills, and predispositions to teach children from diverse racial, ethnic, language, and social class backgrounds' (Weinstein et al., 2003, 270; Mirza and Meeto, 2012). In the misguided ascription of stereotypes, it is conceivable that culturally responsive teaching, more so than a diverse teaching force, can offer an intervention. To refer back to the earlier example from Carter's (2003) work, a culturally responsive teacher would have disentangled students' potential from performances of Blackness.

Examples of negative experiences with Black teachers also brought to the fore the flaws in the assumptions that a more diverse workforce, alone, would offer the solution. This is exemplified by a respondent in Tikly et al.'s (2004, 48) research, who recalled an incident with a Black teacher:

> We [teacher and pupil] was like arguing at the classroom, and she wants to start cussing me, so I cussed her back, and she said at least she's fully Black or something like that.

Not only does this trouble the assumption that more staff of colour will offer an absolute solution but it also reminds us that there are times when specific provisions need to be made for Black mixed-race pupils.

Further concerns were raised over the tokenism of Black representation. 'Making sure the teaching force is simply 'representative' could be seen just as tokenism—making sure there are enough black faces around' (Maylor, 2006, 2). Concerns over such tokenism were evident in participants' experiences,

> I remember we got this black guy coming in … I don't know what his role was actually, he was just there … he just came out of nowhere; they just dropped a black guy in. (Isaac)

Jermaine shared a similar experience:

> This Black guy called Earl, he was supposed to be a mentor but he really didn't do much, didn't really have a proper role, he was just there … You're meant to 'relate' and to 'build a bridge' but it just doesn't work like that.

For both participants the authenticity of the integration was important. It became clear that merely recruiting more staff of colour would not automatically meet their needs. In the two instances above tokenism could be seen as counterintuitive transmitting the idea that Black staff are not worthy of a 'proper role'. This therefore runs the risk of such ideas being internalised by pupils. As Tyrone observed in an earlier excerpt, this can not only fail to break down barriers but can actually create a barrier 'subconsciously giving the message that we're not good enough'. Although Tikly et al. (2004) recognise such mentoring and role model schemes as positive interventions participant responses suggest experiences are more complex. Whilst Diane Abbott's claim that by having a 'critical mass of black teachers in the workforce you get a more culturally literate workforce overall' may be true, this offers far from a holistic picture (Asthana, 2007). Indeed, given that many of the teachers of colour will have been educated and raised in a white supremacist society, it should not be taken for granted that they will not perpetuate hegemonic Whiteness. Training and the raising of teacher awareness, alongside a continued drive to recruit staff of colour, offers the way forward. As a focus group member in Williams (2011, 41) advises, schools should 'give teachers more training on understanding the needs of mixed-race students'. This point is of fundamental importance; culturally relevant pedagogy must recognise the complexity of what it means to be Black mixed-race.

CONCLUSION

This chapter has attempted to highlight some of the needs of a significant, yet massively under researched, proportion of the Black British population. The chapter has considered the role of low teacher expectations, the handling of racist incidents, and to what extent a more diverse workforce might offer an intervention. Whilst the great commonalities between Black males and Black mixed-race males must be considered, there remain unique aspects of mixedness that are unaccounted for in work on Black male educational experiences. It is hoped that this chapter will help us move towards a more nuanced understanding that simultaneously recognises the Black mixed-race male as part of the Black population, and recognises the unique aspects of their mixed identities. As Williams (2011, 17) notes:

> There are times when it is expedient to view black and mixed-race as one group, as there are some obvious and pertinent connections to be made with pupils of black British heritage. However common stereotypes and assumptions made about mixed-race pupils should mean there are also distinct strategies employed for the mixed-race group.

Further work needs to consider the impact of social class on the racialisation of the Black mixed-race male (Aspinall and Song, 2013). There also needs to be consideration given to the Black mixed-race female in education. Finally, work needs to look more closely at the way in which Blackness and mixedness interact to create unique and specific barriers for the Black mixed-race male.

NOTES

1.   This term is used here to refer to the male population of mixed Black and white parentage.

2.   General Certificate of Secondary Education (GCSE) is an academic qualification gained by pupils at the age of 14–16. GCSE attainment is traditionally used as a determinant for further study.

3.   His position was so extremely conservative that he was dubbed a 'modern day Uncle Tom' by activist group, the Organisation of Black Unity (2015).

REFERENCES

Anderson, C. (2015) What are you? A CRT perspective on the experiences of mixed race persons in 'post-racial' America. *Race Ethnicity and Education*, 18(1): 1–19.

Andrews, K. (2014) Toward a Black Radical Independent Education: Black Radicalism, Independence and the Supplementary School Movement. *The Journal of Negro Education*, 83: 5–14.

Aspinall, P. and Song, M. (2013) *Mixed Race Identities*. Basingstoke: Palgrave Macmillan.

Asthana, A. (2007) More black teachers will end underachievement, says MP. *The Observer*, December 2.

BBC. (2002) Male Black teachers needed. *News,* http://news.bbc.co.uk/1/hi/education/1747096.stm

BBC. (2008) 'Stereotype' fear from race data. *News,* http://news.bbc.co.uk/1/hi/education/7746004.stm

Bourdieu, P. (1974) 'The School as a Conservative Force: Scholastic and Cultural Inequalities'. In J. Eggleston (ed.) *Contemporary Research in the Sociology of Education*. London: Routledge.

Caballero, C. and Edwards, R. (2010) *Lone Mothers of Mixed Racial and Ethnic Children: Then and Now*. London: The Runnymede Trust.

Carter, P. (2003) "Black" Cultural Capital, Status Positioning and Schooling Conflicts for Low-Income African American Youth. *Social Problems*, 50(1): 136–155.

Coard, B. (1971) *How the West Indian Child is Made Educationally Subnormal in the British School System: The Scandal of the Black Child in Schools in Britain*. London: New Beacon Books.

Delgado, R. and Stefancic, J. (2001) *Critical Race Theory: An Introduction*. New York: New York University Press.

DfE. (2014a) *GCSE and Equivalent Attainment by Pupil Characteristics in England 2012/2013*, https://www.gov.uk/government/publications/gcse-and-equivalent-attainment-by-pupil -characteristics-2012-to-2013.

DfE. (2014b) *Permanent and Fixed Period Exclusions in England: 2012 to 2013: Statistical First Release*. London: Department for Education, Children, Education and Skills.

DfE. (2013) *'School Workforce in England'*. November 2012, SFR 15/2013.

DfES. (2003) *Aiming High: Understanding the Needs of Minority Ethnic Pupils in Mainly White Schools*. London: Her Majesty's Stationery Office.

Fletcher, M.E. (1930) *Report on an Investigation into the Colour Problem in Liverpool and Other Ports, Liverpool*. Liverpool: Association for the Welfare of Half Caste Children.

Freire, P. (2005) *Pedagogy of the Oppressed: 30th Anniversary Edition*. New York: Continuum International Publishing.

Gay, G. (2000) *Culturally Responsive Teaching: Theory, Research, and Practice*. New York: Teachers College Press.

Gillborn, D. (2014) Racism as Policy: A Critical Race Analysis of Education Reforms in the United States and England. *The Education Forum*, 78: 26–41.

Gillborn, D. and Gipps, C.V. (1996) *Recent Research on the Achievements of Ethnic Minority Pupils*. London: HMSO.

Gordon, J. (2002) *The Color of Teaching*. London: Routledge.

Griffin, J. (2012) *Striving for Greatness: Living, Learning, Loving*. Bloomington: iUniverse Books.

Hall, S. (1996) 'New Ethnicities'. In Chen, K. and D. Morley (eds.) *Critical Dialogues in Cultural Studies*. London: Routledge.

Ladson-Billings, G. (1995) Toward a Theory of Culturally Relevant Pedagogy. *American Educational Research Journal*, 31(3): 465–491.

Maylor, U. (2006) *Black Teachers in London*. Institute of Education: The University of London.

McNamara, O., Howson, J., Gunter, H. and Fryers, A. (2009) *The Leadership Aspirations and Careers of Black and Minority Ethnic Teachers*. NASUWT.

Menter, I., Hextall, I. and Mahony, P. (2003) Rhetoric or Reality? Ethnic Monitoring in the Threshold Assessment of Teachers in England and Wales. *Race Ethnicity and Education*, 6: 307–330.

Merton, R.K. (1968) *Social Theory and Social Structure*. London: Simon and Schuster.

Mirza, H.S. and Meetoo, V. (2012) *Respecting Difference: Race, Faith and Culture for Teacher Educators*. Institute of Education, University of London.

Morrison, S. (2008) How important are role models? *The Guardian*, November 11.

ONS. (2011) *Ethnic Groups, Local Authorities in England and Wales*: Table KS201EW.

Organisation of Black Unity (2015) Beware the modern day Uncle Tom. *Make it Plain,* http://www.blackunity.org.uk/make-it-plain/

Osler, A. (1997) *The Education and Careers of Black Teachers: Changing Identities, Changing Lives*. Buckingham: Open University Press.

Osler, A. and Hill, J. (1999). Exclusion from School and Racial Equality: An Examination of Government Proposals in the Light of Recent Research Evidence. *Cambridge Journal of Education*, 29(1): 33–62.

Phillips, T. (2015) Explosive truths about race we're not allowed to talk about: The political class's failure to confront unpalatable facts has had appalling consequences, says ex-head of equality watchdog. *Daily Mail,* March 15.

Phoenix, A. (2014) *Black and Minority Ethnic (BME) in the Academe*. Sussex University.

Richardson, R. (2005). *Race Equality and Education: A Practical Resource for the School Workforce*. Association of Teachers and Lecturers.

Root, M. (ed.) (1996) *The Multiracial Experience: Racial Borders as the New Frontier*. London: Sage.

Ross, A. (2001) Ethnic Minority Teachers in the Teaching Workforce. *Institute of Policy Studies Occasional Paper*. London: London Metropolitan University.

Sewell, T. (1997) *Black Masculinities and Schooling: How Black Boys Survive Modern Schooling.* Stoke-on-Trent: Trentham Books.

Stonequist, E.V. (1961). *The Marginal Man: A Study in Personality and Culture Conflict.* New York: Russell & Russell.

Tikly, L., Caballero, C., Haynes, J. and Hill, J. (2004). *Understanding the Educational Needs of Mixed Heritage Pupils.* London: Department for Education and Skills.

Tizard, B. and Phoenix, A. (2002) *Black, White or Mixed Race?: Race and Racism in the Lives of Young People of Mixed Parentage.* London: Routledge.

Tomlinson, S. (2008) *Race and Education: Policy and Politics in Britain.* Maidenhead: McGraw-Hill International.

Twine, F.W. (2010) *A White Side of Black Britain: Interracial Intimacy and Racial Literacy.* Durham, NC: Duke University Press.

Warmington, P. (2014). *Black British Intellectuals and Education: Multiculturalism's Hidden History.* London: Routledge.

Weinstein, C., Curran, M., and Tomlinson-Clarke, S. (2003) Culturally Responsive Classroom Management: Awareness into Action. *Theory into Practice*, 42(3): 269–276.

Williams, D. (2011) *Mixed Matters: Mixed-race Pupils Discuss School and Identity.* Troubador Publishing.

PART 3C

RACISM AND EMPLOYMENT

The chapters in this section address an essential part of the experience of a racialized existence—the search for livelihood. The chapters suggest that the salience of racial hierarchies strike at the very heart of the experience of membership in society for racialized minorities in metropolitan societies, a condition that is identified as both historical and contemporary. Work is central to the process of citizenship and so the inequalities that racialized minorities are subjected to undermine their ability to aspire to full citizenship and create a condition of social exclusion that threatens the entire society as they corrode the glue that should keep it together.

FURTHER READING

Bonacich, Edna. 1972. "A Theory of Ethnic Antagonism: The Split Labour Market." *American Sociological Review* 37(5): 547–559.
In "A Theory of Ethnic Antagonism," Edna Bonacich argues that ethnic antagonism or inter-group conflicts are a key source of the split labour market in the United States. In discussing the wage and labour disparities between Blacks and whites, Bonacich cautions that attributing the differences in the price of labour to race or ethnicity alone is highly simplistic; it neglects the complexity of economic processes.

Das Gupta, Tania. 1996. *Racism and Paid Work.* Toronto: Garamond Press.
Race, gender, and class are traditionally defining features of employment systems and processes. In *Racism and Paid Work*, Tania Das Gupta shows how the interactions of racism, sexism, and capitalism serve to oppress and marginalize ethnic minority and female workers. Writing from a Marxist, feminist, and anti-racist framework, Das Gupta explores the lived experiences of workers in the garment manufacturing and health care sectors in Ontario, Canada, and shows how racism and sexism are deeply entrenched in paid work.

Dipboye, Robert L., and Adrienne Colella, eds. 2005. *Discrimination at Work: The Psychological and Organizational Bases.* Mahwah, NJ: Lawrence Erlbaum Associates.
Discrimination at Work is an eclectic compilation of research, theories, and perspectives on discrimination in the workplace. As a part of the Organizational Frontier Series, this volume explores workplace discrimination at the individual, group, and organizational levels,

identifying its manifestations based on race and ethnicity, religion, sexual orientation, age, disability, personality, as well as physical appearance. The result is a comprehensive volume that integrates the varied disciplines, literatures, and bodies of research that address workplace discrimination, and lays the foundation for a general model of an important issue.

Galabuzi, Grace-Edward. 2006. *Canada's Economic Apartheid: The Social Exclusion of Racialized Groups in the New Century.* Toronto: Canadian Scholars' Press.
In this book, Galabuzi provides an engaging account of the experiences of racialized groups in the Canadian labour market. Rich in theoretical and empirical analysis, the book shows how racialized groups, albeit highly educated and a vital source of much-needed population growth, continue to experience significant disadvantages and social exclusion in the Canadian labour market, and in the "democratic" Canadian state in general.

Macedo, Donald, and Panayota Gounari, eds. 2006. *The Globalization of Racism.* Boulder, CO: Paradigm Publishers.
Addressing ethnic cleansing, culture wars, human suffering, terrorism, immigration, and intensified xenophobia, this book explains why it is vital that we gain understanding of how ideology underlies all social, cultural, and political discourse and racist actions. The authors look at recent developments all over the globe and use examples from the mass media, popular culture, and politics to address the challenges faced by democratic institutions.

Oreopoulos, Philip. 2011. "Why Do Skilled Immigrants Struggle in the Labour Market? A Field Experiment with Thirteen Thousand Resumes." *American Economic Journal: Economic Policy* 3(November): 148–171.

Although most immigrants to Canada today are highly educated and professionally qualified, they are severely underemployed in the labour market. Scholars have argued that a number of factors have contributed to this, including racism on the basis of devaluation of non-Canadian educational degrees, absence of "Canadian work experience," and perceived official language skills. This article focuses on a controlled experiment conducted by the author involving thousands of mock resumes of candidates with English, Greek, Chinese, Indian, and Pakistani names educated in their countries of origin in internationally recognized educational institutions with varied levels of Canadian education and work experiences. These resumes were sent to potential employers, and based on a statistical analysis of their responses, the author concludes that employers discriminate among candidates based on their names, assuming that those with Indian, Pakistani, and Chinese names would lack official language and communication skills, and therefore would not consider hiring them. Interestingly, those with Greek names were also eliminated by employers in the same way. Moreover, those with non-English names would not be hired even when they acquired education from well-known institutions in their countries of origin and in Canada upon arrival. The author recommends that in order to minimize or eliminate this racial discrimination at the point of screening job applicants, employers should initiate hiring procedures in which the applicants' names would be masked prior to short listing them.

Chapter 29

Colour Coded Labour Markets

Sheila Block and Grace-Edward Galabuzi

In this chapter, Block and Galabuzi (2011) discuss the racially segmented nature of the Canadian labour market and its implications for racialized poverty. The study found that, despite years of significant economic growth, an increasingly racially diverse population was not participating in the benefits of the economic expansion.

   The data show that while racialized Canadians have a slightly higher level of participation in the labour market than other Canadians (they are working or available to work even when unemployed), they experience a significant double-digit income gap stemming from racial disparities in the distribution of good pay, secure jobs, and labour market opportunities. They are also disproportionately subject to precarious forms of work, are subject to racially defined segmentation in the labour market, and are underrepresented in unionized core manufacturing, public services, and the financial sector. The authors encountered a persistent colour code in the way racialized people are incorporated into the Canadian labour market that blocks them from realizing the benefits of their investment in education, internationally obtained credentials, and experience.

EXECUTIVE SUMMARY

The last available census data before the federal government cancelled the country's mandatory long form Census reveals a troubling trend in Canada.

Despite years of unprecedented economic growth and an increasingly diverse population, this report confirms what so many Canadians have experienced in real life: a colour code is still at work in Canada's labour market.

Racialized[1] Canadians encounter a persistent colour code that blocks them from the best paying jobs our country has to offer.

This report uses the 2006 long form Census data to compare work and income trends among racialized and non-racialized Canadians during the heyday of the economic boom.

It finds that even in the best of economic times, the pay gap between racialized and non-racialized Canadians is large: Racialized Canadians earn only 81.4 cents for every dollar paid to non-racialized Canadians.

The income gap stems from disparities in the distribution of good paying, more secure jobs.

The data show racialized Canadians have slightly higher levels of labour market participation, yet they continue to experience higher levels of unemployment and earn less income than non-racialized Canadians.

The work they're able to attain is much more likely to be insecure, temporary, and low paying. For example, this report shows that racialized Canadians are over-represented in a range of traditionally low-paid business services ranging from call centres to security services to janitorial services, while non-racialized Canadians are not.

The data show that if there is work to do, racialized Canadians are willing to do it: 67.3% of racialized Canadians are in the labour force—slightly higher than non-racialized Canadians (66.7%).

Though they're more willing to work, all racialized groups—except those who identify as Japanese and Filipino—tend to find themselves on the unemployment line more often than non-racialized Canadians. Racialized men are 24% more likely to be unemployed than non-racialized men. Racialized women have it worse: They're 48% more likely to be unemployed than non-racialized men. This may contribute to the fact that racialized women earn 55.6% of the income of non-racialized men.

The Census data makes clear: Between 2000 and 2005, during the one of the best economic growth periods for Canada, racialized workers contributed to that economic growth but they didn't enjoy the benefits.

On average, non-racialized Canadian earnings grew marginally (2.7%) during this period—tepid income gains considering the economy grew by 13.1%. But the average income of racialized Canadians *declined* by 0.2%.

And this was before recession hit Canada in 2008.

The findings raise troubling questions about one of the fastest growing groups in Canadian society. The demographic composition of Canada is quickly changing, but labour market policies are lagging. In the 1980s, racialized groups accounted for less than 5% of Canada's population. By the 2001 Census, racialized Canadians made up 13.4% of the population. Between the 2001 and 2006 Census taking, that population had grown by 27%—five times faster than the rate of growth for the broader Canadian population. In 2006, 16.2% of the population came from a racialized group. By 2031, it's estimated racialized Canadians will make up 32% of the population.

The country's demographic composition is undergoing major transformation. If the labour market continues to relegate workers from racialized groups to the back of the pack, the number of Canadians left behind will only accelerate—calling into question the promise that Canada is a fair and caring society committed to equal opportunities, no matter who you are and where you come from.

Default explanations like "it takes a while for immigrants to integrate" don't bear out. Even when you control for age and education, the data show first generation racialized Canadian men earn only 68.7% of what non-racialized first-generation Canadian men earn, indicating a colour code is firmly at play in the labour market. Here, the gender gap—at play throughout the spectrum—becomes disturbingly large: Racialized women immigrants earn only 48.7 cents for every dollar non-racialized male immigrants earn.

The colour code persists for second generation Canadians with similar education and age. The gap narrows, with racialized women making 56.5 cents per dollar non-racialized men earn; while racialized men earn 75.6 cents for every dollar non-racialized men in this cohort earn.

While noting many similarities across different racialized groups, the report also high-lights some differences. For example, the gap in earnings ranges from 69.5 cents per dollar for those who identify as Korean to 89 cents per dollar for those who identify as Chinese.

This report captures the ongoing racialization of poverty in Canada. Poverty rates for racialized families are three times higher than non-racialized families. In 2005, 19.8% of racialized families lived in poverty, compared to 6.4% of non-racialized families.

Finally, the report makes the links between low-income jobs, the racialization of poverty, and the impacts both have on the health of racialized Canadians.

THE GAP FOR RACIALIZED WORKERS: CANADA'S COLOUR CODED LABOUR MARKET

In recent decades, the profile of the Canadian population has changed dramatically. It has become one of the more racially diverse nations on the planet. Census data shows that between 2001 and 2006, over three quarters of immigrants to Canada came from the global South or countries with racialized majority populations. By 2006, the long form Census enumer-ated 5,068,100 individuals who belonged to the racialized population—16.2% of the total population—in Canada. Between 2001 and 2006, the racialized population increased at a much faster pace than the total population. The rate of growth was 27.2%, five times faster than the 5.4% increase for the Canadian population as a whole.[2]

By 2006, the six largest racialized groups in Canada were, in order of size:

1. South Asian (1,262,900 or 25% of racialized groups)
2. Chinese (1,216,600; 24%)
3. Black or African Canadian (783,800; 15.5%)
4. Arab & West Asian (422,200; 8.3%)
5. Filipino (410,700; 8.1%)
6. Latin American (304,200; 6%)

Statistics Canada estimates racialized groups will make up a third of Canada's population—one in three Canadians—by 2031.[3] This transformation has been rapid, from less than 5% of Canada's population in the 1980s to a projected 32% 20 years from now. It results from both changes in immigration patterns and higher birth rates among racialized Canadians. The racialized population will continue to be younger than the rest of the population, with 36% under age 15 in 2031 and only 18% predicted to be over 65.

The Colour Coded Nature of Work: Who's Working?

Table 29.1 shows the participation, employment, and unemployment rates for racialized and non-racialized Canadians in 2006, the last year of reliable long form Census data available. These data show racialized Canadians have slightly higher participation rates in Canada's paid job market than those who are not racialized. The participation rate for racialized Canadians was 67.3%, compared to 66.7% for non-racialized Canadians. Though they tend to be more willing to work, racialized workers also experience higher unemployment rates—2.4 percentage points higher than non-racialized Canadians. The gap is worse for racialized women, whose unemployment rate was 1.5 percentage points higher than racialized men and 3 percentage points higher than non-racialized men.

TABLE 29.1: EMPLOYMENT, UNEMPLOYMENT, AND PARTICIPATION RATES (PERCENT), CANADA, 2006

	RACIALIZED			NON RACIALIZED		
	MEN	WOMEN	TOTAL	MEN	WOMEN	TOTAL
Participation rate	73.1	62.0	67.3	72.2	61.5	66.7
Employment rate	67.3	56.2	61.5	67.7	57.8	62.6
Unemployment rate	7.8	9.3	8.6	6.3	6.1	6.2

Source: Statistics Canada, 2006 Census—Catalogue Number 97-562-XCB2006013.

Table 29.2 shows a great deal of consistency in the experience of work and unemployment across racialized groups. The majority of racialized Canadians, more than 60% of the adult racialized population, have higher labour force participation rates than non-racialized Canadians. Those who identify as Japanese, Chinese, Korean or Arab/West Asian have lower labour force participation rates than non-racialized Canadians. However, all racialized communities, except those who identify as Japanese or Filipino, have higher unemployment rates than non-racialized Canadians. Of those remaining racialized communities, the differences in unemployment rates from the non-racialized population are significant. The unemployment rate for those who identify as Chinese was 21% higher than non-racialized Canadians. The unemployment rate was 95% higher for those who identify as West Asian/Arab and 73% higher for those who identify as Black.

TABLE 29.2: EMPLOYMENT, UNEMPLOYMENT, AND PARTICIPATION RATES (PERCENT), BY RACIALIZED GROUP, CANADA, 2006

	PARTICIPA-TION RATE	EMPLOY-MENT RATE	UNEMPLOY-MENT RATE
Total Racialized population	67.3	61.5	8.6
Chinese	62.0	57.3	7.5
South Asian[1]	68.5	62.6	8.6
Black	70.7	63.2	10.7
Filipino	76.6	72.8	5.0
Latin American	71.9	65.4	9.0
Southeast Asian[2]	68.9	63.1	8.5
Arab/West Asian	64.1	56.3	12.1
Korean	54.8	50.1	8.5
Japanese	61.6	58.5	5.1
Visible minority, n.i.e.[3]	71.1	65.6	7.8
Multiple visible minority[4]	72.7	66.5	8.5
Non Racialized[5]	66.7	62.6	6.2

1. For example, 'East Indian', 'Pakistani', 'Sri Lankan', etc.
2. For example, 'Vietnamese', 'Cambodian', 'Malaysian', 'Laotian', etc.
3. The abbreviation 'n.i.e.' means 'not included elsewhere'. Includes respondents who reported a write-in response such as 'Guyanese', 'West Indian', 'Kurd', 'Tibetan', 'Polynesian', 'Pacific Islander', etc.
4. Includes respondents who reported more than one visible minority group by checking two or more mark-in circles, e.g., 'Black' and 'South Asian'.
5. Includes respondents who reported 'Yes' to the Aboriginal identity question (Question 18) as well as respondents who were not considered to be members of a visible minority group.

Source: Statistics Canada—2006 Census. Catalogue Number 97-562-XCB2006013.

Racialized Inequalities in Paid Work

Tables 29.3 and 29.4 show the distribution of racialized and non-racialized groups in the labour force by occupation and by industry. The *all industries* and *all occupations* figures at the top of the table show the racialized share of the total labour force, 7.7% for racialized men and 7% for racialized women. Any occupation or industry that has a racialized labour force share lower than 7% shows an under-representation of racialized women workers. Any that has a higher share has an over-representation of racialized women workers. Similarly, any occupation or industry that has a racialized labour force share lower than 7.7% has an under-representation of racialized male workers; any that has a higher share has an over-representation of racialized male workers.

Racialized men are highly over-represented in natural and applied sciences occupations and in processing, manufacturing, and utilities occupations but also over-represented in management and trades, transport, and equipment operators. Racialized women are highly over-represented in health occupations, and in processing, manufacturing, and utilities occupations, and over-represented in business, finance, and administrative, and sales and service occupations. On the other hand, racialized women are under-represented in management; art, culture, recreation, and sport; trades, transport, and equipment operators; and occupations

TABLE 29.3: LABOUR FORCE BY OCCUPATION, CANADA, 2006 (PERCENT)

	RACIALIZED		NON RACIALIZED	
	MEN	WOMEN	MEN	WOMEN
All occupations	7.7	7.0	45.0	40.3
Management	8.2	4.6	55.1	32.1
Business, finance, and administrative	5.4	9.8	23.2	61.6
Natural and applied sciences and related	15.8	4.8	62.4	17.1
Health	4.3	12.0	15.6	68.1
Social science, education, government service, and religion	4.2	7.3	27.7	60.8
Art, culture, recreation, and sport	5.2	5.2	39.6	49.9
Sales and service occupations	7.4	9.1	35.1	48.4
Trades, transport, and equipment operators and related	9.5	0.9	83.6	6.0
Occupations unique to primary industry	3.3	1.8	74.4	20.5
Occupations unique to processing, manufacturing, and utilities	14.0	11.2	52.7	22.1

Source: Statistics Canada—2006 Census. Catalogue Number 97-564-XCB2006009 and authors' calculations.

in primary industry. Racialized men are under-represented in business, finance, and administrative; health; art, culture, recreation, and sport; as well as occupations unique to primary industry. It is important to note that these data do not reveal the vertical distribution of racialized women and men within these occupations.

Table 29.4 breaks down racialized and non-racialized groups by industry. Racialized men are highly over-represented in manufacturing, and transportation and warehousing, but also over-represented in wholesale trade, administrative, support, and waste management and remediation services as well as professional, technical, and scientific services. Racialized men are highly under-represented in agriculture, forestry, fishing, mining, oil and gas extraction, health care and social assistance, educational services, arts, entertainment and recreation, and public administration. Racialized women are highly over-represented in finance, insurance, health care and social assistance, accommodation and food services, and the category of activities covered by 'other services'. They are highly under-represented in mining, oil and gas extraction, agriculture, forestry, fishing, utilities, construction, transportation, warehousing, but also under-represented in public administration, the arts, entertainment and recreation, and educational services. Similarly here, we are not able to address the vertical distribution of racialized women and men in these industries.

Because these data are at a very broad industrial and occupational level, and includes all racialized groups, they do not provide the clearest picture of the racial segmentation in Canada's labour force.[4] However, some gender and race patterns are evident.

Both racialized women and men are over-represented in administrative support, waste management, and remediation services, while non-racialized men and women are not. This industry grouping covers a range of traditionally low-paid business services, ranging from call centres to security services to janitorial services. These jobs also tend to be precarious, insecure, low-paid jobs with few or no benefits.

The data show that both racialized and non-racialized men are over-represented in Canada's manufacturing sector. However, racialized men tend to land in lower paying processing and manufacturing occupations more than non-racialized men. At the same time, more non-racialized men tend to land jobs in the higher paid trades occupations than racialized men.

Even at this level of aggregation, it is possible to see the differences in the construction of gendered labour for racialized and non-racialized women. Racialized women are more likely to work in manufacturing and processing jobs than non-racialized women. Conversely, non-racialized women are more likely to work in educational services than racialized women. Racialized men are more likely to work in natural and applied sciences than non-racialized men. Racialized women are more likely to work in natural and applied sciences than non-racialized women; although, all women are under-represented in these jobs.

From a public policy perspective, the under-representation of racialized workers in public administration is of grave concern. Both racialized men and women appear to be experiencing significant barriers to access to employment in this sector. This has implications for good policy development and suggests a need to review the effectiveness of equitable hiring programs practices in the public service.

Inequalities in Employment Income

Racialized Canadians face barriers to jobs compared to non-racialized Canadians, but they also experience a significant gap in pay. As Table 29.5 shows, racialized Canadians earn 81.4 cents for every dollar paid to non-racialized Canadians.

Looking at employment earnings by gender, we see a pronounced gendered dimension to Canada's racialized income gap. The gap is at its worst when comparing the earnings of racialized women to non-racialized men.

TABLE 29.4: LABOUR FORCE BY INDUSTRY, CANADA, 2006 (PERCENT)

	RACIALIZED		NON RACIALIZED	
	MEN	WOMEN	MEN	WOMEN
All industries	7.7	7.0	45.0	40.3
Agriculture, forestry, fishing, and hunting	2.9	2.2	67.5	27.4
Mining and oil and gas extraction	3.8	1.7	78.0	16.5
Utilities	5.6	2.5	69.7	22.2
Construction	6.2	0.9	81.6	11.2
Manufacturing	12.2	6.9	58.7	22.3
Wholesale trade	10.3	6.5	56.6	26.6
Retail trade	7.2	7.9	37.6	47.3
Transportation and warehousing	11.9	3.3	63.1	21.7
Information and cultural industries	9.4	7.0	44.5	39.0
Finance and insurance	8.3	12.2	28.5	51.0
Real estate and rental and leasing	8.6	6.6	46.0	38.8
Professional, scientific, and technical services	10.2	7.0	45.2	37.6
Management of companies and enterprises	7.5	7.9	43.2	41.4
Administrative and support, waste management, and remediation services	10.2	8.7	45.3	35.9
Educational services	4.3	6.0	28.7	60.9
Health care and social assistance	3.1	11.3	14.8	70.7
Arts, entertainment, and recreation	4.2	4.3	47.1	44.3
Accommodation and food services	10.2	10.5	29.4	49.9
Other services (except public administration)	6.5	8.9	40.3	44.3
Public administration	4.0	4.1	48.8	43.1

Source: Statistics Canada—2006 Census. Catalogue Number 97-564-XCB2006009 and authors' calculations.

Racialized women earned 55.6 cents for every dollar non-racialized men earned in 2005. The gap narrows a bit when comparing the earnings of racialized and non-racialized men. Racialized men made 77.9 cents for every dollar that non-racialized men earned. The gap narrows even further when comparing racialized and non-racialized women. Racialized women earned 88.2 cents for every dollar that non-racialized women earned.

The impact of sexism on both racialized and non-racialized women may partly explain this smaller gap, as all Canadian women's earnings are depressed compared to men's earnings.

The overarching result along the dimensions of race and gender: the earnings of the three groups—racialized men, racialized women, and non-racialized women—all trailed those of non-racialized men.

The data in Table 29.5 show differences in employment income for all workers. Generally, when trying to measure the impact of discrimination, it is more appropriate to compare incomes of full-time, full-year workers. These comparisons can help isolate the impact of race and gender. However, this represents a partial picture of the racialized labour market experience, since unequal access to full-time, full-year employment is one of the barriers that racialized workers and non-racialized women workers face in the labour market.[5]

In Table 29.6 we isolate the full-time, full-year earnings of racialized workers and find that the gap shrinks somewhat to 84 cents for each dollar that non-racialized workers earn. The gap between racialized women and non-racialized men also shrinks from 55.6 cents to 63.2 cents, while those between racialized and non-racialized men goes to 81 cents.

Often, differences in outcomes in the labour market are attributed to differences in educational attainment, immigration status, or factors other than race. To control for differences in educational attainment and in age structure, Table 29.7 compares incomes for 25- to 44-year-old workers who have completed university education, by immigration generational status.

The data show a wide gap in earnings between first-generation racialized and non-racialized workers. Racialized male immigrants make 68.7 cents for every dollar that non-racialized male immigrants make. This suggests a differential impact of immigration on the two groups. We also note the significant income differential between racialized women and non-racialized men. Racialized women immigrants make 48.7 cents for every dollar that non-racialized male immigrants make.

The earnings gap persists for second-generation workers, with racialized men in this generation earning just 75.6 cents for every dollar non-racialized men make.

The data shows a sharp drop in the gap in following generations. However, comparing this group of workers requires some caution, since the sample size for racialized workers is much smaller and therefore the standard for error much larger. Moreover, the racial income gap still persists among men, although it is almost erased among women.

Income Gap Variations among Racialized Groups

There are also important variations among workers in racialized groups. Table 29.8 shows average employment incomes of various racialized groups by gender.

TABLE 29.5: AVERAGE EMPLOYMENT INCOME ($), CANADA, 2005

	RACIALIZED	NON RACIALIZED
Men	35,329	45,327
Women	25,204	28,584
Total	30,385	37,332

Source: Statistics Canada—2006 Census. Catalogue Number 97-563-XCB2006060.

TABLE 29.6: AVERAGE EMPLOYMENT INCOME: FULL-TIME, FULL-YEAR ($), CANADA, 2005

	RACIALIZED	NON RACIALIZED
Men	48,631	60,044
Women	37,932	41,872
Total	43,979	52,345

Source: Statistics Canada—2006 Census. Catalogue Number 97-563-XCB2006060.

TABLE 29.7: AVERAGE EMPLOYMENT INCOME ($), 2005, BY GENERATION, 25–44, UNIVERSITY DEGREE OR CERTIFICATE

	RACIALIZED		NON RACIALIZED		DIFFERENTIAL (%)	
	MEN	WOMEN	MEN	WOMEN	MEN	WOMEN
1st generation	45,388	32,165	66,078	39,264	68.7	81.9
2nd generation	57,237	42,804	75,729	46,391	75.6	92.3
3rd or more generation	66,137	44,460	70,962	44,810	93.2	99.2

Source: Statistics Canada—2006 Census. Catalogue Number 97-563-XCB2006060.

Employment earnings for racialized workers are lower than non-racialized workers across all racialized groups—except for the small number of Canadians who identify as Japanese. A number of groups fare particularly poorly, including:

- Those who identify as Korean: They earn 69.5 cents for every dollar a non-racialized worker earns, with an annual earnings gap of $11,403
- Those who identify as Latin Americans: They earn 70.3 cents for every dollar a non-racialized worker earns, with an annual earnings gap of $11,091
- Those who identify as West Asian: They earn 70.4 cents for every dollar a non-racialized worker earns, with an annual earnings gap of $11,053
- Those who identify as Black: They earn 75.6 cents for every dollar a non-racialized worker earns, with an annual earnings gap of $9,101

- Those who identify as South East Asians: They earn 77.5 cents for every dollar a non-racialized worker earns, with an annual earnings gap of $8,395
- Those who identify as Chinese do better: They earn 88.6 cents for every dollar a non-racialized worker earns, for an annual gap of $4,251

Table 29.9 looks at the change in earnings between 2000 and 2005. It reveals an alarming trend during what was among the best of economic growth periods for Canada: racialized workers in Canada didn't enjoy the benefits of this economic growth. Indeed a growing economy was not a solution to the income inequalities that racialized groups face. They lost ground in that period.

On average, non-racialized Canadian incomes grew marginally, by 2.7%, between 2001–05—tepid growth, given that GDP grew by 13.1% during this time period. But the average income of racialized workers in Canada declined by 0.2%. Only three racialized groups—those who identify as Latin American (0.8%), Chinese (1.9%), and Filipino (3.0%)—gained ground. All other racialized groups in Canada lost ground; particularly Korean (–4.6%), Arab (–3.3%), and those that fall under the category 'not included elsewhere' (–6.6%).

Racialization of Poverty

The racial barriers to Canadian jobs and the resulting racialized income gap has a deep impact on the health and well-being of racialized Canadians. It influences the nature of poverty in Canada and the experience of health and well-being among its citizens.

The data emerging from the last long form Census survey point to an entrenchment of the racialization of poverty. The racialization of poverty refers to a phenomenon where poverty becomes disproportionately concentrated and reproduced among racialized group members, in some cases inter-generationally. The emergence of precarious work as a major feature of Canadian labour markets is an important explanation for the racialization of poverty.

The impact of these forces accentuates historical forms of racial discrimination in the Canadian labour market and creates a process of social and economic marginalization. The result of this marginalization is a disproportionate vulnerability to poverty among racialized communities. The racialization of poverty is also linked to the entrenchment of privileged access to the economic resources in Canadian society by a powerful minority. This access explains the polarizations in income and wealth in Canada as a whole.[6]

The 2006 Census data bolsters previous evidence that racialized Canadians are disproportionately among Canada's poorest, particularly in the urban centres. Table 29.10 shows the differences in poverty rates between racialized and non-racialized Canadians. It shows poverty rates for those living in economic families and for single individuals.[7]

As Table 29.10 shows, poverty rates for racialized families are three times higher than non-racialized families. Only 6.4% of non-racialized families lived in poverty in 2005, but three times that number, 19.8% of racialized families, lived in poverty in that same year. These higher poverty rates cut across all racialized groups. Families who identify as Arab,

TABLE 29.8: AVERAGE EMPLOYMENT INCOME BY RACIALIZED GROUP ($)

	MEN	WOMEN	TOTAL
Arab	34,171	21,874	29,441
Black	31,233	25,336	28,231
Chinese	38,342	27,745	33,081
Filipino	33,141	26,960	29,491
Latin American	31,187	20,802	26,241
Japanese	60,004	32,647	45,116
Korean	30,474	21,122	25,929
Visible minority (n.i.e.)	35,414	25,938	30,666
Multiple VM	37,995	27,081	32,528
South Asian	36,904	24,081	31,102
South East Asian	34,270	23,325	28,937
West Asian	30,173	21,234	26,279
Total Racialized	35,329	25,204	30,385
Non-racialized	45,327	28,584	37,332

Source: Statistics Canada—2006 Census. Catalogue Number 97-564-XCB2006009.

TABLE 29.9: EARNINGS BY RACIALIZED GROUP, 2000 AND 2005 (IN CONSTANT 2005 DOLLARS)

	2000	2005	PERCENT CHANGE
Arab	30,452	29,441	-3.3
Black	28,215	28,012	-0.7
Chinese	32,354	32,981	1.9
Filipino	28,542	29,393	3.0
Latin American	26,034	26,241	0.8
Japanese	42,579	42,177	-0.9
Korean	27,149	25,892	-4.6
Visible minority (n.i.e.)	32,841	30,666	-6.6
South Asian	31,486	31,103	-1.2
Southeast Asian	28,958	28,880	-0.3
West Asian	27,101	26,279	-3.0
Total Racialized	30,451	30,385	-0.2
Non-racialized	36,353	37,332	2.7

Source: Statistics Canada—2006 Census. Catalogue Number 97-563-XCB2006010.

West Asian, and Korean have poverty rates above 30%—a shocking figure given the rate of economic growth during this time period. Only two groups, those who identify as Japanese and those who identify as Filipino, have poverty rates in the single digits. And those are still more than 25% higher than the poverty rate for non-racialized families.

A Question of Racial Disparities in Health

A wealth of international data makes the link between jobs, income, health, and well-being. A social determinants of health approach (SDOH) considers the full range of modifiable economic and political conditions that lead to poor health outcomes and systemic health disparities. The World Health Organization (WHO) Commission on the Social Determinants of Health states

> Employment and working conditions have powerful effects on health and health equity. When these are good they can provide financial security, social status, personal development, social relations and self-esteem and protection from physical and psychological hazards—each important for health. In addition to the direct health consequences of tackling work-related inequities the health equity impact will be even greater due to work's potential role in reducing gender, ethnic, racial and other social inequities.[8]

Work affects our health through a number of different pathways. These include the nature of work we do—whether it is full-time, part-time or contract—the income we draw, the physical or psychological strain, and the conditions of work.

A recent report from Statistics Canada provides a stark Canadian example of the impact of income and income inequality on health outcomes. It showed a clear socio-economic gradient emerged for life expectancy at age 25 for both men and women, based on data from 1991 to 2001. The difference in life expectancy between the poorest 10% and the richest 10% of Canadians was 7.4 years for men and 4.5 years for women.[9] While these differences are striking, an equally important finding is that life expectancy increases with each and every decile. The more you earn, the longer your life expectancy in Canada.

When the study considered health-related quality of life, it found the gap got worse. The richest 10% of men enjoyed 14.1 more years of healthy living than the poorest 10% of men. The richest 10% of women enjoyed 9.5 more years of healthy living than the poorest 10% of women. Among those in the middle of the income scale, the upper middle enjoyed an extra 4.7 years of health-adjusted life expectancy for men and 2.7 years for women.[10]

Unemployment, precarious work, and job strain have a negative impact on health.[11] In the Canadian context, a growing number of studies exploring the link between unemployment, underemployment, precariousness, and poor health establish an increase in health risks among poor Canadians.[12] Given the large share of racialized workers who are immigrants, the interaction between immigration status, occupation, income, low income, and health is worth noting here as well.

TABLE 29.10: AFTER-TAX LOW INCOME RATE BY RACIALIZED GROUPS (PERCENT), CANADA, 2005

	IN ECONOMIC FAMILIES			NOT IN ECONOMIC FAMILIES		
	MEN	WOMEN	TOTAL	MEN	WOMEN	TOTAL
Arab	32.0	33.1	32.5	56.5	56.2	44.3
Black	22.3	25.5	24.0	41.6	47.3	54.3
Chinese	19.6	19.4	19.5	53.8	54.7	42.3
Filipino	8.0	8.3	8.2	31.4	45.5	51.0
Latin American	19.8	21.3	20.6	46.5	57.5	41.4
Japanese	8.5	10.1	9.4	35.1	45.6	70.3
Korean	38.1	38.2	38.2	69.5	71.0	42.0
Visible minority (n.i.e.)	15.0	16.3	15.7	39.0	45.0	37.3
Multiple VM	14.0	14.6	14.3	38.0	36.8	44.0
South Asian	16.1	16.6	16.4	42.4	46.3	49.4
Southeast Asian	17.7	19.1	18.5	45.1	54.8	55.2
West Asian	31.5	33.4	32.4	52.6	60.1	48.7
Total Racialized	19.4	20.1	19.8	46.8	50.8	28.3
Non-racialized	5.9	6.9	6.4	25.8	26.5	

Note: Non-racialized/Not in economic families/Total data for this table was left blank in original and as a result was purposely left blank here, too.

Source: Statistics Canada—2006 Census. Catalogue Number 97-564-XCB2006009.

According to a recent systemic review, the majority of studies showed that immigrant workers are at high risk for occupational injuries, diseases, and death.[13] While these studies did not deal directly with the social distinction related to race, they provide an indication of the health impacts of the outcomes of labour market inequality for racialized Canadians. This is an area that requires future research to deepen our understanding of the problem of racialized poverty, barriers to good jobs in Canada, and their impact on the health of racialized Canadians.[14]

Conclusion

The makeup of Canadian society has changed rapidly in recent years. The past two long form Census surveys indicate a significant and rapid increase in the number of racialized Canadians. Census data also indicates ongoing discrimination in the workforce maintains barriers to good paying jobs and fuels a significant income gap between racialized and non-racialized Canadians.

As this study shows, racialized Canadians continue to face differential labour market experiences, which include higher levels of unemployment and lower employment earnings. The report suggests that racialized groups face a labour market in which racially defined outcomes persist and considers discrimination in employment as a contributing factor to these racial disparities in labour market outcomes.

The changing nature of the labour market is another factor responsible for the unequal outcomes. Precarious employment is on the rise—contract, temporary work arrangements with low wages, limited job security, and no benefits. Racialized groups are disproportionately represented in sectors of the economy where these forms of work are a major feature. This may be because of their vulnerability to employment discrimination and the barriers to access to professions and trades, particularly for those who are immigrants. The material implications are that racialized groups experience different socio-economic status, which has an impact on their well-being. These experiences are increasingly crystallized in the vulnerability to low income and what we have come to know as the racialization of poverty.

The unequal patterns of labour market outcomes and the vulnerabilities to racial discrimination that racialized group members and recent immigrants suffer do not only lead to disproportionately higher levels of low income. They structure a racialized experience of poverty that creates social alienation, powerlessness, marginalization, voicelessness, vulnerability, and insecurity both in the workplace and in the community. This combination of factors results in higher health risks for the racialized population.

These material conditions have the effect of both disadvantaging the racialized population but also undermining the legitimacy of the promise of multiculturalism as a regime of diversity management that can ensure equal access to opportunities for all Canadians.

NOTES

1. The term racialized is used to acknowledge 'race' as a social construct and a way of describing a group of people. Racialization is the process through which groups come to be designated as different and on that basis subjected to differential and unequal treatment. In the present context, racialized groups include those who may experience differential treatment on the basis of race, ethnicity, language, economics, religion (Canadian Race Relations Foundation, 2008). This paper uses data from the 2006 Census on visible minority status. Visible minority status is self-reported and refers to the visible minority group to which the respondent belongs. The Employment Equity Act defines visible minorities as 'persons, other than Aboriginal peoples, who are non-Caucasian in race or non-white in colour'. Census respondents were asked 'Is this person ... white, Chinese, South Asian, Black, Filipino, Latin American, Southeast Asian, Arab, West Asian, Japanese, Korean, Other (specify)'.

2. Statistics Canada, *The Daily*, April 2, 2008.

3. Statistics Canada, *The Daily*, March 9, 2010.

4. Teelucksingh, Cheryl and Grace-Edward Galabuzi, *Working Precariously: The Impact of Race and Immigrant Status on Employment Opportunities and Outcomes in Canada* (Canadian Race Relations Foundation, 2005), Table 20, p. 17.

5. Cranford, Cynthia J. and Leah F. Vosko, 'Conceptualizing precarious employment: Mapping wage work across social location and occupational context' in *Precarious Employment: Understanding Labour Market Insecurity in Canada*, Leah Vosko, ed. (Montreal and Kingston: McGill-Queen's University Press, 2005), pp. 61–66.

6. Kunz, Jean Lock, A. Milan, and Sylvain Schetagne, *Unequal Access: A Canadian Profile of Racial Differences in Education, Employment and Income* (Toronto: Canadian Race Relations Foundation, 2000); Ruth Dibbs and Tracey Leesti, *Survey of Labour and Income Dynamics: Visible Minorities and Aboriginal Peoples* (Statistics Canada, 1995); Grace-Edward Galabuzi, *Canada's Economic Apartheid: The Social Exclusion of Racialized Groups in the New Century* (Toronto: CSPI, 2006); Andrew Jackson, *"Poverty and Racism" Perception* (Canadian Council on Social Development, 24, 4, 2001); Armine Yalniyzian, *The Rich and the Rest of Us: The Changing Face of Canada's Growing Gap* (Ottawa: Canadian Centre for Policy Alternatives, 2007).

7. Statistics Canada data classifies single individuals as 'not in economic families'.

8. Commission on Social Determinants of Health. (2008). *Closing the Gap in a Generation: Health Equity through Action on the Social Determinants of Health*. Geneva: Author, p. 72.

9. McIntosh, C., P. Fines, R. Wilkins and M. Wolfson, 'Income disparities in health-adjusted life expectancy for Canadian adults, 1991 to 2001', *Health Reports* 20, no. 4 (2009), p. 58.

10. McIntosh, C., P. Fines, R. Wilkins, and M. Wolfson, 'Income disparities in health-adjusted life expectancy for Canadian adults, 1991 to 2001', *Health Reports* 20, no. 4 (2009), p. 58.

11. Block, Sheila, *Work and Health: Exploring the Impact of Employment on Health Disparities* (Toronto: Wellesley Institute, 2010).

12. Lewchuk, W., A. deWolff, A. King, and M. Polanyi, 'The hidden costs of precarious employment: Health and the employment relationship', in *Precarious Employment: Understanding Labour Market Insecurity in Canada*, Leah Vosko, ed. (Montreal and Kingston: McGill-Queen's University Press, 2005), pp. 141–162; Access Alliance, *Racialised Groups and Health Status: A Literature Review Exploring Poverty, Housing, Race-Based Discrimination and Access to Health Care as Determinants of Health for Racialised Groups* (Toronto: Author, 2005).

13. Ahonen, E.Q., F.G. Benavides, and J. Benach, 'Immigrant populations, work and health—A Systemic literature Review', *Scandinavian Journal of Work, Environment & Health* 33, no. 2 (2007), 96–104; cited in J. Benach, C. Muntaner, H. Chung, and F. Benavides, 'Immigration, employment relations and health: Developing a research agenda', *American Journal of Industrial Medicine* 53 (2010), 338–343.

14. Arundel, C., *How Are Canadians Really Doing? A Closer Look at Select Groups* (Toronto: Institute of Wellbeing, 2009); Grace-Edward Galabuzi, 'Social Exclusion', in *Social Determinants of Health: Canadian Perspectives, Second Edition*, Dennis Raphael, ed. (Toronto: Canadian Scholars' Press, 2009), pp. 252–268.

Chapter 30

The Integration of Racism into Everyday Life: The Story of Rosa N.

Philomena Essed

Essed (1991) discusses the experience of racism in the workplace with regard to the everyday activities that define the existence of racialized citizens in places such as the Netherlands. Essed's exploration includes identifying the impact of racialization in the processes of entry into the labour market and mobility within it, as well as its impacts on the conditions of work and quality of working life through its manifestation in everyday activities and situations.

Using the example of Rosa, a geriatrician in training, Essed explores the strong pressures to assimilate into Dutch society, only to suffer the indignities of a marginalized existence all the same because of the social significance of race and gender in everyday life. She argues that structures and processes of racialization play out both in the macro and micro dimensions of lived experiences of racialized people, and particularly women who are subject both to racial discrimination and patriarchy. She presents Rosa's life as defined by exclusion, underestimation, and inequality, all representing forms of oppression felt daily as they assault her dignity and material aspirations.

In discussing the method of understanding accounts of racism, it was shown how Black women expose clues and hidden messages enclosed in situations. Overemphasis on situational evidence, however, and insufficient inference from knowledge of the general processes of racism may depoliticize evidence of racism (Essed, 1990a, 1990b). The reader must bear in mind that reconstructions of events are always embedded in more complex and elaborate clusters of knowledge and social processes. The processes involved in the experience of everyday racism are further addressed in this chapter. For that purpose the focus of analysis moves from heuristics of understanding to understanding as experience and from events to interrelated experiences.

To conceptualize and to analyze racism as a process, it is relevant to look at the different dimensions of experience. In real life personal confrontations with racism merge with the experiences with racism of Black friends and family and others who are not even personally known. Furthermore racism operating in interactions with colleagues, supervisors, fellow students, or shop attendants overlaps and reinforces other experiences with racism, such as viewing negative portrayals of Blacks in the media or large-scale discrimination on the labor market. Racism experienced today reminds one of similar past experiences and influences one's expectations about tomorrow. If one unravels complex processes involving different situations and agents, as well as both personal and vicarious experiences, a coherence between practices and experiences can be revealed. [...] [I]ntrasubjective comparisons are made to give insight into simultaneous and sequential instances of racism in personal biographies. Obviously it would be too time-consuming to analyze in detail the infusion of racism into the everyday experiences of each woman. Therefore, one detailed example is given, based on the accounts of one woman, Rosa N., from the Netherlands.

Rosa N. is a geriatrician in training, the only Black in her group. In some respects her story is typically Dutch. [...] Black women in the Netherlands are subjected to strong pressure to assimilate culturally. They also sketch a more elaborate system of ideological repression, in which dominant consensus operates not only to impede equal participation but also to suppress protest against racism. We will see later that the story of Rosa N. is consistent with those of other Black women. Thus the experience of Rosa N. forms a microcosm of everyday racism. I shall demonstrate that these situations are everyday situations and that each experience acquires meaning relative to other experiences.

To examine whether the reported experiences represent everyday racism, they must be tested against the definition and main features of everyday racism. To recapitulate, everyday racism has been defined as a process in which socialized racist notions are integrated into everyday practices and thereby actualize and reinforce underlying racial and ethnic relations. Furthermore racist practices in themselves become familiar, repetitive, and part of the "normal" routine in everyday life. With these presuppositions in mind, let us now turn to the story of Rosa N.

A FRAGMENTARY REPRESENTATION OF EVERYDAY RACISM

Rosa N. was born in Suriname in 1951. She lost both of her parents before she was 10 years old. Her mother's sister adopted her, and Rosa N. was raised with four other children, all girls. After finishing high school in Suriname, she got a scholarship to study medicine in the Netherlands. After graduation she further specialized in geriatrics. In the period when she was interviewed, she was doing her internship at a modern complex for medical research. Four years earlier she had married a Dutchman, Rob, an architect. The following account, recorded in 1986, represents a moment of reflection upon some of her experiences of racism as a Black woman, trainee, and young doctor. The presentation of the story of Rosa N. is largely faithful to the order in which it was told. This may give us an impression of the way experiences of racism in different contexts and situations are associated and related to each other in accounts of racism in everyday life.

Why tell the story of Rosa N.? In many respects this reconstruction of everyday racism challenges (Dutch) commonsense notions of racism (see also Essed, 1987). Rosa N. has never been physically molested, her life has not been threatened. She hardly has to deal with blatant "bigots." She has not been fired. She has been called a Black "whore" only once. She is gifted, she has a job, and she is pursuing a promising career. She is a "successful Black." So one might ask: What is the problem? The problem is exactly that which is at the heart of everyday racism: the invisibility of oppression and the imperceptibility of Rosa N.'s extraordinary perseverance, despite multiple forms of oppression. Rejection, exclusion, problematization, underestimation, and other inequities and impediments are regularly infused into "normal" life, so that they appear unquestionable. This is a story of oppression in the fabric of everyday life. Some of her experiences are obvious indications of racism. Many others are concealed and subtle. Their understanding requires a certain degree of general knowledge of racism. To prevent any misinterpretations, I will clarify in detail why specific seemingly nonracial experiences can only be explained as forms of racism.

A relevant question concerns why we should believe Rosa N. The idea that Blacks are "too sensitive" is popular enough. Therefore, it may be expected that some readers think she just has a "chip on her shoulder" and that she is just as prejudiced against the Dutch as she thinks the Dutch are against Blacks. Suppose that she perceives racism where it is not present. Theoretically this may be the case, which would imply that Rosa N. has little knowledge of racism. This would mean that she is only expressing her common sense about race to account for a range of negative experiences. These crucial questions must be attended to carefully.

"Common sense" is a problematic notion. However, for my purposes the Gramscian (Gramsci, 1971) interpretation, as applied by Lawrence (1982b) in race relations theory, is relevant. Lawrence (1982b, p. 89) discusses common sense in relation to racist ideologies, which he argues have been elaborated from "taken-for-granted" assumptions. Here my concern is not with "racist ideas" but with "ideas about racism." More specifically it must be emphasized that Black women's notions about racism cannot be seen as "common sense" about racism. These notions are not based in taken-for-granted assumptions but, as I demonstrated earlier (see Chapter 3), comprehension of racism is acquired through deliberate problematization of social reality. Lawrence (1982b, pp. 48–50) argues that common sense is basically unsystematic, inconsistent, and contradictory and that it consists of notions that are taken for granted. In other words, common sense lacks reflective underpinning. [...]

[P]roof that she is careful and knowledgeable may be derived from the consistency of evidence. If Rosa N. has recollected just any negative experience to present as racism, we shall not be able to find consistency and coherence in her story. As noted before, everyday racism does not exist in the singular but only in the plural form, as a complex of mutually related, cumulative practices, and situations. [...]

[T]he Rosa N. story is also consistent in another sense, as may be inferred by the absence of the ultimate attribution error (Pettigrew, 1979). Unlike prejudiced interpreters Rosa N. does not dismiss evidence of positive behavior by dominant group members as a means of sustaining previous expectations about racism. This will be illustrated shortly. [...]

The Story of Rosa N.

> I came to Holland in 1969. My life was hard: work, study. My main friends were Dutch, the typical medical students. I had a time when I started to notice more things, such as, I have no home here, but a Dutch person does. I always had a very close friend—Ida, my father's younger sister. She was able to keep me from feeling lonely, from being homesick for Suriname. We gave each other a lot of support without ever consciously knocking the Dutch. That never entered your mind.

Even when Rosa N. did not explicitly feel different than the Dutch, fellow students reminded her that she was not like the Dutch.

> I can remember once making a phone call in a dorm when a Dutch boy said: "There's Rosa with that laugh of hers." And I thought: What does he mean? Strange! Because I was laughing very loud. But that doesn't happen anymore, only when I'm with Rob. [I felt like] I had to get rid of a lot of the Suriname in me. Not consciously. Not at all. I certainly had to lose a lot of my spontaneity. I think too I might have done it because I was always getting it thrown in my face, like with the boy who said, "Why are you laughing like that?" I must say, I've got some of that back now. I'm rediscovering my own culture. That's fantastic.

As for many other Black women in the Netherlands, the 1980s represents a period in which Rosa N. developed a deeper understanding of racism in her daily experiences. Vague feelings of oppression, of Eurocentrism, and cultural deprivation make way for a focused understanding of related practices of racism. Rosa N. preludes her accounts of a range of situated practices of racism by remembering: "How I loathed the Dutch. I saw all those depressed Moroccans, depressed Turks. And I saw all kinds of discrimination and racism. How people reacted, how people treated you." She continues with some examples:

We were in a surgery class. It was taught by a plastic surgeon whose name I've forgotten. If it were now, I'd certainly report that man. I was really angry. [He told us about an industrial accident] in a food processing plant where a Turk working on a cutting machine had sliced open his hand. And he even started the story with: "the stupid Turk." Yeah, that's how he started, "the stupid Turk. His hand is not a can!" He said I didn't really have much confidence, but still, I wanted to save the man's hand, because, he said, you know what it costs the Dutch government if that man loses his hand! He gets social security. So, he had to save the man's hand. He showed us another series of slides [about] how he'd operated on the hand. It looked really weird, but he must and he would save that hand, for it would cost the government too much. But eventually, the hand started to die anyway. It looked really terrible. The surgeon left the hand alone until it was completely black, like a hand of coal. His hand was amputated, after all. And then he showed the next picture. Someone's heel gone, that's another stupid foreigner in a factory, he says then. He talks about there being so many accidents. Only with foreigners. And he doesn't understand it, that's just how he tells the class the story. But he [doesn't add] that it's foreigners who do this kind of work and that they are the highest risk group for having an accident. The students thought it was real funny. They don't really give it much thought, because it arouses a kind of hilarity when it's told that way. Then everyone laughs about it. But I find such humor out of place, actually.

I waited until the man was finished. The lights went on, I told him he shouldn't make remarks like that again because they are offensive, and I chose that attitude because I thought: I must not become uncontrolled, agitated, or aggressive. [...]

And then one time in a general health class, this extremely stupid civil servant blamed the foreigners for overpopulation. I said something about that then, but what struck me was that someone said: oh, there's Rosa with that racism again. And I thought: what a prick! I thought: I'll turn in a complaint. But—and that really disappointed me—when I asked a few people I got on well with if they would testify, the one said, like no, because I have a child and a job I don't want to lose. One girl said she would testify. Then I spoke with my adviser, and he gave me some literature which showed that it has never been demonstrated that foreigners cause overpopulation. I very politely sent the man a letter. He sent such a nasty letter back. It was a totally degrading letter that said more about him than me, because he attacked me on personal points: that I had used my boss's FAX number—while my boss had even approved my letter. That I had not written "personal" on the letter and the secretary and other people had read it.

All these experiences took place when Rosa N. was doing her internship. This is a special situation in which study and work overlap. Thus people who are fellow students in one situation are her colleagues in other situations. Therefore, the distinction between the context of education and work is made only for the purpose of the analysis.

Now at my work, they find me oversensitive, probably because I just can't let certain things pass. And I can absolutely not do that. I do not want to and I will not. So I always respond [against racism], because now I just can't keep quiet. Here's another example. A student [presented] a patient—and I'm the only Surinamese present as doctor. He [introduced the patient with] she is from Suriname. He looked at me and said: sorry. I thought, what's all this? Why in god's name does he say "sorry"?! But to make things worse, when in my confusion I did this [very astonished face], another person started patting me on the back. Then I was completely at a loss.

The patient [being presented] had herpes genitalis. And the student said, oh, yeah, women in Suriname do have more than one man. Then I jumped in immediately with, then everyone in Suriname must have herpes!

[…] Rosa N. mentions that she has been confronted with racism from patients, but, because the patients are ill or demented, she is less worried about this than when it comes from her colleagues:

A patient, a woman told me afterward that during a psychosis, she had thought I was a whore. Then I think once more, yeah, a Black is a whore.… You know, this reminds me of one of the first times that I came into the hospital, I was with [a] demented woman. I gave her my hand. "I don't want the hand of a foreign worker, I don't want that hand." She went on [with] a heap of racist language.

I take a lot of time for things [because] I have the idea that I must work very scrupulously, must not fail. It's the same with everyone, so this isn't so exceptional, but with me there's another dimension. I may not make as many mistakes as the others. I must not do things wrong when with the Dutch. Absolutely not, I don't want to be their lesser. You've got to be better.

In this respect Rosa N. feels that the stress to prove herself as a Black woman is, in fact, the continuation of her past. In comparison with her cousins—the four daughters of her mother's sister—she was darker. She always felt treated as the "nigger" of the family. […]

Reviewing her life at the hospital, Rosa N. says:

I'm not safe at G. [name of hospital]. Like, I can never in my life bring up the subject of racism. That just can't be, because they'll only trip me up.

If you want to say anything about racism, you've got to state your case very well. Otherwise … they tackle you and lay down a thousand pieces of evidence to prove the opposite, and they make you ridiculous.

Because I'm Black, I'm more vulnerable [as a woman]. I always have the idea, if men see a Black woman … then they've got a good chance. You also see this on television. Then there's this stupid commercial where a White man wants a Black [woman], and he plays with her, and suddenly he reaches under her skirt. And then it seems something or the other comes out. I've forgotten what.

The above summary of racism in everyday situations portrays a story in which the woman is constantly fighting against racist opposition—a lonely struggle to keep breathing in a racist climate with an almost overwhelming degree of suppression. In this respect that story of Rosa N. is representative for the story of many other women in the Netherlands. [...] Thus she concludes the interview with the following statement:

> I used to think, when I am a doctor, this will be in the past, then I'll have proved myself, but no such thing. Then the long, hard road begins. Then you start to notice that you aren't there yet, that the fight has just begun. I would really like for it to be over, because I'd like to just be able to live. I'd find it wonderful if I could just feel good with my job and not have a third-rate position in the job. If you spend all your time competing, then it never stops. I participate in this consciously and take care that I don't backslide. I think: just keep it up.
>
> I read at lot more about discrimination now—but then, not so much about Holland, because you don't get any further if you keep on thinking only about they do that and they do that and they do that. Now I would like to know much more about how I can deal with it. My first 10 years in Holland, I found it much too painful to see what was going on in South Africa. The slaughter there. It also has to do with being ready to let that penetrate. I find that positive. I think too that Rob has certainly learned from me. He has learned to look; he gives me support, accepts criticism, while he used to go into a discussion about it.

THE PROCESS OF EVERYDAY RACISM IN THE EXPERIENCE OF ROSA N.

The reader must bear in mind that the story of Rosa N. is not a representation of the whole interview with Rosa N., of which the transcript has 54 pages, but only a compilation of experiences she presented as illustrations of racism. Therefore, one must not see this summary as a general bias against the Dutch, as an indication that she only has negative experiences with the Dutch, or as evidence that she does not know how to distinguish between racism and injustice for other reasons. Space limitations prevent detailed analysis of the experiences not included here, but it may be useful to give a brief impression. On various occasions Rosa N. distinguishes positive aspects of Dutch individuals from practices of racism. To give a few examples: She feels culturally oppressed from the very beginning of her stay in the Netherlands. Yet she has quite positive memories of the group of (Dutch male) friends she spent time with early on. They were "real old fashioned, even brazen in a certain way, but they were also quite straightforward," which is what she "really liked about them." At work she experiences racism from her supervisor in some situations, yet she otherwise appreciates that he is often "very perceptive" about her needs as a trainee. Her comprehension of racism—that is, the fact that she qualifies practices, rather than individuals, as racist—is particularly important. [...]

Rosa N. is also self-critical, as she realizes that on some occasions, in the first period of her stay, she was wrong about the Dutch because she "did not know" enough about their cultural styles and about the way they "socialized among themselves." In other words, Rosa N. realized there were certain gaps in her understanding of Dutch culture that made it difficult to make reliable interpretations of her own experiences with the Dutch. This is consistent with my theory that comprehension of racist events requires knowledge of dominant or subcultural codes of behavior. The consequence is that examples in which Rosa N. was not sure herself whether she was confronted with racism are either excluded or presented with due reservation. Finally, some comments are in order about the criteria against which are assessed the accounts of Rosa N. Her experiences are examples of everyday racism if they are consistent with the definition of (experiences of) everyday racism. Thus it may be assumed that the experiences of Rosa N. represent everyday racism if they are consistent with the following presuppositions:

1. Everyday racism is reflected in different types of experiences.
2. Everyday racism presupposes everyday situations.
3. Everyday racism involves repetitive practices.
4. Experiences of everyday racism are heterogeneous.
5. Everyday racism involves specifications of general processes of racism.

Different Types of Experiences

The story of Rosa N. shows a relatively high frequency of direct experiences of racism. She connects her personal experiences with those of other Blacks and of other oppressed groups such as Turks and Moroccans. [...]

Cognitive experiences. What you feel, know, or believe is happening continuously, or what you expect may happen any day, constitute permanently felt pressures lingering beneath the surface of social reality. Some of these pressures have been activated so many times they are presented as generalized experiences in memory. In the experiences of Rosa N. one of these forms of permanently felt racism is the pressure to assimilate culturally under conditions of Eurocentrism. Apparently she has been harassed or criticized so many times that she has gotten "rid of a lot of the Suriname" in her. Because the Dutch explicitly adhere to the norm of tolerance, pressures on Blacks to assimilate often operate covertly (Jong, 1989). This probably explains why Rosa N. was "not" even "conscious" herself that she was losing much of her genuine cultural identity. [...]

Underestimation is another constant form of racism that must have been activated so many times that Rosa N. feels she cannot afford to be less than perfect. It is interesting to note that Rosa N. is perfectly well aware that all her colleagues work under pressure to perform ("I must not fail. It's the same with everyone, so that is not so exceptional, but with me there is another dimension"). In other words, she is not trying to hide any personal incompetence behind the explanation of racism. She only makes a qualitative difference when she suggests that, if she fails, it will not be seen as personal failure but as failure of a Black woman. In fact Rosa N. points here to a general problem that has been confirmed in many experiments in intergroup attribution (e.g., Hewstone, 1989). I shall return to the behavioral implications of this important aspect when I discuss dominant group actions against Black women who aspire to achieve and who are competent in their fields.

These three forces of racism experienced by Rosa N. symbolize the framework in which all her other experiences may be placed: (a) *Eurocentrism*; (b) the dominant group impeding the efforts of Blacks to achieve (which is rationalized with, among other things, *attribution of incompetence*); and (c) Whites exercising covert pressure with the aim of enforcing cultural *assimilation*. Eurocentrism marginalizes Blacks; low expectations legitimize marginalization; and pressure to assimilate is a form of control. Assimilation is not just a question of state policy, which is how this is usually identified. This "need for control" (Dijker, 1989, p. 87) expressed by individual members of the dominant group, who demand that Blacks adapt to Dutch ways of living, is a dominant feature of Dutch racism. The story of Rosa N., and as we shall see the stories of other women as well, demonstrate that assimilative forces work through everyday situations and practices. These forms of racism all presuppose that difference is organized hierarchically, whether it concerns culture or structure.

Vicarious experiences. Among the most characteristic differences between the experiences of Black women in the United States and those in the Netherlands are those associated with identification with other groups who are targets of racism. The tendency among Black women in the Netherlands to transcend the boundaries of ethnicity when antiracism is concerned is remarkable in light of the prevailing forces on the side of the dominant group to generate and maintain rigid ethnic differentiation in the context of a pluralist model of society. [...] This can also be inferred from Rosa N., who says about the period when she became "aware" of racism that she "loathed the Dutch" because of the depressed conditions of Turks and Moroccans and all of the kinds of racism she began to recognize. [...] A form of commitment is Rosa N.'s protest against the lectures of a plastic surgeon who jokes about the medical experiment he did on a Turkish worker.

Rosa N. says that no matter how polite specific Whites may be to her because she is a doctor, when they intimidate another Black because he is "just" a worker, "they are doing it to you" too. Rosa N. does not only identify with other targets of racism because she feels a commitment to challenge racism. If this were the case, any active opponent of racism, including Whites, would vicariously experience racism through knowledge of the oppression of Blacks. Individual Blacks also experience racism through the experiences of others because of the very nature of racism. It is not directed against any one person but against every Black. For these reasons, vicarious experiences represent a major component of the experience of everyday racism. The notion of vicarious racism underscores the fact that, in the reproduction of racism, agents and subjects are of secondary importance. Whether or not agents indulge in racist practices depends on many factors, among others the degree of saturation of racist ideologies in the individual's social cognitions, the interests involved, the personality of the agent, and expectations about reactions of Blacks or White group members. However, the characteristics of the situation determine the specific forms racism takes. To give an example, the professor abuses the authority attached to his profession by infusing his teaching with racist statements after he had used the power attached to the medical profession to physically abuse a Turkish patient. Another teacher may do the same in a teaching situation, as can be inferred from the experiences of Rosa N. The content of the racist statements that are made may be determined by other factors, such as the role of the speakers in other situations (the surgeon makes racist remarks related to surgery, and the guest speaker comes with racist ideas developed in the context of his work at the Ministry of Public Health). To avoid misunderstanding the primacy of situation over agents and subject does not mean that racism is just situationally construed. It will be shown in the course of this study that the major forms racism takes are ideologically structured; the specific manifestations of these forms, however, are situationally created.

Comparisons between the direct and the vicarious experiences of Rosa N. show that there are similarities in the forms racism takes. Here particular attention is paid to the pathologizing of Blacks. Various studies have focused on the process by which racist notions of difference translate the behavior of Blacks into "maladjusted" behavior while "maladjusted" behavior becomes subsequently "pathological" behavior (Baratz & Baratz, 1972/1977; Lawrence, 1982a). These notions constitute part of commonsense thinking (Lawrence, 1982b).

Pathologizing is in many respects worse than inferiorizing because pathological behavior needs to be cured for one to become "normal" again. Furthermore, it is relevant to make a distinction between ideas of cultural pathology and attribution to Blacks of pathological personalities. The first form represents cultural deterministic explanations of "social disadvantage." The second form perceives reactions of Blacks to oppression in general or to racism in particular as pathological. This line of thinking is important in the story of Rosa N. as it draws upon the idea that, due to "social deprivation," Blacks develop damaged personalities with symptoms such as "oversensitive" and "overemotional" reactions to their social surroundings.

Rosa N. is repeatedly confronted with Whites who think that her perceptions of racism are pathological. This ideological form of racism structures direct and vicarious experiences and is expressed in specific situations according to the characteristics of the situation and the interests involved. In this process both Black professionals and patients are subjected to the same process of pathologizing so that it becomes legitimate to disqualify Rosa N. as a doctor. The story of Rosa N. holds good illustrations of the intricate relation between acts of racism directed against Rosa N. herself and racism embedded in the way doctors discuss their Black patients in the presence of Rosa N. [...]

Everyday Racism Presupposes Everyday Situations

The story of Rosa N. does not deal with racist ideologies of organized racist or fascist movements. She is just reporting about her day-to-day experiences in routine situations involving "normal" people. Due to her profession a proportionally high number of dominant group members with whom she has to deal in daily interactions belong to the Dutch-educated "elite." Relations between Rosa N. and dominant group members are racialized because they are structured by the wider stratifications in society. However, this racialized dimension, which Rosa N. described so well when she referred to "another dimension" compelling her to pursue perfection, is not constantly activated. Dominant group members may relate to her in a nonracist way in some situations but not in others. The racial dimension of the relationship is activated when racist practices are integrated into the situation. All of the situations in which

Rosa N. experiences racism directly constitute routine situations in everyday life. To illustrate I summarize the situations of racism on the job. On the job racism permeates routine situations, formal and informal, through which the institution of a hospital is reproduced:

1. discussing patients with colleagues
2. small talk in the corridors
3. having informal conversation with colleagues
4. having lunch with colleagues
5. discussing patients with the supervisor
6. working with a patient
7. giving a paper in a seminar
8. being disturbed in one's work by the cleaner
9. overhearing the head custodian and the cleaner

Similarly the agents of racism in these situations are part of the natural human fabric of the specific workplace, a medical complex:

1. colleagues: doctors
2. supervisor: doctor
3. patient
4. cleaner
5. head custodian

Recurrent Practices and Heterogeneity of Experiences

Repetition is an indication of the degree of uniformity of practice. [...] In the biography of Rosa N. herself, there is also similarity in the forms of racism she encounters: (a) The same complications arise in similar situations. [...] Also there is repetition of (b) similar forms of racism in different situations. An [...] example concerns the rejection of Surinamese styles of communication by a fellow student in one situation and by Rosa N.'s supervisor in another situation. (c) Similar agents may be involved in similar or in different racist practices. The same colleagues who tolerate racist remarks from the professor during class patronize and pathologize Rosa N. or other Blacks in other situations. [...]

Everyday Racism as Specifications of General Processes of Racism

For practices to occur systematically, there must be certain ideological conditions that both stimulate and legitimize these practices. As stated before, this is not meant to imply that relations between prejudice and discrimination are simple or straightforward. However, the saturation of cognitions with shared notions or consensus on race allows certain practices to happen routinely. This may also be inferred from the experiences of Rosa N. It is explicitly assumed that practices are allowed, rather than that agents always consciously perform racist practices or that others explicitly agree with these practices. Indeed Rosa N. says she also has (situational) allies, among others her husband and a female colleague who she thinks supports her even when she does not take any explicit initiatives against racism. Her boss supported her letter of protest to the representative of the ministry. The tolerance of racism that many other dominant group members display may be a question of indifference, of ignorance, or of mere behavioral conformity (Pettigrew, 1958). In particular in the Netherlands the tradition of establishing harmony through consensus may inhibit individuals from confronting other group members, irrespective of the problem at hand. Whatever the reasons individuals may have, the rule applies that, the more saturated social cognitions are with racist ideological notions, the more likely it becomes that racist cognitions encourage or rationalize specific actions and the more oppressive tolerance of racism becomes. For these reasons it is relevant to reconstruct from the story of Rosa N. the main ideological concepts underlying the racism she experiences.

Problematization. [...] [T]wo structuring concepts underlie ideological racism as reconstructed by Rosa N.: real or imaginary *differences* attributed to Blacks and the subsequent *hierarchical ordering of difference.* Not only is difference organized hierarchically, it is common in—although not only typical of—European thinking for the "superior" to control the "inferior" (Hodge et al., 1975). [...]

Overemphasis on ethnic difference is inherent in various comments and criticisms dominant group members make about (what they presume to be) Surinamese culture. One pertinent example of the fact that difference is inherently perceived in hierarchical terms concerns the situation in which a colleague introduces a patient with "she is from Suriname," after which he immediately looks at Rosa N. and says "sorry." Later the colleague confesses that he apologized because he felt it might have been offensive to his Black colleague to be reminded that she is from the same "inferior background" as the patient. [...]

Another source of problematization Rosa N. experiences derives from the underestimation of Blacks. The idea that Black people are incapable of intellectual advancement probably combines remnants of racist notions of biological determinism (Blacks as genetically less intelligent) and forms of cultural determinism (attributed low drive to achieve). Furthermore it is likely that gender- and race-based ideologies converge in the practice of underrating Black women (Hall, 1982; Piliawsky, 1982; Tomlinson, 1983). The least harmful example Rosa N. mentions is almost too stereotypical to be true: The cleaner comes in and takes the old White male patient for a doctor and the Black young doctor for the patient. [...]

Rosa N. depicts an atmosphere in which difference is exaggerated, reduced to ethnicity, and subsequently pathologized, the prevailing assumption being that Blacks are "emotional." A very good example of this is the reaction of her supervisor when Rosa N. reacts with sarcasm, and then leaves the session, after blatantly offensive remarks one colleague makes about Black female sexuality. First, the supervisor pathologizes her reaction by suggesting that she probably "did not want to react" in that way. And he adds that she "reacted like that because [she] is a Surinamese." Rosa N. is confronted with various other attempts to pathologize Blackness. Being Black in one situation is interpreted as a "disability," in another as an indication of mental instability ("too emotional"), or in another as a condition to be pitied ("another person started patting me on the back"). The pathologization of Blackness can only partly be explained by the environment in which Rosa N. works. However, it is relevant to briefly consider further ramifications of the attribution to Blacks of emotional instability by (mental) health care professionals.

In addition to general knowledge about racism against Black women in society at large, it is relevant to consider general information about racism (class and gender bias) in (mental) health care (Littlewood & Lipsedge, 1982; Miller & Rose, 1986). The overemphasis on differences functions to reduce ethnic behavior to individual traits to justify psychiatric intervention (Mercer, 1986). The case of the "swinging" Surinamese, who, according to Rosa N., should probably not have been hospitalized at all, is an example of this. Racism nurtures the stereotype of Afro-Caribbean (men) as deviant, aggressive, and "dangerous" and as a group that potentially undermines the existing order. The "swinging" style of the patient fits the dominant model of deviant (Black male) behavior. It is behavior that mocks "bourgeois" norms and values. This suggests that the Black man is pathologized and admitted as a patient not on medical grounds but because of potential "dangerousness." Therefore, pathologizing must also be seen in its function to control opposition to the existing order. I shall come back to containment of opposition in a moment. [...]

Marginalization. If Rosa N. had been a cleaner rather than a doctor in the hospital, her story would have been one of racism structured by class exploitation and of class oppression permeated by racism. Indirectly she is confronted with the impact of class oppression in everyday racism. The head custodian bullies the Black cleaner, but he would never be anything but polite with Dr. N. Her own struggle, as it relates to the structural position of Black women with higher education, is directed more exclusively toward racial and ethnic marginalization. [...] Colleagues express indifference rather than polite, let alone cordial, interest when she engages in casual conversation with them ("I'd also like ...... to say what I find nice, pretty or whatever, but they never really go into this").

Often Whites *passively tolerate* and probably hardly even notice *racism*. Let me illustrate: When colleagues insult Rosa N. by considering her *incompetent* to judge a Surinamese patient, none of the participants challenges the insult. It is taken for granted that a White male colleague who has been in Suriname once is more competent. [...]

Containment. Rosa N. is not just a "powerless victim" of racism; neither are agents of racism simply maliciously abusing power. It can be inferred from the story of Rosa N. that power is centrally involved in interracial (ethnic) situations. [...]

Almost half of Rosa N.'s experiences concern processes of containment. This suggests that she encounters a relatively high degree of reluctance to change. The message implied in the *humiliation* of the Black cleaner is that he should accept an inferior position. [...] I speak of *intimidation* when lecturers use racist examples in front of Black students because this situation activates group power. In the act of underrating Rosa N. dominant group members confirm racial consensus that allows these things to be said without sanctions being applied. This is even worse when racist statements are used to induce laughter, which is an explicit way to create approval and tolerance of racism. [...]

The function of intimidation is to "keep Blacks in their place." Later I will return to this important function of containment as it presupposes approval for existing relations between "superior" and "inferior" groups. Many forms of rejection of ethnically specific behavior operate in the same way. Stigmatizing the way you laugh or your enthusiasm about your work is giving the message that different behavior is not appreciated. One could argue that these are trivialities not even worth mentioning. Indeed these are trivialities. That is exactly the problem. We can also look at it in this way: Apparently the dominant group refuses to accept even the most trivial manifestations of difference, because they do not want to deal with them. This confirms my earlier stated presupposition that racism penetrates otherwise insignificant situations in everyday life. This introduces another subtle form of suppression, namely, the act of *patronizing*. In this context Rosa N. recalls how her colleagues made it a point to correct her when they detected a Dutch accent in her pronunciation of a US name. [...]

If dominant group members are tolerant of racism in many other situations, it is not surprising that Rosa N.'s refusal to tolerate racism induces new forms of control. The final step in the process of denial is the incrimination of Blacks (or others) who make a point of opposing racism. Rosa N. is accused of "malice." A colleague who had first compared Blackness to being "disabled" wants the supervisor to do something about Rosa N.'s. "accusing others of racism." [...]

These indications of pathologizing and denial also confirm that Rosa N.'s position is marginal. She is not (considered) part of the in-group, and racism operates to sustain racialized dimensions of social relations. Rosa N. is tolerated as a student and colleague, but she must not expect her colleagues to be sensitive or feel responsible for problems of racism, for they do not acknowledge it to be a problem. The analysis of everyday racism in the life of Rosa N. is not complete. Many other factors may be looked at, such as the specific consequences of racism from people in positions of authority, gender differences in expressions of racism, and conditions for change. [...]

CONCLUSIONS: ROSA N. AND THE SHARED EXPERIENCE OF RACISM

To examine whether the experiences of Rosa N. are consistent with those of other Black women, it is useful first to reiterate some of the earlier findings about the general processes of racism. [...] Earlier I provided a reconstruction of the main descriptive and explanatory concepts included in Black women's general knowledge of racism. This reconstruction reflects highly abstract knowledge and is based empirically in the categorization of statements about the general nature of racism. The structure of Black women's general knowledge of racism reflects the fact that racism consists of general processes (marginalization, problematization, containment) and various subprocesses (e.g., nonacceptance, pathologizing, patronizing). [...]

The general processes and subprocesses of racism as inferred from the story of Rosa N. are the same as those reported by other Black women. Therefore, the story of Rosa N., though unique in its biographical detail, inherently reflects experience shared by other Black women.

REFERENCES

Baratz, J., & Baratz, S. (1977). Black culture on Black terms: A rejection of the social pathology model. In T. Kochman (Ed.), *Rappin' and stylin' out* (pp. 3–16). Urbana: University of Illinois Press. (Original work published 1972.)

Dijker, A.J. (1989). Ethnic attitudes and emotions. In J.P. van Oudenhoven & T.M. Willemsen (Eds.), *Ethinic Minorities* (pp. 73–93). Amsterdam: Swets & Zeitlinger.

Essed, P. (1990a). The myth of over-sensitivity about racism. In I. Foeken (Ed.), *Between selfhelp and professionalism, Part III* (pp. 21–36). Amsterdam: Moon Foundation.

Essed, P. (1990b). Against all odds: Teaching against racism at a university in South Africa. *European Journal of Intercultural Studies, 1*(1), 41–56.

Gramsci, A. (1971). *Selections from prison notebooks*. London: Lawrence and Wishart.

Hall, R.M. (1982). *The classroom climate: A chilly one for women?* (Project on the Status and Education of Women). Washington, DC: Association of American Colleges.

Hewstone, M. (1989). Intergroup attribution: Some implications for the study of ethnic prejudice. In J.P. van Oudenhoven & T.M. Willemsen (Eds.), *Ethnic minorities* (pp. 25–42). Amsterdam: Swets & Zeitlinger.

Hodge, J.L., Struckman, D.K., & Trost, L.D. (1975). *The cultural bases of racism and group oppression*. Berkeley, CA: Two Riders.

Jong, W. de (1989). The development of ethnic tolerance in an inner city area with large numbers of immigrants. In J.P. Oudenhoven & T.M. Willemsen (Eds.), *Ethnic Minorities* (pp. 139–153). Amsterdam: Swets & Zeitlinger.

Lawrence, E. (1982a). In the abundance of water the fool is thirsty: Sociology and Black "pathology." In Centre of Contemporary Cultural Studies (Birmingham; Ed.), *The empire strikes back: Race and racism in the 70s* (pp. 95–142). London: Hutchinson.

Lawrence, E. (1982b). Just plain common sense: The "roots" of racism. In Centre of Contemporary Cultural Studies (Birmingham; Ed.), *The empire strikes back: Race and racism in the 70s* (pp. 47–94). London: Hutchinson.

Littlewood, R., & Lipsedge, M. (1982). *Aliens & alienists*. Harmondsworth, England: Penguin.

Mercer, K. (1986). Racism and transcultural psychiatry. In P. Miller & N. Rose (Eds.), *The power of psychiatry* (pp. 111–142). Cambridge: Polity.

Miller, P., & Rose, N. (1986). *The power of psychiatry*. Cambridge: Polity.

Pettigrew, T.F. (1958). Personality and sociocultural factors in intergroup attitudes: A cross-cultural comparison. *Journal of Conflict Resolution, 2,* 29–42.

Pettigrew, T.F. (1979). The ultimate attribution error: Extending Allport's cognitive analysis of prejudice. *Personality and Social Psychology Bulletin, 5*(4), 451–476.

Piliawsky, M. (1982). *Exit 13: Oppression and racism in academia*. Boston: South End.

Tomlinson, S. (1983). Black women in higher education: Case studies of university women in Britain. In L. Barton & S. Walker (Eds.), *Race, class and education* (pp. 66–80). London: Croom Helm.

Chapter 31

Diversity Management in the Canadian Workplace: Towards an Anti-racism Approach

Vanmala Hiranandani

Hiranandani (2012) discusses the nature of government responses to discrimination in employment faced by racialized populations in Canada and the growing shift from affirmative action programs such as employment equity towards diversity management programs. The focus is on the way diversity management programs reflect the neo-liberal bias towards market regulation of work and the shift away from social equity considerations in the design of these programs. The chapter points to the limits of the diversity management approach and suggests a need to utilize an anti-racism approach that is action-oriented and addresses the need for institutional and systemic change in order to attain greater inclusion of racialized people in informal workplace networks and formal organizations.

1. INTRODUCTION

Human resource management has always been challenged with managing diversity although the exact nature of these challenges has varied over time. While the concern in earlier stages of industrialization was on managing class divisions, with increasing cultural diversity in contemporary times, the focus has shifted to managing diverse identity groups in the urban workplace [1–4]. "Diversity management" has emerged as a more popular alternative compared to employment equity and affirmative action. As a voluntary corporate approach that is perceived to enable organizations to capitalize on the benefits of workforce diversity, diversity management is less controversial. Indeed, diversity management has become a popular term, often under the rubric of corporate social responsibility (CSR), in many multinational corporations, and largely refers to hiring visible minorities and increasing cross-cultural awareness and communication. It is viewed as playing an important role in reducing turnover and absenteeism, attracting competent workers, enhancing creativity and innovation, bringing about attitudinal changes, and creating greater inclusion of all employees into organizational structures [5].

In today's global urban business environment, building a more diverse workforce that brings in different perspectives, experiences, insights, and international and multicultural contacts is increasingly being recognized as crucial to enhancing organizational competitiveness and effectiveness (e.g., [2, 6, 7]). A diverse workforce can maximize talent and creativity and foster innovation, which can ultimately lead to increased profits and positive public image for a successful business enterprise. While diversity has various meanings, the focus of this paper is on racial and ethnic minorities and their treatment in the workplace in the Canadian context[1]. Canada is known for its multiculturalism and for being a refuge for people from diverse cultural backgrounds. Although business literature points to the fact that increasing diversity makes business sense, visible minority employees continue to face discrimination in the Canadian workplace.

This paper reviews various strands of diversity management in Canada: it is found that the business imperative for diversity and strategies to enhance workforce diversity form the bulk of diversity management literature in the country. While recent years have seen an increase in diversity and cultural competence initiatives, these strategies do not address racism in the workplace, and their impact has been limited in terms of retaining visible minority employees. Following a critique of current diversity management initiatives in the Canadian context, this paper examines the strengths and limitations of the emerging anti-racism approach that has been tried in several urban locales and is considered more potent to tackle racism in the workplace and in the larger society of which the workplace is a part. After assessing the major principles underlying the anti-racism framework, the paper ends with suggestions for its nuanced adoption in the Canadian context to create a more inclusive and non-discriminatory work environment.

2. DIVERSITY MANAGEMENT IN CANADA: AN OVERVIEW

The concept of diversity management originated in the USA in the 1990s following the growing need to manage cross-cultural and individual differences in an increasingly diverse demographic workforce [8, 9]. Diversity management has been embraced by many organizations in the USA where it has become multimillion dollar consulting business. As in the USA, in Canada, immigration and large numbers of women entering the workforce promoted diversity management efforts since the 1990s, although the workplace composition differs from that in the USA [10]. While several definitions of diversity management have been posited, the most common definition is that put forth by Gilbert et al. ([11, page 61]): "Diversity management is a voluntary organizational program designed to create greater inclusion of all individuals into informal social networks and formal company programs." A more practice-oriented definition is provided by Bassett-Jones [12] for whom diversity management refers to systematic efforts and planned commitment on the part of organizations to recruit and retain employees with various backgrounds and abilities.

The concept of "diversity" refers not only to demographic and cultural differences, but "a workforce made … distinct by the presence of many religions, cultures or skin colors, both sexes (in non-stereotypical roles), differing sexual orientations, varying styles of behavior, differing capabilities, and usually, unlike backgrounds" (Canadian Institute of Chartered Accountants and Society of Management Accountants of Canada, 1996 quoted in [10, page 307]). Contrary to the USA, where consultants initiated the discourse on diversity, in Canada, government agencies have taken the lead in enhancing public awareness of diversity issues [10]. And in contrast to the USA that has espoused the "melting pot" approach, Canada adopted the policy of multiculturalism in 1971 [13]. The multiculturalism policy stresses the importance of providing services in languages other than English and French, "celebrating" diversity, and challenging dominant norms about dress code, food habits, accents, and other overt forms of prejudice. The policy of multiculturalism did, therefore, officially recognize Canada's mosaic of cultures and espouse the idea that racial/ethnic minorities have the right to maintain their cultural heritage. Multiculturalism resulted in organizations hiring visible minorities in entry-level positions primarily since they spoke a language that was required to serve a particular community.

Another initiative by the Canadian government to enhance labor force diversity is the federal Employment Equity Act (EEA) which is akin to Affirmative Action in the US and was first passed in 1986. The EEA covers the public sector as well as any private sector firm that contracts with the government and has more than 100 workers in Canada and government contracts valued at more than $200,000 [14]. The EEA requires efforts by employers in covered sectors (e.g., communications, transportation, and banking) to reduce disparities in employment and workforce representation between designated groups (such as women, visible minorities, aboriginal peoples, and people with disabilities) and the general workforce [15].

While these policies laid the foundations for diversity management, the business sector's engagement with diversity management revolves around the twin rationale of the "business imperative" and the need to address shortages of skilled labor force. The "business imperative" argument lists several compelling reasons for increasing diversity in Canadian organizations.

i. *Fostering creativity and innovation*: in the present-day urban business environment, characterized by globalization, rapid change, and uncertainty, companies must adapt, change, and learn at an unprecedented pace in business history. In such a rapidly shifting milieu, creative ideas, knowledge, and innovation are the only stable sources of capital [16]. Developing a more diverse workforce assumes enormous significance in a competitive market situation due to its potential to harness a variety of perspectives, experiences, and insights, which is vital to business success. Diversity in the workforce has been considered essential to maximize access to the pool of talented people [6, 17].

An organization's capability to innovate provides the cutting edge in today's competitive world. Researchers have found that groups composed of people from diverse cultures are more likely to bring a wider range of perspectives to the table that can generate more ideas and alternatives than a homogenous group ([6, 16], Rousseau, 1995 cited in [7]). Oliver cites the example of Xerox Canada research center in Mississauga, Ontario, that employs 150 personnel from 36 different countries. The company's diversity has attracted the top scientific talent from around the world which has enabled it to capture more than 100 US patents. Additionally, since a diverse group tends to understand and communicate with each other differently, it is forced to proceed more carefully to reach a consensus. The outcomes are more carefully deliberated decisions and improved results.

ii. *Tapping new global markets*: in an era of the globalized economy, businesses no longer operate in the national base. Global business is not limited to exports and imports; many companies depend on vendors, service businesses, and alliances and mergers in other parts of the world [2, 18]. Enhancing workforce diversity has the potential to capture new global markets and thereby boost corporate success. Oliver [16] and Trichur [19] mention that foreign-born visible minorities living in Canada have knowledge of and connections to other countries which can be an invaluable asset in accessing overseas markets. Oliver [16] reasons that since currently more than 1 million people in Canada are of Chinese origin, tapping into this community could enable Canadian companies to gain greater access to Chinese markets, which today comprise only about five percent of Canada's exports.

iii. *Entry into ethnic markets*: given Canada's changing racial and ethnic demographics, a company with a workforce that resembles its customer base is considered more competitive to gain greater entrée in the country's burgeoning ethnic markets. Oliver [16] provides the example of Bank of Montreal, which began to focus specifically on Chinese Canadians, that established Chinese branches across the country by hiring Chinese-speaking employees to understand the community's cultural nuances and as a result saw its business among this market segment increases by 400 percent over a 5-year period.

Thus, the bulk of Canadian diversity management literature views diversity in the workforce as a business imperative to foster corporate and organizational success in the competitive global market. Shortage of labor is another compelling reason that has propelled Canadian companies to address diversity in the workforce. Severe labor shortages are expected in Canada during the next decade due to the retirement of the baby boomers and low birth rates, which will result in a ratio decline from about five workers for each retired person to about 2.5:1 [16, 20]. A pressing demand for labor, particularly skilled labor, exists in all sectors, including retail, manufacturing, and service industries.

The demand for skilled labor has led to liberal immigration laws that admit 200,000 new immigrants to Canada each year. About 70 percent of recent immigrants to urban Canada are visible minorities; people of color make up nearly 50 percent of populations in

Vancouver and Toronto and are the fastest growing communities in Canada's eight largest cities [21, 22]. Fifty-four percent of these newcomers have professional skills, university qualifications, or have met specified business criteria, a rate that surpasses the Canadian-born population [16]. Oliver further informs that while visible minorities constituted less than 11 percent of the labor force on average between 1992 and 2001, they accounted for as much as a third of the labor force's contribution to the country's gross domestic product (GDP) growth. Undoubtedly, Canada's workforce growth and, consequently, a significant share of its economic prosperity have come to depend on new immigrants. This trend has continued and it has been estimated that in 2011, 100 percent of the net labor force growth depended on immigration; visible minorities will comprise about 20 percent of the country's population by 2016 [16, 21].

These factors have led to increasing recognition of diversity by several Canadian companies. For instance, RBC Financial Group has ensured that 22 percent of their workforce is composed of visible minorities, which is laudable. Telecommunication giants, such as Telus and Rogers, have set examples of recruiting diverse employees [21]. Similarly, FedEx has a high proportion of visible minorities (almost 7%) in senior management positions. Its staff represents about 19 nationalities at its Mississauga, Ontario, headquarters [23].

While these efforts are commendable, programs to hire, retain, and treat diverse employees fairly at the workplace are not widely prevalent in Canada. As the next section elaborates, visible minorities continue to face various forms of employment discrimination even in large multicultural cities.

3. ONGOING WORKPLACE DISCRIMINATION AGAINST VISIBLE MINORITIES

Several research studies have reported that labor market outcomes, employment, unemployment, weeks worked, and representation in better-paying jobs for visible minorities are poorer when compared with nonvisible minorities in Canada. Research has shown that access to job opportunities, upward mobility, earnings, and income have also been poorer (e.g., [24–26]). The unemployment rate for visible minorities has been persistently higher than that of the total population [27]. In 2006, visible minorities represented 15.4 percent of the labor force, up from 6.4 percent in 1986 [28, 29].

The disparity in average wages between visible minorities and Caucasian Canadians is alarming. K. Pendakur and R. Pendakur [24] found varying earnings differences for different ethnic groups and confirmed that Blacks experienced the largest earnings gap. Further, K. Pendakur and R. Pendakur [24] note that the earnings gap for visible minority workers aged 25–64 years has not only been persistent but has also been steadily increasing over the past 25 years. Oliver's [16] research showed that visible minorities earned 11 percent less than the Canadian average in 1991. This gap increased to 14.5 percent in 2000. The differences in earnings for visible minority workers were due to fewer weeks of employment and lower earnings per week ([26, 30]).

It is noteworthy that education levels of visible minorities are not translating into comparable returns in employment. Samuel and Basavarajappa [26], drawing on a Canadian Race Relations Foundation report, *Unequal Access*, stating that almost half of visible minority workers aged 25–34 years had university degrees compared to just over a quarter among the nonvisible minority workers of the same ages. About a third of visible minority workers aged 35–64 years had university degrees compared to a fifth among the nonvisible minority workers. Thus, visible minority men and women have higher educational qualifications, but their shares in the top income quintiles were less than those of their nonvisible minority counterparts, demonstrating that their earnings do not match their educational attainments. The Conference Board of Canada [19] estimated that due to their unrecognized learning visible minorities lose between $2.2 billion and $3.4 billion per year.

Furthermore, research reveals that visible minorities are underrepresented in the upper echelons of Canadian organizations [15, 16, 19]. According to the Employment Equity Act Annual Report, only 14.5 percent of individuals employed in the federally regulated communications sector are visible minorities and only 5.1 percent of senior managers working in the federally regulated private sector in 2006 were visible minorities [31]. Only 13 percent of leadership positions in the Greater Toronto Area are held by visible minorities. The greatest number of leadership positions held by visible minorities is in the education sector (20%), while the smallest number of leadership positions held by visible minorities is in the corporate sector (4%) [32].

The Conference Board of Canada's 2004 report titled *The Voices of Visible Minorities: Speaking Out on Breaking Down Barriers* found that, despite 20 years of enacting employment equity legislation, a "sticky floor" limits the opportunities for initial advancement of visible minorities, while a "glass ceiling" stops them from attaining top positions in organizations (cited in [19]). The concept of a "glass ceiling" refers to the phenomenon where the increased numbers of visible minorities in the workforce are not matched by a corresponding rise in their representation in senior levels of management [7]. The Conference Board's report shows hiring and promotion barriers are creating a widening gap between policy and practice, which will adversely affect the Canadian economy in the future. Visible minorities made up only 1.7 percent of the directors on boards of organizations in 2003 despite the fact that skilled visible minorities were widely available in the labor force [19]. Similarly, Oliver's [16] survey found that among the 69 medium and large companies that responded, only three percent have a visible minority CEO and only three percent of about 900 senior executives in the surveyed firms were visible minorities. The research also uncovered that 9 in 10 organizations do not have any plans to recruit visible minorities to the Board of Directors, even though a majority believed that it is important to have representation of visible minorities in decision-making positions in the organization.

The differences in labor force outcomes between the Canadian-born visible minorities and their nonvisible minority counterparts who have similar human capital characteristics, such as education and language skills, seem to point to the existence of discrimination, which is corroborated by several studies. Visible minorities are significantly less satisfied with their careers than Caucasian Canadians and more likely to experience workplace barriers, lack of fairness in talent management practices, lack of role models, and other key factors influencing career advancement [33]. In 2002, almost 1 in 4 visible minority workers reported that they had experienced racial harassment or discrimination in the workplace [24]. In the Ethnic Diversity Survey, Statistics Canada [27] found that 56 percent of participants who perceived discrimination or unfair treatment identified that they most commonly encountered such treatment in the workplace, particularly during job applications and promotions.

The report by Conference Board of Canada suggests that the propensity for sameness, preservation of status quo, and underlying racism lead employers to often cite "lack of fit" as the rationale for not hiring or promoting skilled minority candidates [19]. Overt discrimination has reduced but subtle forms of discrimination continue to exist. Additional employment barriers cited in Conference Board of Canada's report and also in Oliver's [16] research include speaking with an accent; having foreign-sounding names; unfamiliarity with Canadian mores; lack of recognition of foreign credentials; higher performance expectations for minority candidates. Conference Board of Canada estimates that the failure to recognize foreign credentials will cost the Canadian economy $1 billion [21].

In addition to barriers in the hiring process, several research studies have shown that North American organizational culture, with its everyday discrimination, is the main reason for high turnover among visible minorities (e.g., [15, 16, 20, 34–36]). When capable minority employees see no opportunity to advance, they tend to leave the organization. Organizations thus not only lose trained employees, thereby leading to higher costs, but also face the possibility of decreased productivity and increased absenteeism [7, 37]. While companies place a great deal of importance on hiring visible minorities, they do not take adequate steps to retain them, thereby creating the "revolving door" syndrome—this happens when a visible minority person leaves the company when s/he experiences inadequate opportunities to advance due to discriminatory and biased practices and finds the company's environment to be uncomfortable. Oliver [16] summarizes from his findings that Canadian businesses are wasting much-needed talent that will adversely affect Canada's economy. In a similar vein, Conference Board of Canada's report emphasized that these barriers are not only a disservice to minorities, but they will "come back to haunt mainstream Canadians by eventually stalling the economy" ([19, para 1]).

Evidence about discrimination in everyday lives of racialized peoples in Canada is plentiful. Statistics Canada's [27] survey on Ethnic Diversity reported that more than 1.4 million Canadians reported being subject to racial discrimination. An Ipsos-Reid Survey of 2005 found that 17 percent of Canadians have been victims of racism at some point [38]. Oliver [16] mentions 1 in 5 visible minority persons reported experiencing discrimination or unfair treatment in the last 5 years. The actual figures could be higher. The Canadian Human Rights Commission reported that race-based complaints represent 36 percent of all complaints filed under Canada's Human Rights Act (cited in [39]). The workplace is the most common location where racism is experienced [21].

4. DIVERSITY MANAGEMENT IN CANADA: CRITICAL PERSPECTIVES

Given that workplace discrimination and poor labor market outcomes persist for visible minorities despite diversity programs and initiatives by the Canadian government and several businesses, it is crucial to critically examine the official multiculturalism policy and existing diversity management efforts. Despite its proclaimed merits, Canada's official multiculturalism policy did not reduce racial inequality [22, 40]. Critics of multiculturalism have long observed that the policy of multiculturalism is superficial and does not question the more covert forms of control and ways of maintaining power in the workplace [40, 41]. Boyd [42] observes multiculturalism policy merely grants cultural identities equal footing in the private sphere, but it receives a very low level of government funding for multicultural activities including anti-racist educational initiatives. Multiculturalism maintains the myth that all cultures in Canada are equal, despite the power of the dominant culture to shape Canadian norms, values, and policies [22]. Writing about White Canadians' thoughts about multiculturalism, Yee and Dumbrill [22] cite interviewee comments that Canadian culture should "be first" and that multiculturalism was "dividing the country" (page 110). These anecdotes point to the larger, historical, collective structures embedded in Canadian consciousness. Homi Bhabha points to the unstated meaning underlying multiculturalism as "sham universalism that paradoxically permits diversity [and] masks ethnocentric norms, values and interests" (quoted in [43, page 485]). Multiculturalism, thereby, takes discussions on race and racism off the agenda, consequently further obscuring critical reflections on historical and contemporary privilege, power, and racial oppression.

Furthermore, research indicates that the Employment Equity Act has been ineffective in meeting its goals for ethnoracial minorities [14, 15, 20, 39]. Unlike the disabled or aboriginal population, ethnoracial minorities who are new immigrants constitute a moving target since their population has been growing and varies across provinces. Attaining equity for ethnoracial minorities in the workforce is, therefore, more challenging than equity for other designated groups. Employment equity policy has been disapproved by both the White male majority and intended beneficiaries including women and minority groups. Ng and Burke [5] note that White males perceive employment equity practices as compromising the principle of merit in pursuit of numerical targets, while women and minorities have disassociated themselves from equity policies due to the stigma associated with the perceptions that people hired under employment equity are incompetent and less qualified.

Moreover, while studies have established that large companies have higher levels of employment equity attainment, ethnoracial minorities continue to be disadvantaged in management, sales and service, and technical positions as well as in certain sectors covered by federal legislation, such as transportation and communication [15].

Even in the public sector, the federal government admitted that efforts to recruit more visible minorities are falling short, although targets for other designated groups (aboriginal people, women, and people with disabilities) are largely being met [14, 44]. In the private sector, Trevor

Wilson, president of diversity consulting firm TWI and author of *Diversity at Work: The Business Case for Equity*, commented that many organizations doing work for the federal government "either find ways to get around the law or simply ignore the requirements" (quoted in [14, page 9]). Wilson mentions private sector firms sign EEA compliance certificates every year hoping that they will not get audited. The government does not have an adequate number of auditors, which enable these firms to get away from the law. Moreover, it has been recognized that, with changing times, the business imperative for diversity and equity is far greater than the goals and expectations specified in the EEA [14, 15]. As such, recruiting and maintaining a diverse workforce needs to go well beyond the targets mandated in the legislation. Besides, the EEA is limited to government organizations and private sector firms that enter into contracts with the government. As such, the Act does not cover all organizations, leaving diversity initiatives to the business and/or equity sense of employers. Thus, few Canadian companies have efficient programs to build and utilize the talents of a truly diverse workforce. Again, most initiatives only attract visible minorities (some of them to comply with Employment Equity legislation); many of them are inadequate in *retaining* minority employees.

To its credit, the Canadian government initiated the Racism-Free Workplace Strategy (RFWS) as a key part "A Canada for All: Canada's Action Plan Against Racism" in 2005. Aiming to augment the effectiveness of the EEA, the goal of the RFWS is to remove the systemic discriminatory barriers faced by both visible minorities and aboriginal peoples. RFWS focuses on increasing awareness about racism-related issues in the workplace and building strong partnerships with organizations, employers, and unions [45]. In 2007, RFWS delivered 75 Racism-Free Workplace workshops to 515 private sector employers throughout Canada [46]. In 2008 9 regional Racism Prevention Officers were hired to work with employers and stakeholders directly.

Evaluation of the program is still ongoing and in progress; hence it is too early to assess the outcomes. Results from workshops have shown the need for tools to address racism (OAS, undated).

In the business sector, most diversity management programs involve cross-cultural training to understand differences in cultures, religions, and customs. In the global economy, increasing emphasis is being placed on the need to develop "cultural competence" defined as "the skill to bridge the cultural dimensions of human behavior" ([2, page 210]). The importance placed on the need for managers to be equipped with knowledge about diverse ethnoracial communities emanates from the belief that ignorance and prejudice about cultures different from one's own can lead to cultural insensitivity and discrimination. Hence "cultural competence" programs are based on the belief that if one can better understand the behavior, culture, and perspectives of another ethnoracial group, then cultural respect and acceptance should follow.

Although cultural competence models are well intentioned, in the diversity literature reviewed for this paper, many writers who advocate for diversity in the business field do not question institutional and societal racism of which the workplace is a part. The underlying assumption of most diversity and cultural competence initiatives appears to be that corporate leaders and managers need to be persuaded that people who look or act differently can be of much use to the organization, and, therefore, managers only need to educate themselves about "others" [22, 40]. Educational sessions in diversity programs are seen as the way to provide "socially dominant groups in the organization with selected pieces of information about others, so that they can be brought into an organization, which remains essentially unchanged" [40, page 12]. Information on differences between cultures is highlighted and imparted in cross-cultural training sessions often conducted by White people. A focus on understanding culture creates several problems. Firstly, this approach diverts attention from the lived experiences of minority groups since their voices easily become secondary to the dominant culture that presents itself as nonideological, fair, and neutral but retains the power to define societal and behavioral norms against which minority cultures are compared [22]. Secondly, although a focus on culture and diversity can make us feel good about acquiring knowledge regarding another culture, this approach undermines the shared responsibility to dismantle systemic, individual, and discriminatory barriers in the workplace. Finally, at its worst, diversity training and cultural competence programs can be reductionist by relegating "culture" to a static concept that is reduced to celebration of dress, cuisine, customs, and behaviors of various cultural groups.

Moreover, Wong et al. [47] observe that a review of literature on cultural competence reveals a few common conceptions of culture. Culture frequently refers to "the sum total" or "totality" of "ways of life" or "life patterns": Henry, Tator, Mattis, and Rees (1995) define culture as "the totality of ideas, beliefs, values, knowledge, and way of life of a group of people who share a certain historical, religious, racial, linguistic, ethnic or social background" (quoted in [47, page 150]). However, as Dean [48] reminds us, culture is individually and socially constructed, and cultural identities are fluid and dynamic since they are continually changing and evolving. From this perspective, the growing popularity of cross-cultural aware-ness sessions runs the risk of stereotyping cultures, which can be as damaging as ignorance, as Locker and Findlay [2] admit. Becoming "culturally competent," then, becomes a challenging prospect since it is questionable if one can become truly competent at the culture of another. Dean [48], therefore, proposes a model based on acceptance of one's lack of competence in cross-cultural matters, which acknowledges that our knowledge is always partial. From this perspective, our goal must be not as much to achieve competence as to participate in the ongoing processes of building relationships and understanding the contexts and histories within which cultures develop.

The assumption of cultural "totality" in the conceptualization of values, beliefs, and behaviors of various cultural groups also masks the ambiguous, conflicting, and contradictory meanings of culture that are mediated by power. Understanding power relations is, thus, crit-ical to understanding culture [49]. Dean [48] emphasizes that it is not just rituals, traditions, norms, values, and beliefs that influence the functioning of a member of a cultural group, but also the way that group is treated within the larger society. This treatment emanates from various racial ideologies prevalent in the larger society that attribute particular cultural traits to certain groups. This sociopolitical analysis necessitates an inquiry into the various forms of oppression that have resulted in racial and economic stratification and limited opportunities for ethnoracial minorities in the workplace. A limited focus on gaining "competence" in the beliefs, customs, and historical traditions of different cultural groups can veil the oppressive power relations between groups and the ways in which dominant groups are positioned to control other groups in society. The fervor with which theories of cultural competence are adopted in contemporary organizations while racism remains unnamed is a reminder that culture is treacherous ground to travel in an oppressive society [50].

Racism in Canadian society is important to name, recognize, and understand to build a truly inclusive workforce and nondiscriminatory work environment. Racism is defined as those aspects of society that "overtly or covertly attribute value and normality to White people and Whiteness and that devalue, stereotype, and label racialized communities as other, different, less than, or render them invisible" ([40, page 270]). According to Sintonen and Takala [18], a certain ideology is at the core of racism—this ideology states that the outward appearance of people defines their capabilities and position in society, with skin color as the most important signifier. The hidden function of this kind of ideology is to secure and guarantee the prevailing social order and division of power ([18, 40, 50, 51]). Actions, language, and behaviors that are ideologically based on racism entail discriminating practices in organizations and society. These discriminating practices isolate visible minorities from the resources provided by society and the economy [18].

Boyd [42] emphasizes that attitudes say little about levels of discriminatory behavior: she mentions Canadian politeness may simply ensure that discrimination is hidden or covert. Overt racial slurs and derogatory remarks are not frequently heard in current times; however, blatant racism (although not completely nonexistent) has been replaced by more subtle forms of racism in terms of institutional practices [34, 35]. Institutional racism is defined as "the network of institutional structures, policies, and practices that create advantages for White people and discrimination, oppression and disadvantage for racialized people" ([40, page 270]). These subtle forms of racism allow individuals to hold discriminatory views while defending such views with nonracially based rationales. Brief et al. [34] give an example where a Black candidate is not rejected for a sales position based explicitly on the employer's distaste for working with Blacks; rather the employer rationalizes that a Black salesperson may not be a "good fit" for a White customer population. Because people do not view themselves as "racists," they are unlikely to engage in overt expressions of prejudice, such as racial slurs, but they do engage in more subtle discriminatory behaviors, such as avoidance of visible minorities and closed and unfriendly verbal and nonverbal communication. Thus, the modern nature of racial attitudes suggests that focusing only on blatant discriminatory acts is inadequate to fully understand the experience of discrimination [35]. Overall, critical writings on diversity management and multiculturalism in the Canadian context resonate with emerging international and critical literature that suggests that the discourse of diversity as a corporate social responsibility obfuscates race relations and power, that it reproduces social hierarchies and representations of identities based on binaries and that it is merely a business imperative for attracting global capitalism and exploiting hitherto untapped market segments (see [52–55]).

5. AN ALTERNATIVE FRAMEWORK: THE ANTI-RACISM APPROACH

Most diversity discourse and research in North America have been instrumentally driven and mainly focused on advocating the business case for diversity: the more sophisticated diversity management programs view employees as strategic assets in organizations, while aligning diversity values with the organization's goals and business strategies [53]. With the focus on the benefits of diversity to organizations, current diversity management practices are not intended to guarantee the integration of minorities in a dominant culture.

Keeping in mind the limitations of current diversity and multicultural initiatives, critical theorizing on diversity, particularly originating from the European Union, has begun to question the business case strategies, particularly the assumptions regarding the nature of diversity, approaches to "manage" diversity, and the argument that diversity must be "capitalized" upon (Walby, 2007 quoted in [53]). One strand of this critical theorizing questions the essentializing of sociodemographic categories, such as race, ethnicity, and gender. These scholars maintain that representing sociodemographic categories as fixed essence and binaries (e.g., male/female; able-bodied/disabled; ethnoracial minorities/Caucasians) marginalizes the differences of specific categories and pays inadequate attention to individual or within-group variation. Hence, these writings emphasize the fluidity of diverse identities in organizations and the importance of social and organizational contexts and how they shape the dynamics of managing diversity (e.g., [52, 56, 57]). A second and related strand emphasizes the need to examine diversity within existing interlocking power structures and relations and in differing social constructions of diversity values and priorities [53]. Risberg and Søderberg [54] note that their research and several Danish studies point to a social responsibility aspect of diversity management that is rarely found in North American or British literature. Several discourses of human rights, justice, antidiscrimination social responsibility and diversity as a business case are intertwined in the diversity policies of frontrunner Danish firms, which emphasize care, peer support, and personal development together with the business advantages of diversity. However, Risberg and Søderberg also point to the need to distinguish between the discourse of diversity in strategic corporate communication and the actual implementation in a company's daily social practices pertaining to diversity.

Within the antidiscrimination framework, several Canadian scholars and consultants on equity in the workplace have advanced the concept of anti-racism that poses pointed questions about power disparities and other forms of inequity (e.g., [40]). Dei [58] puts forth a comprehensive definition of anti-racism as an action-oriented strategy for institutional systemic change that addresses racism and other interlocking systems of social oppression. It is a critical discourse of race and racism in society that challenges the continuance of racializing social groups for differential and unequal treatment. Anti-racism explicitly names the issues of race and social difference as issues of power and equity, rather than as matters of culture and ethnic variety (page 252).

While the concrete steps of an anti-racism approach would depend on the workplace culture and dynamics of each organization, there are certain common principles underlying this framework. Firstly, the anti-racism approach asks unsettling questions about the emphasis placed on people's ethnocultural differences and interrogates the ways in which organizations are structured to reinforce inequities [40]. In contrast to "cultural competence," the growing anti-racism movement scrutinizes "systemic racism"—a term used to refer to the ways in which racism is produced and reproduced by seemingly normal ways in which work is structured, monitored, and rewarded. Racism is, thus, seen as a by-product of apparently neutral procedures of doing business. For example, studies have shown that recruitment processes often screen out people of color who do not have the same background as White people who were recruited in the past [7].

Anti-racism acknowledges that inequitable power relations exist in society and permeate every sphere. True and lasting equity can be possible only by taking a reflective, honest, and critical look at the ways in which the normal, apparently neutral mechanisms of most organizations benefit the dominant group and disadvantage visible minorities [40]. Analyzing an organization's systems is thus an invitation to take an honest look at various aspects of the organization such as hiring, promotion, allocation of job responsibilities, employee satisfaction, turnover rates, organizational culture, and other everyday practices. This process of self-analysis recognizes that employment systems may not always reward competence and hard work and may be vulnerable to favoritism and bias.

Secondly, the anti-racism framework believes that modern racism exists in ways that may be hard for those who do not experience it to fully understand. Members of the dominant culture often discourage alternative perspectives by simply ignoring or denying the relevance of other groups' experiences with racism [7, 22, 50]. Anti-racism educators firmly believe that the dominant group must be educated to recognize that they do indeed live in a different world than racial minorities and that the latter's experiences may be fundamentally different from their own. This can trigger dialogue instead of shutting down conversations about racism. Through dialogue the visible majority and minority groups can become more aware of each other and themselves, which enhances the possibilities for working together toward common goals.

Thirdly, and arising from the second principle, anti-racism equips the dominant group with the knowledge and skills to acknowledge their own privilege and to work towards social change. In the Canadian context, a focus on White identity is the crux of anti-racism work, according to Yee and Dumbrill [22] who explain "to examine Whiteness is to identify how race shapes the lives of both White people and people of color" (page 100). Elaborating on the dimensions of Whiteness, Frankenberg (1993 cited in [22, page 103]) noted that firstly, Whiteness is a location of structural advantage or privilege. Secondly, it is a "standpoint"—a place from which White people look at themselves, at others, and at society. Thirdly, Whiteness refers to a set of cultural practices that are usually unmarked and unnamed. The essence of Whiteness, thus, lies in its potency to maintain a silent assumption that equates normality with White culture, which becomes the taken-for-granted norm.

Therefore, proponents of an anti-racism approach believe that any racial equity work must ensure that people with power have opportunities to examine their own experiences of unearned privilege. Peg MacIntosh defines unearned privilege as "the invisible knapsack of unearned assets which White people can count on cashing in each day, but about which they are meant to remain oblivious" (quoted in [40, page 272]). Examples include the ability to be unaware of race; the assurance that police will not stop or harass them because of their race; the assurance that they will not be followed in a store; the assurance that they will not be harassed, hated, or intimidated in the community; the assurance that they will not experience surveillance from their neighbors or police; and the assumption that getting hired or promoted is due to their competence and not because of their race. Lopes and Thomas [40] further mention that White people must also grapple with the difficult question of why they would want to share the power they hold. This can lead to innovative solutions to address the discriminatory work culture.

Finally, this approach mobilizes the skills and knowledge of White and racialized people gained through anti-racism deliberations to question the status quo and work towards a redistribution of power in organizations and society. For instance, White people can challenge employers on the number of White people hired as a result of networks and friendships. Racism, thus, is seen not only as a problem to be resolved by those it targets; it is also the responsibility of White people who benefit from this system to reject it [59]. Lopes and Thomas [40] inform us that although this approach can lead to tensions and discomfort, the dilemmas that arise as a result can be used productively to build alliances and common cause among White and racialized workers.

The anti-racism approach has been applied in several settings in North America and elsewhere (see [60]). Here, four such initiatives—Dismantling Racism; Project Change at Levi Strauss Foundation in the USA; Seattle City Government Race and Social Justice Initiative; and Undoing Racism, New Orleans, USA—are reviewed and pertinent lessons are drawn for the Canadian milieu.

5.1. Dismantling Racism

Dismantling Racism (DR), coordinated by *dRworks* (originally called Change*work*), was initiated in the US as a systems change intervention strategy to address institutional racism in organizational settings. DR is a collaborative effort between anti-racism trainers, researchers/evaluators, community organizers, and leaders working in partnership with organizations and communities. The pivotal characteristic of DR is that it is a process to assist leaders and organizations to understand and address racism, both within their organization and also in the community where the organization operates or is located [61, 62]. The DR framework addresses institutional racism at three levels of an organization:

i. at the individual level in terms of individual employee attitudes, beliefs, and behaviors;
ii. at the intraorganizational level through the organizational structure, climate, and culture, including relationships between staff and organizational policies and procedures; and
iii. the extraorganizational level that includes the influence of external social, economic, political, and cultural factors that impact the organization.

More specifically, DR aims to increase the accountability of individuals and systems in monitoring health care inequalities and to develop a shared analytical framework to understand the underlying problems (see http://www.dismantlingracism.org/about-drworks.html for details). A key element of the DR intervention is incorporating a change team, which is multiracial in composition consisting of a cross-section of employees within the organization, who work alongside DR consultants, evaluators, community representatives, and other stakeholders. The change team is responsible for monitoring and evaluating the impact of the intervention in terms of organizational policies, procedures and practices, allocation of resources, relationship structures, organizational norms and values, and individual skills and attitudes of staff.

5.2. Project Change

Developed by the Levi Strauss Foundation in 1991, Project Change is an initiative to address racial prejudice and institutional racism in four communities in the USA where Levis Strauss operates its facilities: Albuquerque (New Mexico), El Paso (Texas), Valdosta (Georgia), and Knoxville (Tennessee). Although Project Change has concluded, several of its anti-racism activities and networks continue to operate, both within some of the communities, as well as at a national level [63]. The organizing structure of Project Change included the formation of taskforces consisting of volunteer members from diverse groups. The initial goals of Project Change were to

i.   dismantle institutional policies and practices that promote racial discrimination;
ii. ease tensions between minority and majority groups and reduce interethnic conflict;
iii. promote fair representation of diversity in the leadership of community institutions; and
iv. stop overt or violent acts of racial or cultural prejudice (Batten and Leiderman, 1995 cited in [60]).

According to the evaluation undertaken by the Centre for Assessment and Policy Development (CAPD), Project Change succeeded in changing policies and practices in some institutions, including the composition of boards and governing bodies. Tackling institutional racism was the project's biggest challenge, due to lack of clarity and significant resistance from some institutions. Taskforce leaders felt limited in their ability to reduce institutional racism. These challenges were compounded, given limited resources and the broader economic and political context for addressing institutional racism [63].

On the positive side, Project Change enhanced the national and internal dialogue on institutional racism by disseminating information to organizations, corporations, funding bodies, policy makers, and at meetings and conferences. The project also resulted in a number of publications and resources, including an online network and clearing-house for anti-racism news and activities [63].

5.3 The Race and Social Justice Initiative (RSJI)

The Race and Social Justice Initiative was initiated by the Seattle City Government in 2004 to address institutional racism in the city. The program is ongoing with the following aims:

i.   to assess the impact of race on organizational culture, policies, practices, and procedures;
ii. to transform business practices towards race and social justice goals;
iii. to conduct outreach and create public engagement opportunities; and
iv. to provide training and build the capacity and skills of city staff to address institutionalized racism (Potapchuk and Aspen Institute Roundtable for Community Change, 2007 cited in [60]).

The RSJI initiative requires all city departments to develop a work plan to undo institutionalized racism and support multiculturalism; it requires that activities and findings must be reported directly to the mayor. In the first year of the program, review of department plans identified five common concerns: workforce equity, economic equity, immigrant and refugee services, public engagement, and staff capacity building [64]. RSJI developed a comprehensive organizing framework to manage and implement specific activities arising from these central concerns across departments. The Office for Civil Rights is responsible for managing implementation of RSJI: it reviews departmental plans, provides support to change teams, coordinates training and manages the staffing of the core team. The core team consists of approximately 30 employees who receive training to provide strategic planning, lead training/ workshops for other city staff, and work on issues specific to the initiative. Change teams have been created within each department and they are responsible for implementing the RSJI plan supervised by a senior leader. The central concerns committee coordinates efforts across various departments, enables sharing of best practices, and develops tools and policies to address concerns raised within departmental plans (Potapchuk and Aspen Institute Roundtable for Community Change, 2007 cited in [60]).

An evaluation of the initiative found that the broad goals of the RSJI were disseminated and adequately understood by department managers and change team members. Most departments embraced the initiative and established change teams to develop and implement work plans [64]. The mayor's commitment resulted in increased reporting, development, and implementation of a capacity building and anti-racism training program targeted at change team members and managers [64]. Workforce equity activities were enhanced and these included the recruitment of people from diverse backgrounds at every level, particularly entry-level positions such as laborers and administrative assistants. However, the city has expressed its commitment to increase upward mobility and professional development opportunities for employees.

From 2009 to 2011, the City of Seattle expanded its commitment to racial equality: RSJI received the full endorsement of all elected City officials. RSJI has been integrated as a core value into all the mayor's programs and priorities. The City's budget office requires departments to use Racial Equality as a basis to analyze every budget proposal in terms of impact of policy and program decisions, as well as unintended consequences. Seattle City Council requires all City departments to report on the progress of their annual Race and Social Justice Initiative work plans [65]. The City's 2012–2014 plan expands the RSJI to focus on ending racial inequality in the community and to strengthen partnerships across institutions and the community [66].

5.4 Undoing Racism

Undoing Racism is workshop offered by the People's Institute for Survival and Beyond, which is a national, multiracial, anti-racist network based in New Orleans, USA, dedicated to eradicating racism and other forms of institutional oppression (http://www.pisab.org/). The institute provides training, consultation, and leadership development to organizations nationally and internationally. Workshops aim to enable participants to unpack racism, where it comes from, how it manifests and why it persists, and how to dismantle racism. Training materials include learning from history, developing leadership, ensuring accountability, establishing networking, undoing internalized racism, and understanding the role of organizational gatekeepers in perpetuating racism. Under the Undoing Racism program, the Community Organizing Strategy Team (COST) works with community activists to assess their organizations, roles, and relationships in terms of racial and cultural diversity. The Reflection, Assessment, Evaluation Team (RAE) enables the organization or group to articulate its vision, values, and goals and to measure outcomes in terms of the stated objectives.

In the evaluations conducted, participants have rated Undoing Racism highly, with many participants expressing commitment to address institutional racism. For instance, Mack Burch et al. (2005) cited in Trenerry et al. [60] conducted an evaluation of Undoing Racism, undertaken as part of the *Seven Principles* project which conducted workshops with staff from health and social service agencies with the goal of eliminating disparities in African American infant mortality in San Francisco, USA. While 80 percent of participants rated the workshops highly, 90 percent agreed to undertake some form of action to tackle the effects of institutional racism. Many participants also mentioned that the workshops had impacted them on a personal level, and a number of them have adopted practices to improve cultural competency within their organization and to decrease institutional racism. Another evaluation of Undoing Racism was conducted by Johnson et al. [67] to evaluate training for community service providers to address disparities in child welfare. This evaluation found a high level of participant satisfaction with the training, increased knowledge of issues of race and racism, and increased awareness of racial dynamics [67].

Since organizations differ in their internal cultures, no cookbook recipes can be suggested for dealing with racism; however, there are significant commonalities in the aforementioned case studies in terms of intervention strategies, outcomes, and key learnings. It is interesting to note that although several of these interventions included diversity training as one of their components, authors such as Yee and Dumbrill [22] and Lopez and Thomas [40] maintain the distinction between the anti-racism approach and diversity training and cultural competence models: they emphasize that the anti-racism approach must acknowledge that racism exists in society and that conflicts between ethnoracial minorities and the dominant group are not due to lack of understanding between groups, but rather a manifestation of power differentials between the dominant group and racialized minorities.

In terms of positive outcomes, anti-racism initiatives have recorded improved representation of diverse employees; better staff seniority profiles; increased sales and productivity; increased retention of visible minority employees; more diverse composition of boards; improved awareness, knowledge, and skills; perceived fair treatment; acceptance of ethnic differences; and reduced racial tension [60].

Several key learnings deserve attention. One of the most salient themes that emerged from the aforementioned initiatives is the need to be cognizant of resistance from some institutions as the effort required to reduce institutional racism becomes evident. Leadership was underscored as key to supporting institutional change, ensuring adequate resource allocation and persistent efforts, and engaging with those resistant to and/or fearful of change. Training for managers and staff emerged as significant in recognizing and addressing race-based discrimination and its consequences. The case studies also demonstrate that transforming the values and culture of individuals and the organization is a time-consuming process and requires long-term commitment.

Importantly, the anti-racism approach has been criticized for creating psychological discomfort for the dominant group. Strong emotions such as guilt, humiliation, sadness, shame, and embarrassment can result, leading to increased prejudice [68]. As this educator and author of the present paper experienced in her classrooms in USA and Canada, students from the dominant culture may disengage from anti-racism discussions as they become overwhelmed with discussions of race.

Another risk entailed in the anti-racism approach is that it can mistakenly portray racism as mainly perpetrated by the dominant group, thereby creating a simplistic binary between visible minorities and the dominant culture and perpetuating an "us-versus-them" perspective. The atmosphere of alienation and bias against White people thus engendered can further widen the schism. The generic label of an "oppressor" may lead dominant culture participants to avoid interracial contact completely, deny their race, or resist learning about race and racism [69].

Likewise, discussions of the "unearned privilege" of the dominant group require considerable sensitivity as it may result in feelings of guilt, sadness, and embarrassment, which can lead to increased prejudice [69]. Where relevant, it is important to focus on the privilege itself rather than painting the entire dominant group with one stroke of brush as inherently racist. Similarly, evidence of racism committed by members of minority ethnic groups should be acknowledged, rather than being hushed or denied. An anti-racism approach must encourage everyone regardless of racial, ethnic, cultural, or religious background to engage with experiences of privilege across other facets of their identity (e.g., gender and social class). This is particularly significant in a diverse and multicultural country such as Canada where intersecting differences and interlocking forms of oppression and privilege persist across race, gender, class, ethnic and religious backgrounds, aboriginal/non-aboriginal status, age, disability, and so on.

Moreover, an anti-racism approach tailored to the Canadian context must be cognizant of the country's history in terms of colonial legacy, multiculturalism, and immigrant-led growth. As such, firstly it is imperative for the Canadian version of an anti-racism approach to build solidarity with the decolonization struggles of the original inhabitants—aboriginal peoples [70, 71]. Secondly, given the high rates of immigration and racism faced by new immigrants [27], educating participants about the geopolitical reasons for contemporary out-migration from other countries can reduce racism in the society and contribute to a better understanding of immigrants and their cultures. Finally, anti-racism in the Canadian context must also debunk common myths, such as that immigrants are taking away the jobs of the dominant group [72]. As stated earlier, visible minorities have contributed significantly to the country's economic prosperity [16]. Even today, Canada faces a shortage of skilled workers; moreover, many immigrants are employed in unskilled and low-paid jobs such as meat packing that are not filled by the dominant group.

6. CONCLUDING COMMENTS

Despite the fact that diversity makes astute sense for organizational success, visible minorities face discrimination in the hiring process. They are paid less than the dominant group, and they face blocked opportunities in addition to racism in the larger society and community. While employment equity and diversity and cultural competence initiatives exist in many companies and organizations, they have largely failed to ensure equity and fairness in hiring, retention, and treatment of visible minorities. Most diversity programs in Canadian workplaces are limited in their scope. Attempts to increase the number of minority hires are inadequate unless they are also coupled with programs to deal with racism in the workplace. Discrimination continues to permeate organizations in subtle, nearly invisible forms due to stereotypical assumptions prevailing in organizational norms and everyday practices.

The importance of the anti-racism approach for organizational success cannot be overstated. The anti-racism framework takes up the challenge of building healthy, inclusive, and antidiscriminatory work environments. However, the anti-racism approach is not without challenges. This paper has highlighted the key dilemmas faced by anti-racism practice, and it has briefly suggested several directions to make this approach more suitable to the Canadian situation. Undoubtedly, further research and development in anti-racism work in Canada are an urgent priority. Additionally, as Brief et al. [34] and Sintonen and Takala [18] remind us, organizations are not solely responsible for anti-racism efforts. Anti-racism initiatives in the workplace must be supplemented by efforts on a national scale with government officials, educators (including those in business, commerce, and management disciplines) and popular media taking the initiative to debunk the notions of skin color, ethnicity, or religious background as markers of inferiority or superiority.

ENDNOTES

1. While diversity in the workforce originates from many sources such as gender, race and ethnicity, regional and national origin, social class, religion, age, sexual orientation, and abilities [2, 7], for the purpose of this paper the terms "diverse" and "diversity" refer to the inclusion of ethnoracial minorities. Given the space constraints in this paper, it is suggested that workforce participation of other diverse groups are important and complex topics that merit detailed and separate reviews of their own.

REFERENCES

1. K. Hutchings, "Book review: managing diversity: toward a globally inclusive workplace," *Asia Pacific Journal of Human Resources*, vol. 43, pp. 430–431, 2005.

2. K.O. Locker and I. Findlay, *Essentials of Business and Administrative Communication*, McGraw-Hill Ryerson, Toronto, Canada, 2006.

3. G. Palmer, "Diversity management, past, present and future," *Asia Pacific Journal of Human Resources*, vol. 41, no. 1, pp. 13–24, 2003.

4. D.J. Terry, "Social identity and diversity in organizations," *Asia Pacific Journal of Human Resources*, vol. 41, no. 1, pp. 25–35, 2003.

5. E.S.W. Ng and R.J. Burke, "Person-organization fit and the war for talent: does diversity management make a difference?" *International Journal of Human Resource Management*, vol. 16, no. 7, pp. 1195–1210, 2005.

6. A. Ferner, P. Almond, and T. Colling, "Institutional theory and the cross-national transfer of employment policy: the case of 'workforce diversity' in US multinationals," *Journal of International Business Studies*, vol. 36, no. 3, pp. 304–321, 2005.

7. M. Hamlet, *The Underrepresentation of Blacks in the Executive Suite in Corporate America* [Ph.D. dissertation], Walden University, 2000.

8. T.H. Cox and S. Blake, "Managing cultural diversity: implications for organizational competitiveness," *Academy of Management Executive*, vol. 5, no. 2, pp. 45–56, 1991.

9. S. Nkomo and T. Cox, "Diverse identities in organizations," in *Handbook of Organizational Studies*, S.R. Clegg, C. Gardy, and W.R. Nord, Eds., Sage, London, UK, 1996.

10. G.E. Miller and J.I.A. Rowney, "Workplace diversity management in a multicultural society," *Women in Management Review*, vol. 14, no. 8, pp. 307–315, 1999.

11. J.A. Gilbert, B.A. Stead, and J.M. Ivancevich, "Diversity management: a new organizational paradigm," *Journal of Business Ethics*, vol. 21, no. 1, pp. 61–76, 1999.

12. N. Bassett-Jones, "The paradox of diversity management, creativity and innovation," *Creativity and Innovation Management*, vol. 14, no. 2, pp. 169–175, 2005.

13. R.L. Tung, "The cross-cultural research imperative: the need to balance cross-national and intra-national diversity," *Journal of International Business Studies*, vol. 39, no. 1, pp. 41–46, 2008.

14. D. Brown, "Feds miss minority hiring targets," *Canadian HR Reporter*, vol. 17, no. 11, pp. 1–9, 2004.

15. H.C. Jain and J.J. Lawler, "Visible minorities under the Canadian Employment Equity Act, 1987–1999," *Relations Industrielles*, vol. 59, no. 3, pp. 585–609, 2004.

16. D. Oliver, "Achieving results through diversity: a strategy for success," *Ivey Business Journal Online*, vol. 69, no. 4, 2005.

17. D.A. Thomas and R.J. Ely, "Making difference matter: a new paradigm for managing diversity," *Harvard Business Review*, vol. 74, no. 5, pp. 79–90, 1996.

18. T.M. Sintonen and T. Takala, "Racism and ethics in the globalized business world," *International Journal of Social Economics*, vol. 29, no. 11, pp. 849–860, 2002.

19. R. Trichur, *Conference Board of Canada Report. Employment Equity Still Failing Minorities*, Canadian Press Newswire, Toronto, Canada, 2004.

20. F. Henry and C. Tator, *The Color of Democracy: Racism in Canadian Society*, Nelson, Toronto, Canada, 2006.

21. V. Dugale, "The changing color of Canada," *Our Times*, vol. 25, no. 5, pp. 24–28, 2006.

22. J.Y. Yee and G.C. Dumbrill, "Whiteout: looking for race in Canadian social work practice," in *Multicultural Social Work in Canada: Working With Diverse Ethno-Racial Communities*, Al-Krenaw and J.R. Graham, Eds., pp. 98–121, Oxford University Press, Don Mills, Canada, 2003.

23. R. Robin, "Delivering diversity," *Canadian Business*, vol. 77, no. 7, p. 38, 2004.

24. K. Pendakur and R. Pendakur, "Colour my world: have earnings gaps for Canadian-born ethnic minorities changed over time?" *Canadian Public Policy*, vol. 28, no. 4, pp. 489–511, 2002.

25. A. Jackson, *Poverty and Racism*, Canadian Council on Social Development, Ottawa, Canada, 2001.

26. J. Samuel and K. Basavarajappa, "The visible minority population in Canada: a review of numbers, growth and labor force issues," *Canadian Studies in Population*, vol. 33, no. 2, pp. 241–269, 2006.

27. Statistics Canada, *The Ethnic Diversity Survey: Portrait of a Multicultural Society*, (Section on Visible Minority and Discrimination or Unfair Treatment), Catalogue No. 89-593-XIE, StatsCan, Ottawa, Canada, 2003.

28. Statistics Canada, Visible minorities in the Canadian labor force, 1991, http://www.statcan.gc.ca/studies-etudes/75-001/archive/1991/5018456-eng.pdf.

29. Statistics Canada, Labor force activity, visible minority groups, immigrant status and period of immigration, highest certificate, diploma or degree, age groups, and sex for the population 15 years and over of Canada, provinces, territories, census metropolitan areas and census agglomerations, 2006 census—20% sample data, 2006, http://www12.statcan.gc.ca/census-recensement/2006/dp-pd/ tbt/Rp-eng.cfm.

30. CLC (Canadian Labor Congress), *A Workplace that Works*, Canadian Labor Congress, Ottawa, Canada, 2002.

31. Human Resources and Skills Development Canada (HRSDC), Employment Equity Act: annual report, 2008, http://www.hrsdc.gc.ca/eng/labour/equality/employmentequity/tools/annualreports/2008/docs/2008report.pdf.

32. The Diversity Institute in Management and Technology, DiverseCity counts: A snapshot of diversity in the Greater Toronto Area, 2009, http://www.ryerson.ca/diversity/news/CountsReport CONFIDENTIAL.pdf.

33. Catalyst Canada and the Diversity Institute, Career advancement in corporate Canada: A focus on visible minorities-survey findings, 2007, http://www.ryerson.ca/diversity/media/Full%20 Report.pdf.

34. A. P. Brief, R.T. Buttram, R.M. Reizenstein et al., "Beyond good intentions: the next steps toward racial equality in the American workplace," *Academy of Management Executive*, vol. 11, no. 4, pp. 59–72, 1997.

35. E.A. Deitch, A. Barsky, R.M. Butz, S. Chan, A. P. Brief, and J.C. Bradley, "Subtle yet significant: the existence and impact of everyday racial discrimination in the workplace," *Human Relations*, vol. 56, no. 11, pp. 1299–1324, 2003.

36. S. Fox and L.E. Stallworth, "Racial/ethnic bullying: exploring links between bullying and racism in the US workplace," *Journal of Vocational Behavior*, vol. 66, no. 3, pp. 438–456, 2005.

37. S. Jeanquart-Barone and U. Sekaran, "Institutional racism: an Empirical Study," *Journal of Social Psychology*, vol. 136, no. 4, pp. 477–482, 1996.

38. The Dominion Institute, *Ipsos-Reid Survey*, Dominion Institute, Toronto, Canada, 2005.

39. U. Vu, "Feds hiring racism officers," *Canadian HR Reporter*, vol. 19, no. 16, pp. 6–7, 2006.

40. T. Lopes and B. Thomas, *Dancing on Live Embers: Challenging Racism in Organizations*, Between the Lines, Toronto, Canada, 2006.

41. S. Bertone and M. Leahy, "Multiculturalism as a conservative ideology: impacts on workforce diversity," *Asia Pacific Journal of Human Resources*, vol. 41, no. 1, pp. 101–115, 2003.

42. M. Boyd, "Diverse fortunes in different countries? Earnings of White and Black immigrant generations in Canada and the United States," in *Proceedings of the Annual Meeting of the Population Association of America*, Philadelphia, USA, March 2005.

43. G. Jordan and C. Weedon, *Cultural Politics: Class, Gender, Race and the Postmodern World*, Blackwell Publishers, Oxford, UK, 1995.

44. S. Klie, "Public service falls short on hiring minorities," *Canadian HR Reporter*, vol. 20, no. 3, pp. 1–2, 2007.

45. Human Resources and Skills Development Canada, Racism-free workplace strategy website. The Government of Canada Labour Program, 2010, http://www.hrsdc.gc.ca/eng/labour/overviews/workplace equality/rfws.shtml.

46. OAS (Organization of American States), Executive Secretariat for Integral Development—SEDI, Racism-free workplace strategy, 2012, http://www.sedi.oas.org/ddse/doc-umentos/TRABAJO/new portfolio/Canada-DF-Racism-Free%20Workplace%20Strategy-ING.pdf.

47. R.Y. Wong, S. Cheng, S. Choi et al., "Deconstructing culture in cultural competence," *Canadian Social Work Review*, vol. 20, no. 2, pp. 149–167, 2003.

48. R.G. Dean, "The myth of cross-cultural competence," *Families in Society*, vol. 82, no. 6, pp. 623–630, 2001.

49. C. James, *Seeing Ourselves: Exploring Race, Ethnicity and Culture*, Thompson Educational Publishing, Toronto, Canada, 2nd edition, 1999.

50. S. Razack, *Looking White People in the Eye*, University of Toronto Press, Toronto, Canada, 1999.

51. J. Solomos and L. Back, *Racism and Society*, St. Martin's Press, New York, NY, USA, 1996.

52. R. Bendl, A. Fleischmann, and C. Walenta, "Diversity management discourse meets queer theory," *Gender in Management*, vol. 23, no. 6, pp. 382–394, 2008.

53. B.D. Metcalfe and C. Woodhams, "Critical perspectives in diversity and equality management," *Gender in Management*, vol. 23, no. 6, pp. 377–381, 2008.

54. A. Risberg and A.M. Søderberg, "Translating a management concept: diversity management in Denmark," *Gender in Management*, vol. 23, no. 6, pp. 426–441, 2008.

55. J. Wrench, "Diversity management can be bad for you," *Race & Class*, vol. 46, no. 3, pp. 73–84, 2005.

56. A. Lorbiecki and G. Jack, "Critical turns in the evolution of diversity management," *British Journal of Management*, vol. 11, no. 3, pp. S17–S31, 2000.

57. P. Zanoni and M. Janssens, "Deconstructing difference: the rhetoric of human resource managers' diversity discourses," *Organization Studies*, vol. 25, no. 1, pp. 55–74, 2004.

58. G.J. Dei, "Critical perspectives in antiracism: an introduction," *Canadian Review of Sociology and Anthropology*, vol. 33, no. 3, pp. 247–267, 1996.

59. J. Sorenson, "I'm not a racist, and nobody I know is either. A worthy statement which invites discussion of 'color-blindness'," in *Culture of Prejudice*, J.C. Blackwell, M.E.G. Smith, and J.S. Sorenson, Eds., pp. 47–52, Broadview Press, Peterborough, Canada, 2003.

60. B. Trenerry, H. Franklin, and Y. Paradies, *Preventing Race-Based Discrimination and Supporting Cultural Diversity in the Workplace (An Evidence Review: Full Report)*, Victoria Health Promotion Foundation, Melbourne, Australia, 2012.

61. D.M. Griffith, E.L. Childs, E. Eng, and V. Jeffries, "Racism in organizations: the case of a county public health department," *Journal of Community Psychology*, vol. 35, no. 3, pp. 287–302, 2007.

62. D.M. Griffith, M. Yonas, M. Mason, and B.E. Havens, "Considering organizational factors in addressing health care disparities: two case examples," *Health Promotion Practice*, vol. 11, no. 3, pp. 367–376, 2010.

63. S. Leiderman and D.M. Dupree, *Looking Back: Project Change From 1991–2005*, Center for Assessment and Policy Development (CAPD), Conshohocken, Pa, USA, 2005, http://www.capd.org/pubfiles/pub-2005-04-01.pdf.

64. Seattle Office for Civil Rights, Race and social justice initiative report 2008: Looking back, moving forward, 2008, http://www.seattle.gov/rsji/docs/090120rsjiReport.pdf.

65. Seattle Office for Civil Rights, *Race and Social Justice Initiative: Accomplishments 2009–2011*, Office for Civil Rights, Seattle, Wash, USA, 2011, http://www.seattle.gov/rsji/docs/RSJIAccomplishments2009-2011.pdf.

66. Seattle Office for Civil Rights, *RSJI'S New Three-Year Plan: 2012–2014 Plan focuses on Community Partnerships*, 2012, http://www.seattle.gov/rsji.

67. L.M. Johnson, B.F. Antle, and A.P. Barbee, "Addressing disproportionality and disparity in child welfare: evaluation of an anti-racism training for community service providers," *Children and Youth Services Review*, vol. 31, no. 6, pp. 688–696, 2009.

68. Y. Paradies, L. Chandrakumar, N. Klocker et al., *Building on Our Strengths: A Framework to Reduce Race-Based Discrimination and Support Diversity in Victoria—Full Report*, Victorian Health Promotion Foundation, Melbourne, Australia, 2009, http://www.vichealth.vic.gov.au/Programs-and-Projects/Freedom-from-discrimination/Building-on-our-strengths.aspx.

69. A.N. Miller and T.M. Harris, "Communicating to develop white racial identity in an interracial communication class," *Communication Education*, vol. 54, no. 3, pp. 223–242, 2005.

70. J. Blackwell, M. Smith, and J. Sorenson, "Indians shouldn't have any special rights: belief that aboriginal peoples are 'just another minority group," in *Culture of Prejudice: Arguments in Critical Social Science*, pp. 121–126, Higher Education University of Toronto Press, Toronto, Canada, 2008.

71. L.T. Smith, *Decolonizing Methodologies: Research and Indigenous Peoples*, Zed Books, London, UK, 1999.

72. J. Blackwell, M. Smith, and J. Sorenson, "Immigrants are threatening our way of life," in *Culture of Prejudice: Arguments in Critical Social Science*, pp. 53–58, Higher Education University of Toronto Press, Toronto, Canada, 2008.

Chapter 32

Local Produce, Foreign Labour: Labour Mobility Programs and Global Trade Competitiveness in Canada

Kerry Preibisch

Preibisch (2007) tackles the ways in which formalized regimes of temporary visa workers are becoming a feature of the Canadian labour market, particularly in agriculture; the conditions under which they are incorporated into the labour market; and the implications for both those workers and domestic labour. She sees them as an important part of a globalized set of production relations that are highly racialized. She uses the Canadian Seasonal Agricultural Worker Program (SAWP) as a case study to explore the ways in which unfree labour is increasingly essential to the competitive posture of Canadian agricultural producers in a competitive globalized environment. Preibisch sees these workers as representing a comparative advantage for employers often dealing with high turnover of domestic labour because of the conditions of work, an advantage rooted in the racialized patterns of "economic displacement and forced migration" and "unfree labour" in a globalized labour market. Apart from ethnographic research material, the chapter contains data from semi-structured interviews that the author conducted with SAWP workers, administrators, growers, and employers.

The significant and growing role of foreign workers in the U.S. economy has been generally well-researched. In the case of Canada, however, less is known about this social trend despite a number of indicators that suggest similar processes are in play, albeit on a different scale and through different mechanisms. Temporary visa workers in particular are increasingly taking on a heightened profile in the "Great White North," finding work in numerous sectors of the economy. Many of the sectors employing foreign workers are geographically immobile—they cannot relocate their production abroad—and include construction, hospitality, and agriculture. In this paper, I focus on the incorporation of foreign workers in the horticultural industry under the Seasonal Agricultural Workers Program (SAWP). I argue that foreign labor is one of the planks of the global competitiveness of Canadian horticulture and that the industry's comparative advantage rests, in part, on limiting the rights of foreign workers who cannot move out of the sector. I suggest that migration controls, such as so-called "labor mobility" programs, are an integral part of Canada's global restructuring and trade competitiveness. In order to build this argument, I present data on the use of foreign workers historically and the growth of horticulture. Based on qualitative research with employers, administrators, and workers, I show how foreign workers have become the preferred and, in some cases, core workforce for horticulture operations and detail the basis for growers' preference. Further, I explore the increasingly permanent nature of this "temporary" labor mobility program and the ways in which it provides an ever more flexible workforce. [...]

CHANGES IN GLOBAL AGRIFOOD SYSTEMS

Over the last 30 years, but particularly in the last decade, the global agrifood system has experienced significant transformations. Busch and Bains (2004), in their overview of these changes, argue that "the expansion and consolidation of food retailers and the shift towards private standards are dramatically reshaping social, political, and economic relationships on a global scale" (342). A central arena in which the restructuring of the global economy is reshaping these relationships is the labor market serving global agriculture (ILO 2004; McMichael 1996). Recent studies in developing countries on contemporary changes in the global agrifood system have observed a number of trends in production relations with respect to labor, including a growth in informal, contingent employment in horticulture (Barrientos, Dolan, and Tallontire 2003); the proliferation of production contracts for small-holders, often involving the exploitation of unpaid, household labor (Dolan 2002; Raynolds 2002); and the increased use of piece-rate wage schemes to increase production yields (Barrón and Rello 2000). Yet, as Kritzinger, Barrientos, and Rossouw (2004) argue, the trend towards flexible employment in the agricultural sector is also galvanizing in the North. Significant changes to the social relations of agrifood production have also implied important shifts in the ways people are incorporated into wage labor in high-income countries.

One of the most striking trends in this regard is the growing use of foreign workers. In particular, the numbers of people working in high-income countries without status or under temporary work visas is central to the trends differentiating global migration flows from past historical periods. In the case of the United States, perhaps the most prominent example, approximately 90 percent of the migrants who work seasonally on farms producing fruits and vegetables were born abroad, and the share of irregular or unauthorized workers among all hired crop workers rose from less than 10 to over 50 percent through the 1990s (Martin 2004 cited in ILO 2004). The European Union's agricultural sector employs close to 500,000 seasonal workers from countries outside the EU-15, including some 100,000 workers in Britain alone (ILO 2004; Rural Migration News 2004). In Germany, agriculture employs 54 percent of the country's registered seasonal workers (Cyrus 1994 in Hoggart and Mendoza 1999). Most surprising are the changes taking place in the formerly labor-sending countries of the Mediterranean, who have become migrant receivers and permanent migrant destinations in the last 15 to 20 years, particularly in agriculture (Kasimis and Papadopoulos 2005). In Greece, for example, migrants have become the principal contributors of agricultural wage labor (Kasimis and Papadopoulos 2005). Similarly in Italy and Spain, non–European Union migrants are taking on an increasing role in the production of wine grapes, tomatoes, tobacco, and market gardening (Hoggart and Mendoza 1999). There is evidence to suggest that (im)migrant labor has served as an important factor in both the maintenance of farms as well as the expansion of dynamic crops. In Greece, for example, the availability of foreign workers has allowed the maintenance of farm activity in extensive or EU subsidized agricultural systems and stimulated dynamic, export-oriented agriculture (Kasimis, Papadopoulos, and Zacopoulou 2003).

The use of (im)migrant workers to achieve labor market flexibility has emerged as a central aspect of accumulation in the contemporary economy (Sassen 2000; Sharma 2006). With the increasingly evident wealth gap between poor countries in the South and the high-income countries in the North, state citizenship becomes an ever more relevant basis for inequality among workers in labor-receiving states (Stasiulis and Bakan 2003). The granting or withholding of citizenship rights through immigration policy serves as a powerful tool at the disposal of labor-receiving states in determining incorporations in labor markets specifically, and society in general, often rendering both legal and legitimate discriminations based on the social relations of race, class, and gender (Ball and Piper 2004; Sharma 2006; Stasiulis and Bakan 2003). Immigration policy has thus become an increasingly important arena for regulating the labor markets of high-income economies and ensuring their position within the global political economy (Rai 2001; Sharma 2006; Stasiulis and Bakan, 2003). In the case of Canada, Sharma (2006) contends that increasingly restrictive immigration policies have not necessarily served to exclude people per se, but rather to create greater competition within the national labor market. This, she argues, has been achieved principally through the growing admission of foreign workers under conditions that restrict their rights relative to immigrants and Canadian citizens. Accordingly, immigration policy has played a critical role in satisfying employers and maintaining the Canadian economy as globally competitive.

The growing incorporation of (im)migrant workers has also led to a deepening of labor segmentation in labor-receiving countries. As Persaud (2001:379) observes, "new patterns of accumulation have been increasingly built on a deepening of labor segmentation, both in the global division of labor and in national social formation" that rest on social relations that separate categories of workers as protected (primary) or contingent (secondary) in terms of race/ethnicity, gender, and citizenship. In the agricultural sector, foreign workers fill those jobs that most domestic workers with labor mobility and other employment options can avoid (Hoggart and Mendoza 1999; Kasimis and Papadopoulos 2005). The availability of this workforce, which often lacks full citizenship rights and remains socially excluded, allows agriculture to remain as an occupational niche that, despite the existence of some dynamic industries, is contingent, low-waged, and highly flexible. In the remainder of this paper, I describe the employment of foreign workers in Canadian horticulture and how this industry has fared under globalization. I then explore the comparative advantage of foreign workers supplied under the SAWP and argue that the competitiveness of this sector relies, in part, on the provision of this flexible workforce.

FOREIGN WORKERS IN CANADIAN AGRICULTURE

Temporary visa workers have become a pervasive feature of the Canadian labor market. Not only are they employed in a wide range of industries, including mining, construction, hospitality, private homes, and agriculture, they represent an increasingly significant share of Canada's (im)migrant workforce. Indeed, recent research shows that the numbers of people working in Canada under temporary work visas has grown much more rapidly than permanent immigration by foreign workers (Sharma 2006). The growing use of temporary employment visas by the Canadian state since 1973 has "repositioned the balance" between immigrant and non-immigrant people recruited to work in the country, whereby the majority of migrants entering the labor market do so as temporary workers rather than permanent residents[1] (Satzewich 1991; Sharma 2006). While 57 percent of all people classified as workers entering Canada arrived as permanent residents in 1973, sharing most of the same rights as Canadian citizens, by 1993 the percentage of workers entering the country with this status had fallen to 30 percent, with 70 percent entering as foreign workers on temporary employment authorizations (Sharma 1995). By 2004, while the share of temporary visa workers as a percentage of workers entering Canada (65%) next to permanent residents (35%) was similar to that in the 1990s, their actual numbers had risen considerably, from 153,988 to 228,677 (Sharma 2006). Furthermore, if just the group of people entering Canada who were specifically recruited for labor market needs is examined (i.e., those entering under Canada's points system as independent or skilled workers), only 22 percent of (im)migrants in 2004 received permanent resident status and rights while 76 percent were recruited as migrant workers (Sharma 2006). This supports the contention that "temporary" visa workers are gradually becoming a permanent facet of the Canadian labor market.

Agricultural workers account for approximately 20 percent of temporary visa workers entering Canada (CIC 2004). The main mechanism moving foreign workers into agriculture is the Caribbean and Mexican Seasonal Agricultural Worker's Program (SAWP), implemented within bilateral frameworks of agreement between Canada and Jamaica (1966), Barbados

(1967), Trinidad and Tobago (1967), Mexico (1974), and the Organization of Eastern Caribbean States (OECS) (1976–1982). The SAWP has experienced accelerated growth since its inception, from 264 workers in 1966 to close to 20,000 in 2006. The establishment and growth of the program reflect transformations in the character of Canadian agriculture, including a shift away from the family farm. Over the last half-century, Canadian farms have become larger in size and fewer in number, as well as more specialized, intensive, and productive (Agriculture and Agri-Food Canada 2001; Statistics Canada 2007).[2] Further, the size of growers' households has decreased with a declining interest among growers' children to farm as an occupation (Basok 2002). [T]he SAWP experienced two recent periods of growth, one in the late 1980s and a second in the late 1990s. The first can be explained by the simultaneous lifting of the annual quota on the number of foreign workers who could be admitted and the handing over of the program's administration from Human Resources and Skill Development Canada (HRSDC) to the private sector in 1987 (Rural Migration News 2003). In 1986, the year before the quota restriction was lifted and the direct government administration of the program ended, the program had grown to 5,166 workers; by 1989, it had more than doubled to 12,237 (AFL 2003). The more recent period of SAWP expansion can be explained by its extension to new operations that were formerly excluded, such as floriculture, as well as the increased global competitiveness of Canadian horticultural products. [...]

There is some evidence to suggest that foreign labor may be replacing domestic workers in Ontario and Quebec, the provinces employing 95 percent of SAWP workers, where employment of foreign workers has grown appreciably while Canadian wage labor has declined. Weston and Scarpa de Masellis (2003) note that total Canadian employment in the horticultural industries that received foreign workers in Ontario and Quebec declined from 20,380 in 1983 to 14,778 in 2000, while the number of hourly employees fell from 13,748 to 9,518. Over the same period, the number of SAWP workers grew from 4,564 to 16,269. Further, in 2000, SAWP workers accounted for 53 percent of total employment and an estimated 45 percent of total person hours in the agricultural industries using foreign workers (Weston and Scarpa de Masellis 2003). In Manitoba, there is also evidence that SAWP workers have displaced members of the domestic workforce, in particular First Nations groups (Mysyk 2002).

GLOBALIZATION AND CANADIAN HORTICULTURE

The growth in the SAWP is directly linked to the expansion of Canada's horticulture industry. In Ontario, between 1994 and 2000 the labor force supplied by the SAWP grew 60 percent while in value terms the horticulture industry expanded 90 percent (FARMS 2003). Although Canadian agriculture is most well-known for grain production, today the horticulture sector is larger than the grains sector in 7 out of 10 provinces (Agriculture and Agri-Food Canada 2003). Nationally, horticulture ranks second only to cattle, leading all agricultural sectors valued at $6.8 billion, and before grains valued at $4.3 billion (Agriculture and Agri-Food Canada 2003).[3] The horticulture sector contributes between $5 and $7 billion to Canada's trade balance annually, accounting for 12 percent of the total trade surplus and 15.4 percent of all annual farm cash receipts in 2002 (Agriculture and Agri-Food Canada 2003). Floriculture and nursery is the largest horticultural category by value at $1.9 billion (Agriculture and Agri-Food Canada 2003). The horticulture sector contributes significantly to Canada's role globally as the world's third largest agrifood exporter (Agriculture and Agri-Food Canada 2003).

Although globalization has led to intensified competition in global fruit and vegetable markets, many Canadian horticultural commodities have benefited from trade liberalization, particularly greenhouse flowers and vegetables (Agriculture and Agri-Food Canada 2003; Statistics Canada 2004b). During the 1990s, the total area under glass more than doubled to nearly 1,500 hectares, and by 2003 it had reached nearly 1,900 hectares (Purdy 2005). Revenue from greenhouse sales reached a record high of almost $2.1 billion in 2003, nearly double what it had been just six years earlier (Purdy 2005). In 2003, flowers accounted for about 70 percent of greenhouse sales (Purdy 2005). Over the period 1991 to 2001, production in the floriculture, nursery, Christmas tree, and sod sectors increased in value by an average of 9 percent per year, with Canada becoming a net exporter of floriculture products in 1997 (Agriculture and Agri-Food Canada 2003). The farm gate value of floriculture products grew from $245.9 million in 1990 to $745 million in 2002, or an average of 10 percent per year (Brown and Murphy 2003). In Ontario alone, exports of greenhouse floriculture products increased from $63.3 million in 1991 to $228.7 million in 1998 (360% increase in seven years), placing the province only behind California and Florida as the third top North American producer (White, Bills, and Schluep 2002).

Vegetables account for the remaining 30 percent of greenhouse sales nationally, of which tomatoes represent over half of rates revenue (Purdy 2005). In 2003, Statistics Canada reported that the farm gate value of the four main vegetable crops produced under glass amounted to $605.8 million, or more than three times higher than the value of field production of the same four vegetable crops ($171.7 million) (Purdy 2005). Greenhouse tomatoes in particular have experienced spectacular growth, with Canada shifting from being a net importer of tomatoes to a net exporter in the last decade. Since 1996, greenhouse tomato production by volume and value has more than doubled (Agriculture and Agri-Food Canada 2005). In 2002, Ontario's total greenhouse vegetable area was larger than the entire United States greenhouse vegetable industry (Purdy 2005). [...]

Canadian horticultural producers operate in a highly competitive landscape, driven primarily by changes in global trade such as liberalization and deregulation. The trade regime promoted by the General Agreement on Tariffs and Trade (GATT) and the World Trade Organization (WTO) set the stage for large supermarket chains to extend globally and consolidate their market share, to the extent that they now exert market power over the large food processing companies that formerly dominated the food industry, as well as other actors within the commodity chain (Busch and Bains 2004). This is true for Canada: the Canadian food retail market is among the most concentrated in the world, with the top six retailers controlling more than 80 percent of retail food sales (Janoff 2001). Two firms alone have a market share of 55 percent (Janoff 2001). In Canada and elsewhere, supermarkets began to expand in scale during the 1990s such that the larger chains were able to exert market power over upstream actors (Busch and Bains 2004). In addition, food processors and the transnationals that dominate the farm input and technology market have also become more concentrated (NFU 2003; Winson 1996). When farming is left out of the equation, less than a dozen large transnational companies dominate the agrifood chain in Canada (NFU 2003). Another force driving increasing competition is trade liberalization in agrifood products. Canada's principal competitor in this respect is the United States, whose horticultural sector relies heavily on the use of immigrants or unauthorized workers. According to Canada's National Farmer's Union, "trade and investment agreements [...] have thrust all the world's farmers into a single, hyper-competitive market" (2003:17). [...]

THE COMPARATIVE ADVANTAGE OF FOREIGN WORKERS

The horticulture industry fiercely defends the use of foreign workers as the "keystone of the industry" providing a reliable workforce in the face of chronic domestic labor shortfalls (Colby 1997). Industry reports argue that, without foreign workers, most seasonal, labor intensive crops would cease to exist and over half of the Canadian horticulture market would be lost to imports (see for example, FARMS 2003). Industry groups and growers emphasize labor issues as a key concern for horticulture operations with turnover as an ongoing, costly process. As exemplified in the comments by a flower grower: "[Foreign labor] is extremely important because it provides a stable labor force whereas the Canadian labor force—no one wants these kinds of jobs. It's the same story in Leamington[4] or anywhere else you go that Canadians are not willing to do this type of work." With a national unemployment rate of 6.3 percent, employers in the principal horticultural labor markets (Ontario, Quebec, and British Columbia) struggle to find workers, competing with industry and tourism.[5] As one greenhouse nursery employer stated:

> [We hired foreign workers because] the biggest thing that we wanted is reliable labor, because we have 40 positions and when we were working with the local people we found that as the years went by, and the economy got better, we would sometimes have 30 people in the morning, we would sometimes have 35, and we would sometimes have 28. And you can't function a business like that.

[...] In addition to the labor sources above, growers are also able to access an expanding pool of undocumented workers. The *Globe and Mail*, a leading Canadian newspaper, estimates the undocumented population at 200,000 to 300,000 persons (Jiménez and Den Tandt 2005). Although there are no precise estimates of the number of people without status working in agriculture, 15 percent of Barrón's (2004) informants in rural Ontario were working without visas.

High turnover exists among the domestic workforce because these workers are likely to remain in agriculture only until they find better paying and less physically demanding work, or are able to access the social safety net.[6] Domestic workers with other livelihood options simply do not choose to work in agriculture or use it only to supplement their income from full-time jobs. Throughout the twentieth century, farming operations in Canada were notorious for their inability to retain workers and their continued reliance on historically unfree[7] or marginalized sources of labor, including British orphans[8], interned Japanese Canadians, German prisoners of war, conscientious objectors, and First Nation peoples (Bagnell 2001; Basok 2002; Mysyk 2002; Satzewich 1991; Wall 1992). Little appears to have changed: agriculture continues to persist as an unattractive employment opportunity for Canadian citizens. Grower associations and others often argue that domestic workers prefer to avoid strenuous, dirty work:

> The reality is that [farm work] is difficult work. It's deemed to be grunt work, so there's a lot of bending and stooping and you're in the elements and you must work when nature dictates … Canadian mentality is such that we as a nation don't have a desire to do that so this is why we use the offshore[9] workers. (Canadian civil servant)

While in this respect farm work may be less attractive than some jobs, other worksites that continue to attract domestic workers, including meat-packing, factory work, or landscaping, involve similar conditions. It is other characteristics, in addition to the physically demanding nature of agriculture, that constitute the occupation as undesirable. To begin with, farming is considered among the most dangerous occupations in terms of work-related injury[10], yet agricultural workers in many provinces[11] do not enjoy the same labor protections as workers in other sectors. In Ontario, farm workers were excluded from health and safety regulations governing other industries until 2005 and remain excluded in Alberta. Further, since some types of farm work receive more protection than others and workers can change jobs even in the interval of a single day, employees can become confused regarding their rights (Cook 2004). Seasonal harvesters often face the worst conditions and the least protections. In British Columbia's berry industry, the absence of latrines and hand-washing facilities is the norm for hand harvesters (BC Federation of Labour 2004). Farm workers in Ontario, furthermore, are legally prevented from unionizing.

Another reason that explains the high rate of turnover in agriculture is wage rates, which are often lower than those found in other sectors. In some provinces, farm workers are not subject to minimum wage guarantees (Ferguson 2005).[12] In Ontario, farm laborers are on average the lowest paid occupational group of workers (Cook 2004). A recent national wage survey of seasonal workers in the horticulture sector found that domestic workers were earning an average hourly wage of $8.74, with the lowest in Saskatchewan ($7.64) and the highest in British Columbia ($9.44) (Statistics Canada 2004a). While these wages are above the legal minimum wage, they are insufficient to satisfy workers' social reproduction. As one field vegetable grower put it:

> There is no way a Canadian would work for that kind of money [paid to foreign workers]. I almost wouldn't expect Canadians to work for that kind of money because the cost of living is so much higher here [than in Mexico]. There's no way they could support a family at that kind of money.

The SAWP purportedly operates under a labor market policy designed to prevent employers from exploiting foreign workers as a source of cheap labor, driving local wages down, or displacing domestic workers. Prior to the hiring of foreign workers, for example, employers must prove that they attempted to recruit Canadian citizens and permanent residents but were unsuccessful. Further, SAWP policy stipulates that foreign workers are to be paid the greater of the provincially determined minimum wage, the prevailing provincial agricultural wage rate as determined annually by HRSDC, or the rate being paid by the employer to domestic seasonal workers performing the same type of work. Despite the existence of this labor market policy, critics have long argued that the current wage needs to be revised upwards and have reported incidences of Canadians receiving higher wages for equal work (Preibisch 2003; UFCW 2004; Verma 2003). Unsurprisingly, a recent survey aimed at identifying the prevailing wages paid to seasonal horticultural workers in laborer or manual occupations revealed that foreign workers are, on average, paid less than domestic workers.[13] While discrepancies are often justified by employers through the contention that the associated costs of the SAWP imply additional costs, the criteria for establishing a wage rate under the Program's policy does not include any calculation for subsidizing employer-borne costs by the employee.[14] Since the SAWP's established wage rate is considered depressed, the only way foreign workers are able to increase their earnings is through working longer hours.

Although foreign workers may be cheaper, the main factor that constitutes them as "reliable" is the denial of labor mobility (Basok 2002; Sharma 2006). The work permits foreign workers are granted are only valid with their designated employer; they cannot move to more attractive, better-paying work sites. Although the Canadian government refers to the SAWP as a "labor mobility program," it is precisely the lack of labor mobility that differentiates foreign workers from their domestic counterparts. Dismissal is tantamount to deportation. For example, the coordinator of one social justice group noted:

> We've had a number of cases where workers have complained about their housing situation …
> and within hours they'll be on the plane. I have seen it happen over the last two years and
> we have documented facts where a worker indicated to us, 'you watch, I am going in to talk
> to the farmer and the consulate tomorrow about my housing situation' and before the guy
> could even phone to tell us what happened, he was on the plane back (Preibisch 2003:47).

Since foreign workers have been repatriated for falling ill, refusing unsafe work, or raising complaints, the threat of repatriation itself constitutes an effective mechanism of control (Basok 2002; Binford 2002; Preibisch 2004). The following comment from a Canadian administrator is illustrative in this regard: "There are some cases where the grower will call and say, 'my workers won't get out of bed; what do I do?' I say, 'tell them they're going home.' I mean if they're not good, you fire them like anybody else." Foreign agricultural workers, clearly, are not like anybody else—losing one's job means losing the opportunity to work in Canada for that year, if not completely. Since SAWP applicants must be landless agricultural workers or land poor farmers in order to qualify for the program, the economic need to retain their jobs is significant.[15] Indeed, Basok (2002) estimates that Mexican workers' yearly earnings in Canada are five to six times what they would earn at home.

Foreign workers are normally housed on their designated employer's property. Foreign workers' lack of labor mobility coupled with their residential arrangements grants their employer increased access to, and control over, their lives (Wall 1992). One grower boasted about how having his workers housed on the farm allowed him to kick them out of bed when they were late for work. These residential arrangements allow employers to overcome a key constraint they face with domestic workers: transportation. Most entry level domestic workers in agriculture do not have access to their own vehicle (OATI Learning Group 2004). The distance from workers' home to the farm may be great, particular if they live in urban centers, as do most immigrants to Canada. Further, public transportation in rural areas is non-existent. Foreign workers thus represent savings to employers in terms of recruitment, transport costs, and time. The Ontario Fruit and Vegetable Growers Association have openly claimed that their members "prefer migrants from abroad who live on their farms while in Canada rather than Canadian workers who drive from Canadian homes to work everyday" (Rural Migration News 1999). Even when employers provide transport to and from the farm, domestic workers cannot be guaranteed to show up for work everyday:

> Having them [the foreign workers] housed here, knowing that they're going to be here when you get here in the morning is just so much better than sitting here waiting for somebody who is going to drive in themselves. Some people are chronically late so you wind up holding back so many other guys because one person is late or they don't show up at all. (Preibisch 2003:42)

Further, the SAWP residential arrangements allow growers to extend the work day. This point is vividly expressed by a producer of greenhouse flowers:

> Because they live right on the premises, they get out of bed, have breakfast and step out of the trailer and they're at work. It's not a two hour time loss going to and coming back, they're right there. So really working 11 or 12 hours a day for six days a week is perfectly acceptable.

The assertion that foreign workers provided under the SAWP work longer hours and for more days of the week than Canadians has been well-established elsewhere (Basok 2002; Binford 2002). Recent surveys with SAWP participants have recorded work weeks ranging from 60 to 80 hours, with workers regularly working one or both days of the weekend. Russell (2003) found Jamaican SAWP workers averaging 6.7 days per week and 9.5 hours per day. Similarly, Verduzco and Lozano (2003) found Mexican workers regularly working seven days a week, laboring 9.3 hours per day on average, and some reports of shifts up to 17 hours long. Furthermore, Carvajal, Preibisch and Henson's study (2007) reports the average weekly hours among Mexican SAWP workers as 64.2, ranging from 56.3 hours per week in periods of low production to 74.2 in the high season. These findings contrast strikingly to Statistics Canada data for 2005 that estimates the average usual hours worked by employees in Ontario's agricultural sector to range between 31.3 hours per week in January to a high of 42.8 in September (Statistics Canada 2006).[16] In interviews, growers repeatedly indicated the willingness of foreign workers to work significantly longer hours than domestic labor. As one vegetable grower stated: "To have a Canadian work here is to say: how are you going to get a fella to work 60 hours? The whole Canadian philosophy is different. I can't imagine you're going to find somebody to work that amount of hours for minimum wages." In many provinces agricultural workers are not paid overtime, providing little incentive for domestic workers to agree to work longer than a standard working day.

SAWP workers are similarly not paid overtime, which indicates that there are other mechanisms operating that account for their long work days. One of these is the fact that they migrate as individuals, not as families. While domestic workers have families to care for and other social responsibilities, foreign workers leave these behind in their countries of origin; SAWP workers enter the country as single applicants, although they must prove that they have dependents in order to qualify for the Program. This preference in recruitment is an attempt by Canadian administrators to deter SAWP participants from attempting to secure permanent residency through marriage or seeking to remain in Canada illegally. It also results in a workforce more willing (and able) to work additional hours. As growers explained:

> Farming is a dirty job, a tough job. The locals have their own families, so they don't want to work weekends. And at harvest time, we're going seven days a week. The locals just wouldn't do it. (Field vegetable grower)

> With the exception of Vietnamese[17] we are completely dependent on offshore. In some years we've employed them [Vietnamese] for upwards of three and half months. Again we're running into the same problems as we did with the locals; kids go back to school, mothers have to stay home. (Tender fruit grower)

Foreign workers, as physically divorced from their own social reproduction, tied to the job, and eager to improve their living conditions in their countries of origin, thus constitute an attractive labor force for an expanding horticultural industry.

The SAWP also allows employers to use discriminatory hiring practices that would arguably contravene provincial and federal human rights codes protecting Canadians. It allows employers to choose, on an annual basis, the countries that will supply them with labor as well as the gender of each worker. The ability to choose the gender and source country of one's workforce provides the scope for employers to execute gendered and racialized labor strategies designed to promote productivity and impede worker solidarity. For example, it is not uncommon for fruit growers to hire both male and female foreign workers and assign them different tasks. Rather than hire workers from the same country, however, employers will request English-speaking men from the Caribbean and Spanish-speaking women from

Mexico. Employers were very candid about these strategies. As one fruit grower stated: "[previously] it had just been Jamaican men but we did not want to get into a situation with Jamaican women, just for the simple fraternization aspect, so that's why we went with Mexican women."[18] Other employers have hired two groups of workers differentiated by country of origin and/or indigenous or non-indigenous identity in order to inhibit worker unity and breed competition in efforts to speed up production (see also Binford 2002, 2004).[19]

Most significantly, the policy that allows employers to choose the country of origin of their workers grants them considerable power over the participating labor-sending states and leads to heavy competition between their officials to deliver productive, disciplined workers. Sending countries seek to maintain and expand their share of placements in the SAWP. These labor placements are highly valuable, particularly given the role remittances play in the economies of the SAWP sending countries where they account among the principal sources of foreign exchange and, especially in the Caribbean nations, a vital proportion of the GDP.[20] Indeed, a further benefit of the foreign workforce is that it is managed by a sophisticated labor service that is increasingly tailored to grower specifications and "just-in-time" supply, funded not by Canadian taxpayers but those of the labor-sending countries. Canadian growers have long lost state-funded labor recruitment and supply services under neoliberal reform. Although employers pay a user fee per worker to the grower association that administers the SAWP, a much greater portion of the costs of recruitment and administration is borne by the labor supply countries that recruit, prepare, and dispatch workers. They also provide government agents—consular personnel (Mexico) or Liaison Officers (the Caribbean)—to serve as worker representatives in Canada and, in the case of Jamaica and Mexico, have even established satellite consular offices in areas of high worker concentration.[21] In order to secure positions in Canada, sending countries strive to provide "better" workers and better service than their competitors. According to growers' perceptions, a labor supply country is deemed to be providing good recruitment service when they deliver obedient, skilled workers who return to their home countries following the end of their contracts (Preibisch and Binford 2007).[22] The ability to recruit docile workers is a clear criterion by which countries' recruitment services are judged. One Caribbean administrator, explaining his region's diminishing share of placements, stated:

> Caribbean people tend to question things and they don't back down on what they perceive to be their rights. That could be a negative because some employers don't want that. They want a peaceful life, a guy who comes and works hard and doesn't mind if he gets a ten minute break or not.

One grower expressed this issue bluntly: "The Jamaicans are no good because they complain a lot, and spend their time partying. A lot go AWOL." One of Mexico's strategies to discipline their workers consists of a yearly evaluation completed by employers that SAWP candidates must submit in order to participate in the following season. Many workers fear a negative evaluation will compromise their continuity in the program (Basok 2002) or result in reassignment to a less attractive placement.

In order to supply "better" workers, labor supply countries are also seeking SAWP candidates beyond traditional sending areas. In the case of Mexico, this has included a technologically-sophisticated decentralization program that has extended a number of administrative functions, including recruitment, beyond the nation's capital into the most far-flung states, including the indigenous-populated south. Labor supply countries discipline SAWP recruits in other ways. Jamaica froze recruitment from one entire parish when three workers from the area were caught smuggling drugs into Canada.

As important as proper worker selection is the ability to deliver workers "just in time." One Canadian administrator explained how growers factor in worker delivery time when deciding on a source country:

> Once the request goes through, it's getting the worker here on time. So the turnaround time
> to replace that worker in the case of emergency, when a worker decides not to work or gets
> ill, or has to go home for personal reasons, or for the employer to get additional workers [...]
> is a very big telling factor.

Indeed, labor-sending country administrators pride themselves on their ability to respond quickly to employer demands. One official related how they were able to mobilize and send 40 workers within 3 days of receiving the employer's requisition. In recent years, the agreements signed between Mexico and Canada have reduced the number of days HRSDC must request workers before they are needed in Canada and increased the number of workers that Mexico must have in reserve to respond to any sudden demand (Verduzco and Lozano 2003).

Growers also praise foreign country government agents' ability to solve any problems that occur during workers' tenure in Canada, ranging from labor disputes to homesickness. Good service includes the timely response of government agents to these concerns, in order to limit interruptions in production. One field vegetable grower expressed praise for a government agent in solving his particular problem:

> [Caribbean workers] have more attitude. They were out drinking and partying all the time,
> then disappearing for days at a time [...]. We had this one guy from Dominica, who met
> some friends from his own country working on the railway and then expected the same
> benefits and salaries as Canadians! But [the labor sending country official] straightened it
> out. One year, three [workers] got sent back, and we got other ones.

It is important to note that, because government agents have the dual role of defending workers and securing more labor placements in Canada (i.e., remittances), workers' genuine representation before their employers is compromised. Indeed, sending country officials recognize that "too much" representation may result in the loss of the farm to a competitor nation. [...]

CONCLUSIONS

Changes in the global economy have had profound effects on the social relations of agricultural production throughout the world. These transformations have held significant implications for the ways in which people are incorporated into wage labor. In high income countries, a striking development has been the increasing employment of foreign workers in agricultural labor markets, with notable examples including North Africans in Spain, Eastern Europeans in the United Kingdom, and Latin Americans in the United States. While in this context the changes taking place in Canada may appear modest at least in terms of the numbers of foreign workers employed, the case provided in this paper provides further illustration of this social phenomenon. Farm operators, facing serious challenges competing for domestic and export markets with the deepening of trade liberalization and the tightening grip of retail concentration, have sought out more flexible labor arrangements as part of their strategies to remain competitive. Foreign workers provided by the Canadian federal government's SAWP have been instrumental to this strategy.

The benefits to growers include an on-site workforce that cannot move out of the sector or even change employers. Given the class background of participants and the limited livelihood alternatives in their home countries, it is also a workforce more likely than domestic workers to accept the eroded working conditions and variable hours characterizing the industry. Moreover, because SAWP workers must migrate as single applicants, leaving their families in their communities of origin, they are also more likely to agree to work longer hours when required. The Program delivers these workers in a more timely fashion than is possible in a freely functioning labor market due to the competition created between remittance-seeking supply countries who vie for farm placements, including on the basis of fulfilling employer requests promptly. Finally, labor supply countries provide considerable administrative support in selecting, dispatching, and disciplining workers at no cost to employers. Since many of the agricultural supports provided by the Canadian state to growers in terms of their labor needs have long been extinguished, this support is no doubt valuable. It is thus unsurprising that SAWP numbers are rising, that contracts have lengthened, or that growers are instituting strategies to employ farm workers year round; in sum, that the "seasonal" or "temporary" aspects of the Program beg interrogation.

More fundamentally, the SAWP provides an example of how immigration policy, specifically through temporary visa programs, regulates the labor markets of high income countries and maintains their position within the increasingly competitive global political economy. Foreign workers fill those places in the labor market that most domestic workers with labor mobility and other employment or social welfare options can avoid and, by providing a cheapened and unfree source of labor to their employers, create greater labor market competition in general. While the competitiveness of Canadian horticulture is undoubtedly the result of a number of factors, the availability of temporary visa workers has played a critical and acknowledged role in fueling the dynamism of this industry. Indeed, Canadian horticulture—particularly in greenhouse crops and floriculture—has experienced spectacular growth in recent years, despite intensified competition in global markets. The trend among horticultural enterprises in high income countries to turn to foreign workers in order to remain competitive is an interesting phenomenon that deserves further attention in our understanding of global agrifood networks. A close watch is also needed of other sectors to see if and how the experiences of agriculture are replicated and non-citizen labor becomes integral to the wider political economy.

NOTES

1. Permanent residents have almost all of the rights accorded Canadian citizens. The three key exceptions are the right to vote in provincial and federal elections, to serve in federal public office, and to hold political positions. Unlike temporary visa workers, they can move freely in the labor market.
2. The agriculture sector underwent major restructuring in the 1990s. Between 1990–98, the number of small and medium farms combined declined 11.1 percent while commercial farms increased 25.9 percent—with very large farms doubling in number, and large farms increasing by 19.6 percent (Agriculture and Agri-Food Canada 2001).
3. All prices are in Canadian dollars, unless indicated.
4. Leamington, a town located in southwestern Ontario, hosts the largest concentration of greenhouses in North America (Purdy 2005).
5. In Ontario, the expansion of the auto parts industry has captured a significant portion of the labor force in rural (and urban) areas (Winson and Leach 2003).
6. Domestic labor shortages in agriculture have also been aggravated, paradoxically, by neoliberal tightening on social programs such as Employment Insurance that no longer allows people receiving benefits to engage in seasonal employment.
7. A number of scholars have theorized temporary visa workers as a contemporary example of unfree labor within capitalist economies because the visas that bind them to a single employer deny them labor market mobility; that is, they cannot sell their labor power freely (Basok 2002; Satzewich 1991; Sharma 1995, 2006).
8. At the turn of the century, thousands of impoverished British children were sent to Canadian farms as "apprentices" in exchange, upon reaching adulthood, for citizenship (Bagnell 2001).
9. Canadian administrators, industry representatives, and growers use the word "offshore" to refer to foreign farm workers.
10. Farmers and farm workers account for 13 percent of all occupational fatalities in Canada (Hartling, Pickett and Brison, 2000).
11. Workplace legislation falls under provincial jurisdiction.
12. In 1997, hand harvesters picking blueberries in British Columbia were earning between $12 to $40 a day, depending on the harvest. The hourly minimum wage at the time was $7.00 per hour (BC Federation of Labour 2004).
13. The survey focused specifically on foreign and domestic workers hired in the categories of farm laborers or harvesters, and nursery or greenhouse laborers.

14. This has been calculated for FARMS at an average of $2.54 per hour per employee (FARMS 2003).

15. Basok (2002) notes that Mexican participants are landless and poorly educated, with fewer economic resources than U.S.-bound migrants. Indeed, the Program is a migration-based livelihood available to a poorer segment of the rural population who cannot afford the escalating costs of migrating illegally to the United States: there is no smuggler to pay, and employers even bear some of the immediate costs of visas and airfare, a portion of which is gradually recovered. In addition, the Mexican government has begun providing a subsidy to first-time SAWP applicants roughly equivalent to US $300 to defray some of the initial costs associated with the application process.

16. The national average ranges from a low of 35.9 hours in January to 42.7 in September (Statistics Canada 2006).

17. Canadian citizens or permanent residents who are ethnic Vietnamese.

18. Migration flows to Canada through the SAWP are highly masculinized; only 2 to 3 percent of the workforce is female. The gendering of the program has been detailed elsewhere (Bécerril 2003; Preibisch and Hermoso 2006) but suffice to mention here that gender plays a role in the organization of the horticultural industry, most notably on the "shop-floor."

19. A number of authors have suggested that Mexicans represent a more vulnerable source of labor than Caribbean workers because they do not speak either of Canada's official languages (Basok 2002; Preibisch 1998). In the last five years, however, the labor movement and a number of other organizations have made considerable gains in providing resources and support to Spanish-speaking workers. Labor organizers believe the recent emergence of workers who do not speak Spanish is an attempt to counteract these organizing efforts.

20. Jamaica received US $1.6 billion in remittances in 2005, more than double the sum of overseas development assistance (ODA) and foreign direct investment (FDI), and representing 19 percent of the country's GDP (IADB 2006). Mexico received US $20 billion that year, exceeding the country's revenue from tourism and all its agricultural exports (IADB 2006).

21. Verduzco and Lozano (2003) estimate the costs to the Mexican Ministry of Labor as at least US $219 per worker, not including the US $300 economic support to new participants to cover their travel costs that applying incurs, nor the costs borne by the Ministry of External Affairs who supply the diplomatic personnel in Canada.

22. One principal reason explaining the displacement of workers from the Caribbean by Mexicans is the increasing numbers of SAWP participants from the island states who go AWOL, finding refuge among the large Caribbean diaspora residing in Toronto (Preibisch and Binford 2007). Mexican workers who lack proximate social networks within Canada are more likely to desert to the United States, a significantly riskier endeavor following stepped up border controls since 9/11.

REFERENCES

Alberta Federation of Labour (AFL). 2003. *Migrant Agricultural Workers in Alberta*. Policy Paper, Alberta Federation of Labour. Retrieved July 7, 2005 (http://www.afl.org/ publications-research/policy-papers/pp-migrant.pdf).

Agriculture and Agri-Food Canada. 2001. "All Farms." *Economic Overview of Farm Incomes*. Publication No. 2048/B, 2(1):1–27, Ottawa, ON: Agricultural Division, Statistics Canada.

———. 2003. "2002–2003 Canadian Vegetable Situation and Trends." Retrieved July 7, 2005 (http://www.agr.gc.ca/misb/hort/sit/pdf/veg02_03_e.pdf).

———. 2005. "Profile of the Canadian Greenhouse Tomato Industry." Retrieved July 7, 2005 (http://www.agr.gc.ca/misb/hort/index_e.cfm?s15prof&page5tom).

Bagnell, K. 2001. *The Little Immigrants: The Orphans Who Came to Canada*. Toronto: Dundurn Press.

Ball, R. and N. Piper. 2004. "Globalisation and Regulation of Citizenship: Filipino Migrant Workers in Japan." *Political Geography* 21:1013–34.

Barrientos, S., C. Dolan, and A. Tallontire. 2003. "A Gendered Value Chain Approach to Codes of Conduct in African Horticulture." *World Development* 31:1511–26.

Barrón, A. 2004. "Diasporas of Globalization: Labor Markets and Working Conditions of Women Farm Workers: Mexico, USA, and Canada." Presented at the Congress of the Canadian Association of Latin American and Caribbean Studies, October 28–31, Guelph, Ontario.

Barrón, A. and F. Rello. 2000. "The Impact of the Tomato Agro-Industry on the Rural Poor in Mexico." *Agricultural Economics* 23:289–97.

Basok, T. 2002. *Tortillas and Tomatoes*. Montreal & Kingston: McGill-Queens University Press.

Bécerril, O. 2003. "Relación de Género, Trabajo Transnacional y Migración Temporal: Trabajadores y Trabajadoras Agrícolas Mexicanos en Canadá." Presented at the Primer Coloquio Internacional Sobre Migración y Desarrollo: Transnacionalismo y Nuevas Perspectivas de Integración, October 23–25, City of Zacatecas, Mexico.

Binford, L. 2002. "Social and Economic Contradictions of Rural Migrant Contract Labor between Tlaxcala, Mexico and Canada." *Culture and Agriculture* 24:1–19.

———. 2004. "Contract Labour in Canada and the United States: A Critical Appreciation of Tanya Basok's Tortillas and Tomatoes: Transmigrant Mexican Harvesters in Canada." *Canadian Journal of Latin American and Caribbean Studies* 29:289–308.

BC Federation of Labour. 2004. *Hand-Harvesters of Fraser Valley Berry Crops: New Era Protection of Vulnerable Employees*. Retrieved July 7, 2005 (http://www.bcfed.com/Where+We+Stand/Publications/Archives/2004-handharvesters.htm).

Brown, W. and G. Murphy. 2003. "A Profile of the Ontario Greenhouse Floriculture Industry." Ontario Ministry of Food and Agriculture Report. Retrieved July 7, 2005 (http://www.gov.on.ca/OMAFRA/English/crops/facts/greenflor.htm).

Busch, L. and C. Bains. 2004. "New! Improved? The Transformation of the Global Agri-food System" *Rural Sociology* 69:321–46.

Carvajal, L., K. Preibisch, and S. Henson. 2007. "Farm-Level Impacts of Rural Migration: The Case of Mexican Participation in the Canadian Seasonal Agricultural Workers Program." Presented at the Second International Conference of the Interdisciplinary Social Sciences, July 10–13, Granada, Spain.

Citizenship and Immigration Canada (CIC). 2004. "2004 Foreign Worker Overview." *The Monitor.* Summer 2005. Retrieved May 29, 2007 (http://www.cic.gc.ca/english/monitor/issue10/05-overview.html).

Colby, C. 1997. *From Oaxaca to Ontario: Mexican Contract Labor in Canada and the Impact at Home.* Davis, CA: The California Institute for Rural Studies.

Cook, V. 2004. *Workers of Colour within a Global Economy.* Research Paper on Migrant Workers. Ottawa: Canadian Labor Congress.

Cyrus, N. 1994. "Flexible Work for Fragmented Labour Markets: The Significance of the New Labour Migration Regime in the Federal Republic of Germany." *Migration* 26:97–124.

Dolan, C. 2002. "On Farm and Packhouse: Employment at the Bottom of a Global Value Chain." *Rural Sociology* 69:99–126.

Foreign Agricultural Resource Management Services (FARMS). 2003. *The Quest for a Reliable Workforce in the Horticulture Industry.* Mississauga: Foreign Agricultural Resource Management Services.

Ferguson, D. 2005. "B.C. Farmworkers' Union Eyes Alberta." *MetroValley News.* February 16, p. 25.

Hartling, L., W. Pickett, and R. Brison. 2000. "The Canadian Agricultural Injury Surveillance Program: A New Injury Control Initiative." *Chronic Diseases in Canada* 19. Retrieved June 21, 2005 from the Public Health Agency of Canada (http://www.phac-aspc.gc.ca/publicat/cdic-mcc/19-3/d_e.html).

Hoggart, K. and C. Mendoza. 1999. "African Immigrant Workers in Spanish Agriculture." *Sociologia Ruralis* 37:538–62.

Inter-American Development Bank (IADB). 2006. *Remittances 2005: Promoting Financial Democracy.* Washington, DC: Inter-American Development Bank.

International Labor Organization (ILO). 2004. *Towards a Fair Deal for Migrant Workers in the Global Economy.* Report VI, International Labor Conference, 92nd Session. Geneva: International Labor Organization.

Kasimis, C. and A.G. Papadopoulos. 2005. "The Multifunctional Role of Migrants in the Greek Countryside: Implications for the Rural Economy and Society." *Journal of Ethnic and Migration Studies* 31:99–127.

Kasimis, C., A.G. Papadopoulos, and E. Zacopoulou. 2003. "Migrants in Rural Greece." *Sociologia Ruralis* 43:167–84.

Kritzinger, A., S. Barrientos, and H.M. Rossouw. 2004. "Global Production and Flexible Employment in South African Horticulture: Experiences of Contract Workers in Fruit Exports." *Sociologia Ruralis* 44:17–39.

Janoff, B. 2001. "Face Off." *Progressive Grocer* 80:14–19.

Jiménez, M. and M. Den Tandt. 2005. "How to Repair the Welcome Mat." *The Globe and Mail.* April 22, p. A13.

Martin, P. 2004. *Migrant Wages and Working Conditions: Comparisons by Sector and Country*. Paper prepared for ILO/MIGRANT, January 3.

McMichael, P. 1996. "Globalization: Myths and Realities." *Rural Sociology* 61:25–55.

Mysyk, A. 2002. "The Role of the State in Manitoba Farm Labour Force Formation." Pp. 169–83 in *The Dynamics of Hired Farm Labor: Constraints and Community Responses*, edited by J.L. Findeis, A.M. Vandeman, J.M. Larson, and J.L. Runyan. Oxon, OX: CABI Publishing.

National Farmers Union (NFU). 2003. "The Farm Crisis, Bigger Farms, and the Myths of 'Competition' and 'Efficiency.'" Unpublished document.

OATI Learning Group. 2004. *The Ontario Greenhouse Alliance Human Resources Survey*. Guelph: The Ontario Greenhouse Alliance.

Persaud, R. 2001. "Racialized Assumptions in Global Labor Recruitment and Supply." *Alternatives* 26:377–99.

Preibisch, K. 1998. "Land of the Unfree: Temporary Migration Mexico-Canada and Two Fields of Economic Restructuring." Presented at the Latin American Studies Association XXI International Congress, September 24–26, Chicago, IL.

———. 2003. *Social Relations Practices between Seasonal Agricultural Workers, Their Employers, and the Residents of Rural Ontario*. Research Report. Ottawa, ON: The North-South Institute.

———. 2004. Migrant Agricultural Workers and Processes of Social Inclusion in Rural Canada: *Encuentros* and *Desencuentros. Canadian Journal of Latin American and Caribbean Studies* 29:203–39.

Preibisch, K. and L. Binford. 2007. "Interrogating Racialized Global Labour Supply: An Exploration of the Racial/National Replacement of Foreign Agricultural Workers in Canada." *Canadian Review of Sociology* 44:5–36.

Preibisch, K. and L. Hermoso. 2006. "Engendering Labour Migration: The Case of Foreign Workers in Canadian Agriculture." Pp. 107–30 in *Women, Migration and Citizenship: Making Local, National and Transnational Connections*, edited by E. Tastsoglou and A. Dobrowolsky. London: Ashgate Press.

Purdy, J. 2005. "High-Tech Vegetables: Canada's Booming Greenhouse Vegetable Industry." *VISTA on the Agri-food Industry and the Farm Community*. Catalogue no. 21- 004-XIE, March. Ottawa, ON: Statistics Canada.

Rai, S. 2001. *Gender and the Political Economy of Development*. London: Polity Press.

Raynolds, L. 2002. "Wages for Wives: Renegotiating Gender and Production Relations in Contract Farming in the Dominican Republic." *World Development* 30:783–98.

Rural Migration News. 1999. "Canada, Guest Workers." October 1. Vol. 5, no. 4. Retrieved January 7, 2004 (http://migration.ucdavis.edu/rmn/more.php?id5409_ 0_5_0).

———. 2003. "Canada: Guest Workers." April 16. Vol. 9, no 2. Retrieved August 17, 2005 (http://migration.ucdavis.edu/rmn/more.php?id59_0_4_0).

———. 2004. "Europe: Migrants, Enlargement." April 20, Vol. 10, no. 2. Retrieved August 17, 2005 (http://migration.ucdavis.edu/rmn/more.php?id5851_0_5_0).

Russell, R. 2003. *Jamaican Workers' Participation in Canada's Seasonal Agricultural Workers' Program and Development Consequences in Their Rural Home Communities*. Research Report, Ottawa, ON: The North-South Institute.

Sassen, S. 2000. "Women's Burdens: Counter-Geographies of Globalization and the Feminization of Survival." *Journal of International Affairs* 53:503–24.

Satzewich, V. 1991. *Racism and the Incorporation Foreign Labour: Farm Labour Migration to Canada Since 1945*. London and New York: Routledge.

Sharma, N. 2006. *Home Economics: Nationalism and the Making of Migrant Workers in Canada*. Toronto: University of Toronto Press.

———. 1995. "The True North Strong and Unfree: Capitalist Restructuring and Non-Immigrant Employment in Canada, 1973–1993." MA thesis, Department of Sociology, Simon Fraser University.

Stasiulis, D. and A. Bakan. 2003. *Negotiating Citizenship: Migrant Women in Canada and the Global System*. Toronto: University of Toronto Press.

Statistics Canada. 2004a. *Wage Survey of Seasonal Workers in the Horticultural Sector*. Ottawa, ON: Statistics Canada.

———. 2004b. *Canadian Agriculture at a Glance*. Ottawa, ON: Statistics Canada Agriculture Division.

———. 2006. "Table 282-0019." *Labour Force Survey*. Retrieved September 12, 2006 (http://estat. statcan.ca).

———. 2007. "Snapshot of Canadian Agriculture." *2006 Census of Agriculture*. Retrieved May 29, 2007 (http://www.statcan.ca/english/agcensus2006/articles/snapshot.htm).

UFCW. 2004. *The Status of Migrant Workers in Canada: National Report 2004*. Toronto: United Food and Commercial Workers Union.

Verduzco, G. and M. Lozano. 2003. *Mexican Workers' Participation in CSAWP and Development Consequences in the Workers' Rural Home Communities*. Research Report. Ottawa, ON: The North-South Institute.

Verma, V. 2003. *CSAWP Regulatory and Policy Framework, Farm Industry-Level Employment Practices and the Potential Role of Unions*. Research Report. Ottawa, ON: The North-South Institute.

Wall, E. 1992. "Personal Labour Relations and Ethnicity in Ontario Agriculture." Pp. 261–75 in *Deconstructing a Nation: Immigration, Multiculturalism and Racism in 90s Canada*, edited by V. Satzewich. Halifax: Fernwood Publishing.

Weston, A. and L. Scarpa de Masellis. 2003. *Hemispheric Integration and Trade Relations— Implications for Canada's Seasonal Agricultural Workers Program*. Research Report. Ottawa, ON: The North-South Institute.

White, G., N. Bills, and I. Schluep. 2002. "Impacts of Trade Liberalization on the New York Horticultural Sector." Staff Paper. Ithaca, NY: Cornell University.

Winson, T. 1996. "In Search of the Part-Time Capitalist Farmer: Labour Use and Farm Structure in Central Canada." *Canadian Review of Sociology and Anthropology* 33:89–110.

Winson, T. and B. Leach. 2003. *Contingent Work, Disrupted Lives: Labour and Community in the New Rural Economy*. Toronto: University of Toronto Press.

PART 3D

RACISM, THE MEDIA, AND POPULAR CULTURE

> *White supremacists have recognized that control over images is central to the maintenance of any system of racial domination.... Stuart Hall emphasizes that we can properly understand the traumatic character of the colonial experience by recognizing the connection between domination and representation.*
> —bell hooks (1992, 2–3)

Representation in popular culture and in the mainstream media has to do with power. Those who can represent have social, economic, and cultural power. Those who are colonized and racialized rarely have the power to represent themselves unless they find alternative modes and media for self-representation. Such alternative representations can contest the dominant images. But, generally speaking, members of society are depicted in such a way that racial discourses of superiority and inferiority are confirmed and reproduced through overt and hidden meanings, story lines, images, and language. The three chapters in this section are elaborations on the insight of bell hooks, illustrating how representation and domination have interacted in the cases of Indigenous Canadians, Muslim women, Jews under Nazism, and Black people.

FURTHER READING

Brader, Ted, Nicholas Valentino, and Elizabeth Suha. (2008). "What Triggers Public Opposition to Immigration? Anxiety, Group Cues and Immigrant Threat." *American Journal of Political Science* 52(4), 959–978.

There is a strong correlation between media images, audience responses, and the formation of their opinions on controversial issues, such as immigration. In this article, the authors report on experiments they conducted with white members of the public as far as their opinions and political actions regarding immigration are concerned when the images they see are those of immigrants of colour as opposed to white immigrants. The authors demonstrate that when the images are those of non-white South Americans as opposed to Europeans, white viewers experience anxiety and therefore express oppositional views on immigration, no matter what the facts indicate.

Deloria, Philip J. (1998). *Playing Indian.* **New Haven and London: Yale University Press.**
This book explores the ambiguous relationship that has existed between Indigenous peoples in the United States and white colonial men attempting to develop a new "American" national identity that is different from a European one, emphasizing freedom and rebelliousness. The author argues that the "noble savage" trope encapsulates this tension between desiring indigeneity and rejecting it. This, Deloria argues, has led to the twin strategies of either destroying or assimilating Indigenous people, both of which have led to similar results. The ambiguous relationship that has existed between destroying and desiring the Indigenous subject has resulted in a variety of spectacles, customs, and practices that have included white men "playing Indian," wearing furs, feathers, and face paint. The author examines several such examples where American revolutionaries built on European traditions of carnival and misrule, combining these with a constructed "Indianness" to develop a new and unique identity.

Hellwig, Tineke, and Suneral Thobani, eds. (2006). *Asian Women: Interconnections.* **Toronto: Women's Press.**
The second half of this book contains six interesting chapters, divided into two sections: "Imagining Asian-ness in the Diaspora" and "Asia Viewing." All six chapters are comparative analyses of representations of "Asian" women in literature, cinema, newspapers, and popular television. While use of the identifier *Asian* may imply homogenization and essentializing of a variety of different populations on the Asian continent, the editors problematize the term in the introduction, recognizing "Asia's multidimensional existence." The chapters combine comparative and diasporic perspectives on the representation of Chinese and South Asian women in Asian, Canadian, and American media and popular culture, reflecting complex issues encountered in a globalized and transnational world. Continuities and departures from eighteenth- and nineteenth-century colonial images are pointed out.

hooks, bell. (1992). *Black Looks: Race and Representation.* **Toronto: Between the Lines.**
This book is a seminal collection of essays on the representations of Black people in popular music, advertising, literature, television, and film. It calls for a critical and subversive

spectatorship, interpretation of images, and understanding of how these images affect Black femininities and masculinities. Above all, these essays are a call to resist hegemonic images and practices and imagine empowering and revolutionary representations and subjectivities of Black people as a process of decolonization. Towards this goal, hooks argues for the need to love blackness, rather than to see it as an inferior condition, a condition that is often internalized by Blacks themselves. She exposes the futility of the cultural appropriation that can result from the apparent desire for blackness in popular culture. In addition, she points out the vestiges of oppressive discourses (sexism and/or racism) in apparently transgressive cultural practices. Finally, hooks explores differences among Black women on the basis of different locations and experiences through an examination of Black women's writings and urges the development of a revolutionary Black female subjectivity on the basis of a recognition of differences.

Said, Edward W. (1997). *Covering Islam: How the Media and the Experts Determine How We See the Rest of the World.* **New York: Vintage Books.**
Building on his classic work *Orientalism*, Said explores in depth how the "West," in particular the United States, views "Islam" as its Other, especially in the post–Cold War era. The media play a key role in constructing the West and Islam as polar opposites and the latter as anti-modern, dangerous, fascist, and hateful. The images of Islam that are projected by the media are not based in history or real live interactions, but on stereotypical writings, some produced as far back as the eighteenth century and others as recently as the 1990s, such as the writings of Samuel P. Huntington and Bernard Lewis. Said argues against a conspiratorial thesis and asserts that ethnocentric portrayals of Muslims come out of the rules and conventions of media institutions that exist within a specific political and ideological context and are fundamentally ruled by the profit motive. Despite a certain level of variation in views disseminated in the American media, in the end there is a certain consensus about the position of the United States and the West in relation to Islam or countries constructed as "Islamic." This consensus is maintained by setting certain limits as to what can and cannot be said. Chapters 1 and 2 are particularly relevant to the topic of racism in the media, including a detailed discussion of how the American media covered the Iranian student occupation of the American Embassy on November 4, 1979.

Van Dijk, Teun A. (2002). "Denying Racism: Elite Discourse and Racism." In *Race Critical Theories: Text and Context*, edited by Philomena Essed and David Theo Goldberg. Malden, MA: Blackwell Publishers.

This chapter examines the discourse of denial of racism within mainstream media and parliamentary exchanges as examples of elite discourse. The author argues that by denying racism in a variety of ways, elite discourses confirm that elites do not practise racism or think in a racist way, thus that there is no racism and that what anti-racists are saying is invalid. Denial discourses establish in-group solidarity, ethnic consensus, and dualities of "us" and "them," and reproduce racism.

Chapter 33

The Imaginary Indian: The Image of the Indian in Canadian Culture

Daniel Francis

This chapter by Daniel Francis is an excerpt from a work that the author describes as "a book about the images of Native People that white Canadians manufactured, believed in, feared, despised, admired, taught their children" (1992, 3). He cautions that it is not a matter of "fraudulent" versus "real" images, but a matter of understanding that images represent power relations and have real implications in terms of one's access to social, political, economic, and cultural resources and relationships. In the context of the imaginings of "the Orient," Edward Said argued that dominant representations are as much about constructing the "self" as they are about constructing the "other." In this vein, Francis shows how "the Indian" was imagined through an examination of Canadian paintings, including works by Benjamin West, Paul Kane, and Emily Carr. He suggests that these paintings not only reflect the white imaginary but also white people's ambivalent desire to "be the other."

TAKING THE IMAGE

One of the most famous historical paintings ever done on a Canadian theme is "The Death of General Wolfe" by Benjamin West. The huge canvas depicts the English general, James Wolfe, expiring on the Plains of Abraham outside the walls of Quebec City. In the background, his triumphant army is capturing Canada for British arms. Wolfe lies prostate in the arms of his grieving fellow officers. A messenger brings news of the victory, and with his last breath the general gives thanks. The eye is drawn to the left foreground where an Iroquois warrior squats, his chin resting contemplatively in his hand, watching as death claims his commander. The light shimmers on the Indian's bare torso, which looks as if it might be sculpted from marble.

From its unveiling in London in the spring of 1771, "The Death of Wolfe" was a sensation. It earned for its creator an official appointment as history painter to the King, and became one of the most enduring images of the British Empire, reproduced on tea trays, wall hangings and drinking mugs. West himself completed six versions of the painting. Today it still appears in history textbooks as an accurate representation of the past. Yet as an historical document, it is largely a work of fiction. In reality, Wolfe died apart from the field of battle and only one of the men seen in the painting was actually present. Other officers who were present at the death refused to be included in the painting because they disliked General Wolfe so much.

And the Indian? According to his biographers, Wolfe despised the Native people, all of whom fought on the side of the French, anyway. Certainly, none would have been present at his death. But that did not matter to Benjamin West. Unlike Wolfe, West admired the Noble Savage of the American forest. And so he included the image of a Mohawk warrior, posed as a muscular sage—a symbol of the natural virtue of the New World, a virtue for which Wolfe might be seen to have sacrificed his life.

[...] When White Canadians of earlier generations asked themselves what is an Indian, how did they know what to respond? What information did they have on which to base an answer? By the end of the nineteenth century, there were about 127,000 officially designated Indians living in Canada. Non-Natives had little exposure to these people, most of whom lived on reserves isolated from the main centres of population. They were pretty much a forgotten people. When they gave Native people any thought at all, White Canadians believed they were quickly disappearing in the face of disease, alcohol abuse and economic hardship.

For the vast majority of Whites, Indians existed only as images like that of the Mohawk warrior in Benjamin West's painting. These images originated with a handful of artists, writers and photographers who made the arduous journey into "Indian Country" and returned to exhibit what they had seen there. These image-makers to a large extent created the Imaginary Indian which Whites have believed in ever since. [...]

THE VANISHING CANADIAN

Paul Kane was the first artist in Canada to take the Native population as his subject. "The principal object of my undertaking," he later wrote, "was to sketch pictures of the principal

Figure 33.1: Benjamin West (1738–1820), *The Death of General Wolfe*, National Archives of Canada, C12248.

chiefs and their original costumes, to illustrate their manners and customs, and to represent the scenery of an almost unknown country."[1] What made him decide to paint the Indians? Not even his biographer can say for sure. "There is no clear evidence to explain Kane's almost instant conversion at this time to the cause of painting Indians," writes Russell Harper. "A cynic might suggest that he saw a good thing and anticipated fame and fortune coming to him by means of a gallery of Canadian Indians."[2] Kane himself left no explanation for embarking on his great project.

Kane had had little personal exposure to Native people when he commenced his endeavour. As a youngster in Toronto, then the town of York, he saw a few Natives about the streets. But he did not take much interest in them until he travelled to Europe to study painting. There, in London, in 1843, Kane met the American artist George Catlin, whose canvases struck him with the force of a revelation. Catlin had ventured into the trans-Mississippi West during the 1830s to record the lifestyles of the Indians. After his return, he assembled six hundred paintings, along with a large collection of ethnological material, into a mobile display which toured the United States and Europe. In 1841, he published his first book about the Indians, the two-volume *Letter and Notes on the Manners, Customs and Condition of the North American Indians*. When Kane saw what Catlin had accomplished, he determined on the spot to give up portraiture, which had so far been his artistic bread and butter, return home, and do for Canada what Catlin had done so successfully south of the border.

Kane reached Red River by canoe in the middle of June, 1846, where he witnessed a Métis buffalo hunt. "The half-breeds are a very hardy race of men, capable of enduring the greatest hardships and fatigues," he wrote, "but their Indian propensities predominate, and consequently they make poor farmers, neglecting their land for the most exciting pleasures of the chase."[3] Kane crossed Lake Winnipeg to the trading post at Norway House where he remained for a month. Then he set off up the Saskatchewan River, the historic canoe route of the fur brigades, reaching Fort Edmonton towards the end of September. Travelling as he was in the company of Hudson's Bay Company men, Kane not unnaturally formed a positive impression of the company and its trading monopoly. Allowing free traders to enter the country to compete with the HBC would be akin to signing the death warrant of the Indians, he warned. "For while it is the interest of such a body as the Hudson's Bay Company to improve the Indians and encourage them to industry, according to their own native habits in hunting and the chase ... it is as obviously the interest of small companies and private adventurers to draw as much wealth as they possibly can from the country in the shortest possible time, altho' in doing so the very source from which the wealth springs should be destroyed."[4] Kane was referring here to the debilitating effects of the liquor trade with the Natives, which he blamed on the free traders.

With winter fast approaching, Kane and his party hurried to cross the Rocky Mountains, then descended the Columbia River to Fort Vancouver where they arrived early in December. Fort Vancouver remained Kane's headquarters during his stay on the West Coast. He sketched several portraits of the local Flathead people, who were not quite sure how to interpret what they saw. "My power of portraying the features of individuals was attributed entirely to super-natural agency," reported Kane, "and I found that, in looking at my pictures, they always covered their eyes with their hands and looked through their fingers; this being also the invariable custom when looking at a dead person."[5] In the spring of 1847, Kane went on a three-month sketching trip to Vancouver Island. There would not be another artist interested in recording the Native people of the Pacific Northwest until Emily Carr over fifty years later.

That summer Kane left Fort Vancouver for the East. Travelling back up the Columbia River, he made an arduous crossing of the Rockies and did not arrive at Fort Edmonton until December. He remained there for the next six months sketching on the prairie and waiting for the spring canoe brigade to depart with the season's trade of furs. Descending the Saskatchewan River, he crossed Lake Winnipeg and northern Ontario and reached Sault Ste. Marie on the first day of October. Two weeks later a steamboat carried him into Toronto harbour, home again after more than two years wandering the wild Northwest.

Kane's arrival home stirred up great interest. Within a month he mounted an exhibit much like Catlin's, including some of the five hundred sketches prepared on his travels and a selection of Indian "souvenirs." Response was enthusiastic. People flocked to the exhibit to see powerful portraits of Native hunters, scenes of the buffalo chase, and depictions of exotic pagan rituals. Critics remarked on the authenticity and exquisite detail of the work. "A striking characteristic of Mr. Kane's paintings ... is their truthfulness," reported the *British Colonist* newspaper. "Nothing has been sacrificed to effect—no exaggerated examples of costumes—no incredible distortions of features—are permitted to move our wonder, or exalt our conceptions of what is sufficiently wild and striking without improvements."[6] The Ontario public was just beginning to wake up to the existence of the far Northwest, and was already predisposed to romanticize the western Native. In Kane's paintings of picturesque Indians in elaborate costumes of feathers and buffalo hide, his audience found confirmation of a fascinating wilderness world inhabited by fiercely independent, entirely mysterious people. Everyone agreed that Kane, their own local hero, had done even better than Catlin.

Kane's ambition was to complete a series of one hundred large canvases depicting the Northwest frontier from the Great Lakes to the Pacific Coast. After closing his one-man show in Toronto, he set to work on this task. As well, he had to prepare another fourteen paintings which he had promised George Simpson. In 1850, Kane asked the House of Assembly for financial help to complete his project and the next year the provincial government agreed to buy a dozen canvases. After much prompting, these were completed in 1856 and now reside with the National Gallery in Ottawa. Meanwhile, a wealthy Toronto lawyer, George W. Allan, purchased the entire set of one hundred paintings, which were by then almost finished. Together with Kane's Indian artifacts, Allan displayed the works for many years in his home, Moss Park. After his death in 1901, the paintings were sold to Sir Edmund Osler, who in turn donated them to the Royal Ontario Museum in Toronto, where they remain.

Kane was a documentary artist, but he worked within certain conventions and manipulated his images to suit the demands of these conventions. Though he was praised for his accuracy, he often added details of setting and landscape to highlight the romantic flavour of the scenes, and he sometimes "cheated" by adding clothing and artifacts foreign to the Indians in the paintings. His most famous "forgery" is a depiction of an Assiniboine buffalo hunt which was actually modelled on an Italian engraving of two young men on horseback chasing a bull. Recently Kane has been accused of exploiting the Indians by using them as "exotic curiosities" instead of painting them realistically.[7]

But I don't think Kane can be expected to have conveyed a realistic sense of the Native cultures he visited. He was essentially a tourist among the Indians. He spoke no Native languages; he had a superficial understanding of Native customs. Despite his sympathy for what he saw to be their plight, he showed little concern for Native people after his expedition and he was surprisingly narrow-minded about many aspects of their culture. Nonetheless, the power, the beauty and above all the uniqueness of his paintings established him as the pre-eminent artistic interpreter of the Indian for many years to come. Even today it is hard to find a history textbook that does not contain at least one of Kane's renderings of Indian life. For most of us, the Indian of nineteenth-century Canada is Paul Kane's Indian.

Like Catlin, Kane described his western adventures in a popular memoir. *Wanderings of an Artist among the Indians of North America* appeared in 1859 to laudatory reviews. A bestseller in English, it spawned French, Danish and German editions within four years. In the preface, Kane laments the inevitable disappearance of the Indian, and though the rest of the book does not deal with this subject in any detail, most reviewers took it as their theme. "One must make haste to visit the Red Men," said a typical review. "Their tribes, not long since still masters of a whole world, are disappearing rapidly, driven back and destroyed by the inroads of the white race. Their future is inevitable.... The Indians are doomed; their fate will be that of so many primitive races now gone."[8]

In their conviction that the Native people were doomed to disappear, Kane and his admirers were completely representative of their age. If any single belief dominated the thinking about Canadian aboriginals during the last half of the nineteenth century, it was that they would not be around to see much of the twentieth. Anyone who paid any attention at all to the question agreed that Natives were disappearing from the face of the earth, victims of disease starvation, alcohol and the remorseless ebb and flow of civilizations. "The Indian tribes are passing away, and what is done must be done quickly," wrote the missionary John Maclean, a noted Indian authority, in 1889. "On the western plains, native songs, wafted on the evening breezes, are the dying requiem of the departing savage."[9] Any number of other writers made the same point. Some believed that it was the Indian's traditional culture that was being eradicated by the spread of White settlement, while others believed the Indians themselves literally to be dying out. Some found the idea appalling; some found it regrettable; some found it desirable. But all were agreed that the Indian was doomed. [...]

The "fact" that Indians were a vanishing breed made them especially attractive to artists. The pathos inherent in the subject appealed to White audiences. It also gave an urgency to the work. Artists like Paul Kane who chose to portray the Indian believed they were saving an entire people from extinction; not literally, of course, but in the sense that they were preserving on canvas, and later on film, a record of a dying culture before it expired forever.

This sense of urgent mission controlled the way Indians were portrayed in the work of White artists, who became amateur ethnographers seeking to record Indian life as it was lived before the arrival of White people. Artists ignored evidence of Native adaptation to White civilization and highlighted traditional lifestyles. Often the result was an idealized image of the Indian based on what the artist imagined aboriginal life to have been before contact. [...]

At about the same time as Edmund Morris was recording the Plains Indian chiefs, Emily Carr was undertaking a similar project among the tribes on the coast of British Columbia. "I am a Canadian born and bred," she told the audience at a huge exhibit of her paintings in Vancouver in April, 1913. "I glory in our wonderful West and I hope to leave behind me some of the relics of its first primitive greatness."[10]

"These things," she continued, referring to the totem poles, house fronts and village scenes in her paintings, "should be to we Canadians what the ancient Briton's relics are to the English. Only a few more years and they will be gone forever, into silent nothingness, and I would gather my collections together before they are forever past."[11]

As these remarks reveal, Carr initially cast herself very much in the same mould as Paul Kane; that is, a documentary artist making a visual record of a condemned people. Carr conceived her Indian project in 1907 during a summer steamer excursion to Alaska with her sister. The two women spent a week at the Native settlement of Sitka where they visited the famous Totem Walk, a collection of poles erected as a tourist attraction. While she was at Sitka, Carr met the American artist, Theodore J. Richardson, who had been painting in the village every summer for many years. She viewed his work and showed him some of the watercolours she had done of the poles. Richardson praised her abilities and Carr decided on the spot to dedicate herself to recording the heritage of British Columbia's Native peoples before it vanished.

At this time Emily Carr had been studying painting for more than a decade, in California and London, and was teaching art in Vancouver as well as pursuing her own career as a painter. Her exposure to Native people was limited to the Indians she saw around Victoria when she was growing up, and to the visit she had made in 1898 to the Native villages near Ucluelet on the west coast of Vancouver Island. Yet even as a child, she felt a strong fascination for the Indian; "often I used to wish I had been born an Indian," she later wrote. Her biographers speculate that Carr, alienated from her own family and from polite Victorian society, was attracted by the apparent freedom and unconventionality of the Indians who inhabited the fringes of her world.[12] A bit of a misanthrope, she idealized Indians as outsiders, misfits like herself.

Having resolved to paint the Indian "like a camera" for posterity, Carr set about her project with great energy. Between 1907 and 1912, interrupted by a year of study in Paris, she visited Native villages all along the coast, from Campbell River and Alert Bay on Vancouver Island to the Haida settlements of the Queen Charlotte Islands and the Tsimshian villages in the Skeena River Valley. These were arduous expeditions, especially for a woman travelling alone. They involved long voyages by steamship and open boat, toilsome hikes with heavy packs through dense forest, overnight camping in leaky tents in isolated villages. Through it all, her commitment to the project was total.

Carr's Indian painting came to a head in 1913 with the Vancouver exhibition. It contained almost two hundred pieces—oils, watercolours, sketches—covering fourteen years' worth of excursions. The long public lecture which she gave twice during the exhibition explained how totem poles were made and the role they played in the life of the Native people. In her talk, Carr revealed her strong affection and admiration for the Natives of the coast. Unlike Kane and the other artists who had set out to paint the Indian, Carr felt a deep personal bond with her subject. She was recording for posterity, but she was also striving for understanding.

Like many of her contemporaries, Carr interpreted contact between Native and non-Native in Christian terms. Before the White man came, she believed that the Indian lived in harmony with nature in something approaching a Garden of Eden. "In their own primitive state they were a moral people with a high ideal of right," she told her listeners. "I think they could teach us many things." When Whites arrived, they offered Indians the "apple" of a new way of life. But the apple had a worm in it. "They looked up to the whites, as a superior race whom they should try to copy. Alas, they could not discriminate between the good and bad, there was so much bad, and they copied it."[13] As a result, she believed, Indians had lost touch with their traditional culture which was speedily disappearing from the coast.

Carr's 1913 exhibition was well received, but she failed to win a hoped-for commission from the provincial government and had to return to Victoria where she assumed the life of a boarding-house keeper. Without encouragement, she could not afford to go on painting and eventually she abandoned her Indian project. Her "retirement" lasted until 1927, when a visit from Eric Brown, director of the National Gallery in Ottawa, suddenly elevated her and her Indian paintings into national prominence. Brown was looking for canvases to include in an upcoming show of West Coast Indian art at the National Museum. Stunned to discover the cache of paintings Carr had completed so many years before, he convinced her to contribute several to the exhibition. What followed—Carr's trip back east to the opening, her meeting with Lawren Harris, her discovery of the Group of Seven and their discovery of her—is one of the legends of Canadian art history.

The exhibition opened in Ottawa on December 2, 1927. A combination of Native art and modern paintings on Native themes, the show was hailed in the press as an historic occasion, the first of its kind anywhere in the world. "What a tremendous influence the vanishing civilization of the West Coast Indian is having on the minds of Canadian artists," reported the *Ottawa Citizen*. Carr received particular praise. "She is a real discovery," wrote the *Citizen* critic. Her work was "the greatest contribution of all time to historic art of the Pacific slope."[14] Early in January, the exhibition moved on to Toronto where the critic in the *Daily Star* described it as "a revelation" comparable to the discovery of a "Canadian tomb of Tutankaheman." The Native art and artifacts were among the country's greatest cultural treasures, he wrote, as important as the art of the Aztecs, the Mayans or the Incans.[15] It is noteworthy that he made the comparison not to a living tradition but to other vanished Americans.

A cynic might have taken a more jaundiced view of the exhibition. After all, the art seemed to be valued chiefly as examples of a Native tradition long dead. The death of that tradition was both the theme of the work and the necessary precondition of its sudden popularity. While artists like Emily Carr lamented the fate of the Indian, their success was predicated on it. Having first of all destroyed many aspects of Native culture, White society now turned around and admired its own recreations of what it had destroyed. To the extent that they suffered any guilt over what had happened to the Native people, Whites relieved it by preserving evidence of the supposedly dying culture. Whites convinced themselves that they were in this way saving the Indians. By a curious leap of logic, non-Natives became the saviours of the vanishing Indian.

Carr returned from the East with her confidence as an artist restored. She immediately resumed her painting career, and in the summer of 1928 made another excursion north to the villages of the Skeena and Nass rivers and the Queen Charlotte Islands. This trip resulted in some of her finest paintings, but it also marked an end to her Indian project. Under the encouragement of Lawren Harris, she began to feel that she had gone as far as she could as an interpreter of Native art and that it was time to concentrate on her own vision of the forest wilderness, unmediated by Native monuments.

But Carr's interest in Native people remained strong. As her health deteriorated in the late 1930s, she devoted more of her time to writing. She wrote stories about her odd assortment of pets, about her days as a landlady, about her childhood and about her early excursions to the coastal Indian villages. A group of the latter were collected and published in 1941 as *Klee Wyck*.

The book received a warm critical reception—"there is nothing to be said in dispraise of her work," commented Robertson Davies—and the next year it won a Governor General's Award for non-fiction.

Carr's style in *Klee Wyck* is unique and charming, at its best when she describes her deep affection for the coastal forest, "the twisted trees and high tossed driftwood."[16] With few exceptions, though, her Indians lack individual character. They are noble figures, living in tune with forest and sea. But they are exotics—servants, street pedlars, subsistence fishermen who speak broken English—living outside White society and apparently having no place in it. Carr is never patronizing. She herself was alienated from mainstream Canadian society and her stories romanticize the poverty and dignity of the social outcast. She describes the harsh reality of life for the contemporary Native, but she is no social worker. Her stories ask the reader to admire the character of the Indian, just as her painting asks the viewer to admire the spirituality and art. Nowhere does she ask her audience to confront social reality. As a result, although she had great personal sympathy for the Indian, she nevertheless belongs to the tradition of artists who took for granted that Indians were vanishing and sought to preserve and idealized image of them, and not the reality of Native people. [...]

GUNS AND FEATHERS

The last two decades have seen a revolution in public thinking about the Indian. Raised on *Howdy Doody* and *The Lone Ranger,* I have seen the Native peoples of the North defend their way of life against southern megaprojects which threaten their land. I have watched Elijah Harper change the constitutional direction of the country with a wave of his feather, and I have seen the tanks roll at Oka. It is a long way from Chief Thunderthud to the Mohawk Warriors.

In 1968, during the discussions leading up to his government's controversial White Paper on Indian policy, Prime Minister Pierre Trudeau wrote: "In terms of *realpolitik*, French and English are equal in Canada because each of these linguistic groups has the power to break the country. And this power cannot yet be claimed by the Iroquois, the Eskimos, or the Ukrainians."[17] In Canada, Trudeau was saying, political power depends on your ability to destroy the country: if you do not have that ability, you do not have real power. No one thought for a moment in 1968 that Native people had the ability, so why should they enjoy the power?

Now the country is twenty-five years older and we have learned how wrong we were. With the Meech Lake constitutional debacle, and the armed standoff at Oka, Native people proved that they, too, could break the country. If this is what it took—confrontation, roadblocks, constitutional impasse, threats of secession—Natives proved as adept at it as any White politician. The result? Now, suddenly, they enjoy unprecedented political power. Their representatives sit with the prime minister and the provincial premiers. Aboriginals are now recognized as one of the founding peoples of Canada. Constitutional talks are incomplete without Native people present.

All of this came about because Native people refused to live within the stereotypes White people fashioned for them. They would not disappear; they would not be obedient children and assimilate; they would not go away. But even as these events unfold before us, it is clear that our response to them, as non-Natives, is still conditioned by the image of the Imaginary Indian.

There is a simple test which people who study stereotyping like to perform. Ask a child to draw a picture of an Indian. Even though they can see Native people in ordinary clothes on the television news almost every night, youngsters invariably draw the Wild West Indian, in feathers and buckskin, usually holding a weapon. But then take the test yourself. When I did I discovered the first image that occurred to me was a photograph I remembered from the early 1970s of a young Ojibway man taking part in a roadblock at Kenora, Ontario, sitting on the hood of a car cradling a rifle. (Of course, for most of us this image was updated by the powerful photographs of Mohawks and soldiers confronting each other across the barricades at Oka.) And the second image that occurred to me was of Elijah Harper, seated at his desk in the Manitoba legislature, calmly twitching his eagle feather and bringing the process of constitutional change in the country to an abrupt halt. The warrior versus the wise elder; it turns out that the images of Indians we are offered today are not much different from what they have always been. [...]

Sometimes we thought it was simply a matter of conquering the Indians, taking their territory and absorbing them out of existence Then America would be ours. Sometimes we thought just the opposite, that we had to become Indians in order to be at home here. This myth of transformation lies at the heart of Canadian culture—Canadians need to transform themselves into Indians. In this sense Grey Owl was the archetypal Canadian, shedding his European past and transforming himself into an Indian in order to connect through the wilderness with the New World. This is the impulse behind the appropriation by White society of so many aspects of Native culture, trivial as this cultural poaching often seems to be. It also explains the persistent desire by non-Natives to "play Indian," whether by dressing up in feathers and moccasins at summer camp, or by erecting another totem pole as a representative symbol of Canada, or by roaring an Indian chant from the bleachers at a baseball game. This behaviour, repeated over and over, reveals a profound need on the part of non-Natives to connect to North America by associating with one of its most durable symbols, the Imaginary Indian.

There is an ambivalence at the heart of our understanding of what Canadian civilization is all about. On the one hand, the national dream has always been about not being Indian. Since the days of the earliest colonists, non-Natives have struggled to impose their culture on the continent. Indians were always thought of as the Other, threatening to overwhelm this enterprise. Noble or ignoble, it didn't really matter. There was no place for the "savage" in the world the newcomers were building. Canadian history, as Stephen Leacock said, was the struggle of civilization against savagery. There was never any question on which side Indians stood.

On the other hand, as a study of the Imaginary Indian reveals, Euro-Canadian civilization has always had second thoughts. We have always been uncomfortable with our treatment of the Native peoples. But more than that, we have also suspected that we could never be at home in America because we were not Indians, not indigenous to the place. Newcomers did not often admit this anxiety, but Native people recognized it. "The white man does not understand the Indian for the reason he does not understand America," said the Sioux Chief Standing Bear. "The roots of the tree of his life have not yet grasped the rock and soil. The white man is still troubled with primitive fears; he still has in his consciousness the perils of this frontier continent...."[18] As we have seen, one way non-Natives choose to resolve this anxiety is to somehow become Indian.

In the jargon of the day, Canadians are conflicted in their attitudes toward Indians. And we will continue to be so long as the Indian remains imaginary. Non-Native Canadians can hardly hope to work out a successful relationship with Native people who exist largely in fantasy. Chief Thunderthud did not prepare us to be equal partners with Native people. The fantasies we told ourselves about the Indian are not really adequate to the task of understanding the reality of Native people. The distance between the two, between fantasy and reality, is the distance between Indian and Native. It is also the distance non-Native Canadians must travel before we can come to terms with the Imaginary Indian, which means coming to terms with ourselves as North Americans.

NOTES

1. Paul Kane, *Wanderings of an Artist*, in J. Russell Harper, ed., *Paul Kane's Frontier* (Toronto: University of Toronto Press, 1971), p. 51.

2. Ibid., p. 14.

3. Ibid., p. 68.

4. Ibid., p. 74.

5. Ibid., p. 98.

6. Cited in ibid., p. 28

7. Barry Lord, *The History of Painting in Canada* (Toronto: NC Press, 1974), p. 95.

8. Cited in J. Russell Harper, *Paul Kane's Frontier* (Toronto: University of Toronto Press, 1971), p. 41.

9. John Maclean, *The Indians of Canada: Their Manners and Customs* (Toronto: William Briggs, 1889), p. 339.

10. Public Archives of Canada, Emily Carr Papers, MG30D215, Vol. 10, "Lecture on Totems," April 1913, p. 52.

11. Ibid., p. 53.

12. Maria Tippett, *Emily Carr: A Biography* (Toronto: Oxford University Press, 1979), p. 29; Doris Shadbolt, *Emily Carr* (Vancouver: Douglas and McIntyre, 1990), p. 87. Also useful is Paula Blanchard, *The Life of Emily Carr* (Vacouver: Douglas and McIntyre, 1987).

13. "Lecture on Totem," pp. 40–41.

14. *Ottawa Citizen*, 2 December 1927.

15. *Toronto Daily Star*, 9 January 1928.

16. Emily Carr, *Klee Wyck* (Toronto: Clarke, Irwin and Co., 1941), p. 19.

17. Sally M. Weaver, *Making Canadian Indian Policy: The Hidden Agenda, 1968–70* (Toronto: University of Toronto Press), p. 55.

18. Cited in Richard Drinnon, *Facing West: The Metaphysics of Indian Hating and Empire Building* (Minneapolis: University of Minnesota Press), p. 230.

BIBLIOGRAPHY

Blanchard, Paula. *The Life of Emily Carr*. Vancouver: Douglas and McIntyre, 1987.

Carr, Emily. *Klee Wyck*. Toronto: Clarke, Irwin and Co., 1941.

Drinnon, Richard. *Facing West: The Metaphysics of Indian Hating and Empire Building*. Minneapolis: University of Minnesota Press, 1980.

Harper, J. Russell. *Paul Kane's Frontier*. Toronto: University of Toronto Press, 1971.

Jackson, A.Y. *A Painter's Country*. Toronto: Clarke, Irwin and Co., 1958.

Lord, Barry. *The History of Painting in Canada*. Toronto: NC Press, 1974.

Maclean, John. *The Indians of Canada: Their Manners and Customs*. Toronto: William Briggs, 1889.

Public Archives of Canada. Emily Carr Papers, MG30D215.

Shadbolt, Doris. *Emily Carr*. Vancouver: Douglas and McIntyre, 1990.

Tippett, Maria. *Emily Carr: A Biography*. Toronto: Oxford University Press, 1979.

Weaver, Sally M. *Making Canadian Indian Policy: The Hidden Agenda, 1968–70*. Toronto: University of Toronto Press, 1981.

Chapter 34

Doubling Discourses and the Veiled Other: Mediations of Race and Gender in Canadian Media

Yasmin Jiwani

In this article, Jiwani (2010) discusses how Muslim women have been represented in Canadian media, drawing on Orientalist images of Islam, Muslims, and Arabs. The veil itself is seen as a floating signifier that can be represented in different ways depending on the political context and the strategic need. The discourse of the "Muslim victim" can be mobilized to rationalize the need to "save" Muslim women from their purported hyper-patriarchal culture, a rationale strong enough to justify military invasion or occupation of sovereign nations, such as Afghanistan. In these portrayals, Muslim men are simultaneously depicted as hyper-patriarchal while the (Christian) West is drawn as the saviours. Also, there is often an evaluative juxtaposition of "veiled" Muslim women in Canada and in their country of origin. Two case studies are provided by the author: a *Globe and Mail* week-long series on the lives of Afghani women run in 2009, and the CBC TV sitcom *Little Mosque on the Prairie*.

In this chapter, I focus on media representations of the female Muslim body, paying particular attention to the veiled discourses that construct her. The analysis focuses on Canadian mainstream media and its coverage of Muslim women within the domestic and international contexts. By centring the analysis on the strategic use of the hijab and the burqa as signifiers of the Muslim woman, my intent is to emphasize the relational dynamics that are at play in the contrasting oppositions and doubling discourses that frame representations of Muslim women "over here" and "over there."

I begin this chapter with a general overview of the mediated constructions of Muslim women in the West, focusing on the Orientalist gaze, underscoring the doubling discourses that are inherent within them. I then proceed to examine contemporary representations of Muslim women in both "soft" media (entertainment) and "hard" media (news) within the context of their portrayals "over there," as in Afghanistan, and their representations "over here" in the Canadian context. I conclude by linking these representations to an economy that prevails within the mainstream Western media, demonstrating how these representations serve to buttress strategies of exclusion, expulsion, containment, and commodification. But first, I provide a general backdrop to the main arguments of this essay—the terrain of mediated representations of race and gender signified through the bodies of women of colour within the theatre of the Western mass media, a context which is characterized by intense media concentration and conglomeration.

MEDIATIONS OF RACE AND GENDER

In the dominant media, strategies of exnomination, naturalization, and universalization become the tools whereby dominance is affirmed as the normative frame of reference and whereby explanations that privilege race thinking are proffered as having the most explanatory value. The power of exnomination consists of the "power not to be named."[1] This is also the power of whiteness that forms the invisible backdrop against which stigmatized and valorized Others are profiled. As John Fiske eloquently argues, "The power to see while remaining unseen, the power to put others into discourse while remaining unspoken, is a particularly effective form of power."[2]

This power to define the situation and yet remain unnamed is materially grounded in the corporate concentration and convergence that characterizes the media landscape today,[3] most especially in Canada.[4] The Canadian context is marked by a handful of corporations that control most of the media outlets and publications across the country.[5] In such a situation, it is not unusual to find journalists and editors who are compelled, through threat of losing their jobs, to toe the corporate line and privilege the ideologies of those in power.[6] Indeed, commenting on his media empire and its explicit political position, CanWest founder "Izzy" Asper openly stated that an "anti-Israel bias is a cancer affecting Western media organizations,"[7] indicating that his papers (which at the time were the major dailies in most provinces and one national daily) would not take a pro-Palestinian position. Journalist Patricia Pearson commented, upon her resignation from the *National Post* (CanWest's national daily), that "when CanWest, controlled by the Asper family, acquired the paper from Conrad Black, I no longer dared to express sympathy for Palestinians."[8]

In light of the biases inherent in media monopolies and cartels, it is not surprising then that contemporary news portrayals of Arabs, Muslims, and Islam fare so negatively.[9] That aside, there is a long and entrenched history of negative representations that are circumscribed within a tradition of Orientalism, and thus, as Stuart Hall affirms, contemporary discourses bear these past traces.[10] However, just as Orientalist framings are pervasive in the media, so too are colonial tropes representing racialized groups in general. The economy of media representations works to privilege some groups over others, define particular groups in specific ways, and construct discrete groups as signifying distinct threats. Thus, Black males are often linked to crime in Canadian, British, and American newspapers,[11] and Muslim men are now associated with terrorism. Pnina Werbner argues that these representations signify different forms of racism, each drawing on specific historically inscribed stocks of knowledge.[12]

Stuart Hall's influential work on race and representations anchors this grid within a framework of colonial relations.[13] He argues that the binary relations of Manichean oppositions that constitute racist discourse are predicated on a base grammar of race. This grammar, he maintains, revolves around the following power co-ordinates manifest in colonial discourses about colonized Others: the naturalization of differences; the evacuation of history; and the fixed relations of power, wherein the dominance of one is secured by the inferiorization of the Other. Hall further argues that while this colonial form of "active" racism has now mutated into a more inferential form of racism, the premises on which it is based reflect continuity with previous discourses.[14] Contemporary representations of racialized groups thus bear the traces of previous histories, connoting relations of power, as well as naturalizing and dehistoricizing difference.

However, these representations are not "flat" and unidimensional. Rather, they are marked by an inherent ambiguity, a tension or a contradiction. Thus, Hall argues, within each representation, the ambivalence manifests itself in the tension between the "positive" and "negative" aspect of that representation.[15] The rebellious field slave forms one counterpart to the obedient and submissive house slave, yet both are contained within the representational construct of the slave as a subordinated object of possession. The figure of the "jezebel" is the inverse of the mammy, but both are circumscribed within relations of power. In his analysis of the representations of Indian women in Kipling's literary works, John McBratney also draws attention to this inherent tension conceptualizing it as a "doubling discourse."[16] In this context, the doubling occurs with the concurrent representations of Indian women as weak and helpless and in need of rescue, and at the same time, as evil temptresses that use white male colonizers for their own ends. Chandra Mohanty[17] and Ann McClintock[18] make similar arguments demonstrating the use of these representations in legitimizing conquest and colonization.

Abdul R. JanMohamed suggests that these internal tensions make it possible to experience both desire and repulsion, avowal and disavowal.[19] It is this doubling that enables the media to seize on particular representations at specific points in time, without contradicting the basic grammar of race. A representation of a racialized Other can be positively valorized as a state of exceptionalism at one point, but other representations of the same racialized group can be negatively constructed. In either case, the representations underpin and are contained within relations of power. However, the ideological purchase of these representations is contingent and relational: it is contingent on the ideologies framing the group at a specific historical juncture and it is relational insofar as it is reflective of the larger economy of representations prevailing within the mass media at a given time. This is why race is, as Hall remarks, a "floating signifier."[20] [...]

ORIENTALIST FRAMINGS

In his now classic text, *Covering Islam*, Edward Said makes the argument that representations of Arabs, Islam, and Muslims have tended to be conflated.[21] Muslim communities and nations are constructed as static and homogenized entities. Drawing on his earlier work, Said points to the Orientalist frame as the organizing lens through which the West views the East, indicating that he has "not been able to discover any period in European or American history since the Middle Ages in which Islam was generally discussed or thought about outside a framework created by passion, prejudice, and political interest."[22] This situation has, one could argue, intensified with the events of September 11, which have come to represent a Rubicon, paving the way for the invasion of Afghanistan and subsequently Iraq.

Karim H. Karim's analysis of Orientalist representations of Islam and Muslims in the contemporary media coverage reiterates Said's central points, indicating that representations of Muslim men as "having fabulous but undeserved wealth (they have not earned it), being barbaric and regressive, indulging in sexual excess," and as "violent" are increasingly commonplace.[23] His findings are corroborated by Jack Shaheen's extensive analysis of Hollywood films, wherein figures of the veiled Muslim woman as the sexualized and evil Other are similarly pervasive.[24] Orientalism articulates with and encapsulates the grammar of race that Hall identified as underpinning colonial discourses of the Other. It is noteworthy that, as with colonial discourse, Orientalism posits Islam and Muslims as abstracted from history, their differences being naturalized and inferiorized in the process.

Feminist critiques of Said's work have noted the absence of women's subjectification, their role and complicity in shaping Orientalist discourse, and the muted emphasis placed on sexuality.[25] Said, for his part, did emphasize the feminization of the Orient, underscoring its designation as a zone of sexual conquest.[26] For the purposes of the present analysis, these critiques shed light on the importance of examining representations of women both as complicit facilitators of colonialist projects and imperial adventures, as well as subjected women whose material bodies and discursive representations are contested by patriarchal forces within both dominant and colonized groups. Here I draw on Claude Levi-Strauss's argument,[27] which is also echoed by Floya Anthias and Nira Yuval-Davis,[28] concerning women's role as reproducers of the nation and therefore as critical sites on which the discourses of race and nation are inscribed.[29]

It is in this light that representations constitute the anticipatory ground fertilizing and nurturing subsequent actions that, through such processes, perpetrate a symbolic and discursive violence. This is not to suggest that representations are overdetermined and that audiences lack agency. Rather, in communicating preferred and dominant meanings that are privileged through the selection and combination of particular representations, the media legitimize certain actions and inactions, authorize particular ways of seeing the world, and lend credibility to specific interlocutors.

REPRESENTATIONS OF MUSLIM WOMEN IN WESTERN MEDIA

Considerable literature has documented the stereotypical representations of Muslim women in the Western mainstream media. Here, what I wish to emphasize is the consistent media obsession with Muslim women's practices of veiling in contemporary settings. In previous eras, as for example during Hollywood's beginnings and later during its heyday, the veiled Muslim, Arab, Turkish, and Syrian woman—or whoever fit the notion of "Middle Eastern" woman at the time—was portrayed as a highly sexualized figure. Generally figured as the sensual belly dancer, or the princess (who often converts), or the quarrelsome queen, the Middle Eastern veiled woman represented the elusive, sexually tantalizing, and more often than not the wicked, duplicitous woman.[30] While this representation is still alive in some quarters, the tendency within the news media and current affairs programming has been to project representations of the veiled woman as essentially an abject and victimized Muslim figure.

In the sections below, I turn to the larger, current Western context within which the veil functions as a synecdoche for all manner of things associated with Islam and Muslims. By tracking the discourse surrounding the veil across international, national, and local contexts, we can understand its continuity as well as its symbolic values and the semiotic chains of signification that are amplified through the mass media. But for now I want to distinguish between representations of Muslim women and the hijab "over there"—as in Afghanistan, for example—and their representations "over here." I draw this distinction from Shahnaz Khan's work by the same title.[31] Khan makes the argument that the binaries between the oppressed Afghan women under Taliban rule and the liberated women in the West work to reinforce an ideological divide, elide the historical conditions and structures of power that connect them, while simultaneously suggesting that oppression only exists "over there." However, if this is a first order binary, the second level of the myth is the homogenization of all Muslim women—over here and over there.[32] As Khan puts it: "Such homogenized accounts often present the reader with a series of women who in a sense have been ripped out of their contexts, resulting in a re-plastering of their narratives onto Afghan women and other Muslim women in North America."[33] This "re-plastering" is the organization of Muslim women's representations within the same template of an oppressive, patriarchal Islam. However, I want to suggest another complicating layer—that of the mediating agent between "over here" and "over there." This is the native informant, and more often than not, the ex-pat or diasporic Afghan, a citizen of the West who is now relocated to the East. This assimilated figure, situated in the hyphen that bridges West and East, brings to the East the benefits of the West. Drawing from various examples, I will attempt to demonstrate the various layers of the myth of the veiled woman.

VEILED INTENTIONS—MUSLIM WOMEN "OVER THERE"

As numerous scholars have documented, the veil in the West is weighted with semiotic significations that predate the War on Terror and that are installed within Orientalism.[34] To put it another way, the veil itself has become an iconic sign of difference, but one that is reified to the extent that its strategic use, within Western ways of seeing, veils the intentions or motivations of the definer. The veil thus comes to stand in for the mute, passive, and oppressed Muslim woman, a representation that discursively functions as a countersign to the liberated Western woman.[35] In speaking to the recent genre of documentaries that have been released about the veil and Muslim women, Sunera Thobani makes the argument that such representations can be described as "veilomentaries," in that "they are more about the constitution of the Western woman as an emancipated gendered subject, a constitution that relies on the Othering of Muslim women as gendered hypervictims."[36] And as Joan Scott has observed, the obsessive focus on the veil makes it seem "as if patriarchy were a uniquely Islamic phenomenon!"[37]

It is not surprising, then, that Western powers quickly harnessed the veil to legitimize their interventions into Afghanistan. As Eric Louw[38] has observed and Ann Russo[39] has corroborated, the Western feminist concern with the oppression of Afghan women emerged shortly after the Taliban came to power. Yet it was not until 2001 when the War on Terror was unleashed and the "coalition of the willing" exercised its intervention in Afghanistan that the veiled Afghan woman became a strategic pawn in the current geopolitical context. As I have detailed elsewhere, representations of Afghan women as helpless victims of the Taliban and as weak refugees fleeing war remain commonplace in the Canadian print media—so much so that the burqa (the full-body veil) has come to stand for all Afghan women—a metonym that is still in currency.[40] Sherene Razack argues that the imperilled Muslim woman, the barbaric Muslim man, and the white civilized European have become the stock-in-trade characters in the national and international imaginative landscape.[41]

Despite the "intervention" of the international coalition, the reluctance of Afghan women to unveil—in spite of the forces of "liberation" freeing them from the tyranny of the Taliban— was not used to dismantle this stereotype of the veiled woman as a "gendered hypervictim" but rather to reinscribe it in the dominant discourse. Here, as Sedef Arat-Koç[42] points out, the culturalist argument was invoked to suggest that these women could not be liberated because they were so contained or imprisoned by their culture.

The veiled Afghan woman, as a symbol of oppression under Taliban Islam on the one hand and a victim of culture on the other, has become a floating signifier.[43] She remains mute in one instance and yet, in another, is the voice ventriloquizing a particular reality that fits Western preoccupations and assumptions. The real question, as Lila Abu-Lughod asks in her article on the subject, is: "Do Muslim women really need saving?"[44] But this raises the question as to how this floating signifier, in its gendered formation, is communicated discursively. In other words, what are the markers by which the victim status of Muslim women becomes apparent in ways that resonate with common-sense knowledge? In what contexts is the notion of victimhood made intelligible and how does the victimhood of Muslim women constitute them as "deserving" or "undeserving," worthy or unworthy, of Western benevolence and intervention?

Clearly, the answers to these questions depend on the context. As Jasmin Zine has argued, drawing from Mohja Kahf's historical analysis, Muslim women's representations were not always confined to a victim status.[45] Rather, these representations changed in conjunction with Europe's relationship with Islam, from the crusades to the contemporary stages of globalization. With colonization, the representations of Muslim women became increasingly condensed around this victim status such that it is now an entrenched signifier of difference replete with its associated identifier, the hijab. Miriam Cooke succinctly summarizes this link when she writes about the "four-stage gendered logic of empire."[46] This logic, she suggests,

> genders and separates subject peoples so that the men are the Other and the women are civilizable. To defend our universal civilization we must rescue the women. To rescue these women we must attack these men. These women will be rescued not because they are more "ours" than "theirs" but rather because they will have become more "ours" through the rescue mission.... In the Islamic context, the negative stereotyping of the religion as inherently misogynist provides ammunition for the attack on the uncivilized brown men.[47]

Dana Cloud asserts that, "In times of war, images of enemy Others, represented as helpless and savage, are foils for the image of the national self,"[48] One could argue that the "national self," in this regard, also changes in relation to the now-altered projection of the Other. If this is indeed the case, then as the War on Terror continues and as public support for it waxes and wanes, one can expect the discourse surrounding the representations of Afghan women to shift. [...]

In a seven-year study of these representations that I conducted between 2000 and 2007, it was evident that Afghan women had become noticeably more "worthy," making the transition from victims to survivors.[49] In the *Globe and Mail* (Toronto), for example, the women were given more voice, their heroic efforts were underscored, and their emerging entrepreneurship was taken as a positive sign of "them" becoming more like "us."

It would seem that Western liberation through micro-business entrepreneurship, including that initiated by Beauticians Without Borders, served to make Afghan women worthy victims of rescue.[50] [...]

In September 2009, the floating signifier of the veiled Afghan women reappeared again, this time in the *Globe and Mail*'s week-long series entitled "Behind the Veil: Inside the Lives of Afghan Women." The series ran in both the online and print edition, and promised to unveil the lives of these women through online interviews, podcasts, and discussions.[51] The online version featured six stories about Afghan women. At the bottom of the website, one can scroll through various other links, which provide the reader with an introduction; a "behind the scenes" view (offering unedited footage); the foreign news editor's rationale for undertaking the series; the methodology and "creative journalism" used to get this information; a glossary of keywords; a discussion with Paula Lerner, the freelance photographer, and Jessica Leeder, the *Globe* reporter; an archive of previous stories about Afghanistan published by the *Globe*; a help link that offers a list of other charities and organizations "that can help you help Afghan women"; and a section called "The Observers," which covers the discussions between Sarah Hampson, a columnist, and Sally Armstrong, a well-known author who has written on Afghan women's issues before and who has also written opinion pieces for the *Globe and Mail*.[52] [...]

Through this series, just as in crime drama serials, we as the audience are invited to be first-person voyeurs, watching the risks and dangers that Afghan women face from the safety of our chairs at home. In the introduction to the series, Jessica Leeder appears on screen and, through her voiceover, recounts to us what compelled her to engage in this venture of uncovering the lives of Afghan women. In her words:

> My name is Jessica Leeder and I am a journalist for *The Globe and Mail*. In the past year, I have travelled twice to Afghanistan for the newspaper to work rotations in our Kandahar bureau. While female correspondents working in strict Islamic countries face many barriers that our male colleagues do not, we often gain a rare upper hand when it comes to accessing local women. In the conservative Afghan south, cultural and religious practices prevent females from talking to males who are not their relatives. That means the stories of what it is like to be a woman in this almost prehistoric slice of Afghan society have largely gone untold.
>
> Last spring, I arrived in Kandahar to find security in a more precarious state than it was five months earlier at the end of my first trip. I wondered what this meant for the day-to-day lives of women in the city. While that question was still percolating, I found myself writing about the sad and gruesome public assassination of Sitara Achakzai, one of Kandahar's rare female politicians. I telephoned some of her colleagues that I had quoted before. But this time, they begged me through tears not to quote them, so terrified they had become for their lives. By now, I understood that Kandahar's women were even further from shedding their burqas than I had thought. Instead they were scrambling to put them back on. With the help of a local videographer and translator, the *Globe* set out to find out why.
>
> Over the course of a month, we interviewed ten average women in the city who allowed us to film them, offering a rare window into both disturbing and mundane aspects of daily female life. For reasons of security and domestic obedience, some asked us to obscure their faces. But as our series unfolds this week, you'll meet all of them—widows, mothers, working women, and even a child bride. They'll tell you how improbable it seems that women will ever drive cars in Kandahar. You will hear what its like to be sold like livestock and you'll hear about hopes and far-off dreams.[53]

[...] What is most interesting about Leeder's introduction is how she situates herself as a female reporter having more access to Afghan women than her male counterparts. Here, her discursive strategy of invoking a comparison with male reporters serves two functions. First, it legitimizes her as a credible authority (a working journalist returning to Kandahar) and her special status as a woman who can penetrate into the zones that men cannot, akin to the woman anthropologist who can enter a Zenana or harem, a space forbidden to men.

Leeder thus has the kind of access that her male counterparts do not have, but this is also what highlights her special status: She is a woman like these Afghan women are and, hence, she can identify with them, bring out their stories in a way that resonates with the construction of a universal womanhood.[54] This stance is reminiscent of the imperial feminists who would publicize the oppression of their Third World sisters in a way that would also underscore their own superior status.[55] [...]

Leeder's references to Kandahar as a "prehistoric slice of Afghan society," and a place where women beg through tears and are subordinated to "security and domestic obedience," invoke representations of Afghan society as ultrapatriarchal and Afghan women as fearful, submissive, and caught in the bind of tradition. These women are subject to "death by culture" as Uma Narayan describes it.[56] To recount Sitara Achakzai's assassination in April 2009 as "sad and gruesome" summons images of other Afghan women's murders under the Taliban, notably those that have circulated in popular culture.[57] Take, for example, *Beneath the Veil* (2001), an undercover documentary by British-Afghan filmmaker Saira Shah that focuses on women being executed by the Taliban, and *The Death of a Princess* (1980), a British docudrama that recounts the story of a love affair between a princess and her lover, an affair that resulted in their executions. These resonances raise the question as to whether the *Globe* was in fact mimicking Shah's documentary *Beneath the Veil* when it titled its series *Behind the Veil*.

Undoubtedly, the Taliban are patriarchal. My analysis above is not to suggest otherwise, but to underscore the perception that is being cultivated, a perception that effectively elides the patriarchal nature of Western societies and that of other non-Islamic societies. [...]

Leeder's final and tantalizing promise to her viewers is that they will get to meet these women, all of whom are average, and even a "child bride." This effectively erases the sexualized violence that prevails against children in the West—children also who are not married but are nonetheless subjected to violence, sexual and otherwise. However, it is the tone of her voice when she says that we, as the audience, will actually meet one of these exotic creatures that introduces the element or sensationalism—the layers that invoke a certain structure of feeling, an emotional combination of anticipation and pity.[58] Interestingly, it is the picture of the child bride that viewers first got to see when they visited the website at the time when the series began.

Leeder's introduction paves the way to the individual interviews with each of the ten "average" women, who are interviewed with the aid of an interpreter. Most of them are wearing veils or burqas. We only see their faces when they are in an all-women's group doing work. Aside from the translator, the only other voice that is featured in some depth is that of Rangina Hamidi, a human rights activist working in Kandahar. Hamidi is described by Leeder as an "an Afghan-born woman who abandoned a comfortable ex-pat life in Virginia six years ago to pick up the fight for women's rights in Kandahar." Here again, the contrast between Afghan women who are born in Afghanistan and Afghan women who have come from elsewhere in the diaspora is accentuated. Unlike the other women who speak through the interpreter, Hamidi is well versed in English and able to recount the situation of women in Kandahar. She emphasizes the lack of security and the constant threat that women face on a daily basis. This strategic use of the diasporic voice to tell the stories and struggles of Afghan women raised and living in Afghanistan is similar to the manner in which the *Globe* has covered Afghan women's stories in the years preceding this series. As I have noted elsewhere, diasporic Afghan women are often used to portray the "civilizing" influence of the West as evident in their role of bringing Western notions of equality to their homeland.[59] They also become the native informants who model the "benefits" of the West and who provide insights into the world and lives of the colonized.[60] [...]

Overall, the message one gleans from these webcasts is that "we" (Canadians) need to remain in Kandahar to restore order, and that the order that exists is extremely fragile. Women are the ones suffering the most and, hence, it is "our" duty as concerned citizens (and as Canadians with an army stationed there) to remain in Kandahar. The worthiness of the Afghan women victims comes through and is facilitated by the website's link to charities and organizations to which "we" can donate in order to save our Afghan sisters. What is carefully elided in the *Globe's* coverage is the continuing question of Canada's involvement in Afghanistan and the emerging reports of Canadian forces as being complicit in transferring Afghan prisoners to be tortured.[61] These questions are part of the larger context that is significantly muted by the media's obsessive focus on the veil.

I turn now to the representations of Muslim women in the veil "over here."

VEILED INTENTIONS—MUSLIM WOMEN "OVER HERE"

By far, the most popular and well-known iconic representation of the veiled Muslim woman in contemporary Canadian popular media can be found in the figure of Rayyan (played by Sitara Hewitt, a non-Muslim), the second-generation, feminist Muslim physician featured in the popular and highly celebrated CBC comedy sitcom *Little Mosque on the Prairie*. However, Rayyan represents an exception to the normative treatment of veiled Muslim women in the Canadian press or in other television crime dramas.[62] More than that, she is the doubled Other—the inverse side of the oppressed veiled Muslim woman. Though wearing the hijab, she is sufficiently assimilated to be consumed as an exotic Other.[63] Through her representation, "we" as the audience get to see past the stereotype, but at the same time, we also see that Rayyan is constrained by the patriarchal logic of the mosque (as evident in the episode concerning gender segregation within the mosque) and its male congregants.[64]

Little Mosque on the Prairie represents a form of "soft power"[65]—clothing its messages about the diversity of the Muslim *ummah* in a language that is at once appealing, comical, and humane.[66] The show stresses the universality of the everyday problems facing all groups, whether they are Muslims, Christians, or secularist zealots. In other words, through this universalizing discourse, the show enfolds and levels off the differences between these groups while, at the same time, underscoring and deconstructing the popular image of Muslims as threats, rendering their differences as peculiar. In the end, as Cánas emphasizes, "the form of the cultural text—a television comedy—can only use satire, parody, and mimicry in comedic ways that, while challenging orientalist discourse of the Muslim Other, produces its own silences."[67] These silences, as she points out, have to do with the deep cleavages within the *ummah*, the particularities and specificities of the different characters, and the notion of resolution as easily achieved through the forging of a harmonious multiculturalism. More to the point, these silences, I contend, have to do with the particular ways in which Muslim women are represented in a television show. The foil to Rayyan, the assimilated Muslim woman, is her mother, who is a Muslim convert, and not a "good Muslim" at that. Rayyan is the "hybrid" figure reflective of a mix between whiteness and Arabness (from her father's side). As a hybrid, she is "more like us" and, as I have pointed out in my analysis of Asian heroines, this strategy becomes one way in which to defuse or neutralize the threat of race.[68] She is then the figure "in-between"—mediating the links between the oppressed Muslim woman and her liberated white, Western, and secularized counterpart. As well, she mediates the contrasts between the "good" and "bad" Muslim woman (in the case of this sitcom, these figures are represented by Fatima, the African Muslim woman who tends to be more traditional, and Rayyan's mother, the "bad" Muslim convert).

While *Little Mosque on the Prairie* is emblematic of "soft power" in that the format is a situation comedy presented as a half-hour series and intended for familial consumption, news, as in television news programming, press reports, and current affairs magazines, which are laced with considerable credibility and legitimacy, can be construed as a form of hard power. This is not to suggest that all forms of "soft power" convey positive or benign representations of Muslim women.[69] Rather, "hard" news has an aura of authenticity that makes it more amenable to being incorporated within regimes of truth. Nonetheless, as I have shown in an analysis of the popular CBC crime drama *The Border*, Muslim women within this genre still occupy that zone of otherness—as the exotic, the erotic, and the dangerous.[70] Here, they are often portrayed as mute, passive, burqa-clad women or as white women who have "gone native" and therefore pose a substantial danger to domestic security. The only "in-between" figure is the hybrid Muslim woman—assimilated into Western ways but still retaining her Muslim religious allegiance and identity, and terribly conflicted by it all.[71]

Most representations of veiled Muslim women that are communicated through news and documentaries (those formats constitutive of "hard power") tend to cohere around the negative end of the binary, underscoring the entrenched media template of the oppressed Muslim woman living under ultrapatriarchal Islam. Since 9/11, there have been several events within Canada that have secured considerable press and television coverage concerning Muslim women; events that have centred on the veil, honour killings, and forced marriages. This has paralleled corresponding and heightened media coverage of terrorist attempts resulting in Muslim men held in confinement under suspicion. Razack has fittingly described the situation as one where Muslims are "cast out," bereft of any legal protection and held in a state of exception.[72] In a like manner, Shiraz Dossa has described the contemporary Canadian media representations of Muslim males as "Lethal" Others.[73] [...]

CONCLUSION

The story of Afghanistan continues, as all war stories do. But this time, there is no clear victor; just a country of victims whose continual rescue has to be legitimized under different guises. Women, it seems, have become the quintessential victims in this geopolitical war, but their worthiness as victims can only be assured by their constant demonstration of struggle against the odds and their ability, through time, to become more like "us." In the meantime, the discourse has shifted to allow for the construction of "moderate" Talibans who can be trusted to look after their women. That this is so opportune at a time when Western military forces are seeking ways to leave Afghanistan is not surprising. The veiled Afghan woman remains the quintessential "floating signifier": ready to be called forth to legitimize another invasion or, more conveniently for the current situation, to legitimize the abandonment of a "failed state."

Representations of the veil in the Canadian domestic context point to the weight of the template of Islamic oppression which has so easily shifted terrains—from "over there" to "over here"—as evident in the furor generated over the sharia law debate and the quick and easy frame imposed on the murders of Aqsa Parvez and Shemina Hirji. Finally, the threat that the Muslim woman signifies in the case of the Hérouxville Citizens' Code, as in other European instances concerning the banning of the hijab, can be located in her role as reproducer of the culture. In this case, it is her role as reproducing Islam that invokes the paranoia of the cultural dilution on the part of the sovereign state (premised as it is on fictional blood lines and a presumed homogeneity). The threat of the veil is then the threat of an engulfing Islam, a threat that resonates with the historical archive of the crusades and that has to be contained somehow if not neutralized.

In terms of the economy of representations that prevail within the mainstream Canadian media, then, it can be surmised that the veiled Muslim woman remains the abject and passive Other in contrast to her purposive and aggressive male counterpart. Just as she is the gendered hypervictim, he is the ultrapatriarchal figure. However, each of these representations is organized around a doubling discourse. Whereas the traditional Muslim woman is constrained by her allegiance to Islam and imprisoned by her culture (as signified by her veil), the assimilated and Westernized Muslim woman is her doubled counterpart, reflecting the benefits of the West as they are embodied in liberated representations. She is "more like us." However, this liberated Other continues to play the role of a mediating agent, often as a native informant and, at other times, as the foil against which the traditionalism of the abject Muslim woman can be highlighted. The assimilated Other can be commodified and, through such commodification, consumed by popular media.

Whether as the gendered hypervictim in the East or the woman bound and killed by her culture in the West, the veiled Muslim woman has considerable currency in contemporary times. As a floating signifier, her representation can be corralled to fit particular hegemonic designs. And through her liberated, Westernized, and assimilated counterpart, the veiled Muslim woman "over here" or "over there" can be taught the benefits of the West, so that she, too, can become "more like us."[74]

NOTES

This research was supported by the Social Sciences and Humanities Research Council.

1.   John Gabriel, *Whitewash: Racialized Politics and the Media* (London: Routledge, 1998), 13.

2.   John Fiske, *Media Matters: Race and Gender in U.S. Politics*, rev. ed. (Minneapolis: University of Minnesota Press, 1996), 217.

3.   Edward S. Herman and Robert W. McChesney, *The Global Media: The New Missionaries of Corporate Capitalism* (Washington: Cassell, 1997).

4.   Leslie R. Shade and Michael Lithgow, "The Cultures of Democracy: How Ownership and Public Participation Shape Canada's Media Systems," in *Mediascapes: New Patterns in Canadian Communication*, 3rd ed., ed. Leslie R. Shade (Toronto: Nelson Publishers, 2010), 200–20.

5.   James Winter, *Democracy's Oxygen: How Corporations Control the News* (Montreal: Black Rose Books, 1997); James Winter, *Media Think* (Montreal: Black Rose Books, 2002).

6.   Robert A. Hackett, Richard Gruneau, Donald Gutstein, Timothy A. Gibson, and NewsWatch Canada, *The Missing News: Filters and Blind Spots in Canada's Press* (Onawa: Canadian Centre for Policy Alternatives and Toronto: Garamond Press, 2000).

7.   Irwin Block, "CanWest Chief Attacks 'Cancer' in the Media: Anti-Israel Bias 'Destroying Credibility,' Fundamental Precepts of Honest Reporting Have Been Abandoned, Israel Asper Says," *The Gazette* (Montreal), October 31, 2002, A3.

8.   Patricia Pearson, "See No Evil, No More," *The Globe and Mail* (Toronto), April 19, 2003, A19.

9.   See Karim H. Karim, *Islamic Peril* (Montreal: Black Rose Books, 2000); Sina Ali Muscati, "Arab/Muslim 'Otherness': The Role of Racial Constructions in the Gulf War and the Continuing Crisis with Iraq," *Journal of Muslim Minority Affairs* 22,1 (2002), 131–48; Sherene H. Razack, *Casting Out: The Eviction of Muslims from Western Law and Politics* (Toronto: University of Toronto Press, 2008).

10.   Stuart Hall, "The Whites of Their Eyes: Racist Ideologies and the Media," in *The Media Reader*, ed. Manuel Alvarado and John O. Thompson (London: British Film Institute, 1990), 9–23.

11.   Travis L. Dixon and Daniel Linz, "Race and the Misrepresentation of Victimization on Local Television News," *Communication Quarterly* 27,5 (2000), 547–73; Travis L. Dixon and Daniel Linz, "Television News, Prejudicial Pretrial Publicity, and the Depiction of Race," *Journal of Broadcasting & Electronic Media* 46,1 (2002), 112–36; Travis L. Dixon, Cristina L. Azocar, and Michael Casas, "The Portrayal of Race and Crime on Television Network News," *Journal of Broadcasting & Electronic Media* 47,4 (2003), 498–523; Robert M. Entman, "Modern Racism and the Images of Blacks in Local Television News," *Critical Studies in Mass Communication* 7,4 (1990), 332–45; Fiske, *Media Matters*; Stuart Hall, Chas Critcher, Tony Jefferson, and Brian Roberts, *Policing the Crisis: Mugging, the State, Law and Order* (London: MacMillan Press, 1978); Mary Beth Oliver, "African American Men as 'Criminal and Dangerous': Implications of Media Portrayals of Crime on the 'Criminalization' of African American Men," *Journal of African American Studies* 7,2 (2003), 3–18.

12. Pnina Werbner, "Islamophobia: Incitement to Religious Hatred—Legislating a New Fear?" *Anthropology Today* 21,1 (2001), 5–9.

13. Hall, "The Whites of Their Eyes"; Stuart Hall, ed., *Representation: Cultural Representation and Signifying Practices* (London: Sage and The Open University, 1997).

14. See also Cornel West, "A Genealogy of Modern Racism," in *Race Critical Theories*, ed. Philomena Essed and David T. Goldberg (Malden, MA: Blackwell Publishers, 2002), 90–111.

15. Hall, "The Whites of Their Eyes."

16. John McBratney, "Images of Indian Women in Rudyard Kipling: A Case of Doubling Discourse," *Inscriptions* 3,4 (1988), 47–57.

17. Chandra Talpade Mohanty, "Cartographies of Struggle: Third World Women and the Politics of Feminism," in *Third World Women and the Politics of Feminism*, ed. Chandra T. Mohanty, Ann Russo, and Lourdes Torres (Bloomington: Indiana University Press, 1991), 1–47.

18. Anne McClintock, *Imperial Leather: Race, Gender and Sexuality in the Colonial Context* (New York: Routledge, 1995).

19. Abdul R. JanMohamed, "The Economy of Manichean Allegory: The Function of Racial Difference in Colonial Literature," *Critical Inquiry* 12,1 (1985), 59–87.

20. Stuart Hall, "Race: The Floating Signifier (Transcript)," Media Education Foundation, 1997, (http:www.mediaed.org/assets/products/407/transcript_407.pdf) accessed October 7, 2009.

21. Edward Said, *Covering Islam: How the Media and Experts Determine How We See the Rest of the World* (New York: Pantheon Books, 1981).

22. Ibid., 23.

23. Karim, *Islamic Peril*, 62; emphasis in the original.

24. Jack G. Shaheen, *Reel Bad Arabs: How Hollywood Vilifies a People* (New York: Olive Branch Press, 2001).

25. Lisa Lowe, *Critical Terrains: French and British Orientalisms* (Ithaca, NY: Cornell University Press, 1994); Reina Lewis, *Gendering Orientalism: Race, Femininity and Representation* (New York: Routledge, 1996); Meyda Yeğenoğlu, *Colonial Fantasies: Towards a Feminist Reading of Orientalism* (Cambridge: Cambridge University Press, 1998).

26. For instance, Said argues that "the relation between the Middle East and the West is really defined as sexual: The association between the Orient and sex is remarkably persistent. The Middle East is resistant, as any virgin would be, but the male scholar wins the prize by bursting open, penetrating through the Gordian knot despite 'the taxing task.'" Edward Said, *Orientalism* (New York: Random House, 1978), 309. See also, Sherene H. Razack, "Race, Space and Prostitution: The Making of the Bourgeois Subject," *Canadian Journal of Women and the Law* 10,2 (1998), 338–76.

27. Claude Lévi-Strauss, *Structural Anthropology*, trans. C. Jacobson and B.G. Schoepf (New York: basic Books, l963); Claude Lévi-Strauss, *The Savage Mind* (Chicago: University of Chicago Press, l966).

28. Floya Anthias and Nira Yuval-Davis, *Racialized Boundaries: Race, Nation, Gender, Colour and Class and the Anti-Racist Struggle* (London: Routledge, 1992).

29. Such a depiction is, as Himani Bannerji notes, dehumanizing as it objectifies women as no more than "handmaidens of god, priest, and husband." Himani Bannerji, *The Dark Side of the Nation* (Toronto: Canadian Scholars' Press, 2000), 160.

30. See, for instance, the documentary *Hollywood Harems*, writ. and dir. Tania Kamal Eldin, 25 min., Women Make Movies, New York, 1999, VHS/DVD; Shaheen, *Reel Bad Arabs*; Ella Shohat and Robert Stam, *Unthinking Eurocentrism, Multiculturalism and the Media* (London: Routledge, l994).

31. Shahnaz Khan, "Between Here and There: Feminist Solidarity and Afghan Women," *Genders Online* 33 (2001), (http://www.genders.org/g33/g33_kahn.html) accessed June 15, 2003.

32. Here I draw on Roland Barthes's discussion of the myth as an ideological sign constructed from the striations of different signifiers and signified. See Roland Barthes, *Mythologies*, trans. Annette Lavers (London: Paladin Press, 1973).

33. Khan, "Between Here and There," para 45.

34. Sedef Arat-Koç, "Hot Potato: Imperial Wars or Benevolent Interventions? Reflections on 'Global Feminism' Post-September 11th," *Atlantis: A Women's Studies Journal* 26,2 (2002), 433–44; Katherine H. Bullock and Gul Joya Jafri, "Media (Mis)Representations: Muslim Women in the Canadian Nation," *Canadian Women's Studies* 20,2 (2000), 35–40; Dana L. Cloud, "'To Veil the Threat of Terror': Afghan Women and the 'Clash of Civilizations' in the Imagery of the U.S. War on Terror," *Quarterly Journal of Speech* 90,3 (2004), 285–306; Myra Macdonald, "Muslim Women and the Veil: Problems of Image and Voice in Media Representations," *Feminist Media Studies* 6,1 (2006), 7–23; Valentine Moghadam, "Afghan Women and Transnational Feminism," *Middle East Women's Studies Review*, l6,3/4 (2001), 1–12; Meghana Nayak, "Orientalism and 'Saving' U.S. State Identity after 9/11," *International Journal of Feminist Politics* 8,1 (2006), 42–61; Christine Noelle Karimi, "History Lessons: In Afghanistan's Decades of Confrontations with Modernity, Women Have Always Been the Focus of Conflict," *The Women's Review of Books* 19,7 (2002), l, 3–4; Carol A. Stabile and Deepa Kumar, "Unveiling Imperialism: Media, Gender and the War on Afghanistan," *Media, Culture & Society* 27,5 (2005), 765–82; Bradford Vivian, "The Veil and the Visible," *Western Journal of Communication* 63,2 (1999) 115–39; Yeğenoğlu, *Colonial Fantasies*; Jasmin Zine, "Muslim Women and the Politics of Representation," *American Journal of Islamic Social Sciences* 19,4 (2002), 1–23.

35. Mary Ann Franks, "Obscene Undersides: Women and Evil between the Taliban and the United States," *Hypatia: A Journal of Feminist Philosophy* 18,1 (2003), 135–56.

36. Sunera Thobani, "Gender and Empire: Veilomentaries and the War on Terror," in *Global Communications: Toward a Transcultural Political Economy*, ed. Paula Chakravartty and Yuezhi Zhao (Lanham, MD: Rowman and Littlefield, 2008), 221.

37. Joan Wallach Scott, *The Politics of the Veil* (Princeton: Princeton University Press, 2007), 4.

38. Eric P. Louw, "The 'War against Terrorism': A Public Relations Challenge for the Pentagon," *Gazette: The International Journal for Communication Studies* 65,3 (2003), 211–30.

39. Ann Russo, "The Feminist Majority Foundation's Campaign to Stop Gender Apartheid," *International Feminist Journal of Politics* 8,4 (2006), 557–80.

40. Yasmin Jiwani, "War Talk—Engendering Terror: Race, Gender and Representations in Canadian Print Media," *International Journal of Media & Cultural Politics* 1,1 (2005), 15–21.

41. Sherene H. Razack, "Imperilled Muslim Women, Dangerous Muslim Men and Civilised Europeans: Legal and Social Responses to Forced Marriages," *Feminist Legal Studies* 12,2 (2004), 129–74.

42. Arat-Koç, "Hot Potato: Imperial Wars or Benevolent Interventions?"

43. Uma Narayan, *Dislocating Cultures: Identities, Traditions and Third World Feminism* (London: Routledge, 1997).

44. Lila Abu-Lughod, "Do Muslim Women Really Need Saving? Anthropological Reflections on Cultural Relativism and Its Others," *American Anthropologist* 104,3 (2002), 783–90.

45. Zine, "Muslim Women and the Politics of Representation."

46. Miriam Cooke, "Saving Brown Women," *Signs: A Journal of Women in Culture and Society* 28,1 (2002), 468–70.

47. Ibid., 468.

48. Cloud, "'To Veil the Threat of Terror,'" 290.

49. Yasmin Jiwani, "Helpless Maidens and Chivalrous Knights: Afghan Women in the Canadian Press," *University of Toronto Quarterly* 78,2 (2009), 728–44.

50. Beauticians Without Borders is a charitable organization funded by Clairol, Revlon, L'Oreal, and MAC, with many of these cosmetics companies supplying the products. The aim is to teach Afghan women how to be skilled beauticians. (Sec Hamida Ghafour, "Beauticians Without Borders Teach Basics to Afghan Women," *The Globe and Mail*, February 24, 2004, AL.) This presupposes that Afghan women had no such skills before, as attested by the first-hand accounts of the Western beauticians who went over to train Afghan women. As Said has noted of Orientalism in general, the lens through which the Other is viewed bears no traces of history. Afghan women are suddenly discovered as needing beauty treatments and lacking beautifying skills. Said, *Covering Islam.*

51. Online, the podcasts and interviews can be found at (http://www.theglobeandmail.com/news/world/behind-the-veil/). At the time when I began writing this paper, all the information on this website was freely accessible. However, since October 19, 2009, access to the different links has been suppressed and is only available to the GlobePlus members—those who have paid to subscribe to the online version of the paper.

52. Sally Armstrong, "Veiled Threat: Afghanistan's Women under Taliban Rule," *Homemaker's* (1997), 16–29; "Shrouded in Secrecy," *Chatelaine* (May 2001), 131; and *Veiled Threat: The Hidden Power of the Women in Afghanistan* (Toronto: Penguin Canada, 2003).

53. Jessica Leeder, "Behind the Veil" (September 2009), (http://www.theglobeandmail.com/news/world/behind-the-veil/) accessed September 20, 2009.

54. Chandra Talpade Mohanty, "Under Western Eyes: Feminist Scholarship and Colonial Discourses," in *Third World Women and the Politics of Feminism*, ed. Chandra T. Mohanty, Ann Russo, and Lourdes Torres (Bloomington: Indiana University Press, 1991); Russo, "The Feminist Majority."

55. Valerie Amos and Pratibha Parmar, "Challenging Imperial Feminism," *Feminist Review* 17 (1984), 3–19; Antoinette M. Burton, "The White Woman's Burden: British Feminists and the 'Indian Woman,' 1865–1915," in *Western Women and Imperialism: Complicity and Resistance,* ed. Nupur Chaudhuri and Margaret Strobel (Bloomington: Indiana University Press, 1992), 137–57; McClintock, *Imperial Leather.*

56. Narayan, *Dislocating Cultures.*

57. Achakzai was shot dead by four gunmen outside her home in Kandahar.

58. On the topic of sensationalism, see Joy Wiltenburg, "True Crime: The Origins of Modern Sensationalism," *American Historical Review* 109,5 (2004), 1377–404.

59. Yasmin Jiwani, "The Great White North Encounters September 11: Race, Gender, and Nation in Canada's National Daily, *The Globe and Mail,*" *Social Justice* 32,4 (2005), 50–68.

60. Marnia Lazreg, "The Perils of Writing as a Woman on Women in Algeria," *Feminist Studies* 14,1 (1988), 81–107.

61. At present, there are 2,800 Canadian soldiers in Afghanistan, mostly concentrated in Kandahar. See the NATO International Security Assistance Force report at (http://www.nato.int/isaf/docu/epub/pdf/isaf_placemat.pdf).

62. See for instance, Yasmin Jiwani, "Soft Power—Policing the Border through Canadian TV Crime Drama," in *The Political Economy of Media and Power,* ed. Jeffery Klaehn (New York: Peter Lang, 2010), 275–93.

63. Suren Lalvani, "Consuming the Exotic Other," *Critical Studies in Mass Communication* 12,3 (1995), 263–86.

64. Jasmin Zine, Lisa K. Taylor, and Hilary E. Davis, "An Interview with Zarqa Nawaz," *Intercultural Education* 18,4 (2007), 379–82.

65. The distinction between "hard" and "soft" power is drawn from Nye and Owen's framework that focuses on the role of the media in promulgating hegemonic ideologies within international contexts. They argue that this is "soft" power in contrast to the "hard" military power of the state. See Joseph S. Nye, Jr. and William A. Owens, "America's Information Edge," *Foreign Affairs* 75,2 (1996), 20–36. However, my use of "hard" and "soft" also combines Bird and Dardenne's insight about the differences between "hard" news as factual reportage versus "soft" news, which includes columns and human interest stories. See Elizabeth S. Bird and Robert W. Dardenne, "Myth, Chronicle, and Story: Exploring the Narrative Qualities of News," in *Mass Communication as Culture,* ed. James Carey (Beverley Hills: Sage, 1988), 67–87.

66. *Ummali* or *uma* refers to the larger Muslim community.

67. Sandra Cãnas, "The Little Mosque on the Prairie: Examining (Multi) Cultural Spaces of Nation and Religion," *Cultural Dynamics* 20,3 (2008), 209.

68. Yasmin Jiwani, "The Eurasian Female Hero(ine): Sydney Fox as the Relic Hunter," *Journal of Popular Film and Television* 32,4 (2005), 182–91.

69. See, for instance, Catherine Burwell, "Reading Lolita in Times of War: Women's Book Clubs and the Politics of Reception," *Intercultural Education* 18,4 (2007), 281–96; Amira Jamarkani, "Narrating Baghdad: Representing the Truth of War in Popular Non-Fiction," *Critical Arts: A South-North Journal of Cultural and Media Studies* 2,1 (2007), 32–46; Cynthia Weber, "Not Without My Sister(s): Imagining a Moral American in Kandahar," *International Feminist Journal of Politics* 7,3 (2005), 358–76.

70. Jiwani, "Soft Power."

71. I am referring specifically to the first season of *The Border.* By the second season, this Muslim woman, played by Nazneen Contractor, has been killed and replaced by another, this time a woman of mixed racial heritage.

72. Razack, *Casting Out.*

73. Shiraz Dossa, "Lethal Muslims: White-Trashing Islam and the Arabs," *Journal of Muslim Minority Affairs* 28,2 (2008), 225–36.

74. See Cooke, "Saving Brown Women," 468.

Chapter 35

Races, Racism, and Popular Culture

John Solomos and Les Back

John Solomos and Les Back, in this chapter from 1996, ask the question "How is racism made popular?" They address this question by examining four examples. First, they show how racialized and gendered images were popularized in the colonial period of the eighteenth and nineteenth centuries, through such images as the "white male explorer" and "the warrior queen Britannia." These images served to produce the adventurous, benevolent, and overall "good" colonial white subject whose destiny was to control the world. The second example is from Nazi Germany, where propaganda, including popular paintings, theatre, music, dance, posters, and cartoons, juxtaposed racialized and gendered images of the "wholesome Aryan German" in idyllic rural settings with the "decadent Jewish metropolis" and "monstrous and immoral Americans." Resistance to such images is also examined, for instance in the swing subculture.

Solomos and Back's third example is that of the representation of Blacks in British newspapers in the post-war period, a period dominated by popular anxieties around Black sexuality and later the racializing of urban crime. Black Britons are portrayed as "outsiders" who threaten the nation. The final example discussed is the advertising of clothes manufacturers such as Benetton and Levi Strauss, whose images are consistent with white supremacy, but have the potential to "unsettle the valence of racism within popular culture." This potential for duality makes representational politics very complex.

The currency of contemporary racisms cannot be fully comprehended without understanding their relationship to the various cultural mechanisms that enable their expression. Yet there is surprisingly little analysis of how race and cultural difference are represented in popular culture. Although some research has been done on the role of the media in shaping our images of race, there has been relatively little discussion of the other complex forms in which popular culture has helped to produce much of the racial imagery with which we are familiar today. This is why in this chapter we want to shift focus somewhat and explore the following two issues: how is racism made popular? What kind of technical infrastructure exists which transmits racist ideas and what are its origins? With these key questions in mind we want to look at how conceptions of race have been shaped by popular cultural forms. The key aim is to examine the ways in which racism intersects with the meanings, images and texts that furnish the banal aspects of everyday life.

A good example of how the new visual media began to have a major impact on questions about race can be seen in the development of the cinema. The power of film in the representation of racial issues became evident from a very early stage. The controversy surrounding D.W. Griffith's film *The Birth of a Nation*, which was first screened in 1915, is a case in point (Simmons, 1993). The film portrayed southern blacks after the end of slavery as ignorant, uncouth and driven by sexual lust. It represented the Ku-Klux-Klan as the saviours of southern whites, and in particular as the protectors of white women from the desires of black men. What is important to note, however, is that *The Birth of a Nation* also constituted a major development in the art of filmmaking. Edward de Grazia and Roger Newman (1982) argue that no other single motion picture has had as important an impact on the history of the cinema. It was Griffith who mastered what others developed in terms of building scenes and creating imagery. While *Birth of a Nation* celebrated and romanticised southern racism, it brought new techniques of film-making including fade-outs, close ups and long shots that were all assembled to constitute a powerful and elaborate narrative.

Griffith's film demonstrated vividly the power of the new form of cultural expression, yet it was banned more often than any other in the history of motion pictures and remains controversial to this day. The dissension surrounding this film shows that from their very inception the twentieth century's new electronic media became a crucial context in which racism could be both expressed and contested (Kisch and Mapp, 1992). A central theme of this chapter is the degree to which the elaboration of racist ideas has gone hand in hand with technological advancement. [...]

The core sections of this chapter focus on four examples that show how historically situated racisms were expressed through the mass media. We start with an examination of the ways in which iconic representations of nationhood were produced within printed and commercial cultures in Britain during the eighteenth and nineteenth centuries. This leads into an examination of the relationship between racism, popular culture and propaganda in Germany during the Third Reich. The aim of these two sections is to demonstrate the significance of commercial cultures and the media in maintaining the cultural hegemony of imperialism and Nazism. This is followed by a discussion of the ways in which black minorities have been represented in the media in the post 1945 period. The final example looks at the complex and shifting nature of contemporary media representations of race, culture and difference. Here the ambivalent nature of racial imagery in popular culture is examined with particular reference to the sophisticated coding of current racisms.

ICONS OF NATIONHOOD: BRITANNIA AND EMPIRE

[...] A number of historical studies have highlighted the ways in which from the earliest stages of European exploration and settlement images of the "body" and "soul" of the "native" became part of popular culture (Jordan, 1968). However, it was in the late nineteenth and early twentieth centuries that the "mechanical reproduction of culture," to use Walter Benjamin's (1968) famous phrase, took on an unprecedented complexity. It was also during this period that the powerful role of visual culture in reproducing images of race became most evident. This has been illustrated in a number of recent studies of the changing images of Africa and Africans and how these were represented through popular culture (Appiah, 1992; Pieterse, 1992; Coombes, 1994; Mudimbe, 1994).

[...] John MacKenzie has demonstrated that imperialist propaganda was produced in Britain by a large number of imperial agencies in the late nineteenth century. The notion of propaganda here is defined as the transmission of ideas and values from dominant groups who control the means of communication, with the intention of influencing the receivers' attitudes and thus enhancing and maintaining their position and interests. [...] Imperial propaganda was disseminated in two distinct forms via the institutions of church and state and the new and popular forms of culture and communication. The extraordinary explosion of advertising was coupled with the growth of commercial ephemera targeted particularly at young men (Richards, 1990). These took the form of cigarette cards that were collected and swapped, picture postcards and a wealth of juvenile journals. These texts became "the prime source of news, information, and patriotic and militaristic propaganda" (MacKenzie, 1984, p. 17).

[...] Through these means the colonial subject was represented through a restricted grammar of images that included a range of archetypes from the tamed servant, the obliging bearer to the dangerous and primitive savage (Pieterse, 1992). As Stuart Hall has noted this restricted grammar was to provide the "base images" of twentieth-century British racism (Hall, 1981).

Advertising represented the excitement of an expansionist age where colonial campaigns, exploration of remote territories and missionary endeavour dominated the public imagination. An important feature of this process was the way these representations articulated race and nation with images of gender. The explorer was always presented as a white man suffering adversity for the national interest. The advertisers sometimes coupled figures from the pantheon of English heroes with incongruous and unlikely commodities, as in the case of "Stanley Boot Laces" and "Kitchener Stove Polish." Commercial images of exploration in the colonies rarely included references to white womanhood. This omission was underscored by the connection between colonial contexts, white womanhood and danger (Ware, 1992). This was symptomatic of a wider moral and political preoccupation with defending the national character and the purity of the race.

One exception to this was the iconic representation of Britannia. While the image of Britannia as a warrior queen equipped with trident and shield is a pervasive emblem of nineteenth-century advertising, the origins of this representation of nationhood lay in the Georgian era. The patriotic anthem "Rule, Britannia" made its first appearance in 1745 alongside "God Save the King" that was also written during this time. Britannia is represented in the prints of the time as a personification of the nation, which is being threatened by the French. The paranoid intensity of the gallophobia that was rife during this time is extraordinary even in comparison to modern racisms. The French are presented in the prints of Hogarth and Gillray as "tonnish apes," lesser breeds with unspeakable intentions. Gerald Newman, commenting on a particular cartoon, describes one common racist stereotype of the French: "In scenes truly nightmarish to behold, [the French] dismember the fair Britannia, administer emetics to her and force her to vomit English possessions into basins held by apish Frenchmen" (Newman, 1987, p. 79). Here the image of the "French apemen" also doubles as a symbol of the devil. What is interesting, however, is the degree to which these images invoke moral outrage through deploying the image of Britannia and thus coding the nation feminine. In his study of the graphic prints of the era, Atherton suggests that Britannia is an image of "Virtue, especially those virtues relevant to national and public life: love of country, dedication, honesty, selflessness, discipline, simplicity" (Atherton, 1974, p. 266). The violation of Britannia thus becomes a violation of those virtues. This form of ideography works to produce powerful and stirring emotions precisely because it crosses attributes associated with the feminine and national vulnerability.

Beyond this the nation from the mid 1750s onwards was modelled on the family, or more correctly an extension of it. The British character was constructed through invoking ties of shared blood that claimed that they were "immutably the same." As Stella Cottrell suggests, "The King was the loving father. The country, as Britannia, was the mother" (Cottrell, 1989, p. 264). The traces of this gendered nationalism are found quite clearly in the popular culture of the nineteenth century, where references to Britannia are invariably presented in connection with "domestic imagery." An obeying lion is also commonly paired with Britannia as both her protector and an emblem of the violent potency of the nation (Colley, 1992). More often Britannia is portrayed sitting on a green landscape modelled in the shape of the British Isles looking out to sea, sometimes with white cliffs or a gun boat within her regal view. Manufacturers of cleaning products took these links a stage further by presenting Britannia "polishing" her shield or even the globe (Opie, 1985).

[...] This iconic figure embodied the nation in a racialised skin with phenotypic features and national attributes. It is with some irony then that [the] commodity [...] being sold through invoking primal allegiances should claim that it "Cleans and whitens without scratching."

[...] In summary, imperial propaganda established some of the core symbols of British racism. It was also integrally connected with the fashioning of a national subject that possessed a distinct racial character, an imperial destiny and a standing in the world. [...]

It was, however, in the fascist regimes of the twentieth century that the deadly impact of electronic technologies, national symbolism and popular culture became fully clear. Propaganda and popular culture under fascism provided the key weapon for establishing and maintaining its appeal and acceptance.

NAZISM, PROPAGANDA AND VISUAL CULTURE

A key and enduring part of the power of racism is the way in which it helps to account for specific social relations in a simple manner. This process of rendering the abstract concrete is a function of all ideologies. What is important in relation to the morphology of racist ideas is that they intrinsically involve the production of a visual culture. […]

This process of rendering human beings via a repertoire of visual stereotypes was perhaps most clearly exemplified in the representations of Jews within Nazi posters and cartoons. However, the popular culture of the Nazis was also preoccupied with the reinvention of the Aryan character within art, film, sculpture and architecture. […]

The art of the Third Reich attempted to present an image of Aryan Germans into which the individual could project him or herself. It espoused an eternal racial character through images of idyllic rural Germany and simple peasant family life. Through these images of heroic endeavour on the land an imaginary Germany was visualised. Nazi painting presented the peasantry as frozen stereotypes of undisturbed racial perfection in harmony with nature and eternally rooted in the land and soil. This connection was invariably achieved by using the plough, seed and scythe as key symbols of honest toil within the context of fashioning a sense of racial identity (Adam, 1992). It is striking that few references were made to Nazism's "others" within their popular art, this representational space was given over to images of everything that was good and wholesome in the newly found Aryan culture. For most Germans who were living in conditions of urban poverty the consumption of these images meant their individual misfortune could be lost in the alluring racial fantasies of "heimat" and the promise of a better future. This media-generated "virtual home" provided Nazism with the antidote to the excesses of modernity often expressed through references to the decadent Jewish metropolis. The Nazis took their art to the German masses, they sent theatre groups to every village, orchestras played concerts of Wagner, Brahms and Beethoven in factories, and it was through the new technologies of the newsreel and the radio that their message was broadcast to every German home. […]

Nazism produced an image of the German "Volk" into which individuality could be dissolved and where human conscience could be drowned by the deafening sound of the mass rally. Physical exercise along with dance and marching took on a kind of messianic fervour. Nazi dance organised its participants within a geometric discipline: "It place[d] a grid over the mass of bodies, which both arranged individuals and separate[d] them from one another. Clear lines confine[d] them to their places and prevented them from escaping" (Servos, 1990, p. 64). The spectacular rituals of mass dancing recorded during the Olympic Games in 1936 and the display of Stormtroopers marching in perfect cohorts through the Brandenburg Gate anchored

Nazism in the rhythm of the body. These public demonstrations were Hitler's rejoinder and stood as an answer to the very different rhythms that occupied the metropolitan night-clubs where his Volkish reverie was less secure.

During the Nazi period jazz was embraced by German young people much to the chagrin of the white supremacists. Nazi musicologists attacked jazz and justified their opposition to it by arguing that its rhythm was unsuitable. They complained that unlike Germans "Negro tribes do not march" [sic] (Kater, 1992, p. 31). This was also coupled with an attempt to show that jazz was the product of an abominable collaboration between "Negroes" and "Jews" with racially corrosive implications for Aryan Germans. While characterising jazz as another form of "degenerate culture" the Nazis also attempted to develop their own saccharine form of jazz. These moves did not stop the development of a vibrant subculture of *jazz defiants*, known as "Swing youth" after the jazz dance genre. [...]

The dance-hall provided a context in which to explore alternative forms of femininity and masculinity and offered opportunities for gaining sexual experiences. The import of American styles of feminine beauty was viewed as particularly abhorrent by the Nazis and the incorporation of Anglo-American styles by "swing girls" posed a serious challenge to the femininities associated with Nazi ideology and the state youth organisations. Equally for young men their urban style challenged the dominant uniform of Nazi masculinity that combined the Aryan warrior hero with images of the responsible peasant patriarch. The Swing subculture was not a selfconsciously radical movement, despite the vicious suppression meted out to them by the Gestapo and the Hitler Youth. It was estimated that from 1942 to 1944 75 Swing youths were sent to concentration camps by the SS who classified them as political prisoners. Within the context of the metropolitan night-clubs themselves jazz dancing allowed for counter-hegemonic forms of bodily expression and individuality that was so emphatically repressed within Nazi popular culture, music and dance.

Nazi representations of the racial "other" were principally confined to propaganda posters and cartoons (Rhodes, 1976). This included predictable portrayals of "money grabbing" Jewish businessmen, alongside representations of the modernist decadence of Jewish Bolsheviks. During the war years Nazi propaganda combined anti-Semitic images with references to the "black Allied soldier." The propagandists deployed images of black soldiers to stand as a measure of Allied racial decay and a symptom of the mongrelisation of American society. The presence of the black soldier was thus turned into a corrosive threat to European civilisation. The black soldier as a moral threat has a particular history within the wartime German psyche. In the aftermath of Germany's defeat in 1918 the Belgian and French armies used black colonial troops in their occupation of the Rhineland territories. This produced a moral panic within Germany and a sense of outrage that this was the ultimate insult to the vanquished nation's pride. The presence of black soldiers was stereotyped through the image of "Jumbo," a monstrous sexual predator who threatened the moral chastity of white German women. The preoccupation with miscegenation was taken to considerable lengths and Afro-German children and their mothers were subject to ostracism and attack. The Society for Racial Hygiene that was founded in 1905 began conducting sterilisations of Afro-Germans in 1919. Eugenics provided the rationale for these barbaric

Figure 35.1: Monstrous Regiment: Nazi poster portraying the GI as a jitterbugging marauder. Poster in Holland, 1944

acts that were explained as necessary for the protection of the Volk and the elimination of "racial diseases." After 1937 Hitler inherited this mission and hundreds of sterilisations were conducted (Opitz, Oguntoye and Schultz, 1992). [...]

The poster entitled "Liberators" reproduced here was also displayed in Holland prior to the Allied invasion (Figure 29.1). In one image it registered all that Nazi popular culture despised and attempted to expunge. This figure of cultural invasion stands for everything that is decadent in American life. Somewhere between Frankenstein and King Kong the invader brings together the antithesis of the Nazi ideals of racial purity and their attendant versions of manhood and womanliness. The "Statue of Liberty" and the New York skyline can be seen in the distance (bottom left-hand corner) which gives this monster a distinctly urban origin and reinforces the connection between the city and race: New York of all the great metropolises is the most strongly associated with Jewishness. There are other references that reinforce the association between the deviant city life and the Jew. Behind the boxer's glove on the right-hand side of the image hides a Jewish businessman peering over a bag full of dollars and a Star of David hangs between the monster's legs. These images are coupled with other representations of urban delinquency, the set of white arms represents on one side criminality through the manacle and the striped prison uniform and on the other brandishes a stick bomb. These are accompanied by series of confused images relating to US racial politics.

The torso of the monster constitutes a cage that holds an apeman and apewoman associated with black music and dance—the caption reads "Jitterbug—Triumph of Civilisation." References to black masculinity are coded via the monster's top set of arms which are black and muscular. In one hand is a record that signifies the decadent music of jazz while on the other is a boxing glove, a symbol of brute strength. These images, which draw on relatively common racist themes, are then combined with a reference to domestic American racism. The head of the monster is hidden by the mask of the Ku-Klux-Klan and a hangman's noose is wound around one of the black arms as a reference to the practice of lynching black Americans in the South. The tragic irony is that this piece of propaganda was authored by a regime that exterminated a million Jews by this point in the war. The implication seems to be that the culture of the European mainland would be threatened by an Allied invasion because it would bring American racism to the continent.

Also signalled within this image is the potential import of immoral forms of femininity that revealed the sexual depravity of the Americans. The representations of the two white beauty queens on either arm of the monster register this abhorrence of the artificial femininity of white American women and the fetish for such beauty. This is also supported by the female coded right leg of the monster that has a tape measure around its calf and thigh and the ribbon that is tied above its knee announces it as the "world's most beautiful leg." We cannot read the significance of this image without a prior knowledge of the ideal models of Aryan femininity. Nazi art and popular culture stressed the importance of women as the safe keepers of life whose form should be admired as a thing of natural beauty. The caricature presented here of "Miss America Femininity" constitutes the absolute antithesis of Aryan female beauty which was defined by its perfection in nature.

While the monster includes female elements as a whole the figure is gendered male. Its left male formed leg is presented in the form of a bomb that is suspended like a sword of Damocles over the monuments of Western civilisation. It is through these references that it also represents the Allied war machine complete with the wings of a bomber. As the monster stands suspended before trampling over Europe the caption reads: "The 'liberators' will save European culture from its downfall." Reference to a common European culture is being invoked in an attempt to summon sympathy and support within the occupied territories. The use of cultural references here are significant because as we have shown similar forms of pseudo-cultural logic became a core feature of the "new racisms" of the late twentieth century.

These examples of Nazi propaganda demonstrate the role that racism played managing periods of crisis where control was being lost over the occupied lands of Western Europe. They also show the clear vocabulary of race that was at the disposal of these propagandists. [...]

RACISM AND REPRESENTING THE BLACK PRESENCE IN BRITAIN

Throughout the twentieth century the black presence in Britain has been viewed by public commentators as constituting a serious moral and cultural problem; a central anxiety focused on the issue of "race mixing" and the impact of immigration on the social and cultural fabric of British society. Clive Harris has shown that black people in seaports such as Liverpool and Cardiff posed a serious moral and political problem for the politicians and bureaucrats of the day (Harris, 1988). Documenting the survey conducted in 1935 by the British Social Hygiene Council, Harris demonstrates how this organisation was preoccupied with inquiring into black sailors' "sexual demands" with regard to their white partners, their promiscuity and the suggestion that white women became addicted to the "black sailor's sex." In addition to this black men were also connected with the transmission of venereal disease and seen as leading white women into prostitution. Harris goes on to show how the growth in so-called "half-caste children" became another significant feature of the discourse of state officials, particularly in Cardiff and Liverpool and ultimately at the Home Office. These young people were constructed as being "marked by a racial trait" and to "mature sexually at an early age" (ibid., p. 24). This moral panic was to be revisited within a more public arena when, after the Second World War, a number of stories were published about children born to white women and black American and West Indian servicemen. These children were viewed as a "casualty of war." One of the Home Office's proposed solutions to "this problem" was to send these children to America to be brought up with "other coloured children" (quoted in ibid., p. 37). In the face of opposition from within Britain's black population this proposal was never implemented. There are troubling similarities here between these sentiments and Nazi propagandists' attempts to exploit images of black Allied soldiers in order to engender white panic and anxiety.

Harris argues that what is telling about the preoccupation with miscegenation is the degree to which the racist discourse of this period is preoccupied with skin colour as the prime signifier in the subjectification of black people. The preservation of the English racial character was to be achieved by preserving its hue. [...]

During the 1970s media discourses produced a significant shift away from a preoccupation with miscegenation and the early more clearly colour-coded racisms, and became centrally preoccupied with covering emerging forms of "racial crime." The most sophisticated critique of this conjuncture was produced by Stuart Hall and his associates in their book entitled *Policing the Crisis* (Hall et al., 1978). This study attempted to demonstrate among other things how the moral crisis over the street crime that became known as "mugging" was related to managing a wider crisis in British society. Hall et al. argue that the designation of mugging as a black crime provides a vehicle for engendering divisions:

> [Mugging] … provides the separation of the class into black and white with a material basis, since, in much black crime (as in much white working-class crime), one part of the class materially "rips off" another. It provides the separation with its ideological figure, for it transforms the deprivation of the class, out of which crime arises, into the all too intelligible syntax of race, and fixes a false enemy: the black mugger. (Ibid., p. 395)

They conclude that during the 1970s British society managed a crisis in social hegemony through the twin strategies of creating and amplifying the "mugging moral panic" and moving towards a more authoritarian law and order ideology. The symbolic location of "black crime" connects with associated racial discourses that construct black communities as being incompatible with the "British way of life" (Gilroy, 1987). "Black youth" are thus defined as constituting a social problem (Solomos, 1988).

[…] Like many other racialised discourses such responses demonstrated a profound historical amnesia. Britain has a long history of civil unrest. The Gordon riots in 1780 resulted in 285 deaths and a further 25 were hanged for taking part in them. During the 1930s there were frequent clashes between the unemployed and the police and during demonstrations against Oswald Mosley's British Union of Fascists. What is distinctive about the press reporting of urban conflict in the 1980s is that these events were represented as "race riots." There had been previous incidents during the 1950s that represented disorder through a racial lexicon (Miles, 1984) but this mode of representation hardened during the outbreak of violent protest in 1981 and 1985 (Solomos, 1986). […]

We have suggested that media stereotyping of Britain's black population has shifted in the last 60 years. These popular representations have adapted and taken on new characteristics while retaining an interconnected quality. In his study of racism and the news media Teun van Dijk concludes:

> The structure and style of headlines not only subjectively express what journalists or editors see as the major topics of new reports, but also tend to emphasise the negative role of ethnic minorities … [who] continue to be associated with a restricted number of stereotypical topics, such as immigration problems, crime, violence (especially "riots"), and ethnic relations (especially discrimination), whereas other topics, such as those in the realm of of politics, social affairs, and culture are under-reported. (van Dijk, 1991, p. 245)

The thing that remains constant in this reporting is that black people are seen as constituting a social problem, while at the same they are seen as experiencing forms of injustice and discrimination that are "morally offensive." Splitting of this type is a central feature of racist culture and is what Peter Hulme refers to as a "stereotypical dualism" (Hulme, 1986).

Michael Keith in his insightful discussion of the male Bengali street-rebel has described the operation of this dual process within the contemporary urban setting of London's East End (Keith, 1995). He argues that racist discourses make sense of Bengali youth through cartographies of race and power, which map so-called Asian gangs within particular sites of street criminality. This is compensated by a white leftist notion of "the youth" as an agent of insurrection and street revolt. Keith makes the telling point that both of these urban narratives are respectively the product of fear and desire. The street rebel appears as a remixed and recoded urban insurgent, "the result of both collective action and the manner in which such actions were framed by the mass media" (ibid., p. 366). There is a direct lineage between the Asian street rebel of the 1990s and the connections made between race, crime and locality in the 1970s and 1980s which produced the black mugger and rioter: it is only the racial patina that is exchanged.

In summary, we have argued that the British news media has represented the black presence through identifiable motifs. These have shifted in terms of their content and this dynamism demonstrates the necessity of understanding racism in its historical moment. However, it is equally important to understand the continuities that are maintained as these media discourses change. The media racism in post-war Britain can be characterised as possessing two core features in that: (i) the black presence is seen to have a racially corrosive effect on British culture; and (ii) the race/cultural difference of black people makes them incompatible with the British way of life. As we have shown this deploys the idea that alien traditions of criminality and association have been imported into the British social formation from the ex-colonial periphery.

From the Nazi propagandist to the newspaper editors the printed and electronic media have provided means whereby racist constructions of social reality are made popular. We have, however, characterised the relationship between popular culture and racism as unstable and dynamic. [...] In the following section we want to focus on recent examples of how cultural difference is represented within popular culture and the implications this has for understanding contemporary racisms.

CORPORATE MULTICULTURALISM: RACISM, DIFFERENCE AND MEDIA IMAGES

[...] It is important to note that we have seen quite important transformations in recent years in how race is represented through the popular media. For example, advertisers and other media producers are including images of cultural difference within their repertoire of symbols. Within truly global markets some advertisers have attempted to associate their products with the transcendence of racism and cultural barriers. [...]

[W]hat we have seen in recent times is an attempt by some multinational corporations to develop a transnational advertising aesthetic. Perhaps the best and most perplexing example of this is the clothes manufacturer Benetton. Through the camera of Oliviero Toscani, Benetton have attempted to promote a message of human unity and harmony in their advertising. Starting in 1984 they attempted to represent the world's diverse people and cultures as synonymous with the many colours of Benetton's produce. Since then their campaigns have provoked unparalleled controversy, winning them awards and adulation alongside accusations of hypocrisy and opportunism.

One of the striking features of the Benetton campaigns is the degree to which their message of transcultural unity is predicated upon absolute images of racial and cultural difference. The initial campaigns alluded to past and present conflicts through the presentation of archetypal images of Jews and Arabs embracing the globe. What is intriguing about this move is that Benetton's products do not have to be shown in order to convey meanings about the brand quality; the message is simply resolved by the motif juxtaposed over the images of boundaries and conflicts. The "United Colors of Benetton" becomes the antithesis of conflict, the expression of unity, the nurturer of internationalism (Back and Quaade, 1993). However, what is more troubling about this strategy is the degree to which it is reliant on racism's very categories of personhood and the stereotypes which run from these. The example reproduced here (figure 35.2) shows three young people poking their tongues out at the viewer. This advertisement was used in a poster campaign in 1991. The message of transcendence encapsulated in Benetton's slogan only makes sense if it is superimposed on a representation of clear difference. These three figures are coded through a grammar of absolute racial difference: the blue-eyed blonde white Aryan figure, flanked respectively by a "Negroid" black child and an "Oriental" child. This message of unity can only work if it has a constitutive representation of absolute racial contrast. The danger with such representations is that they rely on a range of racial archetypes that are themselves the product of racism and as a result make racial atavism socially legitimate forms of common-sense knowledge: the concept of race is left unchallenged.

One of the most interesting things about Toscani's photography is the ways in which he plays with ambiguity. The most dramatic example of this included a picture showing the hands of two men, one black and the other white, handcuffed together; and a picture of the torso of a black woman breast-feeding a white baby released in 1989. The reactions to these ads varied according to national context. In the United States, they were withdrawn following public complaint. The later image conjured the historical experience of slavery and the position of black women within a gendered and racialised system of exploitation, including their designation as objects of white sexual desire. In the United States and Britain, the image of handcuffed hands evoked notions of black criminality; far from suggesting two men, united in incarceration. The advertisement was associated with the daily reality of young black men arrested by predominantly white law enforcement agencies. In Britain, *The Sun* ran the headline, "Di's sweaters' firm in 'racist ads' row," referring to the fact that Princess Diana had patronised Benetton products for some years. London Transport refused to display the ads on the London Underground, justifying their decision by the suggestion that the ads had racist overtones. The most extreme response to the campaign came in France. In Paris, neo-fascist agitators, opposing what they saw as miscegenation, threw a tear-gas canister into a Benetton shop shortly after the posters appeared. While generating controversy these images were embraced by the media more broadly and won prizes in France, Holland, Denmark and Austria. How can we make sense of this diversity of responses? Perhaps the first point to make here is to foreground the importance of understanding these iconic global images within particular contexts. The images invoked different histories of racist discourse in the United States, Britain, France or Japan. The simple point here is that the social composition of the audience affects the range of intertextual reference (histories, representation, symbolic codes, form of racism) that are used

UNITED COLORS
OF BENETTON.

Figure 35.2: United Colors? Benetton billboard poster, 1991

to make sense of any particular image (Mercer, 1992). These images are ambiguous because they activate the histories and cultural features of racism through connotation.

While Benetton were very much in the vanguard of this type of imagery during the 1980s, other companies have also embraced the idea of imbuing their brand quality with a transnational ethos. [...] Philips uses a blonde haired white girl and a black boy alongside the caption "THE UNIVERSAL LANGUAGE OF PHILIPS." Again the two children are united through their consumption of the commodity, with a black and white thumb sharing the control panel. This advertisement actually appeared in the newspaper that Benetton produce called *Colors*. *Colors* is an extraordinary publication because it effectively turns news items into Benetton advertising (Back and Quaade, 1993). [...] What is common to these campaigns is that they all, in various ways, espouse common humanity and harmony while reinforcing cultural and racial archetypes. At worst they steer a symbolic course that is perilously close to a legacy of crude racist images and associations.

Corporate multiculturalism has not only been confined to the espousal of a saccharin version of internationalism, black style and music have also been used as a means to appeal to a youthful audience. The jeans company Levi Strauss provides a particularly interesting example of this strategy, transforming their 501 jeans from workaday industrial apparel into an essential fashion accessory. From 1984 their campaigns in the United States used black music as a marker of urban authenticity and an expression of individual heartache and freedom. In particular the ads focused on "the Blues." Like Benetton, Levi's attempted to blur the commodity forms with an advertising message and also a state of emotional well-being. In Benetton's case the logic of this strategy ran: united colours of people, united colors in garments—"I wear unity." Levi's attempted to establish an interplay between the commodity and a message of alienated individualism, and it elided blues jeans with the Blues as a celebration of solitude, alienation and solace. These forms of slippage mean that 501's not only shrink to fit your body but they also convey a kind of identity. This is summed up in their slogan: "501 Blues Shrink to Fit My Body—I got the Blues." Music becomes the connective device through which social quotations are made and in turn bolster the product's identity with a cultural dowry. A whole range of black artists were used in these campaigns including Taj Mahal, the Neville Brothers, Bobby McFerrin and Tiger Haynes. Beyond this the inner city provided the context for staging their story lines often producing romantic images of ghetto life: "Blacks who appear on the screen seem 'connected' and 'in tune' with their total social space. Levi's sell the ghetto—a space which transcends social convention, restraint and repressiveness" (Goldman, 1992, p. 191). In some of the advertisements black Americans are presented teaching their white counterparts how to dance, play instruments and express themselves. The 501 advertisements offer their audience instruction in a particular version of blackness via the references to the Blues and the ghetto, where black music is equated with the body, expression, emotionality and ultimately sexuality. Through this "injection of negritude" young whites in particular are offered a fleeting liberation from the strictures of whiteness. [...]

These notions of exotic innocence are no less stereotypical than the idea that the Negro is less civilised and more barbaric. This kind of identification is locked within the discourse of absolute difference which renders blackness exotic and reaffirms black people as a "race apart." It was this danger which Frantz Fanon outlined when he argued that those Europeans who blindly adore the difference of the other are as racially afflicted as those who vilify it (Fanon, 1986). [...]

Before moving on we want to clarify our argument. We are making two related points. First, what we have referred to as corporate multiculturalism possesses a dual quality. While it espouses the goal of transcultural unity it does so through reinforcing crude cultural and racial archetypes. These images operate within what Stuart Hall (1981) called a "grammar of race." The overpowering reference point is that race is real: racial archetypes provide the vehicle for the message, and racial common sense is overbearingly present such that the reality of race is legitimated within this media discourse. Second, the valuation and repackaging of cultural difference within contemporary media result in little more than a process of market driven recolonisation, where the fetish for the exotic reaffirms these various "global others" as distinct and separate types of humankind. In this context the veneration of difference need not be in any contradiction with white supremacy. Quite the contrary: it can be integrally connected with the formation of contemporary cultures of racism. Yet, we also want to argue that these shifts do create important ambivalences and tensions which can unsettle the valence of racism within popular culture.

Kobena Mercer has explored the ambivalences found in racial fetishism through an analysis of the white gay photographer Robert Mapplethorpe (Mercer, 1994). In his initial reading of the photographs of black nude men found in *Black Males* and *Black Book*, Mercer offers an analysis of Mapplethorpe's "line of sight" in which:

> Black + Male = Erotic/Aesthetic Object. Regardless of the sexual preferences of the spectator, the connotation is that the "essence" of black male identity lies in the domain of sexuality ... black men are confined and defined in their very being as sexual and nothing but sexual, hence hyper sexual. (Mercer, 1994, p. 174)

He argues that the regulative function of stereotypes polices the potential for generating meanings, and as a result the spectator is fixed within the position of the "white male subject." However, in a later rereading Mercer changes his mind and points to the ways in which these images actually undermine the conventions of the spectator and the stereotypes which furnish this way of seeing. Mercer argues that once we understand the political specificity of Mapplethorpe's practice, we can see in his aesthetic use of irony disruptive elements which challenge Eurocentred representative regimes. Black men constitute perhaps the most social and politically marginalised group in the United States, but in Mapplethorpe's photographs the men who come from this social location are raised "onto the pedestal of the transcendental western aesthetic ideal. Far from reinforcing the fixed beliefs of the white supremacist imaginary, such a deconstructive move begins to undermine the foundational myth of the pedestal itself" (ibid., p. 200). Mercer's argument suggests that through the use of subversion and aesthetic irony racist regimes of representation are propelled into a state of crisis and erasure. It is with these suggestive comments in mind that we want to return to the iconography of Benetton advertising.

Our intention here is not to merely reproduce a parallel argument to Kobena Mercer's insightful and reflective reading of Mapplethorpe's photography. However, if we look closely at Toscani's photography we can see similar—although not comparable—ambivalences at work. In this sense we need to revise partially the analysis offered earlier (Back and Quaade, 1993) and suggest that there are moments within Benetton's advertising imagery when the racial grammar of these representations is unsettled. Toscani has specialised in blurring photographic conventions, turning news photographs into advertising and advertising into the news. Both he and Luciano Benetton have also indulged in self-parody. In the spring 1992 edition of *Colors* their own faces are superimposed on to one of their ads. This notorious image represented two children embracing, one depicted as a white cherub angel and the other a black child devil. In this reworked version Luciano Benetton is cast as the angel and Toscani as the devil. Returning to the original image one might think of it as a moment where racial anxieties are being displayed. Is Toscani forcing the viewer to confront the racist connotations of such an image or is he merely reproducing and activating these racial ideologies? This question captures the core ambivalence found within Toscani's photography. McKenzie Wark has argued that the Benetton campaigns open up a wealth of meaning and that to reduce these advertisements to a moral narrative or any one meaning does more violence than the image itself (Wark, 1992).

In the aftermath of the Los Angeles riots, in an atmosphere of heightened fears of the possibility of further racial conflict, a whole edition of *Colors* was given over to the issue of race. The editorial captured the impulse to deal with this issue: "If there's one topic COLORS was destined to address, it's racism and the devastation caused by racism. Not just in Los Angeles, Germany or South Africa but everywhere that people are assaulting and killing each other over genetic, linguistic or cultural differences" (*Colors*, no. 4, 1993, p. 68). What is remarkable about this publication is its complete deconstruction of the "idea of race." The journal undermined the racial categories so abundantly deployed in the "United Colors" campaigns since 1984, concluding:

> Finally it occurred to us that while the physical differences between peoples and individuals are real ... the monoliths called races are a purposeful invention, once used to make Europe's slavery and colonial conquests seem moral and inevitable.... What's going on, we believe, is that people continue to live their lives as if the myths about race were fact. Why? Because it's simpler for those in positions of power if those without power vent all their anger on others without power.... As long as our actions are guided by fear, as long as we regard the myths of race and racism as truth none of us is truly safe. (Ibid, p. 70)

The special issue tackled questions ranging from racial harassment, phenotypic difference, neo-Nazi youth culture and mixed relationships. The reflexive and quite extraordinary deconstructivist turn is also embodied within the imagery used in this edition. In a section entitled "What if...?" Toscani presented a series of famous people with transformed racial characteristics, these included a black Arnold Schwarzenegger, a Semitic Spike Lee, an Oriental John Paul II, and an Aryan Michael Jackson. This striking image, challenges the common sense of race and nation which in Britain has constructed blackness and Britishness as mutually exclusive categories. The photograph challenges the reader to ask why s/he finds it implausible. What is exposed is the association between race and nation within the ideology of British, or more precisely, English nationalism.

The "What If..." photograph of the "Black Queen" identifies the mutually inclusive nature of the relationship of whiteness and Englishness. Through this "altered image" racial common sense is unsettled and the implicit, "taken for granted quality" of what it means to look "English" phenotypically is rendered obvious. In the terms of this ideology the Queen cannot be "black" because to be English is to be "white." [...] However, the ideologies of race and nation make the recognition of such heterogeneity impossible, ridiculous and out of question. What is asserted instead within the language of nationalism is the compulsory whiteness of English identity. The photograph of the black Queen invites the reader to ridicule these associations and opens up a representational space which challenges the orthodoxies of race and nation.

The ambivalences and traces of anti-racism found within these examples are important for us to appreciate when evaluating the contemporary politics of race. In many respects these examples force us to move beyond the dualism of "good and bad images" and challenge us to think through the complex interplay of meaning and the ambivalences registered within the representation of race and difference. What we have shown is that any sophisticated understanding of the contemporary relationship between popular culture and racism needs to be alert to the coupling of fear and desire that produces the complex representations of difference we have analysed here.

POPULAR CULTURE AND DIFFERENCE

We began this chapter by asking the question of how is racism made popular? We have attempted to show how both printed and electronic media have been crucially implicated in providing the technical infrastructure for the creation and dissemination of the cultures of racism. Racism is connected integrally to the history of modernity and modern technologies have provided a key means in the establishment of racial supremacy. Popular culture provided the means whereby the masses within any particular modern social formation participated in the domination of others. We have also argued that racist formulations and ways of seeing can also be challenged within these representational spaces. Popular culture has provided a key means for reproducing racism but this is not inevitably the case. The instability of historically inflected racisms makes it important to stress the ideological battles that are being waged within this domain of vernacular culture. [...]

REFERENCES

Adam, P. (1992) *The Arts of the Third Reich* (London: Thames and Hudson).

Appiah, K.A. (1992) *In My Father's House: Africa in the Philosophy of Culture* (London: Methuen).

Atherton, H.M. (1974) *Political Prints in the Age of Hogarth: A Study of the Ideographic Representation of Politics* (Oxford: Oxford University Press).

Back, L. and Quaade, V. (1993) "Dream Utopias, Nightmare Realities: Imaging Race and Culture with the World of Benetton Advertising," *Third Text*, 22: 65–80.

Benjamin, W. (1968) "The Work of Art in the Age of Mechanical Reproduction," in W. Benjamin, *Illuminations* (London: Harcourt, Brace and World).

Colley, L. (1992) *Britons: Forging the Nation, 1707–1837* (New Haven: Yale University Press).

Colours, no. 4, 1993.

Coombes, A. (1994) *Reinventing Africa* (London: Yale University Press).

Cottrell, S. (1989) "The Devil on Two Sticks: Franco-phobia in 1803," in R. Samuel (ed.), *Patriotism: The Making and Unmaking of British National Identity. Volume 1: History and Politics* (London: Routledge).

Fanon, F. (1986) *Black Skin, White Masks* (London: Pluto Press).

Gilroy, P. (1987) *There Ain't No Black in the Union Jack* (London: Hutchinson).

Goldman, R. (1992) *Reading Ads Socially* (London: Routledge).

de Grazia, E. and Newman, R.K. (1982) *Banned Films: Movies, Censors and the First Amendment* (New York: R.R. Bowker).

Hall, S. (1981) "The Whites of Their Eyes: Racist Ideologies and the Media," in G. Bridges and R. Brunt (eds.), *Silver Linings: Some Strategies for the Eighties* (London: Lawrence and Wishart).

Hall, S., Critcher, C., Jefferson, T., Clarke, J. and Roberts, B. (1978) *Policing the Crisis: Mugging, the State, and Law and Order* (London: Macmillan).

Harris, C. (1988) "Images of Blacks in Britain: 1930–60," in S. Allen and M. Macey (eds.), *Race and Social Policy* (London: Economic and Social Research Council).

Hulme, P. (1986) *Colonial Encounters: Europe and the Native Caribbean* (London: Methuen).

Jordan, W. (1968) *White Over Black: American Attitudes Towards the Negro, 1550–1812* (New York: W.W. Norton).

Kater, M.H. (1992) *Different Drummers: Jazz in the Culture of Nazi Germany* (New York: Oxford University Press).

Keith, M. (1995) "Ethnic Entrepreneurs and Street Rebels: Looking Inside the Inner City," in S. Pile and N. Thrift (eds.), *Mapping the Subject: Geographies of Cultural Transformation* (London: Routledge).

Kisch, J. and Mapp, E. (1992) *A Separate Cinema: Fifty Years of Black-Cast Posters* (New York: Noonday Press).

MacKenzie, J.M. (1984) *Propaganda and Empire: The Manipulation of British Public Opinion 1880–1960* (Manchester: Manchester University Press).

Mercer, K. (1992) "Skin Head Sex Thing: Racial Difference and Homoerotic Imagery," *New Frontiers*, 16: 1–23.

Mercer, K. (1994) *Welcome to the Jungle: New Positions in Black Cultural Studies* (London: Routledge).

Miles, R. (1984) "The Riots of 1958: Notes on the Ideological Construction of 'Race Relations' as a Political Issue in Britain," *Immigrants and Minorities*, 3, 3: 252–75

Mudimbe, V.Y. (1994) *The Idea of Africa* (Bloomington: Indiana University Press).

Newman, G. (1987) *The Rise of English Nationalism: A Cultural History, 1740–1830* (London: Weidenfeld and Nicolson).

Opie, R. (1985) *Rule Britannia: Trading on the British Image* (Harmondsworth: Viking).

Opitz, M., Oguntoye, K. and Schultz, D. (eds.) (1992) *Showing Our Colours: Afro-German Women Speak Out* (London: Open Letters Press).

Pieterse, J.N. (1992) *White on Black: Images of Africa and Blacks in Western Popular Culture* (New Haven and London: Yale University Press).

Rhodes, A. (1976) *Propaganda: The Art of Persuasion in World War II* (London: Angus Robertson).

Richards, T. (1990) *The Commodity Culture of Victorian England: Advertising and Spectacle* (London: Verso).

Servos, N. (1990) "Pathos and propaganda?: On the Mass Choreography of Fascism," *Ballet International Handbook*: 63–6.

Simmons, S. (1993) *The Films of D.W. Griffith* (Cambridge: Cambridge University Press).

Solomos, J. (1986) "Polititical Language and Violent Protest: Ideological and Policy Responses to the 1981 and 1985 Riots," *Youth and Policy*, 18: 12–24.

Solomos, J. (1988) *Black Youth, Racism and the State* (Cambridge: Cambridge University Press).

van Dijk, T.A. (1991) *Racism and the Press* (London: Routledge).

Ware, V. (1992) *Beyond the Pale: White Women, Racism and History* (London: Verso).

Wark, M. (1992) "Still Life Today: The Benetton Campaigns," *Photophile*, 36: 33–6.

PART 3E

RACISM IN THE JUSTICE SYSTEM AND POLICE FORCE

A longstanding social fact of colonialism is that, despite the pretention of nation-states to tolerance, diversity, and multiculturalism, the complex networks of policing agencies and criminal justice institutions, discourses, and practices disproportionately punish people of colour and Indigenous peoples. They are disproportionately singled out and treated with suspicion, disregard, and even hostility. Certainly, some of this is the result of consciously racist attitudes and practices of those employed in the criminal justice field. However, a strong case can also be made that the disproportionate impact on people of colour and Indigenous peoples results from longstanding and largely unconscious discourses and practices that comprise "business as usual" in the day-to-day operations of the Canadian justice system and the policing agencies they are linked to.

FURTHER READING

Comack, Elizabeth. 2012. *Racialized Policing: Aboriginal People's Encounters with the Police.* Halifax: Fernwood Press.
In this book, Comack explores the relatively understudied phenomenon of racial profiling of Indigenous people by policing agencies. Situating these policing practices within a broader lens of institutional/structural racism and engaging with interviews in inner-city Winnipeg, Comack argues that these interactions are powerfully framed by police attitudes that position Indigenous people as "troublemakers" and, as such, requiring responses more aggressive in nature. She goes on to detail the kinds of social "order" this produces, and makes a clear and compelling argument for the institutional reconfiguration of the very nature of policing.

Gabor, Thomas. 2004. "Inflammatory Rhetoric on Racial Profiling Can Undermine Police Services." *Canadian Journal of Criminology and Criminal Justice* 46: 457–466.
Gabor argues that while in some locations good data exists to prove the presence of racial profiling, many definitions of racial profiling fail to distinguish between "bigotry" and good, solid police work. In other words, they fail to differentiate between "good" and "bad" racial profiling. "Bad" profiling is the simple result of police officials relying on racial stereotypes to make decisions about whether, for example, to stop a Black motorist (e.g., "He or she is driving a nice car, it must be stolen"). "Good" racial profiling, by contrast, is the result of solid police work that uncovers crime patterns in (for example) predominately Black neighbourhoods.

Monchalin, Lisa. 2016. *The Colonial Problem: An Indigenous Perspective on Crime and Injustice in Canada*. Toronto: University of Toronto Press.

The vast overrepresentation of Indigenous people in all facets of Canada's criminal justice apparatus is often framed ahistorically as a result of individual-level characteristics of Indigenous offenders or, slightly more sophisticatedly, as the inevitable outcome of Canadian colonialism's impact on Indigenous communities. In *The Colonial Problem*, Monchalin instead undertakes a broad structural analysis of the numerous connected historical and contemporary factors—including assimilation policies, dishonoured treaties, draconian legislation, and intergenerational systemic racism—that have played a role in this overrepresentation. Her argument, in short, is that the issue isn't an "Indian problem" (at least, in the way it has been framed) but rather a "colonial problem."

Rankin, Jim, and Patty Winsa. 2012. "Known to Police: Toronto Police Stop and Document Black and Brown People Far More than Whites." *Toronto Star*, March 9.

Part of a broader *Toronto Star* series, this feature article uses Toronto police stop data from 2008 to mid-2011 to demonstrate the disproportionate extent to which young people of colour (and men in particular) are stopped, questioned, and documented by the Toronto police. The story includes interviews from different actors involved in these dynamics—including the Toronto Police Service (and the chief of police), the Toronto Police Services Board, academics, and youth workers—to discuss the policing practices that have led to these statistics. This is part of a larger series, also titled "Known to Police," that is well worth reading.

Wortley, Scot, and Julian Tanner. 2004. "Discrimination or 'Good' Policing? The Racial Profiling Debate in Canada." *Our Diverse Cities* 1: 197–201.

Written following the *Toronto Star*'s stories on racial profiling and the over-policing of Black males, Wortley and Tanner lay out a discussion of racial profiling, speak to some of the concerns of policing agencies regarding the collection of "racial data," and suggest that Canadian policing agencies across the country collect their own police stop data. They suggest that the existence of such data could go a long way towards monitoring police behaviour in ways that might decrease the current over-policing of people of colour.

Chapter 36

In Their Own Voices: African Canadians in Toronto Share Experiences of Police Profiling

Maureen Brown

Maureen Brown (2008) uses narrative analysis to explore the voices of African Canadians in greater Toronto, Ontario, as they shared their experiences in being racially profiled by the various policing agencies of the city. Her interlocutors believed that race played a strong role in being singled out by policing agencies, that this profiling was pervasive, that it affected numerous policing agencies in and outside of Toronto, and that it was in need of some kind of official intervention that would not only count it but manage it. Perhaps equally important, however, Brown documents the deep sense of unease that many Black people felt in their interactions with policing agencies and the feelings of disrespect they were left with following their encounters.

Stories reconfigure the past, endowing it with meaning and continuity, and so also project a sense of what will or should happen in the future. (Davis 2002, 12)

Narrative is one of the most powerful tools available to paint a multidimensional portrait of a community's experience. I found this especially true as I interviewed African Canadians in the Greater Toronto Area for a study on racial profiling by the police. The study was commissioned by the African Canadian Community Coalition on Racial Profiling (ACCCRP), an ad hoc group formed in the wake of widespread allegations that police single out Blacks for negative treatment. Youth and adults, city dwellers and GTA residents, wealthy suburbanites and inner-city poor—all told me that, from their own experience, they believed firmly that the police use race as a factor in determining who is likely to commit or has likely committed a crime. All of these people spoke of their anger, pain, and loss of innocence, as well as their haunting fear that as Blacks, they could not expect the same treatment or benefit of the doubt as others receive in this society. Their stories, taken together, sketch a group of people forged by soul-searing experiences that only they, the tellers, can truly appreciate.

The following points guided the study:

1. African Canadians believe that as a group they are singled out by police, who stop and question them as they go about their business. They complain of police body searches, verbal abuse, name calling, and the apparent assumption that if they are driving a 'nice' car, it could well be a stolen car.
2. Racial profiling is *not* the problem of a single police service. Respondents were drawn from across the GTA, and at least one of them told of being stopped by the Ontario Provincial Police while he was driving on the highway.
3. Racial profiling as a societal issue needs to be chronicled. We cannot manage what we cannot measure, nor can we deny what we have not documented.

One African-Canadian police officer told me that racial profiling is not an academic issue. 'When you experience it,' he said, 'you know it.'

Through their stories, the respondents were challenging society to think about the experiences that African Canadians have with the police, and to let those experiences serve as a catalyst for increased police accountability, which they believed would strengthen the Black community's confidence in the law enforcement system. *In Their Own Voices* did not set out to 'prove' that racial profiling exists, nor did it examine the motives of individual officers in their encounters with African Canadians.[1] The report avoided the question, 'Does racial profiling by police happen?' Instead, through narrative, it explored this question: 'What is it about the experiences that Blacks are having with the police that can leave them often feeling disrespected, targeted, and victims of racial profiling, also known as racially biased policing?' In their responses, people shared stories that offered a glimpse of the unease that many African Canadians feel when their sons, daughters, and spouses go through the door. Even for the most ardent supporters of the police, the issue was not whether their loved ones stood a chance of being unreasonably questioned by police, but rather how these incidents should be regarded and handled.

The Interviews

The respondents entered the study through a variety of doors. Community organizers and municipal recreational workers paved the way for me to interview youth. Also, I randomly interviewed people at local basketball courts and other hangouts, as well as participants at conferences. Many interviewees saw profiling as an inseparable part of being Black. The point of these interviews was not to establish through numbers the extent of racial profiling of African Canadians. Rather, it was to show what profiling—or 'racially biased policing'—looks like through the eyes of African Canadians who have experienced it.

GETTING TO THE TRUTH

Sceptics will challenge the oppositional narratives I present in this chapter by asking one of two questions (or both): Are the interviewees telling the truth? And are these just 'a few' people who 'occasionally' have negative encounters with maverick police officers? The answers to both questions should interest all sectors of society, from community workers who advocate on behalf of profiled community members; to faith groups who, increasingly, are weighing in on the issue; and to lawmakers charged with maintaining our social fabric of justice and equity. The stories should be of particular interest to police services. If in the course of their duties ('to serve and protect'), police are using race as a factor in determining 'criminality' or 'criminal propensity,' and if these practices are being 'unintentionally systemically facilitated' by police organizations and by society—a belief held by the Association of Black Law Enforcers (ABLE) and many others—we should all *want* to hear the voices of community members whose experiences differ from what police services contend. And we should be prepared to accept the validity of these voices.

The stories I heard during the interviews were consistent among themselves; they were also consistent with stories from jurisdictions beyond the GTA. Still, to make sure I was not 'putting words in people's mouths,' I invited the respondents to share positive experiences with the police as well, if they felt that these more appropriately defined their experiences with the police. Some did share positive experiences. Some—very much the minority—even offered narratives that others would read as profiling, but which they saw as professional, by-the-book police work. I felt it was important to include *all* voices, since the dominant discourse is not exclusive to Whites.

PERCEPTION VERSUS REALITY

A powerful weapon sometimes used to challenge narratives about racial profiling involves the old 'perception versus reality' argument. Are African Canadians really being profiled? Or do they merely *perceive* that they are? Interestingly, some experts see nothing wrong per se with describing one's life experiences as a function of perception. The question, though, is 'Whose perception is to be believed?' For that matter, 'Whose perceptions enter the public "transcript" that we all take for granted?'

The interviews suggested a simple answer: 'Perception *is* reality.' This does not mean that every perceived act of profiling is in fact so. The trouble with perception, though, is that it plays a significant role in interactions between African Canadians and the police. Perception affects *both* sides of these encounters. It seems that police, like other members of society, are affected by popular notions of what to expect from African Canadians just as much as African Canadians are affected by popular notions of what to expect from police. The result is a lethal brew of fear, posturing, suspicion, and distrust that can ratchet even a simple encounter up to levels that lead to arrest, resistance, a criminal record, and 'confirmation' that police dislike African Canadians and/or that African Canadians are 'predisposed to crime.' Perhaps the best way to demonstrate how this can happen is through the following scenario involving Marlon, Tariq, and Officer Smith (these people are composites based on my interviews).

THE STORIES

Marlon, Tariq, and Officer Smith

Parents, friends, and his own experience have taught Marlon that the police are his friends and that he should feel free to approach them. He therefore has no second thoughts when Officer Smith approaches him as he walks home from a party and asks him for his name and identification. He does not react 'with attitude' when the officer asks him to empty his pockets and his backpack. In fact, he does not even question what Officer Smith means when he says that this is a 'routine check' and a 'routine pat-down.' The term racial profiling does not cross his mind.

Officer Smith has a job to do—a job he loves and of which he is proud. He has chosen his profession because he believes in an ordered society. But he also finds fulfilment in helping lost children, protecting seniors from muggers, raising funds for charity, and protecting the community from dangers seen and unseen. Officer Smith has no particular philosophy about African Canadians as a group. What he does have is an 'instinct' for crime and, from experience, a gut sense of the types of people likely to commit particular crimes.

Tariq did not have the upbringing Marlon did. Actually, he did, but his experience led him to change his view of the police by the time he was fifteen. A bright, perceptive young man, Tariq loves his high school law course and plans to become a lawyer. So when Officer Smith approaches him and a couple of his friends one night and orders them up against the wall for a search, he has many questions, which he asks the officer: 'Why are you doing this?' 'What did we do wrong?' 'Don't you have to have reasonable and probable grounds to stop us like this?'

Officer Smith is in no mood to engage in a social science lesson with a fifteen-year-old. 'It's a routine pat-down,' he replies, adding, 'You people think you're bad, don't you?' Reluctantly, Tariq submits to the search. His friends seem undisturbed as they do the same. Later, they laugh the incident off. They have seen and experienced this type of treatment before. They actually scold Tariq for talking back to The Man. 'Don't do that next time,' they admonish him. The Man does not like to be challenged. It's the quickest way into the back seat of a cruiser and onto the path away from law school. Tariq's questions turn to anger, especially when other friends at school to whom he recounts the incident react with the same kind of 'so where have you been' attitude his friends demonstrated that night.

Are Marlon and Tariq victims of racial profiling? In the term proposed by a Joint Working Group of the Toronto Police Services Board, were they targets of 'racially biased policing'? Was Officer Smith merely doing his job, or was he a racist maverick who under cover of a dark uniform engaged in the uncommon act of racial profiling? Does it matter what label society places on the exchanges that night? Should we be concerned about Tariq's growing anger?

About Officer Smith's policing methods? About Marlon's blitheness? About the acceptance on the part of Tariq's friends that they live in a society in which they have no right to ask why they are being randomly searched by a police officer? Who is the victim, and who is the villain?

Strangers in a Foreign Land

Perception (or misperception), whatever its source, serves as a great divide when racial profiling is discussed. Many of the respondents believed they were on the losing side of that divide. From their perspective, they may often be viewed as a threat to society, but it is the police, they said, who are equipped with guns, batons, Tasers, and two-way radios. It is the police who can easily summon an army of scout cars for back-up, and who have a powerful union and—most critically—the public's good will. For African Canadians who see things this way, police racial profiling is merely an extension of society's desire to keep them in their place.

Their reactions to police, then, are woven into the overall landscape of their lives. They filter police behaviour towards them through 'lenses' such as those used by a group of youth who put together a recent African-Canadian submission to the UN Rapporteur on Race in 2004:

> I am The African Canadian Youth ... feared by some, reviled by others, misunderstood by even many who try to help me, regarded with hope by those who believe I can Rise. The first thing you need to know about me is that like all other Canadians I am offered protections under the laws of this country. As a matter of fact, the Government Official will show you the policies, programs [and] initiatives that she will say are designed for youth. I am a youth and in her eyes there is nothing stopping me from reaching out and taking my share of the pie. Even my parents sometimes chide me for not taking my share of what [African-Canadian author Cecil Foster] says is, in the eyes of an immigrant generation, 'a place called heaven.' And when I marvel at the gleam of Corporate Canada; when I see the Good Life in TV ads; when I hear of scholarship programs and opportunities to travel and [of] an offer of a second chance under the *Youth Criminal Justice Act,* I see why to some this is a place called heaven. But there is another side of Paradise that you need to visit. This side is not included in The Guided Tour. It's not on the map. As a matter of fact, were it not for me and for those who fight on my behalf, you wouldn't even know it existed. It's our own little family secret ... our Secret Garden of weeds, underbrush and Unacknowledged Spaces.

A DEEP AND COMPLEX RAGE

Forever seared in listeners' minds is the broken voice of an African-Canadian businessman as he described to a joint ACCCRP-OHRC focus group the treatment he received at the hands of security personnel and later the police after a seemingly simple act of returning merchandise went horribly wrong. It's difficult to watch a grown man cry. It's gut-wrenching to watch a tall, distinguished-looking African-Canadian businessman hang his head as he tries to fight back tears. 'They've broken me,' he says softly. 'They've broken me.' What the businessman described that day was not just a debatable act of racial profiling—debatable as in 'Was I treated this way because I'm Black, or because I deserved it?' He was placing the treatment meted out to him by law enforcement officers in the context of shattered expectations of how a person *should* be treated in such an incident. He was echoing Tariq's disillusionment with the vision of courtesy one normally expects when one is angry while dealing with the police, though not necessarily rude.

The businessman was expressing the same feelings as held by Dudley, who agreed to be interviewed for *In Their Own Voices* only after much persuasion. Dudley had buried the memories of the night he was accosted by a police officer while he and his friends were leaving a nightclub. He told his story hesitantly, brushing away the memories as one would an invisible fly. Dudley's calm exterior belied a deep and complex rage, which nevertheless seeped out through his words and through his body language. His rage was deep because he had tied his experiences with the police to other disappointments in life—disappointments he attributed partly to his status as a Black man in society, and partly to his failure to listen to his mother and to the bad choices he had made as a result. In Dudley's eyes there were few socially acceptable ways of expressing how he felt. His rage was complex because, at twenty-seven, his encounters with the police were colliding with the dawning reality that he would never be an NBA star. Dudley had no marketable skill, and he felt like a failure.

The respondents placed clear responsibility for police misbehaviour at the feet of the police services themselves—although some felt that those who feel targeted 'must have' done something to attract police attention. At the same time, interviewees on both sides of the fence saw solutions in the form of a partnership among the police, African-Canadian youth, local African-Canadian communities, and society at large. The stories were sometimes heart breaking. Some reflected wilful acts on the part of police officers. Others suggested that 'how things are done' has a unique impact on African-Canadian communities—a clear reflection of the 'unintentional systemic facilitation' that ABLE speaks about.

The African-Canadian respondents *did not* expect police to overlook it if they were carry-ing drugs when stopped. They *did* expect that—as per the law—they would be stopped only if officers had reasonable and probable grounds to believe they were carrying drugs. They knew that if the licence plates were missing from their car they could be stopped and that once stopped they could be asked for ID. They *did not* expect that while they were walking along the street, the police would pull up and ask for ID as part of a 'routine check.' They *did not* deny that African Canadians had their share of lawbreakers among them, as with any other subgroup in society. They *did* wonder what others—who are not stopped and searched as often—have in *their* backpacks and cars as they pass smugly by. In the end, the respondents sought fair and equitable treatment, not special treatment.

NOTE

1. For a copy of *In Their Own Voices* and its companion report, *Crisis Conflict and Accountability*, contact the African Canadian Legal Clinic in Toronto.

REFERENCE

Davis, J. (Ed.) 2002. *Stories of change: Narratives and social movements.* Albany: State University of New York Press.

Chapter 37

The Street Gangs in Prison: "It's Just a Revolving Door"

Elizabeth Comack, Lawrence Deane, Larry Morrissette, and Jim Silver

People of colour and Indigenous peoples are disproportionately at the receiving end of punishment-based interventions by the Canadian justice system. Indigenous people in particular are more likely to receive custodial sentence and less likely—for a wide variety of reasons—to receive bail. These and a host of other factors have meant that a disproportionate number of Aboriginal people end up in Canada's jails and prisons. Likewise, the same array of dynamics that produce these high prison numbers have also resulted in the rise of Aboriginal gangs in Canada, and jails and prisons have become a primary recruiting ground for gang members. Elizabeth Comack, Lawrence Deane, Larry Morrissette, and Jim Silver (2013) place the voices of current and former gang members front and centre in the relationship between and the role of prisons in Aboriginal gang production and reproduction, noting in particular their mutually constituted nature. The street gang Indian Posse, also known as IP in jail, are further discussed in the chapter.

Given the overrepresentation of Aboriginal people in the criminal justice system, prison has become another part of the normal in the lives of many Aboriginal families. As one of the men commented:

> It was always a normal thing to say, "Oh, my brother's locked up" or, "Oh, man, your uncle's locked up" or "Oh, my cousin's locked up," you know. It was, you heard that every single day, "Oh, he got locked up today and I don't know how long he's going to be gone" or "oh, he's gone for thirty-six months," "oh, he's gone for nine years" or "oh, he got twelve years." Like, it was always, there's not a day that goes by where, you know, someone's getting locked up or someone's getting out. When that someone gets out there's someone to take his place. It's just a revolving door.

For many of the young gangsters, making it to the penitentiary was a mark of status, a means of gaining respect and a reputation within their gang culture. As one of the men told us:

> When I was younger, all I looked up to was gang members, right, 'cause of my family and my older cousins and uncles. And I wanted to be something, you know. But I didn't only want to be part of it. I wanted to be someone…. So I thought that if I went there [the penitentiary] that it would help me, help out my record of, you know, gangsters, you know what I mean?

And another:

> You looked up to all these older guys, you know, they were the ones getting three years, five years, ten years. It was like they had the status. It's what me and my young friends wanted…. And they always talked about, you know, "Oh, you got a TV in your cell, you got a game in your cell, you got this in your cell, you know, if you want weed you got weed." Basically, they glorified it.

In this respect, prisons have become an important site for the production and reproduction of street gangs. While some of the literature on gangs makes a distinction between "street gangs" and "prison gangs" as if they were two completely separate phenomenon (see, for example, Grekul and LaBoucane-Benson 2007; Fleisher and Decker 2001; Skarbek 2012), our discussions with the gang members make it clear that this is a false dualism: the barriers between the prison and the outside community are permeable. If you are not a street gang member when you are sentenced, you will become one for protection once you reach the prison. And when you leave the prison, usually with no money in your pocket, the gang will be there to assist with the transition back to the street. But the role of the prison in the production and reproduction of street gangs runs much deeper.

Even before they became involved in street gangs, the men were involved in dealing drugs and committing other crimes on the street. As one of the guys said, "Dealt drugs, robbed, stole, that's always what we did." But it was in prison where their power and control, especially over the drug trade, was realized.

> And then we went to prison, like, Stony Mountain and that, and you know we learnt from guys in there how it's not about just being in a gang and having colours and being cool. It's about money. It's about power. So then, you know … drugs is power…. You got drugs, you got money, you got power, anywhere you go, anywhere.

Because "drugs is power," one of the guys explained how IP was able to exert its influence within the prison, and how that extended out into the street:

> In there too we made our connections, you know, these are the crooks that are the drug dealers. We made better connections and we're smarter. We're already doing pen time. We've already got people under us. And we know what kind of power we hold. So we basically, us guys in the joint, started just taking dope off of other guys in the joint through their contacts in the street and we'd set up deals through there and—boom! We put a couple of people [on the street] and we just, you know, we controlled the outside from the inside. Dope deals had to be done by us. Dope had to be sold by ours.

That was in the early 1990s. Another man, who was released from Stony two months before we met with him in 2011, affirmed that IP was still running the prison. "The IP are what they call 'the shit' in there. They are the toughest and the craziest and I consider the most ruthless."

Gaining control in the prison involved pushing out the bikers, who had previously been running the drug trade. In the view of an IP leader, the bikers were "the white guys"; it was "all race." As he told us: "You know when us young guys started being the [Indian] Posse we brought in a couple of these older guys … that have done pen time, like, before us." Referring to the American Indian Movement (AIM), he said, "They were all into this Indian movement shit." The older guys wanted to be warriors, to act as Indians, and as activists. But the young Indian Posse guys did not want to be warriors in that way. They treated that aspect of Indian-ness disdainfully. "They want to save the Indian." The IP guys did not. The IP leader said, instead, "I want to be a warrior … like, a gang warrior, like a warrior gang." So in a sense the IP perverted what the older, more politicized AIM guys were talking about. But the idea that they were Indians and should act as Indian—acting on the basis of a racialized resistance identity that they were now claiming—was still there.

> And so they kind of instilled some of that stuff in our heads too. Don't be letting these white people run you, you know, fuck the bikers, you know, why are you going to let a bunch of white people run your 'hood, you know. So we got that mentality too, about we're Indians and, you know, fuck these guys, why should they oppress us.

This particular IP member said that "when we did finally get to the pen and we did make it like that … the guys would come in and they would literally kiss our ass and thank us that we made it like that so they could come to jail and do time." In other words, for the IP guys coming into prison, doing time was made easier because they had the collective power of their gang to draw upon—as long as those entering prison adhered to what the gang leadership said.

The Indian Posse members, then, made it their mission to exert their collective power on the inside, and they did so as *Indians,* and with force. They claimed the racialized space inside the prison. As one of the guys told us, a sign once scrawled on the wall in Stony Mountain Penitentiary read, "Tread softly, Whitey. You're in Indian Country now."

For the gang leaders, doing time had its privileges. One leader told us:

> It's like going home. You know, you walk into jail it's—especially somebody like me, you know what I mean, jail is like a fuckin' reunion. You know, my cell's fuckin' made up before I get there. There's canteen in the cell. There's a radio in there. And the bed's made. Everything's done before you get there … You walk on the range, it's "Hey, man." Everybody's hugging and kissing you. "What's happening." You know?

The younger guys also benefitted from going to prison. They made contacts and were protected while inside (so long as they did what they were told), and they earned status and respect on the street when released.

But prison can also be a nightmare, a violence-filled horror show. The close quarters of the prison would set the stage for power struggles between the street gangs, and for settling disputed and long-standing beefs. That was certainly the experience of one of the men. Like many of the other young gangsters, he had aspirations to do pen time:

> It was always a mission to try and get to Stony. And I think about it and I laugh nowadays. Like, it wasn't trying to get your diploma. It wasn't trying to get your graduation present. It was trying to get to the big house. Because, you know, you wanted to be the big man and, like, basically, it was just a really fucked up way of thinking. Our train of thoughts weren't the same as some individuals who'd want to finish high school and get their diploma and move on to university and everything else.

This man realized his mission at the age of eighteen. His lawyer told him he was getting an eighteen-month sentence. "And in my head I was like, okay, yeah, right on. You know, I wasn't, 'Ah fuck, you know, I'm not going to see the street for eighteen months' … Our train of thought wasn't, 'Ah fuck, you know, I'm not going to see my mom, I'm not going to see my girlfriend.' It was basically, 'Okay, yeah, okay, let's go.'" He was initially sent to Headingley, the provincial jail. But when the chance to transfer to Stony Mountain Penitentiary emerged he jumped at it. That's when he learned what it really was like there:

Like, what it had grown into in the past, you know, from 1991, '92, to '99 was crazy, it was insane, 'cause you had Native Syndicate, you had Indian Posse, you had Los Bravos, who were still Los Bravos, they weren't Hell's Angels yet, and then you had the Manitoba Warriors, and then you had the Asians, the Asians stuck together.

Given his street connections, he was able to join up with one of the gangs when he arrived at Stony Mountain.

They were the guys that we looked up to and they knew exactly who we were ... there was always that phone call, there was always that, you know, like, we always kept in touch basically through their girlfriends.... And whenever one of us would get sentenced it was basically okay, so and so is getting this amount of time, he's coming up, expect him, so take care of him. So that's basically what it was.

He described walking into the main dining hall on his first day at the prison:

It's like a huge cafeteria. You walk in and all's you can see is your own people, Aboriginal people. It's crazy. It blew my mind how many gangs you can see. As soon as you first walk in, it's IP, IP, IP, IP, IP, and IP. They had, I think it was six, seven tables. You have fifteen to twenty guys to a table. And the tables were like maybe two of these tables [pointing to the large one we were sitting at]. And then it would be NS and then it would be Manitoba Warriors and then there'd be two tables of Asians in the corner. And then you'd have your general population—so it was pretty much arranged seating. So you walk in and then you went and sat as to where your gang was.

Members of another street gang knew who this particular man was. "We were at war with them during my teen years, and there was times where we have confronted each other on the streets, and there was times where things happened where people got shot." So when he walked into the prison dining hall on that first day, he was singled out: "This one guy starts pointing at me," the man said. The guy was sitting at a particular gang's table and he made a threatening gesture. One of the members of the newcomer's own gang told him, "The only thing we can do is you guys got to go one-on-one." But he was reassured: "You know, like he's, 'Don't worry,' and he's like, 'No one's going to jump you, you're with us.'" He was told he would have to fight three of the other gang's members. "So yeah, that's how I spent my first day in jail."

What happened next was "an arranged fight." The older members of the newcomer's gang went with him to the washroom. "There was was two of their guys.... So it was pretty much just like, you know, like a gladiator, like a gladiator fight." He had to fight three guys in succession. "It was pretty, pretty bad. I lost a tooth, you know, my eyes were like this [gestures] and whatever." But afterward, he said that he "didn't have no problem with the [other street gang] guys" because of his particular gang association. "I guess, it was pretty much the only reason why I am alive today because, you know, they really wanted me dead."

One of the strategies the prison system has used to respond to the tensions and conflicts between the street gangs is to separate them into different ranges. For the gang members, this means that it became easier to do time. As one of them said, "It makes time a lot faster, yeah. It does 'cause you have your own buddies to joke around with or whatever, right." This strategy means that non-gang members who enter prison have to choose which gang they will associate with. As a former biker told us:

> If you want to survive, if you don't want to get beat every day and be charged tax or rent on your own fuckin' cell that you're getting for free anyway, right? They charge you, the gangs will charge you. You want to stay on this range you're going to have to pay twenty dollars a week in canteen, right. They'd muscle you. So you decide who you want to roll with or who you might know in some gang. That's why they got the fish tank now, hey. It's called the fish tank, Unit One. Anybody that goes to Stony Mountain goes to the fish tank and they evaluate you there for three months to see where you're going to survive the best. So they pretty much tell you what gang you're going to join.

Surviving in prison means being prepared to fight. As one gang member said:

> Everyone from Stony that gets out will tell you, you know, it doesn't matter how big or small you are as long as you know how to fight in a gang, you know, you'll be alright. Like, in some prisons my brothers would be outnumbered a lot, four of my homies and twelve other guys, right, different gang, and my four bros rolled on all these twelve guys and actually took them all out and made a good name for ourselves in prison that time.

How accurate this particular story is we don't know, but its telling exemplifies the competition that exists between the street gangs in the prison system and the violent means by which that competition is played out.

Sometimes the violence is not just between gangs, but within them. One of the men was betrayed by his own gang members when he was in Headingley on remand. His gang set him up for a beating; "All because I told this guy his old lady's acting like a bitch." A fight was arranged between members of opposing Aboriginal street gangs during recreation time:

> They were supposed to be over by the ping pong table because it was all set up where this was all going to be done. So my dumb ass being one all for the brothers, the six of us walked in there, we seen them over by the ping pong table. I walked over there and just started smacking a guy right in the face. And here I didn't know it was a setup on me by my own guys. The minute I turned around to see where my guys were, they were all walking away from me. I ended up getting two broken ribs, they cracked my cheekbone, took almost six to seven months before I could hear out of my right ear. And that's when I decided I'm done with this shit.

When this same man was sent to Stony, he ended up in the fish tank. "To me it's just they want to see how bad you're going to get punched out before you go to population, 'cause all the fish tank is, is nothing but the strong preying upon the weak." While he was there he "took a beating" from one of the street gangs and eventually ended up on the range of another gang, where he spent the remainder of his sentence. He talked about what was involved in surviving prison:

> You do what you gotta do, man. It's not a point of pride. Your pride goes out the window the minute you started doing federal time. A person who's got pride is the person who gets punched out. You suck up your pride. You suck up any fuckin' morals you have and you become a slave to the institutions—and by me meaning a slave to the institution, the institution is the gangs 'cause the gangs run the institution, one hundred percent.

Doing time in prison as a gang member means "doing hard time." If you are a gang member, we were told, you do not benefit from programs or schooling while you are in prison: "You can't do none of that in jail if you're a gangster. You're totally cut off from everything … as soon as you're labelled a gang member in jail you're basically off of the reform list and now you go into the warehouse list." But then again, pressures to avoid rehabilitation emanate from the gang itself. As one of the IP members explained to us: "See you guys got to understand, too, IP doesn't let a lot of those things happen anyways, like, you know, what I mean … programs, schools, traditional things, shit like that.… It's a criminal organization, bottom line. It's all about crime." In other words, if a gang member was to partake in prison programs—to "be legit"—they would be seen as suspect by the gang because their loyalty would be called into question:

> Why be around us? Why have that thought in your head? And why, when you're sitting in the fuckin' cop shop in that seat and you know about this murder and that murder, and the cops are asking you about it and they're saying, "Well, we can give you this, we can offer you this." Well, you were already trying to go that way and live that life anyways and be legit. So now here's your chance. Maybe you'll rat. We don't need people around like that, you know. We don't need people around that have different thoughts and different—you're either in for the full ride or you're out, you know what I mean?

For those who are committed to the gang, the support they receive continues on their release. As one of the gang members explained, "A lot of our boys don't have to bus, you know"—that is, catch a bus back to the city. "We'll go get them, right." Back on the street, the leaders will also ensure that their crew members have what they need:

> When I got started that's what I used to do. Guys would get out of jail and you know, buy him whatever he needs and he'll just pay me back later. I wouldn't rush him or nothing. As long as I see him doing good, you know. That's kind of what my job was, make sure everybody's well and making money so we look good, so people are not dissing us or anything.

The men leaving prison are, then, brought back into the gang lifestyle. There is no other way to pay the rent or make money. And the cycle continues.

BIBLIOGRAPHY

Fleisher, Mark and Scott Decker. 2001. "An Overview of the Challenge of Prison Gangs." *Corrections Magazine Quarterly* 5(1): 1–9.

Grekul, Jana and Patti LaBoucane-Benson. 2007. *An Investigation into the Formation and Recruitment Processes of Aboriginal Gangs in Western Canada.* Ottawa: Public Safety Canada.

Skarbek, David. 2012. "Prison gangs, norms, and organizations." *Journal of Economic Behaviour & Organization* 82(1): 96–109.

Chapter 38

Indigenous Girls and the Violence of Settler Colonial Policing

Jaskiran Dhillon

In this chapter, the author focuses on the manner in which Indigenous women and girls are surveilled, harassed, and criminalized by various local, regional, and national policing agencies in Canada. In particular, Jaskiran Dhillon (2015) focuses on the ways that colonialism and its various structural imperatives impose themselves upon and thus intervene into the daily realities that many Indigenous girls are forced into. She highlights the voices of the Indigenous girls themselves in their interactions with policing agents and agencies.

PRAIRIE POLICING

The story of police violence recounted by this young Indigenous woman is consistent with my longstanding work as a youth advocate and ethnographer researching state interventions in the lives of urban Indigenous youth in Saskatoon.[1] In the remainder of this section, I share snapshots of my ethnographic fieldwork that reveal the gravity of settler colonial policing in the lives of Indigenous girls in this prairie city. To be clear, my interest here is in prioritizing the state's ongoing and manifold strands of assault on Indigenous girls in order to *make visible* the profound restrictions and harm that comes from everyday, routinized violence inherent in particular social, economic, and political formations, and in this case, specifically settler-colonial ones.[2]

Indigenous girls carry history, memory, and otherwise futures within their bodies, within their varied experiences of colonial occupation and their resistance to it. This came across loud and clear one morning when I entered a community and youth organization in Saskatoon where I was conducting a portion of my fieldwork. I walked into the office space that serves as a sort of headquarters for a program supporting Indigenous youth in custody (both open and secure). Case workers are assigned to each youth file and the case worker is supposed to offer support to the youth as she or he transitions from youth detention out into the "real world." This support can take the shape of assistance in enrolling into community education programs, finding housing, attending probation meetings, and seeking employment. On this particular morning, a young Indigenous woman named Sherry[3] was seated next to a desk when I stepped in the room. I had seen Sherry a few times before, but on this day she looked visibly different. There was a large, blackish bruise on her face, although her long brown hair concealed a part of it, and her arm was in a sling. She was dressed in jeans and a simple t-shirt, some kind of mobile device was clutched in her hand. She looked visibly upset, her eyes were narrowed, her mouth in a frown. She wasn't speaking. Sherry's caseworker, Pauline, was sitting behind her desk sipping coffee and typing on her keyboard.

When I saw Sherry, I immediately, of course, asked what happened. Pauline responded in a matter of fact tone, "Oh, it's the cops. They are harassing her again. It happens all the time once you get involved with Corrections and Public Safety." I learned that Sherry had been out walking in the Westside, later in the afternoon the previous day, when she was stopped by two male police officers and accused of breaching her probation orders. According to Pauline, Sherry had tried to explain that she was not in breach of her probation orders but the cops didn't believe her and started accusing her of lying. The situation "escalated," that is how Pauline described it, and Sherry eventually contacted Pauline from St. Paul's Hospital, where she ended up to get her arm and face examined after the altercation with the police. "They let her go, but they roughed her up before they did," Pauline told me. When I asked Pauline what she was going to do to take this matter up, she told me that the only recourse she had was to go to the police station and file a formal complaint. But that, she said, would be very time consuming and often didn't result in anything being done. During this conversation Sherry simply sat still. Dead silent.

What can we make of Sherry's silence? Was her silence imposed from above, from below? What is our role in witnessing these events and making sense of them? All of these questions are fundamental to how we think about what it means to place Indigenous girls' experiences at the centre of critical investigations into settler colonialism. At the moment in which all of this was unfolding, I did not feel like it was my place to ask Sherry to speak or to share her viewpoint on her violent interaction with the city police. I opted not to scratch at the surface of her silence, to be respectful of her decision to remain quiet on the matter. But, I also did not assume that her response reflected stoicism or a lack of awareness about what was happening. I did not assume that there was not a powerful eloquence about the situation that would be uttered if I ever had the opportunity to listen to her. My prior experiences alongside youth in the past suggested quite the opposite. In fact, this entire exchange further reinforced in my mind why it is so important to create avenues for Indigenous girls to speak out safely and with all of the necessary supports. The last thing I wanted to do in this situation was increase this Indigenous young woman's vulnerability and exposure. Nonetheless, I was left thinking about what we might learn from youth like Sherry about the ways Indigenous girls are creatively navigating and negotiating the terrain of state violence if there were more spaces for them to share their knowledge. How might this allow us to interrogate settler colonialism in more complex ways and, in turn, reveal different pathways to decolonization?

Reflecting further on this encounter, I would also like to suggest that the violence Sherry experienced in this instance contains two discrete parts. The first one relates to the violence she has endured at the hands of the Saskatoon City Police, an egregious violation in its own right. And the second is wrapped up in Pauline's individuation and dismissal of Sherry's encounter with settler colonial violence, thereby legitimating it as part of routine behavior and mis-recognizing (Bourdieu & Wacquant, 2004) it because of its predictability and familiarity. In *Violence and War and Peace*, Scheper-Hughes and Bourgeois (2004) describe how "structural violence is generally invisible because it is part of the routine grounds of everyday life and transformed into expressions of moral worth" (p. 4). For Pauline, the experience of this young woman had become entirely normalized to the point that it did not warrant additional time or attention—or even a report to her Director of Programming. It was expected. It was simply what happened. Even when I pressed the issue further, asserting that this was happening to other Indigenous girls too, she didn't seem to think there was anything she could do. She offered no explanation beyond acknowledging that this was "the way things were," nor did she consider the possibility that her own actions of turning a blind eye to the young woman's experience may, in some way, be contributing to a lack of police accountability and in turn, the relentless and vigilant policing of Indigenous youth in the Westside. At best, the underlying message communicated to this young woman was: exercise fortitude when challenged by the onslaught of racist police provocation and coercive force. Suppress your feelings of anger and vulnerability. Keep your head down. Stay out of trouble.

My point here is not to direct all of the blame towards Pauline—she is one caseworker operating within a system of structural, colonial violence—but instead to draw attention to the blatant acceptance of violent policing practices enacted against Indigenous young women in Saskatoon and to redirect us back to the importance of looking at settler colonial gender violence through the social dynamics of everyday practices, which reveal how larger orders of social force come together with micro-contexts of local power to shape material realities on the ground (Kleinman, 1997). In fact, the violation of personal liberty and insidious debasement of human dignity recounted by this Indigenous young woman, in addition to her experience of racism and public humiliation, was not news to me. Having done research and advocacy in Saskatoon for years, this story while stunning in its level of injustice is also stunningly prosaic in its *repeated* occurrence as an act of settler colonial surveillance. On numerous occasions, I have found my senses met with the following scene: a Saskatoon City Police cruiser pulled over on the side of 20th Street (or on more isolated roads, in back alleys, next to forsaken train tracks) with an Indigenous youth standing in the shadow of circulating red and blue lights, arms raised above the head or clasped behind the back. Personal belongings, sometimes broken, have been strewn about the unforgiving ground. One or two police officers are usually engaged in some form of rough "questioning," voices are often raised. The interminable power of the criminal justice system well evidenced by the material presence of guns, slash resistant gloves, bulletproof vests, handcuffs, batons, and split second radio back up. Sometimes there are dogs. The potential use of deadly force by these public-safety sentries, in instances of perceived threat, imagined or otherwise, looms large. They hold the authority to trigger the deployment of lethal violence to maintain the safety and protection of a white Canadian citizenry, to shut down by any means necessary those whose very presence threatens the social, political, and economic structures that have birthed white power and privilege.[4] They are the city's front line drones of white settler defense. And in moments like these, time becomes dilated. Anything can happen.

Numerous youth workers have corroborated the high incidence of racial profiling and surveillance by city police that has been revealed, anecdotally, by Indigenous youth in Saskatoon. When I interviewed a Cree worker involved in counselling Indigenous youth approaching the end of their prison sentence, he told me it was commonplace for Indigenous youth to recount instances of being stopped by the police to the point of feeling deeply harassed because of the style of their clothing and the colour of their skin. He revealed, "If you live in the *core*, it's almost a certainty. They [Indigenous youth] always seem to be conscious of the presence of police. It doesn't matter where we go in the city, they are always looking out for them."

The reference this youth worker made to the geographical specificity of heightened police surveillance also signals the way that the "core neighbourhood" in Saskatoon has become coded as "Indigenous space," a frontier where "law has authorized its own absence and where the police can violate Indigenous peoples with impunity" (Razack, 2015, p. 23). Idylwyld Drive is the borderline that cuts the city longitudinally, bisecting Saskatoon into the east associated with prosperity and wealth, and the west (also known as Alphabet City because the Westside avenues have no names, just letters) associated with poverty, crime, and suffering—often tagged "ghetto territory." "This spatialized relationship," remarks Joyce Green (2011) "maintains the focus on the [I]ndigenous as needing to be controlled, for racism suggests they are ultimately not fit for civilized society" (p. 238). The targeting of Indigenous girls, and Indigenous youth more generally, by police, then, is interlinked with a criminalization of the neighbourhoods where Indigenous families live, and a deliberate categorization of these communities as simultaneously "native and degenerative" (Razack, 2002). Whiteness is able to move freely into these "projected crime zones" as a matter of exercising power over "Indigenous deviance" and ensuring the quarantining of Indigenous bodies. In the words of Razack (2015), "to mark and maintain their own emplacement on stolen land, settlers must repeatedly enact the most enduring colonial truth: the land belongs to the settler, and Indigenous people who are in the city are not of the city. Marked as surplus and subjected to repeated evictions, Indigenous people are considered by settler society as the waste or excess that must be expelled" (p. 24). In Saskatoon, the processes of gentrification, the spatial politics of safety, and the ongoing displacement of Indigenous peoples on *Cree territory within the city*, have further fuelled white invasion into Indigenous urban space.[5]

Bringing the propensity of this ongoing domination into razor sharp focus, a Métis youth worker and activist disclosed the following during one of our interviews in 2007. His recitation of how the criminal justice system works as a mechanism of settler state control, and the ways Indigenous girls are particularly susceptible to the violence of this institution, warrants being quoted at length:

> When it comes to the city police and the Aboriginal youth I have worked with for close to fifteen years, or even longer… well, I have seen the abuse from city police. I've seen the ego, the attitudes, the complete injustice. I understand why young Indigenous people don't trust the police. It's all right to take some Aboriginal girl into a back alley and get a blowjob from her because what is she going to do? Because with most of these kids it's always us against them, it's us against the system. The judges don't care. The cops are a big part of the problem. The majority of the justice system in this province, in this city, is broken. I would love to see what would happen if a 14-year-old Aboriginal girl told a white judge that it was me against the white cop. The cop is always going to win.

And of growing concern is the now swarming police presence in community spaces where Indigenous youth are *supposed to feel safe* through the model of "crime prevention through social development." Bronwyn Dobchuk-Land's (2015) research in Winnipeg lends considerable insight into this more recent configuration of settler colonial state power. Analogous to Winnipeg in this regard, community organizations in Saskatoon, including Indigenous organizations, are increasingly being asked to welcome police into the spaces they are trying to construct as "safe spaces" for youth.[6] Ironically, this means that Indigenous girls, and youth more generally, are encountering settler police agents even in the places where they are supposed to access youth programming—initiatives ostensibly designed to "help" them. Youth community organizations, emergency rooms, the office of a social worker, the corridors of school, recreational centres, and the street are all fair game. In Saskatoon, you can even find police, the very same state entity that was created to aid Indigenous extermination, *leading* rallies and discussions on murdered and missing Indigenous women and girls.

Thus, the persistent sensation of being hunted, of monitored movement, of freedom being truncated through institutional caging *is central to* the daily reality of being a young Indigenous woman in Saskatoon. It is not an anomaly. It is not the fictitious creation of a youthful imagination on overdrive. Through their existence as *Indigenous* girls, these young people constitute a direct threat to an already existing settler social order. A large part of the way this threat becomes contained is through state mechanisms of criminalization, policing, and incarceration that function as both regulators and producers of socially constructed notions of normativity and deviance against which Indigenous youth sociality can be measured. Judith Butler (2015) argues, within the context of black conquest in the United States, that "one way that this [white dominance] happens is by establishing whiteness as the norm for the human, and blackness as a deviation from the human or even as a threat to the human, or as something not quite human" (para. 22). Similarly, young Indigenous lives have been constituted by the Canadian state as "throw aways," lives that are expendable in the quest to maintain settler control, subaltern lives that represent everything Canada does not want to become. Racism's ratification as a way of seeing, as a mode of dominant "public perception" (Butler, 2015, para. 6) that is both recurrent and customary, everyday and systemic, gendered and sexualized (Jiwani, 2006), fuels the construction of these binaries of value on human life and, in turn, standardizes heinous state techniques of subjugation. Settler colonies are heavily reliant on the reproduction of this longstanding controlling technology because of their need to consistently extinguish Indigenous alterity—to stand firm in the march toward the endpoint of successful "elimination."

Hence, it comes as no surprise to anyone working with Indigenous girls that incidents of "conflict" with law enforcement agents are common markers of lived experience—this is where criminalization and caging enter the picture. In urban centres where Indigenous youth come into more direct and frequent contact with state institutions, clashes with the criminal justice system take on even more heightened levels. According to a report presented to The Commission on First Nations and Métis Peoples and Justice Reform:

> For Saskatchewan Aboriginal youth, conflict with the justice system was primarily urban. Similar to the Canadian data, most Aboriginal youth in Saskatchewan committed their offence or alleged offence in a city, and most planned on relocating to a city upon release. Many of the Aboriginal youth experienced conflict with the justice system in the city even though they lived on reserve. (Government of Saskatchewan, 2004, p. 104)

Incarceration rates mirror the intensity of settler colonial confrontation between Indigenous youth and the criminal justice system, although it is important to reinforce that incarceration is part of a *continuum of violence* in the criminal justice system as a whole, which begins with initial police "contact," followed by arrest, detainment, court proceedings, sentencing, jail time, and, eventually, probation orders. In 2004, the Canadian Department of Justice conducted a snapshot of Indigenous youth in custody. The report confirmed the disproportionate representation of Indigenous youth in prison, although scholars and youth advocates have been reporting this phenomenon for some time.[7] While they comprise only 5% of the population, Indigenous youth make up 33% of young people in custody. The highest rates of incarceration are in northern and central Canada, and Saskatchewan is among the most punitive provinces, second only to the Northwest Territories (and Saskatchewan, along with Manitoba, holds the greatest number of police per capita across all of the provinces). In Saskatchewan, an astounding 87% of Indigenous women and girls make up the female prison population (Native Women's Association of Canada, 2012) and *young Indigenous youth are more likely to go to prison than finish high school* (Assembly of First Nations, 2012). Neve and Pate (2005) have argued, in fact, that the prairie provinces have witnessed some of the most egregious examples of criminalization of Indigenous women and girls. They note:

> Aboriginal women continue to suffer the devastating impact of colonization. From residential school and child welfare seizure, to juvenile and adult detention, Aboriginal women and girls are vastly over-represented in institutions under state control … in the Prairie Region most of the women and girls in prison are Aboriginal. (p. 27)

The concluding remarks emerging from Canada's 2012 periodic review, with regards to the country's adherence to the United Nations Convention on the Rights of the Child, also reiterated the criminal justice crisis signalled by the over-representation of Indigenous youth in Canadian jails (United Nations, 2012).

And the violence does not stop there. […]

NOTES

1. This ethnographic research has culminated in my first book titled *Prairie Rising: Indigenous Youth, Decolonization and the Politics of Intervention*. Toronto: University of Toronto Press, 2017.
2. I am being attentive here, to Eve Tuck's (2009) important words about the danger of producing "damage-centered" research (p. 409). My aim in this article is to indict the state—not to create portraits of damage.
3. All names in this section have been changed to preserve anonymity.
4. As Albert Memmi (1965) asserts, "privilege is at the heart of the colonial relationship" (p. xii).
5. For a brief glimpse into gentrification on the Westside of Saskatoon, see Casey (2014).
6. This movement has intensified with police programs such as the Serious Habitual Offender Comprehensive Action Plan (SHOCAP)—read targeted enforcement. The Saskatoon Police Service SHOCAP Unit, in partnership with agencies serving youth throughout the city, "*tracks* [emphasis added] the activity of a select group of young persons" (Saskatoon Police Service, n.d.).
7. For a list of publications regarding the criminalization and incarceration of Indigenous girls in Canada, please see Justice for Girls (n.d.).

REFERENCES

Assembly of First Nations. (2012). *A portrait of First Nations and education*. Retrieved from: http://www.afn.ca/uploads/files/events/fact_sheet-ccoe-3.pdf

Bourdieu, P. & Wacquant, L. (2004). Symbolic violence. In N. Scheper-Hughes & P. Bourgois (Eds.), *Violence in war and peace: An anthology*. Malden: Blackwell Publishing.

Butler, J. (2015, January 12). What's wrong with all lives matter? *The New York Times*. Retrieved from: http://opinionator.blogs.nytimes.com/2015/01/12/whats-wrong-with-all-lives-matter/?_r=0

Casey, A. (2014). Reviving Riversdale. *The Walrus*. Retrieved from: http://thewalrus.ca/reviving-riversdale/

Dhillon, J. (2017). *Prairie rising: Indigenous youth, decolonization and the politics of intervention*. Toronto: University of Toronto Press.

Dobchuk-Land, B. (2015, April). *Making settler colonial violence invisible: Fantasies and failures in western Canadian crime policy*. Paper presented at the Cityscapes Workshop, New York, Columbia University.

Government of Saskatchewan. (2004). *Legacy hope: An agenda for change.* Retrieved from: http://www.justice.gov.sk.ca/justicereform/volume1.shtml

Green, J. (2011). From *Stonechild* to social cohesion. In M. Cannon & L. Sunseri (Eds.), *Racism, Colonialism, and Indigeneity in Canada* (pp. 234–241). Ontario: Oxford University Press.

Jiwani, Y. (2006). *Discourses of denial: Mediations of race, gender, and violence.* Vancouver: UBC Press.

Justice for Girls. (n.d.). *Publications and positions.* Retrieved from: http://www.justiceforgirls.org/publications/index.html

Kleinman, A. (1997). The violence of everyday life: The multiple forms and dynamics of social violence. In Das, V., Kleinman, A., Ramphele, M., & Reynolds, P. (Eds.), *Violence and Subjectivity.* Durham: Duke University Press.

Memmi, A. (1965). *The colonizer and the colonized.* Boston: Beacon Press.

Native Women's Association of Canada. (2012). *Information sheet for Youth Justice Workers.* Retrieved from: http://www.nwac.ca/wp-content/uploads/2015/05/Information-Sheet-for-Youth-Justice-Workers.pdf

Neve, L. & Pate, K. (2005). Challenging the criminalization of women who resist. In J. Sudbury (Ed.), *Global lockdown: Race, gender, and the prison industrial complex* (pp. 19–34). New York: Routledge.

Razack, S. (2002). Gendered racial violence and spatialized justice: The murder of Pamela George. In S. Razack (Ed.), *Race, space, and the law: UnMapping a white settler society* (pp. 121–156). Toronto: Between the Lines.

Razack, S. (2015). *Dying from improvement: Inquest and inquires into indigenous deaths in custody.* Toronto: University of Toronto Press.

Saskatoon Police Service. (n.d.). *Serious habitual offender comprehensive action plan.* Retrieved from: http://police.saskatoon.sk.ca/pdf/brochures/SHOCAP.pdf

Scheper-Hughes, N. & Bourgois, P. (Eds.) (2004). *Violence in war and peace: An anthology.* Malden: Blackwell Publishing.

Tuck, E. (2009). Suspending damage: A letter to communities. *Harvard Educational Review*, 79(3), 409–427.

United Nations. (2012). *Convention on the Rights of the Child.* Retrieved from: http://rightsofchildren.ca/wp-content/uploads/Canada_CRC-Concluding-Observations_61.2012.pdf

PART 4

PRIVILEGES, MARGINALIZATION, AND RESISTANCE

© Jalani Morgan, 2016

PART 4A

RACE, PRIVILEGE, AND IDENTITY

In the now classic 1995 book *How the Irish Became White*, Noel Ignatiev illustrates the social construction of race—as he says, race is not biological, it is assigned. Furthermore, that the Irish were able to *become* white is indicative of the capacity of some minoritized groups to surmount their assigned status. To use Ignatiev's question, "How did the Catholic Irish, an oppressed group in Ireland, become part of an oppressing race in America?" (1995, 1). This example illustrates the shifting materiality of whiteness, and how over time some ethnoracial groups are able to move into the political, economic, and social power sphere, thereby gaining opportunities and possibilities that come with proximity to whiteness. So, as Ignatiev points out, in *entering* the white race, the Irish were able to gain a competitive advantage in the US over groups such as African and Latinx people, who had long before resided in the country. Being "white" and having race privilege also meant that Irish people were able to work in all sectors of society outside of the segregated labour market. The chapters in this section build on Ignatiev's discussion of the ways in which identification is experienced and makes possible and/or limits opportunities. They also alert us to the realities of race and to the fact that, despite the neo-liberal colour-blind discourse, there is evidence that in racially diverse stratified societies, race does matter.

REFERENCES

Ignatiev, N. 1995. *How the Irish Became White*. New York: Routledge.

FURTHER READING

Aveling, Nado. 2004. "Being the Descendent of Colonialists: White Identity in Context." *Race, Ethnicity and Education* 7(1): 57–71.
In this journal article, Aveling, a white woman, explores "being white" with a small group of young, well-educated Australian women. Taking whiteness to be "a given set of locations that are historically, socially, politically and culturally produced," she notes that whites do not define themselves by skin colour; nevertheless, her respondents did give some thought to being "white" and talked of their unearned privileges and their feelings of guilt,

fear, and alienation. The author concludes by suggesting that becoming aware of racial positionality is "not quite enough," especially if one is to address the implications of whiteness for the work that one does.

Hill, Lawrence. 2001. *Black Berry, Sweet Juice: On Being Black and White in Canada.* **Toronto: HarperCollins.**
Starting with personal and family stories and then reporting on interviews he conducted with mixed-race respondents, Hill, son of a white mother and Black father from the United States, writes about forging a sense of identity growing up in the suburbs of Toronto. He discusses such things as "border crossing," hair issues, the "N-word," and the usual question—Who are you?—that is often asked to ascertain identity, nationality, place, and other such locations.

Hirabayashi, Lane R., Akiemi Kikumura-Yano, and James A. Hirabayashi, eds. 2002. *New Worlds, New Lives: Globalization and People of Japanese Descent in the Americas and from Latin America in Japan.* **Stanford, CA: Stanford University Press.**
In this book, contributors explore the question of the historical background and current status of *nikkei*—persons of Japanese descent—in seven countries in the Americas: Argentina, Bolivia, Brazil, Canada, Paraguay, Peru, and the United States. The contributions cover such areas as identity, community life, language, education and schooling, immigration, the family, religion, politics, and economics. The book also provides insights into the special circumstances of the many Japanese people who, in recent decades, have immigrated or returned to Japan seeking employment. Readers are able to note the similarities and differences among the Japanese in various countries over the years.

Hunter, Margaret L. 2005. *Race, Gender, and the Politics of Skin Tone.* **New York: Routledge.**
Making use of survey and interview data, this book describes how "colourism" operates and leads to discrimination against dark-skinned African Americans and Mexican Americans, resulting in them achieving lower levels of education, lower incomes, and lower-status partners compared to their lighter-skinned counterparts.

Ignatiev, Noel. 1995. *How the Irish Became White*. New York: Routledge.
In his book, Noel Ignatiev writes about how assimilation operates in the Unites States. He explains how the Irish peasants who immigrated to the Unites States in the eighteenth and nineteenth centuries, "fleeing caste and a system of landlordism" in Ireland, moved from being a "different race of people" to being "white." His argument indicates how race travels or gets named and lived in different contexts.

Lund, Darren E., and Paul R. Carr, eds. 2015. *Revisiting the Great White North?: Reframing Whiteness, Privilege, and Identity in Education*. 2nd ed. Rotterdam: Sense Publishers.
Employing "the heavy might of whiteness" as a frame, editors Lund and Carr have produced a book that tells of the enduring need for the critical examination of whiteness. As this is the second edition, the two white male editors reflect on the responses of anger, defensiveness, curiosity, and bemusement that resulted from the first edition published in 2007. They note that these responses indicate that there is still much resistance to white privilege—especially from white people. The racially diverse group of contributors offer significant and useful perspectives on the problematic realities of whiteness both in Canada and elsewhere, noting how whiteness intersects with power, history, and contexts, and remains invisible in society's prominent institutions. Indeed, Donald Trump's presidency in the United States, the post-Brexit UK, and the ascendency of Marine Le Pen's right-wing politics in France provide evidence of the consistency—if not the growing tide—of racism, xenophobia, and Islamophobia (all of which are in part fuelled by fear of racialized people and refugees) in North America and Europe, and that whiteness remains at the core of all of these geopolitical circumstances.

Chapter 39

Identity, Belonging, and the Critique of Pure Sameness

Paul Gilroy

Paul Gilroy (2000) writes that we cannot take the impact of race for granted. Indeed, "we have seen," as Gilroy writes, "that the uncertain and divided world we inhabit has made racial identity matter in novel and powerful ways. But we should not take the concept of identity and its multiple association with 'race' and raciology for granted." Identity, Gilroy argues, is both theoretically and politically a complex subject that is useful "to explore if we can only leave its obviousness behind."

When first he opens his eyes, an infant ought to see the fatherland, and up to the day of his death he ought never to see anything else. Every true republican has drunk in love of country, that is to say love of law and liberty, along with his mother's milk. This love is his whole existence; he sees nothing but the fatherland, he lives for it alone; when he is solitary, he is nothing; when he has ceased to have a fatherland, he no longer exists; and if he is not dead, he is worse than dead.
    —Rousseau

If things aren't going too well in contemporary thought, it's because there's a return …
to abstractions, back to the problem of origins, all that sort of thing.… Any analysis
in terms of movements, vectors, is blocked. We're in a very weak phase, a period of
reaction. Yet philosophy thought that it had done with the problem of origins. It was
no longer a question of starting or finishing. The question was rather, what happens
"in between"?

    —Gilles Deleuze

We have seen that the uncertain and divided world we inhabit has made racial identity matter in novel and powerful ways. But we should not take the concept of identity and its multiple associations with "race" and raciology for granted. The term "identity" has recently acquired great resonance, both inside and outside the academic world. It offers far more than an obvious, common-sense way of talking about individuality, community, and solidarity and has provided a means to understand the interplay between subjective experiences of the world and the cultural and historical settings in which those fragile, meaningful subjectivities are formed. Identity has even been taken into the viscera of postmodern commerce, where the goal of planetary marketing promotes not just the targeting of objects and services to the identities of particular consumers but the idea that any product whatsoever can be suffused with identity. Any commodity is open to being "branded" in ways that solicit identification and try to orchestrate identity.[1]

In this chapter I want to show that there is more at stake in the current interest in identity than we often appreciate. I would also like to uncover some of the complexities that make identity a useful idea to explore if we can only leave its obviousness behind and recognize that it is far from being the simple issue that its currency in both government and marketplace makes it appear to be. Where the word becomes a concept, identity has been made central to a number of urgent theoretical and political issues, not least belonging, ethnicity, and nationality. Racialized conflicts, for example, are now understood by many commentators as a problem of the incompatible identities that mark out deeper conflicts between cultures and civilizations. This diagnosis sets up or perhaps confirms the even more widespread belief that the forms of political conflict with which racial division has been associated are somehow unreal or insubstantial, secondary or peripheral. This is something I intend to dispute. The new popularity of identity as an interpretative device is also a result of the exceptional plurality of meanings the term can harness. These diverse inflections—some of which are adapted from highly specialized academic usage—are condensed and interwoven as the term circulates. We are constantly informed that to share an identity is to be bonded on the most fundamental levels: national, "racial," ethnic, regional, and local. Identity is always bounded and particular. It marks out the divisions and subsets in our social lives and helps to define the boundaries between our uneven, local attempts to make sense of the world. Nobody ever speaks of a human identity. The concept orients thinking away from any engagement with the basic, anti-anthropological sameness that is the premise of this book. As Judith Butler puts it in her thoughtful reflection on the concept: "it seems that what we expect from the term *identity* will be cultural specificity, and that on occasion we even expect *identity* and *specificity* to work interchangeably."[2]

The same troubling qualities are evident where the term has been employed to articulate controversial and potentially illuminating themes in modern social and political theory. It has been a core component in the scholarly vocabulary designed to promote critical reflection upon who we are and what we want, identity helps us to comprehend the formation of that perilous pronoun "we" and to reckon with the patterns of inclusion and exclusion that it cannot help creating. This situation is made more difficult once identity is recognized as something of a problem in itself, and thereby acquires an additional weighting. Calculating the relationship between identity and difference, sameness and otherness is an intrinsically political operation. It happens when political collectivities reflect on what makes their binding connections possible. It is a fundamental part of how they comprehend their kinship—which may be an imaginary connection, though nonetheless powerful for that.

The distinctive language of identity appears again when people seek to calculate how tacit belonging to a group or community can be transformed into more active styles of solidarity, when they debate where the boundaries around a group should be constituted and how—if at all—they should be enforced. Identity becomes a question of power and authority when a group seeks to realize itself in political form. This may be a nation, a state, a movement, a class, or some unsteady combination of them all. Writing about the need for political institutions and relationships at the dawn of our era, Rousseau drew attention to the bold and creative elements in the history of how disorganized and internally divided groups had been formed into coherent units capable of unified action and worthy of the special status that defined the nation as a political body. Reflecting on the achievements of heroic individual leaders as builders of political cultures that could "attach citizens to the fatherland and to one another," he noted that the provision of a unifying common identity was a significant part of this political process. Significantly for our purposes, his example was taken from the history of the Children of Israel:

> (Moses) conceived and executed the astonishing project of creating a nation out of a swarm of wretched fugitives, without arts, arms, talents, virtues or courage, who were wandering as a horde of strangers over the face of the earth without a single inch of ground to call their own. Out of this wandering and servile horde Moses had the audacity to create a body politic, a free people ... he gave them that durable set of institutions, proof against time, fortune and conquerors, which five thousand years have not been able to destroy or even alter.... To prevent his people from melting away among foreign peoples, he gave them customs and usages incompatible with those of other nations; he over-burdened them with peculiar rites and ceremonies; he inconvenienced them in a thousand ways in order to keep them constantly on the alert and to make them forever strangers among other men.[3]

In outlining elements of the political technology that would eventually produce the nation as a fortified encampment, Rousseau drew attention to the old association between identity and territory. Moses' achievement is viewed as all the more impressive because it was accomplished without the binding power of shared land. Rousseau underlined that the varieties of connection to which our ideas of identity refer are historical, social, and cultural rather than natural phenomena. Even at that early point in the constitution of modernity, he recognized that work must be done to summon the particularity and feelings of identity that are so often experienced as though they are spontaneous or automatic consequences of some governing culture or tradition that specifies basic and absolute differences between people. Consciousness of identity gains additional power from the idea that it is not the end product of one great man's "audacity" but an outcome of shared and rooted experience tied, in particular, to place, location, language, and mutuality.

When we think about the tense relationship between sameness and difference analytically, the interplay of consciousness, territory, and place becomes a major theme. It affords insights into the core of conflicts over how democratic social and political life should be organized at the start of the twenty-first century. We should try to remember that the threshold between those two antagonistic conditions can be moved and that identity-making has a history even though its historical character is often systematically concealed. Focusing on identity helps us to ask in what sense the recognition of sameness and differentiation is a premise of the modern political culture that Rousseau affirmed and which his writings still help us to analyze.

The dizzying variety of ideas condensed into the concept of identity, and the wide range of issues to which it can be made to refer, foster analytical connections between themes and perspectives that are not conventionally associated. Links can be established between political, cultural, psychological, and psychoanalytic concerns. We need to consider, for example, how the emotional and affective bonds that form the specific basis of raciological and ethnic sameness are composed, and how they become patterned social activities with elaborate cultural features. How are they able to induce conspicuous acts of altruism, violence, and courage? How do they motivate people toward social interconnection in which individuality is renounced or dissolved into the larger whole represented by a nation, a people, a "race," or an ethnic group? These questions are important because, as we have seen, grave moral and political consequences have followed once the magic of identity has been engaged tactically or in manipulative, deliberately oversimple ways. Even in the most civilized circumstances, the signs of sameness have degenerated readily into emblems of supposedly essential or immutable difference. The special appeal of individuality-transcending sameness still provides an antidote to the forms of uncertainty and anxiety that have been associated with economic and political crises. The idea of fundamentally shared identity becomes a platform for the reverie of absolute and eternal division.

The use of uniforms and other symbols to effect the sameness that identity only speaks about has sometimes been symptomatic of the process in which an anxious self can be shed and its concerns conjured away by the emergence of a stronger compound whole. The uniforms worn in the 1930s by fascists (and still worn by some fascist groups today) produced a compelling illusion of sameness both for members of the group and for those who observed their spectacular activities. The British Union of Fascists, one of the less-successful black-shirted organizations from that period, argued that their garb was all the more attractive to adherents when contrasted with the conflict and bitterness created by class-based divisions that were tearing the nation apart from within:

> (The "blackshirt") brings down one of the great barriers of class by removing differences of dress, and one of the objects of Fascism is to break the barriers of class. Already the blackshirt has achieved within our own ranks that classless unity which we will ultimately secure within the nation as a whole.[4]

We will explore below how the ultranationalist and fascist movements of the twentieth century deployed elaborate technological resources in order to generate spectacles of identity capable of unifying and coordinating inevitable, untidy diversity into an ideal and unnatural human uniformity. Their synthetic versions of fundamental identity looked most seductive where all difference had been banished or erased from the collective. Difference within was repressed in order to maximize the difference between these groups and others. Identity was celebrated extravagantly in military styles: uniforms were combined with synchronized body movement, drill, pageantry, and visible hierarchy to create and feed the comforting belief in sameness as absolute, metaphysical invariance. Men and women could then appear as interchangeable and disposable cogs in the encamped nation's military machine or as indistinguishable cells in the larger organic entity that encompassed and dissolved their individuality. Their actions may even be imagined to express the inner spirit, fate, and historicality of the national community. The citizen was manifested as a soldier, and violence—potential as well as actual—was dedicated to the furtherance of national interests. That vital community was constituted in the dynamic interaction between marchers moving together in austere time and the crowds that watched and savored the spectacle they created. In disseminating these valuable political effects, identity was mediated by cultural and communicative technologies like film, lighting, and amplified sound. These twentieth-century attributes were only partly concealed by the invocation of ancient ritual and myth.

The biblical stories of nation-building that demonstrate divine favor and the moral sanctions it supplies to worldly political purposes have been invoked by many different nationalist groups. The Afrikaners of South Africa provide one especially interesting and unwholesome example of how Rousseau's "peculiar rites and ceremonies" need not always serve a benign purpose. Their ethnically minded ideologues systematically invented an Afrikaner identity during the period that saw the rise of fascist movements elsewhere. They provided their political community with its own version of Christianity and a repertory of myths that were the basis for the elaborate political drama that summoned their historic nation into racialized being:

> The most dramatic event in the upsurge of Afrikaner nationalism was the symbolic ox-wagon trek of 1938, which celebrated the victory of the Great Trek. Eight wagons named after voortrekker heroes such as Piet Retief, Hendrik Potgeiter and Andres Pretorius traversed South Africa by different routes ... before they converged on a prominent hill overlooking

Pretoria. There, on 16th December 1938, the centenary of the battle of Blood River, which marked the defeat of the Zulu kingdom, more than 100,000 Afrikaners—perhaps one tenth of the total Afrikaner people—attended the ceremonial laying of the foundation stone of the Voortrekker Monument. Men grew beards, women wore voortrekker dress, for the occasion … (they) knelt in silent prayer.… The ceremony concluded with the singing of *Die Stem van Suid Afrika; God Save the King* had been excluded.[5]

Today's ubiquitous conflicts between warring constituencies that claim incompatible and exclusive identities suggest that these large-scale theatrical techniques for producing and stabilizing identity and soliciting national, "racial," or ethnic identification have been widely taken up. The reduction of identity to the uncomplicated, militarized, fraternal versions of pure sameness pioneered by fascism and Nazism in the 1930s is now routine, particularly where the forces of nationalism, "tribalism," and ethnic division are at work. Identity is thus revealed as a critical element in the distinctive vocabulary used to voice the geopolitical dilemmas of the late modern age. Where the power of absolute identity is summoned up, it is often to account for situations in which the actions of individuals and groups are being reduced to little more than the functioning of some overarching presocial mechanism. In the past, this machinery was often understood as a historical or economic process that defined the special, manifest destiny of the group in question. These days, it is more likely to be represented as a prepolitical, sociobiological, or biocultural feature, something mysterious and genetic that sanctions especially harsh varieties of deterministic thinking.

In this light, identity ceases to be an ongoing process of self-making and social interaction. It becomes instead a thing to be possessed and displayed. It is a silent sign that closes down the possibility of communication across the gulf between one heavily defended island of particularity and its equally well fortified neighbors, between one national encampment and others. When identity refers to an indelible mark or code somehow written into the bodies of its carriers, otherness can only be a threat. Identity is latent destiny. Seen or unseen, on the surface of the body or buried deep in its cells, identity forever sets one group apart from others who lack the particular, chosen traits that become the basis of typology and comparative evaluation. No longer a site for the affirmation of subjectivity and autonomy, identity mutates. Its motion reveals a deep desire for mechanical solidarity, seriality, and hypersimilarity. The scope for individual agency dwindles and then disappears. People become bearers of the differences that the rhetoric of absolute identity invents and then invites them to celebrate. Rather than communicating and making choices, individuals are seen as obedient, silent passengers moving across a flattened moral landscape toward the fixed destinies to which their essential identities, their genes, and the closed cultures they create have consigned them once and for all. And yet, the desire to fix identity in the body is inevitably frustrated by the body's refusal to disclose the required signs of absolute incompatibility people imagine to be located there.

Numerous cross-cultural examples might be used to illustrate this point. Reports from the genocide in Rwanda repeatedly revealed that identity cards issued by the political authorities were a vital source of the information necessary to classify people into the supposedly natural "tribal" types that brought them either death or deliverance. There, as in several other well-documented instances of mass slaughter, the bodies in question did not freely disclose the secrets of identity:

> Many Tutsis have been killed either because their ID cards marked them out as a Tutsi or because they did not have their card with them at the time and were therefore unable to prove they were not a Tutsi.... To escape the relentless discrimination they suffered, over the years many Tutsis bribed local government officials to get their ID card changed to Hutu. Unfortunately, this has not protected them.... The Tutsi give-aways were: one, being tall and two having a straight nose. Such criteria even led hysterical militias to kill a number of Hutus whose crime was "being too tall for a Hutu." Where there was doubt about the person's physical characteristics or because of the complaints that too many Tutsis had changed their card, the Interahamwe called upon villagers to verify the "tutsiship" of the quarry in question.[6]

Similar events were still being reported four years later when the genocidal assault against the Tutsis had been rearticulated into the civil war in Congo—a conflict that had already drawn in several other states and that appeared to provide the key to stability in the region. Under the presidency of Laurent Kabila, people whose physical characteristics made them suspect were still being openly murdered.[7] It is important to remember, however, that the linguistic markers of residual colonial conflict between anglophone and francophone spheres of influence were also implicated in sustaining the killing.

These fragments from a history of unspeakable barbarity underline how the notion of fixed identity operates easily on both sides of the chasm that usually divides scholarly writing from the disorderly world of political conflicts. Recently, identity has also come to constitute something of a bridge between the often discrepant approaches to understanding self and sociality found on the different sides of that widening gulf. As a theme in contemporary scholarship, identity has offered academic thinking an important route back toward the struggles and uncertainties of everyday life, where the idea of identity has become especially resonant. It has also provided the distinctive signatures of an inward, implosive turn that brings the difficult tasks of politics to an end by making them appear irrelevant in the face of deeper, more fundamental powers that regulate human conduct irrespective of governmental superficialities. If identity and difference are fundamental, then they are not amenable to being re-tooled by crude political methods that cannot possibly get to the heart of primal ontologies, destinies, and fates. When the stakes are this high, nothing can be done to offset the catastrophic consequences that result from tolerating difference and mistaken attempts at practicing democracy. Difference corrupts and compromises identity. Encounters with it are just as unwelcome and potentially destructive as they were for Houston Stewart Chamberlain. They place that most precious commodity, rooted identity, in grave jeopardy.

When national and ethnic identities are represented and projected as pure, exposure to difference threatens them with dilution and compromises their prized purities with the ever-present possibility of contamination. Crossing as mixture and movement must be guarded against. New hatreds and violence arise not, as they did in the past, from supposedly reliable anthropological knowledge of the identity and difference of the Other but from the novel problem of not being able to locate the Other's difference in the common-sense lexicon of alterity. Different people are certainly hated and feared, but the timely antipathy against them is nothing compared with the hatreds turned toward the greater menace of the half-different and the partially familiar. To have mixed is to have been party to a great betrayal. Any unsettling traces of hybridity must be excised from the tidy, bleached-out zones of impossibly pure culture. The safety of sameness can then be recovered by either of the two options that have regularly appeared at the meltdown point of this dismal logic: separation and slaughter.

IDENTITY, SOLIDARITY, AND SELFHOOD

The political language of identity levels out distinctions between chosen connections and given particularities: between the person you choose to be and the things that determine your individuality by being thrust upon you. It is particularly important for the argument that follows that the term "identity" has become a significant element in contemporary conflicts over cultural, ethnic, religious, "racial," and national differences. The idea of collective identity has emerged as an object of political thinking even if its appearance signals a sorry state of affairs in which the distinctive rules that define modern political culture are consciously set aside in favor of the pursuit of primordial feelings and mythic varieties of kinship that are mistakenly believed to be more profound. At the same time, individual identity, the counterpart to the collective, is constantly negotiated, cultivated, and protected as a source of pleasure, power, wealth, and potential danger. That identity is increasingly shaped in the marketplace, modified by the cultural industries, and managed and orchestrated in localized institutions and settings like schools, neighborhoods, and workplaces. It can be inscribed in the dull public world of official politics where issues surrounding the absence of collective identity—and the resulting disappearance of community and solidarity from social life—have also been discussed at great length by politicians on different sides of the political divide.

Other aspects of identity's foundational slipperiness can be detected in the way that the term is used to register the impact of processes that take place above and below the level at which the sovereign state and its distinctive modes of belonging are constituted. The growth of nationalisms and other absolutist religious and ethnic identities, the accentuation of regional and local divisions, and the changing relationship between supranational and subnational networks of economy, politics, and information have all endowed contemporary appeals to identity with extra significance. Identity has come to supply something of an anchor amid the turbulent waters of de-industrialization and the large-scale patterns of planetary reconstruction that are hesitantly named "globalization."[8] It would appear that recovering or possessing an appropriately grounded identity can provide a means to hold these historic but anxiety-inducing processes at bay. Taking pride or finding sanctuary in an exclusive identity affords a means to acquire certainty about who one is and where one fits, about the claims of community and the limits of social obligation.

The politicization of gender and sexuality has enhanced the understanding of identity by directing attention to the social, familial, historical, and cultural factors that bear upon the formation and social reproduction of masculinity and femininity. Two groups of agents are bound together by the centripetal force of the stable, gendered identities that they apparently hold in common. But the anxious, disciplinary intensity with which these ideas are entrenched seems to increase in inverse proportion to the collapse of family and household structures and the eclipse of male domestic domination. In these important areas, the concept of identity has nurtured new ways of thinking about the self, about sameness, and about solidarity. If abstract identity and its thematics are on the verge of becoming something of an obsessive preoccupation in the overdeveloped countries, this novel pattern communicates how political movements and governmental activities are being reconstituted by a change in the status and capacity of the nation-state.[9]

This transformation also reveals something important about the workings of consumer society.[10] The car you drive and the brand of clothing or sports shoes that you wear may no longer be thought of as accidental or contingent expressions of the arts of everyday life and the material constraints that stem from widening inequalities of status and wealth. Branded commodities acquire an additional burden when they are imagined to represent the private inner truths of individual existence or to fix the boundary of communal sensibilities that have faded from other areas of public or civic interaction. Though it involves some over-simplification, we can begin to unpack the idea of identity so that it reveals several overlapping and interconnected problems that are regularly entangled in the more routine contemporary uses of the term. The first, of these is the understanding of identity as subjectivity. Religious and spiritual obligations around selfhood were gradually assimilated into the secular, modern goal of an ordered self operating in an orderly polity.[11] This historic combination was supplemented by the idea that the stability and coherence of the self was a precondition for authoritative and reliable truth-seeking activity. That idea has itself been queried as truth has emerged as something provisional and perspectival that is seldom amenable to the application of place-less, universal laws. The forms of uncertainty that characterize our more skeptical time still emphasize the perils that flow from the lack of a particular variety of self-consciousness and self-cultivation.

When subjectivity is placed in command of its own mechanisms and desires, a heavy investment is made in the idea of identity and the languages of self through which it has been projected. The demise of the certainties associated with religious approaches to understanding oneself and locating oneself in a properly moral relationship to other selves endowed with the same ethical and cognitive attributes has had lasting consequences. The idea of a pre-given, internal identity that regulates social conduct beyond the grasp of conscious reflection has been valuable in restoring elements of increasingly rare and precious certainty to a situation in which doubt and anxiety have become routine. It has also been closely associated with the consolidation of a genomic raciology that promotes forms of resignation in which we are encouraged to do nothing while we wait for those decisive natural differences to announce their presence. These specifications are contradicted by the effects of technological acceleration arising from digital processing and computer-mediated communications. They mean that individual identity is even less constrained by the immediate forms of physical presence established by the body. The boundaries of self need no longer terminate at the threshold of the skin.[12]

The distance that an individual identity can travel toward others and, via technological instruments, become present to them has increased and the quality of that interaction has been transformed by a culture of simulation that has grown up around it. No longer finding uniformity and unanimity in symbols worn on or around the body, like the black shirt, the fascistic political identity cultivated by today's ultranationalist and white supremacist groups can be constituted remotely and transnationally over the Internet through computerized resources like the Aryan Crusader's Library, an on-line networking operation run from the United States but offered worldwide to anyone with a computer and a modem. Governments and corporations are promoting these technological resources as engines of modernized commerce and tools of democracy, but access to them is sharply skewed by poverty, inequality, and a variety of cultural and political factors.[13] That does not, however, mean that the cultural processes they animate and encourage remain confined to the privileged layers where they are most obviously apparent. They can be situated in their wider social setting:

> In the story of constructing identity in the culture of simulation, experiences on the Internet figure prominently, but these experiences can only be understood as part of a larger cultural context. That context is the story of eroding boundaries between the real and the virtual, the animate and the inanimate, the unitary and the multiple self, which is occurring both in advanced fields of scientific research and in the patterns of everyday life. From scientists trying to create artificial life, to children "morphing" through a series of virtual personae, we shall see evidence of fundamental shifts in the way we create and experience human identity.[14]

This uncertain, outward movement, from the anxious body-bound self toward the world, leads us to a second set of difficulties in the field of identity. This is the problem of sameness understood here as intersubjectivity. Considering identity from this angle requires recognition of the concept's role in calculations over precisely what counts as the same and what as different. This in turn raises the further question of recognition and its refusal in constituting identity and soliciting identification. The theme of identification and the consequent relationship between sociology, psychology, and even psychoanalysis enter here and add layers of complexity to deliberations about how selves—and their identities—are formed through relationships of exteriority, conflict, and exclusion. Differences can be found within identities as well as between them. The Other, against whose resistance the integrity of an identity is to be established, can be recognized as part of the self that is no longer plausibly understood as a unitary entity but appears instead as one fragile moment in the dialogic circuits that Debbora Battaglia has usefully called a "representational economy":

> ... there is no selfhood apart from the collaborative practice of its figuration. The "self" is a representational economy: a reification continually defeated by mutable entanglements

with other subjects' histories, experiences, self-representations; with their texts, conduct, gestures, objectifications.[15]

Building on this insight, the argument below takes shape around a third line of questioning: How does the concept of identity provide a means to speak about social and political solidarity? How is the term "identity" invoked in the summoning and binding of individual agents into groups that become social actors? For these purposes, considering identity requires a confrontation with the specific ideas of ethnic, racialized, and national identity and their civic counterparts. This departure introduces a cluster of distinctively modern notions that, in conjunction with discourses of citizenship, have actively produced rather than given a secondary expression to forms of solidarity with unprecedented power to mobilize mass movements and animate large-scale constituencies. The full power of communicative technologies like radio, sound recording, film, and television has been employed to create forms of solidarity and national consciousness that propelled the idea of belonging far beyond anything that had been achieved in the nineteenth century by the industrialization of print and the formalization of national languages.[16]

Contemporary conflicts over the status of national identity provide the best examples here. To return to the South African case for a moment, Nelson Mandela's historic inaugural speech as State President illustrated both the malleability of nationalist sentiment and some of the enduring tensions around its radical constitution. Working to produce an alternative content for the new nonracial, postracial, or perhaps antiracial political identity that might draw together the citizenry of the reborn country on a new basis beyond the grasp of racializing codes and fantasies of favored life as a people chosen by God, President Mandela turned to the land—common ground—beneath the feet of his diverse, unified, and mutually suspicious audience. Significantly, he spoke not only of the soil but of the beauty of the country and offered the idea of a common relationship to both the cultivated and the natural beauty of the land as elements of a new beginning. This, for him, was the key to awakening truly democratic consciousness. A transformed relationship between body and environment would transcend the irrelevancies of Apartheid South Africa's redundant racial hierarchies:

> To my compatriots, I have no hesitation in saying that each one of us is as intimately attached to the soil of this beautiful country as are the famous jacaranda trees of Pretoria and the mimosa trees of the bushveld.
>
> Each time one of us touches the soil of this land, we feel a sense of personal renewal.... That spiritual and physical oneness we all share with this common homeland explains the depth of pain we all carried in our hearts as we saw our country tear itself apart in a terrible conflict.[17]

Whether these laudable claims were a plausible part of rebuilding South African nationality remains to be seen. What is more significant for our purposes is that territory and indeed nature itself are being engaged as a means to define citizenship and the forms of rootedness that compose national solidarity and cohesion. President Mandela's words were powerful because they work with the organicity that nature has bequeathed to modern ideas of culture. In that blur, Mandela constructed an ecological account of the relationship between shared humanity, common citizenship, place, and identity. The speech subverted traditional assumptions with its implication that Apartheid was a brutal violation of nature that could be repaired only if people were prepared to pay heed to the oneness established by their connection to the beautiful environment they share and hold in common stewardship.

The alternative argument set out below recognizes the socioecological dynamics of identity-formation. However, it asks you to consider what might be gained if the powerful claims of soil, roots, and territory could be set aside. You are invited to view them in the light of other possibilities that have sometimes defined themselves against the forms of solidarity sanctioned by the territorial regimes of the nation-state. We will see that the idea of movement can provide an alternative to the sedentary poetics of either soil or blood. Both communicative technology and older patterns of itinerancy ignored by the human sciences can be used to articulate placeless imaginings of identity as well as new bases for solidarity and synchronized action. With these possibilities in mind, I want to suggest that considering the de-territorialized history of the modern African diaspora into the western hemisphere and the racial slavery through which it was accomplished has something useful to teach us about the workings of identity and identification and, beyond that, something valuable to impart about the claims of nationality and the nation-state upon the writing of history itself.

Shut out from literacy on the pain of death, slaves taken from Africa by force used the same biblical narratives we have already encountered to comprehend their situation and, slowly and at great emotional cost, to build what might be understood as a new set of identities. They, too, imagined themselves to be a divinely chosen people. This meant that the suffering visited upon their proto-nations in bondage was purposive and their pain was oriented, not merely toward heavenly freedom, but toward the moral redemption of anyone prepared to join them in the just cause of seeking political liberty and individual autonomy. These themes are nowhere more powerfully articulated than in the work of Martin Luther King, Jr. Writing amid the conflicts of the 1960s that would eventually claim his life, about the difficulties experienced by black Americans whose allegiance to America was broken by their lack of political rights and economic opportunities, he had the following to say about what we would now recognize as identity. (He, too, mobilized the biblical mythology of the chosen people to articulate his political choices and hopes):

> Something of the spirit of our slave forebears must be pursued today. From the inner depths of our being we must sing with them: "Before I'll be a slave, I'll be buried in my grave and go home to my Lord and be free." This spirit, this drive, this rugged sense of somebodyness is the first and vital step that the Negro must take in dealing with his dilemma.... To overcome this tragic conflict, it will be necessary for the Negro to find a new self-image.... The Pharaohs had a favorite and effective strategy to keep their slaves in bondage: keep them fighting among themselves.... But when slaves unite, the Red Seas of history open and the Egypts of slavery crumble.[18]

We must be cautious because there are now considerable political gains to be made from being recognized as possessing an identity defined exclusively by this and other histories of ineffable suffering. Dr. King did not exploit that association, but those who followed in his wake have not always been so scrupulous. The identity of the victim, sealed off and presented as an essential, unchanging state, has become, in the years since his murder, a prized acquisition not least where financial calculations have sought to transform historic wrongs into compensatory monies.[19] This problem has not been confined to black politics with its demands for reparations and other forms of financial restitution for slavery in the Americas. From Palestine to Bosnia, the image of the victim has become useful in all sorts of dubious maneuverings that can obscure the moral and political questions arising from demands for justice. And yet, for all its pragmatic or strategic attractions, the role of the victim has its drawbacks as the basis of any political identity. With characteristic insight, James Baldwin described some of them in a discussion of the meaning of racial terror and its impact upon identity:

> I refuse, absolutely, to speak from the point of view of the victim. The victim can have no point of view for precisely so long as he thinks of himself as a victim. The testimony of the victim as victim corroborates, simply, the reality of the chains that bind him—confirms, and, as it were consoles the jailer.[20]

Baldwin cautions us against closing the gap between identity and politics and playing down the complexities of their interconnection. His words locate the trap involved in hoping that what is lazily imagined to be shared identity might be straightforwardly transferred into the political arena. With his help we can apprehend the many dangers involved in vacuous "me too-ism" or some other equally pointless and immoral competition over which peoples, nations, populations, or ethnic groups have suffered the most; over whose identities have been most severely damaged; and indeed over who might be thought of as the most deracinated, nomadic, or cosmopolitan and therefore more essentially "modern" or paradigmatically "postmodern" peoples on our planet. However, with Baldwin's warning still in mind, there is much to be learned by foregrounding that experience of being victimized and using it to challenge the willful innocence of some Europe-centered accounts of modernity's pleasures and problems. That difficult operation yields more than a coda to the conventional historical and sociological stories of modern development. Perhaps a changed sense of what it means to be a modern person might result from this reassessment?

The careful reconstruction of those half-hidden, tragic narratives that demonstrate how the fateful belief in mutually impermeable, religious, racial, national, and ethnic identities was assembled and reproduced was briefly addressed in the previous chapter. It fits in well with the archaeological work already being done to account for the complex cultures and societies of the New World and their relationship to the history of European thought, literature, and self-understanding.[21] The significance of colony and empire is also being reevaluated and the boundaries around European nation-states are emerging as more porous and leakier than some architects of complacently national history would want to admit. These discoveries support the demand for a decisive change of standpoint. Again it seems that to comprehend the bleak histories of colonial and imperial power that besmirch the clean edifice of innocent modernity and query the heroic story of universal reason's triumphal march, we must shift away from the historiographical scale defined by the closed borders of the nation-state. If we are prepared to possess those histories and consider setting them to work in divining more modest and more plausible understandings of democracy, tolerance for difference, and cross-cultural recognition than currently exist, this historical argument can redirect attention toward some of the more general contemporary questions involved in thinking about identity in the human sciences. Histories of the violence and terror with which modern rationality has been complicit offer a useful means to test and qualify the explanatory power of theories of identity and culture that have arisen in quieter, less bloody circumstances. Perhaps those theories also derive from the more complacent scholarly ways of thinking about power common to temperate climes. The idea that possessing a particular identity should be a precondition or qualification for engaging in this kind of work is trivial. The intellectual challenge defined here is that histories of suffering should not be allocated exclusively to their victims. If they were, the memory of the trauma would disappear as the living memory of it died away.

This proposed change of perspective about the value of suffering is not then exclusively of interest to its victims and any kin who remember them. Because it is a matter of justice, it is not just an issue for the wronged "minorities" whose own lost or fading identities may be restored or rescued by the practice of commemoration. It is also of concern to those who may have benefited directly and indirectly from the rational application of irrationality and barbarity. Perhaps above all, this attempt to reconceptualize modernity so that it encompasses these possibilities is relevant to the majority who are unlikely to count themselves as affiliated with either of the principal groups: victims and perpetrators. This difficult stance challenges that unnamed group to witness sufferings that pass beyond the reach of words and, in so doing, to see how an understanding of one's own particularity or identity might be transformed as a result of a principled exposure to the claims of otherness.[22] [...]

DIASPORA AS A SOCIAL ECOLOGY OF IDENTIFICATION

The idea of diaspora offers a ready alternative to the stern discipline of primordial kinship and rooted belonging. It rejects the popular image of natural nations spontaneously endowed with self-consciousness, tidily composed of uniform families: those interchangeable collections of ordered bodies that express and reproduce absolutely distinctive cultures as well as perfectly formed heterosexual pairings. As an alternative to the metaphysics of "race," nation, and bounded culture coded into the body, diaspora is a concept that problematizes the cultural and historical mechanics of belonging. It disrupts the fundamental power of territory to determine identity by breaking the simple sequence of explanatory links between place, location, and consciousness. It destroys the naive invocation of common memory as the basis of particularity in a similar fashion by drawing attention to the contingent political dynamics of commemoration.

The ancient word diaspora acquired a modern accent as a result of its unanticipated usefulness to the nationalisms and subaltern imperialisms of the late nineteenth century. It remains an enduring feature of the continuing aftershocks generated by those political projects in Palestine and elsewhere. If it can be stripped of its disciplinarian associations it might offer seeds capable of bearing fruit in struggles to comprehend the sociality of a new phase in which displacement, flight, exile, and forced migration are likely to be familiar and recurrent phenomena that transform the terms in which identity needs to be understood. Retreating from the totalizing immodesty and ambition of the word "global," diaspora is an outer-national term which contributes to the analysis of intercultural and transcultural processes and forms. It identifies a relational network, characteristically produced by forced dispersal and reluctant scattering. It is not just a word of movement, though purposive, desperate movement is integral to it. Under this sign, push factors are a dominant influence. The urgency they introduce makes diaspora more than a voguish synonym for peregrination or nomadism. As the biographies of Equiano and Wheatley suggest, life itself is at stake in the way the word connotes flight following the threat of violence rather than freely chosen experiences of displacement. Slavery, pogroms, indenture, genocide, and other unnameable terrors have all figured in the constitution of diasporas and the reproduction of diaspora consciousness in which identity is focused, less on the equalizing, pre-democratic force of sovereign territory and more on the social dynamics of remembrance and commemoration defined by a strong sense of the dangers involved in forgetting the location of origin and the tearful process of dispersal.

The term opens up a historical and experiential rift between the locations of residence and the locations of belonging. This in turn sets up a further opposition. Consciousness of diaspora affiliation stands opposed to the distinctively modern structures and modes of power orchestrated by the institutional complexity of nation-states. Diaspora identification exists outside of and sometimes in opposition to the political forms and codes of modern citizenship. The nation-state has regularly been presented as the institutional means to terminate diaspora dispersal. At one end of the communicative circuit this is to be accomplished by the assimilation of those who were out of place. At the other a similar outcome is realized through the prospect of their return to a place of origin. The fundamental equilibrium of nature and civil society can thus be restored. In both options it is the nation-state that brings the spatial and temporal order of diaspora life to an abrupt end. Diaspora yearning and ambivalence are transformed into a simple unambiguous exile once the possibility of easy reconciliation with either the place of sojourn or the place of origin exists. Some, though not all, versions of diaspora consciousness accentuate the possibility and desirability of return. They may or may not recognize the difficulty of this gesture. The degree to which return is accessible or desired provides a valuable comparative moment in the typology and classification of diaspora histories and political movements.

"Diaspora" lacks the modernist and cosmopolitan associations of the word "exile" from which it has been carefully distinguished, particularly in the Jewish histories with which the term is most deeply intertwined.[23] We should be careful that the term "history" retains its plural status at this point because diaspora has had a variety of different resonances in Jewish cultures inside and outside of Europe, both before and after the founding of the state of Israel.

Equiano's sense of an affinity between blacks and Jews stands behind the work of many modern black thinkers of the western hemisphere who were eager to adapt the diaspora idea to their particular post-slave circumstances. Many of them developed conceptual schemes and political programs for diaspora affiliation (and its negation) long before they found a proper name for the special emotional and political logics that governed these operations. The work of Edward Wilmot Blyden in the late nineteenth century represents another important site of similar intercultural transfer. Blyden was a "returnee" to Africa from the Danish West Indies via the United States. He presented his own redemptive involvement with the free nation-state of Liberia and its educational apparatuses, along lines suggested by an interpretation of Jewish history and culture forged through a close personal and intellectual relationship with Jews and Judaism. In 1898, awed by what he described as "that marvelous movement called Zionism," he attempted to draw the attention of "thinking and enlightened Jews to the great continent of Africa—not to its northern and southern extremities only, but to its vast intertropical area" on the grounds that they would find there "religious and spiritual aspirations kindred to their own."[24]

Earlier on, in assessing the power of roots and rootedness to ground identity, we encountered invocations of organicity that forged an uncomfortable connection between the warring domains of nature and culture. They made nation and citizenship appear to be natural rather than social phenomena—spontaneous expressions of a distinctiveness that was palpable in deep inner harmony between people and their dwelling places. Diaspora is a useful means to reassess the idea of essential and absolute identity precisely because it is incompatible with that type of nationalist and raciological thinking. The word comes closely associated with the idea of sowing seed. This etymological inheritance is a disputed legacy and a mixed blessing. It demands that we attempt to evaluate the significance of the scattering process against the supposed uniformity of that which has been scattered. Diaspora posits important tensions between here and there, then and now, between seed in the bag, the packet, or the pocket and seed in the ground, the fruit, or the body. By focusing attention equally on the sameness within differentiation and the differentiation within sameness, diaspora disturbs the suggestion that political and cultural identity might be understood via the analogy of indistinguishable peas lodged in the protective pods of closed kinship and subspecies being. Is it possible to imagine how a more complex, ecologically sophisticated sense of interaction between organisms and environments might become an asset in thinking critically about identity?

Imagine a scenario in which similar—though not precisely identical—seeds take root in different places. Plants of the same species are seldom absolutely indistinguishable. Nature does not always produce interchangeable clones. Soils, nutrients, predators, pests, and pollination vary along with unpredictable weather. Seasons change. So do climates, which can be determined on a variety of scales: micro as well as macro and mezzo. Diaspora provides valuable cues and clues for the elaboration of a social ecology of cultural identity and identification that takes us far beyond the stark dualism of genealogy and geography. The pressure to associate, like the desires to remember or forget, may vary with changes in the economic and political atmosphere. Unlike the tides, the weather cannot be predicted accurately. To cap it all, the work involved in discovering origins is more difficult in some places and at some times.

If we can adopt this more difficult analytical stance, the celebrated "butterfly effect" in which tiny, almost insignificant forces can, in defiance of conventional expectations, precipitate unpredictable, larger changes in other locations becomes a commonplace happening. The seamless propagation of cultural habits and styles was rendered radically contingent at the point where geography and genealogy began to trouble each other. We are directed toward the conflictual limits of "race," ethnicity, and culture. When a diaspora talks back to a nation-state, it initiates conflict between those who agree that they are more or less what they were, but cannot agree whether the more or the less should take precedence in contemporary political and historical calculations.

The reproductive moment of diaspora raises other uncomfortable issues. In a discussion of some recent approaches to the diaspora idea and its relationship to masculinism,[25] Stefan Helmreich has identified the processes of cultural reproduction and transmission to which diaspora draws attention as being radically gender-specific. He underlines the close etymological relationship between the word diaspora and the word sperm as if their common tie to the Greek word meaning sow and scatter still corrupts the contemporary application of the concept as it were, from within. This argument can be tested and contextualized by the introduction of another family term, the word spore: the unicellular vector for supposedly "asexual" reproduction.[26] Could that alternative, gender-free linkage complicate the notion that diaspora is inscribed as a masculinist trope and cannot therefore be liberated from the quagmire of androcentrism, where it has been lodged by modern nationalisms and the religious conceptions of ethnic particularity that cheerfully coexist with them? Though still contested, diaspora lends itself to the critique of absolutist political sensibilities, especially those that have been articulated around the themes of nation, "race," and ethnicity. It seems unduly harsh to suggest that it is any more deeply contaminated by the toxins of male domination than other heuristic terms in the emergent vocabulary of transcultural critical theory. There is no reason descent through the male line should be privileged over dissent via the rhizomorphic principle.[27] Diaspora can be used to conjure up both.

Where separation, time, and distance from the point of origin or the center of sovereignly complicate the symbolism of ethnic and national reproduction, anxieties over the boundaries and limits of sameness may lead people to seek security in the sanctity of embodied difference. The new racisms that code biology in cultural terms have been alloyed with still newer variants that conscript the body into disciplinary service and encode cultural particularity in an understanding of bodily practices and attributes determined by genes. Gender differences become extremely important in nation-building activity because they are a sign of an irresistible natural hierarchy that belongs at the center of civic life. The unholy forces of nationalist biopolitics intersect on the bodies of women charged with the reproduction of absolute ethnic difference and the continuance of blood lines. The integrity of the nation becomes the integrity of its masculinity. In fact, it can be a nation only if the correct version of gender hierarchy has been established and reproduced. The family is the main device in this operation. It connects men and women, boys and girls to the larger collectivity toward which they must orient themselves if they are to acquire a Fatherland. Minister Louis Farrakhan of the Nation of Islam typified the enduring power of this variety of thinking about nation and gender in his description of the 1995 march of African-American men to Washington. He saw that event as an act of warfare in which the condition of their alternative national manhood could be gauged:

> No nation gets any respect if you go out to war and you put your women in the trenches and the men stay at home cooking. Every nation that goes to war tests the fiber of the manhood of that nation. And literally, going to Washington to seek justice for our people is like going to war.[28]

If the modern nation is to be prepared for war, reproducing the soldier citizens of the future is not a process it can leave to chance or whim. Again, the favored institutional setting for this disciplinary and managerial activity is the family. The family is understood as nothing more than the essential building block in the construction and elevation of the nation. This nation-building narrative runs all the way to fascism and its distinctive myths of rebirth after periods of weakness and decadence.[29] Diaspora challenges it by valorizing sub- and supranational kinship and allowing for a more ambivalent relationship toward national encampments.

These non-national proclivities have triggered other de-stabilizing and subversive effects. They are amplified when the concept of diaspora is annexed for anti-essentialist accounts of identity-formation as a process and used to host a decisive change of orientation away from the primordial identities established alternatively by either nature or culture. By embracing diaspora, theories of identity turn instead toward contingency, indeterminacy, and conflict. With the idea of valuing diaspora more highly than the coercive unanimity of the nation, the concept becomes explicitly antinational. This shift is connected with transforming the familiar unidirectional idea of diaspora as a form of catastrophic but simple dispersal that enjoys an identifiable and reversible originary moment—the site of trauma—into something far more complex. Diaspora can be used to instantiate a "chaotic" model in which shifting "strange attractors" are the only visible points of fragile stability amid social and cultural turbulence.

The importance of these nodes is misunderstood if they are identified as fixed local phenomena. They appear unexpectedly, and where diaspora becomes a concept, the web or network they allow us to perceive can mark out new understandings of self, sameness, and solidarity. However, they are not successive stages in a genealogical account of kin relations—equivalent to branches on a single family tree. One does not beget the next in a comforting sequence of ethnic teleology; nor are they stations on a linear journey toward the destination that a completed identity might represent. They suggest a different mode of linkage between the forms of micropolitical agency exercised in cultures and movements of resistance and transformation and other political processes that are visible on a different, bigger scale. Their plurality and regionality valorize something more than a protracted condition of social mourning over the ruptures of exile, loss, brutality, stress, and forced separation. They highlight a more indeterminate and, some would say, modernist mood in which natal alienation and cultural estrangement are capable of conferring insight and creating pleasure, as well as precipitating anxiety about the coherence of the nation and the stability of its imaginary ethnic core. Contrasting forms of political action have emerged to create new possibilities and new pleasures where dispersed people recognize the effects of spatial dislocation as rendering the issue of origin problematic. They may grow to accept the possibility that they are no longer what they once were and cannot therefore rewind the tapes of their cultural history. The diaspora idea encourages critical theory to proceed rigorously but cautiously in ways that do not privilege the modern nation-state and its institutional order over the subnational and supranational patterns of power, communication, and conflict that they work to discipline, regulate, and govern. The concept of space is itself transformed when it is seen in terms of the ex-centric communicative circuitry that has enabled dispersed populations to converse, interact, and more recently even to synchronize significant elements of their social and cultural lives.

What the African-American writer Leroi Jones once named "the changing same"[30] provides a valuable motif with which to fix this supplement to the diaspora idea. Neither the mechanistic essentialism that is too squeamish to acknowledge the possibility of difference within sameness nor the lazy alternative that animates the supposedly strategic variety of essentialism can supply keys to the untidy workings of diaspora identities. They are creolized, syncretized, hybridized, and chronically impure cultural forms, particularly if they were once rooted in the complicity of rationalized terror and racialized reason. This changing same is not some invariant essence that gets enclosed subsequently in a shape-shifting exterior with which it is casually associated. It is not the sign of an unbroken, integral inside protected by a camouflaged husk. The phrase names the problem of diaspora politics and diaspora poetics. The same is present, but how can we imagine it as something other than an essence generating the merely accidental? Iteration is the key to this process. The same is retained without needing to be reified. It is ceaselessly reprocessed. It is maintained and modified in what becomes a determinedly nontraditional tradition, for this is not tradition as closed or simple repetition. Invariably promiscuous, diaspora and the politics of commemoration it specifies challenge us to apprehend mutable forms that can redefine the idea of culture through a reconciliation with movement and complex, dynamic variation.

Today's affiliates to the tradition for which Equiano and Wheatley operate as imaginary ancestors find themselves in a very different economic, cultural, and political circuitry—a different diaspora—from the one their predecessors encountered. Live human beings are no longer a commodity, and the dispersal of blacks has extended further and deeper into Europe, where elements of the scattering process have been repeated once again by the arrival of Caribbean peoples and other formerly colonial folk in the post-1945 period. Several generations of blacks have been born in Europe whose identification with the African continent is even more attenuated and remote, particularly since the anticolonial wars are over. Both the memory of slavery and an orientation toward identity that derives from African origins are hard to maintain when the rupture of migration intervenes and stages its own trials of belonging. However, the notion of a distinctive, African-derived identity has not withered and the moral and political fruits of black life in the western hemisphere have been opened out systematically to larger and larger numbers of people in different areas.

The black musicians, dancers, and performers of the New World have disseminated these insights, styles, and pleasures through the institutional resources of the cultural industries that they have colonized and captured. These media, particularly recorded sound, have been annexed for sometimes subversive purposes of protest and affirmation. The vernacular codes and expressive cultures constituted from the forced new beginning of racial slavery have reappeared at the center of a global phenomenon that has regularly surpassed—just as Wheatley's complex poetry did long ago—innocent notions of mere entertainment. What are wrongly believed to be simple cultural commodities have been used to communicate a powerful ethical and political commentary on rights, justice, and democracy that articulates but also transcends criticism of modern racial typology and the ideologies of white supremacy. The living history of New World blacks has endowed this expressive tradition with flexibility and durability.

Bob Marley, whose recordings are still selling all over the world more than a decade after his death, provides a useful concluding example here. His enduring presence in globalized popular culture is an important reminder of the power of the technologies that ground the culture of simulation. Those same technological resources have subdued the constraints of nature and provided Marley with a virtual life after death in which his popularity can continue to grow unencumbered by any embarrassing political residues that might make him into a threatening or frightening figure. But there is more to this worldwide popularity than clever video-based immortality and the evident reconstruction of Bob Marley's image, stripped of much of its militant Ethiopianism—yet another chosen people and another promised land to set alongside those we have already considered.

Bob's life and work lend themselves to the study of postmodern diaspora identity. They help us to perceive the workings of those complex cultural circuits that have transformed a pattern of simple, one-way dispersal into a webbed network constituted through multiple points of intersection. His historic performance at the Zimbabwe independence ceremony in 1980 symbolized the partial reconnection with African origins that permeates diaspora yearning. Like so many others, he too did not go to Africa to make his home. He chose instead, as many other prominent pan-Africanists had done before and since, a more difficult cosmopolitan commitment and a different form of solidarity and identification that did not require his physical presence in that continent.

His triumph not only marks the beginning of what has come to be known as "world music" or "world beat," an increasingly significant marketing category that helps to locate the transformation and possible demise of music-led youth-culture. It was built from the seemingly universal power of a poetic and political language that reached out from its roots to find new audiences hungry for its insights. Bob became, in effect, a planetary figure. His music was pirated in Eastern Europe and became intertwined with the longing for freedom and rights across Africa, the Pacific, and Latin America. Captured into commodities, his music traveled and found new audiences and so did his band. Between 1976 and 1980 they crisscrossed the planet, performing in the United States, Canada, the United Kingdom, France, Italy, Germany, Spain, Scandinavia, Ireland, Holland, Belgium, Switzerland, Japan, Australia, New Zealand, the Ivory Coast, and Gabon. Major sales were also recorded in market areas where the band did not perform, particularly Brazil, Senegal, Ghana, Nigeria, Taiwan, and the Philippines.

Marley's global stature was founded on the hard, demanding labor of transcontinental touring as much as on the poetic qualities he invested in the language of sufferation that he made universal. In conclusion, his transnational image invites one further round of speculation about the status of identity and the conflicting scales on which sameness, subjectivity, and solidarity can be imagined. Connecting with him across the webs of planetary popular culture might be thought of as an additional stage in the nonprogressive evolution of diaspora into the digital era. Recognizing this requires moving the focus of inquiry away from the notions of fixed identity that we have already discovered to be worn out and placing it instead upon the processes of identification. Do people connect themselves and their hopes with the figure of Bob Marley as a man, a Jamaican, a Caribbean, an African, or a Pan-African artist? Is he somehow all of the above and more, a rebel voice of the poor and the underdeveloped world that made itself audible in the core of overdeveloped social and economic life he called Babylon? On what scale of cultural analysis do we make sense of this reconciliation of modern and postmodern technologies with mystical antimodern forces? How do we combine his work as an intellectual, as a thinker, with his portrayal as a primitive, hypermasculine figure: a not-so-noble savage shrouded in ganga smoke? Are we prepared now, so many years after his death and mythification, to set aside the new forms of minstrelsy obviously promoted under the constellation of his stardom and see him as a worldly figure whose career traversed continents and whose revolutionary political stance won adherents because of its ability to imagine the end of capitalism as readily as it imagined the end of the world?

In Bob Marley's image there is something more than domestication of the other and the accommodation of insubordinate Third Worldism within corporate multiculturalism. Something remains even when we dismiss the presentation of difference as a spectacle and a powerful marketing device in the global business of selling records, tapes, CDs, videos, and associated merchandise. However great Bob's skills, the formal innovations in his music must take second place behind its significance as the site of a revolution in the structure of the global markets for these cultural commodities. The glamour of the primitive was set to work to animate his image and increase the power of his music to seduce. That modern magic required Bob to be purified, simplified, nationalized, and particularized. An aura of authenticity was manufactured not to validate his political aspirations or rebel status but to invest his music with a mood of carefully calculated transgression that still makes it saleable and appealing all over the planet. Otherness was invoked and operates to make the gulf between his memory and his remote "crossover" audiences bigger, to manage that experiential gap so that their pleasures in consuming him and his work are somehow enhanced.

It is only recently that the long-ignored figure of Bob's white father has been brought forward and offered as the key to interpreting his son's achievements and comprehending the pathological motivation to succeed that took him out of Trenchtown. In that sense, the phase in which Bob was represented as exotic and dangerous is over. We can observe a prodigal, benign, almost childlike Bob Marley being brought home into the bosom of his corporate family. All this can be recognized. But the stubborn utopia projected through Bob Marley's music and anticolonial imaginings remains something that is not de-limited by a proscriptive ethnic wrapper or racial "health-warning" in which encounters with otherness are presented as dangerous to the well-being of one's own singular identity. Music and instrumental competence have to be learned and practiced before they can be made to communicate convincingly. This should restrict their role as signs of authentic, absolute particularity. Perhaps, in the tainted but nonetheless powerful image of Bob Marley's global stardom, we can discern the power of identity based, not on some cheap, pre-given sameness, but on will, inclination, mood, and affinity. The translocal power of his dissident voice summons up these possibilities and a chosen, recognizably political kinship that is all the more valuable for its distance from the disabling assumptions of automatic solidarity based on either blood or land.

NOTES

1. Mark Leonard, *Britain™* (Demos, 1997).
2. Judith Butler, "Collected and Fractured," in *Identities*, ed. Kwame Anthony Appiah and Henry Louis Gates, Jr. (University of Chicago Press, 1995).
3. J.-J. Rousseau, "Considerations on the Government of Poland," in *Rousseau Political Writings*, trans. and ed. Frederick Watkins (Nelson and Sons, 1953), pp. 163–164.
4. *The Blackshirt* (November 24–30,1933), p. 5; quoted in John Harvey, *Men in Black* (Chicago University Press, 1995), p. 242.
5. Leonard Thompson, *The Political Mythology of Apartheid* (Yale University Press, 1985), p. 39.
6. African Rights, *Rwanda Death, Despair and Defiance* (London, 1994), pp. 347–354. See also Sander L. Gilman, *The Jew's Body* (Routledge, 1991), especially chap. 7, "The Jewish Nose: Are Jews White? Or, The History of the Nose Job."
7. Arthur Malu-Malu and Thierry Oberle, *Sunday Times*, August 30, 1998.
8. William Greider, *One World, Ready or Not: The Manic Logic of Global Capitalism* (Simon and Schuster, 1997); Jerry Mander and Edward Goldsmith, eds., *The Case against the Global Economy and for a Turn toward the Local* (Sierra Books, 1996); Benjamin R. Barber, *Jihad vs. McWorld: How the Planet Is Both Falling Apart and Coming Together and What This Means for Democracy* (Random House, 1995).
9. Jean-Marie Guéhenno, *The End of the Nation State* (University of Minnesota Press, 1995).
10. Zygmunt Bauman, *Freedom* (Open University Press, 1988).
11. Charles Taylor, *Sources of the Self* (Harvard University Press, 1989); William Connolly, *Identity/Difference* (Cornell University Press, 1991).
12. Chris Hables Gray, ed., *The Cyborg Handbook* (Routledge, 1995).
13. Amy Harmon, "Racial Divide Found on Information Highway," *New York Times*, April 10, 1998.
14. Sherry Turkle, *Life on the Screen: Identity in the Age of the Internet* (Simon and Schuster, 1995), p. 10.
15. Debbora Battaglia, "Problematizing the Self: A Thematic Introduction," in D. Battaglia, ed., *Rhetorics of Self-Making* (University of California Press, 1995), p. 2.

16. Benedict Anderson, *Imagined Communities: Reflections on the Origin and Spread of Nationalism* (Verso, 1982).

17. President Mandela's inaugugural speech was reprinted in *The Independent*, May 11, 1995, p. 12.

18. Martin Luther King, Jr., *Where Do We Go From Here: Chaos or Community?* (Harper and Row, 1967), p. 124

19. Donald G. McNeil, Jr., "Africans Seek Redress for German Genocide," *New York Times*, June 1, 1998.

20. James Bladwin, *Evidence of Things Not Seen* (Henry Holt and Co., 1985), p. 78.

21. Peter Hulme, *Colonial Encounters* (Metheun, 1986); Anthony Pagden, *European Encounters in the New World: From Renaissance to Romanticism* (Yale, 1993); Richard Taylor, *Sex and Conquest* (Cornell University Press, 1995).

22. Charles Taylor, "Understanding and Ethnocentricity," in *Philosophy and the Human Sciences, Philosophical Papers 2* (Cambridge University Press, 1985).

23. Elliott P. Skinner, "The Dialectic between Diasporas and Homelands," in Joseph E. Harris, ed., *Global Dimensions of the African Diaspora* (Howard University Press, 1982).

24. Edward Wilmot Blyden, *On the Jewish Question* (Lionel Hart and Co., 1898), p. 23.

25. Stefan Helmreich, "Kinship, Nation, and Paul Gilroy's Concept of Diaspora," *Diaspora* 2, 2 (1993), pp. 243–249.

26. Londa Scheibinger, *Nature's Body* (Beacon Press, 1993).

27. "To be rhizomorphous is to produce stems and filaments that seem to be roots, or better yet connect with them by penetrating the trunk, but put them to new uses. We're tired of trees. We should stop believing in trees, roots and radicles. They've made us suffer too much. All of arborescent culture is founded on them, from biology to linguistics." Gilles Deleuze and Felix Guattari, "Rhizome," in *A Thousand Plateaus* (University of Minnesota Press, 1988), p. 15.

28. Louis Farrakhan, "A Call to March," *Emerge*, vol. 7, no. 1 (October 1995), p. 66.

29. Roger Griffin, *The Nature of Fascism* (Routledge, 1993).

30. Leroi Jones, *Black Music* (Quill, 1967), pp. 180–211.

Chapter 40

How Jews Became White Folks and What That Says about Race in America

Karen Brodkin

In writing "How Jews Became White Folks," Karen Brodkin (1998) explains how over time the social construction of Jews in American society shifts to make them acceptable to that society. As Brodkin writes, "I want to suggest that Jewish success is a product not only of ability but also of the removal of powerful social barriers to its realization." Accordingly, she shows how the "institutional nature of racism and the centrality of state policies" operate to create and change races and the social construction of racial groups.

> *The American nation was founded and developed by the Nordic race, but if a few more million members of the Alpine, Mediterranean and Semitic races are poured among us, the result must inevitably be a hybrid race of people as worthless and futile as the good-for-nothing mongrels of Central America and Southeastern Europe.*
> —Kenneth Roberts, "Why Europe Leaves Home"

It is clear that Kenneth Roberts did not think of my ancestors as white, like him. The late nineteenth century and early decades of the twentieth saw a steady stream of warnings by scientists, policymakers, and the popular press that "mongrelization" of the Nordic or Anglo-Saxon race—the real Americans—by inferior European races (as well as by inferior non-European ones) was destroying the fabric of the nation.

I continue to be surprised when I read books that indicate that America once regarded its immigrant European workers as something other than white, as biologically different.

My parents are not surprised; they expect anti-Semitism to be part of the fabric of daily life, much as I expect racism to be part of it. They came of age in the Jewish world of the 1920s and 1930s, at the peak of anti-Semitism in America.[1] They are rightly proud of their upward mobility and think of themselves as pulling themselves up by their own bootstraps. I grew up during the 1950s in the Euro-ethnic New York suburb of Valley Stream, where Jews were simply one kind of white folks and where ethnicity meant little more to my generation than food and family heritage. Part of my ethnic heritage was the belief that Jews were smart and that our success was due to our own efforts and abilities, reinforced by a culture that valued sticking together, hard work, education, and deferred gratification.

I am willing to affirm all those abilities and ideals and their contribution to Jews' upward mobility, but I also argue that they were still far from sufficient to account for Jewish success. I say this because the belief in a Jewish version of Horatio Alger has become a point of entry for some mainstream Jewish organizations to adopt a racist attitude against African Americans especially and to oppose affirmative action for people of color.[2] Instead I want to suggest that Jewish success is a product not only of ability but also of the removal of powerful social barriers to its realization.

It is certainly true that the United States has a history of anti-Semitism and of beliefs that Jews are members of an inferior race. But Jews were hardly alone. American anti-Semitism was part of a broader pattern of late-nineteenth-century racism against all southern and eastern European immigrants, as well as against Asian immigrants, not to mention African Americans, Native Americans, and Mexicans. These views justified all sorts of discriminatory treatment, including closing the doors, between 1882 and 1927, to immigration from Europe and Asia. This picture changed radically after World War II. Suddenly, the same folks who had promoted nativism and xenophobia were eager to believe that the Euro-origin people whom they had deported, reviled as members of inferior races, and prevented from immigrating only a few years earlier, were now model middle-class white suburban citizens.[3]

It was not an educational epiphany that made those in power change their hearts, their minds, and our race. Instead, it was the biggest and best affirmative action program in the history of our nation, and it was for Euromales. That is not how it was billed, but it is the way it worked out in practice. I tell this story to show the institutional nature of racism and the centrality of state policies to creating and changing races. Here, those policies reconfigured the category of whiteness to include European immigrants. There are similarities and differences in the ways each of the European immigrant groups became "whitened." I tell the story in a way that links anti-Semitism to other varieties of anti-European racism because this highlights what Jews shared with other Euro-immigrants.

EURORACES

The US "discovery" that Europe was divided into inferior and superior races began with the racialization of the Irish in the mid-nineteenth century and flowered in response to the great waves of immigration from southern and eastern Europe that began in the late nineteenth century. Before that time, European immigrants—including Jews—had been largely assimilated into the white population. However, the 23 million European immigrants who came to work in US cities in the waves of migration after 1880 were too many and too concentrated to absorb. Since immigrants and their children made up more than 70 percent of the population of most of the country's largest cities, by the 1890s urban America had taken on a distinctly southern and eastern European immigrant flavor. Like the Irish in Boston and New York, their urban concentrations in dilapidated neighborhoods put them cheek by jowl next to the rising elites and the middle class with whom they shared public space and to whom their working-class ethnic communities were particularly visible.

The Red Scare of 1919 clearly linked anti-immigrant with anti-working-class sentiment—to the extent that the Seattle general strike by largely native-born workers was blamed on foreign agitators. The Red Scare was fueled by an economic depression, a massive postwar wave of strikes, the Russian Revolution, and another influx of postwar immigration. [...]

Not surprisingly, the belief in European races took root most deeply among the wealthy, US-born Protestant elite, who feared a hostile and seemingly inassimilable working class. By the end of the nineteenth century, Senator Henry Cabot Lodge pressed Congress to cut off immigration to the United States; Theodore Roosevelt raised the alarm of "race suicide" and took Anglo-Saxon women to task for allowing "native" stock to be outbred by inferior immigrants. In the early twentieth century, these fears gained a great deal of social legitimacy thanks to the efforts of an influential network of aristocrats and scientists who developed theories of eugenics—breeding for a "better" humanity—and scientific racism.

Key to these efforts was Madison Grant's influential *The Passing of the Great Race*, published in 1916. Grant popularized notions developed by William Z. Ripley and Daniel Brinton that there existed three or four major European races, ranging from the superior Nordics of northwestern Europe to the inferior southern and eastern races of the Alpines, Mediterraneans, and worst of all, Jews, who seemed to be everywhere in his native New York City. Grant's nightmare was race-mixing among Europeans. For him, "the cross between any of the three European races and a Jew is a Jew." He didn't have good things to say about Alpine or Mediterranean "races" either. For Grant, race and class were interwoven: the upper class was racially pure Nordic; the lower classes came from the lower races.[4]

Far from being on the fringe, Grant's views were well within the popular mainstream. Here is the *New York Times* describing the Jewish Lower East Side of a century ago:

> The neighborhood where these people live is absolutely impassable for wheeled vehicles other than their pushcarts. If a truck driver tries to get through where their pushcarts are standing they apply to him all kinds of vile and indecent epithets. The driver is fortunate if he gets out of the street without being hit with a stone or having a putrid fish or piece of meat thrown in his face. This neighborhood, peopled almost entirely by the people who claim to have been driven from Poland and Russia, is the eyesore of New York and perhaps the filthiest place on the western continent. It is impossible for a Christian to live there because he will be driven out, either by blows or the dirt and stench. Cleanliness is an

unknown quantity to these people. They cannot be lifted up to a higher plane because they do not want to be. If the cholera should ever get among these people, they would scatter its germs as a sower does grain.[5]

Such views were well within the mainstream of the early-twentieth-century scientific community.[6] Madison Grant and eugenicist Charles B. Davenport organized the Galton Society in 1918 in order to foster research, promote eugenics, and restrict immigration.[7] [...]

By the 1920s, scientific racism sanctified the notion that real Americans were white and that real whites came from northwest Europe. Racism by white workers in the West fueled laws excluding and expelling the Chinese in 1882. Widespread racism led to closing the immigration door to virtually all Asians and most Europeans between 1924 and 1927, and to deportation of Mexicans during the Great Depression.

Racism in general, and anti-Semitism in particular, flourished in higher education. Jews were the first of the Euro-immigrant groups to enter college in significant numbers, so it was not surprising that they faced the brunt of discrimination there. The Protestant elite complained that Jews were unwashed, uncouth, unrefined, loud, and pushy. Harvard University President A. Lawrence Lowell, who was also a vice president of the Immigration Restriction League, was open about his opposition to Jews at Harvard. The Seven Sister schools had a reputation for "flagrant discrimination." [...]

Columbia's quota against Jews was well known in my parents' community. My father is very proud of having beaten it and been admitted to Columbia Dental School on the basis of his skill at carving a soap ball. Although he became a teacher instead because the tuition was too high, he took me to the dentist every week of my childhood and prolonged the agony by discussing the finer points of tooth-filling and dental care. My father also almost failed the speech test required for his teaching license because he didn't speak "standard," i.e., nonimmigrant, nonaccented English. For my parents and most of their friends, English was the language they had learned when they went to school, since their home and neighborhood language was Yiddish. They saw the speech test as designed to keep all ethnics, not just Jews, out of teaching.

There is an ironic twist to this story. My mother always urged me to speak well, like her friend Ruth Saronson, who was a speech teacher. Ruth remained my model for perfect diction until I went away to college. When I talked to her on one of my visits home, I heard the New York accent of my version of "standard English," compared to the Boston academic version.

My parents believe that Jewish success, like their own, was due to hard work and a high value placed on education. They attended Brooklyn College during the Depression. My mother worked days and went to school at night; my father went during the day. Both their families encouraged them. More accurately, their families expected it. Everyone they knew was in the same boat, and their world was made up of Jews who were advancing just as they were. The picture for New York—where most Jews lived—seems to back them up. In 1920, Jews made up 80 percent of the students at New York's City College, 90 percent of Hunter College, and before World War I, 40 percent of private Columbia University. By 1934, Jews made up almost 24 percent of all law students nationally and 56 percent of those in New York City. Still, more Jews became public school teachers, like my parents and their friends, than doctors or lawyers. Indeed, Ruth Jacknow Markowitz has shown that "my daughter, the teacher" was, for parents, an aspiration equivalent to "my son, the doctor."[8]

How we interpret Jewish social mobility in this milieu depends on whom we compare them to. Compared with other immigrants, Jews were upwardly mobile. But compared with nonimmigrant whites, that mobility was very limited and circumscribed. The existence of anti-immigrant, racist, and anti-Semitic barriers kept the Jewish middle class confined to a small number of occupations. Jews were excluded from mainstream corporate management and corporately employed professions, except in the garment and movie industries, in which they were pioneers. Jews were almost totally excluded from university faculties (the few who made it had powerful patrons). Eastern European Jews were concentrated in small businesses, and in professions where they served a largely Jewish clientele. [...]

My parents' generation believed that Jews overcame anti-Semitic barriers because Jews are special. My answer is that the Jews who were upwardly mobile were special among Jews (and were also well placed to write the story). My generation might well respond to our parents' story of pulling themselves up by their own bootstraps with "But think what you might have been without the racism and with some affirmative action!" And that is precisely what the post–World War II boom, the decline of systematic, public, anti-Euro racism and anti-Semitism, and governmental affirmative action extended to white males let us see.

WHITENING EURO-ETHNICS

By the time I was an adolescent, Jews were just as white as the next white person. Until I was eight, I was a Jew in a world of Jews. Everyone on Avenue Z in Sheepshead Bay was Jewish. I spent my days playing and going to school on three blocks of Avenue Z, and visiting my grandparents in the nearby Jewish neighborhoods of Brighton Beach and Coney Island. There were plenty of Italians in my neighborhood, but they lived around the corner. They were a kind of Jew, but on the margins of my social horizons. Portuguese were even more distant, at the end of the bus ride, at Sheepshead Bay. The *shul*, or temple, was on Avenue Z, and I begged my father to take me like all the other fathers took their kids, but religion wasn't part of my family's Judaism. Just how Jewish my neighborhood was hit me in first grade, when I was one of two kids to go to school on Rosh Hashanah. My teacher was shocked—she was Jewish too—and I was embarrassed to tears when she sent me home. I was never again sent to school on Jewish holidays. We left that world in 1949 when we moved to Valley Stream, Long Island, which was Protestant and Republican and even had farms until Irish, Italian, and Jewish ex-urbanities like us gave it a more suburban and Democratic flavor.

Neither religion nor ethnicity separated us at school or in the neighborhood. Except temporarily. During my elementary school years, I remember a fair number of dirt-bomb (a good suburban weapon) wars on the block. Periodically, one of the Catholic boys would accuse me or my brother of killing his god, to which we'd reply, "Did not," and start lobbing dirt bombs.

Sometimes he'd get his friends from Catholic school and I'd get mine from public school kids on the block, some of whom were Catholic. Hostilities didn't last for more than a couple of hours and punctuated an otherwise friendly relationship. They ended by our junior high years, when other things became more important. Jews, Catholics, and Protestants, Italians, Irish, Poles, "English" (I don't remember hearing WASP as a kid), were mixed up on the block and in school. We thought of ourselves as middle class and very enlightened because our ethnic backgrounds seemed so irrelevant to high school culture. We didn't see race (we thought), and racism was not part of our peer consciousness. Nor were the immigrant or working-class histories of our families.

As with most chicken-and-egg problems, it is hard to know which came first. Did Jews and other Euro-ethnics become white because they became middle-class? That is, did money whiten? Or did being incorporated into an expanded version of whiteness open up the economic doors to middle-class status? Clearly, both tendencies were at work.

Some of the changes set in motion during the war against fascism led to a more inclusive version of whiteness. Anti-Semitism and anti-European racism lost respectability. The 1940 Census no longer distinguished native whites of native parentage from those, like my parents, of immigrant parentage, so Euro-immigrants and their children were more securely white by submersion in an expanded notion of whiteness.[9]

Theories of nurture and culture replaced theories of nature and biology. Instead of dirty and dangerous races that would destroy American democracy, immigrants became ethnic groups whose children had successfully assimilated into the mainstream and risen to the middle class. In this new myth, Euro-ethnic suburbs like mine became the measure of American democracy's victory over racism. Jewish mobility became a new Horatio Alger story. In time and with hard work, every ethnic group would get a piece of the pie, and the United States would be a nation with equal opportunity for all its people to become part of a prosperous middle-class majority. And it seemed that Euro-ethnic immigrants and their children were delighted to join middle America.

This is not to say that anti-Semitism disappeared alter World War II, only that it fell from fashion and was driven underground. [...]

Although changing views on who was white made it easier for Euro-ethnics to become middle class, economic prosperity also played a very powerful role in the whitening process. The economic mobility of Jews and other Euro-ethnics derived ultimately from America's postwar economic prosperity and its enormously expanded need for professional, technical, and managerial labor, as well as on government assistance in providing it.

The United States emerged from the war with the strongest economy in the world. Real wages rose between 1946 and 1960, increasing buying power a hefty 22 percent and giving most Americans some discretionary income. American manufacturing, banking, and business services were increasingly dominated by large corporations, and these grew into multinational corporations. Their organizational centers lay in big, new urban headquarters that demanded growing numbers of clerical, technical, and managerial workers. The postwar period was a historic moment for real class mobility and for the affluence we have erroneously come to believe was the American norm. It was a time when the old white and the newly white masses became middle class.[10]

The GI Bill of Rights, as the 1944 Serviceman's Readjustment Act was known, is arguably the most massive affirmative action program in American history. It was created to develop needed labor force skills and to provide those who had them with a lifestyle that reflected their value to the economy. The GI benefits that were ultimately extended to 16 million GIs (of the Korean War as well) included priority in jobs—that is, preferential hiring, but no one objected to it then—financial support during the job search, small loans for starting up businesses, and most important, low-interest home loans and educational benefits, which included tuition and living expenses. This legislation was rightly regarded as one of the most revolutionary postwar programs. I call it affirmative action because it was aimed at and disproportionately helped male, Euro-origin GIs.[11] [...]

EDUCATION AND OCCUPATION

It is important to remember that, prior to the war, a college degree was still very much a "mark of the upper class," that colleges were largely finishing schools for Protestant elites. Before the postwar boom, schools could not begin to accommodate the American masses. Even in New York City before the 1930s, neither the public schools nor City College had room for more than a tiny fraction of potential immigrant students.[12]

Not so after the war. The almost 8 million GIs who took advantage of their educational benefits under the GI Bill caused "the greatest wave of college building in American history." White male GIs were able to take advantage of their educational benefits for college and technical training, so they were particularly well positioned to seize the opportunities provided by the new demands for professional, managerial, and technical labor.

> It has been well documented that the GI educational benefits transformed American higher education and raised the educational level of that generation and generations to come. With many provisions for assistance in upgrading their educational attainments, veterans pulled ahead of nonveterans in earning capacity. In the long run it was the nonveterans who had fewer opportunities.[13]

[...] Even more significantly, the postwar boom transformed America's class structure—or at least its status structure—so that the middle class expanded to encompass most of the population. Before the war, most Jews, like most other Americans, were part of the working class, defined in terms of occupation, education, and income. Already upwardly mobile before the war relative to other immigrants, Jews floated high on this rising economic tide, and most of them entered the middle class. The children of other immigrants did too. Still, even the high tide missed some Jews. As late as 1973, some 15 percent of New York's Jews were poor or near poor, and in the 1960s, almost 25 percent of employed Jewish men remained manual workers.[14]

The reason I refer to educational and occupational GI benefits as affirmative action programs for white males is because they were decidedly not extended to African Americans or to women of any race. Theoretically they were available to all veterans; in practice women and black veterans did not get anywhere near their share. Women's Army and Air Force units were initially organized as auxiliaries, hence not part of the military. When that status was changed, in July 1943, only those who reenlisted in the armed forces were eligible for veterans' benefits. Many women thought they were simply being demobilized and returned home. The majority remained and were ultimately eligible for veterans' benefits. But there was little counseling, and a social climate that discouraged women's careers and independence cut down on women's knowledge and sense of entitlement. The Veterans Administration kept no statistics on the number of women who used their GI benefits.[15]

The barriers that almost completely shut African American GIs out of their benefits were even more formidable. In Neil Wynn's portrait, black GIs anticipated starting new lives, just like their white counterparts. Over 43 percent hoped to return to school, and most expected to relocate, to find better jobs in new lines of work. The exodus from the South toward the North and West was particularly large. So it was not a question of any lack of ambition on the part of African American GIs. White male privilege was shaped against the backdrop of wartime racism and postwar sexism.

During and after the war, there was an upsurge in white racist violence against black servicemen, in public schools, and by the Ku Klux Klan. It spread to California and New York. The number of lynchings rose during the war, and in 1943 there were antiblack race riots in several large northern cities. Although there was a wartime labor shortage, black people were discriminated against when it came to well-paid defense industry jobs and housing. In 1946, white riots against African Americans occurred across the South and in Chicago and Philadelphia.

Gains made as a result of the wartime civil rights movement, especially in defense-related employment, were lost with peacetime conversion, as black workers were the first to be fired, often in violation of seniority. White women were also laid off, ostensibly to make room for jobs for demobilized servicemen, and in the long run women lost most of the gains they had made in wartime. We now know that women did not leave the labor force in any significant numbers but, instead, were forced to find inferior jobs, largely nonunion, part-time, and clerical.[16]

The military, the Veterans Administration, the US Employment Services (USES), and the Federal Housing Administration effectively denied African American GIs access to their benefits and to new educational, occupational, and residential opportunities. Black GIs who served in the thoroughly segregated armed forces during World War II served under white officers. African American soldiers were given a disproportionate share of dishonorable discharges, which denied them veterans' rights under the GI Bill. Between August and November 1946, for example, 21 percent of white soldiers and 39 percent of black soldiers were dishonorably discharged. Those who did get an honorable discharge then faced the Veterans Administration and the USES. The latter, which was responsible for job placements, employed very few African Americans, especially in the South. This meant that black veterans did not receive much employment information and that the offers they did receive were for low-paid and menial jobs. "In one survey of 50 cities, the movement of blacks into peacetime employment was found to be lagging far behind that of white veterans: in Arkansas ninety-five percent of the placements made by the USES for Afro-Americans were in service or unskilled jobs."[17] African Americans were also less likely than whites, regardless of GI status, to gain new jobs commensurate with their wartime jobs. For example, in San Francisco, by 1948, black Americans "had dropped back halfway to their prewar employment status."[18]

Black GIs faced discrimination in the educational system as well. Despite the end of restrictions on Jews and other Euro-ethnics, African Americans were not welcome in white colleges. Black colleges were overcrowded, but the combination of segregation and prejudice made for few alternatives. About 20,000 black veterans attended college by 1947, most in black colleges, but almost as many, 15,000, could not gain entry. Predictably, the disproportionately few African Americans who did gain access to their educational benefits were able, like their white counterparts, to become doctors and engineers, and to enter the black middle class.[19]

SUBURBANIZATION

In 1949, ensconced in Valley Stream, I watched potato farms turn into Levittown and Idlewild (later Kennedy) airport. This was the major spectator sport in our first years on Long Island. A typical weekend would bring various aunts, uncles, and cousins out from the city. After a huge meal, we'd pile into the car—itself a novelty—to look at the bulldozed acres and comment on the matchbox construction. During the week, my mother and I would look at the houses going up within walking distance.

Bill Levitt built a basic, 900–1,000 square foot, somewhat expandable house for a lower-middle-class and working-class market on Long Island, and later in Pennsylvania and New Jersey. Levittown started out as 2,000 units of rental housing at $60 a month, designed to meet the low-income housing needs of returning war vets, many of whom, like my Aunt Evie and Uncle Julie, were living in Quonset huts. By May 1947, Levitt and Sons had acquired enough land in Hempstead Township on Long Island to build 4,000 houses, and by the next February, he had built 6,000 units and named the development after himself. After 1948, federal financing for the construction of rental housing tightened, and Levitt switched to building houses for sale. By 1951, Levittown was a development of some 15,000 families.[20]

At the beginning of World War II, about one-third of all American families owned their houses. That percentage doubled in twenty years. Most Levittowners looked just like my family. They came from New York City or Long Island; about 17 percent were military, from nearby Mitchell Field; Levittown was their first house, and almost everyone was married. Three-quarters of the 1947 inhabitants were white collar, but by 1950 more blue-collar families had moved in, so that by 1951, "barely half" of the new residents were white collar, and by 1960 their occupational profile was somewhat more working class than for Nassau County as a whole. By this time too, almost one-third of Levittown's people were either foreign-born or, like my parents, first-generation US-born.[21]

The Federal Housing Administration (FHA) was key to buyers and builders alike. Thanks to the FHA, suburbia was open to more than GIs. People like us would never have been in the market for houses without FHA and Veterans Administration (VA) low-down-payment, low-interest, long-term loans to young buyers. [...]

The FHA believed in racial segregation. Throughout its history, it publicly and actively promoted restrictive covenants. Before the war, these forbade sales to Jews and Catholics as well as to African Americans. The deed to my house in Detroit had such a covenant, which theoretically prevented it from being sold to Jews or African Americans. Even after the Supreme Court outlawed restrictive covenants in 1948, the FHA continued to encourage builders to write them in against African Americans. FHA underwriting manuals openly insisted on racially homogeneous neighborhoods, and their loans were made only in white neighborhoods. I bought my Detroit house in 1972, from Jews who were leaving a largely African American neighborhood. By that time, restrictive covenants were a dead letter, but block busting by realtors was replacing it.

With the federal government behind them, virtually all developers refused to sell to African Americans. Palo Alto and Levittown, like most suburbs as late as 1960, were virtually all white. Out of 15,741 houses and 65,276 people, averaging 4.2 people per house, only 220 Levittowners, or 52 households, were "nonwhite." In 1958, Levitt announced publicly, at a press conference held to open his New Jersey development, that he would not sell to black buyers. This caused a furor because the state of New Jersey (but not the US government) prohibited discrimination in federally subsidized housing. Levitt was sued and fought it. There had been a white riot in his Pennsylvania development when a black family moved in a few years earlier. In New Jersey, he was ultimately persuaded by township ministers to integrate. [...]

The result of these policies was that African Americans were totally shut out of the sub-urban boom. An article in *Harper's* described the housing available to black GIs.

> On his way to the base each morning, Sergeant Smith passes an attractive air-conditioned, FHA-financed housing project. It was built for service families. Its rents are little more than the Smiths pay for their shack. And there are half-a-dozen vacancies, but none for Negroes.[22]

Where my family felt the seductive pull of suburbia, Marshall Berman's experienced the brutal push of urban renewal. In the Bronx, in the 1950s, Robert Moses's Cross-Bronx Expressway erased "a dozen solid, settled, densely populated neighborhoods like our own.... [S]omething like 60,000 working- and lower-middle-class people, mostly Jews, but with many Italians, Irish, and Blacks thrown in, would be thrown out of their homes.... For ten years, through the late 1950s and early 1960s, the center of the Bronx was pounded and blasted and smashed."[23]

Urban renewal made postwar cities into bad places to live. At a physical level, urban renewal reshaped them, and federal programs brought private developers and public officials together to create downtown central business districts where there had formerly been a mix of manufacturing, commerce, and working-class neighborhoods. Manufacturing was scattered to the peripheries of the city, which were ringed and bisected by a national system of highways. Some working-class neighborhoods were bulldozed, but others remained. In Los Angeles, as in New York's Bronx, the postwar period saw massive freeway construction right through the heart of old working-class neighborhoods. In East Los Angeles and Santa Monica, Chicana/o and African American communities were divided in half or blasted to smithereens by the highways bringing Angelenos to the new white suburbs, or to make way for civic monuments like Dodger Stadium.[24]

Urban renewal was the other side of the process by which Jewish and other working-class Euro-immigrants became middle class. It was the push to suburbia's seductive pull. The fortunate white survivors of urban renewal headed disproportionately for suburbia, where they could partake of prosperity and the good life. [...]

If the federal stick of urban renewal joined the FHA carrot of cheap mortgages to send masses of Euro-Americans to the suburbs, the FHA had a different kind of one-two punch for African Americans. Segregation kept them out of the suburbs, and redlining made sure they could not buy or repair their homes in the neighborhoods in which they were allowed to live. The FHA practiced systematic redlining. This was a practice developed by its predecessor, the Home Owners Loan Corporation (HOLC), which in the 1930s developed an elaborate neighborhood rating system that placed the highest (green) value on all-white, middle-class neighborhoods, and the lowest (red) on racially nonwhite or mixed and working-class neighborhoods. High ratings meant high property values. The idea was that low property values in redlined neighborhoods made them bad investments. The FHA was, after all, created by and for banks and the housing industry. Redlining warned banks not to lend there, and the FHA would not insure mortgages in such neighborhoods. Redlining created a self-fulfilling prophecy.

> With the assistance of local realtors and banks, it assigned one of the four ratings to every block in every city. The resulting information was then translated into the appropriate color [green, blue, yellow, or red] and duly recorded on secret "Residential Security Maps" in local HOLC offices. The maps themselves were placed in elaborate "City Survey Files," which consisted of reports, questionnaires, and workpapers relating to current and future values of real estate.[25]

The FHA's and VA's refusal to guarantee loans in redlined neighborhoods made it virtually impossible for African Americans to borrow money for home improvement or purchase. Because these maps and surveys were quite secret, it took the civil rights movement to make these practices and their devastating consequences public. As a result, those who fought urban renewal, or who sought to make a home in the urban ruins, found themselves locked out of the middle class. They also faced an ideological assault that labeled their neighborhoods slums and called them slumdwellers.[26]

CONCLUSION

The record is very clear. Instead of seizing the opportunity to end institutionalized racism, the federal government did its level best to shut and double-seal the postwar window of opportunity in African Americans' faces. It consistently refused to combat segregation in the social institutions that were key to upward mobility in education, housing, and employment Moreover, federal programs that were themselves designed to assist demobilized GIs and young families systematically discriminated against African Americans. Such programs reinforced white/nonwhite racial distinctions even as intrawhite racialization was falling out of fashion. This other side of the coin, that white men of northwest European ancestry and white men of southeastern European ancestry were treated equally in theory and in practice with regard to the benefits they received, was part of the larger postwar whitening of Jews and other eastern and southern Europeans.

The myth that Jews pulled themselves up by their own bootstraps ignores the fact that it took federal programs to create the conditions whereby the abilities of Jews and other European immigrants could be recognized and rewarded rather than denigrated and denied. The GI Bill and FHA and VA mortgages, even though they were advertised as open to all, functioned as a set of racial privileges. They were privileges because they were extended to white GIs but not to black GIs. Such privileges were forms of affirmative action that allowed Jews and other Euro-American men to become suburban homeowners and to get the training that allowed them—but much less so women vets or war workers—to become professionals, technicians, salesmen, and managers in a growing economy. Jews and other white ethnics' upward mobility was due to programs that allowed us to float on a rising economic tide. To African Americans, the government offered the cement boots of segregation, redlining, urban renewal, and discrimination.

Those racially skewed gains have been passed across the generations, so that racial inequality seems to maintain itself "naturally," even after legal segregation ended. Today, I own a house in Venice, California, like the one in which I grew up in Valley Stream, and my brother until recently owned a house in Palo Alto much like an Eichler house. Both of us are where we are thanks largely to the postwar benefits our parents received and passed on to us, and to the educational benefits we received in the 1960s as a result of affluence and the social agitation that developed from the black Freedom Movement. I have white, African American, and Asian American colleagues whose parents received fewer or none of America's postwar benefits and who expect never to own a house despite their considerable academic achievements. Some of these colleagues who are a few years younger than I also carry staggering debts for their education, which they expect to have to repay for the rest of their lives.

Conventional wisdom has it that the United States has always been an affluent land of opportunity. But the truth is that affluence has been the exception and that real upward mobility has required massive affirmative action programs. [...]

NOTES

1. Gerber 1986; Dinnerstein 1987, 1994.
2. On the belief in Jewish and Asian versions of Horatio Alger, see Steinberg 1989, chap. 3; Gilman 1996. On Jewish culture, see Gordon 1964; see Sowell 1981 for an updated version.
3. Not all Jews are white or unambiguously white. It has been suggested, for example, that Hasidim lack the privileges of whiteness. Rodriguez (1997, 12, 15) has begun to unpack the claims of white Jewish "amenity migrants" and the different racial meanings of Chicano claims to a crypto-Jewish identity in New Mexico. See also Thomas 1996 on African American Jews.
4. M. Grant 1916; Ripley 1923; see also Patterson 1997; M. Grant, quoted in Higham 1955, 156.
5. *New York Tunes*, 30 July 1893, "East Side Street Vendors," reprinted in Schoener 1967, 57–58.
6. Gould 1981; Higham 1955; Patterson 1997, 108–115.
7. It was intended, as Davenport wrote to the president of the American Museum of Natural History, Henry Fairfield Osborne, as "an anthropological society … with a central governings body, self-elected and self-perpetuating, and very limited in members, and also confined to native Americans [sic] who are anthropologically, socially and politically sound, no Bolsheviki need apply" (Barkan 1992, 67–68).
8. Steinberg 1989, 137, 227; Markowitz 1993.
9. This census also explicitly changed the Mexican race to white (US Bureau of the Census 1940, 2:4).
10. Nash et al. 1986, 885–886.
11. On planning for veterans, see F.J. Brown 1946; Hurd 1946; Mosch 1975; "Post-war Jobs for Veterans" 1945; Willenz 1983.
12. Willenz 1983, 165.
13. Nash et al. 1986, 885; Willenz 1983, 165. On mobility among veterans and nonveterans, see Havighurst et al. 1951.
14. Steinberg 1989, 89–90.
15. Willenz 1983, 20–28, 94–97. I thank Nancy G. Cattell for calling my attention to the fact that women GIs were ultimately eligible for benefits.
16. Willenz 1983, 168; Dalfiume 1969, 133–134; Wynn 1976, 114–116; Anderson 1981; Milkman 1987.
17. Nalty and MacGregor 1981, 218, 60–61.
18. Wynn 1976, 114, 116.
19. On African Americans in the US military, see Foner 1974; Dalfiume 1969; Johnson 1967; Binkin and Eitelberg 1982; Nalty and MacGregor 1981. On schooling, see Walker 1970, 4–9.
20. Hartman (1975, 141–142) cites massive abuses in the 1940s and 1950s by builders under the Section 608 program in which "the FHA granted extraordinarily liberal concessions to lackadaisically supervised private developers to induce them to produce rental housing rapidly in the postwar period." Eichler (1982) indicates that things were not that different in the subsequent FHA-funded home-building industry.

21. Dobriner 1963, 91, 100.
22. Quoted in Foner 1974, 195.
23. Berman 1982, 292.
24. On urban renewal and housing policies, see Greer 1965; Hartman 1975; Squires 1989. On Los Angeles, see Pardo 1990; Cockcroft 1990.
25. Jackson 1985, 197. These ideas from the real estate industry were "codified and legitimated in 1930s work by University of Chicago sociologist Robert Park and real estate professor Homer Hoyt" (Ibid., 198–199).
26. See Gans 1962.

REFERENCES

Anderson, Karen. 1981. *Wartime Women*. Westport, Conn.: Greenwood.

Barkan, Elazar. 1992. *The Retreat of Scientific Racism: Changing Concepts of Race in Britain and the United States Between the World Wars*. New York: Cambridge University Press.

Berman, Marshall. 1982. *All That Is Solid Melts into Air: The Experience of Modernity*. New York: Simon and Schuster.

Binkin, Martin, and Mark J. Eitelberg. 1982. *Blacks and the Military*. Washington, DC: Brookings Institution.

Brown, Francis J. 1946. *Educational Opportunities for Veterans*. Washington, DC: Public Affairs Press American Council on Public Affairs.

Cockcroft, Eva. 1990. *Signs from the Heart: California Chicano Murals*. Venice, Calif.: Social and Public Art Resource Center.

Dalfiume, Richard M. 1969. *Desegregation of the U.S. Armed Forces: Fighting on Two Fronts, 1939–1953*. Columbia: University of Missouri Press.

Dinnerstein, Leonard, 1987. *Uneasy at Home: Anti-Semitism and the American Jewish Experience*. New York: Columbia University Press.

———. 1994. *Anti-Semitism in America*. New York: Oxford University Press.

Dobriner, William. M. 1963. *Class in Suburbia*. Englewood Cliffs, NJ: Prentice-Hall.

Eichler, Ned. 1982. *The Merchant Builders*. Cambridge, Mass.: MIT Press.

Foner, Jack. 1974. *Blacks and the Military in American History: A New Perspective*. New York: Praeger Publishers.

Gans, Herbert. 1962. *The Urban Villagers*. New York: Free Press of Glencoe.

Gerber, David, ed. 1986. *Anti-Semitism in American History*. Urbana: University of Illinois Press.

Gilman, Sander. 1996. *Smart Jews: The Construction of the Image of Jewish Superior Intelligence*. Lincoln: University of Nebraska Press.

Gordon, Milton. 1964. *Assimilation in American Life: The Role of Race, Religion and National Origins*. New York: Oxford University Press.

Gould, Stephen J. 1981. *The Mismeasure of Man*. New York: Norton.

Grant, Madison. 1916. *The Passing of the Great Race: Or the Racial Basis of European History*. New York: Charles Scribner.

Greer, Scott. 1965. *Urban Renewal and American Cities*. Indianapolis: Bobbs-Merrill.

Hartman, Chester. 1975. *Housing and Social Policy*. Englewood Cliffs, NJ: Prentice-Hall.

Havighurst, Robert J., John W. Baughman, Walter H. Eaton, and Ernest W. Burgess. 1951. *The American Veteran Back Home: A Study of Veteran Readjustment*. New York: Longmans, Green and Co.

Higham, John. 1955. *Strangers in the Land*. New Brunswick, NJ: Rutgers University Press.

Hurd, Charles. 1946. *The Veterans' Program: A Complete Guide to Its Benefits, Rights and Options*. New York: McGraw-Hill Book Company.

Jackson, Kenneth T. 1985. *Crabgrass Frontier: The Suburbanization of the United States*. New York: Oxford University Press.

Johnson, Jesse J. 1967. *Ebony Brass: An Autobiography of Negro Frustration Amid Aspiration*. New York: The William Frederick Press.

Markowitz, Ruth Jacknow. 1993. *My Daughter, the Teacher: Jewish Teachers in the New York City Schools*. New Brunswick, NJ: Rutgers University Press.

Milkman, Ruth. 1987. *Gender at Work: The Dynamics of Job Segregation by Sex During World War II*. Urbana: University of Illinois Press.

Mosch, Theodore R. 1975. *The GI Bill: A Breakthrough in Educational and Social Policy in the United States*. Hicksville, NY: Exposition Press.

Nalty, Bernard C., and Morris J. MacGregor, eds. 1981. *Blacks in the Military: Essential Documents*. Wilmington, Del.: Scholarly Resources, Inc.

Nash, Gary B., Julie Roy Jeffrey, John R. Howe, Allen F. Davis, Peter J. Frederick, and Allen M. Winkler. 1986. *The American People: Creating a Nation and a Society*. New York: Harper and Row.

Pardo, Mary. 1990. "Mexican-American Women Grassroots Community Activists: 'Mothers of East Los Angeles.'" *Frontiers* 11, 1:1–7.

Patterson, Thomas C. 1997. *Inventing Western Civilization*. New York: Monthly Review Press.

"Postwar Jobs for Veterans." 1945. *The Annals of the American Academy of Political and Social Science* 238 (March).

Ripley, William Z. 1923. *The Races of Europe: A Sociological Study*. New York: Appleton.

Rodriguez, Sylvia. 1997. "Tourism, Whiteness, and the Vanishing Anglo." Paper presented at the conference "Seeing and Being Seen: Tourism in the American West." Center for the American West, Boulder, Colorado, 2 May.

Schoener, Allon. 1967. *Portal to America: The Lower East Side 1870–1925*. New York: Holt, Rinehart, and Winston.

Sowell, Thomas. 1981. *Ethnic America: A History*. New York: Basic Books.

Squires, Gregory D., ed. 1989. *Unequal Partnerships: The Political Economy of Urban Redevelopment in Postwar America*. New Brunswick, NJ: Rutgers University Press.

Steinberg, Stephen. 1989. *The Ethnic Myth: Race, Ethnicity and Class in America*. 2d ed. Boston: Beacon Press.

Thomas, Laurence Mordekhai. 1996. "The Soul of Identity: Jews and Blacks." In *People of the Book*, ed. S.F. Fishkin and J. Rubin-Dorsky. Madison: University of Wisconsin Press, 169–186.

US Bureau of the Census. 1940. *Sixteenth Census of the United States*, V.2. Washington, DC: US Government Printing Office.

Walker, Olive. 1970. "The Windsor Hills School Story." *Integrated Education: Race and Schools* 8, 3:4–9.

Willenz, June A. 1983. *Women Veterans: America's Forgotten Heroines*. New York: Continuum.

Wynn, Neil A. 1976. *The Afro-American and the Second World War*. London: Paul Elek.

Chapter 41

Between Black and White: Exploring the "Biracial" Experience

Kerry Ann Rockquemore

In this chapter, Kerry Ann Rockquemore (1998) explores the complexity of racial identity, noting that race and ethnicity function differently due to visibility. Two questions guide her discussion: what does being "biracial" mean to individuals? And what factors may lead to differences in the way these individuals interpret their racial identity? On the basis of interviews, Rockquemore reports on the multiple ways in which individuals experience, understand, and respond to their "biracialness" and illustrates the role physical appearance and socio-economic status play in individuals' capacity to access different types of social networks.

Public debate concerning proposed modifications to the 2000 Census has recently focused on the addition of a "multi-racial" category. Proponents argue that the dramatic increase in interracial marriages over the past three decades[1] has caused a biracial baby boom. These rising numbers of biracial and multi-ethnic Americans, advocates argue, should be recognized by the government as "multi-racial." They believe a multi-racial category is necessary because all people of mixed parentage identify themselves as "biracial" or "mixed" and, if given the opportunity to identify this way on government documents, they would do so.

Despite advocates claims, biracialness[2] is not a newly emergent social phenomenon (Williamson, 1980). The Census debate is merely the latest manifestation of the ongoing socio-historical problematic of classifying mixed race people in the United States. Given the historical stratification of racial groups, supported by an ideological belief in genetic differentiation between races, society has continually had to develop norms to classify individuals who straddle the socially constructed boundaries of "Black" and "White" (White, 1948; Williamson, 1980; Davis, 1991; Zack, 1993). The "One Drop Rule,"[3] historically articulated in legal statutes, mandated that a mixed race child be relegated to the racial group of the lower status parent. This norm has survived despite the removal of its various legal codifications. The One Drop Rule dictated that children of Black/White unions were considered part of the African-American community. While biracials have had varying statuses within that community,[4] they have always been considered, by both Whites and Blacks, as part of the "Black race" (Davis, 1991).

The Census issue provides a contemporary variation on the classification dilemma. Advocates demand separate group recognition and membership for mixed race people and are essentially arguing for a nullification of the cultural norm of hypodescent. In this context, it is not surprising that the movement is led, not by biracial people themselves, but by White mothers on behalf of their children. In this sense, they are arguing for a separate status for their children in the socio-racial hierarchy. The status of "mixed-race" would afford their children more privileges than being Black, but not quite as many as being White (Spencer, 1997). This separate status argument is framed as an attempt towards self-definition on behalf of biracial people who, advocates assume, do not consider themselves Black.

The assumption that biracials have a singular understanding of their racial identity (i.e., as biracial) masks the fact that numerous individuals who are biracial identify themselves as African-American and would continue to do so even if presented with the mixed-race category as an option[5] (Jones, 1994; McBride, 1996; Scales-Trent, 1995; Williams, 1995). The belief that biracial identity has a singular meaning to members of this population begs numerous questions. What does "biracial identity" mean? Is there a singular way in which people with one Black and one White parent understand their racial identity or does "biracial" have multiple meanings? If there are, in fact, multiple ways in which biracial people understand themselves and their group membership, then what types of social factors influence the differences in an individual's choice of racial identity? This article explores what mixed-race people say about the meaning of "biracial" identity and how social factors have influenced their identity construction and maintenance.

THEORETICAL FRAMEWORK OF IDENTITY FORMATION

The conceptual framework of this argument rests on the three classic assumptions of symbolic interactionism: (1) that we know things by their meanings, (2) that meanings are created through social interaction, and (3) that meanings change through interaction (Blumer, 1969). Given these basic assumptions, it is necessary to clearly delineate the conceptual terminology to be used in the following discussion. First and foremost, what is meant by the term "identity"?

Social actors are situated within societies that designate available categories of identification, how these identities are defined, and their relative importance. The term identity refers to a validated self-understanding that situates and defines the individual or, as Stone (1962) suggests, establishes *what* and *where* an actor is in social terms. These are processes by which individuals understand themselves and others, as well as evaluate their self in relation to others. Identity is the direct result of mutual identification through social interaction. It is within this process of validation that identity becomes a meaning of the self. I utilize the term identity interchangeably with self-understanding throughout the discussion.

By situating identity within an interactionist framework, biracial identity may be understood as an emergent category of identification. If identity is conceptualized as an inter-actionally validated self-understanding, then identities can only function effectively where the response of the individual to themselves (as a social object) is consistent with the response of others. In contrast, individuals cannot effectively possess an identity which is not socially typified, or where there exists a disjuncture between the identity an actor appropriates for him/herself and where others place him/her as a social object. In other words, an individual cannot have a realized identity without others who validate that identity. The challenge of research on biracial identity then is twofold. First, it is necessary to understand how individuals understand their social location as "biracial," and secondly, to explore what social and interactional factors lead to the development of this identity and how these individuals try to realize their appropriated identities in social context.

DATA AND METHODS

Data was collected through in-depth interviews with biracial undergraduates at a Catholic university in the Midwest. This type of research methodology was selected due to the exploratory nature of the study and the researcher's desire to generate understanding about a growing group (Root, 1992; Taylor and Bogdan, 1984; Marshall and Rossman, 1989). The selection criterion were that students have one Black self-identifying biological parent and one White self-identifying biological parent. While the argument can be made that within the Black population, many people are of mixed race ancestry, the researcher chose to focus on the particular social circumstances, which are generated from having one Black and one White parent. Therefore, in the limited definition of this study, the biracial experience is exclusively a one-generation phenomenon.

It has been noted by many researchers that there exist inherent problems in engaging a sample of biracial respondents (Root, 1992). The primary dilemmas are (1) the sensitive nature of the subject matter and (2) the difficulty in identifying potential respondents. To address these particular difficulties, a biracial interviewer and snowball sampling were used (Bertaux, 1981). Fourteen biracial students were located and agreed to be interviewed. They ranged in age from eighteen to twenty-two and came from ten different states in the US. All respondents were Catholic, middle to upper-middle class, and came from families where at least one parent had a college education.

Interviews were audio taped and ranged between one and three hours in length. Each respondent filled out a one-page demographic questionnaire at the end of the interview, and each respondent's picture was taken. The taped interviews were transcribed and content analyzed to construct a descriptive map of the various ways in which the respondents understood their racial identity.

WHAT DOES "BIRACIAL IDENTITY" MEAN?

What does "biracial identity" mean to members of this population? If we conceptualize the term identity to mean an interactionally validated self-understanding, then the question, more specifically, is how do the individual selves interpret biracialness and respond to it. My data suggest some tentative descriptive categories of the way that individuals with one Black and one White parent understand their biracialness. Being biracial can be interpreted as: (1) a border identity, (2) a protean identity, (3) a transcendent identity, or (4) a traditional identity.[6]

A Border Identity

Anzaldua (1987) terms biracial identity as a "border identity" or one which lies between predefined social categories. Some individuals viewed the location of their existence between Black and White as defining their biracialness. These individuals stressed their in-betweenness, and highlighted that unique status as the grounding for their identity. In other words, they did not consider themselves to be *either* Black *or* White, but instead had a self-understanding that incorporated both Blackness and Whiteness into a unique category of "biracial." It was their location of difference that served as the substantive base of what it meant to be biracial. Kara, a first year student, explained that it was not only the location of being on the border of socially defined categories, but that the border status itself brought with it an additional dimension:

> It's not that just being biracial is like you're two parts [White and Black], you know, you have two parts but then there is also the one part of being biracial where you sit on the fence. There's a third thing, a unique thing.

The extreme border identity was exemplified by individuals who took their border status to a political level. Those who most consistently identified as biracial across all social contexts were likely to parallel their identity as biracial with a perception of shared struggle unique to their social location. They perceived their position as one of both oppression and advantage. For some, it spanned more than the case of Black-White biracials, and included all who exist between races and ethnicities. These individuals found it difficult to discuss their self-identification without mentioning the problem of bureaucratic racial categorization and their negative feelings of having to select a singular category of identification (particularly if that category is Black or African American). Jessica, a second year student illustrates this difficulty when she stated:

I think there should be a mixed race category, or at least it shouldn't say "choose one" … I just want to put my race down. I don't see what the problem is, acknowledging what your are and I'm mixed! I don't know because I also have this whole problem with the way society says it's okay [if you are biracial] to say that you're black but not to say that you're White because you're both! How can you deny one or the other?

A Protean Identity

For others, biracial identity referred to their protean capacity to move among cultural contexts (Lifton, 1993). Their self-understanding of biracialness was directly tied to their ability to cross boundaries between Black, White, and biracial, which was possible because they possessed Black, White, and biracial identities. These individuals felt endowed with a degree of cultural savvy in several social worlds and understood biracialness as the way in which they were able to fit in, however conditionally, in varied interactional settings. They believed their dual experiences with both Whites and Blacks had given them the ability to shift their identity according to the context of any particular interaction. This contextual shifting lead actors to form a belief that their multiple racial backgrounds were but one piece of a complex self that was composed of assorted identifications which were not culturally integrated.

A student named Mike was able to provide an example in which his dual cultural competencies allowed him to function as an "insider" in differing social groups. He grew up in an all-White neighborhood and attended predominantly White private schools his entire life. He did have, however, frequent contact with his Black extended family. Mike felt that his particular circumstances growing up helped him to not only develop both middle-class White and Black cultural competencies, but also simultaneous multiple identities. In the following excerpt from our conversation, he uses table manners to illustrate his perception of the subtleties of contextual shifting:

Because of their [his parents] status, I always learned, you know start with the outside fork and work your way in, and this one is for dessert, you know. So I know, I know not to eat like this [puts his elbows on the table]. But then again, at the same time, [respondent shifts to Black Vernacular] when it comes picnic time or some other time and some ribs is on the table, I'm not afraid to get my hands dirty and dig on in and eat with my hands and stuff like that. [respondent shifts back to Standard English] I mean I guess my, the shift is when I'm not afraid to function in either world.

While his depiction may be exaggerated and stereotypical, it reveals his understanding of biracialness as having the ability to contextually shift his self-label between what he perceives as Black and White cultural contexts. When the topic of racial identification was initially broached with Mike he stated: "well shit, it depends on what day it is and where I'm goin."

A Transcendent Identity

A third way of understanding biracialness is reminiscent of Robert Park's, "Marginal Man" in its original context (Park, 1950). Park discussed the qualities of the cosmopolitan stranger, an individual who was bicultural (as opposed to biracial), and whose marginal status enabled an objective view of social reality. I refer to this as a "transcendent identity" because like Park's "stranger," individuals with this self-understanding view their biracialness as a unique marginalization, one that enables an objective perspective on the social meaning of race. These individuals discount race as a "master status" altogether. This self-understanding is uniquely and exclusively available to individuals whose bodily characteristics have a high degree of ambiguity (i.e., those who look White). This type of self-understanding of biracialness results in an avoidance, or rejection of any type of racial group categorization as the basis of personal identity. These individuals responded to questions about their identity with answers that were unrelated to their racial status, such as in the following example:

> I'm just Rob, you know. I never thought this was such a big deal to be identified, I just figured I'm a good guy, just like me for that, you know. But, when I came here [to college] it was like I was almost forced to look at people as being White, Black, Asian, or Hispanic. And so now, I'm still trying to go "I'm just Rob" but uh, you gotta be something.

This respondent stated that if required in particular contexts, he would accept the racial categorization thrust upon him. Given the persistence of hypodescent as a cultural norm, the result was his somewhat grudging acceptance of categorization as Black. I refrain from saying that he accepted a Black identity because it was only the label "Black" that was accepted.

This self-understanding was unique in several ways. First, it was available only to those whose appearances fit into the common perception of "White" or "Caucasian." Secondly, these individuals differed from the protean identity group because they did not have the ability, or the desire, to manipulate their identity before others in various social contexts. Finally, racial group membership did not play any significant role in their self-understanding because they socially experience race in a different way than those with a non-White appearance. Instead, they perceive that their biracialness provides them with a location to view and discard race as a meaningful category of their existence.

A Traditional Identity

Finally, there are individuals with one Black and one White parent whose racial identity falls into the category I term "traditional." In this case, the self-understanding is exclusively as African-American. The meaning of biracialness is merely an acknowledgment of the racial categorization of their birth parents. At the extreme, individuals simply do not deny the existence of their (White) parent. However, it is not salient in defining their self-understanding and may not be offered as identifying information unless specifically requested. Interestingly enough,

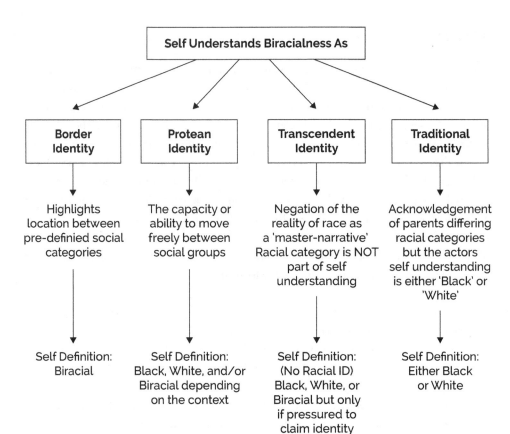

Figure 41.1: The multiple meanings of biracial identity

there were no respondents in the pilot study that identified exclusively as Black. However, we can conceptually formulate this category based upon the historical norm of hypodescent.

The voices of biracial people reveal that there are varying understandings of what "biracial identity" means to individuals within this population. Individuals' selves have not one, but several ways in which they interpret and respond to biracialness. These divergent self-understandings are grounded in differential experiences, varying biographies, and crosscutting cultural contexts. This multiple meaning perspective breaks from the singular conception of Park's Marginal Man, the assertions of multiracial advocates, and much recent research on the biracial population that rests on the unquestioned assumption that biracial identity has a singular and widely agreed upon meaning with which an actor either does or does not understand (Bradshaw, 1992; Fields, 1996; King and DaCosta, 1996). Figure 41.1 provides a schematic representation of this typology.

THE EFFECTS OF APPEARANCE AND SOCIAL NETWORKS ON IDENTITY FORMATION

Mary Waters' (1990) work focuses on ethnic options for individuals with multiple White-ethnic heritages. Waters was interested in why individuals with multiple ethnic backgrounds chose to emphasize one of their ethnicities over others. The factors involved in resolving White ethnic options included: (1) knowledge about the ethnicity; (2) surname; (3) appearance; and (4) general popularity of ethnic groups. She concluded that ethnicity was largely "symbolic," in that it had no consequences for an individual's life chances or everyday interactions and that it was characterized by the existence of choice either to assume the ethnic identity or not.

Waters' findings are instructive because they reveal the symbolic basis of White-ethnicity and explicitly differentiate it from race. The symbolic ethnicity of Whites differs from non-Whites because race is not an option from one situation to the next and race has both immediate and real consequences. In Waters' framework, identity options are either non-existent, or function differently, for members of racial groups compared to Whites because racial and ethnic categories are socio-culturally stratified. Her work implies that race and ethnicity function differently due to visibility, the capacity of individual choice, and a history of stratification based on racial group membership.

The Influence of Appearance on Identity

Appearances provide information about individuals that helps others to define the self as situated. This information enables others to know in advance what they can expect of an actor and what the actor can expect of them (Goffman, 1959). Appearances provide the first information (albeit constructed) about an individual to others in the context of face-to-face social interaction. It helps to define the identity of the individual and for him/her to express their self-identification. It is in this process that identities are negotiated and either validated or invalidated.

Appearance is critical in understanding how individuals develop and maintain racial identities (Stone, 1962). I limit my use of appearances to the following: physical features, language, and clothing. The physical characteristics of biracial individuals range widely in skin color, hair texture, and facial features. At one extreme are individuals who physically possess traits that are socially defined as belonging to the Black race; at the other are those who are visually unidentifiable as Black, or possess no features which are associated with African descent. Because racial categories are defined by appearances, the logic and enactment of racial categorization becomes questionable if individuals cannot be identified on sight. One's skin color, hair, and facial features are strong membership cues in socially defined racial groups. Figure 41.2 is a schematic representation of the proposed explanatory factors.

In addition to physical features, language and clothing have important functions as supporting interactional cues in establishing the identity of an individual. Language is particularly salient in the case of cueing one's membership to a racial group. Individuals may speak

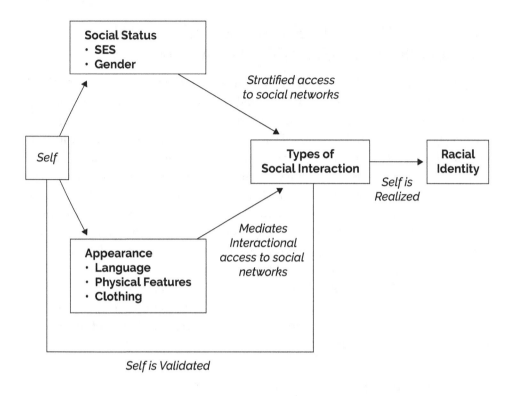

Figure 41.2: Factors influencing biracial identity

exclusively Standard English, Black Vernacular, or code switch between both (Smitherman, 1986; Delpit, 1988; Fanon, 1952). Clothing can work in a similar way as a signifier of racial group membership. Clothing and language differ from physical features, however, in the degree to which they can be manipulated. For example, one of the respondents reported frequenting a tanning salon to make her skin appear darker. In addition, women's hairstyles can decidedly signify group membership and are subject to degrees of manipulation. While certain physical features can be manipulated, some cannot without plastic surgery. Clothing and language on the other hand, may be strategically used by the individual to gain support from others for a particular identity (Goffman, 1959).

Mike told a story, which illustrates the link between appearances and identity. He has light brown skin, brown eyes, freckles, and short kinky hair. His physical appearance can be termed as ambiguous in that he doesn't appear to be White, yet his features do not necessarily fit into any easily definable category. Mike talked about negotiating his identity with a (White) girlfriend in the following way:

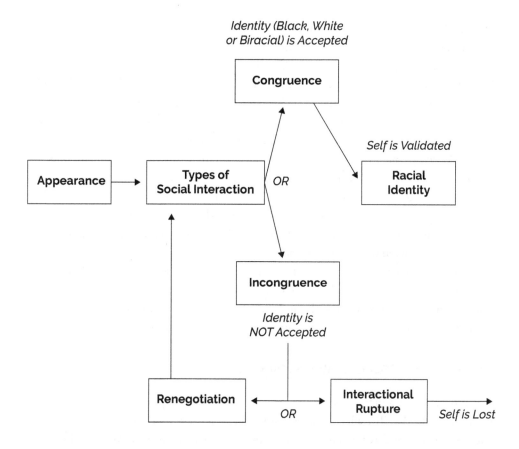

Figure 41.3: The effects of appearance on identity

I worked at a big national meeting thing here and I spoke on my experience here at Notre Dame, being Black. And afterwards, she came up and was like "hi," really cool, and we started talking and everything. And then she goes, "but you're Irish aren't you?" and I'm like "yeah." She says, "you got so many freckles!" And from then on we were like, tight, we still are.... She pulled me out, she was like "no, you're not JUST black" like, "you're not special" and I'm like, "yeah, put me in my place."

This story is interesting because it expresses the tension when others' definition of one's physical appearance fails to be consistent with self-definition (Goffman, 1963). In this case, Mike's physical features and use of Standard English were incongruent (for the future girl-friend) with his professed identity as a Black student speaking about the Black experience on a predominately White college campus. This caused the woman to approach him later and call into question his racial identity. The exchange resulted in the renegotiation of his racial identity, at which time he stated that he was "really" biracial, she accepted the renegotiated identity, and they were able to proceed with the interaction.

This type of experience, when a biracial individual's identity is called into question, or the "what are you?" experience, is a commonly reported phenomenon within the biracial population (Williams, 1996). Questioning an individual's identity reflects two types of problematics involving the link between identity and appearance. First, the "what are you?" question can be a result of an ambiguous appearance. Biracial individuals who look neither Black nor White may be questioned by random strangers about their racial or ethnic background. Williams interpret this as a failure by the other to place the biracial person into one of their cognitive categorizations for members of particular racial groups. The second type of problematic is that addressed by the above example, which could better be termed the "what are you really?" question. In this case, others may approach the question of the biracial individual's racial background to clarify a discrepancy between the appearance and the professed identity. In this case, there can either be a renegotiation of the identity, or an interactional rupture can take place in which no shared meaning can be agreed upon.[7] Because individuals do not create and maintain an identity in isolation, others in their interactional context must support or validate their self-understanding as Black, White, or biracial. Figure 41.3 maps the effect of appearance on identity.

The Influence of Social Status on Identity

It is too simplistic a picture to say that biracial individuals' appearance alone determines their racial identity. The effect of social networks in which an individual is situated must additionally be considered in order to understand their choice of identity. An individual actor is socially located in a system of networks, or social relationships, which are directly related to their social status. Status brings access to different types of social networks. For biracial individuals, the higher the status of one's parents, the more likely that an individual is to have contact with White peer groups. The more time that individuals spend interacting with White peer groups, the less likely they are to develop an understanding of their biracialness as a singular (Black) identity. More specifically, the more time that an individual spends in White peer groups, the more likely they are to cultivate a degree of cultural savvy to fit in with their peers and to see both Whiteness and Blackness in their self-understanding and interactional presentation of self.

The preceding statement suggests that it is merely the access to different types of networks that influences the directionality of one's biracial identity. It is important to note, however, that it is not merely the amount of contact an individual has with either White or Black peers or family members (Hall, 1980), nor is it exclusively which group the individual uses as a reference group (Fields, 1996; Kerckhoff and McCormick, 1995). Instead, it is the type of contact that an individual has with others, or the way in which an individual socially experiences race, that mediates the relationship between one's social status and their biracial identity.

An additional case may illustrate this argument. Kristy is a biracial woman from New Jersey. She is White in appearance, with fair skin, long curly light brown hair, freckles, and green eyes. She attended public schools, which were 50% Black, until the 10th grade. She stated the following in reference to her relationships with Black students:

> I was always rejected by the Black women. I just shied away from the Black males because they were a little intimidating and a little too aggressive I thought. So then when I transferred sophomore year, I went to a Catholic school that only had maybe, about ten Blacks counting the four biracial students, so when I got there I was really taken in by these people and it was just a totally different world. It was like, [in public school] I was really never accepted by these Black females because well, you probably been told this too, they were jealous because you have good hair and light eyes. I remember thinking what were they jealous of? I didn't choose to be like this, I don't mind it, you know what I mean, so it was really their problem I think. Then I went to Catholic school.... I didn't really know anybody, and I was just like hopefully, it will be better. Of course it was better because there was less Black people for me to contend with.... Maybe because it was a Catholic prep school that was $4000.00 a year, that made people really appreciate education and different cultures and you know, and these people really took me in and it was nice. So we [the Black and biracial students], it was a close knit group, it was kind of like family within that high school....

She said about her college transition:

> When I came here it was like, I'm gonna go to [college] and it's gonna kind of be the same as my high school. Cuz you know, here there's not many Black people—it's on a larger scale, but its the same kind of ratio. So I was asked to do a program [specifically for minority students] the summer before freshman year, and naturally you're friends with thirty Black people right away. So that was great and you know, finally it was like oh, they don't care that I'm so light-skinned or whatever, so that was nice. Especially freshman year, I totally identified with the Black population here. And I was telling my parents, this is so opposite of what I've been running away from all my life because finally these people are like, "you're just a person," you know what I mean.

Kristy's experience is interesting specifically because it provides a critical case that defies the simplicity of using the number of Black social networks for understanding her biracial identity. In this case, Kristy underwent the greatest degree of rejection by her Black peers when she was in an environment with a large number of Blacks. Attending a school where 1/2 of the students are Black provided her with numerous opportunities to form friendships with other Black students (as compared to a school with lower numbers of Black students). It was in this environment however, that she reports being "rejected" by Black women and avoiding interaction with Black men. Here, her self-understanding as a Black woman was not validated. In fact, the incongruence between her appearance and identity caused numerous interactional ruptures (such as gum being thrown in her "good" hair and fistfights). This "rejection" by Black women was counterbalanced by friendship from her White peers with whom she had a common economic status. It was in the context of this simultaneous failure to be accepted as Black, by Blacks, and acceptance by Whites as biracial, that Kristy developed her self-understanding of what it means to be biracial.

Once Kristy transferred to a predominately White school, however, with fewer Blacks to "contend with," her closest network of friendships shifted from exclusively White to inclusive of Black and biracial students. This environment was substantively different than her previous school with different "types" of students. Specifically, the Black students at her new school were exclusively middle to upper-middle class and, because they were in an environment which made them a visible minority, they had a strong vested interest in mutual self-acceptance. It was in this group, composed of Blacks that accepted her, and several other biracial peers, that she found further validation for her biracial identity.

Finally, her movement to college further illustrates the importance of examining the type of social interaction an individual has within any given social network. Again, Kristy was in an environment in which Blacks were a small and highly visible minority (less than 2% of the student body). Here, the pattern of her high school relationships was repeated, facilitated by ties made during the summer program. She was accepted by a small cohesive group of Black students at a predominately White institution while maintaining her core group of White friends. These experiences solidified her understanding of biracialness as a border identity.

Specific socio-demographic factors may enable an individual to have access to differing types of social networks than would be available to others. Social networks provide the terrain in which identities may be negotiated, particularly where non-existent identities may emerge in order for the participants to understand an individual's presence within a particular network. It is precisely in these networks that the key process of interactional validation occurs and contributes to the differential choices in identification of biracial individuals.

DISCUSSION

This article questions the assumption, that underlies the push to add a multi-racial category to the 2000 Census, that most biracial people identify as biracial and that "biracial" identity has a singular meaning. The cases presented reflect a homogeneous and highly skewed group of respondents. All came from middle- to upper-middle-class families, all were raised in predominately White social contexts, none could describe incidents of experiencing discrimination by Whites, and yet many talked about feeling "rejected" by Blacks. These students had a singular set of experiences, which led to their strong identifications as biracial. Possibly it is individuals such as these that multiracial advocates believe an additional Census category will represent. We must ask however, if it is not also exclusively these individuals that would be represented by such a change. Is it possible that biracial identity is largely a middle-class phenomenon? Is this particular self-understanding created and validated by those with a specific and privileged set of social experiences? Would we find a different type of identity amongst those who have strong ties in Black social networks, who live in exclusively Black neighborhoods, and attend predominately Black schools?

One final case may help to both support the conceptual model presented and extend our understanding of the diverse meanings of "biracial" identity. Gregory Howard Williams (1995) has written an autobiographical text that explores his social experience of race. Williams grew up in the south believing that both he and his parents were White. At the age of 12, his parent's marriage dissolved and he moved back to their hometown of Muncie, Indiana with his father. On the bus ride to Muncie, Williams' father revealed that he had been "passing," that he was in fact African-American, and that once they arrived in Muncie, Williams and his younger brother would also be Black. This was a shocking realization to Williams and the rest of the book depicts his experiences as a White-appearing Black child, his shift into extreme poverty, and his entry and gradual acceptance within Muncie's Black community.

In Williams' case, once he moved to Muncie, his social status changed drastically. He went from a relatively comfortable middle-class existence to a life of poverty. His social networks shifted from exclusively White to exclusively Black. In fact, his White grandparents also lived in Muncie but Williams was no longer allowed to visit them (as he had when he was "White"). Despite his White appearance, Williams experienced severe discrimination by Whites. It was this experience of discrimination that solidified his self-understanding as Black (i.e., not as biracial or White). His social experience of race was characterized by prejudicial treatment by Whites and seeing other Blacks systematically discriminated against. Once Williams arrived in Muncie, he could no longer have a White identity because it was not validated by any others in his social environment. In contrast, his identity as African-American was cultivated, protected and nurtured by a significant other who came to be a surrogate mother for Williams and his younger sibling.

This case illustrates how an individual's social status and appearance affect both their access to different types of social networks and influence their interactions within those networks. Identity, as an interactionally validated self-understanding, is by definition a result of these ongoing interactions. It becomes clear how certain types of social contexts, such as those exhibited by the students in this study, may provide the terrain on which an individual is able to develop and cultivate a meaningful identity which is "biracial." It also becomes clear, however, when we consider the case of Gregory Howard Williams that there exist alternative social contexts in which "biracial" has no significant meaning. Social status and appearance are mediated by the types of social interactions an actor experiences. These interactions set the parameters of meaning, from which the biracial individual identity is constructed, negotiated, challenged, reshaped, validated, and ultimately sustained.

NOTES

1. Interracial marriages increased from 150,000 in 1960 to 1.5 million in 1990 (US Bureau of the Census, 1993).

2. No terminology currently exists to accurately describe mixed race individuals or to reflect the diversity of possible combinations. While recognizing this limitation, throughout this paper I will utilize the general term "biracial" to describe individuals who have one Black self-identifying biological parent and one White self-identifying biological parent.

3. The American answer to the question "who is Black?" has been anyone who has any African ancestry whatsoever (Davis, 1991; Myrdal, 1962; Williamson, 1980). The term "one drop rule" originated in the South where one drop of "Black blood" designated an individual Black. This has also been known as the "one Black ancestor rule," the "traceable amount rule," and the "hypodescent rule." This definition of Blackness that emerged from the South became the rest of the nation's definition and was accepted by both Blacks and Whites.

4. Williamson (1980) provides a thorough discussion of the shifting statuses of mulattos (within the Black community) during various periods of US history.

5. A Current Population Survey Supplement was conducted to assess the effects of adding a multi-racial category to the 2000 Census. The findings indicated that less than 1.5 percent of all those surveyed identified themselves as multiracial. The addition of the category as an option affected the proportion of those identifying as American Indian/Alaska Native (which dropped) but it had no effect on Blacks (Tucker and Kojetin, 1996).

6. These categories of self-understanding are not necessarily mutually exclusive; instead they represent ideal types.

7. An illustration of interactional rupture can be drawn from a case presented in Funderberg (1994). The individual is a White appearing woman, who changed her given name to Zenobia Kujichagulia, and self-identifies for the most part as Black, but occasionally as Black and Cherokee. She tells the following story: "This was an all-black environment, and as they introduced me to this woman, one friend says to me, 'Zenobia, tell her what you are.' So I knew what was coming, although I didn't expect this woman to go all the way off.

    "I said, 'I'm black and Cherokee.' Like I told you, I always leave the last part off [that she's also White].

    "The woman looked at me and said, 'Like hell you are.'

    "I said, 'Yes. Like hell I am.'

    "And she said, 'No, I mean'—like I didn't know what she meant—'I mean you are not black. You might be Cherokee but you are not black.'

    "And I said, 'I'll be sure to tell my daddy you said so.' And she just started cussing, ranting and raving, and I looked at her and I looked at the friend and said, 'I think I'll go now,' and just went across the room."

REFERENCES

Anzaldua, Gloria. 1987. *Borderlands/La Frontera: The New Mestizo*. San Francisco: Spinsters/Aunt Lute Foundation.

Bertaux, Daniel. 1981. *Biography and Society: The Life History Approach in the Social Sciences*. Beverly Hills, CA: Sage Publications.

Blumer, Herbert. 1969. *Symbolic Interactionism: Perspective and Method*. Englewood Cliffs, NJ: Prentice-Hall.

Bogdan, Robert, and Sari Knopp Biklen. 1982. *Qualitative Research for Education: An Introduction to Theory and Methods*. Boston: Allyn and Bacon.

Bradshaw, C.K. 1992. "Beauty and the Beast: On Racial Ambiguity." In *Racially Mixed People in America*, edited by M.P.P. Root. Newbury Park, CA: Sage.

Davis, F.J. 1991. *Who is Black?* University Park, PA: Pennsylvania State University Press.

Delpit, Lisa. 1988. "The Silenced Dialogue: Power and Pedagogy in Educating Other People's Children." *Harvard Educational Review* 58(3):280–298.

Fanon, Frantz. 1952. *Black Skin, White Masks*. New York: Grove.

Fields, L. 1996. "Piecing Together the Puzzle: Self-Concept and Group Identity in Biracial Black/White Youth." In *Racially Mixed People in America*, edited by M.P.P. Root. Newbury Park, CA: Sage.

Funderberg, Lise. 1994. *Black, White, Other*. New York: Morrow.

Goffman, Erving. 1959. *The Presentation of Self in Everyday Life*. New York: Anchor Press Doubleday.

———. 1963. *Behavior in Public Places: Notes on the Social Organization of Gatherings*. New York: Free Press of Glencoe.

Hall, C.C. 1980. "The Ethnic Identity of Racially Mixed People." Unpublished doctoral dissertation, University of California, Los Angeles.

Jones, Lisa. 1994. *Bulletproof Diva: Tales of Race, Sex, and Hair*. New York: Doubleday.

Kerckhoff, C., and T. McKormick. 1995. "Marginal Status and Marginal Personality." *Social Forces* 34:48–55.

King, Rebecca, and Kimberly DaCosta. 1996. "Changing Face, Changing Race: The Remaking of Race in the Japanese American and African American Communities." In *Racially Mixed People in America*, edited by M.P.P. Root. Newbury Park, CA: Sage.

Lifton, Robert. 1993. *The Protean Self: Human Resilience in an Age of Fragmentation*. New York: Basic Books.

Marshall, Catherine, and Gretchen B. Rossman. 1989. *Designing Qualitative Research*. Newbury Park, CA: Sage.

McBride, James. 1996. *The Color of Water: A Black Man's Tribute to His White Mother*. New York: Riverhead Books.

Myrdal, G. 1962. *An American Dilemma* (20th ed). New York: Harper & Row.

Park, R. 1950. *Race and Culture*. Glencoe, IL: Free Press.

Root, Maria P. 1992. "Back to the Drawing Board: Methodological Issues in Research on Multiracial people." In *Racially Mixed People in America*, edited by M.P.P. Root. Newbury Park, CA: Sage.

Scales-Trent, J. 1995. *Notes of a White Black Woman*. University Park: Pennsylvania State University Press.

Smitherman, Geneva. 1986. *Talkin and Testifyin: The Language of Black America*. Detroit: Wayne State University Press.

Spencer, J. 1997. *The New Colored People*. New York: New York University Press.

Stone, Gregory. 1962. "Appearance and the Self." In *Human Behavior and Social Processes*, edited by A.M. Rose. Boston: Houghton Mifflin.

Taylor, Steven J., and Robert Bogdan. 1984. *Introduction to Qualitative Research Methods: The Search for Meanings*. New York: Wiley.

Tucker, C., and B. Kojetin. 1996. "Testing Racial and Ethic Origin Questions in the CPS Supplement." *Monthly Labor Review*.

US Bureau of the Census. 1993. *We, The American*. Washington, DC: Government Printing Office.

Waters, Mary. 1990. *Ethnic Options: Choosing Identities in America*. Berkeley: University of California Press.

White, Walter Francis. 1948. *A Man Called White: The Autobiography of Walter White*. New York: Viking Press.

Williams, Gregory. 1995. *Life on the Color Line: The True Story of a White Boy Who Discovered He Was Black*. New York: Dutton.

Williams, T. 1996. "Race as Process." In *Racially Mixed People in America*, edited by M.P.P. Root. Newbury Park, CA: Sage.

Williamson, Joel. 1980. *New People: Miscegenation and Mulattos in the United States*. New York: Free Press.

Zack, Naomi. 1993. *Race and Mixed Race*. Philadelphia: Temple University Press.

Chapter 42

Language Matters

Vijay Agnew

With attention to the ways in which race intersects with ethnicity, class, gender, and immigrant status to influence the privileges and opportunities of individuals, Vijay Agnew (2005) highlights the complexity of identity with reference to South Asian immigrant women in Canada. She notes that these identification factors, along with English-language ability, not only help in the construction of her respondents' identities, but also in their capacity and courage to deal with the difficulties of settling into a new country and trying to realize their dreams.

Imagine a fall day in Toronto. Let me help you, in case you've never been here. Multicoloured leaves in red, yellow, brown mixed with some green lie on the roads, but as cars drive by they scatter, some flying high into the air while others, entangled in a mass, rise slowly and soon fall to lie in a heap by the wayside. Long-time residents of Toronto would describe the weather for this day as warm and pleasant, but for me—an immigrant from India—it is cold. I am bundled up in a black woollen coat, with socks and shoes, ready to hop into my car. I drive through wide boulevards laid out in a grid while listening to classical Western music on my radio. But somewhere, deep in my heart, lurks a nostalgia for loud film music, pedestrians, vendors, and the noise, soot, and dust of Mumbai (formerly Bombay), rather than these clean, quiet, and well-marked Toronto roads.

I reach a church, one of many such churches that dot residential neighbourhoods in Toronto, and carefully scrutinize its exterior to get my bearings. I see a side entrance with a poster stuck on the door and walk with deliberate steps towards it, and it directs me to the English as a Second Language (ESL) class that I have come to observe. The class is being held in the basement in a room that is large, simple, and functional; there are no pictures, decorations, or plants. In the centre of the room about thirty chairs are lined up in rows, and a flip chart with a chair for the teacher next to it faces the students. On a table against the wall sit an aluminum coffee urn, milk, sugar, styrofoam cups, and a plate of cookies.

A grass-roots community-based organization of South Asians[1] has brought together about twenty-five new immigrants for an introductory class in the English language. The women are wearing *salwar kamiz*,[2] or saris, the dress of South Asians, but in this basement in Toronto they present a curious amalgamation of the needs of the present and the norms of the past. In the tropical heat and dust of South Asia, the salwar kamiz that are worn during the day are made of light cotton fabric and are comfortable to wear and easy to maintain. Usually women wear sandals with them. In Toronto, it is cold, and thus the women are also wearing colour-coordinated heavy cardigans over their salwar kamiz. They're also wearing shoes with socks.

The women's dress marks them as immigrants and newcomers. To my South Asian eyes, this mixture of East and West—light textures with heavy sweaters—represents a curious hodgepodge of styles. But perhaps other white Canadians who are unfamiliar with South Asian dress see the outfits not as an attempt by the women to accommodate themselves to the weather but as foreign and different. After having lived in Canada and studied immigrants for about twenty years, I still have ambivalent feelings about such clothing, and am uncertain what South Asian women would ideally wear in Toronto, and, more generally, in Canada. Sometimes I think these women ought to retain their traditional dress as a symbol of their cultural identity, but at other times I want them to discard their salwar kamiz and adopt pants and jeans and be done with it.

I am jostled by memories that remind me that in the present, as opposed to the past, the ideal is for a multicultural Canada, and that Canadians do not wish to impose any one kind of clothing on the women. Immigrants are free to choose—or so it is said. Sombrely, I wonder how the women are responding to the impolite stares and frowns from some people in public places, people silently expressing disapproval of their dress. Perhaps such stares make the women uncomfortable, and they begin to think about wearing jeans and pants so that they will not, so obviously, attract attention to themselves. But perhaps their lack of confidence and insecurity in their new environment makes them content with the small adjustments in their dress that they must make. Perhaps family norms and religious precepts make them reluctant to adopt new ways of dressing. I hope the women are warm. Their demeanour suggests that they are feeling uncertain, awkward, and ill at ease.

A palpable sense of anxious anticipation fills the room. All of us, with the exception of the teacher, are South Asian. The South Asian counsellor from the area's community organization gives me a brief rundown on the identities of the women present and introduces me to the teacher, Jane, as a professor who is collecting material for a book on immigrant women in Canada. I talk to Jane, who is dark-haired, fair-skinned, and middle-aged, but my eyes roam restlessly among the other women hoping to make eye contact with them. The women, however, avoid looking in our direction and no one responds by looking or smiling back at me. The women seem to be taking a bit more interest in each other, and some have started making conversation with the person seated next to them, but most are quiet as they wait for the class to begin. The counsellor encourages the women to get themselves some coffee, and, although the women glance toward the table, none gets up. I had expected that the contrast between the larger, culturally alien Canadian environment and the people who look like oneself, despite their social differences, might create a sense of immediate comfort and familiarity. Yet the usual hesitancy and reserve among people who are strangers to one another are still present.

This is the first class in the program of introductory conversational English that is funded by the government as part of its settlement service to new immigrants. Attending the program is free (COSTI 2004). The class is being held in Scarborough, where a large proportion of immigrants from South Asia have settled. In the 1990s, most South Asian immigrants came from India, Sri Lanka, Bangladesh, and Pakistan, and a large proportion of Punjabis from India and Tamils from Sri Lanka settled in Scarborough. Most were economic migrants, like their predecessors throughout Canadian history, while a small proportion were refugees from Sri Lanka escaping ethnic and religious violence there. Judging from the appearances of the women, their style of dress and ornamentation, I would say the class reflects this population mix.

Before long, Jane moves to the front of the class to begin the day's lesson in conversational English, and I walk to the side of the room in the hope of catching the expressions on the women's faces, but otherwise wish to be forgotten by them. Jane tries to put the women at ease by smiling broadly, but their body language reveals their tension as they gaze anxiously at her and focus entirely on what she is about to say and do. Jane tells them slowly and in carefully enunciated English that she has two goals for the class: first, to teach them how to ask a bus driver for directions, and how to tell him or her where they wish to get off; and, second, how to buy a coffee and ask for milk and sugar in it. Jane breaks down the tasks into small segments, providing the words that go with each, and interjecting jokes that the women sometimes respond to with nervous smiles.

Jane asks the women to introduce themselves to the class and to say where they are from. She smiles encouragingly, and the women, who seem terrified, mumble softly, "My name is Harjeet, Ludhiana, Punjab," or "My name is Santosh, Jullunder, India," or "Shahnaz, Karachi, Pakistan," or "Swarna, Colombo, Sri Lanka," and so on. The names and places are familiar to me, and they give me clues about the women's regional, religious, and linguistic identities. I follow the women with my eyes as each one introduces herself, and, almost reflexively, I find myself fleshing out a picture of each by mentally adding other details of her social background and identity.

Canadian immigration criteria in the post–Second World War period favoured those South Asians who were upper or middle class. The 1967 immigration policy, which laid the framework for later developments, required immigrants, among other things, to have a certain level of education, knowledge of English or French, and job-related skills, and to be in a profession or occupation that was in demand in Canada (Li 2003, 14–37). Only those with substantial economic, social, and psychological resources were motivated to take on the risks of emigrating and had the financial resources to go through the process of applying for immigration to Canada and leaving their homes.

The ability to immigrate to a new country is a privilege for a few and is vied for and envied by others in South Asia. Although the criteria are weighed heavily in favour of the upper and middle classes, other ideals embedded in immigration policies—such as "family reunification" and "humanitarian and compassionate grounds"—vary the picture. [...] In addition to immigrants, refugees have come from Sri Lanka, though a very small percentage are from the Punjab. The Tamil women in the room are dependants of male refugee claimants, such as fathers, brothers, and husbands. These criteria have spawned a diversified South Asian population in Toronto: some are professional, English-speaking immigrants, while others have limited education and knowledge of English. Consequently, South Asian immigrants are found at both ends of the labour market (Basavarajappa and Jones 1999). The immigration status of the individual is significant because it entitles her/him to an array of social services, such as this ESL class (Boyd, DeVries, and Simkin 1994). [...]

The age, clothes, and jewellery of some of the women in the class suggest that they are recent brides who have come to Canada consequent to an arranged marriage, while others are older and have come with their families. All the women present are part of the "family class" of male immigrants, the sponsored dependent relatives of brothers and sisters already here. There are no senior citizens in the class, although they too would be eligible for free language training. The women may have several valuable job-related skills, but their lack of ability to speak English disadvantages them in locating good jobs. Besides, their social integration is impeded by their inability to speak English, and there is some danger of their becoming isolated and feeling alienated. Community groups, such as the one that organized this class, act as mediators between the women and the larger society, and they create venues for them to network with others of their own linguistic and regional communities (Agnew 1998).

All the South Asians in this ESL class had lived in multilingual environments "back home." The dominant national language in India is Hindi; in Pakistan it is Urdu; and in Sri Lanka it is Sinhala. There are innumerable regional languages in all these countries. For example, India has seventeen official languages recognized by its constitution; there are thirty-five languages spoken by more than a million people; and in addition there are 22,000 dialects. "People write books and letters, make films, produce plays, print newspapers, talk, teach, preach, fight, make love, and dream in all those languages" (Kumar 2002, 7). In the class that day, only Hindi, Punjabi, and Tamil were represented.

Since many countries in South Asia were colonized, some European languages have been absorbed locally and have become part of their cultures as well. India, Pakistan, and Bangladesh share a common history of British colonization, and the English language is still used there in governmental institutions, in education, and, to a large extent, in politics as well. The Dutch colonized Sri Lanka, but since knowledge of English provides social and class mobility, it has been widely adopted. In India, language has been a contested issue and there have been disagreements over the use of English, acceptance of Hindi as a national language, and the division of territory between states (Khilnani 1997, 175). The status of English vis-à-vis the local languages is further complicated because English is identified as the "idiom of modernity," and the "proliferating, uncontainable vernaculars with the 'natural' state of things in India" (Chaudhuri 2001, xx). Nevertheless, historically English is the language of the elite and the privileged in India, and continues at present to be a requisite for social and class mobility. Official counts peg the number of English-speaking people at 2 per cent, but others argue that a realistic estimate is closer to 15 per cent (Kumar 2002, 6).

As a young girl, I spoke Hindi, Derawali, and English, and could understand Punjabi, Sindhi, and Urdu. I gave no conscious thought to my knowledge of these different languages, and since many Indians are familiar with several languages I thought it to be unexceptional. In Toronto, when I was required to fill in forms at the university and identify the languages that I could read, write, or speak, I understood the question to pertain to European languages and thus left the space blank. Yet in one incident, a white Canadian professor was annoyed with me for not identifying the languages that she assumed correctly that I knew. Her words made me reflect on how I had unconsciously imbibed the biases of the larger Canadian society, how I had voluntarily declined to take or give credit to people like me for being bilingual and even trilingual. My action can be characterized as a telling example of internalized racism. The women in the ESL class were all bilingual and they knew their regional and national language—almost a necessity in South Asia—but were not conversant with English.

The social and cultural alienation that some Indian women experience in Canada is most easily explained by their inability to speak English. However, in documenting the experience of the women in this ESL class, I am attempting to show how race, class, and gender, along with an inability to speak English, constructs the identity of these women in Canada.

Identity, feminist theorists contend, is socially constructed and it changes with time, place, and context. The process of moving from one country to another and learning to get along in a new society changes the self-perception of immigrant women; however, their inability to speak English takes on significance that is quite unlike that which they had experienced in India. The self-perception of the women is at odds with the way white Canadians know and understand them. Social identity, however, is "principally the identity which is recognized and confirmed by others"; consequently, it does not matter how strenuously "individuals may disavow or evade it" (Andermahr, Lovell, and Wolkowitz 2000, 124). Social actions and interactions become meaningful, and although they can be interpreted, much like a text, in many different ways, yet they indicate to the individual "how to go on," and give them valuable clues about how to participate in the culture in which they are now living (249). Social actions and interactions thus affect the individual in immediate and tangible ways.

Ethnic groups have conventionally been constructed in ways that homogenize their experiences and erase the many distinctions, such as those of social class and gender, within them. There are commonalities of experience, no doubt, but at the same time there are vast differences that stem from the different identities. The social construction of an ethnic group may emphasize a particular aspect of its identity, such as language or religion (e.g., head scarf), which not only subsumes its other attributes but also blames the victims for the difficulties they encounter in integrating themselves with Canadian society. Yet, as postcolonial feminists argue, women have had to "negotiate the precarious balance between the tenacious forces of integration and the desire to maintain a sense of their cultural identity as a strategy of self-preservation in their country of adoption" (Code 2000, 396).

Indian women, like other racialized women, experience racism when white Canadians encounter their "difference" from the norm, whether it is skin colour, different clothing, or an inability to speak English. Everyday racism "expresses itself in glances, gestures, forms of speech, and physical movements. Sometimes it is not even consciously experienced by its perpetrators, but it is immediately and painfully felt by its victims—the empty seat next to a person of colour, which is the last to be occupied in a crowded bus; the slight movement away from a person of colour in an elevator; the overattention to the black customer in the shop; the inability to make direct eye contact with a person of colour; the racist joke told at a meeting; and the ubiquitous question 'Where did you come from?'" (Henry et al. 1995, 47).

Indian women's community-based organizations give the lie to the stereotype that constructs women from their group as passive. Community-based organizations lobby for and hold ESL classes for new immigrants from their communities despite constant threats of non-renewal of funds and government cutbacks (Agnew 1996, 1998). They wish to help individuals adjust to their new environment, and to lessen their cultural alienation by bringing them together in supportive environments such as an ESL class. Working-class, non-English-speaking women have the double burden of not speaking English and not having the language—words—to articulate their dissatisfaction with their marginality and oppression. Consequently, we may well ask, why do they come? I answer this question in the next section.

IMAGINATION AS A SOCIAL PRACTICE

"I left them all and walked briskly towards the aeroplane, not looking back, looking only at my shadow before me, a dancing dwarf on the tarmac" (Naipaul 2003, 78). Naipaul's description of the first time he left Trinidad to study at Oxford catches the sense of hope and excitement that immigrants experience on leaving their homes to begin a new and different stage in their lives. The process of leaving home is difficult and painful, but at first it is mitigated by hopes, dreams, and fantasies of a new life in affluent Canada.

> We often think of ourselves as unique individuals with distinct hopes and dreams, yet our imagination is profoundly influenced by the social context in which we live. The images that float in our minds germinate as a result of where we have been and what we have seen and read. Jawaharlal Nehru, in a letter to his daughter Indira Gandhi, writes: For many years now I have been traveling in these oceans of time and space.... It is a fascinating journey ... when the past and present get strangely mixed together and the future flits about like an insubstantial shadow, or some image seen in a dream. The real journey is of the mind; without that there is little significance in wandering about physically. It is because the mind is full of pictures and ideas and aspects of India that even the bare stones—and so much more our mountains and great rivers, and old monuments and ruins,

and snatches of old song and ballad, and the way people look and smile, and the queer and significant phrases and metaphors they use—whisper of the past and the present and of the unending thread that unites them and leads us all into the future. When I have a chance … I like to leave my mind fallow and receive all these impressions. So I try to understand and discover India and some glimpses of her come to me, tantalize me and vanish away. (Gandhi 1992, 121)

Imagination, writes Appadurai (1996), is a social practice that is central to all forms of agency, a key component of the new global order, while the imaginary is a "constructed landscape of collective aspirations" (31). Appadurai has developed the concepts of "Ethnoscapes, ideascapes, and mediascapes" to show how media and travel fuel our imagination in the practice of our everyday lives, and he argues that our identities, localities, and communities are shaped by travel and images projected by the media: "The story of mass migration (voluntary and forced) is hardly a new feature of human history. But when it is juxtaposed with the rapid flow of mass-mediated images, scripts and sensations, we have a new order of instability in the production of modern subjectivities" (4). Immigrants' urge to move from one country to another and their settlement in new societies are deeply affected by a mass-mediated imagination that transcends national space.

As an English-speaking woman who lived in Bombay in the 1960s before I immigrated to Canada in 1970, the way I imagined the West was stimulated by the English-language books and magazines that I read, the Hollywood films that I watched, and the music of Pat Boone and Elvis Presley that I heard. (There was no television in those days in India, and the use of personal computers and the Internet was still in the future—even in the West.) Then there were regular stories about America that came in letters from my English-speaking physician brother who worked in New York City. My dream of studying in North America and living away from my family was an unconscious product of the glamorous images that I consumed from the mass media and the ideas that I garnered from English-language books and magazines. In Canada, I began to re-imagine and reinvent myself, although I did so unknowingly.

The imagination and the subjectivity of the Hindi-, Punjabi-, Urdu-, Sinhala-, and Tamil-speaking women who were in the ESL class must certainly be different than mine because they had lived in India, Pakistan, and Sri Lanka during a different period and in different social and political contexts. By the 1990s, television had become a well-established medium of entertainment throughout South Asia among the middle classes, including those who lived in smaller towns and cities. In India, the number and range of programs in different languages (Hindi, English, and regional languages) continued to expand, and television regularly broadcasted English-language serials produced in the West. Television programs and advertising came to be supplemented, as time progressed, by the Internet and cyberspace, new ways to produce and distribute images that inflected the imagination of the people as well. Furthermore, globalization generated a much greater and more constant flow of ideas and goods between countries, and that had an impact on the subjectivities of the people and constructed their sense of self in comparative and relational terms.

Time and social context distinguished the women in the class from me, but their identities were also different from the contemporary English-speaking professional and the entrepreneurial South Asian transnational migrant. These latter migrants leave their countries in pursuit of education, travel, and employment, but they are mobile and may over time live in many different countries to take advantage of the available economic, educational, and social opportunities for themselves and their families (Ong 1999). A vast array of electronic and print images penetrate and inform their imaginations and identities, the possibilities that are available to them in the present, and what and who they might become in the future.

As a student in Delhi, Amitava Kumar was enamoured of the idea of becoming a writer in the West, and his fantasies of life in London were fed by a returning Indian student, a Rhodes scholar from Oxford:

> I imagined trips to libraries, museums, lectures, theatres, parks. I got a gift from him: a pack of postcards showing scenes of life at Oxford. Sunlight slanted across the narrow brick street; bicycles were propped against walls covered with ivy; cricket was being played on the immaculate greens.... Our visitor from London had come bearing other gifts too: shaving cream and disposable razors and duty-free cigarettes. Tepid tea with toast and omelette in the Hindu College canteen on winter mornings had never tasted so good before because awaiting me at the end of the meal were imported Silk Cuts that I had just received. The London that the Oxford man described seeped into the winter mornings and became a part of my dream.... I wanted to be there. (Kumar 2002, 81–82)

The enormous popularity of Hindi-language Bollywood films (i.e., the Indian film industry located primarily in Mumbai) makes them one of the most significant cultural forms in national and transnational South Asian cultural practices (Desai 2004, 35). Mumbai is named after a local deity, Mumbadevi, but "the real propitiatory deity of the city is Lakshmi, the goddess of wealth. Bedecked in silk and jewels, standing on a lotus flower, a smile on her lips, gold coins spilling from her outstretched hand, pretty Lakshmi beckons her devotees. Glittering and glamorous, she holds out the promise of fortune but extracts cruel sacrifice from her worshippers even as she entices them" (Kamdar 2001, 131). Bollywood "brings the global into the local presenting people in Main Street, Vancouver, as well as Southall, London, with shared 'structures of feeling' that produce a transnational sense of communal solidarity" (Mishra 2002, 238).

Images and values propagated by Bollywood films and picked up in television and advertising filter into the imagination of people living in South Asia and the diaspora, creating thereby a "community of sentiment" that begins to imagine and feel things together (Appadurai 1996, 8). These everyday cultural practices mean that although people have disparate social identities and live in different social contexts, yet because they engage with the same media and its images, they come to share, to some extent, a similar set of social values and norms. These images and values that pervade popular culture play a role in constructing the dreams and fantasies of people living in different locations (Desai 2004).

People in the movie industry, Mehta argues, are "big dreamers" and their films give life to the "collective dreams" of a billion people (Mehta 2004, 340). One message that is often highlighted in Hindi-language films and television is that the "good life" comprises materialism and consumerism. The West is the epitome of consumerism, and the imagery associated with the West symbolizes wealth, influence, and power. Bollywood films have formulaic plots and elaborate song and dance routines that ask nothing more from the audience than they suspend their disbelief and enter a world of love and romance, wealth and power, and watch individuals who espouse ideal values emerge victorious (Kumar 2002, 30; Desai 2004). For example, a Bollywood movie may evoke fantasy and desire in audiences when they see the handsome and rich hero and his glamorously dressed heroine cavorting on the Swiss Alps. Such images, writes Appadurai (1996), become "scripts for possible lives to be imbricated with the glamour of film stars and fantastic film plots" (3).

A conventional, if simple, binary distinction is between the materialistic West and spiritual India. (Another similar and not unrelated cliché identifies India as innocent and America as the den of evil.) Such categorizations are often evoked as an apologetic defence of India's poverty, and what can be termed its lack of development. Indians, writes Sunil Khilnani (1997), have over the last century come to "see themselves in mirrors created by the West" (196). The Orientalist gaze of the Westerner defines India and Indians as the "Others" (i.e., they use their own culture and society as the norm and define other cultures in comparative terms, perceiving them not only as different but also as inferior; Said 1979).

Although it is discussed more rarely, India and other countries in South Asia have also helped shape the self-images of other cultures. According to Khilnani (1997) Western cultures have

> recurringly used India as a foil to define their own historical moments: to reassure or to doubt themselves. And Indians have also, on occasion, tried to work out their own "indigenous" ways of knowing the West. It is impossible to sever these twisted bonds of mutual knowingness and ignorance: the plunder is constant, and neither side can retreat into a luxurious hermeticism. Any discussion of India is thus inescapably forced on to the treacherous fields of the politics of knowledge. These must be navigated, like any political activity, by one's wits. There is no privileged compass, no method, or idiom that can assist. (197)

The middle classes in India, in the post-independence era, have abandoned their "traditional moorings" in their avid pursuit of social and class mobility based on the consumption of material goods. Some argue that these goals result from a thoughtless imitation of Western values, particularly among the younger, middle-class generation. Conspicuous consumption has become necessary for enhancing the self-esteem of the individual. "In a situation where things are difficult to get, and there are so many people around you defining their very existence by the ability to obtain them, the act of acquisition tends to disproportionately dominate the perception of self-esteem" (Varma 1998, 136). The materialistic goals of the middle classes can seem vacuous, debilitating, and immoral in a society where the vast majority of people are poor.

Images of a "good life" at one level threaten to homogenize the values of South Asians living "there" and "here"—in South Asia and in the diaspora. Yet they are consumed and interpreted in local settings and in particular ways that resist standardization and universalism. Furthermore, interpretations of a "good life" are relative and contextual; a "good life" for a middle-class Punjabi immigrant in Scarborough may entail access to and the availability of goods and services and a standard of living that differs from a Punjabi woman living in Ludhiana or Jullunder.

Dreams of affluence and well-being mitigate the heartache of emigrating and leaving behind family, friends, and home. In the post-1967 period, individuals who migrated to Canada often had personal contacts that acted as magnets in a process described as chain migration. Once a family left a village, town, or city, they in turn encouraged friends and relatives to migrate as well, by spinning dreams for them of jobs, educational opportunities, and economic security. For example, working- and middle-class Punjabi immigrants living in Canada still write letters and send photographs to their relatives in Ludhiana and Jullunder that describe their lives in terms of the availability of a good education for the children, well-paid jobs for themselves, and the ownership of consumer household goods for the family. They also return home periodically, bearing gifts for friends and family. While at home, they tell their family and friends of owning houses and cars, and, since there is no norm in those societies concerning mortgages and consumer loans, it is imagined that these individuals have no debts. In comparison with the lives of middle-class people in cities like Ludhiana and Jullunder, returning migrants have discretionary incomes that enable them to consume goods and travel and reinforce the image of the affluent West.

Migrants who return for a visit with their extended families after having lived in the West, the Middle East, or the Far East have some social and economic cachet among the middle classes in South Asia. Furthermore, their children speak fluent English. Given the class and social prestige still associated with that language in South Asia, this accomplishment signals the family's social mobility and well-being. The women in the ESL class undoubtedly had hopes and dreams for themselves and their families when they emigrated. They dreamed of a "good life" that was perhaps both different and similar to that of the other migrants. If not for the dreams, why would they dismantle their homes and think of rebuilding them elsewhere? Given the option of staying put or leaving, they made a choice according to their own limitations and potentials.

I wonder if the imaginations of the women in this ESL class ever carried them to this church basement where they are now sitting in an alien environment feeling anxious and nervous about learning English? I think not. The trials and tribulations of these new immigrants to Canada bring to mind my very different experiences with the language, despite being an English-speaking immigrant at the university. The words of Azar Nafisi (2004) resonate with me: "Other people's sorrows and joys have a way of reminding us of our own; we partly empathize with them because we ask ourselves; What about me? What does that say about my life, my pains, my anguish?" (326). [...]

LANGUAGE AND IMMIGRATION

At present, there are vast inequalities by region, urban or rural residence, social class, and gender in the availability and accessibility of schools and colleges. Thus, the question that Jane asked the women in the ESL class, "Where do you come from?", yields only the minimum facts and does not tell us of the uneven distribution of educational opportunities in the countries of origin that make English-language education available to some and not to others. These differences show up in the mix of immigrants that comes to live in Toronto and becomes part of the larger entity of South Asians. The disparities and disadvantages that originate in the country of origin are thus perpetuated and further aggravated in Canada.

Class and gender biases of Canadian immigration policies favour English-speaking immigrants; thus, women from India come to Canada predominantly as "dependants" (an immigration category) of their spouses or other male relatives. Their entry status as dependants further heightens the class and gender disadvantages experienced in their countries of birth, since immigration status determines access to social services such as ESL classes. Although all non-English-speaking immigrants have access to some introductory language training, only those who are considered to be destined for the labour market have extended opportunities for advanced learning. Since women have formally entered the country as dependants, it is assumed they will not be joining the labour market and thus will have access to only basic training in the English language. However, most Indian women, like other immigrant women, do take up paid employment, but the lack of language proficiency results in lower economic integration of women into the labour market and imposes what Li refers to as a "net income penalty" on the women (Li 2003). Often they end up working on the low rung of the occupational ladder in job ghettos such as the garment industry, working longer hours in more insecure work, and earning lower wages (Fincher et al. 1994). Further, it wastes the skills that the women have acquired with great difficulty and persistence on their part in their countries of birth, and have brought with them. This is a loss both to the individual and to the country.

Gender, race, place of origin, and language facility are cumulative disadvantages that have economic and social repercussions on women's lives. In Toronto, the inability to speak English deters the women from using public transportation, going out alone to buy groceries, or to do other errands for the family, such as driving, or making and keeping appointments at medical clinics and doctor's offices. (There are some community health clinics, such as Access Alliance or Women's Health in Women's Hands, which specifically cater to a multilingual clientele.) The children quickly learn English in school and sometimes act as interpreters for their mothers, but the consequent loss of authority is problematic. Their inability to speak English isolates the women, robs them of autonomy, and reinforces their dependence on their spouses. One positive interpretation of this ESL class might be to view it as indicative of the women's determination to become independent, productive, and contributing citizens of Canada.

The women in this ESL class are intently focused on the instructions Jane gives them. Their tongues get entangled in the strange sounds they are expected to make, the words roll out of their mouths awkwardly, and, though embarrassed, they struggle on bravely, repeating the words that Jane encourages them to say. They are hesitant and self-conscious, yet they carry on.

LINGUISTIC AND CULTURAL HOMES

Language is embedded in cultural norms. Lack of proficiency in the English language crystallizes many other forms of cultural alienation and discomfort experienced by new immigrants, but almost all racialized immigrants have subtle difficulties with the language despite their ability to speak English fluently. The linguistic and cultural experience of a new male immigrant from India to the United States (before vegetarianism became a fad) is described by his daughter:

> "I would like to eat ve-ge-tables. Do you serve ve-ge-tables?" asked my father. (He pronounced the second half of the word like the word "table" with a long "a.")
> "Huh?"
> "Ve-ge-tables."
> "Oh, ya want vegebles? Why'n ya say so? We don got no vegebles. Ya wanna sanwich?"
> "Cheese sandwich? Do you have cheese sandwich?"
> "Ya don wanannie meat?"
> "I don't eat meat. I am a vegetarian. I only eat ve-ge-tables."
> "Okay, kid, I'll make ya a cheese sandwich." (Kamdar 2001, 181)

Although everyone speaks English in the accent that is common to their place of origin and determined by their social class and education, new immigrants from South Asia often feel belittled when they speak English and others have difficulty understanding them. V.S. Naipaul (2000) felt apologetic that he spoke English in a "foul manner" after he first arrived in London. He confides in a letter to his sister, "but now my English pronunciation is improving by the humiliating process of error and snigger" (73). English-speaking South Asians (and other racialized groups) feel disgruntled when they are asked to repeat words and sentences or when white, English-speaking Canadians turn their ears towards the individual to more easily catch his or her words. The latter act is sometimes experienced as a form of racism.

In this ESL class, Jane writes the words *north*, *south*, *east*, and *west* on the flip chart and attempts to gauge from the expression on the students' faces whether they understand the concept. She then goes on to tell them to ask the driver of the bus to let them off, for example, at the northwest corner in front of the mall. The cultural lesson for the students is the use of this terminology, for in South Asia they would normally use landmarks, such as a temple, a grocery store, or a bus stop to find their way and to locate themselves. Even I, as a new immigrant, was bewildered when friends asked me to use such terminology to fix a meeting place. Similarly, in South Asia, tea and coffee are commonly brewed with milk, except when requested otherwise. Thus, being served coffee and tea made with plain water was a new experience as well (at least until some coffee shops popularized Chai as a menu item). The ESL class was about language, but social and cultural lessons were being imparted simultaneously as well.

Cultural differences, or the sense of being an outsider or a foreigner, can make the individual feel alienated and heighten feelings of sadness, nostalgia, and create a longing for home. After having been in London for a few weeks that coincided with the Christmas season, Naipaul (2000) wrote to his family in Trinidad:

> I have been thinking more and more about home.... Christmas never meant much to me or to any one of our family. It was always so much of a glorious feeling of fun we felt existed somewhere, but we could never feel where it was. We were always on the outside of a vague feeling of joy. The same feeling is here with me in London. Yet there is so much more romance here. It gets dark about half past three and all the lights go on. The shops are bright, the streets are well lit and the streets are full of people. I walk through the streets, yet am so much alone, so much on the outside of this great festive feeling.
>
> But I was thinking of home. I could visualize every detail of everything I knew—the bit of the gate, for instance, that was broken off, the oleander tree and the withering roses. Sometimes the sound of a car starting in the road rouses me. The uncertain hesitant beat of the engine brings back No. 26 [their home] back to me, smells and all. It makes me feel sad. Don't misunderstand. It makes me think about you people in a way I thought of you only rarely at home. (43)

Immigrants, particularly those who are racialized, have raised questions about the nature of Canadian identity and the expectations of the population already here about how subsequent arrivals ought to become Canadians. In the early and mid-twentieth century, the ideal of assimilation and Anglo-conformity was held up as necessary and the only way to become a Canadian. But the continued attachment of immigrants to their culture and their disillusionment with the ideal of assimilation led them to express doubts and raise questions politically. Eventually, the policies of bilingualism and multiculturalism were introduced, but they were critiqued for attempting to separate language from culture. Since the focus of these policies was culture, they left undisturbed the unequal distribution of power and prestige among different ethnic and racial groups in Canada (Fleras 2004). At present, South Asians, along with other racialized groups, increasingly focus on anti-racism and human rights activism. Rushdie argues that a creative imagination can give us the power to construct a better world. He writes that imagination can transform and instill a "confidence in our ability to improve the world" and "imagination is the only weapon with which reality can be smashed so it may be subsequently reconstructed" (cited in Needham 2000, 69).

Throughout Canadian history, South Asian women (along with other racialized populations), whether they speak English or not, have encountered formidable structural barriers of race, class, gender, and heterosexuality (Agnew 1996). Although oppressed and victimized, they have survived by exercising their wits. Monica Ali's (2003) novel *Brick Lane* is about the conflicts and tensions that define the immigrant experience. Nazneen, the main character in the novel, is an eighteen-year-old girl from Bangladesh who has an arranged marriage and comes to live in London. On her arrival, she knows only three words in English—*sorry* and *thank you*—and does not know a soul. She lives with her husband, Charu, in Brick Lane, an area exclusively inhabited by immigrants from Bangladesh, whose reference points and values are those that exist "back home." Charu sees no reason for Nazneen to learn English, and she accepts his dictum without protest. Nazneen's lack of English is seldom depicted in the novel as being problematic; rather, it is one of the many characteristics that shape and determine her immigrant experience. Nazneen's life is entirely confined to Brick Lane, where she is happy to make friends, start a family, maintain a correspondence with her sister at "home," while she cautiously adapts to the "strange new contours of life as an outsider in London" (Lehmann 2003).

Nazneen's baby dies, and she is lonely, but in the face of these disappointments she shows courage and initiative in overcoming difficulties. When Charu becomes unemployed, she locates a job sewing garments on a piecemeal basis. She has an affair with the middleman, Karim, who brings her the garments, and through him she is introduced to some young Islamic activists. Nazneen's horizons slowly expand, and when she finally goes on a sightseeing trip to London with Charu and their daughters and utters aloud the word *sorry*, she is taken aback at her own boldness. She picks up English from her daughters and from watching television. Ice skating fascinates her and represents "exhilarating freedom, frozen false emotion and finally a new world of possibilities" (Maslin 2003). Eventually, Charu desires to return "home," but Nazneen is ambivalent and resists him. At the end of the novel, the reader is presented with two epigraphs, one from Heraclitus, "A man's character is his fate," and the other from Turgenev, "Sternly, remorselessly, fate guides us." Ali's book raises the question, "Do we, can we, control our own lives?" and "Should [Nazneen] submit to her fate or make it?" (Gorra 2003).

Immigration is a quest for a better life as defined and imagined by the individual. But for Rushdie (2002), the particulars of the imagined life are less significant than the quest to realize the dream. "In all quests the voyageur is confronted by terrifying guardians of territory, an ogre here, a dragon there. So far and no farther, the guardian commands. But the voyageur must refuse the other's definition of the boundary, must transgress against the limits of what fear prescribes. [She] steps across that line. The defeat of the ogre is an opening in the self, an increase in what it is possible for the voyager to be" (350–351).

Immigration requires the crossing of frontiers—physical and metaphorical, visible and invisible, known and unknown—and the line that is drawn is fluid and unstable. Language is one such frontier that involves "shape-shifting or self-translation" (Rushdie 2002, 374). Learning and adopting a new language changes the individual because all languages permit slightly varying forms of thought, imagination, and play. Crossing frontiers can be arduous, and there are innumerable risks, but the quest to do so transforms the individual, shapes identity, and enables him or her to realize his or her strengths. The individual changes and his or her presence changes the society. "The frontier both shapes our character and tests our mettle" (381).

NOTES

1. "South Asia includes a number of sovereign nations—India, Pakistan, Bangladesh, Sri Lanka—with ethnically diverse populations. In Sri Lanka, Tamils and Sinhalese; in Pakistan and Bangladesh, Hindus and Muslims; in India, Sikhs, Tamils, and Parsees (to name only a few). Immigrant women in Canada exhibit vast social, cultural, regional, religious, and lingusitic differences.… The identity of South Asian women in Canada is partly a social construction by hegemonic practices and processes. South Asian women are categorized as a group on the basis of physical appearance (especially skin-colour), with the cultural differences among them disregarded" (Agnew 1998, 118–119).
2. An outfit comprising a long, loose shirt and baggy pants.

REFERENCES

Agnew, Vijay. 1996. *Resisting Discrimination*. Toronto: University of Toronto Press.

———. 1998. *In Search of a Safe Place*. Toronto: University of Toronto Press.

Ali, Monica. 2003. *Brick Lane*. London: Scribner.

Andermahr, Sonya, Terry Lovell, and Carol Wolkowitz. 2000. *A Glossary of Feminist Theory*. London: Arnold.

Appadurai, Arjun. 1996. *Modernity at Large: Cultural Dimensions of Globalization*. Minneapolis: University of Minnesota Press.

Basavarajappa, K.G., and Frank Jones. 1999. Visible Minority Income Differences. In *Immigrant Canada: Demographic, Economic, and Social Changes*, ed. Shiva Halli and Leo Driedger, 230–257. Toronto: University of Toronto Press.

Boyd, Monica, John DeVries, and Keith Simkin. 1994. Vol. 2. Language, Economic Status and Integration. In *Immigration and Refugee Policy: Canada and Australia Compared*, ed. Howard Adelman, Allan Borowski, Meyer Burnstein, and Lois Foster, 549–577. Toronto: University of Toronto Press.

Chaudhuri, Amit, ed. 2001. *The Picador Book of Modern Indian Literature*. Basingstoke, Oxford: Picador.

Code, Lorraine. 2000. *Encyclopedia of Feminist Theories*. London: Routledge.

COSTI. 2004. www.costi.org.

Desai, Jigna. 2004. *Beyond Bollywood: The Cultural Politics of South Asian Diasporic Film*. New York: Routledge.

Fincher, Ruth, Wenona Giles, and Valerie Preston. 1994. Gender and Migration Policy. In *Immigration and Refugee Policy: Canada and Australia Compared*, ed. Howard Adelman, Allan Borowski, Meyer Burnstein, and Lois Foster, 14–186. Toronto: University of Toronto Press.

Fleras, Augie. 2004. Racializing Culture/Culturalizing Race: Multicultural Racism in a Multicultural Canada. In *Racism, Eh?: A Critical Interdisciplinary Anthology on Race and Racism in Canada*, ed. Camille Nelson and Charmaine Nelson, 429–443. Toronto: Captus.

Gandhi, Sonia, ed. 1992. *Two Alone, Two Together: Letters Between Indira Gandhi and Jawaharlal Nehru 1940–1964*. London: Hodder and Stoughton.

Gorra, Michael. 2003. East Ender. *New York Times*, 7 September.

Henry, Francis, Carol Tater, Winston Mattis, and Tim Rees. 1995. *The Colour of Democracy: Racism in Canadian Society*. Toronto: Harcourt Brace.

Kamdar, Mira. 2001. *Motiba's Tattoos: A Granddaughter's Journey from America into Her Indian Family's Past*. New York: Plume.

Khilnani, Sunil. 1997. *The Idea of India*. London: Penguin.

Kumar, Amitava. 2002. *Bombay London New York*. New Delhi: Penguin.

Lehmann, Chris. 2003. A Long and Winding Road. *Washington Post*, 16 September.

Li, Peter. 2003. *Destination Canada: Immigration Debates and Issues*. Toronto: Oxford University Press.

Maslin, Janet. 2003. The Flavors of a New Land Can Leave a Bitter Taste. *New York Times*, 8 September.

Mehta, Suketu. 2004. *Maximum City: Bombay Lost and Found*. New York: Alfred A. Knopf.

Mishra, Vijay. 2002. *Bollywood Cinema: Temples of Desire*. New York: Routledge.

Nafisi, A. 2004. *Reading Lolita in Tehran: A Memoir in Books*. New York: Random House.

Naipaul, V.S. 2000. *Letter between a Father and Son*. London: Abascus.

———. 2003. *Literary Occasions: Essays*. Toronto: Alfred A. Knopf.

Needham, Anuradha Dingwaney. 2000. *Using the Master's Tools: Resistance and the Literature of the African and South Asian Diasporas*. New York: St. Martin's Press.

Ong, Ahiwa. 1999. *Flexible Citizenship: The Cultural Logics of Transnationality*. Durham, NC: Duke University Press.

Rushdie, Salman. 2002. *Step Across This Line: Collected Non-fiction 1992–2002*. Toronto: Alfred A. Knopf.

Said, Edward. 1979. *Orientalism*. New York: Vintage.

Varma, Pavan. 1998. *The Great Indian Middle Class*. New Delhi: Penguin.

Chapter 43

How Gay Stays White and What Kind of White It Stays

Allan Bérubé

The reactions of white males to living, working, circulating, and socializing in a racially diverse society are analyzed and interrogated in this chapter by Allan Bérubé (2001). In doing so, he challenges the "generic" representation of gay males as "mostly white," and argues that this representation is founded on an "unexamined investment in whiteness and middle-class identification," which functions to divide the community. Bérubé reports on a number of anti-racism activities in the gay community, relating the frustrations, discouragements, difficulties, contradictions, and challenges experienced by those who engage in these activities.

THE STEREOTYPE

When I teach college courses on queer history or queer working-class studies, I encourage students to explore the many ways that homosexuality is shaped by race, class, and gender. I know that racialized phantom figures hover over our classroom and inhabit our consciousness. I try to name these figures out loud to bring them down to earth so we can begin to resist their stranglehold on our intelligence. One by one, I recite the social categories that students have already used in our discussions—immigrant, worker, corporate executive, welfare recipient, student on financial aid, lesbian mother—and ask students first to imagine the stereotypical figure associated with the category and then to call out the figure's race, gender, class, and sexuality. As we watch each other conjure up and name these phantoms, we are stunned at how well each of us has learned by heart the same fearful chorus.

Whenever I get to the social category "gay man," the students' response is always the same: "white and well-to-do." In the United States today, the dominant image of the typical gay man is a white man who is financially better off than most everyone else.

MY WHITE DESIRES

Since the day I came out to my best friend in 1968, I have inhabited the social category "gay white man." As a historian, writer, and activist, I've examined the gay and the male parts of that identity, and more recently I've explored my working-class background and the Franco-American ethnicity that is so intertwined with it. But only recently have I identified with or seriously examined my gay male whiteness.[1]

Several years ago I made the decision to put race and class at the center of my gay writing and activism. I was frustrated at how my own gay social and activist circles reproduced larger patterns of racial separation by remaining almost entirely white. And I felt abandoned as the vision of the national gay movement and media narrowed from fighting for liberation, freedom, and social justice to expressing personal pride, achieving visibility, and lobbying for individual equality within existing institutions. What emerged was too often an exclusively gay rights agenda isolated from supposedly nongay issues, such as homelessness, unemployment, welfare, universal health care, union organizing, affirmative action, and abortion rights. To gain recognition and credibility, some gay organizations and media began to aggressively promote the so-called positive image of a generic gay community that is an upscale, mostly male, and mostly white consumer market with mainstream, even traditional, values. Such a strategy derives its power from an unexamined investment in whiteness and middle-class identification. As a result, its practitioners seemed not to take seriously or even notice how their gay visibility successes at times exploited and reinforced a racialized class divide that continues to tear our nation apart, including our lesbian and gay communities.

My decision to put race and class at the center of my gay work led me as a historian to pursue the history of a multiracial maritime union that in the 1930s and 1940s fought for racial equality and the dignity of openly gay workers.[2] And my decision opened doors that enabled me as an activist to join multiracial lesbian, gay, bisexual, and transgender groups whose members have been doing antiracist work for a long time and in which gay white men are not the majority—groups that included the Lesbian, Gay, Bisexual, and Transgender Advisory Committee to the San Francisco Human Rights Commission and the editorial board of the now-defunct national lesbian and gay quarterly journal *Out/Look*.

But doing this work also created new and ongoing conflicts in my relationships with other white men. I want to figure out how to handle these conflicts as I extend my antiracist work into those areas of my life where I still find myself among gay white men—especially when we form new activist and intellectual groups that once again turn out to be white. To do this I need "to clarify something for myself," as James Baldwin put it, when he gave his reason for writing his homosexual novel *Giovanni's Room* in the 1950s.[3]

I wanted to know how gay gets white, how it stays that way, and how whiteness is used both to win and attack gay rights campaigns.

I want to learn how to see my own whiteness when I am with gay white men and to understand what happens among us when one of us calls attention to our whiteness.

I want to know why I and other gay white men would want to challenge the racist structures of whiteness, what happens to us when we try, what makes me keep running away from the task, sometimes in silent despair, and what makes me want to go back to take up the task again.

I want to pursue these questions by drawing on a gay ability, developed over decades of figuring out how to "come out of the closet," to bring our hidden lives out into the open. But I want to do this without encouraging anyone to assign a greater degree of racism to gay white men, thus exposed, than to other white men more protected from exposure, and without inviting white men who are not gay to more safely see gay men's white racism rather than their own.

I want to know these things because gay white men have been among the men I have loved and will continue to love. I need them in my life and at my side as I try to make fighting racism a more central part of my work. And when students call out "white" to describe the typical gay man, and they see me standing right there in front of them, I want to figure out how, from where I am standing, I can intelligently fight the racist hierarchies that I and my students differently inhabit.

GAY WHITENING PRACTICES

Despite the stereotype, the gay male population is not as white as it appears to be in the images of gay men projected by the mainstream and gay media, or among the "out" men (including myself) who move into the public spotlight as representative gay activists, writers, commentators, and spokesmen. Gay men of color, working against the stereotype, have engaged in long, difficult struggles to gain some public recognition of their cultural heritages, political activism, and everyday existence. To educate gay white men, they've had to get our attention by interrupting our business as usual, then convince us that we don't speak for them or represent them or know enough about either their realities or our own racial assumptions and privileges. And when I and other gay white men don't educate ourselves, gay men of color have done the face-to-face work of educating us about their cultures, histories, oppression, and particular needs—the kind of personal work that tires us out when heterosexuals ask us to explain to them what it's like to be gay. Also working against their ability to put "gay" and "men of color" together in the broader white imagination are a great many other powerful *whitening practices* that daily construct, maintain, and fortify the idea that gay male means white.

How does the category "gay man" become white? What are the whitening practices that perpetuate this stereotype, often without awareness or comment by gay white men? How do these practices operate, and what racial work do they perform?

I begin by mining my own experience for clues.[4] I know that if I go where I'm surrounded by other gay white men, or if I'm having sex with a white man, it's unlikely that our race will come up in conversation. Such racially comfortable, racially familiar situations can make us mistakenly believe that there are such things as gay issues, spaces, culture, and relationships that are not "lived through" race, and that white gay life, so long as it is not named as such, is not about race.[5] These lived assumptions, and the privileges on which they are based, form a powerful camouflage woven from a web of unquestioned beliefs—that gay whiteness is unmarked and unremarkable, universal and representative, powerful and protective, a cohesive bond. The markings of this camouflage are pale—a characteristic that the wearer sees neither as entirely invisible nor as a racial "color," a shade that allows the wearer to blend into the seemingly neutral background of white worlds. When we wear this everyday camouflage into a gay political arena that white men already dominate, our activism comes wrapped in a *pale protective coloring* that we may not notice but which is clearly visible to those who don't enjoy its protection.

I start to remember specific situations in which I caught glimpses of how other gay whitening practices work.

One night, arriving at my favorite gay disco bar in San Francisco, I discovered outside a picket line of people protesting the triple-carding (requiring three photo ID's) of gay men of color at the door. This practice was a form of racial *exclusion*—policing the borders of white gay institutions to prevent people of color from entering. The management was using this discriminatory practice to keep the bar from "turning," as it's called—a process by which a "generically gay" bar (meaning a predominantly white bar) changes into a bar that loses status and income (meaning gay white men with money won't go there) because it has been "taken over" by black, Latino, or Asian gay men. For many white owners, managers, and patrons of gay bars, only a white gay bar can be *just gay*; a bar where men of color go is seen as racialized. As I joined the picket line, I felt the fears of a white man who has the privilege to choose on which side of a color line he will stand. I wanted to support my gay brothers of color who were being harassed at the door, yet I was afraid that the doorman might recognize me as a regular and refuse to let me back in. That night, I saw a gay bar's doorway become a racialized border, where a battle to preserve or challenge the whiteness of the clientele inside was fought among dozens of gay men who were either standing guard at the door, allowed to walk through it, or shouting and marching outside. (The protests eventually made the bar stop the triple-carding.)

I remember seeing how another gay whitening practice works when I watched, with other members of a sexual politics study group, an antigay video, "Gay Rights, Special Rights," produced in 1993 by The Report, a religious right organization. This practice was the *selling* of gay whiteness—the marketing of gays as white and wealthy to make money and increase political capital, either to raise funds for campaigns (in both progay and antigay benefits, advertising, and direct-mail appeals) or to gain economic power (by promoting or appealing to a gay consumer market). The antigay video we watched used racialized class to undermine alliances between a gay rights movement portrayed as white and movements of people of color portrayed as heterosexual. It showed charts comparing mutually exclusive categories of "homosexuals" and "African Americans," telling us that homosexuals are wealthy, college-educated white men who vacation more than anyone else and who demand even more "special rights and privileges" by taking civil rights away from low-income African Americans.[6] In this zero-sum, racialized world of the religious right, gay men are white; gay, lesbian, and bisexual people of color, along with poor or working-class white gay men, bisexuals, and lesbians, simply do not exist. The recently vigorous gay media promotion of the high income, brand-loyal gay consumer market—which is typically portrayed as a population of white, well-to-do, college-educated young men—only widens the racialized class divisions that the religious right so eagerly exploits.

During the 1993 Senate hearings on gays in the military, I saw how these and other whitening practices were used in concentrated form by another gay institution, the Campaign for Military Service (CMS).

The Campaign for Military Service was an ad hoc organization formed in Washington, DC, by a group composed primarily of well-to-do, well-connected, professional men, including billionaires David Geffen and Barry Diller, corporate consultant and former antiwar activist David Mixner (a personal friend of Bill Clinton), and several gay and lesbian civil rights attorneys. Their mission was to work with the Clinton White House and sympathetic senators by coordinating the gay response to hearings held by the Senate Armed Services Committee, chaired by Sam Nunn. Their power was derived from their legal expertise, their access to wealthy donors, and their contacts with high-level personnel inside the White House, Senate, and Pentagon. The challenge they faced was to make strategic, pragmatic decisions in the heat of a rapidly changing national battle over what President Clinton called "our nation's policy toward homosexuals in the military."[7] [...]

The CMS used a set of arguments they called the *race analogy* to persuade senators and military officials to lift the military's antigay ban. The strategy was to get these powerful men to take antigay discrimination as seriously as they supposedly took racial discrimination, so they would lift the military ban on homosexuals as they had eliminated official policies requiring racial segregation. During the Senate hearings, the race analogy projected a set of comparisons that led to heated disputes over whether sexual orientation was analogous to race, whether sexual desire and conduct were like "skin color," or, most specifically, whether being homosexual was like being African American. (Rarely was "race" explicitly discussed as anything other than African American.) On their side, the CMS argued for a qualified analogy—what they called "haunting parallels" between "the words, rationale and rhetoric invoked in favor of racial discrimination in the past" and those used to "exclude gays in the military now." "The parallel is inexact," they cautioned, because "a person's skin color is not the same as a person's sexual identity; race is self-evident to many whereas sexual orientation is not. Moreover, the history of African Americans is not equivalent to the history of lesbian, gay and bisexual people in this country." Yet, despite these qualifications, the CMS held firm to the analogy. "The bigotry expressed is the same; the discrimination is the same."[8] [...]

During the race analogy debates, the fact that only white witnesses made the analogy, drawing connections between antigay and racial discrimination without including people of color, reduced the power of their argument and the credibility it might have gained had it been made by advocates who had experienced the racial discrimination side of the analogy.[9]

But without hearing these voices, everyone in the debate could imagine homosexuals as either people who do not experience racism (the military assumption) or as people who experience discrimination only as homosexuals (the progay assumption)—two different routes that ultimately led to the same destination: the place where gay stays white, the place where the CMS chose to make its stand. [...]

What would the gay movement look like if gay white men who use the race analogy took it more seriously? What work would we have to do to close the perceived moral authority gap between our gay activism and the race analogy, to directly establish the kind of moral authority we seek by analogy? What if we aspired to achieve the great vision, leadership qualities, grass-roots organizing skills, and union-solidarity of Dr. Martin Luther King Jr., together with his opposition to war and his dedication to fighting with the poor and disenfranchised against the deepening race and class divisions in America and the world? How could we fight, in the words of US Supreme Court Justice Harry A. Blackmun, for the "fundamental interest all individuals have in controlling the nature of their intimate associations with others," in ways that build a broad civil rights movement rather than being "like" it, in ways that enable the gay movement to grow into one of many powerful and direct ways to achieve race, gender, and class justice?[10]

These, then, are only some of the many whitening practices that structure everyday life and politics in what is often called the "gay community" and the "gay movement"—making *race analogies*; *mirroring* the whiteness of men who run powerful institutions as a strategy for winning credibility, acceptance, and integration; *excluding* people of color from gay institutions; *selling* gay as white to raise money, make a profit, and gain economic power; and daily wearing the *pale protective coloring* that camouflages the unquestioned assumptions and unearned privileges of gay whiteness. These practices do serious damage to real people whenever they mobilize the power and privileges of whiteness to protect and strengthen gayness—including the privileges of gay whiteness—without using that power to fight racism—including gay white racism.

Most of the time, the hard work of identifying such practices, fighting racial discrimination and exclusion, critiquing the assumptions of whiteness, and racially integrating white gay worlds has been taken up by lesbian, gay, bisexual, and transgender people of color. Freed from this enforced daily recognition of race and confrontation with racism, some prominent white men in the gay movement have been able to advance a gay rights politics that, like the right to serve in the military, they imagine to be just gay, not about race. The gay rights movement can't afford to "dissipate our energies," Andrew Sullivan, former editor of the *New Republic*, warned on the Charlie Rose television program, by getting involved in disagreements over nongay issues such as "how one deals with race ... how we might help the underclass ... how we might deal with sexism."[11] [...]

For those few who act like, look like, and identify with the white men who still run our nation's major institutions, for those few who can meet with them, talk to them, and be heard by them as peers, the ability to draw on the enormous power of a shared but unacknowledged whiteness, the ability never to have to bring up race, must feel like a potentially sturdy shield against antigay discrimination. I can see how bringing up explicit critiques of white privilege during high-level gay rights conversations (such as the Senate debates over gays in the military), or making it possible for people of color to set the agenda of the gay rights movement, might weaken that white shield (which relies on racial division to protect)—might even, for some white activists, threaten to "turn" the gay movement into something less gay, as gay bars "turn" when they're no longer predominantly white.

The threat of losing the white shield that protects my own gay rights raises even more difficult questions that I need to "clarify ... for myself": What would *I* say and do about racism if someday my own whiteness helped me gain such direct access to men in the centers of power [...]? What privileges would I risk losing if I persistently tried to take activists of color with me into that high-level conversation? How, and with whom, could I begin planning for that day?

Gay white men who are committed to doing antiracist activism as gay men have to work within and against these and other powerful whitening practices. What can we do, and how can we support each other, when we once again find ourselves involved in gay social and political worlds that are white and male?

GAY, WHITE, MALE, AND HIV-NEGATIVE

A few years ago, in San Francisco, a friend invited me to be part of a new political discussion group of HIV-negative gay men. Arriving at a neighbor's apartment for the group's first meeting, I once again felt the relief and pleasure of being among men like me. All of us were involved in AIDS activism. We had supported lovers, friends, and strangers with HIV and were grieving the loss of too many lives. We didn't want to take time, attention, and scarce resources away from people with AIDS, including many people of color. But we did want to find a collective, progressive voice as HIV-negative men. We wanted to find public ways to say to gay men just coming out that "We are HIV-negative men, and we want you to stay negative, have hot sex, and live long lives. We don't want you to get sick or die." We were trying to work out a politics in which HIV-negative men, who are relatively privileged as not being the primary targets of crackdowns on people who are HIV-positive, could address other HIV-negative men without trying to establish our legitimacy by positioning ourselves as victims.

When I looked around the room I saw only white men. I knew that many of them had for years been incorporating antiracist work into their gay and AIDS activism, so this seemed like a safe space to bring up the whiteness I saw. I really didn't want to hijack the purpose of the group by changing its focus from HIV to race, but this was important because I believed that not talking about our whiteness was going to hurt our work. Instead of speaking up, however, I hesitated.

Right there. That's the moment I want to look at—that moment of silence, when a flood of memories, doubts, and fears rushed into my head. What made me want to say something about our whiteness and what was keeping me silent?

My memory took me back to 1990, when I spoke on a panel of gay historians at the first Out/Write conference of lesbian and gay writers, held in San Francisco. I was happy to be presenting with two other community-based historians working outside the academy. But I was also aware—and concerned—that we were all men. When the question period began, an African American writer in the audience, a man whose name I later learned was Fundi, stood up and asked us (as I recall) how it could happen, at this late date, that a gay history panel could have only white men on it. Awkward silence. I don't trust how I remember his question or what happened next—unreliable memory and bad thinking must be characteristics of inhabiting whiteness while it's being publicly challenged. As the other panelists responded, I remember wanting to distance myself from their whiteness while my own mind went blank, and I remember feeling terrified that Fundi would address me directly and ask me to respond personally. I kept thinking, "I don't know what to say, I can't think, I want to be invisible, I want this to be over, now!"

After the panel was over I spoke privately to Fundi. Later, I resolved never to be in that situation again—never to agree to be on an all-white panel without asking ahead of time why it was white, if its whiteness was crucial to what we were presenting, and, if not, how its composition might be changed. But in addition to wanting to protect myself from public embarrassment and to do the right thing, that writer's direct challenge made me understand something more clearly: that only by seeing and naming the whiteness I'm inhabiting, and taking responsibility for it, can I begin to change it and even do something constructive with it. At that panel, I learned how motivating though terrifying it can be as a white person to be placed in such a state of heightened racial discomfort—to be challenged to see the whiteness we've created, figure out how we created it, and then think critically about how it works.[12]

In the moment of silent hesitation I experienced in my HIV-negative group, I found myself imagining for the first time, years after it happened, what it must have been like for Fundi to stand up in a predominantly white audience and ask an all-white panel of gay men about our whiteness. My friend and colleague Lisa Kahaleole Hall, who is a brilliant thinker, writer, and teacher, says that privilege is "the ability not to have to take other people's existence seriously," the "ability not to have to pay attention."[13] Until that moment I had mistakenly thought that Fundi's anger (and I am not certain that he in fact expressed any anger toward us) was only about me, about us, as white men, rather than also about him—the history, desires, and support that enabled him to speak up, and the fears he faced and risks he took by doing it. Caught up in my own fear, I had not paid close attention to the specific question he had asked us. "The problem of conventional white men," Fundi later wrote in his own account of why he had decided to take the risk of speaking up, "somehow not being able, or not knowing how, to find and extend themselves to women and people of color had to be talked through.... My question to the panel was this: 'What direct skills might you share with particularly the whites in the audience to help them move on their fears and better extend themselves to cultural diversity?'"[14] I'm indebted to Fundi for writing that question down, and for starting a chain of events with his question that has led to my writing this essay.

I tried to remember who else I had seen bring up whiteness. The first images that came to mind were all white lesbians and people of color. White lesbian feminists have as a movement dealt with racism in a more collective way than have gay white men. In lesbian and gay activist spaces I and other gay white men have come to rely on white lesbians and people of color to raise the issue of whiteness and challenge racism, so that this difficult task has become both gendered as lesbian work and racialized as "colored" work. These images held me back from saying anything to my HIV-negative group. "Just who am I to bring this up?" I wondered. "It's not my place to do this." Or, more painfully, "Who will these men think I think I am?" Will they think I'm trying to pretend I'm not a white man?"

Then another image flashed in my mind that also held me back. It was the caricature of the white moralist—another racialized phantom figure hovering in the room—who blames and condemns white people for our racism, guilt-trips us from either a position of deeper guilt or holier-than-thou innocence, claims to be more aware of racism than we are, and is prepared to catalog our offenses. I see on my mental screen this self-righteous caricature impersonating a person of color in an all-white group or, when people of color are present, casting them again in the role of spectators to a white performance, pushed to the sidelines from where they must angrily or patiently interrupt a white conversation to be heard at all. I understand that there is some truth to this caricature—that part of a destructive racial dynamic among white people is trying to determine who is more or less responsible for racism, more or less innocent and pure, more or less white. But I also see how the fear of becoming this caricature has been used by white people to keep each other from naming the whiteness of all-white groups we are in. During my moment of hesitation in the HIV-negative group, the fear of becoming this caricature was successfully silencing me.

I didn't want to pretend to be a white lesbian or a person of color, or to act like the self-righteous white caricature. "How do I ask that we examine our whiteness," I wondered, "without implying that I'm separating us into the good guys and bad guys and positioning myself as the really cool white guy who 'gets it' about racism?" I needed a way to speak intelligently from where I was standing without falling into any of these traps.

I decided to take a chance and say something.

"It appears to me," I began, my voice a little shaky, "that everyone here is white. If this is true, I'd like us to find some way to talk about how our whiteness may be connected to being HIV-negative, because I suspect there are some political similarities between being in each of these positions of relative privilege."

There was an awkward pause. "Are you saying," someone asked, "that we should close the group to men of color?"

"No," I said, "but if we're going to be a white group I'd like us to talk about our relationship to whiteness here."

"Should we do outreach to men of color?" someone else asked.

"No, I'm not saying that, either. It's a little late to do outreach, after the fact, inviting men of color to integrate our already white group."

The other men agreed and the discussion went on to other things. I, too, didn't really know where to take this conversation about our whiteness. By bringing it up, I was implicitly asking for their help in figuring this out. I hoped I wouldn't be the only one to bring up the subject again.

At the next month's meeting there were new members, and they all appeared to be white men. When someone reviewed for them what we had done at the last meeting, he reported that I'd suggested we not include men of color in the group. "That's not right," I corrected him. "I said that if we're going to be a white group, I'd like us to talk about our whiteness and its relation to our HIV-negative status."

I was beginning to feel a little disoriented, like I was doing something wrong. Why was I being so consistently misunderstood as divisive, as if I were saying that I didn't want men of color in the group? Had I reacted similarly when, caught up in my own fear of having to publicly justify our panel's whiteness, I had misunderstood Fundi's specific question—about how we could share our skills with other white people to help each other move beyond our fear of cultural diversity—as an accusation that we had deliberately excluded women and men of color? Was something structural going on here about how white groups respond to questions that point to our whiteness and ask what we can do with it?

Walking home from the meeting I asked a friend who'd been there if what I said had made sense. "Oh yes," he said, "it's just that it all goes without saying." Well, there it is. That is how it goes, how it stays white. "Without saying."

Like much of the rest of my gay life, this HIV-negative group turned out to be unintentionally white, although intentionally gay and intentionally male. It's important for me to understand exactly how that racial *unintentionality* gets *constructed*, how it's not just a coincidence. It seems that so long as white people never consciously decide to be a white group, a white organization, a white department, so long as we each individually believe that people of color are always welcome, *even though they are not there*, then we do not have to examine our whiteness because we can believe it is unintentional, it's not our *reason* for being there. That may be why I had been misunderstood to be asking for the exclusion of men of color. By naming our group as white, I had unknowingly raised the question of *racial intent*—implying that we had intended to create an all-white group by deliberately excluding men of color. If we could believe that our whiteness was purely accidental, then we could also believe that there was nothing to say about it because creating an all-white group, which is exactly what we had done, had never been anyone's intent, and therefore had no inherent meaning or purpose. By interrupting the process by which "it just goes without saying," by asking us to recognize and "talk through" our whiteness, I appeared to be saying that we already had and should continue to exclude men of color from our now very self-consciously white group.

The reality is that in our HIV-negative group, as in the panel of the Out/Write conference and in many other all-white groupings, we each did make a chain of choices, not usually conscious, to invite or accept an invitation from another white person. We made more decisions whether or not to name our whiteness when we once again found ourselves in a white group. What would it mean to make such decisions consciously and out loud, to understand why we made them, and to take responsibility for them? What if we intentionally held our identities as white men and gay men in creative tension, naming ourselves as gay *and* white, then publicly explored the possibilities for activism this tension might open up? Could investigating our whiteness offer us opportunities for reclaiming our humanity against the ways that racial hierarchies dehumanize us and disconnect us from ourselves, from each other, and from people of color? If we took on these difficult tasks, how might our gay political reality and purpose be different?[15]

When I told this story about our HIV-negative group to Barbara Smith, a colleague who is an African American lesbian writer and activist, she asked me a question that pointed to a different ending: "So why didn't you bring up the group's whiteness again?" The easy answer was that I left the group because I moved to New York City. But the more difficult answer was that I was afraid to lose the trust of these gay men whom I cared about and needed so much, afraid I would distance myself from them and be distanced by them, pushed outside the familiar circle, no longer welcomed as white and not belonging among people of color, not really gay and not anything else, either. The big fear is that if I pursue this need to examine whiteness too far, I risk losing my place among gay white men, forever—and then where would I be?

PALE, MALE—AND ANTIRACIST

What would happen if we deliberately put together a white gay male group whose sole purpose was to examine our whiteness and use it to strengthen our antiracist gay activism?

In November 1995, gay historian John D'Emilio and I tried to do just that. We organized a workshop at the annual Creating Change conference of activists put on that year in Detroit by the National Gay and Lesbian Task Force. We called the workshop "Pale, Male—and Anti-Racist." At a conference of over 1,000 people (mostly white but with a large number of people of color), about thirty-five gay white men attended.[16]

We structured the workshop around three key questions: (1) How have you successfully used your whiteness to fight racism? (2) What difficulties have you faced in doing antiracist activism as a gay white man? And (3) what kind of support did you get or need or wished you had received from other gay white men? [...]

Some men talked about how tired they were of being called "gay white men," feeling labeled then attacked for who they were and for what they tried to do or for not doing enough; about having to deal with their racism while they didn't see communities of color dealing with homophobia; and about how after years of struggling they felt like giving up. Yet here they all were at this workshop. I began to realize that all our frustrations were signs of a dilemma that comes with the privileges of whiteness: having the ability to decide whether to keep dealing with the accusations, resentments, racial categorizations, and other destructive effects of racism that divide people who are trying to take away its power; or, because the struggle is so hard, to walk away from it and do something else, using the slack our whiteness gives us to take a break from racism's direct consequences.

Bringing this dilemma into the open enabled us to confront our expectations about how the antiracist work we do should be appreciated, should be satisfying, and should bring results. One man admitted that he didn't make antiracist work a higher priority because "I [would have to face] a level of discomfort, irritation, boredom, frustration, [and] enter a lot of [areas where] I feel inept, and don't have confidence. It would require a lot of humility. All these are things that I steer away from."

Over and over the men at the workshop expressed similar feelings of frustration, using such phrases as "We tried, but …," "No matter what you do, you can't seem to do anything right," and "You just can't win." These seemed to reflect a set of expectations that grew out of the advantages we have because we are American men and white and middle-class or even working-class—expectations that we *can* win, that we should know how to do it right, that if we try we will succeed.

What do we—what do I—expect to get out of doing antiracist work, anyway? If it's because we expect to be able to fix the problem, then we're not going to be very satisfied. When I talk with my friend Lisa Kahaleole Hall about these frustrations, she tells me, "Sweet pea, if racism were that easy to fix, we would have fixed it already." The challenge for me in relation to other gay white men—and in writing this essay—is to figure out how we can support each other in going exactly into those areas of whiteness where we feel we have no competence yet, no expertise, no ability to fix it, where we haven't even come up with the words we need to describe what we're trying to do. For me, it's an act of faith in the paradox that if we, together with our friends and allies, can figure out how our own whiteness works, we can use that knowledge to fight the racism that gives our whiteness such unearned power.

And whenever this struggle gets too difficult, many of us, as white men, have the option to give up in frustration and retreat into a more narrowly defined gay rights activism. That project's goal, according to gay author Bruce Bawer, one of its advocates, is "to achieve, acceptance, equal rights, and full integration into the present social and political structure."[17] It's a goal that best serves the needs of men who can live our gayness through our whiteness and whose only or most important experience with discrimination is as homosexuals. James Baldwin, who wrote extensively about whiteness in America, noticed long ago the sense of entitlement embedded in a gay whiteness that experiences no other form of systematic discrimination. "[Y]ou are penalized, as it were, unjustly," he said in an interview. "I think white gay people feel cheated because they were born, in principle, into a society in which they were supposed to be safe. The anomaly of their sexuality puts them in danger, unexpectedly."[18] [...]

When John and I asked the workshop participants our last question—"What would you need from each other to be able to continue doing antiracist work?"—the room went silent.

When push comes to shove, I wondered, holding back a sense of isolation inside my own silence, do gay white men as *white* men (including myself) have a lasting interest in fighting racism or will we sooner or later retreat to the safety of our gay white refuges? I know that gay white men as *gay* men, just to begin thinking about relying on each other's support in an ongoing struggle against racism, have to confront how we've absorbed the antigay lies that we are all wealthy, irresponsible, and sexually obsessed individuals who can't make personal commitments, as well as the reality that we are profoundly exhausted fighting for our lives and for those we love through years of devastation from the AIDS epidemic. These challenges all make it hard enough for me to trust my own long-term commitment to antiracist work, let alone that of other gay white men. [...]

STAYING WHITE

By trying to figure out what is happening with race in situations I'm in, I've embarked on a journey that I now realize is not headed toward innocence or winning or becoming not white or finally getting it right. I don't know where it leads, but I have some hopes and desires.

I want to find an antidote to the ways that whiteness numbs me, makes me not see what is right in front of me, takes away my intelligence, divides me from people I care about. I hope that, by occupying the seeming contradictions between the "antiracist" and the "gay white male" parts of myself, I can generate a creative tension that will motivate me to keep fighting. I hope to help end the exclusionary practices that make gay worlds stay so white. When I find myself in a situation that is going to stay white, I want to play a role in deciding what kind of white it's going to stay. And I want to become less invested in whiteness while staying white myself—always remembering that I can't just decide to stand outside of whiteness or exempt myself from its unearned privileges.[19] I want to be careful not to avoid its responsibilities by fleeing into narratives of how I have been oppressed as a gay man. The ways that I am gay will always be shaped by the ways that I am white.

Most of all, I want never to forget that the roots of my antiracist desires and my gay desires are intertwined. As James Baldwin's words remind me, acting on my gay desires is about not being afraid to love and therefore about having to confront this white society's terror of love—a terror that lashes out with racist and antigay violence. Following both my gay and antiracist desires is about being willing to "go the way your blood beats," as Baldwin put it, even into the heart of that terror, which, he warned, is "a tremendous danger, a tremendous responsibility."[20]

NOTES

1.   "Caught in the Storm: AIDS and the Meaning of Natural Disaster," *Out/Look: National Lesbian and Gay Quarterly* 1 (fall 1988): 8–19; "'Fitting In': Expanding Queer Studies beyond the *Closet* and *Coming Out*," paper presented at Contested Zone: Limitations and Possibilities of a Discourse on Lesbian and Gay Studies, Pitzer College, 6–7 April 1990, and at the Fourth Annual Lesbian, Bisexual, and Gay Studies Conference, Harvard University, 26–28 October 1990; "Intellectual Desire," paper presented at La Ville en rose: Le premier colloque Québécois d'études lesbienne et gaies (First Quebec Lesbian and Gay Studies Conference), Concordia University and the University of Quebec at Montreal, 12 November 1992, published in *GLQ: A Journal of Lesbian and Gay Studies* 3, no. 1 (February 1996): 139–57, reprinted in *Queerly Classed: Gay Men and Lesbians Write about Class*, ed. Susan Raffo (Boston: South End Press, 1997), 43–66; "Class Dismissed: Queer Storytelling Across the Economic Divide," keynote address at the Constructing Queer Cultures: Lesbian, Bisexual, Gay Studies Graduate Student Conference, Cornell University, 9 February 1995, and at the Seventeenth Gender Studies Symposium, Lewis and Clark College, 12 March 1998; "I Coulda Been a Whiny White Guy," *Gay Community News* 20 (spring 1995): 6–7, 28–30; and

"Sunset Trailer Park," in *White Trash: Race and Class in America*, ed. Matt Wray and Annalee Newitz (New York: Routledge, 1997), 15–39.

2. *Dream Ships Sail Away* (forthcoming, Houghton Mifflin).

3. Richard Goldstein, "'Go the Way Your Blood Beats': An Interview with James Baldwin (1984)," in *James Baldwin: The Legacy*, ed. Quincy Troupe (New York: Simon and Schuster/ Touchstone, 1989), 176.

4. Personal essays, often assembled in published collections, have become an important written form for investigating how whiteness works, especially in individual lives. Personal essays by lesbian, gay, and bisexual authors that have influenced my own thinking and writing about whiteness have been collected in James Baldwin, *The Price of the Ticket: Collected Nonfiction, 1948–1985* (New York: St. Martin's, 1985); Cherrie Moraga and Gloria Anzaldua, eds., *This Bridge Called My Back: Writings by Radical Women of Color* (Watertown, Mass.: Persephone Press, 1981); Cherrie Moraga, *Loving in the War Years* (Boston: South End Press, 1983); Audre Lorde, *Sister Outsider* (Freedom, Calif.: Crossing Press, 1984); Elly Bulkin, Minnie Bruce Pratt, and Barbara Smith, *Yours in Struggle: Three Feminist Perspectives on Anti-Semitism and Racism* (Brooklyn: Long Haul Press, 1984); Essex Hemphill, ed., *Brother to Brother: New Writings by Black Gay Men* (Boston: Alyson, 1991); Mab Segrest, *Memoir of a Race Traitor* (Boston: South End Press, 1994); Dorothy Allison, *Skin: Talking about Sex, Class and Literature* (Ithaca, NY: Firebrand, 1994); and Becky Thompson and Sangeeta Tyagi, eds., *Names We Call Home: Autobiography on Racial Identity* (New York: Routledge, 1996).

5. For discussion of how sexual identities are "lived through race and class," see Robin D.G. Kelley, *Yo' Mama's Dysfunktional!* (Boston: Beacon, 1997), 114.

6. Whiteness can grant economic advantages to gay as well as straight men, and gay male couples can sometimes earn more on two men's incomes than can straight couples or lesbian couples. But being gay can restrict a man to lower-paying jobs, and most gay white men are not wealthy; like the larger male population, they are lower-middle-class, working-class, or poor. For discussions of the difficulties of developing an accurate economic profile of the "gay community," and of how both the religious right and gay marketers promote the idea that gay men are wealthy, see Amy Gluckman and Betsy Reed, eds., *Homo Economics: Capitalism, Community, and Lesbian and Gay Life* (New York: Routledge, 1997).

7. David Mixner, *Stranger among Friends* (New York: Bantam, 1996), 291. For accounts of how the Campaign for Military Service was formed, see Mixner's memoir and Urvashi Vaid, *Virtual Equality: The Mainstreaming of Lesbian and Gay Equality* (New York: Anchor, 1995). Preceding the ad hoc formation of the Campaign for Military Service in January 1993 was the Military Freedom Project, formed in early 1989 by a group composed primarily of white feminist lesbians. Overshadowed during the Senate hearings by the predominantly male Campaign for Military Service, these activists had raised issues relating the military's antigay policy to gender, race, and class; specifically, that lesbians are discharged at a higher rate than are gay men; that lesbian-baiting is a form of sexual harassment against women; and that African American and Latino citizens, including those who are

gay, bisexual, or lesbian, are disproportionately represented in the military, which offers poor and working-class youth access to a job, education, and health care that are often unavailable to them elsewhere. Vaid, *Virtual Equality*, 153–59.

8. "The Race Analogy: Fact Sheet comparing the Military's Policy of Racial Segregation in the 1940s to the Current Ban on Lesbians, Gay Men and Bisexuals," in *Briefing Book*, prepared by the Legal/Policy Department of the Campaign for Military Service, Washington, DC (1993).

9. For brief discussions of how the whiteness of those making the race analogy reduced the power of their arguments, see Henry Louis Gates Jr., "Blacklash?" *New Yorker*, 17 May 1993; and David Rayside, *On the Fringe: Gays and Lesbians in Politics* (Ithaca, NY: Cornell University Press, 1998), 243.

10. Quoted from Justice Blackmun's dissenting opinion in the US Supreme Court's 1986 *Bowers v. Hardwick* decision. "Blackmun's Opinions Reflect His Evolution over the 24 Court Years," *New York Times*, 5 March 1999. I wish to thank Lisa Kahaleole Hall for the conversation we had on 24 October 1998, out of which emerged the ideas in this essay about how the civil rights movement analogy works and is used as a strategy for gaining unearned moral authority, although I am responsible for how they are presented here.

11. "Stonewall 25," *The Charlie Rose Show*, Public Broadcasting System, 24 June 1994. I wish to thank Barbara Smith for lending me her videotape copy of this program.

12. For Fundi's reports on this panel and the entire conference, see "Out/Write '90 Report, Part I: Writers Urged to Examine Their Roles, Save Their Lives," *San Diego GLN*, 16 March 1990, 7; "Out/Write Report, Part II: Ringing Voices," *San Diego GLN*, 23 March 1990, 7, 9; and "Out/Write Report, Part III: Arenas of Interaction," *San Diego GLN*, 30 March 1990, 7, 9.

13. Lisa Kahaleole Chang Hall, "Bitches in Solitude: Identity Politics and Lesbian Community," in *Sisters, Sexperts, Queers: Beyond the Lesbian Nation*, ed. Arlene Stein (New York: Plume, 1993), 223, and in personal conversation.

14. Fundi, "Out/Write Report, Part III," 7, 9.

15. I wish to thank Mitchell Karp for the long dinner conversation we had in 1996 in New York City during which we jointly forged the ideas and questions in this paragraph.

16. I have transcribed the quotations that follow from an audio tape of the workshop discussion.

17. Bruce Bawer, "Utopian Erotics," *Lambda Book Report* 7 (October 1998): 19–20.

18. Goldstein, "Go the Way," 180.

19. I wish to thank Amber Hollibaugh for introducing me to this idea of "staying white" during a conversation about how a white person can be tempted to distance oneself from whiteness and escape the guilt of its privileges by identifying as a person of color. I was introduced to the idea that white privilege is unearned and difficult to escape at a workshop called White Privilege conducted by Jona Olssen at the 1995 Black Nations/Queer Nations Conference, sponsored by the Center for Lesbian and Gay Studies at the City University of New York. See also Peggy McIntosh, "White Privilege: Unpacking the Invisible Knapsack," *Peace and Freedom* (July/August 1989): 10–12.

20. Goldstein, "Go the Way," 177.

BIBLIOGRAPHY

Allison, Dorothy. 1994. *Skin: Talking about Sex, Class, and Literature*. Ithaca, NY: Firebrand.

Baldwin, James. 1985. "White Man's Guilt." In *The Price of the Ticket*. New York: St. Martin's Press.

Bawer, Bruce. 1998. "Utopian Erotics." *Lambda Book Report* 7 (October): 19–20.

Bérubé, Allan. Forthcoming. *Dream Ships Sail Away*. New York: Houghton Mifflin.

———. 1997. "Intellectual Desire." In *Queerly Classed: Gay Men & Lesbians Write about Class*, ed. Susan Raffo. Boston: South End Press.

———. 1997. "Sunset Trailer Park." In *White Trash: Race and Class in America*, eds. Matt Wray and Annalee Newitz. New York: Routledge.

———. 1995 and 1998. "Class Dismissed: Queer Storytelling Across the Economic Divide." Keynote address at Constructing Queer Cultures: Lesbian, Bisexual, Gay Studies Graduate Student Conference, Cornell University, 9 February and at 17th Gender Studies Symposium, Lewis and Clark College, 12 March.

———. 1995. "I Coulda Been A Whiny White Guy." *Gay Community News* 20 (spring): 6–7.

———. 1990. "'Fitting In': Expanding Queer Studies beyond the *Closet* and *Coming Out*." Paper presented at Contested Zone: Limitations and Possibilities of a Discourse on Lesbian and Gay Studies, Pitzer College, 6–7 April, and at the Fourth Annual Lesbian, Bisexual, and Gay Studies Conference, Harvard University, October 26–28.

———. 1988. "Caught in the Storm: AIDS and the Meaning of Natural Disaster." *Out/Look: National Lesbian and Gay Quarterly* 1 (fall): 8–19.

"Blackmun's Opinions Reflect His Evolution Over the 24 Court Years." 1999. *New York Times*, 5 March.

Bulkin, Elly, Minnie Bruce Pratt, and Barbara Smith, eds. 1984. *Yours in Struggle: Three Feminist Perspectives on Anti-Semitism and Racism*. Brooklyn: Long Haul Press.

Fundi. 1990. "Out/Write '90 Report, Part I: Writers Urged to Examine Their Roles, Save Their Lives." *San Diego GLN*, 16 March.

———. 1990. "Out/Write Report, Part II: Ringing Voices." *San Diego GLN*, 23 March.

———. 1990. "Out/Write Report, Part III: Arenas of Interaction." *San Diego GLN*, 30 March.

Gates, Henry Louis, Jr. 1993. "Blacklash?" *New Yorker*, 17 May, 42–44.

Gluckman, Amy, and Betsy Reed, eds. 1997. *Homo Economics: Capitalism, Community, and Lesbian and Gay Life*. New York: Routledge.

Goldstein, Richard. 1989. "'Go the Way Your Blood Beats': An Interview with James Baldwin (1984)." In *James Baldwin: The Legacy*, ed. Quincy Troupe. New York: Simon and Schuster.

Hall, Lisa Kahaleole Chang. 1993. "Bitches in Solitude: Identity Politics and Lesbian Community." In *Sisters, Sexperts, Queers: Beyond the Lesbian Nation*, ed. Arlene Stein. New York: Plume.

Hemphill, Essex, ed. 1991. *Brother to Brother: New Writings by Black Gay Men*. Boston: Alyson.

Kelley, Robin D.G. 1997. *Yo' Mama's Dysfunktional! Fighting the Culture Wars in Urban America*. Boston: Beacon.

Legal/Policy Department of the Campaign for Military Service. 1993. "The Race Analogy: Fact Sheet Comparing the Military's Policy of Racial Segregation in the 1940s to the Current

Ban on Lesbians, Gay Men and Bisexuals." In *Briefing Book*, Washington, DC: Legal/Policy Department of the Campaign for Military Service.

Lorde, Audre. 1984. *Sister Outsider*. Freedom, CA: Crossing Press.

McIntosh, Peggy. 1989. "White Privilege: Unpacking the Invisible Knapsack." *Peace and Freedom* (July/August): 10–12.

Mixner, David. 1996. *Stranger among Friends*. New York: Bantam.

Moraga, Cherrie. 1983. *Loving in the War Years*. Boston: South End Press.

Moraga, Cherrie and Gloria Anzaldua, eds. 1981. *This Bridge Called My Back: Writings by Radical Women of Color*. Watertown, MA: Persephone Press.

Rayside, David. 1998. *On the Fringe: Gays and Lesbians in Politics*. Ithaca, NY: Cornell University.

Segrest, Mab. 1994. *Memoir of a Race Traitor*. Boston: South End Press.

"Stonewall 25." 1994. *The Charlie Rose Show*. Public Broadcasting System, 24 June.

Thompson, Becky, and Sangeeta Tyagi, eds. 1996. *Names We Call Home: Autobiography on Racial Identity*. New York: Routledge.

Vaid, Urvashi. 1995. *Virtual Equality: The Mainstreaming of Lesbian and Gay Equality*. New York: Anchor Books.

PART 4B

RESISTING RACISM

In the concluding section of this book, we present works on decolonization, anti-racism, and migrant rights activism, in which the authors relate how historical, political, economic, social, and cultural contexts inform the principles, activities, and actions constituting this activism. As Cathie Lloyd relates in the second reading, depending on the context and analyses of racism, anti-racist responses take different forms, especially in the contemporary context of globalization. Activism can include large public actions, such as the Idle No More movement, a drive to organize a labour union such as the Canadian Farmworkers' Union, or it could include micro-resistance on an everyday basis, such as migrant workers in Canada who are subject to deportations if deemed to be engaging in any kind of resistance. Decolonization, a necessary process of anti-colonial and anti-racist action, as described by Māori scholar Linda Tuhiwai Smith, involves a process of critiquing colonial histories and retelling stories from Indigenous perspectives.

FURTHER READING

Aylward, Carol A. 1999. *Canadian Critical Race Theory: Racism and the Law*. Halifax: Fernwood Publishing.
In this book, Carol Aylward looks at the origins of critical race theory in the United States and Canada and the failure of the legal system to place race as a question and/or issue within legal discourse. The author analyzes the complex relationships among race, racism, and the law and discusses how Canadian lawyers are moving towards developing strategies that consider the role of race in litigation.

Choudry, Aziz, and Smith, Adrian. 2016. *Unfree Labour?: Struggles of Migrant and Immigrant Workers in Canada*. Oakland, CA: PM Press.
This anthology centres the working conditions and struggles of migrant workers in Canada, the captive labour pools of the most precarious and marginalized members of the working classes. The book points out how this labour force fits into a neo-liberal, globalized marketplace where migrant workers provide cheap and just-in-time labour and are constructed as "docile" chiefly due to their non-citizen status and resultant denial of rights. Nonetheless, they have organized at some personal cost. Each chapter is a case study of how migrant workers have struggled and organized.

Coulthard, Glen. 2014. *Red Skin White Masks: Rejecting the Colonial Politics of Recognition*. Minneapolis: University of Minnesota Press.

A classic work and a critique of "politics of recognition," which includes a range of settler colonial state practices that recognizes and reconciles with the destruction caused by a colonial "past." Coulthard argues that such a politics of recognition still reproduces colonial relations in the present and serves to advantage the colonial state. Thus, colonial hegemony is maintained in liberal democratic states not just through violence and coercion but also through its "productive power." He proposes the alternative of an "Indigenous resurgence," an example of which is the Idle No More movement in Canada. He centres contributions from Indigenous scholars, particularly Indigenous women, and also critically utilizes the writings of Karl Marx and Frantz Fanon.

Kino-nda-niimi Collective. 2014. *The Winter We Danced*. Winnipeg: ARP Books.

This is a compilation of poetic, artistic, and reflective writings, as well as historical and academic pieces, all connected to the Idle No More movement of winter of 2012–2013. It is said that the movement was free flowing with no singular leadership structure, although it was very organized. The book is similar in that it seems to be free flowing, with no apparent structure, and yet it is powerful and effective. The spontaneous round dances characterizing the movement are present in the book through pictures and appear symbolically in the juxtaposition of diverse genres of writing by individuals, each of whom participated in the actions or was inspired by them.

Kivel, Paul. 2002. *Uprooting Racism: How White People Can Work for Racial Justice*. Gabriola Island, BC: New Society Publishers.

In this book, Paul Kivel explores individual and institutional factors that maintain and perpetuate racism. He focuses on the role of white people in the existence of racism and argues that they have an important role to play in actively "uprooting racism." The author provides a number of questions and exercises, including questions pertaining to particular ethnoracial groups, which are useful for bringing awareness to issues of racism.

Chapter 44

Imperialism, History, Writing, and Theory

Linda Tuhiwai Smith

With reference to Indigenous peoples, Linda Tuhiwai Smith (1999) writes about how concepts of imperialism, history, writing, and theory inform their ideas and issues. She makes the point that "imperialism still hurts, still destroys and is reforming itself constantly." Activism among Indigenous peoples "as an international group," Smith continues, goes beyond the level of text and literature to include challenging and talking with a "a shared language" about "the history, the sociology, the psychology and the politics of imperialism and colonialism as an epic story telling of huge devastation, painful struggle and persistent survival."

The master's tools will never dismantle the master's house.
    —Audre Lorde[1]

Imperialism frames the indigenous experience. It is part of our story, our version of modernity. Writing about our experiences under imperialism and its more specific expression of colonialism has become a significant project of the indigenous world. In a literary sense this has been defined by writers like Salman Rushdie, Ngugi wa Thiong'o and many others whose literary origins are grounded in the landscapes, languages, cultures and imaginative worlds of peoples and nations whose own histories were interrupted and radically reformulated by European imperialism. While the project of creating this literature is important, what indigenous activists would argue is that imperialism cannot be struggled over only at the level of text and literature. Imperialism still hurts, still destroys and is reforming itself constantly. Indigenous peoples as an international group have had to challenge, understand and have a shared language for talking about the history, the sociology, the psychology and the politics of imperialism and colonialism as an epic story telling of huge devastation, painful struggle and persistent survival. We have become quite good at talking that kind of talk, most often amongst ourselves, for ourselves and to ourselves. "The talk" about the colonial past is embedded in our political discourses, our humour, poetry, music, story telling and other common sense ways of passing on both a narrative of history and an attitude about history. The lived experiences of imperialism and colonialism contribute another dimension to the ways in which terms like "imperialism" can be understood. This is a dimension that indigenous peoples know and understand well.

[…] Decolonization is a process which engages with imperialism and colonialism at multiple levels. For researchers, one of those levels is concerned with having a more critical understanding of the underlying assumptions, motivations and values which inform research practices.

ON BEING HUMAN

The faculty of imagination is not strongly developed among them, although they
permitted it to run wild in believing absurd superstitions.
    —A.S. Thompson, 1859[2]

One of the supposed characteristics of primitive peoples was that we could not use our minds or intellects. We could not invent things, we could not create institutions or history, we could not imagine, we could not produce anything of value, we did not know how to use land and other resources from the natural world, we did not practice the "arts" of civilization. By lacking such virtues we disqualified ourselves, not just from civilization but from humanity itself. In other words we were not "fully human"; some of us were not even considered partially human. Ideas about what counted as human in association with the power to define people as human or not human were already encoded in imperial and colonial discourses prior to the period of imperialism covered here.[3] Imperialism provided the means through which concepts of what counts as human could be applied systematically as forms of classification, for example through hierarchies of race and typologies of different societies. In conjunction with imperial power and with "science," these classification systems came to shape relations between imperial powers and indigenous societies.

Said has argued that the "oriental" was partially a creation of the West, based on a combination of images formed through scholarly and imaginative works. Fanon argued earlier that the colonized were brought into existence by the settler and the two, settler and colonized, are mutual constructions of colonialism. In Fanon's words "we know each other well."[4] The European powers had by the nineteenth century already established systems of rule and forms of social relations which governed interaction with the indigenous peoples being colonized. These relations were gendered, hierarchical and supported by rules, some explicit and others masked or hidden. The principle of "humanity" was one way in which the implicit or hidden rules could be shaped. To consider indigenous peoples as not fully human, or not human at all, enabled distance to be maintained and justified various policies of either extermination or domestication. Some indigenous peoples ("not human"), were hunted and killed like vermin, others ("partially human"), were rounded up and put in reserves like creatures to be broken in, branded and put to work.

The struggle to assert and claim humanity has been a consistent thread of anti-colonial discourses on colonialism and oppression. This struggle for humanity has generally been framed within the wider discourse of humanism, the appeal to human "rights," the notion of a universal human subject, and the connections between being human and being capable of creating history, knowledge and society. The focus on asserting humanity has to be seen within the anti-colonial analysis of imperialism and what were seen as imperialism's dehumanizing imperatives which were structured into language, the economy, social relations and the cultural life of colonial societies. From the nineteenth century onwards the processes of dehumanization were often hidden behind justifications for imperialism and colonialism which were clothed within an ideology of humanism and liberalism and the assertion of moral claims which related to a concept of civilized "man." The moral justifications did not necessarily stop the continued hunting of Aborigines in the early nineteenth century nor the continued ill-treatment of different indigenous peoples even today.

Problems have arisen, however, within efforts to struggle for humanity by overthrowing the ideologies relating to our supposed lack of humanity. The arguments of Fanon, and many writers since Fanon, have been criticized for essentializing our "nature," for taking for granted the binary categories of Western thought, for accepting arguments supporting cultural relativity, for claiming an authenticity which is overly idealistic and romantic, and for simply engaging in an inversion of the colonizer/colonized relationship which does not address the complex problems of power relations. Colonized peoples have been compelled to define what it means to be human because there is a deep understanding of what it has meant to be considered not fully human, to be *savage*. The difficulties of such a process, however, have been bound inextricably to constructions of colonial relations around the binary of colonizer and colonized. These two categories are not just a simple opposition but consist of several relations, some more clearly oppositional than others. Unlocking one set of relations most often requires unlocking and unsettling the different constituent parts of other relations. The binary of colonizer/colonized does not take into account, for example, the development of different layerings which have occurred within each group and across the two groups. Millions of indigenous peoples were ripped from their lands over several generations and shipped into slavery. The lands they went to as slaves were lands already taken from another group of indigenous peoples. Slavery was as much a system of imperialism as was the claiming of other peoples' territories. Other indigenous peoples were transported to various outposts in the same way as interesting plants and animals were reclimatized, in order to fulfil labour requirements. Hence there are large populations in some places of non-indigenous groups, also victims of colonialism, whose primary relationship and allegiance is often to the imperial power rather than to the colonized people of the place to which they themselves have been brought. To put it simply, indigenous peoples as commodities were transported to and fro across the empire. There were also sexual relations between colonizers and colonized which led to communities who were referred to as "half-castes" or "half-breeds," or stigmatized by some other specific term which often excluded them from belonging to either settler or indigenous societies. Sometimes children from "mixed" sexual relationships were considered at least half-way civilized; at other times they were considered worse than civilized. Legislation was frequently used to regulate both the categories to which people were entitled to belong and the sorts of relations which one category of people could have with another.

Since the Second World War wars of independence and struggles for decolonization by former parts of European empires have shown us that attempts to break free can involve enormous violence: physical, social, economic, cultural and psychological. The struggle for freedom has been viewed by writers such as Fanon as a necessarily, inevitably violent process between "two forces opposed to each other by their very nature."[5] Fanon argues further that "Decolonization which sets out to change the order of the world is, obviously, a programme of complete disorder."[6] This introduces another important principle embedded in imperialism, that of order. The principle of order provides the underlying connection between such things as: the nature of imperial social relations; the activities of Western science; the establishment of trade; the appropriation of sovereignty; the establishment of law. No great conspiracy had to occur for the simultaneous developments and activities which took place under imperialism because imperial activity was driven by fundamentally similar underlying principles. Nandy refers to these principles as the "code" or "grammar" of imperialism.[7] The idea of code suggests that there is a deep structure which regulates and legitimates imperial practices.

The fact that indigenous societies had their own systems of order was dismissed through what Albert Memmi referred to as a series of negations: they were not fully human, they were not civilized enough to have systems, they were not literate, their languages and modes of thought were inadequate.[8] As Fanon and later writers such as Nandy have claimed, imperialism and colonialism brought complete disorder to colonized peoples, disconnecting them from their histories, their landscapes, their languages, their social relations and their own ways of thinking, feeling and interacting with the world. It was a process of systematic fragmentation which can still be seen in the disciplinary carve-up of the indigenous world: bones, mummies and skulls to the museums, art work to private collectors, languages to linguistics, "customs" to anthropologists, beliefs and behaviours to psychologists. To discover how fragmented this process was one needs only to stand in a museum, a library, a bookshop, and ask where indigenous peoples are located. Fragmentation is not a phenomenon of postmodernism as many might claim. For indigenous peoples fragmentation has been the consequence of imperialism.

WRITING, HISTORY AND THEORY

A critical aspect of the struggle for self-determination has involved questions relating to our history as indigenous peoples and a critique of how we, as the Other, have been represented or excluded from various accounts. Every issue has been approached by indigenous peoples with a view to *re*writing and *re*righting our position in history. Indigenous peoples want to tell our own stories, write our own versions, in our own ways, for our own purposes. It is not simply about giving an oral account or a genealogical naming of the land and the events which raged over it, but a very powerful need to give testimony to and restore a spirit, to bring back into existence a world fragmented and dying. The sense of history conveyed by these approaches is not the same thing as the discipline of history, and so our accounts collide, crash into each other.

Writing or literacy, in a very traditional sense of the word, has been used to determine the breaks between the past and the present, the beginning of history and the development of theory.[9] Writing has been viewed as the mark of a superior civilization and other societies have been judged, by this view, to be incapable of thinking critically and objectively, or having distance from ideas and emotions. Writing is part of theorizing and writing is part of history. Writing, history and theory, then, are key sites in which Western research of the indigenous world has come together. As we saw at the beginning of this chapter, however, from another perspective writing and especially writing theory are very intimidating ideas for many indigenous students. Having been immersed in the Western academy which claims theory as thoroughly Western, which has constructed all the rules by which the indigenous world has been theorized, indigenous voices have been overwhelmingly silenced. The act, let alone the art and science, of theorizing our own existence and realities is not something which many indigenous people assume is possible. Frantz Fanon's call for the indigenous intellectual and artist to create a new literature, to work in the cause of constructing a national culture after liberation still stands as a challenge. While this has been taken up by writers of fiction, many indigenous scholars who work in the social and other sciences struggle to write, theorize and research as indigenous scholars.

IS HISTORY IMPORTANT FOR INDIGENOUS PEOPLES?

This may appear to be a trivial question as the answer most colonized people would give, I think, is that "yes, history is important." But I doubt if what they would be responding to is the notion of history which is understood by the Western academy. Poststructuralist critiques of history which draw heavily on French poststructural thought have focused on the characteristics and understandings of history as an Enlightenment or modernist project. Their critique is of both liberal and Marxist concepts of history. Feminists have argued similarly (but not necessarily from a poststructuralist position) that history is the story of a specific form of domination, namely of patriarchy, literally "his-story."

While acknowledging the critical approaches of poststructuralist theory and cultural studies the arguments which are debated at this level are not new to indigenous peoples. There are numerous oral stories which tell of what it means, what it feels like, to be present while your history is erased before your eyes, dismissed as irrelevant, ignored or rendered as the lunatic ravings of drunken old people. The negation of indigenous views of history was a critical part of asserting colonial ideology, partly because such views were regarded as clearly "primitive" and "incorrect" and mostly because they challenged and resisted the mission of colonization.

Indigenous peoples have also mounted a critique of the way history is told from the perspective of the colonizers. At the same time, however, indigenous groups have argued that history is important for understanding the present and that reclaiming history is a critical and essential aspect of decolonization. The critique of Western history argues that history is a modernist project which has developed alongside imperial beliefs about the Other. History is assembled around a set of interconnected ideas which I will summarize briefly here. I have drawn on a wide range of discussions by indigenous people and by writers such as Robert Young, J. Abu-Lughod, Keith Jenkins, C. Steadman.[10]

1. The idea that history is a totalizing discourse

The concept of totality assumes the possibility and the desirability of being able to include absolutely all known knowledge into a coherent whole. In order for this to happen, classification systems, rules of practice and methods had to be developed to allow for knowledge to be selected and included in what counts as history.

2. The idea that there is a universal history

Although linked to the notion of totality, the concept of universal assumes that there are fundamental characteristics and values which all human subjects and societies share. It is the development of these universal characteristics which are of historical interest.

3. The idea that history is one large chronology

History is regarded as being about developments over time. It charts the progress of human endeavour through time. Chronology is important as a method because it allows events to be located at a point in time. The actual time events take place also makes them "real" or factual. In order to begin the chronology a time of "discovery" has to be established. Chronology is also important for attempting to go backwards and explain how and why things happened in the past.

4. The idea that history is about development

Implicit in the notion of development is the notion of progress. This assumes that societies move forward in stages of development much as an infant grows into a fully developed adult human being. The earliest phase of human development is regarded as primitive, simple and emotional. As societies develop they become less primitive, more civilized, more rational, and their social structures become more complex and bureaucratic.

5. The idea that history is about a self-actualizing human subject

In this view humans have the potential to reach a stage in their development where they can be in total control of their faculties. There is an order of human development which moves, in stages, through the fulfilment of basic needs, the development of emotions, the development of the intellect and the development of morality. Just as the individual moves through these stages, so do societies.

6. The idea that the story of history can be told in one coherent narrative

This idea suggests that we can assemble all the facts in an ordered way so that they tell us the truth or give us a very good idea of what really did happen in the past. In theory it means that historians can write a true history of the world.

7. The idea that history as a discipline is innocent

This idea says that "facts" speak for themselves and that the historian simply researches the facts and puts them together. Once all the known facts are assembled they tell their own story, without any need of a theoretical explanation or interpretation by the historian. This idea also conveys the sense that history is pure as a discipline, that is, it is not implicated with other disciplines.

8. The idea that history is constructed around binary categories

This idea is linked to the historical method of chronology. In order for history to begin there has to be a period of beginning and some criteria for determining when something begins. In terms of history this was often attached to concepts of "discovery," the development of literacy, or the development of a specific social formation. Everything before that time is designated as prehistorical, belonging to the realm of myths and traditions, "outside" the domain.

9. The idea that history is patriarchal

This idea is linked to the notions of self-actualization and development, as women were regarded as being incapable of attaining the higher orders of development. Furthermore they were not significant in terms of the ways societies developed because they were not present in the bureaucracies or hierarchies where changes in social or political life were being determined.

Other key ideas

Intersecting this set of ideas are some other important concepts. Literacy, as one example, was used as a criterion for assessing the development of a society and its progress to a stage where history can be said to begin. Even places such as India, China and Japan, however, which were very literate cultures prior to their "discovery" by the West, were invoked through other categories which defined them as uncivilized. Their literacy, in other words, did not count as a record of legitimate knowledge.

The German philosopher Hegel is usually regarded as the "founding father" of history in the sense outlined here. This applies to both Liberal and Marxist views.[11] Hegel conceived of the fully human subject as someone capable of "creating (his) own history." However, Hegel did not simply invent the rules of history. As Robert Young argues, "the entire Hegelian machinery simply lays down the operation of a system already in place, already operating in everyday life."[12] It should also be self-evident that many of these ideas are predicated on a sense of Otherness. They are views which invite a comparison with "something/someone else" which exists *on the outside,* such as the oriental, the "Negro," the "Jew," the "Indian," the "Aborigine." Views about the Other had already existed for centuries in Europe, but during the Enlightenment these views became more formalized through science, philosophy and imperialism, into explicit systems of classification and "regimes of truth." The racialization of the human subject and the social order enabled comparisons to be made between the "us" of the West and the "them" of the Other. History was the story of people who were regarded as *fully human.* Others who were not regarded as human (that is, capable of self-actualization) were prehistoric. This notion is linked also to Hegel's master–slave construct which has been applied as a psychological category (by Freud) and as a system of social ordering.

A further set of important ideas embedded in the modernist view of history relates to the origins (causes) and nature of social change. The Enlightenment project involved new conceptions of society and of the individual based around the precepts of rationalism, individualism and capitalism. There was a general belief that not only could individuals remake themselves but so could societies. The modern industrial state became the point of contrast between the pre-modern and the modern. History in this view began with the emergence of the rational individual and the modern industrialized society. However, there is something more to this idea in terms of how history came to be conceptualized as a method. The connection to the industrial state is significant because it highlights what was regarded as being worthy of history. The people and groups who "made" history were the people who developed the underpinnings of the state—the economists, scientists, bureaucrats and philosophers. That they were all men of a certain class and race was "natural" because they were regarded (naturally) as fully rational, self-actualizing human beings capable, therefore, of creating social change, that is history. The day-to-day lives of "ordinary" people, and of women, did not become a concern of history until much more recently.

CONTESTED HISTORIES

For indigenous peoples, the critique of history is not unfamiliar, although it has now been claimed by postmodern theories. The idea of contested stories and multiple discourses about the past, by different communities, is closely linked to the politics of everyday contemporary indigenous life. It is very much a part of the fabric of communities that value oral ways of knowing. These contested accounts are stored within genealogies, within the landscape, within weavings and carvings, even within the personal names that many people carried. The means by which these histories were stored was through their systems of knowledge. Many of these systems have since been reclassified as oral traditions rather than histories.

Under colonialism indigenous peoples have struggled against a Western view of history and yet been complicit with that view. We have often allowed our "histories" to be told and have then become outsiders as we heard them being retold. Schooling is directly implicated in this process. Through the curriculum and its underlying theory of knowledge, early schools redefined the world and where indigenous peoples were positioned within the world. From being direct descendants of sky and earth parents, Christianity positioned some of us as higher-order savages who deserved salvation in order that we could become children of God. Maps of the world reinforced our place on the periphery of the world, although we were still considered part of the Empire. This included having to learn new names for our own lands. Other symbols of our loyalty, such as the flag, were also an integral part of the imperial curriculum.[13] Our orientation to the world was already being redefined as we were being excluded systematically from the writing of the history of our own lands. This on its own may not have worked were it not for the actual material redefinition of our world which was occurring simultaneously through such things as the renaming and "breaking in" of the land, the alienation and fragmentation of lands through legislation, the forced movement of people off their lands, and the social consequences which resulted in high sickness and mortality rates.

Indigenous attempts to reclaim land, language, knowledge and sovereignty have usually involved contested accounts of the past by colonizers and colonized. These have occurred in the courts, before various commissions, tribunals and official enquiries, in the media, in Parliament, in bars and on talkback radio. In these situations contested histories do not exist in the same cultural framework as they do when tribal or clan histories, for example, are being debated within the indigenous community itself. They are not simply struggles over "facts" and "truth"; the rules by which these struggles take place are never clear (other than that we as the indigenous community know they are going to be stacked against us); and we are not the final arbiters of what really counts as the truth.

It is because of these issues that I ask the question, "Is history in its modernist construction important or not important for indigenous peoples?" For many people who are presently engaged in research on indigenous land claims the answer would appear to be self-evident. We assume that when "the truth comes out" it will prove that what happened was wrong or illegal and that therefore the system (tribunals, the courts, the government) will set things right. We believe that history is also about justice, that understanding history will enlighten our decisions about the future. *Wrong.* History is also about power. In fact history is mostly about power. It is the story of the powerful and how they became powerful, and then how they use their power to keep them in positions in which they can continue to dominate others. It is because of this relationship with power that we have been excluded, marginalized and "Othered." In this sense history is not important for indigenous peoples because a thousand accounts of the "truth" will not alter the "fact" that indigenous peoples are still marginal and do not possess the power to transform history into justice.

This leads then to several other questions. The one which is most relevant to this book is the one which asks, "Why then has revisiting history been a significant part of decolonization?" The answer, I suggest, lies in the intersection of indigenous approaches to the past, of the modernist history project itself and of the resistance strategies which have been employed. Our colonial experience traps us in the project of modernity. There can be no "postmodern" for us until we have settled some business of the modern. This does not mean that we do not understand or employ multiple discourses, or act in incredibly contradictory ways, or exercise power ourselves in multiple ways. It means that there is unfinished business, that we are still being colonized (and know it), and that we are still searching for justice.

Coming to know the past has been part of the critical pedagogy of decolonization. To hold alternative histories is to hold alternative knowledges. The pedagogical implication of this access to alternative knowledges is that they can form the basis of alternative ways of doing things. Transforming our colonized views of our own history (as written by the West), however, requires us to revisit, site by site, our history under Western eyes. This in turn requires a theory or approach which helps us to engage with, understand and then act upon history. It is in this sense that the sites visited in this book begin with a critique of a Western view of history. Telling our stories from the past, reclaiming the past, giving testimony to the injustices of the past are all strategies which are commonly employed by indigenous peoples struggling for justice. On the international scene it is extremely rare and unusual when indigenous accounts are accepted and acknowledged as valid interpretations of what has taken place. And yet, the need to tell our stories remains the powerful imperative of a powerful form of resistance.

IS WRITING IMPORTANT FOR INDIGENOUS PEOPLES?

As I am arguing, every aspect of the act of producing knowledge has influenced the ways in which indigenous ways of knowing have been represented. Reading, writing, talking, these are as fundamental to academic discourse as science, theories, methods, paradigms. To begin with reading, one might cite the talk in which Maori writer Patricia Grace undertook to show that "Books Are Dangerous."[14] She argues that there are four things that make many books dangerous to indigenous readers: (1) they do not reinforce our values, actions, customs, culture and identity; (2) when they tell us only about others they are saying that we do not exist; (3) they may be writing about us but are writing things which are untrue; and (4) they are writing about us but saying negative and insensitive things which tell us that we are not good. Although Grace is talking about school texts and journals, her comments apply also to academic writing. Much of what I have read has said that we do not exist, that if we do exist it is in terms which I cannot recognize, that we are no good and that what we think is not valid.

Leonie Pihama makes a similar point about film. In a review of *The Piano* she says: "Maori people struggle to gain a voice, struggle to be heard from the margins, to have our stories heard, to have our descriptions of ourselves validated, to have access to the domain within which we can control and define those images which are held up as reflections of our realities."[15] Representation is important as a concept because it gives the impression of "the truth." When I read texts, for example, I frequently have to orientate myself to a text world in which the centre of academic knowledge is either in Britain, the United States or Western Europe; in which words such as "we," "us," "our," "I" actually exclude me. It is a text world in which (if what I am interested in rates a mention) I have learned that I belong *partly* in the Third World, *partly* in the "Women of Colour" world, *partly* in the black or African world. I read myself into these labels *partly* because I have also learned that, although there may be commonalities, they still do not entirely account for the experiences of indigenous peoples.

So, reading and interpretation present problems when we do not see ourselves in the text. There are problems, too, when we do see ourselves but can barely recognize ourselves through the representation. One problem of being trained to read this way, or, more correctly, of learning to read this way over many years of academic study, is that we can adopt uncritically similar patterns of writing. We begin to write about ourselves as indigenous peoples as if we really were "out there," the "Other," with all the baggage that this entails. Another problem is that academic writing is a form of selecting, arranging and presenting knowledge. It privileges sets of texts, views about the history of an idea, what issues count as significant; and, by engaging in the same process uncritically, we too can render indigenous writers invisible or unimportant while reinforcing the validity of other writers. If we write without thinking critically about our writing, it can be dangerous. Writing can also be dangerous because we reinforce and maintain a style of discourse which is never innocent. Writing can be dangerous because sometimes we reveal ourselves in ways which get misappropriated and used against us. Writing can be dangerous because, by building on previous texts written about indigenous peoples, we continue to legitimate views about ourselves which are hostile to us. This is particularly true of academic writing, although journalistic and imaginative writing reinforce these "myths."

These attitudes inform what is sometimes referred to as either the "empire writes back" discourse or post-colonial literature. This kind of writing assumes that the centre does not necessarily have to be located at the imperial centre.[16] It is argued that the centre can be shifted ideologically through imagination and that this shifting can recreate history. Another perspective relates to the ability of "native" writers to appropriate the language of the colonizer as the language of the colonized and to write so that it captures the ways in which the colonized actually use the language, their dialects and inflections, and in the way they make sense of their lives. Its other importance is that it speaks to an audience of people who have also been colonized. This is one of the ironies of many indigenous peoples' conferences where issues of indigenous language have to be debated in the language of the colonizers. Another variation of the debate relates to the use of literature to write about the terrible things which happened under colonialism or as a consequence of colonialism. These topics inevitably implicated the colonizers and their literature in the processes of cultural domination.

Yet another position, espoused in African literature by Ngugi wa Thiong'o, was to write in the languages of Africa. For Ngugi wa Thiong'o, to write in the language of the colonizers was to pay homage to them, while to write in the languages of Africa was to engage in an anti-imperialist struggle. He argued that language carries culture and the language of the colonizer became the means by which the "mental universe of the colonized" was dominated.[17] This applied, in Ngugi wa Thiong'o's view, particularly to the language of writing. Whereas oral languages were frequently still heard at home, the use of literature in association with schooling resulted in the alienation of a child from the child's history, geography, music and other aspects of culture.[18]

In discussing the politics of academic writing, in which research writing is a subset, Cherryl Smith argues that "colonialism, racism and cultural imperialism do not occur only in society, outside of the gates of universities."[19] Academic writing, she continues, is a way of "'writing back' whilst at the same time writing to ourselves."[20] The act of "writing back" and simultaneously writing to ourselves is not simply an inversion of how we have learned to write academically.[21] The different audiences to whom we speak make the task somewhat difficult. The scope of the literature which we use in our work contributes to a different framing of the issues. The oral arts and other forms of expression set our landscape in a different frame of reference. Our understandings of the academic disciplines within which we have been trained also frame our approaches. Even the use of pronouns such as "I" and "we" can cause difficulties when writing for several audiences, because while it may be acceptable now in academic writing, it is not always acceptable to indigenous audiences.[22]

Edward Said also asks the following questions: "Who writes? For whom is the writing being done? In what circumstances? These it seems to me are the questions whose answers provide us with the ingredients making a politics of interpretation."[23] These questions are important ones which are being asked in a variety of ways within our communities. They are asked, for example, about research, policy making and curriculum development. Said's comments, however, point to the problems of interpretation, in this case of academic writing. "Who" is doing the writing is important in the politics of the Third World and African America, and indeed for indigenous peoples; it is even more important in the politics of how these worlds are being represented "back to" the West. Although in the literary sense the imagination is crucial to writing, the use of language is not highly regarded in academic discourses which claim to be scientific. The concept of imagination, when employed as a sociological tool, is often reduced to a way of seeing and understanding the world, or a way of understanding how people either construct the world or are constructed by the world. As Toni Morrison argues, however, the imagination can be a way of sharing the world.[24] This means, according to Morrison, struggling to find the language to do this and then struggling to interpret and perform within that shared imagination.

WRITING THEORY

Research is linked in all disciplines to theory. Research adds to, is generated from, creates or broadens our theoretical understandings. Indigenous peoples have been, in many ways, oppressed by theory. Any consideration of the ways our origins have been examined, our histories recounted, our arts analysed, our cultures dissected, measured, torn apart and distorted back to us will suggest that theories have not looked sympathetically or ethically at us. Writing research is often considered marginally more important than writing theory, providing it results in tangible benefits for farmers, economists, industries and sick people. For indigenous peoples, most of the theorizing has been driven by anthropological approaches. These approaches have shown enormous concern for our origins as peoples and for aspects of our linguistic and material culture.

The development of theories by indigenous scholars which attempt to explain our existence in contemporary society (as opposed to the "traditional" society constructed under modernism) has only just begun. Not all these theories claim to be derived from some "pure" sense of what it means to be indigenous, nor do they claim to be theories which have been developed in a vacuum separated from any association with civil and human rights movements, other nationalist struggles or other theoretical approaches. What is claimed, however, is that new ways of theorizing by indigenous scholars are grounded in a real sense of, and sensitivity towards, what it means to be an indigenous person. As Kathie Irwin urges, "We don't need anyone else developing the tools which will help us to come to terms with who we are. We can and will do this work. Real power lies with those who design the tools—it always has. This power is ours."[25] Contained within this imperative is a sense of being able to determine priorities, to bring to the centre those issues of our own choosing, and to discuss them amongst ourselves.

I am arguing that theory at its most simple level is important for indigenous peoples. At the very least it helps make sense of reality. It enables us to make assumptions and predictions about the world in which we live. It contains within it a method or methods for selecting and arranging, for prioritising and legitimating what we see and do. Theory enables us to deal with contradictions and uncertainties. Perhaps more significantly, it gives us space to plan, to strategize, to take greater control over our resistances. The language of a theory can also be used as a way of organising and determining action. It helps us to interpret what is being told to us, and to predict the consequences of what is being promised. Theory can also protect us because it contains within it a way of putting reality into perspective. If it is a good theory it also allows for new ideas and ways of looking at things to be incorporated constantly without the need to search constantly for new theories.

A dilemma posed by such a thorough critical approach to history, writing and theory is that whilst we may reject or dismiss them, this does not make them go away, nor does the critique necessarily offer the alternatives. We live simultaneously within such views while needing to pose, contest and struggle for the legitimacy of oppositional or alternative histories, theories and ways of writing. At some points there is, there has to be, dialogue across the boundaries of oppositions. This has to be because we constantly collide with dominant views while we are attempting to transform our lives on a larger scale than our own localized circumstances. This means struggling to make sense of our own world while also attempting to transform what counts as important in the world of the powerful.

Part of the exercise is about recovering our own stories of the past. This is inextricably bound to a recovery of our language and epistemological foundations. It is also about reconciling and reprioritizing what is really important about the past with what is important about the present. These issues raise significant questions for indigenous communities who are not only beginning to fight back against the invasion of their communities by academic, corporate and populist researchers, but to think about, and carry out research, on their own concerns. One of the problems discussed in this first section of this book is that the methodologies and methods of research, the theories that inform them, the questions which they generate and the writing styles they employ, all become significant acts which need to be considered carefully and critically before being applied. In other words, they need to be "decolonized." Decolonization, however, does not mean and has not meant a total rejection of all theory or research or Western knowledge. Rather, it is about centring our concerns and world views and then coming to know and understand theory and research from our own perspectives and for our own purposes.

As a site of struggle research has a significance for indigenous peoples that is embedded in our history under the gaze of Western imperialism and Western science. It is framed by our attempts to escape the penetration and surveillance of that gaze whilst simultaneously reordering and reconstituting ourselves as indigenous human beings in a state of ongoing crisis. Research has not been neutral in its objectification of the Other. Objectification is a process of dehumanization. In its clear links to Western knowledge research has generated a particular relationship to indigenous peoples which continues to be problematic. At the same time, however, new pressures which have resulted from our own politics of self-determination, of wanting greater participation in, or control over, what happens to us, and from changes in the global environment, have meant that there is a much more active and knowing engagement in the activity of research by indigenous peoples. Many indigenous groups, communities and organisations are thinking about, talking about, and carrying out research activities of various kinds. In this chapter I have suggested that it is important to have a critical understanding of some of the tools of research—not just the obvious technical tools but the conceptual tools, the ones which make us feel uncomfortable, which we avoid, for which we have no easy response.

> *I lack imagination you say*
> *No. I lack language.*
> *The language to clarify*
> *my resistance to the literate....*
> —Cherrie Moraga[26]

NOTES

1. Lorde, Audre (1979), "The Master's Tools Will Never Dismantle the Master's House," comments at "The Personal and the Political" panel, Second Sex Conference, reproduced in Moraga, C. and G. Anzaldua (1981), *This Bridge Called My Back*, Kitchen Table Women of Color Press, New York, pp. 98–101.

2. Thompson, A.S. (1859), *The Story of New Zealand: Past and Present, Savage and Civilised*, John Murray, London, p. 82.

3. Goldberg, D.T. (1993), *Racist Culture: Philosophy and the Politics of Meaning*, Blackwell, Oxford. See also Sardar, Z.A. Nandy and W. Davies (1993), *Barbaric Others: A Manifesto of Western Racism*, Pluto Press, London.

4. Fanon, Frantz (1990), *The Wretched of the Earth*, Penguin, London.

5. Ibid, pp. 27–8.

6. Ibid., p. 27.

7. Nandy, A. (1989), *The Intimate Enemy: Loss and Recovery of Self Under Colonialism*, Oxford University Press, Delhi.

8. Memmi, A. (1991), *The Coloniser and the Colonized*, Beacon Press, Boston, p. 83.

9. For a critique of these views refer to Street, B.V. (1984), *Literacy in Theory and Practice*, Cambridge University Press, New York.

10. I have drawn on a wide range of discussions both by indigenous people and by various writers such as Robert Young, J. Abu-Lughod, Keith Jenkins and C. Steadman. See, for example, Young, R. (1990), *White Mythologies: Writing, History and the West*, Routledge, London; Abu-Lughood, J. (1989), "On the Remaking of History: How to Reinvent the Past," in *Remaking History*, Dia Art Foundation, Bay Press, Seattle, pp. 111–29; Steadman, C. (1992), "Culture, Cultural Studies and the Historians," in *Cultural Studies*, ed. G. Nelson, P.A. Treicher and L. Grossberg, Routledge, New York, pp. 613–20; Trask, *From a Native Daughter*.

11. Young, *White Mythologies*.

12. Ibid. p. 3.

13. Mangan, J. (1993), *The Imperial Curriculum: Racial Images and Education in the British Colonial Experience*, Routledge, London.

14. Grace, P. (1985), "Books are Dangerous," paper presented at the Fourth Early Childhood Convention, Wellington, New Zealand.

15. Pihama, L. (1994), "Are Films Dangerous? A Maori Woman's Perspective on *The Piano*," *Hecate*, Vol. 20, No. 2, p. 241.

16. Ashcroft, B., G. Griffiths and H. Tiffin (1989), *The Empire Writes Back: Theory and Practice in Post-colonial Literatures*, Routledge, London.

17. Thiong'o, Ngugi Wa (1986), *Decolonizing the Mind: The Politics of Language in African Literature*, James Currey, London.

18. Ibid.

19. Smith, C.W. (1994), "Kimihia Te Matauranga: Colonization and Iwi Development," MA thesis, University of Auckland, New Zealand, p. 13.

20. Ibid, p. 13.

21. van Dijk, T.A. (1989), *Elite Discourses and Racism*, Sage Publications, Newbury Park, California.

22. Smith, L.T. (1994), "In Search of a Language and a Shareable Imaginative World: E Kore Taku Moe, E Riro i a Koe," *Hecate*, Vol. 20, No. 2, pp. 162–74.

23. Said, E. (1983), "Opponents, Audiences, Constituencies and Community," in *The Politics of Interpretation*, ed. W.J.T. Mitchell, University of Chicago Press, Chicago, p. 7.

24. Morrison, T. (1993), *Playing in the Dark: Whiteness and the Literary Imagination*, Vintage Books, New York.

25. Irwin, K. (1992), "Towards Theories of Maori Feminisms," in *Feminist Voices: Women's Studies Texts for Aotearoa/New Zealand*, ed. R. du Plessis, Oxford University Press, Auckland, p. 5.

26. Moraga, Cherrie (1983), quoted by G. Anzaldua in "Speaking Tongues: a Letter to 3rd World Women Writers," in *This Bridge Called My Back*, p. 166.

Chapter 45

Anti-racism, Social Movements, and Civil Society

Cathie Lloyd

In this chapter, Cathie Lloyd (2002) examines the ways in which anti-racism as a movement has been developing in Europe, specifically Britain and France, noting how the movement and its effectiveness must be understood within the context of the historical, economic, and political conditions of the respective nation-states. She argues that European unification and globalization are likely to "increase precariousness among migrants and ethnic minority populations" in Europe.

This chapter examines the ways in which anti-racism is developing in civil society and as a social movement at a time of momentous change. European economic, social and political integration has had a major impact on the issues facing anti-racists and the way in which they organise. While the main themes of the 1990s have been the increase in racism and xenophobia and the harmonisation of immigration controls, attention must now turn to the democratic deficiencies of the new systems of global governance.

Globalisation theory suggests that there has been a diminution in the scope of political activities as effective power shifts away from the sovereign nation state (Bauman 1998). This process is echoed in the decline in influence of and identification with traditional centres of political activity, particularly political parties and trade unions (Cloonan and Street 1998; Johnson and Pattie 1997). This chapter explores some of ways in which anti-racism has been developing within European nation-states and suggests new ways in which broader activities can take place through forms of networking within social movements.

We need to situate anti-racism within a historical and political context in order to be clear about what is at stake. A contextualised approach can help us to see the complexities behind the dualism racism/anti-racism suggested by the term anti-racism. The problem is that using the racism/anti-racism formulation involves taking anti-racism for granted and subordinating it to racism, which means that in theorising racism, anti-racism has been eclipsed. There is an implicit, yet unacknowledged recognition that anti-racism is always attempting to become something but is not always successful. The name "anti-racism" suggests a realised project of how to overcome racism, whereas anti-racists are often groping towards an adequate response. In the next section I consider how analyses of racism have given rise to different forms of anti-racist response within the contemporary context of globalisation, which presents us with challenges but also new opportunities.

RACISM AND ANTI-RACISM IN THE CONTEMPORARY CONTEXT

With the discrediting of pseudo-scientific biological ideas of "race" after 1945, a consensus was established around the idea that education, culture and social environment were the main determinants of differences between human groups (Kuper 1975; Unesco 1951). It was thought that racial prejudice could be educated out of existence. However the economistic left tended to focus on class struggle and migrant labour as the "reserve army of labour" which served to postpone tackling the problem of racism (Castles and Kosack 1973). An important difference between the liberal and Marxist perspectives on "race" and racism lies in the insight that ideologies of racism are not just matters of individual prejudice but can permeate structures. This gave rise to the concept of institutional racism which has opened up a wider field of possible social action against covert attitudes and structural forms of discrimination. Such an approach requires us to pay attention to the wider context in which anti-racist policies and initiatives operate.

Anti-racism therefore operates in a wide arena through public policy and legislation, within institutional structures, in civil society and social movements. My account here focuses on anti-racism which operates within civil society, through social movements, grass-roots organisations and the mobilisations of ethnic minority communities. I seek to explore who are anti-racists, how they organise and what they do (Lloyd 1998b). This gives rise to a further series of questions about the future of anti-racism. How will the traditional themes of anti-racism—opposition to racial discrimination, representation of and solidarity with people who experience racism, and the attempt to establish an anti-racist common sense (or hegemony, in the Gramscian sense)—fit into the political discourses of the twenty-first century, marked by post-colonialism and globalisation?

Globalisation and anti-racism both have a paradoxical relationship to universalism and particularism. In the processes of globalisation, increased consciousness of the international is accompanied by yearnings for the recognition of difference and identity (Held 1991: 149). The political aspects of globalisation involve an apparent loss of control of key aspects of sovereignty by the nation-state, leading to a focus on the control of its own population and its borders. Under these conditions it is thought that power leaves traditional political channels leading to opaque areas of decision-making, which involves political demobilisation and a loss of faith in the main political parties, a growth of social insecurity and a paradoxical swing between universalising and particularistic impulses. This presents social movements with new possibilities: if it is no longer useful to focus on individual states, instead movements may bypass their own target state and rely on international pressure and the transnational human rights movement to support them (Keck and Sikkink 1999).

These views are not uncontested: research points to a continuing high level of political participation in most countries of Western Europe; this is quite distinct from political identification or loyalty, which does appear to be increasingly unstable (Johnson and Pattie 1997; Wilkinson and Muglan 1995). Some commentators suggest that globalisation is used to paralyse reforming strategies, and that these developments are used by states to control the movement of poor people across their borders (Hirst and Thompson 1996).

Globalisation may indeed offer an opportunity to anti-racists since "modern communications form the basis for an international civil society of people who share interests and associations across borders" (Hirst 1997: 180). This emerging international civil society, expressed through a growing number of transnational NGOs, such as Amnesty International or the International League for Human Rights, collect and publish information about abusive behaviour in order to challenge offending parties (mainly national governments). These initiatives have been sustained by the validation of human rights conventions by the majority of governments. Thus "the global spread of political democracy, with its roots in constitutionalism, makes those persons within the territorial space controlled by the sovereign state increasingly aware of their political, moral and legal option to appeal to broader communities in the event of encroachment on their basic human rights" (Falk 1995: 164). These developments may also be understood as transnational networks seeking to mobilise through international NGOs, such as Amnesty International or Anti-Apartheid, and which often operate like oppositional grass-roots movements.

A central feature of anti-racism is its diversity. Studies of anti-racism generally agree that it is a "difficult issue" which is not easily accommodated within the policy-making process partly because its constituency is relatively powerless (Heineman 1972; Lloyd 1994, 1998a; Stedward 1997). As a political movement anti-racism may be best understood as occupying different points on a continuum between well-organised, bureauratic organisations, pressure groups and protest or social movements which challenge dominant social practices and preconceptions. An assessment of its effectiveness as a constellation of pressure groups makes it clear that it does not fit neatly into any one category. For instance, in traditional pressure group theory, anti-racist groups fall somewhere between sectional or representational and promotional or universalist organisations (Finer 1958). A view of the over-arching themes of anti-racist discourse helps to show how anti-racists can be a more clearly defined lobby. Most groups campaign on a variety of different issues: against unjust immigration controls, police harassment, racist violence, or information gathering. Some offer legal services; all tend to vary according to the social and political context in which they operate (Coutant 1997). For instance, in the UK, the existence of a (relatively) well-funded statutory body committed to enforcing the law against racial discrimination, the Commission for Racial Equality (CRE), has limited the priorities and scope of anti-racist organisations. In France, designated anti-racist associations, with tiny budgets, working with a largely voluntary legal advice service, are mainly responsible for the enforcement of the laws against racism.

The relationship between anti-racist organisations and policy-makers is not an easy one. While decision-makers may not always regard anti-racists as respectable or responsible, there may also be pressure from within the anti-racist movement to maintain a distance from the authorities. Both sides may be highly conscious of the disparity in terms of access to material resources and power. The nearer one approaches the social movement end of anti-racism, the more there is suspicion, antagonism and distance towards authority. These attitudes are bound up with analyses of the ways in which racism is rooted in institutional practices and cultures (Macpherson 1999). Anti-racist protest groups face the dilemma of wanting to make a practical impact on policy and keeping faith with their grass roots who are the receiving end of racism (often exacerbated by government policies). Vitriolic debates may take place over co-operation with official inquiries (as with the Scarman inquiry in 1981) or the politics of accepting government grant aid.

Not all anti-racist organisations are equally distant from centres of decision-making. In Britain, Race Equality Councils (RECs) are tied in to a structure funded by a mix of local authority and Home Office money through the CRE. In France some organisations have received large government grants: for instance SOS-Racisme and France-Plus had a very comfortable relationship with the Socialist government during the 1980s. The main focus of these grants was to organise major campaigns which were directed at young people, including lavishly produced "rock" concerts and a national week of education against racism. These organisations carried out important campaigns during this period to encourage young people from immigrant backgrounds to register to vote. There are similar relationships between some anti-racist groups, political parties and churches in other European countries. Governments have increasingly recognised that civil society provides solidarity in a situation of social fragmentation, but this carries with it all the problems attendant on alliances or partnerships: in particular the risk of political manipulation and of co-option. Anti-racist groups' agendas may be distorted because funds may be available for one type of activity rather than another. Or they may become embroiled in political disputes which have little to do with their immediate concerns.

While groups may differ in their ability to benefit from subsidies and grants, another important factor of difference lies in the different resources at their disposal. While some groups may have few resources other than strongly motivated members, others such as the Joint Council for the Welfare of Immigrants (JCWI) in Britain or the Groupe d'Information et de Soutien des Immigrés (GISTI) in France may have slender financial means, but benefit from supporters' professional activities based in law or social work. They are able to formulate demands in ways that policy-makers can understand and use, forming a sort of bridge between protest/social movement groups and policy-makers.

It is important to establish some of the broad characteristics of the different approaches to anti-racism in Europe before we can identify the ways in which wider transnational co-operation might be possible. The next sections of this chapter draw on research and participation in anti-racist activity in Britain and France, enabling this discussion to move from the debate about differences and similarities in approaches to anti-racism in both countries to an assessment of recent attempts to build a European-wide anti-racism.

BRITAIN

In Britain, debates about anti-racism have focused on the problem of conflict between different types of political actors within anti-racist organisations, especially participation, representation and entitlements. Some studies have considered how to surmount the oppositional characteristics of anti-racism by broadening or expanding anti-racist issues, and establishing alliances. Historically anti-racism is associated with movements in support of decolonialisation, anti-fascism and struggles against discrimination and for immigrants' rights. What are the links between these different aspects and do they make some kind of coherent whole which constitutes anti-racism?

Anti-colonialism and anti-fascism were the most prevalent forms of anti-racism in the first part of the twentieth century. Anti-colonialism was so important that it was one of the central characteristics of the British left in the period 1918–64, according to Stephen Howe (1993). It marked an important transition between traditional radical attitudes towards international issues and the orientation of "new left" politics of the 1960s. It also shaped the activity and forms of organisation of early black British political groups, many of which originated in the metropolitan activity of exiled or student anti-colonial leaders (Howe 1993: 25). Anti-fascism was another defining feature of the left, particularly between the 1930s and 1950s. It was however limited by the use of a restricted concept of racism as one among other features of the broader problem of fascism (Knowles 1992). This approach left a legacy which limited the scope for the recognition of ethnic mobilisation as part of anti-racism, and frequently reduced anti-racism to an aspect of anti-fascism. Anti-colonialism, anti-fascism and anti-apartheid involved activists in broader, international struggles which provided a world-view which could be adapted to accommodate the problems raised by globalisation (Seidman 2000).

In the 1950s and 1960s anti-racists began to turn to preoccupations closer to home, in particular the problem of racism against immigrants who had come to work in the UK (as in much of Western Europe) in response to the demand for labour for post-war reconstruction. These concerns tended to be dealt with by anti-racists on a country-by-country basis, although there was some international co-operation. In the UK the point of reference tended to be the USA.[1]

The Campaign Against Racial Discrimination (CARD) provided a base for activists in the 1960s who attempted to promote the cause of social equality and to organise the political representation of immigrants in Britain. In so doing it fell prey to conflicts over the power relations between the black and white liberals and the more radical community-based organisations (such as the West Indian Standing Conference, the National Federation of

Pakistani Associations in Great Britain and the Indian Workers' Association). The CARD anti-racists were attracted to solutions which had developed in the very different conditions of the USA. CARD took its cue from the US civil rights movement to press for legislation against discrimination at the moment when this tactic was being superseded across the Atlantic by community action and Black Power. Consequently, the US experience can be seen to have distorted and undermined the British anti-racist movement, encouraging it to develop goals without fully relating them to specific British conditions (Heineman 1972: xi; Sooben 1990).

[...] During the mid-1970s when the extreme right National Front (NF) appeared to be making electoral headway, anti-racists found themselves negotiating two schools of thought, one (epitomised by the Anti-Nazi League) emphasising the importance of destroying the NF as an electoral force, and the other (perhaps best epitomised by the magazine collective CARF) emphasising the importance of a layered response to racism, which was in tune with experiences of the black community at the grass-roots while maintaining a critique of national policies (Lloyd 1998a; Sivanandan 1982).

From this point onwards, for anti-racists to be able to claim any sort of legitimacy they needed to show that they took their cues from the demands of ethnic minority groups and to work with them in some kind of alliance. In the UK the question of "who are anti-racists" centres on this relationship. However, this is not a simple interface. John Rex has pointed out that ethnic mobilisation is wider and more ongoing than much anti-racism because "at all times, and not only at moments of economic crisis, collective political actors emerge" (Rex and Drury 1994: 3; Rex 1996). Similarly the equation of anti-racism and the struggle for black liberation has been challenged by Paul Gilroy, who argues for a distinction between such struggle and responses to the everyday problems of black people (Gilroy 1987: 115). Ethnic minority groups mobilise for different reasons; their lives are not solely determined by racism and the need to counter it. Such groups do not just mobilise to oppose racism and their choice to ally with other groups is one option among others. Ethnic mobilisation cannot be reduced to anti-racism or vice versa, but they are closely intertwined.

The race relations "industry" in the 1980s, which was dominant in local authority politics, did tend to equate its anti-racist activities with the struggles of the black community in ways that led to bitter divisions and competition (Cain and Yuval-Davis 1990). Community representatives were co-opted onto committees to act as advocates in the process of consultation, with doubtful consequences. One of the central problems associated with these practices was an unproblematic construction of the central concept of the community. This policy tended to construct the black community as solely concerned with racism, which led to a too-rigid dichotomy between victims and oppressors as critiqued in the Burnage report on anti-racism in Manchester schools (MacDonald et al. 1989). The report emphasised the need for all sectors of the local community to take responsibility to oppose racism.

In the 1990s there has been increased awareness of the complexity and heterogeneity of ethnic mobilisation. Further, ideas of hybridity and plurality have undermined the idea of the unitary "black" subject (Goldberg 1990: xiii; Hall and du Gay 1996: 113). The concept of "black" as a universal category denoting the experience of oppression is challenged from a different position by Tariq Modood, who points to the way in which this discourse excludes certain groups, specifically Muslims (Modood 1996).

Feminist analyses of anti-racism have drawn attention to the gender and class differences which run through the black and ethnic minority communities (Anthias and Yuval-Davis 1992; Brah 1996). Women's role in anti-racism has all too often been ignored. Feminist analyses confronted the differences between black and white women over the role of the family in their oppression, the difficulties posed for women attempting to discuss questions of domestic violence, and the policing of young women's sexuality by the family. Clara Connolly (1990) describes the failure of a young women's project attempting to be anti-racist which was working with the structures and concepts of multiculturalism, racism awareness training and fostering cultural identity. She suggests that a feminist anti-racism would involve a recognition of the nature of racism while also acknowledging the separate interests of women, and it would involve black and white women organising together (Connolly 1990: 63). [...]

Given this fragmented field of action, the question of alliances between different groups with different motives for combating racism is raised. Caroline Knowles and Sharmila Mercer acknowledge that first-hand experience of racism confers a privileged position within anti-racist struggle while arguing that "anti-racist politics needs to be built around issues and ... the only qualification for membership needs to be a practical commitment to challenging racism" (Knowles and Mercer 1990: 137). They see "temporary links between groups of subjects with interests and positions" (84) as constantly reconstructing anti-racist politics according to specific circumstances. In this they anticipate what Italian feminists and French activists term "transversal politics" in which each participant in the dialogue brings with her the rooting in her own membership and identity but at the same time tries to shift in order to create an exchange with women who have different membership and identity (Yuval-Davis 1997a: 130). [...]

The British debate has been largely organised around the assumption that anti-racist activity is about opposition to colour-based racism (Brown 1984; Daniel 1968). There has been much less awareness about racism directed against different groups of people (such as the Jews or the Irish), even though their concerns have been covered in much anti-racist practice (Hickman and Walter 1997; Lloyd 1995). The scope of anti-racism has been largely determined by the central role of the CRE, which has responsibility for enforcing the law against racism and for conducting formal investigations into possible areas of racist practice. This has meant that anti-racist civil society focuses on areas which are essentially conflictual and problematic. At the same time anti-racism needs to build alliances and campaign around different *ad hoc* issues.

This self-limiting stance gives rise to two sets of problems: first that anti-racism risks remaining ineffective and tokenistic, unable to do more than make gestures in favour of lasting reforms, and second that it becomes embroiled in fragmentary politics without the benefits of alliance, which only serves to block its access to the political mainstream. Groups which are based mainly in the white left and which attempt to mobilise separately have been criticised in the past, as in 1993 when rival marches were organised by the white-led Anti-Nazi League and black-led Anti-Racist Alliance. Such rivalries have in the past posed serious problems for the establishment of national anti-racist coalitions in Britain, which have encountered problems due to London-centrism (which gives national status to groups without a broad-based implantation), divided or sectarian leadership, a tendency towards formalism and instrumentalism, and "resolution politics" (Huq 1995).

While still viewing anti-racism as essentially defensive, Cambridge and Feuchtwang seek to understand how to go beyond ideas of resistance which involve "emergent political forces which might combine to reduce and eliminate racist practices" (1990: ix). Feuchtwang argues that 'the politics of civil liberty and universal rights ... are the starting position in contesting racism within the discourse and politics of government, civil society and population" (1990: 21). For him, anti-racism begins "with the re-assertion of humanity, citizenship and social being.... The politics of demands for justice, against racialist exclusions and licence to scapegoat excluded populations, point in the direction of new concepts of sovereignty and of public policy" (1990: 21–4).

Developments in the late 1990s suggest that the anti-racist movement in Britain is beginning to reap some successes. Most notable was the campaign surrounding the murder of Stephen Lawrence, illustrating how anti-racist work, which has often operated at the margins, painstakingly collecting data about police racism and racist violence, and forming networks between anti-racist lawyers and campaigners, could bear fruit, given a window of opportunity with the Macpherson Report (Lloyd 1999). Similarly after many thwarted attempts to form a nationally anti-racist co-ordination, the National Assembly Against Racism has shown considerable stability.

I will now turn to a discussion of approaches to anti-racism in another European country, France, in order to draw attention to some of the common issues and to highlight some important differences.

FRANCE

An overview of approaches to anti-racism in France can help us to understand continuities because there are several long-standing organisations which have existed since before the Second World War (or, if one includes the Ligue des Droits de l'Homme, the turn of the century).[2] French anti-racists claim to trace their antecedents back to the Enlightenment and the Revolution of 1789, pointing to precursor anti-racist views among some of the philosophers and the abolition of slavery and emancipation of the Jews during the Revolution (Lloyd 1996). The battles for social justice during the Dreyfus affair and opposition to anti-Semitism and fascism in the 1930s and 1940s were early forms of anti-racist activity, while as in Britain, anti-colonialism and struggles for the rights of immigrant workers have also played a large part in building the bases of resistance (Bouamama 1994; Noiriel 1992).

In the early 1980s anti-racists debated issues about who comprised the main body of activists. One of the key questions related to their affirmation of the positive aspects of the "droit à la différence." Commentators warned that this idea needed to be carefully qualified because it was open to misinterpretation and it was used to advocate segregation and oppose immigration by "new right" groups (Guillaumin 1992; Taguieff 1979, 1980, 1991: 15).

[...] Alain Touraine's theory of "class struggle without classes" challenged the determinism of structural theories, and drew attention to the way in which political conflict could be neutralised if it became entrenched in institutions such as political parties (Touraine 1969). [...] Influenced by the growth of racism in the form of the Front National (FN), urban riots and perhaps his own participation in the Commission of Experts on the Nationality Code (Long 1988; Silverman 1988: 10–16), Touraine turned his attention to questions of immigration and integration. Responding to riots against police harassment in the housing estates of Vaulx en Velin and Les Minguettes in 1990, he argued that "ethnic categories are almost the only ones at present to produce collective action" (*Libération*, 15 October 1990). The social is increasingly viewed in cultural terms in fragmenting post-industrial societies, and people are defined by their ethnicity rather than their occupation or class.

Touraine's associates have taken this focus further: Michel Wieviorka focuses on popular racism, Jazouli on the mobilisation of suburban youth, and Dubet on the problems of life in the suburbs, particularly the "galère."[3]

Michel Wieviorka sees racism as a perversion of social action, a "social anti-movement" which is incapable of structuring society. Anti-racism, however, offers an alternative social vision. He maintains that anti-racist action is only really effective if it involves those directly affected by racism rather than more detached groups acting in the name of democracy, human rights, humanist or religious values (Wieviorka 1993: 418). This form of anti-racist mobilisation is based on the affirmation of identity grounded in racial categories produced by the very processes of racialisation which it is seeking to counter. Anti-racist action by groups who are not mobilising in terms of their own identity may play a useful political, legal or educational role but might also have to contend with racialised identities surfacing within the organisation (Wieviorka 1993: 419). Thus the familiar binary opposition between universalist anti-racism/relativist-differentialist anti-racism reappears in Wieviorka's characterisation of anti-racist actors (Wieviorka 1993: 426).

Wieviorka does not discuss how anti-racism operates in practice. Empirical research suggests that Wievorka's two types of anti-racist actor are rarely found separately from one another. While the problems he highlights may be present in organisations, they are often found in more complex forms than he suggests. Furthermore, this defensive model of anti-racism does not fully acknowledge the positive social project which he sees as central to anti-racism as a social movement.

Catherine Neveu recognises the complexity of anti-racist mobilising as placing different organisations on a continuum between the poles of universalism and particularism (Neveu 1994: 103). Empirical research reveals a much more complex picture over time, with sometimes the same organisation articulating discourses which at different moments veer more or less to one or the other position (Lloyd 1998b). Anti-racists operate in an ambivalent field, caught between the universal and the particular: at one level they appeal to universal values of human equality and the application of social justice; at the other, in opposing discrimination, in representing or practising solidarity towards certain groups of people, they are also working within a particularist agenda (Lloyd 1994).

During the 1980s there was a great deal of proactive mobilisation by young people from immigrant families who established defensive networks against the "double peine."[4] Adil Jazouli highlights the failure of established "left" organisations or existing "immigrant" associations to respond to the changing articulation of their demands in the late 1970s (Jazouli 1986). They developed their own collective identity with a strong grass-roots orientation, and they were anti-institutional and highly critical of the role of the organised left.

The March for Equality of 1983 fitted this social movement paradigm of anti-authority, anti-institutional-grass-roots activity, articulating broad, universalist demands and protesting against the social exclusion of young people from immigrant families in the call for equality. For Jazouli this identification of grassroots demands with universal aspirations epitomises the ethical nature of the mobilisation (Jazouli 1992: 53). While the March was the "founding historical act" of a movement of suburban youth, its very success enabled well-funded and more institutionalised anti-racist organisations such as SOS-Racisme and France-Plus to emerge. Their success marked the political defeat of the more radical grass-roots activists who were replaced by people with experience of "left" organisation who managed spectacular youth mobilisations around concerts against racism. Jazouli argues that the grass-roots mobilisation found it difficult to move from the local to the national level, and that in doing so it was co-opted, even aborted. He implies a rather stark dichotomy between the social corporatist organisations operating at a policy and associational level and the broader grass-roots social movement.

Etienne Balibar argues that in order to be broad-based an anti-racist strategy should promote the autonomous organisation of immigrants and mobilise communal traditions of resistance to exploitation. Pointing to the increasing fragmentation of working-class identity and politico-ideological systems of beliefs, he identifies the challenge to anti-racists to prevent sections of the working class and petite bourgeoisie from drifting towards a defensive, xenophobic ideology. Important anti-racist mobilisations by young people from North African backgrounds in the 1980s could, he suggests, form the backbone of a broad movement of associations, organised groups, parties, churches and trade unions, which could join the struggle against segregation and racism and for the recognition of the multiracial pluralist France (Balibar 1984).

As we have seen, some aspects of anti-racist campaigning involve elements of ethnic mobilisation, since ethnic minorities form an important constituency and their organisations may play a leading role in defining the issues, in demonstrating in public, negotiating and debating. In many ways anti-racists depend on them in claiming legitimately to represent a constituency. Groups from the "dominant culture" may also be involved in anti-racist mobilisation but their action is often dependent in important ways on the first, "ethnic" form of mobilisation. In a sense, and in some circumstances, anti-racist activity can be a transmission belt between ethnic minority groups and the wider political arena.

A central weakness of the writings of the Touraine school, which has been so influential in the French debate about anti-racism, is that they find it difficult to conceptualise an anti-racism which might operate simultaneously on several different levels, at grass-roots, in the associations of civil society and with allies in government. This approach obstructs any exploration of the connection between anti-racist social movements, anti-racist associations and policy initiatives, and closes off an important area of work on anti-racism in the labour movement (Castells 1975; Gorz 1970; Phizacklea and Miles 1980; Wrench 1995). At the same time, the Tourainian social movement analysis makes a number of valuable contributions to the study of anti-racism. It emphasises the change in consciousness which comes about with participation in such movements and draws attention to the issues of racialisation, and of who is mobilised and represented. The question of power relations in alliances and the danger of co-optation is a central problem for anti-racists.

Balibar sees anti-racism as intervening where the nation-state "reflects racism back" to society (Balibar 1992: 85). This is a "virtual" transaction which only becomes tangible when the mechanism is challenged, as when North African families were introduced into social housing, Habitations à Loyer Modéré (HLM), or when the Socialist Party discussed extending the right to vote to migrants with residence qualifications. If the "virtual" process of delegation seems to fail, citizens may take it upon themselves to force racialised groups back "into their place," or pressure the state to do so. Because racism is located in relations of domination and oppression and operates through mutually reinforcing relations between public opinion and the political class, it follows that anti-racism must intervene in both arenas and articulate a discourse of democratic rights.

Balibar argues that anti-racist politics is still in its infancy and that "anti-racist movements of opinion will become genuinely political only when they organise or co-ordinate their efforts at a European level" (Balibar 1991a: 18). Minorities experiencing discrimination will need to find a political voice and pose the question of a wider citizenship in Europe, thereby raising issues of democratic control and cultural equality (Balibar 1991a: 19).

There are many differences between anti-racism in Britain and France. Leadership has been less of a contentious issue in France, and anti-racist activity tends to be more centralised on Paris (although grass-roots campaigns are important). This centralisation has made it easier for major political parties to co-opt anti-racist organisations, as was the case with SOS-Racisme and the Socialist Party. During the 1980s reform to the law made it much easier to form associations and there was an enormous growth in what has been described as the "associational movement" which mobilised large numbers of young people against racism (Barthelemy 2000; Lloyd 2000; Wihtol de Wenden 1997).

Inherent to the anti-racist project is some concept of international action and relatedness. It is not surprising then that anti-racism has been deeply affected by the processes associated with globalisation. European unification has been of particular concern to campaigners since the late 1980s through campaigns connected to the harmonisation of immigration laws and to the growth of the extreme right in Europe.

EUROPEAN ANTI-RACIST ACTIVITY

The central aim of the Single European Act of 1986 (SEA) was free movement of capital and labour for nationals of states of the European Union. "Third country nationals" were not included in these measures, which therefore involved the establishment of tighter external frontier controls (Geddes 1995). Immigration controls (along with issues like national security, terrorism and crime) were discussed by intergovernmental structures and were not subject to democratic debate or control. The Schengen agreement of 1985 was initially signed by France, Germany and the Benelux countries, but has had a much wider impact on the rest of Europe.

Many of the measures introduced since the mid-1980s by national governments actually originated from these meetings. The Ford report of the European Parliament argued that by defining immigrants as a special kind of problem, associated with a threat to national security, European governments served to legitimise the racist discourses of the extreme right (Ford 1992). Following the Palma document (1990) on the crossing of external frontiers, a uniform visa and carriers liability legislation was introduced for all European countries.

In an associated development, the rights of asylum have been restricted: in Germany and France this involved changes to constitutional law, in other countries (such as the UK) restrictive legislation. This gave rise to changes in the rights of many third country residents, including their claims to social benefits to work, and an increase in the power of the police to control identities in public places.

At different levels and in different ways anti-racist movements have protested against these new restrictions and the undemocratic way in which they have been planned and introduced. Some protests have focused on immigration controls and particularly the plight of undocumented migrants and asylum-seekers, while others have concentrated on the need to stop the growth of racism which is seen as a by-product of this new Europe.

In the context of the new Europe, as in globalisation more generally, there has been an increase in interest in civil society; The European Commission (DGV) has been attempting to stimulate a European civil society, acknowledging the need for voluntary and other representative organisations to have a role in a wide range of social issues at European level (*Social Europe* 1997: 17) In March 1996 the European Forum on Social Policy brought together a range of organisations to develop "mutual understanding about the respective roles, responsibilities and capacities of the various actors in civil society in developing a strong civil dialogue, involving both social partners and NGOs" (ibid.).

The efforts to build anti-racist co-operation is an example of the construction of this international civil society. At one level it may make sense to understand the developing consciousness of the European dimension of the problem of racism and of the existence of a common anti-racist agenda in terms of a pan-European social movement of shared values and objectives. Anti-racists are faced with two broad and related problems: first, how to work together and second how to gain access to the relevant power structures in order to make their case heard.

Issues of identification and representation, key aspects of social movements, are crucial to anti-racism where matters of one's identity are at stake. Differences between analyses of racism and anti-racism can lead to more intractable problems, especially when they impinge strongly upon group identity which may be tied up with national differences as in France and Britain. As I suggested earlier, we may understand the different ways in which this is expressed in terms of a continuum between groups with a strongly universalist orientation through to those who are highly particularist.

Attempts by anti-racist groups to establish the Anti-racist Network for Equality in Europe in 1991 foundered over these kinds of difficulties. There was a debate, led by the British-based Anti Racist Alliance (ARA) and the Standing Conference on Racism in Europe (SCORE), over the priority to be given to black leadership in the organisation. This revealed very different analyses of the causes and extent of racism. It illustrated the uniqueness of the British analysis of anti-racism and of "race relations" in Europe at the time. In the context of meetings between French and British anti-racist activists it became clear that the British had difficulties in accepting that there could be a situation where (according to Catherine Neveu) "the dominant terminology is not a racialised one, … [and] groups most subjected to racism and discrimination are hardly (physically) distinguishable from the indigenous population" (1994: 99). While the British framed the debate in highly racialised terms, the French tended to think in what they saw as more "universal" categories of equality and rights. Furthermore, it was argued that the black/white race relations paradigm was inadequate for explaining a situation where there are multiple sites of racism, for instance against African migrant workers but also Yugoslavs, Chinese, Turks, and Muslims in general. This meant that there could be different criteria for the establishment of anti-racist alliances: the British focusing on identity based on phenotype and ethnic identity rather than experience and similar political economic and social position in forming anti-racist alliances, which tended to be the basis of other European groupings (Neveu 1994: 98).

Other difficulties were involved in the formulation of the Migrants Forum, a DGV-funded organisation to represent all migrants (King 1995). The term "migrant" was unacceptable to ethnic minority citizens, who nevertheless wanted to be represented at European level. Protracted negotiations drew attention to the British exception, where ethnic minority citizens' access to political rights does not end discrimination. For the majority of "migrants" in other European countries who enjoyed second-class citizenship at best, the British case was hard to understand. Yet for British anti-racists this problem was crucial. "Citizenship may open Europe's borders to black people and allow them free movement, but racism cannot tell one black from another, a citizen from an immigrant, an immigrant from a refugee and classes all third world people as immigrants and refugees and all immigrants and refugees as terrorists and drug dealers" (Sivanandan 1995).

To the extent that anti-racists recognise a similar agenda and share parallel concerns and approaches to their work, there may be no need to construct a formal set of anti-racist institutions at European level. After all, informal cooperation has already given rise to spontaneous and joint demonstrations as for instance in co-ordinating campaigns or opposing European meetings of the extreme right. The European Commission and Parliament does however find it useful to have organised interlocutors and has continued to attempt to create anti-racist structures.

During the European Year against Racism DGV moved to set up the European Union Network Against Racism. This arises from the Union's own need to have some sort of organised lobby to which the bureaucracy can relate (for instance in co-operating with the European Commission Against Racism and Intolerance in the run up to the European Conference

Against Racism, itself preparatory for the UN World Conference Against Racism in 2001). In debating how to respond to these developments, anti-racists were caught between the reluctance to compromise dearly held positions and the danger that the European bureaucracy would promote a structure with its own chosen groups and its own programme which would make it more difficult for anti-racist groups to determine their own agenda. [...]

Co-operation is more difficult for the more protest-oriented, reactive types of anti-racist group, which share many of the characteristics of social movements. They nearly all suffer from a lack of resources, and their supporters identify strongly, even emotionally, with the goals of the movement, which raises the question of representation, and a tendency to define themselves in terms of what they oppose rather than what they support. Let us examine these questions one by one.

Informal, voluntary, militant types of anti-racist groups or coalitions such as the British-based Assembly against Racism, the MRAX (Movement against Racism and Xenophobia) in Belgium, the MRAP (Movement against Racism and for Friendship between Peoples) in France and Nero e no solo in Italy have relatively few resources and rely heavily on members' contributions and small project grants for their functioning. Such organisations have few resources to fund travel to meetings, time and personnel, people with the necessary pluri-language skills. Organisations with meagre resources are at a disadvantage in competing for funding, co-operating with well-endowed partners and insisting upon their priorities.

The second major problem is access to institutions. The structures of the EU have been frequently criticised in terms of their opaqueness and emphasis on control measures rather than actions against racism. The important difference is between the intergovernmental structures (such as the Council of Ministers) and the European Commission and Parliament. Key individuals in both the latter institutions have sought to expand their roles in developing anti-racist initiatives.

Following the Vienna Conference in October 1993, the Council of Europe set up the European Commission Against Racism and Intolerance (ECRI) to formulate general policy recommendations for member states on issues of racism. ECRI's responsibilities encompass the collection and publication of data, the publicising of examples of good practice and the analysis of legal measures against racism.[5]

The European Parliament's Evregenis (1985) and Ford (1992) reports established that the rhetoric by which immigration controls are introduced and their content have helped to legitimise racism, and may partly account for the electoral success of the far right (Ford 1992). The European Parliament called for EU ratification of the European Convention on Human Rights and the Geneva Convention on Refugees, and criticised the control of movements of third country nationals by unaccountable intergovernmental groups. However, its call for the establishment of a European body against racism on the lines of the CRE and a European residents' charter was rejected by the Social Affairs commissioner Vasso Papandreou, who argued in 1992 that the Commission had no influence over the criminal law of its members.

Member governments of the EU have resisted the establishment of European policies against racism despite their endorsement of international statements condemning racism, such as the European Convention on Human Rights or the preamble to the Social Charter which acknowledges the need to combat all forms of discrimination "on the grounds of sex, colour, race, opinions and belief." National provisions against racism vary considerably across Europe (Costa-Lascoux 1990; Geddes 1995: 211; MacEwen 1995). Faced with mounting evidence of the growth of the extreme right, and pressure from the European Parliament and the Commission, the Council of Ministers set up a Consultative Commission on Racism and Xenophobia in 1994, charged with "making recommendations, geared as far as possible to national and local circumstances, on cooperation between governments and the various social bodies in favour of encouraging tolerance, understanding and harmony with foreigners" (Kahn 1995).

The Kahn Commission argued that the Treaty of Rome should be amended to cover racial discrimination. The European Parliament and Commission have taken up its proposals in taking initiatives against racism and xenophobia at European level. At the forefront, exerting pressure is the Starting Line Group which includes the CRE, the Churches Committee for Migrants in Europe, the Dutch National Bureau Against Racism and the Commissioner for Foreign Affairs of the Senate of Berlin, supported by over thirty national and European organisations. They argue for unambiguous legal competence in the Treaty of Rome and an EU directive for the elimination of racial discrimination. The group organises among other NGOs and targets the Commission and political parties in the European Parliament. This is an important development in that it illustrates how groups can pool resources, expertise and their access to decision-makers, through forming an "advocacy coalition" (Kingdon 1984; Sabatier 1988; Stedward 1997). [...]

CONCLUSION

This chapter has focused on a set of issues with both general and specific implications. In general terms, I have addressed some of the problems of establishing democratic structures within civil society at a supra-national level. European unification and globalisation may increase precariousness among migrants and ethnic minority populations. Providing they have the resources, groups can exploit the enhanced opportunities presented for rapid communications by means of the internet and e-mail. While globalisation has not closed off political action either within civil society or at the level of the nation-state, it does pose problems of scale and structures in alliance-building. Who should be driving the formation of alliances? How can small, under-resourced organisations ensure that they are not sidelined? The establishment of European policies and structures on migration and asylum have produced new problems and new interlocutors for anti-racists, whilst also opening up new opportunities for intervention. This chapter has examined some of the difficulties which under-resourced organisations may experience in responding to political opportunities at the transnational level. This raises a problem inherent in globalisation, which while creating uniformity also stimulates particularist agendas, for example identity politics, but also racism and extreme forms of nationalism. This is a difficult problem for anti-racists because they are not outside the dynamics they are trying to control.

The factors which prevent anti-racists from responding to the opportunities for co-operation in the new Europe are inseparable from the political dynamics of globalisation itself. Anti-racism is muitifaceted and various. It cannot be wholly separated from ethnic mobilisation because in some instances the two are closely intertwined, and depend on one another. If we separate out different levels of mobilisation (European, national, civil society, grass-roots), we can distinguish some of the factors which divide groups from one another. For instance, organisations vary in terms of their distance from policy-makers. Groups with close relationships to centres of power benefit from funding and may find some of their priorities taken up by decision-makers. This may, however, be at the expense of their credibility with the grass-roots sections of the anti-racist movement who may suspect that their concerns are being diluted. This question of co-option is important for anti-racists because of the centrality of their claims to legitimately represent their constituency.

A central feature of the problem is its imbalance. Decisions about immigration have been taken away from democratic fora and made behind closed doors. There is a widely perceived link between the harmonisation of immigration and asylum controls and the rise of racism and xenophobia. These problems are not outweighed by the scope of opportunities presented to anti-racists by the European Parliament and the European Commission. The opportunities also contain the danger that the anti-racist agenda could be co-opted by these powerful organisations and that groups could become dependent on European funding and lose touch with their grass-roots support, which is a crucial resource.

Even if anti-racist organisations accept the need to form pan-European structures, they still face a number of problems. Racism takes a multiplicity of forms, depending on historical, political, social, cultural and economic contexts: for similar reasons (not simply because it is a response to racism) anti-racism is also muitifaceted. Serious study of anti-racism does reveal common themes: anti-racists all work with changing perceptions of discrimination, attempt to represent people who experience racism and develop solidarity actions. Underpinning these themes is a wider social project about social justice, equality and social cohesion. In different ways at different moments and in different contexts, anti-racists have sought to build consent for their ideas by promoting an anti-racist common sense, through broad campaigning, legislation and education.

If instead of focusing on the issues which divide them, anti-racists look at what they have in common, it may become clearer that some joint projects at European level may be possible. There are often as many difficult divisions between groups within countries as between countries. We know surprisingly little about these features of anti-racism in Europe, and this is an important theme for future research. There is a need for detailed study of the main organisations and also of the way in which they co-operate with other groups in civil society like political parties, trade unions and religious organisations. How do they co-operate within specific political campaigns for the defence of public services and welfare for example?

A central issue is that of understanding alliances and how they work. My study of the way in which anti-racist groups have worked together within France has shown that in spite of cultural and generational differences, a "transversal" way of working was sometimes possible, based on recognition of common aims and respect for the positions of different participants. As a system of "alliances" transversal collectives are unstable over a long period of time, but they also offer a more open, tolerant and pluralist way for pressure groups and social movement type organisations to work together (Foucault 1977; Yuval-Davis 1997b). This is the sort of loose, perhaps *ad hoc* co-operation which may be most effective at European level and points to forms which global civil society may take in the future.

NOTES

1. There was regular contact with anti-racists elsewhere, however. For instance there were attempts to co-ordinate lobbying for legislation against racism between Fenner Brockway and the MRAP in France. See Lloyd 1998b.

2. The Ligue des Droits de l'Homme (LDH) was established in 1898. The Ligue contre l'Anti-Semitisme et Racisme (LICBA) was set up under a different name (Ligue contre les pogroms) in 1928, while the Mouvement Contre le Racisme et Pour l'Amitié entre les Peuples (MEAP) was formed in 1949 from Resistance organisations. All three are still active.

3. This is the state of aimless existence of the unemployed poor and marginalised in contemporary France: "the extreme point of domination, an experience of survival which is wholly dominated by the convergences of the forces of domination and exclusion." See Dubet 1987, p. 13.

4. The "double peine" or double penalty was used against mainly young men from migrant backgrounds. A criminal conviction (sometimes very minor) would be punished by imprisonment compounded by a deportation order.

5. ECRI's web address is http://www.ecri.coe.int

REFERENCES

Anthias, F. and Yuval-Davis, N. 1992. *Racialized Boundaries: Race, Nation, Gender, Colour and Class and the Anti-racist Struggle*, London: Sage.

Balibar, E. 1984. "La société rnétisée," *Le Monde*, Paris.

———. 1991a. "Es gibt keinen staat in Europa: racism and politics in Europe today," *New Left Review* (March/April): 5–19.

———. 1992. *Les frontières de la démocratie*, Paris: La Découverte.

Barthelemy, M. 2000. *Associations: Un Nouvel Age de la Participation?*, Paris: Presses de Sciences Po.

Bauman, Z. 1998. *Globalization: The Human Consequences*, New York: Columbia University Press.

Bouamama, S. 1994. *Dix ans de marche des Beurs: Chronique d'un mouvement avorté*, Paris: Desclée de Brouwer.

Brah, A. 1996. *Cartographies of Diaspora: Contesting Identities*, London/New York: Routledge.

Brown, C. 1984. *Black and White Britain: The Third PSI Survey*, London: Heinemann.

Cain, H. and Yuval-Davis, N. 1990 "The 'equal opportunities community' and the anti-racist smuggle," *Critical Social Policy* (Autumn): 5–26.

Cambridge, A. and Feuchtwang, S. 1990. *Anti-racist Strategies*, Aldershot: Avebury.

Castells, M. 1975. "Immigrant workers and class struggles in advanced capitalism: the western European experience," *Politics and Society* 5(1): 33–66.

Castles, S. and Kosack, G. 1973. *Immigrant Workers and Class Structure in Western Europe*, Oxford: Oxford University Press/IRR.

Cloonan, M. and Street, J. 1998. "Rock the vote: popular culture and polities," *Politics* 18(1): 33–8.

Connolly, C. 1990. "Splintered sisterhood: anti-racism in a young women's project," *Feminist Review* 36, (Autumn): 52–64.

Costa-Lascoux, J. 1990. *Anti-discrimination in Belgium, France and the Netherlands*, Strasbourg Committee of Experts on Community Relations, Council of Europe.

Coutant, P. 1997. "L'anti-racisme en crise," *M* (janvier-fevrier): 50–4.

Daniel, W. 1968. *Racial Discrimination in England*, London: PEP/Penguin.

Dubet, F. 1987. *La Galère*, Paris: Fayard.

Evregenis, D. 1985. "Committee of Inquiry into the Rise of Fascism and Racism in Europe, Report on findings of the inquiry," Strasbourg: European Parliament.

Falk, R. 1995. "The world order between inter-state law and the law of humanity: the role of civil society institutions," in D. Archibugi and D. Held (eds) *Cosmopolitan Democracy*, Cambridge: Polity.

Feuchtwang, S. 1990. "Racism: territoriality and ethnocentricity," in A. Cambridge and S. Feuchtwang (eds) *Anti-racist Strategies*. Aldershot: Avebury.

Finer, S. 1958. *Anonymous Empire*, London: Pall Mall Press.

Ford, G. 1992. *Europe: The Rise of Racism and Xenophobia*, London: Pluto.

Foucault, M. 1977. *Language, Counter-memory, Practice: Selected Essays and Interviews*, Oxford: Blackwell.

Geddes, A. 1995. "Immigrant and ethnic minorities and the EU's democratic deficit," *Journal of Common Market Studies* 33(2): 197–217.

Gilroy, P. 1987. *There Ain't No Black in the Union Jack*, London: Hutchinson.

Goldberg, D. 1990. *Anatomy of Racism*, Minneapolis: University of Minnesota Press.

Gorz, A. 1970. "Immigrant labour," *New Left Review* (May): 28–31.

Guillaumin, C. 1992. "Usages theoriques et usages banals du terme 'race,'" *Mots* 59–65.

Hall, S. and du Gay, P. 1996. *Questions of Cultural Identity*, London: Sage.

Heineman, B. 1972. *The Politics of the Powerless: A Study of the Campaign Against Racial Discrimination*. London: Institute of Race Relations, Oxford University Press.

Held, D. 1991. "Between state and civil society," in G. Andrews (ed.) *Citizenship*, London: Lawrence & Wishart.

Hickman, M. and Walter, B. 1997. *Discrimination and the Irish Community in Britain: A Report of Research Undertaken for the CRE*, London: Commission for Racial Equality.

Hirst, D. 1997. "Terror zealot is tamed by market force," *The Guardian* (26 September): 17.

Hirst, P. and Thompson, G. 1996. *Globalisation in Question*, Cambridge: Polity.

Howe, S. 1993. *Anticolonialism in British Politics: The Left and the End of the Empire 1918–1964*, Oxford: Oxford University Press.

Huq, R. 1995. "Fragile alliance," *Red Pepper* (February): 10–11.

Jazouli, A. 1986. *L'Action collective des jeunes maghrébins de France*, Paris: CIEMI/L'Harmattan.

———. 1992. *Les Années Banlieues*, Paris: Seuil.

Johnson, R. and Pattie, C. 1997. "Fluctuating party identification in Great Britain: patterns longitudinal study," *Politics* 17(2): 67–77.

Kahn, J. 1995. *Final Report of the Consultative Commission on Racism and Xenophobia*, Brussels: Permanent Representatives Committee/General Affairs Council 6906/1/95.

Keck, M. and Sikkink, K. 1999. "Transnational advocacy networks in international and regional politics," *International Social Science Journal* 51(1): 89–101.

King, J. 1995. "Ethnic minorities and multilateral European institutions," in A. Hargreaves and J. Leaman (eds) *Racism, Ethnicity and Politics in Contemporary Europe*, Aldershot: Edward Elgar.

Kingdon, J. 1984. *Agendas, Alternatives and Public Policy*, Boston: Little Brown.

Knowles, C. 1992. *Race, Discourse and Labourism*, London: Routledge.

Knowles, C. and Mercer, S. 1990. "Feminism and anti-racism: an exploration of the political possibilities," in A. Cambridge and S. Feuchtwang (eds) *Anti-racist Strategies*, London: Gower.

Kuper, L. 1975. *Science and Society*, London: UNESCO, Allen & Unwin.

Lloyd, C. 1994. "Universalism and difference: the crisis of anti-racism in Britain and France," in A. Rattansi and S. Westwood (eds) *On the Western Front: Racism, Ethnicity, Identities*, London: Polity.

———. 1995. *The Irish Community in Britain: Discrimination, Disadvantage and Racism: An Annotated Bibliography*, London: University of North London Press.

———. 1996. "Anti-racist ideas in France: myths of orgin," *The European Legacy: Towards New Paradigms* 1(1): 126–31.

———. 1998a. "Anti-racist mobilisations in France and Britain in the 1970s and 1980s," in D. Joly (ed.) *Scapegoats and Social Actors: The Exclusion and Integration of Minorities in Western and Eastern Europe*, London: Macmillan.

———. 1998b. *Discourses of Anti-racism in France*, Aldershot: Ashgate.

———. 1999. "Une enquête policière mise en accusation," *Différences* 207 (mai): 8.

———. 2000. "Cent ans de vie associative: table ronde avec Jean-Michel Belorgey, Martine Bartelemy et Catherine Wihtol de Wenden, *Différences* (décembre): 8–10.

Long, M. 1988. *Etre Français aujourd'hui et demain*, Paris: 10/18.

MacDonald, I., Bhavnani, R, Kahn, L. and John, G. 1989. *Murder in the Playground: The Report of the MacDonald Inquiry into Racism and Racial Violence in Manchester Schools*, Manchester: Longsight Press.

MacEwen, M. 1995. *Tackling Racism in Europe*, Oxford: Berg.

Macpherson, W. 1999. "Inquiry into the matters arising from the death of Stephen Lawrence on 22 April 1993," London: Stationery Office, http://www.officialdocments.co.uk/document/cm42/4262/4262.htm.

Modood, T. 1996. "'Race' in Britain and the politics of difference," in D. Archard (ed.) *Philosophy and Pluralism*, Cambridge: Cambridge University Press.

Neveu, C. 1994. "Is 'black' an exportable category to mainland Europe? Race and citizenship in a European context," in J. Rex and B. Drury (eds) *Ethnic Mobilisation in a Multi-cultural Europe*, Aldershot: Avebury.

Noiriel, G. 1992. *Le creuset Français: Histoire de l'immigration XIXe–XXe siècle*, Paris: Seuil.

Phizacklea, A. and Miles, R. 1980. *Labour and Racism*, London: Routledge and Kegan Paul.

Rex, J. 1996. *Ethnic Minorities in the Modern Nation State*, Aldershot: Avebury.

Rex, J. and Drury, B. 1994. *Ethnic Mobilisation in a Multi-cultural Europe*, Aldershot: Avebury.

Sabatier, P. 1988. "An advocacy coalition framework of policy change and the role of policy-oriented learning therein," *Policy Sciences* 21: 129–68.

Seidman, G. 2000. *Adjusting the Lens: What do Globalizations, Transnationalism, and the Anti-Apartheid Movement Mean for Social Movement Theory?*, Michigan: University of Michigan Press.

Silverman, M. 1988. "Questions of nationality and citizenship in the 1980s," *Modern and Contemporary France* 34 (July): 10–16.

Sivanandan, A. 1982. *A Different Hunger: Writings on Black Resistance*, London: Pluto.

——. 1995. "La trahison des clercs," *New Statesman* (14 July): 20–1.

Sooben, P. 1990. "The origins of the Race Relations Act," Research Paper in Ethnic relations, CRER, University of Warwick.

Stedward, G. 1997. "Agendas, arenas and anti-racism," unpublished PhD thesis, Department of Politics, University of Warwick.

Taguieff, P.-A. 1979 "La nouvelle droite à l'œil nu," *Droit et Liberté* 386 (décembre): 21–3.

——. 1980. "Présence de l'héritage nazi: des 'nouvelles droites' intellectuelles au 'revisionnisme,'" *Droit et Liberté* 387 (janvier): 11–17.

——. 1991. *Face au racisme*, Paris: La Découverte.

Touraine, A. 1969. *La société post-industrielle*, Paris: La Découverte.

Unesco. 1951. *Race and Science*, New York: Columbia University Press.

Wieviorka, M. (ed.). 1993. *Racisme et modernité*, Paris: La Decouverte.

Wihtol de Wenden, C. 1997. "Que sont devenues les associations civiques issues de l'immigration," *Hommes et Migrations* 1206 (mars–avril): 53–66.

Wilkinson, H. and Muglan, G. 1995. *Freedom's Children*, London: Demos.

Wrench, J. 1995. "Racism and occupational health and safety: migrant and minority women and 'poor work,'" Coventry: Centre for Comparative Labour Studies, University of Warwick.

Yuval-Davis, N. 1997a. *Gender and Nation*, London: Sage.

——. 1997b. "Women, citizenship and difference," *Feminist Review* 57: 4–27.

Chapter 46

Struggling against History:
Migrant Farmworkers Organizing in BC

Adriana Paz Ramirez and Jennifer Jihye Chun

Maintaining a focus on British Columbia, Ramirez and Chun (2016) reveal the labour conditions of farmworkers that have been described as "indentureship" or "modern-day slavery." South Asian Sikh immigrant men and women were employed in British Columbia in the 1970s and 80s, while today the ranks of farmworkers consist of migrant workers from Mexico who come under Temporary Foreign Worker Programs. Agricultural work is a sector generally not protected under labour laws given the "unfree" conditions of work, the "temporary residency" status of migrants, and their vulnerability to being fired, blacklisted, and deported if they resist. Despite that, migrant and immigrant agricultural workers have organized, the first case being the formation of the Canadian Farmworkers Union (CFU) in 1980 and its eventual demise through employer backlash. Secondly, the authors discuss the ongoing activism of Justicia for Migrant Workers (J4MW), the first author being a long-time organizer for them. Both organizations are examples of community unions, marked by an intense involvement of the larger immigrant community around the workers.

On July 26, 2006, the British Columbia (BC) chapter of the grassroots collective Justicia for Migrant Workers (J4MW) hosted a film screening of *El Contrato* about the plight of migrant farmworkers under Canada's Seasonal Agricultural Worker Program (SAWP).[1] J4MW activists sought to raise money for Mexican workers facing deportation and a potential lifetime ban from SAWP program after walking off their jobs. Although Canadian labour laws protect workers' right to strike, these workers faced immediate retaliation from employers and the Mexican Consulate for openly challenging their unjust living and working conditions. At the time there was little public understanding of the restrictive and dehumanizing conditions of guest worker programs in BC, which joined SAWP in 2004, nearly five decades after Ontario as part of the province's aggressive expansion of the Temporary Foreign Worker Program (TFWP) in a variety of low-paid occupations. Much to the surprise of the J4MW activists, the event was packed, including people from Abbotsford, Delta, Chilliwack, and other Fraser Valley farming towns located over seventy kilometres from Vancouver.

Former leaders of the Canadian Farmworkers Union (CFU), the first farmworker union, which was established in Canada in 1980, also attended. Few people knew about the CFU's history. According to local historian Sadhu Binning (1986, 14–15), the CFU was not just "another union"; it was a "moral" force that galvanized a broad base of unions, community organizations, religious leaders, women's groups, progressive lawyers, political party officials, artists, academics, and students to support BC farmworkers, who then consisted primarily of South Asian immigrants from Punjab, India. Charan Gill, who still serves as CFU secretary treasurer—an entirely symbolic position—and moved on to lead one of the largest immigrant-serving agencies in BC's Lower Mainland, commended the "young people" of J4MW, yet expressed deep pessimism. [...]

This chapter explores past and current organizing efforts in BC's farmworker movement. We examine the relationship between CFU's efforts to organize the predominantly South Asian migrant workforce under the farm labour contract system in the 1970s and 1980s and the current dilemmas of migrant farmworker organizing under temporary workers programs. On the surface, this relationship can be understood in terms of capitalist dynamics and the power of capital to perpetually thwart worker resistance. Faced with threats to capital accumulation by unions, farm owners reorganized production relations and enacted classic "divide and conquer" tactics between two groups of racialized workers: South Asian immigrants with full residence and citizenship rights, and Mexican migrants with highly restrictive temporary work permits under SAWP. While employer backlash certainly explains the extreme difficulties that workers face in mounting resistance and sustaining victories over time, it provides little insight into the ongoing resistance of workers, especially racially subordinated groups, to ongoing commodification and exploitation.

Drawing upon Foucault's (1980) notion of subjugated knowledges—that is, entire histories of struggle against dominant ways of understandings that have been erased, masked, and disqualified as insufficient—we propose another starting point. We ask how such largely unrecorded acts of resistance waged from subordinated groups, often hidden and submerged, become reactivated at different historical moments by different social actors. [...]

First, we discuss CFU's struggles during the late 1970s and early 1980s, examining the CFU's efforts to challenge the exploitative and discriminatory conditions of farm work for a predominantly South Asian immigrant workforce. This section draws primarily from the extraordinary digital historical archive of over 700 CFU publications, documents, and records housed at Simon Fraser University's special library collections.[2] Second, we analyze the daily lives and struggles of migrant workers under the SAWP program in BC, drawing upon in-depth qualitative interviews and participant observation conducted by Adriana Paz Ramirez (2013) and her work as a long-time J4MW organizer. We conclude by exploring the insights that analyzing worker resistance through the lens of subjugated histories has on current organizing efforts, and the political urgency and necessity of challenging both systemic racism and capitalist exploitation.

SOUTH ASIAN FARMWORKERS IN BC'S AGRICULTURAL INDUSTRY, 1970S AND 1980S

The history of labour migration in BC's agricultural industry is tied to the history of racial exclusion and subordination in a newly forming white settler society. After early Chinese migrants were subject to an exorbitant head tax restricting entry into Canada in the late 1800s, white settlers' demands for cheap labour resulted in new flows of migrants from India, primarily from Punjab. […] Growing fears of a "Hindu invasion" and intensifying anti-Asian violence by white workers, however, quickly halted migration. The passage of the 1908 Continuous Journey Act, which remained in effect until 1947, imposed a de facto ban on all Indian immigrants. […]

The second wave of South Asian labour migration to BC occurred during the 1970s after the removal of race and national origins quotas in federal immigration and citizenship policies. The family preferences category, which allowed people to sponsor family members to immigrate, created a flow of South Asian immigrants to BC's saw mills, canneries, garment factories, and farms, the few sectors that hired racialized workers. A gendered pattern of employment emerged in many South Asian households during this period. Men tended to work in forestry, which provided union jobs, while women and children tended to work in lower-paid domestic work and farm work, sectors which were excluded from most provincial labour protections including the Minimum Wages Act, the Hours of Work Act, the Annual and General Holidays Act, and the Payment of Wages Act. In the Fraser Valley, just east of Vancouver, approximately 80 to 90 percent of all farmworkers were from Punjab and an estimated 60 to 70 percent were women (Binning 1986: 9).[3]

The concentration of South Asian immigrants in the Fraser Valley was linked to an ethnic-dominated farm labour contract system that first appeared in 1969 and began to flourish in 1976 (Chouhan et al. 1983, 3). Fruit and vegetable growers, mostly family farms and some of which were owned by members of the Punjabi community, contracted out their labour needs to intermediary contractors that hired Sikh Punjabi workers through kinship networks, social ties, and foreign-language newspapers. Contractors paid farmworkers by the piece, often delayed compensation until the end of the season to ensure that workers would not quit midseason, and subtracted an additional 25 to 40 percent from workers' earnings.

The farm labour contract system was exploitative and dehumanizing on and off the fields. Many workers became physically ill after pesticide exposure. Few if any growers and contractors sought medical assistance for workers who fell ill. Substandard housing conditions resulted in high rates of sexual violence, injury, and sometimes death. Worker accommodation, often consisting of barns converted into living quarters, lacked running water, privacy, and security. Stories circulated about rampant sexual harassment and violence by contractors. Workers, who depended on labour contractors for transportation to as many as twenty different farms during the four to five month harvesting season, were also victims of traffic accidents due to the lack of auto safety on poorly maintained vehicles. Housing and transportation accidents were particularly lethal for workers and the many children who accompanied their mothers to the farms (CFU 1980).

Farmworkers had little recourse to improve their working and living conditions as new immigrants with limited English skills and few social networks outside their ethnic community. Not only were farmworkers excluded from basic legal protections against employer abuse and workplace health and safety accidents, but labour contractors also designated themselves as interpreters for all matters pertaining to wages, housing, and unemployment contributions, leaving workers with extremely limited access to independent information and alternative sources of support. When a crisis occurred, be it a sexual assault or a tragic accident, workers tended to rely on trusted family and community members rather than the law or mainstream institutions. This began to change in the late 1970s when South Asian community members, including Raj Chouhan, Charan Gill, and Harinder Mahill, began to challenge the exploitation and injustice of BC's agricultural industry.

THE CANADIAN FARMWORKERS UNION (CFU)

We are proud to be farmworkers
we sweat like all the rest of the toilers
as they do in the factories and mills
yet you say in the eyes of your law
we are not workers
      —Sadhu Binning, "Farmworkers are Workers Too" (poem)

On April 6, 1980, around two hundred workers attended the CFU's founding convention in New Westminster, approximately two years after Chouhan and others began going door-to-door to workers' homes and Sikh temples. One of the first acts of business was the passage of a resolution demanding that the BC government recognize farmworkers as legitimate workers entitled to basic labour protections such as minimum wage standards and protection against wage theft, employer fraud, and dangerous working and living conditions. In his convention speech, Chouhan (1980, 3), who was elected CFU President, avowed: "As long as the provincial government does not extend labour laws to farm and domestic workers, it is guilty of discriminatory action through inaction. It is maintaining areas of oppression into which people can be driven through societal discrimination."

For Chouhan and the CFU, the legislative discrimination of farmworkers under provincial labour laws was tied to the long history of legal racism enacted against people from India and other colonized regions. [...] Drawing parallels with the David and Goliath fight of the United Farm Workers (UFW) which represented highly exploited groups of Mexican and Chicano farmworkers in California, the CFU stated that it "regarded the struggle of farmworkers in California as its own."[4]

Cross-racial solidarity was a central principle of the CFU's political vision and organizing strategy. CFU leaders were keenly aware of the interconnections between labour exploitation and legal racism, and recognized the "divide and conquer" strategies that farm owners used to pit racially oppressed groups of workers against each other. In the first issue of their newsletter, the Farm Worker Organizing Committee (FWOC), the organizational predecessor of the CFU, publicly welcomed to Canada Vietnamese refugees who were displaced by the war, yet denounced owners' efforts "to reap profit from the misery of a people cast away from their own homeland" (FWOC 1979, 3) by recruiting them into exploitative and unregulated farm labour. FWOC rebuked owners' attempts to "stimulate hostility and suspicion between the two sections of the working class with racist ideas like: 'Immigrant workers take away jobs from Canadian workers'" (ibid., 11).

Through grassroots organizing and an antiracist platform, the CFU successfully unionized over one thousand farmworkers in under two years at some of BC's largest farms, and sparked a broader social movement. The union collected thousands of signatures petitioning the BC government to extend basic labour protections to farmworkers. It garnered the support of numerous unions and labour organizations, including financial contributions from the Canadian Labour Congress (CLC) and the BC Government Employees' Union (BCGEU). It established the BC Organization to Fight Racism (BCOFR), a multiracial coalition which brought together BC Indigenous communities with Chinese-, Filipino-, and Indo-Canadian communities to fight anti-Asian violence and white supremacy. It also mobilized community allies to attend public protests and solidarity events, volunteer as tutors for the union's "ESL Crusade" and legal clinics, and attend plays and documentary films about the plight of BC farmworkers, including *A Time to Rise*, produced by Anand Patwardhan and Jim Munro.

As the farmworkers' movement gained momentum, growers escalated their counterresponse, hiring external consultants and lawyers to challenge union certification campaigns, prolong strikes and collective bargaining negotiations, and dismantle the efficacy of union contracts. Growers also fought against legal gains that included farmworkers in provincial employment standards and health and safety protections, reversing the 1982 decision to extend the BC Workers Compensation Act to farmworkers and reinstating restrictions to farmworkers' ability to claim unemployment insurance in 1983. Their efforts to revise the provincial labour code in 1984 "created the biggest single legislative block to organizing new Canadians" (Boal 1987, 4–5). According to CFU's next President, Sarwan Boal, this measure gave employers "at least one week (between application and vote) to harass and intimidate the workers" which was particularly detrimental to "new Canadians" who feared the arbitrary power of white Canadian growers and male Punjabi labour contractors (ibid.).

The growers' intense counteroffensive took a tremendous toll on the CFU's ability to sustain and grow their organization. In reports issued during their sixth and seventh National Conventions, the CFU described many obstacles and setbacks: "The year 1985 was especially a killer, when we had lost almost all the certified units except one, and our overall membership had dropped to only twenty" (CFU 1987). Although the CFU's renewed commitment to grassroots organizing and their new emphasis on "community unionism," a strategy that "organizes farmworkers in their communities around community and political issues" (Boal 1987, 6), helped rebuild its membership in the late 1980s, the CFU faced an uphill battle to sustain its organizational activities in the context of limited legal victories, continued employer backlash, and a deepening economic recession (see also Binning 1986). Unable to pay full-time staff salaries, rent, and the publication of its *Farmworker* newsletter after 1991—the year the CFU lost funding support from the Canadian Labour Congress—the union gradually waned and CFU supporters redirected their attention towards advocacy, community service provision, and formal politics.

THE SEASONAL AGRICULTURAL WORKER PROGRAM IN BRITISH COLUMBIA

Despite its attempts to collectively organize farmworkers, the CFU was unable to withstand the antiunion backlash. Provincial labour authorities supported employer counteroffensives by allowing labour contractors and growers to engage in ongoing worker abuse with little consequence. The provincial and federal governments took additional steps in the early 2000s to depress working conditions by enacting regressive revisions to employment standards protections (Fairey et al. 2008) and restricting entry through the family reunification provision of Citizenship and Immigration Canada (CIC), the main avenue of entry for South Asian immigrant farmworkers. The most decisive changes, however, took place in 2002 and 2004 when BC's powerful agribusiness lobby convinced the provincial government to authorize temporary visas to alleviate purported "labour shortages" under SAWP and the Stream for Lower-Skilled Occupations. SAWP on the West Coast started as a "pilot program" with forty-seven Mexican workers. The following year two hundred workers were recruited to work in the Fraser Valley. SAWP now brings thousands of workers annually to the Fraser Valley and Okanagan Valley.

Migrant workers under the SAWP are regulated by a distinct set of labour and immigration rules that creates a two-tiered legal system for citizen and noncitizen workers (Basok 2004; Preibisch 2007). Temporary migrant workers do not enjoy the same political citizenship rights and social benefit programs afforded to Canadian citizens or permanent residents such as provincial employment standards legislation and unemployment insurance (UI). [...]

The restriction of workers' rights and mobility constitutes an apartheid-like system of labour control and domination built on "unfree labour" (Paz Ramirez 2013). Sharma

(2006, 125) writes "like past forms of apartheid, its global manifestation is not based on keeping differentiated people apart but instead on organizing two (or more) separate legal regimes and practices for differentiated collectivities within the same nationalized space." Conventionally, apartheid has been regarded as an intensification of race-based segregation policies; however, while the role of racial supremacy was a prominent element in the formation of apartheid, it cannot be reduced to racial domination alone. In the case of South African apartheid, Harold Wolpe (1972) argues that race operated as a political construct that enabled capital and the state to deny fundamental rights and freedoms to racially subordinated groups to guarantee the reproduction and maintenance of cheap labour power for capital accumulation. Although the SAWP does not explicitly contain race-based exclusions and restrictions, following a guiding policy in line with the de-racialization of the Canadian immigration system since 1960 (Shakir 2007), it enacts racialized forms of governing and disciplining of migrant labour through seemingly "raceless" mechanisms such as the denial of political and economic rights, the denial of citizenship, spatial segregation, restrictions on territorial movement and movement within the labour market, family separation, and prohibition of intimate sexual relations.

By subjecting temporary migrant workers to multiple forms of political, cultural, and spatial exclusion, state-sponsored migrant labour programs exercise racialized forms of labour discipline and control that seek to transform displaced groups of migrant workers into disposable populations of cheap labour. Just as growers and employers used ethnicity-based "divide and conquer" strategies in the 1980s with South Asian, white, and Vietnamese farmworkers, SAWP employers engage in similar "divide and conquer" tactics, hence preventing cross-racial alliances that can result in farmworkers organizing. The SAWP and the Agricultural Stream for Lower-Skilled Occupations can be seen as part of employer and provincial government backlash to the organizing efforts of the CFU two decades ago that threatened to undermine the profit-making of the agricultural industry. If the CFU challenged what they called "legislated racism," temporary workers programs now operate through more covert and subtle expressions of racism under a system of labour apartheid.

RESISTING LABOUR APARTHEID THROUGH EVERYDAY ACTS OF RESISTANCE

While most studies suggest that migrant farmworkers in Canada consent to their own oppression and engage in "performances of subordination" as a survival strategy to succeed in the program (Basok 1999; McLaughlin 2010) and while that assertion is partially true from a liberal understanding of freedom under the rule of law, workers *do* resist against powers that oppress them. However, they do so in ways that are not commonly recognized. Resistance has typically been conceptualized in two ways: either as disengaging or not participating, or as participation in organized forms of collective opposition such as strikes and union campaigns. SAWP workers' resistance does not fall neatly into either category. It could be said that migrant farmworkers "choose" to return to Canada year after year through SAWP, mostly with the same employer, and thus consent to an oppressive system of labour control. Nonetheless, this does not imply nor should it mean that workers do not resist and push back against labour apartheid conditions. What it does mean is that we need to engage deeper into their everyday lives and reframe our notions and ways of measuring resistance.

Migrant farmworkers' acts of labour, resistance, courage, survival mechanisms, and expressions of political subjectivity speak directly to the kinds of oppressions and restrictions they face. Unlike acts of resistance that are open and loud manifestations of opposition to power, migrant farmworkers engage in "hidden transcripts"—veiled, disguised, and often unspoken forms of resistance that cannot be openly expressed or articulated because of the extreme imbalances in power between the dominant and oppressed (Scott 1990). Workers exercise subtle forms of resistance such as "stealing" products of the farm produce to give out to friends or to exchange, filing workers' compensation claims or parental benefits, or even visiting a doctor against their employer's wishes. Workers also challenge employers' racially divisive strategies to pit workers of different racial and ethnic backgrounds against each other. A Mexican worker on a Chilliwack farm explained, "The supervisor is always finding ways to make us to compete with the South Asian [workers]. Since we found out and understood his strategy, we decided to slow down the pace and we agreed that none will 'run' anymore because that only benefits no one else than the *patron* [boss] while we break our backs."[5]

For racialized workers, class solidarity is often mediated and articulated through race, gender, and place of origin, opening the potential for cross-racial and multilingual alliances (see Lowe 1996). This was the case with the first Mexican workers' wildcat strike in 2005. South Asian farm coworkers shared chapatis with striking Mexican workers as a gesture of support, sympathy, and solidarity during the days of the conflict. Even though these solidarities are not expressed or articulated in terms of class identity and can be sporadic, they point to the recognition of intersections of class- and race-based economic exploitation. Based on practices and networks of solidarity mediated through aspects of their identities such as race, class, and nationality, workers develop ethics of community care for each other that become evident in cases of aggression or overt inhumane treatment from the employer.

How migrant farmworkers frame and make sense of their acts of resistance differs from the typical "labour disputes" that are mediated through labour unions or political institutions. For racialized migrant farmworkers, these acts of resistance help workers regain control over the conditions of their lives and their relationships with one another, rather than wage an overarching "working-class struggle." Migrant workers rarely identify themselves as part of the Canadian working class because their struggles are specific to their conditions of "temporariness" and the intersections of race, gender, immigration, and employment status that prevent them from enjoying essential freedoms. Unlike unionized (white) workers' struggles, which often revolve around better wages and benefits under union collective agreements, for migrant farmworkers these are not the primary concerns. From their specific localities their salaries are actually good and are precisely the reason why they want to come to Canada. This was articulated by a group of workers who were invited to join Vancouver's "Living Wage Campaign" led by the Hospital Employees Union (HEU).[6] According to Juan, who attended the meeting:

It would be good to have higher wages but to begin with it would be good if employers would start by following the contract as it says that we [SAWP workers] enjoy same rights as Canadians; that we can refuse unsafe work, have vacations to visit family, and so on.... That is not true. Our contract is a dead letter, a dead paper. Nobody follows it. We are imposed under each employer's rules. (Paz Ramirez 2013, 76).

Because workers' immediate concerns generally have more to do with health and safety issues, living conditions, limited and insufficient access to health care, unpredictable work hours, and long periods of family separation, issues such as wage increases are often less salient.

For transnational migrant farmworkers, what ultimately matters is to preserve a sense of dignity and to regain their humanity as they struggle to support themselves and their families in an unjust global economic system. For example, as in the blueberry workers' wildcat strike, twenty workers ended up being deported to Mexico by their employer with the assent of the Mexican consulate. Workers' demands to improve housing and working conditions were not met; however, from the workers' point of view, this was considered neither a failure nor a victory. Daniel, one of the strike's main organizers, said, "We are going back to Mexico with broken illusions and with no money but we are leaving with our heads up and that is what we will tell to our families. We could not keep living [in the farm] as animals with no dignity" (Paz Ramirez 2013, 78).

In the same way that resistance must be reconceptualized from the specific location of temporary migrant workers, the notion and meaning of what constitutes victory and failure must also be reconceptualized. As Kelley (1994, 10) puts it, "Politics is not separated from lived experience or the imaginary world of what is possible; to the contrary, politics is about these things." For migrant farmworkers, resistance sometimes looks like open challenges to authority, but it more often looks like finding cracks and openings in a highly exploitative and dehumanizing system of unfree labour where resistance can be waged in both direct and indirect ways.

RETHINKING THE POLITICS OF ORGANIZING AND SOLIDARITY

Migrant farmworkers' political subjectivities and resistance strategies provide insight into the complex workings of power. We must be willing to delve beneath the surface to appreciate seemingly innocuous or futile acts of resistance. Challenging and transforming the current racial labour apartheid regime means first developing a language and vocabulary that ties the economic exploitation and sociopolitical marginalization of migrant farmworkers to the logics and practices of racial oppression. This necessitates demystifying the neoliberal discourse used by states, employers, and even academic literature that analyzes the program as purely a consequence of the rise of neoliberal hegemony. By creating a counternarrative that names the program as a form of de facto racial labour apartheid, we can begin to develop cultures of resistance that connect and speak to the particular concerns, needs, and demands of racialized migrant farmworkers. Second, we must be willing to reflect upon questions such as: Why after more than forty years in Canada do migrant farmworkers remain at the margins of established political movements and organized labour organizations? How do migrant farmworkers struggle outside of established organizations and social movements? What kind of impact do migrant workers' hidden struggles and daily concerns have on movements that claim (or attempt) to speak for the dispossessed? Workers' acts and strategies of daily resistance contain the seeds for a new political vision of social change. The challenge is how much *we* engage in understanding and making sense of *their* struggles and meet them where they are at, instead of trying to engage workers in our visions and perspectives of their struggles. Third, we need a multipronged strategy that tackles the multiple levels and fronts where workers face oppression, control, and domination. This was clear for the CFU that adopted a "community unionism" approach to organize farmworkers not only in their workplaces but in their communities where they faced racial and socioeconomic exclusions.

In contrast to the United States, the plight of farmworkers in Canada is less known, perhaps due to the absence of a civil rights or immigrant rights movement that mobilizes communities around racial justice issues. Yet radical left, Marxist working-class, environmental, and feminist struggles have had an impact on mobilizing marginalized sectors, and have created languages and cultures of resistance. Racialized communities have been (and still are) subjects of the creation of political and cultural organizations and have mobilized around their cultural, class, race, and gender identities. Examples include the Chinese community, who created the Coalition of Chinese Head Tax Payers to connect historic exclusions and ongoing injustices against Chinese immigrants. South Asian immigrant farmworkers in BC carried forward a momentous struggle over decades resulting in the founding of the CFU. Similar are the organizing efforts of the Filipino community that fight for a "genuine and just integration" stemming from their experiences as temporary workers under the Live-in Caregiver Program (LCP). Yet these narratives of resistance largely remain part of the "hidden history" or, in the language of Foucault, stay as part of subjugated narratives and knowledge.

Grassroots groups such as J4MW that seek to build their analyses and organizing efforts with migrant farmworkers draw from the sources of collective sites of memory rooted in working-class immigrant communities. Lisa Lowe (1996, 21) calls these experiences "sites of collective memory" that act as "collective critical consciousness" and remain sceptical of liberal democracies' values and notions of fairness, equality, and citizenship. J4MW links the histories of indentured servitude inflicted upon im/migrant communities, and emphasizes the need to stand in solidarity with migrant farmworkers at the intersection of class and antiracist struggles. J4MW organizers take the time to approach workers in the places where they live, work, dance, shop, eat, pray, and have fun. Some organizers also visited workers' families and communities in their home countries and carried out our small projects with migrant communities. By engaging with multiple dimensions of workers' lives and working across borders, J4MW members have learned multiple lessons together, especially that organizing and resisting, even when they "lose" a fight, can still make a difference.

Organizations and movements that start with the daily struggles, concerns, desires, and dreams of disenfranchised communities are the seeds of a new political vision. The building blocks of their vision are workers' everyday hidden transcripts of resistance, the subjugated narratives, the sites of collective memory, and the accumulated experiences found in the multifaceted lives of marginalized im/migrant workers. What to do next with these building blocks remain the question and the challenge that lies ahead.

NOTES

1. J4MW, which has chapters in BC and Ontario, organizes and advocates for the rights of migrant farmworkers who come to Canada under temporary workers programs. *El Contrato* (2003) was produced and directed by Minsook Lee.

2. The Canadian Farmworkers Union Project can be found at: lib.sfu.ca/special-collections/canadian-farmworkers-union.

3. The BC Federation of Agriculture reported that approximately thirteen thousand farmworkers were employed in BC's agricultural sector during the 1970s and 1980s; the vast majority consisted of East Indian, Chinese, and Japanese workers (Jhappan 1981, 20).

4. See information on CFU support of UFW boycott of Chiquita Bananas (FWOC 1979, 3).

5. Migrant farmworkers' group interview conducted by Adriana Paz Ramirez, April 2011.

6. At the time of writing, the living wage for Metro Vancouver is $19.14 an hour. SAWP workers' wage is the minimum wage, $9.25 an hour, before government deductions, housing, health insurance, and passport and visa fees.

REFERENCES

Basok, Tanya. 2004. "Post-National Citizenship, Social Exclusion and Migrants Rights: Mexican Seasonal Workers in Canada." *Citizenship Studies* 8, no. 1.

———. 1999. "Free to Be Unfree: Mexican Guest Workers in Canada." *Labour Capital and Society* 32, no. 2.

Binning, Sadhu. 1986. "The Canadian Farmworkers Union: A Case Study in Social Movements." MA Thesis, Simon Fraser University. <content.lib.sfu.ca/cdm/compoundobject/collection/cfu_2/id/2354>.

Boal, Saran. 1987. "Discussion Paper on New Strategies for Organizing Canadians." <content.lib.sfu.ca/cdm/ref/collection/cfu_2/id/300>.

Canadian Farmworkers Union (CFU). 1987. CFY 7th National Convention Documents, National Executive Report. <lib.sfu.ca/object/cfu>.

Chouhan, Raj. 1980. [Canadian Farmworkers Union Public Meeting] Speech, Surrey, BC, May 31. <content.lib.sfu.ca/cdm/ref/collection/cfu_2/id/4671>.

Chouhan, Raj, Sarwan Boal, Judy Cavanagh and David Lane. 1983. "1983 CFU Report—Draft 2." Canadian Farmworkers Union Internal Report. <content.lib.sfu.ca/cdm/ref/collection/cfu_2/id/2781>.

Fairey, David et al. 2008. *Cultivating Farmworker Rights: Ending the Exploitation of Immigrant and Migrant Farmworkers in BC*. Vancouver: Canadian Centre for Policy Alternatives BC, Justicia for Migrant Workers, Progressive Intercultural Community Services, and the BC Federation of Labour.

Farm Worker Organizing Committee. 1979. "Press Release, August 3, 1979." *FarmWorker* 1, no. 1. <content.lib.sfu.ca/cdm/ref/collection/cfu_2/id/3692>.

Foucault, Michel. 1980. *Power/Knowledge: Selected Interviews and Other Writings, 1972–1977.* Colin Gordon (ed.). New York: Pantheon Books.

Jhappan, Carol Rhada. 1981. "Resistance to Exploitation: East Indians and the Rise of the Canadian Farmworkers Union." MA thesis, University of British Columbia. <content.lib.sfu.ca/cdm/compoundobject/collection/cfu_2/id/4542/rec/6>.

Kelley, Robin D.G. 1994. *Race Rebels: Culture, Politics and the Black Working Class.* New York: Free Press.

Lowe, Lisa. 1996. *Immigrant Acts.* Durham and London: Duke University Press.

McLaughlin, Janet. 2010. "Classifying the 'Ideal Migrant Worker': Mexican and Jamaican Transnational Farm Workers in Canada." *Focaal—Journal of Global and Historical Anthropology* 57 (Summer).

Paz Ramirez, Adriana. 2013. "Embodying and Resisting Labour Apartheid: Racism and Mexican Farm Workers under Canada's Seasonal Agricultural Workers' Program." MA Thesis, University of British Columbia. <hdl.handle.net/2429/45530>.

Preibisch, Kerry. 2007. "Local Produce, Foreign Labor: Labor Mobility Programs and Global Trade Competitiveness in Canada." *Rural Sociology* 72, no. 3.

Scott, James C. 1990. *Domination and the Arts of Resistance: Hidden Transcripts.* New Haven: Yale University Press.

Shakir, Uzma. 2007. "Demystifying Transnationalism: Canadian Immigration Policy and the Promise of Nation Building." In Luin Goldring and Sailaja Krishnamurti (eds.), *Organizing the Transnational: Labour. Politics, and Social Change.* Vancouver: UBC Press.

Sharma, Nandita. 2006. "White Nationalism, Illegality and Imperialism: Border Control as Ideology." In Krista Hunt and Kim Rygiel (eds.), *(En)Gendering the War on Terror: War Stories and Camouflaged Politics.* Burlington: Ashgate Publishing Ltd.

Wolpe, Harold. 1972. "Capitalism and Cheap Labour-Power in South Africa: From Segregation to Apartheid." *Economy and Society* 1, no. 4.

Chapter 47

Idle No More

Pamela Palmater and Sylvia McAdam (Saysewahum)

Few social movements have been as dynamic and effective as the Idle No More movement that emerged in 2012 out of grassroots Indigenous communities (initiated by Indigenous women) in Saskatchewan and that spread across Canada and other parts of the world. These two short articles by Palmater and McAdam are not exhaustive but are meant to entice readers to read more about the Idle No More movement.

Pamela Palmater, who wrote this article in 2012, contextualizes the movement within the longer history of Indigenous resistance to the breaking and dishonouring of treaties by the Canadian state in its continuing colonial and capitalist quest for land and resources and the parallel desire to assimilate Indigenous communities out of existence. She characterizes Idle No More as "a coordinated, strategic movement, not led by any elected politician, national chief, or paid executive director."

In this excerpt from her book *Nationhood Interrupted: Revitalizing nêhiyaw Legal Systems*, published in 2015, Sylvia McAdam (Saysewahum) relates her personal "journey" of being one of the founders of the movement. Then Prime Minister Harper's Omnibus Bill C-45 was one of the catalysts. Through the use of social media, she contacted a group of women from which this movement grew, and utilized a variety of actions, including letters to MPs, teach-ins, rallies, drumming, dancing (involving hundreds of Canadians in public sites across the country), marches, and blockades.

WHY ARE WE IDLE NO MORE? BY PAMELA PALMATER

The Idle No More movement, which has swept the country over the holidays, took most Canadians, including Prime Minister Stephen Harper and his Conservative government, by surprise. That is not to say that Canadians have never seen a native protest before, as most of us recall Oka, Burnt Church, and Ipperwash. But most Canadians are not used to the kind of sustained, coordinated, national effort that we have seen in the last few weeks—at least not since 1969. 1969 was the last time the federal government put forward an assimilation plan for First Nations. It was defeated then by fierce native opposition, and it looks like Harper's aggressive legislative assimilation plan will be met with even fiercer resistance.

In order to understand what this movement is about, it is necessary to understand how our history is connected to the present-day situation of First Nations. While a great many injustices were inflicted upon the indigenous peoples in the name of colonization, indigenous peoples were never "conquered." The creation of Canada was only possible through the negotiation of treaties between the Crown and indigenous nations. While the wording of the treaties varies from the peace and friendship treaties in the east to the numbered treaties in the west, most are based on the core treaty promise that we would all live together peacefully and share the wealth of this land. The problem is that only one treaty partner has seen any prosperity.

The failure of Canada to share the lands and resources as promised in the treaties has placed First Nations at the bottom of all socio-economic indicators—health, lifespan, education levels, and employment opportunities. While indigenous lands and resources are used to subsidize the wealth and prosperity of Canada as a state and the high-quality programs and services enjoyed by Canadians, First Nations have been subjected to purposeful, chronic underfunding of all their basic human services like water, sanitation, housing, and education. This has led to the many First Nations being subjected to multiple, overlapping crises like the housing crisis in Attawapiskat, the water crisis in Kashechewan, and the suicide crisis in Pikangikum.

Part of the problem is that federal "Indian" policy still has, as its main objective, to get rid of the "Indian problem." Instead of working toward the stated mandate of Indian Affairs "to improve the social well-being and economic prosperity of First Nations," Harper is trying, through an aggressive legislative agenda, to do what the White Paper failed to do—get rid of the Indian problem once and for all. The Conservatives don't even deny it—in fact Harper's speech last January at the Crown-First Nation Gathering focused on the unlocking of First Nations lands and the integration of First Nations into Canadian society for the "maximized benefit" of all Canadians. This suite of approximately 14 pieces of legislation was drafted, introduced, and debated without First Nation consent.

Idle No More is a coordinated, strategic movement, not led by any elected politician, national chief, or paid executive director. It is a movement originally led by indigenous women and has been joined by grassroots First Nations leaders, Canadians, and now the world. It originally started as a way to oppose Bill C-45, the omnibus legislation impacting water rights and land rights under the Indian Act; it grew to include all the legislation and the corresponding funding cuts to First Nations political organizations meant to silence our advocacy voice.

Our activities include a slow escalation from letters to MPs and ministers, to teach-ins, marches, and flash mobs, to rallies, protests, and blockades. The concept was to give Canada every opportunity to come to the table in a meaningful way and address these long-outstanding issues, and escalation would only occur if Canada continued to ignore our voices. Sadly, Prime Minister Harper has decided to ignore the call for dialogue just as he has ignored the hunger-striking Attawapiskat Chief Theresa Spence.

Although Idle No More began before Chief Spence's hunger strike, and will continue after, her strike is symbolic of what is happening to First Nations in Canada. For every day that Spence does not eat, she is slowly dying, and that is exactly what is happening to First Nations, who have lifespans up to 20 years shorter than average Canadians.

Idle No More has a similar demand in that there is a need for Canada to negotiate the sharing of our lands and resources, but the government must display good faith first by withdrawing the legislation and restoring the funding to our communities. Something must be done to address the immediate crisis faced by the grassroots in this movement.

I am optimistic about the power of our peoples and know that in the end, we will be successful in getting this treaty relationship back on track. However, I am less confident about the Conservative government's willingness to sit down and work this out peacefully any time soon. Thus, I fully expect that this movement will continue to expand and increase in intensity. Canada has not yet seen everything this movement has to offer. It will continue to grow as we educate Canadians about the facts of our lived reality and the many ways in which we can all live here peacefully and share the wealth.

After all, First Nations, with our constitutionally protected aboriginal and treaty rights, are Canadians' last best hope to protect the lands, waters, plants, and animals from complete destruction—which doesn't just benefit our children, but the children of all Canadians.

ARMED WITH NOTHING MORE THAN A SONG AND A DRUM, BY SYLVIA MCADAM (SAYSEWAHUM)

I woke up during the night and heard the familiar constant rumble of logging trucks rolling down the Stoney Lake road right by my little shelter. I suppose it shouldn't surprise me that they're hauling out the trees from my people's territory as fast as they can like thieves in the night.

Like anything, a journey begins somewhere perhaps even before a person realizes their path. Idle No More resistance began long before in different names, different locations through the generations since the arrival of Europeans. My own personal journey began when I was writing a chapter in my new book about land. I felt disconnected from my collection of fond childhood memories out on the territory of my people. I decided to return after a lengthy absence, so leaving the city behind I headed to my parents' traditional lands and waters.

Returning to the land didn't just mean a physical return; it had to be done through the eyes and words of my people's history and ceremony. Returning meant visiting the graves of my people who were nearly wiped out from disease, starvation, and residential school. I sat by the graves hearing once again that horrible history and much more. It also meant a spiritual and emotional return to lands in the process of being devastated by logging activities and other developments.

I felt such grief for the devastation and development I was witnessing; I began to feel a profound and protective love for the lands in which my people were buried and have hunted since time immemorial. Throughout the spring and summer, I explored a vast area often camping in various places. I would find old cabins which would trigger sadness and interest for the abandoned hunting equipment and glimpses of a past life immersed in indigenous knowledge as I took pictures of old sweat lodges and wood stoves. Sometimes I would fall asleep and dream at those cabins and lands.

Soon I had many questions that led me to the offices of Saskatchewan Environment which I won't detail here; needless to say the logging of my people's trees will not stop. As it turns out, that was a minor issue compared to what was to come.

Someone tagged me on Facebook about Omnibus Budget Bill C-45 in the fall of 2012 and I was not very interested … at first. Then I went back and took a second look and began reading. Needless to say, I was angry and stunned. Fortunately, the other ladies and I connected; we realized we had the same concerns, so we made a decision not to stay silent. We had to reach people. Sheelah came up with the idea of sharing this information in a form of a teach-in. So on November 10 in Saskatoon we had our first teach-in and invited as many people as possible to come and hear what Bill C-45 was about, as well as the other bills.

Shortly after that, I made arrangements to talk to elders; they gave us their support and prayers to try and reach as many people as possible. They also said we must use our own laws; one of our most sacred and peaceful laws is "nahtamawasewin." This law is invoked in times of crisis and great threat. "Nahtamawasewin" means to defend for the children, all human children; it's also a duty to defend for the non-human children from the trees, plants, animals, and others. The Elders said, you ladies must invoke this law and let it guide your actions. We must always be prayerful and peaceful.

With this information guiding and directing Idle No More we reached out to people on social media, and fortunately our call for help was answered by grassroots people. We had hoped to reach people but Idle No More seemed to resonate to all people from many different lands.

Through the ensuing months Idle No More became a global grassroots movement. Even with all of our resounding "no consent" protests, rallies, and teach-ins, the Canadian state passed almost all the bills aimed at privatizing Treaty lands, extinguishing Treaty terms and promises as well as Indigenous sovereignty.

However, it has awakened Nations of people to their surroundings; questions and information about the environment, treaties, and Indigenous sovereignty are posted and tweeted—constantly, something that has long been silent.

Canadian laws are constantly changing; a gun law was recently repealed after millions of dollars was spent. These bills can be repealed; Indigenous Nations have stated they will not recognize Bill C-45 or the other bills.

In the meantime, the extraction of Indigenous resources goes unfettered under the guise of "consultation and consent." For the Indigenous people, the ceremonies and lodges continue to pray for the healing of the lands and waters.

Amazingly, more and more settler people are recognizing and understanding that as a people we cannot continue to devastate the very things needed to sustain humanity—our lands and waters—for the generations to come.

Idle No More has taken me to different lands where I have met other Indigenous peoples. I had an opportunity to speak at the United Nations in Geneva, Switzerland. I declared in my language "We are Nehiyawak, we are still here and we need your support to stop the genocide of Indigenous people." While there, I heard other Indigenous people weep recalling the horror and death they are enduring because of their lands and resources. I made a commitment to myself I would defend the lands and waters to the best of my ability. I do not want to return to the United Nations weeping for my lands and waters.

I am forever changed by Idle No More. This journey has not ended; it's still unfolding as I write this. My journey takes me back to my people's lands and waters; it is in the lands and waters that Indigenous people's history is written. Our history is still unfolding; it's led by our songs and drums.

Chapter 48

We Will Win: Black Lives Matter – Toronto

Sandra Hudson and Yusra Khogali

In this chapter, the co-authors, who are activists from Black Lives Matter – Toronto, reflect on their origin and their emergence in fighting anti-Black racism in Toronto, whose reverberations have been felt across the province and country. They discuss their achievements, membership, principles and visions, activities and achievements, connections with a larger movement against anti-Black racism in North America, and their alliances with Indigenous movements. They argue that the institution of slavery and its presence today in the form of anti-Black racism, particularly in the policing and criminal justice systems, continues to be an integral feature of settler colonialism.

It is our duty to fight for our freedom. It is our duty to win. We must love each other and support each other. We have nothing to lose but our chains.
    —Assata Shakur[1]

INTRODUCTION

As recently as 2014, popular discourse regarding anti-Black racism in the settler entity mislabelled Canada did not exist. Popular white culture had accepted the singular narrative of Canada's race tolerance that had been propagandized since the 1960s.[2] Through the passing of the Charter of Rights and Freedoms in 1982, Canada cemented its inaccurate self-assessment as a tolerant multicultural haven in popular discourse. Canada's nation-building project constructed itself in contrast to its intolerant neighbour to the south; it sees itself as the anti-America. Black community activists struggling for justice knew and know better than to trust this false history. In addition to the history of enslavement, segregation, displacement, exploitation,[3] and violent anti-Black racism that is inextricably part of the climate of Canada's colonial genesis,[4] Toronto's Black communities in the late 1970s and early 1980s were struggling against a centuries-old tradition of violent interactions with the police, and, in particular, the police killings of Buddy Evans and Albert Johnson. By 1988, after the killing of Lester Donaldson, members of Toronto's Black community had created the Black Action Defense Committee to fight against executions of Black people carried out by police.[5]

Today, popular discourse has shifted through Black struggle and resistance. Lawmakers and those in power consistently reference anti-Black racism in their commitments to justice.[6] Mass media references anti-Blackness when referring to issues Black community activists have raised.[7] Justice-minded organizations across the city are educating themselves on the impacts of anti-Black racism across their ranks. This is largely due in part to the efforts by Black Lives Matter – Toronto to mobilize power in Toronto's Black communities, and to make it impossible to ignore or deny anti-Black racism's destructive existence and its impact on the Black people of Canada. In this chapter, we will give a brief history of Black Lives Matter – Toronto, and document important lessons learned while struggling against anti-Black racism locally and beyond. It is our hope that you can glean new knowledges from our experiences, and integrate them in your anti-racist praxis.[8]

ORIGINS: OUR HERSTORY

Black Lives Matter is an ideological and political intervention in a world where Black lives are systematically and intentionally targeted for demise. It is an affirmation of Black folks' contributions to this society, our humanity, and our resilience in the face of deadly oppression.
    —Alicia Garza, Black Lives Matter[9]

Black Lives Matter is an international organization for Black liberation that is a continuation of a long tradition of Black resistance against white supremacy and anti-Black racism. At its core, Black Lives Matter is a contemporary manifestation of the ever-blazing abolitionist movement.[10] The organization developed in the wake[11] of the brutal slaying of 17-year-old Trayvon Martin by murderer George Zimmerman in 2012. George Zimmerman would never face punishment for the heinous crime he committed against Trayvon Martin; he was acquitted by a legal system that routinely protects those who brutalize Black people.[12] When the verdict was announced in the summer of 2013, Alicia Garza penned a "Love Letter to Black People" on Facebook that ended with the phrase, "Black people. I love you. I love us. Our lives matter, Black Lives Matter."[13] Together with Opal Tometi and Patrisse Khan-Cullors, she co-founded the Black Lives Matter movement amidst a renewed wave of agitation for Black liberation.

As the movement organized demonstrations against incidents of anti-Blackness, the events that attracted the most attention by mass media were those that directly challenged the use of force and violence—and thus the very structure—of the state. Black Lives Matter was becoming known as the organization challenging police violence against Black people. In 2014, demonstrations were taking place across the world to protest the killing of Michael Brown by Ferguson, Missouri, police officer Darren Wilson.[14] Black communities across the world were experiencing widespread devastation at what many have concluded was an extra-judicial summary execution of this 18-year-old Black man. It was this moment, along with the police killing of Jermaine Carby by police officer Ryan Reid in Brampton, Ontario,[15] that would inspire a Black Lives Matter movement in Toronto.

Jermaine Carby was killed by police officer Ryan Reid on September 24, 2014. Unlike in the case of Michael Brown's killing, however, the public would not find out the identity of the police officer until 2016, due to weak laws enforcing transparency in law enforcement in Ontario. Ruled a homicide by a subsequent coroner's inquest, Jermaine Carby was killed just over a month after Michael Brown.[16] Canadian news media widely covered the Michael Brown case that occurred in the United States. But even though the details surrounding Jermaine Carby's killing were suspect, it was not as widely covered as Michael Brown's case. This is typical of the way that the media is complicit in Canada's false vision of itself as a tolerant, multicultural, racism-free haven compared to the United States. Jermaine Carby's killing should have been newsworthy simply because it happened, and even more so because some of the details in the case suggested that police officers may have planted a knife near Jermaine Carby after slaying him. Concerns were raised about why Carby, who had been the passenger in a car that was stopped by police, was carded.[17] Even still, the Canadian media refused to dedicate time to discussing Jermaine Carby's slaying.

We do not raise this comparison to suggest that Michael Brown's case should not have been covered by Canadian mass media, or to suggest that mass media should only focus on local concerns. What we are pointing to is the ease with which Canadian news media will look in the other direction when the subject matter would force the Canadian public to look within itself and uncover something reprehensible within, the knowledge of which would force any decent person to action. Mass media and the broader public would rather avoid such stories that wrench at the very heart of those who would claim a Canadian cultural identity.

In November of 2014, a grand jury was set to decide whether or not to indict police officer Darren Wilson for killing Michael Brown. Black Lives Matter activists were calling for widespread response regardless of the decision. In Toronto, folks in Black community had been affected by Michael Brown's case, including the authors of this piece. As Sandra stated:

> While searching for a solidarity action occurring in Toronto, my brother taught me one of the most important lessons I have learned in my social justice praxis. My young brother, Michael Hudson, asked me if anyone was doing anything about these issues locally. Had I found a solidarity action we could join? My brother was distraught. He insisted that something had to be done, by someone. It was then, in recognition of his distress, that I

realized there was no reason for me to wait and hope for someone else to do what I already knew needed to be done. One of the most heinous things about anti-Blackness is that it makes us feel isolated and powerless. But I had known after years of organizing and through my knowledge of the history of Black organizing in the city through organizations such as the Black Action Defense Committee that true power comes from an organized community. I contacted dozens of Black organizers that I knew; mostly women, mostly queer; and we got to work organizing a vigil.

On November 24, 2014, a St. Louis County grand jury rendered its decision; they would not indict Darren Wilson. Ferguson was burning, and there was widespread public condemnation. In Toronto, we were distraught, and we got to work. Meeting at Toronto's Black Coalition for AIDS Prevention office, we organized the vigil in the heart of Toronto that occurred on November 25 across from the United States consulate building.

We decided that we did not want to contribute to Canada's national myth-making exercise. We knew about Jermaine Carby's case, and we were furious that the injustice done to him was being ignored, so we involved his family. We decided we would hold a vigil not only to demonstrate in solidarity with the protestors in Ferguson, but also to hold a mirror up to the Canadian public and make non-Black Canada aware that here, too, existed a vile and reprehensible form of anti-Black racism that was constantly interrupting Black life through law enforcement. Each of our materials said "From Ferguson to Toronto, Black Lives Matter/Stop Police Brutality Against Black Lives Everywhere/From Mike Brown to Jermaine Carby." We made literature to educate attendees about the issue of anti-Blackness locally. We organized a vigil for what we thought would be in the realm of 50–100 people in under 24 hours.

We organized with principles. We were against the violent colonial absenting of Blackness and Black degradation under Canadian colonization. We ensured that the elements of our vigil were borne out of a principled refusal to accept both the violence of colonization and how such violence impacts Black and Indigenous people across the lands now referred to as North and South America. We were critical of border politics and the myths it creates of reified lines where racism ends. We made our vigil about Black unity across white supremacist colonial borders. We wanted attendees to know that this was a vigil that demanded justice, dignity, and liberation for all Black lives. We foregrounded Black trans organizers, queer organizers, and Black women. We wanted to show that our struggle could hold everyone and be accessible. We provided free food, handwarmers, public transit tokens, gloves, child care, and mental health supports. We wanted to show that there was beauty in coming together to hold one another in grief and mourning while building our community power. We foregrounded spiritual leaders and artists. And we wanted to centre Black people. We asked any allies attending ahead of time to stand to the periphery and make space for Black folks to come together and mourn.

We expected 50 attendees, but over 3,000 people attended this first vigil. More vigils were held in Edmonton, Vancouver, Montreal, Ottawa, and other major cities. Though we had not set out to become an organization, we knew that it would be irresponsible for us to disappear; Black communities had come forward in droves and made it clear that there was a need for a public mobilizing force for Black people in the city. Shortly thereafter Patrisse Khan-Cullors contacted us from Black Lives Matter's national organization, and she made it official; we were to formally join the Black Lives Matter network. Our vision? To be a platform upon which Black communities across Toronto can actively dismantle all forms of anti-Black racism, liberate Blackness, support Black healing, affirm Black existence, and create freedom to love and self-determine. Our mission? To forge critical connections and to work in solidarity with Black communities, Black-centric networks, solidarity movements, and allies in order to dismantle all forms of state-sanctioned oppression, violence, and brutality committed against African, Caribbean, and Black cis, queer, trans, and disabled populations in Toronto.[18]

COMMUNITY POWER

We are the ones we have been waiting for.
—June Jordan[19]

In the three years of our existence, we have created a powerful social movement mobilizing our communities against anti-Blackness in government, education, health care, and social services. We engage in "open source" organizing, ensuring that we uphold transparency and accessibility in our activism. Our work is grounded in ethics and radical care. When we organize around an issue, we bring the impacted Black communities together and craft a response informed through our communities. For example, if we are aware of a situation where someone in the Black community has been killed by the state, we first contact the family members of that person to get their consent prior to elevating the issue in the media. We do this to ensure that our work will not unduly contribute to the trauma of the Black people left behind in the wake of police violence. We make sure, first and foremost, to offer support where we can give it, and to provide resources for support where we can. The affected families and community members are always a part of our organizing, strategizing, and mobilizing, at every stage. In this way, our work is thoughtful and reflective.

As activists, we must be studied and knowledgeable of the terrain in which we are resisting. But more than that, as Black people, we are often challenged to name and explain our social conditions in order for our claims of anti-Blackness to be considered legitimate by those in power. For this reason, our work provides critical analysis and alternative forms of public education for our different communities. We explore and share with our communities multiple histories of oppression, racism, and resistance in Canada within larger imperial colonial forces. We unpack the nuance of Black bodies and souls surviving within oppressive white supremacist systems. We demand decolonization and reparations. These demands inform our unapologetic, expressive Black resistance, knowledge, and teachings.

We are composed of a steering committee with varied lived experiences in Blackness. We are queer, trans, gender non-conforming, Muslim, women, femme, disabled, parents, educators, students, artists, academics, working class, descendants of enslaved people, Indigenous, migrants, refugees, diasporic, and continental. By the nature of who comprises our team we engage in a praxis of intersectionality[20] in our resistance work. We refuse the relentless attempts to absent the pluralities of Blackness outside of Black communities by exploring the ways different colonial histories and geographies inform our sociocultural complexities, experiences of violence, and experiences of trauma through anti-Black manifestations.

We are keenly invested in creating the conditions and infrastructure that hold our entire complexity as Black people in every space that we make to build community power. This model of organizing operates with the principle of, "all of us, or none of us"—no one gets left behind. This principle directly challenges hetero-patriarchy, ableism, classism, and the idea of a singular Black experience. Our work is an intervention; it disrupts the myth that Black cisgendered men are the sole victims of state violence by elevating the oft-absented experiences of Black trans women in particular, who have been of the state's most systematically brutalized victims. When we say Black lives matter, we mean all Black lives.

Our movement is intergenerational and linked to our predecessors. Our elders guide our strategy through past experiences and are direct participants in our work as healers, advocates, and active listeners. We also carve out space to build with and protect young Black people in our movement. We provide child care that doubles as a space for political education and political education spaces for youth; we manifest actions developed and designed by children and youth, and we provide opportunities to nurture self-affirming, queer-positive growth and leadership for our youth every time we gather. It is our duty to honour African traditions in communal love, respect, dignity, and care in how we engage with one another for our collective breathing. Everyone—young, middle aged, or old—has a place in our movement.

We have different ways in which we communicate our knowledge and messages of resistance. At times we present formally, in ways that normative white culture would expect. But we make a point of intentionally refusing to code-switch, and perform the Black grammars of Black youth culture through our chants and speeches.[21] We combine language from our mother tongues with street lingo birthed from our hoods in the east and west ends of Toronto when we publicly speak with our communities. For Yusra, growing up both immigrant and diasporic as a young East African Muslim woman in Regent Park, this syncretism is how we survive state violence waged on our bodies. This is an act of subversion, and a refusal to be the white supremacist system's "perfect" Black figure in order to be worthy of attention from legitimate sources of power. Unapologetic, creative Black expression is part of the soul of our movement. From dabbing, to voguing, to twerking and milly rockin', we shut it down on every block.

In this section, we tried to give you a sense of who we are. On a final note, we want to give you our thoughts on our position as academics who struggle both within and outside of the academy. We deliberately use our positions in higher education as a method to document Black thought, to produce knowledge that reflects our communities, and to take the time to theorize our current conditions. We intend to give such knowledge to our communities in our resistance projects. The knowledge that we build and the power that we gain from it come directly from our community; it is both ethical and necessary that we return it. Building community power from the grassroots makes different ways of knowing accessible and informs a deep and humane understanding of Black life. We are directed by the everyday lived experiences of our varied and intersecting communities. The importance of Black theory when naming the colonial forces that produce the weather we are in is crucial.[22] It is a liberatory practice that articulates our evolving Black consciousness and lays the groundwork for the development of further strategies for action. We insist that the theory that we engage in cannot remain in abstraction, in inaccessible jargon, or inaccessible for community praxis.[23] Such a Eurocentric form of knowledge production becomes a tool that serves the settler colonial corporate state, not those of us who are under its heel. This element of praxis is a necessary form of resistance. We acknowledge that the revolution will not manifest from within the ivory tower. But we are committed to mobilizing our intellectual work to politicize our community and give the liberatory power of transgressive knowledge back to our communities.[24]

THE METHOD: MOBILIZING POWER

Our resistance tactics in all areas must work against the compelling tide of pressures that seek to individualize us and to reward us individually for good work.
—Akua Benjamin, Black Action Defense Committee[25]

Our organizing method seeks to build power directly from the communities to whom we belong; we are unconcerned with representative models that consolidate power in a few people who eventually, inevitably disappoint the community. We want our communities to represent themselves. This principled orientation allows us to reject the tactics of our political opponents. For example, the City of Toronto has argued in the media that they have attempted to meet with Black Lives Matter to resolve our issues with anti-Blackness, but we have been unreasonable and refused, so cannot do anything. Our community has flatly refused this argument because of a mobilizing strategy that refuses to meet with the city without our community. We will not accept a meeting behind closed doors. We do not claim to be a representative group. No one elected us; we cannot pretend to be a legitimate representative body. What we seek to do is to create spaces where our communities can advocate for themselves.

That being said, we are disciplined. We are very aware that organizing for Black liberation has a history of attracting swift state repression across the Western world. Those in power would rather eliminate Black people building power rather than shift the system to guarantee our dignity. They do this through public attempts to delegitimize us and embarrass us, launching legal battles against us, threatening our employment, incarcerating us, poisoning us, or murdering us. Some of us on the steering committee have been subjected to very targeted campaigns to malign our character. As a result, we have to be very disciplined and careful in our strategy. We are constantly rotating our media representatives so as to avoid creating a singular target, and to ensure that there are a variety of identities that reach a mass audience. We are constantly checking in with our elders, asking for advice, leaning on them for support, and soliciting feedback. Perhaps most importantly, we are always reflecting on the manner in which we completed any given initiative, assessing if we failed our own expectations and how, and how we could have used different strategies to better support our communities.

We also try to be disciplined in the ways in which we take care of one another. This is a skill that must be practised and cultivated in a society such as ours that so strongly privileges individuality. The work that we do is very difficult and hard on the psyche. In our discussions about how we could support one another through our work, we decided to develop a new model of community-focused care. In an idea that can be attributed to fellow co-founder Janaya Khan, we implemented a spiral model of organizing. Inspired by the way that penguins self-organize to shield themselves from the elements, Janaya suggested a model of care in which we constantly shift rotate who is being cared for at the centre of the spiral, shielded from the difficulty of the community tasks, and who are at the tendrils of the spiral, exposed to the work and protecting our family in the centre. This idea of a community model of care has the potential to seriously shift the amount of burnout activists often reference as their reason for giving up on their difficult, revolutionary work.

SHUT IT DOWN: MAKING OUR STRUGGLES PUBLIC

I've never been interested in being invisible and erased.
—Laverne Cox, actress[26]

When we take our struggles public it is a deliberate act of rebellion. Reclaiming public space and shutting down the very streets where we experience brutality is not only an interruption to the capitalist business-as-usual order of white supremacy, it is also a refusal to allow dominant society to look away as we reveal what it really is. Our insistence on public acts of engagement that resist our current conditions and perform our Black joy and care for one another is a significant rupture of the ways in which we are framed by dominant society. Below, we submit brief retellings of some of our public struggles to this point.

Action for Eric Garner

Midday on Saturday, December 13, 2014, Yonge-Dundas Square, one of the busiest intersections in downtown Toronto, was silent. You could hear a pin drop. Thousands of protesters occupied this major economic epicentre performing a die-in, one of several demonstrations happening across the world in protest of the police killing of Eric Garner. The chokehold by New York City police officer Daniel Pantaleo, who killed this Black father for selling untaxed cigarettes, left us with his last words immortalized in our chants—"I Can't Breathe"—reminiscent of the words of anti-colonial activist Frantz Fanon: "When we revolt it's not for a particular culture. We revolt simply because, for many reasons, we can no longer breathe."[27] We created a list of demands that were sent to Toronto City Council detailing measures that could be taken to address anti-Black violence by the city. We called on our city to condemn the actions of the New York Police Department, and we demanded that the city commit to taking action to ensure that Black people are not subject to disproportionate policing, surveillance, and punitive action by Toronto Police Services. We encouraged those who could not participate in our action in person to share their own stories of what it means to be Black in Toronto archived in social media through the hashtag #AliveWhileBlackTO.

Black History Month Interruption

During Black History Month in 2016, we decided to visit Mayor John Tory at City Hall. We heard that he would be "celebrating" Black History Month through a hypocritical ceremony in Council Chambers. He had ignored requests for a public meeting with Black communities for the better part of a year regarding our demands. We interrupted his public relations exercise and demanded that he address Black communities and the unacceptable Black deaths that occurred under his reign while mass media cameras were rolling. This event occurred during City Council's budgeting exercise. We used the media presence to publicize our message: while there was a $27 million increase to police services and a proposal on the table to militarize Toronto front line police officers with $2,000 assault rifles,[28] social services, education, and anti-poverty strategies were severely underfunded. Our public actions increased interest in what would have been an otherwise routine news story.

Black Liberation Collective – Canada

In the fall of 2015, the Black Liberation Collective – Canada came into formation, inspired by actions by Black students occurring across the United States, sparked by the resistance to anti-Blackness at the University of Missouri.[29] But the foundation for the Black Liberation Collective in Canada started the year before, in 2014. Inspired both by events organized to provide space for Black students to articulate the experience of being Black at the University of Toronto, and a podcast elevating first-hand narratives of Black students created by the authors of this piece,[30] a Black student movement in Canada was rebirthed. The Black Liberation Collective consists of Black students dedicated to transforming postsecondary institutions through the same principles as Black Lives Matter. We became affiliated with the broader Black Liberation Collective through a solidarity action with Black students at the University of Missouri. The resistance to the anti-Blackness at Mizzou[31] resulted in the resignation of the University of Missouri's president and chancellor.

In Canada, students from University of British Columbia, Guelph University, Carlton University, University of Ottawa, Ryerson University, and the University of Toronto used the heightened awareness of anti-Blackness in post-secondary education to design campus-specific actions to resist anti-Black racism through direct action. This movement became a branch of Black Lives Matter – Toronto due to overlapping membership and reliance on Black Lives Matter for support. Since its inception, the Black Liberation Collective – Canada's founding chapter at the University of Toronto has demanded institutional changes aimed at significantly interrupting the manner in which anti-Blackness operates in the ivory tower.[32] Demands include increased representation of Black students and faculty, culturally relevant mental health services, targeted scholarships for Black students, free tuition, and divestments from corporations who invest in the prison industrial complex[33] as well as mining companies that brutalize African people.[34] The University of Toronto was one of the first Canadian universities to commit to collecting disaggregated race-based data on students, faculty, and staff as a result of the work of this Black student organizing.

Allen Road Shutdown

In July 2014, Andrew Loku, a South Sudanese immigrant, recent graduate at George Brown College, and father of five was killed within seconds of police arriving at his apartment complex. The apartment complex in Little Jamaica on Eglinton West was leased by a mental health organization that Andrew Loku was affiliated with. Our team connected with the community that had come to serve as his family to offer our support. His blood relations were still in South Sudan; he had hoped to help them migrate to Canada in the future. We held a vigil in the parkette close to his home, and we called for the immediate release of the names of the police officers that killed Andrew and video footage in the apartment complex that we suspected captured the moment he was killed. We consulted the community and held a day of protest in the same park where we held the vigil. There was chanting, painting, music, poetry, and speeches.

We also knew we had to escalate. Inspired by Indigenous protestors and the Tamil protests in Toronto in 2009, we took to the streets and shut down Allen Road, a major artery highway in the centre of Toronto, right in front of a police station. For three hours, we blockaded the road and demanded accountability for Andrew's death. As mass media arrived on the scene, we were told that Mayor John Tory was live in studio at 24-hour news channel CP24. Tory was forced to answer to Jermaine Carby's cousin, La Tanya Grant, live on television when we convinced a reporter to call the studio from the blockade. After a year of attempting to avoid us, we forced the mayor to answer to us in a public forum while the city could watch.

#BLMTOTentCity

A year later in March, we drastically shifted the discourse on anti-Black racism in mass Canadian culture through our #BLMTOTentCity action. We were coming to terms with the announcement that week that AfroFest, the largest free African music festival in North America,[35] would be reduced from two days to one day due to noise complaints from the wealthy residents of the Beaches community where the festival takes place, when we were hit with two devastating news stories: Alex Wettlaufer, a 21-year-old Black man, was killed by Toronto police; and the officer who murdered Andrew Loku would not be charged following an investigation of the circumstances surrounding his slaying. We responded with a community recreation of AfroFest that culminated in a 15-day occupation in front of the Toronto Police Services Headquarters (TPS HQ).

We were calling for an overhaul of the Special Investigations Unit, the Ontario police watchdog that allow officers who kill in Ontario to escape accountability, and the elimination of carding. We did not initially intend to occupy TPS HQ. We intended to occupy the outside of Toronto City Hall. When we set up there, we were met with intense police reaction. They brought horses and riot gear to confront the 50 of us who had decided to engage in the overnight action. When we raised concerns about safety with our community, we were emboldened by their reaction. Despite the freezing cold temperatures, our community insisted that we must continue.

We decided that we would confront the police directly by moving our protest to the TPS HQ. We pitched tents that bore the names of our community members that had been killed by police, and the names of Black spaces in Toronto that had been absented through various manifestations of anti-Blackness.

On the second day of our occupation we were brutalized by the police. They waited until they thought all the media had left, and attacked the hundreds of people who had gathered at the camp on Monday, March 21, 2016. Fortunately, one cameraman was amongst the crowd, and the attack was widely publicized. The way in which the community took care of one another immediately following the attack inspired the creation of an alternative world we called #BLMTOTentCity. Here, we imagined what a community that truly valued Black people could be.

We became a family organized by Black and Indigenous solidarity, feeding, clothing, and sheltering all who came to the space. Tent city was a hub of political education, self care, Black art, body work, dance, healing, child care, spirituality, cultural production, and entertainment. We were a community who truly took care of one another. We ended our demonstration after a march to Queen's Park, and left with a hanging banner across the entrance of the police headquarters stating "You are on notice, We are not finished." The event prompted a number of policy initiatives by the Ontario government, which we will discuss in greater detail in the next section.

Pride

Today's worldwide Pride demonstrations can be traced back to an uprising led by Black and non-Black trans women of colour resisting police brutality and violence in New York City. Today, Pride Toronto has become a corporatized event where the police have significant visibility as they and other organizations engage in "pinkwashing," or associating themselves with the queer and trans community in order to erase their violence toward other communities. In the 2016 parade, there were 13 different police contingents in the Toronto Pride Parade. Blaring their sirens and carrying their guns and dressed in the uniforms they wear when they brutalize our communities, the police represented the largest contingent in the parade. There were more police than unions, political organizations, student groups, or any other discernable group.

There had long been controversy over police participation in the parade, and for good reason. Toronto's history of the police violence against trans and queer communities runs deep. From the 1980s bathhouse raids, to the Pussy Palace raids in the early 2000s, to the targeting of trans sex workers during the G20 summit of 2010,[36] queer and trans community members had raised concerns about police participating in Pride in the past.

This is the context in which Pride announced to the world in May 2016 that Black Lives Matter – Toronto would be Pride Toronto's "Honoured Group." To add insult to injury, we were aware of the way Pride Toronto was systematically marginalizing Black spaces at Pride through funding cuts to Blockorama, a longstanding public party at Pride organized by Blackness Yes!, and the spatial marginalization of the showcase stage organized by Black Queer Youth. In effect, Pride Toronto was "honouring" us while deeply disrespecting Black queer and trans communities. We consulted our community about the status we were conferred and decided to use the title we had been given to agitate for change in the way Pride Toronto was engaging with Black communities, Indigenous communities, other communities of colour, and the deaf community. When we raised our concerns, Pride attempted to pacify us, but would not make any commitments.

Again turning to our Black community, we collectively decided to use our honoured group status as a way to publicly draw attention to the hypocrisy inherent in "honouring" Black Lives Matter – Toronto in a transparent exercise to build social capital, while continuing to marginalize Blackness within Pride. In the middle of the parade, and with the support of our community, we sat at the intersection of Yonge and College and refused to move until we were seriously addressed by Pride Toronto. Our list of demands were all agreed to and led to a significant shift in the leadership of Pride. The Executive Director of Pride Toronto resigned in the weeks following the action, and Pride Toronto's annual meeting of members overwhelmingly confirmed its commitment to our demands in January of 2016, including a demand to refuse to allow the police to march as a contingent in the parade.

When we shut down Pride, the world was watching. This action has inspired similar organizing across the country and across the United States. Because of our work, other organizations are beginning to contend with important questions. How could they implicitly endorse the police when they are known to brutalize Black communities with impunity? What does it mean to ignore this reality, and give them space in a celebration?

To date, the loudest and most vicious anti-Black responses to our work have been generated in the aftermath of this action. It was after this action that we could no longer safely travel in public, as we were being physically attacked and stalked. After this action, Black politicians, police boards, city counsellors, and journalists across the country obsessively debated the ideas of inclusion and exclusion with respect to the police, after never having once considered Black community inclusion in this city in the same way. To witness the uproar that this caused, especially compared to the lack of uproar Black death causes, has been particularly painful for us.

Freedom School

On July 30, 2016, the Freedom School—a three-week-long summer program for Black children created by Black Lives Matter – Toronto steering committee member Leroi Newbold—ended with a closing action opposite the United States consulate to demonstrate against ending immigration detention and abolishing prisons. The school was created in response to a lack of humanizing, self-affirming, queer-positive educational opportunities for Black children in the Greater Toronto Area. Black children ranging in ages 4 to 10 were accompanied with their parents in child-friendly action with visual art, drummers, speeches, and a letter-writing activity to support 60 men on hunger strikes in prisons in Ontario. The immigration detainees have been calling for an end to indefinite imprisonment with a 90-day limit on detentions as an initial step to ending incarcerations.[37] This action concluded a curriculum, offered through Freedom School, designed to teach children about Black Canadian and diasporic history, to engage children in political resistance against anti-Black racism and state violence through an anti-colonial trans feminist lens, and to offer children an entry point into the Black Lives Matter – Toronto.[38] This action was taken up by Canadian corporate media, drawing comparisons to our Pride parade interruption in an attempt to narrate our liberation movement as extreme, despite widespread support from parents and community members.

Black Arts

Black visual artists and photographers within our movement have also insisted that our work exist as a public interruption of space. These artists have had their work documented in galleries across the city, and have created events to continue the public intervention that our live work is known for. Some of the art created during #BLMTOTentCity was exhibited by Harlem Underground restaurant in an art exhibit. The collection included pieces by Black Lives Matter – Toronto steering committee member Syrus Marcus Ware, visual artist Amber Williams-King, and photographer C.J. Cromwell. Syrus Marcus Ware also worked to curate a two-week residency installation with other guest artists to honour the one-year anniversary of #BLMTOTentCity and fundraise for the Freedom School in an exhibit called Black Art City at the Gladstone Hotel. In May 2017, prolific Toronto-based photographer and visual historian Jalani Morgan, who has been central in documenting the Black Lives Matter movement in Toronto, exhibited a public installation entitled *The Sum of All Parts* at Toronto's Metro Hall. The exhibit included photos taken at some of our actions. This public art exhibit is an especially significant interruption of public space, featuring enlarged images of various actions led by Black Lives Matter – Toronto, portraits of Black community members, and images of Indigenous presence at sites of our resistance. This exhibit in particular reinserts our resistance and visibility back into the streets of Toronto.

WE WILL WIN: THE VICTORIES

I think the importance of doing activist work is precisely because it allows you to give back and to consider yourself not as a single individual who may have achieved whatever but to be a part of an ongoing historical movement.
    —Angela Y. Davis[39]

We have, at times, been overwhelmed by what we have accomplished. Our work has been a site of critical interventions from the academy to the streets. To hear it told by mass media, our victories are the stuff of recognition by politicians, promises of consultation, reviews, and recommendations. These moments certainly point to an important shift that those in power feel they have had to make as a result of our work, but these are not victories per se. These are public relations exercises by a power structure that is losing their base as a result of our very strategic and targeted work. These are important moments on the journey toward victory, but they are not victory itself. The victories from power will come from below; from struggle in our communities. They will never be gifted from the benevolence of white supremacist power structures above us. But we have had victories.

The victories we have had will not be televised.[40] Mass media could never truly understand them. One of the most rewarding victories we have realized is how we have been able to build community through our work. One of the ways that anti-Blackness works so insidiously is to isolate us in our pain and make our traumatic experiences detached from a community familiarity. We are made to feel that our experiences with anti-Blackness are irrational; that we are imagining it, or "pulling" some sort of imaginary "race card" as though our entire life experience is some sort of game that we ourselves do not take seriously. By design, anti-Blackness makes it difficult for us to name our pain and to seek out support from the only other people who could understand it.

But as extensively detailed above, our work is intentionally carried out using a very public approach. In this way, our community members can see for themselves that our traumatic and anti-Black experiences are indeed heinous, that other Black people also recognize the atrocities that we go through with too much regularity, and that we can come together in a group to resist it. In creating space to elevate community voice, we have seen a community come together and draw power from that coming together. As an example, one of the most labour-intensive demonstrations that we put together was our #BLMTOTentCity occupation of Toronto Police Services headquarters. As described above, the protest lasted 15 days. The hundreds of people who participated did not simply experience an encampment, but a possibility for what a community that takes care of one another could look like. Participants organized food, shelter, health care, child care, safety protocols, educational activities, cleanliness schedules, wellness activities, entertainment, and art programming, among other initiatives. This was truly an experience in building a community in resistance where a person could, through being a member of this community, contribute to the movement against anti-Blackness.

When we demanded that Pride Toronto address issues that community members had raised for years and years, we saw queer and trans communities recognize that they had the power to force change within the organization. New organizations were formed with the purpose of holding Pride Toronto accountable to the community, and engaging queer and trans community members on issues of police brutality and anti-Blackness. This victory has had reverberations across the country and internationally.

These examples of community building are arguably our most important victories, because once the power of community building is felt, it cannot be unfelt. These experiences could lead others to organize against anti-Blackness in other areas. Since we began organizing, we have seen increased struggle against anti-Blackness in health care, the child welfare system, migration, education, and post-secondary education. Our methods have inspired actions in Indigenous communities and in the struggle against Islamophobia and white supremacy. The empowerment that comes from building a community that believes that they can win is immeasurable.

We have also significantly shifted culture. In 2014, it was not possible to discuss anti-Blackness with a mass audience; today, we have introduced the concept into mass consciousness. Our refusal to engage with media in the ways that they expect us to has forced them to learn and use our language. We have effectively used mass media as a tool to educate mass culture on what anti-Blackness is and why it must be addressed. Anti-Blackness has even been a topic of discussion in bourgeois, white publications like *Toronto Life*. Their readership may not be our audience, but our presence in their world reveals that we have made it acceptable to discuss anti-Blackness in popular discourse in our almost three years of existence.

This shift in mass culture has precipitated the masses to demand change from politicians. When Toronto Mayor John Tory and Police Chief Mark Saunders attempted to respond to us in the ways that white supremacist anti-Black institutional actors often do—by deeming us irrational, unreasonable, and juvenile—they were met with furor. When Premier Kathleen Wynne attempted to criminalize us by creating a media narrative about needing to call in the bomb squad after we left what she deemed "unknown substances" at her home (we had simply left a wreath and a photo of Andrew Loku), again, she was met with furor. These politicians now know that, at bare minimum, they must engage with our message.

Beyond these intangible victories, we have also been able to secure a number of commitments from those in power, which tells us that we are consolidating power on the ground in such a way that those who hold power within the system feel they must respond. This includes a commitment from the Toronto District School Board to implement anti-racism training for all staff across the school board; the public release of all future reports of Ontario's police watchdog, the Special Investigations Unit; a commitment to end carding; the removal of police floats and armed police officers in the Toronto Pride Parade; collecting race-based data in policing, incarceration, education, and the health care system; a province-wide, three-year plan to address racism; and a province-wide, four-year, $47 million commitment to implement an Ontario Black Youth Action Plan, a plan that acknowledges that Black youth are disadvantaged by systemic anti-Blackness.

Our victories are numerous, but what we consider victories is not what some would expect. Ultimately, our goals are to eliminate anti-Blackness, white supremacy, and build a liberated Black future. Anything that is not directly connected to these ends are simply gains that shift the system, and tell us about mass discourse. We do not want to diminish these gains; a gain that amounts to the end of carding is the difference between life and death for our communities. But we must not lose sight of our larger goals, as history tells us how fleeting these gains can be.

CONCLUSION: LOOKING BACK

I am deliberate and afraid of nothing.
        —Audre Lorde, poet[41]

All that you touch
You Change.
All that you Change
Changes you.
The only lasting truth
Is Change.
God
Is Change.
        —Octavia Butler, poet[42]

Our work is deliberate and afraid of nothing. We are constantly reflective and principled in our approach. In our reflexive practice, our work is constantly shifting. We critique one another. We listen to our communities. We shift when required. For example, we are currently reflecting on our practice of receiving consent from family before elevating in mass consciousness violent interactions with police. What if we cannot contact the family? What if all other known members of the family are institutionalized in such a way that it is impossible to contact them? What are the ethics that we need to stand by that honour both our community and our principles? These are questions that we are currently working through.

When we say that we are afraid of nothing, we do not mean that we do not experience fear. Rather, our goals are untarnished by mitigating personal motivations. No one on our team is acting out of personal gain. We are not planning to run for office, and we are not attempting to enhance any capitalist venture. Our work is only concerned with Black liberation. This frees us to be bold and creative in the ways that we engage. We need not play by any established rules for how we "should" act; we only need to imagine that we can be successful in our goals, and do whatever it takes to get us to that place.

Finally, our method and creativity necessitates constant change. What we have discussed is a snapshot of who we are, what we have done, and how we have done it at this moment in time. But we expect that this will shift and change as we move through our work. This is something that we believe that all anti-oppressive movements should espouse. We cannot continue to use the same tactics that those in power are used to ignoring and adapting to. This is just one reason why our work has been able to reach so many people. Our creativity and commitment to change is not solely about the society in which we live. It is also about changing ourselves.

This work for change and for Black liberation is long, hard, arduous work. But it is instructive; it is a necessity for community care, and it is a gift for other communities who can learn from it. And there is joy. We insist upon joy in the struggle. It is this joy that keeps us resilient when anti-Blackness attempts to destroy us. We are inspired by our ancestors, our predecessors, and the possibilities for our future; and finally, of course, our belief that we will win.

Black Lives Matter.

And they always will.

NOTES

1.   Shakur, A. 1973, July 4. To My People. Retrieved from http://www.thetalkingdrum.com/tmp.html.

2.   The 1960 Canadian Bill of Rights was the Canada's first federal law to protect human rights and fundamental freedom. It can be viewed in its entirety here: http://laws-lois.justice.gc.ca/eng/acts/C-12.3/page-1.html. It was eventually replaced by the 1982 Canadian Charter of Rights and Freedoms.

3.   Cooper, A. 2007. *The Hanging of Angélique: The Untold Story of Canadian Slavery and the Burning of Old Montréal.* Athens, GA: University of Georgia Press.

4.   Sharpe, C.E. 2016. *In the Wake: On Blackness and Being.* Durham, NC: Duke University Press.

5.   Sharpe, C.E. 1988. Black Action Defense Committee. Retrieved from http://blackactiondefence.weebly.com.

6.   City of Toronto Receives Feedback on Toronto Action Plan to Confront Anti-Black Racism. 2017, May 17. Retrieved from http://www1.toronto.ca. See also Province of Ontario. 2017. *A Better Way Forward: Ontario's 3-Year Anti-Racism Strategic Plan* (pp. 1–60, Rep.). Retrieved from http://ontario.ca/antiracism.

7.   Hong, J. 2017, May 1. TDSB Director Commits to Anti-Racism Training at Black Lives Matter Walkout. *Toronto Star.* Retrieved from https://www.thestar.com/news/gta/2017/05/01/tdsb-director-commits-to-anti-racism-training-at-black-lives-matter-walkout.html; Yang, J. 2017, May 4. Program for Black Youth in Crisis at Heart of Bitter Dispute. *Toronto Star.* Retrieved from https://www.thestar.com/news/gta/2017/05/04/program-for-black-youth-in-crisis-at-heart-of-bitter-dispute.html; Draaisma, M. 2017, April 24. Black Students in Toronto Streamed into Courses Below Their Ability, Report Finds. *CBC News.* Retrieved from http://www.cbc.ca/news/canada/toronto/study-black-students-toronto-york-university-1.4082463; Gooch, T. 2017, May 10. Don Meredith Should Have Quit a Long Time Ago. *Globe and Mail.* Retrieved from https://www.theglobeandmail.com/opinion/don-meredith-should-have-quit-a-long-time-ago/article34944072.

8.   Freire, P., Ramos, M.B., & Macedo, D. 1993. *Pedagogy of the Oppressed.* New York: The Continuum International Publishing Group Ltd.

9.   Garza, A. 2017. *Guiding Principles.* Retrieved from http://blacklivesmatter.com.

10. Davis, A. 2011. *Are Prisons Obsolete?* Seven Stories Press.

11. Sharpe, C.E. 2016. *In the Wake: On Blackness and Being.* Durham, NC: Duke University Press.

12. Davis, A. 2011. *Are Prisons Obsolete?* New York: Seven Stories Press.

13. Garza, A. 2013, July 13. A Love Letter to Black People [Letter]. Facebook.com, Oakland, California.

14. St. Louis County Health Office of the Medical Examiner. 2014. *Brown, Michael: Narrative Report of Investigation. Exam Case 2014-5143*. Retrieved from: http://www.documentcloud.org/documents/1371268-2014-5143-narrative-report-01.html.

15. Office of the Chief Coroner. 2016, May 26. Verdict of Coroner's Jury. Retrieved from https://www.mcscs.jus.gov.on.ca/english/Deathinvestigations/Inquests/Verdictsandrecommendations/OCCInquestCarby2016.html.

16. Ibid.

17. Similar to the Stop-and-Frisk program in the City of New York, carding is a process by which Toronto police officers stop civilians and ask for their personal identification. They then record the data on the individuals they stop in a database. Black people are disproportionately more likely to be carded in the City of Toronto, and their inclusion in police databases can affect their ability to access certain types of employment and services. See Gillis, W. 2016, May 12. Peel Cop Sought to Card Jermaine Carby Before Slaying, Inquest Hears. *Toronto Star.* Retrieved from https://www.thestar.com/news/crime/2016/05/12/peel-cop-sought-to-card-jermaine-carby-before-slaying-inquest-hears.html.

18. Black Lives Matter – Toronto. 2015. Retrieved from http://blacklivesmatterto.ca.

19. Jordan, J. 1978, August 9. Poem for South African Women. Retrieved from http://www.junejordan.net/poem-for-south-african-women.html.

20. Crenshaw, K. 1991. Mapping the Margins: Intersectionality, Identity Politics, and Violence against Women of Color. *Stanford Law Review*, 43(6), 1241–1299. doi:10.2307/1229039.

21. Walcott, R. 2003. *Black Like Who? Writing Black Canada*. Toronto: Insomniac Press.

22. Sharpe, C.E. 2016. *In the Wake: On Blackness and Being*. Durham, NC: Duke University Press.

23. Freire, P. 1993. *Pedagogy of the Oppressed*. New York: The Continuum International Publishing Group Ltd.

24. hooks, b. 1994. Theory as a Liberatory Practise. *Teaching to Transgress: Education as the Practice of Freedom* (pp. 59–75). New York: Routledge.

25. Benjamin, A. 2011. Doing Anti-Oppressive Social Work: The Importance of Resistance, History, and Strategy. In *Doing Anti-Oppressive Practice* (2nd ed). Retrieved from http://interface.thekatnip.com/conflicts-individualism-part-right-motivations-activist-writing.

26. The New School. 2014, November 7. Public Programs Express: bell hooks and Laverne Cox Discuss Transgender Politics [YouTube]. Retrieved from https://youtu.be/Xuspy9vYMBA.

27. Fanon, F. 1961. *The Wretched of the Earth*. New York: Grove Press.

28. Lancaster, J., & Fowler, J. 2016, January 19. Toronto Police to Get Military-Style Assault Rifles. *CBC News*. Retrieved from http://www.cbc.ca/news/canada/toronto/toronto-police-rifles-1.3409707.

29. Eligon, J., & Perez-Pena, R. 2015, November 9. University of Missouri Protests Spur a Day of Change. *The New York Times*. Retrieved from https://www.nytimes.com/2015/11/10/us/university-of-missouri-system-president-resigns.html.

30. Boundless Whiteness Bounded Blackness [Audio Blog Interview]. 2015, April 1. Retrieved from https://soundcloud.com/sandy-hudson-6/boundless-whiteness-bounded-blackness-yusra-khogali-and-sandra-hudson.

31. A colloquial term for the University of Missouri.

32. Black Liberation Collective: University of Toronto Demands. 2015. Retrieved from http://www.blackliberationcollective.org/our-demands/#utoronto.

33. Davis, A. 2011. *Are Prisons Obsolete?* New York: Seven Stories Press.

34. Peter Munk is chairman and founder of the mining company Barrick Gold, the world's largest gold-mining corporation. The University of Toronto is closely affiliated with Peter Munk and invests in his mining companies. Barrick Gold is implicated in killings, rapes, toxic spills, fraudulent reporting, land theft, and the militarization of entire communities across the globe. Amnesty International, Human Rights Watch, Harvard Law Clinic, Mining Watch, NYU Law School, and many others have documented this abuse. See Peter Munk out of UofT. 2016, April 26. Retrieved from https://munkoutofuoft.wordpress.com.

35. City Says it Received Just Eight 311 Complaints about Afrofest. 2016, March 17. *City News.* Retrieved from http://www.citynews.ca/2016/03/17/city-says-it-received-just-eight-311-complaints-about-afrofest.

36. Toronto police have routinely violently attacked sites of queer expression in Toronto. For more information on the instances referenced, see http://rabble.ca/toolkit/on-this-day/toronto-bathhouse-raids.

37. End Immigration Detention Network. 2016, July 25. *#Migrant Strike Week 2—Detainees Running Out of Time, CBSA Trying to Break the Strike.* Retrieved from https://endimmigrationdetention.com/category/hunger-strike.

38. BLM-TO Freedom School. 2016. Retrieved from http://freedomschool.ca.

39. Angela Davis [Interview by Frontline]. 1997. *Public Broadcasting Service.* Retrieved from http://www.pbs.org/wgbh/pages/frontline/shows/race/interviews/davis.html.

40. Gil Scott-Heron. 1971. *Small Talk at 125th and Lenox* [Vinyl recording]. RCA Studios: Bob Thiele.

41. Lorde, A. 1973. New Year's Day. *From A Land Where Other People Live.* Detroit, MI: Broadside Press.

42. Butler, O.E. 1993. Earthseed. *Parable of the Sower.* New York: Four Walls Eight Windows.

Copyright Acknowledgements

Chapter 44: Linda Tuhiwai Smith, "Imperialism, History, Writing, and Theory," from *Decolonizing Methodologies* (London and New York: Zed Books, 1999), 25–40. Reprinted by permission of Zed Books Ltd.

Chapter 45: From: "Anti-Racism, Social Movements and Civil Society," from *Rethinking Anti-Racisms: From Theory to Practice,* Cathie Lloyd, ed. Floya Anthias and Cathie Lloyd, Copyright 2002 Routledge, reproduced by permission of Taylor & Francis Books UK.

Chapter 46: Adriana Paz Ramirez and Jennifer Jihye Chun, "Struggling against History: Migrant Farmworkers Organizing in B.C.," from *Unfree Labour? Struggles of Migrant and Immigrant Workers in Canada,* ed. Aziz Choudry and Adrian Smith (Oakland, California: PM Press, 2016), 87–104. Reprinted by permission of PM Press. www.pmpress.org.

Chapter 47: Pamela Palmater, "Why Are We Idle No More?" from *The Winter We Danced,* ed. Kino-nda-niimi Collective (Winnipeg: ARP Books, 2014), 37, 39–40. Reprinted by permission of ARP Books.

Sylvia McAdam (Sayswahum), "Armed with Nothing More Than a Song and a Drum," from *The Winter We Danced,* ed. Kino-nda-niimi Collective (Winnipeg: ARP Books, 2014), 65–67. Reprinted by permission of ARP Books.

Photographs

Part 1 by uschools/iStock
Part 2 by Paul McKinnon/iStock
Part 3 by oneclearvision/iStock
Part 4 by Jalani Morgan, Toronto, Canada, 2016.